D1597048

The Life of Shabkar

SUNY Series in Buddhist Studies
Matthew Kapstein, editor

The Life of Shabkar

The Autobiography of a Tibetan Yogin

The King of Wish-granting Jewels That Fulfills the Hopes
of All Fortunate Disciples Who Seek Liberation

The detailed narration of the life and liberation
of the great vajra-holder Shabkar Tsogdruk Rangdrol,
refuge and protector for all sentient beings of this dark age

with a Foreword by
His Holiness the XIVth Dalai Lama

Translated from the Tibetan
by Matthieu Ricard,
Jakob Leschly, Erik Schmidt,
Marilyn Silverstone, and Lodrö Palmo

Edited by
Constance Wilkinson
with Michal Abrams, and other members of the
Padmakara Translation Group

STATE UNIVERSITY OF NEW YORK PRESS

Published by
State University of New York Press, Albany

For information, address the State University of New York Press,
State University Plaza, Albany, NY 12246

Production by Bernadine Dawes
Marketing by Nancy Farrell

Cover photo credit: J. Biancamaria
Cover design: Marjorie Corbett

The cover illustration is a watercolor on silk painted by the eighth Dugu
Choegyal Gyantso Rinpoche for this publication. The artist is a renowned
Tibetan lama and yogin whose work combines traditional style with a free,
expressive manner.

Library of Congress Cataloging-in-Publication Data

Shabkar Tsogdruk Rangdrol, 1781–1851.
    The life of Shabkar : the autobiography of a Tibetan yogin /
translated from Tibetan by Matthieu Ricard . . . [et al.] : edited by
Constance Wilkinson (poetry),   with Michal Abrams . . . [et al.]
        p. cm. — (Suny series in Buddhist Studies)
    ISBN 0-7914-1835-9 (hc). — ISBN 0-7914-1836-7 (pb)
    1. Shabkar Tsogdruk Rangdrol, 1781–1851. 2. Lamas—China—Tibet—
Biography. 3. Yogins—China—Tibet—Biography. I. Ricard,
Matthieu. II. Wilkinson, Constance. III. Abrams, Michal.
IV. Series.
BQ986.A38A3   1994   93-26127
  294.3'923'092—dc20   CIP
B]

Contents

The Life Story

Foreword

*By His Holiness
the XIVth Dalai Lama*

The vast religious literature of Tibet can be divided into two kinds of books: those dealing with Buddhist teaching in a technical, analytical way, intended for those who have trained in logic and philosophy, and those which contain advice. The latter category consists of works which present the Dharma in a way that is accessible to people without special training. It includes, on the one hand, books which deal with the Stages of the Path, Mind Training, and so forth, and, on the other, books of an inspirational nature containing the lives of great practitioners, spiritual songs, and so forth. The special quality of these books lies in their universal appeal. The *Life of Milarepa* and his *Hundred Thousand Songs*, for example, are treasured in almost every Tibetan household and also would often be the only additional book that meditators took into retreat with them.

I am, therefore, delighted to know that the life-story of another more recent great practitioner, Shabkar Tsogdruk Rangdrol, is also to be published in English. Regarded by many as the greatest yogi after Milarepa to gain enlightenment in one lifetime, he also lived the life of a wandering mendicant teaching by means of spiritual songs. Shabkar is particularly celebrated for the absolute purity of his approach to his lama and his personal practice, which freed him from the snare of sectarianism. He is also affectionately remembered for the kindness of his gently teasing humor.

This work will undoubtedly make a great contribution to the growing store of Tibetan literature translated into English, providing a source of inspiration to Buddhist practitioners and general readers alike. I am glad of this opportunity to express my gratitude and admiration to Matthieu Ricard and other friends who have labored long under expert guidance to produce it.

Preface

The autobiography of Shabkar Tsogdruk Rangdrol is one of the classics of Tibetan Buddhist literature and may be counted among the spiritual classics of humankind. Like St. Francis, Jalal-ud-din Rumi, Sri Ramakrishna, or the Hasidim, Shabkar exemplifies through his life and legacy the excellence of a particular religious tradition, while transcending particularity and touching the divine in all.

In Shabkar's life and songs, we receive a privileged and intimate view of the world of the Buddhist adept, a world of intense self-discipline, but also of humor, vision and joy. It is owing to these qualities, and the simple yet elegant form in which they are here expressed, that Shabkar's work has come to be especially beloved among the people of his native province of Amdo, in northeastern Tibet, who find in these pages a companion offering continual wisdom, solace, and the courage needed to face the trials of life.

The mixed prose and verse in which Shabkar's autobiography is written is in some respects reminiscent of the *campu* style of classical Sanskrit poetry, which influenced Tibetan literature primarily through the *Jatakamala* of Aryasura, a work with which Shabkar was certainly familiar. Shabkar, however, is no mere imitator of Sanskrit *kavya*; it is his eschewal, in fact, of literary artifice, in favor of the clear and rich idiom of colloquial speech, folk song and traditional folk oratory, that lends his writing much of its distinctive flavor. Shabkar's wit and playfulness, his magnificent flights of imagination, his persistence in exposing all hypocrisy—these are the qualities that suffuse his work, overriding the niceties of literary style alone.

The gentle and kind personality illuminating these pages should not, however, be regarded as an airy proponent of love and light, a New Age prophet before his time. Shabkar's lightness disguises, to some extent, the intense moral rigor of the ascetical ethos he propounded: Shabkar was an effective apostle of vegetarianism among carnivores, of teetotalism among the lush, of renunciation among the worldly. He wins our respect and sympathy not because we always concur with, much less adhere to, the standard upon which he insists, but because his insistence takes the form not of the moralist's harangue but of the songster's jest, and of teaching through his own good example. For above all, Shabkar practiced what he preached.

In addition to its religious and literary value, the autobiography of Shabkar presents an exceptional record of many dimensions of Tibetan life during the early part of the nineteenth century. The author's remarks on pilgrimages, on the donation and redistribution of wealth in connection with religious affairs, on brigands and thieves, and occasionally on politics, all contribute to our understanding of and receptiveness to a now vanished world.

In offering to us the present translation, the Padmakara Translation Group, inspired by H.H. the late Dilgo Khyentse Rinpoche, and headed for this work by Gelong Konchog Tendzin

(Matthieu Ricard), has magnificently contributed to our knowledge of Tibetan Buddhism. Their achievement is a highly accurate, but at the same time pleasant and readable, rendering of a work the many difficulties of which might well have frustrated the effort. The background material they have assembled here, represented in the notes and appendices, by itself represents a major contribution to Tibetan Studies that will be welcomed by scholars in many differing areas of specialization: religion, history, anthropology, literature, etc.

The SUNY Series in Buddhist Studies is pleased to present this unparalleled addition to the body of Buddhist literature now available in English translation.

MATTHEW KAPSTEIN
Series Editor

Acknowledgments

This work was translated and edited by the Padmakara Translation Group under the guidance of: H.H. Dilgo Khyentse Rinpoche, Tulku Urgyen Rinpoche, Dza Trulshik Rinpoche, Taklung Tsetrul Pema Wangyal Rinpoche, Dagpo Tulku, Dugu Tulku Choegyal Rinpoche, Alak Zenkar Rinpoche (Thubden Nyima), Tulku Thondup Rinpoche, Senge Trakpa Rinpoche, Khetsun Sangpo Rinpoche, Shangpa Tulku, and Tulku Sangnak Tendzin.

Translators
Matthieu Ricard (Konchog Tendzin), Jakob Leschly (Tashi Chöpel), Erik Schmidt (Pema Kunzang), Marilyn Silverstone (Bhikshuni Ngawang Chödrön), and Linda Talbot (Lodrö Palmo)
Editor
Constance Wilkinson
Assistant editors
Michal Abrams (Pema Yeshe), Jeffrey Miller (Surya Das), Daniel Staffler, John Canti, Dana Chubb, Wyatt Benner, Jody Vernon, and Maggie Westhaver
Illustrations:
The eighth Dugu Choegyal Gyamtso Rinpoche
Raphaele Demandre

We would like to thank all those who made valuable contributions during the various stages of the translation, editing, and proofreading of this work: Ani Jinba Palmo (E. De Jong), Ani Samten (Casandra Calo), Ronald Barnstone, Shelagh Byron, David Christensen, the late Terry Clifford, Wulstan Fletcher, Michael Friedman, Shirin Gale, Gelong Tsultrim Gyatso, Janis Joculvar, Dolores Katz, S. Lhamo, Hetty MacLise, Tim Olmsted, Nur Richard, and Pam Ross.

Special thanks are due to Professor Matthew Kapstein (Columbia University, USA) for his invaluable help, and to Dr. Franz-Karl Ehrhard (Kathmandu, Nepal) and Toni Huber (University of Canterbury, New Zealand), whose suggestions brought about significant improvements during the final stages of preparation; to Chris Gianniotis for his long-term technical guidance; and to Vivian Kurz and Bernadine Dawes for their dedicated and careful attention to all the matters related to the publication of this work.

We also thank all those who were kind enough to make maps and other useful information available to us: Katia Buffetrille (Paris, France), Keith Dowman (Chabahil, Kathmandu), Mike Farmer, Peter Kessler (Rikon, Switzerland), Bradley Rowe (Exeter, U.K.), Cyrus Stearns (Bodhnath, Kathmandu), and Tashi Tshering (Library of Tibetan Works and Archives, Dharamsala, India).

Translator's Introduction

The autobiography of Lama Shabkar, a work known and loved throughout Tibet, is probably second only to that of Jetsun Milarepa[1] in popularity. It is a simple and moving account of the life of a wandering hermit from childhood until his ultimate spiritual realization.

Shabkar describes all the steps of his spiritual path, culminating in the teachings of the Great Perfection, Dzogchen. Like Milarepa, of whom he was said to be an incarnation, his teachings, advice, and accounts of spiritual experiences are expressed in the form of songs. In Amdo, his native province, excerpts of Shabkar's life were often read to the dying instead of the *Bardo Thödrol*, the so-called *Tibetan Book of the Dead*.

The story of Shabkar's life illustrates the complete path of Buddhist practice. To begin with, he demonstrates the exemplary path of a perfect practitioner: having become disillusioned with worldly activities, he seeks a spiritual master, develops confidence in him and follows his instructions. By practicing with complete dedication, in the end he himself becomes an enlightened master capable of contributing immensely to the welfare of other beings. Shabkar's account of his progress along the spiritual path is so straightforward, heartfelt, and unaffected that one is encouraged to believe that similar deep faith and diligence would allow anyone else to achieve the same result.

Shabkar was born in 1781 among the Nyingmapa yogins of the Rekong region in Amdo, the remote northeast province of Greater Tibet. These yogins were renowned for their mastery of the Secret Mantrayana practices and gathered in their thousands to engage in meditations and rituals. They were much admired, and sometimes feared, for their magical powers. The yogins of Rekong were also famous for their hair, often six feet long, which they wore coiled on the top of their heads.

From a very early age, Shabkar showed a strong inclination toward the contemplative life. Even his childhood games were related to the teachings of Lord Buddha. By the age of six or seven, he had already developed a strong desire to practice. Visions, similar to those experienced in advanced Dzogchen practice, came to him naturally.

At fifteen years of age, Shabkar felt a strong desire to "pray to the precious master Guru Padmasambhava, the source of blessings." He recited one million Vajra Guru mantras[2] and had auspicious dreams, such as of flying through the air, seeing the sun and moon rising simultaneously, finding jewel treasures, and so forth. "From then on," he wrote, "by the grace of Guru Rinpoche, I became filled with intense devotion to the guru, affection toward my Dharma friends, compassion for sentient beings, and pure perception toward the teachings. I had the good fortune to accomplish without obstacles whatever Dharma practice I undertook" (chap. 1, fol. 19a).

At the age of sixteen, he completed a one-year retreat during which he recited the mantra of Manjushri ten million times and experienced auspicious dreams and signs. "Through the blessing of this practice," he said, "I gained a general understanding of the depth and breadth of the teachings." Shabkar then met Jamyang Gyatso, a master whom he venerated greatly and of whom he later had visions and dreams.

Despite his deep affection for his mother and respect for his family, Shabkar managed to resist their repeated requests that he marry. He eventually left home in order to pursue whole-heartedly his spiritual aims. Determined to re-nounce worldly concerns, Shabkar received full monastic ordination at the age of twenty and entered a meditation retreat. He let his hair grow long again, as was customary for retreatants, who did not waste time in nonessential activities; as a sign of having accomplished certain yogic practices, he wore a white shawl rather than the traditional red shawl, although he continued to wear the patched lower robe characteristic of a fully ordained monk. This rather unconventional attire occasionally attracted sarcastic comments from strangers, to whom Shabkar would reply with humorous songs.

Shabkar left his native land behind and trav-eled south of Rekong to meet his main teacher, the Dharma King Ngakyi Wangpo. Ngakyi Wangpo was a learned and accomplished Mon-golian king, said to be an incarnation of Marpa the Translator,[3] who had renounced the rem-nants of the vast kingdom of Gushri Khan and become a prominent Nyingmapa master. (Details about Ngakyi Wangpo's ancestry are given in Appendix 3.)

As Shabkar says of him, "He had crossed the ocean of the knowledge of the scriptures and sciences and realized the natural state, the pro-found and luminous vajra essence. Because I saw all his actions as pure and did whatever he asked, he came to think of me as a heart-son. There-fore, he gave me all the pith instructions of the Old and New Translation schools, as if filling a vessel to the brim."

After receiving complete instructions from the Dharma King, Shabkar practiced for five years in the wilderness of Tseshung, where his meditation experiences and realization flourished. He then meditated for three years on a small island, Tsonying, the "Heart of the Lake," in the

Kokonor, the Blue Lake of Amdo. There he experienced numerous dreams and visions of gurus and deities.

His search for sacred places took him to many other solitary retreats: the glaciers of Machen, the sacred caves of the White Rock Monkey Fortress, the arduous pilgrimage of the Ravines of Tsari, Mount Kailash, and the Lapchi Snow Range. He spent many years in the very caves where Milarepa and other saints had lived and meditated.

Shabkar's given names were Jampa Chödar, "The Loving One Who Spreads the Dharma," and Tsogdruk Rangdrol, "Self-liberation of the Six Senses." He became renowned as Shabkar Lama, the "White Footprint Lama," because he spent years in meditation at Mount Kailash above Milarepa's[4] Cave of Miracles, near the famous White Footprint, one of the four footprints said to have been left by Buddha Shakyamuni when he traveled miraculously to Kailash. It is also said that Shabkar was called "White Foot" because wherever he would set his feet, the land would become "white," meaning that through his teachings the minds of the people would be turned toward the holy Dharma.

Wandering as a homeless yogin, teaching all beings from bandits to wild animals, Shabkar's pilgrimages brought him as far as Nepal, where, in the Kathmandu Valley, he covered the entire spire of the Bodhnath stupa with the gold his devotees had offered him.

In 1828, at the age of forty-seven, Shabkar returned to Amdo, where he tirelessly helped others through his extraordinary compassion. He spent the last twenty years of his life teaching disciples, promoting peace in the area, and prac-ticing meditation in retreat at various sacred places, primarily at his hermitage in Tashikhyil.

Oral traditions recount even more stories of this great yogin's life than the present autobiog-raphy. For instance, they say that Shabkar fed hundreds of beggars, asking them to gather stones to make stupas[5] in return. When invited to teach, Shabkar would agree to come, provided that the benefactors also fed all the beggars who accom-panied him. The horde of beggars would usually arrive first, followed by Shabkar himself on foot, leaning on the famous walking stick he used to call his "horse," which itself was the subject of some of his songs.

The reputation of Shabkar, the perfect hermit, spread far and wide, inspiring another great renunciate, Patrul Rinpoche,[6] to travel from Kham to Amdo to meet him. Unfortunately, after Patrul had gone only halfway he heard that Shabkar had passed away, whereupon he prostrated himself a hundred times in the direction of Amdo and sang a supplication for Shabkar's swift rebirth. He then added, "Compassion and love are the root of Dharma. I think that there was no one more compassionate than Shabkar in this world. I had nothing special to ask, no teachings to request from him, no teaching to offer him; I simply wanted to gather some merit by seeing his face."

Two successive incarnations of Shabkar were recognized in Amdo, but neither had the spiritual charisma of its predecessor.[7] Once, when H.H. Dilgo Khyentse Rinpoche[8] went to Shohong, Shabkar's birthplace, to bestow the empowerments of the *Treasury of Rediscovered Teachings*,[9] he sat on a stone seat under a particular tree where Shabkar had often sat to sing spiritual songs. While Khyentse Rinpoche himself sat and sang there, a rain of flowers fell on him from the tree. He felt this signified a special karmic connection between himself and Shabkar. Many people thought that he was perhaps Shabkar's incarnation.

Shabkar lived at a time in Tibetan history when many spiritual lineages were on the verge of extinction. Bitter religious sectarianism and tribal feuds divided monasteries and peoples.[10] Transcending these differences, Shabkar exemplified religious tolerance, altruism and "pure perception,"[11] the foremost characteristics of a genuine Buddhist practitioner.

A vision of Guru Padmasambhava he experienced toward the end of his life is typical of Shabkar's Rimey (nonsectarian) approach to the four main schools of Tibetan Buddhism. During the vision, Shabkar tells Guru Padmasambhava, "I have prayed to you all my life and have been blessed by visions of many other deities and spiritual masters, but only now do you appear to

me." Guru Padmasambhava replied, "Do you remember when, on the island of The Heart of the Lake, you had a vision of Tsongkhapa, who gave you the teaching on the *Graded Path*? That was I." In *The Emanated Scriptures of Orgyen*, in which Shabkar recounts this vision, he expresses his faith in the inseparability of Guru Padmasambhava, Atisha, and Tsongkhapa, a triad of teachers who dominated Shabkar's life, practice, and teaching.[12]

The core of Shabkar's practice was the Great Perfection, Atiyoga, the summit of the nine vehicles, the extraordinary treasure of the Nyingma tradition. Yet his realization of the Great Perfection was firmly grounded in the impeccable precepts of the Kadampa masters, which inspire practitioners to have few needs and desires; authentic feelings of renunciation, humility and inner calm, loving-kindness, compassion and, above all, the precious Bodhicitta—the intense resolve to bring all sentient beings to the perfect freedom of enlightenment.

Shabkar did not merely receive teachings from all traditions of Tibetan Buddhism, but he actively taught "pure perception" and openmindedness. Moreover, he eloquently elucidated how all the many different Dharma teachings of the various *yanas* form one coherent, noncontradictory whole. He contributed greatly to the nonsectarian movement that flourished in the nineteenth century and that culminated in luminaries such as Jamgön Kongtrul, Jamyang Khyentse Wangpo, Patrul Rinpoche and Lama Mipham.[13] Gathering teachings from all areas of Tibet and from masters of all spiritual traditions, these teachers—themselves all authentic masters, scholars, poets, commentators, and accomplished yogins— saved the heritage of Tibetan Buddhism from decline and restored its vitality, a heritage still benefiting us today. The essential teachings were compiled into major collections, such as Jamgön Kongtrul's *Five Great Treasuries*, so that they could be practiced and transmitted to future generations.

As was often the case with spiritual leaders in Tibet, Shabkar became an active force in mediating peace. In Amdo, which had known centuries of conflict among the disparate elements of the Tibetan population, Mongolian nomads, and Chinese invaders, time after time he served as a mediator in order to bring bloody feuds to an end and establish peace. He inspired highwaymen to give up banditry and crime, and even persuaded Chinese Muslims to rebuild the Buddhist temples they had burned down.

Shabkar's many didactic songs teach us the value and significance of human life, the meaning of death and impermanence, the law of karma, and the suffering inherent in samsara. He often extols the benefits of renunciation, the need to rely upon a qualified teacher and to cultivate devotion, the view of emptiness imbued with the heart of great compassion, and finally, the realization of the Great Perfection—the primordial, unchanging purity of all phenomena, the innate Buddha-nature. Not only does Shabkar explain all this, but he urges and inspires us to make these teachings a living experience, a part of ourselves.

These songs and teachings do not necessarily appear in the biography in the same order as they would in a systematic exposition of the stages of the path. Therefore, an overview of this path, according to the nine vehicles of the Nyingma tradition, can be found in Appendix 1.[14]

In addition to his biography, Shabkar left numerous clear and inspiring teachings, among which is the famous *Flight of the Garuda*. His vast realization and knowledge, remarkable memory, matchless faculty of improvisation, pure perception of all spiritual traditions, and above all his heartfelt compassion and constant wish to benefit others, yielded many volumes of writings that have now (for the most part) been reprinted in India and in Tibet (see Appendix 5 and the excellent review of Shabkar's writings by Pal Gyalkar, 1993)

The distinctive characteristics of Shabkar's works include directness, simplicity, profundity, and the power to encourage the reader to engage in spiritual practice. He does not write to flaunt his knowledge or to gain fame as a philosopher, but rather to turn readers' minds toward the Dharma, sustain their enthusiasm, and prevent them from becoming sidetracked or falling into the pitfalls that lie along the path to liberation.

Shabkar's sources of inspiration are many and various, reflecting the breadth of his training and his almost unique openness to all traditions. In his songs are themes and verses that have their roots in the writings of Longchen Rabjam[14] and other masters of the Nyingma tradition such as Karma Lingpa (1326–?; see chap. 1, note 62). Constant inspiration is provided by the songs of Jetsun Milarepa, as well as Lord Atisha and his spiritual heirs, the masters of the Kadam tradition.

Shabkar died in 1851. His life-story can move one to tears or to laughter; but above all, as H.H. Dilgo Khyentse Rinpoche said, "As one reads it, one's mind cannot resist being turned toward the Dharma."

Buddhism in Tibet
The Buddhist teachings originated in India in the sixth century B.C.E. with Buddha Shakyamuni. and spread to Tibet in the fifth century C.E. when King Lhathori Nyentsen (b. 433) brought the first Buddhist scriptures to the Land of Snows. However, it was during the reigns of King Songtsen Gampo (617?–50) and King Trisong Detsen (b. 730 or 742) that the teachings of the Buddha actually took root and flourished in Tibet.[16]

Wishing to establish a large monastery, King Trisong Detsen invited the Abbot Shantarakshita from India. After vainly attempting to subdue the negative forces and mountain gods averse to the propagation of Buddhism, Shantarakshita declared that only Padmasambhava, the "Lotus-born Guru," could succeed in this task. This powerful tantric master—also known as Guru Rinpoche, the "Precious Teacher," and revered by the Tibetans as the second Buddha—was invited to Tibet, and Samye Monastery was then constructed and consecrated.

Shantarakshita introduced to Tibet the unbroken lineage of monastic ordination, while Guru Padmasambhava bestowed Vajrayana initiations and imparted essential instructions. At the behest of the King, the Abbot Shantarakshita and the Master Padmasambhava, Tibetan translators, led by Vairocana, along with Indian *panditas* led by Vimalamitra, translated into Tibetan the entire Tripitaka—the "Three Baskets" of the Buddha's words—as well as countless tantras, commentaries, and ritual texts used in meditation practice. For the sake of future generations, Padmasambhava, the dakini Yeshe Tsogyal, and his other chief disciples concealed countless teachings in the form of spiritual treasures, or *termas*.[17]

Despite a period (841–46) of intense persecution by King Langdarma, the Buddha's Dharma flourished. New waves of translations brought even more scriptures to Tibet from India, and numerous schools bloomed, following the appearance of many remarkable saints and scholars.

Principal among these schools are the renowned "eight great chariots of the practice lineages" (see Appendix 1). From these, four main traditions emerged—Nyingma, Kagyu, Sakya, and Geluk—which continue to this day to foster the rich contemplative and philosophical heritage of Tibet.

The ancient indigenous Tibetan religion, known as Bön, has also survived, heavily influenced by the advent in Tibet of Buddhist doctrine. Tibetan Buddhism itself transmuted and incorporated some local Bön customs, as traditional Buddhism in spreading has done within the culture of each new country it has encountered.[18]

Tibetan sacred literature, one of the richest in the world, abounds with treatises on religious history and practice, philosophy, hagiographies, and instructions for contemplative life. As His Holiness the XIVth Dalai Lama often stresses, the Tibetan tradition appears to be the only culture in which all the various aspects of Buddhism—Hinayana, Mahayana and Vajrayana —have not only been preserved, but can be practiced in an integrated, harmonious and effective way. These three *yanas*, or "vehicles," correspond to the three fundamental aspects of the Buddhist teachings: renunciation, compassion and "pure vision."

Renunciation, the foundation of the Hina-

yana and therefore the root of all subsequent vehicles, implies the strong wish to free oneself not only from the current sorrows of life but from the seemingly unending sufferings of samsara, the vicious cycle of conditioned existence. Renunciation accompanies a profound weariness, a dissatisfaction with the conditions of samsara, and a heartfelt disillusionment with worldly concerns.

Compassion, the driving force of the Mahayana, is born from the realization that both the individual "self" and the appearances of the phenomenal world are devoid of any intrinsic reality. To misconstrue the infinite display of illusory appearances as permanent entities is ignorance, which results in suffering.

An enlightened being—that is, one who has understood the ultimate nature of all things—naturally feels boundless compassion for those who, under the spell of ignorance, are wandering and suffering in samsara. From similar compassion, the Mahayana student on the spiritual path does not aim for his own liberation alone, but vows to attain Buddhahood in order to gain the capacity to free all sentient beings from the suffering inherent in samsara.

"Pure vision," the extraordinary outlook of the Vajrayana or Adamantine Vehicle, is to recognize Buddha-nature in all sentient beings and to see primordial purity and perfection in all phenomena. Every sentient being is endowed with the essence of Buddhahood, just as oil pervades every sesame seed. Ignorance is nothing more than lack of awareness of this very Buddha-nature, as when a pauper does not see the golden pot buried beneath his own hut. The spiritual path is thus a rediscovery of this forgotten nature, just as one sees again the immutable brilliance of the sun once the clouds that were masking it have been blown away.

The remarkable feature of the Tibetan tradition of the three *yanas* is how each step of the gradual path is enhanced with the practice of the next. Just as an alchemist might transform a piece of iron, first into copper and finally into gold, so the renunciation of the Lesser Vehicle is ennobled and widened by the universal compassion of the Great Vehicle, which itself becomes infinitely vast and profound when suffused by the view of the Adamantine Vehicle.

Shabkar appeared at a time when the integrity of the doctrine had eroded and many invaluable teachings were on the verge of disappearing. Sectarian bitterness often prevailed over pure perception and mutual respect. Amdo was mainly a Gelukpa stronghold, strewn with smaller monasteries and retreat centers founded by highly realized Nyingmapa yogins such as Do Drupchen Trinley Öser, Dola Jigme Kalzang, and Chöying Topden Dorje.

In this situation, which often led to narrow-mindedness, Shabkar, transcending all sectarianism, perceived the deep unity of all traditions. He made fruitful use of the extraordinary potential inherent in combining the altruistic Mind Training taught by Atisha (and developed by Tsongkhapa as the foundation of the gradual path) with the most profound practices of the Nyingma tradition. Tibetan masters often say that understanding the teachings of all Buddhist traditions to be noncontradictory is the sign of true knowledge. Shabkar says,

In the snow ranges of Tibet,
Owing to the kindness of sublime beings of
    the past,
Many profound teachings were taught.

These days most practitioners
Hold the various teachings to be contradictory,
Like heat and cold.
They praise some teachings and disparage
    others.

Some holy beings have said that
Madhyamika, Mahamudra, and
    Dzogchen
Are like sugar, molasses, and honey:
One is as good as the other.
For this reason, I have listened to
And practiced all of them without
    partiality.

Shabkar can thus be compared to the other masters of the nonsectarian (Rimey) movement who, in the nineteenth century, restored the spiritual integrity and vigor of Tibetan Buddhism and saved it from sinking into a quagmire of doctrinal contention, far removed from spiritual realization and pure perception.

Shabkar's Biographies

Tibetan hagiographies are called *namthar*, which means "perfect, or complete, liberation." A *namthar* is not only the detailed account of a saintly person's life, but the description of his or her journey to liberation: a narrative and a teaching as well (see Willis 1985). More than any other teaching in fact, a *namthar* leaves a deep impression on the reader's mind. Far from abstract considerations, it puts in our hands a chart to guide us on the journey, a testimony that the journey can be accomplished, and a powerful incentive to set out swiftly on the path. *Namthars* of recent masters remind one that these accounts are not ancient fairy tales; they demonstrate that, even in our time, there are accomplished beings who are living examples of enlightenment.[19]

This volume, entitled *The King of Wish-granting Jewels That Fulfills the Hopes of all Fortunate Disciples who Seek Liberation, the detailed narration of the life and liberation of the great vajra-holder Shabkar, refuge and protector for all sentient beings of this dark age* is a translation of Shabkar's autobiography describing the events of his life up to the age of fifty-six. It constitutes the 970-page first part of volume Ka of Shabkar's *Collected Writings*.

Fine wooden blocks of this work had been carved at Tashikhyil Hermitage, Shabkar's seat in Amdo, but were destroyed after the Chinese invasion of 1959. A few prints made from these were brought from Tibet and a two-volume reprint was made in India in 1983 under the auspices of H.H. Dilgo Khyentse Rinpoche. In 1985, the Qinghai Nationalities Press also published a 1097-page edition in book form.

A second, 684-page autobiographical volume (Ka, part 2), not translated here, covers Shabkar's life from the age of fifty-six until his death at the age of seventy. It contains spiritual songs and teachings, interspersed with brief descriptions of Shabkar's travels in Amdo and his meetings with his disciples and with other teachers. This later work ends with a section in which Changlung Tulku Khyapdal Longyang,[20] one of Shabkar's closest disciples, recounts important events and miracles performed by Shabkar that are not included in the autobiographies, and describes the last moments of the master's life.

Reprints of volume Ka, part 2, were also made in India (as vol. 3 of the *Collected Writings*) and in Tibet by the Qinghai Nationalities Press (TS 2). Valuable biographical information can also be gathered from Shabkar's *Collection of Songs* and from his other writings.

According to reliable Tibetan sources, a manuscript of Shabkar's *Secret Autobiography (gsang ba'i rnam thar)*, for which wooden blocks were never carved, has been preserved in Amdo.

Genesis of the Autobiography
Between 1806 and 1809, while he was staying at Tsonying Island, Shabkar wrote down some of his early life-story at the request of Pema Rangdrol and other disciples. A manuscript of this first autobiography has been found in northern Nepal (see Appendix 6, *rnam thar dngos*). It is clear that Shabkar must have referred to this first version when compiling the initial chapters of the complete autobiography, since much of the material is identical. Curiously enough, a few anecdotes and details mentioned in the first version do not appear in the more exhaustive final version.

Pema Rangdrol also composed a biography covering the events of his master's life up to Shabkar's pilgrimage to central Tibet (1810).[21] This work has not survived.

At Lapchi (1819–22), Shabkar recounted his life-story to a group of disciples, who then wrote down what they had heard. Finally, in 1837, acceding to the persistent requests of his disciples, Shabkar himself began composing the first section of his complete autobiography.

Insight into the composition of the final version may arise through examination of a set of three manuscripts (DOL 1, 2, 3) discovered in the Tarap Valley of Dolpo, in Nepal.[22] These texts reveal that the majority of the material in chapter 11 and all of the songs and teachings in chapter 12 already existed in final form as early

as 1814–24. The Dolpo manuscripts end abruptly with an appeal to generous patrons to contribute to the restoration of the Tashi Gomang stupa of Chung Riwoche which occurred in 1824.[23] After the restoration, Shabkar left western Tibet. For these and other reasons,[24] it is logical to assume that the Dolpo manuscripts, or perhaps the texts from which they were copied, were compiled during the time Shabkar lived in western Tibet (1814–24). The remaining songs from the Dolpo manuscripts which were not used in the 1837 autobiography form part of the second volume of Shabkar's *Collected Songs* (TS 4), which was compiled after he returned to Amdo.

Chapters 11 and 12 of the autobiography are thus a vivid account, written down in 1837, of the events of Shabkar's life at Kailash and in Nepal. They are interspersed with songs he had sung and teachings he had given, and which had been written down at the very time those events took place (1814–24). These songs and teachings are therefore much more likely to be an accurate rendering of Shabkar's words than if they had merely been reconstructed from memory twenty years after the events had occurred.

In other cases as well, it is clear that Shabkar kept written records of his songs and teachings. From Tsonying Island, for instance, Shabkar sent a collection of a thousand songs to his friends and disciples at Rekong.[25]

There are also collections of songs related to each of the main sacred places where Shabkar lived and meditated (see Appendix 5). One may thus infer that Shabkar chose to incorporate into his final 1837 autobiography a selection of the many songs he had composed throughout his life, the rest being compiled into his *Collected Songs*.

Shabkar's Former Incarnations
In chapter 14, at the request of a disciple, Shabkar writes a prayer that recounts his previous incarnations within all the main schools of Buddhism in Tibet:

> Many, many aeons ago,
> Having swiftly attained perfect
>   Buddhahood,

To benefit sentient beings and the Dharma
 of the Buddha,
He manifested in whatever manner was
 appropriate to transform beings.

At the time of the Buddha he was
 Avalokiteshvara,
In the land of India he was Manjush-
 rimitra,
In the center of Tibet he became Trenpa
 Namkha,
In the Kagyu tradition he was Milarepa,
In the Kadampa lineage he was the
 Glorious Gyalse Thogme,
In the Ganden lineage he was the Lord
 Lodrö Gyaltsen,
In the nonsectarian lineage he manifested
 to beings as Thangtong Gyalpo.

Now he is the protector of beings,
 Shabkarpa.
In future, in the presence of the Lords of
 the Five Families,
In Manifest Joy and every other
 Buddhafield,
He will be a supreme son
Who will lead all those who have made a
 connection with him
To whichever Pure Land they desire.

Fundamentally, Shabkar was considered to
be an emanation of Avalokiteshvara, the Buddha
of compassion,[26] which would account for the
strong emphasis which he places on compassion
and Bodhicitta in his practice and teachings.

Shabkar was also an emanation of Manjushrimitra (in Tibetan Jampel Shenyen),[27] one of
the main patriarchs of the Nyingma tradition.
Manjushrimitra was a disciple of Garab Dorje
(the first master of the Dzogchen lineage) and the
teacher of Shri Singha and Guru Padmasambhava.

According to Buddhist sources, Trenpa
Namkha was a Bönpo master who embraced
Buddhism and became one of the twenty-five
main disciples of Padmasambhava. Having
attained realization, he was able to manifest various miraculous powers. In particular, he was
able to tame the fierce wild yaks of the northern
plateaus of Tibet. As related in a short biography
by Jamyang Khyentse Wangpo written according to traditional Bönpo sources, Trenpa Namkha
was an extraordinary being.[28] He was said to be
the father of Pema Thongdrol, a name given to
Padmasambhava by the Bönpo, who considered
him to have been born of a human mother
rather than from a lotus.

However, it is as an emanation of Jetsun
Milarepa, the cotton-clad yogin (1040–1123),
that Shabkar is chiefly celebrated. His life of
renunciation and solitary practice, the large following of renunciate disciples he had in the later
part of his life, and his inexhaustible faculty for
teaching through improvised songs are strikingly
reminiscent of Milarepa's life. Shabkar's principal teacher, the Mongolian king Chögyal Ngakyi
Wangpo, was himself considered to be an incarnation of Marpa the Translator, Milarepa's spiritual master.

When Shabkar went to the Cave of the
Subjugation of Mara in Lapchi where Milarepa
had spent a long period in solitary retreat, he
indicated the existence of a second entrance to
the cave. The entrance was unearthed and the
remnants of Milarepa's stone hearth were rediscovered. All those assembled there were con-
vinced by these events that Shabkar was in fact
the incarnation of Milarepa (see chap. 13).

Shabkar is frequently depicted as a yogin
who is posed like Milarepa, his right hand cupped
behind his ear—a gesture which signifies listening to the celestial voices of the dakinis. A few
details, however, distinguish the two masters.
Shabkar's long hair is not loose on his shoulders
like that of Milarepa, but is coiled and knotted
above his head in the fashion of the yogins of
Rekong. Also, Shabkar holds a skull-cup in his
left hand and has a walking stick at his left side;
his upper garb is indeed the white cotton shawl
of a *repa*,[29] but his lower robe is the patched red
skirt of a fully ordained monk.

In the Kadampa and Sakya lineages,
Shabkar was considered to have been the incarnation of Ngulchu Gyalse Thogme (1295–1369),
a great Bodhisattva and teacher who exemplified compassion in all his actions and embodied

the Kadampa ideal of exchanging one's own happiness for the suffering of others (as can be seen in his biography by Palden Yeshe).[30] Gyalse Thogme was the author of the well-known *Thirty-Seven-fold Practice of a Bodhisattva*, which presents the essence of the Bodhisattva path, and of commentaries on *Engaging in the Bodhisattva's Activity* (*Bodhicaryavatara*) and several other major Mahayana texts.

In the Ganden, or Geluk, lineage (the New Kadampa tradition), Shabkar was considered to have been the Lord Chen-ngawa Lodrö Gyaltsen (1402–72), a disciple of Je Tsongkhapa belonging to the Phagmo Drupa family; he was the author of many teachings on Lojong practice, including the famous compendium *Opening the Door to Mind Training*.[31]

In the nonsectarian lineages, Shabkar was Thangtong Gyalpo (1361–1485), the "King of the Empty Plain,"[32] an incarnation of Avalokiteshvara and of the mind-aspect of Guru Padmasambhava.[33] This famous Tibetan *siddha* practiced and taught Buddhist teachings from all the traditional lineages, although his own special realization came from the practice of the Northern Treasures[34] of the Nyingma tradition and of the Shangpa Kagyu teachings, which he received in three visions from the wisdom dakini Niguma.[35] In a vision, Thangtong Gyalpo also traveled to the Glorious Copper-colored Mountain where he received teaching from Guru Padmasambhava himself. He is famous for his meditation practice for achieving longevity, probably the most popular of its kind in Tibet.[36] Following a vision of Vajravarahi, he wrote a set of vajra verses which were later elaborated by his spiritual heirs into a complete cycle of spiritual practices known as the *Oral Transmission of Thangtong*.[37] He is also remembered for building fifty-eight iron suspension bridges, many of which still span the rivers of Tibet and Bhutan. Among the native people he is beloved for having created the well-known Ache Lhamo dance rituals, colloquially known as Tibetan Opera. He passed away at Chung Riwoche, in western Tibet, at the age of 125 years.

His Teachers and Lineage

Although Shabkar sought the blessing and instructions of numerous teachers throughout his life, three were, by his own account (see TN 4, p. 823), central to his spiritual development: Jampel Dorje, Jamyang Gyatso and, above all, Chögyal Ngakyi Wangpo.

At eleven Shabkar entered the community of *ngakpas* of Shohong, "a community known for their pure *samaya*[38] and unshakable faith in the Secret Mantra tradition of the Early Translation school." At twelve he was introduced to basic Nyingma practice by the master Orgyen Trinley Namgyal (see chap. 1, fol. 18a).

Shabkar's first Dzogchen master was Jampel Dorje Rinpoche (d. 1817?)[39] who gave him the initiation of the *Dzogchen Ati Zabdon*[40] of the Mindroling tradition and the instructions that introduce one directly to the ultimate nature of mind. These and other transmissions given by this master suggest that he was a holder of the traditions of the two main Nyingma monasteries of central Tibet: Mindroling and Dorje Trak (see chap. 1, fol. 19a).

Around 1797 Shabkar met Jamyang Gyatso Rinpoche (d. 1800), a highly accomplished master thoroughly versed in the teachings of both Nyingma and Sarma, the Old and the New traditions (see Appendix 1). Shabkar revered him greatly and had several visions and dreams of him after this master passed away. From him, Shabkar received many empowerments on the cycles of rediscovered treasures of Ratön Tertön,[41] Tennyi Lingpa (1480–1535),[42] Karma Lingpa (b. 1326), Jigme Lingpa (1729–98),[43] and Lodrak Drupchen Lekyi Dorje (1326–1401),[44] as well as teachings on Mind Training and meditation.

The list of the Nyingma teachings Shabkar received from Jamyang Gyatso, and later from Chögyal Ngakyi Wangpo and other masters, shows close connections between the lineages of these two spiritual masters, as it appears in tables 1, 2, and 4.

At the age of twenty, Shabkar received the full monastic ordination at Dobi Monastery[45] from Arik Geshe Rinpoche Jampel Gelek Gyaltsen (1726–1803), also known as Gyaltsen Öser, a famous Gelukpa scholar-saint considered to be an emanation of Nagarjuna.[46] He gave Shabkar the monastic name Jampa Chödar, *The Loving*

One Who Spreads the Dharma, and advised him to
meet the great Nyingma master Chögyal Ngakyi
Wangpo.

The dominant inspiration of Shabkar's spiritual life, his root teacher, was Chögyal Ngakyi
Wangpo (1736–1807), said to be an emanation
of both Guru Padmasambhava and Marpa the
Translator.

His full name was Pöntsang Dalai Tai Chingwang Ngawang Dargye Pal Zangpo, the "Great
Oceanic King, Glorious and Excellent All-Blooming Lord of Speech." There is no known biography of this master; however, a few details about
his life can be gathered from Shabkar's autobiography, from the *Ocean Annals* (*a mdo chos 'byung
deb ther rgya mtsho,* the *Amdo Chöjung* abbreviated
below as AC), and from oral tradition.

Ngakyi Wangpo's predecessors were influential rulers, and one of them had donated the
land to Jamyang Shepa[47] for the construction of
Labrang Tashikhyil Monastery, founded in
1708/10. (Ngakyi Wangpo's complex ancestry
is summarized in table 3 and in Appendix 3.)

Although his family had been connected
with the Gelukpa lineage, Ngakyi Wangpo
became a Nyingma practitioner. He was a disciple of Orgyen Tendzin, the spiritual heir of the
great tertön Kunzang Dechen Gyalpo (see
Appendix 4). Ngakyi Wangpo became one of
the main holders of Dechen Gyalpo's rediscovered treasures, although it is uncertain whether
he met the tertön himself. Ngakyi Wangpo was
also a disciple of the first Do Drupchen, Jigme
Trinley Öser, the principal Dharma heir of
Rigdzin Jigme Lingpa's *Longchen Nyingthig* lineage.[48]

Chögyal Ngakyi Wangpo, better known as
a ruler under the name of Ngawang Dargye, was
one of the two kings who governed the Kokonor
region.[49] He was a descendant of Gushri Khan
(1592–1654), a Qosot Mongol king called Tendzin Chögyal by the Tibetans. His tribal group
had migrated from their Urumchi grazing land,
in what is today Xinjiang, to new territories
south of Lake Kokonor, near the Machu River
(the upper reaches of the Huang Ho, the Yellow
River of China).

In Shabkar's autobiography, "Mongolia" (*sog
po*) refers to the area that might be called "Little
Mongolia," a district south of Rekong in Amdo
where many tent-dwelling Mongolian tribes had
settled two centuries before. Thoroughly assimilated, they spoke only the local Amdo Tibetan
dialect.

Urgeh, Chögyal Ngakyi Wangpo's seat in
this nomadic area, was a large encampment of
tents. There was, however, at least one major
monastery in the area, called Urgeh Tratsang
Sang-ngak Mingyeling. It was founded under
the patronage of one of Ngakyi Wangpo's ancestors, Dar Gyalpo Shoktu. Ngakyi Wangpo further enhanced the monastery's prosperity; he
had 108 monks reside there, and arranged that
large ceremonies be performed every year. The
monastery initially belonged to the Gelukpa
school but, probably under the inspiration of
Ngakyi Wangpo, it later turned to the Nyingma
tradition.[50]

Beginning with teaching *Lobjong* teaching on
Mind Training, Ngakyi Wangpo gradually taught
Shabkar the complete path of the three vehicles.
His teachings focused on the Vajrayana empowerment of the *Wish-fulfilling Gem, Hayagriva and
Varahi,* a spiritual treasure (*gter ma*) revealed by
Tertön Kunzang Dechen Gyalpo that was to
become Shabkar's main practice. It was during
this empowerment that Shabkar received the
name Tsogdruk Rangdrol, "Self-liberation of the
Six Senses," which refers to the natural liberation of ordinary dualistic perception (which occurs
by means of the perceptions associated with each
of the five sense organs and with the sixth sense,
intellectual cognition) into the ultimate nature of
emptiness and awareness.

Since the practice of the *Wish-fulfilling Gem,
Hayagriva and Varahi* occupies a central place in
Shabkar's spiritual practice and in his lineage, its
origin is described in Appendix 4.

The Dharma King Ngakyi Wangpo then
gave Shabkar teachings on the development stage,
related to the Vase Empowerment. Next, he
taught about the channels and energy practice of
tummo, related to the Secret Empowerment. Then
he gave teachings on the bliss-void practice of
the *mudra,* related to the Wisdom Empowerment; and finally, he gave teachings on Trekchö

and Thögal, related to the Word, or Symbolic Empowerment.

On subsequent occasions, he imparted to Shabkar the transmission of teachings from Lodrak Drupchen Lekyi Dorje; teachings on Mahamudra; the *Dzogchen Yeshe Lama*[51] of Jigme Lingpa; Nyima Trakpa's (1647–1710) Dzogchen teaching; and the *Khandro Nyingthig*,[52] the chief Dzogchen teachings of Guru Padmasambhava as revealed by Pema Ledrelstel.

Ngakyi Wangpo inspired Shabkar to study the *Seven Treasuries*, the *Three Great Chariots*, and other writings of Longchen Rabjam, a corpus of works that form the quintessence of the Nyingma tradition. He also requested one of his own teachers, Lama Jimba, to teach Shabkar the Vinaya, the rules of monastic discipline.

Until his death in 1807, Ngakyi Wangpo guided Shabkar with great love and tenderness, and considered him his spiritual heir. After his guru passed away, Shabkar had several visions of him. It is said that before leaving this world Chögyal Ngakyi Wangpo showed his disciples a rosary on which he had recited the Vajra Guru mantra of Guru Padmasambhava one hundred million times (see AC, vol. 2, p. 123). He told them, "Once I am dead, don't remove this rosary from my neck; cremate it with my body." After the cremation, the rosary was lying still intact in the ashes, and images of the Buddha Shakyamuni and of other deities were found on the Dharma King's skull as well as on the bones of his hand. Shabkar had many other teachers, the most important of whom are listed in Appendix 2.

Shabkar's lineage still flourishes today. Not only are his writings extremely popular among Tibetans, but Dechen Gyalpo's esoteric *Wish-fulfilling Gem, Hayagriva and Varahi*, which was transmitted through Shabkar, is still practiced today (see Appendix 4). There has rarely been a lama who traveled around Tibet as much as Shabkar did, and inspired so many disciples over the entire country. At the end of the autobiography Shabkar says:

I had a hundred and eight great spiritual children, wise and accomplished,

Who, having perfected themselves, were able to benefit others;
Over three hundred practitioners who, having attained
Consummate loving-kindness, compassion and Bodhicitta, ceased eating meat;
One thousand eight hundred great meditators, men and women,
Who gave up all concern for this life and practiced in solitary places;
Tens of thousands of monks and nuns dwelling in monasteries
Who worked hard at prostrations, offerings, circumambulations and other virtuous actions;
And countless *ngakpas*, village practitioners and householders
Who fasted, completed extensive recitations and sadhanas, and chanted the *mani*.

I ransomed the lives of several hundred thousand animals[53]—
Goats, sheep, birds, fish, and other wild animals.
I protected and saved the lives of five hundred people
Afflicted by hunger, cold, sickness, evil influences and enemies.
I settled eighteen major feuds that were killing men and horses,
Thus halting the line of those who were going to hell.

In brief, by the compassion of my gurus and the Three Jewels
Great benefit was brought to the Dharma and all beings.
To conclude every action I did in accordance with Dharma,
I offered vast dedications and prayers.

A brief survey of Shabkar's most important disciples is given in Appendix 6.

Conventions Used in this Work
In the body of the text itself, Tibetan names and terms appear in an approximate phonetic tran-

scription to provide the reader with a notion of the way in which the Tibetan words are pronounced. Exact transliterations appear in the notes and indexes. Because Sanskrit terms are not common in our translation, we have omitted diacritical marks for the sake of simplicity. Specialized scholars will have no difficulty identifying the Sanskrit terms and phrases that do occur. The page numbers of the Tibetan text are given within square brackets and correspond to the Tibetan numbering of the Tashikhyil wood-block prints. Thus "[21a]", for instance, refers to the recto of the twenty-first folio.

Several indexes were compiled. The indexes of names of persons, places, and scriptures also contains the transliteration all of Tibetan names according to the Wylie system. The general index is a thematic index of topics and concepts. A list of the abbreviations used in the work is given at the end of the main text. For readers interested in more details about Shabkar's teachers, writings, and disciples, several appendices are provided.

Shabkar usually follows the traditional format, which appends a lengthy verse summary to the end of each chapter. Since these summaries appear redundant in an English translation, we have omitted them.

About the Translation

The first impulse to undertake this translation occurred in the early eighties to a few Dharma friends over a cup of tea at Shechen Monastery, near the Great Stupa of Bodhnath in Kathmandu Valley. We were speaking of the unique enchantment of Shabkar's autobiography and found that all of us cherished the wish to translate it into Western languages, but hesitated to embark on such a vast project. One person said, "Let's just do it!" and everyone present agreed.

The text was divided up among the translators, some taking large sections, and others single chapters. After a few months, first drafts appeared. Then, the author of this introduction began to review the drafts that he and the others had prepared. Over a longer period of time, he prepared the subsequent drafts, notes, and appendices, in constant collaboration with

learned lamas and with the main editor who reworked extensively the songs and poems. This work was carried out mainly in the East, which enabled the translators to consult learned and accomplished masters of all schools of Tibetan Buddhism. Not only the guidance of these lamas, but the help of shepherds, painters, doctors, house-builders, and cooks was solicited to elucidate the meaning of some obscure words and phrases. Wiser translators would doubtless have done better, but we did our best within our capacities. The main aim in translating this autobiography was a wish to share with others its depth and beauty, as a remarkable source of inspiration for finding meaning in one's life. To conclude with Shabkar's own prayer:

> For all who read my life-story and songs
> May the doors to the three lower realms
> be shut.
> May all who hear my life-story and songs
> Obtain in their next life a human or
> celestial birth.
> May all who remember or simply touch
> my life-story and songs
> Be reborn in the same realm where I will
> have been reborn.
>
> May all those who, when asked, recite my
> life-story and songs
> Be filled with blessings and achieve
> liberation.
> May the aspirations of those who act
> according to my life-story and songs
> Be accomplished in harmony with the
> Dharma.
> Wherever my life-story and songs are
> found, in monasteries and villages,
> May they fulfill all needs and aspirations
> like a Wish-fulfilling Jewel.
> Wherever my life-story and songs are
> carried,
> May the Dharma, general auspiciousness,
> and excellent virtue blossom.

MATTHIEU RICARD
Shechen Tennyi Dargyeling Monastery
Bodhnath, Nepal, 24 January 1994

Notes

1. Jetsun Milarepa, Shepai Dorje ("Laughing Vajra," *rje btsun mi la ras pa bzhad pa'i rdo rje*, 1040–1123), the most famous of all Tibetan ascetics. Disciple of Marpa Lotsawa, father of the Kagyu lineage, he was the archetype of the perfect disciple, practitioner, and teacher. See Bacot (1925), Chang (1962), and Lhalungpa (1984).

2. The twelve-syllable mantra of Guru Padmasambhava: OM AH HUM VAJRA GURU PADMA SIDDHI HUM.

3. Marpa Lotsawa Chökyi Lodrö (*mar pa lo tsa ba chos kyi blo gros*, 1012–97). The first Tibetan patriarch of the Kagyu lineage. Born in Lodrak, southern Tibet, he first studied with Drogmi Lotsawa and then traveled to India three times to meet his root teacher, the great *pandita* and *siddha* Naropa, as well as his other gurus, Jnanagarbha, Kukuripa, and Maitripa (1012–97), spending seventeen years in India and bringing the Mahamudra lineage and teachings to Tibet. See *The Life of Marpa the Translator* (Prajna Press, 1982).

4. On the origin of the name *zhabs dkar*, see TS 4, p. 703. On the Cave of Miracles, see chap. 11, note 9.

5. On the architecture and symbolism of stupas, see SD, p. 210.

6. Patrul Rinpoche, Orgyen Jigme Chökyi Wangpo (*dpal sprul o rgyan 'jigs med chos kyi dbang po*, 1808–87), also known as Dzogchen Palge Tulku *(rdzogs chen dpal dge sprul sku)*. Uncompromising in his interpretation of the teachings, Patrul Rinpoche lived as he taught, wandering all over eastern Tibet, taking shelter in mountain caves or under forest trees, free of all the trappings of wealth, position and self-importance. A prolific author and commentator, his teachings are still very much alive today, offering a constant source of inspiration to all practitioners of Tibetan Buddhism. The story of Patrul Rinpoche going to meet Shabkar is found in Patrul Rinpoche's short biographies by Do Drupchen Tenpai Nyima (*rdo grub bstan pa'i nyi ma*, 1865–1926) and by Khenpo Kunzang Palden (*mkhan po kun bzang dpal ldan*, c. 1870–c. 1940), and was augmented here by an oral tradition recounted by Tulku Urgyen Rinpoche (b. 1919).

7. The two recognized successive reincarnations of Shabkar were Thekchog Tenpai Nyima (*theg mchog bstan pa'i nyi ma*) and Yeshe Tenpai Gyaltsen (*ye shes bstan pa'i rgyal mtshan*). See RO, p. 646.

8. Dilgo Khyentse Rinpoche (*dil mgo mkhyen brtse rin po che*, 1910–91) was one of the greatest Nyingma masters of our times, and the most exemplary present-day exponent of the nonsectarian movement (*ris med*). He was blessed shortly after his birth by the great Mipham Rinpoche (1846–1912), was recognized by Jamyang Loter Wangpo (1847–1914), and enthroned by Shechen Gyaltsap Pema Namgyal (1871–1926) as the mind-emanation of Jamyang Khyentse Wangpo (1820–92). Dilgo Khyentse Rinpoche spent twenty-two years in contemplative retreat, and studied with more than fifty of the most eminent teachers of his time. His two principal spiritual masters were Shechen Gyaltsap Pema Namgyal and Jamyang Khyentse Chökyi Lodrö (1893–1959, the activity-emanation of Khyentse Wangpo), both of whom considered him as their chief disciple. A treasure discoverer (*gter ston*), a great poet, a scholar with unfathomable knowledge, and a tireless and compassionate teacher with whom luminaries, including the fourteenth Dalai Lama, studied, he was widely renowned for his ability to transmit the teachings of each Buddhist lineage according to its own tradition.

9. The *Treasury of Rediscovered Teachings* (*rin chen gter mdzod*) is a sixty-three-volume collection of spiritual treasures (*gter ma*, see Appendix 1) collected by Jamgön Kongtrul Lodrö Thaye (see note 13 below) in the nineteenth century.

10. Regarding the political situation and the sectarian rivalries in eighteenth-century Amdo, see Pal Gyalkhar (1989) and M. Kapstein (1989).

11. "Pure perception" or "pure vision" (*dag snang*) implies not only to respect the various schools of the Buddhist tradition as being authentic holders of the Buddha's teaching, but also, in a wider perspective, to perceive the entire phenomenal world, including all sentient beings, as being primordially pure and perfect.

12. Jowo Je Palden Atisha (*jo bo rje dpal ldan a ti sha*), Dipamkara Sri Jnana (982–1054). Born in Bengal on the outskirts of the present-day Dacca, he was of royal descent and first studied in India with great Vajrayana masters including Maitripa, Rahulagupta, Virupa, Guru Dharmarakshita (a great master of compassion, who gave his own flesh in generosity), and Maitriyogin (*'byams pa'i rnal 'byor*), who could literally take others' suffering upon himself. He then crossed the sea to Sumatra, where he studied for twelve years with Serlingpa Dharmakirti (*gser gling pa chos kyi grags pa*). On his return to India he became the abbot of the famous Buddhist University of Vikramashila. He was invited to Tibet by King Yeshe Ö (*ye*

shes 'od) and his nephew, Changchup Ö *(byang chub 'od)*. In accordance with a prediction he had received in a vision of Arya Tara, he reached Tibet in 1040. He lived there until passing away at the age of seventy-three at Nyethang Drolma Lhakhang, south of Lhasa. Atisha was nicknamed "the Refuge *Pandita*," because he brought so many Tibetans onto the Buddhist path through bestowing refuge and related teachings. His particular teaching, known as Mind Training *(blo sbyong)*, became the core practice of the Kadampa lineage, of which he is the founder. Atisha had countless disciples, among whom the main ones in Tibet were Khutön Tsöndru Yundrung *(khu ston brtson 'grus g.yung drung)*, Ngok Lekpai Lodrö *(rngog legs pa'i blo gros)*, and the layman Drom Tönpa *('brom ston pa)*. On the biographical tradition concerning Atisha, see H. Eimer (1982).

Tsongkhapa Lobzang Trakpa *(tsong kha pa blo bzang grags pa*, 1357–1419) was born in the Tsongkha region of Amdo province. Gifted with exceptional intellectual and spiritual abilities, he studied with more than a hundred teachers of various lineages. Having been blessed by visions of Manjushri, the Buddha of wisdom, he wrote numerous treatises, collected in eighteen volumes. The emphasis Tsongkhapa put on the graded approach to the spiritual path, on monastic discipline, and on extensive philosophical studies and epistemological debate as a prerequisite to contemplative practice, has defined the Gelukpa school. This lineage is also known as the New Kadampa tradition or as the tradition of Ganden, from the name of the monastery that Tsongkhapa founded near Lhasa, and where he passed away. He had many disciples, among whom were Gyaltsap Je *(rgyal tshab rje*, 1364–1432), Khedrup Je Gelek Palzang *(mkhas grub rje dge legs dpal bzang*, 1385–1438), who succeeded him on the throne of Ganden, and Gedun Drub *(dge 'dun grub*, 1391–1474), who is counted as the first Dalai Lama. Regarding the senselessness of sectarianism, see H.H. Dudjom Rinpoche in NS, pp. 887–940.

13. See G. Smith (1970). Jamgön Kongtrul Lodrö Thaye, Yonten Gyatso *('jam mgon kong sprul blo gros mtha' yas, yon tan rgya mtsho*, 1813–99); Jamyang Khyentse Wangpo *('jam dbyangs mkhyen brtse'i dbang po*, 1820–92), Patrul Rinpoche, see note above; and Lama Mipham Chogle Namgyal *(mi pham phyogs las rnam rgyal*, 1846–1912), also known as Mipham Jamyang Gyatso *(mi pham 'jam dbyangs rgya mtsho)* or Jampel Gyepai Dorje *('jam dpal dgyes pa'i rdo rje)*. These masters and others inspired a remarkable movement known as Rimey *(ris med)*, "nonsectarian," which encouraged followers of the different traditions not to remain confined in the particular philosophical viewpoints espoused by their own schools, but to study and practice all the traditions of Tibetan Buddhism with respect and pure perception in order to gain a profound conviction of the unity of the teachings.

14. For exhaustive presentations of the view, meditation, and action of the nine vehicles, see H.H. Dudjom Rinpoche's *Nyingma School of Tibetan Buddhism: Its Fundamentals and History*, translated and edited by Gyurme Dorje and Matthew Kapstein (1991), abbreviated as NS; and Tulku Thondup's *Buddha Mind* (1989), abbreviated hereafter as BM.

15. Chiefly from the *Seven Treasuries (mdzod bdun)* and the *Trilogy of Natural Ease (ngal gso skor gsum)*, the famous treatises of Gyalwa Longchen Rabjam Drime Öser *(rgyal ba klong chen rab 'byams dri med 'od zer*, 1308–63), the foremost teacher of the Nyingma tradition. For accounts of his amazing life-story, see NS, pp. 575–96 and BM, pp. 144–88. A disciple of teachers of all schools and, above all, the Dharma heir of the great vidyadhara (awareness-holder) Rigdzin Kumaradza Yeshe Shonnu *(rig 'dzin kumaradza ye shes gzhon nu*, 1266–1343), he was the first to commit to writing the oral traditions of the complete explanation of the nine vehicles in general and of the Great Perfection in particular, thus elucidating the meaning of the *Seventeen Tantras of the Great Perfection (rdzogs chen rgyud bcu bdun)*. For translations and anthologies of his writings, see Guenther (1975 and 1976) and BM.

16. See NS, vol. 1, pp. 510–22.

17. Skt. Guru Padmasambhava, or Padmakara (Tib. *padma 'byung gnas)*. As recorded in the *Sutra of Great Nirvana* and in other prophecies, Buddha Shakyamuni said, shortly before passing into nirvana, that since he had been born as a human being in this life, he had not taught extensively the esoteric teachings of the tantras. He predicted that he would return to this world after twelve years by means of a miraculous birth in order to expound the tantric teachings. This rebirth was Guru Padmasambhava, who emanated from the heart of Buddha Amitabha and miraculously appeared in the form of an eight-year-old child upon a lotus at Danakosha Lake in Oddiyana. On *termas*, see NS and Appendix 1, p. 555.

18. For a traditional approach on the relation between Buddhism and Bön, see BM, pp. 106–12 and NS, pp. 936ff.

19. On the nature and general definition of *namthar (rnam thar)*, see J. Willis (1985).

20. For Changlung Tulku Khyapdal Longyang

(*spyang lung sprul sku khyab brdal klong yangs*), see Appendix 6. He was the reembodiment of Changlung Namkha Jigme (*spyang lung nam mkha' 'jigs med*, 1769–1833).

21. This work of Pema Rangdrol has not been found.

22. DOL 1, 2 and 3: These manuscripts are now in the hands of disciples of Kekar Do-ngak Norbu (*skas dkar mdo sngags nor bu*) and Pema Thongdrol (*padma mthong grol*) in Dolpo, northern Nepal. Do-ngak Norbu was a student of Orgyen Tendzin (*o rgyan bstan 'dzin*), himself a disciple of Jimba Norbu (*shyin pa nor bu*). The latter was one of Shabkar's chief disciples in western Tibet (see chap. 11 and Appendices 5 and 6).

23. Tashi Gomang stupa (*bkra shis sgo mang*): the stupa of Chung Riwoche (*cung ri bo che*). See chap. 14, fol. 396a, and Vitali (1990).

24. There would have been little purpose in calligraphing these manuscripts, which are often corrupt and abound in spelling mistakes, after the composition of the autobiography, for which excellent wooden blocks were carved at Tashikhyil while Shabkar was alive. If the compilation of the Dolpo manuscripts had been posterior to or contemporary with the biography, one would not expect it to be limited to events that happened before 1824. Moreover, the colophon of DOL 1 states that this volume of songs was produced by Orgyen Tendzin, Jimba Norbu's student. Jimba Norbu met Shabkar at Kailash and was also with him at Lapchi and Lhasa, but did not follow him to Amdo (see chap. 15, fol. 424b). Songs and teachings from chapter 11 are found in DOL 1 and 2. All the songs and teachings of chapter 12, together with a few songs of chapter 13, are found in DOL 3. (See Appendix 5.)

25. See chap. 6, fol. 124b. These songs are included the *Flight of the Garuda* (see Appendix 5).

26. Although Avalokiteshvara is often counted as one of the eight main Bodhisattvas, according to the Vajrayana tradition he is a a fully enlightened Buddha manifesting in the form of a Bodhisattva to benefit the beings according to their needs.

27. Jampel Shenyen (*'jam dpal bshes gnyen*) was one of the "eight vidyadharas of India" (*rgya gar rig 'dzin brgyad*). See NS, vol.1, pp. 490–94.

28. Trenpa Namkha (*dran pa nam mkha'*). See GC, vol. 1, p. 466 and TN, pp. 345–46. For a detailed study of this master according to a spiritual treasure (*gter ma*) of the *bsgrags pa bon* lineage, see Blondeau (1985).

29. A *repa* (*ras pa*), or "cotton-clad one," is a yogin skilled, like Milarepa, in the practice of "inner heat" (*tummo*). Such a yogin wears only a cotton garment even in the coldest weather.

30. The hagiography of Gyalse Ngulchu Thogme Zangpo Pal (*rgyal sras dngul chu thogs med bzang po dpal*, 1295–1369), known as the *Drop of Ambrosia; or, The Perfect Liberation of the Precious Bodhisattva Thogme* (*rgyal sras rin po che thogs med pa'i rnam thar bdud rtsi'i thigs pa*, 23 folios), was written by one of his close disciples, Palden Yeshe. Most of this biography has been translated as an introduction to H.H. Dilgo Khyentse Rinpoche's oral commentary on the *Thirty-Seven-fold Practice of a Bodhisattva* (*rgyal sras lag len so bdun ma*); Padmakara Translation Group, under publication.

31. The history of the *phag mo gru pa* line is recounted in a text called *rlangs kyi po ti bse ru rgyas pa*, of which there are several modern editions available (Dolanji 1975, Delhi 1974, Lhasa 1986 and 1989). See Chabpel Tsewang Phuntsok (1986).

For *Opening the Door to Mind Training* (*byang chub lam gyi rim pa la blo sbyong ba la thog mar blo sbyong chos kyi sgo 'byed*), see DZ, vol. 3, pp. 459–544.

32. See C. Stearns (1980) and J. Gyatso (1981, pp. 1–18, abbreviated below as TH). Several biographies of Thangtong Gyalpo are known, among which the main one is entitled *grub pa'i dbang phyug chen po lcags zam pa thang stong rgyal po'i rnam thar ngo mtshar kun gsal nor bu'i me long gsar pa*. It was written by Lochen Gyurme Dechen (*lo chen 'gyur med bde chen*, 1540–1615). Wood blocks of this biography have been carved at Thubten Chöling Monastery in Nepal under the inspiration of Dza Trulshik Rinpoche.

About the name "King of the Empty Plain," see TH, p. 37: While Thangtong Gyalpo was engaged in meditation in the Gyede Plain (*rgyas sde thang*) in Tsang, he had a vision of five dakinis, who approached him and sang verses of praise. One of the verses says,

> On the great spreading plain
> The yogin who understands emptiness
> Sits like a fearless king.
> Thus we name him King of the Empty Plain.

33. Enlightened beings may continue compassionate activities for sentient beings through various emanations, such as those of their body, speech, mind, enlightened qualities, and activity. Here Thangtong Gyalpo is said to have been an emanation of the mind-aspect of Guru Padmasambhava.

34. For Northern Treasures (*byang gter*), see chap. 1, note 48.

35. Shangpa Kagyu (*shangs pa bka' brgyud*), a branch of the *bka' brgyud* lineage, which originated with

Khyungpo Naljor (*khyung po rnal 'byor*, late eleventh to twelfth centuries). He traveled to India, where he received teachings from the dakini Niguma, the sister of Naropa (eleventh century), and the wisdom dakini Sukhasiddhi. See Kapstein (1980).

36. This longevity practice is known as *tshe sgrub 'chi med dpal gter*. See TH.

37. *Oral Transmission of Thangtong* (*thang stong snyan brgyud*). See TH, pp. 160–85.

38. *Samaya* (Skt.), in Tibetan *dam tshig*, meaning "pledge." *Samaya* entails taking the vows of the Vajrayana, and forms the sacred bond between disciple and spiritual master. When these vows, related to body, speech, and mind, are kept unsullied, spiritual realization is swiftly achieved. When they are damaged or broken, however, major obstacles and suffering are to be expected, hampering further progress on the path.

39. See chap. 11, fol. 290a. In the second half of the year 1817, Shabkar learns that Jampel Dorje has passed away, and sings a beautiful song of mourning. See also DOL 3, fols. 25b and 26b.

40. For *Dzogchen Ati Zabdon* (*rdzogs chen a ti zab don*), see chap. 1, note 44.

41. For Ratön Tertön, Topden Dorje (*rwa ston gter ston stobs ldan rdo rje*), see GC, vol. 3, p. 209, and TN, p. 608). An incarnation of Langchen Palgyi Senge (*rlangs chen dpal gyi seng ge*), he was born in Gyantse in the Tsang province of central Tibet (*gtsang rgyang rtse*). He was a descendant of Ra Lotsawa Dorje Drak (*rwa lo tsa ba rdo rje 'grags*), eleventh century. Topden Dorje's main teacher was Chöling Dewai Dorje (*chos gling bde ba'i rdo rje*); eventually he became the spiritual heir of this master's *termas*. When the Dzungar Mongols invaded Tibet, Topden Dorje followed his teacher to the sacred hidden land of the White Lotus (*sbas yul padma dkar po*). After Dewai Dorje passed away, Topden Dorje came back to Tsang; later he went to India and Sikkim as a wandering yogin. At Onphu Taktsang ('on phu stag tshang), near Samye in central Tibet, he revealed a large *terma* cycle of Vajra Kilaya. In the later part of his life he was honored by the regent Pholha Sonam Topgyal (*pho lha bsod nams stobs rgyas*, 1689–1747).

42. A look at the lineage and the successive reincarnations of Tennyi Lingpa is helpful for understanding the connections between the various masters from which Shabkar's lineage originated. (See tables 1 and 4). One will notice the connections between the lineages of Dechen Gyalpo's *termas* and of Jigme Lingpa's *Longchen Nyingthig*.

According to ND, p. 239 and BD, pp. 447–55, Tennyi Lingpa Pema Tsewang Gyalpo (*bstan gnyis gling pa padma tshe dbang rgyal po*, 1480–1535), born at Rongden (*rong ldan*) in Tsang, was the reincarnation of Lacham Nuchin Sale (*lha lcam nus 'byin sa le*). He revealed many *termas*, including the *Kunzang Nyingthig* (*kun bzang snying thig*), which is often quoted in Shabkar's writings. According to NG, Tennyi Lingpa is counted as one of the eight main *Lingpa*s. Among all of Tennyi Lingpa's revelations, the *Shitro Yeshe Thongdrol* (*zhi khro ye shes mthong grol*) is still widely practiced today in northern Nepal along with the Northern Termas (*byang gter*) of Rigdzin Gödem. Shabkar received the empowerment for the *Kunzang Nyingthig* from Jamyang Gyatso. Ngakyi Wangpo often quotes this cycle in his *Torch of Wisdom* (see Appendix 4). A later rebirth of Tennyi Lingpa was Namchak Tsasum Lingpa (*gnam lcags rtsa gsum gling pa*), Ratön Tertön's teacher and the father of Rigdzin Thukchog Dorje. According to a prayer to his own former incarnations (*o rgyan gter bdag gling pa'i 'khrung rab bsdus pa bcu gsum ma snang gsal me long*, in *Rediscovered Treasures of Namchag Tsa Sum Lingpa*, vol. 10, p. 28) by Tsasum Lingpa, Tennyi Lingpa would be the reincarnation of Drime Kunga. However, according to GC, vol. 2, p. 741. Drime Kunga was the teacher of Karpo Kunga Trakpa (*dkar po kun dga'i grags pa*), who himself was a teacher of Chogden Gonpo (b. 1497) and a contemporary of Pema Lingpa (1450–1521). This indicates that Drime Kunga antedated Tennyi Lingpa and was probably born in 1404 (see table 4).

Rigdzin Thukchog Dorje (*rig 'dzin thugs mchog rdo rje*; see GC, vol 3, p. 212), also known as the great treasure rediscoverer Hum Nag Drodul (*gter chen hum nag 'gro 'dul*). Thukchog Dorje was an emanation of Guru Padmasambhava's disciple Namkhai Nyingpo (*nam mkha'i snying po*). Born near Samye Chimphu (*bsam yas mchims phu*), he studied at Palri Monastery (*dpal ri dgon*). There he became known as Kyirong Chödze (*skyid grong chos mdzad*), although his real names were Ngawang Lapsum (*ngag dbang bslab gsum*) and Kunzang Trinley Dorje (*kun bzang phrin las rdo rje*). Thukchog Dorje's chief masters were Chöje Lingpa (*chos rje gling pa*), Ratön Tertön Topden Dorje (*rwa ston stobs ldan rdo rje;* see note 41), and especially the great *siddha* Chubri Drupchen Ngawang Kunzang Rangdrol (*lcub ri grub chen ngag dbang kun bzang rang grol*), from whom he received the transmission of the *Yangti Nagpo* (*yang ti nag po*) of Dungtso Repa (*dung mtsho ras pa*), a cycle of teachings that is often mentioned in Shabkar's biography (see chap. 4, note 17). Thukchog Dorje practiced in solitary places, achieved signs of accomplishment, and revealed several spiritual treasures. He had four main disciples: Jigme Lingpa (*jigs med gling pa*, 1729–98, see below), Kunzang Dechen Gyalpo (*kun bzang bde chen rgyal po*, b. 1717), Thekling Karma Drodön Tarchin (*theg gling karma 'gro don mthar phyin*), and the powerful yogin Trati Ngakchang (*mthu chen kra ti sngags 'chang*), also known as the Mad Yogin of Kongpo (*kong smyon*).

43. Rigdzin Jigme Lingpa (*rig 'dzin 'jigs med gling pa*, 1729–98) was considered to be an emanation of the great pandit Vimalamitra, of King Trisong Detsen, of Longchen Rabjam (*klong chen rab 'byams*, 1308–63), of Ngari Panchen Pema Wangyal (*mnga' ris pan chen padma dbang rgyal*, 1487–1542), and of many other sages. He was, as well, the immediate reembodiment of Chöje Lingpa (*chos rje gling pa*), also known as Orgyen Rogje Lingpa (*o rgyan rog rje gling pa*, 1682–1725).

In his childhood he had many visions of past saints. At the age of six, he entered the monastery of Palgi Riwo (*dpal gi ri bo*), the "Glorious Mountain," where he received the name of Pema Khyentse Öser, "Lotus Glowing with Wisdom and Love." At the age of thirteen, he met his root teacher, Rigdzin Thukchog Dorje (*rig 'dzin thugs mchog rdo rje*), who gave him the main Nyingma teachings.

Through his inner realization, Jigme Lingpa effortlessly mastered the whole corpus of the Buddha's doctrine. At twenty-eight he did a three-year retreat, during which, in a vision, he was blessed by Guru Padmasambhava, who named him Pema Wangchen (*padma dbang chen*), "Lotus of Great Power." Other profound visions revealed to him the mind treasure (*dgongs gter*) of the Longchen Nyingthig (*klong chen snying thig*), one of the most widely practiced cycles of the Nyingma tradition. During another three-year retreat at Samye Chimphu (*bsam yas mchims phu*), he had three visions of Gyalwa Longchen Rabjam. Following a prediction from Tsele Natsok Rangdrol (*rtse le sna tshogs rang grol*, 1608–?), Jigme Lingpa went to Tsering Jong (*tshe ring ljong*), where he founded the hermitage of Pema Ösel Thekchog Chöling (*padma 'od gsal theg mchog chos gling*). His main spiritual heirs were the four "fearless ones" (*jigs med*): Jigme Trinley Öser (*'jigs med phrin las 'od zer*, 1745–1821, the first Do Drupchen); Jigme Gyalwai Nyugu (*'jigs med rgyal ba'i myu gu*); Jigme Kundrol (*'jigs med kun grol*); Jigme Gocha (*'jigs med go cha*); and many others.

Jigme Lingpa's writings were collected in nine volumes, among which the *Treasury of Spiritual Quali-* ties (*yon tan rin po che'i mdzod*) condenses the essence of the nine vehicles of Buddhism. His immediate reincarnations were Jamyang Khyentse Wangpo (*'jam dbyangs mkhyen brtse'i dbang po*, 1820–92), the emanation of his body; Patrul Rinpoche Orgyen Jigme Chökyi Wangpo (*dpal sprul o rgyan 'jigs med chos kyi dbang po*, 1808–87), the emanation of his speech; and Do Khyentse Yeshe Dorje (*rdo mkhyen brtse ye shes rdo rje*, 1800–1859?), the emanation of his mind. See also GC, vol.3, pp. 365, and NS, vol. 1, pp. 835–48.

44. Lodrak Drupchen Lekyi Dorje (*lho brag grub chen las kyi rdo rje*), also known as Namkha Gyaltsen (*nam mkha' rgyal mtshan*, 1326–1401). See chap. 1, note 61.

45. *rdo bis*, also spelled *rdo sbis* (RO, p. 146).

46. Arik Geshe Jampa Gelek Gyaltsen, also known as Gyaltsen Özer (*a rig dge bshes 'jam dpal dge legs rgyal mtshan*, or *rgyal mtshan 'od zer*, 1726–1803), was a preeminent teacher in the Rekong area. Born in Arik Kyep (*a rig khyeb*), at the age of seventeen he went to central Tibet, where he studied for thirteen years with some of the important Gelukpa masters of his time, including Phurchok Ngawang Jampa (*phur lcog ngag dbang byams pa*, 1682–1762). He became renowned for his erudition and gave the oral transmission of the Tripitaka (*bka' 'gyur*). At the instructions of the sixth Panchen Lama, Lobzang Palden Yeshe (*blo bzang dpal ldan ye shes*, 1738–80), he returned to Amdo. There, he saw the site of Ragya as the one prophesied in the *Volumes of the Kadampas* (*bka' gdam glegs bam*), and having obtained there a large piece of land from the ruler Jasak Wangchuk Rabten (see Appendix 3), he founded Ragya Monastery, Tashi Kunde Ling (*rwa rgya bkra shis kun bde gling*), in 1769. After teaching there for many years, in 1792 he entrusted the monastery to his chief disciple Shingsa Choktrul Lobzang Dargye (*shing bza' mchog sprul blo bzang dar rgyas*, 1752–1824), and became a hermit, wandering from one mountain retreat to another. He passed away at Gomeh Belwon (*sgo me bal won*) in 1803. He was considered to be an incarnation of Avalokiteshvara, Nagarjuna, Dombhi Heruka, Pandita Gunaprabha, Thonmi Sambhota, Drom Tönpa, Sachen Kunga Nyingpo, Drigung Jikten Gonpo, and Drupkhangpa Gelek Gyatso (*sgrub khang pa dge legs rgya mtsho*, 1641–1713). See Jigme Gyaltsen, pp. 4–8 and AC, vol. 2, pp. 139–46.

47. The first Jamyang Shepa, Ngawang Tsondru (*'jam dbyangs bzhad pa ngag dbang brtson 'grus*, 1648–1722), was the founder of Labrang Tashikhyil in Amdo and the author of the textbooks used at Gomang College and at Drepung Monastery.

48. Do Drupchen Jigme Trinley Öser (*rdo grub chen jigs med phrin las 'od zer,* 1745–1821), also known as Dzogchenpa Kunsang Shenpen (*rdzogs chen pa kun bzang gzhan phan*), the first Do Drupchen (*rdo grub chen*). He was the foremost Dharma heir of Jigme Lingpa and, along with Jigme Gyalwai Nyugu (*jigs med rgyal ba'i myu gu*), the holder of the Longchen Nyingthig (*klong chen snying thig*) lineage. In gratitude for the teaching he received from Do Drupchen Trinley Öser, Ngakyi Wangpo presented him with a pearl umbrella, which, as communicated by Tulku Thondup, was kept at Do Drup Monastery in Tibet until recently. See TN, p. 736.

49. According to Sumpa Khenpo (see Bibliography), in 1786 the other king, who ruled on the left side of the Machu River, was Wang Sonam Dorje (*dbang bsod nam rdo rje*).

50. Urgeh Tratsang Sang-ngak Mingyeling (*u rge grwa tshang gsang sngags smin rgyas gling*), founded by *dar rgyal po shog thus.* See Appendix 3 and AC, vol. 2, pp. 124–30.

51. *Dzogchen Yeshe Lama (rdzogs chen ye shes bla ma),* the *Unsurpassable Primordial Wisdom,* is a famous guide (*khrid yig*) to the Great Perfection practice, written by Rigdzin Jigme Lingpa (see note 43). It expounds the condensed meaning of the *Vima Nyingthig (bi ma snying thig)*; see chap. 15, note 75.

52. For *Khandro Nyingthig (mkha' gro'i snying thig),* see chap. 3, note 16 and table 2 in Appendix 2.

53. Nomads of the high plateaus of Tibet rely chiefly on meat and other animals products to subsist. They are, however, well aware of the evil involved in harming and butchering animals. It is therefore common practice among Tibetans to ransom the lives (*srog bslu*) of animals. Buddhists from all over the world traditionally buy fish, birds, and other animals from the marketplace and set them free. In Tibet, it is often the owners themselves who mercifully spare a certain fraction of their livestock. In the case of sheep and yaks, they will cut the tip of one of the animal's ears and tie to the remaining part of the ear a red ribbon as a sign that the animal should never be slaughtered; the animal is then set free among the rest of the herd. The owner usually strings together all the ear-tips thus obtained and offers them to a lama, requesting him to dedicate the merit accrued through this compassionate act. Lamas and devotees also often give large sums of money to herders, asking them to spare in the same way the lives of a given number of their animals.

A Celebration
of Shabkar

"The Melody of Pure Devotion"

*A song spontaneously arisen when remembering
the lord of yogins, Shabkar Tsogdruk Rangdrol*

Authentic emanation of Lord Mila, eagle
on the great pillar, you are the one who
was[1]

Best of the accomplished renunciates from
the Land of Snows.

Completely immaculate, like the cam-
phor-white moon, the nectar that is the
story of your life[2]

Dispels the thick darkness of ego—your
excellent qualities come to my mind.

Eight worldly concerns,[3] noisy fame—all
these you cast to the four winds like
dust.

For attire, as a *mantrika* you dressed in
white and wore long hair.

Getting drunk, drinking tea to excess, eating meat—you remained unstained by
all such kinds of inferior behavior. I am
inspired by your superior conduct,

High as the sky, brilliant as the autumn
moon.

In the lush *tala* tree forests of Nepal, and at
Mount Kailash, and while

Journeying through various sacred places
like a wandering deer, the

Kingdom of nonduality you were able to
reach in a single lifetime:

Looking at the perfect example that is your
life-story, Lord Shabkar, I bow down to
you with devotion again and again.

Moved by the wondrous awakening of
your heart, pure as the morning star,

Numerous beings have been tamed and
transformed through your compassion.

Onto the path of liberation you guided
many people who had been living their
lives like oblivious cattle.

Paragon of loving-kindness, you were like
a mother who greatly cherished her
children.

Questing through the snow peaks at Tsari,
the sacred gathering-place of the
dakinis,

Remaining unperturbed by hardships like
heat and cold, accompanied by your
many disciples,

Similar to the Victorious One who went
to live at the Jeta Grove,[4]

To many beings who had been living lives
no better than those of jackals, you
taught the adamantine path.

Uninfluenced by sectarianism based on
schools, hats, dresses, and shoes (only
foolish causes of hatred and attachment), and having

Vowed to forsake all flattering schemes
inspired by coveting fine food and fine
possessions,

Without pretense, you manifested renunciation, devotion and perseverance.

*X*traordinary were the learned and
    accomplished disciples who gathered
    round you like a garland of stars.
*Y*ou revealed to your students the naked,
    ultimate nature of mind, free from all
    obscurations, and, thus, like a fresh, cool
*Z*ephyr, the fame of your perfect libera-
    tion swept through the mountain passes
    and valleys of Tibet.

*A*cting from compassion, you tamed even
    the fiercest demons and ogre-like spirits.
A lord of the tenth *bhumi*, you are, in
    actuality, the Lotus-holder.
*A*s if entering a forest of *hari* sandalwood,
*A*ho . . . seeing and listening to the story of
    your life,
*A*roused by utmost faith and reverence, I
    have voiced this song of praise—
A kind of superficial amusement this is not:
    this poem arose spontaneously, out of
    sheerest joy.

written by Mangala
(Tashi Paljor, H.H. Dilgo Khyentse Rinpoche)

Notes

1. This is an alphabetical song. The arrangement of the first letters of each verse follows the
sequence of the Tibetan alphabet (*ka, kha, ga, nga,*
etc.). We have tried to do the same with the English
alphabet, while keeping the order of the Tibetan
verses. The first verse refers to the prophetic dream
of Marpa the Translator, in which he saw four lofty
pillars with a different bird on each, symbolizing his
four main disciples. The vulture, the king of birds for
Tibetans—here translated as "eagle"—was Jetsun
Milarepa.

2. "Camphor-like" is a name for the moon in
Tibetan poetry.

3. The eight worldly concerns are happiness and
suffering, gain and loss, praise and criticism, fame
and obscurity.

4. The Jeta Grove at Shravasti, where the Buddha and his disciples spent their yearly rainy season
retreat *(dbyar gnas)* for nineteen years.

The Life Story

Author's
Introduction

Om svasti!

Lord of the Dharma, Teacher, Bhagavat,[1]
In the perception of extraordinary
    disciples,
You were enlightened countless aeons ago.
To you who perpetually turn the Wheel of
    Dharma, I bow down [2a].

First of the Buddhas of the three times,[2]
You manifested as Samantabhadra,[3] the
    teacher.
To you who turned the wheel of the Great
    Perfection
For Vajrasattva and his assembly, I bow
    down.

In the dharmadhatu palace of the
    Unexcelled Realm,[4]
You manifested as Vajradhara.
To you who turned the wheel of the Secret
    Mantrayana
For the Lord of Secrets[5] and his assembly, I
    bow down [4b].

In the perception of ordinary disciples
You first aroused Bodhicitta,[6] gathered the
    two accumulations,[7]
And, finally, reached true and complete
    enlightenment.
To you who set in motion the wheel of the
    Sutras, I bow down.[8]
Lord Padmakara,[9] heart emanation of all
    the Buddhas,

You turned the wheel of sutra and mantra.
To you, most kind Orgyen,
Who came to Tibet and established the
    great tradition of the Dharma,
I bow down.

When the teachings degenerated due to
    changing times,
Padmakara took birth again as Lord
    Atisha.[10]
To you, most compassionate lord,
Who kindled to greatest brightness the
    torch of the sutra and mantra,
I bow down.

Lobzang,[11] the second Buddha,
Manifestation of Lord Atisha in this
    degenerate age,[12]
To you who spread the teachings of the
    Victorious Ones
And made them bloom like the sun rising
    in the sky, I bow down.

Chögyal Ngakyi Wangpo,[13] you revealed
    in its entirety
The Dharma taught by the Victorious
    Ones.
To you, most gracious root guru,
Who was kinder to me than the Buddha
    himself,
I bow down.

Kind masters, according to the needs of
    beings,

You were emanated as spiritual teachers in
  this dark age
By all the past Buddhas [5a].
To you, who taught me the sutras and
  tantras,
The treatises and pith instructions,
I bow down.

My masters, thinking of your kindness,
I make this offering: to fulfill your every
  command.
Grant your blessings that my life-story and
  songs
May benefit the minds of whoever hears
  them.

For the benefit of those who will come in
  the future,
I shall now tell my whole tale,
From my birth until this very day.
Listen with joy!

In the highlands is the sacred mountain, Machen
Pomra,[14] Lord of the Tenth *Bhumi*,[15] graced
with auspiciousness and prosperity. In the midlands is Trakar Drel Dzong, White Rock Monkey Fortress, the place sacred to the Lord of
Great Compassion,[16] the source of blessings and
siddhis. In the lowlands is the sacred place called
Tsonying Mahadeva, The Heart of the Lake,
which induces well-being, happiness, and fame.
I once spent time engaged in profound meditation in the secluded, pleasant groves of Tsonying
Island, in the middle of Lake Kokonor, the lake
of abundance where the essence of the whole
Mongolian land is gathered—a lake where waves
ripple gently and the calls of water birds constantly resound.

While I was staying there, Lama Pema
Rangdrol ("Self-liberated Lotus," my fortunate
and supreme heart-son, who is diligent, intelligent, and compassionate) [5b], Kunzang Rangdrol
("All Perfect Natural Liberation") Alak Dechen[17]
("Great Bliss"), and Shanye Genpo Lama came to
stay for a year. One day they came to me, prostrated
themselves many times, and, offering a silk scarf of
immaculate whiteness, made this request:

"Great vajra-holder, lasting refuge and protector of all beings in this and future lives, kindly
heed our request: to nourish our devotion and
that of future disciples, as well as to benefit all
beings, please tell us in detail the story of your
life—from the time you lived at home until
now."

They accompanied their request with this
seven-branch supplication:

Jetsun, lord guru, emanation of the
  Victorious Ones,
We bow down with great devotion at your
  lotus feet,
Singing songs of praise and supplication.

We offer you this excellent wealth:
Our body, our speech, and the fulfillment
  of your every command.

We confess whatever breaches and errors
  we have committed,
And henceforth will refrain from committing them.

Protector, we rejoice with great delight
In the life-example you gave with your
  three mysteries.[18]

For our benefit and that of future disciples,
Set in motion the Dharma-wheel that is
  the story of your life.

Protector, for the sake of the Dharma and
  all beings,
Please remain in your bodily form for a
  hundred aeons.

We dedicate the merit gathered by
  ourselves and others
So that we may be able to follow perfectly
  your life's example [6a].
Refuge and protector of beings in this dark
  age,
Out of great kindness,
Tell us the story of your life
From the time you were living at home
Until the present day.

I replied:

> Fortunate heart-son endowed with faith,
> Zeal, intelligence, and compassion,
> Lama Pema Rangdrol, and you fortunate
>   ones,
> Listen!
>
> You must open and behold the treasury
> Of the life-stories of the Buddhas and
>   Bodhisattvas.
> What is the point of rummaging through
>   the rat's nest
> Of the life of a practitioner like me?
>
> If I were to tell you how that ass, Tsogdruk
>   Rangdrol,
> Painfully trailed behind the hoof prints
> Left by those sublime steeds,
> The Buddhas and Bodhisattvas of the past,
> On the vast plain of their perfect lives,
> It would only cause laughter.
>
> There is little need for my life-story,
> So you had better keep to the examples of
>   our forefathers,
> And allow this yogin to rest peacefully
> In his quiet mountain retreat.

Yet, they insisted:

> E ma! Protector of beings living in this dark
>   age,
> Tell us how first you abandoned the
>   concerns of this life,
> How next you followed a qualified master,
> How finally you practiced in secluded
>   places,
> And how meditation experiences and real-
>   ization have now dawned in your mind.
> Protector, your life-story is wonderful
>   indeed!
>
> When the light rays of the sun shine,
> The whole world benefits.
> Likewise, if you tell your life-story,
> It will benefit the whole Dharma and all
>   beings.

> Thus, don't think it unimportant,
> And, from great kindness, tell us the story
>   of your life [6b].

In response to their insistence, I wrote down notes on my life, from the time I lived at home until my stay at Tsonying Island. When I told them my story, they were pleased, did many prostrations, and went away with the notes. Later, Lama Pema Rangdrol composed a biography covering the events of my life up to my pilgrimage to the Pure Realm of U and Tsang.[19] Since it was well-written and was of a suitable length, I thought it would suffice to inspire devotion in present and future disciples.

Later I came to live in Lapchi Snow Range, one of the most sacred places of the body, speech, and mind of Chakrasamvara.[20] The place sacred to Chakrasamvara's body is the abode of the White Lion-faced Dakini at Mount Kailash in Upper Tibet, the famed king of glaciers. The place sacred to his speech is the abode of the Striped Tiger-faced Dakini at Lapchi in Middle Tibet. The place sacred to his mind is the abode of the Black Sow-faced Dakini, matchless Tsari, in Lower Tibet. Among these, the highlands of Lapchi, perpetually wreathed in cloud banks and mist, are the perfect dancing ground of celestial *mamos* and dakinis,[21] the place where Jetsun Milarepa once stayed.

One day, as I was turning the Wheel of Dharma there for many faithful disciples, Kalden Rangdrol ("Self-liberated Fortunate One"), my close spiritual son who had great faith, generosity and intelligence, accompanied by Lama Jimba Norbu ("Jewel of Generosity"), Tendzin Nyima ("Sun of the Doctrine"), Yeshe Wangchuk ("Endowed with Wisdom"), Tsultrim Namgyal ("All-Victorious Discipline"), Lobzang Dargye ("Vast and Excellent Intelligence"), Nyene Khepa ("The Learned Attendant"), and many other close disciples offered me a mandala of gold and silver on a silken scarf, and said [7a]:

"Lord who embodies the Three Jewels, our precious and lasting refuge in this life and in all our lives, heed our supplication. If you tell the story of your life as did the learned and accomplished sages of the past, it will set a supreme example for the Dharma and all beings.

"Therefore, tell us first, lord, where you were born; your father and mother's names; whether they were rich or poor; how many brothers and sisters you had—in short, beginning with your birth, tell us your wondrous life year after year.

"Tell us how, having come to feel revulsion for samsaric affairs, you gave up this life's concerns, followed many learned and accomplished masters, studied and contemplated the sutra and tantra teachings, and, in accordance with the meaning expressed in them, stayed in secluded mountain retreats, persevering in profound meditation.

"Tell us how meditation experiences and realization took birth in your being; how you manifested miracles and the higher perceptions and brought immense benefit for the Dharma and all beings in Upper, Lower and Middle Tibet. Without holding anything back, tell us the outer, inner, and secret stories of your life."

Kalden Rangdrol repeated this request in verse:

Wish-fulfilling gem, refuge and protector,
I have but one request:
In the way of our spiritual forefathers,
Please tell us the story of your life.
This will greatly benefit the Dharma,
Your present disciples, and all beings in the
    future.

Precious refuge and protector,
First, tell us where you were born, the
    names of your parents, and then
What you have done, year after year, since
    your birth.

Tell us the wondrous deeds you have
    accomplished [7b];
How, having given up the affairs of this life
    for the sake of Dharma,
You followed learned and accomplished
    masters;
How you practiced in secluded places

And gave rise to meditation experiences
    and realization;
How you vastly benefited sentient beings
    and the Dharma,
Displaying prescience and miraculous
    deeds.

Please tell us all, not withholding anything,
And grant your blessing that we, your
    fortunate disciples,
May be able to follow thoroughly
The example of the outer, inner, and
    secret aspects of your life.

I answered:

"Since you ask with such insistence, I have no reason to keep my life-story secret. So, I shall tell you all I did from my birth until now—where I have been, where I stayed, and all I have done in accordance with the Dharma. Listen joyfully!"

I then told them all that I could remember. Delighted, they did many prostrations and circumambulations, and then returned to their hermitages. Although no notes were taken at the time, later, a few of the close disciples, who feared they might forget the details, wrote some down.

Following this, I went on to Domey, where I could be of help to beings.

Nine years later, I happened to stay in retreat at Tashikhyil,[22] a perfect secluded place covered with forests and flowers, and filled with the melodious calls of birds of all kinds. At that time, the faithful disciples and *ngakpas* [23] said among themselves, "If our precious refuge and protector would tell his life-story in detail [8a], it would strengthen our faith and be of invaluable benefit for future disciples."

Soon after, Khen Rinpoche dreamed that I was seated outside on a throne at the east side of the Dewachen Temple on the top of Tashikhyil Mountain, telling a great crowd of human beings and celestial beings the life-stories of many Buddhas, Bodhisattvas, and learned and realized beings of India and Tibet. In his dream he thought, "Who knows when I'll die? I must ask

Lama Shabkar to tell his life-story." At that moment, he woke up. The next day, he came, presented me with a white scarf, and made this request:

> Precious protector, our refuge in this life
>   and lives thereafter,
> You have now grown old.
> Almost all the great disciples who earlier
>   asked
> That you tell your life-story
> Have now passed away.
> I, too, am an old man close to death;
> Who knows when I shall die?
> I may never have another opportunity
> To ask you to tell the story of your life.
> If I don't ask this while I live,
> Once I'm dead, even if you tell it,
> I won't be there to hear it.
> So, now while I am still of this world,
> Please tell the whole story of your life.
> It will enhance faith, respect, and pure
>   perception
> In all of us, your disciples;
> And set a perfect example
> For the Dharma and beings in the future
>   [8b].
> From today, and throughout all of my
>   lives,
> May I follow your life-example
> And practice the divine Dharma.
> May my aspiration be fulfilled!

Thereafter, some of my disciples, who always did as their master asked, such as Nyangkyi Tsampa ("The Hermit of Nyang"),[24] Lhakhang Umdze ("The Chant Master"), Yeshe Tendzin ("Holder of the Wisdom Teachings"), Sönam Rinchen ("Jewel of Merit"), my attendant Drupchen ("Great Siddha"), Pema Kardri ("Fragrance of the White Lotus"), Neten ("the Elder"), Sangye ("The Buddha"), Kunga ("All Joy"), Rabjung ("The Renunciate"), Phuntshok ("All-Perfect"), and many devoted patrons, pleaded that, just as there were many biographies of the past and present masters, I should certainly tell my life-story, too.

Although they kept insisting, I thought that there was little need for it. I did not pay much attention to this, and stayed in strict retreat.

One day during my retreat, it occurred to me, "While keeping in mind the practice of Dharma, I have now reached old age, and death is approaching. I do not know how much time I have left for joys and sorrows. At present, my illusory body is fit and free of illness. If, as the Khenpo said, I were to write the story of my life and leave it behind, in the future it might somehow benefit faithful and fortunate disciples who strive for liberation." Thus I began to feel inclined to write down the events of my life from my birth until the present.

Like a wish-fulfilling gem, the spiritual master is the source of all well-being, bliss, and excellence [9a]. For those who are now asking that their master's life-story be told and for the fortunate disciples of the future, it is first of all essential to develop faith and respect toward the spiritual master, perceiving the master as the Buddha in human form. Why is this so? In the perception of extraordinary disciples, Buddha Shakyamuni, the matchless son of Suddhodana, the sublime guide of all beings, men, and gods, realized the unsurpassable state of enlightenment at the very beginning of samsara and nirvana. He then manifested in various forms to tame sentient beings, limitless as space, in accordance with their needs, and ceaselessly turned the Wheel of Dharma.

As is said in *The Sutra of Compassion's White Lotus:*[25]

> Throughout inconceivable billions of aeons,
> Infinite, innumerable—
> I have attained sublime enlightenment,
> And have continuously expounded the
>   Dharma.

In the perception of ordinary disciples, Buddha Shakyamuni first awakened his aspiration, then gathered the two accumulations, and finally attained perfect and true enlightenment. Having displayed these wondrous deeds, he set in motion the Wheel of Dharma. These are the deeds that he will display again and again in the future, as it is stated in the sutra called *The Meeting of Father and Son:* [26]

> Great hero of great skill,
> You manifested in billions of universes
> As the Victorious One, the Buddha,
> To bring sentient beings to full maturity,
> You, the guide [9b],
> Will manifest again as numerous Buddhas.

In this degenerate age, the Buddha manifests as various spiritual masters and spiritual friends who train beings—whoever is in need of taming, by whatever means are needed.

In *The Great Drum Sutra* [27] the Buddha says:

> Do not despair, Ananda!
> In the future I will
> Emanate as spiritual friends
> To benefit you and others.

In the *Salty River Sutra* [28] he also says:

> During the last five-hundred year period
> I will emanate as spiritual friends.
> Regard them as you would myself
> And respect them.

In the *Vajra Tent Tantra* [29] it is said, too:

> Assuming an ordinary appearance,
> The one known as Vajrasattva
> Emanates as spiritual masters
> To benefit all sentient beings.

Considering the Buddha's words as the canon of truth, perceive the master as the Buddha in person; regard all he does as perfect, and feel devotion just by remembering the way he sits, acts, and talks, and even more by remembering the vast and wondrous deeds of his life. Whoever has complete faith and devotion will soon give

rise to all the good qualities of the sacred Dharma, accomplish all activities and attain all the *siddhis* of the Buddhas.

As it is said in *The Sutra of the Ten Dharmas:* [30]

> Those possessed of faith
> Will perform the deeds of the Buddhas.

Likewise, in *The Magical Net* [31] it says:

> The one possessing faith [10a]
> Will naturally achieve all accomplishments.

And Gyalwa Karmapa said:

> The faithful disciple gifted with devotion
> Will soon give rise to the qualities of
>   Dharma.

Machik, [32] the "Sole Mother," said too:

> All those who have faith
> Will see their aspirations fulfilled.

You may wonder whether there had been predictions about me. There had. In the *Description of the Great Stupa Jarung Khashor*, or Bodhnath, [33] one finds among the great master Padmasambhava's predictions:

"Several emanations of the Lords of the Three Families, of the Frowning One, and of Arya Tara will restore the stupa. [34] At that time, someone with fortunate karma—the result of his past deeds—will come; if, having forsaken all concern for this life, he conceives the supreme intention to restore the stupa and undertakes the work, he will succeed. If he does so, this world, the southern continent of Jambudvipa, will enjoy good years and happiness for twenty-five human years; the three lands of India, Nepal, and Mön will enjoy the same for thirty-five years; the Land of Snows, Tibet, will ward off the invaders from Upper Mongolia [35] for sixty years, and there will be good years and happiness for forty years." [36]

It is also said in the *General Predictions for the Dharma* made by Tertön Dudul Dorje, [37] "Adamantine Subduer of Evil":

Glorious Vajra will fly to the east.
One with the name Rangdrol, wise in the
	true meaning,
Will give splendor to Jarung Khashor.
All fortunate and noble beings will have
	faith in him [10b].

In the *Secret Predictions* of Karmapa Rolpai
Dorje,[38] "Adamantine Display," one finds:

Jetsun Shepai Dorje, "Laughing Vajra,"[39]
Will reappear in Dokham, in the east.
He will make excellent restorations
At the Snow Range of Lapchi.

Taksham Nuden Dorje,[40] "Powerful Diamond," made predictions concerning the holders of his teachings:

When the Central Temple,[41] built in three
	styles, is damaged by fire,
A "wheel gathering the profound mean-
	ing" will appear from the east.
If he meets with this deep teaching of
	mine,
Obstacles will be dispelled and immense
	benefit will ensue for beings.
You, great compassionate one with a mole
	above your eye,
Do not harbor doubts; practice and propa-
	gate these teachings.

Likewise in the predictions of Dzogchenpa
Kunzang Shenphen, "Ever-excellent Benevolent
One,"[42] a lord among *siddhas*, one can read:

The Lord, the "Wheel of the Doctrine,"
	will appear in Upper Tibet,
As the magical display of the divine Lotus-
	holder.[43]
He will manifest there and in other places.

According to the prophecies received by the
great awareness-holder Palden Tashi,[44] it is said:

On the mountain that resembles a
	standing elephant

Is a forest shrouded in dark clouds.
This place, known as Tashikhyil,
Will become a place of practice.
There, like the sun and moon
Encircled by a host of stars,
Will appear several realized beings
And secret practitioners of great bliss.

Others say that if someone endowed with
faith and respect were to look through the scriptures of the sutras and tantras, the volumes of the
Kadampas, and the ancient and recent revealed
treasures of Orgyen Rinpoche, there are many
instances where one would wonder, "Isn't this a
prediction, too?" [11a].

For these reasons, if in the future someone
tells or listens to the story of my life with a pure
mind filled with faith and respect, and thinks,
"This is a holy person predicted by our holy
forefathers," great benefit could result.

As it is said in the *Golden Garland of the Kagyu
Lineage:*[45]

Merely hearing of the life-stories, the wondrous deeds and virtues of the Buddhas and
Bodhisattvas and of their emanations, the masters of the precious Whispered Lineage and all
the other holy and supreme emanated beings,
purifies limitless negative karma, evil deeds, and
obscurations, while perfecting an equally limitless accumulation of merit.

Once the seeds of virtue have been sown in
your being, you will always be reborn in the
presence of spiritual masters and take delight in
the teachings of the Mahayana; you will be able
to bear austerities and hardships, while mental
strength and understanding will naturally
develop.

These life-stories teach the Dharma. So if
you hear them many times and keep them in
mind, they will help you to understand what to
do and what not to do. You will know which
path to follow, without any mistake. Faith will
be born in those with no faith and be enhanced
in those who have faith; diligence, intelligence,
revulsion toward samsara, and other excellent
qualities will grow effortlessly.

Your fervent devotion will enable you to receive the blessings of the true lineage; meditation experiences and realization not yet born will arise, and those already born will increase [11b].

When you think, 'May I perform the same wondrous deeds as these Bodhisattvas!' Bodhicitta will arise. When you rejoice in their great virtuous acts, you will gain the same merit as if you had performed them yourself.

When you hear the profound accounts of the Bodhisattvas' wondrous deeds, your attachment and aggression and other negative thoughts, together with suffering of all kinds, will stop, while your joy and pure deeds will blossom. Even if you are criticized and slandered by people with wrong views, you will be welcomed by great beings, and, having been accepted as their disciple, you will put an end to samsara.

In short, these life-stories are a source of benefit for both yourself and others. To read, hear, or reflect on them is very meaningful; you should read, copy, listen to, memorize and reflect upon them with diligence. Keep them in mind and put them into practice with ardent devotion and respect.

Unlike the life-stories of the past Buddhas, Bodhisattvas, and great learned and realized sages of India and Tibet, my own life-story does not have much to offer to my disciples for their practice. Nevertheless, keeping my eyes fixed on the examplary lives of the past masters, I shall relate all that I have done in accordance with the Dharma [12a].

How will this story be told? To make it pleasant to those of superior, middling, and lesser capacities, I shall (as a few learned and accomplished persons have done in the past) alternate prose and verse. This account will be related in fifteen chapters:

The first chapter tells how and where I took birth, as a result of good karma and of pure prayers made in my past lives.

The second tells how, having reflected on the vanity of worldly affairs, I left home for the homeless life.

The third tells how, leaving my homeland behind, I came into the presence of the Dharma King, Chögyal Ngakyi Wangpo.

The fourth tells how, in keeping with the prophecy of my master, I persevered in profound meditation practices in the pleasant solitude of Tseshung Grove.

The fifth tells how I went to practice in other nearby places such as Takmo Dzong, Göpo Dzong, and Getho.

The sixth tells how I went to practice at Tsonying Mahadeva, The Heart of the Lake, the renowned sacred place that induces well-being and happiness.

The seventh tells how I went to practice at Machen Pomra, the mountain of the Lord of the Tenth *Bhumi*, auspicious and magnificent.

The eighth tells how I went to practice at Trakar Drel Dzong, the White Rock Monkey Fortress, the source of all blessings and accomplishments.

The ninth tells how, following the death of my mother, I went to the Pure Realm of central Tibet, U and Tsang.

The tenth tells how I made the pilgrimage through the Ravines of Tsari, and how I practiced at the place sacred to the Mind of Black Varahi, unequaled in Lower Tibet.

The eleventh tells how I went to western Tibet and practiced at Mount Kailash, the famed king of mountains, the place sacred to the Body of the White Lion-faced Dakini.[12b] .

The twelfth tells how I went to the celestial realm of Nepal, and paid homage at the two great stupas.

The thirteenth tells how I went to the authentic place of Lapchi, the place sacred to the speech aspect of the Striped Tiger-faced Dakini, and meditated there.

The fourteenth tells how, coming back to the Pure Realm of U and Tsang, I wandered on, benefiting beings.

The fifteenth tells how, returning to lower Do-kham, I worked to benefit the Dharma and all beings.

Notes

1. Bhagavat is rendered in Tibetan by *bcom ldan 'das*, literally the one who "has vanquished" (*bcom*) the obscuring emotions, is "endowed" (*ldan*) with the excellence of enlightenment, and is "beyond" (*'das*) suffering.

2. Present, past, and future.

3. Skt. Samantabhadra (*kun tu bzang po*), the "Ever-perfect" primordial Buddha. In the primordial universal ground, there are neither sentient beings, nor Buddhas; neither ignorance, nor enlightenment. It is a state of natural, unchanging perfection beyond conditions and concepts. When the first manifestation of phenomena arises from the primordial ground, to recognize that this arising is the display of one's own awareness leads instantaneously to the primordial Buddhahood of Samantabhadra. Not recognizing this to be the case, and taking phenomena and beings to be real entities distinct from oneself, leads instantaneously to the ignorance of sentient beings.

4. Akanishtha (*'og min*), literally "which is not below," the Unexcelled Buddhafield. There are several kinds of *'og min;* see the commentary on Jigme Lingpa's *Treasury of Spiritual Qualities (yon tan mdzod)* by Khenpo Yonten Gyatso, hereafter abbreviated as YZ, vol. 40, pp. 742–43.

5. The Lord of Secrets (*gsang ba'i bdag po*), a synonym for Vajrapani, the compiler of the tantric teachings.

6. Bodhicitta (*byang chub gyi sems*), thought or mind of enlightenment, is defined as the intention to achieve Buddhahood for the sake of all beings. It has two aspects, relative and absolute. The relative mind of enlightenment is itself divided into two steps: the wish to attain ultimate perfection to become able to free all beings from suffering, and the entry into spiritual practice to actualize this wish. The absolute mind of enlightenment is the realization of emptiness, the recognition that the Buddha-nature abides in every sentient being.

7. These two accumulations of merit and wisdom (*bsod nams* and *ye shes kyi tshogs*) lead respectively to the realization of the two kayas, the dharmakaya (*chos sku*, absolute body) and the rupakaya (*gzugs sku*, manifested body) of a Buddha.

8. This verse refers to Lord Buddha Shakyamuni.

9. Skt. Padmakara (*padma 'byung gnas*), the "One Who Arose from the Lotus," or Guru Padmasambhava (see Translator's Introduction, note 17). Known by many names, in this life-story he is referred to as Guru Rinpoche, Orgyen Rinpoche, the Precious Master, or the Lake-born Vajra.

10. For Atisha, see Translator's Introduction, note 12.

11. Lobzang refers to Tsongkhapa Lobzang Trakpa. See Translator's Introduction, note 12.

12. The "age of residues" (*snyigs dus*), which is characterized by a degeneration in (1) the life span (*tshe*), (2) the general karma (*las*), (3) the view (*lta ba*), and (4) the faculties of beings (*sems can*), as well as by (5) an increase of the obscuring emotions (*nyon mongs*).

13. Chögyal Ngakyi Wangpo (*chos rgyal ngag gi dbang po*, 1736–1807), Shabkar's main teacher (see Translator's Introduction and Appendices 3 and 4). In the course of this life-story he is referred to by various names: the precious Dharma King, Chögyal Rinpoche, Chögyal Wang (*chos rgyal wang*), Pöntsang Rinpoche (*dpon tshang rin po che*), and Chingwang Rinpoche (*ching wang rin po che*).

14. The details about this and the other sacred places mentioned will be found in the following chapters and their related footnotes.

15. Skt. *bhumi*, the ten spiritual stages through which a Bodhisattva passes before attaining full Buddhahood, the eleventh *bhumi*. See SD, p. 21.

16. The Great Compassionate One (*thugs rje chen po*) is a name of Avalokiteshvara.

17. Alak (*a lag*) is an honorific title given to lamas and notables in Amdo.

18. *gsang ba gsum*, literally the "three secrets," refer to the body, speech, and mind of an enlightened being.

19. This work of Pema Rangdrol (d. around 1837; see Appendix 6) has not been found. U and Tsang (*dbus* and *gtsang*), the two main provinces of central Tibet, are often described as being a "Pure Realm" because of the presence in U of the Dalai Lama, the living embodiment of Avalokiteshvara, the Buddha of Compassion, and the presence in Tsang of the Panchen Lama, the embodiment of Amitabha.

20. According to tantric cosmology, enlightened qualities of the body, speech, and mind of various deities are manifested in sacred places. Tantric practitioners therefore go to practice in these places where spiritual progress is said to be swifter than elsewhere.

21. Dakinis are female celestial beings of varying levels of realization. The wisdom dakinis are fully enlightened deities. *Mamos* are wrathful dakinis.

22. In 1837, since Shabkar returned to Amdo in

1828. Tashikhyil Hermitage (*dben pa'i bkra shis 'khyil*), where Shabkar spent most of the latter part of his life, is not to be confused with the great monastery of Labrang Tashikhyil (*bla brang bkra shis 'khyil*). This retreat place, also known as Yama Tashikhyil (*g.ya' ma bkra shis 'khyil*; see RO, p. 644), was founded by Gyal Khenchen Gedun Tenpai Nyima (*rgyal mkhan chen dge 'dun bstan pa'i nyi ma*). Shabkar built new temples and hermitages; since then, the place has been taken care of by Shabkar's successive reembodiments and disciples. The Dewachen Temple was recently restored under the guidance of Alak Sherap (d. 1992).

23. A *ngakpa* (Tib. *sngags pa*, Skt. *mantrin*) is a practitioner of the Secret Mantrayana.

24. The Hermit of Nyang, Lobzang Tenpai Nyima (*nyang mtshams pa blo bzang bstan pa'i nyi ma*, 1811–61) was a learned and influential master in the Rekong area and at the Five-peaked Mountain in China (Wu Tai Shan). See RO, pp. 533–43.

25. *The Sutra of Compassion's White Lotus* (Skt. *mahakaruna-pundarika-sutra*, Tib. *snying rje chen po padma dkar po'i mdo*, T 111–12).

26. *The Sutra of the Meeting of Father and Son* (Skt. *pitaputra-samagamana*, Tib. *yab dang sras mjal ba'i mdo*, T 60), which is part of the Ratnakuta.

27. *The Great Drum Sutra* (Skt. *mahabheriharaka-parinirvana*, Tib. *rnga bo che chen po'i mdo*, T 222).

28. The Salty River Sutra (Tib. *ba tshwa can gyi chu klung gi mdo*) is not found in the list of contents of Derge Kangyur (*sde dge bka' 'gyur*). This declaration may be one of those verses which are found as quotes in translated commentaries, whereas the original sutras to which they belong have been lost, or were never translated into Tibetan.

29. *The Vajra Tent Tantra* (the full title of which is in Skt. *dakini-vajra-panjara-mahatantraraja-kalpa*, in Tib. *mkha' 'gro ma rdo rje gur zhes bya ba'i rgyud gi rgyal po*, T 419).

30. *The Sutra of the Ten Dharmas* (Skt. *dasadharmaka-sutra*, Tib. *chos bcu pa'i mdo*, T 53).

31. *The Tantra of the Magical Net* (Skt. *mayajala-mahatantraraja*, Tib. *rgyud kyi rgyal po chen po sgyu 'phrul drwa ba*, T 466).

32. The Sole Mother, Machik Labdrön (*ma gcig lab sgron*, 1055–1153), who, with Padampa Sangye (*pha dam pa sangs rgyas*, d. 1117), initiated in Tibet the lineage of the practice of Chöd (*gcod*), which means "cutting through" ego-clinging and other attachments. In this practice, based on the view of the *Prajnaparamita*, one visualizes offering one's body to the "four classes

of guests" (*mgron po bzhi*), which are: (1) the Three Jewels, the Buddhas and Bodhisattvas who elicit faith and respect, (2) the protectors of the Dharma who are endowed with good qualities, (3) sentient beings who deserve our compassion, and (4) negative harmful spirits to whom we must repay karmic debts. On the history of Chöd, see J. Gyatso (1989). On translations of Machik's biographies, see A. Tempa Gyaltsen et al. (1990) and J. Edou (1993).

33. Jarung Khashor (*bya rung kha shor*), the Great Stupa of Bodhnath in the Kathmandu Valley in Nepal. On its history, see chap. 12, note 23.

34. The Lords of the Three Families (*rigs gsum mgon po*) are Manjushri, Avalokiteshvara, and Vajrapani. The Frowning One (*khro gnyer can ma*) is a wrathful aspect of Tara.

35. According to Trulshik Rinpoche, *dur kha* refers to Upper or Outer Mongolia (*stod sog*) and *mu dur kha* to Lower or Inner Mongolia (*smad sog*). This could also very well refer to Turkey.

36. This story will be told in chap. 13.

37. Rigdzin Dudul Dorje (*rig dzin bdud 'dul rdo rje*, 1615–72), a great tertön reincarnation of Khyeuchung Lotsawa (*khye'u chung lo tsa*), one of the twenty-five disciples of Guru Rinpoche. See GC, vol. 3, pp. 161ff. and NS, pp. 813ff.

38. Karmapa Rolpai Dorje (*karma pa rol pa'i rdo rje*, 1340–83), the fourth Karmapa. See Karma Trinley (1978).

39. Shepai Dorje is Jetsun Milarepa (see Translator's Introduction, note 1). Shabkar's sojourn and restoration work in Lapchi are described in chap. 13.

40. Taksham Nuden Dorje (*stag sham nus ldan rdo rje*, born in 1682), also known as Samten Lingpa (*bsam gtan gling pa*), was a great tertön and an emanation of Atsara Sale, Yeshe Tsogyal's Nepalese consort. See ND, pp. 301–2.

41. The main temple of Samye, the three stories of which were each built in a different style—Indian, Tibetan, and Khotanese (*li yul*).

42. Dzogchenpa Kunzang Shenphen (*rdzogs chen pa kun bzang gzhan phan*), the first Do Drupchen (see Translator's Introduction, note 48), thus called because he was a master of the teachings of the Great Perfection (*rdzogs chen*).

43. Lotus-holder, Padmapani, a name of Avalokiteshvara.

44. Rigdzin Kachupa Palden Tashi (*rig 'dzin bka' bcu pa dpal ldan bkra shis*): this master from Rekong traveled to central Tibet and became a geshe at Drepung monastery. He then embraced the Nying-

mapa tradition at Mindroling Monastery. He also became the disciple of Terchen Nyima Trakpa (*gter chen nyi ma grags pa*, 1647–1710) and of his son Gyalse Orgyen Tendzin (*rgyal sras o rgyan bstan 'dzin*, 1701–7/8) from whom he received the complete transmission of Nyima Trakpa's *termas*. He then returned to Amdo where he taught these widely. (See GC, vol. 4, p. 444, and RO, p. 615). Among the descendants of Palden Tashi was the famed Gedun Chöpel (*dge 'dun chos 'phel*, 1905–51). See RO, p. 647.

45. *The Golden Garland of the Kagyu Lineage* (*bka' brgyud gser phreng*). A collection of hagiographies of Kagyu saints. There are several such collections, related to the different branches of the Kagyu lineage.

1

Early Years

First, I will describe the place and circumstances of my birth,
which were the result of my past good karma and pure aspirations

Within the realm tamed by the peerless Buddha Shakyamuni, north of the Diamond Throne of India,[1] the center of the southern continent of Jambudvipa, lies the Golden Valley of Rekong where Jetsun Kalden Gyatso,[2] "Fortunate Ocean," an emanation of the sublime Avalokiteshvara, benefited countless beings. To the west lie the Pure Realms of U and Tsang where the Buddhas Amitabha and Padmapani emanated as the saffron-clad Victorious Ones—Father and Son.[3] To the north, in Domey, stands the mountain Tsongkha Kyeri, the birthplace of the Second Buddha, the great Tsongkhapa, who reigns supreme over the three worlds.

There are many villages of the Golden Valley of Rekong, and the inhabitants are intelligent, courageous, and skilled in the sciences of religious art, medicine, and astrology. All take delight in practicing the Dharma [13a].

Nearby are Rekong's Eight Places of the Accomplished Ones[4] and many hallowed spots where Lord Kalden Gyatso once practiced. The most eminent of these sacred places is Shohong Lakha, the actual palace of Chakrasamvara, located near the temple of Chuchik Shel.[5] Both farmers and nomads live in this land of cliffs, forests, and flower-filled meadows. Here, by following the practice of Chakrasamvara and Vajrayogini, the great tantric practitioner known as Kawa Dorje Chang Wang, who had come from Eastern Kathok, attained the vajra rainbow body in a single lifetime.[6]

In this region, ten villages of various sizes lie scattered in all directions. Among these is Nyen-gya, a village at the foot of the local god Jadrön's mountain abode. This is my homeland, the place of my birth.

My ancestral line is Cho. Its history and genealogy follow. Close to the banks of the Machu River is the mountain range abode of Machen Pomra,[7] the Lord of the Tenth *Bhumi,* who first conceived the thought of enlightenment in the presence of the omniscient guide, Buddha Shakyamuni. Machen Pomra is the patron deity of the whole region; among the spirits of his retinue is the powerful Trika, a spirit as real as any person.

In this area which carries the name of Trika, there were many large tribes, which abided by the laws of the kingdom and were favorably inclined toward the Dharma. One clan called Megya began a feud with the rich and powerful Namkhai Gyalpo and his household, and forced them to leave the province. They settled at Nyengya and, because they worshiped the local deities, their property and wealth flourished still further [13b]. Namkhai Gyalpo, "King of the Sky," had three sons whom he named "Lion": Nyima Senge ("Sun Lion"), Dawa Senge ("Moon Lion"), and Changchup Senge ("Lion of Enlightenment"). Each of these sons had many male descendants, multiplying the family tree so that eventually there were established three paternal bloodlines called Ngakor, Damtsang, and Gongpa. I am from the family branch called Damtsang, descended from Changchup Senge.

My ancestor, Changchup Senge, had a son, a grandson, and a great-grandson. In the fourth generation, a handsome boy was born. Gifted with a pleasant voice and a good heart, he was named Apo Yag, "Good Fellow." As a young boy, while herding cattle at a place known as Gyang Yaktser, he found a large vase filled with gold and other precious things. Even after three generations had passed, his descendants were still showing the vase to their sons, saying, "Should our descendants ever be faced with hard times, all they need do is help themselves to some of this gold."

This ancestor of mine fathered a son named Tashi Gyal, "Victorious Goodness," who was expert in both religious and secular affairs. Tashi Gyal had a son called Tsewang, "Lord of Life," a man of great merit who lived to a ripe old age. Tsewang's son, Ngawang, "Lord of Speech," was an honest and guileless man skilled in song and storytelling. This Ngawang was my mother's father. He had five daughters followed by one son whom he named Kyabgo, who was inclined toward the Dharma. My mother was third of the five daughters [14a].

Before my mother was born, my grandparents had sponsored a reading of the *Tashi Tsekpa*,[8] a sutra of the Victorious One, in hopes that a boy might be born. Not a boy, but a girl was born, my mother. They named her Tashi Tsek, "Heap of Goodness," and later she was affectionately nicknamed Tsekgo.

> Taking birth neither in a rich family
> Nor in a poor one
> But in a family of moderate wealth,
> May I thus be able to renounce my home.[9]

In accordance with this prayer made by Shariputra,[10] my mother's family was neither rich nor poor, but of average means. My grandparents had only one son, their youngest child. Among their many daughters, my mother proved to be the most capable, and so enjoyed greater consideration than did the others. She was intelligent, and became adept at managing the household and taking care of the family and servants. Her parents decided to keep my mother at home to care for their only son while her sisters were given away in marriage [14b].

As my mother grew older, she met many lamas and spiritual masters of the area and listened to teachings on the karmic law of cause and effect and other subjects. Inspired by their instructions, she took delight in the Dharma and refrained from misdeeds. On each full moon, new moon, and on the eighth day of each month, she observed the eightfold precepts of lay ordination.[11] Reciting praises to Tara daily, she did prostrations. Eventually she completed a hundred thousand such praises as well as a million prostrations. In short, my mother was both skilled in the activities of daily life and eager to practice virtue.

My father's identity was never openly revealed, but almost everyone agreed that it was Tsodu Khen Rinpoche,[12] also known as Ngakchang Dorje Namgyal, the "All-Victorious Adamantine Yogin," an emanation of the Bodhisattva Khyeu Chubeb, "The Youth who Brings Water."[13] Born in a noble family, he had attained perfection in the five sciences.[14] A great lord among *siddhas*, he could make rain fall when needed.

Before my conception, my mother dreamed that the village chief, Uncle Ngaktruk,[15] brought her a statue. Handing it to her, he said, "Keep this image in your home for a while. But you won't keep it forever, for someday it is destined to be placed upon everyone's head." She also dreamed of finding a white lotus flower with which she adorned her hair, and a white conch that she blew. Later, she dreamed that a resplendent image of Avalokiteshvara, about an inch in size, entered the crown of her head and dissolved into her. It was then that I entered my mother's womb, filling her mind and body with boundless bliss.

Causing my mother little pain, I was born in the year called Pharwa, the Female Iron Ox.[16] Just after birth, I opened my eyes and thereafter grew faster than most other infants. Without crying, I would lie on my bed with a joyful expression that endeared me to everyone [15a].

At this time, a relative named Kyablo calculated my astrological chart. He said, "The placement of the stars at his birth is good. Because this boy was born on the day known as the 'One

Man Who Makes a Hundred Take Flight,' if he leads a worldly life, he will become a hero who can defeat a hundred men. However, should he practice the Dharma, he will become a *siddha* who can defeat the eighty-four thousand obscuring emotions."[17] On hearing this, our village chief, Ngaktruk, made offerings to the divinities associated with my birth and freed animals that were about to be slaughtered. I was given the name Ngawang Tashi, "Auspicious Lord of Speech."

The year I was born, the entire country enjoyed good fortune and an abundant harvest. When a feast was held to celebrate my birth, the wise elders who had gathered for the occasion said, "Calling the boy 'Auspicious Lord of Speech' was an excellent choice. He truly deserves his name." The local people rejoiced and gave me other names, "Auspicious Long Life" and "Auspicious Prosperity."

From early childhood, I never told lies or spoke harshly, and I avoided any kind of cruel games or mischief. I preferred to recite prayers, sing the mantra *Om mani padme hum*, and beat a drum or play other temple instruments. In this way, I found entertainment through activities inspired by the Dharma. Naturally honest and good-hearted, I was kind to my playmates. When I ate even a handful of *tsampa*,[18] I divided it up and shared it with others.

At night, lying on my mother's lap and looking into the darkness, I sometimes saw many rainbow lights, circles, and the images of deities like the paintings in temples. I told my mother about this, saying, "Mother, when I look into the air, I see many different-colored things" [15b]. She answered, "Don't tell fibs—how can anyone see such things in complete darkness? Just quiet down." A few days later, I saw the same things again and told her about them. She asked, "You're not making it up, are you?" I replied, "Really, I'm not lying." Mother told Ngaktruk, the village chief, about this. "It could be true," said he. "You must keep this child clean and guard him from defilements. If he is the incarnation of a good practitioner and practices the Dharma, he will benefit both himself and others." Years later, when I was practicing Thögal[19] in

mountain retreats and many similar things manifested, I wondered if what I had seen as a child was a reawakening of previous tendencies.

Once, when I was six or seven years old, after the spring fields had been sown and the days were growing longer, our village chief sat down in a warm, sunny spot with a copy of the *Sutra of the Wise and the Foolish*.[20] A crowd gathered around him while he gave teachings on the karmic law of cause and effect. I had come to listen, too. He said:

"Listen! In future times, beyond this lifetime, it will be difficult to find a precious human birth, free and well-favored. We must therefore try hard to practice Dharma, now that we have this precious body. The time of our death is uncertain. Who knows? We might even die tonight.

"After death, we will enter the presence of Yamaraj, Lord of Death, who will weigh our good and evil deeds. Those who have done wrong will be sent to suffer the pains of hell, while those who have acted with virtue will enjoy the happiness of the higher realms. Is it not therefore foolish to do wrong? [16a].

"Of all misdeeds, taking the life of a sentient being is the most heinous, and cannot fail to lead you to the hell realm. Avoid this at all costs!

"Do what is good. Serve the Sangha respectfully, make offerings, be generous. Prostrations, circumambulations, reciting mantras, and keeping a good heart lead to rebirth in the Blissful Realm.[21] Work hard at them! The reasons are explained in the *Sutra of the Wise and the Foolish*, which I shall now read."

While reading it, Ngaktruk would pause from time to time to explain the meaning. In this way, he benefited the minds of those who had gathered there. I, too, gained some understanding, and resolved that, from then on, I would refrain from any wrongdoing and practice only virtue.

As I grew older, I never forgot this vow and even avoided crushing the tiniest of earthworms. I didn't allow others to kill the horseflies that had settled on meat and gave them my own blood to drink. Whenever my mother did prostrations, I prostrated myself, too. I offered incense and flowers at our altar, and recited whatever mantras and prayers I knew, like the *mani* and the *Mik-tsema Prayer*.[22]

One autumn, the harvest was excellent. Both rich and poor families said this was something to celebrate, and thus many scores of sheep were slaughtered. This grim spectacle horrified me and filled me with compassion. I couldn't bear to remain at the slaughtering-place and had to go and wait elsewhere. When the killing was over, I returned, and I saw the sprawled carcasses of the sheep being carved into pieces. I thought, "These people are doing evil, even though they know they will experience the results in their next life. When I grow up, I will turn away from evil actions and only practice Dharma." I reaffirmed this promise again and again [16b].

At this time, my old grandfather, Ngawang, was teaching the alphabet to my cousin Nam Lhajam. I used to sit behind them and, just by looking on, I learned the letters with little difficulty. When, after a long time, Nam Lhajam hadn't learned, Grandfather scolded him, saying, "Though I am teaching you, you still haven't learned. Your little cousin has learned without being taught. What is to be done with you?" To me he said, "You are quite bright," and treated me very kindly. In the same way, I learned to read by looking on while other children were being taught. Thus, without formal training, I mastered both printed and cursive scripts.

Then my old grandfather and a nun living with us died. Following this, my mother's young brother, Kyabgo, died suddenly at the age of twenty-one. The strain of these and other difficulties caused my mother to age prematurely.

By the age of nine or ten, I had learned the liturgy used by the community of *ngakpas* living in Shohong Lhaka,[23] as well as printed and cursive script calligraphy. Thus, for a child my age, I had mastered reading and writing quite well.

When I turned eleven, I joined that community of *ngakpas*, a community known for their pure *samaya*[24] and unshakable faith in the Secret Mantra tradition of the Early Translation school.[25] I became good at chanting the rituals, thus pleasing most of the older *ngakpas* who commented, "This young *ngakpa* really sings well!" They called me Tashi Tsering, "Auspicious Long Life" [17a].

One day, a relative of ours, an old spinster by the name of Ayi Lumo Pal, was sitting alone in a warm, sunny spot near her door. I went over to her and said, "Don't feel sad. When I grow up, I will help you in any way I can." I went home, took some butter from our kitchen—without my mother knowing it—and gave it to the old woman. As I grew older, from time to time I helped Ayi Lumo Pal. This made her very happy; she would call me whenever she saw me and often share with me whatever nice food she had. Even now, I remember how she treated me with the affection she would have shown to her own child.

One day, the root guru and crown jewel of the Sangha and of everyone in our district, Gedun Tashi Gyatso Chumar Rinpoche[26] arrived. To many monks and lay people he gave the refuge vows and the oral transmission for the *Confession of Misdeeds*, the *Hundred Deities of Tushita*,[27] the *Miktsema Prayer*, and the *mani*. He gave general teachings on the difficulty of obtaining a precious, free, and well-favored human birth, on death and impermanence, on the karmic law of cause and effect, and on the defects of samsara in as much detail as necessary, benefiting everyone. At this time he advised:

"Parents, if you have several children, don't let them all become householders. How excellent if some of them became ordained and practiced the Dharma! [17b]. Our teacher, the Buddha Shakyamuni, was saddened at the sight of the suffering of old age, sickness, and death, but was pleased at the sight of a monk. Forsaking his kingdom, he renounced the world in front of the Stupa of Great Purity.[28]

"Then, after practicing austerities on the banks of the Nairanjara River, he attained complete enlightenment, seated under the Bodhi-tree at Vajrasana, the Diamond Throne of India. In the light of his example, consider the good fortune of practicing Dharma in this way."

After hearing this, I returned home. We had seven *thangkas* that illustrated the twelve great deeds of the Buddha's life.[29] Considering them deeply, I thought, "This is what was meant." My heart was filled with the aspiration to become like the Buddha.

This precious master instituted chanting of the *mani* in our area.[30] Turning everyone's mind toward the Dharma, this venerable lama showed great kindness to the people there. From this time on, without fail, I observed the eightfold precepts on each eighth lunar day as well as on the days of the full and new moons.

When I grew older, I painted frescoes depicting stories from *A Drop of Nourishment for the People*[31] on either side of the lama's door; they pleased him greatly. Even now, I can remember the spiritual conversations we had in those days. When he was about to die, he left his final testament:

> Unfailing refuge for whoever relies on you,
> Source of all excellence in this and future
> lives,
> Treasury of all accomplishment, gracious
> lords,
> Teachers whom I have met and those of
> the lineage,
> Sustain me until enlightenment.
>
> You beings, who have continuously
> wandered in samsara
> Like a river flowing on and on,
> Consider the sufferings of old age, sickness,
> and death [18a].
> Give up the ten evil actions and try to
> practice the ten virtuous deeds.[32]
> Always keep in mind that you are walking
> into the maw of the Lord of Death.
>
> Don't let your mind be too involved with
> outer phenomena;
> Turn it inward—better to ascertain
> The true nature of mind within.
>
> Though you may be unable to experience
> the vajra-feast
> That is naked, brilliant emptiness,
> If you don't have some certainty about the
> real meaning,
> Guiding others is like the blind leading the
> blind.
>
> When the time comes to enter the mouth
> of the Lord of Death,
> If you lack the small but crucial shield of
> this oral instruction,
> Other instructions, like dull instruments,
> Won't be much help at that crucial
> juncture.
> Don't miss the main point!
>
> Visualize the Great Compassionate One
> above your head.
> With your voice, recite the six-syllable
> mantra.[33]
> With your mind, generate compassion for
> all suffering beings,
> So that this and future lives may be filled
> with virtue and excellence.
>
> Devoted people of future generations,
> Keep this in mind.
> Had you met me in person,
> I would have nothing to say beyond this.
> May all faithful men and women
> Who have some connection with me
> Take rebirth in the paradise Arrayed in
> Turquoise Petals.[34]
> May this region be endowed
> With auspiciousness and abundant
> harvests,
> And its people enjoy fulfillment and
> prosperity.

There was great meaning in his words.

Some time later, when I was about twelve or thirteen years old, I went to Orgyen Trinley Namgyal, "All-Victorious Activity of Orgyen," a lama living at lower Tashikhyil who was skilled in the practices of pacifying, enriching, magnetizing, and subjugating[35] according to the Nyingmapa school of the Secret Mantra. I received teachings from him on the ritual liturgies of the *Eight Commands, Union of the Sugatas*,[36] the *Most Secret and Unsurpassable Dagger*,[37] the *Lord of the Dead Who Destroys Arrogant Spirits*,[38] *Hayagriva*, and others [18b]. He also taught me how to make *tormas*[39] and draw *chakras*[40] for protection and for averting evil according to these traditions. Since I learned these without difficulty, he was pleased with me.

When I asked him for some oral transmissions for my daily practice, he said, "If you want the Dharma, I will give it to you, but first you must be able to withstand some hardships." I replied, "I can," and, from then on, I fetched water up to thirteen times each day to make mud for the walls of his retreat hut. I beat the mud, and he applied it to the hut. After many days of carrying water, my back ached. "My back is sore now," I told him. But he replied: "Haven't you heard how, in the past, the great Jetsun Milarepa carried enormous quantities of earth and stones— much more than you've done—and three terrible sores broke out on his back?" "That's true," I thought, and after I had brought water for fifteen more days, he was pleased and gave me all the transmissions I wanted. These included the daily practices of the *White Path of Liberation*, the *Guru Yoga of Orgyen Rinpoche*,[41] the meditation and recitation practice of *Peaceful Manjushri*, the smoke-offering *Spiral of Auspiciousness*,[42] and the general *torma* offering to the *samaya*-holding protectors.[43]

"Now, avoid a worldly life, lead a life of pure Dharma practice and you will succeed," he said. I asked, "What is the best way to practice the Dharma?" He replied, "If you genuinely wish to practice, look at the life of Jetsun Milarepa. The best way of all would be to follow his example."

When I was fourteen I met Jampel Dorje Rinpoche, "Adamantine Gentle Glory," the great lord of *siddhas* who had attained full realization in the development and completion stages, and in the Great Perfection of the Diamond Vehicle of the Secret Mantra [37]. When the *ngakpas* of Shohong received the empowerment of Vajrasattva and seven days of teachings on the oral instructions of the *Dzogchen Ati Zabdon*, the *Profound Unsurpassable Meaning of the Great Perfection*,[44] I, too, sat in the gathering and listened.

When he explained the more general teachings, renunciation and weariness with samsara grew in everyone's minds. When he reached the main part of the teachings, he had us look for the nature of mind. He called each *ngakpa* up before him, and questioned him. At one point, I, too, was called on. He asked, "What is mind like?" I said, "I could find nothing at all." He replied, "You're still very young. If you weren't able to find it, that's fine."

Then, when all the *ngakpas* had gathered and he gave the "pointing-out" instruction, I recognized that the nature of mind is like the sky: empty, luminous, and beyond duality. The master and most of the elderly *ngakpas* said to each other, "This is surely someone with good karmic potential from his former lives."

After that, every year when the community of *ngakpas* and the practioners who perform the offerings of the tenth day[45] received teachings, I also went to listen. Thus I received the empowerment of *Vajra Kilaya*[46] and the permission-blessing for the practice of Khecari, the *Sky Dweller*,[47] as well as the transmission for the *Supplication to Guru Rinpoche in Seven Chapters*, the *Prayer for the Spontaneous Fulfillment of Aspirations*, the *Sadhana of the Lineage of Awareness-Holders*,[48] the *Praises to Tara the Savioress*, the *Sutra of the Heart of Wisdom*,[49] the dharanis of the *White Umbrella* and of the *Lion-faced Dakini*,[50] the *Long-Life Dharani*, and others. From then on, my character became more gentle. I had meditation experiences of bliss, clarity, and nonthought, and was able to get on well with whomever I met [19b].

At the age of fifteen, I thought, "I should pray to the precious Master [Padmasambhava], the source of blessings. I recited one million Vajra Guru mantras,[51] based on the ritual of the *Lineage of Awareness-Holders*. I dreamed of flying in the sky, seeing the sun and moon, walking uphill, finding jewel-treasures, and so forth. From then on, by the grace of Orgyen Rinpoche, I became filled with intense devotion toward the guru, affection toward my Dharma friends, compassion for sentient beings, and pure perception toward the teachings. I had the good fortune to accomplish without obstacles whatever Dharma practice I undertook.

After that, at the age of sixteen, I thought I should do some practice on a meditation-deity of knowledge. So, I stayed in retreat for a year, reciting the mantra of the peaceful Manjushri according to the spiritual treasure of Minling Terchen. My mother helped me during the retreat. Having recited the Arapatsa mantra[52] ten million times, I dreamed of finding books written in gold and silver; I dreamed of wheels, swords, the vajra and bell, and so forth. From then on, by the grace of the noble Manjushri, my intelligence increased, and I acquired a general understanding of most of the vast and profound teachings.

At seventeen, I learned religious painting from Tenpa Dargye, "One who Spreads the Dharma," a religious artist from Ling Gya, and became able to make good drawings. I drew many of the *chakras* and *lingas*[53] that are in general use among the holders of the mantra teachings for protection and for averting evils. I also made many icons and amulets that liberate the wearer, and gave them away to Dharma friends and faithful people. I copied many books for myself and others [20a], and I became so skilled at writing that, on a single spring day, I wrote a hundred folios. People were amazed.

Around this time, I met Jamyang Gyatso Rinpoche, "Ocean of Gentle Melody," a lord among accomplished beings, who was thoroughly versed in the teachings of both the Old and the New Traditions, Nyingma and Sarma. He had been invited to Tashikhyil by the venerable Gyal Khenchen, the "Great Victorious Abbot." With the congregation of *ngakpas* I received the empowerment of *Taktsang Phurba;*[54] I received the oral instructions on the Great Perfection teachings of the *Heart Essence of Samantabhadra*[55] three times.

Moreover, when many monks and *ngakpas* requested further teachings from him, I received them as well. These included the empowerment of the *Hundred Supreme Peaceful and Wrathful Families*[56] and of the *All-Embodying One,*[57] as well as the oral transmissions and instructions on the *Offering to the Gurus,*[58] the *Condensed Meaning of the Graded Path,*[59] the *Seven Points of Mind Training,*[60] the *Supreme Medicinal Nectar of the Garland of Questions and Answers,*[61] the *Liberation Through Hearing,* the pointing-out instruction *Awareness Seen in its Nakedness,*[62] *Cutting off Errors and Deviations;*[63] the *Oral Teaching of the Omniscient One called the Drop of Amrita*[64] and also the instructions on *tummo,*[65] inner incandescence, based on the *Sole Ornament of the Five Families of Vajrasattva.*[66]

I completed the required number of recitations in the preliminary practices of the Great Perfection, and through their blessing acquired some understanding of the meaning of the teachings of the Victorious Ones.

One day, at eighteen, I thought, "Food and wealth have no real essence; I must practice the Dharma." Just then, a goldsmith came by with a golden image depicting Orgyen Rinpoche seated upon a lotus flower on a lake and accompanied by the divine lady Mandarava and the princess Yeshe Tsogyal. Although I owned only two *dzomos,*[67] I offered him these along with some silver coins[68] as payment; it pleased him [20b]. For the consecration, I invited my kind root master, Jetsun Jamyang Gyatso Rinpoche. Together with many *ngakpas,* he threw the flowers of consecration. I held a great feast, and the local people rejoiced. Afterward, Kashul Nyengyal and others called upon the goldsmith, who as a result received commissions for many more gilded statues.

While my kind root master, Jamyang Gyatso, was staying at Tashikhyil, I went to visit him many times and offered him whatever I possessed. Because I did exactly as he asked, he treated me with great affection.

Notes

1. The Diamond Throne of India (Skt. Vajrasana, Tib. *rgya gar rdo rje gdan*), now called Bodhgaya: the place where Lord Buddha Shakyamuni attained enlightenment and where the thousand Buddhas of this aeon attain enlightenment.

2. Jetsun Kalden Gyatso (*rje btsun* or *grub chen skal*

ldan rgya mtsho, 1607–77) is the author of beautiful songs and poems on contemplative practice, and he was a great source of inspiration to Shabkar. A highly venerated master, he was considered to be an emanation of Lord Buddha's disciple Shariputra. The example of his life and teachings had a wide influence in the Rekong area, where he founded Tashikhyil retreat center (*bkra shis 'khyil sgrub sde*) in 1648. He was also known as Kalden Repa (*skal ldan ras pa*) and Kachu Rinpoche (*bka' bcu rin po che*, RO, p. 185). A hagiography of Kalden Gyatso, entitled *grub chen skal ldan rgya mtsho'i rnam thar yid bzhin dbang gi rgyal po*, is mentioned by Vostrikov (1970). A short biography can also be found in RO, pp. 164–88. Kalden Gyatso was a disciple of another famous hermit, Chöpa Rinpoche Lobzang Tenpai Gyaltsen (*chos pa rin po che blo bzang bstan pa'i rgyal mtshan*, 1581–1659).

3. The Victorious Ones, Father and Son: the Dalai Lama and the Panchen Lama.

4. The Eight Places of the Accomplished Ones (*grub thob gnas brgyad*), in the Golden Valley of Rekong, are eight places prophesied by Guru Padmasambhava where eight great yogins of his lineage practiced, attained realization and performed many miracles. In AC, vol. 2, pp. 304–12, the eight (or nine) places are identified as follows:

In the center is Balgi Khargong Lakha (*'bal gyi mkhar gong la kha*) the meditation place of the Bodhisattva of Bol (*'bol gyi byang chub sems dpa'*).

In the east is Taklung Shelgi Riwo (*stag lung shel gyi ri bo*), the meditation place of Shelgi Odeh Gung Gyal (*shel gyi 'o de gung rgyal*).

In the southeast is Lhadrak Karpo, in the Upper part of Chang (*spyang phu'i lha brag dkar po*), where Kalden Gyatso had a vision of Kasarpani and one of the Sixteen Arhats. In the vicinity is Ratse Phug (*rwa rtse phug*), the meditation place of Masö Shili Urwa (*ma gsod zhi li 'ur ba*).

In the south, in Dambu, is Drakar Serkhang (*'dam bu'i brag dkar gser khang*), the meditation place of the great Brahmin Litrö (*bram ze chen po li khrod*).

In the southwest is Thamug Dzongmar Gonpa (*mtha' smug rdzong dmar dgon pa*), the meditation place of Athu Ngakpa Yu Ngok (*a mthu'i sngags pa g.yu rngogs*).

In the west is Sheldel Chökyi Potrang (*shel del chos kyi pho brang*), the meditation place of Tönpa Odeh Shampo (*ston pa 'o de sham po*). AC mentions that this is an extra, or ninth, place.

In the northwest is Kyagang Nemö Bangwa or Dori Palkyi Ritse (*skya sgang gnas mo'i bang ba*, or *do ri dpal gyi ri rtse*), the meditation place of Seyi Gyalwa

Changchup (*bse yi rgyal ba byang chub*), where there are many images that have appeared naturally on the rocks.

In the north is Gongmo Gurkhang Draktsa (*gong mo'i gur khang brag rtsa*), the meditation place of the Bönpo master Drenpa Namkha (*dran pa nam mkha'*).

In the northeast is Chuchik Shel (*bcu gcig shel*), the meditation place of Kathok Dorje Wangpo (*ka thog rdo rje dbang po*, see note 6), Chöpa Rinpoche and Jetsun Kalden Gyatso (see note 2).

In RO, pp. 46–58, nine places where eight *siddhas* meditated are identified in a slightly different way. The spelling of the names of the places and of the *siddhas* also vary.

5. Chuchik Shel (*bcu gcig shel gi dgon pa bde chen chos kyi pho brang*, see note 4, and RO, pp. 47. and 545), lit. the "Dharma Palace of Great Bliss, the Crystal Monastery in Eleven," is thus called because of the "Crystal Monastery" located in the lower part of a valley named "Eleven." Crystals in the shape of deities, such as Chakrasamvara, Guru Padmasambhava and the eight Bodhisattvas, and of stupas, conches, vajra and bell, etc., are found in abundance on the boulders around the monastery.

6. Kawa Dorje Chang Wang (*ka ba rdo rje 'chang dbang*), also called Kathok Dorje Wangpo (*ka thog rdo rje dbang po*), is one of the Four Sons of Kathok (*ka thog bu bzhi*), who were contemporaries of King Trisong Detsen. Dorje Chang Wang came to Amdo and meditated at Chuchik Shel, where he attained the rainbow body.

7. Machen Pomra (*rma chen spom ra*). See details n chap. 7.

8. Tashi Tsekpa (Skt. *Mangala-kuta-sutra*, Tib. *bkra shis brtsegs pa*), a sutra recited to bring auspiciousness. It is found in the *gzungs 'dus* (a collection of dharanis and short sutras used to perform ceremonies), in vol. Wam, folios 249b–254b of the Lhasa edition, but is not included in any of the eleven known editions of the Kangyur. (Communicated by Peter Skilling.)

9. To be born into a rich family is the source of great attachment, while to be born into a poor family is the source of great difficulties. The former circumstance hinders one's aspiration to renounce the world, and the latter hinders one's ability to practice the Dharma. To be born into a family that is neither very rich nor very poor thus offers the best conditions to further one's Dharma practice.

10. Shariputra, one of the two disciples always depicted at the side of Buddha Shakyamuni.

11. The eightfold precepts of lay ordination (*bsnyen gnas yan lag brgyad pa*) or one-day vows, are taken for

twenty-four hours, from dawn to dawn. These include avoiding 1) taking life; 2) taking what is not given; 3) sexual intercourse; 4) telling lies; 5) drinking liquor; 6) dancing, wearing garlands, using perfumes, and playing worldly music; 7) sleeping on a high and ornamented bed; and 8) eating after midday.

12. Ngakchang Dorje Namgyal (*sngags 'chang rdo rje rnam rgyal*), was the second incarnation of Tsodu Khenchen Lobzang Trinley (*'tsho 'du'i mkhan chen blo bzang phrin las*). According to RO, p. 555, he had several sons, of whom Shabkar was one. Further incarnations of Lobzang Trinley were recognized. Tsodu (*tsho 'du*) is one of the five grasslands of the nomad area of Rekong (*rong 'brog tsho lnga;* see RO, p. 560). The name of a Dorje Namgyal also appears in the lineage of the Mindroling tradition that Shabkar received from his Dzogchen master Jampel Dorje (*'jam dpal rdo rje*). See fol. 19a of this autobiography. On Shabkar's lineage for the Khandro Nyingthig, see Appendix 2, table 2, and F. K. Ehrhard, *Flügel-schläge des Garuda*, p. 37.

13. The Youth Who Brings Water (*khe'u chu 'bebs*): the Bodhisattva, the Buddha Shakyamuni in a former birth. As a sea merchant, by uttering the names of the Buddhas he used to free the fish and other creatures living in the ocean.

14. The five sciences (*rigs pa'i gnas lnga*): grammar, crafts, medicine, astrology, and philosophy.

15. Not necessarily her real uncle. "Aku" is used to address a paternal uncle, but is also used for a monk or a priest, independent of any family ties. Similarly, "Ashang" is used to address a maternal uncle but is also used for any layman.

16. The year 1781. The Tibetan calendar is based on a sixty-year cycle, based on twelve different animal signs combined with five elements. In addition, each year of this cycle also has a specific name of its own.

17. Obscuring emotions (Skt. *kleshas*, Tib. *nyon mongs*), the eighty-four thousand kinds of confusions that obscure the mind, prevent the realization of the lack of existence of individual self, or ego, and of phenomena, and thus perpetuate suffering in samsara. They can be condensed into five: anger, desire, ignorance, pride, and jealousy, which are often called the "five poisons."

18. *Tsampa* (*rtsam pa*) is a flour made of roasted barley. It is the staple food among Tibetans.

19. Thögal (*thod rgal*), the most advanced practice of the Great Perfection (*rdzogs chen*, see Appendix 1).

20. *Sutra of the Wise and the Foolish* (Skt. *damomurkha-nama-sutra*, Tib. *mdza' blun zhes bya ba'i mdo*, T 341) is a

sutra that contains fifty-one narratives of the previous lives of the Buddha. For a translation into English, see Frye (1981).

21. The Blissful Realm, Sukhavati (*bde ba can*), is the paradise of Buddha Amitabha.

22. *Miktsema* (*dmigs brtse ma*), a prayer to Je Tsongkhapa (1357–1419), considered as inseparable from Avalokiteshvara, Manjushri, and Vajrapani.

23. The monasteries around Rekong, including Shohong (*zho 'ong*, spelled *zho 'phong* in RO), are famous for the number, spiritual accomplishment, and power of their *ngakpas* (Skt. *mantrin*), who dress in white and keep their hair, sometimes more than six feet long, coiled on top of their heads.

24. *Samaya.* See Translator's Introduction, note 38.

25. The Early Translation school (*snga 'gyur rnying ma*), often simply called Nyingma, is the earliest tradition of Tibetan Buddhism (see Appendix 1).

26. Also known as Chumar Chungwa Ngawang Gedun Tashi Gyatso (*chu dmar chung ba ngag dbang dge 'dun bkra shis rgya mtsho*). Born in Shohong Lakha, he studied under both Geluk and Nyingma masters, such as Chöying Tobden Dorje (*chos dbyings stobs ldan rdo rje*, c. 1787–1848, see Appendix 2 and RO, pp. 549–50).

27. The *Confession of Misdeeds* (*ltung bshags*) is part of the *triskandhaka sutra* (*phung po gsum gyi mdo*, T 284). *The Hundred Deities of Tushita* (*dga' ldan lha brgya*), written by the fifth Dalai Lama. It is a Guru Yoga practice which starts with the words, "*The hundred deities of Tushita . . .*" and is focused on Tsongkhapa being emanated from Amitabha's heart and coming before one on a milk-white path.

28. The Stupa of Great Purity (*mchod rten rnam dag*) is the stupa in front of which Shakyamuni cut his hair and vowed to renounce the world. Some place it near Ramagama, east of Kapilavastu (see Lamotte, 1958), and others near Mankapur in Uttar Pradesh (see NS, vol. 2, p. 30 n. 400), or near Bodhgaya itself.

29. The twelve deeds performed by fully enlightened Buddhas (*mdzad pa bcu gnyis*):

1) Descending from Tushita Heaven (*dga' ldan gnas nas 'pho ba*).
2) Entering the womb of his mother (*lhums su bzhugs pa*).
3) Taking birth (*sku bltams pa*).
4) Becoming skilled in worldly arts and demonstrating physical prowess (*bzo la mkhas par ston pa dang gzhon nu'i rol rtsed*).
5) Enjoying his retinue of queens (*btsun mo'i 'khor gyis rol pa*).

6) Renouncing the world (*rab tu 'byung ba*).
7) Practicing austerities and then renouncing them (*dka' ba spyad pa*).
8) Going to the Bodhi-tree (*byang chub snying por gshegs pa*)
9) Subduing Mara (*bdud btul*).
10) Attaining full enlightenment (*mngon par sangs rgyas pa*).
11) Turning the Wheel of the Dharma (*chos kyi 'khor lo bskor*).
12) Passing into the ultimate peace beyond suffering (Skt., *parinirvana*, Tib. *mya ngan las 'das pa*).

30. Traditionally, once a year the whole population of a village and its surroundings would gather and recite together a hundred million *mani* mantras. (i.e., the mantra of Avalokiteshvara, OM MANI PADME HUM). During this time, a lama would give daily teachings on the Dharma.

31. *A Drop of Nourishment for the People* (Skt. *nitasastra-jantuposanabindu*, Tib. *lugs kyi bstan bcos skye bo gso ba'i thig pa*, T 4330), a short collection of didactic metaphors written by Nagarjuna. See Frye (1981).

32. *Ten virtuous deeds:*
Three of the body:
(1) To protect life, (2) to be honest, and (3) to maintain proper sexual conduct.
Four of speech: (1) To tell the truth, (2) to avoid gossip, (3) to avoid slander, and (4) to speak gentle words that bring happiness to others.
Three of the mind: (1) to rejoice in the good fortune of others, (2) to have only thoughts that are beneficial to others, and (3) to have correct views.

33. OM MANI PADME HUM (see note 30).

34. The paradise Arrayed in Turquoise Petals (*g.yu lo bkod pa'i zhing*), the Buddhafield of Arya Tara.

35. These are the four main activities performed for the sake of others by accomplished yogins: *pacifying* sickness, obstacles, mental obscurations, and ignorance; *enriching* merit, life span, glory, prosperity, and wisdom; *bringing under control* the spiritual qualities, life force, and all the powerful energies of the three worlds; and *subjugating wrathfully* the outer and inner negative forces.

36. *The Eight Commands, Union of the Sugatas* (*bka' brgyad bde gshegs 'dus pa*), rediscovered by Nyang Ral Nyima Öser (*nyang ral nyi ma 'od zer*, 1136–1204). This is the first and most important of the *terma* cycles based on the Eight Commands (*sgrub pa bka' brgyad*). On the life-story of Nyang Ral, see NS, pp. 755–59.

37. *The Most Secret and Unsurpassable Dagger* (*phur pa yang gsang bla med*): rediscovered by Chögyal Ratna

Lingpa (*chos rgyal ratna gling pa*, 1403–78). Ratna Lingpa is said to be the only tertön who always met with perfectly auspicious circumstances (*rten 'brel*) and could thus find the complete set of *termas* that were prophesied to him. On the life-story of this master and the account of his revelations, see *Collected Rediscovered Teachings of Ratna gLing-pa*, vols. 1 and 2, as well as NS, pp. 793–95.

38. *The Lord of the Dead Who Destroys Arrogant Spirits* (*gshin rje dregs 'joms*) is a *terma* that was rediscovered by Minling Terchen Terdak Lingpa, Gyurme Dorje (*smin gling gter chen gter bdag gling pa 'gyur med rdo rje*, 1646-1714). A disciple as well as a teacher of the fifth Dalai Lama, Terdak Lingpa revealed major *termas*, compiled the canonical scriptures of the Nyingma tradition (*rnying ma bka' ma*), and, with his brother Minling Lochen Dharma Shri (*smin gling lo chen dharma shri*, 1654-1718), played a major role in ensuring the continuity of the exegetical tradition of the *Guhyagarbha Tantra* (*Tantra of the Secret Quintessence*, see NGB, vol. 14, no. 187). See NS, pp. 825–34.

39. A *torma* (*gtor ma*) is a symbolic ritual object often made of flour, wood, or precious metal, which, depending on circumstances, can be visualized as an offering, as the deity, as a blessing, or as a weapon hurled against negative forces.

40. Skt. *chakras* (Tib. *'khor lo*) are symbolic "wheels," or circular diagrams, upon which are written mantras and formulae meant for protection, for helping one to attain liberation, and for accomplishing any of the four activities (see note 35) for the sake of sentient beings.

41. *The White Path of Liberation* (*thar lam dkar po*). This text could not be identified.

The Guru Yoga of Orgyen Rinpoche (*o rgyan rin po che bla ma'i rnal 'byor*): a practice of guru devotion focusing on Guru Padmasambhava.

42. *The Spiral of Auspiciousness*: the *lha rnams mnyes par byed pa'i bsangs mchod bkra shis 'khyil ba*, written by the fifth Dalai Lama. This is a text for the ritual of smoke-offering (*bsangs*), which is made by burning leaves and branches of fragrant trees such as juniper and rhododendron, mixed with blessed ingredients. Boundless offerings, filling the sky, are visualized in the smoke and are offered to the "four classes of guests" (see Author's Introduction, note 32).

43. The general *torma* offering to the *samaya*-bound protectors (*dam can spyi gtor*) is a condensed offering ritual to the protectors of the Mindroling tradition, written by Terdak Lingpa (see above).

44. *The Profound Unsurpassable Meaning of the Great Perfection* (*a ti zab don snying po*): a *terma* cycle rediscov-

ered by Terdak Lingpa. The explanation for its practice was written by Jetsun Mingyur Paldrön (*rje btsun mi 'gyur dpal sgron*, 1699–1769), one of his daughters, who became the main holder of his teachings. See RT, vol. 58 (Si) and the *a ti zab don* cycle published by Kocchen Tulku, Dehra Dun, 1977.

45. The offering on the tenth day (*tshes bcu*) of the lunar month is dedicated to Guru Padmasambhava, who promised that he would come from the Buddhafield of the Glorious Copper-colored Mountain, Zangdopalri (*zang mdog dpal ri*), and bless the disciples who pray to him and offer a *ganachakra* ritual feast (*tshogs 'khor*) on that day.

46. Dorje Phurba (*rdo rje phur pa*), or Vajra Kilaya. One of the main meditational deities, or *yidam*, of the Nyingma and other traditions, whose specific quality is to dispel all obstacles on the path of enlightenment.

47. Khachöma (*mkha' spyod ma*, Skt. Khecari) is an aspect of the wisdom dakini extensively practiced in the Sakya and Geluk traditions.

48. *The Supplication to Guru Rinpoche in Seven Chapters* (*gsol sdebs le'u bdun ma*), the *Prayer for the Spontaneous Fulfillment of Aspirations* (*bsam pa lhun grub ma*), and *The Sadhana of the Lineage of Awareness-Holders* (*rig 'dzin gdung sgrub*) belong to the cycle of practices focused upon Guru Padmasambhava rediscovered by Rigdzin Gödem (*rig 'dzin rgod ldem*, 1337–1408) and are part of what is known as the Northern Terma (*byang gter*). See NS, pp. 780–83.

49. *Sutra of the Heart of Wisdom* (Skt. *prajnaparamitahridaya*, Tib. *mdo shes rab snying po*, T 21).

50. The White Umbrella (Skt., *Sitatapatra*, Tib. *gdugs dkar*) is a deity said to be born from the protuberance (*usnisha*) on the Buddha's head. The dharanis and mantras of the *White Umbrella* and the *Lion-faced Dakini* (*seng ge gdong can*) are among the chief recitations used to avert obstacles and negative forces.

51. The twelve-syllable mantra of Guru Padmasambhava, OM AH HUM VAJRA GURU PADMA SIDDHI HUM.

52. The root mantra of the peaceful Manjushri, OM A RA PA TSA NA DHI.

53. *Linga*: Representation of the forces of evil as a figure in chains, with destructive mantras written upon it.

54. *Taktsang Phurba* (*stag tshang phur ba; see* RT, vol. 31, Ki) is the cycle of teachings focused on Vajra Kilaya, rediscovered by Ratön Tertön (*rwa ston gter ston*, see Translator's Introduction, note 41) at Onphu Taktsang (*'on phu stag tshang*) near Samye in central Tibet. Onphu Taktsang is the cave where Guru Padmasambhava gave the Vajra Kilaya initiation to Tashi Kyidren (*bkra shis khyi 'dren*) and Yeshe Tsogyal

(*ye shes mtsho rgyal*). It is also one of the thirteen "Tiger Dens" (*stag tshang*) of Tibet and Bhutan.

55. *Kunzang Nyingthig* (*kun bzang snying thig*), a *terma* of Tennyi Lingpa (*bstan gnyis gling pa*, 1480-1535). See Translator's Introduction, note 42, and table 4.

56. The Hundred Supreme Deities (*zhi khro dam pa rigs brgya*) are the forty-two peaceful and fifty-eight wrathful deities that correspond to the enlightened aspects of the psychophysical components of a sentient being.

57. Vairocana (*kun rigs rnam par snang mdzad*) is a deity who embodies the five Buddha families.

58. *Offering to the Gurus* (*bla ma mchod pa*): the ritual of offering to the gurus of a spiritual lineage. Each school of the Tibetan Buddhist tradition has its own *bla ma mchod pa*.

59. The *Condensed Meaning of the Graded Path* (*byang chub lam gyi rim pa'i nyams len bsdus don*), written by Tsongkhapa.

60. The *Seven Points of Mind Training* (*blo sbyong don bdun ma*) written by Geshe Chen-ngawa (*spyan snga ba*, also known as *tshul khrims 'bar*, 1038–1103) according to the oral instructions on loving-kindness, compassion, and Bodhicitta that he had received from Drom Tönpa (*'brom ston pa*, 1005–64), the chief disciple of Atisha (982–1054). The latter had received these instructions from the great Bodhicitta master Serlingpa (*gser gling pa*).

61. The *Supreme Medicinal Nectar of the Garland of Questions and Answers* (*zhu len sman mchog bdud rtsi phreng ba*) was written by Lodrak Drupchen Lekyi Dorje (*lho brag grub chen las kyi rdo rje*), also known as Namkha Gyaltsen (*nam mkha' rgyal mtshan*, 1326–1401; see GC, vol. 3, pp. 282–96). This great Nyingmapa siddha had many visions of Guru Padmasambhava and Vajrapani, whom he used to meet as though meeting real people. He was the Dzogchen master of Tsongkhapa (*tsong kha pa*, 1357–1419). These *Questions and Answers* are those that were put by Tsongkhapa to Lodrak Drupchen. The latter would, in turn, ask Vajrapani and then give the answers to Tsongkhapa. On these history and contents of these dialogues, see Ehrhard (1992) and NS, pp. 923ff. Lodrak Drupchen's embalmed body was kept in the Stupa Vase of Lodrak (*lho brag bum pa*) at Taphu (*rta phu*), below Ganden monastery. The stupa was erected at a crossroads, on the spot where the master had passed away, lying facing the ground to suppress the influence of the nagas and other negative forces that cause leprosy and other diseases.

62. The *Liberation Through Hearing*, the *Bardo Thödrol* (*bar do thos grol*) and *The Self-liberation through Awareness*

Seen in its Nakedness (*rig pa ngo sprod gcer mthong rang grol*) belongs to the famous cycle of rediscovered teachings of Karma Lingpa (1326?, see GC, vol. 2, pp. 714–18 and NS, pp. 800-801), known as *The Peaceful and Wrathful Deities, Self-liberated Wisdom Mind* (*zhi khro dgongs pa rang grol*).

63. *Cutting Off Errors and Deviations, the Lion's Roar* (*gol shor tshar gcod seng ge'i nga ro*) is a text from the cycle of the *Longchen Nyingthig* (*klong chen snying thig*). The cycle was rediscovered in a vision by Rigdzin Jigme Lingpa (see Translator's Introduction, note 43). This text explains the various deviations through which a practitioner may go astray in his meditation.

64. *The Drop of Amrita*: probably the *bdud rtsi'i thig pa'i rtsa tshigs* of Lodrak Drupchen. See note 61.

65. One of the Six Yogas, *tummo* (*gtum mo*), which corresponds to the Sanskrit *candali*, means literally the "wild one." It refers to the practice of the inner heat, which is related to the mastery of the spiritual channels, energies and essences (*rtsa, rlung,* and *thig le*).

66. The *Sole Ornament of the Five Families of Vajrasattva* (*rdor sems rigs lnga rgyan gcig*) is the peaceful aspect of the *Taktsang Phurba* cycle. See RT, vol. 31 (Ki) and note 54 above.

67. *Dzomo*, the female offspring of a yak and a cow.

68. Throughout this biography various Tibetan coins and measures are mentioned. These measures correspond to quantities of silver and gold, since banknotes were issued only at the beginning of the twentieth century. In Shabkar's times one *sho* (*zho*) was the equivalent of 3.7 g. of silver and nine *sho* were roughly equivalent to one *sang* (*srang*). Various Nepalese coins (called *tamka*, Tib. *tangka*, from a Muslim name) equivalent to one-and-a-half *sho* circulated in Tibet at the same value, although some were made of pure silver and some of 50 percent alloy. The issue of debased coins caused repeated conflicts with Nepal (see chap. 13, note 46). Chinese coins of fine silver equivalent to one *sho* were also common. The *karma* (*skar ma*) is the smallest monetary unit and is roughly equivalent to one-tenth of a *sho*. A *che-gye* (*phyed brgyad*) is half of a cut *tanka*. A *dotse* (*rdo tshad* = stone-size) is the weight, or collection of fifty *sangs*. A Chinese *tamik* (*rta rmig* = horse hoof) is a silver ingot cast in the shape of a horse's hoof. There are two sizes: a large one weighing 165 *tolas* of silver (that is, about 2 kg.) and a small one weighing about 500 gms. On the development of currency in Tibet, see Rhodes (1990).

2

Renouncing the World

How, understanding that worldly things are without essence,
I left home for the homeless life.

One day, when I came into the presence of my root guru, Jamyang Rinpoche, he asked, "What do you intend to do? Aren't you going to take a wife?" I answered, "I have no desire to be reborn in samsara. Having seen the troubles that come with having a home, I have no desire to have a wife; my sole desire is to give up all the concerns of this life, as the spiritual masters advise, and to stay in the pleasant groves of a mountain retreat, drinking the nectar of the holy Dharma."

Pleased with my answer, he went on, "Well, my son, if that's so, you're not wrong. Meat, liquor, sense pleasures, worldly enjoyments—the best things of samsara are temporarily beguiling. Young brides in the full bloom of youth and beauty are expert at leading one astray. Therefore, even if you have as your companion a young daughter of the gods, have no attachment, have no desire. Why? Speaking generally, because all the things of this world are without essence, impermanent, unreliable, and by their very nature lead to suffering [22b]. In particular, because domestic life is like a pit of fire, a cannibal island, a nest of poisonous snakes. Enjoying the entire array of samsaric perfections, wealth, and pleasures is like eating food mixed with poison, like licking honey on a razor blade, like the jewel on a snake's head: a single touch destroys.

"Consider this and keep in mind that all spiritual beings, from the fully enlightened Buddha down to the masters of the present, cast away the preoccupations of this life. They received the nectar of the sacred teachings on sutra and mantra at the feet of a holy master, and drank it in the cool shade of solitary mountain forests until they were satisfied. When their spiritual experience and realization had grown to full maturity, they were able to bring benefit to themselves and to others. Should you, too, succeed in emulating the life of liberation of the past sages, there is not the slightest doubt that in this very life you will fulfill your aspirations and those of others." He then sang these verses:

> Supreme guru, remain like a diadem
>   above my head.
> Look with compassion on myself and all
>   beings.
>
> Son, son!
> You're right!
> What good is a wife?
>
> A wife is like a black noose tying you to
>   samsara,
> Like an adversary who attracts all kinds of
>   undesirable things.
>
> Once you've taken a wife,
> There's no time or chance for bliss.
>
> Taking a poisonous snake onto your lap—
> Is that bliss?
>
> Right now, not changing your noble inten-
>   tion,
> Persevere in the holy Dharma—
> It gratifies whoever attains it.

Persevere in the Dharma,
And real happiness will naturally come
   about.

May the perfect lord guru, the diadem
   upon my head,
Bless the mind-stream of this devoted son
   with wisdom.

His eyes half-closed, he added, "Son, at twenty,
having met the sublime master [23a], staying in
the refreshing shade of mountain seclusion, you
will sit just like this." Having said this, he straightened his back, looked straight ahead, eyes wide
open, and rested evenly for a while in the natural
state. Then, he broke into laughter.

When I think of it now, these were prophetic words, for just as he had said, I later had
the good fortune to practice meditation in solitary mountain retreats.

Meanwhile, the boys from my father's side kept
telling me, "It's time for you to marry." My
mother and relatives echoed them, saying that I
should take as my wife either the young widow of
my maternal uncle, who had died at the age of
twenty-one, or a certain other girl. "Choose between these two," they said. I replied, "Listen,
kind mother and you, my relatives. I am determined to practice the Dharma. I do not want a
wife."

"By all means you must take one," my
mother insisted, "for who will take care of our
land and house? If you don't, then what is the
difference to me between having you and having
no son at all? If you want to practice the Dharma,
you can do so very well in your homeland. All
your uncles practice the Dharma that way."
They went on with many examples, and gave all
sorts of reasons.

I replied, "I want nothing to do with that
kind of Dharma. I would rather not practice the
Dharma at all! If I were to take a wife, she would
have to be a peerless woman, beautiful to look at,
pleasant to listen to, easy to be with, harmonious,

agreeable—one who would gladden everyone's
mind. What's the point of marrying a slovenly,
bellicose woman who likes to gorge herself and
fall asleep?" [23b].

A few people nearby smiled and laughed.
One of my relatives pressed me further: "Then
you should take a perfect wife, one just like you
described. We will add whatever you may need
in the way of wealth and food."

But I ended the discussion by saying, "Well,
I was just teasing you. In this world, there might
be such a rare woman, a beautiful daughter from
a wealthy family, with a sweet voice and noble
character, like a daughter of gods come into the
human realm, like a fresh lotus flower in bloom
that one never tires of looking at—in short, an
object of desire for both men and gods.

"When such a peerless woman is wed to a
man who is like a celestial prince, who comes
from a rich and powerful family, both of them
are dressed up in elegant robes and bedecked
with jewels, corals dangling from their ears. As
all eyes are focused on them, they think, 'How
fine if it could be like this forever, without sickness, without growing old.'

"But some years later, after a few prized
boys and less-prized girls[1] have been born to
them, and after they have undergone illness and
misfortunes, their many troubles quickly age
them. If someone then says, 'They were once
that young couple,' who would believe it?

"When I see beautiful people who, as the
years pass, turn into an elderly pair who no
longer look appealing to anyone, I realize that, if
I took a young wife now, a time would eventually
come when we would be just another grimy, wiz-
ened old couple, and I cannot but feel dismay.

"Even if all of you got together to give me a
heavenly wife [24a], I wouldn't want her. While
still young, my only prayer is to practice the
Dharma just as the masters of the past have
done, so that, in future lives, I may be reborn not
in samsara but in the Blissful Pure Land. There,
in the company of those freed from birth and
death, I will enjoy the feast of the sublime
Dharma." Again, in verse, I said:

Lord, root guru, Vajradhara,
Bless this beggar

That he may accomplish the divine
Dharma.
Now I will give myself some advice;
All of you, listen a bit, as well.

In general, when you examine carefully
Outer things, whatever they may be,
You see them to be impermanent and
without essence.
In particular, when I think of family life in
samsara,
I feel sadness deep from within.

Seeing old people, burdened with their
years,
I realize that, if I took a young bride,
A time would come when she would fade,
as they have.
Thinking of this, I feel sadness deep from
within.

Seeing the sorrows of others in my village,
I realize that, if I set up a worldly home,
A time would come
When I would encounter the very same
sorrow.
Thinking of this, I feel sadness deep from
within.

Considering the perfect lives of past
masters,
I realize that, if I could practice the holy
Dharma,
A time would come when I would be
happy, like them.
Thinking of this, I feel great faith deep
from within.

I pray that I may be able to practice the
holy Dharma
Following the example of the victorious
lords of the past.

Lord, root guru, Vajradhara,
Bless this beggar
That he may accomplish the holy Dharma!

Thus, by various means, I was able to avoid
accepting anyone's daughter [24b]. As for the

particular young woman I had been asked to
marry, she ended up happily married to the son
of one of my relatives. For my Dharma practice,
she had indirectly been a great help.

Once, Bendhe, my relative and Dharma friend,
had some disagreement with my mother. I inter-
vened, and thus their *samaya* was not damaged.
Later, when Bendhe's irritation had subsided, he
invited me to come to his home, and, as we were
discussing various religious and worldly matters
over a cup of tea and a glass of *chang*,[2] he con-
fided, "Anger just brings harm to oneself, doesn't
it? You were good to me." In that way, he
complimented me.

During the time I spent at home, I cannot
remember ever having said a malicious word to
anyone. At break times during religious gatherings and when we were listening to the Dharma,
in order to relieve people's tiredness and wake
them up a bit, I used to tell amusing stories, and
they would all break into laughter. Some, remembering these stories, could not stop laughing. I
only needed to open my mouth and most of
them would start to laugh. Even some of the
older yogins asked me to their tea breaks, saying,
"Ngawang Tashi, tell us a joke," and they would
be amused. I would say witty things that hurt no
one's feelings, at which people could not help
laughing. During feasts and popular gatherings I
would joke and clown, increasing everyone's good
humor and cheerfulness. They even say that a
long time after I had renounced this life, old
people recalled my pleasantries and laughed.

Sometimes I would sing the spiritual songs
of the revered Lord Kalden Gyatso to old people
and inspire them to recite the *mani* [25a]. Explaining to them the meaning of these songs as
best I could, I turned the minds of these old
people toward the Dharma. In one of these
songs it says,

If you aspire to mountain solitudes
Under peaks wrapped in mist,

There are natural caves in steep, rocky
    cliffs.
To stay in such places will bring immediate
    and ultimate joy.

Whenever I sang praises of mountain
retreats, I would make a wish that the day might
come when I would have the good fortune to
stay in mountain solitudes.

One day my root guru, Jamyang Gyatso
Rinpoche, showed the signs of illness, and, leaving Tashikhyil, he went to a place known as
Meditation Cave. Although he was given all
kinds of attention during his sickness, and
although many prayers were offered for his long
life, nothing helped, and he left for other realms.
I was overcome by great sadness. Returning
home, I told my mother what had happened,
and, overwhelmed by grief, I sang a song of
despair:

The sole object of hope of all celestial
    beings,
The wish-fulfilling tree,
Has suddenly been felled.

When the wish-fulfilling tree
Lies on the ground
What will become of the desolate gods?

The sole hope of the poor,
The wish-fulfilling jewel,
Has been stolen away.

Without the wish-fulfilling jewel
What will become of the desolate poor?

The gracious guru, the sole hope of his
    disciples,
Has departed for other Buddhafields.

Once the genuine guru has gone
What will become of his desolate students?

Even if, riding a miraculous horse,
I could roam over the whole earth,
Where could I find such a teacher?
Where can I now meet the guru? [25b].

I wept a long time. In tears, too, my mother
consoled me with the words:

My only son, for whom I've cared since
    birth,
Listen to your mother's words: do not
    despair.
I need not say
How great his kindness was to you.

For me, as well, he was the lama
With whom I had the deepest connection.
Although the guru's sudden departure
Has broken our hearts,
What good does it do to stay prostrate with
    despair?
To offer whatever we can for his funeral
    rites
Is the best way to fulfill his enlightened
    wishes.

As my mother spoke, my grief subsided.
    Among our possessions was one fine *dzomo*.[3]
I thought we should offer her for the funeral
ceremonies and mentioned it to my mother,
who agreed, saying that she had just been thinking the same thing. The next morning, a relative
came by and said, sympathetically, "People say
that you are going to offer your *dzomo* for the
funeral. Is that true?" "Yes," I said, "it is." "Well,"
he replied, "you should see what the whole company of yogins is going to offer. Offer a fraction
of that; it would be quite enough. After all, this
isn't the funeral of your father or mother. Keep
your *dzomo*." I answered him in this way:

Brother, your advice came from your
    heart,
But my thoughts are just the reverse.

You're right—he was neither father nor
    mother,
But his kindness was more than a mother's
    or father's.

Whatever deep and vast teachings I
   wanted,
Freely he poured them forth to me.

If I can practice these teachings,
I will reach the higher realms,
And the state of ultimate excellence.
This makes me a fortunate being.

Even if I filled the triple universe with gold,
And offered it to him, it would be hard
To pay back my master's kindness,
The kindness of the one who bestows last-
   ing happiness.

Even if, lacking this one *dzomo*,
From today our family went into ruin,
I would have no regret.
How could I regret it, my dear relative?
   [26a].

The Victorious Ones of the three times
Have all said in a single voice
That to make offerings
To a single hair of one's own master
Surpasses making offerings to a thousand
   Buddhas.

My relative then said, "I spoke with pure
intention, thinking that you, mother and son,
might not be able to sustain yourselves; but if you
don't take my advice, there is no point in trying
to hinder your virtuous act." With that, he left.

I went, with the *dzomo*, and offered it as a
contribution for the funeral. I did it with the wish
to fulfill my guru's wisdom intentions, praying
over and over again for his swift return. A senior
yogin, Tsebum Gyal, offered seven hide bags of
wheat, and my other yogin friends offered together one hide bag containing whatever flour
and roasted barley they had gathered. With all
this, alms, tea, bread, flour, and barley were
presented to a hundred monks of Shohong, and
the funeral offerings were made in a complete, ample
way. Gyal Khen Rinpoche also made offerings, and
so did the people of Mongolia when they came to
know the news. Nearly everyone who heard of it
went about saying, "It is wonderful that Ngawang
Tashi offered his only *dzomo*."

Not long afterward, having copied a holy
book, I received a *dzomo*. Then, having given a
sister in marriage, we received another *dzomo*
and, having recited some holy scriptures, I
received one more. I thought that this was due to
the guru's blessings.

On the day of the cremation, the sky was
perfectly clear, yet on the eastern side of the
funeral stupa there appeared a vivid five-colored
rainbow, predominantly white. All the heart-
sons gathered there saw it. The conviction that
the guru was a real Buddha grew naturally in our
minds [26b]. These signs, we thought, indicated
that he had gone to the eastern Buddhafield of
Manifest Joy.[4]

Grieved by my guru's departure to another
realm, I could not stay home peacefully; so,
accompanying a Dharma companion, the hermit of Tongsa, as well as Topzang Lama and a
few other friends, I went on a pilgrimage.

We visited the great sacred places of Dentig,
Yantig,[5] and Jampa Bumling—the abode of the
Hundred Thousand Maitreyas[6]—and places
where images of several deities had appeared by
themselves in the rock (the Chakrasamvara of Logya,
the Great Compassionate One of Gegosu, and the
Hayagriva of Agang)[7] as well as the White Stupa,[8]
the Valley of Buddhas, and some holy places in
China, too. Coming upon these miraculously
formed images that had great blessings, and all
these holy places, I prayed again and again to be
able to perfect every aspect of spiritual life.

The following year, I went to Tashikhyil
Monastery in the first month, on the occasion of
the Great Prayer Festival, and in the seventh
month for the scholastic gathering. There I did
many prostrations and circumambulations, and
offered butter-lamps before the image of the
Crowned Buddha of the Golden Pagoda. I made
an ardent prayer that I might be able to practice
the Dharma perfectly. As Panchen Lobzang
Yeshe[9] said:

The various doctrinal views found in the
   provinces of U, Tsang, and Ngari
Are all the very teachings of the Victorious
   One.
How fine if, not allowing the demon of
   sectarianism to ignite animosity,

The radiance of the jewel of pure perception would encompass all.

In accordance with these words, I always cultivated respectful devotion toward the teachings and teachers, seeing them all as pure.

From the nonsectarian master of the Dharma, Ngawang Tashi Rinpoche, abbot of Sey, I received the transmission of the prayer for offering prostrations, as well as the prayer for taking rebirth in Dewachen, *Blissful Paradise*, composed by Chagme Raga Asya [27a].[10]

From Ngawang Lobzang Tendzin Rinpoche,[11] an emanation of Langdro Lotsawa, I received the empowerments of *The Lord of the Dead Who Destroys Arrogant Spirits*;[12] of the *Lord of Secrets, Subduer of Arrogant Ones*;[13] and of the *Eight Classes of Spirits*,[14] and I received the transmission of many ritual texts.

From Beu Thang Palden Rinpoche, a learned and accomplished teacher, I received the empowerment of the *Eleven-faced Great Compassionate One*[15] and the transmission for the practice of fasting.

From the great abbot and powerful *siddha* of Tsodu, I received the transmissions for the meditation of Vajrapani,[16] for the *Multicolored and the Black Garudas*,[17] the collection of mantras known as the *Adamantine Armor*,[18] and the *torma* offering related to Shasa Horma.[19]

From Gedun Tsogphel Rinpoche, master of healing, I received the *Great Oral Transmission of the Mind Training*,[20] the *Repairing Confession*, the *Sur* burnt offering,[21] the *Hundred Tormas*, the water-offering related to Vaishravana,[22] and the fire-offering connected with Zache Khandro.[23]

From Nyangpai Rabjampa I received the transmission for the transference practice known as *The Hero Entering the Battle* and the prayer that starts with the line, "The absolute and unsurpassable self-arising paradise . . . " From the religious sculptor Jamyang, I received the transmission of the Mahasiddha Jahabira teachings on *prana*.[24]

Having received a great number of initiations and transmissions from many teachers of the Ancient and New Traditions,[25] when I turned twenty-one I thought, "Now I must begin to practice Dharma right away, and do so in a perfectly pure way. In order to urge those who cling to permanence to do spiritual practice, even my most kind root guru Jamyang Gyatso Rinpoche has shown the passing into nirvana of his physical manifestation. Someone like me is bound to die soon, needless to say. Abandoning concern for my native land, for my family and friends, and for this life's affairs, I must go to some place far away, and practice the Dharma truly [27b]. I must do this, and it is already late." An unbearable sadness arose in my mind, and I told my mother:

"Mother, death comes suddenly, and one cannot predict its arrival. I must practice Dharma now, genuinely. The sutras say, 'Samsara is like the sharp point of a needle, on which no happiness can ever be found.'

"No matter where we are reborn on the wheel of existence, there is nothing but suffering; whoever we befriend is but our companion in suffering; whatever we enjoy is but an enjoyment of suffering; whatever things we do are but the means to attract suffering.

"Especially, as Lord Buddha said, domestic life is nothing but a source for suffering—like a pit of fire, a cannibal island, a nest of venomous snakes. I must now become completely homeless. Whatever happens, I must practice the Dharma. But for this, mother, I need your permission."

She replied: "Son, we are now living in dark times; in this Rekong province, if I do not have a son living at home, I will be mistreated by everyone.

"You are my only son—I have no other. When I grow old I will be unable to care for myself. If you have compassion for your mother, take a wife and practice the Dharma at home. Thus, our well-being will increase."

I answered her with these verses:

Most kind mother of mine, listen a bit.
Remaining in the world that is samsara,
There is no contentment,
And within that, this home—a pit of live
   coals;
A wife—a sorceress stealing the life force of
   liberation.
So I ask you, with all your loving-kindness,

To give me permission to give up my
   home [28a],
And devote my life to the holy Dharma,
So that we, mother and son,
May win the citadel of lasting content-
   ment.

My mother conceded, saying, "My son, if I
don't give my permission, it will hinder your
practice. If I do give it, I, your mother, will come
upon hard times." Weeping, she added, "But
even though I shall have to endure hardship, I
give you my permission, praying that you may
reach your ultimate goal."

Filled with joy, I said, "Kind mother, you
are so good! Don't be sad. I am confident that
the wishes and aims of us both, mother and son,
will be accomplished, in this and future lives."

My mother's spirits brightened.

Then I went to Tashikhyil, an isolated place
of retreat. I met Gyal Khenchen Rinpoche
and told my whole story to him. Very pleased,
he said, "We are inviting Yongdzin Arik Geshe
Rinpoche[26] to Doby Monastery to give full
ordination to Kusho Lakha Tulku. It would
be very auspicious if you were ordained at the
same time. After that, it would be excellent for
you to go to meet the Dharma King, Pöntsang
Chögyal Ngakyi Wangpo. I shall take you
there. But don't change your mind! Most of
these yogins have very changeable minds.
Don't change yours."

At that instant, hearing the name of the
supreme Dharma King, my hair stood on end
and tears of devotion filled my eyes. My longing
to meet him became like that of a man thirsting
for water. From that moment, the urge to go to
him, whatever might happen, never left my mind
[28b].

Then Gyal Khenchen Rinpoche asked me,
"Have you got anything with which to make
yourself some robes?" I answered, "No, I haven't,
but I shall manage something."

"You don't need to look elsewhere," he said.

"I will provide you with robes. After that, what
sort of Dharma you practice will be up to you."

Then I returned home. To mark my gratitude to my mother and my relative, Topzang
Bendhe, who had always been kind to me, I
drew for each of them a "*chakra* that liberates on
contact," of the kind known as *Liberating the Cities*,[27]
and put one around each of their necks. After this, I
went to Doby Monastery and had robes made.

In those days my hair was about three feet
long. One of the monks at the hermitage seized a
sharp wool-shearing knife and teased me, saying,
"Eh, what a nice sheep from Shohong! Looks
like he's ready to be sheared!" Everyone around
burst into laughter.

That night, I dreamed that as I was going up
a lofty mountain I came to a boulder obstructing
the path. A man cleared it away, and as I reached
the summit the sun was rising. On the summit, in
a hermitage, I beheld an image of Lord Atisha.

On the morning of the auspicious eighth
day of the waxing moon in the fifth month of the
female Iron Bird Year,[28] I was ordained. Arik
Geshe Rinpoche, the emanation of Arya Nagarjuna, the supreme leader of the Chariot of the
Teachings, the great holder of the Vinaya, endowed with the three virtues of being learned,
pure, and noble-minded, whose name—Jampel
Gelek Gyaltsen Pal Zangpo—I hardly dare to
pronounce, acted as main abbot. He was sec-
onded by the supreme luminary of the teachings,
Gyal Khenchen Gedun Tenpai Nyima Rinpoche
[29a], who, acting as auxiliary abbot, asked the
secret questions.[29]

Following the traditional procedure, with
Lakha Tulku Rinpoche and many others, in the
midst of the requisite number of monks, I
received, in order, the novice vows and those of a
fully ordained monk.

I received the name of Jampa Chödar, "Kind
One who Spreads the Dharma." Seeming very
pleased, the abbot said, "There will be great
benefit for sentient beings and for the Dharma."

At the request of the whole congregation,
the abbot also bestowed the empowerment of
Kunrik, the *All-Knowing One*, and the transmission
of the *Blissful Path*.[30]

It is said: "Just as the earth supports both the
animate and the inanimate, discipline is the sup-

port of all good qualities." Having understood that the precious monastic training was the foundation of all virtue and excellence, I thereafter behaved according to the Vinaya, eating only before noon, taking off shoes in the temple, drinking blessed water, and so forth.

On my way home, I encountered Grandmother Lumoya, a relative of mine. She was a woman well-versed in worldly chatter, with marked likes and dislikes concerning others. She had been very fond of me. Not recognizing me, she called out, "Who are you?" "I am Ngawang Tashi," I answered.

"Ay! What a wicked thing you've done!" she exclaimed. "It looks like your father Ngawang Tsewang's lineage is finished now! You don't deserve to be called a man! Later, when people see your poor old mother deprived of everything, you will have set an infamous example!"

In reply I sang these verses:

Dear loving grandmother, listen to me.
Aren't the words you've said today mistaken?
Having given up wickedness of all kinds [29b],
I have now gone forth toward excellence.

Remaining in samsara, where there is no contentment—
To desire and be attached to samsara:
Now *that's* wicked!

Falling into the prison that is one's homeland—
Clinging to the father and mother and wife
That bind one to samsara:
Now *that's* wicked!

Taking part in all sorts of nonvirtuous deeds
Just to feed and clothe one's family:
Now *that's* wicked!

Human life is over in an instant.
To leave for the next life without Dharma:
Now *that's* wicked!

Approaching one's next rebirth,
The impulsive force of negative acts
Hurls one down into the three lower realms:
Now *that's* wicked!

Having thrown down a layman's rags,
My body wears excellence, the beauty of saffron robes.

Having given up all useless talk,
My speech remains in excellence,
Making prayers and reciting mantras.

Having cast away all nonvirtuous thoughts,
My mind rests in excellence, conceiving pure thoughts.

I got away from a worldly home
As though from a pit of live coals
And inherited the cool pavilion of homelessness:
This is the excellence of my action.

Happy in this life, when going on to the next
I shall ascend, higher and higher:
This is the excellence of my career.

She replied, "Right now you look all right, walking along, all decked out in your robes. I am an old grandmother, not long for this world, but should I live a few more years, I'd like to see what becomes of you. I've seen a good many of those who used to practice the Dharma. To reach the ultimate point of it is not so easy. Well, well, all the best! *Om mani padme hum . . .* "

So saying, she went away, mumbling her *mani*. Although at the moment the old grandmother's words were not very pleasant, later they proved helpful to me. When other faithful old people saw me, they exclaimed: "Fortunate one!" [30a]. And when I reached home, my mother and sister rejoiced greatly.

Notes

1. This reflects the general attitude in a patriarchal society. However, the question of the role of women in Tibetan society and religion is a complex one. In the Vajrayana, for instance, women are praised as the symbol and source of wisdom. For recent studies in feminine imagery and symbolism in Tibetan Buddhism, see J. Willis (1987).

2. *Chang*: the most common Tibetan fermented beverage, prepared with millet.

3. *Dzomo*. See chap. 1, note 67.

4. The Buddhafield of Manifest Joy (*mngon par dga' ba*) is the eastern Buddhafield of Vajrasattva.

5. Dentig (*dan tig*), where Lhachen Gongpa Rabsel (*lha chen dgongs pa rab gsal*, 892–975 or 832–915?) spent thirty-five years and passed away. Gongpa Rabsel was the disciple of the three monks known as the "three learned men from Tibet" (*bod kyi mkhas pa mi gsum*), who fled from central Tibet to escape the persecution waged by King Langdarma (841–46). With the help of two monks from China, they ordained Gongpa Rabsel, who in turn ordained the ten monks from U and Tsang. Thus the monastic lineage survived in Tibet. At Dentig, there are famous images of Jetsun Drolma, Chenrezi, and other deities naturally formed in the rock; there is also a cave blessed by Guru Padmasambhava.

   The "doors" of the sacred place of Yantig (*yang tig*) were opened by the third Dalai Lama, Gyalwa Sonam Gyatso (*rgyal ba bsod nams rgya mtsho*, 1543–88), who had a vision of Guru Padmasambhava and revealed a spiritual treasure there (*gter ma*). See AC, vol. 2, pp. 70–73.

6. Jampa Bumling (*byams pa bum gling*), the Monastery of One Hundred Thousand Maitreyas, which sheltered a huge statue (said to be eighty meters high) and a hundred thousand smaller molded images of Maitreya. Some say that the large Maitreya statue was erected by the Chinese princess Wengchen, on her way to Lhasa to wed King Songtsen Gampo; some say that it was a Bönpo statue of Tönpa Shenrap (*ston pa gshen rab*), which has been turned into a Buddhist image. See AC, vol.1, pp. 311–17.

7. Agang Monastery (*a 'gang*), at Machuka (*rma chu kha*). There is a miraculously formed image of Hayagriva known as *rma khar rta mgrin rang byung*.

8. After Kublai Khan (1215–94), founder of the Mongol dynasty in China, became the disciple of the great Sakya master Chögyal Phagpa (*chos rgyal 'phags pa*, 1235–80), on the occasion of receiving the Hevajra empowerment he offered to his master sovereignty over Tibet up to the White Stupa (*mchod rten dkar po*). Since then, this stupa became the border-mark between Tibet (Amdo province) and China. Eight years later, the Mongol Kublai Khan conquered China.

9. Lobzang Yeshe (*blo bzang ye shes*, 1663–1737), the fifth Panchen Lama (second to hold the title).

10. Karma Chagme Raga Asya (*ka rma chags med ra ga asya*, 1613–78), an inspired writer and visionary master who belonged to both the Nyingma and Kagyu traditions. He was said to be an emanation of Guru Padmasambhava's disciple Luyi Gyaltsen. His prayer for taking rebirth in Dewachen (*bde ba can smon lam*) is one of the prayers most commonly recited by Tibetans. It is said that Karma Chagme's writings bear special blessings, because in most cases he received permission to compose them in visions of his tutelary deities (*yi dam*). See GC, vol. 3, pp. 347ff.

11. Ngawang Lobzang Tendzin (*ngag dbang blo bzang bstan 'dzin*, 1745–1812), born in Dzogeh (*mdzod dge*) district in Amdo, was a descendent of a highly realized Nyingmapa *siddha* from Kathok, Ngakchang Dorje Senge (*sngags 'chang rdo rje seng ge*). He went to central Tibet where, at Mindroling Monastery, he received from Khenchen Orgyen Tendzin (*mkhan chen o rgyan bstan 'dzin*, b. 1742) the empowerments of the Mindroling tradition, which he conferred here upon Shabkar.

12. Concerning *The Lord of the Dead Who Destroys Arrogant Spirits* (*gshin rje dregs 'joms*), see chap.1, note 38.

13. For *The Lord of Secrets, Subduer of Arrogant Ones* (*gsang bdag dregs pa kun 'dul*), see *Rinchen Terdzö*, vol. 28 (Sa), a *terma* focused on Vajrapani revealed by Pema Ledreltsel (1291–1315, see chap. 3, note 16).

14. The eight classes of spirits (*sde brgyad*)); see NG, pp. 255–56.

15. The Eleven-faced Great Compassionate One (*thugs rje chen po bcu gcig zhal*). Once, as a Bodhisattva, Avalokiteshvara was able to liberate all the beings reborn in the hell realms, instantaneously causing these realms to be emptied. Yet, when he looked again, there were as many new beings in the hells as there had been before. Overwhelmed by the infinite sufferings of beings, his head burst into a thousand pieces. Amitabha put these pieces back together into eleven heads, and Avalokiteshvara renewed his promise to work for the sake of beings until the very end of samsara. Avalokiteshvara also has a thousand hands with an eye on each. These symbolize that he continually sees the suffering of every being in the universe and that he is the source of the thousand Buddhas of this present aeon.

16. Vajrapani (*phyag na rdo rje*), here the wrathful aspect of the Buddha of the "mind family."

17. Black and multicolored garudas (*khyung nag* and *khyung khra*). Sadhanas related to these can be found in RT, vol. 46 (Mi).

18. *The Adamantine Armor* (*sngags 'bum rdo rje go khrab*) is a collection of mantras for protection and for repelling obstacles. It was revealed by Dorje Lingpa (*rdo rje gling pa*, 1346–1405). See RT, vol. 42 (Ni).

19. Shasa Horma (*sha za hor ma*). According to Kyabje Dilgo Khyentse Rinpoche this is the same as Shasa Khamoche (*sha za kha mo che*), a wrathful female wisdom protector who was entrusted by Guru Padmasambhava at Samye Chimphu to guard the Nyingma teachings in general and the Lama Gongdu (*bla ma dgongs 'dus*) cycle in particular (a *terma* rediscovered by Sangye Lingpa, 1340–96).

20. *The Great Oral Transmission of the Mind Training* (*blo sbyong snyan brgyud chen mo*) is the collection of the writings of Gyalse Ngulchu Thogme Zangpo Pal (*rgyal sras dngul chu thogs med bzang po dpal*, 1295–1369), compiled by Drogön Palden Yeshe (*'gro dgon dpal ldan ye shes*), who was also the author of Gyalse Thogme's biography.

21. *Sur*, burnt offering (*gsur*): an offering of smoke produced by burning *tsampa* (barley flour) mixed with the "three whites" (milk, butter, and cheese), the "three sweets" (sugar, molasses and honey), and blessed substances. This smoke, accompanied by a meditation upon Avalokiteshvara, the Buddha of Compassion, in the form of Khasarpana, and the recitation of his mantra, OM MANI PADME HUM, relieves the pangs of hunger and thirst of the *pretas* (*yi dwags*), or hungry ghosts.

22. The water-*torma* offering (*chu gtor*) is an offering of pure water made to the "four classes of guests," (see Author's Introduction, note 32).

23. Zache Khandro (*za byed mkha' 'gro*) is a wrathful dakini related to a purification practice. One makes a fire and visualizes Zache Khandro in it with her mouth wide open. One then throws into the fire black sesame seeds and one thinks that as the seeds enter the mouth of Zache Khandro and are burned, all one's defilements, which had been absorbed in the seeds, are purified. Zache (*za byed*), "the devourer," is a synonym of fire.

24. The teachings on *prana* of the Indian *mahasiddha* Jahabira are instructions on the vital energies (*rlung*) and on taking the essence of the elements (*rasayana* or *bcud len*); through them one can ultimately transform one's ordinary physical aggregates into a

rainbow body (*'ja' lus*). These instructions, gathered by Jamyang Khyentse Wangpo, can be found in volume 30 (A) of RT, pp. 311–564, and in the *Compendium of Sadhanas* (*sgrub thabs kun btus*, vol. 11). Instructions on these teachings are also found in the *termas* of Garwang Dorje (*gar dbang rdo rje*, 1640–85). A disciple of the *mahasiddha* Mahanatha (who was considered to be an emanation of Guru Padmasambhava), Jahabira himself had hundreds of disciples, among whom, in Tibet, were Manikanatha and Nesar Jamyang Khyentse Wangchuk (*gnas gsar 'jam dbyangs mkhyen brtse dbang phyug*, 1524–1568). Jahabira eventually attained the rainbow body.

25. The Ancient (*rnying ma*) and the New (*gsar ma*) Traditions correspond to the "early" and the "later" stages of translating Buddhist scriptures into Tibetan. See Appendix 1.

26. Concerning Arik Geshe (*A rig dge bshes*), see Translator's Introduction, note 46.

27. The "Wheel that Liberates the Cities" (*grong khyer grol ba'i 'khor lo*). See *sgrub thabs kun btus*, vol. 13, p. 689. Once, Atisha pondered the terrible state of suffering of beings in general and of the Tibetan people in particular. He shed tears and wondered if there could be a way to ease these sufferings. One night a dakini appeared in his dream and told him to go to Vajrasana in India (Bodhgaya). Atisha transported himself there miraculously and prayed ardently in front of the place where the Buddha had attained enlightenment. At that moment a beautiful dakini appeared in the sky before him in a mass of light and showed him the "Wheel that Liberates the Cities." She told him that if he had that "wheel," or *chakra*, drawn in Tibet it would relieve immense suffering. So Atisha had this done. The *chakra* depicts Atisha at the center, with mantras written around him. It is said that it liberates from rebirth in the lower realms of samsara the whole population of the place where it is kept. Shabkar was famous for drawing such *chakras*, writing tiny letters, and drawing in miniature. Some of these were kept at his birthplace, Shohong, until recently.

28. The year was 1801. Shabkar was then twenty.

29. The secret questions, which are asked of the candidates before they receive full monastic ordination, concern conceivable obstacles to the keeping of the vows, such as not having permission from one's parents, and so forth.

30. *The Blissful Path to Omniscience* (*byang chub lam gi rim pa'i khrid yig thams cad mkhyen par bgrod pa'i bde lam*) is one of the so-called Eight Great Scriptures on

the Graded Path (*lam rim*). This commentary was written by Lobzang Chökyi Gyaltsen (*blo bzang chos kyi rgyal mtshan*, 1570–1662), also known as Lobzang Chögyen (*blo bzang chos rgyan*), the fourth Panchen Lama and the first to hold this title. (He was declared by the fifth Dalai Lama to be the fourth tulku of Khedrup Je, 1385–1438, one of Tsongkhapa's main disciples). A great scholar, Chökyi Gyaltsen wrote many commentaries and ritual texts; his *Offering to the Gurus* (*bla ma mchod pa*) is one of the major offering rituals used in the Geluk tradition.

3

Meeting My Teacher

*How, leaving my homeland behind, I came to stay at the lotus
feet of the Dharma King, Chögyal Ngakyi Wangpo*

After my ordination, I went home; the next day I set out for a place called Gonphuk, which lay in a forest on the other side of the mountains bordering our village. There, I paid homage at a clay stupa containing the relics of my kind root guru, Jamyang Gyatso Rinpoche. Offering many flowers that I had brought from home, I prayed, "Precious teacher! Grant your blessing that, forsaking my homeland, I may find a qualified master and have the good fortune to practice the profound Dharma" [31b].

On the way back to my village, at a place called Dobum Nyagkha, I recognized a friend named Poma walking some distance away. From afar, I called out mischievously, "Brother Po! Where is Upper Nyengya? Where is the Tsekgo family house? Is their son, the *ngakpa*, around?"

He answered, "The place you're looking for is up there. The Tsekgo house is the lower one. Whether the fellow you mention is there or not, I couldn't say. Where are you from?" As he came closer, Poma recognized me, and we started to laugh. We sat and talked for a long time. Before we parted, I said:

E ma!
Listen, fortunate, dearest friend!

I, Ngawang Tashi,
To practice the essence of Dharma
Have given up actions without essence.

Having taken up robes,
I am now called Jampa Chödar,
"Kind One Who Spreads the Dharma."

With my mind intent on pure Dharma,
I'll practice at Tashikhyil
And other secluded spots.

While you are young,
Don't let yourself get carried away
By the activities of this life.
Practice meditation and recitation of the
    yidam deity;[1]
Establish spiritual connections with holy
    masters;
Keep *samaya* with your vajra brothers and
    sisters;
Be kind to the poor;
And, keeping in mind that all actions have
    their results,
Act in the right and proper way.

In short, keep your three doors[2] in
    harmony with the Dharma,
To make sure you have no regrets at the
    moment of death.
May we both have long, healthy lives,
And may we meet again and again.

He replied, "You are a fortunate fellow. Don't go too far away!" With that, we parted [32a].

As I approached my house, Dorje Tseten, "Adamantine Life," a close friend, invited me into his home nearby. We drank tea and discussed my ordination and other things. Finally I told him, "I plan to go to Mongolia to see the Dharma King, Chögyal Chingwang Rinpoche, and do retreat there."

Dorje replied, "May all your aspirations be fulfilled. You are a person with good karma. I will try to follow in your footsteps. It is impossible now, but I vow to do so someday."

When I arrived home, I said to my mother, "Mother, thank you for letting me practice the Dharma all these years. Now, I would like to do something truly worthwhile. I must go and attend a qualified master who lives far away and, having received his profound instructions, seek a solitary place where I can practice meditation.

"Though one of my sisters has married and left, the other is still at home. Mother, I am thinking of going to another land for some years. Please, give me your consent."

She replied, "I have already given you my consent to your practicing the Dharma. But I would be happy if you would stay nearby until I die." Then she said:

Son, so dear to my heart,
I have cared for you since you were small.

Leaving your mother, where will you go?

Even young animals never stray from their
    mothers.
Son, how can you leave me?

Son, you are the very eyes in my head.
If you go far away,
Your mother will be like a blind woman.

Son, you are my very own limbs.
If you go far away,
Your mother will be like a cripple.

Son, you are my very own heart [32b].
If you go far away,
Your mother will be like a corpse.

Whatever you do, stay somewhere near,
So I might see you or just hear of you.

My sister, Lumo Kyi, said, "If I have to stay at home, I won't be able to provide for myself, let alone take care of Mother. And others will call me an old spinster! I won't stay!" Then she said:

Brother, if you have the heart to leave
    Mother,
Why shouldn't I have the heart to leave,
    also?

It is hard for a daughter to run a house
    alone.
I won't stay! I'll find some other household!

In this dark age,
Most girls can hardly fend for themselves;
How can they also take care of their
    mothers?

People will snicker, and call me an old
    maid!

If Mother is happy, or if she suffers—
It's your doing! It's your choice!

Saying this, she began to weep. I answered:

Listen, sister Lumo Kyi!
Don't cry!
No garment is warmer than sheepskin;
No jewelry more beautiful than gold and
    turquoise;
No scent is sweeter than sandalwood;
And no place is more pleasant
Than being at one's mother's side.

Listen, sister Lumo Kyi!
Even if I were to go far away,
What would prevent my protecting
Both you and our mother?

See how the sun, so far away,
Continuously nourishes the lotus gardens.
Just as when there is wheat there is also
    straw,
If you persevere for the sake of future lives
You will reap joy and happiness in this life,
    too.

Listen, sister Lumo Kyi!
Believing you'd be happier in another
    household
Is like thinking you'd be happy in a ditch.

Your mother-in-law wouldn't give you
    enough to eat and drink.
Your father-in-law would contradict and
    criticize every word you say.
Your husband would beat you with sticks
    and stones,
And your neighbors would say you
    deserved it! [33a].
You'd reap neither thanks nor a day of rest,
But only drudgery and abuse.

Listen, sister Lumo Kyi!
There's no more pleasant place than your
    own home.
It is pleasant to be free from domestic
    slavery.
It is pleasant to be free to do as you please.
It is pleasant to be free to eat what you like.
It is pleasant to be free to wear your own
    clothes.
It is pleasant since you're free to sleep in
    comfort, without worry.

Listen, sister Lumo Kyi!
Stay in your own country;
There's no better service
Than caring for your mother.
As you and mother ask,
I won't go too far off.

I thought, "If I tell my mother and sister the
truth, they aren't going to let me go. But, if I stay
nearby, how can I do much practice? I'm going
to have to lie. Surely, lying for the sake of the
Dharma can only be a minor offense."

I told my mother and sister that this year I
would accompany Gyal Khenchen Rinpoche to
Mongolia and promised that, having gathered
provisions, I would return and settle at Tashikhyil.

My mother said she had no objection to this
plan. But my sister argued, "If he goes, he will
never come back! Please, mother, don't let him
go!" My mother finally said, "It's up to him."

I decided that I would leave.

I stayed at home for another week. During
that time, I gave my mother and sister some
beneficial teachings and some advice about
worldly affairs.

The night before I left, I visited my friend
Dorje Tseten and told him, "Tomorrow I'm
leaving. From now on you must stay away from
chang and not practice black magic. Keep your
mind in harmony with the Dharma and inspire
others to follow the Dharma, too. Hold religious
gatherings and constantly enrich your observance
of the tenth-day feast. Always cultivate a good
heart" [33b]. In reply he said many affectionate
words. Sad to part, we shed many tears. Finally I
said:

Born from the eagle, the king of birds,
We two fledglings, together since
    infancy,
Are now ready to spread our wings.
Feeling no attachment to the nest
I'll fly off to another land.
You stay here and be happy!
I pray that we will meet again.
You'll see: I'll soon return.

Born from the spotted wild yak,
We two yak-calves, together since
    infancy,
Are now mature and strong.
Feeling no attachment to the rocky cliffs,
I'll make my way to the meadows.
You stay here and be happy!
I pray that we will meet again.
You'll see: I'll soon return.

We two friends, together since infancy,
Have listened to teachings from the same
    lama.
Now, while still young,
Feeling no attachment to my country,
I'll leave to practice the sacred Dharma.
You stay here and be happy!
I pray that we will meet again.
You'll see: I'll soon return.

Like birds that gather at night on tree
    tops,
Scattering in all directions at sunrise,
Phenomena are impermanent.
Remembering this, practice the sacred
    Dharma.

He replied:

> I, your evil companion, am a domestic
>   fowl
> Left at home in utter despair.
> You, my excellent companion, are an
>   eagle.
> For the sake of the Dharma,
> May you safely reach Mongolia.
>
> I, your evil companion, am an old bull
> Left at home, in utter gloom. [34a]
> You, my excellent companion, are a wild
>   blue yak.
> For the sake of the Dharma,
> May you safely reach Mongolia.
>
> Parting is unbearable
> For two close friends.
> Alas! Though such is the nature of
>   samsara,
> May we swiftly meet again.

After this last farewell, we parted with unbearable sadness. I spent the remainder of the evening with my mother. The next morning, before my departure, my mother made some delicious tea. While we sat enjoying it, she turned to me and said, "Son, be very careful when you're traveling!" I smiled, and she went on, giving more motherly advice. Then, growing somber, she said, "Look at this wrinkled, withered face. I'm old now, and death is close at hand. Keep in mind the old mother you've left behind. Have pity on me and come back quickly."

She began to weep. My sister, too, burst into tears.

My mother and sister accompanied me outside. As I turned to leave, a great tear fell from each of my mother's eyes and I thought, "The birth and death of beings is so uncertain. Now I am about to leave my mother, having lied to her. Who knows if we will ever meet again?" I, too, became very sad; unable to control myself, I began weeping. "Mother, you need not come further; stay here, don't cry, I will come back ."

Overwhelmed by sorrow, I walked away, looking back again and again, tears streaming down my cheeks.

Heartbroken that her only son was leaving, my mother stood there weeping, and watched, transfixed, until I disappeared from sight [34b]. My friend Dorje Tseten lit a smoke-offering on his roof and then stood in his doorway watching me.

Reaching Lablung Khaso, I looked back and saw my mother and Dorje Tseten still standing in their doorways. When I continued into Lablung and could no longer see my mother, I stopped, grief-stricken, and considered going back to see her for just a moment. I had the feeling we would never meet again.

When I had vanished from view, my mother, still grieving, went back into her house.

I continued on my way, accompanied by Rinchen Gyal, "Victorious Jewel," a childhood friend to whom I had taught writing and *torma*-making. When we reached Tashikhyil, I asked him, "Could you please look after my mother and sister? I am on my way to Mongolia to study the Dharma and will probably stay there for several years. Meanwhile, would you help look after them?" He promised to do the sowing, the harvesting, and whatever else he could do to help them. As he added that he needed some guidance in the Dharma, I told him:

> Childhood friend, Rinchen Gyal,
> This precious human body, so difficult to
>   obtain,
> Vanishes as easily as a flash of lightning in
>   the sky.
> On our journey to the far shore after
>   death,
> All is useless but the Dharma.
>
> Whether or not you practice is your
>   choice.
> But if you do decide to practice the holy
>   Dharma,
> Request oral instructions from an authentic master,
> Supplicate the meditation deity,
> Keep pure *samaya* with your vajra brothers
>   and sisters [35a],

Make offerings to the Three Jewels,
And, principally, watch your mind.

Be charitable to the poor,
Be sympathetic with the weak,
Serve the learned, disciplined, and honest,
And respect your parents.
May your life be long and free from illness.
May all be auspicious.

Having said this, I asked him not to tell my mother and sisters of my plans.

I left with a group of Gyal Khenchen Rinpoche's attendants. We crossed into Little Mongolia[3] at a place where a narrow gorge leads into a wide open plain. We felt light-hearted, as though a new day was breaking. After some time we arrived at Kusho Rinpoche's [Gyal Khenchen's] tent camp, not far from Urgeh, the seat of the precious Dharma King.[4]

A gentle rain fell, after which the sun shone warm and bright and a rainbow appeared. Interpreting this as an auspicious omen meaning that the sun of happiness would rise, I felt joyful.

When I appeared before Kusho Rinpoche, he smiled and said, "Marvelous! This rainbow must be a sign that Pöntsang Rinpoche will accept you."

The great Orgyen [Padmasambhava] made the following prophecy about Pöntsang Rinpoche:

In the direction of the great lake
Will appear an emanation of Karma
    Guru,[5]
The Subduer of Demons.
Should he meet with this teaching,
His prosperity will increase like a lake in
    summer.

As this prophecy says, Pöntsang Rinpoche[6] was an emanation of the great master, Pema Jungne, the Lotus-born Guru, the heart-emanation of the Buddhas of the Three Times [35b]. He had crossed the ocean of knowledge of scriptures and sciences, and had realized the natural state, the profound and luminous vajra essence.

He was a powerful monarch with the beau-

tiful name of Pöntsang Dalai Tai Chingwang Ngawang Dargye Pal Zangpo, the King "Great Oceanic King, All-Blooming Lord of Speech." With Gyal Khenchen Rinpoche, I came into his presence.

We arrived during a feast, just as someone was singing. I prostrated myself three times before the Chögyal, the Dharma King, and offered him a copy of the Dzogchen teaching *Buddha in the Palm of Your Hand*,[7] and a white scarf. I also offered white scarves to his consort and sons and asked after their health.

The very moment I met the Dharma King and his consort, I perceived them as enlightened beings and felt immeasurable devotion and joy. Both the precious Dharma King and his queen spoke kindly to me. He opened *Buddha in the Palm of Your Hand* and read a few passages from it. That evening, he arranged for me to stay in a small tent and told his bursar, "This fellow has come a long way to see me. Take good care of him."

The next morning, just as the sun was beginning to warm up the place, the Dharma King entered my tent with his personal attendant, Zangpo, who carried a copy of the *Graded Path to Enlightenment*,[8] a brilliant teaching by the great master Tsongkhapa which, with its threefold annotation, illuminates the three worlds.

The Dharma King said, "I am glad that you have come here with the intention of practicing the Dharma. Having developed a bit of renunciation, one may turn to practice, but there is the danger that later one's mind might change [36a]. So, to train your mind by studying and contemplating this text is very important. It contains two sections: one meant for individuals of lesser ability and one meant for those of average ability. Train your mind accordingly, be sure to generate a genuine wish for liberation, and be free from the slightest desire for worldly achievements."

Before leaving my tent, he spoke at length about how to rely upon and serve one's spiritual master.

For a month, the precious Dharma King visited me once or twice daily to give lengthy instruction on sections of the text ranging from the difficulty of obtaining a free, well-favored human birth, to how to make progress in meditation on inner calm and insight.

He then told me, "You are intelligent. Now, train your mind according to the methods suited to the higher, middle, and inferior individuals."

As he advised, I spent the next two months training my mind.

Then, Gyal Khenchen, Aku Gelong of Tongsa, and many earnest students, including myself, requested a maturing empowerment of the Secret Mantrayana.

At the beginning of the preparation for the empowerment, I offered this seven-branch prayer:

E ma!
Precious Dharma King!
The faithful students gathered here make
    obeisance.
With genuine devotion, we offer riches,
Both real and imagined,[9]
And confess our wrongdoings, failures, and
    obscurations.

Rejoicing in all noble activity,
We ask that you turn the wheel of the
    highest teaching,
And pray that you never pass into nirvana.
May our accumulated merit ripen all
    beings
So that they swiftly attain Buddhahood.

That night, after Chögyal Rinpoche had given the preparation for the empowerment [36b], I dreamed that my mother gave me a skull-cup filled with *chang* and that I drank all of it.

When I related my dream to him, he said, "This is a good dream. It indicates that you have a connection that will enable you to accomplish all the guru's pith instructions."

At dawn the following morning, he bestowed on us the maturing empowerment of the Victori-

ous One, the *Wish-fulfilling Gem, Hayagriva and Varahi.* This is a profound and extraordinary teaching from the cycle of the new treasures.[10] In heaven, the lineage of *vidyadharas* remains unbroken; on earth, the lines and colors of the mandala have not yet vanished; in between, the heaps of sacred substances have not yet diminished. Unsullied by demons and *samaya*-breakers, it still carries the fresh breath of both the wisdom dakinis and worldly dakinis.

During the empowerment, when I threw my flower[11] it fell toward the north and I received the name Tsogdruk Rangdrol, "Self-liberation of the Six Senses," which refers to the natural liberation of sense-attachments.[12] After Chögyal Rinpoche gave a few oral transmissions, the empowerment ended.

Every day thereafter, he gave a complete explanation of the practices related to each of the four empowerments. First, he gave teachings on the development stage of the deity, related to the Vase Empowerment; next, he gave teachings on the channels and energy practice of *tummo*, related to the Secret Empowerment. After that, he gave teachings on the bliss-void practice of the *mudra*, related to the Wisdom Empowerment; and finally, he gave teachings on Trekchö and Thögal, related to the Word, or Symbolic, Empowerment. He also gave the permission-blessing for the protectors of the teachings.

On subsequent occasions, he conferred on us the maturing empowerments, the liberating instructions, and the support of the transmissions for several practices: the *Nectar-drop of Vajrapani,* which Vajrapani himself gave to the *siddha* of Lodrak, Lekyi Dorje; Mahamudra teachings such as the root text and commentary of the *Precious Vajra-garland of the Holder of Secrets*;[13] the *Dzogchen Yeshe Lama*;[14] Nyima Trakpa's[15] Dzogchen teaching; and the *Heart-drop of the Dakinis* [37a].[16]

Once he said to us: "The Dharma of the Secret Mantrayana relies on interdependent links. When Jetsun Milarepa offered his guru, Lord Marpa, an empty cauldron, he created a link that caused him to have little food when he practiced later on.

"Marpa of Lodrak created yet another link,

however, by filling the cauldron with clarified butter so that, later in his life, Milarepa met with abundance and so did the holders of his lineage. Though you may own nothing, never request a teaching empty-handed."

He gave me a silver mandala plate with gold, silver, coral, pearls, turquoise, jeweled necklaces, grain, brocades, and other things, and told me to use these when making the mandala offering. I did so, and believe that because of this, whenever I had something to accomplish for myself or for others it was never difficult to obtain the resources needed.

Finally, gathering various offerings, we held an elaborate *ganachakra* feast. When offering the first part to the guru and consort, I sang this song:

> My own lord, Dharma King, diadem
> above my head,
> My own pure mind I offer you as a feast.
> My own wish, with all the fortunate dis-
> ciples, is that you shower teachings on
> us, according to
> My own and others' capacities.
>
> Abhe Rinpoche,[17] I offer this feast to you,
> too.
> Ati Dakini, you who have realized the
> meaning of the letter
> A—the sign of the uncreated, in the tradi-
> tion of the Great Perfection,
> Ama—mother—care for us with a
> mother's love.

As I sang this song, the Dharma King, his consort, sons, ministers and the whole assembly were amused and laughed [37b]. I thought, "Offerings of gold and silver don't make them laugh. Perhaps making the guru, his consort and sons laugh may also cause them to accept me with love."

Just as in the past the mother Dagmema[18] cared for Jetsun Milarepa, so the precious mother Abhe, vastly knowledgeable about worldly and religious matters, took care of me with the greatest loving-kindness, providing food, clothing, and whatever else I needed.

One night I dreamed that I held in my hand a two-sided mirror, the size of a gong. In the sky overhead both sun and moon had risen. When I held the mirror toward the sky a second moon rose to the left of the sun. Many monks and laypeople assembled on the plain and cried out, "Look! Another moon has risen to the left of the sun and moon." I thought, "These people don't realize that it is just a projection of my mirror." As I tilted the other side of the mirror toward the ground, white light filled the whole place.

I reported this dream to Chögyal Rinpoche, who said, "It is a very good dream, a sign that, if you meditate, experiences and realization will occur."

I stayed for some time at a place above Urgeh, where I studied the *Seven Treasuries*, the *Three Great Chariots*,[19] and other essential writings of Longchen Rabjam. I went over the difficult points with the Dharma King until I had gained a clear understanding of the different stages on the path, according to the views of both my own and other traditions.

Chögyal Rinpoche requested that Lama Jimba, whom he regarded as supremely worthy of veneration, teach me the monastic discipline [38a]. Accordingly, Lama Jimba taught me the *Essence of the Vinaya-Ocean*, complementing it with selections from the *Hundred Thousand Anecdotes on the Origin of the Vinaya* and other works.[20] I gained some understanding from these scriptures; my guru was pleased.

When Chögyal Rinpoche gave teachings on the four medical tantras to Lama Pema Rangdrol, "Self-liberated Lotus," and others, I was allowed to come and listen. I also studied a little and learned to diagnose hot and cold diseases. Later, when I was staying in mountain retreats and working for the benefit of others, I was able to help many sick people.

As it is said, "On a golden mountain everything becomes gold," and just by living in Urgeh I acquired many qualities. I learned how to show respect to my superiors; how to show kindness to those in humbler positions, and how to get along with my peers. In particular, in my attitude and in my practice, I learned how to attend properly the all-encompassing lord and protector of the mandala, the Dharma King.

Because I saw all his actions as pure and did whatever he asked, he came to think of me as a heart-son. Therefore, as if filling a vessel to the brim he gave me all the pith instructions of the old and new translations that he held, with nothing added or lost.

From the great Chöd practitioner, Konchog Chöpel, "He who Spreads the Doctrine of the Three Jewels,"[21] I received the empowerment for the Chöd practice called *Opening the Door of the Sky*; the empowerment of the *Five Wrathful Black Deities*; the *Chöd Accomplished at One Sitting*;[22] several other transmissions on the practice of *Chöd* [38b], teachings on bliss and emptiness related to the practice of *tummo*, and teachings on the Path of Means according to the *Sole Ornament of the Five Families of Vajrasattva*, which is a part of the *Taktsang Phurba*.[23]

When the incarnation of Jetsun Jamyang Shepa, the precious Losel Jigme Gyatso,[24] "Intelligent Fearless Ocean," was invited to Urgeh, I received from him the oral transmission for the *Protectors of the Three Families*, the *Hundred Deities of Tushita*, and the *Miktsema Prayer*.[25]

Since I had the good fortune to receive countless empowerments, oral transmissions, and instructions from many great masters, my mind became rich with the sacred teachings.

Notes

1. Literally, the "approaching" (*bsnyen*) and "accomplishing" (*sgrub*) of the *yidam* deity. These are two phases of the development stage (*bskyed rim*) during which one visualizes deities and recites their mantras. First one "approaches" the meditation-deity by familiarizing oneself with the practice, and then one "accomplishes" the deity by becoming one with its wisdom nature. The development stage is then fol-

lowed by the completion stage (*rdzogs rim*), with or without formal representations.

2. The three doors: body, speech, and mind.

3. *sog po*. On the name "Little Mongolia," see Translator's Introduction, p. xxii.

4. On Urgeh, see Translator's Introduction, p. xxii.

5. Dudul Karma Guru (*bdud 'dul karma gu ru*) is the name of a wrathful form of Guru Padmasambhava, particularly in the *terma* (see RT, vol 12, Na) revealed by Karma Guru Tashi Topgyal Wangpö Deh (*karma gu ru bkra shis stobs rgyal dbang po'i sde*, 1550–1603), better known as Changdak Tashi Topgyal (*byang bdag bkra shis stobs rgyal*). Chögyal Ngakyi Wangpo himself is also referred to as Karma Guru, in WL for instance.

6. On the various names of Chögyal Ngakyi Wangpo, see Author's Introduction, note 13.

7. *Buddha in the Palm of Your Hand* is probably the famous *rdzogs pa chen po mngon sum snying thig gi gdams pa thod rgal 'od gsal gyi zab khrid sangs rgyas lag 'chang*, from the Dzogchen teachings in vol. 12 of the *Collected Rediscovered Treasures* of Namchö Mingyur Dorje (*gnam chos mi 'gyur rdo rje*, 1645–67). Commentaries on this cycle were written by Namchö's mentor, Karma Chagme Raga Asya (see chap.2, note 10).

8. The *Graded Path to Enlightenment* (*lam rim chen mo*) is Je Tsongkhapa's masterpiece expounding the entire Bodhisattva path.

9. "Real and imagined offerings" refers to visualizing boundless offerings of all kinds filling the sky, in addition to the material offerings one makes.

10. The *terma* rediscovered by Kunzang Dechen Gyalpo. See Appendix 4.

11. This refers to the section of the empowerment ceremony in which one throws a flower onto the mandala to determine the meditation deity with which one has the closest karmic links or affinity.

12. The perceptions of the six senses (*tshogs drug gi snang ba*) are the experiences of sights, sounds, smells, tastes, textures, and mental events.

13. The *Nectar-drop of Vajrapani* (*phyag rdor bdud rtsi'i thig pa*) and the *Precious Vajra-garland of the Holder of Secrets*, root text and commentary (*gsang bdag gces phreng rdo rje rtsa 'brel*) are found in the *Collected Works* of Lodrak Drupchen. See also chap.1, notes 61 and 64.

14. *Yeshe Lama* (*ye shes bla ma*), the *Unsurpassable Primordial Wisdom*, is a famous instruction manual (*khrid yig*) for the practice of the Great Perfection written by Rigdzin Jigme Lingpa (*rig 'dzin 'jigs med gling pa*, 1729–98) on the basis of the *Vima Nyingthig* (*bi ma snying thig*).

15. Rigdzin Nyima Trakpa (*rig 'dzin nyi ma grags pa*, 1647–1710). This lineage is likely to have come through Kachupa Palden Tashi (*bka' bcu pa dpal ldan bkra shis*). See Author's Introduction, note 44.

16. *The Heart-drop of the Dakinis* (*mkha 'gro'i snying thig*) is the Dzogchen teaching that was given by Guru Rinpoche to King Trisong Detsen's dying daughter, Lhacham Pema Tsel (*lha lcam padma rtsal*), at Samye Chimphu. To console the king, Guru Rinpoche revived the princess and gave her these teachings, after which she passed away. Guru Rinpoche also gave those teachings to Yeshe Tsogyal (*ye shes mtsho rgyal*) in the Great Gathering Cave of the Dakinis at Tidro in Drigung (the full name of which is *gzho stod ti sgro brag dkar mkha' 'gro'i tshogs khang chen mo*). The *Khandro Nyingthig* was hidden as *terma* at Dangla Thramo Drak in Dagpo (*ldang lha khra mo brag*) and revealed in 1253 by Pema Ledreltsel (*padma las 'brel rtsal*, 1231–59), who was the reincarnation of Lhacham Pema Tsel. Pema Ledreltsel later reincarnated as Gyalwa Longchen Rabjam (*rgyal ba klong chen rab 'byams*, 1308–63), who incorporated these teachings in his *Nyingthig Ya Shi* (*snying thig ya bzhi*; see chap. 15, note 75). On Shabkar's lineage, see Appendix 2 and table 2.

17. Abhe Rinpoche was Chögyal Ngakyi Wangpo's consort.

18. Dagmema (*bdag med ma*) was Marpa Lotsawa's wife.

19. The *Seven Treasuries* (*mdzod bdun*) and the *Three Great Chariots* (*shing rta rnam gsum*), the commentaries on the Trilogy of Natural Ease (*ngal so skor gsum*). See Translator's Introduction, note 15.

20. *The Essence of the Vinaya-Ocean* (*'dul ba rgya mtsho'i snying po*) is an important text on the Vinaya written by Je Tsongkhapa. The *Hundred Thousand Anecdotes on the Origin of the Vinaya* (*'dul ba'i gleng 'bum*), written by Gedun Drup (*dge 'dun grub*, 1391–1474), is a narration of the events and circumstances that prompted Lord Buddha to formulate the various monastic rules.

21. The Chöd practitioner Konchog Chöpel (*gcod yul ba dkon mchog chos 'phel*, 1767-1834) lived in Urgeh and was the tulku of Pönlop Tashi Gyatso (*dpon slob bkra shis rgya mtsho*).

22. *Opening the Door of the Sky* (*nam mkha'i sgo 'byed*), probably the empowerment from the cycle of the *Oral Transmission of Thangtong* (*thang stong snyan brgyud*). See Translator's Introduction, p. xxi. The *Chöd Accomplished at One Sitting* (*gcod gdan thog gcig ma*) has not been identified. Several known texts bear this title.

23. *Taktsang Phurba*, see chap.1, note 54.

24. The third Jamyang Shepa Losel Jigme Gyatso (*blo gsal 'jigs med rgya mtsho*, 1796–1855), also known as Lobzang Yignyen Thubten Gyatso (*blo bzang dbyig gnyen thub bstan rgya mtsho*).

25. See respectively Author's Introduction, note 34, and chap.1, notes 27 and 22.

4

Retreat at the Hermit's Cave

How, following my guru's prediction, I persevered in the profound
practice of meditation in the pleasant solitude of Tseshung grove

One day the precious Dharma King, peerless in kindness, told me, "To practice, you should go now to the pleasant solitude of Tseshung, a place blessed by the presence of a great being, the *siddha* Karma Tsewang Rigdzin, who displayed many signs of accomplishment such as catching thunderbolts in the folds of his robes. In Tseshung he set many fortunate and worthy disciples on the path of ripening and liberation. This extraordinary site, facing south, sunny in the winter and cool in the summer and autumn, is favorable to clarity of mind. Water, firewood, and all other necessities are available there. There is a pleasant cave called Thayenchi, which in Mongolian means the Hermit's Meditation Cave.[1] Go there, and raise the victory banner of spiritual practice."

On the eve of my departure for this holy place, the revered mother, Abhe Rinpoche, gave me a book cover made of beautifully woven brocade and the lord guru gave me a rosary, each bead of which bore a naturally formed triangle. I took these gifts with me as an auspicious connection.

The treasurer and the bursar gave me enough provisions for a few months and sent two helpers to carry them. Thinking that at first I might be afraid to stay alone, the master said that one of them should stay overnight near the cave and return the next day [40b].

The three of us set out for the cave. When we reached it, my helpers, who were afraid to remain, each said to one another: "*You* stay!" I could see that they would never reach an agreement, so I told them: "Neither of you needs to stay. I'm not afraid. Sweep the inside thoroughly, make a hearth, and then you can both go. If a murderous spirit haunts the place, it can kill me tomorrow night just as easily as tonight; now or later makes little difference. If the precious Dharma King questions you, explain that I told you there was no need to stay, and he won't scold you."

So they happily went back.

After they left, I made a small, square dwelling place in a corner of the cave. First I drew a swastika, symbolizing the unchangeable state, and on top of that I placed some dry grass and my monk's mat. In a high niche, I put a statue of the Buddha, Lord of the Teachings, and arranged some offerings in front of it. After sitting down comfortably, I made the following promise: "In accordance with the words of my guru, I shall not leave this place until definite and genuine meditation experiences and realization arise in my being. At night, I won't sleep in the corpse-like posture of ordinary people but will stay cross-legged and upright. At all times, rather than indulging in idle chatter, I will refrain from speaking. I will eat once a day, at noon. I will live alone. I will think of nothing but my guru's instructions. I will not seek comforts but persevere in the hermit's life and accept its hardships. I will avoid all worldly distractions until I achieve stability in my realization [41a]. In short, not letting my body, speech or mind stray into the ordinary, I shall practice day and night.

May the root and lineage gurus grant their
blessings that I be able to fulfill these
promises!
May the *yidam* deities grant me *siddhis!*
May the dakinis, the Dharma protectors,
and celestial beings who delight in
virtue always remain with me!

I then expressed these promises and prayers
in a song:

Father, root guru, vajra-holder,
Grant your blessing
That I, your son, may keep to this
mountain retreat.
May I be able to practice correctly the
profound Dharma
As did the victorious sages of the past
Throughout their exemplary lives.

During the preliminaries common to all
paths,
May I accomplish the purpose of each
practice.
Then, during the main practice
May all the qualities of meditation
experiences and realization arise.
Having reached the end of the path in this
very life,
May I strive for the benefit of all beings,
my mothers.
When I work for my own and others'
benefit,
May there be neither obstacles nor
interruptions.
May the teachings of the practice lineage
Flourish in this place,
Endowing it with auspiciousness.

Sitting comfortably, I then assumed the
seven-point posture of Vairocana[2] and let my
mind rest in its natural state.

With my mind turned completely toward
virtue, I went through the refuge with prostrations, the generation of Bodhicitta, the recitation
of the hundred-syllable mantra,[3] the offering of
the mandala, and guru yoga. I completed one
hundred thousand repetitions of each of these

practices. Signs related to the twofold accumulation of merit and wisdom, signifying the purification of defilements, occurred in my dreams.

For my main practice I trained with great
perseverance in the whole of the *Graded Path of
Enlightenment* [41b]. Thus I laid the foundation
for an intense spirit of renunciation, of Bodhicitta,
and a perfectly pure view.[4]

Next, I meditated on the development stage
of the sadhana of the *Wish-fulfilling Gem, Hayagriva
and Varahi.*[5] I recited more than the customary
number of mantras. Attachment and ordinary
perceptions were purified, and I perceived all
appearances as the display of the deity. Various
signs appeared that indicated the presence of the
guardian deities of the *terma.*

Then I practiced the completion stage related
to the channels, energies, and vital essences;
through this the blissful warmth of inner heat
blazed forth, and I was able to withstand the cold
wearing just a single cotton garment. Mind and
energy joined, entered into the central channel,
and untied the knots;[6] I continuously experienced the union of bliss and emptiness.

Later, for many months, I concentrated on
the extraordinary preliminary practices of the
Great Perfection. Finally, for about three years, I
concentrated exclusively on the practices of
Trekchö and Thögal. I realized clearly the natural state of Trekchö, and the various visions and
experiences of Thögal arose.

At that point, I returned to the presence of
the precious Dharma King to tell him about my
practice and the various visions and meditation
experiences I had had. He was extremely pleased.
Smiling, his face like the radiant full moon, he said:

"My son! Having persevered with all your
heart in the practice, renunciation, Bodhicitta,
and the correct view have truly taken birth in
your being. You have also had extraordinary
meditation experiences and realization of the
two stages.

"Thus, the fortunate human birth you have
obtained has become meaningful. Above all, you
have realized the view of the natural state through
the Trekchö practice of the radiant Great Perfection, in the tradition of, the victorious Lotus-
born guru, Padmasambhava. Having relied on

the instructions for the Thögal practice of spontaneous presence, the wisdom of the four visions arose; this is indeed wonderful! [42a]. In one of his songs of realization, the omniscient Longchenpa says:

"The meditation of luminosity that is
     naturally present is as follows:
In the mansion of light, the unchanging body,
Is the stainless, hollow crystal channel
Linked to the water-lamp, the 'far-reaching
     lasso'.[7]

Outwardly, the radiance that links jewel
     and ocean
Appears in the cloudless sky.
Inwardly, the five-colored light of the five
     wisdoms
Appears as designs in a dome of brocade,
Adorned by the lamp called 'empty
     spheres'.

Amid all this are the vajra-chains of
     awareness,
Small and large spheres strung together
Like threads made of pure gold from the
     Jambu River,
Adorned with clustered constellations of
     light
Like peacock feathers' eyes.

The appearance of lights arranged as triads
Is the natural appearance called the
     'absolute nature becoming manifest'.

Then comes the vision of 'increasing
     appearances'.
One sees images of wisdom mansions,
Thousand-petaled lotuses of five-colored
     light,
Spokes of light, webs of jeweled beams,
And crystal stupas of five-colored light.
In the mansions of empty spheres
Appear the seeds of awareness—various
     symbols, letters, and complete forms of
     Buddhas
Radiating five-colored light throughout
     space.

In the vision called
'Awareness reaching its greatest
     magnitude',
These displays are seen in groups of five.
Wherever one looks, the universe is filled
     with light;
One sees threads of light entering into
     one's heart.

At that time, if one moves one's body,
The realms of the ten directions quake;
If one's body remains in the equanimity of
     samadhi
All else rests in equanimity as well [42b].

Through the sonorous Brahma-like voices
     of the emanations
The great drum of Dharma resounds;
The qualities of the stages and paths are
     perfected.

By fully integrating the two visions—
The gradual increase of enlightened
     qualities
And the exhaustion of dualistic
     perception—
One reaches the stage called 'exhaustion of
     phenomena in dharmata'.[8]

The gross material body, and the swarms
     of discursive thoughts are exhausted;
Ripening karma and latent tendencies are
     exhausted;
The seeds of ignorance and delusion are
     exhausted;
Clinging to apparent phenomena is
     exhausted;
Materiality is purified; its means of growth
     is exhausted.

In the crystal mansion of the body
Watch the five-colored lights
As they emanate and gather:
However the lights and awareness move,
They dissolve in a state
That is naturally present and primordially
     pure.
In the ground of original simplicity

The citadel is won;
In the inner luminosity
The three kayas are ever present.[9]

The rupakaya presents itself within the
   dharmakaya;
Wherever in the universe there are beings
   to be tamed,
The perfect sambhogakaya and
   nirmanakaya,
Without moving from the expanse of the
   dharmakaya,
Continuously accomplish twofold benefit
   for beings.
These are the instructions for liberation in
   this life."

Having quoted these verses he continued:
"You may wonder which of these stages and
levels you have reached. You have come to the
point of the appearance of complete forms of
Buddhas radiating five-colored light throughout
space. Once you have reached this point, you
have dealt with the *bardo*[10] in this life. As it is said
in the *Clear Space Tantra*:

When the vision of deities has increased to
   fullness,
You have passed through the visions of the
   bardo within this life,
And since you have recognized the
   sambhogakaya,
There will be no further *bardo*.[11]

"Even if you were to die right now, you
would attain enlightenment during the *bardo* in
the body of perfect enjoyment. If you practice as
long as you live, you will be liberated in the
rainbow body within this lifetime, or you will be
liberated in the dharmakaya at the moment of
death. Have no doubt about this."

Such were his predictions.

One night, I dreamed of a lofty crystal mountain
with steps of blue sapphire cut into it [43a].

Climbing the steps, I saw the sun shining in the
south. As its rays struck the crystal mountain, a
white light shone from the northern face, bathing in light the northern plain, where many
people joyfully played.

I related this dream to Chögyal Rinpoche,
who said: "Your dream is excellent. In the past,
Marpa of Lodrak made predictions about
Milarepa by interpreting a dream. Today I will
do the same with your dream." In an amused
tone, he continued in verse:

E ma!
My fortunate only son:
The mountain of immaculate crystal
Is the teaching of the Vajrayana.

The radiant shining sun
Is none other than myself,
This old father of yours.

The steps you climbed symbolize
Your gradual ascent of the paths and
   stages.

The light shining toward the north
Shows that in the north,
You, my son, will benefit beings.

That many beings dance in light
Means that your disciples will be capable
   of practice.

Understand and keep this in mind.

Then he gave me the initiation, transmission, and explanations of the *Long-Life Practice of
the Northern Continent*,[12] with the essential oral
instructions. Following this, both of us, master and
disciple, did that longevity practice for a month.

One day, holding a slate in his hand, the
Dharma King said, "Without thinking, let us
write a four-line stanza." He wrote for me:

Everyone is deceived by delusory samsara.
Persevere in nothing but the holy Dharma
And no doubt you shall escape
The inescapable ocean of samsara.

In turn I offered this reply:

> There is no happiness in samsara [43b];
> Like ripples on the water, suffering follows
>   suffering.
> Thus, in accord with the guru's words,
> I shall persevere in nothing but the holy
>   Dharma.

This was an exceptional and intimate time. Out of his immense compassion, the Dharma King spoke with me on many topics related to both Dharma and the world. These conversations are still vivid in my mind.

Gyal Khenchen Rinpoche, a guru who had always shown me great kindness, arrived on his yearly visit to Mongolia. He presented me with a monastic robe and a woolen shawl, and gave me extensive instructions and advice.

Together we went to Thayenchi, where the great realized being Karma Tsewang Rigdzin had lived as a hermit. Spending the night there, we two, master and disciple, shared our understanding and experiences, discussing various topics related to the supreme words of the Victorious Ones in the sutras and tantras. In an atmosphere of joy our two minds became as one. The next day, as he was leaving, I offered him this farewell song:

> Compassionate guru who helped me enter
>   the Dharma,
> Protector of beings in this dark age,
> Supreme holder of the Dharma
> Who impartially preserves all teachings,
> May you continue happily on your way
> To benefit the teachings and all beings.

The venerable Khenchen replied:

> E ma!
> O powerful yogin who accomplishes great
>   bliss

> Stay happily at this pleasant rocky cave
> In the joyful solitude of Tseshung,
> And we will meet again soon.
> Farewell until then;
> Auspicious links have been created
> In this retreat place today.

Saying this he went away.

I then received a letter from my dear mother urging me to return [44a]. Thinking it over, I decided that my living with her for twenty years had not brought her any benefit—how could I now benefit her by seeing her just once, while, at the same time, abandoning my practice?

With some presents, I sent a letter asking about her health, and telling her that, according to my guru's command, I was now practicing the divine and perfect Dharma for the lasting happiness of both of us, mother and son. I said that I could not come that year but would see her the next.

Soon afterward the glorious and excellent Tertön Sonam Nyentrak, "Famous Merit," an emanation of Drogmi Lotsawa[13] and a fifth-generation descendant of Tertön Dudul Dorje, came to Urgeh. The Dharma King requested many empowerments from him. Along with the Dharma King, I, too, was fortunate to receive the initiations for the *Hundred Supreme Deities*,[14] the *Prayer of the Spontaneous Fulfillment of all Aspirations*,[15] and the *Manifestation of Awareness*,[16] and other initiations, seven altogether. The tertön also granted the transmission and explanations of the cycle of the *Single Golden Syllable of the Black Quintessence*[17] and the cycle of teachings of Tertön Longsal Nyingpo,[18] the treasure discoverer "Essence of Brilliant Space."

Before his departure, the precious tertön came to Thayenchi. There, I questioned him about the sutras and tantras, and specifically about some difficult points of the Trekchö and Thögal practices of the luminous Great Perfection.

Pleased by these queries, he answered them at length. He also gave me many helpful teachings. I begged him for an object of faith for the hermits dwelling there, and he left an imprint of his hand in a rock. (Later, someone took the rock away.) We prayed that we, master and disciple, might meet again and again in all our lifetimes, and, our two minds having merged, he left [44b].

I remained in retreat. One day at noon, when the sky was clear, I walked to the summit of the hill above my cave and sat there alone. Toward the north, I saw a pure white cloud billowing over a mountain peak, as milk does when it is boiled into a froth and spills over. The moment I saw this, the memory of my precious spiritual father, Jamyang Gyatso, overwhelmed my mind, and I sang this song of longing:

To the north,
A single great cloud surges
Over the high mountain peaks—
White as overflowing milk.
When I see this,
I think of my guru's kindness.

Beneath that distant cloud
Rise the solitary heights of Tashikhyil.
The way my perfect guru once lived
In that excellent retreat place
Comes back to my mind.

Thinking of his kindness,
Tears come to my eyes, sorrow into my
   heart.
My mind is dazed,
Perception becomes uncertain;
Everything around me becomes hazy and
   unreal.
How wonderful if he were here again!

I am but an ordinary man,
A man with scant devotion.
Still, I long to meet him once again.

The guru dwells now in the space of
   dharmakaya
And his low, unfortunate son is left behind
In the mire of samsara.

When I see the myriad flowers
Blooming in the meadows,
The authentic guru's form
Comes to mind.

Then I could see his excellent form;
Now I cannot.
Thinking and thinking of him,
The guru's presence fills my mind.

As I listen to the cuckoo's soft and gentle
   call,
The authentic guru's voice, grave and
   sonorous,
Comes to mind.
Then I could hear his deep, melodious
   voice;
Now I cannot.
Thinking and thinking of him,
The guru's presence fills my mind.

As I see the rising sun spreading radiance
   all around,
The authentic guru's wisdom and
   compassion
Come to mind [45a].
Then he tenderly looked after me;
Now that time is gone.
Thinking and thinking of him,
The guru's presence fills my mind.

The authentic guru's presence
When he was with me—
The way he gave empowerments,
Instructions, and explanations—
Comes back to my mind.
Then I could request
Empowerments, instructions;
Now that time is gone.
Thinking and thinking of him,
The guru's presence fills my mind.

I remember the times
When I sat at his lotus feet,
Drinking in the nectar of his words;
I could never hear enough.
Then I could attend him;
Now that time is gone.
Thinking and thinking of him,
The guru's presence fills my mind.

I think of when I went to see him,
Having been away

For months or for years—
The warmth of his welcoming smile
Comes back to my mind.
Then I could see his face; now I cannot.
Thinking and thinking of him,
The guru's presence fills my mind.

No matter in which direction
I go, I think of the guru;
No matter in which solitary place
I stay, I think of the guru;
No matter what signs
I see, I think of the guru—
Always, at all times, I think
Of my authentic master.

When I remember my teacher,
It is almost more than I can bear:
My heart catches in my throat,
Beyond control.
My eyes are blind with tears I can't
   restrain.

Precious one—
From your invisible realm
Do you hear me, father?

If so, from the pure
Spacious sky of dharmakaya
Now—this very moment—
Appear in a form that I can see;
Ease the desolation of your son!

As I sang this plaintive song, the cloud continued to swell until it took the form of a heap of jewels. At the top, in a tent of five-colored rainbow lights, my root guru appeared. Performing a graceful dance, his hands in the gesture of protection, he was more resplendent than ever, peerless in loving-kindness [45b]. He smiled radiantly and spoke these words in a voice like Brahma's:

Noble son,
You who are like my heart,
Do not despair;
Listen to your father's words.
We, father and son, who came together

By the power of past prayers, are
   inseparable
In the state of the luminous absolute
   nature.

Son, from now on,
Let the length of your practice
Equal the length of your life;
Wander from place to place,
In solitary mountain retreats;
By practicing austerities,
May you help all fortunate beings.

In the end, when your life span is
   exhausted,
From the pure, spacious sky of the
   dharmakaya
I, your father, will show you, my son,
The rupakaya that is naturally present
And remind you of the clear light at
   death.
Son, keep this in your mind;
Be happy.

With an amused smile on his face, he added:

In future, do not call on me
With such fierce lamentations!
If the people of this dark age
Were to hear this,
They would not understand.

Don't be sad,
But look toward the mind that feels
   sadness.
The guru is not other than mind.
It is mind that remembers the guru;
It is mind into which the guru dissolves.
Remain in the uncontrived nature of
   mind,
The dharmakaya.

With airy and graceful movements, as though dancing, he rose higher and higher until he vanished like a rainbow into the sky. The clouds too, dissolved into space, and my grief dissolved along with them. I remained for a long while in a serene state beyond thought.

Another day, I went out for some fresh air to a meadow covered with flowers. I was singing *The Inconceivable Arisen of Itself*, the song on the view which Tilopa[19] used to teach the great pandit Naropa [46a].

While singing and remaining in a state of awareness of the absolute view, I noticed among the profusion of flowers spread out before me one particular flower waving gently on its long stem and giving out a sweet fragrance. As it swayed from side to side, I heard this song in the rustling of its petals:

An offering!
My father and mother are the sky and the
    earth;
I am the child nurtured by warmth and
    moisture.
See how beautifully I display my fine
    petals,
Waving them in the ten directions!
They are my offering to the Three Jewels.

Listen to me, mountain dweller:
The yogin for whom all phenomena
    appear as scriptures
Is satisfied with the book of the
    phenomenal world.
You, so-called "hermit," collecting all sorts
    of scribbling,
Stagger under the weight
Of your load of worn-out books.
If these books and instructions
Are not present within your own mind,
Why should you carry such a burden of
    writings?
When you roam around the mountains
To whom can you complain of the
    hardships you endure?

I don't want to hurt your feelings,
But, in fact, you even lack awareness
Of impermanence and death,
Let alone any realization of emptiness.

For those with such awareness,
Outer phenomena all teach
    impermanence and death.
I, the flower, will now give you, the yogin,
A bit of helpful advice
On death and on impermanence.

A flower born in a meadow,
I enjoy perfect happiness
With my brightly colored petals in full
    bloom.
Surrounded by an eager cloud of bees,
I dance gaily, swaying gently with the
    wind.
When a fine rain falls,
My petals wrap around me [46b];
When the sun shines I open like a smile.

Right now I look well enough,
But I won't last long,
Not at all.

Unwelcome frost will dull these vivid colors,
Till turning brown, I wither.
Thinking of this, I am disturbed.
Later still, winds—
Violent, merciless—
Will tear me apart
Until I turn to dust.
When I think about this,
I am seized with fear.

You, hermit born in Lower Rekong,
Are of the same nature.

Surrounded by a host of disciples,
You enjoy a fine complexion,
Your body of flesh and blood is full of life.
When others praise you, you dance with
    joy;
When faithful patrons turn up,
You sit in a dignified manner;
When they shower you with lavish food,
You smile with satisfaction.

Right now, you look well enough.
But you won't last long,
Not at all.

Unwelcome aging will steal away
Your healthy vigor;
Your hair will whiten
And your back will grow bent.
Just thinking about it,
Don't you feel chastened?

When touched by the merciless hands
Of illness and death
You will leave this world
For the next life,
Vanquished and powerless.
Just thinking about it,
Aren't you seized with fear?

Since you, mountain-roaming hermit,
And I, a mountain-born flower,
Are mountain friends,
I have offered you
These words of good advice.

Then the flower fell silent and remained still. In reply, I sang:

O brilliant, exquisite flower,
Your discourse on impermanence
Is wonderful indeed.
But what shall the two of us do? [47a].
Is there nothing that can be done?

The flower replied:

I make this offering,
An offering to the infallible Three Jewels.
We two must now do as I say.

Among all the activities of samsara
There is not one that is lasting.

Whatever is born will die;
Whatever is joined will come apart;
Whatever is gathered will disperse;
Whatever is high will fall.

Having considered this,
I resolve not to be attached
To these lush meadows.
Even now, in the full glory of my display,

Even as my petals unfold in splendor,
I pray that I may swiftly go and meet
The temple of the Three Jewels.

You, too, while strong and fit,
Should abandon your clinging
To the pleasing taste of respect
And the offerings of others;
Meditate in solitude;
Seek the pure field of freedom,
The great serenity.
I pray that you may swiftly
Encounter the Pure Realms.

The flower concluded, "If you want to rest in evenness, maintaining the view of the natural state, you should do this," and it rested unmoving in a clear state free from thoughts.

One night I dreamed of a child, completely white, radiating light an arm's length in all directions. He was so resplendent that I could not take my eyes off him. He stood on a rock in front of me. With his right hand he held his secret vajra and with a smile he spoke to me these words:

Your body, the perfect jewel vase,
Is filled with the nectar of pure great bliss.
By the power of the vase initiation,
May benefit for others increase [47b].

As he spoke, white nectar flowing from his secret vajra fell on my head and entered my body, gradually filling it in a vivid, perceptible way. Eventually, except for the hair and nails, my whole body was filled, and I experienced the taste of great bliss.

With a symbolic gesture of his left hand, the youth pointed toward the sky and said, looking up into space:

Natural awareness is the all-pervading
    absolute expanse.

Natural clarity is like the vastness of the
    sky.
By my bestowing upon you the initiation
Of the wisdom that is naturally arisen,
May your aspirations be naturally fulfilled.

I remained effortlessly in a state of evenness
as vast as the sky, beyond words. The youth then
rose slowly higher and higher into the eastern
sky and disappeared. Such was my dream.

Another night I dreamed that, while seated
cross-legged, I held my breath as in a vase and
flew high into the sky until I reached the level of
the sun and moon. There I saw celestial cities on
the sun in the east and on the moon in the west.
Looking in all directions, I saw the vast architecture of the universe and its various sceneries.

Then I tried to descend but could not, because an ascending wind held me aloft; I
continued floating where I was. Just then, from
amidst the clouds, a young celestial being
emerged, visible from the waist up, and said,
"To descend, unfold your legs, free your breath,
spread your limbs, and fly, like a bird" [48a].
Doing so, I flew down with ease and came to rest
on the top of the mountain behind Tseshung.

I thought these and other good dreams
meant that I would travel the path in this very
life.

One day, one of my benefactors came and said
that divinations and astrological calculations
indicated that an evil charm had been placed in
his home, but he could not find out what it was.
He urged me to do a divination.

I remained evenly in the natural state for a
while, and, within this sky-like evenness, I looked
to see what the cursed object might be. I saw that
under a large wooden case of butter was an old
offering lamp with a short stand and a broken
rim. Curious as to its origin, I saw that it had
been taken out of a pond by the lady of the house
five years before, and because of this, she was
suffering recurrent difficulties with her right hand.
All these images arose clearly in my mind.

As I related this to my patron, his faith grew
stronger and he said, "Grant us your protection—though you keep it hidden, you have
unimpeded prescience." Saying this, he left.

Thereafter, when people insisted on having
me perform a divination, I was able, after
remaining for a while in equanimity, to know the
good and the bad of things. Thinking that such
prescience might prove quite presumptuous and
unreliable, and realizing that all this might invite
disturbances and create obstacles to my practice,
I later kept silent about such matters and claimed
to know nothing [48b].

About that time an epidemic broke out and
decimated the cattle population. Two patrons
living in the vicinity asked for my protection. So,
every morning and evening I visualized the protective tent of my *yidam* and throughout the day I
visualized the luminosity of Trekchö and Thögal
permeating the entire place. As things turned
out, the cattle of that area were spared, and the
two patrons, filled with joy, offered me much
assistance.

One day a poor Mongolian vagabond turned
up. Rifling through my provision bags, he set
about stealing one of them. At that very moment
I said:

Thief, you have come! Wonderful!
We'll see if I, the mountain dweller,
The so-called "renunciate,"
Can behave in keeping with my name.
Let's see if I have really understood
The main point of the Dharma.

We'll make some tea and drink it together.
If you live far away, stay here for the night.
Let's discuss both worldly and spiritual
    things.
Then I shall give you whatever I have.

Accordingly, the thief and I boiled some tea,
and as we were drinking it he asked, "Where is
your native land? In which monastery do you

live? Do you have any family at home? What is your name?" I answered with these words:

My native land is all lands,
In no particular direction.
My monastery is the solitary mountains,
In no particular place.
My family is all the beings of the six
    realms.
My name is "Hermit Protected by the
    Three Jewels."

At this playful reply, the thief burst out laughing and said, "Lama, you are a gifted speaker" [49a]. Then, having given him what little I had, I sang:

I pray to you, father, King of Dharma!
Grant your blessings
That my mind may remain free from
    attachment!

Open your ears, thief, and listen carefully.
I see everything as illusion.
Having neither accumulated wealth nor
    craved it,
I have never owned illusory possessions.
Beyond what you see, I have neither food
    nor riches.
See for yourself!

Now, if you don't know me
I shall tell you frankly—
I was born in Rekong Shohong;
As to my father, I am a disciple of the King
    of Dharma, Chögyal Wang.
I am a practitioner of the Great Perfection;
My name is Tsogdruk Rangdrol.

Having meditated again and again
On all beings as my parents,
I am free of the duality of enemy and
    friend.
Having found the sublime inner wealth,
I am glad to give you whatever outer
    wealth,
Food, and possessions you desire.
Now, just relax and be content.

On the occasion of this virtuous action,
I dedicate all merit accumulated in the
    past,
And all to be accumulated in the future,
So that you and all beings
May achieve supreme Buddhahood—
Such is the way of the Bodhisattvas.

Content, the man did three prostrations, wished me good-bye, and went on his way.

Another day, on my way to Urgeh, one of my Dharma brothers said, "Hey! You're supposed to be in retreat in your cave. Have you come out?" In response, to explain my tradition for doing retreat, I playfully spoke these words [49b]:

I bow down at the feet of the peerless guru,
Protector of beings, whose mind is one
With that of Samantabhadra.

Fortunate friend,
Listen without distraction.
For the yogin of the most secret Great
    Perfection
There is no leaving of retreat,
Neither is there any entering.
In the simplicity that is beyond concepts,
There is no crossing of boundaries.
With all this formal entering and leaving
One cannot really be called a retreatant.

My way of doing retreat is this:
In the retreat hut that is my own body
Endowed with the six characteristics,[20]
With the three pure vows [21]
I sweep away the dirt—negative actions of
    the three doors;
In the stream of the four initiations,
I wash away all defilements.

Seated on my cushion—
The fundamental consciousness,
Coarse and subtle thoughts—

I, the yogin of awareness
That is itself brilliant and cognizant
Remain in the retreat
That is the uncontrived natural state.

Freed from discursive thoughts,
Staying within the limits
Of naturally abiding meditation,
Fearing visitors—mental dullness and
    wildness—
I mark my retreat boundaries
With the poles of undistracted mindfulness.

My retreat helper is emptiness:
Through which whatever arises
Is freed as it appears.

As for my way of practicing the
    development stage:
In the immeasurable palace
Of primordial purity arisen of itself,
The universe and beings arise
As a display of deities, apparent yet unreal.

Since all sounds are the resonance of
    voidness,
Recitation is never interrupted;
Thoughts that are set free just as they arise
Are the utter openness of dharmakaya.

I offer all food and drink
As a feast-offering, a gathering of merit.
To the mouth of the birthless absolute
    state.

Whether walking, sitting, or sleeping,
To blend all actions with contemplation
Is the Mantrayana seal [50a].

Just as no darkness exists in the center of
    the sun,
To a yogin the universe and beings all arise
    as deities—
And the yogin is content.

Just as no ordinary stones exist on an island
    of gold,

To a yogin all sounds resound as
    mantras—
And the yogin is content.

Just as a bird flying through a clear,
    empty sky
Leaves no trace,
To a yogin all thoughts arise as
    dharmakaya—
And the yogin is content.

In the vastness of awareness,
Without any separation into sessions of
    practice,
For a yogin, practice is relaxed and at
    ease—
And the yogin is content.

In the indivisible state in which, from the
    beginning,
Development and completion are
    indissociable,
One may do practice, or leave everything
    just as it is.
Even if one does intensive practice,
There is nothing to be done.

Beyond the workings of mind,
I realize that phenomena are the
    dharmakaya.
You, my friend, should realize this too.
Not putting your trust in intellectual
    teachings,
Master the meaning of the great evenness
    that has no origin.

As for the duration of such a retreat:

When, at death, the net of the body is
    finally torn apart,
And one is freed in the clear light of the
    dharmakaya,
One could call that "taking down the
    boundaries of one's retreat."

The virtuous practice of such lifelong
    retreat,

Beyond fixed periods,
Was the way of great yogins of the past.

Ha! Ha!
Having done no such things myself,
I've just been joking!

When I said this, my friend remarked, "Your way of staying in retreat is admirable indeed. I pray that my mind, like a hermit, may dwell that way in the solitary hermitage that is my body."
Another person asked me: "When you were first a lay yogin in your native land, did you plough fields, sow seeds, and grow crops?" [50b]. I gave him a straight answer at first, then, teasing him, I sang these verses just as they came into my mind:

I bow down at the feet of the Dharma King.
You, friend, listen to the words of the
   yogin:
I, the renunciate Tsogdruk Rangdrol,
Have not worked in the fields of this life;
Again and again, I have worked in the
   fields that are lasting.

I have not sown the seeds of samsara;
Again and again, I have sown the seeds of
   liberation;

I have not plowed ordinary fields back and
   forth;
Again and again, I have plowed through
   attachment to cyclic existence;

In the pristine field of the nature of mind
I uprooted the weeds of the obscuring
   passions.

In the vast sky of primordially pure
   dharmakaya
The southern clouds of the lineage gurus
   gathered;
The turquoise dragon of my fervent prayer
   rumbled;
Red lightning—the hook of compassion—
   flashed;

And the nectar-rain of blessings fell to the
   earth.

Having harnessed the oxen of pure
   perception and devotion,
I set in motion the plow of the guru's
   instructions.
The farmhand, fierce endeavor,
Plowed the field of study and reflection.

Cultivating the crops of the ten white
   virtues,
I cleared away the rocks and stones of
   wrong thoughts
And sowed the seeds of the Great
   Perfection.
Once more, harnessing the ox of
   perseverance,
I took the harrow of meditation
And tilled with undistracted
   mindfulness.
With the mallet—the pith instructions—
I broke up the clods of obstacles and
   deviations.
When the seedlings of experience and
   realization emerged,
The women of the farm—unwavering
   vigilance—
Cleared away the gross and subtle weeds of
   mental dullness and wildness.
As the green blades of uncontrived
   compassion
And the sprouts of unwavering concentra-
   tion flourished
The spontaneous crop of benefit for self
   and others ripened.

If you have to till the soil, do it like this.
If you have to plow a field, do it like this
   [51a].
If you have to sow a seed, do it like this.
This is how I, the renunciate yogin,
Have grown the crops of liberation.

Another time, a layman said, "The people of Rekong are exceedingly cruel. When you were in your homeland, did you fight with any enemies?"

In reply, after giving him a simple answer, I sang
this spontaneous song:

I bow at the feet of the Dharma King.
You, my man, listen to this yogin:

In samsara's narrow Rekong valley,
The cruel robbers of the negative emotions
Were waiting in ambush. As I, the
    renunciate,
"Kind One Who Spreads the Dharma,"
Headed toward the city of liberation
On the path of the supreme Dharma,
My archenemy, ego-clinging,
Gathered the armies of the eighty
    thousand passions
And raised the black-and-white banner of
    the eight worldly dharmas.

As they all were about to barricade the
    road,
I jumped on the horse of renunciation,
Donned the armor of Bodhicitta,
And seized the long lance of the perfect
    view.

Taking the Three Jewels as my allies and
Without a backward glance at this life,
From the high ground of my mountain
    retreat
I galloped into the midst
Of the army of negative emotions.
Moistening my hands with the spit of
    vigilant mindfulness,
I raised the sharp spear—
Freedom from mental dullness and
    wildness—
Pierced the heart of the general, ego-cling-
    ing,
And liberated all my foes into the absolute
    nature.

I enjoyed the illusory show of void
    appearances.
And gained total confidence in the
    undeceiving law of causation.
My allies, the undeceiving Three Jewels

Granted me a reward—happiness in this
    life and the next—
And hailed me as an undisputed hero;
Thus the yogin won the battle [51b].

As I sang, the layman, although he didn't quite
understand the meaning, felt happy for a while.

Notes

1. Thayenchi (known as *rtse gzhung* in Tibetan) is
a mountain retreat in Bakhog area (*ba khog*), near
Chuzang Monastery (*chu bzang dgon*). One speaks of
the big and the small Thayenchi (*tha yan chi che chung*,
see AC, vol. 1, p. 48).

2. The seven-point posture of Vairocana (*rnam
snang chos bdun*):

1) The legs should be crossed in the Vajrasana
    posture, the right one over the left.
2) The hands, closed into fist, with the thumb
    pressing the base of the fourth finger, are
    placed on the thighs at the juncture with
    the pelvis, and the elbows are then locked
    straight. (Two variations of this are to place
    the hands palms up, right over left, on the
    lap, with elbows bent out to the sides, or to
    place both hands palms down, relaxed, on
    the knees).
3) The shoulders should be raised and rolled
    slightly forward.
4) The abdomen should be pushed forward.
5) The spine should be kept straight, "like a
    pile of golden coins.
6) The chin should be tucked in slightly.
7) The eyes should be kept without blinking,
    unwaveringly focused at a distance of twelve
    fingers' breadth ahead of the tip of the
    nose. See Shechen Gyaltsap's *kun mkhyen
    zhal lung*, pp. 41–42.

3. This refers to the hundred-syllable mantra of
Vajrasattva. The five steps described in this para-
graph are those of the preliminaries (*sngon 'gro*) which
lay the foundation for the main practice (*dngos gzhi*).
The main practice goes through the two stages of
development (*bskyed rim*) and completion (*rdzogs rim*),
to culminate in the Great Perfection (*rdzogs pa chen po*).

4. Although one speaks of a "view," this refers to the nonconceptual recognition of the absolute nature of phenomena, the basis for subsequent meditation and action.

5. For *Wish-fulfilling Gem, Hayagriva and Varahi* (*rta phag yid bzhin nor bu*), see Appendix 4.

6. There are twenty-two knots between the central channel and the two lateral channels. As they become freed, pair by pair, the meditator attains the successive *bhumis*, from the first to the eleventh, up to Buddhahood.

7. The "far-reaching lasso" (*rgyang zhags*) is the eye, which can "catch" distant objects. The eye is also called the "water lamp" (*chu'i sgron ma*). These and the following terms used in this song are related to the secret Thögal practice and belong to the section of extraordinary instructions (*man ngag sde*) of Ati yoga (see Appendix 1).

8. Dharmata (*chos nyid*), the absolute nature. At this stage, both ordinary phenomena and the visions experienced in the former stages dissolve in the absolute nature.

9. The three kayas (*sku gsum*) are the dharmakaya (*chos kyi sku*), or absolute body; the sambhogakaya (*longs spyod kyi sku*), or body of enjoyment; and the nirmanakaya (*sprul sku*), or manifested body. They correspond respectively to the void, the luminous, and the compassionate aspects of a Buddha.

10. *Bardo* (*bar do*), "intermediate" or "transition" state, commonly refers to the transitional state between death and the next rebirth. One also speaks of six *bardos*: the *bardos* of birth and life (*skye gnas rang bzhin gyi bar do*), of meditative concentration (*bsam gtan gyi bar do*), of the dream state (*rmi lam gyi bar do*), of the moment of death (*'chi kha'i bar do*), of the absolute nature (*chos nyid bar do*), and of taking a new existence (*srid pa'i bar do*).

11. This means that when a realized person dies, his or her consciousness will merge directly (*zang thal*) with the dharmakaya. Thus, for this person there is no *bardo*.

12. The *Long-life Practice of the Northern Continent* or Uttarakuru (*byang sgra mi snyan gyi tshe sgrub*) can be found in the *Compendium of Sadhanas* (*sgrub thabs kun btus*), vol. 1, p. 417 and RT, vol. 48 (Tshi). This practice was received in a vision of Guru Padmakara by Drigung Chökyi Trakpa (*'bri gung chos kyi grags pa*, 1597–1659).

13. Drogmi Lotsawa (*brog mi lo tsa ba*, 993–1050), who brought to Tibet the Path and Fruit (*lam 'bras*) teachings of the Sakya tradition. Tertön Dudul Dorje

(*gter ston bdud 'dul rdo rje*, 1615-72), a great visionary master of Kathok Monastery in Kham (of whom Sonam Nyentrak was a descendant), was also connected with the Sakya tradition. See NS, pp. 813–17.

14. For the *Hundred Supreme Deities*, see chap. 1, note 56.

15. For the *Prayer of Spontaneous Fulfillment of all Aspirations*, see chap. 1, note 48.

16. The *Initiation to the Manifestation of Awareness* (*rig pa'i rtsal dbang*) is a most profound transmission which introduces one to the nature of awareness beyond conditioned mind and makes one realize that thoughts are the display of this awareness.

17. The *Yangti Nagpo,* or the *Single Golden Syllable of the Black Quintessence* (*yang ti nag po gser gyi 'bru gcig*). This cycle of teachings belongs to the most esoteric section (*yang ti*) of Ati Yoga. It involves practices focused on the Hundred Peaceful and Wrathful Deities and dealing with the stages of the Great Perfection, with some pith instructions for the practice of meditation in complete darkness. The later Dungtso Repa (*dung mtsho ras pa phyi ma*; see G. Smith [1972], GC, vol. 2, pp. 784–86, TN, pp. 518–19, and Yangti Nagpo, vol. 3, p. 267), a disciple of the famed dakini Kunga Bum (*kun dga' bum*), found this *terma* in a tortoise-shaped rock near the Lake of the Black Mandala (*mtsho mandal nag po*), also known as Kala Dungtso (*ka la dung mtsho*). The latter lies across the Kashong Pass (*kha shong la*; see Fletcher 1975, and Huber 1992) near Gampo. The "later" Dungtso Repa is thus called for being the immediate reembodiment of the "earlier" Dungtso Repa (*dung mtsho ras pa snga ma*, 1267–1329?, see GC, vol. 3, pp. 30–31 and TN, pp. 515–16), who also revealed a *terma* (the *sems khrid yid bzhin nor bu*) from the Lake of the Black Mandala. Although the above sources concur consistently, there is a certain amount of confusion between the two Dungtso Repas, since in ND, p. 144b, for instance, Kunzang Ngedön Long Yang attributes the discovery of the Yangti Nagpo to the first Dungtso Repa, and so do other historians who based their works on ND (for instance, BD, vol. 3, p. 424). In his *gter ston chos 'byung*, pp. 65–66, Karma Mingyur Wangyal, too, considers there to be only one Dungtso Repa and attributes to him the *termas* of both the "earlier" and the "later."

18. Rigdzin Longsal Nyingpo (*rig 'dzin klong gsal snying po*, 1625–92), a disciple of Dudul Dorje and a great tertön of Kathok Monastery. See GC, vol. 3, p. 177.

19. On the lives of the great *siddhas* Tilopa and Naropa, see Guenther (1963).

20. Earth, water, fire, and wind, along with the spiritual channels (*rtsa*) and the vital essence (*thig le*), are the six things that make a human being a suitable vessel for receiving the four empowerments (*dbang*, or Skt. *abhiseka*) and consequently able to practice the Vajrayana. Celestial beings from the form realm and the formless realm have subtle elements only, or none, and lack the proper support of the channels, energies (*rlung*), and vital essences for receiving the second and third empowerments.

21. The Three Vows (*sdom pa gsum*) are the Pratimoksha vows, the Bodhisattva precepts, and the Vajrayana *samayas*. See Appendix 1.

5

Meditation at Tigress Fort

How I practiced in other isolated places nearby:
Takmo Dzong, Göpo Dzong, and Getho

Many retreatants began coming to Tseshung Grove, the place where I had first settled into meditation practice, and, due to the increase in commotion, my practice ceased to flourish. When this happened, I thought, "I should go somewhere alone and practice meditation in a quieter place."

I asked the precious Dharma King for advice, and he said, "Take some provisions and go to the retreat place at Takmo Dzong, the Tigress Fort." To repay his kindness, I made a pledge always to do as he told me:

Your understanding
Sees all that can be known
As it truly is.

Your loving-kindness
Grants to beings
The feast of great teachings.

Your actions accomplish
Only what delights the Victorious Ones.

Sublime Bodhisattva, think of me for a
    moment.

Your heart's loving-kindness has held onto
    me
Since I left behind my homeland
To be with you, father.

Through the basic path, you trained
And greatly purified my mind-stream.

My father's kindness has turned my mind
    toward the Dharma.

Having given the empowerments that
    ripen
And the oral instructions that free,
You pointed out absolute, birthless mind:
The natural state, as it is.
Due to my father's kindness,
I don't need to search elsewhere for
    Buddhahood [53b].

In short, your great kindness and affection
In two ways have sustained me:
You've given me empowerments,
Explanations, and oral instructions,
As well as the food and clothing needed to
    live.

It would be hard to repay such kindness
Even if I filled a billion worlds with gold.

But to repay it by means of practice,
I will wander only in mountain solitudes,
Doing practice for the rest of my life.

Father, accept this offering made to please
    you:
The length of my practice
Shall equal the length of my life.

Until I achieve unchanging stability of
    mind,
I won't remain in busy, worldly places,

But will stay alone in isolated places of
  retreat.
Father, accept this offering made to please
  you.

So that I remain true to my renunciate
  name,
I won't own more than the food and
  clothes I need to survive.
Father, accept this offering made to please
  you.

Please make strong prayers
That each of my aspirations
May be accomplished without fail, and
Keep me always within a place of safety
From which I'm never cast out—
The mandala of your primordially pure,
Profound, luminous mind.

After I had made this offering, he gave me this
advice on how to give up concern for this life:

I supplicate the glorious guru
Inseparable from primordial Lord
  Samantabhadra,
Forefather of all the Buddhas of the three
  times:
Bless this son so that he renounces the
  concerns of this life.

E ma!
Listen, fortunate heart-son.
For your benefit,
I'll give you a father's heartfelt advice.
Since it is heart-guidance,
Keep it in the center of your heart.

One's homeland is a wellspring for the
  obscuring emotions [54a]:
Knowing that it is Mara's prison,[1]
Wander only in mountain solitudes, my
  heart-son.
This is loving advice, so do take it to heart.

Sense-pleasures and desirable things are
  prime enemies;

Friends and relations are like a rope
  keeping one tied to samsara.
Leave behind close family and distant
  relatives, my heart-son.
This is loving advice, so do take it to heart.

Servants and followers cause anger and
  attachment.
It's easy to get along without anyone else.
Stay without servants and followers, my
  heart-son.
This is loving advice, so do take it to heart.

Veneration and respect are the snares of
  Mara.
Praise and fame will only lead you astray.
Give up renown and veneration, my heart-
  son.
This is loving advice, so do take it to heart.

Living off food given by the faithful
And food offered on behalf of the dead
Create conditions that hamper efforts
  toward virtue.
Cut your longing for good food at its root,
  and
Just live on whatever comes your way, my
  heart-son.
This is loving advice, so do take it to heart.

A renunciate needs two strengths:
Courage to throw concern for this life to
  the wind; and
Self-reliance, to avoid being led around by
  others.
This is loving advice, so do take it to heart.

When you are in retreat, distractions serve
  as sidetracks
Away from your spiritual practice.
Don't get preoccupied by one thing after
  another, heart-son.
This is loving advice, so do take it to heart.

Base your mind on the Dharma [54b].
Base your Dharma on a beggar's life.
Base your beggar's life on asceticism.

Base your death on a cave.
This is loving advice, so do take it to heart.

Cast yourself out from the company of
  worldly people,
As a corpse is simply cast away;
Keep to the company of dogs, and, with
  no effort,
You will win the company of celestial
  beings.
This is loving advice, so do take it to heart.

One hasn't heard, and one won't hear,
  stories
Of meditators dying of cold and hunger:
Don't let your nerve and courage fail you!
This is loving advice, so do take it to heart.

In short, abandon concern for the activities
  of this life.
Avoid these three things like poison:
  society, wealth, food.
Be a renunciate, a beggar who's left
  everything behind.
This is loving advice, so do take it to heart.

Where you've stayed, leave behind just the
  imprint of your bottom;
Where you've walked, leave behind only
  your footprints;
Once you put on your boots, let there be
  nothing else left to bring along.
This is loving advice, so do take it to heart.

This way of giving up concern for the
  ordinary activities of life
Was the way of many learned and accomplished beings of India and Tibet.
Follow the life-examples of *siddhas* of the
  past, heart-son.
This is loving advice, so do take it to heart.

By this merit, may many worthy beings
Relinquish concern for the ordinary
  activities of life,
And by their diligent practice in isolated
  retreat,

May they reach fruition in this very
  lifetime.

The other oral instructions he gave me can be
found in my *Collected Songs*.[2] When I was about to
leave for the retreat, I offered this song of farewell [55a]:

Dharma King and consort, who bestow all
  excellence,
I, your faithful son, wish that you stay in
  good health
In your encampment, the place of
  contentment,
And ask that you never cast me out
Of your blissful and luminous heart.

Following the advice of the guru
Who is all the Sugatas in one,
I leave joyfully for that excellent abode—
  solitude.
When meditation experiences and
  realization arise,
And with them a confident and truly
  satisfied mind,
I'll return to offer you my best wishes.

Anyone on the path to liberation that is
  great bliss
Who has given up samsara's frustrating
  preoccupations,
Should, like me, go to mountain solitudes
  to find satisfaction,
And the sun of true happiness will arise
  from within.

Chögyal Rinpoche gave me the blessings of body,
speech, and mind, and said:

All the Victorious Ones without exception
In the realms of the ten directions
Arose in the form of the lama
Who appeared to my ordinary eyes.
By means of the supreme medicine of the
  Dharma
He cured the sickness of confusion:
To him I bow down.

Look upon me with great compassion!
This fortunate son, my disciple,
Goes to practice in a solitary place.
Without, may enemies and obstacles not
   come.
Within, may sickness and the disturbing
   emotions not arise.
May the signs of blessings truly come to pass.
May his practice of the profound Dharma
   quickly reach completion,
And may we two soon meet joyfully again.

Then I prostrated myself before the Dharma
King and his consort. Just as I was leaving, I
touched my head to his feet, and made this
prayer that we would soon meet again:

E ma ho!
Root and lineage lamas who grant all
   blessings—
Peaceful and wrathful *yidams* who grant all
   siddhis [55b]—
Dakas and dakinis who dispel all
   obstacles—
Dharmapalas who perform all Buddha-
   activity—
Keep the life of my father-guru firm for a
   hundred kalpas.
Make his son's good qualities, meditation
   experiences, and realization flourish.
May master and disciple quickly meet
   again.
When we meet, grant us the excellent
   happiness
Of never having to part again.

After Chögyal Rinpoche, pleased by my
request, had spoken at length, I set out for my
retreat at Thayenchi.
    There I met my faithful, diligent, intelligent
and compassionate vajra brothers and Dharma
friends: the learned, pure, and noble Kusho
Lakha Rinpoche, the realized yogin Konchog
Chöpel, the great disciple Pema Rangdrol,
Jampel, Rabgye, Dageh, Chödrak, and others. I
gave some advice on clearing away obstacles and
enhancing practice, and, as I was leaving, gave
them this reminder of virtue:

From my heart
With respectful body, speech, and mind
I supplicate the Dharma King, Ngakyi
   Wangpo,
Embodiment of the Three Jewels,
Unfailing objects of refuge:
Grant your blessings so that I and all others
May be ripened and freed.

Fortunate friends who keep stainless
   samaya,[3]
Let this renunciate offer some heartfelt
   advice.

Dharma friends—
Now that you have the excellent support
Of a free, well-favored human birth,
Fulfill its true purpose, enlightenment.

Dharma friends—
Give up concern for the meaningless things
   of life, and
Wander off to solitary places for retreat.

Dharma friends—
Death strikes suddenly; it comes without
   warning—
When it comes, you must have no regrets
   [56a].

Dharma friends—
When you die, you must leave food, wealth
   and belongings behind,
So give up greed.

Dharma friends—
You'll have to go along the *bardo*'s narrow
   pathway all alone,
So give up your attachment to companions.

Dharma friends—
There is not a single sentient being
Who once was not your own parent,
So give up hatred toward enemies.

Dharma friends—
When you've tamed your mind—the inner
   adversary—

There are no outer enemies.
Tame your own obstinate mind!

Dharma friends—
Good and evil actions have inevitable
results:
Give up doing wrong and do what is
right.

Dharma friends—
In samsara there's no chance for
contentment:
Regard it as a pit of fire.

Dharma friends—
Food, wealth, society—all these have no
ultimate meaning:
Don't perform rituals and exorcisms in
villages to earn your keep.

Dharma friends—
The commotion of worldly places
Distracts you from striving, from doing
what is right:
Spend your time alone in isolated places.

Dharma friends—
When you're with friends who practice the
teachings,
Adopt the intention to benefit them
And maintain pure perception.

Dharma friends—
You can be called "renunciate"
Only if you're free from hopes, plans, and
saving face:
Don't fall under the sway of other people.

Dharma friends—
You can be called a *siddha*
Only when you've controlled the stream of
obscuring emotions:
Depart from error by yourself.

Dharma friends—
The signs of accomplishment are
Gentleness and discipline
Of body, speech, and mind:

Give up attachment to those close to you
And aversion toward strangers.

Dharma friends—
The Three Jewels are the unfailing refuge:
Take refuge in them from your heart.

Dharma friends—
The root of Mahayana is generating
Bodhicitta:
Cultivate supreme Bodhicitta, the mind of
enlightenment [56b].

Dharma friends—
The four strengths are the principal means
for purifying obscurations and wrong
actions:
Perform the practice of Vajrasattva.

Dharma friends—
Offering the mandala is the supreme
means for accumulating merit:
Make mandala offerings constantly.

Dharma friends—
Guru yoga is the quickest way to receive
blessings:
Ceaselessly supplicate the master.

Dharma friends—
The words of an authentic master are not
misleading:
Regard what your lama says as perfect.

Dharma friends—
The *yidam* is the basis for the ordinary and
extraordinary *siddhis*:
Practice the development stage of the
yidam.

Dharma friends—
Dakinis and dharmapalas dispel all obstacles:
Hold feast-offerings and offer *tormas*.

Dharma friends—
Trekchö fosters the state of awareness that
of itself is luminous—
Maintain this nondual empty brilliance.

Dharma friends—
Thögal frees the material body as the body
   of light—
Cultivate the luminosity that is naturally
   present.

Dharma friends—
Practicing in this way,
One can achieve the rainbow body in a
   single lifetime:
Practice from your heart, with joy.

These words are spoken honestly and
   unerringly:
Practice in this way, Dharma friends.

By their truth, and by the power of all past,
   present, and future virtue,
May the glorious guru's life be firm and
   long.
May my Dharma friends' meditation
   experiences and realization flourish,
   and
May they realize the *trikaya* in a single
   lifetime.

When I finished speaking, my friends were filled
with joy [57a].

The great spiritual son Lama Pema Rangdrol
(also called Sengzang Gyatso, "Ocean of Leonine
Perfection" and Rigdzin Dawa, "Moon of Awareness") had fortunate karma accrued from practice and training in previous lives. He had received
many instructions and empowerments from
Chögyal Rinpoche. At this time, I gave him
many transmissions and instructions, and personal advice—although this was like using a butter-lamp to light up the daytime.
   Later, after passing through the great monastery at Labrang Tashikhyil, which is like another
U-Tsang,[4] he went on to the Golden Valley of
Rekong. There, in the solitude of the heights of

Tashikhyil, a place predicted by deities and
gurus, he concentrated on practice for many
years. In this way, he produced immeasurable
benefit for the Dharma and for all sentient beings.
The details can be found in his biography.
   I packed up my small tent and supplies,
put them on my back, and set out on the road.
I soon came upon a man who asked where I
was from and where I was going. I first answered him directly, and then I spontaneously
sang a song:

I'm called "Child of White Snow Lioness."
To begin with, I was fed with milk from
   my lioness mother.
Later, I was fed with foods of various kinds.

Now, the three strengths have reached
   perfection in my form:[5]
The lion's great turquoise mane bristles
   through his parents' kindness.

I don't stay in one place now,
But wander across snow peaks:
The snow lion's domain is snow
   mountains.

I'm called "Child of Garuda, King of
   Birds."
To begin with, I was nurtured with
   warmth from my bird-queen mother.
Later, I was fed with foods of various kinds.

Now, my great wings are spread out in
   strength;
The garuda soars in space through his
   parents' kindness.

I don't stay in one place now,
But go wandering across azure heavens.
The garuda's domain is the vast skies
   [57b].

I'm called "Child of Dharma King."
To begin with, I was accepted and given
   instructions.
Later, I went into mountain retreat.

Now, meditation experiences, realization,
    and good qualities have been brought
    forth in me.
The strength to be a wandering
    practitioner
Comes through my master's kindness.

I don't stay in one place now,
But go wandering across high plateaus.
The renunciate's home is wild solitudes.

I went on to Tsang Monastery, where a monk kindly gave me a place to stay, and I paused there for a week or so. I was reading the biographies of the eighty-four *mahasiddhas* (which, among other books, belonged to a certain Kusho Tsangpa), when this occurred to me:

"Most of these *siddhas* attained realization by persevering in a few profound practices of development and completion. If I can devote myself entirely to practice, I won't need a lot of different teachings." My intention to practice was strengthened by reading these biographies.

One day, I went to see Kusho Galgor. I asked for and received from him the transmission of *Opening the Door to Mind Training*.[6] I also met Kusho Tsamgor, and received the transmission for the *mani* and for *Aiming at Loving-kindness*.[7] Following that, I went to see Jamyang Adzi, a hermit who lived on the mountain behind Tsang Monastery, and I stayed with him for several days. I asked him for the transmission of the biography of Jetsun Milarepa, the collected songs of Lord Kalden Gyatso, the *Thirty-Seven-fold Practice of a Bodhisattva*,[8] and the *Seventy Admonitions*.[9] He granted this request and also gave me much good advice. When it was time to leave, I offered him my best wishes and set off for the retreat place at Takmo Dzong, Tigress Fort [58a].

At Takmo Dzong, there were two rock caves. Inside the smaller of the two, I spread out some hay as a mat and stayed there.

The next night, I was in a state halfway between waking and sleeping when I heard a roar like that of an earthquake. Tiny lights shim-

mered like stars in the space around me. A shiver ran from my head to my toes; my body felt weightless, light as fleece. My skin tingled, and a pounding sensation filled my whole body. The noises and lights got louder and louder, brighter and brighter.

I remembered that a certain Lama Parinpa was said to have practiced black magic in this cave, and I figured the trouble probably came from that. I was thinking, "Maybe I should invoke Vajrapani," and just then I realized, "I haven't given up clinging to this ego of mine at all! To say, 'Eat me, drink me!' just once is better than saying 'Protect me, save me!' a hundred times! Without really putting an end to the belief that phenomena are real, what's the point of practicing Dharma?"

I then did a thorough visualization of Chöd, and fell asleep in an empty and clear state like the sky, like the dharmadhatu,[10] the true condition of all things.

In a vivid dream, having left behind my body, my awareness appeared as Vajrayogini. With the hooked knife in her right hand, she carved up my body, which was lying senseless on the ground. She cut off my head and the top of my body, and gave it to a black man, an old lama, and a woman, who devoured it ravenously. Curious as to the taste of human flesh, I considered eating it, and put some in my mouth [58b]. Then I thought, "To eat one's own flesh must be very inauspicious!" I took it out of my mouth, and threw it on the ground. The black man grabbed it in an instant and ate it up. Seeing how hungry they were, I proceeded to carve up the rest of my body and feed it piece by piece to the three of them, until they disappeared, satisfied and pleased.

From that night on, the upheavals in the cave did not recur. I thought, "Once one relinquishes regarding phenomena as real, gods and demons will not only stop making trouble, they will be pleased and helpful."

Later, the monk Thogme from Gartse[11] asked me if the cave was pleasant. In reply, I sang a spontaneous song describing its many good qualities:

Mind-emanation of the Buddhas of the
      three times,
Father, Dharma King, Ngakyi Wangpo,
I supplicate you without ceasing.
Grant your blessings that this vagabond
May be able to keep to mountain retreat.

Making joy and inspiration arise,
This solitary place, Takmo Dzong, and I
      are in complete accord.
I'm of the mountains, my mind is there:
Thus do I sing my song.

"Tigress Fort"—stately and auspicious,
A place where many great beings once
      stayed.
A rocky crag without—within, a home.

Its southern door is bathed in light, even in
      winter.
Spring and fall—the air is cool; mind is
      clear.
Water, wood for fires—everything I need is
      easily found;
My perceptions here are always lofty and
      joyous [59a].

Above, in a sky without boundaries,
Eagles circle, gliding.
Celestial juniper trees ornament
The cliff's back face;
Their scent spices the air.

Before me, six-legged honeybees hum,
      hovering over
Wild flowers spread out across the
      meadow.
From a stream's clear water rushing over
      stones
Come continuous murmurings.

Wild animals bask on the slopes,
Frisking, gamboling; they saunter or stroll
      about.
In the deep green forest, from the highest
      branches,
Various birds chatter and sing.

Rain clouds hang overhead like great
      canopies.
From clouds swirled like scattered white
      silks
And patterned with perfect rainbows
Summer rain falls in a fine mist.

The guardians of this place
Are on the Dharma's side:
Anything wanted is right here.
There are no villages nearby, no temples,
      no noise:
Everything is slow and serene.

Through the lama's blessing,
And by the grace of the place itself,
Meditation experiences and realization
Arise easily in one's mind-stream.

I, a renunciate of these mountains,
Call out the clear tones of my song.

How wondrous if all those who practice,
With minds turned toward the Dharma,
Had the support of a place like this!

To sing like this—
Go into the mountains!
By this merit, may all those practicing the
      teachings
Make use of solitary places for retreat,
And may they become fully perfected.

One day, in a joyful state of mind, I sang a small
song called the *Union of the Sun and Moon of Contentment*:

I bow down at the feet of the authentic
      master.

I, Tsogdruk Rangdrol,
The renunciate who practices the
      Dharma, am singing a song:

The union of the sun and moon of
contentment.

When I relinquished concern for the usual
activities of samsara [59b],
There arose a sun—a mind filled with
weariness and revulsion.
There arose a moon—a real desire for
Dharma.
These were contentment's first sun and
moon.

When I searched for the refuge of the
Dharma and for a master,
There arose a sun—the Dharma, the
profound path of Dzogchen.
There arose a moon—the Dharma King,
lord protector.
These were contentment's second sun and
moon.

When I stayed at the feet of the lord
protector,
There arose a sun—the perception of him
as the actual Buddha,
There arose a moon—a mind filled with
changeless faith.
These were contentment's third sun and
moon.

When I practiced in remote retreats,
There arose a sun—unceasing compassion
for sentient beings,
Each one of whom was once my own
mother.
There arose a moon—excellent meditation
experiences and excellent realization.
These were contentment's fourth sun and
moon.

This small song of the union of the sun and
moon of contentment,
I've sung to lighten my mind.
By this merit, may all sentient beings,
Each one of whom has been my mother,
Be content at all times and in all
circumstances.

One day, when I was thinking about my elderly
mother, I felt such a strong wish to see her again
that I sang this song:

> Most kind master,
> Treasury of all good qualities,
> I supplicate you.
> Grant your blessings that attachment,
>   confusion, and taking things as real
> May be severed at their root.
>
> You, renunciate Tsogdruk Rangdrol,
> Listen well, without distraction!
>
> When you are still yearning for home,
> What's the point of having gone off to the
>   mountains?
>
> When your attachments aren't like pure,
>   empty space,
> What's the point of calling yourself
>   "renunciate"?
>
> When you're not making good use of your
>   free, well-favored birth,
> What's the point of having obtained a
>   human body?
>
> When you still don't behave so as to be free
>   of regret at the time of death,
> What's the point of knowing that death will
>   come?
>
> When you're still not giving up evil and
>   doing what is good [60a],
> What's the point of having understood the
>   law of karma?
>
> When you've still not renounced samsara
>   and its ways,
> What's the point of having understood its
>   imperfections?
>
> When you're not taking refuge with all
>   your heart,
> What's the point of doing it just with your
>   tongue?

When you're still not doing as your master
    says,
What's the point of all those polite *yeses?*

When you're still not practicing with
    diligence,
What's the point of having heard the
    profound instructions?

When you're not intent on practicing for
    all of your life,
What's the point of doing retreat for a few
    months or years?

When you still can't arouse real impartial
    compassion,
What's the point of loving just the mother
    of this life?

When you still can't truly regard all beings
    as once having been your mother,
What's the point of keeping this life's
    mother in mind?

When you still haven't realized samsara
    and nirvana's single flavor,
What's the point of going back to see your
    mother again?

When your thoughts aren't arising as
    dharmakaya,
What's the point of merely suppressing
    them?

When you can't meet face to face beyond
    "coming" or "going"
In the homeland that is the view "one
    taste,"
Just to meet your mother in person is
    pointless,
And might make problems—so forget it!

The way to meet your mother in the
    absolute state
Is to practice through mixing your mind
    and her mind
With that of all sentient beings,
And all these with the mind of your
    master.

Having thus chided myself, I thought, "I *am*
confused. Didn't I come to this solitary place
because I wanted to attain enlightenment for the
sake of *all* sentient beings, each one of whom has
been my mother?" Thinking about my own
mother, an overwhelming sense of compassion
arose in me toward all suffering sentient beings.

Afterward, I gave my new tent to a crippled
old woman who lived outside Tsang Monastery
[60b]. She sold the tent for sixteen lengths of
cotton; with half of that, she bought tea to offer
to the monastic community.

I gave my new long sheepskin coat to a
beggar, who traded it for six lengths of cloth, and
then bought tea, butter, and *tsampa.* He was later
seen doing prostrations, circumambulating the
monastery. I fed a flock of magpies and crows
with much of my food.

After this, I made prayers that all sentient
beings might swiftly attain Buddhahood, and
that they and the teachings might benefit greatly.
Then I began to practice.

At sunset one day I heard a male and a female
crow, cawing and jabbering at each other, and I
wondered what they were saying. I said to myself, "If you're such a good singer, try making a
song of their conversation!"

The male crow said this:

Ah! Ah!
Now it's just the time to go:
The sun has disappeared in the west.
Let's go home to the forest,
To our tree's high branch;
Going to rest,
Let's make our way back home.

I spoke to the crows:

You! Crows who live in the forest!
Listen to this person who lives in a cave!
Don't you know where your home is?
It's not up in some tree.
Not to know your own home is ludicrous.

The male crow looked miffed, and, ruffling his feathers, replied:

> Caw!
> Old monk, what are you talking about?
> My home is certainly right there.
> And if you know better [61a],
> Then speak up, you homeless beggar!

I replied:

> Don't fly off, crow, just sit still.
> Since you don't know about your real,
> Lasting home, I'll tell you—
> But then you must keep it in mind.
>
> This is not home. Home is
> The realm of Samantabhadra.
>
> Just after birth,
> Some old lady relative called Ignorance
> Put mother Samantabhadri's child
> On the horse of karma and kleshas:[12]
> Thus was the child brought into
> Samsara's triple realm.
>
> There's no place that we haven't gone,
> There's no body in which we haven't been
>   born.
> It's really sad that you, homeless pair of
>   crows,
> Don't understand where home is!

The male crow replied:

> Heh! Heh!
> You talk and talk, you homeless beggar,
> But you just make me laugh.
> If you're so smart,
> Homeless beggar, you'll
> Probably go back to that "home" soon,
> But why should we?

I said to him:

> Listen, you skeptical crow:
> Many spiritual friends told me
> That this is not my real home, and
> At that time I begged them

To show me the way.
I made offerings
Of my thoughts and deeds,
With pure perception, my palms
Joined in devotion toward
The guide on the path—the authentic
   lama.

> My master showed the direct path, Dzogchen.
> He placed me on the excellent steed of oral
>   instructions,
> And put in my hand a whip to enhance my
>   practice.
> I used the spur of joyful diligence,
> And rode along the path to liberation.
>
> Because of the steed's good breeding [61b],
> I reached Samantabhadra's realm,
> The permanent homeland, quickly and
>   easily.
> Meeting the mother, Samantabhadri,
> I felt joy beyond duality.
>
> In the primordially pure dharmakaya
>   kingdom,
> I, the child Inherent Awareness,
> Seized the royal throne of changeless
>   samadhi.
> With seven noble riches I filled my
>   treasury.[13]
> Luminosity became my most beautiful
>   queen,
> Whom I accompany with nonattachment.
> Through the joy and contentment that is
>   naturally present,
> I have captured the permanent kingdom.
> What do you think, crow?

The crow replied:

> Hey, if that's true,
> Then you *are* amazing!
> Still, comparing my home to yours,
> Mine is better!
> Sweet wife, let's go!

With a profusion of caws and jabberings, off they flew. As they flew, the female, looking a bit despondent, spoke to the male:

It certainly is amazing that this great
    meditator
Who lives inside a cave
Has discovered his permanent home.
We don't have one:
How depressing to fly aimlessly in samsara!

The male crow said to her:

Listen to me, sweet wife!
There's not the slightest bit of truth
In what he says.
This masterless, servantless man
Is simply shooting his mouth off
Because his belly is full of food:
There's nothing amazing about that!
We two are far more amazing!

Hearing this put her mind at ease, and they flew
further away. I made up this song just to refresh
my mind [62a].

One day, when I went to the spring, I saw that
hundreds of winged insects had fallen into a pool
of water. Some were already dead, and others,
still alive, were struggling on the water's surface.

Seeing this, I felt so sorry for them that I
lifted many of them to safety with a spoon, to let
them dry their wings and fly again. I broke open
the pool's dam and let the water escape. Then I
made this prayer of aspiration:

As I have carried onto dry land
These poor insects who fell into this pool,
So may I save all beings from the sea of
    samsara
And establish them in Buddhahood.

I stayed in the sacred place of Takmo Dzong
for about four months, and, because there were
no people coming and going, I made some
progress in my practice.

I then left for a pilgrimage to Amnye Getho,[14]
the seat of my kind root master, Jamyang Gyatso

Rinpoche. On the way, I first reached Ragya
Monastery, where I met Shingsa Lobzang
Dargye,[15] from whom I received a reading trans-
mission and instructions on taking refuge in the
Three Jewels. He kindly gave me detailed expla-
nations on the general path, which were of great
benefit to me. I also met Trigen Rinpoche, the
elder holder of the throne of Tharshul; from him
I received reading transmissions for both *The
Blissful Path* and *The Swift Path*.[16] I saw Lama
Jampa Trinley Rabgye, holder of the throne of
Arik; at my request, he gave me generous amounts
of tea and butter.

I crossed the Machu River on a boat and
arrived at the mountainside of Amnye Getho
[62b]. I stayed for over a month at the seat of
Jamyang Gyatso. There I found an old hermit
who was reading the collected works of Tsongkhapa and his two spiritual sons.[17] I looked at the
works of these precious masters and, by merely
reading through them quickly, gained much understanding. Later, when I had time to study
them in detail, I understood their prime importance among all the elegant expositions that clarify
the sutra and tantra teachings.

Karmapa Kunkhyen Chökyi Trakpa[18]
wrote:

Once, the seal of the Dharma
Was in the hands of the learned and
    accomplished Sakya masters.
After that, the learned one known as
    Lobzang Trakpa
Clarified the doctrines of sutra and
    mantra.

And as I thought this statement quite true, pure
perception and devotion increased in me.

While I was staying at Amnye Getho, some
Mongolian beggar women of Walgasu came,
asking if anyone had *tsampa* to trade for some
top-quality sweet-roots. I gladly traded with them,
and pleased them by adding some extra *tsampa*.

One day a Mongolian layman told me he
was ill, and asked me to do a *mo*[19] for him. I said
to him, "I don't make divinations. Your sickness
is temporary and not life-threatening, but you

are unaware that you've caught a much worse disease. If you want a divination for *that*, I'll do it."

So I sang for him, with a stately melody, *The Divination Method According to the Buddha's Words*:

Bowing down at the feet of the Dharma
   King,
I, the renunciate Tsogdruk Rangdrol,
Now make the unerring divination
In accord with the Buddha's words.

First, I invoke the truth of the rare,
   supreme ones:
To the Buddha, Dharma, Sangha,
To the guru, deva, dakini,
I entrust this divination
With fervent supplication [63a].

This man has been struck down
Continuously throughout his past lives
In the house of samsara's triple realm,
And has suffered from the diseases
Of karma and of the obscuring emotions.

First, the cause;
Second, the symptoms;
Last, whether his life can be saved
If he quickly does the rituals that protect
And ward off danger:
I trust in you, precious ones,
To give a clear answer to these questions.

I lay out the divination mat of the
   Buddha's words
Right in the palm of my hand.
I throw the dice of clear vision
And perform the divination of insight . . .

Alas!
This *mo* augurs nothing good.
First, you are sick from having eaten
The putrid food of ignorance and
   confusion.
This stuff remains in the belly of your pure
   mind-essence,
Creating pain from attachment to self
And aversion toward others.

Your condition is aggravated by the five
   poisons
As the chief demonic forces,
Reinforced by the eighty-four thousand
   different kinds of lesser harmful spirits.
You've lost your appetite for the food of
   the holy Dharma.
This has increased your pain and suffering,
   and the severity of your illness.
You've thirsted for the water of evil deeds.
These are the diseases and harmful spirits
   that afflict you.

Sick one,
It is certain you've not diagnosed these
   diseases;
Harmful spirits and the obscuring
   emotions
Have left you in anguish and complete
   delirium.
However, if you quickly do the rituals for
   treatment and healing,
There will be no danger to your life.
If you don't quickly cast the protection
   spell of the holy Dharma
Your serious illness will become grave
And will sever liberation's life force.
There is, therefore, a lot at stake.

As to the procedures that can cure this
   disease:
Attend the doctor, your spiritual friend [63b];
Offer him the gifts of virtuous thoughts and
   acts.
To counteract the poisoned meat of igno-
   rance and confusion
First apply learning, contemplation, and
   purification.
As appropriate, then drink the excellent
   medicine of the oral instructions
Of Madhyamika, Mahamudra, or
   Mahasandhi.[20]
Without doubt, you will quickly be free of
   illness.

To avert evil influences
The *ngakpa*—self-control and mindfulness—
Should offer in the proper manner

A talisman of affection
To the spirit-king of anger;

A ninefold thread-cross talisman[21] of distaste
To the spirit-queen of passion;

A freeing ritual of insight
To the nagas and local guardians of
    ignorance;

Many rituals of pure perception for
    neutralizing poisons
To the *rahu* spirits of jealousy;

Many humbling wrathful exorcisms
For the wandering murderous ghost of
    pride;

A talisman of excellent devotion
To the wild *tsen*-spirit[22] of wrong view;

And to the demon of greed who brings
    poverty,
The *ngakpa* should offer generosity.

To counteract all other negative forces
He should perform protecting and repel-
    ling rituals [23] of the ten virtuous deeds.

At the end, he should perform the *yidam*
    practices
Of emptiness and compassion as much as
    he can.

If all these rituals are carried out,
Your suffocation will cease, and
You will be cured and freed of all illness.

If these measures are not applied,
Your disease will become more grave
And you will collapse onto the deathbed
Of samsara's triple world.

With birth and death as your pillow
And joy and sorrow as your cloak,
The excruciating agony of aversion and
    attachment
Will never give you a moment's rest.

Because of all this, sick one,
Wouldn't it be better
To quickly apply the remedies
Now, when you can still be cured? [64a].

By this merit, may all beings beneath the
    skies
Make this "Divination According to the
    Buddha's Word."
May they depend on a spiritual friend as
    their doctor,
May they drink the medicine of profound
    and perfect Dharma,
May they cure the sickness of the passions.

After I said this in a teasing way, the man
was impressed and said, "This divination
according to the Buddha's word is truly excellent! Since I may die any time, please give me the
transmission for the *mani*, and always remember
me in your prayers." I gave him a blessing, the
transmission he'd asked for, teachings on the
general path, and explanations on the benefits of
reciting the *mani*. I sang many songs to him, and
thus turned his mind toward the Dharma. With
genuine respect and devotion growing in his heart,
he went on his way home, chanting the *mani*.

I started on a pilgrimage to the slopes of
Lhanyen Götse, where my supreme spiritual
master, Arik Geshe Rinpoche, had done some
meditation. On the way, I crossed the Machu
River at Getho.

Near Ragya Monastery, I saw an old
Mongolian woman lying in a hollow. The muscles
on one side of her body had atrophied, leaving
her crippled. Her right wrist was infected, and
the stench of the pus and blood that oozed from
it could be smelled from far away. Seeing this
woman, who had nothing to eat or drink, I felt
great compassion. I begged food from the monks
at the monastery, and, having gotten enough for
a month or so, I put it by the old woman's head,
and prayed [64b]:

Compassionate guru,
Compassionate Three Jewels,
Regard this old woman
With compassionate eyes.

There is not a single being
Who has not been my mother—
It's so sad to see this poor old woman!

Now, when she's suffering,
There are no friends or relatives to help
    her.
Now, when she's hungry,
There's no food for her to eat.
Dampness wells up from the ground
    below;
Rain, unwelcome, pours down from
    above.

Her body, stricken with illness,
Has no nourishment.
She is penniless.
She can't move even if she wishes to.
Surrounded by the smell of her pus and
    blood,
There isn't one person to look after her.
She hovers between life and death
On a bed soiled with piss and shit.
Seeing this, my eyes fill with tears.

When I said this, the old woman also started to cry. She asked me, "Where are you from? Where are you going?" and continued, "I had a dear son who died. Your coming here is like meeting him again; it's as if he came back from death." Remembering her son, she wept for a long time; tears came to my eyes as well.

I told her a little about myself, and she said, "Please, protect me in this life, the next, and in the *bardo*."

I gave her a blessed pill containing relics of the Buddha that had multiplied miraculously, the Bodhicitta from Orgyen and consort—the mere taste of which brings liberation—and other precious substances. Explaining to her the miseries of samsara, birth, and death, I did *phowa* [25] for her, and offered this prayer on her behalf to the protector Amitabha and his retinue:

Amitabha—Buddha, lord of limitless light,
Avalokiteshvara—sovereign of the uni-
    verse,
Vajrapani—possessor of great power:
Cast your compassionate gaze day and
    night
Upon this old woman who relies on me.

Protectors and your heirs:
At the time of her death, accompany her
    joyfully [65a]
And guide her to your realm of boundless
    happiness,
The western Pure Realm of Great Bliss.

Having made this prayer, I said, "Now, old woman, continually pray to the protector Amitabha and his retinue, visualizing them vividly on the crown of your head, and at the moment of death your consciousness will be led to the western Pure Realms of Great Bliss."

Two days after I left her, the old lady died.

On the slope of Lhanyen Götse, where the glorious and excellent Gyaltsen Öser,[26] "Radiant Banner of Victory," an incomparable spiritual master, had once practiced, I spread out some hay and sat down.

One night, after I had been there a week, a piercing pain ran three times from the top of my head to the soles of my feet. I began to chant strongly the syllable *hung* with a thorough visualization of "annihilating phenomena and self" according to the special preliminaries of the Great Perfection.[27] After I did that, nothing else happened.

I dreamed that night that many spirits met, and one of them said, "He seems to be neither Buddhist nor Bönpo—it's hard to tell what he is; we've never had anyone at his level of realization staying here before. Tonight I tried to find out, but when he said 'Hung! Hung!' so very many *hungs* came out of his body, it was like bees swarming out of a broken beehive; there was nowhere for me to hide. If he stays on here, we'll have to kill him." He roared with laughter as he said this.

After this, I didn't have a single bad dream [65b]. Over the course of a month, my practice progressed and, especially, great compassion toward sentient beings arose in me. I constantly made prayers that I, in this life, could benefit sentient beings, my mothers in previous lives.

Then, I received a message from Chögyal Rinpoche, which said, "Don't go to another place. Chödpa[28] has built many pleasant retreat huts in the secluded grove of Tseshung. Go soon—you can stay in any one of the huts."

On my way, I spent a day at the entrance to a cave in a rocky place to the right of Lhanyen Götse. That night, I had a vision of many monks and lay people arriving, led by a yellow-hat priest who said, "Hey, old monk! Don't sit on our path!" They all waited. The yellow-hat priest said, "Well, since he won't go when he's told to, let's teach him a lesson!"

Suddenly, two black men came with a big bag of charcoal, which they poured on the ground. They heaped up the charcoal and put a bellows to the right and to the left. Between the bellows they placed a cauldron as big as a man, and heated it till it was red-hot. Both men stood up then and said, "If you're such a good Buddhist monk, sit in there!"

They started to beat the top of the cauldron, screaming war cries, and making a noise that sounded like the cracks of thunder in a summer storm. Splashes of molten bronze flew in all directions, splattering over the entire valley.

I rested evenly in the natural state. When I looked again, the cauldron had become smaller and smaller and the molten bronze was splashing less and less [66a]. Finally, out of love and compassion, I sang this song for them:

I ask that the most kind master
Transform adverse conditions into helpful
    ones.
You devas, demons, and obstacle-makers
Who are gathered here,
Listen a bit to this yogin's song.

In the vast expanse of space, beyond center
    and fringe,

Clouds that gather in the south
Are the sky's adornments.
If there's a little rain,
So much the better.

In the vast ocean, beyond increase or
    decrease,
The waves that interweave there
Are the sea's adornments.
If the surf comes crashing,
So much the better.

On the mountains, which are immovable,
The trees growing in thick forests
Are the mountains' adornments.
If the leaves rustle gently,
So much the better.

For a yogin like me
Who has realized the natural state,
The arrival of gods and demons
Is just adornment for my practice.
If you're a bit vicious,
So much the better.

It's wonderful that you've come today.
Now put on an even better magic show!
Please, stay here until daybreak,
Destroying this old monk
So that not one dust-particle remains.

Having sung this, I rested evenly in the view.

One of the men said, "Don't say anything to that old monk! Let's get out of here!" With much commotion, they left. This event enhanced my understanding of the view.

The next morning, I got up early and went to beg some tea from two camps of nomads from Gartse who were staying in the lower valley. They called me inside and asked where I had spent the night. I said that I'd stayed under the rock overhang at the entrance to Draknaphuk cave.

One elderly patron said, "That's not a place for anyone to stay! They say that two hermits once pitched a tent below that rock, and, at midnight, a fire came out of the side of the cliff [66b]. The next night the fire burned even higher. Finally, a demoness with a long iron beak came and split the door of the tent. When she poked her beak in and looked around, one of the hermits saw it and was terrified.

"At dawn, he told his friend, 'Let's get out of here! This place is haunted!' The friend replied, 'No, it'll be fine,' and they stayed.

"At night, the first of the two hermits lit a butter-lamp and sat chanting the *Miktsema* prayer. The demoness came again and poked her iron beak through the back of the tent where the other hermit was sleeping. She struck him in his heart. He screamed once and died, without even having had time to wake up. The next morning, the other hermit ran away."

The elderly patron then asked, "Did a demoness like that disturb you?" I told him what had happened; he was amazed and faith arose in him. He said, "You are a truly realized being! I take refuge in you!" He offered me some butter; then he escorted me out past the dogs, and I went on.

On the road I met a young man from Gartse who asked me, "Don't you have a horse?" I replied, "Oh, yes! I do!" and I sang a song as if my bamboo walking stick were my horse:

> I bow down at the feet of the Dharma
>   King.
> When Buddha Shakyamuni, sentient be-
>   ings' only friend,
> Milarepa, lord of yogins,
> And the accomplished, learned beings of
>   the past
> Went out to beg,
> They all had horses of excellent breed—
> And I have one of the same bloodline!
>   [67a].
>
> This horse is caparisoned with sashes of
>   five-colored silk!
> On its head—a golden halter!
> On its back—a rug, and a gold-studded
>   saddle cinched with an iron ring!
> Below, its hooves are shod well with iron.

> Steering my horse with my right hand
> I wander at will from wilderness to
>   wilderness,
> My horse never tires—even after months
>   and years!
> No matter where I leave it, it's never
>   stolen!
> My horse does much better than others in
>   mud!
> Against a guard dog, it does best of all!

Thus I sang, and he went away laughing.

I arrived at Urgeh, where I met the precious Dharma King, Chögyal Rinpoche, and his consort. When I told them how I'd practiced and been attacked by gods and demons, Rinpoche was very pleased.

He said, "Dear son, you've done extremely well! By being able to raise the victory banner of practice, you overcame adverse conditions. From now on, no obstructing spirits or obstacles will be able to harm you."

I rested for a few days. Every day I went to my master and asked questions on some uncertainties I had and on various difficult points of the sutras and tantras. He answered me at length, and thus the days passed.

Then I went to the retreat place at Thayenchi where I visited my vajra brothers and Dharma friends; we had many joyous conversations. Following the orders of the Chögyal Rinpoche, I gave them all the teachings and transmissions they asked for, and I sang some songs of realization.

After I had given them the oral instructions, many of the retreatants stayed in their own huts in strict seclusion [67b], concentrating entirely on the practice of the Great Perfection. Thus, they gained confidence that they would actually be liberated in the *bardo*.

I sealed myself in the cave with mud and practiced in complete darkness following the instructions of the *Single Golden Syllable of the Black Quintessence*. I was amazed to see the visions and other signs described in the texts.

One day, it rained lightly and rainbows appeared. High in the sky, eagles were flying; when the sun came out, I took a walk to the mountain peak behind Thayenchi and sang this song of praise to the retreat-place:

E ma!
This extraordinary wilderness!
Here, where so many learned and
    accomplished lamas have stayed,
The gathering-place of dakinis and
    dharmapalas,
Is the place where I stay in solitude.

Tseshung, this secluded mountain place:
Above—a slow, soft rain drizzles down.
Flocks of eagles flying—north, south—
Beaked mothers and their young
Trying their wings—
Rainbows vividly appear.

Below me—the curved necks of geese,
Glancing, and the Tsechu River flowing
    on,
Sinuous. Behind them, deer dance on the
    slope
Of a mountain whose peak penetrates
    space.

On both sides, meadows blaze with wild
    flowers;
Myriad bees whirl above them.
In front, rocks ornament the mountain
    meadows;
A cuckoo's cry fills me with sadness.

Up and down the valley, cattle and sheep
Owned by the faithful
Dot the land. The young girls
Watching over them are busy,
Making up songs and plays and dances.

Today I climbed behind [68a]
This excellent retreat place,
Looking down on such charming scenes
From the mountain's summit.

I raised my head, looking up,
And saw the cloudless sky.

I thought of absolute space, free from
    limits,
The view of dharmadhatu.
I then experienced a freedom
Without center, without end—
All biased views
Completely abandoned.

I lowered my head to look in front of me,
And saw the sun of this world.

I thought of meditation—
Luminous and unobscured.
I then experienced a nondual empty
    clarity.
All meditations that focus the mind
I completely abandoned.

I turned my head, looking south,
And saw a pattern of rainbows.

I thought of all phenomena—
At once both apparent and empty.
I then experienced a natural clarity beyond
    duality.
All nihilist and eternalist viewpoints
Completely abandoned.

Looking above, looking below,
Looking in all directions,
I saw the world and the beings in it—
All reliant on space.

I thought of fruition that is inherent and
    naturally present.
I experienced a state beyond accepting or
    rejecting—
Hope of results and fear of failure
I completely abandoned.

When I finished this song, I felt great joy.

Another time, when relaxing in a place covered with flowers, I sang a song from the *Hundred Thousand Songs of Milarepa:*

The Three Jewels, which are all refuges
   combined,
Are contained within unfabricated
   awareness.
In that state, supplications aren't needed.
Without having to perform recitations,
The yogin is content.

The *yidam*-deity who grants the two *siddhis*
Is contained within radiant clarity,
Without any deity to be accomplished;
In that state there is no need for creative
   meditation.[29]
Experiencing his body as that of the deity,
The yogin is content [68b].

The assembly of dakinis who dispel
   obstacles and adverse circumstances
Is contained within one's own innate
   nature;
In that state there is no need to offer
   tormas.[30]
Leaving the six sense-consciousnesses in
   their natural condition,
The yogin is content.

Discursive thoughts, those troublesome
   demons,
And even the concept of "demon" itself,
Are contained within the absolute nature.
No need, in that state, for exorcisms.
With discursive thoughts arising as the
   dharmakaya,
The yogin is content.

All philosophical logic and language
Are contained in the state of luminosity.
In that state, there's no need for intellectual
   pursuits.
Appearances arising as his books,
The yogin is content.

As I sang this, a small, beautiful, sweet-voiced
bee flew by, saying:

Listen, lucky young one!
Don't brag, just pipe down!
If appearances are really your books,
   yogin,

Make a song about me and what I do!
That will show if you really can read
Appearances like books!

In reply, I sang:

All right, listen here, you lovely bee!
Your body's small; your buzz is loud.
My experience is feeble, but I have a big
   mouth,
So you and I have much in common.
Taking your unreal bee body as a meta-
   phor,
I'll make a song about you and what you
   do.

I, the renunciate yogin-as-bee,
Have a body: primordially pure awareness.
I've two full-grown wings: skillful means
   and insight.
I'm striped with the experience of
   luminosity.
I stand on six feet: the six paramitas.
From meditation experiences and
   realization,
I've grown the antennae of good qualities.
I've eyes that discriminate between
What to accept and what to reject.

Sometimes I visit my patrons, the flowers,
   and
From the jewel-vase of my throat
Flow precious songs of realization
Sweet as a bee's hum.
The patron-flowers' faith blooms fresh and
   bright:
Knowing just how to take the nectar of
   food and clothing [69a],[31]
I do not impair the freshness of their faith.

In old age, when dark clouds gather
And suffering's heavy rain pours down
I unfold my two wings of insight and
   skillful means,
In the sky of empty, luminous
   dharmakaya,
Preparing to fly back to the hive:
The youthful vase-body,[32] the state of
   nonreturn.

"Good bee, did you understand?" I asked. "I did indeed," said the bee, "and I am delighted. What a beautiful song!" It flew respectfully around me, circling to the right, and went off into the distance, not looking back.

When Lakha Tulku's house was being built, a Dharma friend asked me, "Do you know how to pound walls for a meditation hut?" I said that I did, and for fun I sang this song:

I bow down at the feet of the Dharma King!

Listen well to this short tale
Of how a yogin who renounced all worldly
    activities
Performed the ultimate wall-pounding!

My perfect root guru
Tamed the earth of my stubborn mind
By taking up the antelope horn[33] of the
    profound instructions.
Diligence—the good laborer—
Piled up the earth—wholesome virtue—
On the level ground that is virtuous
    thought.
My gracious root guru moistened this
    earth
With the water of the four empowerments.

The foreman—self-existing awareness—
Drew the wall-lines of steady calmness,
Set the wall-forms of the Great Perfection,
And fixed the rods of changeless
    primordial purity.
He bound these with the ropes of
    undistracted mindfulness,
And tightened them with wedges—
    clearing obstacles and enhancing
    practice [69b].
With a mallet—profound perseverance—
Undistracted, he pounded the walls.[34]

The tall earthen house is the view.
The firm foundation is meditation.

The tightly pounded walls are the action:
When these three come together, there is
    an earthen house that lasts forever.

A man once asked me, "In your homeland, do people live in tents or in houses?"

I first gave him a straight answer, and then I sang this song on living in neither a tent nor a building, but a dwelling of light:

At the feet of Chögyal Ngakyi Wangpo
I make this supplication, with veneration.
Grant your blessing that I achieve
A dwelling-place of light,
The source of all the *siddhis* one could
    desire.

In my homeland, the houses are made of
    wood.
But I, who, carefree and content,
Have left behind the things of this life,
Do possess a house:
A house of five-colored light
That, of itself, arose.

Worried that a house like those of my
    homeland would collapse,
I put up an absolute, indestructible house,
One that is free from fear.

The young child, Fresh Awareness, is the
    woodworker;
Various deluded appearances are the
    wood;
By means of the sharp tool of insight,
These are turned into
Substanceless emptiness.

Setting the house foundation is the view;
Placing the pillar stone—the lamp called
    "lasso cast into the distance";[35]
Raising the pillars—the lamp "absolute
    expanse";
Supporting the pillars—the lamp "empty
    spheres";
The covering roof—the various visions.
The canopy—luminous emptiness free
    from taking things as real—
Is the lamp called "insight arisen of itself."

In the house that is naturally present
   luminosity
Are set out the mandalas
Of the peaceful and wrathful deities—
Apparent, yet empty.
My offering is not regarding phenomena as
   real.

These days, even the best worldly houses
Don't last, and soon crumble into ruins [70a].
My house of light, arisen of itself,
Can't fall into ruin; it can't be destroyed
By earth, water, fire, or wind.
An indestructible vajra house—
I have it, but not many do.

So, fortunate disciples,
If you build, make a dwelling of light.

By this merit, may all fortunate disciples
Put up the excellent Thögal mansion.

Another Dharma friend said to me, "It's very
dirty in here; you should sweep and straighten
up the place a bit, and put out some statues and
offerings."
   I said to him, "Following the words of my
father-guru, I've already swept and straightened
up, and I've made an excellent arrangement of
images and offerings according to the tradition
of the Great Perfection." I then sang this song:

   I bow down at the feet of the Dharma King,
   The mind-emanation of the Buddhas of
      the three times.

   Through the blessings of the sublime guru,
   I, the renunciate Tsogdruk Rangdrol,
   A yogin of the Great Perfection,
   Have an inner shrine, not an outer one.

   Here is the way to make shrine-offerings
   That, like the sun, naturally arise
   In the shrine-room of the luminous Great
      Perfection.

   In my body, the shrine-room,
   The temple keeper called "thoughts freed
      as they arise"

Sweeps the dust of thoughts and obscuring
   emotions
Into the unborn expanse of dharmakaya.

In the state that is empty, luminous,
And free from taking things as real,
I set out the deities' images
Of primordial purity and natural
   presence,
Not made by hand, but arisen of
   themselves.

On a shelf: stable calm-state meditation,
   [70b]
I offer water for drinking: clear and empty
   primordial purity.
I offer water for bathing: unchanging
   samadhi.
I offer flowers: natural luminosity, free of
   clinging.
I offer incense: the natural freedom of
   whatever arises.
I offer a lamp: continuous practice
   throughout day and night.
I offer perfume: spontaneous presence, free
   of clinging.
I offer food: simultaneous appearance and
   emptiness.
I offer music: unborn and empty sound.
I offer a mandala: the various visions.

When you set out images, set them out in
   this way.
When you make offerings, make them like
   this.
Most people have outer shrines;
This yogin has an inner one.
This is the kindness of the glorious guru.
Vajra brothers, I am joyful and content.

I don't know how to sew. Once, when one of my
Mongolian disciples was mending my shawl, he
said to me, "You don't seem very good at sewing. Didn't you ever make any clothes when you
were at home?" I answered with this song:

I bow down respectfully at the lotus feet
Of my master, who possesses threefold
    kindness.[36]
Grant your blessings that I may become
    skilled
At sewing the brocade of the four clear-
    light visions.

Worried that clothes made from condi-
    tioned substances would wear out,
I've never sewn any conventional clothing.
But I've made, and now I wear,
The unconditioned clothes of the absolute.

With the shears of study and
    contemplation,
The tailor—all-accomplishing
    intelligence—
Having realized the natural state of all
    things,
Cut out a pattern from luminous
    Dzogchen brocade.

Wearing the thimble of strength and
    perseverance,
I passed the thread of unbroken diligence
Through the needle's eye of the lama's
    instructions [71a].

In the workshop of the primordially pure
    absolute space,
By guiding the seam of the four lamps
With the fingers of the postures and gazes,
I made a brocade robe of radiant light
Which I continually wear day and night.

All you fortunate disciples,
When you sew, make a garment of radiant
    light.
To protect against the heat and cold of the
    obscuring emotions,
This is the best clothing of all.

Light to wear, extremely durable—
It is the superior Dzogchen apparel,
The summit of the nine vehicles.[37]

By this merit, may all beings,
Limitless as the sky,

Wear the brocade of the four visions
Of luminous Great Perfection
To protect against the heat and chill
Of the obscuring emotions.

When I sang this song, the disciple's faith grew
stronger.

A man once asked me, "Are you a doctor? Do
you have medicines?" I answered him with this
spontaneous song:

I bow down to my old father, the Dharma
    King.
I, Tsogdruk Rangdrol, the yogin,
Have a supreme medicine to cure the five
    poisons
Stored within my breast:
Dzogchen, the universal antidote,[38]
And also many other medicines—
The profound sutra and tantra
    teachings.

Following my teacher's oral tradition,
I perfected my skill at composing songs in
    verse.
The young physician—awareness—
With his voice as the golden spoon,
Gives out as required the medicine—
    perfect advice.

If you can drink it with the tongue of
    discernment,
Drinking it from the white porcelain cup of
    devotion and true respect,
It will cure the chronic disease of clinging
    to ego,
And clear the disorders of wind, bile, and
    phlegm
That are caused by the three poisons.

When suffering—anger and attachment—
    has subsided,
An appetite for the food of the holy
    Dharma will increase.

Your physical strength—experiences and realization—
Will grow, and you'll be able to help other sick persons [71b].

Once a *ngakpa* asked me, "Do you know magic? Have you ever done any?" I improvised this song in reply:

I bow down at the feet of the Dharma King!
I, the renunciate Tsogdruk Rangdrol,
Once had an enemy: "Ego-clinging."
Time and again
He made trouble for me.
So I put a spell on him.

How did I cast it?
First I offered the magician—the guru—
The many gifts of faith and respect.
I said I needed magic to destroy my enemy.
My lama was glad to teach me
The many magic spells
Of the sutras and tantras.

In a mountain wilderness retreat hut,
I donned awesome attire—that of a renunciate.
I recited a wrathful mantra—having no wants or needs—
And dug a magic pit—steady inner calm.

Using my power, discriminating insight,
My enemy was brought into my presence.
I dispatched him with my weapon—the pristine wisdom of emptiness—
And tossed him into the maw of the unborn dharmakaya.

If anyone wants to learn
This sort of magic,
I will teach without holding anything back.

Someone else asked me, "When you lived in your homeland, did you have a wife?"
I replied, "I didn't marry a worldly woman, but later I married Lady Dharma," and sang:

I bow down at the feet of the Dharma King.
I, the renunciate Tsogdruk Rangdrol,
Didn't marry a worldly woman, a source of sorrows;
I was too weary.
Listen, and I'll tell you
How I took, instead, a lovely wife,
The holy Dharma.

My lama made the match;
The bride-price was the pleasures of samsara.
The Three Jewels and Three Roots
Served as the elders [72a].
They dressed the lovely, smiling maiden—emptiness—
In ornaments and gowns—bliss, clarity, and non-thought—
And with her dowry—the seven noble riches—
She was led along the path of the dharmadhatu.
Welcomed by teachings on union
She was placed on the seat of constant faith.

We were served meat and wine—devotion and pure perception—
And a feast was laid—the vast and profound teachings.
Speeches were made—the two truths—
Songs were sung—on causal origination—
And dances were danced—on the experience of great bliss.

The matchmaker, my perfect lama,
Dressed me in the wedding robes of inexhaustible blessings,
Requesting for us riches—many *siddhis*.
To my gracious guru, who made this match,
I gave gifts—my thoughts and deeds.
At the end of the feast of the four skilled ways to gather beings[39]—

The guests dispersed into the absolute
    expanse.

With two arms—wisdom and skillful
    means—
I embraced the young maiden who grants
    lasting contentment.
Having made love in emptiness and bliss
We had one son—uncontrived compas-
    sion—
And one daughter—insight arisen from
    practice.

My mind is now at ease,
Having mastered the sky-like treasury
Of inexhaustible virtues—
Meditation experiences and realization.

E ma!
Wondrous good fortune!
All you Dharma practitioners
Should have a wife like this!
I hope that all who hear this song
May marry the Lady Dharma.

A monk said to me, "You're good at drawing.
Are you a *thangka* painter, too?" I sang this song:

I bow down at the feet of the King of
    Dharma.
I, the yogin Tsogdruk Rangdrol,
Picked up a white canvas—noble intention
    [72b].
I stretched it on the frame of the four
    boundless thoughts,[40]
And with pure discipline I primed it.
I applied gesso—changeless faith—
Smoothing it over and over
With an onyx stone—the ten virtues.

First I made the grid—learning.
Then I made a sketch—reflection.
Then I brushed in color—meditation.

Then I painted in the highlights—medita-
    tion experiences and realization.
E ma!
Isn't that good art?

Another monk asked me, "Do you know calligraphy?" First I answered him directly, and then I
sang this spontaneous song:

To my kind, authentic master, I bow
    down.
I, the fellow called Self-liberation of the Six
    Senses,
Took my stubborn mind as the paper
And smoothed it with the stages of the
    path.
I drew the three straight lines—
Development stage, completion stage, and
    Great Perfection.
Sitting on the porch of my retreat hut,
I took a bamboo pen—practice and
    perseverance—
And all day long I inscribed
The golden letters of meditation experi-
    ences.

In these ways, without inhibition, I composed an
almost inexhaustible series of songs, which arose
in my mind as the natural manifestation of
meditation experiences.

The glorious and perfect Arik Geshe, my spiritual guide (whose name, Jampel Gelek Gyaltsen,
I hardly dare say), displayed the appearance of
passing into nirvana. Kusho Gyal Khenchen
Rinpoche wrote me the following letter when he
heard this news:

Kye hu!
Listen—
The great *pandita*, the spiritual guide,
The vajra-holder possessing the Three Vows,
Has left for the Pure Land.

See him as the teacher
Who demonstrates impermanence.
His kindness is greater
Than that of all the guides
In the ten directions [73a].
Offer your vow to practice
In accordance with his commands.
Protect, as you would your own eyes,
All aspects of the three sets of vows he gave
    you.

Let the length of your practice
Equal the length of your life;
Devote yourself to enlightenment.
Thus you will fulfill his wish
And accomplish his intentions—
Now and forever.

Say the *Prayer of Perfect Deeds* [41]
And the *Praise to Tara* as much as possible.

The Dzogchen view is high;
The practice of the development and comple-
    tion stages is deep.
Yet, as a basis for virtue,
The three vows are most powerful.

If you've kept these vows without fail,[42]
It's said in the tantras that you will merge into
The state of unity, without practicing,
To quickly cross the paths and levels.

Not drawn in by the five sense-pleasures,
Search for the actual object of attachment;
By looking directly at their nonexistent nature
Let attachment be naturally freed.

Not angered by the five poisons, your enemies,
Search for the objects of anger.
By looking directly at their nonexistent nature
Let anger be naturally freed.

When, beyond discursive thoughts,
This point of view is continuously present
And is set free in the nondual state,
The Madhyamika view beyond extremes
Dawns, beyond acceptance and rejection,

Beyond proofs and refutations.
Samsara and nirvana
Are of a single taste—
And the two truths appear as aides:
Relative truth and absolute truth,
Skillful means and its result,
Existing only in relation to each other,
And lacking any true existence.

Gather the accumulations;
Purify the two veils;[43]
Do recitations;
Observe even the most subtle aspects
Of the law of karma.

If you behave dispassionately,
In accordance with the conventions of relative
    truth,
The unfailing causal links will operate
And the two kayas will be realized.

The peak of wholesome aims
Will be fulfilled;
Your benefit and aspirations
Will be accomplished.

This was written with a mother's affection for
a friend who is accomplishing lasting contentment by Khenpo Pema, he who roams the passes
and valleys and holds onto nothing but awareness [73b].

When I read this, I offered whatever I had, made
prayers that the master's enlightened wishes be
fulfilled, and recited the *Praises to Tara* and the
Prayer of Perfect Deeds. I sang a song of longing:

The precious lord, incomparable guru,
Set out in his great ship of fathomless merit
On the limitless sea of conditioned
    existence.
He raised the sail of wisdom
Beyond nihilism and eternalism.
Carried on the strong winds of stainless
    aspiration
He has reached the blissful realm
Of boundless happiness,

The vast golden continent
Beyond death and beyond rebirth.

I, his luckless disciple,
Am left behind
On this ocean of samsara.

Father!
Sublime captain!
You who save us from the sea
Of conditioned existence!
Wherever you may be in the infinite pure
    lands
I beg you, listen for an instant!
Listen to the sad song of your son—
Abandoned, without protector,
With no refuge.

Pulled on by your previous aspirations
Like the sun pulled by his emerald steeds
You beautified the sky, the deities'
    pathway,
Above the snow mountains of Tibet:
Sole friend of the lotus-field of
    Buddhadharma,
Lord who shone with a thousand
    interlaced rays
Of Buddha-activity: you, the sun, have
    now set.

Abandoned by the blazing sun,
Abandoned by you, my protector,
I am left alone, inconsolable,
On the peak of a western mountain.

Despair,
The ivory flower that blooms at night,[44]
Opens at the touch of moon-rays,
My ruined happiness.

Sadness rages like a great fire,
Though in mind
There is no wood.

A storm of tears pours down
Ceaselessly
Though in the sky of my eyes
There are no clouds.

Although I want only to follow you,
Protector, I have been brought helplessly
    bound
Into the prison of samsara
By those mighty enemies, the obscuring
    emotions,
And am locked tight in the shackles
Of clinging to self.

I suffer punishment
Daily, again and again—
Sickness, aging, loss of wealth.
When a son's state
Is so desperate,
Won't the father
From his invisible realm
Pay heed? [74a]

All the Victorious Ones of the past
Left for liberation,
Leaving behind those of inferior karma.
Protector, you who have even more
    compassion,
Can you bear to abandon us miserable
    beings,
Like travelers in a perilous place
Abandoned by their guide?

While your mind remains unmoved
In the sky of dharmadhatu,
I ask that, in accord with your former vows
    and aspirations,
You quickly manifest once more
The dazzling sun of a new incarnation.

Nurture the lotus-field of Buddhadharma!
Dispel mind's darkness!
Bring the dawn of virtue and goodness!

Protector—
May all your followers,
In whichever realm you abide,
Protector—
Be reborn in your presence
And never again be parted from you,
Protector—
May we only accomplish
What pleases you,

Protector—
May we taste endlessly
The nectar of your teachings,
Protector—
Constantly striving
To practice like you,
Protector—
May we swiftly become your equals!

Thus I prayed to be accepted by him throughout all my lifetimes.

Notes

1. Mara (*bdud),* the devil—in a Buddhist context, the personification of ego.
2. The Collected Songs of Shabkar, *The Feast of Songs.*
3. *Samaya.* See Translator's Introduction, note 38.
4. The Pure Realm of U and Tsang, central Tibet, where there are many beautiful golden-roofed monasteries to be seen.
5. The three strengths or faculties of the lion (*seng ge'i rtsal gsum*). These three have been suggested: miraculous transformations (*rdzu 'phrul*), swiftness (*myur mgyogs*), and the possession of wings made of wind (*rlung gshog*).
6. For *Opening the Door to Mind Training,* see Translator's Introduction, note 31.
7. The *dmigs rtse ma* prayer. See chap.1, note 22.
8. For the *Thirty-Seven-fold Practice of a Bodhisattva.* See Translator's Introduction, p. xxi.
9. The *Seventy Admonitions,* lit. the *Seventy Verses Ending with "Ang"* (*ang yig bdun bcu pa*), is spiritual advice by Karak Gomchung (*kha rag sgom chung,* 10–11th cent.) that condenses the essence of the Kadampa teachings. Karak Gomchung was the perfect example of the renunciate who has given up all activities other than spiritual practice. Constantly contemplating the imminence of his own death, he would not even bother to remove the thorn bushes blocking the entrance of his cave, thinking what a waste of time this would have been if he were to die that same day. He was renowned for his limitless compassion. He was a disciple of Geshe Gonpa (*dge bshes dgon pa*), and among his own disciples were Ngulton (*rngul ston*) and Dharma Kyap (*dharma skyabs*).

10. Dharmadhatu (*chos kyi dbyings*), the absolute expanse: emptiness pervaded with awareness.
11. Gartse (*mgar rtse,*) a nomad area near Tsang (*gtsang*), under Ragya (*rwa rgya*) Monastery. See AC, vol. 2, p. 283.
12. For *Kleshas,* see chap.1, note 17.
13. The seven noble riches or qualities ('*phags pa'i nor bdun*) are faith, discipline, generosity, learning, a sense of moral shame in front of others, a sense of ethical conscience in regard to oneself, and intelligence. One also speaks of faith, which is like a river; discipline, which is like a flower; generosity, which is like a jewel; learning, which is like an ocean; *samaya,* which is like a crystal; a sense of moral shame, which is undeceiving like one's own parents; and wisdom, which is like the sun.
14. Amnye Getho (*a myes ge tho*): a line of red cliffs inhabited by the mountain god of the Jasa tribe. It is two days walk from Ragya Monastery, through the Sharlung Valley (*shar lung*), across the Machu River. (See Rock 1956).
15. Shingsa Pandita Lobzang Dargye (*shing bza' pandita blo bzang dar rgyas,* 1753–1824). He became the second abbot of Ragya monastery, succeeding its founder, Arik Geshe. He was considered to be the incarnation of, among others, the Kashmir *pandita* Sakya Shri and Tsongkhapa's mother Shingsa Achö (*shing bza' a chos*). See Jigme Gyaltsen, p. 11, and AC, vol. 2, p. 139.
16. For *The Blissful Path* (*bde lam*), see chap. 2, note 30. The *Swift Path* (the full title of which is *byang chub lam gyi rim pa'i dmar khrid thams byang chub*), another of the Eight Great Scriptures on the Graded Path, was written by the second Panchen Lama, Lobzang Yeshe (*blo bzang ye shes,* 1663–1737).
17. Khedrup Je, Gelek Palzang (*khas grub rje dge legs dpal bzang,* 1385–1438) and Gyaltsap Je, Dharma Rinchen (*rgyal tshab rje dharma rin chen,* 1364–1432).
18. Shamar Chen-ngawa Chökyi Trakpa (*zhwa dmar spyan snga ba chos kyi grags pa,* 1453–1524), the fourth Shamarpa, or Red Hat Karmapa. Born in Kangmar in Domey, he became a disciple of the seventh Karmapa Chötrak Gyatso (*karma pa chos grags rgya mtsho,* 1450–1506).
19. *Mo,* a divination.
20. Madhyamika (*dbu ma*), the Middle Way, is the corpus of the highest philosophical view of the Mahayana, free from all limiting concepts. Mahamudra (*phyag rgya chen po*), the Great Seal, is the main system of practice for recognizing the nature of mind

in the Kagyu tradition. Mahasandhi, the Great Perfection or Dzogchen (*rdzogs chen*), is the pinnacle of the Nyingma tradition and the ultimate view of the nine vehicles. It is based on primordial purity (*ka dag*) and spontaneous presence (*lhun grub*). See NS, book 1, parts 3 and 4, as well as Appendix 1 of this volume.

21. Thread-cross talisman (*mdos*): an elaborate structure made of threads of various colors; arranged as a three-dimensional device, it represents the body and its various elements (earth, water, fire, wind, and space). The *mdos*, accompanied by various other objects symbolizing great riches, is offered as a substitute for a person and his or her possessions in a special ritual, the aim of which is to satisfy harmful spirits intent on stealing the person's life or prosperity.

22. The *rahu* and *tsen* spirits are part of the "eight classes of gods and rakshas" (*lha srin sde brgyad*). See Glossary of Enumerations.

23. Repelling rituals (*zlog pa*), intended to reverse, or send back, evil influences or charms cast upon one.

24. Bodhicitta from Orgyen and consort: these are pills, discovered as *terma*, said to be made of the white "Bodhicitta" of Guru Padmasambhava (*byang sems dkar po*) and the red "Bodhicitta" (*byang sems dmar po*) of Khandro Yeshe Tsogyal.

25. Phowa (*'pho ba*): the transference of consciousness, at the moment of death, to a Buddhafield where Buddhahood will ultimately be attained. There exists also a practice known as "*phowa* for the living" (*gson 'pho*) or "*phowa* transmission" (*'pho lung*) in which the method of the transference of the consciousness to a Buddhafield may be given, in association with a blessing to attract longevity (*tshe 'gugs*), to old persons before their death.

26. Gyaltsen Öser (*rgyal mtshan 'od zer*), another name of Arik Geshe. See Translator's Introduction, note 46.

27. An esoteric practice preliminary to the main section of the Great Perfection.

28. Chödpa, a Chöd practitioner, disciple of Chögyal Wang.

29. The practice of the development stage (*bskyed rim*). See chap.3, note 1.

30. *gtor ma*. See chap. 1, note 39.

31. A bee can take the nectar of a flower without doing the flower any harm. Here, Shabkar's metaphor advises the practitioners to receive help and gifts from the faithful in a dignified way, without attachment, so that the benefactors don't lose faith.

32. The youthful vase-body (*gzhon nu bum pa'i sku*)

represents the state of dharmakaya, in which all the qualities of Buddhahood are like an image within a vase: present in their entirety, but not seen outwardly.

33. The extremely hard horn of the antelope (*gtsod*) is used as a tool to break clods of earth.

34. This refers to traditional wall-making in Tibet. Lines are drawn by slapping on the ground, and later on the wall, a taut string impregnated with white chalk. Then forms made out of planks are set. Ropes are tied across the forms on wooden rods that are laid flat against the forms. The forms are tightened by driving wedges between these forms and the rods. After the earth has been carefully and thoroughly pounded, the extremities of the ropes are cut, freeing the rods and forms. The same process is then repeated above the section of the wall just made.

35. These and the following terms are related to the secret practice of Thögal (*thod rgal*; see Appendix 1).

36. According to the Mantrayana, the three kindnesses (*bka' drin gsum*) of a spiritual master are as follows: to mature the disciple with an empowerment (*dbang bskur*), to expound the tantras (*rgyud bshad*), and to bestow pith instructions (*man ngag ston*).

37. The nine vehicles. See Appendix 1.

38. The all-victorious myrobalan (*rnam rgyal a ru ra*, Lat. *Terminalia chebula*), renowned as the panacea, is a dry fruit used in the preparation of many herbal and sacramental medicines.

39. The four attractive qualities of a Bodhisattva, or four ways of gathering beings who need to be benefited (*bsdu ba'i dngos po bzhi*): 1) to please them with presents, 2) to please them by saying gentle things suited to their minds, 3) to teach them in accordance with their needs and capacities, and 4) to behave and practice in accordance with what one teaches.

40. The four boundless thoughts (*tshad med bzhi*) are boundless loving-kindness (*byams pa tshad med*), boundless compassion (*snying rje tshad med*), boundless sympathetic joy (*dga' ba tshad med*), and boundless equanimity (*btang snyoms tshad med*). They are boundless because the number of beings to whom they apply is boundless, the motivation to benefit them is boundless, the virtues of doing so are boundless, and the excellence of the result is boundless.

41. *The Prayer of Perfect Deeds, the King of Prayers* (Skt. *bhadracarya pranidhana raja*, Tib. *bzang po spyod pa'i smon lam gyi rgyal po*), taken from the *Avatamsaka Sutra* (*phal po che*, T 44). A prayer that summarizes the twelve great prayers made by Buddha Shakyamuni on the eve of his enlightenment.

42. Lit. "without the defeating acts *(pham pa),*" namely the four major transgressions, any one of which makes one completely lose one's ordination. These four are: to kill a human being, to steal (take what is not given), to break celibacy, and to tell major lies such as pretending to have attained a high spiritual level, to have experienced visions, etc. There are also thirteen major faults called "remnants" (*lhag ma*) because after commiting any of these, only remnants remain from one's ordination. The "downfalls" (*ltung ba*) comprise thirty important faults that need to be purified through confession.

43. The two veils (*sgrib gnyis*) that prevent one from achieving enlightenment are the veil created by the obscuring emotions and the veil masking ultimate knowledge.

44. Kumud, the water lily (*Nymphea aesculanta*).

6

At The Heart of the Lake

How I practiced at Tsonying Island, the renowned place sacred to Mahadeva that induces well-being and happiness.

The incomparably kind Dharma King, Ngakyi Wangpo [76a], was considering installing his son, Tashi Jungne, "Source of Auspiciousness," as regent, and going to live in a mountain retreat for the benefit of the Dharma and all beings. When he explained his reasons to his queen, ministers and subjects, they all pleaded:

"Precious Dharma King! We rely on you, as does everyone in the whole region, on both banks of the lake; you are our sole protector and refuge. If you retire to a mountain solitude, we will be without protection or refuge, like ants when the rock covering their nest is removed. How could you do such a thing? Especially now that you have grown older, it is hardly advisable that you go to live in seclusion." They objected so strongly that they prevented him from following his wish for solitude.

Several ministers thought it was I who had talked him into retiring to the mountains. They complained to me, saying, "Please don't tell our precious king to go into retreat! Have you no sympathy for his subjects?" Despite my protestations of innocence, they would not believe me, and threatened, "Just you wait!"

At this point I thought it better not to stay there much longer.

The Dharma King himself seemed displeased. I told him, "You reached enlightenment innumerable aeons ago, and, since you consciously came here for the sake of beings in this dark age, you will benefit others no matter where you are. Even if you cannot go to an isolated retreat place, please continue your work

for the Dharma and all beings [76b]. Besides, if you go into retreat in the mountains, your queen, ministers and subjects will all blame me."

For a while he said nothing.

The next day, he began dictating the *Torch of Wisdom That Dispels the Darkness of Ignorance, According to the Great Perfection,*[1] which I had requested earlier. When he finished, he declared, "Here is this old man's testament." With several similar comments he hinted that he was thinking of going to another Pure Realm. "Please don't say that!" I begged him, asking that he remain here a long time for the sake of his disciples.

He replied, "Wherever there is power, there is crime. Nonvirtue naturally follows the attainment of high rank. It is also said that 'after pleasure comes pain.' I have no attachment to the samsaric glories of this life. They appear temporarily as pleasure, but lead inevitably to pain.

"Ever since my trip to central Tibet I have cultivated a completely even attitude in which gold is not more desirable than stone, and stone is not less pure than gold. Ever since I was small, I have longed to go into permanent retreat in the mountains, but because of my past karma and aspirations my life has unfolded differently.

"I have reached a mature age, and according to the predictions made by my tutelary deity and my guru, I have arrived at the limit of my lifetime. Of course, I would be glad to remain in this world a few more years, but why should the remainder of my life be long?"

Apart from this he made no great promises.

Then, as if filling vases right up to their

brims, he gave to Gyal Khenchen Rinpoche, Lakha Tulku [77a], myself, and many other disciples the transmission for the works of Lodrak,[2] the empowerments and transmission for the New Termas,[3] and the cycle of Kilaya teachings, along with the permission-blessing for the protectors of these teachings.

"Now, you must not be lazy!" he warned. He stressed the need for mastering fully the teachings of the Victorious Ones in general, and the old translation tradition of the mighty Victorious One, Padmasambhava, in particular. He insisted on the importance of holding, preserving, and spreading these teachings. He gave all the books to Gyal Khenchen Rinpoche. In the intervals between the teachings, I offered several transmissions of the New Termas to Lakha Tulku.

One day, during a tea break, I told the Dharma King: "Earlier, I intended to stay in your presence as long as you lived. But if I stay, others may create discord and I am afraid that the guru and consort might dismiss me from their hearts.

"At Thayenchi there are many retreatants now, and thus much distraction. As my only wish is to persevere in my practice, I shall go to some isolated place like Tsonying Island.

"Since, for the last five years, you have so graciously sustained me with food, clothing, and teachings, and I have received from you complete oral instructions, everything now depends on my meditation practice."

The exalted Gyal Khenchen added on my behalf, "It would be most kind if you granted permission to this mountain retreatant" [77b].

The Dharma King replied, "Retreatant, if you were to stay here it would benefit others, yet most people would not perceive this. Therefore, it would be better for you to go to Tsonying Island, and that would please me as well." Thus he gave his permission.

Then he added, "Yet, for a while longer, let us, master and disciple, stay together in retreat. During this time, we should clarify whatever questions you have, and we shall discuss both worldly and religious matters. I am an old man, and do not know how many years I have left. You are a homeless wanderer, and do not know

where you will go next. Who knows if we shall meet again?"

We stayed together in retreat for a month and a half. During the tea breaks he gave the transmission of the songs of realization of Kunkhyen Longchen Rabjam, Jetsun Taranatha,[4] and other holy beings, as well as general advice. I listened and engraved it in my mind. Every evening, I did many prostrations and circumambulated his tent several hundred times. I prayed that I would meet him in all of my lives, and be able to see his face and hear his voice—in reality, in meditation experiences, and in dreams—whenever the need might arise.

Noting that his hair and beard had become white, I thought, "If I had met him when he was younger, how happy I would have been! Now, he has grown old and I am ready to go to Tsonying Island. From now on we will be separated by a great distance [78a], and, as birth and death are so unpredictable, who knows if we will meet again? Should he happen to pass away, to which Buddhafield will he go? I must ask him."

Unable to think of anything else, I pleaded with him, "In all my future lives, never leave me without the protection of your spiritual practice! Which Pure Realm are you considering, Rinpoche, for your future birth? Please tell me."

He said: "Oh, son! Pray without ever forgetting me. I will keep you in my mind, and never forget you. Since it is not even possible for me to go into mountain retreat in the present, who knows if it will be possible for me to enter a Buddhafield in the future? Yet, in accordance with a prediction made by the glorious Sakya Dagchen Wangdu Nyingpo,[5] I pray to be reborn in the Pure Realm of Heavenly Enjoyment.[6] If my prayers are successful, I think I will go there for a while."

Then I asked him, "What should be my chief objective for the rest of my life? Please, tell me what I should do."

"Son, what's the use of a lot of talk? Keep in mind all I said before, when we had more time; everything is included in that. In brief: give up all thoughts of this life, as all the Victorious Ones have done to gain liberation. Wander from one solitary mountain retreat to another, without preference. Make your life and your practice one, and through its fruit, benefit the teachings and all beings in every possible way. Especially, train yourself to see all teachings and individuals as pure and perfect [78b]. With love, compassion, and a mind set on enlightenment, care for all weary sentient beings as if they were your own children.

"In whatever you do to bring about good fortune for the teachings and happiness for sentient beings, such as erecting sacred objects related to body, speech, and mind,[7] employ skillful means and great compassion and you will accomplish your aims easily and without hindrance." So saying, he marked a white scarf with the imprint of his two hands moistened with saffron water, gave it to me as an object of faith, and added:

> Samantabhadra and consort,
> Vajrasattva,
> Great wisdom dakini Lekyi Wangmo,
> Humchenkara, Lapkyi Dronma,
> Pejung, Tsogyal, Palseng, Dechen Gyal,
> Orgyen Tendzin and all the other glorious
>   root and lineage gurus,[8]
> With your extraordinary blessings
> Make a rain of *siddhis* fall,
> And bless this fortunate disciple's three
>   doors as the three vajras.
> Assembly of dakinis, protectors, and vowed
>   guardians,
> You, who nurture genuine practitioners of
>   the sacred Dharma:
> Please provide sustenance for him,
> Gather all favorable circumstances,
> Fulfill all his wishes, and
> Dispel all unfavorable circumstances.
>
> In this age when the five degenerations are
>   increasing greatly,[9]
> Beings disregard the consequences of their
>   actions, thus opening the door to lower
>   rebirths.
> They transgress the precepts of the
>   Victorious Ones and their *samayas* with
>   the guru:
> I feel saddened and distraught.

> Consider this for the sake of beings
> Whose number is as vast as the sky,
> And, with kindness, compassion, and the
>   aspiration to free all beings,
> Persevere day and night to attain enlightenment.
>
> What good are many words now?
> Make strong vows of dedication,
> As did the masters of the past,
> And then strive with strong, undistracted
>   diligence.
>
> Whatever virtuous actions you perform,
> Dedicate them to the attainment of
>   enlightenment by all beings [79a].
> To the long life of the great holders of the
>   teachings,
> To the increase of their enlightened
>   activities,
> And to the flourishing of the Great Secret
>   Doctrine.[10]
> May all be auspicious!

The time to leave for Tsonying Island was drawing near. One day I went to see the mother, Abhe Rinpoche, Rigdzin Wangmo, "Great Lady of Awareness," and explained in detail my reasons for going to the island:

> E ma!
> Divine Abhe, you who have been even
>   more kind to me than my own mother!
> Having left behind my homeland,
> I came to stay near the Dharma King and
>   you, his consort.
> When I met you, a joy arose in me like that
>   of attaining the first *bhumi*.
>
> The Dharma King and you, his consort,
> Have cared for me as kindly as if I were
>   your only son.
> Thank you, divine Abhe.
> I shall repay your kindness by offering my
>   practice.
>
> Now I will go to the hill on remote
>   Tsonying Island.

It is certain that I shall return
To see the father and mother and their sons.
I pray that when I come you will care for
    me as kindly as before.

When I would not accept the ten *sang* of silver
that she gave me, she wrapped in blue silk some
relics of the three kinds[11] gathered in central
Tibet, with some fragrant red and white sandalwood and saffron, and gave it to me saying:

When still small, you became weary of
    samsara.
Older, you heard of the fame of the
    Dharma King.
You came before him with the intent
To serve at his lotus feet,
And for five years you attended him well.

You have listened to, reflected,
And meditated upon the Dharma.
You have attained confidence
That you will be liberated in the *bardo* [79b].

Mountain hermit whom we have known
    for so long,
On your way to your distant retreat
Various good and bad experiences
Will arise in your mind.

When on the road and when resting,
Take good care of your body:
You need it for the practice of Dharma.

Don't stay long; come back soon;
The Dharma King is growing older.
Sustenance for your practice
Will be provided as before.
From now on and in all lives,
I pray we shall meet again and again.

She expressed her fondness for me and told
me to come back after three years.

Then I went to see the precious Dharma
King. After a few days, on the evening before I
was to leave, I did many prostrations and circumambulations, went inside, and sat at his feet. He
was digging through a big bag, normally used for

medicine, and pulled out the money and white
scarves that were inside.

"Tonight, now that no one is around, I shall
say farewell to my son!" He then gave me nine
sang of silver and twenty white scarves—long
ones and short ones—and told me, "Take these,
and buy provisions."

I took them in my hands, but I kept only two
white scarves for the sake of our auspicious connection, and offered the rest back to him saying,
"If I had any possessions, I would make a large
offering to repay your kindness, but I don't have
sufficient merit for that. So, of all the gifts you
have given me I shall only accept a token, to
make an auspicious connection.

"The life-stories of the sages tell how they
received pith instructions from their gurus and
then went into solitary retreat [80a]. Giving up
all thoughts of this life, they continuously visualized their guru on the crowns of their heads, and
kept his pith instructions in their hearts. They
took with them into retreat nothing more than a
staff and a small book to remind them of the
teaching. There is no mention of them taking
gold, silver or valuables.

"Following their worthy examples, giving
up all concern for the affairs of this life, I will go
to the mountains without any silver or gold. If
you, Lord, want to give these away, great
would be your compassion if you gave the old
woman who lives near here—to whom you
have often given generously—some money to
buy a *dzomo*."

"Here," he said, giving me five *sang* for that
purpose.

The next morning he got up early and,
while taking tea, said, "So, renunciate, after drinking this tea you will be off?"

"Yes, master," I replied.

He gave me the rest of his tea, and, when I
had finished drinking it, putting his right hand
on my head he gave me his blessing and added,
"This is my last teaching, my last advice:

By the blessings of the Victorious Ones of
    the ten directions,
By the might of having perfected the two
    accumulations,

And by the inconceivable power of the
immaculate dharmadhatu,
May the aspirations of this fortunate disciple be accomplished.

You, fortunate heart-son born from my
mind,
Have given birth in your mind to
renunciation,
And now, for the sake of your Dharma
practice,
You are going to a solitude that delights
the mind.
There sadnesses and joys may stir your mind.
Therefore make excellent prayers at all
times,
And, just as the outline of a hare naturally
appears when the crystal moon waxes
into fullness,[12]
Your prayers will naturally bring white
moonlight rays of benefit and happiness
[80b]
To make blossom the eight-petaled night-
flower of mind."

While he was saying this, I placed his feet
upon my head, and visualized myself receiving
empowerment from him.

I thought, "How can I know if I will ever see
my guru, my spiritual guide, again in this life? If,
after today, I never see him again, what shall I do?"

I wept. Then, looking at his face, I offered
this song of good wishes:

Heart-emanation of the Buddhas of the
three times,
Protector of beings in this decadent age,
farewell!

Foretold by the great Orgyen,
Lord of the transmissions of Dharma, farewell!

You who dispel the darkness of ignorance,
Shining torch, farewell!

You who remove the pain of the obscuring
emotions,
Medicinal tree, farewell!

You who soothe the burning heat of the
five poisons,
Water-crystal moon, farewell!

You who grant all wishes,
Crown jewel, farewell!

You who rescue beings from the ocean of
suffering,
Savior captain, farewell!

Unmistaken guide on the path of
liberation,
Guru endowed with all qualities, farewell!

Establishing all your subjects in
happiness,
King of Dharma, farewell!

My lasting refuge in this and future lives,
Gracious guru, farewell!

I, your disciple who obey your every
command,
Ask that you always care for me as your
own son!

Again I touched my head to his feet, and then
moved back a little.

In this life and in other lives,
Until I attain enlightenment,
Never separating from him,
May I be reborn at the feet of my glorious
guru.

While I recited this prayer, I choked with emo-
tion, tears streaming down my face [81a].

As he saw this, some tears came to Chögyal
Rinpoche's eyes also and, moved, he took out a
fine crystal suffused with rainbow-colored light
that he treasured greatly.

"I give you this," he said, "because, owing to
your past aspirations and prayers, you are a true
disciple. Especially, I give it to you as a sign of the
perfect purity of the spiritual bonds between the
two of us, father and son. Keep this crystal; there
is a special auspiciousness attached to it." Putting

it in my hands, he added, "Don't weep, mountain hermit; father and son, we will meet again."

When I crossed the door of the tent and looked up at his face, seeing it filled with tears, I couldn't bear to go any farther. Finally, resolving to go, I went to the tent of Abhe Rinpoche and of their retinue, wished them good health, and offered ceremonial scarves with these words:

> Crown jewel of all beings, Dharma Queen,
>   farewell!
> Caring perfectly for all the subjects and
>   attendants,
> Sovereign of kindness and love, farewell!
> Your countenance is more beautiful than
>   that of a goddess;
> You, who grant the splendor of every joy,
>   farewell!
> Your kindness has been greater than a
>   mother's,
> Abhe, may your health be strong.
> May you, princes, heirs to the kingdom,
>   fare well
> May you ministers and subjects fare well.

Thus, with unbearable regret, I left.

Proceeding down the road, I kept turning my head to look back at Urgeh [81b]. When it was finally out of sight, I could not bring myself to continue, and turned to look again: there, bright and vivid, was the tent encampment of Urgeh. I longed to go back.

Then I remembered that I had received all the pith instructions and there was no real need for me to return. Thinking that after staying a while at Tsonying Island I would be able to return to see the precious Dharma King, I prayed over and over that I might meet him in all of my lives.

Again I found myself standing still, unable to go any farther. Finally, I proceeded on, with a heavy heart.

I have never felt greater distress in my whole life. It was a sign that I would never see my guru again.

Filled with sadness, I arrived at Thayenchi, the retreat at Tseshung where I had stayed previously. I remained there for several days with all my vajra friends with whom I shared pure *samaya*. I told Lakha Tulku, the Chöd practitioner of Go, Jampel, Rigden, Dageh, and my vajra friends staying there:

"You have crossed the threshold of the Buddha's precious teaching, the source of all benefit and happiness. You have also benefited yourselves through listening, reflecting, and meditating. Now that spiritual experiences, realization, and qualities have blossomed in you, you must help others in a vast way, tirelessly, using the skillful means of the four ways of gathering disciples. Throughout this lifetime, make ceaseless efforts to benefit others and yourselves." I then presented each of them with the symbolic gift of a white scarf, and we exchanged many affectionate words.

On the morning of my departure, my friends gathered early to perform a vast incense smoke-offering [82a], to sound the cymbals, beat the great drum, and blow the copper horns and conch shells, so that auspicious connections would be created for my teachings to become famed throughout the ten directions. Then they accompanied me a short distance to a spot where I addressed them:

"It has been many years since we first met and practiced the Dharma together. Now we must go our own ways and will be separated by great distances. Who knows whether we will meet again in this life? Our hold on life is tenuous; all things are impermanent. Consider this and be diligent in your practice. Maintain devotion to the guru, affection for your Dharma brothers and sisters, compassion for sentient beings, and an open, pure attitude toward all the teachings.

"From today on, if you look, you will not see me; if you listen, you will not hear me; I will have gone far away into the wilderness. Yet you should continue to practice, dedicate the merit, and pray for all of us to meet again, both in this life and later in the Pure Realms. Thus will we attain enlightenment together."

Aku Rigden, Dageh, and most of my friends shed tears, and tears also gathered in my eyes.

After we had prayed to meet again and again, I told them to remain seated. Rising and leaning on my staff, I offered them this farewell song:

On the high coral-tinted cliffs
Young eagles live, nursed by their parents
   [82b];
Until we meet again, farewell!
I, a young eagle, will now
Spread my wings and fly away.

In the forest of deep turquoise green
Tiger cubs live, nursed by their mother.
Until we meet again, farewell!
I, a strong young cub, will now wander off.

In the mountains of striped-agate slate,
Colorful wild yak calves live,
Nursed by their mothers.
Until we meet again, farewell!
I, a young yak with blue-black horns,
Will now amble on.

In the pleasant, wide-open fields of
   Tseshung
My heart-friends live, nursed by the lord
   guru.
Until we meet again, farewell!
I am now leaving for the solitudes of
   Tsonying Island.

I left them with great sadness. That day my escort and I traveled only a short distance and camped on the sunny side of the valley. Some faithful people had given us more *tsampa* and butter than we could carry, so with most of the *tsampa* we made *tormas*, *ganachakra* feast offerings, and a variety of food offerings to the deities.

We melted the butter, filled up a pan and its lid, a lamp and a pitcher, and, inserting many wicks, we offered them that evening as butter-lamps, making prayers to the guru and the Three Jewels. The next morning after awakening, I gave all that was left to my escort and to several beggars.

Continuing my journey, I made my way through the monastery of Tsang to Yudok, and then to Gartse. To the old devoted *ngakpas* Baleh,

Tamdrin, and other disciples and benefactors of that area, I gave teachings on relative truth, such as on cause and effect [83a], as well as on absolute truth, the profound teachings on the void nature of mind. They offered me horses, cattle, and goods, which I returned to them.

When I went to the home of one of these devotees to bless his household, his wife asked if I missed my mother, my friends, and my homeland. I answered with this playful song of the "ten forgotten things":

By the grace of the king of Dharma,
Since I, the renunciate Tsogdruk
   Rangdrol,
Have made my home again and again
On the safe ground of dharmakaya,
My homeland has been naturally
   forgotten.

Since I have contemplated again and again
That each being has once been my
   mother,
Attachment to only one mother
Has been naturally forgotten.

Since I have accumulated again and again
The seven noble riches,
Ordinary food and wealth
Have been naturally forgotten.

Since I have again and again befriended
The absolute nature,
The friends from my childhood
Have been naturally forgotten.

Since I have again and again guarded
The *samaya* oaths,
Deceitfulness
Has been naturally forgotten.

Since I have again and again seen
The display of luminosity,
Worldly entertainments
Have been naturally forgotten.

Since I have again and again tamed
The enemy, the obscuring emotions,

My ordinary enemies
Have been naturally forgotten.

Since I have regarded again and again
All dharmas as illusory,
The eight worldly concerns
Have been naturally forgotten.

Since I have again and again experienced
The samadhi of simplicity,
Complexities have been naturally
    forgotten.

Since I have wandered in remote places
And in mountain solitudes,
This life has been naturally forgotten.

Another woman said, "Tell me about your homeland."

I first gave a simple answer, and then continued with this song of the "thirteen possessions"
[83b]:

Listen, wealthy and devoted lady,
I am a yogin of the luminous awareness
    that arises of itself.
My homeland is primordial purity, the
    dharmakaya.
My father—Samantabhadra
My mother—Samantabhadri,[13]
My paternal uncle—Bodhicitta,
My priests—the Three Jewels,
My maternal uncles—deity and guru,
My wife—the lovely *shunyata*.[14]
My children—meditation experiences,
    realization, and fine qualities.
My brothers—devotion and pure
    perception,
My fields—the ten white virtues,
My riches—the inexhaustible seven noble
    qualities,
My sister—pure *samaya*,
My neighbor—firm faith,
My cousin—great diligence.

"Do you understand?" I asked. All those
present felt great devotion. Several disciples and
householders then accompanied me to Bhel plain.

Just before we parted, in response to their request
that I sing something, I sang this joyful song:

Now that I have won this human body
So hard to obtain,
And have met the authentic guru,
Absorbing myself in one-pointed practice,
I, the renunciate yogin, am happy.

Having sung this sweet song of joy,
I will go to the excellent place of solitude.
If anyone here does as I do,
The sun of happiness will surely dawn.

I have no powerful superior,
I have no powerless servant.
Free from bad company,
I, the renunciate yogin, am happy.

Having sung this sweet song of joy,
I will go to the excellent place of solitude.
If anyone here does as I do,
The sun of happiness will surely dawn.

I have no monastery to look after.
I have no precious things to hoard.
I have no benefactor to impress [84a].
I, the renunciate yogin, am happy.

Having sung this sweet song of joy,
I will go to the excellent place of solitude.
If anyone here does as I do,
The sun of happiness will surely dawn.

I have no enemy to subdue,
I have no family to protect.
Free from biased attachment toward
    friends and family,
Free from aversion toward strangers,
I, the renunciate yogin, am happy.

Having sung this sweet song of joy,
I will go to the excellent place of solitude.
If anyone here does as I do,
The sun of happiness will surely dawn.

When I stay, I have nothing to be attached
    to.

When I leave, I have nothing to leave
  behind.
Wherever I am, no one says, "Where have
  you been? Where are you going?"
I, the renunciate yogin, am happy.

Having sung this sweet song of joy,
I will go to the excellent place of solitude.
If anyone here does as I do,
The sun of happiness will surely dawn.

I have a few essential notes to remember;
I have no stacks of books;
Undistracted from my practice,
I, the renunciate yogin, am happy.

Having sung this sweet song of joy,
I will go to the excellent place of
  solitude.
If anyone here does as I do,
The sun of happiness will surely dawn.

I am fed up with samsara.
I am rich with the seven noble qualities.
Safe from the thieves of the eight worldly
  concerns,
I, the renunciate yogin, am happy.

Having sung this sweet song of joy,
I will go to the excellent place of solitude.
If anyone here does as I do,
The sun of happiness will surely dawn.

Accompanied by Bodhicitta for the sake of
  others [84b],
I have developed unmistaken experience
  and realization.
By benefiting whoever is connected with
  me,
I, the renunciate yogin, am happy.

Having sung this sweet song of joy,
I will go to the excellent place of solitude.
If anyone here does as I do,
The sun of happiness will surely dawn.

These days, in the Land of Snows,
There is no one as happy as I am.

Having sung this sweet song of joy,
I will go to the excellent place of solitude.
If anyone here does as I do,
The sun of happiness will surely dawn.

The singer of this song
Is one called Tsogdruk Rangdrol.

With intense devotion, they offered prostrations
and circumambulations before returning home.

While at Bheldo, I looked up Tsego, a
wealthy Mongolian devotee about whom I had
been told; he invited me to his home. After
receiving his gracious and generous hospitality, I
sang teachings to benefit everyone and turn their
minds to the Dharma.

The next morning, while I was chanting
some auspicious verses, my host offered me a
horse and red saddle bags, which I didn't accept.
Not wanting me to leave his house empty-handed,
he then offered me a deerskin bag filled with
loose tea, as well as much butter and *tsampa*. So
that I would not lose my way, he sent a man to
accompany me to the banks of the Machu. Since
this man was poor, I gave him most of my
provisions and sent him back, keeping only what
I could easily carry.

When I arrived at Ngamong plateau, I saw
that the camp fires of other travelers had set the
grass afire. Scattered over the plateau were perhaps a hundred fires, resembling hundreds of
smoke-offerings [85a]. Curious, I walked around
and discovered that these were anthills that had
caught fire. Flames were consuming the ants; the
ground was aglow with burning embers.

Seeing this, I felt great compassion. There
was no water on that vast plateau, but I stayed
there for the whole day, doing everything I could
to accumulate merit and purify obscurations—
taking refuge, generating Bodhicitta, making the
seven-branch offering, and so on. Visualizing a
rain of purifying nectar, I prayed to the guru and
the Three Jewels, "May you guide these dying
ants to the Pure Realms."

In the evening, I sat with a straight back and
clear awareness, and merged the minds of all the
ants with my own mind. Then, merging my
mind with the wisdom-mind of the guru and the

Victorious Ones of the three times, I remained in evenness in the wisdom-mind, the dharmakaya, the state that is like the sky. Thus, the karma, obscuring emotions, two veils, and habitual patterns of the ants were purified in the unborn absolute expanse.

Just before dawn, arising from this vivid state of luminosity, I visualized the illusory Buddha-body of each dead ant, made of subtle *prana*-mind, arising in the form of the Great Compassionate One[15] with one face and two hands, and glowing with the marks and signs.

Then, just as I shouted, "Phet!" like flinging a stone into the midst of a hundred birds, I visualized that all the ants [85b], now transformed into deities, flew into the sky toward whichever Pure Realm they wished. I then dedicated the merit and said prayers.

Reaching the riverside in the valley below the Old Hang-nga Mountain, I made some tea and sat there. I spent the next day crossing the mountain. That evening I was thirsty. I spotted the black yak-hair tent of some wealthy people; as I approached and asked for tea, a harsh female voice said, "Don't come in—there's no tea!"

A more gentle male voice added, "Wait over there. I'll bring you some." After a long time, he brought me a small clay pot with a liquid that was not quite water and not quite tea, and a plate with a handful of *tsampa*, and a pat of butter the size of two butterfly wings.

"In our area, *tsampa* is quite scarce," he said, apologizing, "and serving it in the evening is unheard of. However, because you've come from far away, I've given you this. Please say some prayers for us and our animals."

I could not help smiling and told the householder that I had taken a vow not to eat at night, so I wouldn't accept the *tsampa*, but would offer the prayers. I drank the tea and, after reciting a few prayers, I sang this loud enough for the householder to hear me:

Great is the compassion of the Victorious
    Ones.
Great is the power of the dharmapalas.
Great is the stinginess of the rich.
Great is the greed of the poor.

Rare is a human body, complete with the
    freedoms and endowments.
Rare is the practice of the holy Dharma by
    those who have gained such a body.
Rare are the householders who make offer-
    ings to Dharma practitioners.
Rare are their offerings of butter and *tsampa*.

For me, a *repa* who looks like neither Bud-
    dhist nor Bön,[16]
This householder, who is neither old nor
    young,
Poured something that was neither tea nor
    water.
All you who are neither gods nor demons
Refrain from harming him! [86a].

My teasing must have hit home, because he went inside smiling, and came back with a sizeable quantity of tea. "Take this for your journey," he said.

Nearby was a poor man who, seeing how much tea I had been given, begged me for some. I took the deerskin bag full of the loose tea other householders had been giving me, turned it upside down, and poured all the tea into the poor man's container.

"If you give me all this," he said, "your mountain retreat will be much more difficult." Taking out several handfuls of tea leaves, he insisted that I take them back, which I did.

I could see he had nothing to wear but an old worn-out sheepskin, so I gave him my sleeveless coat, made of fine new sheepskin, which was soft, light, and warm. In its place, I put on my old woolen coat.

The beggar was moved with faith and began to offer me prostrations and obeisance. "These days a Dharma practitioner with such compassion is rare. From now on, protect me and remember me always in your meditation," he said, with tears in his eyes.

Observing my generosity, the householder and most of the other nomads in the vicinity were also moved, and requested some teachings to make an auspicious connection with me. I gave the transmission for reciting the *mani* mantra and the *Miktsema* prayer.

"To be poor in this life is the result of miserliness in previous lives," I told them, "and to be prosperous in this life is the result of generosity in previous lives. If you want to be happy in your future lives, you must untie the knot of avarice and cultivate pure virtuous actions—offerings, prostrations, circumambulations and recitations [86b]. Particularly, develop compassion for the poor and be generous." I then sang this song:

Kind precious guru,
Look with compassion upon all beings.
Untie the knot of avarice in the rich.
Extend your love to the weary poor.

Having failed to accumulate merit in
     previous lives,
One is born destitute in this life.
If one again fails to accumulate merit,
Again one will be reborn poor;
Thus it is said.
For the rest of this life
Practice the Dharma,
The source of future happiness.

Every being has been our parent.
How sad to see them now destitute!
The rich must not be mean;
Rather, they should give generously to the
     poor.

I, the renunciate Tsogdruk Rangdrol,
In order to attain enlightenment
For the sake of all weary beings,
Have abandoned all futile activities
And now depart to practice
The essential, divine Dharma.

I made my way to the monastery of Lama Gyalu Huthokthu, met the lama, and requested teachings. He gave me the transmission for the *mani* mantra, the *Miktsema* prayer, the *Praises to Tara*, and the *dharani* of long life. He also gave me tea, butter, and *tsampa*. I took a little for my own needs and gave the rest back to him. After requesting his spiritual protection, I went on my way.

I encountered a poor Mongolian woman and her son, and gave them a long white scarf emblazoned with the four verses of auspiciousness that begin, "May all be auspicious in the day. May all be auspicious in the night . . ." I advised them to trade it for some food so that the boy could study Dharma, thus ensuring [87a] both of them, mother and son, happiness in this and future lives. They departed in a most cheerful mood.

On the way to Wobu, I met a Bönpo and a layman from Rekong, who were returning home after herding cattle. They asked where I had come from and, on hearing my story, rejoiced at our having met. They asked for a teaching in order to establish an auspicious connection. I gave the transmission for the *Swift Fulfillment of Wishes*[17] and a short teaching, ending with this song:

Guru, remain always
On the crown of my head
As its ornament.
Bless the mind-stream
Of this faithful one.

The one who roams the mountains
For the sake of Dharma
And the two from Rekong
Who roam the mountains
For the sake of business
Have met on the plain of Wohu.
This must be due to earlier aspirations.

Do you intend to practice the Dharma?
If you are thinking of doing so, consider
     this:

After this teaching, we three will part
And go our separate ways.
Just so, all things are impermanent.
Consider this and practice the divine
     Dharma.

Praise, respect, and make offerings
To the guru and the Three Jewels;
Help those who are suffering,
And always do prostrations,
Recitations and circumambulations.
In this way you will be free of regret
At the time of death.

I will now go to the solitudes of Tsonying
  Island,
I pray that you may return home content,
That your lives be long and free from
  illness,
And your future lives be happy.

I gave them each a long white scarf. Filled with
faith, they left for their homeland.

When I arrived at the south shore of Lake
Kokonor, it was snowing heavily. Not a single
yurt[18] was in sight, my supplies were exhausted,
and my boots were rubbing my feet raw [87b].

With great difficulty I reached the inhabited
area of Arik, on the northeastern side of the lake.
There I met an old man I knew called Dziri, who
provided gracious hospitality; I stayed with him
for two days. Wishing to add to my meager supplies,
he filled a small bag with barley and rock salt, and
added three pounds of butter on top.

When I went to beg in other parts of the
Arik District, I first came across a small, seemingly insignificant tent, which I passed by without stopping. I continued walking and came
upon some more richly appointed tents. I felt
sure I could obtain some provisions there. At the
edge of that encampment were about fifteen
Tibetan mastiffs; they charged at me like an
army. I said to myself:

There is no way that these faithless, evil
  people
Are going to call off their evil guard dogs.
Listen, renunciate Tsogdruk Rangdrol,
What you need is the holy Dharma.
For that you need this body;
And, since this body needs food,
You have had to come here.

Now, these dogs are extremely vicious;
They have their weapons in their mouths.
Following their tan-colored leader,
The pack of mastiffs surges and attacks!

Gather ammunition—
Stones and sticks!
On this very meadow,
Defeat the evil army of dogs!

With that pronouncement, I put down my
pack, gathered a few stones, and stood my ground
as the dogs advanced. I threw one stone; most of
the dogs either stopped in their tracks or fled. But
"Tan-head" caught hold of my shawl and tore it,
while a black dog clamped its jaws around the
shaft of my boot. Feeling sorry even as I did it, I
hit him with a stone. All the dogs then ran away
[88a].

From inside the sheep pen, a man called
out, "Hey! What are you doing out there, making
noise and stirring up the dogs? We don't take in
travelers! Don't come into the sheepfold, fellow!"

The family gave me half a cup of *tsampa*, and
I left, saying to myself:

Renunciate Tsogdruk Rangdrol,
You arrive at a rich man's door
Confident of getting what you need,
And an army of angry dogs attacks.
Now that the old shawl you wear is torn to
  pieces,
You will be in danger tonight
From the cold winter's wind.
You'd better get going with a needle and
  thread!

So I sat in a sheltered spot to sew up the rips in
my shawl.

I then went to beg at the door of the little
yurt I had ignored earlier. An old Mongolian
woman with very brown lips greeted me from
within. She held back her dog, prostrated herself
and, when I entered, presented me with a big
plate of cheese and a measure of freshly churned
butter. I was as happy as if she had given me a
horse, and I said dedication prayers.

I went to another small yurt, where a man
gave me a plateful of *tsampa*. He apologized,
saying, "I don't have much, but there is a rich
family at the end of the valley." As I approached
that place, I was attacked by two dogs. Before
they could bite me, I raised my staff at them

threateningly. Unfortunately, the staff hit against a rock and split in two. The family offered me a plate of *tsampa* and cheese, and I walked back, saying to myself:

> I ventured down this long valley
> For the sake of one plate of *tsampa* and
>   cheese.
> Now, my staff, worth more to me than
>   even a horse, is broken.
> This yogin is left with nothing but his own
>   two legs [88b].

Carrying in each hand a piece of the staff, I continued on my way, laughing. Soon I came upon a group of people performing a ritual for a deceased relative; on receiving a plate of *tsampa* from them, I thought:

> The renunciate rushes on to a land of
>   rituals.
> Even though he takes some abuse,
> He gets to take some food and drink and,
> Happily, no dogs have yet sunk their teeth
>   into him.

A monk at Ngari Monastery named Tendar had a dream in which he was told, "The Indian Padampa Sangye[19] has arrived—you must go and meet him." He went and saw a brown-skinned yogin, hair knotted on top of his head and holding at his waist a golden wheel from which light radiated to people around him. As it shone upon Tendar, he felt bliss pervade his body.

He asked the yogin, "Please turn the Wheel of Dharma again." The yogin replied, "I shall turn it once again in the future; then, you must come."

The next day, when he met me, he remembered his dream. Feeling great faith, he asked me for a song of advice. I sang for him the one that Padampa had sung to Jetsun Mila. Later, he came to Tsonying to listen to the teachings and remained there for many years. Persevering in doing good, he became a fine practitioner.

Then I went to the Upper and Lower Yangön Monastery, where each person gave me a measure of *tsampa*. The year before, a fake hermit had come there and stolen a hundred coins from Zungshul Geshe [89a]. When I arrived, the kind bursar invited me for tea; while I was sitting there, a few monks came in and asked, "Who's he?"

Joking, the bursar said, "He's the hermit who robbed us last year." Everyone laughed. Then I went into the room of a monk, who shouted, "We know how people like you have helped us in the past! Get out! Out! Out!"

Taking a few broken pieces of old, hard, yellow bread, rather than putting them in my hands, he threw them at me and, giving me a dark look, went off. I stood there with a smile and, when leaving, quoted a saying:

> A man will run from a place
> Where a snake once bit him,
> Even though he sees a necklace
> Of gold and silver lying there.
>
> Once harmed by another's malice,
> A man will distrust even the holy.

"I don't blame him," I concluded.

People from Arik asked me many times, "Why do you keep your hair so long, coiled around the top of your head?" I replied:

> At the feet of the gracious guru I bow
>   down.
> Assembled sangha, listen:
> As to the hair I wear coiled on my head,
> The reason I keep it so long is this:
>
> I keep it so that
> When I forget the guru's kindness,
> I am reminded.
>
> I keep it so that
> When I wander to various places,
> I am protected against bandits and thieves.

I keep it so that
When the cold wind of the new year
    comes,
My ears are protected.

I keep it so that
When blinding snows fall day and night,
My eyes are protected.

I keep it so that
When I go out begging [89b],
I'm protected from the enemy, worldly
    distraction.

I keep it so that
When I wander over these vast plains,
I don't fit in with other people.

I keep it so that
When I, wrongly, think in terms of this
    life's concerns,
I remember the life of Milarepa.

"That makes sense," said one old monk.
    Later, as I was begging near Arik, another
old man asked, "Are you a Bönpo, or are you a
yogin? What good is all that long hair? It must be
tiring to carry it with you everywhere!" I replied:

I bow down at the feet of the Dharma
    King.
Keeping my hair like this
Makes everyone doubt and mistrust me.

If they have doubt, they have no faith.
If they have no faith, I don't get offerings.
If I don't get offerings,
I'm not oppressed by possessions.
If I'm not oppressed by possessions,
My practice progresses.

If my practice progresses,
Experience and realization are born.
If experience and realization are born,
I can benefit others.

Such are the reasons for wearing
This long hair that benefits others.

"It seems to me a person like you doesn't need to
beg like this," said a woman who was listening.
"Aren't you living this way because of a divination or some astrological calculation?"[20] I
answered:

I bow down at the feet of the Dharma King!
I, the renunciate Tsogdruk Rangdrol,
Made this calculation for myself:

On the astrological chart—the Dharma of
    sutra and tantra,
I calculated the cycle—the twelve causal
    links.
I set down eight trigrams—the eight
    consciousnesses,
Surrounding it with nine diagrams—the
    nine *yanas.*
I then calculated friends and enemies—
    virtue and nonvirtue [90a].
This chart proved to be ill-starred.

Disease arose like this:
First came an offense to the nagas and
    local deities—deluded ignorant mind.
Then, because of this offense,[21] the
    protector—dharmadhatu wisdom—
    departed,
And because he departed,
The demon—clinging to the notion of
    reality—entered in its place.
It is the nature of this demon
To produce pain—attachment and
    aversion.

Having diagnosed the problem, the chart
    described a cure:
To bring back the protective deity, wisdom,
The excellent realized guru
Must effect a purification
By introducing me to the nature of mind.

To subjugate the demon, clinging to things
    as real,
I must renounce my homeland, and,
Relying on alms for my food and drink,
Wander in the mountains from one soli-
    tary place to another.

I must cultivate the supreme attitude
That holds others dearer than myself,
And preserve recognition of the true
    condition of all things:
The view that one's "self" and phenomena
    are essenceless.
 This is what the chart revealed.

Once I embarked on the path prescribed,
The protective deity of dharmadhatu
    wisdom returned.
Once I was free of the demon, clinging to
    the notion of reality,
The confusion of desire and anger for the
    most part subsided,
Leaving just a small residue behind.
They will never again
Be as harmful as before.

By the time I had finished my speech, faith had begun to arise in the woman, who offered me some excellent *tsampa*.

Thus I wandered on and on, begging until my feet, chewed and bruised by my boots, finally became swollen and infected. Hungry, cold, and tired to the bone, I visited over a hundred families, each of whom donated a few bowls of *tsampa*. Altogether, I received one sack of flour, one skin bag of *tsampa* and one of barley, a quarter of a box of black tea, and nine measures of butter [90b].

On the third day of the first month of the Fire Tiger year,[22] having gotten together sufficient provisions, I arrived at the supreme place renowned as Tsonying Mahadeva, Heart of the Lake. It is an island found in the middle of Lake Trishok Gyalmo,[23] the abode of Naga Bodhisattva, the naga king Anavatapta's minister. It is a natural gathering place of benevolent *mamos* and dakinis, and was blessed by many holy beings in the past. I thought of my great good fortune in being able to stay in such a place, and, in my joy, sang this song:

I bow down at the feet of my father, the
    Dharma King;
Grant your blessing that this lowly one
May keep to mountain retreat.

I, the renunciate Tsogdruk Rangdrol,
Have left behind my native country.
I have given up my loving friends and
    relatives completely.
Relinquishing all desire for a retinue and
    servants,
I have always served the authentic root
    guru with great care,
With pure intention and pure action.
I've received from him empowerments,
Teachings, pith instructions, and advice.

Following the advice of the glorious guru,
I have come to Tsonying Island.
In the beginning of the year, through his
    blessings,
I arrived safely to practice the Dharma.
Encountering neither obstacles nor
    hardship.
I've found a place to stay and everything I
    need.

Singing a spontaneous song of joy,
Dancing, my body at ease,
There is such great bliss!
There is such great wonder!
The realm of the absolute nature
Is filled with delights!

As I explored the sacred place, I met Tendzin Nyima Rinpoche, "Sun of the Doctrine," a *nyungne*[24] practitioner living on the hilltop. I explained to him in detail the reasons for my coming, which [91a] pleased him. That particular year he and his disciple were in short supply of *tsampa* and had only a box and a half of tea. So, we pooled our supplies and then divided them equally.

I stayed alone in a cave facing east.

One day Lobzang Dondrup, renunciate Tendzin Nyima's faithful and intelligent attendant, who was close to his master's heart, asked me to sing a song in praise of the place. In response, I sang this:

I bow down again and again
At the lotus feet of the Dharma King.

To all, according to their wishes,
Even to students who are difficult to tame,
He explains the Dharma of sutra and
    tantra.

Have you never heard of Tsonying
    Mahadeva,
The place unsullied by the eight worldly
    dharmas?
Foretold in the prophecies
Of Dharma King Songtsen Gampo,
And of the Lake-born Vajra,[25]
It has many splendid qualities.

In the middle of wave-tossed Trishok Lake
Stands an immovable mountain;
In the wide-open, clear and empty sky
    above it
Dawns the luminous mandala of the sun.

In the morning the sun rises early;
At night, it sets late.
Wherever one looks,
There are good, solid caves to live in.

There is a good supply of water and wood,
And wild flowers bloom here in abundance
    [91b].
There is plenty of food—
Wild garlic and other edible plants—
To sustain the yogin's body.
Around the bright flowers,
Bees continuously hum their songs.

The trees move with the wind,
Leaves gently rustle.
Small birds in their multicolored plumage
Sing out all sorts of different songs.

When a small breeze blows,
Patterns appear on the water's stainless
    surface.

The air rings with the quiet cries
Of many waterfowl
Nesting near this pure lake.

Fish with golden eyes, searching for food,
Swim gracefully through the water.

Here one never sees thieves outside—
    neither men nor dogs.
Nor is there ever a whisper of thieves
    inside—rats or other vermin.

Around this lake filled with good fortune
Are many rich householders who are full of
    faith.
The local deities give help ceaselessly
To all who practice the holy Dharma here.

The yogin fond of the pleasures of touch
Who stays at this infinitely wondrous lake
Will find grass for a fine cushion.

The yogin fond of the pleasures of sight
Will find golden fish whose dances dazzle
    the eyes.

The yogin fond of the pleasures of smell
Will find the perfumes of a thousand
    flowers.

The yogin fond of the pleasures of taste
Will find wild vegetables of exquisite flavor.

The yogin fond of the pleasures of sound
Will find the intermingled melodies of
    many kinds of birds.

This solitary place,
Complete with all the pleasures of the
    senses,
Rivals the god-realm of desire.
With so many excellent qualities,
A solitary place such as this is rare.

Recognizing the defects of the eight
    worldly concerns,
Holy ones who practice Dharma should
    stay [92a].

All who follow the perfect lives of past
   masters
Of the practice lineage
Should stay, practicing, at this place.
This is a happy and blissful place for retreat;
Those who wish for bliss and happiness
   should use it.

By the merit of this praise,
May all humans and animals here
Be free from famine and disease.
May the Dharma increase
And may all be auspicious!

That night I dreamed I came to a celestial mansion made of precious stones. Inside, on a jewel throne, was a beautiful woman adorned with silks and ornaments. She was seated like a queen and was surrounded by a multitude of young boys and girls. They were holding a great feast, singing, dancing, and playing musical instruments.

At one point the queen looked at me and smiled. Turning to a young servant girl, she said, "Sing the praise that he sang yesterday." "I don't remember it all," the girl said. "Then sing as much as you can remember." The girl sang:

This solitary place,
Complete with all the pleasures of the senses,
Rivals the god-realm of desire.
With so many excellent qualities,
A solitary place such as this is rare.

After she had sung what little she could remember, everyone laughed, and the queen presented me with fruit, sugarcane, and a heap of other sweets [92b]. Having dreamed this, I thought, "Wherever I stay, a song in praise of the place seems to be appreciated even more than the usual ritual offerings."

During that year, except for some tea at noon, I didn't cook much.[26] For eight months I maintained silence and only practiced the least elabo-

rate practice, remaining evenly in the natural state of the Radiant Vajra Essence.[27] While resting in this state, various visions, such as mystical cities and Buddhafields, came into in my mind. I was quite joyful.

The great masters of the past say: "A yogin who has attained stability in calm-abiding and in insight meditation, and in both the development and completion stages, should train in the various modes of transformation[28] if he wishes to give rise to the qualities of the stages of the path." Therefore, each day that summer I practiced different transformations such as these:

From wisdom's own manifestation, which occurred when I was visualizing myself as the deity, an unsaddled white snow lioness appeared, which I mounted. Then, with Vajravarahi leading the way, and the guardians of the four directions each holding a paw of the lioness, I ascended into the sky.

Sometimes I would ride in succession an elephant, a divine horse, a garuda, a dragon, the sun, and the moon, ascending higher and higher into space.

Using my shawl as a pair of wings, I wheeled and soared from one peak to another across the lake. In the sky, I built a long staircase of crystal and beryl and climbed up to the celestial realms and then back down again.

Imagining that all mountains and rocks were like rainbows, clearly visible yet insubstantial, I passed back and forth through them [93a]. Visualizing rocks as mud, I left handprints and footprints in them. I also kneaded rocks like dough and divided them into small lumps.

Sometimes I visualized the upper half of my body as turbulent water, and the lower half as blazing fire—without the water extinguishing the fire. I turned my body inside out without any damage; I fluffed it up like wool, poured it like water, and transformed it into the wish-fulfilling gem, the excellent vase of great wealth, or the wish-granting tree, raining down everything that beings might require.

I visualized deities, transforming one into another, until the last one dissolved like a rainbow in the sky. I then settled into a state beyond images, an emptiness like the sky.

While I performed these and other practices, some people with fortunate karma who lived by the lake saw above the island white lights, rainbow tents pitched in the sky, and many large birds hovering overhead.

Various apparitions were reported by people who had visionary abilities. One, a shepherd, saw me flying from Tsonying Island in the direction of Gonpo Dong-nga, the Five-faced Lion Protector. Another, a carpenter from Shabdrung Tsang, said that during the summer he had actually seen me in the Harawol Cave near the lake, and that I had told him not to cut down the sacred trees in that area.

People expected storms that summer. When the thunder began, I did this protective concentration [93b]: first, I visualized my surroundings as a perfect Buddhafield, in the center of which the immeasurably vast, four-storeyed Mount Meru emerged, composed entirely of jewels and precious stones. On the top was a thousand-pronged iron vajra; its thousand lower prongs reached the solid gold ground below; the central knob rested at the level of the top plateau, and its upper thousand prongs projected into space.

I then visualized myself as Vajrapani seated at the heart of the vajra, and above the topmost prongs I visualized a thousand-spoked golden wheel, resting horizontally. In the hub was seated the Buddha. On the spokes, seated in the defending and protecting posture, the 1,002 Buddhas of this fortunate aeon generated from their hearts a thousand white lions that appeared at the spoke-ends and roared fiercely in the ten directions. Terrified and silenced, the thunder-dragons withdrew and took flight.

Several times, while I was concentrating on this visualization and recited the mantra of Vajrapani, the thunder stopped completely, so I thought that my visualization practice was going quite well.

In the fourth month a cuckoo came. When I heard it singing clear and loud in the forest on the north side of the island, I had mixed feelings of joy and melancholy. Jetsun Nyungnepa,[29] Tendzin Nyima Rinpoche, remarked, "I have been here for ten years. Until today, not one single cuckoo has ever come. This year you've arrived and so has this cuckoo. How wonderful!" [94a].

It flew away after a single day's visit. Intrigued, I thought, "That bird could have been the emanation of a Buddha, a Bodhisattva, or a spiritual teacher, and his song might have been the holy Dharma. You're supposed to be so good at composition—why not compose a teaching on what this bird might have taught?" I came up with this:

> Yesterday's heaven-blue cuckoo sang
>   something like this:
> Listen well, human who dwells here—
>   cuckoo!
> These are a few things I've learned—
>   cuckoo!
>
> When I see lamas traveling around just
>   doing rituals in villages—cuckoo!
> I see that, in their youth, they neither
>   studied nor reflected on the teachings—
>   cuckoo!
>
> When I see how even ordinary worldly
>   laws are disobeyed—cuckoo!
> I understand what will become of the
>   teachings and sentient beings—cuckoo!
>
> When I see how Chöd practitioners can't
>   do much beyond subduing evil spirits—
>   cuckoo![30]
> I understand their motivation for wander-
>   ing in solitudes and cemeteries—
>   cuckoo!
>
> When I see the *ngakpas* making a living by
>   casting their magic spells—cuckoo!
> I understand their motivation for practic-
>   ing the development and completion
>   stages—cuckoo!
>
> When I see the evil deeds of house-
>   holders—cuckoo!

I understand where they'll wind up in
   future lives—cuckoo!

When I see you sound asleep, like a
   corpse—cuckoo!
I understand why you came alone to this
   mountain retreat—cuckoo!

Amazing to watch, the behavior of people
   in this dark age—cuckoo!
It makes me feel like laughing—cuckoo!

The bird laughed, and I replied:

E ma!
Marvelous celestial bird!
Famous, sweet-voiced cuckoo! [94b].
Your eloquent speech is wonderful
   indeed;
Your timely song will help my practice.
Your song exposing the faults
Of worldly people like me
Is, I agree, completely true:
Please elaborate!

The blue cuckoo sang:

Cuckoo! Cuckoo!
You, yogin who hides away in mountain
   solitudes—cuckoo!
Like a wounded mountain animal—
   cuckoo!
Listen to me, a mountain bird—cuckoo!
Who flies over valleys and mountains
   alike—cuckoo!

They pretend to look after their
   monasteries—cuckoo!
They hoard their possessions—cuckoo!
And share with the sangha none of the
   donations—cuckoo!
Such are the monastery lamas—cuckoo!

They listen to malicious advisors—cuckoo!
Who tell them to hound the innocent—
   cuckoo!
And punish hundreds of subjects—cuckoo!
Such are kings and ministers—cuckoo!

Careless about studying Dharma—cuckoo!
Merely showing off in their Dharma
   robes—cuckoo!
They chase after food rather than
   Dharma—cuckoo!
Such are Dharma-less village monks and
   nuns—cuckoo!

Chöd practitioners stretch black sheep-
   skins—cuckoo!
In the houses of black-clad laymen—
   cuckoo!
And beat on their black drums—cuckoo!
Such are the black-hearted Chöd
   practitioners—cuckoo!

Filled with harmful intent toward others—
   cuckoo!
Gathering heaps of harmful ingredients—
   cuckoo!
Performing harmful acts of black magic—
   cuckoo!
Such are the harmful-minded *ngakpas*—
   cuckoo!

To perform inhumane actions—cuckoo!
They use this precious human body, so
   difficult to obtain—cuckoo!
They sadly waste their human lives—
   cuckoo!
Such are ordinary human beings—
   cuckoo!

Failing to maintain undistracted
   diligence—cuckoo!
They fail to attain unsurpassable
   enlightenment—cuckoo!
And fail to achieve anything for this life or
   the next—cuckoo!
Just like you, poor cotton-clad *repa*—
   cuckoo! [95a].

I replied:

A Ah! The Bodhisattvas—
A ro! Who knows where one might appear?
A ka! Do you speak this bluntly to
   everyone?

A ro! Do you know what I mean, royal
bird?

The bird sang:

> Cuckoo! Cuckoo!
> No one but the omniscient Buddha—
>   cuckoo!
> Can judge the virtues and faults of oth-
>   ers—cuckoo!
> I don't say these things to just anyone—
>   cuckoo!
> O Tsogdruk Rangdrol who has renounced
>   everything—cuckoo!

In my turn, I sang:

> Eloquent azure bird,
> Striking in your blue plumage,
> Give three words of advice
> To the one who sits here near you!

Obligingly, he sang:

> Cuckoo! Cuckoo!
> One day, O human, you and I—cuckoo!
> Must cross to the other shore—cuckoo!
> There is no certainty when that will be—
>   cuckoo!
> So don't cling to this world—cuckoo!
>
> If you must speak—cuckoo!
> Don't lie, gossip, or speak harshly—
>   cuckoo!
> Use no words that hurt others—cuckoo!
> Speak gently, like me—cuckoo!
>
> You know why you've come to these
>   solitudes—cuckoo!
> So don't waste time sleeping, but practice
>   your best—cuckoo!
> You'll naturally fly—cuckoo!
> From one happiness to another, like me—
>   cuckoo!
>
> Never forget this—cuckoo!
> Who knows if we will ever, ever meet
>   again?—cuckoo!

> O hermit, be well, my friend, my friend—
>   cuckoo!
> I am leaving you now, right now—cuckoo!

Just as he was about to fly away, I said:

> If I am alive, alive,
> Then a year from now you must, you
>   must,
> Return to this island, surely, surely,
> To voice your song, clearly, clearly.
>
> We'll separate soon, soon [95b];
> Our hearts' core fills with sorrow, sorrow.
> We can't bear parting, truly, truly:
> Such is samsara's nature—oh, oh!
> I pray we will meet again, again;
> My friend, stay in good health, for ever
>   and ever.

He concluded:

> Cuckoo! Cuckoo!
> My friend, look at me—cuckoo!
> One day you will spread your wings—
>   cuckoo!
> The wings of merit and wisdom—cuckoo!
> And just as I soar now—cuckoo!
> You'll soar in the sky of deathless
>   omniscience.
> Watch me; soar as I do—cuckoo!
>
> How sweet is my clear Dharma song—
>   cuckoo!
> Having listened well, now sing it, too—
>   cuckoo!

He flew away with a little song, gazing back
again and again with affectionate glances.

I sang this to inspire myself and others to
practice.

At the end of autumn I visited Nyungnepa
Tendzin Nyima Rinpoche. "Please, sing an edi-

fying song," I asked, and couching my request in verse, I offered my own song:

> E ma!
> Lord, supreme being of this decadent age,
> Spiritual friend linked with me beyond time,
> You took ordination when you were young
>   and kept pure discipline;
> You have attended many authentic gurus,
> You have heard many profound teachings
>   of sutra and tantra,
> You have given up worldly concerns,
>   which are so hard to abandon.
> Along with listening to and reflecting on
>   the Dharma,
> You now absorb yourself in the actual
>   practice, so hard to undertake.
> Please grant me whatever enlightened
>   advice
> Arises in your wisdom-mind.

As I thus tried to persuade him to sing, he pleaded, "I've never tried singing before; at this moment, nothing will come." Again the next day I requested:

> E ma!
> Dear authentic heart-friend,
> There is an ocean of sutra and tantra
>   teachings [96a];
> Nonetheless, with the nectar of clear
>   exposition
> That flows from the crystal vase that is
>   your wisdom-mind,
> Please satisfy the thirst
> Of your friend who yearns to drink.

Out of sheer kindness, he spoke:

> E ma!
> Dear intelligent friend,
> If you are eager to know about the view,
> I, a simpleton,
> Will tell a bit of what I've understood.
>
> If there's bias, that's not the view.
> If there's clinging to things as real, that's
>   not the meditation.

> If there's accepting and rejecting, that's not
>   the action.
> If there's hope and fear, that's not fruition.
>
> "Then what is it?" you may ask.
> The view is empty awareness, without any
>   source.
> The meditation is empty clarity without
>   any concepts,
> The action, like the path of a bird through
>   the sky, is without any traces.
> Whatever arises is freed, just as it arises.
> The fruition is samsara and nirvana,
> Complete within mind itself.
> Does this suit you, dear friend?

I replied:

> O precious supreme being,
> O heir to the Victorious Ones,
> From the crystal vase of your bliss-void
>   wisdom mind
> Pours the nectar of clear exposition,
> Cleansing the wish-fulfilling gem of my mind
> Of the stains of ignorance and emotions.
> And this song, I think, might fulfill the
>   needs of one and all.

We also talked at length about Dharma; our minds mingled as one.

I received from him the transmission of the *Kadampa Teachings of Father and Son*,[31] the *Five Stages of Guhyasamaja Accomplished In One Sitting* written by Je Rinpoche, the *Torch Illuminating the Five Stages*, the *Twenty-one Notes*,[32] and the *Nyungne Ritual* composed by Panchen Lobzang Chögyen and Changkya Rinpoche.[33] From then on, I perceived him as one of my kindest gurus [96b].

Throughout that year, Jetsun Tendzin Nyima Rinpoche's attendant, Lobzang Dondrup, occasionally brought me goat's milk and curd; in the summer some vegetables were to be found. By the end of autumn, however, my supplies were exhausted, and for two months I was reduced to eating only a thin soup of *tsampa*. During this period I honed my patience and fortified my diligence; when I think back on it, I realize what fortunate times those really were.

When the lake was sufficiently frozen to walk on, I went down to the island's shore and found a Mongolian family called Bageh. With them was a package for me from the Dharma King, the queen, and their son. Inside were seven silver *sang*, a box of black tea, and a letter saying that they were all in good health. I felt as happy as if they had arrived in person. For the seven silver *sang*, the local fishermen sold me fifteen hundred live fish, which I set free.

At the beginning of the following summer the immeasurably kind Gyal Khenchen Rinpoche came to Arik District. There, he praised me to the inhabitants of Arik and, adding that I was a person with a special destiny, he made prostrations toward Tsonying, where I was in retreat.

He asked all residents of Arik, of both high and low standing, to help with my supplies. He himself sent me a box of black tea, some butter, a sweet cheese, a white woolen felt blanket, and a letter saying:

Padmasambhava,
Embodiment of the infinite Victorious Ones,
You who look with great love on all the
    vast number of beings,
You have manifested as the great
    nirmanakaya, Ngakyi Wangpo:
With great faith, I take you as my crown-
    Buddha.

On the solitary mountain-island renowned
    as Mahadeva [97a],
Your flawless and excellent Bodhicitta
Takes on the task of freeing all sentient
    beings,
Each of whom was once your mother:
To you, spiritual friend who banishes the
    darkness of ignorance,
I make this request like a child crying for its
    mother.

Although I look like a monk,
In fact I serve the emperor of Ego.

I remain imprisoned by the delusions of
    ignorance,
And thus wander round the impure wheel
    of existence.

E ma!
For a long time, you have traveled the
    excellent path;
Unhindered, you have gathered its fruits.
You have been blessed by the refuge of
    supreme gurus.
To unify your life and your *sadhana*,
You have chosen to retire to remote places.
Unburdened by this austere existence,
You have worn it like an ornament.

Your sacred and harmonious life-story
Is an inspiration to all, high and low;
Because of it, throughout all the mountains
    and valleys,
Faith, respect, and wonderment blossom in
    a hundred directions.

Your old mother, sisters, and Dharma
    friends, the *ngakpas*, and others,
All of us, including Sengzang,[34] are well.
Following your example we devote
    ourselves to practice,
Not just paying lip-service, but penetrating
    its core.

Here is the heart of my request:
To gain an unerring certainty,
You must persevere and let realization
    unfold
On the graded path of the three types of
    individuals,
The path praised in unison by all the
    saints.

Let impartial compassion and the supreme
    intention
To attain enlightenment for the benefit of
    others
Keep you from remaining in nirvana.

As taught in the most supreme and pro-
    found path of the Great Perfection,

Which cuts clinging to the notion of reality,
Let the natural state of Trekchö,
From which you should never stray,
Keep you from remaining in samsara
   [97b].

Achieving the final signs of liberation
   according to the practice of Thögal,
You will thus swiftly arrive at the exhaustion of phenomena in dharmata.[35]
Focusing awareness on the fingernails,[36]
You will manifest the signs of accomplishment with this illusory body,
And liberate the six classes of beings from
   samsara.

O renunciate, for the sake of your disciples,
Consider bringing your practice swiftly to
   fruition.
To make your followers dance with joy,
Share with us in song your experience
Of the paths you have climbed and the
   levels you have reached,
And send us detailed spiritual advice about
   the right way to practice:
I shall place it as an ornament on the
   crown of my head.

Bless me, a humble man,
That I may be soon disentangled from this
   worldly life,
And, following your example,
Raise in secluded places the victory banner
Heralding the tradition of the practice
   lineage.

Should such fortune elude me in this
   lifetime,
Please guide me compassionately in the
   bardo,
And if my karma, obscuring emotions,
And the misuse I might have made of
   religious wealth do not prevent it,
May I tread the supreme path in my next
   birth.

I offer you these bricks of tea, some butter,
   sweet cheese,

And a white felt blanket.
Please accept too whatever the faithful
   ones of Arik,
The mighty and the humble, might offer
   you at my request;
May thus your practice wax like the moon.

This letter is accompanied by a divine
   white scarf,
Which I unfold before you with a loving
   mind and pure white wishes.
So may this reach you on a pure white day
   and month
When the great lake is wearing its white
   mantle.

I felt the same boundless joy as if I had met him
in person.

During this time, both the humble and the
powerful of Arik came to invite me [98a], saying,
"Earlier we did not recognize you as a great
hidden yogin; but after Gyal Khenchen Rinpoche
told us about you last year, we greatly regret our
disrespect. By all means you must come and visit
us."

Accordingly, I went to Arik, where the local
lamas, the chieftains, monks and nuns, laypeople
great and small, old and young, all came to meet
me. I gave some basic Dharma teachings and
the transmission for recitation of the *mani* mantra, the *Miktsema* prayer and the *Praises to Tara*.

Singing songs, I tried to inspire them to
practice Dharma. Many gave up negative acts in
favor of virtuous ones. In particular, each part of
the district vowed to recite together a hundred
million *mani* mantras every year; later I heard
they had accumulated a hundred times that
number.

I established connections with all those who
offered horses, gold, silver, and other valuables
by making prayers and dedications, and then
returning the gifts. Accepting the tea, butter,
tsampa and cheese, I gathered a stock of provisions.

The old lama who had thrown pieces of dry
bread at me the previous year felt guilty, and,
offering me some butter and cheese, expressed
regret for his earlier distrust. I was also invited to

the homes of some women who formerly had been barely hospitable, and to the homes of those who hadn't given anything at all.

Presenting me with tea, butter, and cheese, the latter said "We confess frankly that last year, deluded by our pride, wealth, and our ignorance, we treated you badly. Please be patient with us, and from now on [98b] keep us under your spiritual protection. May you live long! Next year you must come again and let us offer you our warmest hospitality." I promised to come and made some prayers for their good fortune. Everyone was delighted.

I then went to meet Naktsang Tulku Rinpoche, a sage of great learning. He gave me the transmission for the biographies of Jetsun Tilopa, Naropa, Marpa and Rechungpa,[37] the transmission for the *Mind Training on Cutting All Ties of Attachment* by Chen-ngawa,[38] and other teachings on mind training. Pleased by our conversations, he gave me so many presents that on my way back a young man remarked that I should have a horse. At first, I gave him a simple answer, and then teasingly said, "But I *do* have a horse!" and sang this song:

I bow down at the feet of the Dharma
   King!
Though it may not be within everyone's
   reach
I ride a horse that is free of birth and
   death.

I ride a stallion, the foal of a barren mare:
Unborn, all-pervading absolute space.[39]

I sit in a saddle made from rabbit horns:
Without meditation, without tampering—
Mind just as it occurs.

I steer with reins made of tortoise hair:
Free of all efforts to accept or reject.

This horse, which neither comes nor goes,
Canters along the plain of equanimity.

Whoever rides this actionless dharmadhatu
   horse,

Without coming or going,
Will surely reach the land of Buddhahood.

Before returning to Tsonying Island I improvised this song for the chieftain Behu, the householder Datrak, and other male and female devotees:

You, a lofty and solid rock—making one,
I, an eagle who slept here cozily—making
   two;
Our meeting and mutual understanding
   [99a]
Have been excellent.

May you, O lofty rock, remain
   content.
This eagle cannot stay, but must leave,
Soaring through the sky.
I pray that I meet you again and again.
May my prayer be fulfilled.

You, a most delightful meadow—making
   one,
I, an antelope who slept here in comfort—
   making two;
Our meeting and mutual understanding
Have been excellent.

May you, O meadow, remain content.
This brown antelope cannot stay, but must
   leave,
Heading for good grass and water.
I pray that I meet you again and again.
May my prayer be fulfilled.

You, a tree with swaying branches—
   making one,
I, a cuckoo singing at the summit—making
   two;
Our meeting and mutual understanding
Have been excellent.

May you, O tree, remain content.
This cuckoo cannot stay, but must leave,
Flying to another country.
I pray that I meet you again and again.
May my prayer be fulfilled.

You, a patron with pure devotion—
   making one;
I, who have taught the sacred Dharma—
   making two;
Our meeting and mutual benefit
Have been excellent.

May you, O patron, remain content.
This yogin cannot stay, but must leave
And go to the mountain on Tsonying
   Island.
I pray that I meet you again and again.
May my prayer be fulfilled.

All you noble men and women gathered
   here,
Give up evil acts; perform virtuous ones.
Devoted patrons, Datrak, and others [99b],
I have given you some heartfelt advice;
May its merit benefit all.

Reaching the lake's shore, my companions said, "If snow hasn't fallen on the ice by tomorrow, the pack animals won't be able to cross." So I prayed to the guru and the Three Jewels, and made an offering of fragrant incense to Mother Trishok Gyalmo and others, exhorting them to act. In the evening heavy snow fell. In the morning everyone was merry: riding on horseback, they could reach Tsonying Island easily. After circumambulating the sacred place, they returned home.

When I had left Tsonying Island to beg in Arik, only a grass mat and some dried vegetables were left in my cave. When visiting pilgrims saw how few possessions I had, they felt faith and respect; some of them left butter and *tsampa*, with a note saying that they were an offering.

One night, in a dream, I saw that my close disciple Pema Rangdrol had sent from my homeland Gedun Jungne, a monk of the Tob family, to inquire about my well-being and present me with a large bag full of tea, a belt, a letter, and a white scarf. I told those who were staying on the island with me, "Tomorrow someone from my homeland will be coming here."

When it happened just as I had said, everyone's respect and devotion increased. I asked

the messenger for news; he told me that the lamas, Dharma friends, my mother, sisters, and others were all well, but that Aku Dorje Tseten had passed away. The monk had brought his bones to me.

I felt heartbroken that my best childhood friend had died. For his sake, I did some practice to accumulate merit and to purify obscurations. Finally, mingling his mind with absolute mind, I rested in evenness [100a].

From his bones I molded *tsa-tsas*,[40] and prayed he would take rebirth in a Pure Realm. I had an auspicious dream indicating that he had been liberated from samsara.

In his letter, my close disciple Pema Rangdrol requested all the teachings I had been giving here. So, with the monk from the Tob family, I sent many songs I had written down for various worthy disciples and devoted householders, as well for my own edification. In particular, I sent him the Song of the View called *The Flight of the Garuda*,[41] with the sections on Thögal practice. I also sent a long letter of advice.

Later I heard that when it reached them safely, they felt the same joy and devotion as if they had met me in person. I also sent letters in verse and prose to the Dharma King and his queen, and to Gyal Khenchen, who were pleased.

That year I was able to offer my root teacher, Tendzin Nyima Rinpoche, and his disciple all the supplies they needed. I also gave empowerment, instructions, and all sorts of material necessities to Tenpa Phende, Gelong Tendar, Gyupa Kukye of Arik, Rabjampa of Jigme Behla, Alak of Suneh, and the old lama from Shabdrung.

After this, they all stayed in retreat, each in his own cave. I, too, that year, sealed off my cave with mud, and, maintaining silence, persevered constantly in meditation practice [100b].

On the night of the tenth day of the third month, I dreamed of a terrifying black man riding a blue horse. He declared that he had been sent by

Pöntsang,[42] and told me, "Your sole and unfailing refuge in this and future lives, the Dharma King Ngakyi Wangpo, is about to depart for the distant land. Come quickly to see him."

I got behind him on his horse, and, reaching Urgeh in an instant, I saw the Dharma King astride a blue horse decorated with jewels. He was surrounded by many young men and women in the full bloom of youth, who held aloft standards and victory banners.

The Dharma King had reached the foot of a high mountain to the southwest when I caught up with him. The precious Dharma King smiled, and said, "It is good the protector called you. As I told you earlier, I am going to the Pure Realm of Celestial Enjoyment. Don't feel sad; I will come back soon for the sake of beings to be trained." Then he said:

Empty and luminous sky beyond
    attachment,
Remain here.
I, the evening sun ablaze with light,
Shall not remain.

I shall set behind the western ridge,
Soon to reappear
Above the eastern mountains.

Vast, unobstructing space,
Remain here.
I, the five-colored rainbow arc,
Shall not remain.

I shall disappear into the sky,
Soon to reappear again
From the very midst of space.

Cool lake, clear and shimmering,
Remain here.
I, the waterfowl with a sweet song,
Shall not remain [101a].

I will fly off to a distant land,
Soon to reappear again in spring.

Disciple of unwavering faith,
Remain here.

I, the old man from the snow land of
    Tibet,
Shall not remain.

I will pass into the Buddhafield Celestial
    Enjoyment,
Soon to reappear again as another
    incarnation.

With these words, he began to climb; I touched his foot with my head and, with longing, uttered this lament:

Just as in earlier times the teacher,
    Shakyamuni,
Left his following of human and celestial
    beings,
And went on to the Pure Realm of
    Akanishtha,
Will you, too, leave us today, O second
    Buddha?

Just as the Lotus-born, Padmakara,
Who was beyond the sway of birth and
    death,
Left behind the land of Tibet and his
    twenty-five disciples
And went on to Cannibal Island in the
    southwest,
Will you, too, leave us today, O second
    Lotus-born?

Just as Milarepa, the king of yogins,
Left behind his following of many *repas*
And went on to the eastern Pure Realm of
    True Enjoyment,
Will you, too, leave us today, O second
    Mila?

Just as Lobzang Trakpa, Manjushri in
    person,
Left behind his many fortunate disciples
And went on to the Pure Realm of
    Tushita,
Don't leave me today, O second Lobzang!

When I sang these verses to him, he placed his hand on my head and said, "It is not time for you to go. Uniting your life and your *sadhana*, work for the benefit of the Dharma and sentient beings."

Then he ascended a broad white path stretching up the mountain. When he and his disciples and retinue arrived at the top [101b], an inconceivable host of dakas and dakinis emerged from the sky. A white, a yellow, a red, and a green dakini each held a leg of the guru's horse and miraculously lifted it into the sky, rising higher and higher.

Those who had escorted him turned and went back. I stayed there motionless and sang this song of sadness:

In the thirty-three-fold celestial realm,
Indra, the lord of the gods,
Leaves his throne and palace,
Passing through space in comfort and ease.
As he arrives at the pleasure grove,
Great is the god's rejoicing.

The illuminating sun
That benefits all beings,
Sets behind the western mountain peaks,
Leaving in darkness the southern
    continent, Jambudvipa.
As it arrives in the western continent,
Great is people's rejoicing.

The wish-fulfilling jewel
That grants whatever one wishes
Leaves the ocean island,
Removed by a clever seafarer.
As it becomes as an object of offering
On the pinnacle of a victory banner,
Great is people's rejoicing.

The protector of beings of this dark age,
The king of Dharma,
Leaves me behind, unfortunate disciple,
And proceeds along an immaculate white
    highway.
As he arrives in the Pure Realm of
    Celestial Enjoyment,
Great is people's rejoicing.

In my dream, I began crying, and awoke to find my pillow wet with tears. I thought, "I rarely have dreams, not even good ones, and when I do, they rarely come true. Yet, I fear that such an ominous dream as this might really come true." I began to feel cold and uneasy inside.

It later turned out that this dream coincided with the precious Dharma King's passing to the Pure Realm [102a]. This coincidence astonished the heart-sons when they heard of it and strengthened their faith in the Dharma.

In the summertime, in the fifth month, Ngawang Lobzang, the old Shabdrung lama staying in a cave facing north, fell ill. I heard about it and sent this letter:

Listen, heart-son
Who lives in accord with the Dharma:
If your mirage-like body is unwell,
Do all you can to protect it against disease
    and untimely death.
If you do so and are still unwell, I shall
    come.

We have come together in this place
Because of links formed by previous
    actions and aspirations.
When we are practicing the holy Dharma
    purely,
If diseases and demons harmful to our lives
    arise,
We must do all we can to avert untimely
    death.

A few days after I had sent this letter, he became ill to the point of death. Jetsun Tendzin Nyima Rinpoche and I left our retreats and went to his cave. After performing a ransoming ritual,[43] we did the "chasing out of hindrances." A wind arose inside the cave and, rushing out through the cave opening, transformed into a black whirlwind. Swirling across the surface of the lake, it disappeared in the distance, as everyone watched.

Since the old lama's illness ended the next day, the other practitioners thought that it must have been a demon and concluded, "The evil force left, thanks to those two. How amazing!"

Similarly, Rabjampa Kunga Gyaltsen from Jigme Behla was once ill; among other complaints he had heart trouble. He sent me this letter from his retreat:

Wish-fulfilling gem, bestower of all
    happiness!
Experienced guide on the path
Leading to the realm of bliss!
Father, embodiment of all Sugatas,
Listen a little [102b],
And tenderly consider your tormented son.

In my search for happiness,
I follow your instructions
And stay in the seclusion
Of a peaceful, joyous mountain retreat.

Now, while practicing the holy Dharma,
The source of happiness,
I have experienced much suffering.
In suffering or in happiness,
You are my only hope.
Gracious lama, bestower of all bliss,

Never dismiss me from your blissful and
    luminous heart;
Swiftly bestow the feast of happiness and
    joy.

I responded:

E ma!
Having purified yourself in previous lives,
You now have good predispositions.
From childhood, you have listened to
And reflected on the wondrous Dharma.
Now you try to practice accordingly,
Without the least attachment to the taste of
    pleasures.
Heart-son who is free from clinging and
    aversion,
If your heart isn't well,
Practice purely, and you will recover
    quickly.
I who roam through mountains and valleys

Will pray to the Three Jewels, the source of
    well-being.

Heart-son, you have given up worldly
    activities
And, for the sake of future lives,
You practice the Dharma in remote
    mountain places.
May the Buddhas of the three times,
The *yidams*, dakinis, and dharmapalas
Who protect one as a mother does her
    child,
Lovingly watch over you, my heart-son.
May all obstacles and adverse
    circumstances
Vanish like frost at sunrise.

Praying so from the heart,
Until the mighty Lord of Death arrives,
May we all be free from obstacles and
    afflictions,
And practice in solitude,
Making our lives and practice one.

I did practices to protect him, but his illness worsened [103a], and again I left my retreat. After giving him a long-life empowerment, according to the tradition of the Queen of Siddhas,[44] I had a dream: some Chinese were about to kill a sheep and I forbade them to kill it, thus saving the sheep's life. From that very night Rabjampa was free from his illness.

Then we all resumed our strict retreats.

Again I sealed my entrance with mud and, taking a vow of silence, based my practice on the two Bodhicittas,[45] the development and completion stages of the Secret Mantrayana, and the Trekchö and Thögal practices of the most secret Great Perfection. Day and night, I practiced one-pointedly.

On the eighth day of the eighth month, during the midnight session, as I was meditating on great compassion for all sentient beings, our mothers, I thought, "I am practicing to gain enlightenment for the sake of all beings, but since I lack perseverance, Buddhahood won't come about." Contemplating the sufferings of sentient beings, I felt unbearable sadness.

I thought, "I have no ability to relieve be-ings of their suffering. Then who does? Surely the noble Avalokiteshvara, the principal deity of Tibet." With yearning devotion, I recited the *mani* mantra, thinking, "You are aware of the pain and happiness of all beings, each one of whom has been a mother to me."

The cave grew lighter and lighter, until a white radiance pervaded everywhere. Before me in space, in an expanse of rainbow light, appeared the noble great compassionate one, Khasarpana. He had a pure white complexion and a peaceful smiling expression [103b]. His right hand was in the gesture of bestowal, his left hand held the stem of a white lotus. Adorned with silk scarves and jewel ornaments, he was resplendent with the marks and signs of a Tathagata. He sang:

I, mighty Avalokiteshvara, principal deity
  of Tibet,
Always watch over the world with eyes of
  compassion.
You, fortunate one born in the central
  land, Tibet,
And everyone who lives there should do
  this:

Ngakpas should protect their *samaya*
As they would protect their own eyes.
Especially, they should not perform black
  magic or sacrifice animals.
Monks should keep their vows properly,
And, especially, should renounce alcohol
  and women.

Householders should shun the ten
  nonvirtues,
And, especially, should not quarrel, steal,
  fight, or kill.
The rich should not be stingy, but give
  generously.
Dharma-practitioners should not wander
  around
In populated places, but stay in their
  retreats.

Don't mistreat elderly parents; serve and
  respect them.

Don't beat farm animals and watchdogs;
  be kind to them.

Make offerings to the guru and Three
  Jewels; *siddhis* will follow.
Make prostrations and circumambulations;
Negative acts and obscurations of the body
  will be purified.
Recite scriptures and mantras;
Obscurations of speech will be purified.
Anything you do with a good heart will
  become Dharma.

Please act accordingly, disciples of Tibet.
In particular, everyone should pray to me;
Young or old, they should recite
The six-syllable mantra.

I will always be present before those with
  faith.
I have always led those with faith
To the Buddhafield of Sukhavati.
Follow what I have explained here,
And at the time of death
I shall appear in the *bardo*
To guide you to Sukhavati or Mount
  Potala.[46]
Do not doubt this, my disciples.

Having spoken thus, he disappeared [104a]. On other occasions, I frequently saw gurus and deities in reality, in meditation experiences, and in dreams.

At the end of autumn, at the request of some retreatants, Gyupa Kukye Rinpoche gave the transmission and explanation of the *Great Gradual Path to Enlightenment*, by Je Rinpoche.

When the lake froze again in the winter, Tendzin Nyima Rinpoche received some visi-tors who told him that my refuge and protector, the lord of the mandala endowed with the three kindnesses, the precious Dharma King, had passed on to another Buddhafield some months before.

Tendzin Nyima Rinpoche came to see me. His face was sad. After just sitting silently with me for a while, he finally said, "Well, as Jetsun Mila says:

Sometimes one feels the presence of the
    guru.
When this feeling comes,
Merge with his presence,
Visualize him seated on the crown of your
    head,
And pray.
Never forgetting the guru,
Visualize him in the center of your heart.
Beyond that, one should know
That even the guru is a mirage.

"Tsogdruk Rangdrol, this is so. You must
not let yourself become desolate with sadness: I
have heard from a visitor that Chögyal Rinpoche,
the precious Dharma King, has passed away
into another Buddhafield."

For a moment my mind went blank. Then,
suddenly, the thought of my guru vividly surged in
my mind, and my memory became of him so strong
that I was overwhelmed, and began weeping.

Tendzin Nyima took my hand and said:
"Don't let yourself be overcome by sorrow. Make
offerings and prayers to your guru to fulfill his
intentions. He merely displayed the passing of
his physical form into nirvana in order to urge all
of us who cling to permanence to practice Dharma.
In reality, the guru knows no death, yet he must
demonstrate impermanence and death [104b].

"Now, to serve your guru, repay your parents' kindness, and benefit sentient beings, you
should raise the victory banner of practice while
staying in solitude. It is by doing so that you will
fulfill your guru's wishes.

"Later, you will meet him in the Buddhafield
of Celestial Enjoyment. Of course, you know all
this; I am merely mentioning it as a reminder.
Keep what I have said in mind." Then he left.

After he had gone, the living memory of my
teacher became so intense that I wept and wept,
quite uncontrollably. Finally, I sang a song of
lamentation:

Kye-ma! Kye-hu!
Kind lord!

Just to hear your name gives birth to
    devotion.

Just to see your face purifies all
    obscuration.
Just to hear your voice brings blessings into
    one's being.

Prostrating oneself to you and
    circumambulating you,
One perfects the accumulation of merit.
Instead of staying and caring for your
    disciples,
Where have you gone, protector, my
    refuge?

Kye-hu!
Mount Meru has collapsed:
Where shall the *kamaloka* gods now
    abide?[47]

The great ocean has dried up from its
    depths:
How can the fish bear such a thing?

The sun has set behind the western peaks:
How can work in the fields continue?

The full moon has been seized by Rahu:[48]
What can the benighted traveler do?

The lord of birds has lost his wings:
How can he fly with only his claws?

The hollyhock in the garden has withered:
Where shall the bees go now to gather
    their nectar?

The wish-fulfilling gem has disappeared
    into the earth:
Whom shall we petition for our needs and
    wishes?

The parents of the heartbroken child have
    died:
In whom can the poor orphan place his
    trust?

The heart has been torn out of the body:
What can bring the dead back to life?
    [105a].

The head, the most precious part of the
   body,
Has been severed:
What can the body do, alone?

The eyes, finest among senses,
Have lost their sight:
Who will guide the blind?

The guru has passed into invisible space:
Where can I look for protection and
   refuge?

Kye-hu!
The great mansion's pillar has toppled.
The dark continent's lamp has died out.
The ship, the bridge that takes one to the
   river's far shore, has broken apart.
The guide who leads us through hazardous
   places
Has abandoned us, left us to fend for
   ourselves.
The supreme leader, the King of Dharma,
   has passed into nirvana.

Kye-ma! Kye-hu!
What can be done?

My heart, adrift, is torn with grief.
My body trembles like a baby bird.

My perception alternately clears and
   darkens,
And tears fall, beyond control—
The anguished mind has no means by
   which to resist.

With your infinite knowledge of samsara
   and nirvana,
Look upon me from invisible space.
Please show your face; give relief to my
   mind.

Even though I do not have the fortune
To meet you in reality,
Show me your face and give some words
   of advice,
In meditation experiences or else in dreams.

In my coming lives
May I stay near you, O protector,
And become your closest disciple.

Through practicing virtuous acts,
May I perfectly accomplish whatever
   pleases you.
May I always attend you;
May I never part from you.

On that day I felt a hopeless anguish—as if my
heart had been torn from my chest.
   I prepared a vast feast-offering with both
real and imagined offerings [105b]. I arranged
the mandala of my tutelary deity, the *Wish-fulfilling Gem, Hayagriva and Varahi,* and received
empowerment from the guru as inseparable from
the main deity of the mandala. From then on, I
made repeated prayers invoking the guru's compassion, requesting his swift rebirth, and praying
for the fulfillment of his enlightened intentions.
   One day, I went to the peak of the island
and, facing in the direction my guru had lived, I
sang this heartfelt song of sadness:

   Firmly rooted in true concern
   You extended in the ten directions
   The shade of benefit for others.
   Abundant with the fruits of good qualities,
   Celestial, wish-fulfilling tree,
   You have been cut down.
   Kye-hu! I, the *deva*-disciple ask:
   What has become of our cool resting
      place?[49]

   Drawn by the emerald steeds of our past
      prayers,[50]
   You beautified the sky of this world.
   The rays of your activity were
      all-pervading.
   O luminous sun, excellent guide, you have
      disappeared.
   Kye-yu! I, the lotus-disciple, ask:
   Where has my sun-companion gone?

   The stream of your compassion ceaselessly
      ran
   Into the vast pool of the three trainings,[51]

Embellished by the flower of your perfect
  deeds.
The delightful sacred pool is no more.
Kye-ma! I, your swan-disciple, ask:
How can I swim on dry land?

Raised on study, reflection, and meditation,
You rested in the meadow of spiritual
  experience,
Generously giving the milk of pith
  instructions.
Guru, bountiful wish-granting cow,[52] you
  have now departed.
Kye-hu! I, the nursing calf-disciple, ask:
How can I drink the milk of pith
  instructions?

As I sang my lament, remembering the guru
and weeping, before me in the southern heavens
a new white cloud surged up, higher and higher
in the sky, like milk boiling over [106a]. Upon it,
seated astride a white lion adorned with various
precious stones, was seated my root guru, his
body more radiant than ever, attired in silken
scarves and adorned with jewel and bone ornaments. He said:

Without ever moving from the space of
  dharmakaya,
My rupakaya display appears in many
  ways.[53]
You, who pray to me with a melody of
  longing,
My supreme son, Tsogdruk Rangdrol,
  listen to me:

Son, O son,
The human body is rare and easily lost.
Surely, yes, surely,
This will happen to you,
Just as it has happened to me.
Remember this!

Over and over, in the past,
I gave you teachings.
Now do as I said, just as I said,
And whatever you wish shall be
  accomplished.

Saying so, he disappeared. After this, my
grief began to ease.

The admiration I had developed for Jetsun
Tendzin Nyima Rinpoche's practice of sutra
and tantra, and particularly for his practice of
the development and completion stages of Secret
Mantrayana, inspired this song:

Aspiring to benefit yourself and others,
You have served authentic teachers
Through both thought and action.
You received the empowerments and pith
  instructions
Of the development and completion stages.

Praying to develop the propensity for the
  two stages,
With a mind deeply moved by faith and
  devotion,
I join my palms above the crown of my
  head.

Praying that my mind be imbued with
  both the sutras and tantras,
May I become like you, O second Buddha
  [106b].

I offered him this song and he was delighted.
Thus, for two years we, father and son, stayed
together.

On an auspicious day in the first month of
the New Year, just before he was about to depart
on a pilgrimage to the Five-peaked Mountain in
China, I offered him a vajra and bell, a woolen
shawl, and a roll of fine silk as farewell presents. I
then sang this song:

Sole ornament of the southern continent,
  Jambudvipa,
Sun, high in the sky, may you fare well.
Though you will move over the other three
  continents,
I pray that soon I may see your face again.

Sole ornament of the River Ganges in the
  east,
Golden-eyed fish, may you fare well.
Though now you will travel through the
  outermost ocean,
I pray that soon I may see your face again.

Sole ornament of the mighty tree,
Cuckoo bird, may you fare well.
Though now you will travel to distant
  lands,
I pray that soon I may see your face again.

Sole ornament upon the crown of my
  head,
Father guru, may you fare well.
Though now you will travel to distant
  horizons,
I pray that soon I may see your face again.

I offered this, and in return he gave me many
presents and much advice. Just before he left,
he presented me with a long white scarf, and
said:

Stay well, Jambudvipa,
While the sun tours the four continents.
For a short while we shall separate,
But soon the sun and Jambudvipa will
  meet again.

Stay well, Ganges,
While the golden-eyed fish roams the
  ocean.
For a short while we shall separate [107a],
But soon the golden-eyed fish and the
  Ganges will meet again.

Stay well, tree,
While the cuckoo travels to distant
  countries.
For a short while we shall separate,
But soon the cuckoo and tree will meet
  again.

Stay well, my son,
While the old father visits the Five-peaked
  Mountain.

For a short while we shall separate,
But soon we yogins, master and disciple,
Will meet again.

He then gave much advice and taught the
Dharma to all the disciples and patrons assembled there, who had known him for a long
time. Saddened that he was going so far away,
many of them wept. The master crossed on
the white-silk ice covering the crystalline lake,
as if traveling over some celestial path, and then
was gone.

A few days later, his disciples Lharampa and
Thubten Gyaltsen decided to accompany him to
the Five-peaked Mountain and left as well. I
remained, feeling a bit sad for a few days.

Around this time the faithful old Shabdrung
Lama, who lived in this holy place, said, "Years
of meditation must have developed your clair-
voyant perceptions. Tomorrow I shall go and
try to gather supplies for next year—will I
obtain them or not? Will there be any hindrances or obstacles? Can you make a clear
prediction?"

"What will happen to him?" I thought
[107b]. Resting my mind in evenness, I saw that
he would get plenty of provisions; he would load
two yaks borrowed from his home and from a
neighbor, and return with them over the ice. Just
where one begins to see Tsonying Island, the ice
would crack, and the two yaks would be unable
to continue. At that moment, two patrons on
horseback, coming from Arik to see me, would
lend him their horses, enabling the old lama to
bring his supplies across.

This I saw as clearly as seeing a reflection in
a mirror and I described it to him. When things
happened exactly as I had foretold, he developed great faith in me, declaring, "Whoever can
make a prediction like that is someone in whom I
will take refuge!"

Things like this happened a few times, and
so, some people said, "He doesn't talk about it,
but he has unhindered higher perceptions."

During this period, my young disciple from
Arik, Tenpa Phende, was leaving for central
Tibet to study. I gave him good advice and, as a
farewell-present, sang this song:

Gurus, victorious ones, and spiritual sons,
All of you—
Bless your devoted son.

My son, when going to central Tibet,
Travel on, seeing the guru above your
    head.
Travel on, taking to heart all that I've
    taught you.
Travel on, carrying with you the seven
    riches of the noble ones.
Travel the roads with care.

Son, when you reach central Tibet,
Serve an excellent and authentic master
With both your intentions and actions.

And when studying, hearing and reflecting,
Don't fall under the sway
Of distraction by day, or of sleep by night:
Be diligent, son of my heart.

After thoroughly listening to
And reflecting on the meaning of the
    teachings [108a],
As your home take a cave blessed by the
    great sages,
As friends, take the birds and wild animals;
As for food, rely on begging.

Meditate one-pointedly without
    distraction.
Don't meditate for just a little while:
Practice for as long as you live,
And in mountain solitudes quit your
    illusory body.

I won't forget you; I will keep you in my
    mind.
You, on your part, should pray to me.
I wish that you and I may meet again and
    again.

Be on your way now, making prayers as
    you go.
From now on, until enlightenment,
Whenever we, father and son, wish to
    meet,

Wherever we might be,
May we quickly meet once more!

In response, he asked for my spiritual protection, offering me butter, sweet cheese, a white scarf, and this song of wishing me well:

Merciful lord, sovereign of loving-kindness,
You have treated me as a mother treats
    her beloved child.

Since I, your son, am now going to central
    Tibet,
Bless me with your vajra body,
Bless me with your melodious speech of
    Brahma,
Bless me with your undeluded wisdom
    mind.
Until I reach enlightenment,
Protector, do not forsake me!

Wish-granting jewel,
Fulfilling the needs of this life,
Farewell!

Warrior who conquers our enemies—
Obstacles and circumstances adverse to
    Dharma—
Farewell!

Loving friend who appears to us
When we are wandering helplessly in the
    bardo,
Farewell!

Guide who will lead us through future lives
To the city of liberation,
Farewell!

Protector and refuge,
My only hope in this life, in future lives,
And in the *bardo*,
Farewell [108b]!

Father whose kindness can never be
    repaid,
May I, your son, meet you again and again
Until I attain unsurpassable enlightenment.

Thus having asked for my protection, he did prostrations and circumambulations, and left for central Tibet. There he studied logic for many years. Later, when I met him there, he had become an excellent geshe[54] and rendered me good service.

That year the incomparable Jampa Daö Rinpoche, protector of beings in the dark age, came to Tsonying Island. He was the heart-son of the greatly learned, glorious, and excellent spiritual master Jampa Gelek Gyaltsen. Having received and realized many teachings, Jampa Daö was endowed with great qualities.

He gave the transmission of the graded path known as *The Words of Manjushri*.[55] After completing it, he said, "I hear that you can easily improvise songs—let's see. Sing a few verses for me." I sang:

Lord, authentic precious guru,
Consider me with the great love of your
  wisdom mind.

That I am unhindered in song is untrue,
That I have sung many songs is true.

So I, the singer Tsogdruk Rangdrol,
Will now offer you, my protector,
A song of thanks.

Protector, your visit this year
To Tsonying Island's secluded groves
Is very fortunate.

It was most kind of you
To have given us the *Speech of Manjushri*,
The essence of all Dharma.

To practice as best I can
Is my offering to you:
Grant your blessings
That my mind may mix with Dharma.

Protector, may your life be firm and long
  [109a];
May we hear more of the vast and
  profound Dharma.
May this offering of song please you greatly!

Pleased, he replied, "That was excellent. But from your appearance, it's hard to tell whether you are Buddhist or Bönpo." I replied to his teasing with this song:

The great garuda, dwelling on the peak of
  Mount Meru,
Has a body shaped like a man's,
Yet, like a bird, has full-grown feathers and
  wings.
Neither man nor bird: the garuda.

The turquoise dragon, dwelling in space,
Has a body shaped like a serpent,
Yet, like a bird, it soars in space.
Neither serpent nor bird: the turquoise
  dragon.

I, the yogin who stays in deserted mountains,
Have a body dressed like a Buddhist monk,
Yet, like a Bönpo, I leave my hair long.
Neither Ben nor Bön: I am Nyingma.[56]

When he asked to read some of my earlier songs, I first answered:

Learned possessor of supreme accomplishment,
Authentic precious guru!

I, the renunciate Tsogdruk Rangdrol,
Have not studied the sutras and tantras;
My songs are not fit to be read or heard by
  learned ones.
Yet if those with insight were to hear my
  songs,
They would not find them inconsistent
  with the scriptures.

Since I lack meditation experiences,
My songs are not fit to be heard by
  realized ones [109b].
Yet, if realized beings were to hear my
  songs,
They probably wouldn't mind.

As I have not trained in poetry and
  composition,

My language may be inelegant or incorrect.
Yet I've felt they could benefit
A few dull-witted people like myself,
And that, practicing in accord with them,
Even if no one becomes a *siddha*,
Some might at least gain a better rebirth
And, one day, enlightenment.

Therefore, not sparing my body and speech,
Nor sparing ink and paper,
I wrote these songs with sincere intent.
When you read them, please don't scold
    me.

I gave him most of my songs. Upon reading them he pronounced them excellent. I asked him, "Do you ever sing any songs?" He replied, "I once made a song for a disciple." And he sang this:

*A*h! (*ka ye*) Listen my intelligent friend,
*B*ecause your request comes not merely
    from your lips (*kha*), but rather
*C*omes from your heart, I will gradually
    (*ga le*) explain a few words concerning
*D*harma, as best I (*nga*) can, speaking
    simply.
*E*mpty gossip (*ca co*) and plans to gather
    wealth—
*F*or future rebirths, these can't be of the
    least (*cha tsam*) help.
*G*ive up craving for good tea (*ja*) and other
    nice things, and be content.
*H*olding to the teaching like fish (*nya*) who
    keep to their lake,
*I*nfuse your mind with the words of the
    Tathagata (*ta*), and
*J*ust persevere in practice, which is of
    certain and ultimate (*tha mar*) benefit:
*K*now that your having gained a human
    birth is now (*da lta*) meaningful.
*L*ook upon Dharma as the main thing
    you need when meeting with sickness
    (*na*) and death.
*M*ind, when empty of Dharma which is
    white as the morning star (*pa sangs*),[57]
*N*ever sees an end (*pha mthar*) to
    floundering in the ocean of karma
    and obscuring emotions.

*O*ne may expound the Dharma for hours
    on end, not budging even by a hair (*ba
    spu*), and yet [110a]
*P*oorly benefit oneself, let alone help other
    beings, each of whom was once one's
    mother (*ma*).
*Q*uiet mountain retreats such as Tsari
    (*tsa*)[58]—
*R*emain in them. Not caring about heat
    (*tsha*) or cold, give up evil and do what is
    good.
*S*avages (*dza lang*), beings who are driven
    on by the goads of karma and the
    emotions—
*T*oward these foxes (*wa*) and their like,
    always maintain vivid compassion.
*U*pon the western mountain, the sun of
    the yellow-hat (*zha*) doctrine is about to
    set—
*V*ery soon, the devouring (*za byed*) Lord of
    Death may arrive:
*W*ithout making a fuss (*'a 'ur*), meditate
    on renunciation and the two
    Bodhicittas
*X*periencing them as an inseparable (*ya
    ma bral*) unity.
*Y*earn to help all living beings, even goats
    (*ra*) and sheep,
*Z*ealously, without attachment toward
    some (*la*) and aversion toward others.

*A*voiding behaving like a barbarian
    cannibal (*sha za*)
*A*lways care tenderly for beings of the
    three worlds (*sa gsum*), as though they
    were your own children;
*A*ll of them are being tortured by the three
    intense (*ha cang*) sufferings.[59]
*A*spire to free all beings, once your own
    mothers (*A ma*), from the ocean of
    samsara and incomplete nirvana.
*A*ll together, led by your mother of this
    life, may we
*A*ttain swiftly the inseparable three
    kayas.[60]

Whatever virtue there may be in this,
I dedicate to the swift fulfillment

Of the profound intent
Of all the glorious lamas
Who have departed to the Pure Realms,
And to the spontaneous accomplishment
of their wishes.

May the lives of those who hold the
teaching be firm.
May the sangha of study and practice
increase.
May all beings live long, free from illness;
May they prosper.

All temporary and ultimate aims accomplished,
May all beings again and again break out
in joyous song!

In a happy mood, he talked about other things as
well [110b]. To establish a connection with this
sacred place, he stayed a few more days. As he
was about to leave, I offered him this farewell
song:

𝓜any authentic gurus' lotus feet have
you attended;
𝓜any pith instructions from the sutras
and tantras have you heard and contemplated;
𝓜any lonely mountain retreats have you
practiced in;
𝓜any qualities of experience and realization have been born in your mind.

𝓘 wish that you, incomparable guru, may
travel on in perfect health.
𝓘, a silly man, am also leaving, going to
pleasant solitude.
𝓘 will there practice the holy Dharma, and so
𝓘 ask for your spiritual protection, that my
practice may have no obstacles and
may progress.

He replied:

Meditate in solitude on the development
and completion stages, and on the
Great Perfection:

The knots in your central channel will be
quickly untied.

You express in song the meaning of the
sutras, tantras, and shastras:
Singer Tsogdruk Rangdrol, your songs are
delightful!

Until we meet again, stay well.
Though I am unable to sing songs as
delightful as yours,
Out of my joy came this song of well-
wishing.

He then left to visit his disciples at Gomchok Hermitage.

Later in the year, an uninterrupted stream of
Mongolian pilgrims came every day to the island
from Arik, crossing from the southern and eastern banks of the frozen lake. There were so
many people, it looked as if two black lines had
been drawn across the ice.

That year I received all the provisions I
needed and did not have to leave my retreat
[111a]. One day some valuables came my way.
These were accepted by my ego, which began to
speculate about them. However, Wisdom saw
this, and chastised Ego:

You are the one
Who keeps those seeking liberation
Prisoners in the dungeon of samsara,
Forcing them to endure the punishment
Of various unwanted sufferings.

You—evil corrupter, black heart, enemy—
Earlier, I didn't know how to find you.
Today, I can see you clearly.

For all the errors I've made up to now,
You may take all the honors,
But from now on, you cannot stay.
Go away, get out of my sight.

If you don't leave,
Were I to let you hang around,
I, Wisdom, would be a coward.
So off with you! Now!

Ego replied:

Hu! Hu! Ha! Ha! Ya! Ya!
I'm laughing so hard that I'm choking!

Uncle Wisdom, listen to me:
In which muddy swamp have you been
    lying, dead to the world?
You've never come around to where I am!
How wonderful that you've come today!
Don't be in such a hurry to leave;
Relax, stick around,
Let's have a chat.

Uncle Wisdom, listen here:
In the past many like you
Have made up schemes to expel and to kill
    me.
Over and over again they've tried—
But they haven't gotten me yet!

Don't even bother trying—
Nothing will come of it.

Just take it easy, like you usually do.
A good sound sleep is very good for you!

Don't say mean things
That only hurt my feelings!

Your empty threats
Don't bother me a bit! [111b]

However, unless I tell you
The reasons for this, you'll never
    understand.
Therefore I'll explain a little:
First listen, Wisdom;
We can fight later.

In this world,
Who is more influential than I?

Sentient beings in general,
And more so those who are seeking
    liberation,
Are all my serfs.
When I just say the word, they all jump up
    and come.

Even in pouring rain and pitch-black
    darkness they come,
Nervously twitching—like horses' tails
    eluding the jaws of pursuing packs of
    dogs—
 Leaving their grimy footprints
Across immaculate snow-mountain passes:
All these present-day "gurus"
Obey my every command.

Leaving the Dharma communities,
They wander into the villages.
Giving up discipline, they gather up
    wealth.
Giving up vows, they take up wives:
All these present-day "monks"
Obey my every command.

Losing interest in mountain retreat,
They run around in villages, stirring the
    dogs into a frenzy.
They are even busier than the
    householders!
When they move from one solitude to
    another,
They have so much to pack up, so much to
    carry:
All these present-day "renunciates"
Obey my every command.

Having done a tiny bit of practice,
Having had a few feeble meditation
    experiences
And some small shreds of realization,
They are so thrilled that they brag to
    everyone around.
When they are praised in the slightest
They puff up with pride:
All these present-day "great meditators"
Obey my every command.

At first they seem very devoted.
Yet, even after they've been given the
   deepest Dharma,
If one fails, just once, to give them food
   and drink,
They develop wrong views against the guru:
All these present-day "disciples"
Obey my every command [112a].

With their mouths they pretend to ask for
   teachings.
In their hearts they only long for wealth.
They present offerings and service,
But even if they are granted the most
   profound Dharma,
When they aren't also rewarded with
   delicacies and presents,
They develop wrong views against the
   guru:
All these present-day "patrons"
Obey my every command.

For a few measures of cloth,
For a few ceremonial scarves,
They lavish Secret Mantrayana
   empowerments.
For a few mouthfuls of food,
They trade away profound initiations.
For just a single funeral rite,
They sell out their present and future
   lives:[61]
All these present-day "great teachers"
Obey my every command.

In a high place they suspend
Their piece of wood covered with skin;
They beat it incessantly,
Roaring out loud
Hum! Phet! Jo!
Stop! Strike! Kill! Cut!
And make offerings of meat:
All these present-day "monks" and
   "Chöd-practitioners"
Obey my every command.

Not paying the slightest attention
To karmic consequences,

They sell out the law for money.
They let everything unpleasant
Befall the subjects they rule:
All these present-day kings and ministers
Obey my every command.

Even when they reach old age, they think
   they will live on;
They keep busy raising and tending cattle.
They spread out grain to dry and guard it
   against the birds,
Working as the servants of their children:
All the old men of today
Obey my every command.

Never thinking of their lives to come,
Even when they grow old,
Still they fluff the wool and light the fire,
Nurse their grandchildren, great-grand-
   children and their nephew's nephew,
And work as servants for their daughters-
   in-law:
All the old women of today [112b]
Obey my every command.

Never thinking of the sacred teaching,
Killing men and stealing horses,
Keeping busy running farms and making
   profits,
All the men of today
Obey my every command.

Herding cattle and milking cows,
Fetching water, collecting wood, making
   tea,
Sweeping the floor, spinning wool and
   weaving,
Without even a second's leisure:
All the women of today
Obey my every command.

In this decadent age,
All sentient beings in general,
And in particular Dharma-
   practitioners,
Whenever I command them,
Unwind like a ball of wool

Or wind up like a spindle!
Didn't you know that?

Think carefully, Uncle Wisdom,
Does anyone ever listen to what *you* say?

Isn't it obvious that, these days, no one
    respects you?
Don't you see that everyone venerates *me?*

These days, Dharma practitioners
Say they want *you.*
But in their hearts, they all want *me.*
If they had to choose between you and me,
They would choose me!

Why? Because you don't bring quick
    rewards—like food!
You don't bring drink! You don't bring
    clothes!
You might bring benefit in the next life,
But the future is something far away—
The immediate is a juicy steak!

I am of use to everyone:
Are the tea, the beer, the dinner, good or
    bad?
Are the favors big or small?
Are the offerings lavish or niggardly?

All these I acknowledge, and accordingly,
I grant or withold immediate gratification.
I handily oblige both high and low.

Dharma practitioners are the servants
    [113a],
I am the master: didn't you know that?

Though a few, desiring liberation,
Break my commands and join your side,
As soon as I unleash the five poisons,
They become like lice caught between
    one's nails.

How many have ever reached the city of
    liberation?
They are as rare as stars in daytime.

Once upon a time, by a stroke of good
    luck,
A few did escape—but, in this decadent
    age,
If I allow even one single person
To reach the higher states of existence,
Let alone reach liberation,
Then my name isn't "Ego."

In this decadent age
It is I who preside
Over the happiness and suffering of beings
    in general,
And in particular over the lamas, *ngakpas,*
Chöd-practitioners, renunciates, and
    meditators.

These days, in this dark age,
My activity prospers:
From the lamas and rulers
To the most humble beggars,
All are my retinue, my servants.
Who is greater than me?
Wisdom, tell me!

Wisdom replied:

Old tyrant, destroyer of the Dharma,
    listen!
What do I care about your arrogant
    bluster?
I am stronger than you!
Though you've heard just the sound of my
    name,
You are already faint with terror,
    powerless.
When I wield the spear of emptiness
And strike, where will you run off to?

I told you to leave, but you keep hanging
    on,
And now you start raising your voice!
If I don't reduce you to dust this instant
    [113b],
Wisdom might as well be dead.
Do you understand this, Ego, malicious
    schemer?

Ego replied:

> Sure . . . yeah, yeah . . . sure!
> We'll soon find out
> Who is stronger.
>
> Before, you took away some of my
>   servants,
> So I came in search of you many times,
> But I couldn't find you.
> Now I no longer need to look for you!
> I am so very glad that you came!
>
> When I rain down, without letup, the
>   weapons
> Of the eight worldly concerns,
> You'll have no chance to escape.
>
> I have known plenty like you in the past:
> Not one has escaped me.
> If I were now to let you go,
> I might as well be dead! [62]

As Ego finished boasting, Wisdom arose and wielded the long spear of the view. Terrified, old tyrant Ego ran off and disappeared from sight.

I made this up for my own amusement, and for the good of myself and others.

In the beginning of the first month, Pema Rangdrol, my first disciple and heart-son, who possessed a special karma because of his practice in previous lives, came to see me with some of his disciples. He offered me a white scarf and inquired about my health:

> Embodiment of the Buddhas of the three
>   times,
> Sole protector of all beings,
> Precious lama endowed with all the
>   supreme marks,
> Is your rupakaya well?

Melodiously, I sang in reply [114a]:

> I am not unwell; I am well.
> In the space of dharmakaya, the rupakaya
>   is well.
> Worthy son of fortunate karma,
> Did your journey go well?

He answered:

> By the grace of the authentic guru,
> From the beginning of the journey to the
>   end,
> We did not suffer in body or mind;
> Rather, happiness has followed happiness.

Afterward we had a long talk about Dharma. The next day they offered some gold and silver, and insisted I give them empowerments, transmissions, and instruction, for their benefit.

Accommodating their wishes, that same day I gave them the transmission and explanation on the *Mind Training on Cutting All Ties of Attachment*.[63] As they had earlier received many elaborate empowerments, I considered that sufficient. I gave them the essential samadhi-empowerment and the empowerment of the display of awareness. Afterward I gave transmissions and instructions on the luminous Great Perfection and on the *Teachings of the Kadampa Spiritual Sons*.

I sustained them all with food, clothes, and Dharma. That year I stayed on the summit of the hill; my close son, Pema Rangdrol, stayed where I usually lived, and the other eight retreatants each occupied a cave. They all practiced with energy and determination, and developed boundless devotion, seeing the guru as the Buddha himself. Their gross poisons and defilements subsided, while their body, speech, and mind became serene, controlled, and in harmony with the teachings.

I stayed alone, maintaining silence. My principal practice was to remain in evenness free from concepts. In between sessions, I sang many songs for my own and others' benefit [114b].

In the summer we built a tiny shrine on the peak of Tsonying Island, for our own merit and purification and for that of others, as well as for the welfare of the Dharma and living creatures. Whatever work needed to be done, such as fetching stones, was done by the great son Pema Rangdrol and the other retreatants.

When the temple was finished, a statue of the Great Compassionate One with a thousand arms and a thousand eyes was placed inside. On his right was placed a statue of Mahadeva, the lord of this place, and on his left a statue of the goddess Tsomen Trishok Gyalmo. Behind these three were placed the twelve volumes of the Prajnaparamita, sole mother of the Victorious Ones of the three times.

The disciples and Dharma friends offered whatever they had—ritual implements, garments for the statues, and ceremonial scarves. A great consecration feast with prayers and dedications was held. Travelers say that this shrine still stands to this day.[64]

That year, I felt quite at ease and untroubled; my awareness became very clear. We had many talks about the sacred Dharma, through which my close son Pema Rangdrol and all those assembled there developed a strong aspiration for enlightenment, and a firm, unchanging confidence in the teachings of sutra and tantra, and of the old and new translations. They developed a pure, unbiased perception of all practitioners of the Dharma. One day those assembled there requested a song. I came up with this:

Contemplating the kindness
Of the matchless old father, the King of
    Dharma [115a],
The devoted son bows down.

Whatever experiences and realization have
    arisen
In the mind-stream of this yogin—
Bringing them to my throat I will voice
    them a little.

Praying unceasingly to the gracious lama,
I have received his blessing in my mind-
    stream.

Considering again and again samsara's
    defects,
I feel revulsion for society, riches, and food.

Meditating on all creatures as my kind
    parents,
I have developed the wish to attain enlight-
    enment,
While considering others dearer than
    myself.

Preserving the nakedness of unobstructed
    awareness-void,
I have given rise to unmistaken meditation
    experiences and realization.

Practicing Thögal, the special teaching of
    the Great Perfection,
I have discovered that appearances *are* the
    Akanishtha heaven.

I, the yogin who belongs to the lineage of
    the Lake-born Vajra,[65]
Have sung a song of experience and
    realization.
All of you heart-friends who keep pure
    samaya,
If you sing, sing a song like this.

In this sacred solitude, The Heart of the
    Lake,
He who is singing, with a dragon's
    thunder,
Songs of experience and realization,
Seems to be just this yogin, Tsogdruk
    Rangdrol!
Through this merit may all beings attain
    Buddhahood!

Everyone was pleased. Another day I took the collection of my written songs and went to a meadow. Sitting there on my own, I sang them with some pleasant melodies. Suddenly, I heard from the sky a voice exclaiming, "Excellent!" Filled with joy, I thought, "Whoever hears these songs will benefit from them—gods, ghosts, or humans" [115b].

One night I dreamed that a youth of about sixteen with a rose-white complexion appeared to me and said he was the tulku of Jetsun Kalden Gyatso.[66] His countenance was so noble that one never tired of looking at him. He was wearing the robes of a monk and was on his own, without any retinue, carrying only a staff.

I met him in a delightful meadow. When I asked where he was going, he replied he was on his way to meditate in solitude. I thought, "This present incarnation must be in mountain retreat—how kind and wonderful for all! It's good that I met him." Then we both went on our way.

The day after this dream, I recalled the kindness of the first Jetsun Kalden Gyatso and how he had lit the lamp of the Buddha's teaching in the Rekong district, which inspired this song:

> The light-rays of your omniscience
>   pervade all things,
> The warmth of your kindness nurtures all
>   beings:
> Holy sun of good fortune,
> Shine upon me from the sky of the
>   absolute expanse!
>
> In the dark, barbaric valley of Rekong,
> You set alight the torch of the holy teaching,
> So that it shone even brighter
> Than in the holy land of India.
> Miraculous!
>
> Thus, the sun, moon, and stars
> Of the eighteen retreats and other
>   practice-centers
> Appeared across the sky of Rekong,
> Spreading the light of bliss and
>   happiness—
> Miraculous!
>
> On the brocade of the pure land,
> With its caves and mountains,
> Decorated with the designs of sacred places
>   of accomplishment,
> The king- and minister-meditators take
>   their pleasure [116a],

> Drinking the nectar of the holy teachings.
> Miraculous!
>
> The barbaric inhabitants, like wild horses,
> Were well-trained with the reins of the
>   holy teachings.
> They renounced the mad pranks of
>   nonvirtue
> And entered the path of certain liberation.
> Miraculous!
>
> You made available for all
> The wish-granting treasury of your spiri-
>   tual songs,
> Formed on the island in the ocean of your
>   learning,
> And owned by the naga king of your
>   intelligence.
> Miraculous!
>
> From now until we attain enlightenment,
> With love, as a mother for her only child,
> Care for all the disciples of Tibet,
> Particularly for all your followers in
>   Rekong.
>
> O protector—
> By the merit of offering my practice
> In emulation of your life,
> Offering with the hands of my mind
> Something which is merely a droplet
> Compared to the vast ocean of your
>   perfect life,
> May I never be separated from you
> Throughout all of my lives.

One summer day, in a meadow that faced north, I gave extensive explanations on the necessity of first developing faith, respect, and pure vision regarding all teachings and individuals, and then practicing the teaching for which one feels a particular affinity. In the end, I sang this spontaneous song:

In the snow ranges of Tibet,
Owing to the kindness of sublime beings of
    the past,
Many profound teachings were taught.

These days most practitioners
Hold the various teachings to be
    contradictory
Like heat and cold.
They praise some teachings and disparage
    others.

Some holy beings have said that
Madhyamika, Mahamudra, and
    Mahasandhi
Are like sugar, molasses, and honey:
One is as good as the other [116b].
For this reason, I have listened to
And reflected on all of them without
    partiality.

Sectarian practitioners with aversion and
    attachment,
Please don't reprimand me.

When the immaculate white snow
    mountain
Of Madhyamika, Mahamudra, and
    Mahasandhi
Is bathed in the sunlight of pure
    perception,
The stream of blessings will certainly flow.

After I had sung this, all the disciples there developed unbiased pure perception regarding all
teachings and individual practitioners.

One day in autumn, on seeing a layer of
snow that had settled on a mountain peak, I
recalled death and impermanence, and sang this
to myself:

That distant mountain peak
Has now been covered in white snow.
Hey there, Tsogdruk Rangdrol!
Look at the hair on your old grey head!

The blue gentian blossomed;
It now has withered.

Hey there, Tsogdruk Rangdrol!
Look at your own face!

The waterfowl, one by one, have left;
Now the shores of the lake are deserted.
Hey there, Tsogdruk Rangdrol!
Look what's happened to your friends!

What was once a rising sun
Is already setting behind the mountain.
Hey there, Tsogdruk Rangdrol!
Look how old you've grown!

Having sung this, I persevered in my practice.

On the twenty-fifth day of the tenth month,[67]
at night, I lit a butter-lamp, which burned brightly.
After praying to the precious Lord Lama
Tsongkhapa, I went to sleep. I dreamed of a long
crystal staircase on a mountain made from all
kinds of precious stones [117a]. I ascended and,
reaching the top, found myself on a level surface
decorated with sweet smelling flowers. In the
middle of the meadow stood a tent of blue brocade with beautiful designs, held with tent ropes
made from five-colored silks tied to gold and
silver pegs.

Inside was a splendid lofty throne upon which
were piled soft silken cushions. On it sat a lama
of resplendent dignity. One never tired of looking at him, and the mere sight of his face put an
end to mind's delusions.

Surrounded by an innumerable retinue of
noble ones, he was giving the transmission of the
Condensed Meaning of the Graded Path.[68] I sat down
in the assembly, and after having listened to all of
it, I asked if I could borrow the book. "You don't
need to return it, just keep it," he told me. So I
held the book close to my chest and went outside, transported with joy.

Outside, I was able to see throughout the
Snow Land of Tibet and lingered a while, enjoying the view. The staircase leading down seemed
too steep to descend. Someone to my left said,
"Those who have been on this mountain need
not descend by the staircase: they can fly!"

Using my shawl as wings I flew off into the
sky and, while descending, could see all the districts of Tibet.

Inspired by the account of this dream, my close spiritual son, Rigdzin Dawa, offered a golden mandala [117b] and, together with all my worthy disciples, asked for a teaching in verse on the gradual path that is concise, easy to comprehend, and easy to practice in all circumstances. I composed an exposition of the graded path called *Torch That Illuminates the Graded Path.*[69] I gave the transmission and advised them to meditate on it a little every day. They practiced it much to their benefit.

On a certain occasion, I had a vision of the precious lord Manjushri. Light shone forth from his heart and entered mine. I gradually merged into a state of bliss, clarity, and nonthought.

At the very moment it occurred to me to ask for some clarifications on the view, Manjushri melted into light and dissolved into my heart. I then fell asleep and dreamed that I held in my hand a glowing blue vessel made of precious stone. From within the vessel flowed golden liquor, which three people drank. After that came much curd, which many people drank. So I thought: "This seems to be a wish-fulfilling vessel. I must take it where there are many poor people."

One day on the lake shore, I looked into the water from the top of a rock and saw, at the base of each rock, a great many creatures, large and small. Realizing that at every rock's base and from the surface to bottom of the whole lake there lived a multitude of creatures, I thought, "Oh, how sad—there must be a way to do something helpful for their future!" [118a].

I went back, ground up all the blessed relics given to me by Abhe Rinpoche and others, and dissolved them in water. Then, wading into the lake all around the island, I poured the relics into the lake, while making deep prayers.

When I was living at Tsonying, I noticed an eagle[70] that, each spring day, caught three or four of the thousands of baby waterfowl that couldn't fly yet. The eagle tore out and devoured

their hearts while they were still alive. Feeling intense pity, each year during those two spring months, I tried to protect the small waterfowl from the eagle. They soon understood that I was protecting them and would come and gather near me on the shore of the island. Whenever the eagle approached, they all cried out miserably.

One day I ran after the eagle wielding a slingshot; when the eagle saw me it faltered and fell into the water. It lay there flapping in the water, exhausted, and it began to sink, looking right at me. I felt sorry for it, hauled it out of the water, and put it on the shore. When it had dried a little, I tied the slingshot around its neck and scolded it, saying, "When you're killing little birds you're quite brave, aren't you?" I tapped it several times on its beak and claws with a twig, and just left it there for a while, then freed it [118b]. It didn't come back for some time.

One day the eagle came back and caught a fledgling. I rushed after it and, when it landed on a boulder, I hit it with a stone from my slingshot, almost killing it. It flew off, leaving the baby bird sprawled on its back. I thought the little bird's heart had already been torn out, but when I picked it up, I saw it had just lost consciousness out of fear. Upon reviving, it looked at me and then scampered back into the water.

Protecting them in this manner during those two years, I saved several thousand small birds. When they could fly, I used to make this prayer:

> Like these fledglings
> That now can fly about happily,
> Free from fear of the eagle,
> May all beings be freed from all fears
> And be established in happiness.

I told the other retreatants staying in this sacred island to protect the small birds as I had done; later I heard they did so and saved many lives. Wherever I stayed, I would protect fledglings from birds of prey and keep small insects from killing each other. I would always tell others: "Feeling compassion for all suffering beings, I protect their lives in whatever way I can [119a]. Each time I do so, I make a prayer to be able to perform the splendid acts of the Bodhisattvas, the spiritual sons of the Victorious Ones. Through the connection created by such prayers, my strength of mind grew, and now I can benefit many beings. All of you, my disciples, should also make prayers when you perform even the slightest altruistic action; later you will be able to benefit all beings."

Around this time the lake began to freeze once more. All my other provisions were exhausted, and I was eating only *tsampa*. One morning I thought to myself, "This excellent *tsampa!* Even when I have no other provisions, it's enough in itself." I sang this song as it came to mind:

The only guru I require
Is the King of Dharma, Ngakyi Wangpo.

The only friend that I require
Is Pema Shepai Dorje.[71]

The only student I require
Is the renunciate Rigdzin Dawa.

The only solitude that I require
Is Tsonying Mahadeva.

The only clothing I require
Is the soft wool of sheep.

The only food I require
Is fine, fresh, white *tsampa*.

This sweet song of the six contentments
Was sung by Tsogdruk Rangdrol!

That year the retreatants were able to practice well, with few needs and a sense of contentment. When the lake froze over again, some new retreatants came, and patrons I had known before came to visit, along with many new ones [119b]. I foresaw that, with so many people in such a small area, I might become susceptible to distraction, and my practice might not progress.

I felt inclined to go to a more remote, desolate place where there was no living creature to be found, neither men nor dogs. After some thought I decided to go to towering Mount Machen, the king of white snow mountains, the most secluded place of all. I made up my mind that I would leave when summer came.

When I told my disciples and patrons of my plans, my close spiritual son Pema Rangdrol and the other disciples from my native region said, "When we left home to come here, the local lamas, your mother, friends, and relatives—everyone—insisted that we invite you to return home, and we promised to do our best. Your mother and all these people rely on you. Just one visit would fulfill their wishes. Isn't it said that pleasing others is also Dharma?"

The disciples and patrons around the Blue Lake argued there was no place more quiet than Tsonying, so I should continue to stay where I was. I paid them no heed, and confirmed my irrevocable decision to go. My spiritual son Pema Rangdrol then said, "If you won't go home and must go to Mount Machen, at least, please, answer all the letters I've brought." I promised to do so.

My old mother had sent a message: "Son, seven years have passed during which I have been constantly waiting for you to return at least once, but you have not come [120a]. I have often been sick; I would be very sad to die without seeing you. This year you *must* come." There was also a letter from her saying:

You abandoned your homeland
And left behind your family.
You served at the feet of the Dharma King
And received his profound instructions.
You have stayed alone in the wilderness,
    without companions.
Son, you who practice one-pointedly,
Here is a message
From the mother who gave you life:

Son, hearing you are well, I am overjoyed.
The illusory body of your mother
Has felt much sickness and pain.
I am hanging on; I'm just not dead yet.

Even though I haven't the good fortune
To be with you for a lifetime,
Come and let me see you just once more.

I had hoped that we—mother and son—
Could stay together in our homeland until
    I die.
I was pleased to think that in my hour of
    need,
When ill, stricken by old age, and at the
    time of death,
I would have a son unlike others' sons.

Now that I'm old, just to get up,
Sit down, or move at all is difficult.
With only meager food and drink
My health has worsened.

Your mother has no soft, warm clothes:
I'm dressed in ragged clothing.
Many years have passed since you have left
    me;
How can you bear to stay away like this?

When I hear the blue cuckoo, the king of
    birds,
Or see someone practicing Dharma like
    you,
I think of you, and tears flow from my eyes.
Sometimes I can't even sleep at night.

Even though in my previous letters
I've asked you many times to come,
You haven't done so.

Have you become more dull-witted than a
    calf?
When animal mothers call their young,
The young come, instantly! [120b]

Consider the kindness
With which I have cared for you,
And, by all means, come to see me this
    year.

Once we've met, you may go wherever
    you please:
I, your own mother, promise this.

In the past, did I ever once create a single
    obstacle
For your practice of the Dharma?

Now that I am just about to meet with
    death,
Other than meeting you again,
What other wish could I have?

I, your aged mother,
Have grown old; I'm close to death.
Son, if, out of compassion,
You don't pay me even one visit,
All your meditation on kindness and
    compassion toward all beings
Will have been for naught.

As a result of this letter I am sending you,
    son,
May we swiftly meet once more.
May disease, famine, and strife in this
    region subside,
And may virtue, excellence, and
    abundance
Increase like the waxing moon.

In reply I wrote this:

Dear old mother, kinder than any other
    mother I know of,
I have received your letter
And am pleased to hear your illusory body
    is sound.

While I, your son, have been practicing the
    Dharma,
Certainly, you've never caused me the
    slightest obstacle;
Rather, you have helped me.

By the grace of the guru and the Three
    Jewels
My illusory body is well, too,
And my meditation experiences have
    progressed.

That you summoned me before and I
    didn't come

Should not upset you.
As people say, "There's not much
    difference
Between reading in a letter about
    someone's well-being
And meeting him in person."
Before, I didn't come, but I will come,
    soon.

Several years may pass when an only son
Is off performing exorcisms and village
    ceremonies in distant places,
Simply to earn enough to feed his family
    [121a],
Yet the parents he leaves behind don't
    mind.

So why should you feel so unhappy,
    Mother,
That your son has been away all these
    years,
Staying in distant places,
In solitary mountain retreats,
To accomplish your lasting happiness and
    enlightenment?

There might be many children who benefit
Their parents in this life with food, clothes,
    and wealth.
Yet how many parents have children
    staying in the mountains,
Practicing the holy Dharma for the benefit
    of their parents' future lives?

There are difficult children, always
    opposed to their parents,
Who live nearby them all their lives,
    bringing their parents more harm than
    help.
And there are loving children who do
    bring benefit,
Even though they live far away—
Isn't this so? Think about it.

We shall meet again in this life;
Even if we don't, whatever practice I
    undertake
I shall dedicate it to you, Mother.

I pray that, later, we will meet again in the
    Joyful Pure Land
And stay there together, never parting.

I sent this with some relics and a small present. A
letter from the *ngakpas* of Shohong also urged me
to revisit my homeland:

Lama, using the sharp hook of
    compassion,
You bring onto the path of liberation
The mad, rampaging elephant-disciples,
    who,
Intoxicated with the wine of karma and
    emotions,
Are lost in the jungle of samsara [121b].
Compassionate One,
Heed the fierce and desperate cry of our
    community of *ngakpas!*

Weighed down by the heavy load of the
    three sufferings,
Tormented by the burning thirst of the
    three poisons,
Wandering constantly over the arid plains
    of samsara,
Deprived of the food, riches, and clothing
    of liberation,
Crying out with hatred and attachment,
Suffering from multiple afflictions in this
    house of samsara,
All of us impoverished ones
Are longing for the coming of a guide like
    you.

Don't linger on golden Tsonying Island,
But, sailing on the boat of compassion,
    come quickly!
Bring with you the precious gold of
    transmission and realization!
With fierce lamentations, we pray over and
    over again.

Blinded by the cataract of ignorance,
We can't see the pure path;
Driven on by the winds of evil karma
We approach the precipice of the three
    lower realms.

If you do not seize us with your
  compassion, we are lost.
How can you forsake us?

In this boundless ocean of samsara,
We are carried away by the great raging
  waves of karma and kleshas;
If you don't save us from being devoured
  by the sea monster of suffering,
Will you not belie your claim to cherish us?

This lotus garden of your brothers and
  sisters who keep pure *samaya*
Is now fresh, blossoming with hundreds of
  petals.
But unless you, the precious bee, now
  come to visit it,
Once the flowers have been withered by
  the morning frosts of sickness and
  death,
It will be too late!

O king of swans, protector of beings in this
  life and the next,
It is now time for you to come quickly
To the center of the milk-lake of *ngakpas*
And sing the sweet song of the Mahayana.

On this auspicious day of the waxing
  moon,
With an immaculate blue-green silken
  scarf [122a]
We present this letter, a pleasant soft
  meadow
Where the deer of your eyes might frolic
  for an instant.

I wrote in reply:

I bow down at the feet of the Dharma King,
My refuge and protector:
Bestow all excellence upon these friends
And relatives, in this and future lives.

All you *ngakpas* with pure *samaya*
Whom I have known since we were young,
Listen to the words of your friend,
  Tsogdruk Rangdrol:

Not having perfected myself, how can I
  perfect others?
If we stay together, you will see my faults
  and your faith will grow dim,
So there is little reason for us to meet.
The best for all of us is that I engage in
  practice.

Even if we were to meet,
I have nothing more to tell you
Than the instructions I have given you
  before.

Your practicing in accord with these
Will bring me great joy,
And bring you certain contentment and
  bliss.

I pray that, throughout all of our lives,
Whenever we want to meet,
Wherever that might be,
We may meet like a loving mother and her
  child.

When I attain perfect Buddhahood,
May all of you become my first
  disciples.
Until then, throughout all of my lives,
May I be your spiritual guide.

I sent this with a small gift. I also replied in
verse to all those who had written: lamas, relatives, and friends from home. I have not included
them all here, as there are too many, but one can
find them in my *Collected Songs* [122b].

While I was writing these replies, my relative and disciple Ngawang Tashi thought that
perhaps if he tried asking me one more time, I
might agree to go home. Putting into verse all
the reasons why I should visit my homeland, he
said:

Vidyadhara Tsogdruk Rangdrol,
Who, forsaking all activities of this life,
Have secluded yourself in the solitude of
  Tsonying Island,
Here is a request to you from your devoted
  son:

Everyone in our region, young and old,
Headed by your mother and relatives,
Held a meeting and decided
That I should be sent to invite you.

They said that, though last year
You declined their insistent requests,
This year whatever happens, you should
    come.

By now, everyone must be saying:

"The envoy we sent to invite the lama,
 Might have died on the way,
 Or gone off on pilgrimage,
 Or left for Mongolia to do business—
We must find out."

"Maybe he is so happy staying with the
    lama
 That he has forgotten all about us.
 Far from inviting the lama,
 He might even entreat him to stay where
    he is.
 Or maybe the envoy is sick.
 He is not coming—what happened?"

They must be imagining all kinds of
    possibilities,
So please, come home!
Particularly, your dear mother
Has gone without seeing you for seven
    years.
The sun of her life is about to set:
Your old mother is close to death.

She may be happy in future lives,
But she yearns to see you, now, in this
    one.
You ought to visit her once,
Since it would be best if she could be
    happy
Both in this and in future lives.
So please, come home! [123a].

If remote mountains please you,
We have most pleasant mountain
    hermitages,

Free of bustle and diversions.
So please, come home!

If remote forests please you,
We have delightful forest groves
Abundant with nourishing wild fruit,
As you well know,
So please, come home!

All the hermitages nearby
Need to be blessed.
So please, come home!

Your homeland is a wild land
Where beings need to be trained,
So care for us; don't dismiss us from your
    heart!

If you care, show it now,
When everyone is awaiting your arrival.
Please, come home!

No one here creates obstacles to Dharma
    practice.
Emulating your example,
Many practitioners have given up all con-
    cern for this life
And live in secluded mountain hermitages.
So please, come home!

By the power of my sincerity,
May I be able to bring the guru home
And through the guru's coming,
May the whole region experience joy and
    well-being.

May the rain of Dharma fall ceaselessly
On the field of beings who need to be
    transformed.
Practicing according to your instructions,
May all beings attain Buddhahood.

In response to his eager request, I promised to
stay no more than a year in the snows of Machen
and then come home. That comforted him somewhat [123b].

    A faithful patron from the Shabdrung com-
munity told me, "You haven't been home for

many years. Won't your mother think her son is sick or dead, and that people are keeping it a secret?" I answered, "It doesn't really matter if I get sick and die," and I sang this song on the yogin's being ill and being cremated:

> I pray with respect at the feet
> Of the one who has perfected all qualities,
> Dharma King Ngakyi Wangpo:
> Bless me with death—death to
>   ego-clinging.
>
> I, the renunciate Tsogdruk Rangdrol,
> Am a yogin of the Great Perfection.
> Not only sickness, but even death is fine
>   with me.
>
> Listen, I shall tell you all
> About my sickness, death, and cremation.
>
> The aggregate body stemming from cling-
>   ing to "ego"
> Caught the sickness of the lama's blessing
> And was possessed by the demon of
>   unchanging awareness.
> When the agonizing pain of spiritual
>   experience
> And realization struck me down,
> Spiritual songs escaped from my mouth
>   like moans.
> Unable to eat the food of the eight worldly
>   concerns,
> I collapsed on the bed of the sublime
>   Dzogchen teaching.
>
> Not just sickness, but even death is fine
>   with me:
> The demon of natural awareness
> Caught me with the lasso of unwavering
>   samadhi.
> He murdered clinging to the skandhas as
>   real,
> With the weapon of perfect view:
> From the extremities escaped the bodily
>   warmth of hatred;
> From the nose and mouth came the water
>   of attachment;
> The head of ignorance fell forward;

> The limbs of pride collapsed;
> The breathing of jealousy came to an end,
> And I died in the expanse of the unborn
>   dharmakaya.
>
> Not just death, but even cremation is fine
>   with me [124a]:
> The helpers "freed as they arise"
> Built the funeral pyre of the dharmadhatu.
> The firewood of firm *shamatha* was arrayed
> Upon the even plain of pristine simplicity.
> The cremation fire—the five wisdoms—
> Consumed the corpse of ignorance and the
>   other poisons.
> Then the remains were scattered on the
>   ground of the unborn
> And buried in the charnel ground of
>   Samantabhadra.

My song greatly increased his faith. I then gave to Dechen Garwang Tsel, "Powerful Dance of Great Bliss," a staff and a *yantra* that liberates by wearing, and advised him to concentrate on practice in a hermitage near Gomeh. He became a snow lion-like meditator, who, as result of his practice, was able to benefit the Dharma and sentient beings.

I took care of the hermits from Dzogeh—Kunzang Gyurme and Kunzang Rangdrol, Rabjampa Kunga Gyaltsen, Gelong Tendar, the monk from Mangneh, and others—nine practitioners altogether—supplying them with good food and clothing so that they could fly the victory banner of practice on Tsonying Island.

As my representative, I sent back the accomplished yogin Pema Rangdrol with this letter to all the devotees, disciples, and householders in Rekong:

> I bow down to the Dharma King, my
>   refuge and protector:
> Look with compassion on me and those
>   connected with me.
>
> All you devoted fellow countrymen with
>   faith in me
> Should venerate this supreme son of mine,
> Pema Rangdrol, as myself [124b].

Until we meet again, read the songs he will
    bring you
And practice accordingly.
Even if you met me in person,
I would have nothing more to say;
And if I die, I have no further testament.

Now I shall go to whichever place will
    benefit my practice.
My friends, if you give up concern with this
    life
And follow my example, you will attain
    lasting happiness.

I then told Pema Rangdrol: "These songs
are not just fancies that came into my mind.
They are based on the writings of our spiritual
forefathers, such as the *Teachings of the Kadampas,
Father and Sons* (Atisha and his heart-sons), which
are themselves based on the teachings of the
Victorious Ones; on the *Mani Kahbum* of Songtsen
Gampo, the incarnation of the Great Compassionate One; the *Hundred Thousand Songs* of
Milarepa; the *Elegant Sayings* of Jamyang Sakya
Pandita; the *Gradual Path* of Je Rinpoche; the
songs of the omniscient Longchenpa; and the
songs of Jetsun Kalden Gyatso and others. If an
intelligent fellow like you follows the example of
these songs and shares them with others, they
will inspire faithful men and women to practice
the Dharma."

I gave him the manuscript, containing a
thousand songs, and extensive advice on both
immediate and ultimate matters. Just before my
disciples departed, I expressed in this song my
aspiration to meet them again in this and future
lives [125a]:

Wish-fulfilling gem, supreme ornament of
    my crown,
Gracious father guru, I bow down at your
    feet.

May auspiciousness prevail wherever we,
    teacher and disciples, go.
May we be blessed to accomplish all our
    aspirations.

Following sublime gurus,
Accompanied by sublime companions,
I listened to and meditated in accord with
    the sublime teachings,
After which I practiced in sublime places.

Hearing of this you felt faith, devotion,
And a deep urge to come here.
Although many tried to stop you,
You paid them no heed,
Aware that one should heed only Dharma.

Last year you came here and have stayed
    until now.
I, an ordinary man, have taught you
Whatever I know of the holy Dharma,
And you have practiced it all year.
Even if we part now, we have been
    fortunate.

A lifetime is short and strewn with hazards
    and obstacles.
Nobody knows how long it will endure:
Give up thoughts of this life!
Sons, make the length of your practice
Equal the length of your life;
Abide in mountain solitudes, like a wild
    deer.

May your life be free of obstacles;
I pray that we, master and disciples,
May meet again in this life.
Even if we do not meet again,
I pray that we meet for certain in the next.

May we go to Buddhafields never visited
    before,
May we behold Buddhas never seen before,
May we hear sublime Dharmas never
    heard before,
May we see sights never seen before.
May you all have a safe journey [125b].

When leaving for whichever solitude I
    please,
I make a pure prayer that we meet again
In the auspicious harmony of Dharma.

In response to this song, my close spiritual son Pema Rangdrol said:

Your body performs only excellent actions,
Your speech voices clear expositions of the
    Dharma,
Your mind knows no partiality, no
    attachment or hatred.
Father, source of excellence, think of me:

When I was constantly distracted by the
    activities of this life,
You warned me of life's impermanence
    and of the shortcomings of samsara,
And, hearing this, I gave up wealth, food,
    and society.

In the flower-strewn meadow of Tseshung,
I tasted the nectar of the Dharma King's
    words,
And stayed at your feet, my protector, for
    one year.

At this time, following the command of our
    spiritual father and of you, his heart-
    son,
I went to Tashikhyil, in my homeland,
    Rekong.

You told me to raise the victory banner of
    accomplishment,
And I practiced there three years and ten
    months.
For my own sake, I offered my sincere
    practice;
For the sake of others,
I established the faithful in virtuous ways.

During that time,
I was grieved by the death of the Dharma
    King,
And deeply longed to see you, my protec-
    tor.

Last year I came here to meet you,
And joy arose in me—
As in a meeting of mother and son.

For one year I have been with you, like
    your shadow,
And received the vast and profound
    instructions
That ripen and free:
This year has been very fortunate for me.

Furthermore, you have given us so many
    songs
Enabling us to attain higher rebirths and
    liberation.
Wondrous!

I shall now go back to Rekong [126a];
Father guru, may you stay in good health.
I, your son,
The monks, disciples, friends and relatives,
And everyone in your homeland who relies
    on you,
All request that you never leave us without
    your love.

Other than you, we have no source of
    hope.
I pray that it won't be long before we once
    more behold your face.
May these prayers be fulfilled!

After he had offered this, with tears pouring down his cheeks and with the hairs on his body standing on end, backing away respectfully in a state of faith, praying that in our many lives we would not separate, he left with a heavy heart.

In the wake of this, I felt an intense weariness with samsara stronger than before, and a determination to practice stronger than ever; I didn't want to stay on any longer, but felt a strong urge to go deeper into solitude.

One day, while I was circumambulating Tsonying Island, I recalled earlier gatherings with the Dharma King, his queen, their sons and ministers, and my Dharma brothers, and the conversations we used to have about spiritual and temporal matters. I thought how wonderful it would be if the lama were still alive, and how much I longed to see him. Recalling him, my mind filled with his presence. I felt an infinitely strong sadness, and, in tears, I sang this song of the six remembrances of the guru:

South of mighty Mount Meru,
In the center is the southern continent,
    Jambudvipa;
In its northern region is Tibet, the Land of
    Snows.

On this vast plateau [126b],
In a valley meadow, covered with flowers,
In a tent white as a snow peak,
On a throne covered with soft and
    beautiful cushions,
Presiding over a varied gathering of
    subjects and students,
Sits the precious unequaled lord.
Merely to lay one's eyes upon him
Makes happiness and joy well up:
Whoever comes before him
Cannot bear to part from him.

The image of my father, the Dharma
    King,
Comes to my mind. The clear way he
    addressed
The excellent assemblies of silent listeners
Comes to mind. Kinder than other fathers,
Ngawang Wang—how wonderful if he
    were here now!
Although I have little devotion, I long to
    see him.
Although so far apart, I long to be with
    him again.

Thinking again and again, I remember my
    old father,
The Dharma King, his queen, and his
    court:
The image of the Mother Abhe comes to
    my mind.
To the left of the Dharma King, on a pile
    of exquisite soft cushions,

With a graceful form one never tired of
    looking at,
A daughter of the gods descended to the
    human realm—
The sweet way she used to speak to her
    retinue comes to mind.
Abhe, kinder than any mother—how
    wonderful if she were here now!
Although my affection is inadequate, I long
    to see her.
Although the road is hard to travel, I long
    to be with her again.

Thinking again and again, I remember my
    old father,
The Dharma King, his queen, and his court:
I remember the great beings who came
    from all directions,
And also those like me [127a]—
That assembly of the faithful whom you
    accepted with your great loving heart.
With the Dharma of the great Secret
    Vajrayana
And the four empowerments, you ripened
    our mind-streams.
The memory of those occasions comes to
    mind.
These four initiations of the Adamantine
    Vehicle:
How wonderful if those empowerments
    were to be given now!
Although I have done but small service, I
    long to receive them.
Although I have no offerings, I long to
    receive them.

Thinking again and again, I remember my
    old father,
The Dharma King, his queen, and his
    court.
I think of the Secret Mantrayana which
    liberates the mind-stream:
Whoever hears it won't fall into the lower
    realms;
Whoever meditates on it correctly won't
    wander in samsara.[72]
It is rare to hear even one word of such
    teachings, even in a hundred aeons.

His teachings on the development and
completion stages, and the Great
Perfection,
And the way he gave profound instructions
come to my mind.
This Dharma of development, completion
and Great Perfection,
How wonderful if it were being taught
now!
Although my intelligence is small, I long to
hear it.
Although my diligence is feeble, I long to
practice it.

Thinking again and again, I remember my
old father,
The Dharma King, his queen, and his
court.
I remember the great beings who came
from all directions,
The assembly of devoted friends from
Mongolia—
Our occasional meetings were like those of
mother and child;
Joyfully we talked on and on together.
The way we spent time together comes to
my mind.
The holy beings from far away,
And the faithful Mongolian friends [127b]:
How wonderful if they were with me now!
Although my capacity for real affection is
so small, I long to see them.
Although I don't know where they are
now, I long to see them.

Thinking again and again, I remember my
old father,
The Dharma King, his queen, and his
court.
I remember how those who'd gathered in
Mongolia
Have now gone their separate ways,
Like traders going back home from a
marketplace.
The father, the Dharma King, has passed
on to another realm,
Friends with pure *samaya* have returned to
their homelands,

I, the luckless one, am left abandoned here
on the mountain of Tsonying Island.
The feast of the world and the feast of
Dharma have come to an end.

Thinking again and again, I remember my
old father,
The Dharma King, his queen, and his
court.
Remembering my father, the Dharma
King,
My heart breaks with longing—I cannot
bear it.
My breath catches in my throat—I cannot
speak.
Tears, uncontrollable, stream from my
eyes.

Father, in whichever Pure Realm you
dwell,
Listen to this song, and, like a kind mother
Who lovingly responds to the cries of her
infant child,
Look upon your son with the eyes of
wisdom!

I wept again after I had sung this. That
night I had a dream: I arrived in Urgeh and was
invited into Pöntsang Rinpoche's large tent by
an attendant whom I knew well. Inside were the
precious Dharma King, his queen, their sons,
the ministers, subjects, and all my vajra friends,
gathered as before. I felt an immeasurable delight,
and with supreme respect prostrated myself and
approached the Dharma King [128a]. He was
smiling and laughing just as he used to, and he
said, with affection, "Renunciate of the mountains, by thinking of us you have come to pay a
visit. It is good to see you. Now relax and enjoy
yourself!" He had me sit near him.

A big feast was held. From the crowd two
young men stood up and, in unison, sang Tibetan songs with slow, enchanting melodies and
beautiful words. After some Mongolian songs, a
man named Durel Onpo put on a brocade dress
and a beautiful domed hat with a wide brim and
rose from the gathering. Dancing, and singing in
central Tibetan dialect, he had everyone roaring

with laughter. I was having a wonderful time but I laughed so hard that it woke me up. Wide awake, I experienced a clear and joyful state of mind.

At the end of the first month, as I was about to leave Tsonying Island to go to great Mount Machen, all the fortunate heart-disciples nearby held a *ganachakra* feast. At the end of the feast, I told them:

"We have all gathered here, without anyone having requested us to do so. This is due to the pure prayers of aspiration we have made in the past. We have stayed together for two years, but now our ways part. This demonstrates the impermanence of all things [128b]. Therefore, don't be attached to anything; don't cling to anything—bring everything onto the path of Dharma.

"Especially remember that, after this year, you won't be staying on here either. None of you should be left hungry or cold: when winter approaches, those who have plenty should share with those who don't. In this way, share joy and suffering. Treat each other with tenderness, like brothers and sisters, and persevere day and night in whatever teaching you are practicing. This is very important."

I then sang this song of the yogin's departure:

Precious lord guru and the Three Jewels,
Bless the three doors of your sons who
  dwell here.
Lords of this remote land, Heart of the
  Lake,
Assist the practitioners who stay here.

Clear and cool ocean, farewell.
I, the golden duck, will spread my wings
And fly off to another lotus lake.
I pray that I may return
To sing sweet songs.

Wish-granting tree, farewell.
I, the russet laughing-thrush,[73] will spread
  my small wings
And fly off to pleasant blue-green groves.
I pray that I may return
To sing sweet songs.

Faithful children, farewell.
I, the *repa* yogin, staff in hand,

Shall go off to other pleasant solitary
  places.
I pray that I may return,
Singing songs of realization.

All of you, children of my heart who
  persevere in practice [129a]:
There is no need to say much at this time
  of parting.
Do as I instructed you before:
You will gain immediate happiness
And ultimate Buddhahood.

By the merit of singing this song,
May all you renunciates
Endure no hardships while remaining in
  this solitude;
 May you enjoy the good fortune of prac-
  ticing the Dharma.

In reply, my disciple Kunga Gyaltsen offered this song to wish me well and to request spiritual protection:

Upholding a stainless life of liberation,
Like the pure guide Milarepa, the heir of
  the Buddhas,
You are the source of every pure virtue,
Our permanent refuge and protector.

I, Kunga Gyaltsen, an inferior,
Utterly confused, and humble monk,
Opening the ten-petaled lotus of my folded
  hands,
Prostrate myself before you with extreme
  devotion and submit this wish for your
  well-being:

May you be well, sun, jewel of the sky,
And return to shine upon us, the lotus-
  garden.
If I, a small lotus, have not been beaten
  down by hail,
I shall welcome you, my opened petals in
  full bloom.

May you be well, turquoise thunder-
  dragon,
And return to look after us, the peacocks.

If I, a small peacock, have not been seized
   by some great bird of prey,
I shall welcome you, dancing, my feathers
   fanned out.[74]

May you be well, O handsome and
   youthful one,
And return to look after me and other
   monks and disciples [129b].
If I, your small monk-disciple, have not
   been vanquished by sickness or by
   death,
I shall welcome you, my arms outstretched,
   prostrating myself before you.

From now until we reach enlightenment,
May you, our protector, always grace us—
The monks, disciples, and patrons of this
   region
Who have formed a connection with
   you—
And grant your blessings, that we attain
   the ultimate level of omniscience.

By the infallible blessing of the guru and
   the Three Jewels,
The merit of wishing you well-being, and
   the power of requesting your protection,
May I be able to serve the lama for a long
   time
And, uniting my life and my practice,
   attain Buddhahood.

After he offered this, just as I was about to
leave, escorted for a while by the disciples, patrons,
and pilgrims, some beautiful blue clouds—as if
from a smoke-offering—arose in the sky from
the crest of Tsonying Island. They took the shape
of a parasol from which fell snowflakes shaped
like lotuses with four and five petals. I thought,
"This rain of flowers comes from our having
pleased the local deities."

   As we parted, my disciple Kunzang
Rangdrol began to weep profusely, and tears
welled up in the eyes of the assembled pilgrims;
all were moved and filled with faith.

   Thus they stood there, as I went on my way;
and with a sad heart I looked back at them
standing there.

Notes

1. See Appendix 4.

2. *Lho brag bka' 'bum*, the writings of Lodrak Drupchen Lekyi Dorje. See chap. 1, note 61.

3. The *termas* revealed by Kunzang Dechen Gyalpo (see Appendix 4), which were the foremost cycle of practices taught by Chögyal Ngakyi Wangpo.

4. Jetsun Taranatha Kunga Nyingpo (*rje btsun ta ra na tha kun dga' snying po*, 1575–1635). This great saint and outstanding scholar was the holder of the Jonang tradition and one of the leading exponents of the "extrinsic emptiness" view (*gzhan stong*) within Madhyamika philosophy. See Ruegg (1963) and Hookham (1991).

5. Dagchen Wangdu Nyingpo (*bdag chen dbang 'dus snying po*, 1765–1806), the thirty-third holder of the throne of Sakya.

6. Khechara (*mkha' spyod),* the Buddhafield of Vajravarahi. See also chap. 11, note 10 for *mkha' spyod* as a general sky abode.

7. Statues symbolize the enlightened body; books symbolize enlightened speech; and stupas, vajra, bells, and other sacred objects symbolize enlightened mind.

8. This list of teachers refers to the lineage of the *rta phag yid bzhin nor bu* (see Appendix 4).

9. The "age of residues" (*snyigs dus*), which is characterized by a degeneration in 1) the life span (*tshe*), 2) the general karma (*las*), 3) the view (*lta ba*), and 4) the faculties of beings (*sems can*); it is characterized as well as by 5) an increase of the obscuring emotions (*nyon mongs*).

10. The Secret Mantrayana (*gsang sngags rdo rje theg pa*), a synonym for Vajrayana. See Appendix 1.

11. The relics of the three kinds are relics related to the bodies of past saints, such as hair, bones, or clothes; relics related to their speech, such as pieces of their handwriting or pages from their personal books; and relics related to their mind, such as tiny pearl-like relics (*ring bsrel*) found in their ashes, which are the sign that these saints attained ultimate realization.

12. The moon is here poetically referred to by the epithet "water crystal" (*chu shel*). Tibetans see the shape of a hare on the surface of the moon.

13. Samantabhadri (*kun tu bzang mo*), the consort of the primordial Buddha Samantabhadra, the Ever-Perfect (see Author's Introduction, note 3). Their union symbolizes the inseparability of the phenomenal world and emptiness.

14. *Shunyata* (Skt.), emptiness.

15. The Great Compassionate One (Skt. *Mahakarunika*, Tib. *thugs rje chen po*) is a name of Avalokiteshvara.

16. *Repa* (*ras pa*), "cotton-clad," refers to the yogin practitioners who dress in simple white cotton robes even in the bitter cold of winter. Bön refers to the followers of the original Tibetan spiritual culture. See BM, pp. 106–12.

17. *The Swift Fulfillment of Wishes* (*bsam pa myur 'grub ma*). Unidentified.

18. Yurt, a round Mongolian tent. In that area most of the people lived in tents.

19. Padampa Sangye (*pha dam pa sangs rgyas*, d. 1117?), the great Indian *siddha* who came five times to Tibet and introduced there the lineage called "pacification" (*zhi byed*), referring to the pacification of the suffering endured in samsara. See Aziz (1980).

20. It is believed that to adopt a humble appearance and subject oneself to inferior conditions can prevent the fulfillment of a bad omen.

21. *thab gzhob*, a defilement of the hearth (as when a cooking pot overflows into the fire) that offends the local deities and must be repaired immediately through a purification ritual.

22. In 1806.

23. The Blue Lake (in Tibetan, *mtsho sngon po*; in Mongolian, Kokonor; in Chinese, Qinghai, the Blue Sea) is located in the north of Amdo, a province of Greater Tibet presently assimilated to the Qinghai province of China. The lake is also known as Trishok Gyalmo (*khri gshog rgyal mo*), the "Queen who Destroyed Ten Thousand." This name is explained as follows by Kyabje Dilgo Khyentse Rinpoche: "A long time ago the site of the lake was a vast plain; at its center was a spring. There lived an old woman who each day sent her daughter to fetch water from the spring. Knowing that it was not an ordinary spring, she told her daughter always to be careful to put back the flat stone that kept the spring covered. One day, the girl forgot. The water kept on flowing, filled the whole plain and destroyed ten thousand homes, hence the name of the lake."

This account is almost identical to the one given by Sumpa Khenpo (see the Bibliography), who, however, spells the name *khri shor rgyal mo*, the "Queen Who Swept Away Ten Thousand." The legend also says that Guru Padmasambhava came to the lake and miraculously manifested a small hill that covered the spring and stopped the flood. This hill was Heart of the Lake Island, Tsonying Mahadeva (*mtsho snying mahadeva*). Sumpa Khenpo quotes early references to this lake, e.g. in the writings of King Songtsen Gampo, who speaks of the "Bodhisattva Naga Minister from the Ocean that Flooded Ten Thousand" (*khri bshos rgya mtsho'i klu blon byang chub sems*.)

The lake is said to be inhabited by the naga king Bodhisattva and by four naginis, the four Menmo (*sman mo*) sisters, one of whom is Trishok Gyalmo. These four sisters also happen to be, with the White Mahakala (*mgon dkar*) and Vaishravana (*rnam thos sras*), the guardians (*gter srung*) of the *rta phag yid bzhin nor bu* (see Appendix 4).

24. *Nyungne* (*smyung gnas*) is a practice of fasting focused upon the Buddha of Compassion, Avalokiteshvara, in his eleven-faced and thousand-armed form. The main lineage of *nyungne* practice came down through the famed Indian nun Gelongma Palmo (*dge slong ma dpal mo*): Bhikshuni Shri.

25. "Lake-born Vajra" (*mtsho skyes rdo rje*) is one of Guru Padmasambhava's names. In his *Description of Trakar Drel Dzong* (*brag dkar sprel rdzong gi dkar chag*), Drigung Chötrak (*'bri gung chos grags*, 1597–1659) speaks of Guru Padmasambhava blessing Lake Trishok Gyalmo. The *Guide to Tsonying Island* (*mtsho snying ma ha de wa'i gnas yig*), written by Orgyen Samten Lingpa (*O rgyan bsam gtan gling pa*) according to a vision he had, says that 108 great spiritual treasures (*gter ma*) were concealed by Guru Padmasambhava and Vairocana on this blessed island.

26. In accordance with his monastic vows, Shabkar would eat just once a day at noon. He chiefly ate roasted barley flour (*tsampa*), which, mixed with tea, needs no further cooking. This combination of *tsampa* and tea constitutes the diet of most retreatants in Tibet.

27. Ösel Dorje Nyingpo (*'od gsal rdo rje snying po*) is an appellation of the Great Perfection (*rdzogs pa chen po*).

28. *sprul bsgyur*: a meditation practice in which a practitioner visualizes himself or herself going through all possible transformations.

29. *smyung gnas pa*: someone who regularly performs fasting practices (see above, note 24).

30. They try to subdue evil spirits rather than taming their own ego-clinging. In the *Chöd* practice one visualizes one's body being cut into pieces, which are offered to the four classes of guests (see Author's Introduction, note 32). On a higher level the practice of *Chöd* is intended to cut through the belief that the ego and phenomena truly exist.

31. *The Teachings of the Kadampas, Father and Sons* (*bka' gdams glegs bam pha chos bu chos*) is a collection of instructions, questions and answers, stories, songs,

and prophecies given by Atisha (982–1054) to his main spiritual son Drom Tönpa Gyalwai Jungne (*'brom ston pa rgyal ba'i 'byung gnas*, 1004–64) and to other subsequent Kadampa masters. These teachings were collected by Lekpai Sherap (*legs pa'i shes rab*) in two volumes.

32. The *Five Stages of Guhyasamaja Accomplished in One Sitting* (*gsang 'dus rim lnga gdan rdzogs*), the *Torch Illuminating the Five Stages* (*rim lnga gsal sgron*), and the *Twenty-One Notes* (*yig chung nyer gcig*) are works by Je Tsongkhapa related to the practice of the Guhyasamaja tantra (*gsang ba 'dus pa*).

33. Panchen Lobzang Chögyen; see chap. 2, note 30. Possibly the first Changkya, Ngawang Chöden, (*lcang skya ngag dbang chos ldan*, 1642–1714) or the second, Rolpai Dorje (*rol pa'i rdo rje*, 1717–86).

34. Sengzang stands for *seng bzang rgya mtsho*, another name of Pema Rangdrol.

35. The "exhaustion of phenomena in dharmata" (*chos nyid zad pa*) corresponds to the reabsorption of all phenomena into the absolute nature, which occurs simultaneously with ultimate realization and represents the fourth and final stage of Thögal practice.

36. When, through having performed the ultimate practices of the Great Perfection, a yogin is on the verge of dissolving his or her body into rainbow light, he or she may concentrate awareness on the tips of the finger nails (which are considered dead parts of the body). This results in a body of light which remains visible for the sake of all sentient beings, like Vimalamitra and Guru Padmasambhava. This is the wisdom form called the Rainbow Body of Great Transformation (*'ja' lus 'pho ba chen po*). If the yogin chooses not to do this concentration, like Chetsun Senge Wangchuk (*lce btsun seng ge dbang phyug*, 10th–11th cent.), his body will dissolve entirely into light.

37. Tilopa (10th–11th cent.), Naropa (active in the middle of the 11th cent.), Marpa (*mar pa chos kyi blo gros*, 1012–97) and Rechung Dorje Drakpa (*ras chung rdo rje grags pa*, 1084–1161) are the first patriarchs of the Kagyu lineage.

38. *The Mind Training on Cutting All Ties of Attachment*. This refers to the *legs bshad zhen 'khris kun gcod*, one of the many *blo sbyong* teachings written by Chenngawa Lodrö Gyaltsen (1402–72). See Translator's Introduction, p. xxi.

39. These expressions—the "foal of a barren mare," etc.—are classic metaphors for nonexistent things.

40. *Tsa-tsa*s are small stupas molded in clay or other material. When made for the sake of a dead person, funeral ashes are mixed with the clay, and later the *tsa-tsa*s are deposited in holy places or in a clean natural environment.

41. *The Flight of the Garuda* (*lta ba'i mgur mkha' lding gshog rlabs*. (See Appendix 5.)

42. The Dharma King.

43. *glud*, a ritual in which the effigy of a person, together with some offerings, is presented to the Lord of Death as a ransom and substitute for that person.

44. This long-life empowerment, according to the tradition of the "Sole Mother Queen of the Siddhas" (*ma gcig grub pa'i rgyal mo*), is an important longevity practice in the Kagyu lineage. When Rechungpa, Milarepa's heart-disciple, was struck by leprosy he was sent to India to find a cure for his illness. There he met the Indian master known as Guru Balachandra (*bla ma ba la tsan dra*). One day Balachandra told Rechungpa, "Today, you must go to the Happy City (*dga' ba*)." There Rechungpa met an Indian ascetic, wearing a deerskin on his shoulder, who was blowing a thighbone trumpet. Staring piercingly at Rechungpa, the ascetic told him: "You have only seven months more to live." Filled with anxiety, Rechungpa came back to Balachandra and told him what had happened. Balachandra said: "I knew all about it, but so that you would believe it, I sent you there." Then Balachandra went on: "Go to the place called the 'Golden Mandala of Meadows and Woods' (*shing spang gser gyi mandal*) and meet there the dakini called 'The Sole Mother Queen of the Siddhas' (*ma gcig grub pa'i rgyal mo*). She has attained the *siddhi* of Amitayus (*tshe dpag med*), the Buddha of Boundless Life, who blessed her in reality; she alone can save you from dying within seven months." Rechungpa went and made his request to the dakini, who asked: "How much more life do you want?" Rechungpa answered: "Until I feel it's all right to die." So the Sole Mother made the prayer: "May the son live the number of years that separate him from his father," and spoke: "Live forty-four years more!" (Milarepa, 1040–1123, was forty-four years older than Rechungpa, 1084–1161).

When Rechungpa did the longevity practice that the Queen of the Siddhas had taught him, he became cured of his illness. He went back to Tibet and again met Jetsun Mila who, offering a mandala, asked Rechungpa to give him one of the pith instructions that he received in India. Accordingly, Rechungpa offered to Mila this longevity practice, which is focused both on Amitayus to extend life and on Hayagriva to dispel obstacles. The transmission then came down to Gampopa and to all the teachers of the Dagpo Kagyu lineage. It came to the Drukpa Kagyu lineage through Gyalwa Götsangpa (*rgyal ba rgod tshang pa*, 1189–1258) and later to the Gelukpa lineage through Je Tsongkhapa (*rje tsong kha pa*, 1357–1419). See *sgrub thabs kun btus*, vol. 1, pp. 263–309 and 377–90.

45. The absolute Bodhicitta (*don dam byang chub kyi sems*) corresponds to the realization of emptiness. The relative Bodhicitta (*kun rdzob byang chub kyi sems*) is the wish to attain enlightenment for the sake of others and the putting of this wish into action.

46. Sukhavati (*bde ba can*) is the Pure Realm of Buddha Amitabha; Mount Potala is that of Avalo-kiteshvara.

47. The celestial beings (*deva*) dwelling within the *kamaloka*, the realm of desire.

48. Lunar eclipses are said to begin when the demon Rahu swallows the moon and to cease when the moon escapes through the second mouth Rahu has on his stomach.

49. Here four lines are missing in TS 1.

50. A classical metaphor, based on the image of the sun being drawn by seven powerful horses. The color green indicates activity.

51. Three trainings (*bslab pa gsum*): discipline, contemplation, and wisdom.

52. The wish-granting cow (*'dod 'jo'i ba*) is a classical symbol of abundance.

53. Rupakaya, the "form body," which includes both sambhogakaya and nirmanakaya.

54. Geshe (*dge bshes*), a high academic degree in Buddhist philosophy.

55. *The Words of Manjushri* (*lam rim 'jam dpal zhal lung*), one of the eight major teachings on the *Graded Path* (*lam rim*) *to Awakening*. It was written by the fifth Dalai Lama, Ngawang Lobzang Gyatso (*ngag dbang blo bzang rgya mtsho*, 1617–82).

56. *Ben* refers to an orthodox Buddhist monk, *Bön* to a follower of the Bönpo religion.

57. Seen from the earth, the planet Venus is brilliant white; thus, it symbolizes purity.

58. Tsari is a mountain in southern Tibet sacred to the deity Chakrasamvara (see chap. 10).

59. The three sufferings (*sdug bsngal rnam pa gsum*): the suffering upon suffering (e.g. losing one's parents and then falling very sick); the suffering of change (e.g., going to a pleasant picnic and being bitten by a snake); and the all-pervading, latent suffering inherent in all forms of conditioned existence.

60. Although presenting different aspects, the three kayas are not separate within the unity (*zung 'jug*) of appearance and emptiness.

61. Performing such funeral rites and accepting offerings for them without maintaining proper concentration cause one's spiritual practice to degenerate.

62. Literally, "You could go buckle my belt on a dog!"—meaning the belt's owner has died.

63. See above, note 38.

64. Having been destroyed by the Chinese during the Cultural Revolution, this shrine has now been partially restored by devotees.

65. Guru Padmasambhava.

66. On Jetsun Kalden Gyatso, see chap. 1, note 2. According to AC (vol. 2, fol. 175) he had several reembodiments: Ngawang Trinley Gyatso (*ngag dbang 'phrin las rgya mtsho*, 1678–1739), Gedun Trinley Rabgye (*dge 'dun 'phrin las rab rgyas*, 1740–94), and Lobzang Chötrak Gyatso (*blo bzang chos grags rgya mtsho*) who was a contemporary of Shabkar.

67. The twenty-fifth of the tenth lunar month is the anniversary of Je Tsongkhapa's nirvana.

68. The *Condensed Meaning of the Graded Path*. See chap. 1, note 59.

69. *The Torch That Illuminates the Graded Path* (*lam rim gsal ba'i sgron me*); see Appendix 5.

70. Lit. "water-eagle" (*chu glag*). This could be an eagle or an osprey.

71. Pema Shepai Dorje (*padma bshad pa'i rdo rje*). Another name of Gyal Khenchen. See TS 3, pp. 16–25.

72. Here one line is missing in TS 1.

73. Probably the variegated laughing-thrush, *Garrulax variegatum*.

74. According to an ancient myth, all peacocks are in fact female, and the thunder-dragon is their husband. This is the reason peacocks dance when there is thunder: they are happily welcoming their husbands.

7

Meditation at
Mount Machen

How I went to Machen Pomra, the Lord of
the Ten Bhumis, and practiced there

Jetsun Kalden Gyatso said in his songs:

> The lake where the Naga Bodhisattva
>   dwells
> The blue lake, Trishok Gyalmo,
> In winter wears its raiment of pure white
>   ice—
> Like a celestial silken pathway.

In the second half of the first month of the year called "White," the female Earth Snake[1] Year, I set out on the white ice pathway to cross over this lake of immense splendor and auspiciousness.

My boots, however, were giving me blisters. I thought, "I wish I had a piece of cloth!" I asked around, but no one had any. I said in jest, "Ama Tsomen Gyalmo![2] These boots are giving my feet blisters; I can hardly walk. Please give me half a yard of cotton cloth!" As we went on, everyone saw a piece of red cloth that was being blown about by the wind; it landed in front of us.

"This must be a gift from Tsomen Gyalmo," we thought. Everyone was amazed [132a].

Having crossed over the lake, we made tea near Tserpa Mountain and had our lunch. That same day I went to the house of the Mongolian family Bageh. One of my disciples, a skilled physician, translated and explained some thirty songs that I had sung for the householders. He also translated and explained the teachings I gave, turning the minds of all the devoted Mongolian patrons in that area toward the sacred Dharma.

They offered many valuables, including horses and cattle, gold and silver, clothes and brocade. I gave everything back to them, after having made prayers of dedication and aspiration.

The Bageh family would not take back the horse they had given me, so I had to accept it. When I was going to leave to circumambulate the lake, I loaded the horse with clothes and provisions and brought it along. After finishing the circumambulation, I sent the horse back.

Before leaving, I took my walking stick, rose, and slowly sang this song:

> May the lord and master gaze with a
>   loving heart
> And bestow his blessings on you patrons.
> All of you have been most kind
> To me, the wanderer from Rekong.
> My devoted benefactors, farewell—
> Now I'll go to retreat in the mountains.
>
> Just as we, patrons and practitioners,
>   separate,
> So are all things impermanent [132b].
> Without being attached to wealth, food, or
>   clothing,
> Practice the Dharma as much as you can.
>
> Not forgetting you,
> I shall keep you in my heart;
> I shall accomplish whatever I can
> For your present and ultimate benefit.
>
> I pray that we may meet again within this
>   lifetime.

155

But if we do not meet again,
I pray that, whatever happens,
We will meet in future lives.
May my prayer be fulfilled!

I also sang this song:

In the lofty, wide celestial pathway
That is the open sky above,
Sun, moon, and stars, farewell.
I, the turquoise blue thunder-dragon,
Am leaving for the slate mountains,
But will return, with roaring, thunderous
  sounds.

In the vast gardens on this good earth,
May you, sandalwood forests, stay content.
I, the blue cuckoo, am leaving for another
  land,
But will return, calling out sweetly.

Around the lake of great splendor and
  auspiciousness,
May you, devoted patrons, live content.
I, the yogin, am going to Magyal snow
  range,
But I will return, singing songs of
  realization.

May virtue and excellence reign when we
  meet again.
May auspiciousness prevail in this land!

Since I was young and my voice was good,
the Mongolian ladies, though they did not
understand the meaning of the words, were
moved just by the sound of my voice; many of
them began crying. Filled with faith, they made
many prostrations and circumambulations.

In reply to my song, my devoted disciple,
the skillful physician, explained at length why I
should come back again, and finally offered this
song of thanks [133a]:

Lord, qualified and precious master,
Without concern for gifts
Of wealth and material things,
You have been most kind to us,

The householders and ordained sangha of
  the Blue Lake,
Turning our minds toward the Dharma.

May you, the sun, now leave happily,
But still nurture us who live
In the lotus pond far away.
Protector, bestow your blessings
So that, in accordance with your words,
We may practice Dharma and attain
  supreme Buddhahood.

We ask that you return again and again
To this great lake of splendor and
  auspiciousness.
I make the wish that everyone
Who has made a connection with you at
  this place
May meet you, lord and master, over and
  over again.

Overcome with sadness, they were unable
to bear our parting. They walked on with me,
escorting me a long way, their eyes filled with
tears. Then I said, "Now, all of you should go
back. I will come back soon." They prayed to
meet me again throughout all of their lives. They
stayed, watching me go for as long as I was in
sight, not wanting to go back home. Finally,
sadly, they returned home. From then on, they
worked wholeheartedly to give up evil and practice virtue.

We, master and disciples, circumambulated
the lake. Arriving at the northeast side, we camped
on the shore in front of Arik. In Arik there was a
faithful old man who had been suffering from an
abdominal disease and had only a few days to
live. His son came to me and said, "Please be
kind enough to perform the transference of consciousness tonight for my father." I told him,
"Tonight, after everyone has gone to sleep, I will
do *phowa*. At that time, tell your old father to
have faith" [133b].

While I was performing the *phowa* from a
distance, the old man was saying to his son, "I
had an experience of seeing a dark man come to
me. He stuck an iron pipe into my genitals, and I
felt completely cold all the way up to my navel.

Then Lama Shabkar arrived, and the black man pulled out the pipe and ran away. At this point, Lama Shabkar inserted a copper tube from the crown of my head down to my navel, and my entire body became filled with bliss."

Soon after he had related his experience to his son, the old man drew his last breath. This occurred at the same time as I was finishing the transfer of consciousness.

Because of this, an old lama living in their home gained faith in me and came to our encampment with some tea, butter, and *tsampa* as offerings for dedication prayers, and told me the story of the old man's experience. Before going home, the lama made this aspiration, "At the time of my death, may I meet a master like you."

We continued the round of the lake, and many people from Arik and Mongolia came to see us. I gave them teachings and sang spiritual songs to all of them. Out of deep faith they offered many horses and cattle, which I returned to them. A Mongolian who had come a long distance to see me offered, as a meeting gift, an excellent horse, with saddle, rug, and bridle. I did not accept it, but he left it for me anyway, and took off.

The next day I met an utterly destitute beggar from Jigme Behla, with his wife and three children [134a]. When he started to beg from me, I felt strong compassion. I placed the reins of the horse in his hands, saying, "This is for you." He couldn't believe it and asked, "Aren't you teasing me?" "No, I am really giving it to you— take it!" I replied. Then he, his wife, and his children made prostrations and paid me homage; joyfully, they took the horse and left.

Having come around the head of the lake, we reached its southern side. There was a young woman there from the house of Shabdrung who had been suffering from "Chinese wounds"[3] for a year. Her tongue had been cut off, but still she lingered on, unable to die. I performed *phowa* for her and, in less time than the time it takes to boil water for tea, she passed away.

Again I was offered a horse with saddle, rug, and bridle.[4] Having accepted it, I gave it to an old man from Mangneh who had no money or possessions. An old lady who had not many years to live asked me to perform the transference of consciousness for her. When I was performing the *phowa*, she lost consciousness for a moment.[5] When she regained her senses, her son offered a horse to repay my kindness to his mother. I gave it to a poor wandering monk from Dzogeh.

As I was doing *phowa*, giving teachings, and singing songs of Dharma and realization, the pious men and women from the house of Shabdrung came to see me. I gave them teachings on death and impermanence and on the karmic law of cause and effect. Many promised to give up evil actions and perform virtuous deeds [134b].

The people of the Shabdrung clan were prosperous, so they might have offered me a great deal, had I been willing to accept it; however, I accepted hardly anything, and what I did accept, I gave to the poor. Some patrons said, "This is the first and probably the last lama to give away horses to beggars." Thus they showered flowers of praise over me.

I borrowed two yaks from a couple of long-time patrons and loaded our provisions onto them. As I was about to leave, with the old man from Mangneh and the monk from Dzogeh leading the animals, I sang this song of good wishes for all the people gathered there:

The lord, authentic master, wish-fulfilling
    gem,
Provider of all needs and wishes, common
    and supreme,
Adorns the wheel of great bliss on this
    beggar's crown.

From my heart I supplicate you, jewel
    ornament:
Bestow on all the men and women
    assembled here
The *siddhi* of happiness in this and future
    lives!

Farewell, lotus-flower garden,
As I, sun, do not stay, but prepare to leave.
If the dark clouds do not rise against me,

I will return, spreading a thousand rays of
  light.
If you, lotus-garden, are not destroyed by
  hail,
You may welcome me with smiling
  blossoms.

Farewell, garden of night-blooming
  waterlilies,
As I, moon, do not stay, but prepare to
  leave.
If the eclipse-god does not devour me,
I will return, spreading a cool white
  light.
If you, night-waterlilies, are not crushed
  down by snow,
You may welcome me, with swaying,
  dancing blossoms [135a].

Farewell, male and female patrons,
As I, yogin, do not stay, but prepare to
  leave.
If sickness and death do not rise up as my
  enemies,
I will return, with my walking stick in hand.
If you, male and female patrons, have not
  passed away,
You may welcome me, greeting me as I
  arrive.

I, the yogin who practices the sacred
  teachings,
And you, the patrons who provide support,
Have made an auspicious link
So that, together, we may attain
  enlightenment.
Be happy; be joyful!
Through our mutual Dharma practice,
May we meet time and time again.
And when we meet, may auspiciousness
  reign.

Filled with faith and reverence, everyone gathered there prostrated themselves and made
circumambulations. The faithful doctor, a
learned monk who had been my disciple for a
long time, offered this song of good wishes in
reply to mine:

Precious master, protector and source of
  refuge,
Bestow your blessing on us, the faithful
  who have assembled here,
And on all sentient beings, young and old,
So that our minds may turn toward the
  Dharma.

It is so rare to meet a spiritual guide:
Meeting you, we had the good fortune
To taste the nectar of your words.
Lord and rupakaya, go now; be well.
Protect until enlightenment
All of us who are linked with you.

Our present meeting has lasted but an
  instant;
May we meet many, many times again.
In this dark age, one's hold on life is
  tenuous at best [135b];
Thus, if we, master and disciples, do not
  meet again in this life,
I pray that in the next life we may meet
In the Blissful Buddhafield,
The Buddhafield True Joy,[6]
Or any other Pure Realm.
There, may we receive teachings, attain
  enlightenment,
And serve as guides for all the beings of the
  impure realms.

Having presented this song, the benefactors asked
for blessings, and then returned home. A few old
patrons escorted us a little further, until I told
them, "You need not walk any farther." I blessed
them and tied protection cords around their
necks, and they went home. We, myself and two
disciples, set out on the main road leading to
central Tibet.

One afternoon, as we were walking at a leisurely
pace on the way to Mount Machen, in a meadow
below the road we saw eighty wild asses, mothers
and foals, eating grass and frolicking about.[7]

Since I had never seen this before, I watched, thinking, "What a pity! They have never heard the sound of Dharma!" and I sang the *mani* slowly and melodiously. Far from being frightened, they approached and gathered around me. While they remained thus, listening, I sang this song, with the same tune:

In former times, in the noble land of India,
You turned three times the Wheel of
    Dharma.
Buddha, remain at the crown of my head
And regard with compassion all these wild
    asses.

You who have never heard even one word
    of teaching—
You beings were all once my own mother.

Poor wild asses gathered here [136a],
Listen to the true words of the Buddha:

"Doing no evil whatsoever,
Practice virtue perfectly.
Tame your mind absolutely:
This is the teaching of the Buddha."

Compassionate teacher, enlightened one:
By hearing the sound of Dharma,
Their obscurations having been purified,
May these wild asses obtain a human form
    in their next lives
And practice the holy teachings!

Seeing this, my two escorts were filled with faith and, with tears in their eyes, said, "What a great wonder that those wild asses came closer to listen to your teaching instead of running away. You must be Milarepa in person! We have been so fortunate to serve you. From now on, in life and death, please keep us always under your spiritual protection." Having said this, they made many prostrations.

I also thought, "Considering how, through the blessing of my master and the Three Jewels, these animals came to listen to the Dharma, there might also be some benefit if I teach human beings."

Further on, I met some people who asked me who I was, and many other questions. After answering them, I sang this song:

All of you, listen to my song:
I am a wandering hermit of the mountains.
My homeland is any land, without
    preference.
My chieftain is my perfect master,
My paternal uncles are the Buddhas and
    Bodhisattvas,
My maternal uncle is the supreme *yidam*
    deity,
My friends are the dakas and dakinis
    [136b],
My relatives are the protectors and
    guardians of the Dharma,
My neighbors are the local deities and
    local guardians.
My wife is the beautiful maiden Emptiness,
My offspring the innocent child Aware-
    ness.
My house is any remote rocky cave.
My field is unchanging faith,
My crops are the ten spiritual activities.[8]
My wealth is the seven noble riches.
My benefactors are Tibetan, Mongolian
    and Chinese:
These are the particulars of this yogin.

Later, I met some hunters on the road. When they asked me who I was and where I was going, I replied:

I bow down at the feet of the Dharma
    King.
Listen here to the yogin's song of reply!

I am a hermit who has renounced
    mundane activities.
I am a monk possessing the vows.
I am a *ngakpa* whose *samaya* is pure.
I am a meditator who dwells in caves.
I am a practitioner who tames his own
    mind.
I am a spiritual friend who encourages
    others to practice the Dharma.
My name is Tsogdruk Rangdrol, and

I am going to the snowy range of Machen.
Having arrived there, I will strive to attain
    enlightenment.
These are the particulars of this yogin.

They prostrated themselves with faith and
reverence, asked for blessings, and left. We went
on. On the day we first saw the peaks of Machen
Pomra,[9] we made a fragrant smoke-offering and
offered prostrations in the direction of the holy
mountain. Suddenly the sun shone on the clouds:
rainbows appeared and there was a welcoming
rain of orange-red flowers [137a]. On the day
we reached the foot of the snow mountain, a
formidable sound, like that of a thundering
dragon, resounded from the glacier. I looked at
the mountain and felt happiness and joy.

My two escorts stayed on for a couple of
days, during which we built a small stone hut,
just my size, under a rock overhang in a sunny
spot.[10] The escorts then returned home with the
yaks. Once alone, out of sheer joy I sang this
song:

Keeping above my head as an adornment
My perfect and sacred master,
I, Tsogdruk Rangdrol, felt yearning
To go to the mountain of Machen.

The white glacier, Mount Machen,
The stone hut fit for one person,
And I, Tsogdruk Rangdrol, have come
    together:
A perfect meeting—auspicious
    coincidence!

The birds calling out in pleasant tones,
The lovely wild animals with their lovely
    forms,
And I, Tsogdruk Rangdrol, have come
    together:
A perfect meeting—auspicious
    coincidence!

The oral instructions given by my master,
The provisions offered by patrons,
And my illusory body, free of sickness,
    have all come together:

A perfect meeting—auspicious
    coincidence!

Freedom from obstacles and adverse
    conditions,
Enjoying all favorable conditions,
Practicing the divine Dharma correctly:
A perfect meeting—auspicious
    coincidence!

When all these favorable conditions arise
    together,
Now that I stay happily in solitude
I feel like singing a song aloud
From the slopes of the radiant snow
    mountain.

When the same auspicious conditions
    occur again
For me and my fellow practitioners,
We all will experience the same feeling of
    joy [137b].

I then persevered single-mindedly in my meditation practice.

One day I sang this spontaneous song in praise
of the place:

To my master, who embodies the Three
    Jewels,
I bow down in devotion with my body,
    speech and mind.
Now I sing a small song of praise
To this mountain possessing all good
    qualities and no faults.

This ornament of the southern continent of
    the Rose-apple Tree,[11]
The mountain renowned as Magyal Pomra
Has been celebrated as marvelous
By many spiritual forefathers.

This white and majestic snow mountain
Is beautified by a raiment of white silk.

Those seeing this white glacier peak
Have white thoughts and delight in the
    Dharma.

The moment the snow is touched by
    sunlight
The pure glacier water makes trickling and
    splashing sounds.
This water quenches all thirsts and cures
    all illness:
Everyone comes to drink it.

The flow of the famous Machu River
Is unceasing, like that of the Ganges.
By means of this river, all the water
    covering the land
Flows down into the oceans of the world.

On the valley meadows in the mountain's
    foothills,
Wild animals move about at leisure.
Chasing one another, gamboling playfully:
Watching this, one feels like laughing.

Seeing the many thousands of yaks and
    wild asses
That cover the empty plains,
The nomads' claim to own lots of cattle
Just sounds like bragging.

The wild ass foals frisk and roll about
    [138a],
The young wild yaks play, low, and drink
    from their mothers.

As one watches all this, the day passes,
And love and compassion well up in one's
    heart.

The lakes, blossoming with a multitude of
    flowers,
Are adorned with many kinds of wild
    ducks.
With these sights before one's eyes,
One is always joyful and filled with delight.

At the tips of blue, white, scarlet, and
    saffron flowers,

Red and yellow-striped bees soar, hover
    and swirl.
When they buzz and hum, gathering
    nectar from flower to flower,
The yogin longs to wander throughout the
    land.

Here are various kinds of edible plants,
Nettles and chives, and the bodies of wild
    animals that have died natural deaths;[12]
There are so many that one could live on
    these alone, should provisions run out;
One has confidence that sustenance will
    appear.

When one has a stone hut
And a natural abundance of slate, water
    and firewood,
All the necessities are gathered:
It's not true to say one needs attendants.

Here dwells the supreme deva Magyal
Around whom many devas are always
    gathered.
Sympathetic to those who practice the
    Dharma,
They assist all work in accord with the
    teachings.

At this mountain, good fortune and
    prosperity come together;
Nothing inauspicious is ever even heard of.
For those who practice meditation in this
    place
The sun of meditation experiences and
    realization will dawn.

All those who wish to attain the level of
    gods and men
Should stay in this divine abode, Mount
    Magyal.
All those who aim to achieve
    unsurpassable enlightenment
Should live on the matchless Magyal
    range.

When you live here, banish all concern for
    this life.

Simply live here, and happiness, joy, and
   renown will come about.

By the power of this praise of Mount
   Machen,
May all people and animals near this
   mountain range [138b]
Be happy morning, afternoon, evening—
Be happy constantly, throughout the day
   and night.

The following morning at the break of dawn,
I had this experience: a white man came to call
me; I followed him to a camp of hundreds of
white tents, at the center of which was pitched an
enchanting tent, immense and very beautiful.

When I went inside it, I saw a great king
seated on a high throne. In front of him, to the
right, was a throne where I was told to sit. When
I did so, the king stood up and presented me with
a long immaculate scarf and a magnificent hat.

Then he said, "It is very wonderful that you
adhere to the life-style of our holy predecessors,
singing songs of the sacred teachings. I name you
'Bard of the Land of Snows'. It is most kind of
you to leave thousands of songs as the heritage of
Tibet. They will bring immense benefit to faithful
disciples. Please continue to concentrate on meditation practice and benefit the Dharma and all beings.
At the same time, express in song the meaning of the
teachings of the Victorious One; I promise to assist
you with any of your spiritual pursuits."

Following this, I supplicated my masters
every day and visualized receiving the four
empowerments. Letting my awareness rest, open
and relaxed, I merged with the vast sky-like
emptiness [139a].

One day, during my meditation practice, I
saw many valleys, countries and Pure Realms
that I had never seen before. Another time, I saw
clearly a couple of yellow ducks and a wild ass
that lived on the banks of the two lakes nearby.
Wondering whether this could be real, I went
outside and looked. They were right there, exactly as I had seen them in my meditation.

In this way, every day while I was resting in
meditation I had many experiences and visions
as clear as images in a mirror.

One day a bee entered my hut, buzzing
sweetly. In a joyful frame of mind, I sang this
imitation of its buzz:

A ma, A me, my friend the bee—
How do you do? Where are you from?
This yogin is delighted—
His friend has come.

Loneliness—suddenly gone!
The sun of happiness—suddenly come!
Sing now, once more, your long, slow
   song.

As I said this, the bee landed on the edge of
my seat. Folding its wings, bending its head down
and lowering its antennae, it made a gesture like
bowing. Coming closer, it touched its head to my
robe, as if paying homage. Then it flew into the
air and, performing a dance, sang these lines
[139b]:

E ma! Guru!
Are you well?
We bees are very well, indeed!

My father, my father's father,
And his father before him,
All were singers—and so am I!

I've heard stories
That in the past, some of your singers,
Such as Jetsun Kalden and others,[13]
Sometimes made offerings of songs
When they felt happy.

When we bees sing, we sing as we please,
Singing our long, slow songs over the
   empty plains.
If such offerings are pleasing to you, master,
Why should we not sing?

If we sing songs as offerings to the teacher,
The lasting merit of that act will be an
   enduring harvest.

O great Jetsun, please listen a while
To this, our offering of song.

Flying higher up, it continued:

> When this thirsty bee drinks the fine nectar
> From brilliant wildflowers, it spreads its
>   wings
> And performs a joyous dance throughout
>   the air,
> The celestial pathway, to celebrate you,
> Celestial one who sings joyous songs.

> When this bee, once ruled by ignorance,
> Can drink the fine nectar of your
>   wondrous teachings,
> And give rise to real experience and
>   realization,
> It, too, when in secluded places,
> Will wish to sing songs of realization.

The bee came lower again, and continued:

> Now this singer must return to its
>   homeland.
> Until we meet again, farewell.
> From time to time, I shall return,
> And when I'm happy, I'll offer songs
> For you to hear time and again.

> I ask that I be kept in your protection,
> Jetsun—kept safe from obstacles in this
>   very life,
> And throughout all of my lives to come
>   [140a].

In response, I sang:

> My friend the bee, come back again,
> And sing your songs for me, the yogin.
> And once I have reached enlightenment,
> I pray that you, bee, will join my retinue.

> If you must go, circle once around this
>   yogin,
> And be off, fly right back to your home.

Thus I sang to refresh my mind. Delighted, the bee made two circumambulations, one clockwise and one counterclockwise, and flew away without a backward glance.

For my own benefit I also sang about the signs of the path as mentioned in the *King of Samadhi Sutra*,[14] and how these signs arise when one lives in remote mountain retreats farther than one day away from villages, and one practices the sacred Dharma in accordance with the Buddha's words:

> I bow down to the compassionate
>   Buddha:
> Grant your blessings so that I may keep to
>   secluded places.

> If, having understood impermanence
> And the defects of samsara,
> You live alone in isolated places
> To practice perfectly the sacred Dharma,
> There are ten benefits,
> As taught in the *King of Samadhi Sutra*:

> Your activities will be fewer and fewer,
> And you will be far removed from noise
>   and distractions.

> You will be free from quarrels;
> You will be also free from harm.

> You will not let obscuring emotions
>   increase,
> Nor create causes for discord [140b].

> You will always enjoy perfect tranquility,
> Keeping your body, speech, and mind
>   under control.

> Living in a way that is conducive to
>   liberation
> You will quickly reach complete
>   freedom.

> The same sutra further states that
> If you remain in solitary places
> You will attain divine sight and divine
>   hearing,
> The capacity to know the minds of other
>   beings,
> Recollection of your former lives,
> And other miraculous powers.

You will perceive the innumerable
    Buddhas
Of the east, south, west, and north;
And never be parted from them.

Through divine hearing, you will receive
All the sacred teachings that are taught
By these Buddhas throughout the ten
    directions;
Thus you will continuously listen to the
    Dharma.

Never forgetting any of these teachings,
You will teach the sacred Dharma to all
    beings.
Fully comprehending their meaning,
You will know the acts of all sentient
    beings
Throughout the past, present, and future.

As it was taught, so also you, Tsogdruk
    Rangdrol,
Should remain alone in secluded places
And you will surely achieve the great and
    lasting aim.

May everyone who hears this song
Keep to remote places and practice
    Dharma.

After this, my diligence grew stronger and I worked harder at my meditation, merging with the ultimate nature of mind.

One evening I had this experience: a black whirlwind appeared in my room. I shouted, "Go away!" and spat on it. The whirlwind turned into a terrifying black man with long fangs [141a]. Ferociously biting his lip, he looked extremely angry. Raising up a sword with a short double-edged blade, he said, "Until today, no one ever spat on me. In retaliation for being spat upon by you, a disgusting yogin, I will enter your body and stab my knife into your heart. I'll be damned

if I don't kill you!" He instantly turned into a black pea, entered through my mouth, and disappeared inside me.

I thought, "What a weird hallucination! Well, if you're going to do that, here is my answer!" And, in a single moment, I visualized my body as being an indestructible house of meteoric iron. Holding my breath, I focused intensely on the letter *Ram* below my navel, and I visualized an intensely hot fire arising from it. As I did so, the black man made himself grow bigger, gradually filling my chest from the bottom up, until I felt that my body was going to burst.

Still, I increased the flames and kept them burning. Unable to bear it, he cried out, "Don't burn me! A-*tsa tsa*! I'm being burned alive!" and moaned piteously.

I replied, "It seems that you have murdered many meditators who came here and many patrons of this region. Now, there's no escape for you!" and I made the fire blaze even stronger, adding, "I shall roast you alive and send your consciousness into the absolute expanse!"

His voice grew meek as he said [141b], "A-*tsa tsa*! Don't you, a Dharma practitioner, have compassion for me? Don't burn me; let me go! From now on, I shall never harm anyone!" I replied, "Well, then, swear that you will never again harm visitors or local patrons."

After he had sworn many times, I said, "I have never had a revolting ghost like you sneak inside me. I'll let you go out—not through my mouth but through my anus." Holding the upper breath, I forced him down, and I visualized him coming out through my anus. He came out, looking like a corpse the size of a handspan, and fell onto the floor.

He grew to the size of a man: his hair and beard had been scorched and he was nearly dead. After he had recovered for a few moments, he again turned into a whirlwind and went away, spinning slowly.

The following day, my whole body felt wobbly and strange, and my chest uncomfortable, but, by doing the meditation and recitation of Vajrasattva, I felt well again. The next evening a white man appeared to me, laughing, and said, "Last night a bad person from our family went to test you, but you put him to shame. He told us about it, and he will not harm anyone again [142a]. Forgive him for being so rude as to enter you. In the future, please don't forget to keep him under your spiritual protection."

A pair of yellow ducks had been living on the banks of the two lakes in front of my hermitage. One afternoon, an eagle killed one of the ducks and the other duck fled, terrified. Since they had kept me company for so long, I felt saddened, and I sang this song:

> E ma! Marvelous and wonderful birds,
> From your bodies of precious gold,
> Wings of white conch and turquoise
>   opened.
> Your beaks and feet were black as bees,
> And your webbed toes were like a lattice.
>
> Garlands of beryl were draped
> Around the vase of your jeweled necks;
> Duck and drake, you were a pair.
>
> Your wings shone with a dazzling splendor;
> Your melodious voices sounded in clear
>   tones.
>
> When you came, with joyful dancing
>   movements
> On the vast, celestial pathway of the skies,
> You were divine birds, eminent monarchs
>   of fowl,
> Whose qualities, far surpassing those of
>   other birds,
> Captivated irresistibly the minds of those
>   who beheld you.
>
> When you alighted on our aquamarine
>   lakes,
> It was more beautiful than placing a vase
> Made of gold from the Jambu River
> Upon a mandala of white grains and blue
>   turquoise.

> While you remained on the shore of the
>   lakes,
> You delighted the spirit of this yogin
> Even more than the company of Dharma
>   friends.
>
> But today, suddenly, this very afternoon
>   [142b],
> One of you was killed by a wicked eagle;
> One of you flew away.
>
> Alas! The unique jewels of the lake are
>   lost.
> Unadorned, the lake is no better than
>   water in a cauldron.
>
> I, the yogin, am bereft of friends,
> No better off than a widower.
> Left desolate, my grief is fierce indeed.
>
> Compassion for my old companions,
> Those two ducks, brings tears to my eyes;
> This prayer comes to my lips:
>
> "There is no happiness in samsara.
> Birth, old age, sickness, death:
> There is so very much suffering.
>
> "To the west is the Buddhafield called
>   Blissful Realm.
> By the power of whatever merit I possess,
> May my faithful friend,
> The duck who was killed today,
> Not be reborn within samsara,
> But be reborn in the Blissful Realm."
>
> So sad, so sad!
> How strange is samsara!
> Yesterday, the two ducks, male and
>   female,
> Flew and played near the banks of the
>   lakes.
> Today, one was killed by an eagle
> And the other, terrified, flew off to another
>   place.
> The link which once united them
> Has been severed;
> And they have gone apart.

Today this old man, Tsogdruk Rangdrol,
Found a teacher of impermanence.
Understanding the indications given by
    this good teacher
I found certainty in the Buddha's
    teachings.

All things are subject to impermanence,
    and
I myself am also subject to it.
If my clinging to permanence is strong,
It will sever my chance to practice the
    Dharma.
Now I must strive to practice in secluded
    places.

Thus I sang to encourage myself to practice.

One day, when I was living happily, at ease,
a gang of bandits from Golok swept down upon
me [143a]. When they started rifling through
my provision bags, I told them, "You don't need
to look for my provisions; they are here. One of
you can make tea for lunch, and after we have
finished drinking it, if you need some provisions
let's talk it over, and you may have some."

We had the tea and talked about different
things. Afterward, I showed them all my provisions and, giving them half, I sang this song:

Surpassing even the wish-granting gem,
Master, remain as the ornament on the
    crown of my head.

No matter what joy or sorrow befalls
Tsogdruk Rangdrol the yogin,
It is my nature to sing,
So listen to my song.

Though you have now obtained a human
    birth,
It is hard to obtain again and again.
No one can say when you will die:
Death may strike tomorrow.

Good and evil actions
Bring their results without fail.
At death, whatever happens accords
With whatever you have done.

If you have performed wholesome,
    virtuous acts,
There will be happiness, birth in the higher
    realms.
If you have done unwholesome, unvirtuous
    acts,
There will be suffering, birth in the three
    lower realms.

Right now, when there is the choice,
To be happy or to suffer,
Don't indulge yourselves in unvirtuous acts
But strive as best you can
To perform virtuous deeds, great and
    small.
It is wrong to take what has not been
    given,
So refrain from doing that.

In particular, when stolen, the food of a
    practitioner
Is like poison: to eat it will cause your own
    destruction.
If you cannot curtail your cravings and
    learn to be satisfied,
You may take for yourself the wealth of the
    whole country
And still be wanting more.

Once you've become ruled by craving
    [143b],
In the end you will die by the knife.
If you sustain anything, better sustain your
    own life.
Curtail your craving and be content.

Today you have been good to me;
You made me practice generosity and
    patience.
Even ordinary possessions have become
    supreme.
E ma! This yogin is fortunate!

I know nothing of magic and evil spells.
But, by the Three Jewels,
Even if I did, I wouldn't use them.
So, later, if you fall ill or are cursed,
Don't think it was my black magic.

May everyone who has made some
    connection with me,
Either for good or for ill,
Always be happy and joyful.

After I had sung this, the eldest bandit said,
"We took your provisions because we didn't
have any ourselves. Otherwise we would never
have robbed you. If you want some meat, this is
clean and wholesome." Saying this, he gave me
several hunks of meat and prostrated himself.

All of them asked for my blessings and said,
"A good practitioner is someone like you. May
you live for a hundred years! May your health be
good! Don't forget to keep us under your spiritual protection." After they had gone, I sang this
song:

Root teacher, endowed with blessings,
Bless me that I keep impermanence in
    mind.

Yesterday, in the morning,
In the foothills of the snowy ranges of
    Machen,
Wild asses and yaks lay around on the
    plain, at ease.
Some ate grass; the little ones played.

On the lakes, white and golden ducks
    assembled.
Some stretched their wings and cried out
    with melodious voices.
The yellow flowers outside my doorstep
Laughed and danced.

Yesterday, this little hut, my dwelling
    place, was full of food;
Leaving the bigger pieces, I ate the smaller
    ones.
Trouble was something unheard of.
Everyone was happy and joyful [144a].

But this very day, near noontime,
Eight bandits with malicious intent
Who claimed to come from Golok
Appeared suddenly out of an untraveled
    valley,

And hard times fell upon us mountain
    dwellers:

The wild asses and yaks stampeded up and
    down the hills.
The birds flew away to other places.
The flowers at my door were trampled by
    their horses,
And the bandits themselves stole the food
    from my hut.

Today the teacher of impermanence
Came to visit the beggar Tsogdruk
    Rangdrol.
Do you see how all things are
    impermanent?
Don't take them to be permanent,
Renunciate of the mountains!

The next day, thirteen other bandits turned up;
they prostrated themselves with faith and respect,
and having asked for my blessing, presented me
with fresh provisions. I answered their many
questions about where I came from and where I
was heading. When they were about to leave, I
sang this song:

Master and Precious Ones,
Bestow your blessings
Upon my body, speech, and mind, and
    those of others.

You faithful bandits gathered here,
Listen to the song of this yogin.

I am a wandering hermit of the mountains
And my name is Tsogdruk Rangdrol.
My homeland is Lower Rekong,
The name of my village is Shohong.

From childhood, I had faith
In the teachings of the Old and New
    Schools
And I followed many qualified masters.
In particular, for five years without
    interruption
I followed the King of the Dharma,
    Ngawang Wang,

Receiving many oral instructions on the
   sutras and tantras.

By the grace of that immensely kind master,
I, Tsogdruk Rangdrol, have understood
   impermanence,
The defects of samsara, and that all
   sentient beings are my own parents
   [144b].

From deep within me, the yearning welled
   up
To attain Buddhahood for the sake of all
   beings;
And, thinking that for attaining this I
   should do spiritual practice,
I completely gave up the concerns of this
   life.

I wandered from one solitary place to another,
And several years went by.

At the retreat of Tsonying I stayed for
   three years;
Afterward I came to this sacred place.
Such is the story of this yogin.

The faith you all have in me
Is the result of your past karma and
   aspirations.
This precious human birth is difficult to
   find.
Life is short; we soon must die.

Birth in the western Blissful Realm
Will be full of happiness and joy.
If you act virtuously, you will be reborn
   there.
So, you must do that, O faithful ones.

Birth in the eighteen hells below
Will be full of intense suffering.
If you act wrongly, you will be reborn
   there.
So, don't live by banditry, O faithful ones!

I don't know if, in future, I will come to
   your place,

But if I come, you must look after me.
For now, go in peace;
I shall pray that you all have long lives, free
   of sickness.

When I had sung this, they bowed down
and asked for my blessing. As they set out, some
of them said, "How amazing! That man is
Orgyen in person![15] How fortunate to have met
him just once! Among all the unfortunate we are
the most fortunate! Those men who came here
yesterday were not good people! This yogin is
not one of the usual lot who roam around here.
You can tell just by the way he looks at you. He's
not one to come to the Machen Glacier just
because he can't find any place else to stay. Just
see what happens to those other bandits later.
It'll be nothing good!" [145a].
   After they had left, I sang this song:

Master, *yidam*, and dakinis,
I ask that you grant your blessings.

Yesterday, at noontime,
Faithless bandits took away my
   provisions.
But this morning,
Faithful bandits replenished my supplies.
Joy and sorrow are like travelers on the
   roadside—
Suddenly come and suddenly gone.

Before this, I was not eating much;
I wasn't even offering as much as a feast
   torma to the deities.
Those provisions I'd been hoarding at
   great pains
Turned into supplies for all those bandits.

When the food is there, it should be
   eaten;
This, I didn't know before today.
Hermit, if you have it, eat it!

Snow lions don't freeze in snow mountains;
Vultures do not fall out of the sky;
Fish do not drown in water;
Practitioners do not die of hunger.

So, cast away this life's concerns!
Give up plans for the future!

That year, it didn't rain during the summer months, and many of the lakes and pools not fed by streams dried up. This was especially true of the smaller of the two lakes in front of my hermitage.

When I went to that lake, I could see thousands of little creatures, tadpoles and fry, as many as millet seeds in an urn of *chang*. Using my leather bag, I first carried some water from the large lake to the small one. Then, cupping my hands, I lifted the little creatures out of the receding lake, poured them into the bag, and took them to the large lake. I made about thirty trips. I think that in this way I was able to save a myriad lives [145b]. For those that died, I recited many prayers of aspiration, such as:

> By the power of all my meritorious deeds,
>   symbolized by this one,
> May all these dead creatures
> Gain existence as human or celestial beings
>   in their next lives,
> And, by practicing the divine Dharma,
>   may they attain Buddhahood.

An owl used to come every night and perch on a rock above the place where I was staying. Its hooting disturbed me very much.

Late one night, I got some pebbles and hid under a rock overhang near its perch. When the owl came, I could hardly keep from chuckling to myself.

I waited, thinking I would let it hoot and then toss a pebble at it. It stayed silent, and I wondered if it had become aware that I was there. Just as I had decided to toss a pebble whether it hooted or not, it went "Whoo!" loudly.

I let it go "Whoo!" twice, then, just as it was about to do it again, I threw a pebble. It hit the bird at the very moment it was going "Whooooo!" and I dissolved into laughter.

Then I thought, "You say that you are practicing the view, but you can't bear even the irritation caused by the hoot of an owl—that's pathetic! What has become of your 'view'? You think that you meditate on compassion, but what if that owl dies as a result of your throwing a stone at it—how will that be? Perhaps this particular owl was not your mother in a previous life? Perhaps this owl does not require your compassion? [146a].

"You are a practitioner who wanders in the mountains, with no fixed home. Here is one single owl, who is a permanent resident of this place, and tonight, unable to endure a few off-key hoots, you've picked a fight with it!

"Look what you've done! Tonight it has become clear that you have failed to develop even the most meager compassion, realization of emptiness, or any other good quality." Having thus made myself feel utterly ashamed, I returned to my hermitage.

I promised myself that even if the owl came back and hooted right above my head, I would do nothing. But the owl, terrified, didn't come back; I heard him hooting somewhere down in the lower part of the valley.

Following this, after each session of resting in the nature of mind, I would do intense meditation on compassion. Subsequently, without having to cultivate it, a strong, uncontrived, almost unbearable compassion was born in me.

Every day I made ardent prayers to the Three Jewels for the sake of sentient beings, and made many dedication prayers so that I might benefit all beings, my former mothers, in this lifetime.

One day, through the connection that had been created by these prayers, while resting evenly in the true nature of mind, I had a vision. I saw the

Buddha surrounded by all the Buddhas and Bodhisattvas of the ten directions and by many sages and accomplished great beings of India and Tibet. They were all smiling and laughing. From their hearts emanated rays of light that concentrated on one point and turned into a great victory banner, which was put into my hands [146b].

The day following this vision, I sang this song, *The Laughter of the Buddhas and Bodhisattvas*:

Those who are gathered will separate.
Thinking about this—oho!
If you look for an authentic master—aha!
Buddhas and Bodhisattvas laugh in
    delight—ko re!
They'll hand on the victory banner
That is the Buddha's teaching—ya, yi!
Ya yi! Ya yi!

If having rejoiced in the eight freedoms—
    oho!
You endeavor in perfectly pure actions—
    aha!
Buddhas and Bodhisattvas laugh in
    delight—ko re!
They'll hand on the victory banner
That is the Buddha's teaching—ya, yi!
Ya yi! Ya yi!

It's not possible to find anything lasting!
If thinking about this—oho!
You give up clinging to everything—aha!
Buddhas and Bodhisattvas laugh in
    delight—ko re!
They'll hand on the victory banner
That is the Buddha's teaching—ya, yi!
Ya yi! Ya yi!

If having gotten your parents' permis-
    sion—oho!
You shave your head and don the
    monastic robes—aha!
Buddhas and Bodhisattvas laugh in
    delight—ko re!
They'll hand on the victory banner
That is the Buddha's teaching—ya, yi!
Ya yi! Ya yi!

If having trained in all the Buddha's
    teaching—oho!
You follow the life-examples of the
    Kadampas—aha!
Buddhas and Bodhisattvas laugh in
    delight—ko re!
They'll hand on the victory banner
That is the Buddha's teaching—ya, yi!
Ya yi! Ya yi!

If having received the Secret Mantrayana
    teaching—oho!
You, in secret, do the practice—aha!
Buddhas and Bodhisattvas laugh in
    delight—ko re!
They'll hand on the victory banner
That is the Buddha's teaching—ya, yi!
Ya yi! Ya yi!

If having given up incomplete paths—oho!
You practice the complete one—aha!
Buddhas and Bodhisattvas laugh in
    delight—ko re!
They'll hand on the victory banner
That is the Buddha's teaching—ya, yi!
Ya yi! Ya yi! [147a]

If you become completely accustomed—
    oho!
To this complete and excellent path—aha!
Buddhas and Bodhisattvas laugh in
    delight—ko re!
They'll hand on the victory banner
That is the Buddha's teaching—ya, yi!
Ya yi! Ya yi!

If you harbor no bad feelings toward
    others—oho!
And always think of their welfare—aha!
Buddhas and Bodhisattvas laugh in
    delight—ko re!
They'll hand on the victory banner
That is the Buddha's teaching—ya, yi!
Ya yi! Ya yi!

Maybe you'll help others,
Or maybe you won't—oho!
But should you help them greatly—aha!

Buddhas and Bodhisattvas laugh in
    delight—ko re!
They'll hand on the victory banner
That is the Buddha's teaching—ya, yi!
Ya yi! Ya yi!

If you take losses onto yourself—oho!
And leave victories to others—aha!
Buddhas and Bodhisattvas laugh in
    delight—ko re!
They'll hand on the victory banner
That is the Buddha's teaching—ya, yi!
Ya yi! Ya yi!

If you give up evil acts—oho!
And perform perfect deeds—aha!
Buddhas and Bodhisattvas laugh in
    delight—ko re!
They'll hand on the victory banner
That is the Buddha's teaching—ya, yi!
Ya yi! Ya yi!

Another day, in a vision, I saw the faces of
Manjushri, Lord of Knowledge, and Sarasvati,
Mistress of Speech. Smiling and laughing, they
emanated rays of light that filled the sky like
clouds, in the midst of which were flowers, banners, points of light, symbolic letters [147b], forms
of deities, medicines, and all sorts of beautiful
objects of various shapes and colors that I had
never seen before. Falling in a gentle rain, they
dissolved into my body, which became as if
insubstantial, ethereal. I had an inconceivable
realization of bliss-emptiness.

The next day I sang this *Laughter of Manjushri
and Sarasvati*:

Continuously, with great respect—oho!
I bow down to the perfect emanation—
    aha!
Manjushri, the master, will laugh with
    delight—ko re!
And grant all good and wondrous things—
    ya! Ya yi! Ya yi!

Do whatever results in joy—oho!
Renounce whatever results in suffering—
    aha!

Manjushri, the master, will laugh with
    delight—ko re!
And grant all good and wondrous things—
    ya! Ya yi! Ya yi!

Give up your family, lands, and cattle—
    oho!
Stay where the cuckoo flies, in the high
    valleys—aha!
Manjushri, the master, will laugh with
    delight—ko re!
And grant all good and wondrous things—
    ya! Ya yi! Ya yi!

Continuously tame your wild mind—
    oho!
Practice all the Muni's perfect precepts—
    aha!
Manjushri, the master, will laugh with
    delight—ko re!
And grant all good and wondrous things—
    ya! Ya yi! Ya yi!

Hold deep within the silver vase that is this
    body—oho!
This small song gathering the essence of
    Buddha's teaching—aha!
Manjushri, the master, will laugh with
    delight—ko re!
And grant all good and wondrous things—
    ya! Ya yi! Ya yi!

Follow the spiritual friend who brings
    contentment—oho! [148a]
Rely on him, and there will never be
    obstacles or hardships—aha!
Sarasvati, as well, will laugh in delight—
    ko re!
And grant all good and wondrous things—
    ya! Ya yi! Ya yi!

Bodhicitta pleases the Sugatas—oho!
Reap bliss and excellence, virtue's
    harvest—aha!
Sarasvati, as well, will laugh in delight—
    ko re!
And grant all good and wondrous things—
    ya! Ya yi! Ya yi!

Dispel the clouds: obscurations and evil
    acts—oho!
Realize the sun of contentment—aha!
Sarasvati, as well, will laugh in delight—
    ko re!
And grant all good and wondrous things—
    ya! Ya yi! Ya yi!

To tear apart the two veils—oho!
Meditate, concentrating on the two
    stages—aha!
Sarasvati, as well, will laugh in delight—
    ko re!
And grant all good and wondrous things—
    ya! Ya yi! Ya yi!

Teach all men and women who aspire to
    learn the Dharma—oho!
Dedicate the merit—the conclusion of all
    Dharma practice—aha!
Sarasvati, as well, will laugh in delight—
    ko re!
And grant all good and wondrous things—
    ya! Ya yi! Ya yi!

One night I dreamed that I came to a remote mountain wilderness where I had never
been, an exceedingly pleasant place like a celestial land. Sitting there, at ease, I sang many
spiritual songs by Jetsun Milarepa and other
exalted beings. My mind became filled with the
thought of Jetsun Milarepa and his spiritual sons,
and, as I prayed to them with great yearning,
they appeared before me, smiling and laughing.
With great tenderness, Mila placed his two hands
upon my head, and, spat, as a blessing [148b].

At that moment, all my deluded perceptions
ceased, and I rested serenely in the vivid state of
Mahamudra, free of discursive thoughts and
adorned with bliss, clarity, and nonthought.

The next day, I sang this *Laughter of Milarepa
and his Spiritual Sons*:

If having met your teachers—oho!
You train in the teachings of Buddha—
    aha!
Milarepa and his spiritual sons will laugh
    in delight—ko re!

And, like fathers, will care for you
    always—ya! Ya yi! Ya yi!

If having heard the path of the excellent
    Secret Mantrayana—oho!
You recite the mantra of the *yidam* deity—
    aha!
Milarepa and his spiritual sons will laugh
    in delight—ko re!
And, like fathers, will care for you
    always—ya! Ya yi! Ya yi!

If you practice the blazing *A* and melting
    Hang—oho![16]
Until it sets afire the inner heat—aha!
Milarepa and his spiritual sons will laugh
    in delight—ko re!
And, like fathers, will care for you
    always—ya! Ya yi! Ya yi!

If you place your hands in the *mudra* of
    evenness—oho!
And rest evenly in the view—aha!
Milarepa and his spiritual sons will laugh
    in delight—ko re!
And, like fathers, will care for you
    always—ya! Ya yi! Ya yi!

If you strive for enlightenment for yourself
    and others—oho!
Although such striving is difficult—aha!
Milarepa and his spiritual sons will laugh
    in delight—ko re!
And, like fathers, will care for you
    always—ya! Ya yi! Ya yi!

If, having renounced all worldly
    preoccupations—aha!
You become a true renunciate—oho!
Milarepa and his spiritual sons will laugh
    in delight—ko re!
And, like fathers, will care for you
    always—ya! Ya yi! Ya yi! [149a]

If, without any attachment or aversion—
    oho!
You do anything you can to help others—
    aha!

Milarepa and his spiritual sons will laugh
    in delight—ko re!
And, like fathers, will care for you
    always—ya! Ya yi! Ya yi!

If, leaving places unsuited to practice—
    oho!
You stay in places well-suited to practice—
    aha!
Milarepa and his spiritual sons will laugh
    in delight—ko re!
And, like fathers, will care for you
    always—ya! Ya yi! Ya yi!

If, with your right hand placed just behind
    your ear[17]—oho!
You sing sweet songs of experience and
    realization—aha!
Milarepa and his spiritual sons will laugh
    in delight—ko re!
And, like fathers, will care for you
    always—ya! Ya yi! Ya yi!

If, on the White Glacier and on the Red
    Rock—oho![18]
You sing sweet songs to benefit beings—
    aha!
Milarepa and his spiritual sons will laugh
    in delight—ko re!
And, like fathers, will care for you
    always—ya! Ya yi! Ya yi!

When in pleasant meadows and slate
    mountains—oho!
You sing sweet songs of experience and
    realization—aha!
Milarepa and his spiritual sons will laugh
    in delight—ko re!
And, like fathers, will care for you
    always—ya! Ya yi! Ya yi!

When the sonorous thunder-drums of
    summer—oho!
Accompany your excellent songs—aha!
Milarepa and his spiritual sons will laugh
    in delight—ko re!
And, like fathers, will care for you
    always—ya! Ya yi! Ya yi!

When you remain miles away in the
    wilderness—oho!
And your spiritual songs resound in the
    distance—aha!
Milarepa and his spiritual sons will laugh
    in delight—ko re!
And, like fathers, will care for you
    always—ya! Ya yi! Ya yi! [149b].

Another night, in my dream, a man who said
he was the god Brahma appeared, smiling and
laughing. He gave me a beautiful cloth bag filled
with myrobalan and other medicines, saying, "Give
these to everyone; they will be of great help."

The next day I sang the song of the *Laughter
of Brahma*:

With faith in the guru who grants all good
    things—oho!
With great love, give help to your good
    father and mother—aha!
Celestial Brahma will laugh in delight,
And grant all good and wondrous things—
    ya! Ya hi! Ya hi!

The hand of vast vision working in
    wondrous ways—oho!
May beings' bliss be brought to bloom—
    aha!
Celestial Brahma will laugh in delight,
And grant all good and wondrous things—
    ya! Ya hi! Ya hi!

Renounce ruinous wrongheaded
    relationships—oho!
Constantly cultivate correct companions—
    aha!
Celestial Brahma will laugh in delight,
And grant all good and wondrous things—
    ya! Ya hi! Ya hi!

Keep clear of killing, cut down
    concupiscence, et cetera—oho!
Completely conquer conflicting
    emotions—aha!
Celestial Brahma will laugh in delight,
And grant all good and wondrous things—
    ya! Ya hi! Ya hi!

Sing out the sweetest spiritual songs—oho!
To soothe and succor self and others—
    aha!
Celestial Brahma will laugh in delight,
And grant all good and wondrous things—
    ya! Ya hi! Ya hi! [150a].

Thus, in the style of the spiritual songs of Jetsun
Kalden Gyatso, playfully using tongue-twisting
words, with pure intention, I sang these songs for
my own edification and for the benefit of others.
Then, remembering my experiences and visions,
I felt joy and spoke these words:

I bow down at the feet of the Dharma
    King.
E ma! Listen, fortunate spiritual sons!
Mind, once settled in samsara and nirvana,
Experiences various joys and sorrows.
The nature of mind is the entrance
To the great mansion that is the absolute
    expanse.
When this door opens, one sees the true
    face
Of the Buddhas and Bodhisattvas of the
    ten directions;
One actually comes to understand
    everything about
The happiness and suffering of sentient
    beings in samsara.

Following my lama's teachings, I, an old
    monk,
Have tried to open the entrance to the vast
    expanse of mind,
But the door moved just a crack.
For me to say that I've seen the faces of
    Buddhas,
As many as there are stars in the sky,
Would be an enormous lie.
Still, from time to time, I have beheld
The faces of my tutelary deities:
In dreams, in meditation, in reality.

For me to say that I see the happiness and
    suffering,
The good and bad, that happens to all
    beings

Would be an enormous lie.
Still, from time to time, I have seen
Something about people's past and future.

But I wasn't able to open the door all the
    way,
I got just a glimpse through a crack,
Not seeing much—
It waxes and wanes, this old monk's
    clairvoyance!

King of Dharma, grant your blessings that,
In this, the last part of my life,
I may complete the opening of this
    entrance,
And witness wondrous things [150b].

May all spiritual children
Who hear this find benefit in it.

One day, to refresh my spirits, I walked to a
summit of the Machen Range and, relaxing my
mind completely, I looked around in all directions. My mind opened up, becoming clearer
and clearer.

I sat, keeping my back straight, and looked
straight ahead into the infinite expanse of the
sky. My mind blended with the sky, becoming
indistinguishable from it.

Completely at rest in the natural state of
mind—empty, luminous, without taking things
as real—I sang this song, in a state like space, an
unlimited, transparent, all-pervading expanse.

Without a center, without a border,
The luminous expanse of awareness that
    encompasses all—
This vivid, bright vastness:
Natural, primordial presence.

Without an inside, without an outside,
Awareness arisen of itself, wide as the sky,
Beyond "size," beyond "direction,"
    beyond "limits"—

This utter, complete openness:
Space, inseparable from awareness.

Within that birthless, wide-open expanse of
    space,
Phenomena appear—like rainbows, utterly
    transparent.
Pure and impure realms, Buddhas and
    sentient beings,
Are seen, brilliant and distinct.

As far as sky pervades, so does awareness.
As far as awareness extends, so does
    absolute space.

Sky, awareness, absolute space,
Indistinguishably intermixed:
Immense, infinitely vast—
The ground of samsara,
The ground of nirvana.
To remain, day and night, in this state—
To enter this state easily—this is joy [151a].
E ma ho!

Yogin!
In this state,
You must simply remain:
Resting loosely—
Letting yourself open—
Attaining dharmakaya—
Letting nirmanakaya come to pass—

Phet!
A!
Ah!

Then, I rested one-pointedly in the evenness
of a sky-like emptiness. All mental wildness and
dullness, gross and subtle, vanished naturally,
like clouds vanishing in the sky.

Like the sun shining in a clear autumn sky,
the luminous emptiness that is the true nature of
mind was laid bare. In a state without center,
without limits, empty like space, all phenomena—forms and sounds—were present in spon-
taneity, vivid as the sun, moon, planets and stars.
Mind and phenomena blended completely in a
single taste.

Friend and enemy—no difference; gold and
stone—no difference; this life and the next—no
difference; mind and sky—no difference. Having seen this for myself, I was ready to sit among
the glorious sky-like yogins.

One afternoon, I saw, one after the other,
two royal eagles flying high in the sky toward the
abode of my guru. I thought, "If I had a pair of
miraculous wings, I could fly in an instant to my
master's place like those two eagles—but I can't."
Overwhelmed by recollection of my master, his
consort, my Dharma brothers and sisters, and all
my vajra companions, I sang this plaintive song
of remembering the guru [151b]:

I saw two mighty eagles,
Royal birds, flying one after another,
In the direction of my guru's dwelling.
The memory of the place, my guru, and
    my friends
Arises vividly in my mind;
Thinking of our first meeting, tears fill my
    eyes.

U shu!
If only he were here, right now!
The longing to meet him burns in me like
    fire.
Again and again I remember my master's
    excellence,
His great kindness,
And fervent devotion wells up from deep
    within.

His wisdom mind was lofty like the sky,
His compassion was impartial, like the sun
    and moon,
His boundless good qualities were like
    miraculous jewels.
Most kind lord, you fulfilled all aspirations!

He was the reward for having accumulated
    precious merit
For millions and billions of aeons in the past.
Even if I now searched for a million aeons,
How could I ever find such an excellent
    teacher?

Kye ma! Kye hu!
Having found the jewel,
I let it slip from my hands—
What execrable karma!

I am an empty-handed beggar;
Now I will never find an instant's
    happiness.

Before, even if I went on foot, I walked at
    ease,
Knowing that, sooner or later,
I would arrive and meet my master.

Now, when I long to meet him,
Even if I rode the very finest steed,
How could I reach him?

U shu!
Before, for many years, I attended him.
Now, I cannot even look upon his face!
Now, I cannot even hear his voice! [152a].
Again and again such thoughts come to me;
Sadness wells up from deep within.

Kye hu!
Precious teacher,
You, the world's sun,
Have passed behind the western
    mountains
Into the invisible absolute expanse,
Leaving this southern continent in
    darkness.

In the sky of my mind
The dark clouds of distress are gathering;
The turquoise dragon of lamentation
    thunders.
A rainstorm of tears is pouring down my
    face.
My body shudders; a forest of hairs stands
    on end,
The lotus of my hands restlessly opens,
Restlessly closes—
I can think of nothing but my master.

By the power of this yearning song of
    remembrance,

May I, Tsogdruk Rangdrol,
Who was always cared for by my guru,
Continue always to be cared for by him.

Not long after this, over two arm-spans of
snow fell during eight days and nights without
interruption. For many days it was that deep
snow which set the boundaries of my retreat; I
wasn't even able to boil any tea. I drank melted
snow mixed with a little *tsampa*, and rested evenly
in meditation.

In earlier years, during the times when I was
contemplating such things as the difficulty of
obtaining a free, well-favored human birth, the
unpredictability of the time of death, the defects
of samsara, and the fact that all beings were once
my parents—while I was practicing to the best of
my capabilities, roaming through uninhabited
places, glaciers and mountain slopes, trying to
regard others as dearer than myself, keeping to
the most humble station, wearing worn-out
clothes, and forgetting about food, clothing and
conversations [152b]—I did not have very many
strong thoughts about my mother. When
thoughts of her did come to mind while practicing, I was able to use some meditation tech-
niques as antidotes to settle my mind again.

But while I was staying on the slopes of
Mount Machen, I must have had a premonition
that my mother was about to die. One evening,
when eight months and nine days had gone by
and all my provisions were exhausted, I began
thinking about my mother, yearning to see her
again as if thirsting for water. Though I tried and
tried to stop thinking about her, the thoughts
would not subside.

I realized that over nine years had passed
since I had last seen her, and that this year
corresponded to the prediction made by Tertön
Sonam Nyentrak Rinpoche about her life span. I
thought, "Is she still alive? If so, I must go to see
her once more. The last time I saw her, afraid
she might not consent to let me go away, I
purposely lied to her. Because of my lie, when I
left I wasn't even able to say good-bye properly.

"Nothing is sure about birth and death.
Whether or not I actually succeed in seeing her
again, I shall go to her. Not only is it time to go—

it may already be too late. Why didn't I go before? Had I gone last year, I could certainly have seen her."

With this in mind, I left the Magyal Snow Range.

Notes

1. The year 1809.

2. Ama Tsomen Gyalmo (*a ma mtsho sman rgyal mo*), the chief among the four sisters (*sman mo*) who are guardians of the lake. She is the wife of one of Machen Pomra's nephews. See also chap. 6, note 23.

3. "Chinese wounds" (*rgya rma*) refers to syphilis.

4. It is the Tibetan custom to offer a horse to the lama who performs the *phowa* for a deceased person.

5. When a lama performs the "*phowa* for the living" (see chap. 5, note 25) for an old or sick person, it often happens that this person faints for a while because of the power of the ritual.

6. Respectively the Buddhafields of Buddha Amitabha to the west and Buddha Vajrasattva to the east.

7. Kyang (*rkyang*), the swift Asiatic wild ass (Lat. *Equus hemonius pallas*).

8. The ten spiritual or Dharma activities (*chos spyod bcu*): 1) Writing commentaries and spiritual instructions, if one is qualified to do so; 2) making offerings (of the mandala, the seven branches, etc.) 3) giving to the needy; 4) listening to the teachings; 5) reading the holy scriptures; 6) committing their meaning to memory; 7) explaining this meaning to others; 8) reciting one's daily prayers; 9) pondering over the teachings one has received; and 10) assimilating them through meditation. See Kongtrul's *rgya chen bka'i mdzod*, vol. 12, p. 10.

9. The mighty Amnye Machen Range, the "Great Peacock Ancestor" (*a myes rma chen*), also called Magyal Pomra (*rma rgyal spom ra*), or Machen Pomra (*rma chen spom ra*), stands in the great curve of the Machu River (which becomes the Yellow River in China), to the east of two great lakes, known in Mongolian as Tsaring Nor and Oring Nor (Tib. *skya rangs mtsho* and *sngo rangs mtsho*). This sacred mountain is said to be the abode of Machen Pomra, a powerful protector of the Dharma who, after having being subjugated by Guru Padmasambhava, became a Bodhisattva of the tenth spiritual level (*bhumi*).

In his *History of the Dharma Protectors* (*dam can bstan srung rgya mtsho'i rnam thar*, vol. 1, p. 142), Lelung Shepai Dorje (*sle lung bzhad pa'i rdo rje*, b. 1697) presents Magyal Pomra as the chief of 360 surrounding mountain-gods, led by four main ones, one in each of the four directions (among whom is *gnyan chen thang lha*, in the north). Magyal Pomra is said to be married to Gungmen Lhari (*gung sman lha ri*) and to have nine sons and nine daughters.

When, at Samye, Guru Padmasambhava bound under oath the *devas* and *rakshas*, he omitted to subjugate Machen Pomra. The Bönpos rejoiced greatly, but after Guru Padmasambhava made the summoning *mudra*, Machen came, arrogantly putting one foot on top of Hepori at Samye and keeping one foot in Amdo. Guru Padmasambhava bound Machen under oath, yet the latter remained one of the haughtiest among the wild spirits.

There are eight great peaks in the Machen range, of which the three most prominent are Amnye Machen itself, in the center, the lowest of the three, at 6282 meters; Chenrezi (*spyan ras gzigs*), to the south, the medium peak; and Dradul Lung Shok (*dgra 'dul rlung gshog*), to the north, the highest. It takes a week to perform the circumambulation of the whole range on foot, and more than a month when making prostrations the entire way, as many faithful pilgrims do. Pilgrims gather in especially great numbers every twelve years, in the Horse Year. See K. Buffetrille (1992) and Galen Rowell (1984).

10. The ruins of Shabkar's stone hermitage are still clearly recognizable (see Buffetrille, 1992). Pilgrims who perform the circumambulation of Amnye Machen often visit the site, which is located at a place called Mowatowa (*mo ba gto ba*) on the west side of the range, in between the Height of the Supreme Horse (*rta mchog gong pa*) and before the Great Hanging Brocade Image (*gos sku chen mo*), a cliff of various hues, said to be the door curtain of Magyal's palace.

11. The Jambu Riksha, the Rose-apple Tree (*Eugenia jambolana*), is a legendary tree that grew on the banks of the "Ever-cool Lake," Anavatapta or Manasarovar. Its fruit falling into the lake made a sound like "jambu!" This gave the name Jambudvipa to the southern continent.

12. We assume that the text should read *ri dwags thed*, which refers to the carcasses of wild animals.

13. Jetsun Kalden Gyatso; see chap.1, note 2.

14. *The King of Samadhi Sutra* (Skt. *Samadhiraja-sutra*, Tib. *ting nge 'dzin rgyal po'i mdo*, T 127).

15. Guru Padmasambhava.

16. "The blazing *A* and melting *Hang*": this refers to the letters or syllables visualized during *tummo* practice (see chap. 1, note 65). The white letter Hang (*ham*) represents the male aspect, the means of compassion. It is visualized on the top of one's head. From it, drops of amrita fall and fuel the fire which originates from the *A* or *Asheh* (*a shad*), which is visualized below the navel center. For the visualization, only part of the Tibetan letter *Ah* is visualized, the *Asheh*, which is the vertical downward stroke at the far right of the letter. It represents the female aspect, the wisdom of emptiness.

17. Jetsun Milarepa is usually pictured singing with his hand placed behind his ear. This gesture signifies that while singing he was also listening to the celestial songs of the dakinis.

18. The White Glacier (*gangs dkar*) is Mount Kailash; the Red Rock (*brag dmar*) is another place where Jetsun Milarepa meditated.

8

At White Rock Monkey Fortress

How I went to practice at White Rock Monkey Fortress, the holy place of the Great Compassionate One, the source of all blessings and accomplishments

Having done prostrations and offerings to the deities, dakinis and Dharma protectors of the sacred place of Mount Machen, I—the yogin who looking outward has no master, looking inward has no servant; who, when he stays has no work to do; who, when he goes, has nothing he leaves behind; who can do what pleases him, as it pleases him—quickly went on my way.

One day at noon, I came upon a brown bear,[1] a *dremong*, with her cub; the sudden fright that came upon me when I saw them helped to enhance my practice.

Another day, on a plain, a fierce wild yak, a *drong*,[2] suddenly got to its feet in front of me [155a]. Grunting and raising its tail, lightning-quick, it charged at me.

I ran toward it, too.

It rushed headlong at me, its horns lowered, and when it was only a few steps away, it lowered its head even further. Just then, I jumped at it, and landed between its horns.

As the *drong* tossed its head up, I was around its neck, my legs braced against the two horns, my hands clutching at its mane. Praying to the guru and the Three Jewels, aiming at the *drong's* heart I shouted "Ki!" so strongly that the *drong*, startled and terrified, ran about fifty yards[3] with me on its back. It then shook itself with great force, scattering like hay my backpack, my walking stick, a small drum, and one tuft of its hair with me still grabbing onto it. Without a single glance back, the *drong* ran off.

Having suffered no injury, I jumped to my feet. Shouting "Ku!" I chased the *drong*, which took off to the top of a small hillock, stopped, released a turd, and turned around to inspect me. While retying my bundle, I sang this song:

> Master, precious ones, and *yidam* deities
>   [155b],
> Dakinis and Dharma protectors, remain
>   above my head.
> Fierce wild yak, you, the *drong*, turn round
>   and
> Listen to this yogin's song.
>
> First, when you charged like lightning,
>   intending to kill me, an innocent yogin,
> You looked brave
> And I, the yogin, was scared.
>
> Next, when you were on the point of
>   crushing me,
> And I, the yogin, rode on your back
>   unharmed,
> You lost your bravery and were struck with
>   fear.
>
> In the end, like a thieving dog in flight,
> You fled without looking back.
> *Drong*, today you were worse than dead.
> Your great strength has been of little use.
> How embarrassing that you couldn't crush
>   me!
>
> The horns that have grown on your head
> Set you apart, and you live alone.
> Having kept a long plait on my head,

I too live alone.
Don't run away, come back here!
Let's compete in strength and intelligence;
Let's see the difference between man and
    beast.

Great is the compassion of the precious
    ones!
Great is the power of the dakinis and
    dharmapalas!
Today a yogin endowed with intelligence
Defeated a wild yak endowed with
    strength.

I am not sure yet
Whether this is dream or real,
But even if it is a dream, it's a rare one for
    sure
To thus go riding on a *drong!*
If it's real, then anyone who might have
    seen this today
Would have been entirely amazed!

Isn't it astounding and fortunate
To have escaped thus from between the
    horns of a *drong?*

Having sung this, I beat my small drum and
shouted "Ku!" Thereupon the *drong* raised its tail
and ran off to the far end of the valley [156a]. I
put my bundle on my back and set off again.

A little further, I said to myself, "Who knows
when I'll die? I must leave a testament for my
disciples and patrons. What kind of testament
should it be?" And I sang this *Testament of a Yogin:*

May all the Victorious Ones who are free
    from the fear of death
Lead the way for me—a vassal of the Lord
    of Death.
Disciples and patrons who have not yet
    been struck down by death,
Listen to this song, a testament made on
    the eve of death.

The name "death" is proclaimed to all like
    the sound of thunder,
And when the Lord of Death strikes,
    irrevocably, like lightning,

To try and pay him ransom[4] or perform
    healing rituals is of no avail.

Death is certain, but the time it arrives is
    not certain—just like me.
Without being attached to this life, think of
    death, and,
To be joyful at death, put all your strength
    into the sublime Dharma.

On the eve of death I do not need to leave
    a lengthy testament.
The songs I sang when I was healthy and
    spared by death
Are the testament left for the time of death:
    act in accordance with them.

Even the Buddhas who achieved the
    deathless vajra body,
Gave the appearance of death—needless
    to say what will happen to people like
    ourselves.
Think of death as the teacher of
    impermanence,
And do not be afflicted when I fall under
    the power of death.
But until the very moment you meet with
    death, persevere in virtue.

Tsogdruk Rangdrol has now set out on the
    path of death.
Unafraid of death, he goes to the Realm of
    True Joy [156b].

Thus I sang, lighthearted.

With autumn coming, all the mountain
heights became blanketed with snow, and *drongs*
and other wild animals descended to the lowlands. At one point, I had to walk around a
group of dangerous *drongs* who were lying across
the path, blocking it. One night, I stayed in an
empty valley, with deer calling at the upper end,
foxes yapping at the lower end, and owls hooting
in between. It sounded as if I were in the *bardo.*

Traveling on the path that leads to central
Tibet, I came upon the remains of some traders'
pack animals. Exhausted and left behind, they
had just been killed and eaten by wolves. Look-

ing around, I saw about ten wolves moving on a mountain slope. I shouted "Ki!" and they took off, glancing back as they fled.

When I arrived near the White Rock Monkey Fortress,[5] some devout people asked, "Where is your home? What is your name?" I replied with this song:

As a lion cub, I stayed in the den;
When my strength developed,
I followed my lioness mother,
Roaming the glacier's heights.
I fully trained my body
And have no fear of falling over the
    glacier's edge.
Now I live near the crest of white snow
    peaks.
My name is Lion, the king of beasts.

As a little bird, I stayed in the nest;
When my feathers grew, I flew behind my
    mother bird;
High above in the sky, I fully trained my
    wings
And have no fear of falling into the abyss
    below [157a].
Now I live on the cornices of red cliffs.
My name is Eagle, the king of birds.

As a young vagabond, I stayed in my
    homeland,
Then I served at the lotus feet of my
    master.
Having entered the door of Dharma, I
    fully trained my mind
And have no fear of falling to the lower
    realms.
Now I live in mountain solitudes;
My name is Tsogdruk Rangdrol, the
    renunciate.

After I had sung this, everyone became filled with faith.

Upon reaching the White Rock Monkey Fortress, Trakar Drel Dzong, I met the hermit Alak Gonpo, who had come from Labrang Tashikhyil and practiced the ritual of the Six-armed Mahakala, the protector of this holy place. I met too the nun Dechen (who used to recite by

heart the *Sutra of Great Liberation*),[6] a faithful old nun from Gyalu Shabunar, the monk Chökyap of Bongtak with his relative, and all the patrons.

We talked a lot, and when I asked after my mother, they said that, so far as they knew, she was still alive. "If it is so, I shall go to see her again." When I said this, they began to plead with me, arguing, "We are so fortunate that you came to this holy place; you must stay for a few months as the object of our veneration. The dead of winter is not a time for traveling. It will be much better to go and meet your mother after the new year, when the earth warms up, the mountains and valleys become green, and the blue cuckoo sings sweetly" [157b].

Another patron asked how old my mother was. I told him that if she lived, she would be fifty-three at the new year. "Your mother is not very old," he said. "Don't behave like us worldly people; relax, we will take good care of you."

They thus insisted that I postpone my departure; unable to resist, I had to stay. They gave me all I needed. To benefit their minds, I gave them teachings on the law of karmic cause and effect, and sang many spiritual songs as well, which turned everyone's mind to the sublime Dharma. From Alak Gonpo, a person ornamented by the Three Trainings who was living in this holy place, I received the transmission of the texts for the ritual of the Six-armed Mahakala.

Then my spiritual son, Kunzang Rangdrol, arrived from Tsonying. I gave him the various transmissions and explanations that he needed. My kind root teacher Tendzin Nyima Rinpoche had come back from the Five-peaked Mountain and gone to Tserpa Mountain, at the far end of the Blue Lake. He sent me the following letter in verse, a letter worthy of placing above my head.

I take refuge in the excellent Three Jewels.
Bless all mountain-dwelling vagabonds!

Enjoying the excellent fruition of his past
    deeds,
Has my son, the young lion, been well?
Did your experience and realization grow?
Did you feel no more attachment to body
    and life
Than you would to a rotting carcass?

Were you harassed by fierce bandits?
[158a]

Did weariness and renunciation grow in
    your mind?
Did your compassion and loving-kindness
    increase?
Did you meditate, first equating yourself
    with others, then exchanging yourself
    for them?
Did you don the armor of patience?

Did phenomena dawn as your mind?
Did you understand the play of illusion?
Are you sad at the condition of samsara?
Do you bear in mind the qualities of
    liberation?
Did you stop distinguishing between
    enemies and friends?

Does your Dharma keep up with
    circumstances?
Does your Dharma always win?
Did you understand the warnings of
    impermanence?
Did you cut the ties of clinging to
    permanence?

Did you merge space and awareness?
Did you conquer the kingdom beyond
    birth?
Did you have any trouble on the way?
Were there any dangers from wild beasts,
    narrow paths, and rivers?
Did your meditation progress?
Are you well now?

By the compassion of the deities and the
    guru,
We all, master and disciples,
Arrived safely at the Five-peaked
    Mountain,
And thought, "Could we have wished for
    better than this?"

As for my way of wearing the armor,
I thought, at best, to leave there the heap
    of my bones,

Or at least to stay a few years.
But due to karma accumulated in the past
And the conditions we met, one of my
    attendants,
To whom the place and water were not
    suitable,
Was on the verge of death;
Therefore, driven by compassion,
We had to leave.

By the grace of the Three Jewels
We met on the way
A noble official with the pure mind of a
    Bodhisattva.
By the kindness of this good person [158b]
We came back without difficulty or
    fatigue.

At present I dwell at ease
On the mountain at the end of the lake,
And after the Mother has donned her
    mantle[7]
I wish to visit the holy place.
If I feel happy in the Mother's palace
I intend to remain there.
Son, what do you think of this?
If we can meet and converse, that would
    be the best.
If not, tell me clearly your thoughts.

Simply to have something to offer to your
    eyes,
I send you a few presents
And a white scarf of auspiciousness.

In answer to his letter I offered him this song in
verse:

Lord, precious and authentic guru,
Great is my joy that you have returned
    safely.
Your son will now relate to you, lord,
What he did at the Magyal Mountain.

Having left behind my native place, I was
    well,
For at Magyal there were no attachments
    nor aversions.

Since family and friends were far away, I
     was well,
For there was no one for me to look after.

Having offered or given away
All my wealth and possessions, I was well,
For I had nothing to hoard and guard.

Since there was a massive stone cavern
Above my head, I was well,
For I did not suffer from heat or cold.

Since dry yak dung was easy to find, I was
     well,
For I was never short of fuel.

Since my patrons provided me with
     provisions, I was well,
For I was never short of food.

By the blessings of the lord guru and the
     Three Jewels, I was well,
For I never suffered from illness.

Having meditated with diligence, I was
     well,
For I found the confidence that death will
     be joyful [159a].

It is excellent that both father and son are
     alive and well;
In due time we will talk about the Dharma
     and the world.

Through the son having told of his
     well-being to the father,
May all sentient beings, our mothers, be
     well and happy.

E ma! Precious Jetsun Rinpoche,
Protect me until enlightenment!

I shall now relate to you in detail
How I came and stayed at that glacier of
     immaculate whiteness.

Distractions having increased
In the happy secluded grove of Tsonying,

The progress of my spiritual practice
     dimmed
Like moonlight vanishing with the coming
     of sunlight.
I therefore thought to go to the solitudes
Of the white snows of Magyal
To meditate there with my whole being.
So, I left,
Carrying food, clothing, and all necessities.

One afternoon, stopping on the way,
I saw eighty wild asses in a meadow by the
     road,
Something I had never seen before.
While watching them playing, carefree and
     frolicking about,
I thought, "What a pity; none of them has
     ever heard the sound of Dharma."
Then, when I began to sing the *mani*,
Not only did the wild asses not run away,
They came closer and gathered near me.
While they were thus listening to me, free
     of fear,
I proclaimed the Dharma in one verse and
     prayed for them.
My two escorts, filled with amazement and
     faith,
Were moved to tears, and prostrated
     themselves many times.

The day I first saw the summit of the snow
     peak,
The arc of a rainbow appeared in the sky
And a rain of orange flowers fell.

The day I reached the foot of the
     mountains [159b],
Extraordinarily melodious sounds issued
     from the glacier,
Like the roar of a thunder-dragon,
And I felt extreme joy.

After I had stayed there for a month,
One day, as I was meditating,
In a vision a white man invited me to
     come,
And led me to a most beautiful tent
Standing amidst hundreds of white tents.

Inside was a great king sitting on a lofty
    throne.
I was given a seat on a throne to his right,
And the king stood up and presented to me
A long silken scarf of immaculate whiteness
And a hat of great beauty, and said:

"Emulating the lives of the great masters of
    the past,
The way you sing songs of realization is
    wondrous.
I name you: 'Bard of the Land of Snows'.
Continue to persevere in the essential
    practice
And to sing songs to benefit beings.
The collection of your songs will be a great
    legacy for Tibet
And will greatly benefit beings of the
    future."

Three months later, one evening,
I saw in a vision
A black whirlwind swirling in front of me.
I uttered, "Go away!" and spat on it,
And it turned into a black man holding a
    short sword.
When I asked who he was, he became
    furious,
And, transforming himself into a black pea,
Entered my mouth and disappeared inside
    me.

I then visualized my body as an iron house
And at my navel the letter *Ram*, from
    which arose a fire.
As I did so, the black man made himself
    grow bigger,
Gradually filling my chest from the bottom
    up,
So that I felt that my body was going to
    burst.

I made the flames blaze stronger
Until, unable to bear being consumed by
    the fire,
The man shouted, *"Don't burn me!"*
And kept on supplicating me with loud
    lamentations [160a].

Finally, when he had promised that from
    then on he would never harm anyone,
I let him pass out through my lower door.

The next day, the whole inside of my body
    felt a bit uneasy,
So I did some meditation and recitation on
    Vajrasattva and felt well again.

During the fourth month, some Golok
    bandits came
And went away, taking half of my provisions.
Thinking that all beings were my parents
I meditated on compassion over and over
    again,
And considered the bandits as spiritual
    friends
Who had helped me to perfect the two
    paramitas, generosity and patience.
Short of food, I donned the armor of
    endurance;
I regarded all phenomena as dreams,
    illusions.
These words came vividly to mind:

"Give gain and victory to others;
Take loss and defeat upon yourself."

I gained an even stronger certainty, too, in
    the truth of saying:
"Impermanent as the dew on grass,
Wealth and possessions are just invitations,
Attracting enemies and harmful influ-
    ences."

During the fifth month
I had visions of many deities,
And of Buddhas and Bodhisattvas singing
    songs.

In the seventh month snow fell day and
    night
Without interruption for eight days.

As Jetsun Mila said:

"There were big flakes, big as tufts of wool,
That came gliding down, like birds.

There were small flakes, small as spindle
    wheels,
That came swirling down, like swarms of
    bees.
There were tiny flakes, tiny as bean seeds,
That came whirling down, like fine grains
    of hail."

Since two arm-spans of snow had fallen,
For many days I was cloistered inside,
Not even able to boil some tea [160b].

At the end of the eighth month
My provisions were exhausted, and I had
    to leave.

Along the way, one day at noon,
I came upon two brown bears, a mother
    and cub,
And my sudden fright on seeing them
    helped my view to progress.

Another day, in the afternoon,
A fierce wild yak suddenly stood up in
    front of me.
Raising his tail, snorting fiercely,
He ran straight at me, like lightning
    through the sky.
Yet, through a happy combination of
    circumstances,
I managed to find myself riding on his
    neck.
Leaning over his side I shouted, "Ki-ii!"
And, frightened, the wild yak ran away.
It was wondrous that he did not kill me.

At present I am staying, quite content,
At the White Rock Monkey Fortress.
Eight years have gone now since I last saw
    my mother.
The time predicted for her life to end,
Given by my root teacher, the vidyadhara
    Tertön Sonam Nyentrak,
Is drawing near.

Therefore, after the new year,
I shall go to see if the kind mother
Who gave me life still lives.

If she is alive, I shall go back to see her;
If she is dead, I shall go back to pray for
    her.

May mother and son, whose minds are
    one, meet again soon.
May you, the perfect teacher, be pleased
By this news of how I traveled to and lived
    in the snow mountains.

When this detailed letter reached him he was
very pleased—the best offering that I could make
to him.

When entering into retreat I sang these verses in
praise of Trakar Drel Dzong:

With body, speech, and mind [161a]
I bow down, with respect, to the Dharma
    King, Ngakyi Wangpo.

I will sing here a few words in praise
Of this sacred place, White Rock Monkey
    Fortress.

E ma! The Trakar Drel Dzong mountain
Is as beautiful as a heap of precious white
    crystals.
It is a supreme abode of solitude
Blessed by Padmakara, the Lord of the
    Victorious Ones.
There are countless miraculously arisen
    images of deities,
The refuge of all beings, men and gods.
Almost all the practitioners who, after
    renouncing the world,
Meditated in this place, attained realization.

Here, too, came many masters
Who, like the sun, benefited countless
    beings.
Here gather the dakas and dakinis of the
    three planes,
And the local deities revere the Dharma.

The rocky slopes are adorned with trees
and flowers,
And from deep within the rocks, sacred
springs issue forth.
Wild animals, carefree, come and play;
People from central Tibet and elsewhere
come here
To do prostrations and
circumambulations.

Wild edible plants and berries grow here,
The sustenance for many sages.
Celestial juniper trees sway as though dancing,
Celestial birds sing their tunes.
When the mountains and valleys turn lush
green,
The blue cuckoo comes and sings.

No hindrances or hardships
Disturb those who stay in this sacred site.
Food, clothing, everything one needs,
Is found without even being sought.

You who aspire to happiness and
satisfaction in this existence,
Give up concern with ordinary life; stay in
this place.
You who long for ultimate happiness,
Stay continuously in this wilderness [161b].

Through having expressed these few words
of praise,
May obstacles and adverse circumstances
be dispelled!
May all aspirations and favorable circumstances be accomplished!

Again, one day I sang:

I have never defiled the wish-fulfilling gem,
The perfect teacher, with disrespectful
thoughts,
But have brightened it even more, using
the soft cloth of ardent faith,
And now wear it as my crown-ornament.
I shall now sing a melodious song:

Wondrous!
When in the sky of U and Tsang,

The sun and the moon—the two
protectors, the Victorious One
and the Great Pandita[8]—
Send forth the rays of their excellent sayings,
The darkness of ignorance is dispelled
And beings see what is to be done and
what is to be avoided.

When, on the Gold Mountain of Lower
China[9]
The poised white lion, the emperor,
protector of all,
Roars his commands and laws,
Millions of wild animals, his subjects and
retinue, are subdued.

In the Middle Lands, at the top of the
pleasant temple of Rekong,
The most precious Jetsun Kalden Gyatso
left this world.
After that precious one had raised the
indomitable victory banner of the
teaching,
His reincarnation came and raised it even
higher.[10]

At this very moment, I, the renunciate
born in Lower Rekong,
Having drunk the nectar of the sutras and
mantras,
Sing, in the cool shade of a solitary
mountain retreat,
Songs pleasant to hear and satisfying to the
mind.

Wondrous!
You faithful people from the Upper,
Lower, and Middle Lands,
How fortunate you are to be born these
days in Tibet:
Make connections with both the Victorious
Lord and the Great Pandita,
And they will lead you to the Pure Realms
[162a].

Observe the laws proclaimed by the
emperor, the Guardian of the Skies,
And all countries will enjoy happiness and
well-being.

Practice according to the words of Jetsun
Kalden's reincarnation,
And all your aspirations will be accomplished, while the Dharma will spread
more and more in Rekong.

Remaining in solitudes, meditate as I do,
And the sun of happiness will arise from
within.

With a mind as white as a snow mountain,
I, the snow-land bard, have sung this song.
By this merit, may the teachings of the
Buddha spread far and wide,
And may the lives of the teachers be firm
and long.
May all the beings of the three worlds be
happy and peaceful,
And may they, filled with joy,
Practice the Dharma and attain Buddhahood.

I then did strict retreat.

Two months later, the wives of five men from
Derge families came to the door of my retreat
hut, weeping. Their husbands had been arrested
on their journey by some Chinese who accused
them of being thieves and had taken them to
Xining.

I felt bad for them, and I asked them who
was the most influential person in the area. One
of the older women said that the chieftain
Gyaltsen Martri, a member of the Shabdrung
clan, was on good terms with the Chinese; she
added that if he sent a letter stating that the men
were not thieves, and requested their release, the
Chinese would let them go.

I told them, "Don't worry, this chieftain is
one of my most devout patrons [162b]. I shall
ask him to come and he will have your husbands
released." They left, much relieved.

However, since I was alone, there was no
one to go and contact the chieftain. I wondered,
"Could I bring him here simply through meditative concentration?"

I visualized myself as the *yidam*, and visualized myself emanating rays of light that went
from my heart to my patron's heart. I then
imagined that this light generated in my patron's
body and mind a feeling of bliss-void he had never
felt before. I imagined that, in this state, he would
think of me, feel an urge to see me, and come.

I did this visualization repeatedly and, in a
few days, Gyaltsen Martri did come, with a large
group of people. After I explained the matter to
him, he wrote a letter, and the five men from
Derge were released, to the joy of everyone.

Later, whenever I needed to summon a
disciple or a patron, I did the same visualization
and they came. I thought that from then on, I
could easily contact anyone.

For my own edification and that of others, I sang
several satirical songs pointing out my own and
others' shortcomings:

I bow down to all those who,
Having generated loving-kindness,
compassion and Bodhicitta,
Train themselves in the ways of the
Bodhisattvas.

I, an old monk roaming the world, which I
see as a book,
Once took the highway of mind training.
While traveling, I reached the treacherous
path of desire and hatred [163a];
There sat three people, a master and his
two disciples, serene and self-controlled.
They were "Bodhisattva," "Precious
Loving-kindness," and "Boundless
Compassion."

On meeting them I asked: "You three, where
are you from and where are you going?"

They replied:

"We are from the Diamond Throne of
Ultimate Excellence;[11]

We came because a few people of the High
   Realm of Tibet called us.

"Those who called us proclaimed loudly
   our excellence
To all the monasteries and villages around.
But, although they were many, none of
   them asked us to stay.
In this dangerous area filled with high cliffs
   and gorges,
We endured many difficulties,
So, we won't remain; we are going back."

"Well," I said," I am an exceedingly
   fortunate man.
If you are going back,
Take me, an old monk, along with you!"

With a smile, Bodhisattva said:

"Poor old monk, we have already taken
   many people like you,
And most of them, while climbing the pass
Of the Bodhisattva's activity, got tired and
   turned back.
To look at you, it seems that you are one of
   that kind.
The pass of the Bodhisattva's activity is
   very steep
And one must climb up to it; there is no
   way to leap over it.
You had better just stay quietly here, in
   this Higher Realm!"

Having said so, he laughed and left.

May all those who hear this song
Cultivate loving-kindness, compassion, and
   Bodhicitta,
And put them into practice.

   In this way, I tried to point out the defects of
some practitioners who, having first generated a
bit of loving-kindness, compassion, and Bodhicitta
[163b], become disheartened when they comprehend the vastness of Bodhisattva conduct,
and are unable to train in it. Again I sang:

I bow down to those who unite means and
   wisdom in their practice,
And therefore perfect the level of Buddhahood, the ultimate excellence.

One day when I set out upon the main
   road
Of the gradual path and was looking around,
Along came a man carrying a bulky load of
   provisions—skillful means—
But who, lacking a horse—wisdom—was
   going on foot.

I said, "Where are you going, uncle with a
   big load?"
He replied: "I am going to the Central
   Land of Ultimate Excellence."

I asked: "Did your horse die under you on
   the way?
Or was it seized by bandits or stolen by
   thieves?"
"I came from home without a horse," he
   replied.
I went on, "People who come from there
   say, 'Without a horse, it is too difficult—
   you won't reach the Central Land.'"
"To ride on horse is a risky thing," said he,
And, having readjusted his load, he went
   on his way.

After he had gone I thought, "Aho! This is
   not the way to travel; one must have a
   horse."

Then, having gone a little farther,
I saw a man riding swiftly upon a fine
   blue wisdom horse,
Controlling him with the bridle of
   mindfulness
And urging him on with the whip of
   vigilance.

"Where are you going, swift-moving
   uncle?" I asked him.
He replied: "I am going to the Central
   Land of Ultimate Excellence."

I questioned him further:
"Has the horse—skillful means—carrying
    your provisions
Gone ahead or is it following behind?"

"I am but one rider with but one horse; I
    have nothing else."
I replied: "'Without provisions you won't
    reach the Central Land, it is too
    difficult'—that is what everyone says."

"To take along a packhorse is to create
    heavy karmic debts," he said; and
    saying so, he whipped his stallion and
    sped off [164a].

After he had gone I thought:
"Aho! This is also not the way to travel;
    one must have a packhorse!"

After I had rested there for a while,
Someone came riding on a wisdom horse,
Leading the packhorse, skillful means.
He had as guides the Three Jewels and the
    Three Roots,
And was singing songs filled with good
    words.

"Amazing! Where are you going,
    uncle?"
" I am going to the Central Land of
    Ultimate Excellence."

I thought, "This is the right way to travel.
From now, whoever intends to go to the
    Central Land of Ultimate Excellence
Should go in this way, and he will surely
    arrive there easily.
This is how I should go."

Whoever hears this song should never
    separate wisdom from means,
But practice, uniting the two of them.

In this way, I pointed out the defects of those
who separate wisdom from skillful means. Again
I sang:

I bow down to all the great beings of the
    past, endowed with discipline:
May you turn to the Dharma the minds of
    all faithful monks and nuns!

Once, as I was going to a mountain
    solitude
I met a monk, his body dressed in the three
    monastic robes
And his mind filled with serenity and
    composure.

"Amazing! Venerable monk, where are
    you going?
Who gave you your monastic vows?
Considering how many vows there are,
I wonder if you decided on your own to
    take them,
Or if someone else induced you to do so?
Or are there *gelong* ordinations with a
    variable number of vows?[12]

He said: "What's the matter with
    you?"[164b]
"Well," I said, "it looks like you alone are
    keeping more vows
Than a hundred of those other monks
    around here."

He replied: "There are two hundred and
    fifty-three vows,
And I am a *gelong* observing that very
    number,
For when receiving the full ordination,
One must take the full number of vows.
I am now going to my patrons at
    Ganden."
And so saying he continued on his way.

Having seen this fully ordained monk, I
    could not but admire him.

Having gone a little further I met on my
    way
An easy fellow dressed in an old sheepskin,
    walking along with a girl,
Chatting away, with great animation.

"Aro! Eh, you old chap, where are you
      from?
Where are you going like that with your
      wife?"
"I am a *gelong*," said he.

"Aho! Did someone steal your robes?
Or did they run out of robes at the time of
      your ordination?
Or maybe you took your vows so long ago
      that you're all finished with them now?
Or perhaps you thought they were
      pointless and gave them back?"

Angrily, he grumbled:
"What's the matter with you?"

"Well, compared to some other *gelongs*, it
      seems
That you have no vows to keep at all."

After I had said this, he left without saying
      anything.
On seeing such a monk, I felt quite sad.

May all the faithful monks and nuns who
      hear this song
Keep their discipline with joyful
      enthusiasm.

And in this way, I pointed out the defects of some
monks. Again I sang:

I bow to the realized Chöd[13] practitioners
      of the past [165a].
May they turn to the Dharma the minds of
      the faithful ones who practice the Chöd!

Once I went into an empty valley
And reached a pleasant spring.
And there I saw a Chöd practitioner
      playing his drum,
Dro-lo-lo!
Playing and dancing as well.

"Amazing! Dancing Chöd practitioner,
Why must you live in this empty valley?
Can't your Chöd cut anything?

Or is it that, having already finished your
      cutting in the villages,
You wanted to see if there was anything
      else to cut on mountaintops?

"What's the matter with you?" he said.
I went on: "Compared to some of the
      Chöd practitioners around,
It seems that you don't busy yourself going
      here and there
Cutting off the heads of goats, sheep, and
      ewes."

He replied: "I am cutting through
      ego-clinging."
"Well," said I, "and where will you go
      from here?"

"I shall go to a celestial field."
Having said this, he left, playing his drum.

On seeing this Chöd practitioner, I
      became filled with admiration.

Then having gone a little farther, at a
      crossroad,
I met a fellow approaching on a wild
      horse,
Carrying behind the saddle the skins of
      some freshly flayed sheep.
I hailed him:

"Aro! Benefactor, where are you coming
      from?
Has an epidemic broken out among the
      sheep?"

He replied that he was a Chöd practitioner.
I continued: "A-me! Look at how sharp
      your 'cutting' is;
Do you use an axe or a knife?
It seems that you are cutting through
      nothing but the necks of old ewes [165b].
Doing so, aren't you cutting the jugular of
      your own liberation?"

He got upset and retorted angrily:
"What's the matter with you?"

I replied: "How good of you, going around
    like that
Cutting off the heads of goats and sheep!"
Muttering a few threats, he went away.

Seeing this Chöd practitioner I felt quite
    sad.
May all the faithful Chöd practitioners
    who hear this song
Give up skinning animals.

Thus I pointed out the defects of some Chöd
practitioners. Again I sang:

I bow down at the feet of the hermits of
    past who lived in mountain retreats;
Grant your blessings that I and others may
    remain in mountain solitudes.

One day as I was going into the
    wilderness,
I saw, in a pleasant cave beneath an
    overhanging cliff,
A hermit who had given up all worldly
    activities
To stay in retreat in the mountains;
He sat with his back straight,
His two hands resting in meditation
    posture.

"E ma! How wonderful! Mountain hermit,
    are you well?
Why do you need to stay here?
Are you staying on behalf of all the
    'mountain hermits'
Who are roaming about in the villages?
Or are you a villain banned from villages?

"What do you mean?" he answered.
"Well," I went on, "It seems that, when
    you feel hungry and cold,
You stay here and don't go down to the
    villages for food."
"Yes, I stay and practice meditation," said
    he.
"Where will you go from here?"
"I shall slowly move on to the plateaus of
    the pure land of U and Tsang."

On seeing this mountain hermit, I was
    filled with admiration.

Then having gone a little farther, I saw
    approaching, in the distance,
An old monk riding on a horse and hold-
    ing a spear [166a].

"Uncle-with-a-spear, where are you going?
It looks as though you have lost
    something."
"I am a hermit staying in mountain
    retreat," he said.

"Aho! Did you fall sick?
Did some brigand steal all your provisions?
Did you come face-to-face with some
    ferocious beast?
Did hosts of gods and demons show up as
    appalling apparitions?
Was your cave destroyed by lightning?

Upset by these words, he shouted:
"What's the matter with you?"

I went on: "It looks as if rather than staying
And meditating in a mountain retreat,
You go visiting in the villages from
    morning to night."

His lips and voice quivering with anger, he
    grumbled:
"What's that madman saying?" and went
    away.

As he passed I looked closely and I could
    see that his "spear" was only a bamboo
    cane.
"What an odd fellow!" I thought, bursting
    into laughter.

May all the mountain hermits hearing this
    song
Remain cheerfully and happily in
    mountain solitudes.

Thus I pointed out the defects of some who do
so-called "mountain retreats."

Again I sang:

Immaculate guru, remain on the crown of
   my head,
And give your blessing so that, when I
   point out defects,
It may benefit those who have them.

Are the lamas deep in debt to their own
   monasteries?
Why do I ask? Because each year, each
   month
They give out alms and pay out money,
And, in return, get back nothing but
   complaints.

Are the head lamas the domestic servants
   of the monasteries?
Why do I ask? Because they work so hard
   and deal with all the problems,
And even when the work is done it's not
   appreciated.

Are the mountain hermits under attack by
   bandits? [166b].
Why do I ask? Because they don't remain
   up in the mountains,
But keep coming down to the villages,
   looking for food.

Do soothsayers say that elderly monks
   attract evil spirits?
Why do I ask? Because some families don't
   let old monks stay at home
But send them away to distant monasteries.

Do the names of elderly relatives die with
   them?
Why do I ask? Because, when asking lamas
   to pray for their "old uncles,"
People can't remember their actual names.

Are children mistreated by their parents?
Why do I ask? Because, when the parents
   get old,

Their own children give them dark looks,
And may even threaten and beat them.

Are there briars in the cushions of monks
   and nuns?
Why do I ask? Because some monks and nuns
Can't stay in one place
And run restlessly from house to house.

Unless one is given animal hides,
Is it improper to perform village
   ceremonies?
Why do I ask? Because some Chöd
   practitioners and *ngakpas* get so upset
When you do not let them take away
   animal hides.[14]

Is it true that medicine, when given in
   large doses, doesn't cure patients?
Why do I ask? Because some physicians
   administer
Such small spoonfuls of their medicine.

Are family priests the family's servants?
Why do I ask? Because they wear old hats
   and worn-out shoes,
And must go on ahead or trail behind both
   men and cattle.

Does keeping vows make no sense at all?
Why do I ask? Because some monks and nuns
Give back their vows not long after they've
   taken them.

Does everyone think that they have
   something amazing to say?
Why do I ask? Because old people gather
In sunny doorways and do nothing but
   gossip.

Does the breath of the rich reek of shit?
Why do I ask? Because, no matter what
   they've been talking about,
They always end with, "That's bullshit!"
   [167a].

Are people raising horses for slaughter?
Why do I ask? Because some rich people
   don't give any away,

Don't offer them to lamas,
Can't rent them out anyhow,
But own so many of them.[15]

Do rich people have arthritic, crippled
    hands?
Why do I ask? Because when beggars
    come
They are unable to open their fists and give
    alms.

Are maids and servants unable to digest
    rich food?
Why do I ask? Because in some households
They are given such meager fare.

Is the Lord of Death dead and gone?
Why do I ask? Because, heedless of the
    consequences,
Most people commit bad deeds.

Is the Blissful Western Buddhafield so
    unpleasant?
Why do I ask? Because so few people are
    trying to perform the good deeds
That would cause them to be reborn there.

Are the words of the Buddha not quite to
    the point?
Why do I ask? Because people would
    rather listen to soothsayers
Than listen to the supreme scriptures.

Do people worry that others may get
    enlightened?
Why do I ask? Because they don't let their
    friends recite their *mani*
But say, "Come on, let's talk!"

May all men and women who hear these
    admonishments,
And recognize any of these faults in
    themselves.
Be glad to remove them, as one is glad to
    remove thorns.

Again I sang:

I bow down to the supreme gurus

And offer this advice to those who go
    begging for alms [167b].

One day as I went to refresh myself
In the middle of a meadow,
Many goats and sheep came from all sides
And gathered around me.

Among them, an old sheep spoke:
"Old monk, neither virtuous nor sinful,
I have something to tell you."
"Alright," I said. "Come on, tell me."

He went on: "I have a great favor to
    request
Of the 'meritorious' lamas
Who come gathering alms in summer and
    autumn.

"The very moment a short-necked, shiny,
    chubby monk
Arrives at our village door, leading
    packhorses carrying a lama's red
    bundles,
He takes a villager with him and comes
    right toward us sheep.

"The 'protection cord' the lama is going to
    give out
Is for us a noose—
It gets tied around the patrons' necks—
And soon, by our necks, we ourselves are
    caught.

"The fate of goats and old mother ewes[16]
Is thus in the hands of visiting lamas.
In this life, in the *bardo*, and in the next life
There is no other object of hope than the
    guru,
So, at the time of hope, don't betray us,
Take pity on us!

"You should let us live out this life,
Or take us to the higher realms in the next
    one.
Otherwise, if this life is suffering, and so is
    the next,
We are just being slaughtered and slaugh-
    tered one lifetime after another—

Don't let your wisdom, compassion, and
  power be so weak!

"Going on to the next life,
We will call aloud to the lamas
With fierce lamentations,
'Lamas, think of us! Lamas, think of us!'

"Some patrons come, take off their hats,
And say to you lamas:
'Please, come to our houses.'
When they invite you,
Don't pretend you don't know
That your patrons are about to kill us
  sheep.
Rather, come after having said a few kind
  words on our behalf [168a].
Otherwise, the time of a lama's arrival
Means the time for our death.

"So, don't pretend you don't know what's
  happening,
But come to visit after saying, kindly:
'Don't slaughter your sheep; set them free.'

"When some lamas enter someone's
  house
And seat themselves comfortably upon the
  throne,
We are being slaughtered right outside the
  door—
Don't pretend you don't know what's
  going on!
When there is nothing on earth
You lamas don't know,
How can you not know about this?

"A goat or a sheep is thrown down to the
  ground.
All the neighbors around can hear
The goat bleating or the sheep being
  smothered.
Yet people say:
'Sheep and goats are our livelihood,'
And they just recite, *'Om mani padme hum!'*

"We pray to you from the bottom of our
  hearts

That, at that moment, you may say
  something to reprieve us.
When we are gagged and being
  smothered,
If we could but draw a single breath,
It would be the greatest goodness on
  earth.

We have such terrible karma!
When autumn comes, the season for
  slaughtering sheep,
The fate of the old mother ewes is the
  worst of all.[17]
If, at that time the compassion
Of even the lamas, which is said to be
  great, declines,
What will happen to the compassion of
  those who have so little to begin with?
In short:

  When the red lamas come,
  For the sake of red meat and blood,
  They cut our red jugulars,
  And, red, the sun rises."

In answer to this I said:

"Aro! Goats, sheep, and old ewes,
These bodies in which you've taken birth
Will have to be left behind, sooner or
  later.

"If one were to pile up all the flesh and
  bone [168b]
Of all the bodies you've once had and left,
They would make a heap higher than
  Mount Meru;
There would be as many as all the particles
  of dust on the entire earth.

"Not even one of these bodies was used to
  sustain the life of a master—
Every one of those lives was wasted.
By relinquishing this body to sustain a
  lama's life,
You accomplish something worthwhile.
Is it not noble to give up one's body for the
  Dharma?"

As I said that, the goats and sheep
   exclaimed, with one voice:
"Oh, no! He is one of *those* lamas!"
And, terrified, they all ran away.

As they went off, I added:
"Anyway, I shall take your message to a
   few lamas.
But when I do so, some of them
May curse or try to kill me!"

May all alms-seekers who hear this song
Never accept the meat of animals
That have been killed especially for them.

Thus I pointed out the defects of some of the
prosperous lamas who go around gathering alms
in summer and autumn.

Again I sang:

One day I went to the top
Of a mountain where no one lives.
From the unborn expanse there came
The child "He-who-does-not-regard-
   things-as-real."

Alone, he was thinking, "Who would be a
   proper vessel for me?"
Over and over again, pondering
Whether this person or that would be
   more suitable:

"The eminent lamas possess the clear eyes
   of insight,
But they've caught the disease of the eight
   worldly concerns—
I'd just as soon not choose them!

"The monks and the nuns
Have nice costumes and a nice appearance,
But they're prone to catch the 'cold
   disease' of desire and craving—
I'd just as soon not choose them!

"The old monks in the villages
Dwell in the cool pavilion of monastic
   renunciation,
But they've become crazed by poisoned
   water— misusing religious wealth—
I'd just as soon not choose them!

"Laymen and laywomen
May be generous and open-handed when
   giving alms [169a],
But they are devoured by the tumor of
   clinging to ego—
I'd just as soon not choose them!"

When I, the old monk, then exclaimed,
   "Choose me! Me!"
The child said, "You pathetic old monk!
You're shouting out loudly 'Me! Me!'
But you won't do, either!

"If I can't find a healthy, pure being
I won't enter into a defective being!

"I'd rather just go back to the absolute
   expanse."

And having said so, he disappeared.

Thus, to tease and amuse, I sang these criticisms,
aimed at myself and others.

Another time, to brighten the spirits of the
Dharma practitioners, I imitated the style of
Jetsun Milarepa and sang a few songs explaining
my way of having banquets with meat and *chang*.
   First is the slaughter before the meat ban-
quet:

My old father, precious Dharma King,
Remains as the ornament of my *chakra* of
   great bliss.

At harvest time, all Tibetans,
People of the Land of Snow,

Hold meat and *chang* banquets.
I, a yogin, also hold a banquet.

I, the renunciate, "Self-liberation of the Six
    Senses,"
First do a lot of slaughtering for the meat
    banquet:

The young shepherd—awareness—
Comes from the mountain
Of the sublime Dharma of the Great
    Perfection,
Herding the nine yaks of the nine vehicles,
The four sheep of the four tantra sections,
And the three goats of the Tripitaka.

Bringing the goats, sheep, and yaks
Into the center of a large enclosure—the
    vast, absolute expanse—
The butcher—omniscient primordial
    wakefulness—
Sharpens the knife of insight,
Lays one of them down on the ground—
    firm faith—
And ties it up with rope—the accumula-
    tion of merit.
Cutting the belly open by means of the
    accumulation of wisdom [169b],
He swiftly severs the main vein of the two
    veils,
And removes the hide of discursive
    thoughts.

Cutting up the carcass with the
    enlightened meaning of the sutras and
    tantras,
He dismembers it with logic and reason,
And chops it into pieces with the hand-axe
    of the pith instructions.

Then he throws the pieces of the various
    phenomena
Into the vast cauldron of the absolute nature;
And, placing it on the tripod of the natural
    presence of the three kayas,
Lights the fire of the four boundless
    thoughts.
He cooks meditation experiences and
    realization to their ultimate end,

And serves this all on a ground cloth[18]—
    the merging of meditation and post-
    meditation.

Then I explained my way of preparing a *chang*
celebration:

My old father, precious Dharma King,
Look upon us all with the eyes of
    compassion.
I, the renunciate Tsogdruk Rangdrol, will
    now
Brew good *chang* for the party.

Having called the brewer lady—faith—
She places the vast cauldron—
    Bodhicitta—
On the hearth—renunciation.
She pours into the cauldron some water—
    the six *paramitas*.
Then having put in place the wood—inner
    calm meditation—
She lights the wisdom fire of insight.

In the center of the meadow of the four
    perfect empowerments,
She spreads the cloth of pure *samaya*.
Having added yeast—the development
    and completion stages, and the Great
    Perfection—
She blends and spreads it out on the
    ground
Of hearing, reflecting, and meditating.

When the *chang* mash—meditation
    experiences and realization—
    is mixed well,
She pours it in a jar—freedom from conceit,
And, having sealed it with the straw and
    clay of silence,
Stores it in the warmth of mountain
    solitude.

When it has fermented,
She puts it into the cauldron—benefit for
    others—
Sets in place the jug—courage—
And lights the fire of all-distinguishing
    wisdom.

Through the tap of flawless scriptures and
   logic [170a]
The *chang*—expounding, debating, and
   composing— flows in abundance,
And fills many cups—skill in the four ways
   of gathering.

Now follows my way of serving the banquet to
the guests of honor:

My old father, precious Dharma King,
Bless the body, speech, and mind of myself
   and others!
I, the renunciate Tsogdruk Rangdrol,
Shall now offer a banquet of meat:

Guests from many villages
Gather in the fine hall of the vast
   dharmakaya;
And you, skilled servants, the five wisdoms,
   serve them!

To the qualified and authentic teachers,
Serve the sirloin—intention and action.

To the great meditators who have realized
   the unborn,
Serve the leg—the wisdom of emptiness.

To those who practice the path of means
   of the Secret Mantrayana,
Serve the loins—the enjoyment of great
   bliss.

To those whose main activity is to practice
   the supreme Dharma,
Serve the chuck—steadfast aspiration.

To those who are conscious of the law of
   cause and effect,
Serve the shoulder—completely satisfying
   self and others.

To the arhats who preserve the Dharma,
Serve the foreleg—benefit for all.

To those who are not sectarian with regard
   to the various schools,
Serve the jowl —harmony with all.

To those who meditate on
   impermanence,
Serve the breastbone—not planning for
   the future.

To the physicians of the healing Bodhicitta,
Serve the diaphragm—well-being in this
   life and in those to come.

To the faithful who possess great
   diligence,
Serve the two kidneys—wisdom and
   skillful means.

To the disciples who are worthy vessels,
Serve the heart—the vital instructions.

To the monks and nuns who keep the
   Vinaya discipline
Serve the kidney fat—serenity and
   composure.

To those who have just crossed the
   threshold of the Dharma,
Serve the ribs—skillful guidance through
   relative truth [170b].

To the faithful who never part from virtue,
Serve the liver—the infallible law of cause
   and effect.

To the yogins who have devoted
   themselves to spiritual practice,
Serve the duodenum—the nourishing
   instructions."[19]

Now comes the way to distribute the remnants
to the lesser guests:

My old father, precious Dharma King,
Bless the body, speech, and mind of myself
   and others!
I, the renunciate Tsogdruk Rangdrol,
Now offer the remaining bits of meat to the
   lesser guests.

To the lamas and chiefs who make strong
   distinctions between friends and enemies,
Serve the tears of attachment and hatred.

To the teachers who only pay lip service to
Dharma,
Serve the spleen—smooth outside, filthy
within.

To the arrogant masters,
Serve the nape—high up, but with no
meat on it!

To those who cast wrathful spells and
charms,
Serve the gall-bladder of bringing ruin to
self and others.

To the sectarian monks,
Serve the lips of discord and dispute.

To those who constantly run after pleasure
and food,
Serve the nose of wasted meditation.

To these practitioners who just hang out in
villages,
Serve the ears of practices learned, but not
applied.

To the disciples who have little faith and
wrong views,
Serve the pancreas, which does more harm
than good.

To those who sow discord everywhere,
Serve the disgusting cud.

To those who practice just for
appearance's sake,
Serve the lungs—big pieces with no use.

To Buddhists and Bönpos who sacrifice
animals,
Serve the blood and lymph of evil deeds
that lead to suffering.

To the soothsayers who make all sorts of
predictions,
Serve the tongue-tip that can tell all sorts of
lies.

To those who do not believe in the karmic
law of cause and effect,
Serve the tail—the limiting viewpoints of
eternalism and nihilism.

To those who are attached to the
tranquility of *samatha* meditation,
Serve the brains—oblivious unawareness
[171a].

To the children who are unkind to their
parents,
Serve the ganglia, objects of dislike
for all.

To those who neglect both religious and
worldly ethics,
Serve the scraps, neither meat nor fat.

To those who, having little knowledge,
pose as teachers,
Serve the short caecum, of which the
beginning is already the end.

To those who practice Dharma chiefly to
accumulate wealth,
Serve the throat of the path to the lower
realms.

To the viragos whose mouths spit fire and
whose hands are tightfisted,
Serve the constricted anus of avarice.

To those who are very wealthy and very
stingy,
Serve the ruminant pouch that can hold a
lot but can't retain anything.

To the practitioners who crave the things
of this life,
Serve the testicles, excellent outside but
dirty within.

To those women fair on the surface and
black within,
Serve the large intestine—light on the
surface and dark within.

To the women of easy virtue,
Serve the long, thick *vajra*.

To the monks who have given up their vows,
Serve the moist *bhaga*.

To the parents with too many children,
Serve the loose, freshly skinned hide of
     utter exhaustion.

To the improvident householders,
Serve the rectum—which can keep
     nothing now and nothing later.

To those who always postpone,
Serve the leftovers—chronic laziness.

Finally, I shall tell you my way of serving the
chang celebration:

My old father, precious Dharma King,
Bless my body, speech and mind, and that
     of others!
I, the renunciate Tsogdruk Rangdrol,
Shall now offer a *chang* feast:

Get up, skilled *chang*-girls—the five wisdoms!
Offer to the guru of threefold kindness
The ambrosia of accomplishing all that he
     says.

Offer to the *yidam* deities—the peaceful
     and wrathful Buddhas—
The profound ambrosia of recitations and
     sadhana practice.

Offer to the dakas, dakinis, and Dharma
     protectors [171b]
The ambrosia of the *ganachakra* feast and *torma*.

Offer to the companions brought together
     by the Dharma,
The ambrosia of pure *samaya*.

Offer to the parents who gave us life
The ambrosia of respectful offering and
     service.

Offer to all sentient beings of the six realms
The ambrosia of present and ultimate
     happiness.

Offer to the superior, middling, and
     inferior disciples
The ambrosia of the graded path.

Offer especially to those of higher faculties
The ambrosia of the development and
     completion stages, and the Great
     Perfection.

Offer them a little at first, then
Serve them again and again.

I, the yogin, also enjoy meat and *chang*.
All who are full of this meat and drunk on
     this *chang*
Tease each other —*Di ri ri!*
And burst into laughter—Ha! Ha! Ha!
The sun of happiness and peace shines for
     all.
E ma! What wondrous good fortune!

Thus to lighten everyone's spirits, I playfully
spoke these words. Again a few of my ordained
disciples said, "If you would build a small monastery in a nice place it would be useful for all of us,
master and disciples, when we grow old.

I told them, "I don't need a small monastery. I've already built a big one. Build one like
mine, and I promise you a happy old age." I explained in a song how a yogin builds a monastery:

I bow at the feet of the Dharma King.
I, Tsogdruk Rangdrol, installed the
     monastic community of the ten
     religious activities
In the mountain monastery of my body
     [172a].

Having surrounded it with the wall of
     complete renunciation,
I raised the lofty pillars of love and
     compassion,
And put up the assembly hall of Bodhicitta.

There, I offered to all the tea of the ten
   virtuous acts
And distributed the donations of the seven
   noble riches.
I instituted teachings on the sutras and
   tantras;
I declared the rules of conduct of *samaya*
   and vows,
And appointed, as disciplinarian,
   awareness of impending death.

I now hope to enlarge the monastery of
   meditative experiences and realization.

I myself have built a monastery like this;
In the same way should you build one too,
And enjoy happiness now and in time to
   come.

Everyone nodded and said, "That's a remarkable monastery indeed. We may not be
able to build one like yours, but at least let's see if
we can build an ordinary one. Please grant your
spiritual protection to achieve this easily and
without hindrances." Then, having prostrated
themselves and walked round me with devotion
and respect, they left.

After I had finished my retreat, many people
came to see me. I gave them the transmission of
the *mani*, the *Praises to Tara*, the fasting practice,
and the one-day vows. I explained to them the
karmic law of cause and effect and various songs
about impermanence and death. Everyone's
mind turned toward the Dharma.

Many people offered me horses, cattle, sheep,
tea, cloth, and garments. I did not take them;
having made prayers to dedicate the merit of
their offerings, I returned them to the donors,
except for a *dzo* which, moved by pity, I gave
to a woman of the Shabdrung family who had
come to meet me. She was in tears because
her only possession, a bull, had been stolen
[172b].

I also accepted one hundred lengths of cloth
of various colors, with which I made a thousand
prayer flags printed with the *mani*. When I hung
them, there were enough to make five lines of
flags between two hills above my place.

I then went to pay homage, circumambulate,
prostrate myself, and make offerings to the many
self-arisen images which are found in the area of
the White Rock Monkey Fortress.

Then, wondering whether I would be able
to see my mother or not, I crossed the Machu
River on my way. At some point on the journey,
the strong yearning I had felt when I thought of
her vanished, and I no longer felt such a strong
urge to go.

By the banks of the Machu was a pleasant
cave known as Pema Dzong, the Lotus Citadel.
After I had stayed a few days there, Lhundrup
Rigdzin, Gelong Nyungnepa, and a few others
arrived with the news that, a little more than a
month after I had reached at the White Rock
Monkey Fortress, my mother had suddenly fallen
ill. She told my sisters, my cousins Nyingpo Cham,
Alak Bendhe, and others:

"I wasn't well last night. This is the year of
Tertön Rinpoche's prediction[20] and the year
that my son promised that he would come and
see me. Can it be that I shall die this year? My
son once sent me a letter that said, 'This is what
you should do when you are on the point of
death . . .' Look for that letter, and read it to me;
even if I can't see my son again, that will bring
me great peace of mind."

When the letter was read to her, she wept
tears as big as peas, and said, "Since I am dying
now, and since my son hasn't come back to me,
send my bones to him, in accordance with what
he wrote to me [173a]. I have no other request."

Saying this, she died, without much pain.

If I had not succumbed to the persuasion of
my patrons when I was staying at the White
Rock Monkey Fortress, there would still have
been enough time to go to see my mother while
she was living. There would still have been time
for her to be able to hear me ask her, "Mother,
how are you?" But blinded by ignorance and
tangled up in circumstances, I did not have the
good fortune to see my mother one last time in
this life.

When my mother died, the lord of *siddhas*, Pema Rangdrol Rinpoche, was invited to come from Tashikhyil. He set the mandala of the hundred supreme peaceful and wrathful deities, and, making clouds of material and imagined offerings, he prayed to the Three Jewels to lead my mother along the path. He thus made a perfect accumulation of merit and purification of obscurations.

Especially, following the tradition of the Radiant Great Perfection, he performed the purification of the seeds for rebirth in the six realms. Then he visualized clearly the consciousness of my mother as a white letter *A* and merged it with the sky-like dharmakaya of his mind. Remaining evenly in the confident view of the natural state of all things, he purified, in the unborn absolute space, her two veils and their subtle residues.

He then visualized that, from within the expanse of dharmakaya, my mother's mind arose as a wisdom dakini, with one head and two hands, so beautiful that one would never tire of looking at her [173b]. Through her unhindered miraculous power, the dakini transported herself instantly to the Blissful Western Buddhafield. There, she met Lord Amitabha, heard his voice, was graced by his prediction,[21] and reached the level from which one never falls back.

Pema Rangdrol then performed the cremation with a fire offering ceremony, and concluded with prayers and wishes of dedication. My sisters, using all our possessions and the plentiful goods and food that our relatives and all the local devotees had gathered, performed all the traditional meritorious deeds.

On the night of the cremation, my spiritual friend Tsewang Rabten dreamed that my mother, radiant and beautified with various dresses and ornaments, and surrounded by a fabulous retinue of dakas and dakinis, rose in the sky and advanced westward on a great path of light. When he recounted his dream, people said, "Fortunate mother! By the kindness of her son she is now in the Blissful Buddhafield."

After this, according to my mother's last request, my close disciple Pema Rangdrol collected her bones and sent them to me with Lhundrup Rigdzin, Gelong Nyungnepa, and a few others [174a]. When they found me, they told me how my mother had died, what her last will was, and all the other details.

When they placed in my hands my mother's bones, I thought, "Aho! Things of this world really are nothing. In the past, my old mother, overwhelmed by affection and thinking of her only son, used to weep bitterly and send me messages and letters begging, 'Son, come back once again.' But still I did not interrupt my practice. I still thought of my mother as being young, and thought that, even if I did not see her for a few years, she wouldn't die.

"Thus, believing in the permanence of things, I kept putting off my return. I purposely deceived her by continuing to write, saying, 'Next year . . . I'll come to see you next year.' And, in the end, she died without my ever having seen her again.

"Thinking of my mother, I, her bad son, had just set out on my way back to her from a distant place, pack on my back, staff in my hand. I did not have anything of value to bring for her, but I was coming back to her with many comforting words already in mind that would have brought peace to her mind.

"But my merit was insufficient. My mother had already set out on the infamous road called Death. She is no longer in a place where, if I looked, I could see her, or that, if I spoke, she could hear me. She has gone on to the distant land that is the next life.

"Even if, by virtue of having practiced the Dharma, we meet again in our next lives, we did not have the opportunity to meet once again in this life in order to say a few things to one another that would have warmed our hearts." Disconsolate, my sadness was fathomless. Weeping, I sang this song of mourning [174b]:

> Lord guru, enlightened one,
> Please remain on the crown of my head.
> With compassion look upon all sentient
>   beings,
> Each one of whom was once my mother.
> Especially, look upon my mother of this
>   life,
> Whose fate is now in your hands.

I went off, thinking I'd meet
My mother one more time.
I did not meet her—
I met her bones.

Considering, reflecting,
The memory of my mother
Comes to mind.

I went off, thinking of all
The nice things I'd say to her,
But I found that the object
Of the conversation,
My mother, was dead.

Considering, reflecting,
The memory of my mother
Comes to mind.

Her fond hope to meet her son again—
Who can make it come true?
The few things I'd wanted to tell her—
To whom can I tell them?

In my mind, I can see how she was
    before—
Inside, outside our little house.
Considering, reflecting,
The memory of my mother
Comes to mind.

My good mother—I remember so well
What she looked like, how she moved,
The way she spoke to me.

Considering, reflecting,
The memory of my mother
Comes to mind.

If she were here now,
It would be such a joy.
With tender affection,
I long to see her again.

Considering, reflecting,
The memory of my mother
Comes to mind.

If she were here now,
It would be excellent.
There are just a few things
I long to have said to her.
I'd be so happy.

Considering, reflecting,
The memory of my mother
Comes to mind.

Mother and son,
The two of us—
Our thoughts and words
Were in accord.
I am desolate that, in this life,
We will not meet again.

Considering, reflecting,
The memory of my mother
Comes to mind.

It is clear that we two
Shall not meet again in this life,
So, I pray that we will meet in the next.

Considering, reflecting,
The memory of my mother
Comes to mind.

I, the son, shall go to practice
The divine, essential Dharma.
I shall go to the quiet forests
Of mountain solitudes [175a].

Considering, reflecting,
The memory of my mother
Comes to mind.

Vajradhara guru, lord, and refuge,
Be my mother's guide
On the path of liberation;
Grant your blessings that this beggar
Stays in solitudes.

Saying this, I felt intense sorrow. Then I
offered to my gurus and the Three Jewels a vast
cloud of offerings, both real and imagined, and

prayed to them with all my heart to lead my mother on the path.

For my mother's benefit, for a few days I did as much practice as I could to accumulate merit and purify obscurations. I made *tsa-tsas* [22] from her bones. I concluded with prayers and dedications of merit, made with the intense aspiration to benefit her. By the power of this, I had good signs and dreams that, being freed from the sufferings of the lower realms, my mother was reborn in the Western Blissful Buddhafield.

I then hid the *tsa-tsas* among rocks. When I came down to the banks of Machu River, I stopped in a meadow near a forest of Red Gyata [23] and other kinds of trees. There I began to think of the time when my mother was still alive: her physical appearance, her facial expressions, the sound of her voice, and everything about her.

Then I thought, "Such a mother, who was so very kind, is now dead, reduced to a handful of bones. Her bones I have made into *tsa-tsas*. The *tsa-tsas* I have put in places where no one can see them.

"From now on, I shall again wander off to distant places. Not only will I never see my own mother again, I won't even know what becomes of the *tsa-tsas* made from her bones [175b].

"I have no need to meditate any further on impermanence and death. My mother gave me these teachings and vanished. Now, if I don't practice the Dharma—what else is there?" Again, overwhelmed by the memory of my mother, I sang this song about her, weeping, in utter dismay:

Mother who first gave me life,
Mother who fed me and clothed me,
Mother who allowed me to enter into
    Dharma,
Mother who now teaches me
    impermanence:

Having died, you have turned into a
    handful of bones.
Your bones I have turned into *tsa-tsas*.
These *tsa-tsas* I have hidden in a scree.
Now even I can no longer see them.

In times to come, when I am wandering in
    distant places,
I shall never see you again, Mother.
Not only will I never see you again,
    Mother,
I won't even see the *tsa-tsas* of your bones.

Considering this, sorrow surges up from
    deep within me.
Now I do not need to do "meditations on
    impermanence."
My old mother, leaving me, gave me these
    teachings.

With this in mind, I, her disconsolate son,
From now on will practice the holy
    Dharma.

Having sung this, I thought: "My mother, whose memory is like a knife in my heart, no longer exists. What is the point of staying on here any longer? I must go away to some remote and solitary place to practice Dharma in an authentic way."

This longing burned in me like fire.

Notes

1. Dremong (*dred mong*), the Brown or Snow Bear (Lat. *Ursus isabellinus*), of which Tibetans distinguish two kinds: the dangerous steppe dweller (*byang dred*) and the forest dweller (*nags dred*), smaller in size, that does not attack humans unless provoked.

2. *Drong* ('brong, Lat. *Bos grunniens linnaeus*), a very large species of wild yak. Solitary males that have left the herd are considered very dangerous.

3. *thag rgyang gang do*, lit,. "the distance of two rope lengths," corresponding to approximately ten arm-spans, or 150 feet.

4. Ransom ritual (*glud*).See chap. 6, note 43.

5. The White Rock Monkey Fortress (*brag dkar sprel rdzong*) near Hang-nge Chado Monastery (*hang nge bya mdo dgon*), north of Amnye Machen, is said to

be a site filled with blessings equal to those of the sacred land of Tsari. Drigung Chökyi Trakpa (*'bri gung chos kyi grags pa*, 1597–1659) wrote a description (*dkar chag*) of the place. In this, he quotes the following prediction said to be anterior to the coming of Guru Padmasambhava: "In this degenerate age, the Lotus Born Guru, Padmasambhava, will go to Lake Trishok Gyalmo, subdue the 'nine *samaya*-breaking brothers' (*dam sri spun dgu*) at Yerma Thang, hide there many spiritual treasures, and go on to Trakar Drel Dzong. There, while Guru Padmasambhava will remain in deep samadhi in a cave, two fierce Rakshasis will block the top entrance of the cave with a rock. Having removed the rock with his vajra and subdued the Rakshasis, Guru Rinpoche will bind under oath the guardian of this sacred place, a spirit with a human body and a monkey head, and pray that no evil will ever harm people of the locality. Finally he will hide spiritual treasures there, and leave imprints of his feet on the rocks."

At the White Monkey Fortress, beside these hand- and footprints, there are images of Guru Rinpoche and of his eight manifestations, as well as letters and symbols, which are said to have appeared naturally on the surface of the rocks. See AC, vol. 2, pp. 61–68, as well as RO, pp. 699–700.

6. The *Sutra of Great Liberation* (Skt. *ghanaja-maha-bhricaphulakarma avirnasodhaya bhudharakusumasancaya-sutra*, Tib. *thar pa chen po'i phyogs su rgyas pa'i mdo*, T 264).

7. The Mother is the Blue Lake, Trishok Gyalmo, and her mantle is the ice that covers the lake during the winter and allows one to cross from the mainland to the islands. The holy place and the palace mentioned below refer to Tsonying Island.

8. The Dalai Lama and the Panchen Lama.

9. This refers to the palace of the emperor. It looked like a golden mountain, for its roofs were all plated with gold.

10. On Kalden Gyatso's reembodiments, see chap. 6, note 66.

11. The Diamond Throne of Ultimate Excellence (*nges legs rdo rje gdan*) is enlightenment.

12. *Gelong (dge slong,* Skt. *bhikshu)* is a fully ordained monk who takes for life the full set of 253 vows.

13. Concerning Chöd, see Author's Introduction, note 32.

14. In village ceremonies, it was customary for the one performing the rituals to take away the skins of the animals killed for food.

15. In eastern Tibet, horses are not slaughtered or hired out to people, and therefore just to keep many horses—neither setting them free, nor using them, nor offering them to lamas, nor giving them to friends—is mere miserliness.

16. *sha gzan,* a fully grown sheep (i.e., at least three years old).

17. The old ewes are the first to be killed, because they can no longer produce lambs.

18. *phyar ba,* thick and rough material used for many purposes, made of goat or yak hair.

19. *dzi sha,* the large duodenum of ruminants. According to one informant, it could be the same as *dzi mo,* a "delicacy" prepared by stuffing empty lungs with choice pieces of meat cooked in butter.

20. Great lamas often predict the length of a person's life.

21. The Buddha would prophesy under what name someone would become a Buddha and the name of his or her Buddhafield.

22. See chap. 6, note 40.

23. Red Gyata (*gya rta dmar po*) is described as a tree with a tall, straight trunk which grows in sandy ground. Its hard wood with fine grain is used in carving protective amulets. Possibly it is a kind of birch or aspen.

9

Pilgrimage to Central Tibet

*How, after my mother's death, I went
to the Pure Realm of Central Tibet*

One morning at the break of dawn, when I was staying near White Rock Monkey Fortress, a clear blue wisdom dakini appeared in my dream; she was adorned with silk and jewels, and so exceedingly lovely that one could never tire of looking at her.

It occurred to me that she must be an emanation of Arya Tara. Just then, she said: "My son, don't be sad that you left too late to find your mother still alive. The law of impermanence rules all things. You must use difficult circumstances as an inspiration to practice virtue.

"Don't stay here; go to the Pure Realm of U-Tsang and plant the victory banner of practice there. Practicing the Dharma is the most supreme way to repay your mother's kindness and is the most supreme of all virtuous acts you might perform for her benefit." Having made this prophecy, she disappeared.

I thought, "When I was living in remote places, far away from my mother, I had intended to come back to see her, and then stay in a place sufficiently close that she would at least be able to hear news of me. But, as the saying goes, 'A horse does not always run where man wants.' I will never again, in this lifetime, see my mother. While I'm still young, I should go to the Pure Realm of U-Tsang to practice, as indicated in my dream." Thus, I decided to go to U-Tsang.

After I had told some monks, disciples, and patrons of my intentions, I sang the song *Leaving for Central Tibet* [178a]

Before,
When my mother lived,

I did not wish to go to meet her.
Now when I wish to go to meet her,
She no longer lives.
The time never came to pass
For us to meet once more.
I won't remain here;
I'll go on to U.

Before,
I did not wish to stay nearby her.
Now, when I wish to stay near to her,
My mother no longer lives.
The time never came to pass
For us to meet once more.
I won't remain here;
I'll go on to U.

Before,
I did not wish to listen to her words.
Now, when I wish to listen to her words,
My mother no longer lives.
The time never came to pass
For us to meet once more.
I won't remain here;
I'll go on to U.

Now I will go to practice the profound
    teachings
In sacred sites like those where Jetsun Mila
    stayed.

Heart-sons, disciples who follow my example,
Like me, practice for the whole length of
    your lives.

Patrons who put your trust in me,
This vagabond—give up evil acts;
Practice virtue.
May you all have long lives;
May you be free from illness;
May you act in accordance with the Dharma.
I pray that we all will meet again.

After singing this song, I set off toward U-Tsang. From that time onwards, my despair over my mother's death eased.

To mature his mind-stream for the first time, I gave the four empowerments of the "samadhi without concepts" to my supreme heart-son Lhundrup Rigdzin, "Spontaneously Accomplished Awareness Holder," also called Kalden Rangdrol. He was a being of fortunate karma, who had already trained himself in previous lives.

At the time of the Descent of Blessings,[1] Kalden experienced this pure vision: before him in space, in a mass of rainbow light, I was seated as the dharmakaya Buddha, Samantabhadra. From my heart, light radiated and [178b] penetrated his heart, and all his perceptions of his body being substantial ceased. Even my apparent form as Samantabhadra disappeared, and he could just hear the sound of my voice, without understanding any words or meanings. Thus, he remained for a moment in a state like a pure cloudless sky.

Over several days, I gave him the transmission for and detailed explanations on the text called *Dispelling the Darkness of Ignorance*,[2] according to the teachings of the Great Perfection. Finally I gave him this advice:

On a lotus, a sun and a moon
Above the crown of our heads
Is the noble root master,
Possessor of blessings—
Look upon all beings with compassion;
In particular, cherish as your sons
Disciples who live in harmony with the
    Dharma.

Through the power of past pure actions
    and aspirations
We two have taken birth in the same country;
This year we have come together in this
    place;
We are fortunate to have established a
    good connection.

Life is not permanent; it ends in death.
A gathering of relatives does not last—
In the end, they part.

Amassed wealth does not last—
In the end, it runs out.

A high position does not last—
In the end, one falls from it.

Son, if you consider well
How all dharmas are impermanent,
You will cease thinking of this life's affairs,
And will follow the life-examples of past
    saints.

Son, in the future, regardless of where I
    may be,
To accomplish all your aims,
Supplicate the divine Three Jewels
And urge the glorious dharmapalas and
    protectors
To act in fulfillment of their vows.
Until we meet again, remain well and in
    peace.

I make prayers of aspiration
That we meet again soon, not at some
    distant time;
On the auspicious day when we meet once
    more,
May auspiciousness pervade that very
    place [179a].

My disciple, Kalden Rangdrol, who was like my own son, replied with this song:

In a pleasant hermitage, away from all
    society,
You preserve the life-examples of past holy
    beings—

Precious father, Tsogdruk Rangdrol,
Be kind enough to heed your son's
    request.

Protector, through the power
Of your many vast, profound teachings,
The mind of your lowly disciple
Has begun to turn toward the Dharma:
This is your kindness, father guru.

O venerable master of inestimable kindness,
From now on, by remaining in remote
    retreats,
I will dedicate my life to intensive Dharma
    practice.
This is my offering, made to please you,
    father guru.
From now on, until I reach enlightenment,
I have no other hope for refuge
Than you, father guru.

With your unfailing love and compassion,
Please look after me.

Gracious master, travel safely.
I pray that, later, when I long to meet you,
I, the son, will meet you once again.
May virtue, excellence, and auspiciousness
    prevail.

A few days later, when the patrons at Beldo, Jipar and other nearby places heard that I was about to go far away, they all came to see me.

I explained to them in great detail the difficulty of finding a free, well-favored human birth, the uncertainty of the time of death, and the need to believe in the karmic law of cause and effect. Many of them gave up negative actions and practiced virtue [179b]. As I was leaving, I sang this advice:

I pray with fervent devotion
To the guru, the crown ornament
Above the head of this wanderer.
O venerable, glorious guru,
Possessor of blessings,
May the minds of those who have gathered
    here
Be turned toward the sacred Dharma.

Through the power of our previous pure
    actions and aspirations
We, teacher and disciples, though born in
    different places,
Have gathered here this year and made
Both a material and spiritual connection.
Now teacher and disciples
Will go their separate ways—
Impermanent, as are all things.

From now on, all you faithful disciples,
Continuously practice virtue as much as
    you can,
Relinquish, as you would poison,
Lies, harsh words, theft, banditry, fighting,
    and the taking of life.

The cuckoo comes,
His melodious song resounds;
And then he leaves for other lands.

So have I come here
And taught the Dharma,
And so shall I leave
For retreat in distant lands.

Just as the cuckoo returns again,
So shall I come back, again and again.

Until we meet once more,
Farewell and be happy.
May our future meeting bring
Virtue, excellence, and auspiciousness.

Having heard this, filled with faith, they did prostrations and circumambulations, and returned home.

One evening it occurred to me that I should try to find a way to pacify the banditry rampant in Upper Rekong, and the fighting and feuds in Lower Rekong [180a]. I went to sleep, and, in a dream, beheld the face of Tertön Sonam Nyentrak Rinpoche. He made a prophecy that I wrote down and proclaimed to all:

I bow down at the feet of the true
     manifestations
Of Buddhas and Bodhisattvas—the gurus,
Kings and ministers of the past and
     present.

Please look with compassion on all sentient
     beings.
Especially, grant your blessings
To pacify banditry, wars, and feuds
In Upper and Lower Rekong,
Bringing back peace to all.

I, the renunciate Tsogdruk Rangdrol,
Will give you some advice beneficial
For now and for the future.
Devoted men and women,
Listen without distractions;
Keep what I say in mind.

One evening I was wondering
If there might be a way to pacify
The theft and banditry in Upper Rekong
And the feuds in Lower Rekong
That bring ruin and disaster upon all.
With this thought in mind, I went to sleep.

Near midnight, in a dream appeared
My root teacher Tertön Sonam Nyentrak,
Vajradhara, lord of *siddhas*,
Treasury of omniscience, who said:

"The wise lamas and chiefs of Upper and
     Lower Rekong
Have issued edicts to control banditry,
     according to the imperial laws.
If these edicts are heeded, for seven
     generations
Everything will continue to improve.
But if they are disregarded
A Mongolian king of either the Snake Year
     or the Ox Year
Will foster intrigues at the court of the
     Guardian of the Skies;[3]
For seven years there will be great
     unhappiness,
And all will suffer like fish thrown on hot
     sand [180b].

"When the lamas and chiefs of Lower
     Rekong
Use their wisdom to weigh others' faults,
     petty or serious, and make judgments,
Then disputes and lawsuits will be settled.

"Laws must be made to curb fighting:
If no fighting occurs
For twenty, fifteen or, at the very least, ten
     years,
The ravenous, belligerent ghost,
Greedy for the flesh, blood, breath and life
     of humans,
Will go far away to the north or to the
     west,
And for many generations happiness will
     reign.
But should much fighting continue,
Hail, frost, drought, famine, and epidemics
Will increase and become the rule.

"To stop theft and banditry in Upper
     Rekong
And fighting in Lower Rekong
Everyone should commission paintings of
     the Blissful Buddhafield,
Erect statues of the great Compassionate
     One, Avalokiteshvara,
And recite the quintessential six-syllable
     mantra.

"Old and young alike should learn to read
And observe minutely the karmic law of
     cause and effect
Regarding positive and negative acts.
All should cultivate a pure mind.
If this is done, in this life and in future lives
The sun of happiness and well-being will
     shine."
Thus he spoke in my dream.

In these degenerate times
Human life is extremely short.
See how even the young die suddenly.
The time of death is uncertain,
And, when their deaths come,
Robbers, thieves, and warriors
Will fall into the eighteen realms of hell,

And experience unbearable suffering,
With no chance of escape.

Therefore all you devoted people
Of Lower and Upper Rekong, great and
　　small [181a],
Since theft, banditry, and fighting
Are causes for suffering, never commit
　　them again,
Even in the slightest degree:
Perform virtuous deeds as often as possible.

I, Tsogdruk Rangdrol, give this advice
To all the devoted men and women
Of Upper and Lower Rekong.
May whoever hears it benefit!

Put into writing and distributed throughout
Upper and Lower Rekong, this proclamation
helped a great deal.

On the way to Chuzang, in Mangra, we stopped
in a verdant forest grove near Jipar to boil some
tea and take our noon meal. After I had left,
some people with pure vision said they saw my
handprints in the rock table; some saw me flying
across the Machu River from one mountain to
another; some saw me in the form of the great
Compassionate One and of other deities. Because
of this, they considered me as the Buddha in
person, and my renown spread in all directions.

At Chuzang,[4] I met Alak Gedun Sherap of
Botsuk in Kangtsa, a pure, noble and learned
lama. Perceiving me with pure vision, he made
me sit on a high throne. Then, hoping that it
would help to tame the wild tribes of Bhanak
Khasum, the Three Black Camps, he asked me
to teach them the Dharma. He told them all,
"You must listen to his advice," and thus helped
to establish auspicious spiritual connections
[181b].

He built a high throne in the middle of a
plain and made announcements in all directions,
saying, "This lama will be staying only a month,

as he is on his way to U. All those wanting to
meet him must come soon. Out of his great
compassion, he will turn the Wheel of Dharma
for all."

Because, in those days, in the Three Black
Camps and the domain of the Shabdrung clan
the nomads were prosperous, all the men and
women came dressed in their finest clothes and
jewelry, rode their best horses and brought
excellent white tents. Every day thousands came
to see me, filling the plains of Chuzang with
white tents and hearthstones.

Then a few people asked, "Do you drink
kumiss?"[5] When I said I didn't, they asked, "Why
not?" In reply I said, "Actually, I do have a most
excellent kumiss to drink," and sang this song
entitled How a Yogin Drinks Kumiss:

Father, King of Dharma,
I supplicate you.
Grant your blessing so that my mind-
　　stream
May merge with the Dharma.
I, a yogin who has realized the true nature
　　of mind,
I, the awareness-holder, Jampa Chödar,
Have never tasted kumiss made by human
　　beings;
But I have a kumiss that others do not.

With a mind that thirsts for the holy
　　Dharma,
Toward worldly dharmas I felt only
　　weariness.

With money—the glories of worldly
　　existence—
I bought a mare—the Great Perfection,
From whose womb came forth a foal—
　　compassion.
The milk of spontaneous accomplishment
　　naturally appeared.

Then the youthful maiden—emptiness—
Sat in the postures of the three kayas [182a]
And with her fingers—the four lamps—
Did the milking—the experience of the
　　four visions—

Into the milking pail—the crucial points of
the three gates.[6]

She then poured the milk into the vessel of
naked, utter transparency,
Stirred it with the golden spoon of the
practice,
Uniting primordial purity and spontaneous
presence,
And let it rest in the natural state.

Now I shall offer the first fresh part.
You, the young child Awareness,
Stand, vivid, in the natural state
And dip out the first part
With the ladle of undistracted mindfulness.

E ma!
This Dharma, wondrous and
extraordinary,
The fresh, first *kumiss* of liberation from
suffering,
I offer to the lamas and the hosts of *yidam*
deities:
Partake of it from within the state of the
unborn dharmakaya—
This is the joyous feast of gratitude.

Secondly I offer it to the dakinis and
dharmapalas.
Partake of it in the state beyond the
workings of mind—
This is the joyous feast of the
accomplishment of activities!

Then I offer it to all my vajra brothers and
sisters:
Partake of it in the spontaneous,
uncontrived state—
This is the joyous feast of pure *samaya!*

Lastly, the dregs of ambrosia, on the bottom,
Are drunk by me, the fortunate renunciate.

All the guests were cheered by this
excellent ambrosia
And offered toasts to excellent
auspiciousness.
I, the yogin, also became intoxicated.

Deep from within, I savored its taste,
Inexpressible like the blissful ecstasy of a
young maiden.

An experience arose in me—
One that could not be captured in words,
Like the dream of a mute.

I realized the single meaning,
Indivisible, indissociable,
Like raw sugar and its sweet taste.

Ignorance and conflicting emotions
dissolved into the absolute expanse,
Like clouds vanishing in the sky [182b].

I found irreversible confidence,
Like an archer of great skill and strength
shooting arrows.

I felt an immeasurable joy,
Like a beggar discovering his hearthstone
to be gold.

Be blissful and happy,
O vajra brothers and sisters.

This song inspired faith in their minds. Then
from Bhanak Khasum, Trika, Rekong, Marnang,
Tso-nga, the Mongolian area under Shabdrung,
and other places, so many people came to meet
me it that became like a busy marketplace. Having prayed to the Three Jewels and generated
Bodhicitta, with love and compassion, from a
throne erected in a field I taught in detail on the
karmic law of cause and effect, as one can find in
the *Beneficial Sun.*[7]

My close disciple Kalden Rangdrol gave
refuge vows and, according to everyone's need,
the transmissions of the confession prayers, the
mani mantra, the one-day vow and fasting practice, the *Praises to Tara,* the *White Umbrella* mantra, and the *Diamond Sutra.*[8]

Doing so, we could turn toward the pure
Dharma the minds of all the cruel tribes of Bhanak
Khasum who, high and low, had never done
anything but exert themselves in banditry and
wrongdoing, and were renowned for having
remained untamed despite the countless Bud-

dhas who had appeared in the past. All those who killed many wild animals, goats, and sheep stopped their endless sins, and many also renounced robbing and stealing. For many years, most families gave up killing lambs and the calves of *dzomo*[9] [183a]. To everyone's amazement, even the servants who were in charge of slaughtering took vows not to kill. Many men and women pledged to practice virtue.

To many qualified disciples I gave the empowerment of the *Wish-fulfilling Gem, Hayagriva and Varahi,* and the teaching on the Great Perfection called *Dispelling the Darkness of Ignorance.* About twenty of them renounced the world.

So much silk, cotton, clothing, jewelry, sheep, horses, and cattle were offered to me that, had I accepted it all, it seemed that it would not have fit into the valley. Realizing that the northern route I was going to take entailed many difficulties, I returned most of these offerings after having dedicated the merit. Of what I did accept, I used the most valuable things as Dharma offerings and gifts, and to offer in central Tibet put aside one thousand coins, a few white Chinese bowls, some corals and turquoise, and hundreds of scarves with woven designs of Amitayus. With the help of a few monks—Ngawang Dargye and Kunzang Rangdrol from Shabdrung, Alak Tsöndru, Bendhe from Shohong, and Chödpa from Bongtak—all the food, supplies, pack- and riding horses needed for our journey to central Tibet were swiftly and easily prepared.

I offered to Alak Gedun Sherap Rinpoche all the remaining goods and provisions, and requested some teachings to establish a spiritual link. In return, he gave me one horse for the journey to central Tibet [183b]. After we had conversed joyfully for a long time, I offered this song before parting:

You, luminous empty sky, farewell,
While I, earthly sun, make the round of the
    four continents.
Soon, with rays of light, I will return.

You, wish-fulfilling tree, farewell,
While I, cuckoo, king of birds, fly off to
    other horizons.
Soon, with melodious songs, I will return.

You, thousand-petaled flower, farewell,
While I, handsome bee, leave to seek out
    nectar in the ten directions.
Soon, with a bee's humming, I will return.

You, authentic lama, farewell,
While I, fortunate disciple, leave for
    whichever wilderness I please.
Soon, with an offering scarf, I will return.

After I had offered this song, he accompanied me outside his tent, said farewell, and went inside. I then passed through Chuzang, where I gave much advice on religious and worldly matters to all the faithful men and women gathered there; I ended with this song:

Above the crown of my head,
On a lotus, a sun and a moon,
Sits my root lama, the lord Vajradhara:
Grant the accomplishments
To this gathering of men and women
That they may be happy in this and in
    future lives.

You, sky—blue in color, so easy to soar
    through,
Passage of the gods—remain in joy.
I, a white eagle, fly off to other lands
    [184a].

Riding on the high winds,
I will return, time and again.

You, great lake—white in color, easy to
    alight upon,
Ocean of milk—remain in joy.
I, a celestial swan, fly off to other lands.

To savor joyful leisure,
I will return, time and again.

You of pure white minds, so easy to be
    with,
Lamas, monks, and patrons, remain in joy.
I, the yogin, go off to U and Tsang.

To practice meditation,
I will return, time and again.

I, the yogin, will make a long-life prayer
So that you may live one hundred years.
When we meet again on an auspicious
    day,
May excellence pervade that place.

In reply, my close disciple Kalden Rangdrol
offered this song:

Kind lord who emulates the saints'
Life-examples of perfect liberation,
Father lama, Tsogdruk Rangdrol,
Please listen to this beggar's song!

Through the power of pure aspirations
The two of us met here this year.
Whatever was done, was done in accord
    with Dharma—
This is your kindness, excellent father!

When I heard you were going to another
    place
I could not bear to part from you, father
    guru;
But the gathering of close friends always
    ends in parting.
Reflecting on this, what's the use of being
    sad?

When traveling to the Pure Realm of U
    and Tsang
Excellent father, fare well; have a
    comfortable journey.
I, the son, will act according to all your
    instructions
And make prayers that they be quickly
    accomplished.

So that you, holy one [184b],
May continue to look after us, your
    followers,
Please make heartfelt prayers
That we meet again quickly
In this supreme auspicious place.

By the compassion and protection of the
    Triple Gem,
And by the power of the protecting
    deities,

May the aims of all monks and disciples
Be accomplished according to their wishes;
May all be auspicious!

About three hundred monks, disciples, and
patrons accompanied me about halfway across
the lower end of the plain of Chuzang, and then
sat on the ground to receive blessings and protection. I explained:

"Through the potential created by our past
pure aspirations, we met within the auspicious
harmony of the Dharma. We have made profound spiritual and material connections. Now,
within this auspicious harmony, we separate.

"Likewise, the nature of all things is unreliable, impermanent, and essenceless. In particular, sooner or later, little by little, impermanence
will unravel the current gatherings of husbands
and wives, parents and children; it is certain that
you will all have to depart for the next life. From
now on, think of death and impermanence, and
practice the Dharma. Wherever I may go, I will
keep you all in mind, and so throughout my life I
will pray for you."

Then, standing, resting my chin on my walking stick, I gave this heart-advice, called *The
Yogin's Departure*:

Lord, root guru, Vajradhara,
Arise from the *dharmachakra* in my heart
Through the path of the central channel
    [185a],
And remain as my head's crowning
    ornament,
On the *chakra* of great bliss.

May the sicknesses of body and sufferings
    of mind
Of all those gathered here be dispelled.
Grant your blessing that they become
    happy, filled with joy,
And that their minds may turn toward the
    Dharma.

From here and there, all of us have come
And gathered here for but an instant.
We will not stay on long, but will soon
    part—
Impermanent, just as are all things.

Remember how, in the past,
All your neighbors, the old men, the old
   women,
Have already died. Think of how
These young boys and girls
In whom people place such hopes
Will themselves, before long, die.

It's the same for us:
Within the span of eighty human years
   or so,
All of us, without exception, who are
   gathered here today
Will have gone on from this life to the next.

Some, with a remorse that arrives too late,
   will weep.
When leaving for the next life, we must
   leave empty-handed:
How can we take any of the wealth that we
   have accumulated?
How can we take even a good friend to
   accompany us?
We will have to go alone through the long
   and narrow gorge that is the *bardo*.

At that time, our only guide is the lama;
The only real help is the excellent Dharma.
Faithful men and women gathered here,
Remember: no one knows when death
   will come!

Give up the ten unvirtuous acts as if they
   were poison.
Don't be stingy with your wealth—
Offer it to the lama and to the Three
   Jewels,
And give it away to the poor.

Obey and respect your parents and elders
   [185b].
Don't mistreat your servants; give them
   food and clothing.
Don't beat your dogs and domestic
   animals; take good care of them.
Don't quarrel; foster harmony within the
   household.
Don't harm friends or neighbors; try to
   help them.

With your body, don't stay idle, but do
   prostrations and circumambulations.
With your speech, don't be lazy but count
   manis;
From time to time, keep the vows of
   fasting.
And at all times keep a pure mind.

I, as well, wherever I may go
Will not forget you, but will keep you in
   mind.
I will do all I can to dispel your obstacles in
   this life
And in future lives, will guide you on the
   path.

I pray that I, a meditator who dwells in the
   mountains,
And you, monks and laymen with whom
   I've made a spiritual link,
May attain Buddhahood at the same time.
In the same way, you all should pray.

I will pray that, from now until the end of
   this life
We will meet, time and again;
Should we have no chance to meet,
I pray earnestly that we will meet in a
   future life.

Faithful men and women,
I have given you this beneficial advice from
   my heart;
Please remember it from time to time;
Today we have made a profound
   connection.

May you all remain well and in peace.
May whoever sings and listens to this song
Always remain well and happy.

While I sang this song with a slow and melodious tune, immeasurable devotion arose in the people present; tears sprang from their eyes and their hair stood on end.

Then I drew a line on the ground with my walking stick, and told them not to go beyond it. "There is an auspicious meaning to this," I told them [186a]. Like a wall collapsing, everyone fell to their knees doing prostrations; and, having requested my spiritual protection, they returned home.

My close disciple Kalden Rangdrol went in the direction of Trika. I crossed the Machu River in a boat and camped there for a few days. Nearby, at Kangtsa, across Hang-nga Mountain, above the White Rock Monkey Fortress, lived the chiefs Bendhe Thar and Tsering Gyal, two brothers. They offered me many *dzo*, horses, silver, corals, turquoise, food and clothing, which I accepted, dedicating the merit and making prayers for auspiciousness.

Many laymen from the province of Kangtsa accompanied me over one high pass, and when Chief Bendhe and other patrons were on the point of return, I sang this song entitled *Aspiration to Meet Once Again:*

> Upon my crown, in the expanse of a tent
> of rainbow light
> Is the lord, the venerable precious guru of
> supreme grace—
> Grant your blessing that all those gathered
> here
> May have long lives free from illness
> And that we may meet many times again.
>
> You, eastern mountain, farewell,
> While I, the moon, do not stay,
> But go on to another continent.
> If I don't fall prey to the planet Rahu-
> Vishnu,[10]
> I will come again to adorn the eastern
> mountain.
>
> You, northern mountain crags, farewell,
> While I, a small wild yak, do not stay,
> But go off to the mountain meadows.
> If I don't fall prey to tigers or hunters
> I will come again to adorn the rocky
> mountain.
>
> You, the faithful of Domey, farewell,
> While I, the yogin, do not stay

> But go on to the Pure Realm of U and
> Tsang.
> If I don't fall prey to death
> I will return to care for all the faithful
> [186b].
>
> I, the yogin, will pray
> That all those gathered here
> Have long and healthy lives.
>
> May the day and place of our next meeting
> Be bathed in auspiciousness.

After I had sung this, our group reached a ford in the river. There, I told everyone to take care and gave them some beneficial advice. After making prayers that we might meet many times again, I left, accompanied by about ten friends.

There were altogether about fifty other travelers from the province of Bhanak Khasum going to U, including Kharjam and Chador from Dratsa, and Tsering Gyal and others from Kangtsa. All had many packhorses and much luggage.

In the Male Iron Horse year,[11] called Rabnyo, in the sixth month, on an auspicious day of the waxing moon, we set off for the Pure Realm of U-Tsang. When I, someone unattached to horses, was about to mount a white horse that had been given to me by my patron Bendhe Thar, I sang the *Yogin's Horse Race:*

> I supplicate all the father lamas:
> May your blessings ripen and free my
> mind-stream.
>
> I have no attachment to men's horses,
> But, by the kindness of the authentic guru,
> In addition to this man's horse
> I ride a stallion—emptiness.
> Though this man's horse is excellent,
> I am much more comfortable on mine.
>
> On my stallion, emptiness,
> I put a bridle—pure discipline.
> Beneath the Bodhicitta saddle
> I spread the saddle pad—firm faith.
> I fasten the girth—devotion and pure
> vision—

Under the stirrups—the union of emptiness and appearance.

Seated on this excellent horse and excellent
saddle,
I, the young child Awareness Arisen of
Itself [187a],
Am dressed in the brocade of the four
immeasurables,
Bound with the sash of pure *samaya*.
I wear a qualified lama upon my head like
an excellent hat;
I wear boots of angerless patience.

Seated on my horse,
I, the young son Awareness,
Race across the even plain of pristine
simplicity.
Steering with the bit and reins of diligence
I urge my horse on with the whip of my
lama's pith instructions.
Free of doubts, I give it its head.

I enjoy the spectacle of samsara and
nirvana.
When going—I gallop on the path of
enlightenment.
When crossing—I cross through the mud
of samsara,
Not falling to either side—nihilism or
eternalism.

On this tireless excellent horse,
When I flee, I can escape from the jaws of
the Lord of Death.
When I pursue, I can catch up to the wind.

Ho! Fortunate youths!
If you buy a horse, buy an excellent
horse—emptiness!
If you race a horse, race a horse like this!

After singing this song, I mounted the horse and
rode off.

At Dzasorwa, we had to wait more than ten
days for some central Tibetans returning from
Domey to U. We heard that a trading caravan
coming down from U had abandoned a man
from Trika who was near death. After two days

of searching we found him, and gave him food
and clothing. When he had recovered, we sent
him home.

For those who had escorted me up to that
place, I sang a song called the *Auspicious Aspiration
to Meet Again*:

I supplicate the kind master:
Please bless the body, speech, and mind
Of all those who have assembled here
[187b].
Faithful men and women gathered here,
Listen a moment to this yogin's song.

Through the power of previous pure deeds
and aspirations,
All who are assembled here have had the
good fortune
To encounter the Buddha's teachings.
Achieving either a higher state of existence
Or ultimate excellence is up to you.
Now, when you have the choice,
Practice right away the means to attain the
ultimate excellence—enlightenment!

Like the bee that sings a long humming
song
Before flying off to a distant land,
I, the yogin, after singing my song of
contentment
Will go on to the distant land of U.

Like the bee returning
I, the yogin, will soon return.
Until then, may virtue and auspiciousness
Continuously pervade this land.

After I had sung this, everyone did prostrations
and circumambulations with faith and devotion,
then bade me farewell, saying, "Be well till we
meet again!"

At this time we met a leper from Marnang
Be'u Thang, on his way to drink the medicinal
snow waters of Mount Machen. Out of pity, I
gave him a *dzo*, a saddle, ropes, a tent, bellows
and flint, and a month's provisions, and sent him
off. Later, I heard he had been cured and had
returned home singing and riding upon the *dzo*.

While traveling, I ate only before noon and

never interrupted my spiritual practice. I always explained to my fellow travelers that robbing, stealing, and hunting were wrong, and I gave them much advice on right conduct [188a].

During the journey, my devoted disciple, Gelong Ngawang Dargye, asked me to sing, for the benefit of the present and future travelers to U-Tsang, a song that would explain how to behave properly on the road and at home. At his request, I composed the cycle entitled the *Songs on the Path of the Long-Distance Traveler*. First came this song entitled *The Necessity of Giving up Negative Actions:*

I bow down at the feet of the Victorious
    Ones, Father and Son,
The object of all beings' homage and offering.
Please look with compassion
On all the long-distance travelers bound
    for U.

At the start,
The bad traveler puts his bad saddle
Atop the bad saddle-pad of his horse.
He overloads the horse and,
Rushing on, he overworks it.

He takes along with him many sheep,
To be killed for food along the journey.
As he goes, he also hunts wild animals—
    many of them.
When his sheep are all eaten up, he buys
    more on the way.
Thus, committing evil deed after evil deed,
    he travels.

When discussing whether to travel on or to
    set camp,
No matter what anyone says, he disagrees.
Arguing back and forth, he always says no.
Since he never listens to experienced
    travelers,
Almost everything goes wrong;
Mistaking the road, he goes astray.

He doesn't stay awake when he's on guard,
    but is sunk in sleep;

When his possessions are carried off by
    thieves,
He just runs around in circles.

He doesn't let his horse stop to graze,
But forces it to keep going on and on,
And when the horse, exhausted, cannot
    take another step,
He hurls abuse at it.

He lingers near the hearthstone where
    people are cooking,
But can't be bothered to bring back wood
    or water;
When the firewood runs out, he'll blame
    his friends.

When there is nothing to worry about, his
    courage is at its zenith.
He'll say, "No need to stay on guard, there
    won't be any problems."
But when bandits come, his heart shakes
    with fear [188b].
He won't go where there's fighting;
Should he happen to find himself where
    there's fighting, he hides.

When faced with outer enemies, he is
    hopeless;
At creating discord within the party, he is
    peerless.

On the road, he keeps on slandering his
    fellow-travelers behind their backs.
His stomach is gigantic, his appetite insatiable.
He scrutinizes each person's portion;
If someone else takes more than he does,
He throws a fit, eyes ablaze with rage,
While he seizes the choicest, richest food
    for himself.

He won't give away a morsel;
If, by chance, he does, he gives only the
    tiniest sliver,
Saying, "Here, sink your teeth into this!"
Since the sliver isn't even something big
    enough to swallow, much less chew,
The recipient, embarrassed, just slinks off.

He just cannot keep his big mouth shut;
Behind their backs, he'll ape the way some
    people speak or eat—
To make all the others snigger.

On the road, he leaves his servants hungry
    and thirsty.
To the poorer and more humble travelers,
He won't give even a handful of *tsampa*.
And when others give alms, it just stirs up
    his greed.

Not only does he not lend anything to his
    friends,
But he begs to be given, or sneaks off with,
Their belongings, their money, their food,
And even their stakes, rope, and string—
Or else he just steals them.

When his friends say, "Don't you see that
    we're having trouble?"
He shouts back, "Ah, what's eating you?"

And after a while, he wails "Ah! Oh! Oh!"
And grumbles, "I should never have gone
    with these people!"

In the middle,
When the bad traveler
Arrives in U, what does he do?
He buys hats, felt, cups, corals, turquoise,
And other articles for his own enjoyment,
But never makes a single offering of tea or
    distribution of alms.

He never does prostrations or
    circumambulations, but strolls about
    the marketplace.
He never says daily prayers, but gossips
    and tells stories.
He has no faith and devotion and is
    thoroughly warped within.

All the goods in the marketplace—
When he sees them every day, his desire
    increases.
He steals the silver coins of his friends
    [189a],

And when he's caught, says, "I'm *terribly*
    sorry!"

He gives lavish presents to the ladies of the
    evening,
Sleeps with them, and ends up with the clap.

He tells many lies, says divisive things,
And meddles in the affairs of good friends,
Causing discord and ill will.

He backbites his friends, and the represen-
    tatives from his homeland,
Covering the whole of U and Tsang with
    evil rumors.

In the end,
When this bad traveler goes back to his
    region,
He does not bring a single sacred object
    related to Buddha's body, speech, or
    mind,
But sets off loaded down with goods.

On the way, if a weakened packhorse of
    one of his friends dies,
Not only does he not lend him another
    horse,
But he curses his friend, saying, "You just
    bring bad luck!"

On the way, if one of his friends falls ill,
He's irked, and tries to get rid of him.
On the road, he looks at the humble
    dwellings
To see if he could possibly steal something.

Evil speech, evil mind, evil conduct!
Traveling on and on with him, things get
    worse and worse.

As his bad manners become obvious,
No one, from men to dogs, trusts him.

When he arrives anywhere in the vicinity
    of his country
There is no question of accompanying his
    companions a little further,

Of inviting them home, or of even saying
    "good-bye":
He just sheds one after another
Those with whom he has traveled for so
    long.

When his fellow countrymen ask questions
    and news of everyone,
His travelling companions will say:
"This evil man's pilgrimage to U was
    pointless;
He behaved in such an awful fashion
That he made life miserable for everyone
    day after day."

Upon reaching his country, the very next day
He fills the whole land with slander and
    evil tales.
In the future, his countrymen will use him
    as an infamous example.

All of you who travel to central Tibet,
Please don't behave like this!

May this song benefit all those
Who hear or read it on their way to U and
    Tsang [189b].

After that, I sang *How to Conduct Oneself in a Noble Way:*

I bow down at the feet of the divine refuge
    and protector of all beings,
I bow down at the feet of the Victorious
    Ones, Father and Son:
Look with compassion upon all
    long-distance travelers
Bound for central Tibet.
At the start,
The good traveler
Puts a good saddle and a good saddle-pad
On his packhorse, and gives it
A light and comfortable load.
He does not rush his horse, but takes his
    time.

He brings not a single sheep to eat,
And on the way, does not kill a single wild
    animal.

To his traveling companions, he gives good
    advice, saying,
"To have the chance to go to central Tibet
    is rare.
When going, it is difficult to find traveling
    companions.
Even when traveling companions have
    been found,
 At the end of the journey, each goes his
    own way again.
So, for those few months, one should share
    whatever comes,
Good times or bad times,
Helping each other as much as possible,
Without quarreling or fighting."

Regarding how to go and where to stop,
He takes the advice of experienced
    travelers who have taken the road
    before.
Withstanding hardships of cold or hunger,
    he works well—
He pitches tents, unloads and stacks the
    luggage,
Fetches water, collects firewood, and starts
    up the fire with the bellows:
Whatever is needed. While resting or on
    the move, he eagerly says, "I'll do it."
He is always ready to get up and ready to
    go.
When his turn comes to watch the horses,
    he takes good care of them.
When it rains, when crossing rivers, when
    night falls,
He reminds everyone to be careful.

When he sees bandits, he tries to reason
    with them;
If they don't listen, he rushes at them,
    spear in hand:
No question of losing his own things—
He even takes away the bandits' hoard!

Afterward, when they continue, the travel-
    ers excitedly exclaim [190a],
"Today, this good son of his mother has
    shown his courage!"
Everyone calls him a real hero.

If others cannot do something alone, he'll
lend a hand.
He gives food and money to poor and
humble travelers.
If he sees another's possession, big or
small,
That has fallen to the ground, he picks it
up and asks "Whose is this?"
Someone says, "It's mine; what a kind
person you are!"

In the middle,
When the good traveler
Arrives in central Tibet, he offers all he
has,
Making as many tea offerings as he can
afford.
To the Jowo statue he offers a new coat of
gold and a hundred butter-lamps;
To the beggars he gives alms of food and
drink,
From the butchers he ransoms goats and
sheep.

With body he does prostrations and
circumambulations.
With speech he exerts himself in daily
prayers and recitations.
With mind, he keeps faith, devotion, and
pure vision.

He pays homage at all holy statues of
deities.
He requests that all the teachers' lives be
firm and long,
And offers them the symbolic objects of
Buddha's body, speech, and mind.
Because he offers whatever he has to the
Dharma
His good example spreads throughout U
and Tsang.

In the end,
When the good traveler
Returns to his homeland,
He makes prayers to have the chance
again
To visit the Pure Realm of U and Tsang.

He does not bring back ordinary goods,
Only sacred objects related to body,
speech, and mind.

On the way, he helps all his fellow
travelers,
Giving them food and useful things.
More loving than a brother,
He takes special care of those who fall ill.
If, by chance, someone dies,
He cuts open the corpse so vultures can
feed on it.[12]
If there is a lama present, he requests that
he make prayers of dedication.

Kind words, kind heart, kind conduct!
[190b].
The more one travels with him, the more
one appreciates him.

As his good qualities become apparent,
Everyone says, "May you live long, may
everything be auspicious with you!"
And some of his companions even call him
"Kind One."

When arriving at each traveler's
homeland,
He goes on a little farther with each of
them to bid him farewell.
Since it is painful to separate,
Everyone weeps when they must part.
Wishing each other good health,
Good luck and all the best, they leave
exchanging good wishes.

When people at home ask after the news,
His traveling companions will say,
"This fortunate being made a meaningful
journey to central Tibet.
He acted with virtue,
And brought benefit to all along the way."

After arriving in his country, the very next
day
The good traveler has plenty of good
things to say,
And everyone prays to follow his example.

You, travelers bound for central Tibet
Please behave in this same manner.

May all the travelers to central Tibet
Who hear or read this song
Be benefited by it.

Then I sang a song, *How Unsuitable It Is to Commit
Negative Actions on the Way:*

Bowing down to the two Jowo Shakyas[13]
Who shine like the sun and moon rising
    together,
I will give a few words of advice
To the long-distance travelers who wish to
    visit the Precious Jowos.

To load an immense burden on a
    packhorse,
Till it can't budge, to beat the horse with
    sticks and stones
That fill its whole body with pain,
To leave it at night where there is no grass
    or water,
To abandon it to be eaten alive by wolves
    or ravens
When at last its back is covered with sores
And its legs are lame and injured:
There is no crime worse than this.
Please treat your pack animals with
    kindness.

The sheep become attached to the master
Who drives them along on great distances
    [191a].
Wherever he goes, they follow him,
Wherever he stays, they stay as well.
If they don't see their master they start to
    bleat;
When they see him, they joyfully rush
    toward him.
One day, when they are resting, trusting
    their owner and completely at ease,
Their owner grabs one, ties its mouth to
    smother it,
Slits open its belly, and pulls out its red life-
    vein with his hand:
This is just like murdering an old friend.

One cannot conceive of a greater shame.
Though he has made the pilgrimage to
    central Tibet,
Such a man has not gained virtue, but only
    committed sin.
So, please do not take along sheep to
    slaughter for food on the way.

In the wilderness,
Many innocent wild animals live,
Eating free grass and drinking free water.
Even if the sight of such beauty doesn't
    move you,
You must not shoot and kill them.
Wild animals are like the pets of the local
    deities,
And if one kills them, diseases will plague
    men and animals.
Hail, thunder, lightning, snowstorms,
    landslides,
And flash floods will bring suffering to all.
So, don't shoot and kill wild animals!

The Jowo Shakyas, and the Victorious
    Ones, Father and Son,
Look lovingly on each sentient being as
    they would their child.
Therefore, if you take life,
No matter how much wealth you offer
    them, they will never be pleased.

When on the way to pay homage to the
    two Jowos,
If you think there is no harm in doing evil
And you perform unvirtuous deeds,
This is creating bad karma in connection
    with Dharma—
This is the worst possible karma.

Someone who is traveling to the feet of the
    two Jowos
In order to confess his previous negative acts
And commits even more negative actions
    on the way,
Is merely adding evil deeds to evil deeds,
So that nothing ever gets purified.
Therefore, don't commit evil acts at any
    time [191b].

May all travelers who hear this song
Never commit negative actions.

Then I sang *A Brief Advice for the Benefit of All, at Home and on the Way*:

I bow down to the two Jowo Shakyas
Who shine like the sun and moon rising
    together.
I will give a little advice to those travelers
Who come from afar to visit the Jowos.

It is hard to get more than one chance to
    see
The Victorious Ones, Father and Son, the
    two Jowos,
And the sangha of the three monasteries—
    Sera, Drepung, and Ganden.[14]
It is a rare chance in this life
To travel to the distant land of U.

So, if you have possessions to offer, take
    them with you,
For, if you leave them behind,
Thinking to offer them in a future pilgrim-
    age,
This may never happen.

On the journey, unable to bear hardships
    like hunger and cold,
A traveler might grow angry and threaten
    others.
He argues over the size of his share of
    hunks of meat,
His share of *tsampa*, bread, and butter, and
    even over how much tea is poured into
    his cup.
If he has a full stomach, he shows a smiling
    face and chats happily.
If he is hungry, he gives dark looks and
    speaks nastily.

When he is on guard watch, he is
    completely unreliable;
When there is no danger, he shouts out,
    "Wake up! Run! Come!"
But when the danger is real, he sleeps
    more soundly than a corpse,

And though you call his name many times,
    he won't wake up.
Don't behave like this!

Such a bad fellow is only concerned about
    his homeland;
He does not visit pilgrimage places, but
    gossips about home.
He never does prostrations or
    circumambulations;
And even worse, he doesn't even let his
    friends do any either.
When the time approaches to go home, he
    just says, "Let's get out of here!"

When leaving central Tibet, don't say such
    things.

When the travelers arrive in their
    homelands, everyone rejoices,
And rushes up in welcome, asking after
    their travels:
"O mother, O uncle, you lucky ones,
What did you see and what did you visit?
How many prostrations and
    circumambulations did you do?
What religious offerings did you make?
    [192a].
Surely you have collected relics of body,
    speech, and mind; please, give me one!"
How shameful if there is no answer!

For that reason, you, kind pilgrims who
    have visited central Tibet,
Lay on the heads of your neighbors, your
    countrymen old and young,
Sacred relics of the body, speech, and
    mind,
Tie around their necks red and white pro-
    tection cords,
Put in their hands sacred pills of body,
    speech, and mind,
And give them all news they will rejoice in,
Thus making your countrymen happy.
All will say, "Our fortunate uncle
Has made great use of his trip."
Your conduct should be such that it
    arouses the admiration of others.

May this song benefit all those
Who hear or read it on their way to central
    Tibet.

In this way, I tried to create a good motivation in
the minds of those travelers who heard this song.

On the way over the northern plains, Chador
from Dratsa and other singers gathered. Some of
them sang this melancholy song:

When crossing the first valley and river,
Looking back, I think of my father.
And why do I think of my father?
My father and his stallion are both growing
    old.

When crossing the second valley and river,
Looking back, I think of my mother.
And why do I think of my mother?
My mother and her *dzomo* are both greatly
    kind.

When crossing the third valley and river
Looking back, I think of my younger
    brothers and sisters.
And why do I think of my brothers and
    sisters?
My siblings and their colts are all so very
    young.

Then someone else sang:

To take the pommel of a saddle as an
    example,
It is like having Tö and U-Tsang in one's
    lap.
Wielding the stinging whip,
One feels like racing on.

To take the cantle of a saddle as an
    example,
It is like the place and parents one has left
    behind.

Pulling back on the light bit,
One feels like staying on [192b].

To take these three as an example:
The tall wooden saddle, its covering
    carpet,
And the leather pads underneath,
They are like the hearthstones put out by
    three brothers;
Dismounting, one feels like stopping a bit
    to play.

A few of the women shed tears when they
heard these songs, which reminded them of
home. Another singer joined with this happy
song:

Upon a yellow golden throne,
A qualified teacher feels at ease.

Upon a white silver throne,
A meritorious chief feels at ease.

Upon a swift striding horse,
An elegant skilled youth feels at ease.

How do you like this kind of song?

Saying this, they laughed. Someone else sang:

Juniper shrubs cling to the tops of
    mountains, to the tops of cliffs.
Those who live there never lack the
    incense of the gods—that's one happi-
    ness!

Monasteries cling to the waists of
    mountains, to the waists of cliffs.
Those who live there never fall into the
    hells—that's one happiness!

At the base of mountains, in the plains,
Those who live there are never without tea
    and food and *chang*—that's one
    happiness!

He concluded, "I don't know how to sing, I was
just amusing myself." Another sang:

Like the golden sun at its peak
Are the golden roofs of Tö, U and Tsang.
I pray to be reborn there.
Like a constellation of shimmering great stars
Are the three great monasteries of U—
     Sera, Drepung and Ganden.
I pray to see those monasteries.

Like a long line of yaks getting up and
     moving forward
Are the travelers going to central Tibet.
I pray to go there myself.

He concluded, "Say it's a good song, and I'll sing
another." Someone else sang:

In the highlands live the Victorious Ones,
Father and Son, the wellsprings of the
     Dharma:
I pray to encounter these lords [193a].

In the lowlands lives the Manchu ruler,
The life tree of the Dharma:
I pray to encounter his court.

In the midlands live Tibetan and
     Mongolian travelers,
The patrons of the Dharma:
I pray to swiftly reach central Tibet.

Another sang:

In the highlands,
Live the Three Great Lamas:[15]
May the auspiciousness of a hundred
     thousand monks prevail!

In the lowlands
Dwells the Manchu ruler:
May the auspiciousness of a hundred
     thousand wise ones prevail!

In the midlands
Dwells King Gesar, Great Lion of the
     World:
May the auspiciousness of a hundred
     thousand infallible archers of Ling
     prevail!

Then another sang:

I have come from the land of clothes—
May there be everywhere the good fortune
     of never being without clothes on one's
     back.

I have come from the land of food—
May there be everywhere the good fortune
     of never being without food in one's
     mouth.

I have come from the land of Dharma—
May there be the good fortune of never
     being without Dharma in one's mind.

Singing these and many other songs, we traveled
on to the Pure Realm of central Tibet.

Every day my fellow travelers and the chief
merchants killed some of the sheep they had
brought along, and thus the number of sheep
dwindled. Out of compassion, paying three
sang for every sheep, I ransomed the lives of
about thirty-five of them, which I then brought
with me.

One important merchant on his way to central Tibet with his caravan had left behind two
monk escorts of Kumbum Monastery who had
fallen sick and [193b] a Khampa household of
five travelers whose horse and *dzo* had collapsed
from exhaustion. Out of pity, on parting I gave a
horse to the Khampa family, a *dzo* to the monks,
and food and clothing to them all.

Those traveling to central Tibet that year
said it was the best trip they had ever made. After
traveling together for many months, as we
approached Lhasa, everyone gradually left, saying, "Good-bye, farewell," and scattered in every
direction. Realizing the impermanence of all
things, I sang this sad song:

The sun which shines high in the sky at
     noon

By evening descends to hide in the western
    hills.

The lama shows the impermanence of all
    things;
By leaving for other realms,
He demonstrates that the body is
    impermanent.

The pleasant and comforting song of the
    cuckoo
Sounds no more. Where has it gone,
    leaving no trace?

The kind parents who gave rise to this
    body,
Leaving behind their body and wealth,
Have passed on to their next lives.

Outside, under our very eyes, crops and
    berries
Are taken away, day after day.

Old, young, middle-aged—with each
    passing year
One's friends grow fewer and fewer.

The beautiful colors of flowers in bloom
Turn brown as their freshness withers.

When the youth of this illusory body
Is exchanged for age, the body withers.

The flocks of friendly birds that met in
    fields of reeds
With resounding cries fly off in the four
    directions.

The friendly companions who have
    traveled to central Tibet [194a]
With parting words of good wishes, all go
    their separate ways.

Wherever I look, there is impermanence,
Transience, constant change.
Mind is made uneasy;
I long to practice the holy Dharma;
I wish to sing this plaintive song.

My kind parents and the guru I revered
I shall never see again in this life.

But you, friends, monks, disciples, and
    patrons—
I make a wish to see you, in this life, once
    again.

After singing this, we arrived in the Pure Realm
of central Tibet, Lhasa, "the Seat of the Gods"
and my mind became happy and serene. It was
like coming to a Pure Realm and I felt great joy.
We stayed at Jamyang Shar,[16] where the
guestmaster, the chieftain, and the cook were
most hospitable. The Dharma King Songtsen
Gampo said:

> At the end of this age, almost all those
> Who see, hear of, or touch my Rasa
>   Temple,[17]
> Even those who have committed much
>   evil,
> Will be liberated from samsara.
> This stems from the compassion of the
>   noble ones
> And the merit of my Tibetan subjects.
> For that reason, all of you disciples,
> Keep your courage and endeavor growing,
> And see, speak of, or pay homage at my
>   Rasa.
>
> Whatever faults you wish to purify, and
> Whatever good qualities you wish to
>   develop,
> If you worship with devotion at Rasa
> All your aspirations will be fulfilled.

Thus, almost all those who establish an auspicious connection, through seeing, hearing,
touching or thinking about the Jowo Rinpoche,
the statue of the Crowned Buddha, the main
sacred object of the Miraculous Temple of Rasa
[194b], the unique ornament of the universe,
most supreme object of offerings and prostrations, will be benefited.

The very day that I arrived, I went to see the
Jowo. It was like meeting the Buddha himself.
Inconceivable faith and devotion arose in me.

The following day I went to pay homage to the Jowo of Ramoche, the Avalokiteshvara of Five Miracles,[18] and others. I offered butter-lamps and made many prayers.

I made enquiries at the Potala[19] through the secretary and the chief cook to find out if it was possible to behold the golden face of the Dalai Lama Lungthok Gyatso,[20] "Ocean of Scriptures and Reason," the saffron-clad manifestation of noble Avalokiteshvara. Two days went by, and I got word to come to meet him. With many powerful chiefs of Domey and Mongolia, and with Tendzin, the attendant of Jamyang Shepa,[21] I came into presence of the Precious Protector. I offered him a mandala and objects symbolic of the body, speech, and mind of the Buddha, a ceremonial scarf, fifteen *sang*, a crystal rosary ornamented with corals, and a horse with all its gear.

We sat in a line and were given a little of the remainder of the Dalai Lama's tea. The Precious Protector first spoke to the chiefs of lower Kham and Mongolia, and then to Jamyang Shepa's secretary. Finally he said to me, "Amdo lama, you didn't have any trouble on the way, did you?"

Following the others' example, I rose, bowed slightly and, with folded hands, replied, "Precious lord and protector, through your compassion, everything went well" [195a]. It must have been my high voice and Amdo accent that caused the Dalai Lama and some of his attendants to smile.

The chiefs from lower Kham and Mongolia requested the transmission for the Lords of the Three Families. Before receiving the teaching, we offered a mandala. Ceremonial scarf in hand, I offered this long-life supplication in the form of a seven-branch prayer:

Noble Avalokiteshvara, tutelary deity of
    Tibet,
Who deliberately manifested
As the saffron-clad protector and refuge.
Mighty conqueror, Lungthok Gyatso,
I bow down with devotion at your lotus
    feet.

I offer objects symbolic of
Enlightened body, speech, and mind,

And all the gold, silver, and silk brocade
That exists in an ocean of Pure Realms.

All my wrongdoings and those of others,
Before your eyes, prostrating myself, I confess.

With my palms joined, I rejoice in all deeds
    of your body, speech, and mind.

With an offering of a golden Dharma
    Wheel and a white conch with clock-
    wise spiral,
I ask that you turn the Wheel of Dharma.

With an offering of a throne stamped with
    a double vajra
I ask that you live for an ocean of kalpas.

All the virtue accumulated throughout the
    three times,
Symbolized by this present offering,
I dedicate so that you may grant your
    blessing.

Precious refuge, protector for this life and
    the next,
I supplicate you: please bless my mind-
    stream.

I beseech you: please pacify all undesirable
    conditions and obstacles of this life [195b];
In the next, guide me to the Pure Realm of
    Sukhavati.

In this Pure Realm of Tibet, encircled by a
    rampart of snow mountains,
Lives the source of all happiness and
    benefit to beings—
Lungthok Gyatso, Avalokiteshvara in
    person.

May your life be firm and long,
May your lotus feet stand firm till the end
    of samsara.

Throughout all our lives, may we never be
    separated from the glorious master;
May we delight in the glory of Dharma;

May we accomplish the qualities of the
    paths and *bhumis*,
And swiftly attain the state of Vajradhara.

After I offered this, the Dalai Lama, the
precious refuge and protector, with a voice as
sweet as Brahma, sang in a lovely melody some
verses about the proper motivation and conduct
needed to listen to the Dharma, and gave the
transmission. I felt the same immeasurable joy as
if I had arrived at Avalokiteshvara's feet in the
Potala Pure Realm. When we left, he gave us
each a protection cord.

On another day, the Dalai Lama called me
into his presence and gave me a plate, some
woolen cloth, blessed pills, protection cords, and
a white silk scarf. We talked for a long time.

Then, I met the Refuge and Protector
Panchen Rinpoche,[22] the emanation of Buddha
Amitabha in the form of a saffron clad monk. I
offered him a horse, ten *sang*, a long silken scarf,
and a jade rosary ornamented with corals, and
requested his spiritual protection with the following verses:

Sole protector of beings,
In former times you attained Buddhahood
For the sake of all sentient beings, our
    mothers,
And from the sky-like unborn dharmakaya
Displayed an array of forms, vivid as
    rainbows,
Throughout the immensity of pure and
    impure realms [196a].

Especially you have manifested infinite
    emanations
In order to benefit this impure realm.

When your nirmanakaya form was born to
    your mother,
Wondrous auspicious signs appeared.

Remaining for a few months with your
    mother,
Taught by her and your elder sister,
You learned what to adopt and what to
    abandon.

Then, relying on a teacher who was even
    more kind than a mother,
Before long you had mastered almost all
    subjects of study.

Without difficulty you understood the
    Graded Path
That unerringly condenses the essential
    points of Dharma.

Your stainless omniscience ignores
    nothing
About the Secret Mantrayana teachings,
Through which the impure constituents
    of the ordinary body
Are transformed into the pure ones of a
    deity.

Without having to be told,
You know what is in others' minds.

Without having to practice,
You have beheld the faces of many deities.

Hosts of dakinis and dharmapalas
    surround you like your retinue.
You subdue all vicious, perverted foes, and
    hindrance-makers.

Even when you expound the Dharma to a
    single one
Of those beings who, overpowered by
    ignorance,
Does not see what must be done and not
    done,
You begin by praying, "For the sake of all
    beings, each one of whom has once
    been my mother . . ."
This is the sign that, like a mother,
You care continuously for beings.

To the slaughterers of *dri*, yaks, sheep, and
    goats,
You explain, "Don't kill! It is wrong to
    commit such negative actions."

To the ignorant overwhelmed by wrong
    thoughts,

You say, "This is not the way!" and show
   them the excellent path.

When destitute beggars ask for alms,
Filled with compassion, you say, "Poor
   things!" and give them food and
   clothing.

When someone's parent dies,
You tell those who are grief-stricken,
   "Don't be sad! Don't cry!" and console
   them [196b].

When seemingly undeserved harm befalls
   someone,
You advise, "Don't be angry, don't bear
   any grudge—all this is due to your past
   karma."

When someone's lack of sight, knowledge,
   or understanding puts him in difficulty,
Without being asked, you give clear
   information.

When someone has more work than he
   can do,
Without being asked, you help him.

Those who gossip everywhere
You urge to recite the *mani* and say
   prayers.

Those children who are unkind to their
   parents
You admonish by saying, "Don't act in
   such a rude manner."

To those who have committed negative
   actions under the power of ignorance,
You say, "Don't leave it like that—
Confess your faults, take vows, and you will
   purify yourself."

You advise:
"Rely on a teacher, as a child longs for its
   mother,
And, until death, train in heightening your
   good qualities.

Develop Bodhicitta
For the sake of sentient beings, each of whom
Was your mother in a former life.
Never harm anyone and always help
   however you can.
Go and stay, without plans, in isolated
   mountains,
And practice the sutras and tantras without
   distraction."

Through the power of your expounding
   the Dharma
To all sentient beings, who were once our
   mothers,
May the sun of happiness and peace
Shine on all beings!

To you, kind as a mother, all beings should
   offer
Respect and service even more than to
   their own mothers.

Giving up lack of faith and other faults,
I bow down to you with devotion;
I offer you a multitude of perfect, stainless
   offerings;
I confess all wrongdoings and downfalls I
   have, through ignorance, committed;
I rejoice in the immaculate deeds of your
   three secrets;[23]
I ask that you turn the Wheel of Dharma
   for the sake of unrealized beings;
I beg you to remain for a hundred kalpas.
I dedicate to your long life, O Lord,
All merit accrued by all beings, each one
   who has been my own mother [197a].

Kindly take care of me,
Miserable minion of ego-clinging,
And care for all mother-like beings without
   exception,
Until, having entered unerringly the door
   of Dharma,
We all attain the paths and *bhumis*.

After I had offered this, with great affection
he gave me a protection cord, a precious piece of
his handwriting, and various blessed substances.

The next year when he came to Lhasa and was residing in his upper quarters, I went to visit him with Khenpo Shiwa Tsering, who asked of him a long-life blessing. Thus, I was able to meet the Panchen Lama again and to receive the long-life initiation.

I then went to meet Ngawang Nyentrak Rinpoche,[24] the golden throne-holder of Ganden, and offered him one *dzo*, five *sang*, a rosary of precious stones, and an immaculate white scarf. As a request for a Dharma connection, I offered him this song:

Your body never leaves the saffron
    Dharma robes.
Your voice never ceases to speak excellent
    words of Dharma.
Your mind never ceases to rest in the
    Dharmadhatu.

Through the power of listening and
    reflecting on the Dharma tradition
Of the unequalled king of Dharma,
    Tsongkhapa,
You have understood the crucial points of
    the eighty-four thousand sections of the
    Dharma
And every word of this Dharma arose as a
    spiritual instruction.

Since you act in accord with the Dharma,
    everyone venerates you and presents
    you with offerings and praise.
You were enthroned on the golden throne
    of Ganden, the sanctuary of Dharma.

Following the example of Lobzang, who
    knew all Dharmas,[25]
You turn unceasingly the Wheel of Dharma
For millions of fortunate beings who
    manifest affinities with the Dharma
    [197b].

You are highest among those learned in
    Dharma, like the pinnacle of a victory
    banner.
Whatever Dharma you teach, you are just
    like the second Buddha.

Whenever you expound the Dharma, it
    benefits the minds of others.
Though vastly knowledgeable about the
    Dharma, you have not the slightest
    pride.

Never disparaging the Dharma of others,
    you maintain pure vision toward all.
Never committing a single nondharmic
    act,
You love all Dharma practitioners—
    superior, average, and low.

Though Dharma teachers are abundant as
    trees in the forest,
Because you teach the Dharma equally to
    all, high and low,
All those possessed of the eye of Dharma
    became your disciples.

How wonderful: Dharma practitioners
    have filled this land!
If you wish to expound the Dharma, be
    like the golden throne-holder of
    Ganden!

At the time of the Dharma festival, the
    great prayer of Lhasa,
Tens of thousands of Dharma practitioners
    gather at one time.
And when the rain of Dharma falls, every-
    one says, "Excellent!"
All those who are learned in Dharma
    should teach it to others in just this way.

When you see practitioners acting contrary
    to Dharma,
You exhort them to cast out the eight
    worldly dharmas
And cease all other activities opposed to
    the Dharma;
Thus, special devotion arises for you,
    Dharma Lord.

Having crossed the threshold of the
    Dharma,
I have gained the name "Dharma
    practitioner."

Yet, having listened to the Dharma, I
    maligned the teacher.
I did not respect the Dharma connection
And harbored animosity toward Dharma
    friends.

Though dressed in Dharma robes,
I have worked as the slave of the eight
    worldly dharmas.

Slandering other Dharmas, accumulating
    bad karma,
I lost the true Dharma,
I, a fake Dharma practitioner
Who turned his back on the Dharma.

Resolving at last to practice Dharma,
I beg you for some teaching, O Dharma
    lord:
The Dharma I request is the *Pith Instructions
    of the Swift Path* [198a].

Whenever you are able to give these
    Dharma teachings,
I your servant, the dharmaless Jampa
    Chödar, will come.

Please confer these teachings upon me, the
    mere reflection of a Dharma
    practitioner,
And protect me so that, whatever dharmic
    activity I engage in,
I may achieve Dharma's ultimate goal.

Undistracted by the eight worldly
    dharmas.
I long to listen, to contemplate, and
    practice the Dharma.

After I had offered this, I asked about his
health and mentioned a few things about myself.
Pleased, he told me to come back in a few days.
When I did, he gave me the transmission for the
Pith Instructions on the Swift Path, interspersed with
his commentary. On another occasion, he gave
me the transmission for the explanations of
Panchen Lobzang Chögyen on the *Six Yogas of
Naropa*.[26] I would visit him from time to time; we

would sit for a while, happily discussing religious
and worldly matters.

Then I met the great practitioner Khardo
Chökyi Dorje Rinpoche.[27] I offered him a horse,
some brocades, silver, corals, turquoise, a rosary
of precious stones, and this letter resting on a
ceremonial scarf:

You, Buddha Samantabhadra, first among
    all the Victorious Ones,
You, Vajradhara and Shakyamuni,
You, regents of the Buddha—Padmakara,
    Atisha and Lobzang Trakpa—
You Buddhas and Bodhisattvas, grant us
    virtue and excellence.

All the teachers who have explained the
    vast teachings of the Victorious Ones
Have been even more kind than the
    Victorious Ones themselves.
Until I reach the level of the Victorious
    Ones, protect me always,
Just as a king protects his subjects [198b].

Master, heart-son of all the Victorious
    Ones,
Having attained the exalted level of the
    Victorious One himself,
Emanating myriads of incarnations as
    kings, ministers, *panditas* and *siddhas*,
You greatly benefit the world—wondrous!

Here, in this degenerate age, who other
    than you, great *siddha*,
Emanation of the mighty Victorious Ones,
Raises aloft the victory banner of the
    teaching of the Buddha,
And, particularly, the secret teaching of
    Padma, the Lord of Victorious Ones.

Merely your name suffices to pacify
In the minds of whoever hears it—gods,
    men, or demons—
The three coarse, violent, poisonous
    emotions.
Your instructions ripen and liberate the
    body, speech, and mind
Of whoever, gifted or dull, practices them.

You see clearly the infinite display of pure
and impure realms;
You hear clearly all sounds, melodious and
dissonant;
You know clearly all happiness and
suffering,
The good and bad, what must be accepted
or rejected:
For those who are helpless, you, protector,
are a treasury of good qualities.

Whatever you do, you act for the benefit of
the Dharma and sentient beings;
Whatever you say is vast, profound teaching.
However we can, I and others pay homage
with our body, speech, and mind.
Whatever you ask, I shall accomplish—this
is my offering.
Whatever transgressions I have committed
through deeds, words, and thoughts, I
confess.
In your three activities—outer, inner, and
secret—I rejoice.
I ask that you turn the Wheel of Dharma
in three ways—through explanation,
writing, and debate.
I ask that you to remain throughout the
three times.
I dedicate to your long life, O great master,
Whatever virtue I and others have
accumulated.

In all our future lives,
Please look after me and all those
connected with me.

Through using my three doors to practice
diligently the unerring instructions
[199a]
Of the undeceiving master, the
embodiment of the three roots,
Having swiftly attained the unsurpassable
level of the three kayas,
May I guide all beings throughout the
limitless three realms.

Thus I made offerings. I related to him what
I had done until then; he accepted me with great
kindness and compassion.

The Chöd practitioner from Arik Tromtsa
and many other pilgrims from Domey and
Mongolia were also there. Together, we received
the empowerment of the *Great Compassionate King
of the Sky*.[28] On another occasion, Khardo Rinpoche gave me a long-life empowerment from
Thangtong Gyalpo's *Oral Transmission*[29] and, later,
the transmission for several of his own mind
treasures.[30]

Whenever I met him, filled with faith and
devotion I felt it was the same as if I was meeting
the Dharma King Terdak Lingpa and other
tertöns of the past. He gave me some blessed
relics and sacred substances.

Then, I went to meet the regent-king of
Tibet, Demo Rinpoche.[31] I offered him one
horse, five *sang*, and a ceremonial scarf, and
received from him the transmission of the *Six
Yogas of Naropa with the Three Confidences*.[32] I also
met the supreme reincarnation of Yongdzin
Pandita[33] and offered him three *sang*. I requested
the transmission of the *Three-fold Praise*[34] and
Eighty Tsongkhas.[35]

I then met the Vajradhara holder of the
throne of Reting,[36] offered him one *dzo* and a
few *sang*, and asked him for the explanations on
the *Seven Point Mind Training*.[37] I went to meet Tri
Changchup Chöphel Rinpoche,[38] offered him a
few silver coins, some corals, turquoise, and brocades, and [199b] requested from him the empowerment of the *Five Deities of Chakrasamvara* in
the tradition of Drilbupa,[39] and the transmission
and extensive teachings on the *Offering to the Gurus*
and the *Condensed Meaning of the Graded Path*.

I met Dungwa Rinpoche of Mindroling and
received from him the transmission of the *Supplication Prayer Focused on the Life Stories of the Incarnations of the Great Tertön*.[40] I met the great Vidyadhara
of Dorje Drak,[41] presented some offerings, and
requested the transmission of the *Prayer for the
Spontaneous Fulfillment of all Aspirations* and the
Prayer for Dispelling Obstacles on the Path.[42]

I met Chakzam Tulku Rinpoche,[43] presented him some offerings, and requested the
transmission of a few texts belonging to the cycle
of *The Great Compassionate One*, from Thangtong
Gyalpo's *Direct Oral Transmission*.

I met Orgyen Tendzin Rinpoche of Rina
Monastery,[44] the reincarnation of Tertön Dechen

Gyalpo, and offered him a horse, clothes, and silver. He gave me the empowerment for the *Taktsang Phurba* and the transmission of the cycle of new rediscovered treasures.[45]

When the Gyalwa Karmapa[46] came to Lhasa, the Seat of the Gods, I met him, presented him with offerings, and requested the transmission of the meditation and recitation of the *Great Compassionate One*. I met and made offerings to Lelob Pawo Rinpoche's incarnation,[47] and received from him the transmission of the *Mahamudra Prayer*.[48] I met the tulku of Kusho Jamyang Shepa. I offered him nine *sang*, a horse with bridle and saddle, and a ceremonial scarf. He gave me the transmission of the *Praise of Dependent Arising* and the *Glory of the Three Realms*.[49]

I also met many other lamas and abbots of Sera, Ganden, and Drepung and offered them horses, silver, brocades, and rosaries adorned with precious stones; I offered ceremonial scarves of fine silk, woven with images of long-life deities, and requested various Dharma connections. All were pleased [200a].

When paying homage to the sacred objects of body, speech, and mind at the Potala, Lhasa Thil, Chakpori, Ling Sum, Gyu Tö, Gyu Me, Meru, Shi De,[50] Sera, and Ganden, I offered hundreds of ceremonial scarves and made many prayers of aspiration. I offered tea to all those monastic communities and requested their spiritual protection.

I distributed alms and tea to all, and offered a permanent fund to our provincial headquarters.[51] Especially, I offered to the Vaishravana Treasury of the Upper Palace[52] an endowment of eight hundred silver coins and a porcelain cup filled with turquoise and corals. From the Upper Palace, I was given fifty coins of the purest gold. I entrusted these coins to Shiwa Tsering, the goldsmith master from Döpel,[53] and to Chakzam Khenpo for the making of a gold butter-lamp, inscribed with this prayer:

The devoted Tsogdruk Rangdrol, Chador, and others from Domey
Offer this lamp of gold at the feet of Jowo Rinpoche,
The sole ornament of the world, the supreme object of offering and obeisance.

By the power of this offering, may the teaching of the Buddha spread,
May its holders have long life, and
May all beings have happiness in the present,
And ultimately attain Buddhahood.

I presented the lamp before the Supreme Protector at the top of the Potala. Very pleased, he threw auspicious rice to consecrate it, made compassionate prayers, and told me, "You have accumulated merit. When you place this before the Jowo, make fervent prayers," and gave me a long ceremonial scarf [200b].

On the occasion of the Great Prayer Festival of the new year, on the fifteenth day, I took the butter-lamp to the top of the Labrang and showed it to the ministers seated there. I offered it and it was entered in the official register. Almost everyone, gods and men, said, "He surely has accumulated merit," and rejoiced. When the ministers read the inscription engraved on the lamp of solid gold, they put it above their heads and made prayers.

The minister, Kalön Trimön, said, "You have accumulated merit. When you offer it in the temple, dedicate it to the long life of the two Victorious Ones, Father and Son, and the Guardian of the Skies,[54] as well as to the prosperity of the Buddha's teachings and all sentient beings. Conclude with the excellent prayers of dedication and your act will have great meaning." Pleased, he wrapped a ceremonial scarf around the golden lamp and handed it back to me. That same day I filled it with melted butter and offered it at the feet of the Jowo Shakyamuni.

I arranged vast offerings and invited many monks from Lubum Khamtsen. I offered them tea, soup, and a silver coin each. They performed the *Offering to the Gurus* and concluded with many stainless prayers.

All of us, master and disciples, recited the butter-lamp prayer, as can be found in *The Blazing Jewel That Grants All Wishes* [201a].[55] I sent Alak Tsöndru, Gelong Ngawang Dargye, and the Chöd practitioner back home to Domey. Alak Tsöndru went into retreat for life in the Trika mountains. As a result of his practice, he became able to benefit the Dharma and sentient beings.[56] Gelong Ngawang Dargye went to Mangra and other mountain retreats, and through his efforts became an excellent practitioner. The Chöd practitioner gave up "red offerings"[57] and was able to help many sick people by performing rituals in the villages.

My spiritual son Kunzang Rangdrol received many empowerments and teachings from Khardo Chökyi Dorje, Tertön Sala Rinpoche, Chögyal Lhagyari, and many other lamas of U and Lokha. After staying one year in these areas, he returned to Domey. There he practiced the two stages of the Secret Mantrayana and the profound path of Chöd, and became a realized sky-like yogin who brought delusion to an end. Through his Chöd practice he brought great benefit to beings.

Shohong Bendhe was sent on pilgrimage where he visited the three perfect sacred places, met three excellent lamas, and became a renunciate free of clinging and attachment.

I myself did circumambulations and prostrations for a few months, paying over and over again my respects to the Jowo of Lhasa.

One day I stayed in front of the Jowo a long time, making such fervent prayers that I became absorbed in a state of profound samadhi. Afterward, when I was walking along on the outer circumambulation path, I saw many sheep and goats that had been slaughtered [201b]. Feeling unbearable compassion for all animals in the world who are killed for food, I went back before the Jowo Rinpoche, prostrated myself, and made this vow: "From today on, I give up the negative act that is eating the flesh of beings, each one of whom was once my parent."

From then on, although I engaged in many activities to benefit beings, no one ever killed animals as food to offer me. I even heard that, knowing that I was coming, some faithful patrons said, "This lama does not even eat the meat of animals that have died a natural death. Don't leave any meat around where he will see it," and they hid whatever there was. The fact that the lives of animals were no longer being taken on my account was, I thought, due to the compassion of the Jowo himself.

Near Lhasa, at the Upper Chölung Valley, "the Dharma Valley,"[58] was a place called Zhalung, "the Valley of Nettles," where the Lord of Beings, Lama Shang Yudrak,[59] once lived. There was a temple with a statue of the Four-armed Mahakala. I explained to the temple-keeper, named Gonpo, how I happened to have come there, and told him that I wanted to do retreat for a year in that sacred place.

Very pleased, he gave me a place to stay, and turned out to be hospitable and helpful. Later, he became my disciple and, after I gave him empowerments and instructions, he practiced meditation and became a self-liberated yogin.

The next summer I received an invitation from the Lubum Khamtsen of Drepung. I went to Drepung and stayed there a few days. The discussions we held about the Ancient and New Traditions pleased all the geshes. At this time, I also did prostrations and circumambulations at Drepung and Lhasa, and went to pay homage to all the sacred relics [202a].

An epidemic of fever broke out in Lhasa, and Gonpo caught it. When we came back to Zhalung, he became so ill that he was unable to get out of bed for a few days. I gave him blessings and some medicine; after a few days he recovered. When he was better, I fell ill; my fever raged for several days. In my feverish state I had the deluded vision of a temple burning down. The deities inside the temple, far from being burnt, became even more resplendent. I saw Pure Realms in all four directions and when I felt like going to one, an imposing black man stopped me saying, "No, don't go!"

During my sickness, I prayed to my teacher and to the Three Jewels, and visualized a continuous cool stream of cleansing nectar flowing inside my body and purifying me. Gonpo went to Lhasa and brought back medicine from the physician of Doring. With this auspicious help, I quickly recovered. Gonpo and I performed a *ganachakra* feast in front of the Four-armed Mahakala.

I then happened to run out of food. For a few days I ate only a few roasted peas. Gonpo went to perform rituals for some patrons of Chölung, and when he told them that I had exhausted my provisions, the administrator of Kusho Jamyang Shepa, the administrator of the chief merchant Namkhai Dzö, and some local chieftains gave some tea, butter, and *tsampa*, which Gonpo brought to me.

Water had always been scarce in that valley, but from the year I lived there onward, water became plentiful and crops were abundant. This fortunate event increased the faith of the patrons of the Upper Chölung Valley, rich and poor, and prompted them to help me during my stay and when I left [202b].

At that time, the wise, devoted, diligent, and compassionate Gelong Lobzang Öser was on pilgrimage. He had gone from the Lotus Lake in Tö to the Great Stupa of Bodhnath in Nepal. Since all prayers made in front of this stupa are fulfilled, he did prostrations and circumambulations, offered many butter-lamps, and made this wish:

"In this lifetime, as quickly as possible, may I have the good fortune to meet a qualified teacher and receive his profound instructions. Following the example of the holy beings of the past, may I live in retreat in the mountains, making the length of my practice equal to the length of my life."

On the way back, he eventually arrived in Lhasa, where he met Ngawang Nyentrak Rinpoche from Chakyung in Amdo,[60] then throne-holder of Ganden and tutor of the Sovereign of the Upper Palace.[61] By merely hearing about me from this abbot, Lobzang Öser felt great devotion and came straight to meet me. When he arrived I was sitting outside my door, in the shade of a beautiful bush of wild roses. The air was filled with the melodious buzzing of bees and I was singing this song, *Victory Over the Obscuring Emotions:*

E ma!
I, a yogin of Tibet,
The mendicant Tsogdruk Rangdrol,
Sent a proclamation—my faith, devotion
    and prayer—

Gathered an army—the deities of the three
    roots—
Sent off messengers in all directions—study
    and contemplation—
And stored armor and weapons—the pith
    instructions of the sutras and tantras
    [203a]—
On uninhabited glaciers and mountain
    slopes.

Then I fought my archenemy—the army
    of obscuring emotions.

I rode a powerful horse—renunciation.
I spurred it on with an iron-tipped whip—
    the certainty of death.
I wore an armored suit and helmet—love
    and compassion—
And held aloft a long spear—Bodhicitta.

On my bow—the skillful means of
    generosity and the other paramitas—
I placed an arrow—the perfect view—
Drew it tight with fierce diligence and
    endeavor,
And shot into the midst of the enemy
    army—the obscuring emotions.
It struck the heart of the general—
    ego-clinging—
And pierced his vital artery—deluded
    ignorance.
He fell senseless on the ground of
    egolessness,
And the army of the eighty-four thousand
    conflicting emotions
Fled, routed, in complete panic.

Today the yogin won;
He beat the great victory drum—the
    sublime Dharma—
And hoisted the great flag of joy.

The fears of samsara have vanished;
I now relax on the plain of great bliss.

E ma!
I, the son, am so happy!
If my mother knew of this, I'd be glad!

E ma!
I, the heart-son, am so happy!
If the guru heard of this, I'd be glad!

Hearing this song, Lobzang Öser ceased taking illusory phenomena as real, concrete entities, and remained in a state of pristine clarity, free of thoughts. Thinking that the coincidence of his arrival with my song was auspicious, immeasurable faith and joy arose in him. He prostrated himself, and offered me some nutmeg[62] and a silk scarf. With fervent devotion, he explained in detail all he had done until then and asked me to give him empowerments and spiritual guidance [203b].

I said, "You have offered me medicine, so I will offer you medicine—the medicine of the sublime Dharma, the cure for the obscuring emotions." Gradually, I gave him all the empowerments and special instructions.

As an auspicious omen that he might hold the Buddha's teaching, the source of peace and benefit, and be of help to all beings, I gave him the name Tendzin Nyima, "Sun-like Holder of the Teaching." Thus having declared him a son of Shakyamuni Buddha, I gave him this heart-advice:

I supplicate the compassionate Buddha.
Grant your blessings that we may be in
    harmony with the Dharma.

Now listen to a few beneficial words of
    advice
From my heart. Keep them in your heart;
Do not forget them, Shakya son.

Never be apart from the gracious teacher,
The source of blessings and accomplishment.
As your crown ornament,
Keep him always with you, Shakya son.

Give your whole being to the Three
    Jewels;
They never deceive those who rely upon
    them, Shakya son.

Since you have now reached the jewel
    island—

A precious, free, well-favored human
    birth—
Don't come back empty-handed, Shakya
    son.

You won't always have the chance to meet
    the unsurpassable teacher,
The precious Dharma, Shakya son.

The Lord of Death comes unexpectedly:
From now on, be on the alert, Shakya son.

On the day of your death,
Only the Dharma can help you.
Its benefits are certain,
So concentrate on Dharma now, Shakya
    son.

Give up concerns limited to this life;
Cultivate the means for happiness in future
    lives;
This surpasses all other aspirations, Shakya
    son.

The consequences of positive and negative
    acts are inevitable;
Give up evil and practice virtue, Shakya
    son.

Where there is wealth, there is greed;
Be a poor renunciate, Shakya son [204a].

Where there is power, there are evil deeds;
Keep to a humble station, Shakya son.[63]

In the company of noble friends, you too
    will gain excellence;
Associate with virtuous friends, Shakya son.

In the company of degenerate friends, you,
    too, will become corrupted;
Give up evil friends, Shakya son.

If your thoughts and intentions are pure,
The paths and stages will be pure;
Always harbor pure thoughts, Shakya son.

If your thoughts and intentions are impure,
The paths and stages will be impure;

Never harbor negative thoughts, Shakya
   son.

Should someone whisper gossip and
   slander,
Choose not to understand them, Shakya
   son.

Should someone expose your faults in a
   gathering,
Don't bring up his faults in revenge,
   Shakya son.

Should someone you have cherished as
   your own child
Regard you as an enemy,
Don't give rise to hatred, Shakya son.

Should you be blamed when you are
   innocent,
Regard this as past karma ripening,
   Shakya son.

Should an angry hand threaten or even
   beat you,
Do not retaliate with wrath, Shakya son.

All phenomena are illusory—good and
   bad dreams;
Do not let suffering depress or happiness
   elate you, Shakya son.

All sentient beings have been your kind
   parents;
Take on their misfortunes and cherish
   them lovingly, Shakya son.

An open, easy mind meets no arguments
   or quarrels;
Don't be easily depressed or elated, Shakya
   son.

Even if a Bodhisattva feels anger, he does
   not cling to it as real;
Don't harbor resentment at the harsh
   words of others, Shakya son [204b].

The gurus and deities see and know all
   things;

So don't engage in wrong conduct on the
   sly, Shakya son.

The superior practitioner is without
   falsehood or deceit;
Be honest and speak the truth, Shakya son.

Many Buddhas and Bodhisattvas assume a
   humble form;
Never revile or despise anyone, Shakya son.

There are no impure teachings within the
   Buddhadharma;
Don't have prejudice as to "pure" or
   "impure," Shakya son.[64]

Prostrations and circumambulation purify
   the obscurations of the body;
Perform these two from time to time,
   Shakya son.

Prayers and mantra recitation purify the
   obscurations of speech;
Recite them whenever you have time,
   Shakya son.

Fervent devotion and respect purify the
   obscurations of mind;
Generate devotion for your teacher,
   Shakya son.

In isolated places, emulate the life-
   examples of the past saints,
And the sun of happiness will shine,
   Shakya son.

Whether one studies a lot or a little, the
   main point is to practice;
Put the teachings into practice, Shakya son.

I dedicate all merit accumulated in the
   three times, symbolized by the present
   one,
So that I and others may live in accord
   with the Dharma.

I pray that in all lifetimes
We may meet the sublime teaching of the
   Buddha and practice it correctly.

May whoever practices in this way
Always have the auspicious fortune of bliss
    and happiness.

After I gave him these instructions, he became
an excellent lifetime practitioner, who benefited
beings and the teachings.

In the autumn of that year, my close spiritual
sons Kalden Rangdrol and Kunzang Shenpen
[205a] and the patron Tsering Gyal came to
meet me, with many monks, disciples, and faithful men and women. In answer to their greetings
and inquiries about my well-being, I sang this
song entitled *The Yogin's Happiness:*

Venerable master who bestows the
    Dharma,
Source of bliss and excellence,
Rest on the crown of my head in a sphere
    of rainbow light.

Having accumulated some merit,
I obtained a human birth
And gathered wealth and possessions.
Inspired by the deities and by virtuous
    friends,
A wish arose in me to come to U.

Having left behind my homeland, so hard
    to abandon,
I took the long northern route, so difficult
    to traverse,
And I arrived this year, so luckily,
In the Pure Realm of U-Tsang.

Today my joy equals that of the meeting of
    mother and son.
Having banished all concern for this life,
I, the mendicant Tsogdruk Rangdrol, am
    happy.

In joyful, pleasant solitary groves
Alone, at ease, I remain in bliss.

Owing to the compassion of my gracious
    master and the Three Jewels,
I am at peace in body and mind;
I am free from suffering.

Owing to the kindness of my patrons,
I happily enjoy good conditions for
    practicing the Dharma.
Through practicing this profound
    Dharma,
I shall find happiness in this life and in
    future lives.

When I try to describe the happiness,
That I, the yogin, perpetually enjoy,
No words come to me.

It would be difficult even for the gods,
    Brahma and Indra,
To achieve a happiness of body and mind
    like mine.

Faithful monks and disciples
Do as I have done and you, too,
Will enjoy lasting happiness.

By the virtue of singing this song [205b],
May all beings, our mothers, find joy and
    happiness.

In response, my close spiritual son Kalden
Rangdrol offered this song:

Loving protector, Tsogdruk Rangdrol,
Remain as my crown ornament!

May your great love and compassion
Care for me until I reach the essence of
    enlightenment.

Through the ripening of my previous
    karma
The bad conditions of samsaric suffering
    arose as friends.
I saw my homeland as the prison of the
    demon ego-clinging.
World-weariness and renunciation arose in
    my mind, and I came here.

When passing through many countries on
  my far-reaching travels,
I encountered neither enemies nor danger,
  neither fatigue nor despair.

I relied fully upon the Three Supreme
  Ones of the Pure Realm of U,
And upon my lord, the precious and
  qualified guru—
Through their blessings, I have gained
  infinite joy.
Today my aspirations are fulfilled.

O father Jetsun, peerless in kindness,
You sustain the glorious Dharma of the
  Victorious Ones,
Bestowing benefit and peace upon all
  beings to be tamed.
Amazing indeed was your happiness
When you lived like a great *rishi* in
  mountain wilderness!

Upon hearing your melodious spiritual
  songs,
Fusing my mind with yours, I offer many
  prostrations.
I, Kalden Rangdrol, thus establish a
  perfect connection.

Venerable one, I respectfully offer you my
  body and all my possessions.
Please embrace me with your
  loving-kindness
And see that all of us may swiftly attain
  liberation.

I pray to accomplish whatever pleases you,
  father guru.
Pray that we may cut the flow of the eight
  worldly concerns,
Pray that we, beginners, may be able to
  live in isolated retreats [206a].

Please give us the vital core of the
  profound Dharma,
Please dispel the ignorance of our minds,
Please chase away our conflicting
  emotions.

I supplicate you:
May we not stray onto the path of seeking
  salvation for ourselves alone.
May we manifest unlimited compassion for
  sentient beings, our mothers.
May all obstacles and errors be dispelled.
May we quickly reach the ultimate goal of
  spiritual experience and realization.
Please care for us with your unfailing
  compassion!

The two of them offered me all they had—
gold, silver, brocades, cloth, and ceremonial
scarves. The patron Tsering Gyal offered two
young mules and a few silver coins. All the other
monks, disciples and patrons, made many offerings, most of which I exchanged for gold.

Of this gold I used seven large coins for the
casting of a statue of Buddha Shakyamuni, about
a hand-span high. I had his throne and back
support cast in silver, inlaid with turquoise and
corals. After performing the consecration, I placed
the statue on the heads of all, masters and disciples, and prayed that we might attain Buddhahood together. For a few years I kept the statue
constantly with me, and then offered it to Tsemön
Lingpa, the regent-king of Tibet.[65]

Out of the horses, cattle, silver, and cloth
offered to me, I gave enough to Kalden Rangdrol
and Kunzang Shenpen for them to buy themselves provisions for pilgrimage to the Tsari
Ravines. I used the rest as offerings to make
spiritual connections with the two protectors,
Father and Son, with Khardo Chökyi Dorje,
and with other lamas. I offered tea and money to
Sera, Drepung, and Ganden, and to our provincial headquarters, dedicating the merit to the
attainment of complete enlightenment [206b].

Then Kunzang Rangdrol, Kalden
Rangdrol, Tendzin Nyima, Tsöndru Gyatso, and
many other faithful disciples and householders
offered stainless white scarves with this request:

"When you came to Bhanak Khasum, and
to Upper, Lower, and Middle Tibet, you taught
the Dharma, mainly about karma—the law of
cause and effect—in simple, ordinary language.
You taught the monks and householders, you
taught those of superior, middling, and lesser

faculties and, like the sun, you benefited all. Great would be your kindness for future disciples if you could now write down all these teachings!"

They requested this repeatedly. I had no book from which to draw stories and quotes, yet like a generous person who turns his bag inside out and pours all the contents on a cloth spread on the ground, without holding anything back, I wrote down everything that came into my mind and called it *The Beneficial Sun, a Discourse on the Dharma.* My students then took the book to Domey and it proved to be of great benefit to sentient beings.

Notes

1. The descent of blessings (*byin 'bebs*) is a point, during an empowerment ritual, when the master invokes the deities and requests them to shower blessings upon the mandala and the participants in the initiation.

2. The same as *Torch of Wisdom That Dispels the Darkness of Ignorance,* see Appendix 4.

3. The Manchu ruler.

4. Chuzang Monastery (*chu bzang*) or Ganden Mingyur Ling (*dga' ldan mi 'gyur gling*), founded by Chuzang Namygyal Paljor (*chu bzang rnam rgyal dpal 'byor,* 1578–1651). See AC, vol. 1, p. 50.

5. *Kumiss,* a beverage of fermented mare's milk.

6. The three gates (*sgo gsum*) are the body, the speech, and the mind. All these enumerations (the three gazes, the three postures, the four lamps, the four visions and the three crucial points) refer to the esoteric practice of Thögal (*thod rgal*).

7. *The Beneficial Sun ('chos bshad gzhan phan nyi ma*), composed by Shabkar. See Appendix 5.

8. The *Diamond-Cutter Sutra* (Skt. *Vajracchedika-prajnaparamita,* Tib. *'phags pa shes rab kyi pha rol du phyin pa rdo rje gcod pa,* T 16).

9. The *tol bu,* pronounced "tolhu," is the calf born from a *dzomo* (the hybrid offspring of a bull and a *dri,* the female of the yak). The *tolhu* is a feeble animal useless for domestic purposes, and is often killed or left to starve to death.

10. Rahu (*bza'*), another name for Vishnu (*khyab 'jug*), is said to cause stroke and epilepsy, as well as solar and lunar eclipses (see chap. 6, note 48).

11. In 1810.

12. In Tibet corpses are cut up in a special way, so that the vultures can feed on them. It was considered inauspicious if vultures did not come, or came but did not eat the corpse. The corpses are sometimes dismembered by monks or, in populated areas, by professionals.

13. One image of the Crowned Buddha is the Jowo Rinpoche (*jo bo rin po che*), or Jowo Shakyamuni. It is in the Jokhang, the main temple of Lhasa, originally called Rasa Trulnang Tsuklagkhang (*ra sa 'phrul snang gtsug lag khang*). The other image is the Jowo Mikyö Dorje (*jo bo mi bskyod rdo rje*), which is kept in the temple of Ramoche (*ra mo che*). These two precious images were brought to Lhasa by the two wives of Songtsen Gampo, the Nepalese princess Bhrikuti (Tib. *lha gcig khri btsun*), who founded the Jokhang, and the Chinese princess Wengchen Kungchu, who founded Ramoche.

14. Drepung (*'bras spungs*) was founded in 1416 by Jamyang Chöje (*'jam dbyangs chos rje*). Sera (*se ra*) was founded in 1419 by Jamchen Chöje (*byams chen chos rje*), and Ganden (*dga' ldan*) in 1409 by Je Tsongkhapa (*rje tsong kha pa*).

15. The Dalai Lama, the Panchen Lama, and the throne-holder of Ganden.

16. The Eastern Jamyang (*'jam dbyangs shar*) is the name of a large mansion near the Jokhang in Lhasa. It was founded in the fifteenth century by Desi Rinpungpa (*sde srid rin spungs pa*).

17. Rasa Trulnang Tsuklagkhang (*ra sa 'phrul snang gtsug lag khang*), the "Goat Field's Manifested Temple," is commonly known as the Jokhang (*jo khang,* see note 12) from the name of its central chapel. To shelter the most precious statue of Tibet, the Jowo Shakyamuni (see above, note 13), King Songtsen Gampo, through his miraculous powers, had this temple built with the earth carried by a single goat. The "Goat Field" (*ra sa*) is the ancient name of the place; it later was called the "God's [i.e., King's] Field" (*lha sa*). For a detailed history of the Jokhang and its successive renovations, see Vitali (1990).

18. The image of the Five Naturally Arisen Miracles (*rang 'byung lnga ldan*). These five miracles are:

1) King Songtsen Gampo gathered a large amount of jewel powder; wondering how to make a statue out of it, he made fervent prayers. When he awoke the next morning, the jewel powder had turned into a beautiful image of Avalokiteshvara with eleven heads.

2) The king wondered what relics should be enshrined within the statue. The heart of

the statue then emanated Bhikshu Akara-matishila, who went to India and brought back a small, miraculously formed statue of Avalokiteshvara that had been guarded by a powerful elephant. When Akaramatishila arrived back in Lhasa, the small statue dissolved into the big one's heart.

3) When King Songtsen Gampo died, he dissolved into the statue without leaving any mortal remains.

4) When his queen Wengchen died, she dissolved into the right eye of the statue.

5) When his queen Bhrikuti died, she dissolved into the left eye of the statue.

Akaramatishila brought back altogether five statues of Avalokiteshvara, which became among the most venerated ones in Tibet and Nepal. The four others are the Jowo Lokeshvara, which is still kept in the Potala at Lhasa, the Jowo Wati Zangpo of Kyirong (see chap. 12, note 21), the Jowo Jamali at Kathmandu (see chap. 12, note 31) and the Jowo Ukhangpa (*u khang pa*) in Patan (Kathmandu).

19. From the Great Fifth onwards, the Potala Palace has been the home of the Dalai Lamas. Relics of the deceased Dalai Lamas are preserved there in golden stupas.

20. The ninth Dalai Lama, Lungthok Gyatso (*lung rtogs rgya mtsho*), 1806–15.

21. The person mentioned here is probably the attendant (*mgron gnyer*, lit. the "one who looks after the guests") of the third Jamyang Shepa (*blo bzang dbyig gnyen thub bstan rgya mtsho*, 1796–1855).

22. The seventh Panchen Lama, Lobzang Tenpai Nyima (*blo bzang bstan pa'i nyi ma*, 1781–1859).

23. See Author's Introduction, note 18.

24. Ngawang Nyentrak (*ngag dbang snyan grags*), the sixty-sixth throne-holder of Ganden.

25. Lobzang, as well as the "second Buddha" mentioned thereafter, refers to Tsongkhapa, Lobzang Trakpa.

26. The *Pith Instructions on the Swift Path* (*myur lam dmar khrid*) is the *byang chub lam gyi rim pa'i dmar khrid thams cad mkhyen par 'grod pa'i myur lam* by the second Panchen Lama Lobzang Yeshes (*blo bzang ye shes*, 1663–1737).

27. For Khardo Chökyi Dorje (*mkhar rdo chos kyi rdo rje*), see Appendix 2 and chap. 14.

28. Great Compassionate King of the Sky (*thugs rje chen po nam mkha'i rgyal po*), one of the six main names and aspects of Avalokiteshvara.

29. For *Thangtong Gyalpo's Oral Transmission* (*thang ston snyan rgyud*), see Translator's Introduction, p. xxi.

30. Mind treasures (*dgongs gter*) are *termas* concealed by Guru Padmasambhava in the mind-stream of the treasure-discoverer (*gter ston*). They manifest clearly to the tertön at the appropriate time. (See Appendix 1.)

31. Demo Rinpoche, whose full name was *de mo ngag dbang blo bzang thub bstan 'jigs med rgya mtsho*. He acted as regent-king from 1811 until his death in 1819.

32. *The Six Yogas of Naropa with the Three Confidences* refers to the *zab lam na ro chos drug gi khrid rim yid ches gsum ldan* of Tsongkhapa. According to H. H. Khyentse Rinpoche, the three confidences are 1) the confidence that the goal of the practice resides in oneself (*bsgrub bya rang la bzhugs pa yid ches*), 2) the confidence in the extraordinary instructions that allow one to attain this goal (*sgrub byed kyi man ngag la yid ches*), and 3) the confidence in the spiritual master (*bla ma la yid ches*).

33. This must be the third incarnation of Tsechok Ling Yongdzin Pandita Kachen Yeshe Gyaltsen (*tshe mchog gling yong 'dzin pandita bka' chen ye shes rgyal mtshan*, 1713–93), a learned and accomplished sage who lived most of his life as a renunciate and was the founder of Samten Ling Monastery in Kyirong. He was, as well, the tutor of the eighth Dalai Lama, Jampel Gyatso (*'jam dpal rgya mtsho*, 1758–1804).

34. The *Threefold Praise* (*skabs gsum pa*) is a ritual text of praise in use in the Geluk tradition.

35. The *Eighty Tsongkhas* (*tsong kha brgyad bcu pa*) are eighty verses composed in praise of Tsongkhapa by the Kashmiri *pandita* Punya Shri.

36. The second throne-holder, Trichen Lobzang Yeshe Tenpa Rabgye (*khri chen blo bzang ye shes bstan pa rab rgyas*, 1759–1816). Reting or Ratreng (*rwa sgreng*) is the monastery founded by Drom Tönpa (*'brom ston pa*, 1004–64), the foremost disciple of Lord Atisha (see BA, pp. 251ff.). It is there that the Kadampa teachings first flourished. Later, it became the seat of the Reting incarnations, several of whom were regent-kings of Tibet.

37. On *Seven Point Mind Training*, see chap. 1, note 60.

38. Tri Changchup Chöpel Rinpoche (*khri byang chub chos 'phel*, 1756–1838), the first Trijang Rinpoche, and the sixty-ninth holder of the throne of Ganden. He became tutor of the ninth Dalai Lama.

39. Drilbupa (*dril bu pa*) or Vajraghantapada, one of the eighty-four Mahasiddhas of India.

40. The great tertön is Minling Terchen, Terdak Lingpa, Gyurme Dorje (see chap. 1, note 38), who in 1670 founded Mindroling, the main seat of the Nyingma tradition in central Tibet. *Gdung ba* refers to *gdung sras*, the descendant of Minling Terchen, who holds the throne of Mindroling.

41. Possibly the fifth Great Vidyadhara of Dorje Drak (*rdor brag rig 'dzin chen po*), Kalzang Pema Wangchuk

(*skal bzang padma dbang phyug*, also known as *rdo rje thogs med rtsal*). Born in 1719, he is said to have lived to over a hundred. He was the fifth reincarnation of Rigdzin Gödem (*rig 'dzin rgod ldem*, 1337–1408) and the immediate reembodiment of the famed Rigdzin Pema Trinley (*rig 'dzin padma phrin las*, 1641–1717).

42. Respectively the *Prayer for the Spontaneous Fulfillment of all Aspirations* (*gsol 'debs bsam pa lhun grub*), a *terma* of Rigdzin Gödem, and the *Prayer for Dispelling Obstacles on the Path* (*gsol 'debs bar chad kun sel*), probably the prayer revealed by Tertön Bakal Mukpo (*ba mkhal smug po*; see RT, vol. Bi, pp. 189–96, a former incarnation of Chogyur Dechen Lingpa (*mchog 'gyur bde chen gling pa*, 1829–70).

43. Before his death, the famed Tibetan *siddha* Thangtong Gyalpo blessed with his body, speech and mind his close disciple Tendzin Chöje Nyima Zangpo (*bstan 'dzin chos rje nyi ma bzang po*), who was also said to be his son. The latter is therefore considered to be a "reincarnation before death" (*ma 'das sprul sku*). (Communicated by Cyrus Stearns.)

The successive incarnations of Nyima Zangpo are known as the Chakzam tulkus (*lcags zam sprul sku*) and were the heads of Chuwori (*chu bo ri*) Monastery in central Tibet. The lama whom Shabkar met might have been Tendzin Yeshe Lhundrup (*bstan 'dzin yes shes lhun grub*), the seventh and most famous incarnation, or the eighth incarnation, Tendzin Khyenrab Thutop (*bstan 'dzin mkhyen rab mthu stobs*).

44. Rina (*ri sna*) Monastery, in the Kyichu Valley, to the west of Lhasa. See Appendix 4.

45. On the *Taktsang Phurba*, see chap. 1, note 54. The rediscovered treasures mentioned here are likely to be the mind *termas* (*dgongs gter*) of Kunzang Dechen Gyalpo (see Appendix 4).

46. The fourteenth Karmapa, Thekchog Dorje (*theg mchog rdo rje*, 1798–1868).

47. The eighth Pawo Rinpoche, Tsuklak Chökyi Gyatso (*gtsug lag chos kyi rgya mtsho*, 1785–1840).

48. The *Mahamudra Prayer* (*phyag chen smon lam*) written by the third Karmapa, Rangjung Dorje (*rang 'byung rdo rje*, 1284–1339).

49. *Praise of Dependent Arising* (*rten 'brel bstod pa* or more exactly *thub pa'i dbang po'i bstod pa legs bshad snying po*) praises in 58 stanzas the view of the dependent links. Composed by Tsongkhapa while doing a solitary retreat at Olkha (*'ol kha*) in central Tibet, it was the result of a dream in which he met Nagarjuna, Shantideva, Chandrakirti, Aryadeva, and other great Indian *panditas* who were the chief exponents of the Madhyamika philosophy. At the end of the dream

Buddhapalita stood up and blessed Tsongkhapa with a volume of his commentary on the *Madhyamaka-karika*. Following this dream, Tsongkhapa attained a high degree of understanding of the ultimate reality while reading a verse of Buddhapalita that states that "the self is neither different from, nor identical to, the aggregates." The same day, Tsongkhapa wrote this praise to the Lord Buddha, the Awakened One who first realized this truth. The *Glory of the Three Realms* (*dpal ldan sa gsum ma*) was also written by Tsongkhapa.

50. The Potala Palace of Lhasa. Its construction started in 1645 on Marpori at the order of the fifth Dalai Lama. Lhasa Thil is the main part of the city of Lhasa; Chakpori (*lcags po ri*) is the hill near the Potala, on top of which was the medical college.

Ling Sum, "the three residences," are 1) Tsemön Ling (*tshe smon gling*), the seat of Tsemön Ling Rinpoche; 2) Tengye Ling (*bstan rgyas gling*), the seat of Demo Rinpoche (*de mo rin po che*); and 3) Kunde Ling (*kun bde gling*), the seat of Tatsak Rinpoche (*rta tshag rin po che*). These three high lamas would assume by turns the office of the regent-king of Tibet, who took care of the secular and religious matters of state during the minority of the Dalai Lama.

Gyu Me (*rgyud smad*), the Tantric College of Lower Tibet, was founded in 1433 by Sherap Senge (*shes rab seng ge*) and eventually settled near the Ramoche Temple of Lhasa. Gyu Tö (*rgyud stod*), the Tantric College of Upper Tibet, was founded in 1474 by Kunga Dondrup (*kun dga' don grub*) at Jampeling Monastery. Both were dedicated to the practice of the Guhyasamaja Tantra (*rgyud gsang ba 'dus pa*).

Meru (*rme ru*) included the New and Old Residences (*rme ru rnying pa* and *rme ru gsar pa*). The Old Meru was the seat of the Nechung state oracle. Shi De (*bzhi sde*) is the area where Reting Rinpoche (*rwa sgreng*) resided.

51. *khams mtshan*, or "college." Each province of Tibet had a college in each of the main monasteries of central Tibet.

52. The Potala Palace, the residence of H.H. the Dalai Lama.

53. Döpel (*'dod dpal*) was a famous goldsmith and ironsmith workshop at the foot of the Potala.

54. Kalön Trimön is Krimön Dorje Tsering (*khri smon rdo rje tshe ring*), who was minister from 1801 to 1813 (see Petech 1973, 231). The Father and Son, and the emperor, the Guardian of the Skies, are respectively Dalai Lama, the Panchen Lama, and the Manchu ruler.

55. *The Blazing Jewel That Grants All Wishes* (*smon lam 'dod 'byung nor bu 'od 'bar*), a prayer composed by Shabkar.

56. Alak Tsöndru (*a lag brtson 'grus*) is one of the disciples who requested Shabkar to compose the second part of his autobiography (vols. Kha and TS 2).

57. "Red offering" (*dmar chog*): some *Chöd* practitioners gather heaps of the meat and bones of dead animals as a help for their visualization of the offering of the flesh of their own bodies.

58. Chölung (*chos lung*) is located in Olka ('*ol kha*), a hundred kilometers west of Lhasa.

59. Lama Shang, Yudrak Tsöndru Trakpa (*zhang g.yu brag brtson 'grus grags pa*, 1123–93), an influential teacher who founded the Tsalpa Kagyu (*tshal pa bka' brgyud*) lineage. He was a disciple of Dagpo Gomtsul Tsultrim Nyingpo (*dwags po sgom tshul, tshul khrims snying po*, 1116–69), Gampopa's nephew. See BA, pp. 771ff.

60. The "Garuda Monastery," Chakyung Gonpa, Thekchen Yönten Dargye Ling (*bya khyung theg chen yon tan dar rgyas gling*) in Domey (Amdo) was founded by Chöje Dondrup Rinchen (1309–?) following a prediction of Tronyer Chenma (*khro gnyer can ma*), a wrathful manifestation of Jetsun Drolma. (See AC, vol. 2, pp. 1–45). It has eighteen branch monasteries.

61. H.H. the Dalai Lama.

62. Nutmeg (Tib. *dza ti*, Lat. *Myristica fragrans*) is one of the "six excellent ones" (*bzang po drug*) used in many medicinal preparations.

63. This verse is missing in the TS 1.

64. Here six verses are missing in the TS 1.

65. The regent-king from Tsemön Ling in Lhasa (see above note 50; commonly pronounced "Tsomonling"), Ngawang Jampel Tsultrim (*tshe smon gling ngag dbang 'jam dpal tshul khrims*), who ruled from 1819 to 1844.

10

The Ravines of Tsari

How I made the pilgrimage to the Ravines of Tsari, and devoted
myself to meditation practice in the place sacred to the Mind of
Black Varahi, unequaled in Lower Tibet

I thought to make the pilgrimage circumambulating the Ravines of Tsari,[1] when it next occurred, during the Monkey Year. So, at the beginning of the eleventh month of the year of the female Iron Sheep,[2] I left Chölung. I asked Khenpo Shiwa Tsering of Döpel for a letter of introduction soliciting the deputy-treasurer of the supreme protector, Drukpa Rinpoche,[3] to help me in Tsari. I assured him that his kindness would be repaid.

Since Topden, the governor of E Kyilkhor, was returning home from Lhasa, I went with him. On the way, we spent a day visiting all the sanctuaries and sacred images of Samye, the Glorious Immutable Temple that has been praised in countless ways. The great master, Guru Padmasambhava, said:

> Unique under the sun is Samye, "the
>   Inconceivable,"
> Equal to the Diamond Throne of India.[4]
> For whoever sees Samye,
> The gates of lower rebirth are shut;
> Whoever circumambulates Samye, even a
>   butcher,
> Will be reborn in the higher realms;
> Whoever bows down to Samye
> Will rise to ever greater excellence.

On meeting the abbot, I offered him one silver *sang* and requested the blessing of Vajrakilaya [209a]. I made offerings and prayers and went to the houshold of the meritorious patron, the noble-

man Tsachanga, to whom I gave a wild mule. In return, he gave me whatever provisions I needed.

Then I met Tertön Sala Rinpoche of Neuring, who was ill at the time, and offered him a good-natured mule. I asked for a teaching to establish a spiritual connection. For several days I offered prayers for his long life; he gave me some presents and whatever I might need.

Passing through Chögyal Lhagya's[5] pastures, I reached Char Sang-ngak Chöling and entered the presence of the supreme refuge, the omniscient Drukpa. I offered him nine *sang*, and when I told him the circumstances of my coming he was very pleased. I then presented the abbot's letter to the deputy treasurer, who, after reading it, gave me valuable help and offered to look after my personal effects.

A few days later, I passed Chözam and Dotsen rest house,[6] and reached the Mandala Plain of Tsari. I stayed there several days while people from all directions were gathering. Some said prayers and did prostrations, some sang, danced, and played music, and some offered *ganachakra* feasts.

Government officials gave two yaks to the Lhopa tribesmen; they gave one the first day and the other the next. The yaks were tied up; many Lhopas gathered, pulled out knives of all sizes, and cut the legs, hide, and flesh from the yaks' bodies while they were still alive. Each Lhopa then left with his share of meat [209b].[7] Seeing this mixture of good and evil, joy and sadness arose in my mind, and for my own benefit and that of others, I sang this song:

I pray with yearning and devotion
To the deities of the Three Roots, the
    infallible refuge:
Dispel the obstacles of this life for all those
    gathered here;
Lead them to the Pure Realms in their
    next lives.

At the center of the divine circle that is the
    Mandala Plain of Tsari—
Land of excellence, auspiciousness, and
    prosperity—
Through the power of their past good
    deeds and pure prayers,
Many pilgrims, of diverse origins and
    tongues,
Over a hundred thousand faithful men
    and women,
Came together of their own accord,
    without anyone having called them.

For a few days, waiting for their group to
    leave,
Having pitched tents and built grass huts
    all around,
Some engage in prostrations, recitation,
    meditation,
Giving real meaning to the freedom and
    potential of their lives;
Some sing, dance, and play musical
    instruments;
Others please the mother dakinis with
    ganachakra feasts.

Many Lhopas from the barbarian
    borderlands,
Wield weapons and strike down the lives of
    beings.

Looking upon this scene of good and evil
    actions,
Feelings of joy and sadness mingle in my
    mind.

The Lhopas have returned to their
    homeland,
Having forsworn evil actions, promising
    not to attack the pilgrims.

The pilgrims circumambulate the Pure
    Crystal Mountain.[8]
Then, none remaining, they go their
    separate ways,
Like all things—impermanent.

Land, parents, relatives, and friends,
All associations of this life last but an instant.
No one will remain; all will go on to
    another life.
On the eve of your own departure,
It is the Dharma that you need:
Consider this, practice the sacred Dharma,
    and
Even at the cost of your life, refrain from
    evil deeds [210a].
For whoever does so, the sun of happiness
Will shine in this life and the next.

By the merit of having sung this song,
May all these pilgrims, ordained and lay,
    male and female,
Encounter no hardship of body or mind,
And, having made the rounds of the holy
    places,
Meet their kin again.

I pray that the pilgrims, companions from
    all provinces,
May meet again in the next life
In a pure celestial field.
May this prayer be fulfilled!

For the sake of the faithful, I also sang this praise
of the sacred place:

I pray to all the deities of the Pure Crystal
    Mountain,
Please grant your blessings!

I, the vagabond, the renunciate Tsogdruk
    Rangdrol,
Will express in song whatever comes to my
    mind.

Measureless palace of the glorious Heruka,
Celestial field where the mother dakinis
    gather like clouds,

Exalted realm, the glorious Caritra,[9]
Stands supreme among the twenty-four
    holy places.

This marvelous landscape unveils its many
    aspects—
Natural forms of deities and sacred
    letters,[10]
Winters with flowers, verdant grass and
    thickets:
How fortunate to behold such a place!

If you circumambulate it, the two veils are
    lifted;
If you offer a *ganachakra*, the two
    accumulations are perfected;
Meditate, and inner realization dawns—
Rare in the world is such a place!

Practitioners who yearn for meditation
    experiences and realization [210b]
Stay here and persevere in practice!
Men and women who have committed
    great evil deeds and whose obscurations
    are dense—
Circumambulate this place and bow down
    to it.
You who collect the seeds of the two
    accumulations,
Offer all that you can to this sacred site.

May whoever hears or sees this song
Practice meditation and swiftly become a
    Buddha!

On hearing this, all those present acquired
faith and respect for this holy place. Then, in the
male Water Monkey Year,[11] called Angira, on
the third day of the first month, we were divided
in groups[12] and, accordingly, we set off single file
on the pilgrimage of the Ravines.

On the way, I met some sick people on the
verge of death, and came upon some corpses as
well. I offered my spiritual protection to the sick
and performed the transference of consciousness
for the dead.

Some, left behind by their companions, unable to travel further, were simply sitting there

and weeping. Approaching them, I tried to comfort them, saying, "The stream of pilgrims is not
exhausted yet; rest for a few days and continue
on when you feel stronger." Before continuing
my journey, I left medicines and provisions with
them.

Some people carried their ailing friends,
while others carried their friends' burdens. Approaching them, I said, "You have fidelity and
concern. Relax now and rest; we are near the
Shag River." Thus I tried to hearten them.

In other cases as well, I always did my best
to take care of those in difficulty. Nearly everyone faced severe hardships and I felt great pity
for them. When similar difficulties befell me, I
visualized that all my obscurations and negative
acts were being cleansed [211a].

When we finally reached Yulmeh at the end
of the circuit, everyone was cheerful and
relieved. At Chözam[13] all the pilgrims boiled
some tea and drank it. Each person packed
his or her things, and after having put those
aside, most of the pilgrims gathered round
me. They asked me:

"Where will you go? Please visit, at least
once, our homelands—Kongpo and Kham!" I
answered that I was going on pilgrimage to
the three holy places—Tsari, Mount Kailash,
and Lapchi—and added: "I pray to come to
your homelands, yet human birth and death
are unpredictable. If the distance between us
prevents us from meeting again, I shall pray
that you be protected in this and in future
lives.

"Realize that death strikes without warning;
do not be attached to this life; practice some
Dharma for the sake of your next lives. Even if
you are not able to practice a great deal, at least
renounce the evil of killing. When dying, remember your spiritual master and the Three Jewels.
Pray to them, and we will have the good fortune
to meet again in a Pure Realm."

Thus I gave them much advice. As their
hearts were with me, they remained there, transfixed, not leaving. A faithful nun, who said she
had come from near Chagme Monastery in
Kham, prostrated herself, and, with tears in her
eyes, exclaimed:

O lord and protector, wish-fulfilling gem,
I ask that you grant blessings to us all.
Master and disciples, may you travel
In good cheer and good health to the white
    snows of Tö [211b];
We ourselves will now leave for our homes.
Kindly protect us from obstacles and
    hindrances.

May we meet again in this life,
May we meet again in the next life,
May we meet again in the *bardo*;
May we meet over and over again!

Having made many such prayers in verse
and in prose, she set off on her way. Others, too,
most of them unable to contain their tears,
departed one by one for their homelands, the
shadow of impermanence cast upon their faces.
In the end, no one was left.

We, master and disciples, went back to Char
Sang-ngak Chöling, the seat of Drukpa Rinpoche.
We met the great protector himself, the omniscient Drukpa, and received from him the blessing for the *Sadhana of Amitayus and Hayagriva
Combined*,[14] and the oral transmission and complete instructions on the preliminaries and main
practice of Mahamudra.

We stayed there for a month or so, recover-
ing our strength. Then I sent Kalden and my
other attendants and disciples to continue their
retreat practice in the mountain solitudes of U
and Lokha.

Carrying the provisions that the omniscient
Drukpa had given me, I went back to the north
of the glorious pure celestial field of Caritra,
where the wonderful herb known as the Black
Naga's Devil grows.[15] This herb cures leprosy
and other ailments, and brings forth both ordinary and extraordinary *siddhis*. Because meditation experiences and realization occur
instantaneously in this secluded place, it is called
Chikchar, which means "all at once" [212a].[16]

There one finds an extremely beautiful
golden-roofed temple[17] that houses many blessed
objects symbolic of enlightened body, speech,
and mind. Chief among these is a dazzlingly
resplendent image of the two-headed Varahi.[18]
Larger than human size, made of many kinds of

precious jewels, this image seems alive. It was
made by the very hands of the omniscient Pema
Karpo,[19] a manifestation of Padmapani.

On a hillside nearby lies a beautiful meadow
with trees spread out like a lattice of turquoise,
sapphire, and pearls; it is known as Yangön,
which means "completely secluded." I stayed
there in solitary retreat for one year and one
month in a pleasant meditation hut just large
enough for one person.

On auspicious days I experienced visions of
many dakas and dakinis coming and going in the
direction of the Turquoise Lake Palace.[20] I joined
their *ganachakra* feast and listened to their vajra
songs. After this, through the blessings of the
dakinis, I developed spontaneous faith and respect
for the Path of Means relied on by the yogins
who practice the development and completion
stages of the Secret Mantrayana, and for teachings and practitioners of all levels. I saw all of
them as pure.

One day, after having heard all sorts of
curious stories from many places, I sang this:

Some vassal kings of the land of Kancha,
Kill their old fathers before seizing the
    kingdom.

Some savages from a corner of the
    southern land of Mön,
Kill their old mothers before taking a wife.

Some Nepalese, when a husband dies,
Burn the wife alive when they burn the
    husband's corpse [212b].

Some heretic kings
Sacrifice their mothers to Maheshvara.

Some barbarians in the land of Lo
Kill as many animals as they possibly can,
Thinking to benefit their dead parents.

Some people in Kongpo believe that by
    poisoning others
Their own good fortune will increase.

Hearing that in the world so many people
Act in such perverted ways,

I feel pity for those who do not understand
That the fruit of evil deeds is suffering.

A person who is fortunate to be born in an
    age
And place where the highest Dharma
    flourishes,
And who, owing to the kindness of an
    authentic spiritual master,
Is able to differentiate virtue and nonvirtue,
Yet still commits evil actions,
Is like a man who jumps knowingly into an
    abyss.

There is no madness greater than this!
Wise ones, practice virtue!

Having sung this, it became clear to me that
my sound understanding of karma, the law of
cause and effect, was due to my gurus' kindness.
Thereafter, I applied myself more than ever to
giving up evil and to doing what is right. As
Jetsun Mila said:

If I die, I am happy: I didn't do evil.
If I live, I am happy: I will further my
    virtuous practice.

The truth of these verses struck me, and I
felt extremely happy, thinking that even if I were
to die this very moment I would have nothing to
regret.
    Then a devoted and wealthy patroness,
Yidzin Lhamo, "Enchanting Goddess," requested
some advice to remind her of virtue. I offered her
the following words:

Though now you delight in wearing
Ornaments of gold, turquoise, and coral,
When leaving for the next life,
Leaving all that jewelry behind,
You will be sad.

Though now you enjoy the company
Of your friends, beautiful and
    noble-minded,
When leaving for the next life [213a],
Parting with your family,
You will be sad.

Though now you delight at having
    gathered
All the possessions, food, and wealth that
    you need,
When leaving for the next life,
Leaving all these possessions behind,
You will be sad.

Though now you rejoice at having
This jewel-like human body, free and
    well-favored,
When leaving for the next life,
Empty-handed, without Dharma,
You will be sad.

Therefore, Yidzin Lhamo,
Do not assume that you'll live long.
Do not entertain excessive craving or
    attachment
Toward friends, food, and wealth.

Knowing that death will strike without
    warning,
Do not delight in adornments of turquoise
    and coral;
Do not be spiteful to your spouse;
Do not be mean with wealth;
Do not indulge in meaningless distractions.

Use your body to do prostrations and
    circumambulations.
Use your speech to say prayers and
    recitations.
Use your mind to have faith, respect, and
    pure perception.

Cultivate loving-kindness and
    compassion;
Make offerings to the guru and the
    Three Jewels;
Give to those in need;
Serve the members of the sangha;
And be kind in all ways to your servants.

If you do so, in this life you will
Have happiness, well-being, and renown,
And—as the Buddha said—in life after life
You will go from one happy state to
    another.

All of us practitioners, master and disciples,
Have met for a fleeting instant in this
    lifetime.
I pray that in the life hereafter
We may meet again in a Pure Land.

Thus I gave her this advice. She acted accordingly, and by the time of her death, she had entered the Path.

One day, my spiritual son Kunzang Shenpen, "Ever-perfect Benevolence," asked me to sing a praise of the sacred Caritra. My words could only praise a few drops of the ocean of perfections of this glorious place, which fortunate beings with pure perception and karma see as the heavenly realm of Khechara,[21] a vast Buddhafield in which peaceful and wrathful deities dwell, numberless as the sesame seeds in an opened pod [213b]:

White and brilliant, the color of white
    crystal,
The central mountain is like a king on his
    throne,
Surrounded by a host of lesser mountains
    as ministers.

Multicolored flowers blanket the whole
    place.
Blossoms and fruit bedeck the trees.
Its meadows are like golden trays
Carrying their blue lakes like mandalas of
    turquoise;
Its rivers unfold like white silken scarves.

Wild geese sound the sonorous drum of
    their throats,
While, like reed flutes, small birds trill.
Bees are humming, dancing.

Here mind is content and awareness clear.
Here is the dwelling place of many *siddhas*
    of the past,
The fields where dakas and dakinis gather.

Most exalted among the twenty-four holy
    places,
Wondrous as the pure paradise, Khechara,
This is glorious Caritra:

In the center, on the immaculate crystal
    mountain,
Dwell two thousand eight hundred
    deities.[22]
In each of the surrounding hills, rocks, and
    lakes
Are countless dakas and dakinis.
The men and women who live here
Are all of the race of dakas and dakinis.

Whoever stays here to practice the
    Dharma
Will find that meditation experiences,
    realization, and positive qualities blossom.
He or she will see the faces of dakas and
    dakinis
In reality, in dreams, or in visions.

Here, performing a single sacramental
    feast,
Making a single offering, lighting a single
    lamp [214a],
Will increase life and merit.
At the time of death, dakas and dakinis
Will lead one to the pure celestial field of
    Khachö.

To do a single prostration or
    circumambulation
Will shut the doors to the three lower
    realms, and
Even a very sinful person
Will be reborn in the higher realms of gods
    or men.

The living creatures inhabiting this place
Never fall into the hells.
The animals eating its grass and drinking
    its water
Are purified of their obscurations
And are reborn as human beings.

Through seeing, hearing, touching, or
    remembering,

Through faith, offering, praise, and
   respect:
Any connection made with this place is
   meaningful—
Many wise and accomplished sages have
   said so.

If I were to speak for a thousand aeons
   with a thousand tongues,
It would never suffice to describe
The outer, inner, and secret qualities of
   this sacred place.

This is why you, faithful men and women,
Should always pay your respects to it with
   offerings,
Praise, circumambulations, and
   prostrations.

My words are in accord with those of the
sages of the past; therefore you should hold them
to be true, and make offerings, prostrations, and
circumambulations. Thus I exhorted all the pilgrims gathered there.

On one occasion, I received the transmission of the biography and spiritual songs of the
omniscient Padma Karpo from the vajra holder
of Chikchar, Ngaktra Tulku Rinpoche.[23] I also
requested from the great *siddha* Damchö Zangpo
the instructions on the *Six Yogas of Naropa* and on
the *Hundred and Eight Combined Yogic Exercises*
[214b].[24]

To demonstrate the power of *tummo*[25] practice, the thirteen great yogins of Chikchar retreat
center used to go out in the dead of winter,
wearing only a single cotton shawl, and spend a
night in the snow at the edge of the glaciers.
Early the next morning, the *tsulpas*,[26] the patrons
of Tsari, would come to greet them with canopies and banners. Seeing all the yogins approaching, steam rising from their bodies, everyone felt
overwhelming faith in these sons of Milarepa.

Then Kunzang Rangdrol, my fortunate and
excellent spiritual son, endowed with the good
karma accrued through training in his previous
lives, and Kalden Rangdrol, who was rich in the
noble virtues of faith, generosity, and wisdom,
urged me to compose a detailed teaching for the
benefit of the present and future disciples dwell-

ing in mountain retreats. Accordingly, I composed the text called *Beneficial Moon*, ornamenting it with sayings of the saints of the Kagyu
lineage.

Giving many reasons for their request, they
also asked for a teaching according to the nonsectarian point of view, that would generate faith,
respect, and pure perception in everyone's minds.
So, I composed the *Beneficial Jewel* and the *Offering-Cloud of Samantabhadra*,[27] ornamenting these
with scriptural quotations and with my own understanding.

When I gave the transmission for these texts
to my spiritual son Kunzang, I visualized myself
as the Bodhisattva Samantabhadra, emanating
rays of light from my heart, inviting all the Buddhas and Bodhisattvas of the three times and the
ten directions and all other worthy objects of
offering without exception.

I then visualized clouds of offerings, real and
imaginary, filling the whole sky, and offered these
to the Buddhas with praises and prayers. I invoked
their blessings to make me able to benefit the
Dharma and all beings [215a]. I then visualized
all the beings of the billionfold universe in front
of me, imagining that, as the melodious sound of
the Dharma fell upon their ears, they would
understand both the words and the meaning.

I gave the transmission, reading with a clear,
loud voice; at the end I placed the volumes on
Kunzang's head, praying that these teachings
might benefit all those who would see, hear,
remember, or touch them.

At that very moment, by the blessings of the
deities and dakinis of this sacred place—which I
was visualizing as a perfect Buddhafield—in the
sky before me, the Buddhas and Bodhisattvas
appeared vividly, smiling in approval, emanating from their hearts a multitude of light rays
that illuminated the entire universe. They said:

"O son of the Victorious Ones, it will be so!
These wonderful new teachings fulfill the wishes
of the Buddhas and will satisfy the minds of all
beings. Noble son, you are truly the heir of the
Victorious Ones; we enthrone you as protector
and refuge of all beings."

Thus, as they graced and honored me, all
the dakas, dakinis, and guardians of the Dharma
performed graceful dances, and sang "Immov-

able Meru . . ."[28] and other auspicious songs. Clouds of rainbow light appeared, flowers fell like rain, and the sound of cymbals resounded [215b].

Besides this vision, a five-colored rainbow appeared in the sky, a rain of white flowers fell, and the sound of conches, drums, and other instruments resounded. These were seen and heard by almost everyone nearby. It was a most auspicious omen for both of us, master and disciple. The thought that in the future these teachings would help many beings delighted me as much as if I had attained the *bhumi* of Complete Joy.[29] In this mood I sang many more songs of happiness.

Once, some of the great yogins of the retreat center of Chikchar asked me, "Who is your teacher? What instructions did he give you? What practices have you done?" First I answered directly, and then I sang this song:

In the beginning I took the teacher as
    teacher,
In the middle I took the scriptures as
    teacher,
In the end I took my own mind as teacher.

From the teacher who showed the path of
    deliverance,
I received the sacred *pratimoksha* teachings:[30]
My practice was to shun wrongdoing and
    cultivate virtue.

From the Bodhisattva teacher,
I received the sacred Mahayana teachings
    on generating Bodhicitta:
My practice was to cherish others more
    than myself.

From the Vajradhara teacher,
I received the sacred teachings,
Initiations and instructions of the Secret
    Mantrayana:
My practice was to meditate upon the
    development and completion stages,
    and the Great Perfection.

From many other teachers,
I received many sublime teachings,

Thus establishing spiritual connections:
My practice was to cultivate faith, respect,
    and pure perception.

This song pleased them and enhanced their faith. Again, some people said [216a], "It's amazing that your songs seem to burst forth from space, unhindered, whenever you want, without your having to make any effort as others do." In reply I sang this song as it arose in my mind:

The white eagle, the *rishi*,[31]
Having grown feathers and wings in the
    nest,
Flung himself from the cliff and flew out
    into the sky.
Now he soars higher and higher into space.

I, the disciple of an authentic guru,
Having heard the teachings and
Contemplated them in my master's
    presence,
Severed all doubts and misconceptions,
    and then wandered off into the
    wilderness.
Now I persevere in my meditation.

The divine bird, the beautiful snow grouse,[32]
Sought grass and water among the rocky
    crags.
Now it dwells at the edge of the snows,
Sounding its musical call in the misty
    heights.

I, a bard from the Land of Snows,
Sought food and clothing in valleys and
    nomad camps.
Now I dwell in mountain seclusion
Singing songs among my heart-sons.

The fully grown deer with ten-branched
    antlers
Gazing afar from the mountaintop
Descends into the valleys, playing and
    running as it goes,
And again returns to its rocky heights.

I, the yogin with full-grown awareness,
Generated Bodhicitta in mountain retreats.

Descending to the villages, I taught the
    Dharma,
And returned to my solitary dwelling.

The cool cascading waterfall
Requires neither effort nor toil;
It flows freely from the edge of the rock cliff
And relieves the pangs of thirst of whoever
    drinks of it.

These songs, melodious to hear and
    satisfying to the mind,
Require neither effort nor toil;
They flow freely from the yogin's throat
And relieve the pangs of obscuring
    emotions of whoever hears them
    [216b].

Again some asked, "Why did the hermits and
great meditators of the past, and some recent
masters and practitioners, sing so many spiritual
songs?" I answered, "This is a sign that meditation experiences and realization have flowered
within them," and I improvised this song:

On the mountain covered with gleaming,
    golden meadows,
The grazing wild animals, sleek and con-
    tent, sing their song:
It is the sign that they have had their fill of
    grass and water.

In the fields of yellow summer flowers
The six-legged bees sing their song:
It is the sign that they have had their fill of
    honey.

In the midst of the clouds gathered in the
    azure sky,
The first turquoise thunder-dragon of
    summer roars his song:
It is the sign that the elements of cold and
    heat are equal.

On the soft meadows of emerald
The young maidens tending cattle sing
    their songs:
It is the sign of the full bloom of their
    youth.

At the doors of wealthy farmers and
    nomads,
Humble beggars sing the song of the *mani*:
It is the sign they have received plenty of
    food and drink.

At the pillow of the person who has just
    passed away
The revered priest sings his ritual song:
It is the sign that he has been given plenty
    of offerings.

In the solitude of mist-shrouded peaks
The renunciate yogin sings his song:
It is the sign that meditation experiences
    and true realization have dawned.

On another occasion, someone asked, "When
the holy beings of old sang their vajra songs, it
brought great benefit; has the same benefit
accrued from your songs?" In reply, I sang of
how many disciples had been benefited [217a]:

All the wise sages of old, from India and
    Tibet,
Expressed in song the meaning of the
    sutras and tantras,
And, by doing so, immensely benefited
    beings.

I also sang, in accord with the words of the
    holy ones,
Of the way to rely on the father guru;
Many came to follow in this way.

When I sang that a human body complete
    with the freedoms and endowments
Is valuable and difficult to obtain,
Many entered the door of the Dharma.

When I sang that, as the days, months, and
    years slip by,
One's life soon comes to its end, and that
Everyone, sooner or later, will die,
Many gave up concerns limited to this life.

When I sang that constructive and
    destructive deeds bear their inevitable
    fruits,

And must be respectively performed or
  avoided,
Many gave up misdeeds to practice virtue.

When I sang that, deep in samsara's ocean
  of suffering,
There is not the slightest bit of happiness,
Many developed weariness and revulsion.

When I sang that all beings in the six
  realms
Have been, without exception, our kind
  mothers,
Many developed love and compassion.

When I sang of how, having received
  teachings on sutra, tantra, and pith
  instructions,
I practiced meditation to realize these
  teachings,
Many who had listened to the Dharma
  began to practice.

When I sang of the fruit of Dharma
  practice
In mountain retreats where past saints
  lived,
Many went to live in solitary places.

When I sang that all the philosophical
  views
Flourishing in the land of Tibet were pure
  traditions,
Many developed pure perception [217b].

Someone else said, "In central Tibet, we consider that the distinctive sign of a practitioner is
that he wanders alone in cemeteries and remote,
uninhabited mountains." I answered with this
song:

Mighty Vishnu, blessed with miraculous
  powers,
Moves throughout all of space
Fearless of the sun, moon, stars, and
  planets:
This is the distinctive sign of his great
  might.

The golden wild duck, the king of
  migrating birds,
Soars throughout the vastness of the
  sky
Fearless of the most turbulent winds:
This is the distinctive sign of its powerfully
  feathered wings.

The king of beasts with his turquoise
  mane
Roams throughout the hills and valleys,
Fearless of any other animal:
This is the distinctive sign of its consum-
  mate strength.

The pointed white conch, spiraling to the
  right,
Roams throughout the ocean depths
Fearless of fish or sea monsters:
This is the distinctive sign of its ability to
  pierce its enemies.

The yogin engaged in practice
Wanders through cemeteries and moun-
  tain solitudes
Fearless of ghosts or demons:
This is the distinctive sign of his meditation
  experiences and realization.

Someone else said, "Your character and behavior are excellent indeed. Your beautiful songs
benefit the mind and make us long to hear more."
In reply I sang this song:

I am the bard of the Snow Land of
  Tibet,
The yogin Tsogdruk Rangdrol.

When I attended the authentic guru
I obeyed his every command.

When I prayed wholeheartedly,
I was unable to contain my tears.

When I remembered the unpredictability
  of the time of death [218a],
I grew diligent in study, reflection, and
  meditation.

When I considered the flaws of sensory
    enjoyments,
I grew utterly weary of worldly pleasures.

When I stayed in secluded mountains,
Not a thought alien to Dharma passed
    through my mind.

When I remained in the natural state,
I saw a spectacle that I had never seen
    before.

When I rested in samadhi free from
    thoughts,
Those who lived nearby became serene.

When I generated compassion for sentient
    beings,
I unstintingly gave away food and clothing.

When I expounded the teachings on cause
    and effect,
Gods, men, and demons were stirred by
    faith.

When I sang melodious songs,
Even the *gandharvas* smiled.[33]

As I sang this, a yearning faith grew in them.

One day I watched an eagle, the king of birds,
gliding in the sky and, as it soared higher and
higher, this song burst into my mind:

You, royal eagle, soaring in the firmament,
Circling in the midst of the azure sky,
In whichever of the four directions you go,
Carry this message of mine.

If you go toward the east, request
    Vajrasattva
To appear whenever people die
And lead them to the realm of Manifest
    Joy.

Tell the people from the eastern continent
    of Sublime Physical Form
That, since their beauty of face and form
Is the result of having practiced patience in
    earlier lifetimes,
They should practice patience even more!

If you go toward the south, request
    Ratnasambhava [218b]
To appear whenever people die
And lead them to the Glorious Field.

Tell the people from the southern
    continent of the Rose-apple Tree
That, since their ability to recognize right
    and wrong
Is the result of having practiced Dharma in
    former lives,
They should practice the Dharma even
    more!

If you go toward the west, request
    Amitabha
To appear whenever people die
And lead them to the Blissful Buddhafield.

Tell the people from the western continent
    of the Bountiful Cow
That, since their prosperity is the result
Of having been generous in former lifetimes,
They should give in charity even more!

If you go toward the north, request
    Amogasiddhi
To appear whenever people die
And lead them to the celestial field of
    Totally Fulfilled Action.

Tell the people of the northern continent
    of Ominous Sound[34]
That since their longevity is the result
Of having protected the lives of others in
    former lifetimes,
They should protect others' lives even
    more!

As I was singing, the eagle soared higher
and higher in space, gliding toward the east; I

watched him until I could see him no longer. I thought how nice it would be if I had unlimited miraculous powers, and could fly east like that eagle and reach the realm of Manifest Joy.

With full concentration, I prostrated myself many times toward the Buddhafields of the four directions, praying that when death came I might go to these Buddhafields and take with me all the beings with whom I had a connection.

Once, some people asked me, "When you were doing the pilgrimage of the Tsari Ravines, what came into your mind?" In answer, I sang this:

When I made the pilgrimage of the Tsari
  Ravines—
The paradise of Khechara on this earth
  [219a].
The amazing abode of the deities of the
  Three Roots—
These thoughts arose in my mind:

When traversing with difficulty the
  treacherous paths,
The rivers and bridges of the land of Lho,
It occurred to me that it must indeed be
  like this
When traveling the perilous paths of the
  bardo.

When I saw those possessed of food and
  strength
Going along joyfully,
It occurred to me that it must indeed be
  like this
When going to the next life possessed of
  Dharma.

When I saw all those lacking food and
  resources
Struggling along with great hardship,
It occurred to me that it must be indeed
  like this
When going to the next life without the
  Dharma.

When I saw some people continuing on,
Having abandoned their ailing friends,

It occurred to me that the likes of these,
  indeed,
Are what are called shameless friends.

When I saw some people going along,
Carrying their ailing friends on their backs,
It occurred to me that these indeed are
What are called real friends.

When I saw some caring for and giving
  food
To those bereft of everything,
It occurred to me that these indeed are
What are called Bodhisattvas.

When I saw that many who were making
  the pilgrimage
Were dying of starvation and illness,
It occurred to me that those people indeed
Had given their bodies and lives for the
  Dharma.

When I saw pilgrims by the tens of
  thousands
Part from each other and disperse,
It occurred to me that indeed this showed
The impermanence of all phenomena.

At these words, everyone felt sadness and compassion. One day, I sang this spontaneous song of experience [219b]:

In mountain rock mansions,
In the cool shade of forests,
In small huts of green grass,
Under tents of white cotton,
I, the carefree yogin,
Dwell at will.

Here is a cheerful song
From a mind at peace.

Divine authentic guru,
Your kindness to me
Exceeds that of the Buddha!

Entrusting myself to you,
I have understood that all appearances

Are the magical play of the mind—
That the phenomena of samsara and
    nirvana
Are apparent yet unreal.

I realized that the nature of this mind,
The root of samsara and nirvana,
Is an ineffable luminous void
With nothing to cling to.

I stayed in a solitary place
In the continuum of the natural state—
Like releasing a handful of cotton wool,
I let consciousness relax,
And it resumed its natural shape.

The darkness of ignorance
Having naturally cleared,
There arose the vast sky
Of the absolute expanse.

As to whether this is the absolute nature,
Not a question, not a hesitation
Arises in my mind.
Even if all the Buddhas were to appear
    before me,
I would have no doubts for them to clarify.

Buddhafield of the deities of the Three
    Roots,
Celestial Khechara in reality,
This is Tsari, where meditation
    experiences and realization
Arise in an instant.

Staying there are the Mahamudra yogins
Who live up to their names,
The assembly of those who have
    encountered
The true face of the absolute nature—

Transparent as the sky,
Brilliant as the sun,
Bright as a mirror,
And clear-seeing as an eye—

And who, preserving these four
    dharmakaya qualities,

Move together toward
The realm of absolute vastness.

It is a pleasure to hear [220a]
Scholars thoroughly trained
In Madhyamika scriptures and logic
Exchange views at a monastic gathering;
So also it is a pleasure to hear
The yogin of Mahamudra and
    Dzogchen—
The yogin who knows the one thing that
    liberates all—
Singing in solitude his songs of realization.

This song pleased the realized yogins, the
"destroyers of delusion," who dwelled there. Then
someone else asked, "While you were alone in
the mountains, since there was no one to desire
and no circumstances to inspire desire, did lust
arise in your mind?"

I answered, "O yes, many opportunities
came to me, and, not only did desire arise, but I
satisfied it!" and, teasing, I sang this song:

In the pleasure groves of isolated
    mountains,
The six-legged dancing bee
Is embraced and kissed
By the exquisite lotus maiden.

Many young birds,
Bending their graceful necks
And sending each other sidelong glances,
Ride one upon another in their sensuous
    dance.

Seeing this, I, the yogin,
Became inflamed by intense desire.
Uniting inseparably with
The beautiful maiden, the absolute
    expanse,
I became deeply intoxicated
By the enchanting taste of bliss, clarity, and
    nonthought.

Now, even were I to see a daughter of the
    gods,
No lust would arise.

The momentary and misleading company
of the daughters
Of this perishable world is pointless.
Better to have an everlasting companion
like mine,
To grant everlasting happiness.

When someone asked for a song about my meditation experiences, I sang this [220b]:

When relying upon the perfect teacher,
I felt that he was the Buddha himself.

When receiving the profound and vast
instructions,
I felt they were like ambrosia.

When contemplating the imperfections of
samsara,
I felt samsara was like a prison.

When meditating on compassion for all
beings,
I felt like a mother toward her children.

When merging with emptiness,
I felt it was like the vast sky.

When practicing the development and
completion stages, and the Great
Perfection,
It felt like arriving at the Unsurpassable
Buddhafield.

When dwelling in isolated mountains,
I felt I was in a celestial realm.

When staying alone with no companions,
I felt like I was a *rishi*.

When roaming through countries at random,
I felt they were like my homeland.

When meeting any sentient being,
It felt like I was meeting my own kin.

Once my fortunate spiritual son Kunzang
Shenpen asked me, "How should one remain in
the nonmeditation samadhi that is like a continuous stream? What is meant by 'stream'? Is
there any risk of confusing this with another
state?" My answer was this song:

Having received the faultless instructions
on Mahamudra or on Dzogchen,
The unique path traveled by countless
Buddhas and Bodhisattvas,
If you wish to remain uninterruptedly
In the nonmeditation samadhi
That is like a continuous stream,
You must do this:

Keep your body still;
Keep your voice silent;
As to mind, don't bind it: let it rest at ease
[221a].
Let consciousness relax completely.

At this time, attachment to "meditation"'
and "nonmeditation" clears,
And mind remains without any aim or
fabrication
In self-luminous awareness, vast and
transparent.

To remain just like this
Is the view of Mahamudra and Dzogchen.
If intellect does not tamper with this state,
And if you are graced by blessings of your
root and lineage gurus,
The view arises, clear as the sky.

Preserving this view continuously
With awareness undistracted,
In a continuity unbroken like a flowing
stream,
Is what is called "nonmeditation samadhi,
continuous like a stream."

If one has not recognized this,
One might simply let everything go
And lapse into an amorphous, ordinary
state
That cannot be said to be this or that—

To be immersed in an indistinct vagueness.
This would be a mistake.

Although these two states are similar,
Insofar as neither is intentional meditation,
Nonmeditation samadhi that is like a
    continuous stream
Is just remaining in a vivid clarity
That is like a bright, cloudless sky—
Limitless, pervasive, transparent.

The other is merely a dull state of mind
That is nothing in particular:
A constricted, fragmentary, biased state
Lacking lucid clarity,
A vague and hazy stupefaction.

Apart from confusing these two states,
There is no other error to be made.

Kunzang Shenpen went on, "That being the
case, when one is remaining in the nonmeditation
samadhi that is like a continuous stream, what
should it be like?" I replied:

One must remain in a vivid, lucid
    openness,
Like looking out
Into the reaches of the boundless sky
From the peak of a mountain open to
    every direction

The lord of *siddhas*, Jetsun Tilopa [221b],
Directing his gaze toward the sky,
Said to the great *pandita* Naropa:

What supports the sky? On what does
    sky rest?
The Mahamudra of one's mind has
    nothing to rest on.
If you loosen the bonds, liberation is
    certain.
Remain at ease in primordial simplic-
    ity.

The nature of mind is the sky beyond
    the contents of thoughts.
Remain thus at ease,

Not holding on to some thoughts,
Or pushing other thoughts away:
In true Mahamudra mind is undi-
    rected.

The unsurpassable fruition
Is simply to preserve this state.

Thus, through Marpa Lotsawa,
There will come many sky-like yogins,
Sons of the lineage of the great
    panditas Naro and Maitri.

The great awareness-holder, Shri Singha,[35]
Pointing his finger toward the heart of a
    cloudless sky,
Told the Lotus-born Guru:

Ever empty, ever empty; ever void, all
    void;
This crucial absolute truth is a
    treasure
Which shines everywhere—above,
    below, between, in all directions—
Shri Singha made it spring from the
    perfect vessel:
Action inseparable from view.

And with this he dissolved into vajra space.

In the same way the omniscient Longchen
    Rabjam said:

In the infinite sky, there is neither
    meditation or non-meditation.
This is the vast expanse that is
    Samantabhadra's wisdom.

It is also said in the *Miscellaneous Sayings of
    the Kadampas:*

The place for practice must be open
    and spacious;
One's view must be vast and open,
    too;
Even if the whole of samsara and
    nirvana were placed within it,
It would remain as unfilled as ever—

Such should be the immensity of the
view [222a].

He said, "To practice by merely remaining in a
vague, oblivious, ordinary state—that's completely useless for progressing along the paths
and stages, isn't it?" I replied:

The Victorious One, the incarnation of the
Holder of the White Lotus,[36] said:

These days, some say that when mind
is just at rest,
That is the Mahamudra view;
But that is not the true Mahamudra.

And Manjushri incarnate, Sakya Pandita,
said:[37]

Mahamudra as practiced by fools
Usually leads to an animal state.

This is why all the teachers of Madhyamika, Mahamudra, and Dzogchen
Repeatedly warn that just remaining
without awareness in a vague,
oblivious state,
Won't result in progress along the paths
and stages.
This is not merely true, but is a most
profound, crucial point!

If one merges with the evenness of sky-like
samadhi,
At a certain point a real knowledge will
burst forth from meditation.

Boundless clairvoyance, miraculous
powers, and miraculous vision will
manifest,
And ultimately one will realize the
dharmakaya.

Not understanding this, one might go
astray
And remain merely in a dull, amorphous
state—
Then meditation withers and one dozes off.

When absence of mind prevails, there
occur
Dullness, obliviousness, and, finally,
sleep;
After much meditation like this,
One will take rebirth in the animal realm.

All of this, which is said out of affection,
Must be understood.
To practice meditation, confusing these
two states—
Like drinking milk mixed with water—
Is the way of fools;
To practice meditation clearly
distinguishing the two
Is the way of the wise.

Kunzang asked again, "What should one do
when, while remaining in evenness, one does
sink into that oblivious, ordinary state?" I replied:

When clouds form, they obscure the
stainless sky [222b].
If they are blown away by the wind
And scattered in the ten directions,
The natural blue color of the sky
reappears.
In the same way, when a state of vague
oblivion
Obscures one's meditation,
One should straighten one's back,
Raise one's gaze,
Widen one's perspective, heighten
awareness.
Let it extend into infinity,
Then let it be.

Thus one separates the pure essence from
the dross;
This mental haze will clear away like
clouds that just vanish,
Leaving the royal samadhi,
Vividly transparent, like the immaculate
sky.

This is the supreme method
For dispelling difficulties and enhancing
practice.

Rigdzin Shri Singha said:

> The mind of sentient beings remains
>   fragmented,
> While the mind of the Buddhas is all-
>   encompassing;
> To let the mind become vast and
>   open like the sky
> Is the key instruction for enhancing
>   practice.

> From time to time, examine the mind with
>   analytic insight;
> Ascertain that mind is not something
>   graspable—
> That it has neither center nor boundary—
> And let this discovery expand.

> Sometimes, merge mind
> With a clear, cloudless sky;
> Make it vast and lofty;
> Leave it wide open
> As an immense, all-encompassing
>   expanse.

> Doing this, you will avoid the flaws
> Of slackness, obliviousness, and
>   somnolence;
> Your experience of the view will be
>   enhanced.

> Then, when mind contracts again,
> Like an old scroll rolling itself up,
> Examine mind thoroughly, time and
>   again:
> This is a profound instruction.

> Wondrous—remaining in lucid serenity
>   [223a],
> The state of sky-like evenness!

> Joyous—when day or night, indoors and
>   outdoors,
> Eyes open or closed, makes no difference
>   to your awareness.

> Wondrous—when the world of form
>   appears

> Like a rainbow in the unchanging sky of
>   dharmakaya!
> Joyous—to dredge the depths of samsara,
> Bringing all beings to enlightenment!

> All you whose wisdom is vast as the sky,
> Brilliant as the unobscured sun,
> Limpid as crystal, firm as an unshakable
>   mountain—
> To you I pay homage, go for refuge;
> Grant me the waves of your grace.

After I had said this, his understanding of the view progressed greatly and his realization became as vast as space.

The great king of Dharma, Lhagyari Tashi Tsering Pelbar, a true descendent of the luminous celestial beings, asked me to perform a ceremony for his long life, and sent whatever was needed for that purpose. I sent him this letter:

> You observed the exhaustion of vain
>   wealth,
> And took hold of the inexhaustible treasury
>   of the seven noble riches.
> Having extracted from it the wish-fulfilling
>   gem of skill
> With the four ways of gathering retinue
>   and disciples,
> You fulfilled the aspirations of all.

> With the iron claw of scriptural and
>   intellectual authority
> You shed the heart-blood of vile naga-like,
>   evil-minded antagonists.

> The dragon of your strict discipline
>   thundered its voice
> And struck at the heart-vein of the
>   thousand devils of wrongdoing.

> With the supreme medicine of the vast,
>   deep teachings,

You soothed the agonizing pain of the
    passions of beings.

As for myself, the hermit Tsogdruk
    Rangdrol,
Though I obtained all the potential of a
    human being,
Met a perfect teacher, received his vast and
    profound instructions,
And remained in solitudes [223b],
Because I did not have the fortitude to
    persevere in meditation,
The swift path of the Secret Mantrayana
    became for me
As long as the road of the sutras, and
I could not even help myself, much less
    benefit others.

Before the jewel throne supported by
    fearless lions,
On which rest your lotus feet, O matchless
    Dharma King,
From the core of my heart,
Not merely paying lip service,
I respectfully offer this letter,
Presenting it with both hands held high
    above my head.

As I received your perfect letter with its
    seal intact,
Conveying the news of your good health,
    together with your presents,
A delight never known before arose in my
    mind.

By the grace of the Three Jewels
The illusory body of your servant is also
    well:
Not lacking the basic necessities, my body
    and mind are at ease.
I have devoted myself as much as possible
    to virtuous practice,
Adorning it at the outset with Bodhicitta
And at the end with the dedication of merit
    and prayers of aspiration.

O wondrous Dharma King,
I have taken the flowers of your words

As a wreath upon my head;
I have taken the nectar of their meaning
As a treasure to my heart.
I shall accomplish your command,
And present you with the sacred long-life
    substances.

O lord, it is fitting that your efforts
To benefit the Dharma and sentient beings
Should increase a hundredfold.

Do not impose excessive taxes, nor require
    excessive labor;
Show all possible kindness to the poor
    within your domain,
As though they were your children.

O lord, we pray that, like a wish-fulfilling
    tree
Protected by the wall of our good fortune,
Your manifested form, which fulfills the
    aspirations of gods and men,
May ever remain [224a].

This letter, resting upon a pure white scarf,
    I offer to you
From Caritra, the meeting ground of dakas
    and dakinis,
The realm of the Great Glorious Heruka,
The forest where realization dawns all at
    once.

My letter greatly pleased him. As I was
about to leave the area, I stayed for seven days in
the meditation cave of the Guru of Orgyen, near
Lomi Kyimdun, the Seven Households of Lo,
making a spiritual connection with that holy
place. As Ama Khandroma[38] called me to her
home, I went and gave her a long-life empowerment and some teaching. Faith arose in her; she
gave me a good pack-*dzomo* and all the tea and
butter we needed. Palgye, a chieftain from
Kongpo, also gave some tea and butter. With
these I sent from the Phagmo Lhakhang, "The
Varahi Temple," a day's supply of tea and soup
to the great hermits of the Chikchar retreat center. A *ganachakra* feast was offered and religious
dances performed, to everyone's delight.

In farewell, for the benefit of Ama Khandroma Mingyur Paldrön, "Torch of Unchanging Glory," the chief Palgye, and all the faithful patrons of Chikchar and Norbu Khachö, I sang this song:

May the divine assembly of the deities of
    the Three Roots
Bless the body, speech, and mind of all
    those assembled here.

You, faithful patrons of the blissful abode
    of Tsari,
Do not feed yourselves by hunting birds
    and wild animals [224b].
Do not lie and cheat when trading.
Do not kill calves to get more milk from
    dris and *dzomos*.
Do not accumulate wealth by theft,
    robbery, or banditry.
If, in this life, your acts are evil,
Great will be your suffering in the next
    life.

While your body is still healthy, offer
    prostrations and circumambulations.
While your tongue can still move, recite
    prayers and mantras.
While your mind is still clear, listen to the
    Dharma.
While you are still young, hasten to
    practice meditation.
While wealth and possessions are in your
    hands, make offerings; be charitable.
While you are powerful, protect the
    helpless.
If you practice the Dharma while you are
    young and have white teeth,
Your mind will be at peace when you are
    old and have white hair.

All you patrons, men and women, have
    been very kind
To all of us yogins, master and disciples;
I pray that, in the present, you may enjoy
    long and healthy lives,
And that, ultimately, you may attain
    Buddhahood.

May this heartfelt advice sung by a
    departing vagabond
Benefit the mind of whoever hears it.

This song did them some good, and later they did their best to shun wrongdoing and perform only virtuous acts. On the day of our departure, all the great hermits accompanied us for a while on our way. As a farewell prayer I sang this:

Remain, pride of white snow lions,
Living at ease on the splendid snow
    mountains,
Flourishing your extraordinary turquoise
    manes,
While with perfect wings the royal eagle,
Whose eyes see everywhere,
Soars through the azure sky
To distant lands.

Remain, vajra friends, Dharma
    companions.
May your extraordinary meditation
    experiences and realization
Flourish on splendid Tsari Mountain,
While I, the renunciate Tsogdruk
    Rangdrol,
Who travels from place to place with no
    particular destination,
Regarding everything with pure percep-
    tion,
Set out for distant solitudes [225a].

We, vajra brothers with unsullied vows,
Met for a brief instant in this life.
May we meet again in a pure Buddhafield;
May we never again be parted!

At the end of this song, all the elder yogins stayed behind, filled with fervent devotion and respect, while the younger cotton-clad yogins escorted us on a little farther. When the time came to part, so great was our mutual affection that most of them did prostrations with tears streaming down their faces. I prayed that we would meet again and again. Then, although our parting was almost unbearably sad, every-one went on his own way.

After we, master and disciples, reached Dotsen, I went on to the Adamantine Rampart[39] with only my spiritual son Kalden. Having offered purifying smoke of fragrant plants, a *ganachakra* feast, *tormas*, and prayers, I told Kalden, "I feel that many dakas and dakinis have come. If you know any folk songs, sing some to please them." He sang many different songs with beautiful tunes, and accompanied these with dances. We laughed a lot and had the impression that the dakas and dakinis were laughing too [225b].

Past Chözam, we climbed to just below Gongmo La, the Snow Grouse Pass, and spent the night there. Before dawn I had a dream:

Crossing the pass near Dagpo Ganden Rabden, Kalden, Tsultrim, and I were leading a horse carrying food and clothes. On the pass, we saw a very old woman lying there, apparently unable to move. Filled with pity, I asked her if she could get up. She could not, but raised her head and begged us to give her anything we could. I gave her tea, butter, and *tsampa*. She also asked for some clothes, and I gave her some.

Then she said, "You are able to walk; I am unable to do so. It would be most kind and compassionate if you were to give me your horse." Filled with compassion, I gave her the horse as well.

At that moment she got up joyfully and said, "You are said to be the most compassionate one of all, so I thought to see for myself. I have no need of a horse or anything of that sort. Don't you know who I am?"

"No," I said, and she continued:

"If you don't recognize me,
I am Vajravarahi.
I shall bestow a *siddhi* upon you—
If you have doubts, look at this!"

Instantly she transformed herself into Vajravarahi, red, with two heads: her main head, with a wrathful expression, was surmounted by the smaller head of a black sow. She was naked, adorned only with bone ornaments and garlands of dried and fresh skulls [226a]. In her right hand she held a hooked knife, and in her left a skull cup filled with blood. In the crook of her left arm she held a *khatvanga*.[40] Majestically, she danced. From her heart emanated rays of light that penetrated me and brought me into an increasingly clear and vivid expanse of bliss and voidness.

"Here is the *siddhi*," she said, handing me a sack resembling a medicine bag, made of multi-colored cloth. It contained what seemed to be thousands of silver coins of various sizes. "Take this!" she said, "and give these to many fortunate beings with suitable karma; they will all be able to fly." Then she flew into the sky.

Tucking the miraculous bag into the left side of my garment, I, too, could fly. Kalden and Tsultrim were also flying and we rose higher and higher. Seeing us, the people on the ground prostrated themselves. Vajravarahi then said, "It is not yet time for you to come. You must give the *siddhi* to all these beings. Later, when you are dying, pray to me and I shall come to receive you with a myriad dakas and dakinis." Having uttered these words, she rose higher and higher, then disappeared.

Filled with joy, the three of us continued to fly and, watched by all the local people in the valley, alighted on the summit of a mountain. Overwhelmed with faith, the people climbed to meet us and offered abundant food and many presents.

I thought, "Vajravarahi has given us a *siddhi* so that whenever we are without food or resources, we just need to fly" [226b]. Not accepting the offerings, we returned them, and people's faith grew even stronger. Then the three of us came down. In a pleasant place we opened the miraculous bag and found in it round pieces of silver that looked like coins—over a hundred large ones, a thousand medium-sized ones, and ten thousand small ones.

If one held a large coin, one could fly anywhere one wished. If one held a medium-sized coin, one could fly up into space until disappearing from sight. If one held a small coin, one could fly at the height of a four- or five-storey house. I thought joyfully that, later, I would give these to many people so that they too could fly. In this mood, we continued on our way.

Later, reflecting on the meaning of this dream, I thought it predicted that, by giving to my spiritual sons the profound instructions, which are like the warm breath of the mother dakinis, they would attain either the state of celestial and human beings, liberation, or ultimate omniscience, in numbers corresponding to those of the different silver pieces.

The next day we reached the monastery of Ganden Rabden and stayed for the night. We offered tea to the whole community, and did prostrations and circumambulations. The following day we crossed the Tsangpo River in a hide coracle and spent the night at Lungkar Monastery, where we received a warm welcome [227a]. The next day we arrived at the holy place of Dagla Gampo. We visited the chapels of the monastery and made offerings. The day after, we went to the retreat center on the hillside. I was offered use of the hermitage where Shar Dagpo Tashi Namgyal[41] and many other great sages of the past had lived, and I stayed there in retreat for four months.

During this time a drought occurred. The local people asked me to bring rain. I said I did not know how to make rain, but that I would pray to the guru and the Three Jewels. Then I went to a lovely nearby meadow facing south. In the middle, at the foot of a juniper tree, flowed a spring. I performed the consecration of the ground, the invitation to the Buddhas, the cleansing ritual, the offering of the *Hundred Tormas*, and the *torma* offering to the nagas. Then I made this prayer:

"By the blessings of all the Buddhas of the ten directions, the merits gathered by all our mother-sentient beings, and by the good fortune I may have gathered through performing virtuous deeds and meditating with pure motivation, when rain is needed, may the sky fill with clouds and as much rain as desired fall.

"When warmth is needed, may a warm, gentle sun shine and ripen the crops [227b]. When hail threatens, may the air turn into a great fire and melt the hail into a welcome downpour of rain. When hoarfrost threatens, may it be prevented by a gathering of warming clouds. May all the birds, rabbits, and insects that destroy the crops and damage the trees be diverted.

"May every year be an excellent one, and may harvests be so abundant that jars are filled to the brim with grain and overflow into inexhaustible heaps, ensuring prosperity and happiness for everyone, day and night, as in the golden age."

After making this prayer, I returned to my hermitage and visualized first a vast empty sky, then this sky becoming filled with huge clouds. Within a few moments, it began to rain heavily. Since the year thus turned into a good one, people's faith grew, and they kept on bringing me offerings and provisions.

During my retreat, praying to the spiritual forefathers of the Kagyu lineage, I practiced the skillful path of *tummo*, the inner heat, and the clear-light Mahamudra. An ineffable realization of bliss-emptiness dawned in my being [228a].

My close spiritual sons Kalden, Tendzin Nyima, and Kunzang Shenpen chiefly practiced merging with the realization of the vast, all-pervasive expanse of pristine simplicity that crushes delusion into dust:[42] the primordial true nature of one's own mind—nondual, empty, luminous—which is the root of both samsara and nirvana. In between meditation periods they cultivated compassion for all beings under the sky. Doing so, they greatly enhanced their inner experience and realization.

We then received many transmissions from Tendzin Chöwang Rinpoche, "Dharma Lord Holder of the Doctrine," a teacher at the retreat center. Among these were instructions written by Dagpo Tashi Namgyal on the Six Yogas of Naropa, Mahamudra, Guru Yoga,[43] yogic exercises, instructions on isolating the central channel, and on drinking the vajra water.[44]

From Lama Tsondru Chöbar, "Blazing Spiritual Endeavor," we received the transmission of the writings of Dagpo Lharje—Lord Gampopa—and of other texts.[45] From the head lama of the retreat center, I received a few texts from the *Single Golden Syllable of the Black Quintessence*,[46] the rediscovered treasures of Dungtso Repa, which I had not received earlier.

At my request, the hermit Damchö, "Sublime Dharma," and other great practitioners who had mastered the practices of the channels, energies, and yogic exercises showed us the holding of the breath and other exercises, which we enjoyed watching. I was fortunate to learn some new exercises.

One day, Kalden Rangdrol asked me to compose some verses in praise of this supreme place. Granting his request, I said this:

Here is the true palace of the Buddhas of
  the three times
And of the infinity of peaceful and wrathful
  deities;
Here is the gathering field of the dakas and
  dakinis of the three places [228b]⁴⁷
And of the glorious protectors of the
  Dharma.
Here the teaching of the practice lineage
  has flourished;
Here many learned and accomplished
  sages have lived.

Dagla Gampo, the great eastern holy
  place,⁴⁸
The most illustrious, glorious mountain,
One with the Diamond Throne of India,
You are the chief ornament of the Land of
  Snows, Tibet;
You offer to men and gods a basis for
  accumulating merits.

Behind, the summits of the rocky peaks
  reach the sky.
Wherever one looks there is delightful
  beauty.
To the south are vast and verdant forests
In which lovely birds fly and wild animals
  roam.
The scene is a brilliant mingling of
  exquisitely colored flowers
And a great variety of potent medicinal
  plants.
Natural food, fruits, nettles, and other
  edible plants abound.
Down all the hillsides cool streams cascade.
There are many pleasant caves and huts to
  dwell in.
Enchanting place!

Looking out, one sees the vast open sky;
In front, the Tsangpo River⁴⁹ winds, as if it
  were a water-offering;

The trees, with all their many forms and
  foliage, form a mandala.

The local guardians are well-disposed
  toward the Dharma.
Rain falls in due season, crops and cattle
  prosper;
In the winter the sun always shines, giving
  warmth,
While in summer the weather remains cool
  and pleasant.

One's mind is always happy; awareness is
  crisp.
One finds everywhere people who are
  practicing the Dharma
And shrines sheltering sacred objects
  imbued with blessings.
Faithful patrons living on either side of the
  valley
Supply water, firewood, and other
  necessities.
No one here creates obstacles to Dharma
  practice;
Meditation experiences and realization
  grow by themselves [229a].

If one lives in such a place, this life will be a
  happy one;
If one can also practice meditation, the
  next life will be blissful.
Therefore, those who aspire to happiness
  in this life and the next
Should live and meditate in this very place.

Doing so, benefiting themselves and others,
May they all become holders of the
  teachings of the practice lineage.

Everyone was gladdened by these words.

On the eve of our departure, I offered tea to all the monks and a *ganachakra* feast at the retreat center, concluding with many prayers of dedication. Lama Tendzin Chöwang Rinpoche told me, "Last night I dreamed that, sailing on a vast ocean, you reached the far shore. Wherever you go, you will receive much wealth. Without any clinging, use this wealth to make offerings and be charitable, and it won't defile you."

On the morning of our departure, the Dharma brothers with whom I had pure connections, together with many disciples and patrons, accompanied us for a short while. For them I sang this song:

Lord root guru, enthroned above my head
On the *chakra* of great bliss,
I bow down to you with fervent respect.

I, Tsogdruk Rangdrol, who have given up
    all concerns for this life,
Sing these words to urge you to practice
    the Dharma.

You, my spiritual brothers whose *samaya* is
    pure
And my son-like disciples, listen well!

In this decadent age,
Life is short and subject to many hazards.
No one can say when this vulnerable body
    will be destroyed.
Whether we consider it or not, death is
    near [229b].

Even if we had enough provisions for a
    hundred or a thousand years,
Crossing the threshold of death, we leave
    everything behind.

Even if our wardrobe would suffice for a
    hundred or a thousand years,
Crossing the threshold of death, we go on,
    naked.

Even if we owned a hundred or a thousand
    pieces of gold and silver,
Crossing the threshold of death, we go on,
    empty-handed.

Even if we had a hundred or a thousand
    relatives and friends,
Crossing the threshold of death, we go on
    all alone.
So it is!

Spiritual sons and companions,
Do not cling to what will prove useless

At death, in the *bardo*, or in the next life—
Wealth, food, clothing and the like.

Forsake all greed, cravings, and other
    preoccupations centered on this life.
Taking an example from the perfect lives
    of the past saints,
Filled with love, compassion, and the
    aspiration for enlightenment,
Avoid unwholesome acts, accumulate
    merit,
And always seal all virtue with prayers of
    dedication.

If you are able to do as I say,
This life and the next will be fulfilling,
And you will go from Buddhafield to
    Buddhafield.

Auspicious connections have been created
    between us
For meeting in a pure land in our next
    existence.
So, practice with joy in your hearts!

May the minds of all who hear or see this
    song
Turn toward the Dharma!

The minds of all those present became imbued with the spirit of the teachings; with unshakable faith, they implored me to visit this sacred place again and again. When we left, they all remained standing where they were. Full of faith and respect for the lamas, the Dharma brothers and the sublime place we had left behind, we all, master and disciples, went on, looking back, praying that we might meet them many times again [230a].

We then spent one day at Lama Lochenpa's place, and asked him for a long-life blessing to establish a spiritual connection. Next, we visited Dagpo Shedrup Ling;[50] here we offered tea to all, and made offerings and prayers. I made prayers of auspiciousness for the senior and junior treasurers of Dagpo Drumpa and gave a longevity blessing and some teaching to their wives and children. They were very helpful to us and gave us provisions. As offering for the longevity blessing, they gave us a skin bag full of butter and some silver coins.

On our way back, we reached the sacred site of E Rigpai Jungne and met the great King of Dharma, Lhagyari, and his son. I presented them with a *dzomo*, and asked for the initiations for the most profound *Embodiment of the Three Jewels*[51] and for the *Secret Wisdom*,[52] as well as the oral transmission of the rituals related to the *Secret Wisdom* and the mind teaching known as *The Eternal Sky*.[53] In turn, I offered him a longevity empowerment and the oral transmission of the *Life and Songs* of Jetsun Milarepa.

Then I remained in retreat at the place known as Zabmo Ri, Profound Mountain. There I gave some teaching on the nature of mind to the Dharma King's mother. She was introduced to the nature of mind, and offered me various gifts.

I gave a longevity blessing to the chieftains Khangsar and Kyilkhor, to Tsachanga, Yukhang, and other faithful patrons, men and women, and also gave them teachings on the karmic law of cause and effect. Faith grew in all of them. Pleased, Tsachanga offered me a *dotse*[54] of Chinese silver, and others offered much gold, silver, corals, and turquoises.

I accepted these and went to Lhasa [230b]. There I met Theji, the nephew of Abhe—the consort of Chingwang Rinpoche, the Dharma King of Mongolia—as well as the treasurer Darhen, Agyap Delek, and many other devoted patrons who had come from Mongolia. They offered me thirteen *dotse* of silver. I exchanged them for gold and asked the master goldsmith of Döpel to make with it a lamp weighing about fifteen coins.

In the meantime, I stayed for two months in King Songtsen Gampo's meditation cave, Drak Lhalupuk, on the side of Chakpori Hill. I also performed a longevity practice for the benefit of Demo Rinpoche, the regent-king of Tibet.

The son of Topden, the faithful, diligent, intelligent, and compassionate governor of Kyilkhor, came to meet me with the intention of crossing the gateway of the Dharma and renouncing the world. I ordained him and gave him the name Kalzang Tsultrim, "Fortunate Discipline." Breaking with all worldly affairs and devoting his whole life to spiritual practice at Serphuk Gangri, the Golden Cave of the Snow Peak, and at Lapchi, he became an authentic practitioner.

When the gold lamp was finished, the patron Namkha Dzöpa and I went to glorious Samye. Filling the lamp with clarified butter, I lit it and offered it in front of the Jowo Changchup Chenpo, the Great Enlightened Crowned Buddha[55] and, with it, made the "Great Thousandfold Offering." I offered food for one day and a silver coin each to all the monks of Samye. I gave alms to over a hundred beggars. To the most destitute, who were shoeless and half-naked, I gave shoes and clothes. I concluded with many prayers of dedication [231a].

The great protector Oracle of Samye[56] was very pleased, and, manifesting through the trance of the Dharma Lord, called me into his presence and declared, "Great *siddha*, it is excellent that you offered a gold lamp to Samye, for there was none before. You should continue to render as much service as you can, and I shall always protect you, accompanying you like your shadow." So saying, he gave me a long white silken scarf.

The Dharma Lord of Samye, the governor of the fortress,[57] and all the local people were moved with faith. Many of them called me to their homes and presented me with food and other things. I stayed for a few days at the temple on Hepori hill. When I offered a *ganachakra* feast, a girl who could see gods and demons said that she saw celestial beings belonging to the eight classes of gods and rakshas coming to the feast from all directions, gathering in the sky like clouds.

I went to Samye Chimphu to visit the central gathering place of the dakinis of Akanishtha.[58] There I lit a hundred lamps, offered a hundred *ganachakras*, and gave tea and a silver coin to each of the retreatants. From Chimphu I went to the Red Rock of Yamalung,[59] where I met and made offerings to all the pure monks who do retreat in this sacred secluded place [231b].

Following this I proceeded to Ganden. In front of the precious golden reliquary[60] I offered a hundred lamps and tea to all at the monastery.

I also made a general offering to the community of monks from Kham. Since I had two small gold coins, I offered them to the Golden Reliquary and to the Damchen Chögyal, the "Pledgeholder Dharma King."[61]

After making many wishes and prayers, I went to Drak Yerpa.[62] I spent the night there, paid homage, and made offerings to all the blessed objects. In front of the statue of the precious master, Guru Rinpoche, I offered a *ganachakra* feast, and offered tea as well to the whole monastic community.

In Lhasa, I went before the two Crowned Buddhas and offered butter-lamps, prostrations, and circumambulations. I made gifts to all the beggars and ransomed the lives of seven sheep and goats, which I bought and set free, praying that wherever I went I might have a long life free of illness, and be able to practice Dharma purely.

Notes

1. Tsari is identified as both *Caritra* and *Devikota*, two of the twenty-four great sacred places described in the tantras. For an analysis of the identification of Tsari as these two sacred places, see Huber (1992, vol. 2). For a summary of the guidebook to Tsari by the eighth Drukchen, Chökyi Nangwa, see Filibeck (1988).

There are four main gateways to the Pure Crystal Mountain of Tsari *(dag pa shel ri)*: the eastern one is that of Manjushri; the southern, of Vajrapani; the western, of Tara; and the northern, of Avalokiteshvara. According to Kunkhyen Pema Karpo (see Bibliography), the general sequence of human entry into the Tsari mandala is as follows:

Guru Padmasambhava entered through the southern door and remained seven years in the Magnificent Secret Cave *(zil chen gsang phug;* see JK, vol. Da, p. 104). Vimalamitra, too, traveled miraculously to Tsari.

Lawapa *(la ba pa,* or Kambalapada, tenth century), a teacher of Atisha, entered through the eastern door with his disciple Bhusuku, and later departed to the Buddhafield of Khechara *(mkha' spyod)* without leaving his physical body behind.

Kyebu Yeshe Dorje *(skyes bu,* also spelled *skye bo, ye shes rdo rje,* twelfth century), an incarnation of Nyang Ben Tingdzin Zangpo (see TN, p. 515), tried thrice to enter Tsari according to the prediction of Gampopa, his teacher (see JK, vol. Da, p. 104). The third time, Yeshe Dorje was able to enter through the western door and reached the Turquoise Lake *(g.yu mtsho).* He also opened the door to the Lake of the Black Mandala *(mtsho mandal nag po)* in Dagpo; there, together with Gampopa, he concealed as *terma* the *Teaching on Mind, the Wish-fulfilling Gem (sems khrid yid bzhin nor bu).*

Tsangpa Gyare Yeshe Dorje *(gtsang pa rgya ras ye shes rdo rje,* 1161–1211, not to be confused with Kyebu Yeshe Dorje) went to Tsari, following a prediction given to him in a vision by Gyalwa Lorepa *(rgyal ba lo ras pa,* 1187–1250). After Tsangpa Gyare had opened the door of the sacred place he had a vision at the Turquoise Lake Palace in which Chakrasamvara told him, "You will become the Buddha known as The Young Aspirant *(chung mos pa),* the youngest of the 1002 Buddhas of this kalpa, and your teachings will spread far and wide from here, to the distance of eighteen days of a vulture's flight."

Drigung Jigten Gonpo *('jig rten mgon po,* 1143–1217) sent to Tsari first three of his main disciples, headed by Nyö Gyalwa Lhanangpa *(gnyos rgyal ba lha nang pa),* and then a great number of hermits (see chap. 11, note 10).

Finally Sonam Gyaltsen *(bsod nams rgyal mtshan),* from Ralung, entered through the northern door.

2. In 1811.

3. This was the eighth Drukchen, Kunzig Chökyi Nangwa *('brug chen kun gzigs chos kyi snang ba,* 1768–1822).

4. The Diamond Throne of India; see chap. 1, note 1.

5. Chögyal Lhagyari Tashi Tsering Pelbar *(chos rgyal lha rgya ri bkra shis tshe ring dpal 'bar).* The Lhagyari kings, said to be originally descendants of celestial beings *(lha),* are direct descendants of King Trisong Detsen. A prophecy from the State Oracle of Nechung said that if the Lhagyari line flourished, so would Tibet. See also Karsten (1980).

6. Chözam *(chos zam)* is a small village. Dotsen *(rdo mtshan),* or "sexed stones," is so called because of large stones naturally shaped as the *linga* of Chakrasamvara and the *bhaga* of Vajravarahi. They were kept in the Dotsen Temple *(rdo mtshan gtsug lag khang).* Childless couples would come to circumambulate the temple and pray to be blessed with a child.

7. There are three levels at which one can circum-

ambulate the holy mountain of Tsari: upper, intermediate, and lower. The last one, known as Tsari
Rong Khor, the Circumambulation of the Ravines
of Tsari (*tsari rong bskor*), is exceedingly difficult and
was done only once every twelve years, in the Monkey Year.

Because of its blessing and rarity, this event
attracted tens of thousands of pilgrims. These were
confronted by many difficulties. The southern part of
the pilgrimage led through low altitudes and the
pilgrims had to travel under the cover of tropical
forests so thick that the sky could not be seen for
hours on end. The humidity, moreover, was so intense
that their woollen and felt clothing, suited to the dry,
cold climate of the highlands, would rot. Sometimes
the pilgrims had to walk along dangerous cliffs and
cross turbulent rivers on vertiginous ladders or on
bridges made from the slippery trunks of trees.

Another danger came from the savage Lhopa
tribes scattered throughout the forest, who would
attack unaccompanied travelers with poisoned arrows
and often kill them. In an attempt to prevent such
incidents, every twelve years the Tibetan government would send up to a hundred loads of gifts and
offer incentives to the Lhopas to pacify them while
the pilgrimage was taking place. After an agreement
had been reached, a swearing ceremony was held.
(See *House of the Turquoise Roof*, pp. 90–91, summarized below.) A gate made of bamboo was erected
and the meat of two freshly killed yaks was tied to the
post on each side. The Lhopas' representatives would
show their good faith by passing under the gate. In
passing, each Lhopa would cut a small piece of raw
meat from one the carcasses and eat it. But even then
they could not be trusted completely, and the government had to send soldiers to protect the pilgrims and
guides to lead them on their hazardous journey.

8. The Pure Crystal Mountain (*dag pa shel ri*), the
central and holiest snow peak of Tsari. Detailed
descriptions of this mountain are given in Pema Karpo and Chökyi Nangwa's guidebooks. See also Martin
(1988), Sorensen (1990, 14–22), and Huber (1992,
note 110). Around the sacred mountain are four
ravines: the Human Skin Protector Ravine (*mi lpags
mgon po rong*), the Dazzling Ravine (*'od 'bar rong*), the
Tiger's Den Ravine (*stag tshang rong*), and the difficult
and frightening Bear's Den Ravine (*dom tshang rong*).
In these four ravines flow four rivers related to the
four empowerments (*dbang bzhi*).

9. Caritra; see note 1 above.

10. Shapes of deities and of sacred letters which
appear naturally on the surface of rocks.

11. In 1812.

12. The procession of the pilgrims was divided
according to geographical origin into groups called
sho and would proceed in long lines headed by a
group leader (*stong dpon*, as communicated by
T. Huber). The local people would take the lead,
since they knew the place well. Next came the
Bhutanese, since they were good at clearing the way,
followed by the strong Khampas, and finally the
pilgrims from central Tibet. Often the path was so
narrow that the pilgrims had to walk in single file and
if, for some reason, the way was blocked for those in
front, they might have to wait for many hours leaning
against a rock wall above a precipice. Those who
were among the first fifty behind the guide were
considered lucky, for the difficulty and danger were
much greater for those coming further behind in the
line.

The main purpose of the pilgrimage was the
long circumambulation of the sacred Pure Crystal
Mountain. The route followed, which includes in
particular the celebrated "nine passes and nine valleys" (*la dgu lung dgu*), has been described by Bailey
(1957) and Huber (1992). Anyone who had success-
fully completed this pilgrimage, which could take ten
to fifteen days, would find any other pilgrimage relatively easy.

In the lower altitudes, there were no places or
temples of particular interest. In contrast, in the upper
levels of Tsari the way led through pleasant and
beautiful areas such as Chikchar (*cig char*), where
there were many temples and sacred objects to be
visited, and all were accessible throughout the year.
These temples and images were nearly all destroyed
during the Cultural Revolution.

13. Yulmeh (*yul rmad*), a small village at over four
thousand meters, is the main practice place of the
Drigungpas in Tsari. Chözam (*chos zam*) marked the
end of the pilgrimage. See Huber (1992, note 54).

14. The *Sadhana of Amitayus and Hayagriva Combined*
(*nye brgyud tshe rta zung 'brel 'chi med dpal gter*) is a *sadhana*
that was prophesied in a *terma* concealed by Guru
Padmasambhava in the Magnificent Secret Cave (*zil
chen gsang phug*) at Tsari and revealed by the great
siddha Thangtong Gyalpo; see *Compendium of Sadhanas*
(*sgrub thabs kun btus*, vol. 1, p. 439). The *sadhana* texts
presented in the *Rinchen Terdzö* (vol. Tshi, pp.1 91–
204) combine the three traditions of the Canonical
Transmission (*bka' ma*), Spiritual Treasures (*gter ma*)
and Pure Visions (*dag snang*). On this longevity practice, see J. Gyatso (1981, 142–69).

15. The Black Naga's Devil (*klu bdud nag po*), known

in full as the "Supreme Herb, Black Diamond Naga's Devil" (*rtswa mchog klu bdud rdo rje nag po*), is the bonnet bell-flower (*Codonopsis*). According to information received in conversation with Dr. Sherap Jorden, this is a creeping plant with grey-blue flowers and an unpleasant smell. The preparation made from its roots, leaves, flowers, and fruits is said to cure all diseases, especially leprosy and epilepsy; to enable one to fly in the sky and walk on water; and to bring forth all ordinary and extraordinary *siddhis*. It is used in the preparation of a sacramental substance (*dam rdzas*) called the "rainbow light pill" (*'ja 'od ril bu*), the mere taste of which liberates one from rebirth in the three lower realms of samsara. The common *klu bdud* (*Codonopsis nervosa*) is used, associated with eighteen other medicines, as an anti-inflammatory, an analgesic, a tonic, and as a treatment for gout, abscesses, and leprosy. See also T. J. Tsarong (1986).

On the likely identification of the *klu bdud rdo rje* as *Codonopsis convolvulaceae* or *Codonopsis ovata*, and for the detailed description of this plant and its varieties, see Fletcher (1975), Martin (1988, 351–54) and especially Sorensen (1990). According to Tertön Rinchen Lingpa (*gter ston rin chen gling pa*, 1295–1375) this plant is called Diamond Naga's Devil because it is precious like a diamond and because it overcomes the nagas that cause leprosy and other skin diseases (see *gso ba rig pa'i tshig mdzod g.yu thog dgongs rgyan*, p. 18). According to Trogawa Rinpoche, the Diamond Naga's Devil (*klu bdud rdo rje*) should not be confused with the ordinary Naga's Devil (*klu bdud*): only some persons with spiritual capacities can see and find the former at dusk, when the plant is said to emit a faint glow.

16. Chikchar (*cig char*) is a secluded spot in Old Tsari (*tsa ri rnying ma*) on the northern side of the Pure Crystal Mountain. For a history of Chikchar, see also Filibek (1988, 4).

17. The famous Varahi Temple (*phag mo'i lha khang*) was founded by Padma Karpo between the years 1567 and 1574. See Pema Karpo's biography (vol. 3, Ga, pt. Nya of his *Collected Works*, fols. 128–29) and Situ's *Account of a Pilgrimage to Central Tibet*, p. 526.

18. Called "two-headed" because the head of a sow emerges from Vajravarahi's own head.

19. Kunkhyen Pema Karpo (*kun mkhyen padma dkar po*, 1527–92), the "Omniscient White Lotus," was an emanation of Padmapani, the "Lotus-holder," a name of Avalokiteshvara. As the fourth Drukchen (*'brug chen*), the head of the northern branch of the Drukpa Kagyu lineage (*byang 'brug*), he founded the monastery of Char Sang-ngak Chöling (*byar gsang sngags chos gling*). He had two immediate reincarnations. The

first, Gyalwa Pagsam Wangpo (*rgyal ba dpag bsam dbang po*, 1593–1641), occupied the throne of Sang-ngak Chöling. His incarnations were known as Drukchen Rinpoche. The second, Shabdrung Ngawang Namgyal (*zhabs drung ngag dbang rnam rgyal*, 1594–1651) went in exile to Bhutan, where he contributed greatly to the spreading of Buddhism and unified the country as a Buddhist state.

20. The Great Turquoise Lake Palace (*pho brang chen po g.yu mtsho*), two days walk from Chikchar, is south of the Pure Crystal Mountain. It is a magnificent lake "like a mirror of sapphire and the mandala of Chakrasamvara."

21. *mkha' spyod;* see chap. 6, note 6.

22. The two thousand and eight hundred deities who dwell on the central mountain of Tsari, which resembles a large crystal "Stupa with Many Doors of Auspiciousness" (*bkra shis sgo mang mchod rten*). An explanation on how to calculate that number is given in Pema Karpo's description of Tsari.

23. Ngaktra Tulku, which should be written *sngags grwa sprul sku*, means "the Tulku of the Tantric College," and refers to one of the six monastic communities of Sang-ngak Chöling. (Communicated by Sengtrak Rinpoche. See also G. Smith, 1968).

24. *The Hundred and Eight Combined Yogic Exercises* are the yogic exercises related to the Six Yogas of Naropa. *Se-pho* (*bsre 'pho*), "Combination and Transfer," is the basic name of the cycle of teaching of the Six Yogas of Naropa. The instructions on these teachings are found in two main sets of explanations:

1) *rgyud dang 'brel ba thabs lam gyi dbang du byas te bshad pa*, a large and detailed explanation based directly on the texts of the tantras. Its lineage and practice have become extremely rare.

2) *byin rlabs dang 'brel ba snyan rgyud kyi dbang du byas nas bshad pa*. A concise summary of these instructions, according to the oral tradition, has been preserved and is still practiced today.

"Combination" (*bsre*) refers to combining a spiritual practice with any of the many ordinary activities of daily life. "Transfer" (*'pho*) refers to the various kinds of practice of the transfer of consciousness at death.

25. *Tummo* (*gtum mo*); see chap. 1, note 65.

26. The *tsulpas* (*tshul pa*) were local people from Tsari villages outside the Ravines who used to help the pilgrims going to Tsari. They would set up rest houses (*tshul khang*) along the pilgrimage route and provide the pilgrims with water and fuel, but rarely provisions.

27. The *Beneficial Moon* (*chos bshad gzhan phan zla ba*); the *Beneficent Jewel* (*chos bshad gzhan phan nor bu*); and the *Offering Cloud of Samantabhadra* (*chos bshad kun bzang mchod sprin*). (See Appendix 5).

28. Verses of auspiciousness which say:

> May the auspiciousness of the body, immovable as Mount Meru, prevail,
> May the auspiciousness of the Sixty Branches of Speech prevail,
> May the auspiciousness of the mind, the ultimate meaning free from extremes, prevail,
> May the auspiciousness of the body, speech, and mind of the Victorious Ones prevail.

29. *Bhumi*; see Author's Introduction, note 15. The level of Complete Joy is the first *bhumi* of the Bodhisattvas.

30. *Pratimoksha:* The vows of individual liberation (*so sor thar pa'i sdom pa*) are seven sets of precepts intended for lay disciples, novices, and fully ordained monks and nuns. They form the foundation of the Three Vehicles. See Appendix 1.

31. The Sanskrit *rishi* has been translated in Tibetan as *drang srong*, "Straight Ones," and refers to Indian hermits, both Buddhist and non-Buddhist, who were renowned for the rectitude of their conduct and spiritual practice. *Rishis* were dressed in white, hence the analogy with the white vulture. In the Tibetan culture, the vulture is considered to be the king of birds. We have substituted "eagle" for "vulture" in most instances in this translation, since the latter often has a negative connotation for Western readers.

32. The snow grouse or Tibetan partridge (*gong mo*, Lat. *Perdrix Hodgsoniae*).

33. *Gandharvas* (*dri za*), a class of spirit-gods who have exceedingly melodious voices and who feed on odors alone.

34. The continent of Ominous Sound (*sgra mi snyan*), Uttarakuru, so called because when any of its inhabitants reaches the end of his or her very long life, a tree falls down, and in the sound it makes when falling one can hear the words, "You are going to die!"

35. Shri Singha, the great vidyadhara who conferred upon Guru Rinpoche the empowerment of the "Manifestation of Awareness" (*rig pa'i rtsal dbang*). See chap. 4, note 16.

36. The fifth Dalai Lama, Gyalwa Lobzang Gyatso (*rgyal ba blo bzang rgya mtsho*, 1617–82), who wrote this verse in his advice called the *Pearl Garland* (*mu thi la'i phreng ba*).

37. Sakya Pandita, Kunga Gyaltsen (*sa skya pan di ta kun dga' rgyal mtshan*, 1182–1251), wrote this verse in

his *Distinctive Features of the Three Vows* (*sdom gsum rab 'byed*).

38. Ama Khandroma (*a ma mkha' 'gro ma*) was said to be a human descendant of the dakini guardian of Tsari. See Wylie (1962, 94).

39. Adamantine Rampart (*rdo rje ra ba*), or Vajra Horn or Prong (*rdo rje rwa ba*). The two words *ra ba* (rampart, fence, enclosure) and *rwa ba* (horn, prong, tip) are often confused. At the beginning of chapter 13, for instance, the text reads *la phyi gang gi rwa ba*, where it should read *la phyi gangs gi ra ba* (the Lapchi Snow Range, or "enclosure of snow mountains." According to a personal communication by T. Huber, the term *rdo rje ra ba* or *rwa ba* can be understood in different ways in the context of Tsari sacred geography.

1) The Crystal Mountain is considered to be the palace of Chakrasamvara, with all the surrounding hills, valleys, lakes and trees arranged in the shape of a mandala. Every mandala is circumscribed by a rampart or fence (*ra ba*) of standing vajras tightly fit together, which prevents negative forces from entering. Here, the Adamantine or Vajra Rampart is believed to encircle the Crystal Mountain and forms a sacred threshold over which one must pass to enter the mandala. Near the Crystal Mountain, most pilgrims cross the Adamantine Rampart and enter the mandala when they climb up from Chikchar (*cig char*) on the "central" or "middle" circumambulation track (*gzhung bskor*), or at a certain point on the upper circumambulation (*rtse bskor*) around the peak.

2) The guide to Tsari describes the relationship of the three holy places of Chakrasamvara and Vajravarahi in this area as being like a vajra laid down from east to west, with the Pure Crystal Mountain (*dag pa shel ri*) as the western prong (*rdo rje rwa ba nub*), the White Lake (*mtsho dkar*) as the central knob, and New Tsari (*tsa ri gsar ma*) as the eastern prong of the vajra (*rdo rje rwa ba shar*).

3) Another possibility, which fits well with the text of this biography (considering the route which Shabkar took, from Dotsen to *rdo rje rwa ba*, then to Chözam, see map 3), is that Vajra Horn is an alternative name for a site referred to as Vajra Rock (*rdo rje brag*) by inhabitants of Tsari or by pilgrims. The Vajra Rock is a site above Dotsen. The

biography of Doring Pandita, who made a pilgrimage to Tsari in 1794 (see *rdo ring pandita'i rnam thar*, Szechuan edition, p. 1043), refers to Vajra Horn (*rdo rje rwa ba*) as a site which corresponds to the Vajra Rock (*rdo rje brag*).

40. *Khatvanga*, a staff surmounted by a double vajra, by a long-life vase, by three heads—a fresh head, a decomposing head, and a dry skull—and by a vajra (here the vajra replaces the trident usually found on Guru Rinpoche's Khatvanga). This Khatvanga represents Vajravarahi's male consort in hidden form. On the symbolism of the Khatvanga, see Dilgo Khyentse Rinpoche (1989, 23).

41. Dagpo Tashi Namgyal (*dwags po bkra shis rnam rgyal*, 1513–87), a descendant as well as an incarnation of Gampopa and a holder of the throne of Dagla Gampo (*dwags la sgam po*). (See GC, vol. 4, pp. 113–15 and JK, vol. Da, p. 333). He studied with many masters, including Karma Trinlepa (*karma phrin las pa*) and Khenchen Sakya Zangpo (*mkhan chen sha kya bzang po*). He is the author of several commentaries on various aspects of contemplative life, including the famed *Three Cycles of Light-rays* ('*od zer skor gsum*), one of which, the *zla ba'i 'od zer*, has been translated into English by L. P. Lhalungpa under the title *Mahamudra, the Quintessence of Mind and Meditation* (1986).

As communicated by Tashi Tshering, a short biography of Tashi Namgyal is found in folio 83 of the biographies of Gampopa's successors (*gangs can 'dir ston pa'i rgyal tshab dpal sgam po pa'i khri gdung 'dzing pa'i dam pa rnams kyi gtam be durya'i phreng ba*). It was written by one Zangpo (*bzang po*) at Dagla Gampo in 1662 and is presently kept at the library of Rumtek Monastery in Sikkim.

42. "Pristine simplicity which crushes delusion into dust." *zang thal* is a synonym of *ma 'gags pa*, "unobstructed," but according to Taklung Tsetrul Rinpoche (Pema Wangyal) it can also be explained as *zang kha ma thal du 'byung*. *Zang kha ma*, "natural condition," refers to *ma bcos pa'i gdod ma'i gnas lugs*, the unmodified simplicity of the primordial nature; and *thal du 'byung*, "reduce to dust," refers to the annihilation of deluded thoughts, *'khrul pa'i rnam rtog*.

43. The four basic practices of the Kagyu lineage are:

1) The view—of Mahamudra (*phyag rgya chen po*)
2) The meditation—the Six Yogas of Naropa (*naro chos drug*)
3) The action—the Six Cycles of Even Taste (*ro snyoms skor drug*)
4) The profound path—Guru Yoga (*lam zab bla ma'i rnal 'byor*).

The guru yoga mentioned here is likely to be the secret Guru Yoga associated with the yogic exercises.

44. Isolating the central channel (*dbu ma 'dzugs skor*): a yogic exercise in which the central part of the abdomen and the subtle central channel are isolated by making them protrude from the rest of the abdomen. The Vajra Water (*rdo rje chu*) refers to a highly esoteric yogic practice—the first of two practices known as *mdun thur* and *rgyab thur*. (See *Yangti Nagpo*, vol. 2, 273–74).

45. The collected writings of Gampopa, Sonam Rinchen (*sgam po pa bsod nams rin chen*, 1079–1153), comprise two volumes of spiritual instructions, and the famed *Jewel Ornament of Liberation* (*dam chos yid bzhin nor bu thar pa rin po che'i rgyan*). Gampopa was born in Nyal in eastern Tibet. He first trained as a physician, hence his name Dagpo Lharje (*dwags po lha rje*), the Physician of Dagpo (the province in which he spent many years). He renounced the world and became ordained at the age of twenty-six after his wife and two children died in an epidemic. After having studied and practiced the Kadampa teachings, at the age of thirty-two he met and became the foremost disciple of Jetsun Milarepa. His own chief disciples were the first Karmapa Dusum Khyenpa (*dus gsum mkhyen pa*, 1110–93), Phagmo Drupa Dorje Gyalpo (*phag mo gru pa rdo rje rgyal po*, 1110–70), and Dharma Wangchuk (*dharma dbang phyug*, 1100–?).

46. The *Black Quintessence* (*yang ti nag po*); see chap. 4, note 17.

47. The three places (*sa gsum*) are the realms of celestial beings above the earth, of human beings upon the earth, and of the nagas below the earth.

48. Dagla Gampo (*dwags la sgam po*), the place where Gampopa lived. It is said that such was the devotion of Gampopa's disciples that some of them realized the meaning of Mahamudra simply by seeing the Dagla Gampo mountain from afar.

49. The Brahmaputra.

50. Dagpo Shedrup Ling (*dwags po bshad sgrub gling*), a monastic college, seat of the fifth Shamar Konchog Yanlak (*dkon mchog yan lag*, 1525–83). Also the place where the eighth Karmapa, Mikyö Dorje (*mi skyod rdo rje*), passed away in 1554.

51. *The Embodiment of the Three Jewels* (*bka' rdzogs pa chen po dkon mchog spyi 'dus*), the famed spiritual treasure revealed by Rigdzin Jatshön Nyingpo, (*rig 'dzin 'ja' tshon snying po*, 1585–1656), which contains, among other instructions, *sadhanas* focused upon the peaceful and wrathful aspects of Guru Rinpoche (*gu ru zhi ba* and *drag po*), and upon the Lion-headed Dakini (*seng ge gdong ma*).

52. The *Secret Wisdom* (*gsang ba ye shes*) cycle is possi-

bly the cycle of *termas* rediscovered by Kunzang Dechen Gyalpo (see Appendix 4), since, according to GC (vol. 3, 226) a former Lhagyari king was a chief disciple and patron of Dechen Gyalpo (see Appendix 4). This could also refer to the cycles of the same name revealed by Minling Terdak Lingpa (1646–1714; see chap.1, note 38) and elaborated by Lelung Shepai Dorje (*sle lung bzhad pa'i rdo rje*, b. 1697; see chap. 14, note 51).

53. The Eternal Sky (*g.yung drung nam mkha'*). The name could indicate a Bönpo text.

54. *Dotse;* see chap.1, note 68.

55. The central image in the main temple of Samye, the Jowo Changchup Chenpo (*jo bo byang chub chen po*), is a huge stone statue of Lord Buddha taken by Guru Padmasambhava as a *terma* from Hepori Hill.

56. The Protector (*chos skyong*) and the Dharma Lord (*chos rje*) of Samye. At Samye, Guru Padmasambhava subdued all the king-spirits (*rgyal po*) and put them under the power of King Pehar (*pe har*). He did the same with all the Tsens (*btsan*), whom he put under the power of Tsimara (*tsi ma ra*). The Protector of Samye, Gyalpo Pehar, sometimes descends into, or inhabits, a predestined person called the Dharma Lord of Samye. When present in the Dharma Lord, Pehar gives prophecies for the sake of Tibet and the Dharma. When Pehar took the oath not to harm any beings and to guard them and Guru Rinpoche's teachings, he offered his heart to Guru Rinpoche as a symbol of his pledge. Until recently this "heart" was kept in a precious box that only the Oracle was allowed to open. He would do so once a year. When Kyabje Dudjom Rinpoche (1903–87) gave the empowerment of the Rinchen Terdzö (*rin chen gter mdzod*) at Samye, at one point the Oracle went into a trance and showed him this heart, which looked like a fresh heart.

57. The Governor of the Fortress (*rdzong dpon*) was a notable from Lhasa posted at Samye's fortress behind the main temple.

58. The place where Guru Padmasambhava gave the first empowerment (*abhisheka*) in Tibet to King Trisong Detsen and to seven other disciples, each of whom was entrusted with the practice upon one of the Eight Herukas of the Eight Canons of Accomplishment (*sgrub pa bka' brgyad*).

59. Drakmar Yamalung (*brag dmar g.ya' ma lung*), the eighth among the sacred places in Tibet and Bhutan blessed by Guru Padmasambhava for the practice of the Eight Herukas.

These eight places are:

1) Drak Yangdzong (*sgrags yang rdzong*), the place related to the Heruka of the body

family, Jampel Shinje, where Nup Sangye Yeshe achieved realization,

2) Samye Chimphu (*bsam yas mchims phu*), the place related to the Heruka of the lotus, speech family, Tamdrin, where Gyalwa Chöyang attained realization;

3) Lodrak Karchu (*lho brag mkhar chu*), the place related to the Heruka of the mind family, Yandak, where Gelong Namkhai Nyingpo attained realization;

4) Yarlung Sheldrak (*yar lung shel brag*), the place related to the Heruka of the enlightened qualities family, Dudtsi Yonten, where Karchen Yeshe Shonnu attained realization;

5) Mönkha Senge Dzong (*mon kha seng ge rdzong*), the place related to the Heruka of the activity family, Dorje Phurba, where Khandro Yeshe Tsogyal attained realization;

6) Yartö Shambo Khangkyi Rawa (*yar stod sham po gangs kyi ra ba*), the place related to the Mamo Bötong, where Drokmi Palkyi Yeshe attained realization;

7) Paro Taktsang (*spa gro stag tshang bsam grub ke'u tshang*), the place related to Jigten Chötö, where Langchen Palgyi Senge attained realization; and

8) Samye Yamalung (*bsam yas g.ya' ma lung*), the place related to the Möpa Trak-ngak, where the Great Translator Vairocana attained realization.

60. The golden reliquary that contains the remains of Je Tsongkhapa.

61. The Pledge-holder Dharma King (*dam can chos rgyal*) is one of the three main protectors of the Gelukpa tradition. Tsongkhapa received a prophecy that the followers of his lineage must propitiate one of three protectors, and none other, failing which the Gelukpa tradition would decline. These three are: 1) Namsey (*rnam sras*), for beings of lesser faculties, 2) Damchen Chögyal (*dam can chos rgyal*), for beings of medium faculties, and 3) Gonpo Chadrukpa, the Six-armed Mahakala (*mgon po phyag drug pa*), for beings of highest faculties. These three categories of beings correspond to those explained in the *Great Graded Path* (*lam rim chen mo*), written by Tsongkhapa.

62. Drak Yerpa (*brag yer pa*) is the holy place of Guru Padmasambhava related to the speech aspect. It is also said to be the "life tree" (*srog shing*), or spiritual axis, of Lhasa. There are over eighty caves where many great beings from all lineages meditated. On the top are the cave of Guru Padmasambhava, the Rock that is Hard to Reach (*brag gi yang bgrod dka'*),

and Yeshe Tsogyal's Secret Cave (*gsang phug*). Below is the Moon Cave (*zla ba phug*), another cave of Guru Padmasambhava; the Dharma King's Cave (*chos rgyal phug*), King Songtsen Gampo's cave; the great cave where the eighty *siddhas* of Yerpa (i.e., Guru Padmasambhava's disciples) meditated together; and Lord Atisha's cave, the Cave of Auspicious Coincidence (*rten 'brel phug*), thus named because when Atisha entered it, a rain of flowers fell. See Gegyepa Tendzin Dorje (1988) and Dowman (1988, hereafter abbreviated as PP). In some enumerations, instead of Drak Yangdzong (see above, note 59), Trak Yerpa is given as the holy place related to the body aspect of Guru Rinpoche.

11

At Mt. Kailash

*How I went to western Tibet and practiced at Mount Kailash,
the famed king of mountains, the sacred place of the body of the
White Lion-faced Dakini*

I had grown tired of distractions and diversions. I told myself, "Though it looks like you are helping other beings, you have not perfected yourself at all; you run the risk of reaching the end of your life having really benefited no one. You must go to a remote place like Kailash Snow Mountain and practice for the rest of your life. Let's find out if you can attain the rainbow body."

I made up my mind: nothing else mattered. At that time, I met the treasurer of Purang Shephel Ling Monastery and the generous chieftain Depa Wangpo, both of whom had come to Lhasa. They told me about the area around Kailash, and I decided to travel with them. Khenpo Chaksampa entrusted me to the good care of Depa Wangpo. Khenpo Shiwa Tsering and his spouse gave me a tent and other necessities.

In the company of Depa Wangpo, we set off. On the way we visited the Tara of Nyethang[1] and the great Maitreya of Rong, offering butter-lamps and prayers [233b]. At Tashi Lhunpo[2] we paid homage to all the sacred shrines and objects, met the Panchen Lama and his tutor, and requested their protection and teaching to establish spiritual connections.

Further on our journey, I gave to some beggars the twenty-five silver coins that I had. At Saga the governor, a relative of Khenpo Chaksampa, and his devout wife requested a long-life empowerment. They offered me coins, *tsampa*, tea, and butter, which we took with us.

On the way, people would occasionally ask me where I was going. Saying that I was on my way to the Snow Mountain, I would sing verses like these:

> On the summit of great Mount Meru
> Lies the wonderful Mansion of Complete
>   Victory.[3]
> Before I did not have the chance:
> Now I will go and see it.

> In the vastness of distant oceans,
> Lies the marvelous wish-granting jewel.
> Before I did not have the chance:
> Now I will go and get what I desire.

> In the vastness of the snow ranges
> Roams the splendid snow lion.
> Before I did not have the chance:
> Now I will go and ride it.

> At the border of meadows and rocky crags,
> Roams the wild blue-horned *dri*.
> Before I did not have the chance:
> Now I will go and milk it.

> On the white snow mountain Kailash,
> The navel of the world,
> Lies the marvelous palace of
>   Chakrasamvara.
> Before I did not have the chance [234a]:
> Now I will go and visit it.

> Living in that great sacred place
> Are the five hundred marvelous arhats.

Before I did not have the chance:
Now I will go and ask for teachings.

Gathered in that great sacred place
Are exalted dakas and dakinis.
Before I did not have the chance:
Now I will go to be with them.

On the eastern side of this great sacred
    place
Lies the marvelous Cave of Miracles.
Before I did not have the chance:
Now I will go there to become enlightened.

For amusement, I sang whatever came to
my mind, inspiring faith in everyone's mind.
Some threw me the flowers of compliments,
saying, "Excellent!"
    Traveling on, as we left Lhasa and our home-
land farther and farther behind, I pondered the
impermanence and ceaseless change of all things,
and sang this melancholy song:

The valley where I was born
Had times of wealth and times of hardship:
No trace of those now [234b].
I'll never go back again.

My kind old parents
Are gone from this world.
No trace of them now.
I'll never see them again.

My vajra brothers and sisters,
With whom I shared pure *samaya*,
Have gone on the great path of future
    lives.
No trace of them now.
I'll never see them again.

The guru who manifested the three
    kindnesses,
Has gone on to the Pure Realms.
No trace of him now.
I'll never see him again.

Withered with age,
The illusory body of this yogin

Can never be what it once was.
My youth is finished.

Whatever comes to mind,
Everything, is transient;
It is not what it once was.
I can't rely upon this life.

Cut off all attachments!
I will sever all ties to this life
And go to the Snow Mountain,
The very center of the southern continent,
    Jambudvipa.

In the Cave of Miracles, on the glacier,
I will raise the victory banner of practice
As high as samsara's highest point:
This is my prayer.

My weariness and renunciation grew even stronger, my determination to practice even more
fierce [235a].

On the road to Droshö, I met a beggar woman
named Drolma, weeping bitterly by the road.
While she was out begging, some thieves from
the Magar Yalong tribe[4] had entered her small
tent and taken everything, down to the tent poles.
Feeling pity, I gave her ten silver coins and all the
tea, butter and *tsampa* I had. I told her to pray to
Tara. She stayed by the main road, telling everyone passing by, "An accomplished lama, a true
Buddha, has passed by on his way to the Snow
Mountain of Tö." The reputation she made for
me aroused faith in Drungtse, the chieftain of
Droshö, and in most of the wealthy nomads.
They came to meet me and, later, their devotion
grew even stronger and inspired them to come visit
me at the snow mountain, where they helped me.
    When we arrived at Trugolho, the South-
ern Gate of the Thaw,[5] on the shore of Manasarovar, the Ever-cool Turquoise Lake,[6] the
monks there thought we were the party of the
abbot of Shephel Ling,[7] and came to welcome us

in a beautiful procession. That was an auspicious sign!

During the waxing moon of the third month, in the male Wood Dog year,[8] known as "Wealth," we came to the monastery of Purang Shephel Ling. After a few days' stay, we collected our provisions and went to a cave below the White Footprint of the Cave of Miracles,[9] near Kailash, the king of mountains. The first thing I did was to sing this song in praise of the place:

Described in the sutras and tantras,
This mountain is the mansion of infinite
    Jinas [235b].
The gathering place of mother dakinis and
    local guardians,
The abode of celestial beings and sages:
The snow mountain renowned as
    Kailash,[10]
With its ice-peak shaped like a crystal
    stupa.

This is the mountain the Buddha meant
When he spoke of "The Snow
    Mountain."
This crystal-stupa mountain
Is the infinite palace of Chakrasamvara.

The places where many arhats once stayed
Ring the slopes of the mountain.

Here, the Buddhas of the three times
Are gathered like clouds,
With dakinis and dharmapalas
Assembled as their servants,
And in every cave sits a practitioner,
Each like a turquoise set in gold.
Self-arisen forms of deities, footprints of the
    Buddha,
And amazing signs of the miracles
Performed by Lord Milarepa and Naro
    Bönchung—[11]
So many wonders can be seen!

The two great lakes, Manasarovar and
    Rakkas Tal,
Lie before that mountain
Like two lovely water-offerings.

Surrounded by many faithful patrons,
One feels complete contentment;
Everything needed to practice the Dharma
    is at hand.
The call of the golden duck, the king of birds,
And those of other birds delight the mind.

East of the noble Kailash snow peak,
In the solitary Cave of Miracles,
I, the renunciate Tsogdruk Rangdrol,
Have the good fortune to practice the
    Dharma.

Masters of the whispered lineage who have
    stayed here:
Mature me, free me with your blessings!
    [236a].

Victorious peaceful and wrathful *yidam*
    deities,
Grant me the ordinary and extraordinary
    siddhis!

May the dakinis, dharmapalas, and local
    guardians
Help this beggar to attain enlightenment.

I then sealed the entrance to my cave with mud and, in a song, made this vow to practice:

No sentient being who has not been my
    mother!
No happiness when one stays in samsara!
No condition in the lower realms without
    unbearable suffering!
No way to avoid suffering!

Thinking of the pain of sentient beings
I can't help but feel dismay.

Kye ma! Kye hu!
What should one do?
Meditate? Or teach?

There are so many beings!
I may serve as a guide for a few small
    valleys,

Teaching the Dharma, benefiting a few—
But how can that empty samsara?

But if, through practice, I reach enlighten-
  ment,
Every ray of light I emanate
Will guide and liberate an infinity of
  beings—
How can I not empty samsara?

Previously, Buddhas and Bodhisattvas,
Dredging the depths of samsara again and
  again,
Brought to Buddhahood the six classes
Of beings of this billionfold universe.

In the future, at the time of the Buddha
  Aspiration,
The beings of this billionfold universe
Saved from the depths of samsara
Will become Buddhas, the sutras say.

If I practice now,
I will surely reach enlightenment;
With enlightenment [236b],
I can dredge the very depths of samsara.

So, better to meditate than to teach—
I will now dedicate myself to practice,
With the aspiration that, one day,
Emanating infinite forms,
I may dredge the very depths of samsara.

I stayed in retreat and kept silence.

While I was engaged single-mindedly in the excellent practices of the development, completion, and Great Perfection stages, my supreme and worthy heart-son Jimba Norbu and many fortunate disciples gathered in the vicinity like rain clouds in summer. Offering a golden mandala heaped with corals and turquoise, they repeatedly asked me for teachings.

"Should I strive to reach perfection myself, or to help others?" With this question in mind, I prayed to the deities of the Three Roots. One night, towards dawn, the Lion-faced Wisdom Dakini appeared, surrounded by a large retinue of other dakinis. She said:

"Kye! Son of the Victorious Ones, it would be wonderful if, through spending your whole life in practice, you attained the body of rainbow light. But you wouldn't be able to help others very much in this lifetime. Through the vast prayers and aspirations you made previously, the time to care for others has come, and there are many for whom you have already opened the door. You should bring these fortunate beings onto the path of maturation and liberation; this will greatly benefit the Dharma and all beings. We, the dakinis, will accompany you like your shadow" [237a].

Having said this, she vanished. "According to the dakini's prophecy, if I serve the Dharma and all beings, I may not attain the rainbow body, but I will have no regrets." With this in mind, along with my practice, I gave teachings from time to time through a small window in the door of my cave. This is how I came to work for both myself and for others.

One afternoon, thinking of my spiritual master and the place where he used to live, and thinking about my parents, relatives, Dharma friends, and my native land, I sang this melancholy song:

Journeys through marvelous countries
Brought delightful sights to my eyes,
Yet thoughts of my kind guru's home
Again and again come back to mind.

Excellent teachers I encountered
Granted all the teachings I desired,
Yet thoughts of the Dharma King, Ngakyi
  Wangpo,
Arise in my mind, again and again.

Close friends practicing the same tradition
Happily talked with me about Dharma,
Yet thoughts of my heart-friend, Dorje
  Tseten,
Again and again come back to mind.

Faithful patrons, men and women,
Were as kind to me as a mother,
Yet thoughts of my own sweet mother
Again and again come back to mind.

The place where my gracious guru once
    lived
Has fallen victim to impermanence:
There is nothing left there to see—
Yet I long to see it.

The Dharma King, endowed with the
    three kindnesses,
Has passed off into impermanence:
There is no one left to meet—
Yet I long to meet him [237b].

Childhood friends, Dharma companions,
Have fallen victim to impermanence:
There is no way to be with them now—
Yet I long to meet them.

My parents who gave me life
Have fallen victim to impermanence:
There is no way to meet them now—
Yet I long to meet them.

My gracious guru, my friends, my parents,
Everything, everyone—impermanent!
When I think about this thoroughly,
Boundless weariness wells up in me.

My hair turned grey, wrinkles line my face:
Omens of impermanence and death.
Soon I shall be dead—
How can I make plans for some distant
    future?

Eh, you old renunciate!
Give up everything, be attached to
    nothing,
And, in this remote and excellent grove,
Put all your force into practice!

One day I heard heart-breaking news: the refuge
and protector of all Tibetans, the powerful Victorious One Lungtok Gyatso Rinpoche,[12] had
passed on to another Buddhafield. My infinite
sadness arose as this song of lamentation:

A ho!
The sun has set in Tibet, the Northern
    Land.[13]
The master pillar in the great house of the
    Buddha's teaching has fallen.
The torch that dispelled the darkness of
    ignorance has died out.
The jewel that eased the poverty of
    samsara and nirvana has been lost.
The physician who cured the disease of the
    obscuring emotions has passed away.
The ferryman who carried us across
    samsara's river has died.
Our refuge and protector in this life and
    beyond has gone on to another
    Buddhafield.
The good fortune of tasting the nectar of
    his teachings has come to an end
    [238a].

Kye hu!
The anthill's covering rock has been
    removed:
The living creatures of Tibet have no
    refuge or protector now.
Abandoned by our guide on a perilous
    path,
What shall we do?

Kye ma! Kye hu!
You whose vast knowledge encompasses
    samsara and nirvana,
Protector, from your invisible realm,
    consider us with loving-kindness.
We, unfortunate and desolate disciples,
    have no other hope but you,
And with hope and confidence we
    supplicate you.

You who possess such great kindness: don't
    leave us to perish here,
But, fulfilling your vow and aspirations,
Swiftly return as an authentic incarnation.

By the power of the guru, the Victorious
    Ones and their sons,
By the merit I and other faithful ones have
    gathered throughout the three times,

May you swiftly return as an authentic
   incarnation of the Buddhas
And bring your followers onto the path of
   ripening and liberation.

One day as I was recollecting my meeting with
the precious refuge and protector, his physical
appearance and the sound of his voice came
vividly to my mind, and I sang this song:

A body more beautiful than that of a god,
A voice more melodious than Brahma's,
A mind softer than silk—

Gyalwa Lungtok Gyatso,
"Conqueror Ocean of Learning and
   Realization,"
Your lifetime was short.

To spur on those who cling to permanence
   and
Who postpone practicing the sacred
   Dharma,
You have departed for the Pure Realms
   [238b].

I remember our meeting—
The splendor of your presence,
The perfect sweetness of your speech.

Kye hu! From now on,
Supreme nirmanakaya,
Let alone meeting you in reality,
Even in dreams you are hard to meet!

Even if I were to search
Throughout samsara and nirvana
For eighty thousand kalpas,
How could I find such a wondrous
   incarnation?

When the young sun of your new
   incarnation arose,
What joy was born in our minds!
Alas! Even greater is the pain that arises
Now that that sun has set.

What would have become of me,
A slave to this life,

Oblivious of the stark presence of death,
Had I not had such a teaching on
   impermanence?

If even your vajra body so suddenly
   displayed
The manner of impermanence,
How can I, with this body like a fragile reed,
Know with certainty the hour of my own
   doom?

Tsogdruk Rangdrol!
Keep in mind the transience of life!
And now, right at this very instant,
Throw yourself into your practice of the
   Dharma!

Once, I gave the transmission and instructions for the practice of the *Graded Path* and other
teachings on mind training to my fortunate disciple Lama Jimba Norbu and many other spiritual sons. Some of them asked me, "What
practices did you do while wandering from place
to place?" My answer was this song:

I, the renunciate Tsogdruk Rangdrol,
Gave up my homeland, took to other
   countries,
Visited many different places,
And practiced like this:

I went to the east [239a].
And, like a Chinese woman
Gently unraveling threads of silk,
I loosened and relaxed
My own entangled mind.

I went to the south,
And, like a carpenter from the south lands
   of Mön
Straightening a crooked piece of wood,
I unbent and straightened out my mind.

I went to the west,
And, like the sugar traders from the west,
Tasting time and again the flavor of rock-
   sugar,
I practiced, tasting the superior flavor of
   the Dharma.

I went to the north,
And, like the Mongolian shepherds from
    the north plateaus
Who continuously guard their sheep,
I constantly persevered in the practices I
    knew.

I went to the central region,
And, like the chieftains of central Tibet
Struggling their best to vanquish their
    enemies,
I conquered as best I could
Ego-clinging and the obscuring
    emotions.

In short, wherever I went,
Equating happiness and sadness,
I turned pleasure and pain into practice:
This is what you must do.

My song strengthened their aspirations.

In the summer, Lama Neten, who was from
Marmig in the northern steppes and whose secret
name was Gangshar Rangdrol, "Self-liberation
of Whatever Arises," arrived at this sacred place.
He had consciously taken rebirth for the sake of
the nomads of the northern steppes who had
neither protector nor refuge. He performed offerings to the Snow Mountain and asked me for
a mind teaching in the tradition of the Great
Perfection [239b]. I offered him what I knew
about clarifying and enhancing practice, and
removing obstacles.

    After all his doubts were cleared away, his
realization became vast as the sky. Offering seven
sho of gold, he asked for some profound advice. I
sang this:

Handsome body—
Like a rainbow in space.
Sweet voice—
Like Brahma's song.
Vast mind—

Like the wide expanse of sky:
To the guru's body, speech and mind, I
    bow down.

Look with stainless wisdom-eyes
On myriad beings, each one once our
    mother.
Grant your blessing that,
Having swiftly realized the absolute body,
I may manifest the body of form.

I, the yogin Tsogdruk Rangdrol,
Will now sing some essential advice:

Fortunate ones, you wish to reach
    Buddhahood
In this very life, with this very body:
Listen with respect.

The root of all that exists,
Samsara and nirvana, is one's own mind.
Primordially, mind is emptiness.

Merge into the sky-like absolute expanse,
Empty, luminous, beyond clinging.

Outside, inside; eyes open or closed,
Day, night; asleep, awake:
No difference.

During practice, after practice,
Mind, appearances:
Blend them.

Continuously, without wavering,
Merge completely with this vibrant,
    sky-like state.

Even if you died right now,
You would have no regrets.
Death is release into the luminosity of
    dharmakaya;
Out of the expanse of the absolute body
The body of form arises.

Although on this path there can be no
    mistakes,
Don't be complacent [240a].

Once you've achieved stability in
    meditation,
Do not remain satisfied with that alone.
If you persist, practicing the instructions
To transmute the body of this life into a
    body of light,
You'll become like the deathless Lotus-
    born One.

Therefore, fortunate heart-son,
Practice the development stage of the *yidam*
    deity.
Consider your body as the *yidam*, apparent
    yet empty;
Consider the outer world as a Pure Land, a
    celestial palace,
And all beings as gods and goddesses.

In the center of your divine body,
Visualize the three channels and the *chakras*,
The *Ah* and the *Hang*.[14]
Holding *prana* in the vase,
Practice *tummo* meditation,
The main practice of the completion stage.

Abandoning the nine actions of the three
    doors,[15]
Using the postures and the crucial points
Of the sense-doors, the sense-fields, energy,
    and awareness,[16]
Meditate on the Dzogchen practice of
    Thögal.

The distance covered by a great ship
Pulled on land by a hundred men for a
    hundred days
Can be covered in a day when it is put to sea.

In the same way, a single day of meditation
Performed with real stability of mind
Brings more progress than a hundred days
Practicing the development and comple-
    tion stages
Before stability of mind has been attained.

If you persevere in practice,
Your *skandhas* will be freed in a body of
    rainbow light
In this very lifetime, with this very body.

If you lack diligence,
Even though you don't achieve the
    rainbow body in this life,
Your death will occur without suffering
And be accompanied by marvelous signs
    and miracles.

Practice the development and completion
    stages,
And practice Thögal [240b];
Beyond doubt, you will be liberated
Into the sambhogakaya during the *bardo*.

Even if you are not liberated in the *bardo*,
You will reach the Buddhafield of Manifest
    Joy,
Or whichever Pure Realm you prefer:
You need not fear rebirth in samsara.

Fortunate heart-son!
Do not long for formal knowledge;
See if, through practice,
You can attain the *siddhis*.

Do not hope to obtain signs of attainment
    very soon,
But let your meditation practice last until
    your death.

When they parted, Marpa said to Mila:
"Hankering after many different teachings
    creates distraction;
Just keep in mind the crucial instructions!"
You, too, should keep this advice in mind.

To enable you to practice in this way,
May the root and lineage gurus grant their
    blessings,
May the *yidam* deities grant *siddhis*,
May the dakinis and dharmapalas perform
    their enlightened actions.

May neither obstructions nor deviations
Hinder your quest for Buddhahood.
May the heart-sons surpass even their father!

Lama Neten practiced in this way, and, at
the time of his death rainbow-light, tiny pearl-
like relics[17] and other pure signs bore witness to

his achievement in the *bardo* of perfect Buddhahood at the *sambhogakaya* level.

Another time, my close disciple Jimba Norbu
asked me for a brief account of my life. I said:

My fatherland: Domey,
An area known as Rekong.
My mother: Heap of Goodness,
A native of that region [241a].
My father: I don't know who he was.

We were three children,
Among whom I was the eldest;
I was called Auspicious Lord of Speech.

From childhood,
I had faith in the Dharma and the lamas;
From the age of seven I could read,
And from ten I attended spiritual masters.
Up to now I've had perhaps a hundred
    teachers.

Among these, my gracious root-lama
Was the Dharma King, Ngakyi Wangpo.
I received many profound teachings,
On Madhyamika, Dzogchen,
    Mahamudra, and Chöd.

At the age of twenty-one,
I gave up all the affairs of this life.
In Domey, U, Tsang, and other regions,
I stayed in many remote retreats.

I meditated without distraction
On the profound instructions
Of the two Bodhicittas,
And on the development and completion
    stages.

By the blessing of my gurus, I recovered
From the illness of the five poisons, the
    obscuring emotions,
And developed loving-kindness,
    compassion, and Bodhicitta.

I know that all phenomena are illusory;
I have lit the blissful fire of *tummo* in my
    body:

The experience of bliss and void is
    uninterrupted.

I have opened the *nadis* in the enjoyment
    chakra in my throat;
Now, my vajra songs flow freely.

I have purified all clinging to ordinary
    perceptions
And experience the natural display of the
    Unsurpassable Pure Land.

In dreams, in meditation, and in reality,
I have beheld marvelous visions of deities
    and Buddhafields.

The eyes of wisdom, clairvoyance,
    miraculous powers, and so forth,
All the signs and qualities of the path, have
    occurred.

I have not the least preferential
    attachment:
To me rocks and gold are quite the same
    [241b].

Such is the brief story of your spiritual
    father's life.
Son, use it as an aid for your devotion.

When I said this, their respect and devotion
increased. I told a pilgrim monk about to return
to Trika in Amdo, "When you return home, tell
the devoted people there that if I live long, I shall
come back to Domey; and show them this letter." It read as follows:

I, the Bodhisattva captain, have safely arrived
At the supreme jewel island.
I am now searching for precious stones.
After finding the wish-fulfilling gem,
If sea monsters spare me,
And if the wind blows fair,
I shall bring back whatever
My relatives and old friends need and
    desire.

I, the cuckoo, messenger of spring, have
    safely arrived

At the deep sandalwood forest;
I am now seeking nourishment.
After gaining full strength,
If birds of prey don't seize me,
I will return with summer and sing sweetly
To my old friends, the assembly of birds,
　　large and small.

I, the renunciate Tsogdruk Rangdrol, have
　　safely arrived
At the great pilgrimage place, Mount
　　Kailash;
I am now practicing to attain enlightenment.
After meditation experiences and
　　realization have arisen,
If I am spared by the Lord of Death,
I shall return with good companions,
Bringing pith instructions to my old
　　friends,
The assembly of the faithful [242a].

I offer this song as a present
To faithful men and women.
Don't be sad;
Soon we will meet:
If not in this life, surely in the next,
In the eastern Buddhafield of Manifest Joy.

One day the devoted, generous, and gifted
Garpön Bentsa Lhopa, governor of Ngari,[18]
offered me a new coat. At first I declined it and
handed it back. But he insisted, saying, "I know
you have no need for this, but please wear it just
for today, so that I can accumulate merit. Later,
give it to whomever you wish." He gave me the
coat. I put it on, and sang this song:

When I was wandering freely from place to
　　place,
When I was living in various distant places,
I, the yogin, Tsogdruk Rangdrol,
Afraid of the cold, made myself a garment.

I lined the light and soft brocade coat—
The splendid deity, apparent yet unreal—
With the soft lambskin fur
Of the vividly clear three *nadis* and five
　　chakras.

I threaded a sharp needle—the *asheh*—
With a fine thread—the letter *Hang*,
And, holding the vase,
I joined the upper and lower energies.

I have worked on this for months and
　　years,
And, through perseverance, it has come
　　out nicely.
Now, wearing it, my body feels completely
　　warm,
And both body and mind are
　　comfortable.

This superior robe of *tummo*'s blissful
　　warmth [242b]
Was the robe worn by the past sages.
Though it's worn, it won't wear out.

Making it just as I did,
You too should wear such a robe.

This fur coat is a fine offering,
Yet, I, a beggar, have little need of it.
Since you are full of faith,
To let you perfect the two accumulations
I shall wear it for a while.

By this merit, may all disciples,
Having perfected the two accumulations,
Attain the body adorned with the marks
　　and signs.

Pleased by my song, he left in a happy
frame of mind. I kept the coat for a while, then
gave it to a disciple, who was delighted.

The yogini Jomo Yudrön, "Turquoise
Lamp," had given up thoughts of this life and,
with great faith and respect for her lama, practiced in secluded places according to his instructions, making her life and *sadhana* one. She asked
me to write a liturgy to help her remember the
qualities of the guru and to develop devotion. "I
don't need to compose one," I told her. "Such a
liturgy already exists. Recite the following verses
from the *Flower Ornament Sutra*[19] and the blessing
of the compassionate Buddha's words will benefit your mind":

The spiritual friend who teaches me the
   Dharma,
Displays for me the excellence of all
   teachings,
Shows me in full the practice of a
   Bodhisattva—
I have come with this in mind.

A mother giving birth to all excellence,
A nurse feeding us with the milk of good
   qualities,
A spiritual friend averting all harm,
He protects the limbs of enlightenment.

A doctor curing old age and death
   [243a],
Mighty Indra showering a rain of nectar,
A full moon nurturing virtues,
A brilliant sun, he illuminates the path of
   peace.

Like a mountain, he is equal to friends and
   enemies,
Like an ocean, his mind is undisturbed,
Like a ferryman, he cares for all—
I, Norzang, have come with this in mind.

He who developed the enlightened mind,
Renowned as a Bodhisattva, a son of the
   Buddhas,
Is my teacher, praised by the Buddhas
   themselves—
I have come with this in mind.[20]

A hero watching over the world,
A guide granting protection and refuge,
An eye revealing all pleasures—
With this in mind, I revere the spiritual
   friend.

I added, "Chant these verses with a nice
tune, reflect on their meaning, and, putting yourself in Norzang's place, remember the kindness
of your guru and an extraordinary devotion will
arise."

While I was staying in strict retreat, I heard that
my devoted, generous and intelligent disciple
Depa Wangpo had arrived, bringing with him
many supplies. As a gesture of welcome, I wrote
him this letter:

You dress in the garment of discipline
Fastened with the sash of mindfulness;
You adorn the crown of your head with
   the jewel of the spiritual friend,
Wearing the earrings of the teachings you
   have heard
Along with the necklace of lucid
   exposition,
And jingling the golden bracelets of
   generosity—
Seeing and hearing this, one forgets about
   ordinary adornments [243b].

When I heard that you, Wangpo,
The disciple who enchants everyone, had
   arrived here,
I was overjoyed as if attaining the level of
   Perfect Joy.

I, your father, terrified of the demon of
   death,
Retreated into my cave and sealed the
   door.
To be victorious when he, my enemy,
   arrives,
I don the armor and wield the weapon of
   the guru's pith instructions,
And train in listening, reflecting, and
   meditating.

Son, aren't you weary with the
   phenomena of samsara?
Isn't that why you've given up thoughts of
   this life and come here?

At present, I am strictly sealed in retreat.
Can we meet after a few days?
But if urgent affairs require that you leave
   soon,
We can meet tonight.

He sent this reply:

Marvelous holder of the Buddhas' wisdom,
   love, and power.
Lord guru, refuge and protector of all
   sentient beings.
Jetsun, how kind of you to expound the
   sacred Dharma
And hold the victory banner of its theory
   and practice.

Owing to your compassion, I am very well.
I have come here hoping I might see your
   face once again.
Tomorrow is the first day of the new year:
I beg you to show me the mandala of your
   smiling face.

Although I do not now have the good
   fortune to stay and practice,
May your protection allow me to return
   soon and follow your advice!

Meanwhile, please give me some
   instructions as to
What to adopt and what to reject
Regarding my conduct and attitude.
There is nothing in my behavior that
   would please you, holy being, but
Merely actions that would make you feel
   ashamed of me.
Yet, accept me, hear me! [244a].
This supplication I offer with a celestial
   white scarf.

In response to this I gave him this advice on
worldly and dharmic affairs:

Supreme son, the same as my heart,
Listen to this heartfelt advice, helpful for
   this and future lives:

Both with powerful enemies and powerful
   river rapids—
Don't overestimate your capacities!
Don't eat food you can't digest.
Don't ask advice from people with white
   tongues and black hearts.
Don't listen to gossip and slander.
Don't make decisions when you can't tell
   what's true or false.

Don't swear on the Three Jewels when you
   know you're lying.
Don't rely on those who have no sense of
   shame or modesty.
Don't deceive those who are reliant on you.
Don't trade with false weights and
   measures.
Don't get rich through theft and robbery.
Don't eat poisoned, polluted, or dirty food.
Don't accept disputed wealth.
Don't kill in the name of the Dharma.
Don't say things that hurt people.
Don't recite mantras that harm
   non-humans.
Don't give arduous work to those
   incapable of it.
Don't overburden animals.
Give up the root-causes of negative actions,
   such as alcohol and women.
Avoid rowdy behavior and venereal
   disease.
If you rely on the advice of elders, you
   won't go wrong.
If you have discussed things with others,
   you'll have few regrets.

When people sicken, perform ceremonies
   for them.
When cattle sicken, make offerings to the
   protectors.
When bad omens occur at home, perform
   repelling rituals.
When someone dies, don't cry; perform
   virtuous deeds [244b].
Ask often after the health of your sick
   friends.
When neighbors lose something, help
   them look for it.
Be compassionate to the weary and the
   helpless.
Console people who are in pain.
Rely upon the unfailing refuges, the guru
   and the Three Jewels.
Dispel sudden difficulties by pleasing the
   local guardians with offerings.
Don't mistreat your elderly parents; repay
   their kindness.
Don't tyrannize your servants and attendants; give them food and clothing.

Don't harm your friends and neighbors;
  help them.
Don't beat dogs and cattle; take good care
  of them.
Don't be stingy; use your wealth for
  offerings and charity.
Don't let your body be idle; do prostrations
  and circumambulations.
Don't let your mouth be idle; recite the
  mani mantra.
Always have pure thoughts towards others.

In brief, keeping death in mind, practice
  the sacred Dharma.

Give up doing wrong, and do what is
  wholesome.
Whatever happiness and sufferings you
  undergo,
Regard them as the result of previous
  actions.
Always act in accord with the Dharma.
Even though I may be far away,
These instructions will remain like my very
  presence:
Keep them in mind!

In response he offered this:

Greatly kind and precious teacher,
Your wisdom knows all that can be known,
  just as it is.
Unawareness, which deludes the six senses,
You have released into its own natural
  state.
At your pure lotus feet, with great
  devotion,
I pay homage with body, speech and
  mind.

I, your rotten-hearted student,
Fettered by my own stupidity,
Ignorant even about human affairs,
Not to mention the divine Dharma,
Am very grateful for your advice, the fruit
  of my request.

I confess whatever wrongdoings I have
  committed

By failing to carry out your words,
  O protector [245a].

From today on, I vow to do my best to
  fulfill your commands,
Particularly giving up killing, sexual
  misconduct, and alcohol.

Today, from the perfect vase of your
  throat, O protector,
I have heard the beneficial teachings of the
  graded path
And have written down all I could.
I ask that, having attained liberation
  myself,
I may become able to teach this to others.

Under your spiritual protection,
And compassionate attention,
Using these teachings,
May I master the qualities of the path,
Attain total enlightenment,
And, like you, become in this lifetime
A supreme guide for sentient beings.

I let him come inside, and I gave the transmission and explanations for the *Graded Path to Enlightenment* that I had composed. With his retinue, he left for home.

I had an attendant called Lobzang Sherap[21] who would always do whatever I asked of him. He didn't speak much, was honest, and had all good qualities.

One day he said to me, "Precious lama, today please sing a song about what makes an attendant good or bad." In response I sang this:

First, the bad attendant:
Unable to get out of bed, he adores
  sleeping.
He's always on the lookout for companions
  to eat with.
He surreptitiously hoards money and
  precious things.

He lies, cheats, and is puffed up with pride.
When newcomers arrive, he is surly.
If they linger, he treats them more rudely
    every day.
When irked, he responds with black looks.
He is contemptuous of those who practice
    virtue;
When he comes upon someone else who's
    the very mirror of himself—
To *that* one, he'll give food and gifts.

He reinterprets what the guru says,
    changing it.
Whatever he says is bent toward the three
    poisons [245b].

He disgraces the teachers above him;
He mistreats the humble;
He dislikes his spiritual peers.
Sooner or later, he'll give himself over
To the ways of the ordinary world.

Such is the bad attendant:
Don't be like that!

Now, the good attendant:
He goes to sleep late and gets up early.
He practices as much as he can
From morning till night.

He moves gently, quickly, without
    clumsiness.
He is very clean and makes good food and
    drink.
He is not a greedy eater and likes to share
    with others.

His thoughts are kind, his conduct
    admirable.
He is broad-minded and kind to those
    below him;
He smiles and speaks gently.
His behavior towards his superiors,
    inferiors, and equals is naturally correct.
He directs the entourage and servants with
    skill and gentleness.
He makes proper use of the offerings given
    by the faithful.

Whatever he does, he asks his guru first;
His conduct is in harmony with the
    Dharma,
And he accomplishes all the master's aims.

Such is the good attendant:
If you want to be good, be like that!

After I sang this, he told me, "Thank you,
that inspired me. All the time I have been here, I
have not offered any valuable service to you, my
guru, union of the Buddhas of the three times—
but at least I have not disgraced you. I might not
have pleased you, but I hope I have not upset
you either. Yet, if my weak intelligence and strong
obscurations have made me act so as to displease
you, please bear with me. Would you kindly
advise me: how I can best serve and please you?"
[246a].

I replied, "Well, to serve your guru, if you
simply conform with what I just explained about
good and bad attendants, that will do. However,
in essence, this is what you should do in your
daily activities: in the morning and evening do
your spiritual practice as much as you can. In the
daytime, avoid whatever would displease or disgrace your lama; instead, render him whatever
services please him. Do not distort anything he
says. Help all your spiritual friends equally, without partiality. Care for the lowly and the poor as
if they were your own children." Putting it into
verse I said:

My dear attendant Lobzang Sherap—
Get up before dawn,
Dress, wash your face and hands,
Take refuge, generate Bodhicitta, and
    recite your daily prayers.
Sweep the room and clean the hearth.
Make a good fire without much smoke,
Carry out your duties with diligence,
And delegate work to others.

When you talk, laugh, or sneeze,
Take care that your saliva does not land in
    the cooking pot.
Be clean with all food and drink;
Prepare it without clumsiness or waste.

When it's ready, serve everyone in proper
   order,
And after that, eat your own food.
When everyone has finished eating and
   drinking,
Clean and wash whatever utensils need it
   [246b].

Invite visitors in as soon as they arrive.
Be hospitable; offer tea and pleasant
   conversation.
Assist them in meeting the lama and asking
   for teachings.
Accompany those who leave and bid them
   farewell with gentle words.

Prepare the dwelling and bedding for new
   disciples;
Welcome them with the flowers of pleasant
   speech.
Even if they stay for a long time, don't
   make them feel uneasy.
When they leave, give them whatever food
   you have,
Accompany them for a short distance,
And with kind words, send them on their
   way.

Don't be intimate with some and distant
   with others,
But care for all equally, whether high or
   low.

At night you should wait to sleep
Until you see the visitors to bed.
When all is finished,
Think about the next day's work.
Consult the lama about the questions you
   have,
And notify others if you have work for them.

Then, go to bed.
Recite the Seven-Branch Prayer,
Do your regular practice as much you can,
And sleep peacefully.

Once you know how to organize your day,
You can simply go on in the same way.

So he did, and as long as he was my attendant,
he was of great help to me. Later he became an
excellent practitioner.

My disciple Thaye Gyatso, "Infinite Ocean,"
was also a true practitioner. He had devotion,
pure perception of his spiritual friends, and great
compassion for living creatures. I taught him the
essential instructions of the sutras and tantras;
through his practice of inner calm and insight
meditation, of *tummo* and *phowa*, he had extraordinary experiences and realization.

   One day, to express his gratitude, he offered
me a woolen blanket, saying, "You have already
been so kind to me; still, please give me some
further advice" [247a]. He presented this request
in verse:

> As gods and men respectfully paid homage
> To the Buddha when he came to this world,
> I, too, with supreme respect
> Bow down to the gracious guru.
>
> As the maiden Sujata
> Joyfully offered milk to the Buddha,
> I, too, present the glorious lama
> With real and imagined offerings.
>
> As King Ajatasatru came before the
>   Buddha
> And offered confession of his sins,
> I, too, before the eyes of the guru,
> Confess all my wrongdoing.
>
> As the beggar rejoiced
> In the virtue of King Prasenajit,
> I, too, rejoice in the activity of the guru
> And the virtuous deeds of the exalted ones.
>
> As Brahma and Indra requested the
>   Buddha
> To turn the Wheel of Dharma,
> I, too request that you, authentic guru,
> Turn the wheel of the teachings.

Just as Depon Zangpo requested
The Buddha not to pass into nirvana,
I, too, supplicate you, glorious guru,
To remain for a hundred kalpas.

As the Buddha dedicated
The merit accumulated by King Prasenajit,
I, too, dedicate all merit, symbolized by the
    merit of this prayer,
So that I and others may attain
    Buddhahood.

Wish-fulfilling gem, refuge and protector!
Consider me with your great kindness.
Jetsun, I have nothing else to ask of you but
    this [247b]:

In this present degenerate age,
Life is short, disease and dangers are
    rampant.
I have known many who died in their
    youth;
Really, one could die tonight.

Even if one lives a long time,
Half of life is wasted
In the meaningless torpor of sleep,
The other half is wasted in eating,
    drinking, and distraction,
Leaving little time for Dharma practice.

When I was young, I didn't think much
    about the Dharma.
I was seduced by monastic wealth.
Now I'm old and unable to practice the
    Dharma.

Though it is late to begin practice now,
I will emulate the householder Palkye.[22]
As death draws nearer,
I intend to practice the Dharma as best I
    can.

Compassionate lama!
Out of your great affection, please teach
    me
How to reject nondharmic acts and
    thoughts,

And how to practice in accord with the
    Dharma.

From now on, until I attain enlightenment,
Keep me close to you;
Even after I attain enlightenment,
May I never be parted from you,
    O compassionate lord.

I replied:

Depend upon an authentic guru, the
    source of all good qualities.
Pray to him continuously and all your
    wishes will be fulfilled.

Until you attain real confidence in
    practice,
Stay in the company of true spiritual
    friends
Whose excellence can help you reach the
    ultimate goal of the Dharma.

Dharma practice makes meaningful
The unique opportunity of your free,
    well-favored human birth.

Death is certain, its time of coming is not;
So, don't bother to accumulate wealth.
Give up worldly dharmas and the divine
    Dharma will come about.

Consider the shortcomings of the
    sense-pleasures;
Sever your clingings and cravings.

If you are weary of attachments, you won't
    need wealth.
Cast away your possessions, and you will
    be done with your relatives as well.
Give up your homeland, and attachments
    and aversions will subside of their own
    accord [248a].

Stay in a hermitage, and your practice will
    naturally increase.
Live alone, and obstacles and adverse
    circumstances will be few.

With a kind heart, all you do will turn into
   Dharma.

If you have a pure heart, you'll never
   quarrel.
If you act in accord with the Dharma,
The compassion of the Three Jewels will
   protect you.
If you practice inner calm and insight,
Clinging to reality and obscuring emotions
   will be controlled.
If your *samaya* is pure, you will be blessed
   by the dakinis.

Meditation on the development stage of
   the *yidam*-deity brings accomplishment.
Ignite the bliss-warmth of *tummo*.
Meditation experiences and realization will
   develop.
When realization occurs,
The phenomenal world will arise as
   teachings.

Give up luxurious Dharma-practice; live
   on alms.
Consider your own defects and always
   yield to others.
Give people what they need, and they will
   gather around you.
Teach the great Dharma of compassion;
   benefit beings.

Doing this, you will realize the
   dharmakaya,
And manifest the rupakaya for the sake of
   beings.

I also gave my kind-hearted, devoted and
generous disciple Jigme Gyaltsen, "Fearless Banner of Victory," some instructions on the nature
of the mind according to Mahamudra. Within
six months of practicing this meditation, he gained
certainty regarding the teaching and unprecedented experiences of bliss, clarity, and non-
thought arose in his mind. "This is due to my
lama's kindness!" he thought. With this in mind,
he offered me some warm winter clothing, some
butter, and this request:

Your face is graceful, your body
   resplendent,
Your gentle speech gives voice to the sweet
   sound of the Dharma [248b],
Your mind dwells permanently in the
   realm of clear emptiness—
Lord Tsogdruk Rangdrol, I bow at your
   lotus-feet.

In times past, within the confines of the
   Snow Land of Tibet,
The incomparable lord, Mila the Cotton-clad,
Roamed about like an unbridled snow
   lion.
How wonderful that he reappears now in
   human form!

From the time my mother bore me until
   this day,
I have prayed to lord Mila, the Laughing
   Vajra,
With devotion and yearning.
O Jetsun, haven't you merely changed
   names?
Now, in this extraordinary place, Mount
   Kailash,
How fortunate that I can see your face!

Most graciously you have accepted me.
You have given me beneficial instructions
And introduced me to mind's absolute
   nature—
This is what I practice with zeal.

I gained certainty about the teachings on
   karma, cause and effect,
And saw the mind-essence in its complete
   simplicity;
Now, the experience of luminous
   emptiness never ceases:
This is your blessing, O lord guru!

This realization from my six months of
   meditation
I present as an offering to please my father
   guru.
From now on, until I achieve
   enlightenment,

Please hold on to me with your compassion, O protector.

To help me tame this tough, wild nature of mine,
Please give me some further advice.

When my illusory body is no more,
Guide me to the Buddhafield where you dwell
And let me be your very first disciple,
Like the Five Excellent Disciples of Lord Buddha.

In response, I said, "I'll give you some advice on the Six Paramitas, since they contain the essence of all the Buddhist teachings." And I sang this [249a]:

Listen, Jigme Gyaltsen, my son,
There are six claims you may make:

When you can give away all your possessions to others,
You may say you are generous.

When you are unstained by the ten negative actions,
You may say you keep discipline.

When you can endure adverse circumstances,
You may say you have patience.

When you can persevere in practice without distraction,
You may say you possess diligence.

When you can rise above the obscuring emotions and discursive thoughts,
You may say you can meditate.

When you understand the guru's pith instructions,
You may say you have insight.

Listen, Jigme Gyaltsen, my son,
There are six claims you shouldn't make:

If you don't even give a little *tsampa*
To the beggars at your door,
Don't claim to be generous.

If you haven't given up lies and deception,
Don't claim to keep discipline.

If you can't endure a single unpleasant remark,
Don't claim to be patient.

If you don't get up before sunrise,
Don't claim to be diligent.

If you can't sit still, even for as long as it takes to drink a cup of tea,
Don't claim to have firm concentration.

If you don't have even a rough idea about the karmic law of cause and effect,
Don't claim to have great insight.

Listen, Jigme Gyaltsen, my son,
In the following six, you should persevere:

Until you have untied the knot of avarice,
Persevere in generosity.

Until you have removed the ulcer of deceitfulness,
Persevere in discipline.

Until you have allayed the sharp pains of anger [249b],
Persevere in patience.

Until you have rid yourself of laziness, your enemy,
Persevere in diligence.

Until you have pacified inner poisons and discursive thoughts,
Persevere in meditation.

Until you have illuminated the darkness of ignorance,
Persevere in wisdom.

As I sang this, the monks and other disciples were inspired. I had another disciple, the hermit Tendzin Rabgye, "Holder and Disseminator of the Teachings." He was well versed in the pith instructions of sutra and tantra, and was determined to accomplish the actual meaning of what he had been taught. One day, with a white ceremonial scarf, he offered me some butter, sweet cheese, a piece of white woven wool, and a few turquoises on behalf of people who had asked for prayers. He respectfully offered me praise like those found in the life-stories of the past sages. Putting it into verse, he sang:

You attained Buddhahood long ago,
Yet, to guide the beings of this degenerate
    age,
You came again as a renunciate yogin.
Lord root guru, think of me.

You took birth in Domey,
Yet your karma and aspirations
Brought you to the Snow Mountain, Kailash.

Here, according to the capacity of each
    individual,
You have offered the feast of Dharma
To all, regardless of rank or lineage.

You have consecrated all holy objects that
    needed consecration;
You have dedicated all merit that needed
    dedication.
You have restored broken vows and
    samayas.
You have given food, wealth, and clothing
    to the poor.
You have taught the ignorant how to
    observe the karmic law of cause and
    effect.
You have set every disciple of Ngari in
    western Tibet
Onto the path to higher realms and
    liberation [250a].

This region is greatly indebted to you.
In particular, I, this saffron-robed devourer
    of offerings,

Understand that what little of my mind is
    turned toward the Dharma
Is due to your kindness .
To repay such kindness will be difficult,
    gracious lord.

From now on until I attain the heart of
    awakening,
Accept me always, protector, never be
    separate from me!

Earlier you gave me profound and
    extensive instructions,
Yet I ask you to give me one more
    reminder.

From now on, and for the rest of my life,
May I only please you, protector,
And accomplish your every command.
Bless me that my wishes may come true.

I replied, "O son, you entered the door of Dharma at a young age and were fortunate to hear many teachings and reflect upon them. In this degenerate time, life is short and the time of death is uncertain. Don't bother with external knowledge; turn your attention inward and practice as I taught you earlier. For that, you must give up all thoughts of this life and stay by yourself in mountain retreats." Having explained all this to him, again, I told him in verse:

Tendzin Rabgye, my son,
You were ordained a novice at a young
    age, and you kept pure discipline.
You served many gurus, well-known and
    unknown,
You received empowerments, transmis-
    sions and instructions:
Son of noble family, you have been
    fortunate indeed!

Now, while you are still young,
If, from the heart, you wish to practice the
    Dharma [250b],
Give up thoughts of this life
And remain constantly in a mountain
    hermitage.

The grace of the precious guru and the
    Three Jewels is swift:
Direct your prayers toward them.

The peaceful and wrathful *yidam*-deities
    bestow *siddhis*:
Endeavor in the approach and
    accomplishment practices.[23]

The ocean of vowed guardians and
    dharmapalas has great power and skill:
Urge them to act.

All sentient beings, weary of suffering, have
    been your parents:
Care for them tenderly.

The inexhaustible Seven Noble Riches are
    your inherent wealth:
Keep them with you always.

Stainless samadhi is your inherent
    sustenance:
Continually feed yourself on it.

The bliss-warmth of *tummo*, which glows of
    itself,
Is your inherent garment: wear it constantly.

The obscuring emotions are the yogin's
    enemies:
Tame them, press them back down as they
    arise.

Your own mind is the root of all
    phenomena,
The greatest of all spectacles:
Watch it continuously.

Regard all countries as your homeland;
Be at ease, happy, wherever you go.

Follow this advice, and you will render
    meaningful
The freedoms and favorable conditions
    you gained by your human birth.

He left, very happy.

Once, I explained the karmic law of cause and
effect to the faithful householder Palleh, the lama-
doctor Tendzin, and other faithful male and
female householders:

"Whatever you have done, good or bad, in
your past lives, ripens in this lifetime; whatever
you do in this life will have an effect on future
lifetimes. So, you must beware of the consequences of your actions. This is explained in the
*Sutra Discriminating between the Path of Virtue and the
Path of Vice*,[24] a flawless teaching of the Bhagavat
Buddha [251a]:

"To be handsome in this life is the result of
meditation on patience. An unpleasant appearance comes from anger and malice. Poverty
comes from avarice. Authority comes from having bowed respectfully to the Buddha. Having a
low status is the result of having been proud and
aggressive. To be tall and well-built comes from
having served others respectfully. To be short is
the result of having been a lazy practitioner.
Stupidity comes from having been a sheep in
one's previous life.

"To be dark and skinny is the result of
staining a representation of the Buddha. Dispro-
portionate lips result from eating the teacher's
food. A twitch in the eyes is the result of having
refused to give light when asked. Night blindness
comes from having gouged out the eyes of a
hawk. Dumbness comes from having slandered
the sacred teachings. Deafness results from dis-
liking listening to the teachings. Protruding teeth
result from having burned bones or marrow.

"A wrinkled nose results from having offered
the Buddha foul-smelling incense. A harelip is
the result of having pierced the mouths of fish.
To be an albino is the result of having plucked
out the hairs of swine. A torn ear is the result of
having pierced others' ears. Resembling a desert
snake comes from having accompanied the Buddha while wearing dirty clothes. A birthmark
comes from having left a Buddha statue in an
ordinary room or passageway.

"To be lame or crippled comes from not

standing up when seeing one's abbot or lama [251b]. To be a hunchback is the result of turning one's back on the Buddha while wearing dirty clothes. A protruding forehead comes from having only joined one's hands at one's forehead instead of prostrating oneself when seeing the Buddha. A short neck is the result of turning one's head down and walking away at the sight of monks and lamas. A diseased liver comes from having cut and pierced the bodies of animals. Leprosy is the result of having taken wealth to which you were not entitled.

"Excessive mucus is the result of having given others cold food and drink in wintertime. To have no children is the result of killing many fledglings. To have many children is the result of caring for many animals. Longevity comes from great compassion; short life comes from killing. Abundance comes from generosity. To own horses and chariots is the result of having made offerings to the Three Jewels.

"Intelligence is the result of diligent study and of recitation of the sutras. Stupidity indicates one has been an animal in a previous life. To be a servant or a maid is the result of not having repaid one's debts. A short temper indicates that one has been a monkey in a previous life. Leprosy also can be the result of having destroyed representations of the Three Jewels. Incomplete limbs are the result of having cut off the legs of animals. Viciousness is the sign of having been a snake or a scorpion in a previous life.

"Unimpaired sense faculties are the result of having kept discipline; impaired sense faculties are the result of having broken it. Untidiness comes from having failed to make offerings to the exalted ones [252a].

"If you like song, dance, and music, you will be reborn as a musician. Great desire indicates you have been a bird in a previous life. To have a goiter comes from having eaten garlic. Weak speech is the result of having spoken harshly. Impotence is the result of having castrated dogs, pigs, and horses. A short tongue comes from having scorned or slandered monks and lamas. If you have illicit sex with another man's wife, you will be reborn as a goose or a duck.

"If you deceive close friends you will be reborn as a sparrow. Even though you know where to find the sutras and scriptures of a temple, if, out of stinginess, you don't allow them to be shown to others, you will be reborn as an earthworm. If you like carrying bows and arrows, or riding horses, you will be reborn as a jackal or a wolf. If you delight in hairdos and head ornaments, you will be reborn as a mosquito. If you are overly fond of sleeping and eating, you will be reborn as a pig. If you delight in dressing in multicolored silks, you will be reborn as a parakeet.[25] If you take pleasure in crude jokes, you will be reborn as a parrot. If you relish gossip, you will be reborn as a six-headed cobra.[26]

"If you are fond of fooling others, you will be reborn as a dazed insect. If you take pleasure in spreading bad news, you will be reborn as a screech owl. To take pleasure in saying harmful and hurtful things brings rebirth as a vixen. If you enjoy frightening others, you will be reborn as a centipede [252b]. If you enter a temple wearing wooden clogs, you will be reborn as a horse. If you fart without restraint you will be reborn as a stinkbug.

"If you use the millstones of the sangha for your own profit, you will be reborn as a flatheaded worm. If you prevent sentient beings from eating, you will be reborn as a woodpecker. If you steal water from the sangha, you will be reborn as a fish, a tortoise, or some other aquatic creature. If you criticize the sangha, you will be reborn as a latrine maggot. If you steal fruit from the sangha, you will be reborn as a liver-eating parasite. If you steal wealth from the sangha, you will be reborn as a donkey or an ox turning millstones. If you borrow from the sangha without repayment, you will be reborn as a pigeon. If you slander members of the sangha and they are expelled, you will be reborn as a worm living on the neck-sore of an ox. If you steal the vegetables of the sangha, you will be reborn as an insect on vegetable roots. If you sit on seats meant for the sangha, you will be reborn as a redheaded worm.

"If you use the possessions of the sangha, you will be reborn as a dust-worm. If you enter a temple wearing bone hairpins, you will be reborn a hoopoe. If you enter a temple showing yourself with powder and rouge, you will be reborn as a rubythroat. If you wear colored silks in a temple you will be reborn as a kingfisher. If, as a couple, you sleep overnight in a temple, you will be reborn as blue-headed worms. If you use a stupa of the Sugatas as a resting place, you will be reborn as a camel [253a]. If you enter a temple wearing shoes and a fancy overcoat, you will be reborn as a frog. If you chatter during a teaching, you will be reborn as a magpie. If you seduce a monk or a nun who has been keeping pure discipline, you will be reborn in a hell of iron-creatures, where your body will be pierced by a wheel of a million swords. So it is said."

I concluded: "Thus it is! Faithful male and female householders, if you desire happiness and freedom from suffering in future lives, give up negative actions and practice wholesome deeds as the compassionate Buddha said." Then I put it into verse:

> I pray to the gracious lamas.
> Grant your blessings that I may under-
>   stand the consequences of actions
> And know what to adopt and what to
>   avoid.
>
> Meditate on patience; you will have a
>   handsome appearance.
> If you are full of hate and anger, you will
>   be ugly.
> If you are stingy with your wealth, you will
>   be poor.
>
> Prostrate yourself before the Buddha; you
>   will have authority.
> If you are proud and arrogant, you will be
>   vile.
> Be respectful; you will obtain a tall and
>   healthy body.
> If you practice the Dharma lazily, you will
>   be short.
>
> To be dull is due to having been a sheep in
>   your previous life.
> If you defile sacred representations, you
>   will be reborn dark and skinny.
> If you eat the food of your Dharma-teacher,
>   you will have disproportionate lips.

> If you refuse to supply light when asked,
>   you will have twitching eyes.
> If you gouge out the eyes of a hawk, you
>   will suffer night blindness.
>
> Slander the teachings: you will be mute.
> Spurn listening to the sacred Dharma: you
>   will be deaf [253b].
> Burn bones and marrow: you will have
>   uneven teeth.
> Offer foul-smelling incense: you will have a
>   wrinkled nose.
>
> Pierce the mouths of fish: you will have a
>   harelip.
> Pluck the hairs of swine: you will be an
>   albino.
> Pierce others' ears: you will have a torn
>   ear.
>
> Fail to stand up when you see the guru:
>   you will be crippled.
> Turn your back on an image of the
>   Buddha: you will be a hunchback.
> Turn your head down and walk away
>   when you see the lama: you will have a
>   short neck.
>
> Cut or pierce others' bodies: you will have
>   a diseased liver.
> Take wealth improperly: you will be a
>   leper.
> Give people cold food in the winter: you
>   will have much mucus.
> Kill fledglings: you will have no children.
> Care for many animals: you will have
>   many children.
> Cultivate great compassion for living crea-
>   tures: you will live long.
> Kill many creatures: your life will be short.
>
> Be generous: you will be wealthy.
> Make many offerings: you will have horses
>   and chariots.
> Recite sutras: your intelligence will be
>   sharp.
> Stupidity comes from having been an
>   animal in your previous life.

Fail to pay your debts: you will be a servant
    or a maid.
A short temper comes from having been a
    monkey in a previous life.
Destroy representations of the Three
    Jewels: you will be a leper.
Cut off others' hands and feet: you own
    limbs will be incomplete.

Viciousness comes from having been a
    snake or a scorpion in your previous life.
The result of having kept discipline is
    obtaining unimpaired faculties.
Break discipline: you will have impaired
    faculties.
Fail to make offerings to the Noble Ones:
    you will have little sense of cleanliness.

If you are fond of singers, dancers, and
    musicians, you will become one yourself.
If you were a bird in your previous life, you
    will have great desires in this one.
If you are overly fond of garlic, you will be
    reborn with a goiter.
Speak harshly: you will be reborn as some-
    one to whom no one listens. [254a]

Castrate animals: you will be impotent.
Slander the lama: you will have a short
    tongue.
Make love with someone else's partner:
    you will reborn as a duck.
Deceive close friends: you will be reborn a
    sparrow.
Be stingy with the Dharma: you will be
    reborn an earthworm.

Delight in archery and horseback-riding:
    you will be reborn a wolf.
Be fond of hair-ornaments: you will be
    reborn a mosquito.
Be fond of eating and sleeping: you will be
    reborn a pig.
Be obsessed with clothes: you will be
    reborn a parakeet.

Take pleasure in making crude jokes: you
    will be reborn a parrot.

Relish gossip: you will be reborn a
    six-headed cobra.
Take pleasure in teasing: you will be
    reborn a dazed insect.
Take pleasure in carrying ill tidings: you
    will be reborn a screech owl.
Find pleasure in saying hurtful things: you
    will be reborn a vixen.
Take pleasure in frightening people: you
    will be reborn a caterpillar.

Unrestrained farting leads to rebirth as a
    stinkbug.
Use the sangha's millstones improperly:
    you will be reborn a flat-headed
    worm.
Prevent others from eating: you will be
    reborn a woodpecker.
Steal water: you will be reborn a fish or
    some other aquatic creature.

Criticize the sangha: you will be reborn a
    latrine maggot.
Steal fruit: you will be reborn a liver
    parasite.
Steal wealth: you will be reborn a donkey
    turning a millstone.
Borrow money without repaying it: you
    will be reborn a pigeon.
Use a stupa as a resting place: you will be
    reborn a camel.
Wear shoes in the temple: you will be
    reborn a frog.
Chat during a teaching: you will be reborn
    a magpie.

In short, every action has its corresponding
    result.
So the Buddha said,
And the Buddha's words never deceive.
Acknowledge their truth and exercise your
    discernment:
This is crucial.

Glorious and precious root teacher [254b],
May I develop the ability to conduct myself
Bearing in mind the karmic law of cause
    and effect.

I concluded, "Recite these verses and reflect on their meaning; it will greatly help you to reckon the consequences of your actions."

Jimba Norbu, "Jewel of Generosity," was the first of the renunciates at Snow Mountain to become my disciple. He was gentle, generous, intelligent, straightforward, full of faith, and compassionate.

As soon as we met, he experienced constant devotion. I gave him all the essential instructions on the uncommon development and completion stages of the Mantrayana. He meditated on these and attained exceptional experiences and realization. After completing his retreat he offered a large *ganachakra* feast and as a gesture of gratitude he offered me some *tsampa*, butter, and other provisions. He also presented me with these verses describing the progress of his inner experience and realization:

Precious guru, embodiment of all Buddhas,
I offer this for your ears:

Jetsun! By your graceful compassion,
I have learned meditation and had the
    good fortune to practice it.

Contemplating the suffering of the cycle of
    birth and death,
I felt a strong, decisive weariness with
    samsara.

Meditating on loving-kindness,
    compassion, and Bodhicitta,
Made me think again and again that
    others were dearer than myself.

When I was practicing inner-calm
    meditation, once the stream
    of thoughts was cut
I could concentrate vividly on any chosen
    object.
At that time, I experienced great physical
    well-being,

Together with bliss, clarity, and
    non-thought [255a].

When I was resting within that inner calm,
I investigated phenomena: insight
    deepened;
I understood the primordially empty nature
Of all that exists in samsara and nirvana;
I saw clearly that phenomena are nothing
    more than
Labels and designations affixed by
    discursive mind.

I understood that the nature of mind
Does not truly begin, remain, or come to
    an end—
It is substanceless;
Its nature is emptiness.

As I examined the one who had this
    understanding,
That "one" also dissolved into emptiness.

I merged with this state of clear emptiness.
Its nature was empty, yet was bright and
    clear.
There arose an experience of luminous
    emptiness beyond words;
And impure perception was purified as
    emptiness.

Within this realm of emptiness, meditating
On the creation of the mandala and its
    deities,
Resting upon the tiers of the four elements,
I experienced again and again clear
    visualization and firm pride.[27]

Through *tummo* meditation—the
    foundation-stone of the completion
    stage—
Bliss-warmth blazed forth within ten days.
I am confident that I could have withstood
    the cold
With a single cotton cloth, if I had one at
    hand.

Yet, I did not experience as much bliss as
    warmth,

So I beg you to teach me
How to make the great bliss blaze forth,
And, when it comes, how to merge bliss
    with emptiness.

I told him that nourishing food would help
and taught him how to increase the flow of
Bodhicitta from the letter *Hang* at the crown of
his head, and how to let Bodhicitta fill his whole
body—as if filling up a leather pouch with milk
[255b]. I taught him the sequences of concentra-
tions that generate almost unbearable bliss. He
meditated accordingly and his experience of bliss
increased. I then instructed him how to bring
down the Bodhicitta to the secret center, draw it
up again, and spread it. He could bring the
Bodhicitta up to the crown of his head, without
losing even a tiny drop, and spread it out. His
bliss blazed stronger than ever and it pervaded
his whole body. Within the realm of bliss, he
experienced directly the view of the natural state
that he had ascertained earlier, and developed
extraordinary experience and realization of bliss-
emptiness. Later he could subsist on samadhi as
his only nourishment; he could take no food or
drink for many days without feeling hunger or
thirst. I thought, too, that his complexion was
more radiant.

The governor Garpön Bentsa Lhopa Tsewang
Topgye, "Mighty Lord of Life," a devoted, generous, and intelligent man, arrived with his
entourage. I gave him and the others many
empowerments, transmissions, and instructions.
His faith became irreversible, and he offered
much gold, silver, jewelry, and clothing, as well
as horses and fifteen bags of rice and *tsampa*.
With these verses, which he had composed, he
requested an elaborate protection-blessing:

I supplicate you, father guru,
Compassionate lord, embodiment of
    Akshobhya:[28]
The happiness and suffering of this beggar
    are in your hands:

Grant me your ceaseless blessings!

I have gained a precious support, a free
    and well-favored human body [256a];
I have met the lord guru, the Buddha in
    person;
I have received the ultimate profound
    Dharma, the Secret Mantrayana:
What could be more marvelous than this?

Gracious lord, compassionate one!
I offer my practice to repay your kindness.
May the life and *sadhana* of this beggar
    become one;
May realization of the absolute lineage be
    born.

I dwell in mountain hermitages and
    monasteries,
Yet my mind-stream has not mixed with
    Dharma
And remains ordinary. Why? Laziness!
Grant your blessing that this beggar
    overcome laziness!

Though I've heard the profound teachings,
    I haven't practiced.
Merely entertaining fantasies about
    practicing the Dharma,
I've frittered my life away.
Why? Because I think my life will go on
    forever!
Grant your blessing that this beggar keep
    death in mind!

Outwardly, I appear to be a practitioner of
    Dharma,
Yet I involve myself in evil actions.
I call myself a renunciate,
Yet I go hunting for food and clothes.
Why? Craving!
Grant your blessings that I relinquish all
    thoughts of this life.

Outwardly, I am good at fooling people,
Yet every daily event in life reveals my
    mediocrity.
Why? I haven't merged the stream of my
    mind with the Dharma.

Grant your blessing that I blend my mind
  with the Dharma.

Inwardly, because I've failed to tame the
  stream of my negative thoughts,
The slightest word sparks desire or hatred.
Why? The obscuring emotions!
Grant your blessing that this beggar tame
  his emotions!

My life is carried away by evil actions,
I am endlessly occupied with wrong
  activities,
Yet I feel no shame.
Why? I haven't really understood the law
  of karma.
Grant your blessing that this beggar
  become aware of the consequences of
  his acts! [256b].

Immersed in samsara's ocean of suffering,
My mind never stops taking things as real.
Why? I don't consider deeply the First
  Noble Truth: suffering.
Grant your blessing that this beggar
  contemplate the truth of suffering!

I had intended to practice the Dharma,
But somehow I never got around to it.
For so many lives, from beginningless time,
I've been wandering in samsara.
Why? Because of the Second Noble Truth:
  the origin of suffering.
Grant your blessings that this beggar put
  an end to the source of suffering!

My mind, completely entangled in
  samsara,
Veers away from the lasting aim of life.
Why? Because of not having renunciation
  in my mind-stream.
Grant your blessing that this beggar
  develop renunciation!

Strongly discriminating between beings,
  each of whom has been my kind parent,
I add to my attachments and aversions
And accumulate bad karma.

Why? Because I've failed to develop
  Bodhicitta.
Grant your blessing that this beggar perfect
  Bodhicitta!

Although striving in acts of relative virtue,
I will never exhaust the seeds of samsara.
Why not? Because I haven't realized the
  pure view.
Grant your blessing that this beggar realize
  the true nature of mind!

Father guru, through the blessing of your
  body,
May I perceive my illusory body as the
  deity.

Father guru, through the blessing of your
  speech,
May my speech become a
  vajra-recitation.[29]

Father guru, through the blessing of your
  mind,
May I behold the innate simplicity of mind.

Father guru, through the blessing of your
  body, speech, and mind,
May my body, speech, and mind become
  one with yours.

For myself, may I conquer the
  dharmakaya citadel.
For others, may I plant the seed of the
  rupakaya.
When the expanse of compassion and
  Buddha-activity unfolds [257a],
May I accomplish great benefit for all
  sentient beings, my mothers.

Revealing the treasure of the two
  accomplishments,
The power of blessings surpasses any other.

May my compassion be unbiased and
  ceaseless,
Enabling me to dredge the depths of
  samsara.

Though I am a worthless man, my guru is
 supreme.
Through his blessings and through the
 infallible truth of karmic cause and
 effect,
May the aspirations of this beggar be
 swiftly accomplished!

When he offered this to me, I dedicated the merit and made prayers; he then returned to his place .

One day, my disciple Jigme Gyaltsen said: "As a result of negative tendencies, I get very angry. What can I do?" I replied:

"For that, nothing is more important than to cultivate patience. In the future age of illness, warfare, and famine, when the average life span of human beings has been reduced to only ten years, the One Robed in Saffron, an emanation of Maitreya, will appear. Amazed, everyone will wonder, 'Has the Buddha Maitreya arrived?' and ask, 'Why is it that you are wearing such beautifully colored Dharma robes? Why are you so beautiful?'

"'Through having cultivated patience,' the emanation will reply and add, 'Give up quarreling; practice patience.' When people do this, their life spans will increase, first from ten years to twenty, then gradually to eighty-thousand years [257b]. Then Buddha Maitreya will come and turn the Wheel of the Dharma.

"Beauty, longevity, and many other pleasant qualities are the results of having cultivated patience: cultivate it as much as possible! The master Shantideva says:[30]

> There is no worse evil than hatred,
> And no better ascetic practice than
> patience:
> So, striving in various ways,
> Cultivate patience.

"Therefore, meditate sincerely on patience." I continued:

> I pray to the gracious root guru:
> Grant your blessings that my anger be
> pacified.

One fit of anger destroys the merit
That one has accumulated over of a
 thousand aeons:
In this life, your anger will only reap anger
 and lack of sympathy from everyone;
When you die, your sole destination will be
 the hells.

If you shun anger and cultivate patience, in
 this lifetime,
Gods and men will love you and gather
 around you.
Wherever you are born again, you will be
 beautiful;
Ultimately, you will obtain the body of a
 Buddha,
Adorned with the major and minor marks
 of perfection.

Thus, there is no enemy like anger.
When it arises, know it to be your real
 enemy, and crush it.

An ordinary enemy is the best catalyst for
 developing patience;
Regard him as a spiritual friend and
 perfect your patience.

O glorious precious root guru,
Grant your blessing that I may cultivate
 patience free from anger.

I dedicate all past, present, and future
 merit
Toward perfecting the *paramita* of
 patience.

From now on, wearing the armor of
 patience,
May I vanquish my archenemy, anger
 [258a].

I added, "Recite these lines whenever anger arises, reflect on their meaning, and anger will subside of its own accord."

Once, I gave this advice to some fifty friends and disciples doing retreat:

Life is short; the time of death uncertain;
Even tonight you may die.

A lot of talking is the source for evil deeds.
A lot of thinking is the work of Mara.
A lot of running around just weakens your
     practice.

The crucial instruction:
Stay on your meditation seat!

Keep to your silent retreat, don't talk;
Obstacles won't come, *siddhis* will.

You who practice the preliminaries,
Persevere throughout day and night.

Meditators resting in samadhi,
Meditate with unwavering body, speech,
     and mind.

Practitioners of *tummo*, the path of skillful
     means,
Be diligent, and bliss-warmth will blaze
     forth.

Even those of you who know only the *mani*,
Don't run around, stay inside; do your
     recitations.

Be ready to starve to death for the sake of
     Dharma;
Be ready to endure hardship for the sake of
     happiness in future lives.

In brief, don't think so much!
Put all your energy into practice!

Thus I exhorted them. Some practiced for one year, some for two. *Ngondro* [31] practitioners had dreams indicating that their obscurations had been purified. Those who trained in relative Bodhicitta [258b] developed kindness, compassion, and the wish to benefit others. Those who meditated on absolute Bodhicitta were able to remain steadily in mind's true condition, the state of simplicity that is like the sky: empty, luminous, and beyond grasping. *Phowa* [32] practitioners had many signs, such as itching, swelling, and secretion of liquid at the top of the skull. Those practicing on *prana* [33] gained extraordinary realization of bliss-emptiness, their bodies blazing with the bliss-warmth of *tummo*. In reality, in dreams, or in meditation, Chöd practitioners had all the appropriate signs: the arising of challenging experiences and their successful termination. Those who prayed to the Great Compassionate One and recited the *mani* mantra were blessed: their obscuring emotions diminished, as did their clinging to reality. They had extraordinary experiences and realization of renunciation, Bodhicitta, and the perfect view.

Konchog Chöden "Upholder of the Dharma of the Three Jewels," was a hermit who had given up the preoccupations of this life to practice pure, virtuous deeds. With Gyalwa Lhundrup, "Spontaneous Victor," a Bönpo inclined toward the Buddhist teachings, he came to me with this request:

"Under the influence of our bad habits, we have been unable to tame our tough minds. Please teach us how to make our minds pliant." They then offered their request in verse:

Your body is resplendent with perfect
     marks and signs.
Your speech voices the unobstructed
     melody of Brahma.
Your mind, void and clear, is a treasury of
     wisdom and love.

Lord, enlightened yogin [259a],
The sun, moon, and stars—
The phenomena of samsara and nirvana—
Appear vivid and distinct
In the sky-expanse of your empty,
     luminous mind.

Lord, sky-like yogin,
When sentient beings, starved for the
     Dharma,
Pray to you with veneration,
You grant whatever Dharma they pray for.

Lord, gem-like yogin,
You clearly show how to take up good and
    avoid evil.
You amply supply food, clothing, and
    Dharma, and
You always look after others with kindness
    and love.

Lord, father- and mother-like yogin:
Though we have entered the door of
    Dharma,
The strong negative habits formed over so
    long
Keep us bound to comforts and to concern
    for this life.

To make true Dharma come alive is
    difficult.
With a full stomach, sitting comfortably in
    the sun,
We might visualize deities down to the
    most minute detail,
And count mantras, our lips mumbling
    diligently:
Outwardly, we look like true Dharma
    practitioners.

But when we encounter the slightest
    difficulty,
Cold, hunger, fatigue, ghosts, or
    enemies,
We can't bear it: our faults are brought
    to light,
And we cease to appear as real Dharma
    practitioners.

We relish delicious foods, comfortable
    clothing:
The precious teaching slips away and is
    lost.

The lama gives teachings but that won't
    suffice:
We expect that he will also give us
    presents.

We may give food and drink to friends,
But we hope for something in return.

We stay in remote and solitary places,
But we hope that others will provide us
    with food and drink.

When everything goes well, we want to
    practice Dharma;
When things go wrong, we feel like giving
    up.

Now we have become aware of thoughts
And actions contrary to the Dharma
    [259b].

Wanting to make it supple,
We've soaked the dry hide that is our mind
In the water of the guru's pith instructions,
And rubbed it with the hands of skillful
    means and wisdom:
Please show us once more how to make
    this hide soft and pliant.

From now on, throughout all of our lives,
May we never be separate from you.
Savoring the nectar of your speech,
May we benefit both others and ourselves.

I answered:

Listen, my two fortunate disciples:
The Lord of Death comes suddenly.
How easy it is to lose this human body you
    have gained!

Wandering in the *bardo*, you will have
    many fears.
The sufferings of the lower realms are
    miserable.

Even in the higher realms there is no
    happiness.
Now is the time to strive for the ultimate
    happiness of enlightenment.

If you strive for this accomplishment, avoid
    the following:
The authentic root guru is the one who
    shows us the way
To the higher realms, to liberation;

Yet, rather than thinking of his good
    qualities,
We contemplate his faults.
"In the beginning, he used to treat me
    nicely,
Now he's changed," we say,
Criticizing him behind his back.

We cannot bear it when he scolds us,
And answer back when he does.
We hold ourselves dearer than the guru.

Our minds fill up with trivial
    preoccupations:
We seek wealth and food by business and
    deceit;
We crave the sinful food of misused
    religious wealth.

We stay in lonely mountain retreats
But don't do our practice: we're just
    distracted.
Far from developing meditative
    experiences and realization,
We develop desires and cravings.

"Wouldn't it be something if people looked
    on us as great practitioners
And gave us offerings and veneration!"
With this in mind, we stay in the
    mountains [260a].

We swear to practice for three years,
But the days seem endless.
We can't bear it any longer.
We entrust our provisions and *tsampa* to a
    friend,
And race down to the village, to be snared
    by attachment and aggression.

If you really want, from the depths of your
    heart, to practice Dharma,
Don't ever do this!

E ma!
Now that you have gained this human body,
Rely upon your lama in thought and deed.

Develop the aspiration toward supreme
    enlightenment,
And continually train in the six
    transcendent perfections.

You must receive the four empowerments
    of the Secret Mantrayana, which ripen
    and liberate,
And meditate according to the pith
    instructions
Of the development and completion
    stages, which bring liberation.

In short, giving up the desire for ordinary
    happiness,
Don't strive for the goals of ordinary
    life.
In an excellent place, a remote mountain
    retreat,
Let the length of your practice equal the
    length of your life.

Tendzin Zangmo, "Noble Holder of the
Dharma," and Döndrup Drölma, "All-accomplishing Savioress," were two nuns with faith in
the guru and the Dharma. They kept pure vows
and *samaya*, zealously practicing wholesome deeds
and abandoning evil. They offered me this song
asking for advice:

O gracious lord guru,
We prostrate ourselves with veneration at
    your feet,
We present a wealth of real and imagined
    offerings,
We confess our previous negative actions
    and downfalls,
We rejoice in the lama's deeds,
We ask that you turn the Wheel of the
    Dharma for sentient beings,
And remain without passing into nirvana.
We dedicate our accumulated merit
    toward the attainment of Buddhahood.

E ma!
Supreme, precious being!
Heed us! Listen to us!

The nuns of this degenerate age [260b]
Rarely live according to the Dharma;
Especially, if we two were to recount our
spiritual careers,
It would surely displease the holy ones.

Thinking mostly about food, drink, and
sleep,
We rarely remember the Dharma.

Having quenched our thirst and filled our
stomachs,
We are just about able to do recitation and
meditation;
But when we don't have butter to go with
our *tsampa*,
Forget about practice—even saying
prayers is hard!

Seeing something beautiful,
Each of us thinks, "I wish I had that."

When we find a piece of thread, we are
thrilled;
When we lose a needle, we are miserable.

Unable to bear a single harsh word,
We destroy all our merit through anger.

We think we are keeping our vows and
samayas,
But they are endangered as soon as bad
times come.

Forgetting that death may come at any
moment,
We plan on living for many years.

Unaware of the flaws of ordinary enjoyments,
We long to accumulate even more food
and wealth.

Unaware that all beings have been our
parents,
We harbor attachment toward some and
hatred toward others.

At night, we sleep in ignorance,
By day, we slave to find food and clothes.

In short, our minds are at odds with the
Dharma.

Compassionate Lama,
Grant your blessing that our minds and the
Dharma may become one.
Although you have given us many
teachings,
Please give us some further advice.

From now on, throughout all of our lives,
May we never be separate from you
And, practicing the Dharma in accord
with your teachings,
May we swiftly attain omniscience.

I replied:

Faithful "Noble Holder of the Dharma"
[261a],
And "All-accomplishing Savioress,"
Listen to this advice
From the renunciate Tsogdruk Rangdrol:

Respectfully attend an authentic guru.
Live with close Dharma friends.
Keep your vows without hypocrisy.
When you hear harsh words, cultivate
patience.
When you have food and money, practice
generosity.
While your illusory body is healthy, do
prostrations and circumambulations.

Meditate while your intelligence is clear.
Eat the food of your funeral now, while
you still have an appetite.[34]
Make your testament now, while you can
still talk.

Have compassion for the destitute.
Meditate on the Great Compassionate
One as your *yidam* deity.
Recite the essential six-syllable mantra.

Now and then, reflect on the fragility of life.
And always watch your mind.

In short, give up thoughts of this life
And practice the sacred Dharma
    according to the lama's instructions.

If the instructions are profound,
You don't need many of them,
But must take them into practice.
So—meditate!

If you practice, you will be happy in this
    life,
And in future lives, you will progress
    toward liberation.

I said to my fortunate disciples, "Between meditation sessions, while cultivating the deep understanding that everything is like an illusion, it will help you to chant from time to time these verses from the *King of Samadhi Sutra*:[35]

Like a mirage, like an illusion,
Like the apparition of a city of *gandharvas*,[36]
Like dreams—
The forms you have been taking for
    realities
Are empty by their very nature [261b]:
Know that all phenomena are like this.

When the moon rises in a clear night sky,
Its reflection appears on the surface of a
    calm lake.
But the moon is not really in the lake, is it?
Know that all phenomena are like this.

When people who are in a rocky gorge
Sing, or laugh, or weep, or shout,
No one pays any attention to the echoes,
    do they?
Know that all phenomena are like this.

These echoes are but the empty resonance
Of those songs, that laughter, weeping,
    shouting:
They have no separate existence in
    themselves at all.
Know that all phenomena are like this.

When someone feels a pleasurable
    sensation in a dream,
And then awakens, there is nothing left.
But, under the enchantment of desire,
A childish person clings to such experience.
Know that all phenomena are like this.

The illusory forms created by a magi-
    cian—
Horses, elephants, and chariots—
Have no real existence whatsoever:
Know that all phenomena are like this.

When a woman dreams that she has given
    birth to a son
And then, in the dream, sees that son
    dying,
She rejoices when he is born and
She is grief-stricken when he dies.
Know that all phenomena are like this.

At night, in a clear, calm lake,
The reflection of the moon
Appears to be there in the water:
Can anyone take hold of that water-moon?
Know that all phenomena are like this.

At noon, in the hottest time of the year,
Someone parched and tormented by thirst
Will perceive a mirage of water [262a].
Know that all phenomena are like this.

In that mirage, there is no water,
Yet that dazed person wants to drink it.
Can anyone drink water that does not
    exist?
Know that all phenomena are like this.

Thinking that the watery trunk of the
    plantain tree
Has a solid core, one may cut it down;
But there is nothing solid there, outside or
    inside.
Know that all phenomena are like this."

I advised them, "Recite the verses of this profound sutra and reflect upon their meaning; your recognition of the illusory nature of phenomena will be heightened."

Hundreds of worthy renunciates and thousands of faithful men and women came from various places. As months and years went by, I turned the Wheel of the Dharma for them at length. I taught stage by stage: first, according to the provisional, relative truth, I taught that actions have inevitable consequences. Then, according to the definitive, absolute truth, I taught that, by nature, even the most subtle particle lacks true existence.

I wrote the *Emanated Scriptures of the Kadampas*,[37] explaining the heart essence of the teaching of the Victorious Ones—the gradual path for the three types of individuals—following the teachings of the Kadampa masters, and illustrating them with various stories.

I also wrote the *Emanated Scriptures of Manjushri*,[38] in the form of questions and answers. Using verse and prose alternately, it explains at length the crucial pith instructions of the graded path [262b], mind training, Mahamudra, Dzogchen, and the Dohas.[39]

When, over many days, I gave the transmission and explanations of these two texts, rainbow canopies formed in the sky, flower-shaped raindrops fell, extraordinary fragrances manifested themselves, and I felt that the sky was filled with celestial beings who had come to attend the teachings.

The explanations I gave enabled fortunate students with sharp intelligence to comprehend the essential teachings of the Victorious Ones. Some became learned, virtuous, and noble disciples who fully benefited themselves and others, and the Dharma as well.

You may wonder what the term "emanated scriptures" means. In the past, the Great Master[40] presented immeasurable outer, inner, secret, and absolute offerings to Manjushri, and prayed fervently to him. Jetsun Manjushri then bestowed upon him the *Great Emanated Scriptures of the Oral Transmission Pith Instructions*,[41] a work which covers the entire body of sutras and tantras.

This Great Master handed these on to the lord of *siddhas* Jampel Gyatso ("Ocean of Tender Glory"), who gave them to Baso Chökyi Gyaltsen ("Victory Banner of the Dharma"), who then transmitted them to the mahasiddha Chökyi Dorje ("Diamond of the Dharma"), who gave them to Gyalwa Wensapa Lobzang Döndrup ("Victorious Hermit 'Fulfilling Intelligence'").[42]

The teaching I composed is not as perfect as its model, but, insofar as it consolidates the important points of the sutras and tantras explained therein, it is similar [263a].

The incomparable Atisha—the patriarch of the Kadampa teachings who perceived each word of the Buddha's as a pith instruction—and his spiritual sons, Drom Tönpa and the others, condensed the essence of the eighty-four thousand approaches to the Dharma into a graded path for the three kinds of individuals, in a way that can be easily practiced. I extracted the instructions and stories contained in these teachings and arranged them as a book. I called them "emanated," to show their authenticity. They are "emanated" by the earlier *Scriptures of the Kadampas,* just as one butter-lamp lights another.

As to the *Emanated Scriptures of Manjushri:* relinquishing his long hair[43] for the sake of the beings who needed care, the precious Manjushri, lord of supreme wisdom, manifested as the saffron-robed great protector Lama Tsongkhapa. Tsongkhapa composed the *Great Graded Path,* a lamp for the three worlds. My work is based on this and other similar works. The title indicates that it is an emanation from a pure source.

The *Emanated Scriptures of the Bodhisattva*[44] is so called because it is inspired by the life-story and writings of the precious Gyalse Thogme, the "Unimpeded Bodhisattva," an emanation of Avalokiteshvara [263b].

The *Marvelous Emanated Scriptures*[45] is based on the teachings and stories found in the discourses of the Victorious One and in various writings of learned and accomplished sages of India and Tibet.

For these reasons, the mere titles of these texts carry, for future disciples, the blessing of the Buddhas of the three times. I told everyone, "Put these teachings into practice; they will surely benefit your minds." The fortunate disciples gathered there felt faith and respect, and valued highly these writings.

To purify their karma and obscurations and

to perfect their provision of merit, my disciples and patrons erected a stone Stupa of Enlightenment. I consecrated it and made prayers.

Soon after, the anchorite Jetsun Sangye Dorje, "Adamantine Buddha," came to this sacred place. I requested from him the transmission of the cycle of the *Formless Dakini* [46] from the oral pith instruction lineage of Lodrak Marpa. I also requested teachings from all the lamas who came, in order to create spiritual links with them. I made the offering and prayers to Mount Kailash many times. One night I had a dream: Dordzin Rinpoche, "Holder of the Vajra," a lama from Kailash, came and said to me, "If you want to visit a sacred place, I shall take you there." I followed him and we arrived at a huge palace, resembling the Great Temple of Sakya [264a],[47] made from a variety of precious stones. In its center was a stainless crystal stupa, brilliant and transparent as though made of light.

Inside, the lord of the mandala was Chakrasamvara, surrounded by the deities of the four classes of tantra. They appeared clear, bright, and distinct, like reflections in a mirror. On seeing this, I prostrated myself and made circumambulations and offerings. Then, as I was praying, light emanated from the hearts of the deities. It touched me, and I experienced an extraordinary bliss-void wisdom.

Another day, while meditating I had a vivid experience: a host of dakas and dakinis appeared in the sky before me and said, "We are circumambulating the palace of Chakrasamvara." I watched them doing circumambulations in the sky around the snow peak of Mount Kailash, carrying a multitude of offerings.

Once, some patrons from the area of the Crystal Peak of Rong[48] insisted that I visit them. "I can't come now," I said. "Have faith and pray; I shall give a blessing just as real as if I had come in person." The patrons guessed that I would come there miraculously, and prayed with great faith. Repeatedly, I visualized myself going to their homes and blessing them [264b]. Through the auspicious link thus created, one day, some wood-collectors and herdsmen with pure vision and good karma saw me flying through the sky. I was coming from the direction

of Mount Kailash, holding in each of my hands a white prayer-flag. They saw me land on the summit of the Crystal Peak, plant the prayer-flags, and fly away. They told the local people, who went to investigate. Everyone could see, on the top of Crystal Peak, a large white prayer-flag that hadn't been there before. This event aroused great faith and created auspicious circumstances for the Dharma to flourish in that area.

During the three years I practiced there, through the combination of my students' deep faith and the blessing of my having meditated on the two Bodhicittas and practiced the development and completion stages, many of my devoted disciples and patrons had pure visions. Handprints and footprints were found in places where I had walked or sat, and became objects of reverence in the mountain monasteries. Spreading the word, faithful people said, "In his sky-like meditation, he flew to the Crystal Snow Peak, and in his post-meditation, seeing all phenomena as illusion, he left footprints in the rock."

Through the combination of the compassion of the lama and the Three Jewels, the faith of the patrons [265a], and the strength of my pure aspirations, a new sun of happiness and well-being dawned: harvests were abundant, cattle were healthy, gold ore was found, and auspiciousness prevailed throughout the region. The local men and women, laypeople and clergy alike, understood that this was due to the kindness of the lama and the Three Jewels. Filled with faith, many had the good fortune to enjoy the sacred Dharma.

I told my disciples, "If the disciples have faith, devotion, and pure perception, even though the teacher has not achieved any special quality of transmission and realization, they will see signs of accomplishment. This shows how important respect, devotion, and pure perception are. I have trained myself in these, and, as a result, I have had many excellent visions. You, too, my son-like disciples, must train yourselves, and your vision will be pure." They all developed devotion, respect, and pure perception.

Then, ten of my spiritual sons, who had renounced all thoughts of this life, spent a year receiving teachings and doing retreat. Among them were Ngawang Senge, "Lion with the Power of Speech," a teacher deeply endowed with Bodhicitta; Tendzin Wangchuk, "Powerful Holder of the Doctrine," a Bönpo whose mind had turned to the Dharma; Trulshik Kunzang Rangdrol, "Self-liberated Samantabhadra, the Destroyer of illusion"; and my attendant Kalzang Sherap, "Fortunate Wisdom." I supplied them with food, clothing, and teachings. After a year, they came to see me. They first offered me a scroll painting of the mandala of the Great Compassionate One [265b], and then, for the sake of making a connection, each made a personal offering of whatever he had. Finally, with great respect they asked:

"Precious Lama, for one year you have given us food, clothing, and teachings. We are extremely grateful. Now, out of your great kindness, please give us some advice on what we should do when we leave here and wander from one secluded place to another." One of them expressed their request as a song:

Your body is the embodiment of all
    Buddhas,
Your speech is the source of the depth and
    breadth of the Dharma,
Your mind is a vast treasury of wisdom,
    love, and strength:
Lord root guru, think of us!

O Protector, though you became
    enlightened long ago,
Your loving heart could not bear
The misery beings must endure in this
    dark age.
Willingly you took another birth in
    samsara, as a human being.

Through the four skillful means of gathering,
You established on the path of higher
    rebirths and liberation
Even those most difficult to train.

All beings of this dark age are in your debt.
We, especially, are in your debt—
We beggars with little merit
Who, in search of the Dharma and a
    teacher,
Have traveled to the ends of the earth and
    met many gurus,
Yet have never met one greater than you,
    O Protector.

With compassion, you've provided us with
Food, clothes, and teachings throughout
    the year.
From the day my mother gave me life,
    until today,
I have never experienced such happiness—
I know this is the work of your grace.

As to material wealth, I have none to
    offer—
Yet, from now on, to please you,
I shall offer you my practice
As long as I live [266a].

Please give some beneficial advice
To help us when we wander from place to
    place
With no particular destination in mind.

Lord root guru, Vajradhara,
Grant your blessing that we may shatter all
    concern for this life.

I answered, "Sons, have you thought well about birth and death, about the defects of samsara? Have you given up attachment to this life? If you strongly aspire to the state of liberation and complete omniscience and decide to practice Dharma genuinely, this what you should do:

"Leave your mind to the Dharma; leave your Dharma to a beggar's life; live your beggar's life until death; leave your death to a cave. These are 'four ultimate aims'.[49]

"Cast yourself out from your place among men and take your place among dogs, and you shall find a place among celestial beings. These three are known as 'casting oneself out, taking, and finding'.

"Start with the vajra of unswerving determination, end with the vajra of indifference to what others may think of you, and, at all times, keep with you the vajra of wisdom. These are the three 'diamond-hard resolutions'.[50]

"Altogether, these ten are known as the 'ten cardinal treasures of the past saints'.

"Faith, generosity, discipline, learning, modesty, sense of shame, and insight: these are the 'seven riches of the noble ones'.

"Simple food, simple clothing, simple dwelling place, simple possessions: these are the 'four preferences of the noble ones'.

"Not returning anger for anger, insult for insult, slander for slander, blow for blow: these are the 'four Dharmas of training in virtue'.

"If you follow these, wherever you may go, you will succeed in the Dharma. Furthermore, to sever all ties and attachments, when you are wandering without preference through different countries you should do this [266b]:

When you wander from place to place,
Traveling at will throughout many regions,
Visualize your root guru on the crown of
    your head
And, in sadness or happiness, pray to him.

When you've found food and clothes and
    Dharma—
Establishing your well-being,
That is the compassion of the guru.

When you face hardships,
It is your residual karma
That has made you needy.

Even if you are lacking food and clothing,
Don't behave in evil, shameless ways.

When you beg for alms and people give
    you nothing,
Don't say harsh, angry things.

Wherever you are happy, make that place
    your homeland.
Rely on whoever is kind to you as if he or
    she were your parent.

Even if you have nothing material to offer,
When you see symbols of the enlightened
    body, speech, and mind,
Offer prostrations and circumambulations.

When you meet a good lama,
Even if you have no present to offer,
Ask him to give you a blessing with his
    hand.

Beware of bandits, thieves, and dogs:
They may harm your body and life.

Avoid meat, wine, women, garlic, and onions;
These are poison for practitioners.

To stay in towns or monasteries is very
    comfortable,
But if you linger there, attachment and
    hatred will increase.

A Dharma practitioner's place is a
    mountain hermitage;
Always remain in the wilderness.

When you see suffering and poverty,
Be compassionate; try to help.

When you perceive faults in others,
Think, "This is my own fault,"
And train in pure perception.

Life is short;
Death constantly confronts us:
Don't bother wondering if you'll have
    enough food
To eat tomorrow or the day after.

If you don't die, and if you seek it out,
You'll find the illusory wealth for what is
    needed—
But even if you did not find what you
    sought,
And you were to die of hunger,
Your next rebirth would be excellent,
Since your death had come to pass
From having sought to practice the
    Dharma.

Always be even-minded about death:
To die practicing Dharma is the best way
     to die.

In conclusion, don't think too much [267a];
Practice according to your master's
     instructions;
Don't be lazy or indifferent:
Have enthusiastic diligence.

After I gave to all my spiritual friends whatever tents, food, clothes, and other things were
needed, they asked me to their hermitages and
offered me tea. I gave them personal advice and
wrapped white scarves around their necks. On
the day they were leaving, we offered an elaborate *ganachakra* feast and I gave a silver coin to
each brother and sister. Then, with a sad heart, I
sang this song to those assembled there:

Lama of unrepayable kindness.
Remain at the *chakra* of great bliss on the
     crown of my head.
In this life, in future lives, and in the *bardo*,
Be my escort and my refuge.

Listen, fortunate disciples
With faith and pure *samaya*,
Who have come from everywhere,
     highlands and lowlands,
Drawn by the power of your karma and
     aspirations.

At Darchen, the village of the Great Flag,[51]
     at Mount Kailash,
Summer sees the traders gather for the
     market;
Autumn sees them depart again,
Each going his separate way.

Likewise, we yogins, master and disciples,
Gathered at this holy place.
Having completed years or months of retreat,
And formed new links of affection,
Are now about to go our separate ways.

Realizing that the day will surely come
When I shall pass beyond this world, alone,

I think about impermanence and death
     [267b].
When I consider this carefully,
I see that nothing at all has any meaning.

Practice the Dharma, which does have
     meaning;
Become a pure renunciate,
And apply yourself single-mindedly to
     practice
In remote mountain retreats.

Even if we, teacher and disciples,
Don't meet again in this life,
I pray that in future lives
We meet again many times in a Pure Realm.

Tears fell from their eyes; touching their heads to
my feet, they offered this song of good wishes:

Peerless king who has conquered
The relentless enemy—the obscuring
     emotions—
Lord, farewell!

Youthful physician who can remove
The cataract of our ignorance—
Lord, farewell!

Authentic guru who gives food, clothing
     and Dharma
To all humble practitioners,
Lord, farewell!

Wish-fulfilling gem
Who grants all ordinary and extraordinary
     siddhis,
Lord, farewell!

Universal monarch
Who leads all sentient beings to the
     Dharma,
Each one of whom was once our own
     mother,
Lord, farewell!

Buddha of the three times
You who have exhausted all faults,

And developed all good qualities,
Lord, farewell!

From now on, until we attain
    enlightenment,
Lord, care for us always.

The disciples who were to depart left in tears, making many prayers. The assembled friends remaining behind were so moved that they wept as well. For some distance, they accompanied their friends who were traveling to Nepal and then intended to wander on from place to place, with no particular destination in mind [268a].

After more than two years had passed in this great sacred place, I often talked to my disciples about leaving, and one day I sang this song:

In a small willow grove
The cuckoo flies happily here and there.
But once he gets entangled in a net,
He regrets his carelessness.

Now he severs his ties to the willow grove
And, freed, flies back into the heavens.
The cuckoo makes his way through the
    blue sky—
The place where the white vulture soars.

In the cool shallow waters,
The fish swims happily here and there.
But once he is caught on a steel-blue hook,
He regrets his carelessness.

Now he breaks out from shallow water,
And swims comfortably in the pure depths.
The fish makes his way to the ocean—
The playground of the great whales.

In the quiet mountain retreat,
The yogin lives happily amid his disciples,
But once he is caught by the Lord of Death
He will regret his heedlessness.

Now, breaking the ties to this life,
Traveling here and there to pleasant
    regions
He will make his way to other solitudes
Where past sages once stayed.

Realizing that I was thinking of leaving, Rabgye and other disciples presented many reasons why I should stay one or two more years to help them, and offered this song:

You are the fire-crystal, the sun,
Born in the land beyond the ocean [268b].
Because you dispel the darkness of the four
    continents,
The beings here are happy;
The wild flowers of this meadow
Will sadden without you.
Please remain in the azure heights,
Continuing to illuminate us.

You are the white snow lioness of the
    glaciers,
Born in the high snow ranges.
Because you rule over the savage beasts,
All other animals are joyful;
The wild creatures of the forest
Will sadden without you.
Please remain on these mountain slopes,
Tossing your turquoise mane.

You are the authentic guru,
Born in Domey.
Because you came to benefit others,
Everyone is joyful;
Your followers and disciples,
Will be saddened without you.
Please remain in this great sacred place,
Granting us your teachings.

When they thus entreated me, I could not resist their pleas; I had to promise to stay on a while longer. I then sang this song:

Roaming the ordinary jungle,
The Bengal tiger longed for the
    sandalwood forest.
Forsaking the ordinary jungle,
He reached the sandalwood forest—

The place where tigers display their
splendid stripes.

Roaming on the glacier's edge
The white lion longed for the heights of the
ice-peak.
Forsaking the glacier's edge,
He made his way to the highest ice peak—
The place where snow lions toss their
turquoise manes.

Roaming at random from place to place,
The yogin longed for the solitude of the
wild mountains [269a].
Forsaking his wanderings,
He made his way to this sublime sacred
place—
The place where yogins practice
meditation.

Pleased with this, the disciples made offerings,
and held a fine *ganachakra* feast. At the end of it
they sang this joyful song:

The fragrant lotus flower
Gives off a most delicious scent,
Even seeming content to do so;
It unfolds itself petal by petal.
Striped like small tigers,
Humming our contentment,
We bees fly easily through space
In joyful celebration of the lotus flower.

The dark and cool southern cloud
Lets fall a gentle rain,
Even seeming content to do so,
It unfolds its varied transformations.
Fanning out ocellated iridescent feathers,
We peacocks arrange ourselves on the solid
earth;
In joyful celebration of the thunder dragon
We dance in our contentment.

The authentic root guru,
Has given profound instructions,
And even seems to enjoy doing so.
His mind replete with the Dharma.
Wc, his fortunate disciples,
Prepare an excellent mansion

To hold a feast with song and dance
In joyful celebration of these teachings.

Jigme Gyaltsen and a few other disciples said:
"Today we are indeed fortunate [269b]. Precious lama, to benefit our minds, please sing a song of spiritual advice, and a short song in praise of this sacred mountain and the two lakes."
I sang this song:

Here is Manasarovar, the great turquoise lake,
The fountainhead of the four great rivers.
Here dwells the naga king,[52]
The Lord who bestows upon this land
Prosperity and auspiciousness.

Here is the Vulture Peak, Kailash,
The center of the world,
Where people of four human races come
and go.
Here dwells the Buddha himself,
The lord who turns the Wheel of Dharma
For the sake of sentient beings.

The wish-granting jewel
Comes from a distant ocean.
To free all beings from poverty.
It is now set at the pinnacle of the victory
banner
And rains down all our needs:
Whoever has a wish, come and fulfill it!

The renunciate Tsogdruk Rangdrol,
Was born in Domey,
Yet to benefit the Dharma and sentient
beings,
From the slopes of the Snow Mountain
He now showers whatever Dharma one
might wish for:
Whoever has an interest, come and listen.

The fragrant, exquisite lotus flower,
Will one day be spoiled by frost,
Its stalk will be wilted, its petals left behind.
Now, while it is still splendid and vivid,
Fortunate bees, gather up the sweet nectar!

This human body, complete with its
freedoms and endowments,

Will one day be vanquished by death;
Its flesh and bone will decompose.
Now, fortunate disciples, while you are
    young,
Meditate according to the vast and
    profound instructions!

Although the fire-crystal sun itself is
    burning hot,
When that very sun comes up,
Its coming is a boon to the waterfowl [270a].
When they go to swim upon the lotus lake,
Calling out sweetly, they are perfectly
    content.
Look at them, playful, almost dancing
In the fresh lotus-leaf groves.

Hard circumstances may well occur,
Yet they can come as boons for
    practitioners.
When practitioners meditate on Bodhicitta,
And traverse the paths and stages,
They are perfectly content.
Look at them, in mountain solitudes,
Seeking to tame their minds!

Palace of Chakrasamvara
Abode of five hundred arhats,
Celestial land of dakas and dakinis,
Seat of the *siddhas* of the past,
Center of this Jambudvipa world—
Here is Kailash, the White Mountain!

Completing a single circumambulation
Of this great sacred place
Will purify the evil actions of one's entire
    life.

Palace of the eight great nagas,
Playground of *mamos* and dakinis,
Gathering place of the gods who take
    delight in virtue,
Growing place of the Rose-apple Tree,
Source of the four great rivers—
Here is the turquoise lake, Manasarovar!

Just bathing here or drinking the water
Will purify negative actions and the
    obscuring emotions.

Make offerings here, do prostrations;
Circumambulate this glacial lake, faithful
    ones!
It will purify your bad karma, unwhole-
    some deeds, and obscurations,
And you will reap blessings and
    accomplishments.

After I sang this, they prostrated themselves with fervent devotion, offered many words of gratitude, and returned to their hermitages.

Almost three years had passed since I had come. I said to all my disciples [270b]:

"In the past, holy beings never stayed in one place for more than one or two years. This was not because they were unable to remain, it was for the exalted purpose of benefiting themselves and others. I have been in this excellent place three years now. I have taught you whatever I know, without keeping anything back. If you practice, you will be able to accomplish your aims.

"Owing to your kindness, disciples and patrons, in these three years, I, too, was able to complete my retreat, thus benefiting myself. Benefit for both self and others having been accomplished, it would be best if we parted now in such excellent circumstances and mutual satisfaction. Now, it is time to go: there is no point in trying to delay my departure."

I explained to them at length why there was no reason to try to dissuade me from leaving, and at the end I sang this song:

Once the proper number of days has passed
No one can keep the moon
From moving on to other continents.
Powerful *mantradharas*, now it is your task
To guard the garden of white lotuses
From the threat of hail!

Once the cold winds and rains have come,
No one can keep the bees
From moving down into the jungles.
Warm southern clouds, now it is your task
To guard the flowers, the meadow's
    ornaments,
From the threat of frost!

Once the time to leave has come [271a],
No one can keep the yogin
From moving on to another place.
Powerful dharmapalas, now it is your task
To guard the assembly of fortunate
    disciples,
From the threat of disease and evil spirits!

My disciples from Toding, Tashigang, and
Purang did prostrations and said to me politely:
    "Precious lama, wherever you go, you do
nothing but benefit others. Yet, the benefit of
helping a single being here, in this dark barbarian country, is far greater than that of helping
one hundred beings in central Tibet, where the
Dharma is well-established. A starving person is
much happier with a handful of plain *tsampa*
than is a well-fed person with a plateful of but-
tery *tsampa*.
    "We are grateful indeed for the teachings
you have given us, but how can we, who are so
stupid, comprehend all these teachings at once?
Please teach us more, until we understand thoroughly what to adopt and what to abandon.
There have been many instances of *siddhas* stopping the sun. Even if it is time for you to leave,
please stay another year or two!"
    They emphasized the reasons I should stay,
finally condensing them into this song [271b]:

When the sun above, the sole ornament of
    the southern continent,
Moves on to the western continent,
Each being of the southern continent feels
    his own sun has set.

Lord, compassionate guru of sentient beings,
If you move on to another country
Each of us, unprotected disciples,
Will suffer as though his own protector has
    gone.

Once, when the sun that dispels darkness
Was to leave for another continent,
It was seized by an ancient *siddha*,
And for many days stood still.

Look at the life-stories of so many *siddhas* of
    the past—

How they prepared to leave for the sake of
    other beings,
And yet would prolong their stay for many
    years
When supplicated by their faithful
    disciples.

Compassionate lord, protector of beings,
You ought to leave and help those
    elsewhere who need your care;
Yet, because of our faith and yearning,
You must stay for at least a year or two
    more.

How can small children learn right away
How to behave—to eat and do things
    properly?
Over and over again, their mother must
    teach them.

How can we disciples with confused minds
Understand properly right away
The causes and consequences of our
    actions
And the depth and breadth of Dharma?
Please teach us the Dharma again and
    again!

I replied, "I have no answer for that; I'll
have to stay." They were all exceedingly happy
and said to me, "Just as a king's statement is
irreversible, since you, our lama [272a], the
Buddha of the three times, have said you will
stay, it would be wrong for you to change your
mind again. On this occasion, please sing a beneficial song." I sang this:

Just as, even having searched and searched,
No one can ever find a royal white eagle
That has died of starvation,
No one will ever find the bones of a
    practitioner
Who died of hunger.

Indians, with their waterwheel,
Bring a river to the top of the hill.
When a practitioner takes to the
    mountains,
Provisions will naturally find their way up.

Just as an old dog asleep in the center of a
    road
Gets hit by lots of stones,
A meditator who comes down to the
    villages
Attracts lots of loose talk.

If there is some meat and there is a cat,
To say the cat won't eat that meat is
    nonsense.
If there are a monk and a nun, near to
    each other,
Sooner or later, they're going to break
    their vows.

For the mouth to eat something very
    delicious,
The hands must work very hard.
To obtain the lasting bliss of Buddhahood,
One must diligently practice Dharma.

Birds and wild animals
Stay wherever they are content.
Practitioners should stay
Wherever their practice progresses.

If the snow lion lives in the snows,
Its turquoise mane grows lavish.
If the meditator stays in remote mountains
His meditation will flourish.

A cat may look like it's fast asleep,
But it hasn't forgotten about mice.
A meditator may stay up in the mountains,
But not forget about food and clothes.

A fish lives in the water,
But a hook pulls it out onto dry land.
A meditator may live up in the mountains,
But his craving drives him back into town.

Hanging around with dogs,
You'll soon get bitten [272b].
Hanging around with coarse companions,
You'll be stained by their bad behavior.

Ants scurrying around here and there
May get stuck in some pine-pitch.

Practitioners running around doing too
    much
May never finish the practices they've
    begun.

When grain has been planted in a field,
Fodder grass will come up as well.
When you practice Dharma from your
    heart,
Food and clothing will come to you as well.

Whoever fights his enemy to the limit of his
    strength
Is called a warrior, a hero.
Whoever endures hardships to the limit of
    his strength
To practice the Dharma,
Enjoys renown among men and gods.

To the noble ones
Gold nuggets and stones are the same.
A practitioner who exhausts desire
Becomes the same as those noble ones.

When, in summer, fruit trees are in bloom,
They are lavishly decked in blossoms and
    fruit.
When, in autumn, the earth pales,
The fruits and flowers vanish.

When you have full youth and vigor,
Your mother and father are at your side.
When you grow old and needful,
These kind parents are gone.

A Chinese woman's silk brocades,
With all their exquisite shades and
    patterns,
Gradually grow older and more worn; in
    the end
They are no different from rags of cotton.

Our own body, radiant with good health
That we owe to the good care of our par-
    ents,
Gradually decays from youth to old age,
Becoming not much different from a
    corpse.

The flowers of summertime,
Troubled with frosts again and again,
Lose their elegant carriage and
Bend their heads toward the earth.

The body of our youth,
Troubled by illness again and again,
Loses its power and strength—
Once erect, it is now stooped and bent.

My hair is getting grey;
I'm losing my teeth;
No matter in what light I look at it,
I am going to die;
I can't help but feel dismay [273a].

When reasoning, the wish-granting tree,
Is shaken by the wind of impermanence,
Its leaves, melancholy songs like this,
Lie scattered everywhere.

This song prompted higher aspirations and a strong feeling of renunciation in many disciples. When I had finished my retreat and was about to set out on a pilgrimage, I sang this:

In the turquoise lake of Manasarovar
Lives the golden-eyed fish;
Circumambulating the lake toward the
    right,
It goes on to the waters of the Ganges.[53]

In the Snow Mountain Cave of Miracles
Lives the renunciate yogin;
Circumambulating the Snow Mountain
    toward the right,
He now goes on to other solitudes.

Glacier-lake, sole ornament of the world,
You are a celestial palace.
Deities and dakinis who dwell here,
Care for beings as if they were your own
    children.

This holy glacier's lake
Was the abode of past sages.
You who wish to practice Dharma,
Live in this sacred place.

From the Ever-cool Lake,
Rivers flow in the four directions:
They will not meet again
Until they merge in the great ocean.

Leaving this sacred place,
Master and disciples travel to the four
    directions:
They will meet not again
Until they meet in the next life.

The luminous sun of our world
Is far away in the sky;
Still, from dawn till dusk,
It benefits the lotus garden.

The authentic root guru
May reside far away;
Still, he benefits the faithful [273b]
In this life and in the next.

Worthy disciples,
We have met but for a moment in this life.
In future lives, when we meet again,
May we remain together for a long time.

Saddened by parting from their teacher, some disciples wept.

During the waxing moon of the fifth month in the year called "Rich with Power,"[54] I circumambulated the Snow Mountain. I first reached Gyangdrak Monastery[55] on the south face. There I performed the offering to the Snow Mountain, and offered donations and tea to the sangha. I met Serphuk Lama Rinpoche and requested from him the transmission of the preliminary practices for the Fivefold Mahamudra of the victorious Drigungpa.[56]

I then traveled on to the western ridge to Nyenpa Ridzong,[57] where I saw the Chöku Rinpoche statue.[58] I performed the offering to the Snow Mountain, and offered donations and tea to the monastic community. There, too, lived Dordzin Rinpoche,[59] a true Bodhisattva. When I first met him, the very sight of him had caused my mind to merge with his. During the three years I spent at Kailash, he had supplied me with whatever I needed and I felt extremely grateful to him. I requested from him the empowerment of the *Thirteen Deities of Chakrasamvara's Mandala*, and presenting him with offerings of gold, silver, and valuables, I asked for his spiritual protection. Before leaving, I offered him this letter of good wishes:

> Your body is the unchanging vajra body;
> Your speech is the free-flowing melody of Brahma;
> Your mind rests in unwavering samadhi.
> Lord, hidden Buddha, think of me.
>
> Long ago, you attained the body of ultimate union,
> Yet you assumed again the form of a vajra holder
> To carry the burden of liberating all beings, our mothers [274a]:
> Your life is the most sublime of all!
>
> Attracted by this holy place, I, a beggar, came.
> For three years, I remained in this perfect place
> And had the good fortune to practice meditation—
> This is all your grace, O lord guru, refuge of beings!
>
> Lord with the sweet-sounding name "Victory Banner of the Dharma,"
> Compassionate refuge, protector of beings,
> I beg you to remain for many years
> As the crown ornament of all the disciples here.
>
> Like hay carried off by a gusty wind,
> I, the renunciate beggar Tsogdruk Rangdrol,
> Was brought here on the strength of my karma and aspirations;
> Now, I shall go on to other countries.
>
> Like the cuckoo that, sweetly singing,
> Flies off to distant places,
> So I, expounding the profound Dharma,
> Go off to distant solitudes.

> Like the eagle that soars higher and higher in the sky
> And flies off to whichever land it chooses,
> So, I, having circumambulated this holy place,
> Go on, as I please, to other holy places.
>
> Protector, never cease to care
> For your disciples in this region.
> In this life and in all my lives,
> May I meet you many times again.

After I offered him this, he spoke to me at length and with great kindness; he gave me provisions and other useful things for my journey.

On the northern face I visited Drithim Phuk, The Cave in which the Dri Vanished,[60] and made offerings to Mount Kailash and to the sangha [274b]. During the *ganachakra* offering, the great accomplished practitioners of this place sang vajra songs and performed Dharma dances in a most joyous manner.

I finally came back to the eastern face. There, too, at the Cave of Miracles, I performed the offering to the Snow Mountain, and made donations and a distribution of tea to the sangha. I gave alms to all the poor people and supplies to the resident monks and disciples for their retreats. Before setting off we held a great *ganachakra* feast, and I blessed all those gathered there, praying that they might encounter no obstacles in their spiritual practice. I ended with these words:

"Worthy disciples, listen carefully and remember these words. The strength of our previous karma and pure aspirations naturally brought us here, without anyone having called us to come together. Now, having spent three years in retreat, we must part. This illustrates the impermanence of this world—everything is transitory, changing more with every year. One cannot count on anything at all. Before reaching the age of eighty, most of us will have already left for our next lives. There is neither order nor fixed time for our deaths.

"Who of us can say that, tonight, he won't leave his relatives and loved ones to wander alone through the *bardo*? To postpone practicing, believing that things last, is to waste the precious opportunity to practice Dharma. Don't crave, don't be attached to anything; dedicate yourself right now to practicing Dharma [275a]. To practice it from the bottom of your heart, follow the instructions of the *Lion's Roar*,[61] which the divine Lord Atisha gave on his departure to Lhatsun Changchup Ö."[62]

I gave them the transmission for this text from memory and, adding, "Here is the conclusion of all my teachings, my parting advice," I sang this:

Lord root guru Vajradhara,
Remain upon the crown of my head,
As the ornament of the *chakra* of great bliss.

I pray that you turn toward the Dharma
The minds of these sons and daughters of mine,
And put an end to all thoughts contrary to the Dharma.

Faithful disciples assembled here,
Listen to this beneficial advice:

At all times, ceaselessly,
Pray to the kind lord guru,
Whose kindness can never be repaid.

This human body is a very rare support to find;
Now that you have found it, practice the essence of Dharma.

It is certain that we will all die, but uncertain when;
Dismiss concern for this life alone.

The sufferings of the lower realms are difficult to bear;
To find protection from fear, take refuge.

The consequences of actions are inevitable;
Give up wrongs acts and perform virtuous ones.

There is no happiness anywhere in samsara;
Strive to find the way out of it.

To do so there are three trainings,
The ground of which is discipline.
You should guard it as you guard your own eyes.

All sentient beings have been your kind parents [275b];
Care for them with kindness and compassion,
And strive for their enlightenment.

The practice of the six *paramitas* encompasses all Dharmas;
Practice these six continuously.

The Secret Mantrayana is the swiftest path;
It is important to practice it in secrecy.

If you wish to practice in this way,
Remain in a remote mountain retreat.

Buddhahood is not gained by practicing for a few months or years;
You must practice the whole length of your life:
This is crucial.

This my ultimate advice;
Were I to die now, I would have no other testament.

Pray that you may put the Dharma into practice,
Free from obstacles and deviations.

They offered me whatever wealth they possessed, with touching words, gestures, and feelings of immeasurable sadness. Requesting an elaborate protection, they offered this song:

You are our unfailing protector—
In this and future lives, and in the *bardo*.
You are our eyes—
The eyes for those of us who have been blinded
By ignorance and unawareness.

Supreme physician
Who clears away the disease of conflicting
    emotions,
Merciful lord, root guru,
If you go somewhere else,
We will be like blind men lost in the
    middle of a plain.

Unable to leave, unable to stay—
What should we disciples do?

Just as a small child who, left behind
By his mother, bursts into tears,
We cannot bear being parted from you;
Yet, having to part, we cannot help weeping.

Like a small child left behind
Who remembers his mother and
Calls out for her again and again [276a],
We, the disciples who have been left
    behind,
Again and again will make prayers to you.

Just like a good mother gone away to the
    mountains
Who does not forget her child,
But keeps him always in her heart—
Protector, wherever you go,
Keep hold of us with your compassion.

May you travel happily, lord,
Ferryman who carries us across this lake of
    samsara.

May you travel happily, lord,
Guide who shows us the path to liberation.

May you travel happily, lord,
Physician-king who cures the sickness
Of the five poisons, the obscuring
    emotions.

May you travel happily, lord,
King of Dharma, who bestows all wealth,
And protects from all miseries.

May you travel happily, lord,
Powerful Indra, displaying your physical
    manifestation

To all beings who are in need of being
    tamed.

May you travel happily, Lord Brahma,
Proclaiming the Dharma with your
    melodious voice.

May you travel happily, lord, omniscient
    Buddha,
You who regard all phenomena within the
    continuum
That is the empty brilliance of your
    realized mind.

May we see your face again and again,
In this life and beyond, and in the *bardo*.

Lord, may we, your disciples, be reborn
In whichever Buddhafield you dwell.

Following their offering, I dedicated the merit,
made extensive wishes for auspiciousness, and
sang a song expressing the prayer that in the
future we, students and disciples, might meet in
the Pure Realms.

Our escort through this life, future lives,
    and the *bardo*,
Protector and refuge, wish-fulfilling gem
    [276b],
Never apart from me, remain on the
    crown of my head,
And rain blessings and accomplishments.

All of us, teacher and disciples,
Gathered from all over Tibet,
Now must go our separate ways:
How can we not feel sad?

All of you white snow lions,
Roaming about in the high snows,
Tossing your beautiful turquoise
    manes,
Stay here in these same snows.

Having circled the mountain once,
The sage, the white eagle,
Glancing back at the Snow Mountain
Continues on toward distant places.

Brother and sister disciples
Who live on the four sides of Kailash,
Stay in this great sacred place
And further your practice.

The renunciate Tsogdruk Rangdrol came
    here
Once in this lifetime;
Regarding everything and everyone with
    pure perception,
He now goes on to distant countries.

You might hear of me later,
But we will never meet again.
This will have been our only meeting.

So, keep my heart's advice in your
    hearts.
Even if we don't meet again in this
    life,
I pray that, in a future life, we come
    together
In the eastern Buddhafield of Pure Joy.

At the end of my song, most of the monks and disciples were in tears; for a moment no one could speak.

Then they all accompanied me down to Dzongdo and, having prostrated themselves before me and circled me with reverence, they remained there [277a]. I walked on, looking back from time to time; as long as they could see me they stood there transfixed, and then slowly returned to their dwellings.

Leaving the snow mountain, I went to teach in nearby Gangsakpa and Barkha Tasam. That night I dreamed that I sailed across a great lake in a boat, that I rode across a plain covered in filth, and that great wealth came to me.

Combining pilgrimage with teaching, I went to Tsegyeh Monastery,[63] to the households of Gopa Rinchen and Nyala Chukpo, to Dochu Monastery, Pretapuri,[64] and Khyung Lung Monastery. In each of these places, I made offerings to all the sacred sites and shrines. After I gave teaching to the patrons, Gopa Rinchen offered me a tent worth forty silver *sang* and five gold *sho*. Other patrons offered me many valuables—gold, silver, clothing, ornaments and food.

I then continued on, visiting the monasteries on the banks of Manasarovar, Serkyi Chakyip Gonpa (the Golden Bird-shelter), Bönri Gonpa (the Monastery of the Bön Mountain), Sera Lung Gonpa (the Monastery of the Hailstorm Valley), and Bön Phuk Gonpa (the Monastery of the Bön Cave).[65] Everywhere, I offered tea, alms, and prayers. Then with some nomads from Hor and Tö, I went on to Rong Limi.

Here many patrons from the Valley of the Crystal Peak came to see me [277b]. Giving them teachings, I was able to turn their minds to the Dharma. Many offered me food and clothing. I went on, visiting the main families on the southern face of the Rong glacier, and having visited successively upper, lower, and central Purang, I gave to several thousand monks, disciples, and householders empowerments of the Great Compassionate One and of longevity, as well as transmissions and instructions for the development and completion stage practices of *yidam* deities.

In all these places I gave appropriate teachings. First, I would ask the disciples to practice the meditation and recitation of Vajrasattva to become suitable recipients for the teachings. Next, they would visualize the lama as Buddha Vajradhara upon the crowns of their heads and receive his blessing. Then, I would give some general teaching like this:

You must attend this teaching with a good heart and think, "As fast as I can, I must attain the precious and unsurpassable level of Buddhahood for the sake of all sentient beings, my mothers, whose number is unfathomable like the sky. For this purpose, I shall first listen to the sacred and profound teaching from this holy and glorious lama, and from today onward, I shall practice them.

The *Vajra Peak Tantra* says:[66]

Gathering your attention,
Listen to the teaching with a pure
    heart.

The *Udanavarga* says:[67]

Giving up dullness and laziness,
Listen with supreme joy.

The *Garland of Rebirths* says:[68]

> As a patient listens to a doctor,
> Listen to the teaching with the
>   intention of applying it [278a].

"According to these words, listen to the teaching with a perfect attitude and respectful manners.

"Now that we have gained this great vessel—this life with its freedoms and endowments—we must cross the vast, awesome ocean of samsara. Why? Owing to virtuous deeds we have performed in the past, we now have the extraordinary good fortune to possess a precious human body with five unimpaired senses; we are able to speak and reflect. We have been accepted by a spiritual teacher, have met the teachings of the Victorious One, and are able to practice them. At this point, knowing what we should do, if we fail to practice the Dharma—the surest way to free ourselves from the wheel of samsara—we will find out how difficult it is to gain such an existence in the future and how exceedingly rare it is to meet the Dharma. The Buddha said:

> Countless realms fill this universe—
> To be born on the continent of
>   Jambudvipa is rare,
> To obtain a sound human body is
>   exceedingly rare.

As it is stated in *The Tantra of the Enlightenment of Mahavairocana*:[69]

> The omniscient ones in this world
> Are like the Udumbara flower:
> In a hundred kalpas, one may or may
>   not appear.
> The Secret Mantrayana tradition is
>   even more rare.

Lord Tsongkhapa said:

> To obtain a human body and meet
>   the Dharma
> Is very rare: it has happened just this
>   once.

> Right now is a unique chance to
>   accomplish something meaningful
>   [278b].
> Consider this, and use this human
>   body for what is essential.

The omniscient Longchen Rabjam said:

> To gain this human body is one
>   chance in a hundred.
> Moreover, to meet the Dharma is as
>   rare as seeing a star in the daytime,
> And to meet the Dharma of the supreme
>   vehicle is next to impossible.
> So *now* is the time to practice the
>   sacred teachings wholeheartedly.

"As these quotations say, we must practice the Dharma. Not to do so would be worse than a seafaring captain returning empty-handed from the treasure-island. It would be like being a living corpse, or like a person having gone insane though not possessed by an evil spirit. It would be more senseless than filling with spit and excrement a vase made of precious jewels. The *Letter to a Friend* says:[70]

> To take rebirth as a human being,
> And still engage in evil acts,
> Is more foolish than to own
> A golden vessel studded with jewels,
> And use it as a dustbin or a chamber
>   pot.

"Thus on top of missing the path of liberation the fool will fall into the abyss of the three lower realms, where, for many millions of kalpas, he won't even hear the word 'happiness' [279a]. In *Engaging in the Bodhisattva's Activity*[71] one finds:

> If I do not practice virtue,
> And instead accumulate negative acts,
> In many hundred millions of kalpas
> I shall not even hear of the higher
>   realms.

"There is no person in the world more foolish than one who, hoping to gain a little food and clothing for this life, accumulates evil deeds and thus cuts himself off from happiness in future lives. Again, in *Engaging in the Bodhisattva's Activity* it is said:

> Having found such freedom,
> If I do not practice virtue,
> There is no greater delusion,
> No greater mistake.

"At death, such degenerate, ignorant, and destructive individuals are just objects of compassion for the Buddhas and Bodhisattvas. The great master Padmasambhava said:

> A free, well-favored human birth is so
>   hard to obtain!
> When the Lord of Death strikes one
>   down in agony,
> How sad for those who are empty-
>   handed,
> Who lack the Dharma!

Men and women, you must discriminate between that which is important and that which is not by asking yourselves, examining any act, large or small, "Is this in accord with the Dharma or not?" Padampa Sangye[72] said:

> One without courage rarely attains
>   Buddhahood;
> Be equal to hardship, Tingri folk!
>
> If you don't have time *now*, you will
>   never find time later;
> This is your one meal in a hundred
>   chances, Tingri folk!
>
> Recognize what is truly important;
> Don't waste your entire lives, Tingri
>   folk!

"As these words say, 'Now that you have been born this time in a land where the Dharma flourishes, don't go empty-handed to your next life.'

"Wise, skillful, and courageous men and women: you have gained a precious human body;

try to make it meaningful and satisfying. You may ask, 'If I just practice when it's convenient, is that enough?' No. That won't do. Why? Because, although you have gained this precious human life, it won't endure; it is subject to death [279b]. The Buddha said:

> When there is birth, there is death;
> When there is growth, there is decay.
>
> Youth does not endure;
> Radiant health is carried off by
>   illness,
>
> Life is carried off by death:
> There are no lasting phenomena.

The great master Padmasambhava said:

> Failing to understand
> That all things are impermanent and
>   unreliable,
> We continue to cling to samsara.
>
> Throughout our lives we are wishing
>   for happiness,
> But our lives are consumed by
>   suffering.
> We fritter away this human birth,
> Wasting its freedoms and endowments
> On the paths of distraction.
>
> A sick man at the point of death
> Is like a lamp running out of oil.
> Once the conditions for maintaining
>   life have been exhausted,
> There is no way to remain.

"Thus, there is not one sentient being who, once having been born, will not die. There are no exceptions; there is no possible doubt. The master Asvaghosha said:

> Have you ever seen, heard, or even
>   suspected
> That there is anyone on this earth or
>   in the higher realms,
> Who, having been born, has not died?

"Great spiritual masters and eminent rulers, fabulously wealthy monarchs and starving beggars, newborn babies and eighty-year-old men—no one escapes the Lord of Death [280a]. Even so, most of you in this village—old parents, young children, beloved spouses and relatives—assume you will stay and make a lot of plans. But when that devil, the Lord of Death, shows up, you won't be able to stay even for an instant longer. Think about those who, without Dharma, walk empty-handed to the land of the next life.

"None of us here is beyond death. Like animals drawing near to the slaughterhouse, taking one step after the other, every year, month, morning, and evening, we draw nearer to the formidable jaws of the Lord of Death. The *Udanavarga* says:

> Those whose fate it is to be butchered,
> Come nearer and nearer to their
>   slaughter
> With each and every step they take.
> So, too, goes the life of man.

"The girl Saleh Ö, 'Brilliant Light',[73] said to Jetsun Milarepa:

> Owing to the merit accrued in
>   previous lives,
> I have, this once, gained a human
>   body.
> Now, years and months push me from
>   behind,
> Days and hours pull me from ahead—
> Each moment I come nearer to the
>   dreaded death.
>
> Thinking about it, this girl feels
>   dismay
> And longs to practice the blessed
>   Dharma.

"Death is certain; when it will occur is not. Today you may have a beautiful, bright countenance, and by tonight, tomorrow, or the day after, have turned suddenly into a stinking, rotting corpse. This has happened to so many beings, yet not one of them thought, 'By tomorrow, I'll be dead.'

"This body, a combination of the four elements, cannot be depended upon to endure even for as long as it takes to eat a meal. Our breath is just vapor, bodily heat a mere spark; at any moment they might vanish [280b].

"Practice the Dharma *now*, when you have the chance to do so, this year rather than next, today rather than tomorrow: there is no time for being idle. The Victorious Kalzang Gyatso[74] said:

> In the morning, you sit there, excited
>   and healthy,
> Talking about how to take care of
>   your friends
> And finish off your enemies.
>
> By dusk, at the sky-burial rock,
> Your corpse is fed to vultures
> And gets eaten by dogs.
>
> Isn't that really what happens?

"And in *Engaging in the Bodhisattva's Activity* it says:

> Don't be heedless, thinking, 'I'm not
>   going to die just yet—at least, not
>   today.'

"And in the *Udanavarga*:

> There is no saying which comes first,
> Tomorrow, or the next life:
> Rather than making plans for tomor-
>   row,
> Work for your future lives.

"When death comes you won't gain much from the achievements of this life—the houses you've built, the wealth you've accumulated, your acquaintances, children, spouse, servants, or possessions: only the Dharma can help you. In the *Sutra of Manjushri's Perfect Emanation*[75] it is said:

> Your parents will be no refuge,
> Neither will your friends or relatives.
> You will leave all of them behind,
> And go on, all alone, to your next life.

"Also, the Great Master, Padmasambhava, said:

Even if the King of Physicians
    appears,
When your life span is exhausted,
He cannot prolong it.
A powerful man cannot prohibit
    death;
A persuasive man cannot not talk his
    way out of it;
A rich man cannot buy his way out of it.

You will have no power to take
    wealth,
Food and possessions with you [281a]:
Despite yourself, you will go,
Like a hair plucked out of butter.[76]

"When death arrives, the power and influence of a universal monarch will not help in the slightest. Rich as Vaishravana, the god of wealth, you won't be able to take as much as a sesame seed with you. None of the parents, brothers, sisters, relatives, and friends who surround you can go with you. This is certain: at one point you will *have* to leave, like a hair pulled from butter. You will go alone, without protection, without refuge, along the long, narrow, unfamiliar, unpredictable track of the *bardo*, where you will experience terrifying hallucinations, beyond imagination.

"Then, except for the holy Dharma and your guides—the lama and the Three Jewels—you will have no other assistance. No help will come from wealth, friends, and relatives of this life. But that's not all: driven on by your karma and obscuring emotions, you will wander through the three realms of samsara; from then on there will not be a moment of happiness, only suffering.

"Born in the hell realms, you will suffer unbearable heat and cold. Born a hungry ghost, you will suffer the pangs of hunger and thirst. Born as an animal you will suffer from stupidity, and from being abused, killed, or eaten alive [281b]. Born as a human you will suffer birth, ageing, sickness, and death. Born as a demi-god you will suffer from rivalry and fighting. Even if born as a celestial being, you will later suffer

from transience when falling from that realm. The possibilities for suffering are limitless. In the *Sutra of Intent Mindfulness*[77] one reads:

Beings in the infernal realms
Must endure being burnt in the fires
    of hell;
Animals must endure being eaten by
    others;
Hungry ghosts must endure hunger
    and thirst;
Humans must endure a short lifespan;
Asuras must endure quarreling and
    fighting;
And gods must suffer from their own
    heedlessness.
Thus in all of samsara there is no
    place—
Even one as small as a needle-tip—
Where real happiness is to be found.

"The Great Master Padmasambhava said:

These sentient beings circle through
The cities of the six realms
From which they never find release,
Like a water-wheel, continuously
Turning round and round—how sad!

"Marpa of Lodrak said:

Son, ponder the miseries of samsara.
Even if I were to manifest miraculously a hundred tongues
And expound the sufferings of
    samsara for myriad aeons,
I could never fully put those sufferings
    into words.
Don't let the holy Dharma go to
    waste!
This is my advice.

"Thus, the suffering in samsara is fathomless. No matter where you are born, high or low, samsara is a place of suffering. Your companions are your companions in suffering; your enjoyments are the enjoyments of suffering. Whatever you do will prove the source for additional suffering.

"Therefore, as if you had discovered yourself to be in a dark prison, you must try to escape from samsara [282a]. You must escape from this immense ocean, the torment of cyclic existence, in which you are driven on by the swelling waves of karma and the obscuring emotions, where the terrifying sea monsters of the three sufferings abound.

"Still, setting yourself free is not enough at all. All beings have been your kind parents in previous lives: you must liberate them from samsara. To do this you need first to attain Buddhahood, in which all defects are exhausted and all enlightened qualities perfected. For that, the Buddha taught infinite approaches to the Dharma. The *Sutra of Individual Liberation*[78] summarizes these:

> Doing no evil whatsoever,
> Practice virtue perfectly,
> Tame your mind completely:
> This is the teaching of the Buddha.

"This means giving up negative acts and performing wholesome ones. 'Negative' means attachment to oneself, aversion toward others, and mental darkness. These three poisons lead to the ten negative acts—killing, taking what is not given, sexual misconduct, lying, slander, harsh words, gossip, greed, harmful thoughts, and wrong views [282b]. You should never commit these ten acts, or induce others to commit them, or rejoice when someone else has committed them. If one fails to reject like poison even the slightest negative action, great suffering will follow. It is stated in the *Udanavarga*:

> Committing even a small misdeed,
> Will lead to great fear and utter misery
> In the next life:
> It is the same as swallowing poison.

"It is most important, therefore, to confess your previous negative acts and vow not to commit them again. For instance, someone may have been poisoned in the morning and be cured in the evening by taking an antidote. Similarly, through confession and vowing to shun future wrongdoing, negative acts can be purified. In this way, even great sinners can have the good fortune to reach the higher realms and achieve liberation. Therefore, until you die, muster your intelligence, confess your negative actions, and vow to amend your conduct.

"Similarly, wanting to give up negative acts and undertake virtuous ones, you may wonder what positive acts are. Positive acts include being aware that all sentient beings have been your kind parents in previous lives. Be sympathetic toward the destitute who come to your door and toward all those who suffer. Show tenderness toward those who are unhappy. Vow to attain enlightenment in order to dispel others' suffering, and establish them in happiness. Resolve that you will practice the Dharma for that very reason.

"With kindness, compassion, and the aspiration to attain enlightenment, cherish all living things, be generous without attachment, maintain discipline, speak the truth, reconcile adversaries, speak gently, celebrate others' good qualities, be content [283a], be kind toward others, and trust the law of karmic cause and effect. In this way practice the ten virtues.

"Also, offer prostrations and circumambulations, sponsor the making of sacred objects symbolic of the enlightened body, speech, and mind, read scriptures, perform offerings, remember the words and meaning of the teachings, contemplate them, explain them to others, and assimilate the ultimate meaning. Perform such virtuous deeds yourself, inspire others to perform them, and rejoice when they do.

"Thus, beginning by doing small virtuous deeds, little by little, like water drops which gradually fill an entire jar, you will eventually attain the level of Buddhahood. The *Condensed Perfection of Wisdom* states:[79]

> Drops of water falling into a jar
> Little by little, fill it;
> The aspiration to enlightenment, the
>   initial seed,
> Eventually blossoms into Buddha-
>   hood,
> Complete with all the pure qualities.

"Whatever positive act you seek to undertake, do not lose courage: be like a heroic warrior hurling himself into battle. Let your positive acts be continuous, like the red wheel of flames made by a whirling firebrand, and unceasing like the flow of the Ganges: you will find happiness in this and in future lives, and in the end you will attain Buddhahood."

Putting into verse these teachings of the Buddha and the gurus, I sang this song, according to the particular dispositions and capacities of the disciples:

Homage to the guru!
I pray to the compassionate teacher [283b]:
Look upon all of us, your followers.

Protector, may your blessings
Enable us to follow your life-example,
And practice according to your instructions.

Lord Buddha, the fourth of the perfect guides,[80]
Displayed infinite deeds in his many lives,
Yet, in essence, he first meditated on kindness and compassion;
He cultivated the wish to attain enlightenment,
And put that wish into practice—the two Bodhicittas.

Next, he abandoned all concern for himself,
Strived for the sake of sentient beings,
Whom he considered to be like mothers,
Swiftly attained Buddhahood,
And now reigns as the crown of all beings.

Taking as examples the lives of the compassionate Buddha,
Cultivate kindness and compassion for sentient beings, your mothers,
And develop the two Bodhicittas— aspiration and action.
Offer gain and success to others,
And take loss and defeat upon yourself.

The complete detailed exposition of the Buddha's
Turnings of the Wheel of Dharma is unimaginable,
Yet the essence is,
"Give up negative actions; do what is good;
Tame your mind and the obscuring emotions."

So, in accord with the compassionate Buddha's words,
Reject as you would reject poison the ten negative deeds:
Killing, stealing, sexual misconduct,
Lying, slander, gossip, harsh words,
Covetousness, ill will, and wrong views.

Practice instead the ten immaculate virtues:
Safeguard living things, be generous,
Keep your vows, speak truthfully,
Reconcile conflicts, speak gently,
Extol the virtues of others, be content [284a],
Be kind to all beings,
And develop conviction in karma, the law of cause and effect.

When the mental poisons arise—desire, anger, ignorance, pride, jealousy, and greed—
Counteract them immediately with antidotes.

May this song of the renunciate Tsogdruk Rangdrol,
An epitome of the teachings of the Compassionate Guide,
Benefit whoever hears it.[81]

I sang other songs and told everyone, "Above all, all beings have been our parents in previous lives; therefore, it is utterly wrong to kill in order to obtain the worst of all foods: the flesh and blood of living beings."

I emphasized this so strongly that all the wealthy families abandoned their evil actions and vowed to refrain from further killing: many goats, sheep, *dris*, and yaks which were meant to be butchered were thus set free. The people of the area then got together and offered a hundred *ganachakras* and a great feast. At the end, they sang a song that went like this:

Refuge, protector, wish-fulfilling gem.
On a jewel seat you are enthroned.

Before your gaze we offer you
These presents of songs and dance.

Atop the peak of Mount Potala,
Reside the Victors, Father and Sons:
Make three rounds about its base,
And the defilements of body are cleansed.

When the Buddha Dalai Lama merely
    turns his horse
Upon the Turquoise Roof Bridge,[82]
The fish swimming beneath that bridge
Won't be reborn in the lower realms
    [284b].

The sun shining down
On the White Peak,
The snow sparkling—
It seems so wondrous!
One, two, three . . .
The ice setting firm
On the lake's surface,
Completely freezing—
It seems so wondrous!
Four, five, six . . .
Leaves, buds, blossoms
Bursting into bloom
On the wish-fulfilling tree—
Wondrous happiness!
Seven, eight, nine . . .

And they performed many dances. Others sang:

As much as we drink our excellent *chang*,
It never runs out!
The storerooms are full of fresh barley
Right up to the lintels.

Even if we are reborn as gods,
We will only get water offerings.[83]
Now that we are born human beings
Let's enjoy—enjoy, and rejoice!

But consider this samsaric world:
There is no meaning in it.
O protector, wish-fulfilling gem,
Please cut the first lock of my hair.[84]

The sun shining down
On the White Peak,
The snow sparkling—
It seems so wondrous!

They also sang and danced to the song that begins, "Earth goddess, earth goddess . . . ," and to others as well. Celebrations were held over many months. The joy of young and old matched the happiness of celestial beings.

Wealth and bounty were showered upon me. I was offered fifty *sho* of gold by Dorje Wangchuk of Limi, fifteen by a wealthy lady of the southern slopes, and between ten and thirty each by the wealthy Logpa and Gyashang, by the general of Kyithang, and by the prosperous families of Purang. Even those who weren't rich offered two or three *sho* of gold, clothes, head ornaments, and whatever precious things they had. Altogether, the gold alone made up a full load for a horse. I was also offered thirty gold *tangka*-coins, one hundred big and small silver reliquary lockets [285a], five large and small mandala offering plates, two silver butter-lamps, three *torma* trays, eighty pearl and coral earrings, a full bag of turquoise, coral, and amber hair ornaments, forty-three rolls of new brocade and woolen cloth, ten rolls of old woolen cloth, twenty-five excellent horses, and two mules. There were also countless persons who offered silver *tangka*-coins, blankets, rolls of woolen and of cotton cloth, and an incalculable number of white scarves.

Since I was born, I had never experienced being surrounded by so much wealth and comfort as in that year. With this wealth, on the roof of the assembly hall of the Shephel Ling monastery, I erected two big victory banners, one *ganjira* pinnacle ornament, and a thousand-spoked Dharma-wheel flanked by a male and a female deer—all made of copper covered with gold. I used seven hundred *sho* of gold for the gilding. Inside, I placed three big silver butter-lamps, made from many *dotse* of silver, which were to remain lit day and night, two long pillar-banners made from "four themed" brocades of various colors,[85] and one thousand brass butter-lamps. With objects worth one thousand *sang*, I created a permanent fund for offerings. I distributed alms and tea to the monks. I requested the empowerment of Bhairava from the abbot, and made him a large offering of gold and other valuables; he was very pleased.

Depa Wangpo undertook building a high stone wall to hold back the water that had been damaging the temple of the silver Jowos of Purang.[86] This took two months, and involved bringing stones on horse-drawn carts from different places. From then on, the water did no damage. Depa Wangpo thus rendered a great service to the three Jowo images [285b].

He also erected two gilded copper victory banners on the roof of the temple, toward which I contributed ten *sho* of gold. I filled a huge brass lamp and a cast-iron cauldron with an ocean of melted butter and made a thousandfold offering, with vast aspiration-prayers.

My close disciple Rigdzin Orgyen Namgyal offered lotus flowers to be held by each of the three Jowo statues and, later, Khampa Tulku offered a volume of scripture and a sword of pure beaten silver.[87] I then prompted my close disciple Jimba Norbu to offer a splendid butter-lamp made from three hundred *sho* of gold.

I spent the winter staying in the Kangyur Lhakhang,[88] where I read the Kangyur, the Tengyur, and the collected writings of Lord Tsongkhapa and his spiritual sons. I wrote a work in which I included many of the stories about the Buddha's life, about the way his followers practiced, and about his teachings on both the Dharma and ordinary life—what should be given up and what should be accomplished. I called this work the *Marvelous Emanated Scriptures*.[89]

Everyone took good care of me. When I was about to leave, the local authorities presented me with a set of clothes, a saddle, a saddle-blanket, a bridle, and one hundred and eight *sho* of gold. I was also invited to visit some monks and some rich people, several of whom offered me six or seven *sho* of gold each.

The next summer, I went to upper Purang with many students and benefactors of Purang [286a]. At Kardung, we met Lama Kalden from Lokha in central Tibet, a Khenpo from Ladakh, Tendzin Nyima, and the Dharma practitioners Kalzang Tsultrim and Rigdrol, who had come up from the Pure Realm of U-Tsang.

Ladakh Khenpo had renounced this worldly life to go wandering from one mountain retreat to another. He offered me five *dotse* of silver, and many brocades of different colors. I gave him the name Jatang Rinchen, "The Precious Renunciate," and made extensive dedication of merit and prayers for him. Drubwang Kalden offered me one *dotse* and many ceremonial silken scarves, short and long. The others also offered me different things, worth seven *dotse* altogether. Out of this, I left one hundred silver *sang* as an offering of a permanent fund at Purang Shephel Ling and the rest as a contribution for a golden lamp for Ganden.

Then we, teachers, patrons, and disciples, reached the shore of Manasarovar, at the Southern Gate of the Thaw. We stayed there many days. I offered money and tea to the monastic community. In the great turquoise lake of Manasarovar, the spiral of auspiciousness and good fortune, I placed an offering of twenty-one vases filled with various kinds of grains and precious stones. I concluded with wishes and prayers that, in all countries, rains be timely, crops be abundant and cattle thrive [286b].

Once when I was relaxing on the bank of the lake, I experienced a state of freedom devoid of any particular object of focus, a state that was clear, vast and open. This inspired me to sing this instruction to my worthy heart-son Orgyen Namgyal:

Omniscient lama
Whose wisdom mind is wider than the sky,
Grant your blessing that
My mind and yours may merge as one.

Like dreams, like apparitions:
All these phenomena of samsara and
    nirvana.

Like the wide sky:
One's own mind.

All the phenomena of samsara and nirvana
Are the natural play of mind—
This I've come to understand.

The source of all phenomena of samsara
    and nirvana
Is the true nature of one's own mind:
An immense expanse that is an empty
    brilliance
Completely free of taking things as real:
This I have realized.

If I look toward the one who realizes this—
One's own awareness—
It is like the sky,
Set free, beyond clinging,
In the unborn expanse of dharmadhatu.

Relaxed, at ease in that very state of
    freedom,
I arrive at the immense sky realm
That is unconditioned dharmakaya.

When it is left to itself, as a vast sky
Utterly transparent and serene,
The poisonous, painful bindings that are
    mental constructs
Loosen by themselves.

When I remain in this state,
Which is like a transparent, empty sky,
I experience joy beyond words, thought, or
    expression.

When I dissolve into that vast expanse—
Empty and clear—
Without end, without limits—
There is no difference between mind and
    sky.

Looking on with the eyes of a wisdom
That is more immense than the
    all-encompassing sky,
The phenomena of samsara and nirvana
Become delightful spectacles.

Within that brilliant continuum,
There is no need for effort.
Everything occurs by itself,
Completely at ease, very naturally:
Complete contentment! [287a].

Not expecting to see anything at all,
I actually did see an empty brilliance
In its nakedness: what was seen
Was, like the sky, unchanging—
Extraordinary!

Signs of progress on the path,
Spiritual qualities, will arise in reality,
In dreams, and in meditation experiences;
What is called "enlightenment in a single
    lifetime"
Can really be achieved, I'm sure of it.

Compassion toward sentient beings
Once my mothers, surged up from deep
    within me—
These aren't just empty words:
Now I'll work to benefit others!

While I was remaining in the natural flow
Of the essence of mind, the absolute
    natural state,
This and similar songs spontaneously
    arose.

Fortunate disciple with a special
    connection,
Sing songs like this while you remain
In the realm of the natural state, and
Meditation experiences and realization will
    blaze forth.

One day, I was relaxing alone in a pleasant meadow on the bank of the lake. My disciple Kalden Rangdrol came along and said, "No one is around. Please sing a song about meditation experiences." I sang a song, just as it arose in a vast, free, and serene awareness:

Your mind, free from taking things as real,
Void, clear, more immense than the sky,
You who see everything with perfect
    clarity—
Saraha, think of me.

The view, free from bias or polarity,
Is the all-pervasive vast expanse.
The meditation, free from mental dullness
    and wildness,
Is the complete transparence of awareness.
The action, without particular intent,
Is a relaxed freedom [287b].
The fruition, beyond hope and fear,
Is samsara and nirvana complete within
    mind.

The excellent path of the Dohas
Is beyond cause and result,
Beyond trying and doing.

Look at such meditation instructions—
Buddhahood without meditation!

Look at my delighted laughter!
The delight of a vast, free mind!
The experience of lightness of being
As when emerging from a narrow gorge
Onto a high, wide mountain pass!

Look at my gaze!
It naturally overpowers samsara and
    nirvana.
It comes from savoring the view of sky-like
    evenness!

Look how, free from mistaking things as
    real,
I am blissful, and yet more blissful,
Enjoying the realm of primordial
    wakefulness,
Blissful yet empty.

Look how, trained on the excellent path,
I now walk on effortlessly toward Buddha-
    hood—
Singing, dancing, playing!

Worthy ones with good karma, come
    along!
Together, in one lifetime, we'll reach
    Buddhahood.

When you are confident that at death
You will be liberated in the dharmakaya,
Whenever the Mara of Death comes—
Just let him come!

I, renunciate yogin, a son of Saraha's
    lineage,
Sing this song as my inner experience
    unfolds.

Meditators wandering from place to place
With no particular destination in mind,
If you're singing a song about joyful
    experiences,
Sing one like this.

Let your awareness become heightened:
Let it spread out into the infinite sky.
From that state of complete openness,
That vast expanse, sing out!

When dullness, drowsiness, obliviousness
Have been cleared away,
The natural condition of one's own mind
Will become manifest: clear, empty,
    naked—
Like the immaculate autumn sky [288a].

This song helped his view and meditation to progress.

Many hundreds of disciples from Ngari who had renounced this life gathered at the Southern Gate of the Thaw, the southern outlet of the lake. I gave them the transmission and explana-

tions for the *Condensed Meaning of the Graded Path,*
the essence of all teachings. Its author, the Lord
of Dharma Tsongkhapa, source of benefit and
happiness, peer of our guide the Buddha, explained
it as a song that had arisen from his inner experience; thus it is also known as the *Song of Experience
of the Precious Lord.*

I also gave the *Three Main Points of the Path,*[90]
and the heart-advice known as the *Lion's Roar*[91]—
the mere sound of it strikes the obscuring emotions and renders them mute like terrified animals.
At the request of Lhatsun Changchup Ö, this
profound advice was given by the peerless Atisha
as he was about to leave Ngari and go back to
India. After that, I taught the *Jewel Rosary of the
Bodhisattvas,*[92] the core of the Kadampa patriarchs' practice.

I gave, too, the *Eighty Pieces of Advice to the
People of Tingri.*[93] Padampa Sangye, the sovereign
of *siddhas,* gave these eighty verses of advice when
he was about to leave this world. The great lama
Char came before him, weeping, and supplicated him, "Dampa, as you will now pass on to
the Pure Realm of Celestial Enjoyment, you are
blissful indeed. Yet you are abandoning us poor
people of Tingri. What shall we do?" This advice,
his testament, was his response [288b].

I also gave the *Seventy Admonitions.*[94] Karak
Gomchung Rinpoche, the paramount ornament
of the Kadampas—for whom every syllable of
the Buddha's word arose as a pith instruction—
understood the complete meaning of the
Buddha's teachings and meditated on them in a
cave in Karak. Teachers such as the matchless
Potowa became devoted to him. With the pure
motivation of bringing benefit to the mind-
streams of his fortunate students, Karak Gomchung wrote these seventy admonitions ending
with the interjection *ang!* (please!) in which he
clearly and openly sets forth his wisdom.

I then gave the *Thirty-seven-fold Practices of a
Bodhisattva,*[95] the direct pith instruction composed
by the glorious and excellent Gyalse Thogme,
an incarnation of the Lotus-holder. This teaching explains how to put into practice the sutras
and the instructions of the past sages. Finally, I
gave the *Emanated Scriptures,* which I had composed

and which are like emanations of the sutras,
tantras, and commentaries of the past sages.

In this way, I gave many transmissions and
teachings on these special and wonderful instructions,
sweet-sounding, and satisfying to the mind. Before
leaving I gave this advice for the benefit of the
renunciates and people of Ngari:[96]

I respectfully prostrate myself before the
  Buddhas and their spiritual sons.
Bless me that I may be able to act in
  accordance with your words.

Now that you have this free, well-favored,
  precious human body,
Study, reflect, and meditate, people of
  Ngari.

In your homeland, the three poisons and
  the obscuring emotions only increase:
Leave your homeland behind, people of
  Ngari [289a].

In mountain solitudes, practice improves
  and the mind becomes clear:
Stay in such places, people of Ngari.

At the time of death you will leave behind
  relatives, friends and wealth:
Give up this life's concerns, people of
  Ngari.

If you keep bad company, the three
  poisons will get stronger;
Listening, reflecting, and meditating will
  get weaker:
Avoid bad company from now on, people
  of Ngari.

If you remain near spiritual friends,
Your faults will lessen and your good
  qualities increase:
Rely on spiritual friends, people of Ngari.

The unfailing source of refuge is the Three
  Jewels:
Take refuge at all times, people of Ngari.

The suffering of the three lower realms
Is the result of having done wrong:
Never act wrongly, people of Ngari.
There is no happiness within samsara:
Strive for liberation, people of Ngari.

To deliver all beings from cyclic existence,
Set your mind on enlightenment, people of
    Ngari.

Don't be concerned with your own happiness;
Hold others dearer than yourself:
Give up your happiness in exchange for
    others' suffering, people of Ngari.

Even if your wealth is taken away by others,
Dedicate all your merit to them, people of
    Ngari.

Even if someone is about to cut off your
    head,
Take his negative karma upon yourself,
    people of Ngari.

Even if someone criticizes you openly,
Applaud that person's virtues, people of
    Ngari.

Even if someone you've cared for
As lovingly as your own child
Regards you as an enemy,
Love him all the more, people of Ngari.

Even if someone points out your faults
In the midst of a crowd,
Show him respect, people of Ngari [289b].

Even if someone seeks your humiliation,
Place him on the crown of your head,
    people of Ngari.

However much you may suffer,
Take on yourselves the suffering of others
And still don't lose heart, people of Ngari.

However happy you may be, see that
    happiness has no real essence

And be free of pride, people of Ngari.

With the armies of kindness and
    compassion,
Always wage war on your true enemy,
    anger, people of Ngari.

You may enjoy all comforts, yet never be
    satisfied,
Always wanting more and more:
Reject all craving as it arises, people of
    Ngari.

The root of all phenomena is mind,
Primordially empty:
Rest in the state of empty clarity, people of
    Ngari.
Attractive things are as insubstantial as
    rainbows:
Give up grasping attachment, people of
    Ngari.

Suffering is like seeing one's child die in a
    dream:
Don't let a dream cause you pain, people
    of Ngari.

To obtain Buddhahood, generously give
    up your body
And all your possessions, people of Ngari.

Discipline is the ground of all virtues:
Observe it at all times, people of
    Ngari.

Even the enemy who harms you has been
    your parent in previous lives:
Cultivate patience toward everyone,
    people of Ngari.

All qualities come from diligence:
Strive diligently in Dharma practice,
    people of Ngari.

Cultivating inner calm weakens the
    obscuring emotions:
Meditate in solitude, people of Ngari.

Developing insight uproots these
    emotions:
Meditate on the wisdom of emptiness,
    people of Ngari.

Continually examining your own mind,
Reject thoughts and actions contrary to the
    Dharma, people of Ngari [290a].

Never broadcast the defects of anyone
Who has entered the Mahayana, people of
    Ngari.

Never be attached to your family home,
Or the homes of your benefactors, people
    of Ngari.

Reject all harsh talk
That upsets the minds of others, people of
    Ngari.

The moment desire and other conflicting
    emotions arise
Crush them at once with antidotes, people
    of Ngari.

Always equipped with mindfulness and
    alertness,
Work for the benefit of others, people of
    Ngari.

Dedicate all merit you accumulate
To the attainment of supreme Buddha-
    hood, people of Ngari.

Doing so you will be happy now,
And ultimately gain enlightenment, people
    of Ngari.

May the minds of all men and women
    hearing this song
Turn to the holy Dharma.

Through these instructions, pure seeds were sown
in the mind-streams of all those present. Spontaneously, they all became diligent renunciates,
who lived only in mountain retreats, in harmony
with the Dharma.

One day Lama Kalden told me, "I heard from a
pilgrim that one of your root-lamas, the compassionate Jampel Dorje[97] from Domey, has passed
on to another Buddhafield." Filled with sadness I
said:

At Kushinagara in India,
    The protector of beings, the Buddha,
        passed into nirvana.

From the Gungthang pass in the Land of
    Mang,
Padmasambhava left for the cannibal
    island to the southwest [290b].

At Nyethang in central Tibet,
Jowo Atisha passed into the realm of the
    invisible.

From the manifest palace of Chubar,
Jetsun Milarepa left for the Buddhafield of
    Pure Joy.

From the monastery of Ganden,
The second Buddha went to Tushita
    heaven.

In the palace that is the Potala on earth,
Our refuge and protector tossed away the
    flower of his life.[98]

Now, in Lower Kham,
My root guru has departed for another
    Buddhafield.

Kye-hu!
The sun, the precious master, has set;
Who will bathe us in rays of
    compassion?

The medicinal tree of Dharma has fallen
    to the ground;
Who will cure the diseases of the obscuring
    emotions?

The snow peak of the four empowerments
   has collapsed;
From what source will the rivulets of
   blessing flow?

The treasury of liberating instructions has
   been emptied;
Who will dispel our poverty?

The great drum of the vast and profound
   Dharma has been rent;
How will the sutras and tantras resound?

The standard of the profound instruction
   has fallen;
How will the flag of the whispered lineage
   wave?

In brief, the crown jewel has been lost;
To whom will we direct our wishes?

Kye-hu!
The blind man, lost in the desert,
In despair calls out for guidance.

The young orphan who can't manage on
   his own,
Crying, thinks of the mother who once
   cared for him.

The fish flopping on dry land,
Stares toward the water and vainly tries to
   leap into it.

I, luckless, sunk in the mire of samsara,
Pray to my lord and guide:

In whichever Buddhafield you may dwell,
Look with compassion upon me, the one
   left behind.

I am now old, close to death;
When death comes, lead me along the path.

I pray to meet you again,
Face to face, in a Pure Realm.
Jetsun, by your blessings,
May my prayer be fulfilled [291a].

I performed some meritorious deeds, praying
that his enlightened intentions might be fulfilled.
Some days later, I sang this song with a sad
mind:

He who frees us from the fears of samsara,
Our escort, the lama, has departed.
Left with no protector,
We are lost in a desert of despair.

The old people of my native region, whom
   I knew for so long,
Have now passed away—
Even my old mother has left this world,
Without the two of us meeting one last
   time!

Where did the years, months, and days go?
Unnoticed, they slipped away in an instant!
My life runs out in meaningless
   distractions;
I feel utterly depressed.

I may have gained this free and fortunate
   human body,
Yet I haven't really practiced the divine
   Dharma.
Most of my relatives and friends have
   passed away,
Yet I am oblivious to death and
   impermanence.

I may bear the marks of grey hair and
   wrinkles,
Yet I don't recognize this as old age.

I may have illness and fever,
Yet the thought that I may die doesn't
   even occur to me [291b].

When the Demon Lord of Death
Comes to me and those like me,
Who take delight only in food and drink,
All we'll do is whine, "What's happening?
   What can we do?"

When, from time to time, I think
Of this and similar truths,

I feel helplessly sad;
And I am not just mouthing words.

Kye-ma!
Life is so short!
When will we die?
If you really want to do something to
    secure the future,
Practice the divine Dharma.

The monks, disciples, patrons, laymen and laywomen, who had been following me on the way, gathered around and we exchanged words of farewell. I gave them my spiritual protection, blessed them, and concluded:

"Supreme among the four continents, where it is difficult to gain rebirth, is Jambudvipa in the south. The Buddha, the Conqueror, has walked on this earth and blessed it as a Pure Realm for his followers. We have taken birth on it, having gained a rare and precious human existence, complete with the eighteen freedoms and favorable conditions, more valuable than the wish-fulfilling gem. We have met the precious teaching of the Buddha, the source of benefit and happiness, rarer than the *udumbara* lotus.

"We have met a lama, a spiritual master, an occasion rarer than a star in the daytime. Persevering in virtuous actions, we must again obtain birth in the higher realms of celestial and human beings and reach the certainty and excellence of omniscience. When one has a boat, one should cross the ocean; when one has gathered an army of heroes, one should defeat the enemy; when one has a wish-granting cow, one should milk it; when one has a superb horse, one should ride it to faraway places. You now have a precious human body and a lama who embodies the Buddhas of the three times. With great joy and enthusiasm think that, traveling the highway of the sacred Dharma [292a], you will come closer and closer to the higher realms and to the ultimate excellence of liberation and omniscience.

"Not attached to your body, to an entourage, to relatives, or to the possessions of this life, right now, concentrating solely on the holy Dharma, embark upon the path of liberation. If you don't, it will be worse than a seafaring mer-

chant returning home empty-handed from an island of jewels. You would be behaving as if you were mad; you would be as good as a corpse, even though you were still breathing.

"Whether or not you have reason, courage, creativity, and intelligence is now clear. Don't waste your precious human existence and end up empty-handed; practice the sacred Dharma according to your lama's instructions. At the time of death, perceive your lama or *yidam* deity coming in reality to guide you to a perfect Buddhafield—the realm of Pure Joy, the realm of Celestial Enjoyment, the Paradise of Bliss, or another—and go there just like a child going home to his parents. A fortunate person who, without delay, joyfully applies himself in this way has all the above qualities.

"Consider someone who does not embrace the Dharma, refuses even to listen to an authentic teacher, and day after day accumulates a full measure of negative actions for the sake of food, clothing, family, and all the rest [292b]. When that person dies, many messengers of Yama will appear—fierce, enraged, merciless, and hideous in color, tying one by the neck with a black rope, striking one's body with sharp weapons—and will lead that person down to one of the three lower realms, the eighteen hells or others, as if tugging that person, terrified and powerless, into a black dungeon. People like that—male or female, high or low—have no hearts in their chests and no brains in their skulls; they are worse than lunatics—cheating, deceiving, ruining themselves.

"Don't return empty-handed from the jewel island. You have been born in a civilized country where the holy Dharma is taught; it is imperative that you practice it. Immediately, vigorously, throw yourself into your practice, since, although you may have gained this rare and precious human body, you won't keep it for long; you will die.

"No one will escape death. All of our countrymen, townspeople, parents, brothers, sisters, friends, lamas, and spiritual companions will be taken away by impermanence. Expecting to stay, they may have made many plans, but when the Mara of Death comes, they have no power to remain even one day longer. They must set out, empty-handed, without Dharma, upon the great road to their future lives. Think about this. None of us is beyond it.

"Life ends, as a pond dries up when water ceases running into it [293a]. Life vanishes, as the shadows of the setting sun vanish into darkness; life becomes exhausted, like an emptied granary. With each passing year, month, day, morning and evening, we are drawing closer and closer to the feared maw of death, like an animal being taken to the slaughterhouse draws closer to its death with every step it takes. Appalling! Horrible! What agony!

"There are means to preserve life—medicine, food, clothes, and so on—but even these, when used wrongly, can become the causes of death. People die while trying to seek food and clothing, infants are smothered under their blankets, people are poisoned by food, die by taking the wrong medicine, are betrayed by intimates, are crushed under their collapsing houses, are dragged on the ground after falling from their horse—all previously helpful conditions that can become causes of death. There are also 404 diseases, 80,000 evil influences, and a multitude of circumstances that are injurious to life and cause death.

"No one who dies suddenly has had the least thought on the previous day that he was about to die. Yet, there is no certainty that the Mara of Death will not strike right now, like a bolt of lightning. Today an eloquent, radiant person; tomorrow a stinking corpse. This happens all the time. No one really thinks that he or she will die tomorrow, yet this body, an aggregate of the four elements, cannot be relied upon to last even for the duration of a meal. Breath is like vapor, body's warmth like a spark: they may be extinguished in an instant.

"Keep in mind that the time and the circumstances of death are unpredictable. If you have the good fortune to practice the Dharma, practice it this year rather than next [293b], today rather than tomorrow, and this morning rather than tonight: *now* is the time to practice, not to sit idle.

"Past generations have died, future generations will die, and so will all of us on earth today.

Old or young, there is no fixed order; male or female, beautiful or ugly, there is no preference: death is certain, and only the time it will occur is not.

"Close friends are left behind, conversations are left unfinished, projects uncompleted, clothes unworn, and food uneaten. Your bed, clothes, dishes—everything is just left behind, discarded. Taken away from your home and companions, you must go. 'He died'; 'she died.' Nothing but these words are left of you.

"In short, life is less enduring than autumn mist, and one is as easily parted from one's spouse, relatives, and companions as from people met in a marketplace. Luxuries and possessions are even less durable than a mirage. That demon, Death, approaches faster than the evening shadows—appalling!

"Like a thunderclap, irreversible as lightning, death strikes suddenly. You may be eminent or powerful, a universal monarch: that won't even help one bit. You may be rich as Vaishravana, the god of wealth: you won't be able to take anything, not even as much as a mustard seed, on the journey to your next life. Like a hair plucked from butter, you will be pulled out alone from among the multitude of your parents, brothers, sisters, and friends.

"Though they cannot bear to be parted for a second from the house they've built [294a], the wealth they've accumulated, their friends, relatives, possessions, and the children and spouses who were like their own hearts, people must leave everything behind. Convulsively clutching at the clothes of their relatives, casting haggard glances at them, whispering one or two last wishes, shedding a tear or two, many have thus gone on to their next lives, empty-handed, without Dharma.

"All of us have seen or heard of this many times, and all of us will have to go to the unknown land of future lives. Yet, we ignore the time of departure: it might well be tonight. We risk leaving bereft of Dharma. For the remainder of this life, which will last no longer than the rays of the sun that have already touched the mountain pass, we should give up plans that assume we will live a long time.

"From this very day, this very sunset, not just paying lip service, but from the core of your heart, the marrow of your bones, right away, practice pure Dharma—as the lasting harvest, the provisions for the next life, the ultimate aim, the means of happiness for yourself and others.

"If you do not, after death, you will wander without refuge or protection in the unfamiliar, tortuous paths of the *bardo*. In the *bardo* myriad hallucinations will occur, surpassing in horror all description, making your very heart quiver with fear [294b]. Apart from the Dharma and your guides—the guru and the Three Jewels—you will not receive any help. There will be none from the wealth, relatives, children, and friends of this life. No brave son will come rushing to your aid, shouting out, 'Ki-hi-hi!' No dutiful daughter will be there to bring along provisions and other useful things. Not only that: the memory of your relatives will merely increase your torment. It is because of such attachment that you are wandering in the three realms of samsara.

"All those who have committed negative actions to satisfy their children and meet their needs for food and clothing will be led down by the gruesome messengers of Yama to suffer in the eighteen hells or in other places of torments in the three lower realms.

"The blessed men and women who have practiced the Dharma will be led to the higher realms and to liberation by a host of gurus and deities appearing before them; they will find happiness and fulfillment.

"Whether you want to drink the nectar of the gods or the molten bronze of the hells, whether you wish to attain Buddhahood or wander in hell: the choice is now in your hands. Think it over, examine well, reason carefully and you will reach this undeniable conclusion: 'I must give up wrongdoing, which leads to the lower realms, and practice the Dharma, which leads to the higher rebirths.' I have explained extensively before how to put aside nonvirtuous actions and cultivate virtuous ones [295a].

"Now, I am leaving; there is no need to say much more. From now on, great distances will separate us. Our hold on life is uncertain; we cannot say whether we will meet each other again on the roads of this life. Here, in verses set to a melody, is the conclusion of all my teachings, my final advice. Thinking, 'Now I have met a guru. Will I ever meet him again?' and aware of the rarity of such an occasion, listen carefully, without letting your mind wander, and from now on put this advice into practice the best you can.

I supplicate the gracious lamas:
Grant your blessings so that
I keep in mind death and impermanence.

Like autumn clouds, this life is transient.
Our parents, our relatives, are like
   passersby met in a marketplace.
Like the dew on grass-tips, wealth is
   evanescent.
Like a bubble on the surface of water, this
   body is fragile, ephemeral.

The dharmas of this samsaric world are
   futile;
The sacred Dharma alone has value.
The chance to practice this Dharma is
   occurring just once, right now.

Faithful men and women here assembled,
Don't, *don't* commit negative deeds.
Do, *do* what is good.

Most wealthy people are too greedy even
   to eat their own food;
How can they endure giving away anything to others, or to the Dharma?
When they die, all their riches will have
   been meaningless.

Wrong! Wrong!
Wealthy misers, you're wrong.

Right! Right!
When you have it, give it away, offer it up!
   [295b].

If you're obsessed by the desires of this life,
You'll always be needy:
When you get a horse, you'll want a
   saddle.

Having all kinds of desires
Is characteristic of life in samsara.
These desires are rarely satisfied,
And even when they are, turn out to be
    meaningless.

Faithful men and women patrons gathered
    here
Don't, *don't* act in this way;
Give up thoughts of this life,
And whatever you do,
Do what brings happiness for future lives.

A person who has acted virtuously
Will ascend the path to the higher realms
    and liberation
A person engaged in nonvirtuous actions
Will head straight down the path to the
    lower realms.

The power to go up or down is now in
    your hands.

All you faithful men and women patrons
    assembled here,
Don't, *don't* do the destructive acts that will
    hurl you down;
Do, *do* positive deeds that will exalt you.

May the faithful men and women who
    hear this
Turn their minds to the holy Dharma!

Lord, root guru, Vajradhara,
Who rests in the *dharmachakra* of my heart,
Ascend through the central channel,
And remain upon my head, as the
    ornament of the *chakra* of great bliss.

By your blessing, may all those present here
Be relieved from physical illness and
    mental suffering;
Healthy in body, joyful in mind,
May they turn their aspirations toward the
    Dharma.

We came here from different provinces,
    east and west;

We have assembled for a brief moment,
And will now disperse, like all phenomena.
This is impermanence!

Our countrymen, neighbors, old people,
Young people as well—in whom all put
    their hopes:
Remember how many have passed away
    without having grown old [296a].
We are all like that.

Within seventy years
All of us, without exception,
Will die, leaving this world,
After which a few affectionate people may
    think of us and weep.

Empty-handed, we will leave for the next
    life:
How can we carry the wealth we have
    amassed?
We may have good friends, but they have
    no power to accompany us;
We will travel the long, narrow path of the
    bardo all alone.

At that time, only the guru, our guide,
And the holy Dharma, which surely benefits,
Can be of help to us.
Men and women patrons, from this
    moment on,
Bear in mind that death may strike at any
    time.

From your heart, supplicate the divine
    guru;
Take refuge in the deities and the Three
    Jewels;
Reject the ten nonvirtuous actions like
    poison.

When a teacher comes, make a spiritual
    connection with him,
When you encounter destitute people, give
    to them generously,
And on your own level, serve and respect
    the sangha.
Serve the parents who gave you life.

Don't quarrel; remain in harmony with
   your family.
Don't abuse servants; give them food and
   clothing.
Don't beat dogs and cattle; look after
   them.
Don't harm friends and neighbors; help
   them.
Don't sit around idly; do prostrations and
   circumambulations.
Don't let your voice be idle; recite the *mani*.
At all times, have kind thoughts.

Wherever I may go, I will not forget you,
And will do my best to dispel your
   obstacles in this life
And guide you on the path of the next
   [296b].

This yogin will go on his way;
Men and women patrons, remain happy.

I pray to meet you again and again,
In what remains of this life.
I pray that if we don't meet now,
We may meet in future lives.

This is my farewell advice,
Given to you, faithful men and women
   patrons.

May all men and women who hear this
   song,
Always be joyous and happy!

My escort in this life, the next, and the
   bardo,
Wish-granting gem, refuge and protector,
Dwell inseparably on the crown of my
   head,
Rain a shower of blessings and
   accomplishments.

Coming from east, west, and everywhere,
We, teacher and disciples, have gathered
   here,
And now scatter in all directions—
How sad we feel!

Assembly of faithful householders
Established in this good land,
May you all enjoy happiness,
Practicing the divine Dharma.

I, the yogin "Self-liberation of the Six
   Senses,"
Making prayers to create a spiritual link
With you, faithful ones with pure *samaya*,
Proceed to foreign lands.

We may hear news of each other
But we will not meet again.
We have just met this once,
So, keep my heart-advice in mind.

Even though we won't meet again in this
   life,
I pray that we shall meet
In our next life,
In the eastern Buddhafield of Pure Joy"
   [297a].

I gave them all ceremonial scarves. Sadness
and renunciation filled everyone's mind; their
respect and devotion grew; the very hairs on
their bodies stood on end, and tears welled up in
the eyes of many people. Again, I said:

"Although we come from different places,
by the power of our previous karma and pure
prayers, traveling for many months I came here
without you needing to call me. You may wonder to which school I belong and be puzzled by
my appearance. Who can tell whether I am a
siddha or an ordinary monk? People might find it
be difficult to conceive any faith in me. I may be
good, I may be bad; however it may be, as a sign
of my having been your lama in a previous life,
you spontaneously felt faith simply through hearing my name or seeing my face. During the three
years I have stayed at the Snow Mountain, you
provided not only for all my needs but also for
the food and clothing of over a hundred disciples
and renunciates. Now, as I leave, you unstintingly
offer me whatever you have—horses to ride,
clothes to wear, food to eat, gold to bring along—
and you accompany me on my way. Thanks to
your kindness, men and women, wherever I go, I

shall be going from one happiness to the next. How could I not be pleased with you?

"My youth is gone, I draw closer and closer to death. Among you, too, men and women, many are advanced in age [297b]. Great distances will separate us. Dear patrons and disciples who attentively listen and practice whatever you are taught—nothing is certain about birth and death, and thus, we may not see each other again in this life. Later, who knows in which of the six realms we may be born, driven on, as we are, by the force of our karma and obscurations? Thinking that this may be our only meeting, I feel sad; tears run down my face.

"Because of the merit you accumulated previously, you enjoy families, wealth, food, happiness, comfort, and renown, and you were able to meet me. On our meeting, you presented me with the threefold offering of wealth, service, and practice. You need not have the slightest regret: not even once did you displease me. To be accepted with love by a teacher is to be like a child who receives his father's inheritance. As if filling a vase to the brim, without hiding or keeping anything secret, I have given you profound and vast instructions. If you are capable of putting them into practice, you will attain freedom and the level of omniscience. Then, even if you met the Buddha in person, he would have nothing to add.

"Now, as I go, you have my blessing, given with great tenderness, and my prayers that I meet you and care for you throughout our future lives. In your next birth, by the compassion of the guru, you will meet me in a Pure Realm [298a]. Not only that, if you pray with faith, you will meet me again in this very life, in reality, in dreams, or in meditation.

"By the compassion of the guru, auspiciousness now prevails in the whole country, blessing has suffused the land, prosperity prevails everywhere, human are free from diseases and cattle from epidemics—everyone enjoys well-being. Beyond that, your lama, the Buddhas of the three times in person, takes leave in good health, after having established his worthy disciples on the path of maturation and liberation. Thinking what good fortune this is, you have only reasons to rejoice, not to be sad.

"Of course you may feel, 'Even if I cannot accompany my teacher—my crown jewel, my refuge in this life, in the *bardo,* and in future lives, he whose kindness has been greater than that of the Buddha—how wonderful if I could at least stay with him for a few more years! Once he has gone far away, there are many other lamas I could meet, but how will I ever meet him, my root lama, the embodiment of the Buddhas of the three times? When will I die? The lama I need at the moment of death is now going far away. From today onwards, how will I ever behold his face? How will I ever hear his voice? How miserable I am!' When such thoughts arise it is true that one feels like crying.

"When I left the Dharma King Ngakyi Wangpo [298b], I wept a great deal, and continued to cry for three days. Later, when thinking of my teacher, I have often cried helplessly. Now, when you remember me and cry, it makes me remember my lama and I also feel like weeping. It is neither like the crying of someone who tells a lama his worldly troubles about food and clothing, nor like the tears caused by one's spouse or relatives. It is said that tears shed while thinking of the guru can close the doors of the Hell of Blisters.[99]

"To cry when parting from one's guru, and when one's father or mother dies, is a noble thing in this world. It is something you should wish for, not something despicable. Those who don't cry need not feel uneasy about the many who do; those who are crying need not feel ashamed, since crying is quite just on this occasion. Anyone who feels like crying should just go ahead and weep—there is nothing wrong with it.

"We may not meet again, but there is no need for you to feel depressed; just maintain unwavering faith. For my part, wherever I go, I will not forget you. I will practice for the sake of all of you. If I attain enlightenment, it will be as though you all had attained enlightenment, too. I shall not abandon you. Even if we don't meet in this life, this life is just an instant. I will do everything so that in our next life we meet in the Buddhafield of Pure Joy, or in any of the Buddhafields of the Five Families. Be joyous!" [299a].

I set out on my way, occasionally looking

back. The monks, disciples, and patrons stood there behind me. There was a whole colorful crowd of people, some people wiping away tears, some doing prostrations while praying aloud, some praying with joined palms. Many poor people whom I had known a long time were crying loudly. Seeing this, I felt strong pity for them, and tears streamed from my eyes. Unable to bear the separation, they just stood there transfixed, looking at me, till they could see me no more. Then they all returned to their respective homes.

Lama Kalden and his disciples, who had renounced the concerns of this life, went to the meditation place of the White Footprint above the Cave of Miracles to the east of Mount Kailash, and raised there for three years the victory banner of spiritual practice. As a result of this, he became able to benefit the Dharma and sentient beings.

Notes

1. The Tara Temple of Nyethang (*snye thang sgrol ma lha khang*), south of Lhasa, was the main residence of Jowo Atisha (see Translator's Introduction, note 12) in Tibet and the place where he died in 1054. Some of Atisha's bones, his Dharma robes, and a statue said to be a true likeness of him are still kept in this temple, along with many other precious relics.

2. Tashi Lhunpo (*bkra shis lhun po*) was founded in 1447 by Gedun Drup (*dge 'dun grub*, 1391–1475), Tsongkhapa's nephew and disciple. He was retroactively designated as the first Dalai Lama and his relics were preserved in a stupa at Tashi Lhunpo. Tashi Lhunpo, which housed up to four thousand monks, is the seat of the Panchen Lamas (see chap. 2, note 30).

3. The Mansion of Complete Victory (*rnam par rgyal ba'i khang bzang*) is the name of the palace of the celestial beings of the thirty-three-fold god realm.

4. The Magars, one of the largest Nepalese tribes. Of Tibetan origin, the Magars are often craftsmen, blacksmiths, bridge makers, salt traders, or warriors.

5. The Southern Gate of the Thaw (*khrus sgo lho*) is thus called because this is the last area of the lake to become frozen and is the first to thaw. It normally

freezes at the beginning of the twelfth Tibetan month and thaws at the beginning of the third month. The Gelukpa monastery built on that shore took this name (*khrus sgo dgon pa*).

6. At 4600 meters altitude, and with 320 square kilometers, Lake Manasarovar is the highest large body of fresh water in the world. Its other names are the Unvanquished Turquoise Lake (*ma pham g.yu mtsho*), Anavatapta, the Ever-cool Lake (*mtsho ma dros pa*), and the Divine Lotus Lake (*padma lha mtsho*). It is called the Unvanquished Lake because when one examines all the other great lakes of Tibet to see if they possess the eight qualities of perfect water (*chu yan lag brgyad ldan*) they are faulty in some respect. It is called Turquoise Lake because its limpid waters resemble a turquoise mandala. It is given the name Ever-cool Lake because it is the palace of the naga king Anavatapta, "Who Never Warms Up." It is called Divine Lotus Lake because it resembles a fully opened eight-petaled lotus. See MK, pp. 65–73 and 109.

7. Purang Shephel Ling (*spu hreng*, or *spu rang*, *bshad 'phel gling*), the main Gelukpa monastery in Purang.

8. In 1814.

9. The Cave of Miracles (*rdzu 'phrul phug*) lies to the southeast of Mt. Kailash and is a few hours' walk from the mountain itself. When Jetsun Milarepa constructed his meditation cave with a few boulders, he first found that the ceiling of the cave was too low. Stretching his body, he pushed the ceiling up, leaving the print of his head in the rock. Then he thought that the ceiling was too high, so he went outside and stepped on the rock from above the cave, leaving prints of his feet in the rock. Shabkar stayed in retreat in a nearby, smaller cave located above the Cave of Miracles.

10. The White Snow Mountain, Kangkar Tise (*gangs dkar ti se*), Mt. Kailash (lit., Silver Mountain), is one of the world's great holy mountains, sacred to Hindus and Buddhists alike. It is one of the so-called "Three Holy Places of Tibet," associated with the body, speech, and mind aspects of Chakrasamvara and Vajravarahi. The other two are Lapchi (*la phyi*) and Tsari *(tsa ri)*. These three are also listed among the "twenty-four sacred places" (Skt. *pitha*) of the world (see Glossary of Enumerations), Kailash being identified as Himavat, Lapchi as Godhavari, and Tsari as both Caritra and Devikota. There are several descriptions of and guides to Mt. Kailash, including one written by Konchog Tendzin Chökyi Lodrö, the sixth Drigung Chungtsang (*'bri gung chung*

tshang dkon mchog bstan 'dzin chos kyi blo gros, 1829–1906), and a recent one composed by Chöying Dorje (1990), hereafter quoted as MK.

It is recounted in the *Chakrasamvara Tantra* and its commentaries (as related in MK) that the world was once ruled by Bhairava, the wrathful form of Mahadeva, who made the land of Magadha the seat of his power. It is said also that four devas and four *gandharvas* descended from the sky and established their dominion in eight places known as the eight Celestial Abodes (*mkha' spyod kyi gnas brgyad*). Likewise, four yakshas and four rakshasas, already on the earth, made their way to Jambudvipa, where they established themselves in eight Earthly Abodes (*sa spyod kyi gnas brgyad*), while four nagas and four asuras came to Jambudvipa from beneath the earth, to settle themselves in eight Underground Abodes (*sa 'og gi gnas brgyad*). They invited Bhairava to visit their dwellings, twenty-four in all, but he, instead of coming personally, manifested in each place as a *lingam* to which these savage beings would make blood sacrifices.

These demonic forces prevailed from the "golden age" until the beginning of our present "era of strife and conflict." It was then, the tantra recounts, that the Blessed One, Vajradhara, knew that the time had come to subdue these unsuitable beings. Without his mind ever wavering from objectless compassion, he arose in the formidable wrathful display of a Heruka with four heads and twelve arms. He danced, and through the power of the nondual wisdom of all the Buddhas, trampled down Mahadeva and his consort together with their retinue, liberating their minds into the absolute expanse and establishing them in great bliss.

The Heruka then blessed each of the twenty-four abodes as a palace of Chakrasamvara and each of the the twenty-four *lingams* as a mandala of sixty-two wisdom deities. The sixty-two are Chakrasamvara, his consort, and his retinue: the twenty-four male and twenty-four female Bodhisattvas, and the twelve goddesses.

At the nirmanakaya level, it is said that Mt. Kailash was miraculously blessed by Buddha Shakyamuni and five hundred arhats. Once, Ravana (*mgon po beng*) and his consort had taken to their palace in Lanka one of the three statues of the Buddha Shakyamuni which the Lord himself had blessed. Desiring to place this statue on a worthy support, Ravana had planned to take Mt Kailash on his back and carry it to Lanka. At the same moment Lord Buddha and five hundred arhats came flying through the sky and alighted to the west of Mt. Kailash,

leaving their footprints in the rock. The Buddha stepped on all four sides of the mountain, leaving footprints in the rock that are known as the Four Immutable Nails of Kailash (*mi 'gyur ba'i gzer bzhi*). Ravana was thus unable to lift the mountain. Then the Buddha sat on a rock in front of the mountain and taught the Dharma to the naga king Anavatapta, the lord of Lake Manasarovar. He then taught the *Lankavatara Sutra* to Ravana, and blessed him and his consort as the Glorious Wisdom Protector, the Great Being and Consort (*dpal ye shes mgon po beng chen lcam dral*).

Mt. Kailash was later blessed by Guru Padmasambhava, and became famous after Jetsun Milarepa lived there in meditation and held his contest of miracles with Naro Bönchung (see below, note 11). Later Gyalwa Götsangpa (see note 60), Lingje Repa (*gling rje ras pa*, 1128–88), and many other great meditators lived ascetic lives at the foot of Mt. Kailash.

In particular, holders of the Drigung Kagyu lineage frequented the place in great numbers. Drigung Jigten Gonpo (*'bri gung 'jigs rten mgon po*, 1143–1217) had a dream in which the guardian deities of the three holy places of Tsari, Lapchi and Kailash came and prostrated themselves before him, requesting him to go and bless their territories. Jigten Gonpo replied that he would send great meditators instead. Accordingly, he dispatched 80 hermits to each place. Some years later, he reputedly sent 900 hermits and finally 55,525 practitioners to each site (see Huber 1989). At Kailash they were under the leadership of the great *pandita* Yakgangpa (*pan chen yag sgang pa*, who is also called, according to MK, p. 59, Dordzin Guhya Gangpa, *rdor 'dzin guhya sgang pa*); at Lapchi the practitioners were led by Geshey Paldrak (*dge bshes dpal grags*, 12th–13th century); and at Tsari they were under the guidance of Dordzin Gowoche (*rdor 'dzin mgo bo che*). In the three sacred places of Kailash, Lapchi, and Tsari, Dordzin (*rdor 'dzin,* "Holder of the Vajra") usually refers to a spiritual master or an administrator sent from Drigung Monastery as representative of the Drigung hierarchs. (See Petech 1978, 317.)

11. When Jetsun Mila and the Bönpo Naro Bönchung held their famous contest of miracles to decide who would retain supremacy over the sacred mountain, they left imprints of their feet in the rocks and many other miraculous signs. See G. C. C. Chang (1962, vol. 1, pp. 215–24).

12. The ninth Dalai Lama, Lungtok Gyatso (*lung rtogs rgya mtsho,* 1806–15).

13. Tibet is often called the "Land to the North,"

referring to the prediction of Buddha Shakyamuni that his teachings would spread to the north. When passing into Parinirvana, the Buddha laid his head toward the north.

14. For "the *Ah* and the *Hang*," see chap. 7, note 16.

15. The nine actions of the three doors (*bya ba dgu phrugs*): all outer, inner, and secret activities of body, speech, and mind, which a yogin will give up when engaging in Thögal practice. Three concern the body: 1) outwardly, all worldly, distracting activities, 2) inwardly, all ordinary virtuous deeds such as prostrations and circumambulations, and 3) secretly, all unnecessary movements that scatter one's practice. Three concern speech: 1) outwardly, all worldly, deluded conversations, 2) inwardly, all liturgies and recitations, and 3) secretly, any talking whatsoever. Three concern the mind: 1) outwardly, all worldly, deluded thoughts, 2) inwardly, all mental activity focused on visualizations of the development and the completion stages, and 3) secretly, all movements of the mind. (See Jamgön Kongtrul's *snying thig ma bu'i khrid yig*, in DZ, vol. Kha, pp. 196–97).

16. Specific points of sense-organ (*dbang po*), sense-field (*yul*), energy (*rlung*), and awareness (*rig pa*).

17. Tiny pearl-like relics (*ring bsrel*). See chap. 6, note 11.

18. Garpön (*sgar dpon*): one of the two commissioners of Tö (*stod sgar dpon*) who supervised the four districts (*rdzong*) and the numerous nomad clans of Ngari (*mnga' ris*). See Petech 1973, 13.

19. The *Flower Ornament Sutra* (Skt. *Gandavyuha-sutra*, Tib. *sdong po bkod pa'i mdo*, T44, part 45).

20. These last four verses are missing in TS 1, p. 554.

21. According the second part of Shabkar's autobiography, Lobzang Sherap remained Shabkar's attendant until his teacher's death.

22. The householder Palkye (*khyim bdag dpal skyes*) renounced his troublesome family life at the age of one hundred to became a monk. The novice monks used to tease him constantly about his age. Weary, he went to a solitary place and practiced with such diligence that he soon became an arhat and came, flying through the air, into the presence of Lord Buddha. There, at Jeta Grove, he became the teacher of the younger monks who had teased him.

23. For approach and accomplishment, see chap. 3, note 1.

24. The *Sutra Discriminating between the Path of Virtue and the Path of Vice* (Skt. *Subhasubhakarmavipaka-nirdesa-sutra*, Tib. *dge ba dang mi dge ba'i lam gyi rnam par smin pa bstan pa'i mdo*, T 355).

25. The names of the various species of birds and insects mentioned in this section have been, for the most part, guessed at from the descriptions given by Tibetan oral sources.

26. Representations of six-headed cobras are common in Hindu iconography.

27. Not ordinary pride, but the unshakable confidence that results in complete identification with the deity, and the certainty of being one with the deity's primordial nature.

28. Akshobhya (*mi bskyod pa*), the lord of the vajra family, dwelling in Abhirati (*mngon dga'*), the eastern Buddhafield.

29. Vajra-recitation (*rdo rje bzlas pa*): the recitation of mantras synchronized with the inhaling, retention, and exhaling of the breath.

30. Shantideva (*zhi ba lha*, 685–763) was one of the eighty-four *mahasiddhas* of India. He composed the famous *Bodhicaryavatara* (*byang chub sems dpa'i spyod pa la 'jug pa*, T 3871), *Engaging in the Bodhisattva's Activity*, from which the verse quoted here is extracted.

31. *Ngondro* (*sngon 'gro*): the preliminary practices of the Mantrayana. For a detail exposition of the *Ngondro* practice according to the Nyingma tradition, see Patrul Rinpoche's *kun bzang bla ma'i zhal lung*, translated by Bruyat et al. (1987 and 1994).

32. *Phowa* (*'pho-ba*) is the practice of transference of consciousness (see chap. 5, note 25). Itching at the top of the head and the other signs show success in the practice and are sometimes accompanied by the opening of a small aperture at the fontanelle in which a stalk of *kusha* grass can be inserted.

33. *Prana* (*lung*) refers to the yogic practices for gaining control over the body's energy flow. *Prana* is the subtle energy compared to a blind horse ridden by the "legless man" of the mind (*sems*). On the different kinds of *prana*, see BM, p. 59, and YZ, vol. 40, p. 334. When ordinary *prana* circulates in the subtle channels it perpetuates the three poisons, desire, hatred and ignorance. After it has been transmuted into wisdom *prana* (*ye shes kyi rlung*), the three poisons become transmuted into their corresponding wisdoms. On Chöd, see Author's Introduction, note 32.

34. When someone dies, according to folk custom, friends and relatives offer food to the dead person for a few days. Here the advice is to make use of one's physical abilities while they exist.

35. The *King of Samadhi Sutra* (Skt. *Samadhiraja-sutra*, Tib. *ting nge 'dzin rgyal po'i mdo*, T 127).

36. The City of the Gandharvas is a curious phenomenon sometimes seen by people with visionary faculties: a city complete with buildings and inhabitants appears, and then disappears again without a

trace, after a few days or just a few moments. It may correspond to the mirages seen in deserts when a city is reflected in an adjacent plain.

37. For *The Emanated Scriptures of the Kadampas (bka' gdams sprul pa'i glegs bam)*, see Appendix 5.

38. For *The Emanated Scriptures of Manjushri ('jam dbyangs sprul pa'i glegs bam)*, see Appendix 5.

39. *Dohas* are the spontaneous spiritual songs of the Indian *mahasiddhas* and other accomplished masters.

40. Tsongkhapa.

41. *The Great Emanated Scriptures of the Oral Transmission Pith Instructions (man ngag sprul pa'i glegs bam snyan brgyud chen mo)*. These esoteric teachings, connected with Tsongkhapa's vision of Manjushri, were never written down.

42. Jampel Gyatso (*'jam dpal rgya mtsho*, 1356–1428); Basowa Chökyi Gyaltsen (*ba so ba chos kyi rgyal mtshan*, 1409–73); Drupchen Chökyi Dorje (*grub chen chos kyi rdo rje*, fifteenth century); and Gyalwa Wensapa Lobzang Dondrup (*rgyal ba dben sa pa blo bzang don grub*, 1504–66). These are four of the "six *siddhas* of the Ganden Mahamudra." See Willis (1985).

43. Meaning that he manifested as a shaven-headed monk clad in saffron robes.

44. For *The Emanated Scriptures of the Bodhisattva (rgyal sras sprul pa'i glegs bam)*, see Appendix 5. As will be seen in chap. 14, Shabkar is considered to be a reincarnation of Gyalse Ngulchu Thogme (see also Translator's Introduction, p. xx).

45. For *The Marvelous Emanated Scriptures (ngo mtshar sprul pa'i glegs bam)*, see Appendix 5.

46. *The Nine Cycles of the Formless* (lit. disembodied) *Dakini (lus med mkha' 'gro'i skor dgu)* were received by Tilopa from the wisdom dakinis at the Gondhala Temple. The teachings were then transmitted to Naropa, and then in part to Marpa, Milarepa and their disciples. Later when Rechungpa went to India he received and brought back to Tibet the entire cycle, which henceforth became part of Rechungpa's lineage. This cycle also became known as the *Surmang Nyengyu (zur mang snyan brgyud)* from the name of Surmang Monastery in Nangchen, Eastern Tibet, where its tradition has been kept alive. See DZ, vol. 8, and NG, p. 305.

47. The seat of the Sakya school (*sa skya*), founded in 1073 by Konchog Gyalpo of the Khön clan. Its main temple, the impressive Great Emanated Temple (*sprul pa'i gtsug lag khang chen mo*), was erected in 1268 and is the only building, among over a hundred temples in Sakya's monastic complex, which survived the Cultural Revolution.

48. The Crystal Peak of Rong (*rong shel mo gangs*), is a sacred mountain in Limi Rong in the district of Dolpo, Western Nepal. There is a guide to this legendary site, *gnas chen shel mo gangs gi dkar chag mthong ba rang grol*, written by one *bla ma padma dngos grub*.

49. These are famous maxims of the Kadampa teachers.

50. As explained by H.H. Dilgo Khyentse Rinpoche, "unswerving determination" means that no matter what our parents, friends, or anyone else may think or say, no matter what adverse conditions may be, nothing can deter us from our resolve to practice the Dharma. "Indifference to what others may think of you" means that once we have achieved our goal—to practice Dharma—even if people have a poor opinion of us, criticize us for "wasting our time," or slander us, we should not care about it in the least. The "vajra of wisdom" is the awareness of the ultimate truth, which should accompany us at all times. See also Shabkar's *Beneficial Moon (chos bshad gzhan phan zla ba)*, fols. 148–49.

51. Darchen *(dar chen)* or Darpoche *(dar po che)*, the Great Flag: a prayer flag that is so huge that a hundred men are required to raise the pole. The pole is raised every year after changing the flag on the full moon of the fourth lunar month (*saga zla ba*), the month of the birth, enlightenment, and parinirvana of the Buddha. There is a small temple and a marketplace—the only one in the Kailash area.

52. The naga Anavatapta, "Who Never Warms Up " (*ma dros pa*). See above, note 6.

53. The small river that links the two lakes, Manasarovar and Rakkas Tal, is also called Ganges.

54. In 1817.

55. Gyangdrak Monastery (*rgyangs grags*, called "Gengta" on old maps). A little above Darchen, Gyangdrak Monastery was founded by Dordzin Guhya Gangpa (see above, note 10), according to a prediction of Drigung Jigten Gonpo (see MK, p. 59) upon a hill endowed with perfect geomantic features.

56. The Fivefold Mahamudra (*phyag chen lnga ldan*) of the Drigungpas consists of : 1) The Great Seal of Bodhicitta (*byang sems phyag chen*); 2) the Great Seal of the Deity's form (*lha sku'i phyag chen*); 3) the Great Seal of Fervent Devotion (*mos gus phyag chen*); 4) the Great Seal of the True Nature (*gnas lugs phyag chen*); and 5) the Great Seal of Dedication (*bsngo ba'i phyag chen*).

57. Nyenpa Ridzong (*gnyan pa ri rdzong*): a monastery founded by Nyenpa Drupchen (*gnyan pa grub chen*, see MK, p. 50) at the feet of an immense cliff that is the dwelling of local protecting deities.

58. Chöku Rinpoche (*chos sku rin po che*) is a precious white statue of Buddha Amitabha. It is one of the five image-emanations of Avalokiteshvara that

originated miraculously from the milk lake of the Dakini Land of Karsha (*gar shwa*, Lahaul northern India). The story of how this image came to Mt. Kailash is related in MK, p. 50. The monastery also housed the white conch and the cauldron of Naropa. These three relics were hidden when the monastery was destroyed during the Cultural Revolution, and reinstalled in the new monastery rebuilt since 1981.

59. For Dordzin Rinpoche (*rdor 'dzin rin po che*), see note 10.

60. The "Cave in which the Dri Vanished" (*'bri thim phug*), also called Drira Phuk, the "Cave of the Dri Horn" (*'bri rwa phug*). When Gyalwa Götsangpa opened the sacred place of Kailash (from 1213 to 1221), he came to the Wild Yak Valley (*'brong lung*), knowing that the hill overlooking it was the palace of the Thousand Buddhas. As he approached, the Lion-headed Dakini (*seng ge dong ma*) appeared to him in the form of the female of the wild yak, or Drong Dri (*'brong 'dri*), and showed him the path to a certain cave. There it vanished into one of the walls, leaving on the rock the visible mark of its horn. Götsangpa meditated for several years in this cave. Above the entrance he, too, left his footprint in the rock. See MK, p. 53.

61. *The Lion's Roar*, the full title of which is *snying gtam lhug par smra ba seng ge sgra dbyangs*, is advice in prose by Jowo Atisha.

62. Lhatsun Changchup Ö (*lha btsun byang chub 'od*) was the nephew of the King of Gu-gey, Lha Lama Yeshe Ö (*lha bla ma ye shes 'od*). Lha Lama sent envoys with offerings of gold to invite Atisha to Tibet so that he could restore the purity of the teachings, which were in decline. But Atisha refused. Meanwhile, Lha Lama was captured by the king of Garlog, who was alarmed at any effort to revive the teachings. The king demanded Lha Lama's weight in gold as ransom. When Changchup Ö brought it, Lha Lama said, "I am now old, and it matters little whether I live or not. Use the gold to bring Pandit Atisha here." So Changchup Ö sent Naktso Lotsawa to India with the invitation. Hearing that the king Lha Lama had sacrificed his life for the sake of the teachings, Atisha said he could not refuse the invitation, although he had received a prediction from Tara that he would live to the age of ninety-two if he remained in India but only to seventy-three if he went to Tibet.

63. Tsegyeh Gonpa (*rtse brgyad dgon pa*), the only monastery on the banks of Rakkas Tal Lake.

64. Seventy-five kilometers west of Darchen, Pretapuri is one of the most sacred of the eight Underground Abodes (*sa 'og gi gnas brgyad*, see note 10). Vajravarahi is the chief deity of the place. According to the *Padma Kathang* (*padma bka' thang*, chap. 6), the

subjugation of Rudra took place at Pretapuri. This site has also been blessed by Guru Padmasambhava and many other saints. (See MK, pp. 81–88). Khyung Lung Monastery is located about thirty kilometers west of Pretapuri. It initially followed the Bönpo tradition and later turned to the Gelukpa school.

65. There were eight monasteries around Manasarovar, five of which have been rebuilt since 1981:

1) *ser ra lung*, "Hailstorm Valley," to the east, founded by the great yogin Drigung Dordzin Konchok Gyudzin (*'bri gung rdor 'dzin dkon mchog rgyud 'dzin*);

2) *mnyes 'go*, "Started with Pleasure," in the southeast, so called because Atisha was overjoyed when he visited the place, remaining there for a few days. Later Ngorchen Kunga Lhundrup (*ngor chen kun dga' lhun grub*) had a vision of Guru Padmasambhava there and built a monastery that was subsequently held by the Sakya school;

3) *khrus sgo*, the "Gate of the Thaw," in the south. See above, note 5;

4) *'go tshugs*, "The Initiator," in the southwest, so called because it was there that, after meditating for three months in a cave, Gyalwa Götsangpa began the propagation at Kailash of the Drukpa Kagyu tradition (*'brug pa bka' rgyud*);

5) *byi'u*, "Little Bird," in the west, built in the form of the Glorious Copper-colored Mountain (*zangs mdog dpal ri*) upon a heart-shaped rock. It was blessed by Guru Padmasambhava, who is said to have spent seven days there on his way to Chamara, when leaving Tibet;

6) *gser gyi bya skyib*, "Golden Bird-shelter," in the northwest, a place said to have been first blessed by the Buddha and his five hundred arhats, afterwards by Drigung Chen-nga Lingpa (*'bri gung spyan snga gling pa*) and his five hundred great meditators, then by Tsang Nyön Heruka (*gtsang smyon he ru ka*, 1452–1507), who established a retreat center there;

7) *glang sna*, "Elephant Trunk," in the north, so called because it was built on a hill shaped like an elephant's trunk. It was founded by two Drigung masters, Drupthob Nyemowa Samten Phuntsok (*grub thob snye mo ba bsam gtan phun tshogs*) and his reincarnation Kunga Lodrö Nyingpo (*kun dga' blo gros snying po*);

8) *bon ri*, "Bön Mountain," in the northeast, a seat of the Gelukpa school. It was founded

by the great meditator Khedrup Lobzang Norbu (*mkhas grub blo bzang nor bu*) on Bönri, the hill which Milarepa had given to Naro Bönchung as a dwelling place after winning the ownership of Mt. Kailash in a contest of miracles. See MK, pp. 73–76.

66. The *Vajra Peak Tantra* (Skt. *Vajrasekhara-mahaguhya-yogatantra*, Tib. *gsang ba rnal 'byor chen po'i rgyud rdo rje rtse mo*, T 480).

67. Skt. *Udanavarga* (Tib. *ched du rjod pa'i mtshoms*, T 326) is a collection of verses from the Buddhist canon compiled by Dharmatrata. The *Udanavarga* is similar in content and style to the famed *Dhammapada* found in the Pali canon.

68. The *Garland of Rebirths* (Skt. *Jatakamala*, Tib. *skye pa'i rabs gyi phreng ba*, T 4150) by Aryasura.

69. The *Tantra of the Enlightenment of Mahavairocana* (Skt. *Mahavairocanabhisambodhi-vikurvitadhisthana-vaipulya-sutranta-raja*, Tib. *rnam par snang mdzad chen po mngon par rdzogs par byang chub rnam par sprul pa byin gyis rlob pa shin tu rgyas pa mdo sde'i dbang po'i rgyal po*, T 494).

70. *Letter to a Friend* (Skt. *Suhrllekha*, Tib. *bshes pa'i spring yig*, T 4182) of Nagarjuna.

71. For *Engaging in the Bodhisattva's Activity*, see above, note 29.

72. For Padampa Sangye, see chap. 6, note 19.

73. Saleh Ö (*gsal le 'od*), the famous female disciple of Jetsun Milarepa. The verses quoted here show slight differences from those found in most editions of the *Hundred Thousand Songs* (*mgur 'bum*).

74. The seventh Dalai Lama, Kalzang Gyatso (*skal bzang rgya mtsho*, 1708–57).

75. The *Sutra of Manjushri's Perfect Emanation* (Skt. *manjusri-vikridita-sutra*, Tib. *'jam dpal rnam par rol pa'i mdo*, T 96).

76. This is a classic Tibetan allusion: a hair removed from butter comes out completely clean—nothing clings to it.

77. The *Supreme Dharma of Intent Mindfulness* (Skt. *Saddharmanusmrityupastana*, Tib. *dam pa'i chos dran pa nye bar gzhag pa*, T 287).

78. The *Sutra of Individual Liberation* (Skt. *Pratimoksa-sutra*, Tib. *so sor thar pa'i mdo*, T 2).

79. The *Condensed Perfection of Wisdom* (Skt. *Prajna-paramita-sancayagatha*, Tib. *'phags pa shes rab pha rol tu phyin pa sdud pa tshig su bcad pa*, T 13).

80. Referring to the fourth among the 1,002 Buddhas who will appear during this kalpa.

81. In DOL 2, p. 18a, Shabkar specifies that he composed these instructions in the Kangyur Temple (*bka' 'gyur lha khang*) of Shepheling Monastery (*bshad 'phel gling dgon*, see note 7).

82. Turquoise Roof Bridge (*g.yu thog zam pa*), a famous bridge in Lhasa erected by Yutok Yönten Gönpo, the famous luminary of Tibetan medicine.

83. The bowls of water offered to the deities daily on every altar.

84. When one takes refuge or monastic vows, the master who gives these vows symbolically cuts a lock of one's hair.

85. Four Ornaments *(rgyan bzhi):* four classical themes of old brocades—the elephant, *hastina*, symbolizing strength; the deer, *sharana*, symbolizing compassion; the sea monster, *patrana* who purified desire; and the Garuda, *karuna*, who purified ignorance.

86. The silver images of the Three Protectors (*rigs gsum mgon po*) of Korchag ('*khor chags*) in Purang, representing the Bodhisattvas Manjushri, Avalokiteshvara and Vajrapani. For a detailed description of the fascinating story of these three statues, see Ngawang Sonam Gyaltsen (1988).

87. The sword and the volume of scriptures—symbolizing, respectively, wisdom and skillful means—are the two symbols held by Manjushri.

88. A temple dedicated to the *Kangyur* (*bka' 'gyur*), the scriptures containing the sermons spoken by the Buddha and gathered by his disciples.

89. For *The Marvelous Emanated Scriptures* (*ngo mtshar sprul pa'i glegs bam*), see Appendix 5.

90. *The Three Main Points of the Path* (*lam gyi gtso bo rnam gsum*), a short text by Tsongkhapa, belonging to the pith instruction section of the Kadampa teachings. The three main points are, as Jamgön Kongtrul says in his commentary, "The gold foundation of renunciation, on which rises the fabulously arranged Mount Meru and continents of Bodhicitta, upon which shines the brilliant sun of the wisdom of the perfect view." (See DZ, vol. 4, pp. 435–88).

91. For *The Lion's Roar*, see above, note 60.

92. *The Jewel Rosary of the Bodhisattvas* (*theg pa chen po'i man ngag bka' gdams glegs bam rin po che'i rtsa tshig byang chub sems dpa' nor bu'i phreng ba*), a short text by Jowo Atisha. (See DZ, vol. 3, pp. 11–14).

93. *Eighty Pieces of Advice to the people of Tingri* (*rje btsun dam pa sangs rgyas kyis ding ri bar zhal chems su stsal ba ding ri brgyad bcu ma* or, in some versions, *brgya tsa ma*) by Padampa Sangye. See DZ, vol. 13, pp. 31–36. There are several versions of these teachings. See H. H. Khyentse Rinpoche's commentary, *La Sagesse aux cents miroirs* (1994).

94. For the *Seventy Admonitions*, see chap. 5, note 9.

95. For the *Thirty-Seven-fold Practice of a Bodhisattva*, see chap. 5, note 8.

96. This advice follows the structure of Ngulchu Thogme's *Thirty-Seven-fold Practice of a Bodhisattva*.

97. Jampel Dorje is the Nyingma master who,

when Shabkar was fourteen, introduced him to the nature of mind. See chap. 1, fol. 118b.

98. The Potala of Lhasa is said to be an earthly version of the celestial Potala Palace (*pho brang ri bo gru 'dzin*), the Buddhafield of Avalokiteshvara. The "pro-tector and refuge" refers here to the ninth Dalai Lama, Lungtok Gyatso, who had passed away in 1815.

99. Hell of Blisters (*chu bur gyi dmyal ba*), one of the eight cold hells.

12

Pilgrimage to Nepal

*How I went to pay homage at the two great stupas of Nepal, the
wondrous land that resembles a celestial realm*

In the eighth month of the male Earth Tiger Year,[1] accompanied by many disciples, I set off for Nepal. There, I explained the Dharma to the Horpa chieftain Truk and other patrons, cutting the stream of negative action and initiating the stream of virtue. People offered me many horses and a lot of silver and gold, tea and butter.

That year, everyone gave up the sin of killing, and the official traders, going back and forth, said that meat had become scarce. Having reached Trochö, I went to the home of Gopa Lobzang Trinley, son of Gopa Trungse. He gave me many ornaments of gold, silver, turquoise, and pearls, as well a large number of silver *dotse*.

The rich people of Trochö too offered me horses, clothes, turquoise, corals, and various precious things. I then gave more than a thousand silver coins' worth of these things to about twenty-five families of hunters who used to kill thousands of antelopes and other game every year [301b]. I taught them the Dharma of cause and effect and made them promise to stop hunting. I also gave them advice about worldly affairs. I collected five or six yak-loads of ropes and trappers' nets and burned them all. I then brought together the hunters and the wealthy families of Trochö, made them sit together, and told them that if the hunters stopped killing, the rich must help them. Later on I heard that the rich people were giving the hunters food and clothing in exchange for some work, and that all were happy.

Then I and a few others went to Gachö Gon, the "Monastery of the Joyous Dharma," where we distributed tea and money and requested spiritual protection. After resting for a few days, we, master and disciples, accompanied by the dignitary Wangpo and a few others, taking gold, silver, and most of our possessions to make offerings, left for the Pure Realm of U and Tsang.

First we met the glorious Sakyapa masters, father and son. I offered them a fine horse and a mandala of silver, arrayed with heaps of turquoise and corals. In the Great Emanated Temple, I offered a lamp made of twenty *sang* of gold, and left a fund of five hundred silver coins so that butter would be continuously replenished.

Then I met the Lord Protector, Panchen Rinpoche. I offered him three good horses and a large mandala of silver with heaps of gold, turquoise, and coral. In front of the precious golden reliquary of Panchen Lobzang Chökyi Gyaltsen [302a][2] I offered a lamp made of twenty *sang* of gold.

Continuing on to Lhasa, I presented three horses and a mandala of silver with heaps of gold, turquoise, corals, and various jewels as an offering to the reliquary of the Dalai Lama Gyalwa Lungtok Gyatso.[3]

I also offered five horses, thirteen *sho* of gold and a mandala of silver with turquoise, corals, and pearls to Demo Rinpoche, the regent of Tibet, requesting his help for making a golden lamp for the monastery of Ganden. For this, I offered one thousand *sho* of gold. The regent having given his command, the two master goldsmiths of Döpel[4] made the design, and the lamp with its support was fashioned by the goldsmith at the bottom of the Potala. The entire thing was thus perfectly designed and executed.

When the lamp was offered in front of the great golden reliquary of Ganden, along with a thousandfold offering, Sertri Rinpoche, the holder of Ganden's golden throne, was extremely pleased and made many prayers. Following this I offered tea and distributed money to the entire monastic community of Ganden, and concluded with stainless prayers of dedication. People said that this lamp weighed approximately one hundred and eighty *sang* of gold.

In those days, a new temple was being built at Samye; as a contribution I offered a hundred *sho* of gold and five horses, as well as turquoise, corals and amber worth one *dotse* of silver. I sent my offering through the regent-king of Tibet.[5] Soon after, the treasurer Depa Wangpo [302b] went to stay for some time at Yerpa Lhari Nyingpo Mountain near Lhasa. Practicing as best he could, he gained peace of mind.

With a few disciples, I then went through Namgyal Lhatse to the southern land of Chumik Gyatsa, the Hundred Springs, where one finds fire coming from stones and fire burning upon the water.[6] On the way I met my close disciple Kunzang Shenpen, who was coming up from the holy place of Tsari, where he lived. He asked me, "When you were living at Mt. Kailash did you give many teachings? Did many of your disciples practice the Dharma?" After giving him a detailed answer in prose, I spoke these verses:

I bow down at the feet of the Jetsun Lama.
Look with compassion upon all your
    followers,
And bless those to whom I have taught the
    Dharma
So that they may practice in accordance
    with it.

This is how I taught the Dharma
To the faithful who lived at the Snow
    Mountain:

I taught the Dharma,
Telling them to make offerings, prayers,
    and render service

To authentic teachers and the Three
    Jewels.

I taught the Dharma,
Telling them the rarity of the freedoms and
    favorable conditions,
To inspire them to use their human
    existence meaningfully.

I taught the Dharma,
Telling them of impermanence and death,
To spur their diligence for the sake of the
    next life.

I taught the Dharma,
Telling them of the suffering of the six
    realms,
To extinguish their thirst for samsara.

I taught the Dharma,
Telling them the defects of the objects of
    desire,
To inspire them to give up craving for
    wealth.

I taught the Dharma,
Telling them how to meditate on
    compassion [303a],
So that they might never forsake sentient
    beings.

I taught the Dharma,
Telling them how arouse great compassion
And generate Bodhicitta.

I taught the Dharma,
Telling them to shun
The ten unvirtuous actions and other
    wrongdoing.

I taught the Dharma,
Telling them to strive
To gather virtue through the six
    perfections and other means.

I taught the Dharma,
Telling them to benefit others as much as
    they could
Through the four ways of gathering.

I taught the Dharma of the profound
   Secret Mantrayana
Through which Buddhahood can be
   attained in one lifetime.

I taught the most secret quintessential
   Dharma
Through which enlightenment can be
   attained effortlessly.

Moreover, I taught the Dharma
To many people, high and low:

I taught the Dharma, telling the teachers
To benefit all traditions without sectarian
   bias.

I taught the Dharma, telling the chiefs
To protect their subjects with
   loving-kindness.

I taught the Dharma, telling the subjects
To serve and respect their leaders.

I taught the Dharma, telling all
To serve their parents, for they are the
   kindest of all.

I taught the Dharma, telling everyone
To abandon killing, for life is dear to all.

I taught the Dharma, telling the rich
Not to be stingy but to make offerings and
   gifts.

I taught the Dharma, telling people
To cultivate pure perception toward all
   traditions and doctrines.

Thus, by the power of having taught the
   Dharma, there appeared:
Many disciples, practitioners, and faithful
   ones,
Many who gave up thoughts of this life
   [303b],
Many who remained in mountain
   retreats,
Many who had great compassion,
Many who had generosity and wisdom,

Many who worked for the sake of others,
   and
Many who had pure perception.

There is no way to recount all that
   happened,
So, for now, this will suffice.

Continuing to expound the Dharma in this
   way,
May I bring benefit to all beings.

This song made Kunzang Shenpen happy.

On the way, I bestowed longevity blessings on Jampel Dradul, king of Lo Mangthang,[7] Trowo Palgön, king of Trithok, Yonten Sangye, governor of Jyulung, and to many other faithful men and women. I also gave them the following teaching:
   "We have now obtained this precious human existence, but we won't stay for long. It is certain that we will all go to the unknown land of the next life, yet when we will go is uncertain. There is a danger that we may even set out this very night on the great path of death and impermanence.
   "At that time, those who have practiced the Dharma will ascend higher and higher to the freedom of the superior realms and experience happiness and bliss. Those who have committed negative actions will go lower and lower to the three inferior states of existence, and suffer there. Right now, when the power to ascend or fall is in your hands, you must give up the negative actions that will lead you to the inferior realms, and by all means accomplish the sublime Dharma that will cause you to ascend.
   "Killing goats, sheep, and other wild animals [304a]; taking wealth from others through stealing, robbing, or deceit; angrily scolding and abusing your servants and others—in brief, all evil thoughts and violence—are negative acts. You must shun them.
   "Offering up to the masters and the Three

Jewels, giving alms to the lowly poor and the beggars, and serving the sangha, your own father, mother, and old people—all these are positive acts. You should perform them.

"Furthermore, with your body do prostrations and make circumambulations; with your speech recite prayers and mantras; and with your mind have faith, respect, and pure perception. Meditate on loving-kindness, compassion, emptiness, and on the deities. If, in accord with this, you abandon negative acts and accomplish positive ones, your present life will be happy and the next one also.

"We have established an auspicious connection so that eventually we may all meet in a Pure Realm and achieve Buddhahood together!" Then I sang this song:

> I bow down at the feet of the lord of men,
>   the Munindra.
> Grant your blessing that my aspirations
> And those of others be accomplished.
>
> Listen while I explain the means to
>   generate happiness both in this
>   life and in the next:
> How to distinguish between what to avoid
>   and what to accomplish.
>
> Although you all have obtained this
>   human life,
> Free and well-favored,
> You will not stay long in this life;
> You must go to the unknown land of the
>   next life,
> Without even knowing when you must
>   leave.
>
> There is great danger that you may set out
>   tonight itself [304b]
> On the highway of impermanence and
>   death.
>
> On the long, unfamiliar, tortuous path of
>   the *bardo*,
> Of which you know nothing at all,
> You must travel alone, without refuge or
>   protector.

> When going along that arduous path,
> Unimaginably fierce delusions will arise.
>
> At that time, only the sublime Dharma,
> The lama and the Three Jewels, your
>   guides,
> Will be of any avail to you—
> Not people, food, and possessions of this
>   life.
>
> Fortunate beings who have practiced the
>   sublime Dharma in this life
> Will ascend to the freedom of the higher
>   realms.
>
> The unfortunate, who have committed
>   unvirtuous acts,
> Will descend to the three lower realms:
>
> You are now at the crossroad, which leads
>   up and down—
> Don't take the wrong path!
>
> Therefore, to give up negative actions,
>   which lead one down,
> And accomplish positive ones, which lead
>   upward, do this:
>
> Have faith and respect in the Three Jewels
>   and the Three Roots.
> Develop compassion for all beings in the
>   three worlds.
>
> Even for the sake of your father and
>   mother, never take life.
> Even at the cost of your own life, never
>   give up the Three Jewels.
>
> Offer flowers, incense, lamps, food,
>   hanging banners[8] and canopies
> To the sacred objects symbolic of
>   enlightened body, speech, and mind.
> Make offerings, prayers and give service to
>   the virtuous communities of the sangha.
> Read and recite the infallible words of the
>   Victorious Ones.
> Give generously to the destitute, for all of
>   them have been your mothers.

Give medicine to the disabled and the
  sick.
Seek reprieve for criminals under sentence
  of death [305a].
Ransom the lives of animals about to be
  slaughtered—
All these serve as the cause for obtaining
  the excellent support
Of a celestial or human existence in your
  next life.

Observe the one-day vows,[9] which entail
  little hardship yet have great meaning.

When you hear harsh words that can
  scorch one's heart and upset others—
Meditate on patience; don't let anger
  develop.

If your laziness is great you won't achieve
  your aims;
Practice the sublime Dharma with strong
  endeavor.

Practice one-pointed samadhi meditation,
Focusing your attention on a statue of the
  Buddha—or on any other object.

Understand that all phenomena are like
  dreams and illusions,
Lacking any real existence.

Do your best to benefit the teachings and
  all beings:
Where you can't be of benefit, at least
  don't do harm.

Work hard at the means to achieve present
  and ultimate happiness:
The visualizations and recitations of the
  yidam deities,
And the rituals of repair and fulfillment for
  the Dharma protectors.

May all those who act in this way swiftly
  achieve omniscience
And lead all sentient beings—their
  mothers—to enlightenment.

These words turned toward the Dharma
the minds of all—kings, ministers and subjects.
By following my advice, they gained the good
fortune of enjoying merit, power, longevity,
descendants, luck and fame in this life, and of
gradually achieving the unsurpassable attainment,
Buddhahood.

They offered me many gold and silver coins,
coral and turquoise ornaments, and other possessions. I reached the Hundred Springs of the
land of Lo and I stayed there for a few days
[305b], making a connection with this holy place,
offering *ganachakra* feasts, and bathing in the
waters. I saw fire burning on the water and fire
burning on stones.

On the way back I visited holy places and
monasteries. In each village I benefited beings
and gave the following teaching to the Abchenpa
nomads and all the faithful men and women of
Ngari Dzongkar:

"All of us have been born in the southern
continent of Jambudvipa, supreme among the
four continents, a place where birth is difficult to
obtain. At this time, when we have a precious,
free and gifted human existence, so difficult to
gain, when we met the teachings of the Buddha
and an authentic teacher, so difficult to meet, we
must strive to do what is good.

"If, right now, we don't practice the sublime
Dharma—the way to travel the far-reaching
path—we won't obtain a free and gifted human
existence again. Even if we were to obtain it, we
might not meet the teachings of the Buddha.
Even if we were to meet these teachings, who
knows if we would have the freedom to practice
the sublime Dharma? Now that we have a choice,
we must give meaning to our freedoms and
endowments. If we don't make efforts immediately, but leave everything for tomorrow or the
next day, simply feeling regret at the time of
death will be useless.

"Why? Because all compounded phenomena are by nature impermanent. This body of
flesh and blood is like a bubble in water; the
universe and beings are in a perpetual cycle of
change; our life, our breath may vanish as easily
as mist on a mountain pass—we can't even have
the least confidence that we will not die tonight

[306a]. The causes for our death may flash at any moment like lightning. There is no way to avoid death, no way to run away.

"When death comes, even if our influence and strength have been equal to those of a universal monarch, it won't help us a bit. Even if we had the riches and possessions of Vaishravana,[10] we won't have the power to take with us even so much as a sesame seed. Even if our father, our mother, many relatives, and friends surround us, we won't be able to take along a single one of them. We will go completely alone, like a hair pulled out of a pat of butter.

"Moreover, we will experience inconceivable, terrifying fears—the delusory appearances of the *bardo*. At that time, only the supreme Dharma and our guides—the spiritual master and the Three Jewels—can be of help. None of the people, wealth, and food of this life can give us an atom of help.

"But that's not all. If, for the sake of food and clothing, or for our sons and daughters, we have committed serious negative actions, we will be reborn in the hells and experience unbearable sufferings, heat or cold. If we have committed negative actions of medium strength, we will suffer thirst and hunger when reborn among the tortured spirits. If we have committed negative actions of small magnitude only, we will experience countless torments when reborn among animals—obscured by stupidity we will be abused, enslaved, and finally slaughtered.

"After these experiences, we will eventually be freed from the three lower realms [306b], but even though we are then reborn in the human realm, if we are sinful, with impure karma, out of a hundred possible misfortunes—short life, constant sickness, death from poison or weapons, being blind, deaf, mute, crippled, enslaved, destitute, or powerless—there's not a single one that we will not encounter.

"Having obtained a miserable existence, lacking even a single opportunity for happiness, the waters of sin, suffering, and defamation will rise; we will accumulate further bad karma and again be hurled like a stone to the bottom of the three lower realms, from whence one can hardly rise again. This is why it is said that one must give up unvirtuous actions.

"If we practice virtuous deeds perfectly and extensively, in the best case we will achieve Buddhahood in this lifetime with this very body, and become able to set forth on the path of ripening and liberating all sentient beings who see, hear, touch, or remember us.

"If we practice virtuous deeds in a medium way, at the time of death our spiritual master and tutelary deities will come in reality to show us the path, enabling us to go to the Pure Buddhafield of Manifest Joy, to the Blissful Buddhafield, or to any other Pure Realm.

"If, in the last case, we have accomplished minor virtuous actions, we will again obtain a free, well-favored human birth and be born in a good family, with a good appearance, wealth, power, intelligence, longevity, health and happiness. Going, we will go on horseback;[11] sitting, we will sit on a carpet; eating, we will eat whatever we like. Acting, we will have the freedom to practice the sublime Dharma [307a], and practicing it joyfully we will eventually reach the level of no return, gaining the good fortune to benefit sentient beings. This is why it is said that one must practice virtuous actions.

"If we have to give up nonvirtue for virtue, what are the unvirtuous actions to be abandoned? They are those committed under the sway of obscuring emotions—desire, hatred, ignorance: taking the lives of many beings, each one of whom was once our parent, stealing the possessions of others, indulging in sexual misconduct, telling lies, slander, speaking harsh words, gossiping, feeling envy, fueling harmful thoughts and false views—in brief, whatever makes the lama and the Three Jewels ashamed of us and causes harm to other sentient beings is a negative action that we must avoid.

"Even minor unvirtuous actions entail grave consequences. In the past, someone who told another, 'You are like a monkey,' was reborn five hundred times as a monkey. A novice monk who once told a fully ordained monk who had an unmelodious voice, 'You sing like a barking dog,' was reborn as a dog for five hundred lives.

A woman who told other women, 'You are like bitches!' was reborn as a bitch for five hundred lives. A monk who told a major lie[12] to the All-seeing One,[13] thus losing his vows, was reborn for five hundred lives as a worm [307b].

"In particular, the moment we merely conceive of killing a goat, a sheep or a wild animal, our life span, good fortune, and merit become exhausted and in a future rebirth we will ourselves be killed. If we have a hundred or a thousand similar thoughts, we will be killed that many times. If we actually kill, in this life we will have a short life filled with many illnesses; after we die we will be reborn in the ever-reviving hell where hundreds of thousands of times a day we will be killed by weapons, revived, and killed again and again.

"If, under some false pretext, we take away others' possessions, in this life we will be stricken by leprosy or some other grave disease; in the next life we will go to a hell realm where our tongue, five hundred miles long, will be ploughed by a thousand ploughs of burning iron. If we speak wicked words to our parents, our tongues will be pierced from beneath the chin by an iron rod, an arm's length long, stuck in the ground. If we are fraudulent traders who cheat people by falsifying weights and measures, flesh will be cut from our bodies until it weighs on the scales the same as the amount we stole.

"Even a single burst of anger destroys the merit accumulated for a thousand kalpas and leads us after death to be reborn in a hell realm. Even if we are eventually reborn a human being, we will have an ugly complexion and be unattractive to all.

"Therefore, having pondered the evil consequences of negative actions—that to have done them is as harmful as having swallowed boiling, poisonous water [308a]—it is of utmost importance to confess them remorsefully and make the firm promise that, even at the cost of our life, we shall never commit them again.

" Someone who has swallowed poison in the morning can be cured by good medicine in the afternoon, and even though we have committed sins in our early life, through confession we can purify them later in our life. Even we sinners will have the fortune to travel to the freedom of the higher realms. Therefore, I entreat you to belief and trust in confession and vows.

"Having given up negative actions, how are we to practice the positive ones—those motivated by loving-kindness, compassion and an enlightened attitude?

"We must familiarize ourselves with the Dharma, make offerings to the Three Jewels, be generous, listen to the teachings, read the scriptures, keep them in mind, explain them to others, say prayers, and meditate earnestly. In brief, all that pleases the heart and mind of the spiritual masters and the Three Jewels, all that benefits others, is virtue. This is what we need to accomplish.

"Even a small virtuous action brings great benefit. Once an old lady offered a single butter-lamp to the Buddha, who then made the prediction that in the future she would become a Buddha named 'Bright Lamp',[14] endowed with the ten powers. The Buddha also prophesied that a village chief who kept the vow of not killing for a single day, would ultimately become enlightened as the Buddha 'Beneficial Speech' [308b].[15] A Brahmin girl offered her needle to a bhikshu; because of that she became the noble Shariputra. A woman offered a meal to a beggar; she was reborn in a mansion made of jewels, where she enjoyed delicious food with a hundred flavors. A pig who happened to make one circumambulation around a stupa because he was chased by a dog took rebirth as the householder Palkye, who attained the level of an arhat. So it is said.

"If we ransom the lives of animals and set them free, in all our lifetimes we will enjoy a long life free from illness. If we offer respect and bow down to our teacher and our parents, we will be reborn into a good family. If we cultivate patience, we will have a beautiful appearance in all our lives and will eventually obtain the major and minor marks of a supreme body. If we make even a single offering, we will enjoy great wealth. Therefore, thinking of the benefits of practicing virtue, we should rejoice in the virtuous actions we have done in the past, and strive to practice them in the future.

"If we do so, in this life itself we will gather people, wealth, and food; we will enjoy happiness, well-being and renown. In the next life we will meet again, like old friends, in the eastern Buddhafield of Manifest Joy or another Buddhafield. There we will delight in joyous conversations, and through our unimpeded miraculous power visit millions of pure and impure realms [309a]. We will make offerings to all the Buddhas and be able to bring there all sentient beings. Such will be our good fortune. Keep that in mind." Then I sang this song:

Lord and master, Vajradhara,
Dwell as an ornament on the crown of my head
And bless all the fortunate men and women gathered here
So that their minds may turn toward the Dharma.

This yogin who roams throughout the land
Sings this melodious song.
All you who have good fortune,
Listen well to my heart-advice.

A human birth, free and well-favored, is hard to find.
It is unlikely that you will obtain it again and again.
Now that you have obtained it once,
Don't return empty-handed, fortunate ones.

Every day that passes, you come closer to death,
Like a sheep dragged off to the slaughterhouse.
You can't be sure you'll be around much longer:
Ponder the fragility of life, fortunate ones.

Wealth is impermanent,
Like dew on the tip of a blade of grass;
Soon exhausted, it won't endure.

Free of greed and stinginess,
Give to the Dharma, fortunate ones.

Like people gathered in a marketplace,
One's family won't stay together for long;
Soon they will pass on to the next life.
For the present, maintain harmony among yourselves, fortunate ones.

Your enemy was your parent in past lives.
Even if he harms you a little in this one [309b],
He must look forward to his own death as well; nothing endures,
So don't nourish hatred, fortunate ones.

When departing for the land of the next life,
If the suffering of the three lower realms
Falls upon you, it will be hard to bear.
So give up unvirtuous actions, fortunate ones.

If you can ascend to the supreme place of freedom of the higher realms,
You will enjoy constant bliss and happiness.
The divine Dharma is the best method for reaching there;
Practice it, fortunate ones.

Morning and evening, at all times,
Take refuge in the Three Jewels—
The infallible refuge.
With a good heart, whatever you do will turn to Dharma:
Develop an enlightened attitude, fortunate ones.

Make efforts in the mandala practice and in reciting the hundred-syllable mantra,
The method for completing the accumulations and purifying all obscurations.
To the lord lama, laden with blessings,
Address your prayers, fortunate ones.

Meditate on the supreme deity, the mighty
    Avalokiteshvara,
The sublime patron Buddha of the Land of
    Snows.
The essence of all Dharmas is the *mani*;
Recite it continuously, fortunate ones.

In the Land of Snows,
Orgyen Pema is the most gracious.
His compassion and blessings are swifter
    than those
    of any other Buddha;
Pray to him, fortunate ones.

Beings of this decadent age have little
    merit.
Wealth is a lure to call enemies and spirits.
Don't be envious of others' wealth,
But be content with what you have,
    fortunate ones.

In these times, it is difficult
To be a person without faults and with
    good qualities.
Without looking at the defects of your
    friends [310a],
Consider everyone as above yourself,
    fortunate ones.

Maintain a low position, perform virtuous
    deeds;
At the end of whatever virtuous act you do,
Dedicate its merit with whichever prayer
    you know:
If you do so, your merit will increase and
    never be exhausted, fortunate ones.

By the virtue of having sung this song,
May all beings, our mothers, be happy and
    well.
May auspiciousness and prosperity be
    established in this place,
And spread throughout the three worlds.

As I sang this, the faith and devotion of everyone
grew stronger than before; many fortunate men
and women renounced evil to practice virtue.

Once Om Phuk Lama and a few disciples and
patrons said to me, "These evil people of Ngari
Dzong[16] behave in accord with neither worldly
nor religious ethics, and engage in many shameless acts. Out of kindness, please give them some
advice that will expose their deep-rooted defects."
In answer, I sang a song for the benefit of all,
high and low:

I pray to the lama, who never deceives:
Grant your blessings that I remember the
    uncertainty of the time of death.

Birth ends in death:
Contemplate impermanence and death,
    Dzongka folk.

See how many young people suddenly die:
The time of death is uncertain, Dzongka folk.

At death, those have done good will climb
    the path to liberation:
Those who have done wrong will fall into
    the hells, Dzongka folk.

Right here is the point where you can go
    up or down [310b];
Great is the danger of taking the wrong
    road, Dzongka folk.

If you want to ascend, not fall,
Here is what you must do and what you
    must avoid, Dzongka folk:

Even if you don't have heartfelt devotion
    to the lama,
At least don't end up rejecting your faith,
    Dzongka folk.

Even if you don't make regular offerings to
    the Three Jewels,
At least offer butter-lamps from time to
    time, Dzongka folk.

Even if you don't fully repay your parents'
    kindness,
At least don't cast them aside when they
    grow old, Dzongka folk.

Even if you don't offer tea and money to
    the sangha,
At least give something to those who beg
    for alms in the autumn, Dzongka folk.

Even if you can't give away all your posses-
    sions,
At least give some *tsampa* to the beggars at
    your door, Dzongka folk.

Even if you can't abandon all ten
    unvirtuous actions,
At least don't slaughter animals for food,
    Dzongka folk.

Even if you can't practice the Dharma day
    and night,
At least don't sleep during the day,
    Dzongka folk.

Even if you can't be patient with your
    enemies
At least don't be angry with your friends,
    Dzongka folk.

Even if you can't meditate in solitary
    places,
At least don't act out every thought that
    comes to mind, Dzongka folk.

Even if you don't know how to meditate
    on wisdom and emptiness,
At least remain aware of the law of cause
    and effect, Dzongka folk.

Even if you are not kind to pilgrims,
At least don't tax or rob them, Dzongka
    folk.

Even if you landlords won't provide all that
    your servants need,
At least don't tyrannize them, Dzongka
    folk.

Even if you must punish your subjects,
At least don't cut off their noses or hands,
    Dzongka folk.

Even if you don't give the nomads clean
    barley in exchange for salt,
At least don't give them barley mixed with
    grass and dust, Dzongka folk.

Even if you have no faith in other
    practitioners [311a],
At least don't speak ill of them, Dzongka
    folk.

Even if you don't get along with your
    neighbors,
At least don't ruin them by taking them to
    court, Dzongka folk.

Even if you, monks, cannot give up doing
    business,
At least don't engage in evil sorts of trade,
    Dzongka folk.

Even if you local people can't come to an
    agreement,
At least don't create scapegoats, Dzongka
    folk.

Even if you don't praise people's virtues,
At least don't gossip about their defects,
    Dzongka folk.

Even if you covet others' wealth,
At least don't crave the possessions of the
    sangha, Dzongka folk.

Even if you don't repay your cattle's labor
    when they grow old,
At least don't slaughter them for food
    when autumn comes, Dzongka folk.

Even if you don't feed your dogs every day,
At least don't let them starve or freeze to
    death, Dzongka folk.

Even if you do not help your neighbors
    and your fellow countrymen,

At least don't think of ways to harm them,
    Dzongka folk.

Even if you can't repay the kindness of all
    those who have been kind to you,
At least repay that of your parents,
    Dzongka folk.

Even if you can't do pilgrimage to other
    holy places,
At least go pay homage to the Jowo of
    Kyirong, Dzongka folk.

Even if you don't make offerings to the
    Jowo,
At least don't steal the offerings of others,
    Dzongka folk.

Even if you can't make many prayers and
    recitations,
At least keep reciting the *mani*, Dzongka
    folk.

Even if you old nuns don't recite the *mani*,
At least don't spend your time scolding the
    young wives, Dzongka folk.

Even if you can't benefit all beings—your
    mothers,
At least train yourself continuously in
    wishing for their benefit,
Dzongka folk [311b].

This heart-advice of the yogin is like gold.
Take it to heart, Dzongka folk.

If you behave accordingly, you will be
    happy in this life and in the next,
And you will ascend to higher and higher
    destinies, Dzongka folk.

May the oath-bound guardians, the
    protectors of the Dharma,
Accompany all who practice the supreme
    Dharma in this way.

It was said that, from then on, in accordance
with my advice, the local governors stopped

inflicting severe punishments on their subjects
and levying tolls or taxes on the pilgrims. The local
people and all the humble pilgrims were very happy.
Many people offered me food and goods.

Then I went to the Luminous Cave, Ösel
Phuk,[17] where Jetsun Milarepa meditated, then
to Kangtsuk Phuk,[18] the cave called "Standing
on my Feet." At his birthplace, Kya Ngatsa,[19] I
saw the stupas built on the ruins of his house,
"Four Pillars and Eight Beams." I also saw his
fields, the "Triangle of Horma" and Trepe
Tenchung, "Small Monkey Mat."

On my way to see the Jowo of Kyirong, I
met some strangers. Seeing me from a distance,
they said, "This one can't be a Nyingmapa,
because he dresses like a monk; he can't be a
Gelukpa, because he has long hair. What a
strange lama; he doesn't look like anything!"
Hearing that, I improvised this song:

Neither a white lion nor a garuda—
I am the son of their union
Known as the Eight-legged Lion.
Not like anyone else,
But in harmony with all—how strange!
    [312a].

Neither a horse nor a donkey—
I am the son of their union
Known as the White-mouthed Mule.
Not like anyone else,
But in harmony with all—how strange!

Neither a nomad's *dri* nor a bull—
I am the son of their union,
Known as the villagers' *dzomo*, White
    Garuda.[20]
Not like anyone else,
But in harmony with all—how strange!

Neither Nyingma nor Geluk—
I am a yogin born of their union,
Known here as Lama Shabkar, White Foot.
Not like anyone else,
But in harmony with all—how strange!

After this, I went down to pay homage to
the Jowo of Kyirong called Wati Zangpo,[21] an

image of Avalokiteshvara made of "snake-essence" sandalwood [22] that miraculously appeared and spoke. I stayed there a few days, making some offerings.

As I was going to leave for Nepal to pay homage to the two great stupas, Bodhnath and Svayambunath,[23] accompanied by an excellent friend, the secretary Yugkawa, I sang this joyful song:

On the islands of the Outer Ocean
There are many jewels,
But there is none greater
Than the Wish-fulfilling Gem [312b].

Having sought it with great longing,
Set it atop the victory banner;
Make offerings, praises, and supplications:
"May all that we desire descend like rain."

In the distant land of Kyirong
There are many sacred objects of body,
    speech and mind,
But there is none
More sublime than Wati Zangpo.

Out of utter faith
Touch your head to his feet,
And pray to him with your whole heart,
"Please bestow blessings and *siddhis!*"

In the expanse of the celestial vault
There are stars and planets without number,
But none like the sun and the moon,
Whose rays pervade all directions.

The corollas of the water lilies
Turn toward you, O sun and moon:
To nurture all the flowers
Send forth your luminous rays.

In the excellent country of Nepal
There are many glorious sacred objects,
But none like the two stupas,
Renowned in the ten directions.

The mind of the yogins, master and
    disciples,

Turns toward the two stupas:
Guardians of the two stupas,
Come and protect us, master and
    disciples.

Roaming without preference through all
    countries,
Free from attachment, I, the yogin, am
    happy.
Having seen the Jowo of Kyirong,
I celebrate my happiness in songs of joy.

With my good friend the secretary,
I go to the fine land of Nepal.
If anyone else wishes to go,
Come along, and together we'll offer
    prayers
Before the two great stupas [313a].

Singing joyful songs, I crossed valley after valley. I first paid homage at *Svayambunath*, Nepal's great stupa. I offered it a coat of whitewash and saffron, which cost more than five hundred silver coins; then, offering lamps and a great *ganachakra* feast, I prayed:

By the strength of this merit
And all other merit,
May all of us practitioners,
Master, disciples, patrons,
Effortlessly, swiftly, easily
Achieve the level of Buddhahood.

From now on,
May auspiciousness prevail
Wherever I go.

May blessings remain
Wherever I stay.

May good qualities be transferred to
Whomever I accompany.

May prosperity be attached to
Whatever I touch.[24]

May all relics of body, speech and mind
That I see be consecrated.

May all the faithful
Who come to meet me be empowered and
blessed.

May the suffering
Of those who think of me in times of fear
Be pacified.

May whatever I do, say, and think
Be of great benefit to the Dharma and all
beings.

May whatever merit I have accumulated
Be the cause of benefiting others [313b]
And of achieving unsurpassable
enlightenment.

May the blessings of the twofold
accumulation
Of the lamas and Victorious Ones,
And all the merit gathered by myself and
others
Throughout the three times
Fully and swiftly mature in me
So that I quickly attain Buddhahood.

May I achieve enlightened qualities
Even more numerous than those of the
body, speech, and mind
Of the infinity of Victorious Ones in the
ten directions,
Multiplied by the number of particles of
dust in the universe.

Through my own efforts,
May I myself establish in Buddhahood,
Leaving not a single one behind,
All beings, my mothers, whom the
Victorious Ones of the past
could not guide.

May I emanate infinite rays of light
That will reach all sentient beings and all
universes throughout the reaches of
space,
And, like the sun dispelling darkness,
Purify all impurities, imperfections, and
faults, leaving no trace.

May I emanate light again toward the
universe and beings,
Which, like the alchemical transformation
of iron into gold,
Will purify the universe into a pure
paradise
And all sentient beings into male and
female deities.

All impure places having become pure
Buddhafields,
And all beings having become deities adorned
with the major and minor marks,
May even the names of the three worlds of
samsara no longer exist,
Just as on an island of gold ordinary stones
do not exist.

Having utterly emptied all samsara,
Having completed all their enlightened
activities [314a],
And totally fulfilled all their
wisdom-intentions,
May all Buddhas and Bodhisattvas happily
remain.

Having established all beings in
Buddhahood,
May I not remain at rest even then,
But as long as absolute space remains,
May I emanate infinite clouds of offerings,
Pleasing all the Buddhas.

By the power of these boundless offerings
Tirelessly made throughout the six periods
of day and night,
May all the Victorious Ones
Cherish me like their only child,
And may I be praised throughout all
celestial fields.

In brief, by giving them all that they desire
May I fulfill the hopes of all beings.
By making inconceivable offerings
May I fulfill the intentions of all Buddhas.

By my perfectly pure prayers,
Made with utterly pure intention,

May all lamas, Buddhas and Bodhisattvas
Grant their blessings that I achieve
   realization
Swiftly and without hindrance.

By the wondrous blessings of the
   Victorious Ones and their sons,
By the truth of infallible interconnections,
And by the strength of my pure motivation,
May all my prayers be accomplished.

I made this and many more aspirations, using
the *Golden Garland of Dedications*.[25] I then went to
pay homage to the Great Stupa of Bodhnath. With
six hundred silver coins, I offered it a garment of
whitewash and saffron and, instead of letting a
water buffalo be killed for the sacramental feast
[314b], I ransomed the life of a water buffalo. I
offered a great *ganachakra* feast and many butter-
lamps, and concluded with this prayer:

By the power of all the merit
Accumulated throughout the three times,
Symbolized by the merit of this prayer,
May we all—I the yogin, disciples and
   patrons,
And all those with whom I have made a
   connection—
Effortlessly attain in this very lifetime
The level of the great Victorious
   Vajradhara.

May I then be able to establish on the path
   of maturation and liberation
All beings who see, hear, touch, or
   remember me.

From now on, may I bring boundless
   benefit to all beings
Through the four ways of gathering.

May I bring boundless benefit to all beings
Through exposition, debate, and
   composition.[26]

May I bring boundless benefit to all beings
Through listening, reflecting and
   meditating.

May I bring boundless benefit to all beings
Through the path of the three trainings.

May I bring boundless benefit to all beings
Through the Tripitaka.[27]

May I bring boundless benefit to all beings
Through the development and completion
   stages, and the Great Perfection.

May I bring boundless benefit to all beings
   [315a]
Through the higher perceptions and
   miracles.

In brief, may I bring boundless benefit to
   all beings
Through my body, speech, and mind.

May all those who see, hear, touch, or
   think of me, the yogin Vidyadhara—
All those whose hairs stand on end with
   ardent faith—
Ripen within themselves
The seeds of supreme enlightenment.

May the physical illnesses
And the mental sufferings
Of all those who see, hear, touch, or think
   of me,
The yogin Vidyadhara,
Be totally pacified.
May they experience
Boundless physical well-being and mental
   happiness.

May all those who see, hear, touch, or
   think of me,
The yogin Vidyadhara,
Turn their minds toward the Dharma
And have the good fortune to practice it
   properly.

May all those who see, hear, touch, or
   think of me,
The yogin Vidyadhara,
Be happy now and, ultimately,
Reach with ease the state of Buddhahood.

May all the Buddhas and Bodhisattvas
Grant their blessings so that these prayers
    may be fulfilled.
May all the *rishis* of the ten directions who
    have accomplished the words of truth
Support whatever prayers I make.

"In the past, a swineherd's son, who had offered a vase to the great stupa, made a prayer of aspiration; through its power, he took rebirth as the Khenpo Bodhisattva and spread the teachings of the sutras.[28] May we yogins, master and disciples, by the power of offering a garment to the Great Stupa, uphold the teachings of the Vinaya and sutras as did the great Khenpo Bodhisattva.

"In the past, the son of a dog keeper, having offered a vase to the Great Stupa, made an aspiration-prayer; by its power, he took rebirth as the great master Padmakara and spread the teachings of the Secret Mantrayana. May we yogins, master and disciples, by the power of having offered a garment to the Great Stupa, uphold, preserve and spread the teachings of the Secret Mantrayana as did the great master Padmakara.

"In the past, the son of a stablehand, having offered a vase to the Great Stupa, made a prayer of aspiration; through its power, he was reborn as the Dharma King, Trisong Detsen, and became the benefactor of the teachings of sutra and mantra. May we yogins, masters and disciples [315b], by the power of having offered a garment to the great stupa, become benefactors of the teachings of sutra and mantra, as did the Dharma King.

"By the blessings of the Buddhas and Bodhisattvas, and the power of all merit accumulated by myself and others throughout the three times, from now on and throughout all of my lives may I become the glory of the teachings and of beings.

"Even when a wish-fulfilling jewel is hidden within a silk wrapping, it brings benefits, happiness and auspiciousness to all. Likewise, even if from now on, and in all my future lives, I remain in solitude, may I always benefit beings.

"Just as the sun and moon never linger but, circling the four directions [316a], bring benefit to beings on the four continents, so, from now on, and in all my future lives, wandering throughout all lands, may I bring benefit to beings.

"By the blessings of the wondrous Victorious Ones and their sons, by the truth of the undeceiving causal links, and by the strength of my pure motivation, may all the aspirations of my pure prayers be swiftly accomplished."

With this, I offered many other prayers, following the *Golden Garland of Dedications*. I also made the following dedications for all the faithful local people and pilgrims who, while I was traveling to the two stupas and staying there, had made offerings in the name of the living and the dead, and had requested prayers:

"Lamas, Buddhas and Bodhisattvas who dwell in infinite, boundless, limitless Buddhafields of the ten directions, think of me and of all sentient beings. Especially, throughout the six times, day and night, gaze with great tenderness upon these faithful benefactors, men and women.

"By the blessings of the Victorious Ones of the ten directions, and by the merit accumulated by myself and others throughout the three times; especially by the merit accumulated by these faithful patrons in the past, and that which they aspire to accumulate in the future, along with the pure connection they have made now through these material offerings [316b], may the Buddha's teaching spread and bring happiness and well-being to all.

"Particularly may all these merits fully ripen in the minds of these faithful men and women and all their families. In their present life may all sickness, evil influences, and obstacles be totally pacified. May their glory, longevity, and good fortune increase. When their lives come to an end, may they be spared suffering the agony of death. As soon as they leave this life, may Avalokiteshvara and the gurus appear before them and guide them to rebirth in the Blissful Buddhafield.

"If such fortunate karma is not theirs, may they again obtain a sound human body and, with its support, may they hear, study and practice the holy Dharma like the Lord of Yogins, Jetsun Milarepa, and attain Buddhahood in one lifetime.

"Moreover, by this merit, may all inauspiciousness be assuaged in this region and throughout the entire kingdom. May auspiciousness, excellence, and happiness pervade the whole country in all directions. May this be so!"

By the blessing of realizing the trikaya of
    the Buddhas,[29]
By the blessing of the truth of the
    unchanging absolute nature [317a],
By the blessing of the virtuous community
    remaining undivided,
May all these prayers be granted!

Having made these dedication prayers for the living, I then made one for the dead:

"Lamas, Buddhas and Bodhisattvas, who dwell in infinite, boundless, limitless Buddhafields of the ten directions, look with great compassion upon myself and all beings; look with compassion especially upon all those who have left this world, wherever they now dwell, in the intermediate state leading to a new existence or in one of the six realms of this universe.

"By the blessing of the Victorious Ones of the ten directions and the merit that I and others have accumulated throughout the three times; especially by the power of all the meritorious acts performed in the past by relatives for the sake of their dead, by the meritorious acts they aspire to perform in the future, and by the connections they have made with me in the present for making dedication prayers—all this symbolizing the merits accumulated throughout the three times—may the Buddha's teachings flourish and spread, and in particular, may all beings obtain happiness. Especially, may these root merits fully ripen in the minds of all those who have left this world.

"Wherever they are now, in the intermediate state leading to a new existence or in any of the six realms of this universe, by the strength of this prayer, may they never be reborn in the three lower realms or in any inferior state of existence [317b].

"May even those who have already been reborn in an inferior state escape from that state and be miraculously reborn from a lotus in the Blissful Buddhafield; may they there behold the face of Buddha Amitabha. Even if such good fortune is not theirs, may they again obtain a sound human body; with its support, hearing, reflecting, and meditating according to the holy Dharma, may they swiftly achieve complete Buddhahood.

"Furthermore, by these merits, may all inauspiciousness be assuaged in this place and in the whole kingdom. May excellence, auspiciousness and happiness pervade the whole country in all directions. May this be so!"

Through the unfailing connection established with
The Lord of the Shakyas, the guide
    Amitabha,
The Invincible One, Manjushri, the Lord
    of Secrets,[30]
Avalokiteshvara, and all the Sugatas and
    their retinues,
And by the truth of these prayers,
May all this swiftly be granted.

Then I was invited to the houses of two devoted merchants of Yambu: the Kashmiri merchant Yolak Tsongshak and a merchant from La Khang Thokshing. I gave them some beneficial teachings and, before departing, made these wishes for auspiciousness:

Deities of the Three Roots, dwelling throughout space, and all local deities of the three realms of existence who delight in virtuous deeds, shower on this place a rain of flowers of auspiciousness and of all desirable wealth, cattle, and grain [318a]; fill the whole space with wondrous fragrances and the sounds of music, poetry and praise.

Namo!
May the auspiciousness of the root and
    lineage gurus prevail.
May the auspiciousness of all the *yidam*
    deities prevail.
May the auspiciousness of all the Buddhas
    and Bodhisattvas prevail.
May the auspiciousness of all the dakas
    and dakinis prevail.
May the auspiciousness of all the Dharma
    protectors and guardians prevail.

May the auspiciousness of all local deities
and owners of the ground prevail.
May the auspiciousness of the unchanging,
Mount Meru-like body prevail.
May the auspiciousness of the sixty
melodious qualities of speech prevail.
May the auspiciousness of the limitless,
immaculate mind prevail.
May the auspiciousness of the body,
speech, and mind
of the Victorious Ones prevail.
May the auspiciousness of people being
free from illness prevail.
May the auspiciousness of cattle being free
from plagues prevail.
May the auspiciousness of fields being free
from hail and frost prevail.
May the auspiciousness of storehouses
always being full prevail.
May the auspiciousness of everyone enjoying longevity and good health prevail.
May the auspiciousness of cattle always
prospering prevail.
May the auspiciousness of fields yielding
timely crops prevail.
May the auspiciousness of treasuries filled
with riches prevail.
May the auspiciousness of gathering
people, wealth, and food prevail.
May the auspiciousness of enjoying well-
being, happiness, and fame prevail.
May the auspiciousness of everyone acting
in accord with the Dharma prevail.
May the auspiciousness of uninterrupted
virtue and excellence prevail.
Thus may auspiciousness, excellence and
happiness pervade the whole land
[318b].

Having said this and thrown consecrated rice throughout the house, everyone in the house-holds of the two chief merchants rejoiced greatly and, filled with great faith, were most respectful.

At that time I could not visit all the holy places of Nepal. Yet, in the vicinity of the two great stupas, I saw the image of the Great Com-passionate One called the Jowo Jamali in the royal city of Yambu.[31] I also visited the Royal

Palace and had a look at the deer, horses, tigers, leopards, elephants, and rhinoceroses that were kept there. I stayed a month, doing prostrations and performing circumambulations around the two great stupas.

Then I returned to Kyirong, where I offered before the Wati Zangpo a lamp made out of thirty-four ounces of gold set with turquoise. I made a thousandfold offering and concluded with this prayer:

"Just as this lamp is perfectly clean within and without, and made out of fine material, may I keep throughout all of my lives perfectly pure vows and *samayas*, and have a good mind filled with loving-kindness and an enlightened atti-tude.

"Just as this lamp is filled with pure clarified butter, may the minds of myself and all beings be filled with many good qualities; may the whole universe be filled with happiness; may all the Buddhafields be completely filled with accumu-lations of offerings.

"Just as this lamp burns, in all my future lives may I have the good fortune to keep con-tinuously burning the great torch of the Buddha's teaching in order to dispel the darkness of the ignorance of beings in the three worlds [319a].[32]

"Just as the light of the lamp enables one to see in all directions, may I and all beings obtain the eyes of wisdom that vividly see all phenom-ena of samsara and nirvana.

"Just as the light of the lamp radiates every-where, may auspiciousness, virtue, and excel-lence pervade all lands.

"Just as in this life I made offerings to the Three Jewels, may I have the good fortune always to be able to make offerings to the infallible Three Jewels throughout all of my lives.

You, the lama and the Three Jewels,
Who cherish others more than yourselves,
Look with compassion on me and on all
beings.

I dedicate to the benefit of the Dharma
and all beings
This merit, symbolizing all merit accumulated throughout the three times.

I made this stainless prayer with pure
intention,
So that the infinite totality of beings may
be benefited.
By the blessings of the undeceiving Three
Jewels,
May my supplication be accomplished
without hindrance.
I ask that the beneficent sages whose
prayers are immediately fulfilled
Join me in this beneficial prayer.

Just as this lamp is clean within and
without [319b],
May our vows, our *samayas*, and our hearts
be pure.

Just as this lamp is filled with melted butter,
May the minds of all beings be filled with
positive qualities.

May the universe be filled with happiness.
May all the Buddhafields be filled with
offerings.

Just as this stainless lamp burns brightly,
May the torch of the Buddha's Dharma
blaze bright.

Just as the light of this lamp dispels
darkness,
May ignorance, karma, emotions and
obscurations be purified.

Just as by the light of this lamp we can see
in all directions,
May we see all phenomena with the eyes
of wisdom.

Just as the light of this lamp radiates
everywhere,
May great auspiciousness pervade in all
directions.

Just as we make offerings to the Three
Jewels in this life
May we make offerings to the Precious
Ones throughout all of our lives."

I also inscribed the following lines at the base of
the golden lamp:

> At the feet of the Jowo Wati Zangpo,
> The unique ornament of this world,
> The supreme object of prostration and
> offering
> This lamp made of gold was offered by
> Tsogdruk Rangdrol, Jampel Delek, and
> other devotees.
>
> By the power of this offering,
> May the Buddha's teachings prevail,
> May the holders of the Dharma live long,
> May all beings be happy at all times, and
> May they ultimately obtain Buddhahood.

I also made vast prayers of dedication for the
sake of the Dharma and all beings.

That year, I went to stay in retreat for a few
months at the hermitage of Tsigpai Gön Nang,
in Mang Yul near Kyirong—the abode of the
miraculously manifested image of Arya
Lokeshvara, Wati Zangpo.

Located at the border between Tibet and
Nepal, where different languages are spoken
[320a], where milk products and crops are always plentiful, where the snows do not melt in
summer, and the flowers do not dry up in winter,
Kyirong is a marketplace where all desirable
things can be found.

Near there, the translator Tsami Lotsawa
Sangye Trak[33] once had a vision of Mahakala,
who told him, "Make your dwelling place over
there on that big square rock." Thus, Drupkhang
Tsigpai Gön Nang, "the Meditation Hermitage
Built at the Order of the Gönpo," was built
where Mahakala had indicated.

It is a solitary mountain dwelling conducive
to practice. In back of it are massive rocks, and in
front of it a mountain surrounded by a garland
of snow peaks. In all directions, clouds of mist
gather, passing beneath the arches of five-col-

ored rainbows. In that place are many different kinds of trees; their branches sway like offering goddesses swaying as they dance. There are many kinds of wild flowers that, like seductive maidens, display smiling faces.

There are streams, murmuring, "I am pure, pure; drink here, drink here." Juniper trees and wild rhododendrons fill the air with their fragrance. Cuckoos, laughing-thrushes, and other sweet-voiced songbirds soar freely.

Because the slope faces south, there is sunlight all day, even in winter. In summer and in spring it remains cool and one's awareness is clear. Water, firewood, and all one needs are here [320b]. In the lower parts of the valley live many wealthy benefactors. In this pleasant place, filled with auspiciousness, with a vast open view, one feels naturally happy, lighthearted, serene and relaxed. It is a wondrous mountain wilderness, as though a celestial grove had been transported to earth.

I stayed there in retreat for several months and my meditation progressed more than in any other solitary place. One day, I sang this song in praise of the place:

I bow down to the guru,
Who in this sacred place
Opened the door to hundreds of samadhis
And saw wondrous visions.

Bless me and others like me,
To remain in mountain solitudes
Where contemplation blossoms.

Wondrous!
Behind are mountain rocks,
Solid and beautiful.
Snow ornaments the summits
Of the amazing mountains in front.
In all directions mist gathers and rainbows
    appear.

In this wondrous sacred place,
The very sounds of rivulets seem to say,
"Swiftly, quickly, like this goes the life of
    man—
Practice meditation without interruption!"

Flowing on continuously, day and night,
    Sweetly murmuring, they seem to say,
"When you meditate upon the *yidam* deity
This is how you should recite
The void sound of mantras."

The trees, when their branches wave
In all directions, seem to say,
"Come to the mountain
You fortunate ones with good karma."

When the branches are still, they seem to
    say,
"When meditating, remain still in one
    place as we do."

The many flowers demonstrate to all
    [321a],
"This is how your meditation experiences
    should bloom."

And when autumn comes, the flowers
    show their transience,
To remind one of impermanence and
    death.

Like a fan that waves back and forth,
The cool breeze tempers the ardor of the
    sun;
The fresh winds as well bring many
    fragrances.
"You, hermit, have no incense."

Without fixation, the wind goes its way.
"Like me, have no attachment to
    anything."

Surrounding me closely,
Singing sweetly,
Birds, large and small,
Dispel my loneliness, as if saying,
"You don't need to hoard;
Food and drink are easy to find."

And, flying on from treetop to treetop, they
    say,
"To eat whatever comes your way
Is the source of happiness.

Without clinging to anything,
Go on your way."

A variety of flowers
In the full bloom of their youth
Sway like seductive maidens.
Young bees come,
Humming their song, and
Embrace the blossoms.
The bees' wings thrum
And seem to say,
"When staying in solitude,
Sing like this."

To an intricate melody, they say,
"Wondrous is the yogin who dwells in
    sacred places."

Having circled around me many times
They touch my robe for blessing,
And flying off without a backward glance,
    say,
"Do not be fascinated
Even by those who seem the most
    desirable of all."

Marvelous!
In this sublime, secluded place of retreat,
Whatever appears points out the teachings.

Like a celestial forest brought to earth,
The wilderness shelters all kinds of natural
    beauty.

In this remote and wondrous forest [321b],
Outside, the nurturing sun:
My illusory body is content.

Within, primordial clarity:
My mind is content.

In between, I sing songs:
My voice is content.

If he found out about the complete
    contentment
Of my body, speech, and mind,

Even the king of Nepal himself
Might feel envious and restless—
Let alone anyone else!

"Practitioners who roam the villages
Instead of staying in such a retreat place—
What are you doing?"
This I proclaim everywhere.
May fortunate beings with good karma
    understand!

Thus, one day I spontaneously sang this song.

Another day, at that pleasant retreat, I was walking alone on the mountainside to refresh myself. These thoughts arose in my mind, "I am old, my hair has turned white. Now, on the eve of death, it's no good to move around too much, it's better to stay in mountain retreats. Stricken by years, even if I feel like going, I can't get around much. It's almost certain that I won't meet again most of my disciples and benefactors, who live far away." Reflecting on joining and parting, birth and death, and all the miseries of samsara, I felt sad and sang this melancholy song:

Essence of all the Buddhas,
Source of the eighty thousand sections of
    the Dharma,
Sole ornament of the supreme assembly of
    the Sangha—
Most kind root lama, think of me.

Enduring the drought of the three months
    of summer,
The crops seem inconsolable.
Turquoise thunder-dragon,
Come with your refreshing rain
To console the sadness of the fields [322a].

Crushed by the heat of the three months of
    spring
The golden-eyed fish seems inconsolable.

Torrent whose source is the melting snows,
Come with your sharp icy freshness
To console the sadness of the fish.

Stricken with so many years,
I, your son, am inconsolable.
You, my master, come, bestow your
    blessings
To console the sadness of this vagabond.

For as long as a rainbow is sustained
By the rains falling down from thick
    summer clouds,
Its appearance is very beautiful.
But, even though it is so very beautiful,
When the cold, strong winds sweep through,
The rainbow will have to go.

For as long as a blossom is sustained
By sunlight and by moisture
Its appearance is very beautiful.
But even though it is so very beautiful,
When the frosts of autumn come
The blossom will have to go.

For as long as this transitory body is
    sustained
By clothing and by nourishment,
Its appearance is very beautiful.
But even though it is so very beautiful,
When the Demon Lord of Death arrives,
This body will have to go.

Omens of danger to the lives of fish,
The nets are set along the coast;
Don't go to feed at the ocean's edge,
But stay out at sea, in the deep!

Omens of danger to a vulture's life
The noose is set, covered over with earth;
Don't come to feed on the carcasses of
    village horses,
But stay atop lofty cliffs!

Omens of danger to the hermit's life
Gods and demons dwell in towns and
    villages;

Don't come into villages to exorcise
    demons,
But remain in mountain solitudes!

As I sang this, from above, the sky-gods enveloped me in the soft warm sun; from beneath, the earth goddesses laid out a smooth carpet of blue-green grass and flowers; and in between, the wind-gods brought sweet fragrances [322b]. The wind was pleasant and refreshing, filling my mind and body with well-being. I said to the wind-god:

E ma!
Wind-god—you go from place to place,
Not clinging to anything—wondrous!
You came today, bringing with you
Sweet fragrances—I am so happy!

It is hard for this old man,
Stricken with so many years,
To get around now from place to place.
You can travel around with great ease:
You would serve as an excellent
    messenger,
Carrying news in all directions.

I have a message that needs to be sent
Everywhere, in all directions:
Please take it for me.

Tell them that I have become an old man.
Tell them that my hair has now turned
    white.
Tell them that, while this tongue still
    functions,
I am sending this message to my country-
    men,
To my neighbors and to all faithful men
    and women everywhere:

Tell them to have respectful devotion to
    the guru;
Tell them to have affection for their friends;
Tell them to cultivate compassion for all
    beings;
Tell them to have pure perception towards
    all traditions;

Tell them to avoid negative actions;
Tell them to practice virtue as much as
    they can;
Tell them to tame their untamed natures.

Go and tell them
That I have said this earnestly again and
    again.

Tell them I pray to meet them many times
Before the end of this life.

Tell them that even if we don't meet in this
    life
I shall always keep them in mind.

Tell them that as soon as I depart from this
    life
I shall go to the Buddhafield of Manifest Joy.

Tell them that, from there,
I shall to the Glorious Buddhafield
And then to the Blissful Buddhafield.

Tell them that, from there,
I shall go to the Buddhafield of
    Consummate Activity [323a],
And ultimately to the Unsurpassable
    Buddhafield.

Tell them that, from there,
I shall come back to fetch them
And bring them all to these Pure Realms.

Tell them that I shall also come again
To this very universe, in many emanations.

Tell them that,
Even if we met again in this life,
I would have nothing more to add.

Tell them that, if I die without seeing them
    again,
This is my testament; there is nothing left
    unsaid.

Tell them not to be sad, even if we don't
    meet;

We will meet again in the next life.
Tell them that, in a Pure Realm,
We will continue our present
    conversations.

Tell them that I shall see that all this
    happens—
And so, be joyful!

To this, the wind-god replied:

Well said, supreme and precious being!
I shall convey to everyone
The messages you have given me—
Whether they listen or not
Is up to them!

Again and again I will come
Bringing offerings of fragrances.
Pray that we may meet again soon.
At that meeting, I shall bring you detailed
    news.
Till then, farewell!

Then, with a great, sweeping sound, leaving no
trace at all, attached to nothing, the wind left. I
thought that this was the way I, too, should go.
    During my stay in this sublime and pleasant
place, a few patrons and disciples asked after my
well-being; I answered:

Wondrous—
On this mountainside blanketed in
    blue-green grass,
Above me are wild animals,
Below, downhill, are grazing cattle.

Mountain streams cascade: splashing,
    murmuring.
The branches of the many trees are moving,
Just as if dancing; sweet birds are singing
    out
Sweet melodies; new buds present their
    smiling faces [323b].

Striped honeybees buzz their small songs;
Wild rhododendrons and junipers exude
    sweet fragrances.

On the mountain slopes of this
	extraordinary wilderness,
The yogin sings a song of happiness:

I have given up my homeland—
Free of attachments, I am happy.

I have given up friends and relatives—
Free of attractions and aversions, I am
	happy.

I have given up possessions—
Free of worries, I am happy.

I have given up the company of visitors—
Free of distractions, I am happy.

I visualize my physical aggregates as
	deities—my body is happy.
I recite the essential mantra of the deity—
	my speech is happy.
I have merged with the state of luminous
	emptiness—my mind is happy.

In short, in this life I am happy in body,
	speech, and mind;
In the next life I shall be happy,
Since I am perfecting the two
	accumulations.

This present and future happiness
I owe to my guru's kindness;
To repay his kindness,
I ceaselessly offer him my practice.

Disciples and patrons, rejoice at this song
Expressing the yogin's happiness.

When I finished, everyone rejoiced.

One day, during my stay at that excellent place, I
gave the following teaching for the benefit of
some fortunate disciples, including my close spiritual sons Kunga Lekpa, Kalzang Trinley,

Kalzang Dondrup, Lobzang Sherap, Lobzang
Tsultrim, and Jamyang Rangdrol:

"All of you, fortunate sons and daughters,
listen without distraction and keep this well in
mind:

"Time out of mind we have taken countless
rebirths in samsara, particularly in the lower
realms [324a]—more times than the number of
hairs on the body of a black animal. Now that we
have, for once, obtained a precious human birth,
free and well-favored, it is like one single white
hair on that beast's forehead, amidst all of the
black ones. If, this time, we fail to take advantage
of this human birth, and fail to prepare the
ground for lasting happiness by practicing the
Dharma properly, it will be exceedingly difficult
to come upon such an existence again. As it is
said in *Engaging in the Bodhisattva's Activity:*

A free, well-favored human birth
Is extremely hard to find.
How can those who do nothing
To give their lives real meaning
Encounter such favorable conditions ever
	again?

"However you may reflect on these words,
using metaphors or numerical comparisons,
human existence is something very hard to obtain.
Not only is it rare, but it can be made truly
meaningful as well by using it to practice
Dharma—to reach the highest realms and ultimate excellence.

"Think about this, and, without clinging to
society, wealth, food, and other things of this life,
persevere solely in practicing the sublime
Dharma. At death, the best practitioner will be
joyful, the medium one will be free from fear,
and the worst one will have no regrets—so it is
said. Even if, when you die, you are neither
joyful nor free from fear, at the very least you
should have no regrets. Otherwise, can you
endure not having repaid your kind parents for
having fostered you? Can you bear not having
repaid your master for all the empowerments
and instructions he has given you?

"With your head in your hands,[34] consider
this: for all of us, master and disciples, birth will

end in death, joining will end in parting, accumulating things will end in their being exhausted [324b], holding a high position will end in its loss. No one escapes these. Most important of all, on the very day of our birth we begin traveling on the road towards death. It is said in the *Prior Lives of the Buddha*:[35] 'From the very evening of entering our mother's womb, we set out on the path of this world, a path that leads us directly into the presence of the Lord of Death.'

"Our life is shorter than a sheep's tail; our plans for the future longer than a horse's tail. There is no certainty as to when the Lord of Death will turn up; we don't know whether dawn or death will come first. Therefore, being aware of death, make only short-term plans and abandon, one after another, all the activities of this life.

"Alas! Who knows if I will still be alive another year, another month, another day? I am not even sure that I won't die tonight. What is the point of thinking of things to be done next year, next month, tomorrow? Right now I must practice the Dharma to ensure a happy frame of mind at the time of death!' It is essential always to think in this way, and cut short all speculation about the future.

"After death, those who have acted positively will be reborn in the higher realms of freedom and enjoy happiness. Those who have committed negative acts will be reborn in one of the three lower realms and enjoy suffering. For example, if one sows the seed of a sweet plant, one will harvest sweet fruit; if one sows the seed of a bitter plant, the harvest will be bitter—there is nothing more true than the karmic law of cause and effect [325a].

"Yet nowadays there are people who claim, 'To be too meticulous about the law of cause and effect is the way of the Hinayana—the Sravakas and the Pratyekabuddhas. We who have realized the view of the Mahayana have no need to be so punctilious about the laws of karmic cause and effect.' For them it is said, 'Erring too much on the side of emptiness is the downfall of those with weak intellects.'

"It is vital not to lean to the side of those who declare, 'The practice of the Mahayana overrides the Hinayana,' and not to become like them. The Great Master Padmasambhava said:

> One's view may be higher than the sky,
> But attention to one's actions and their
>   results
> Must be even finer than barley flour.
>
> I am the Lotus-born Guru,
> I hold the instructions that differentiate
> In accord with the laws of cause and effect.

"Similarly, the precious Physician of Dagpo[36] said, 'Even if your view is higher than the sky, it is vital that your behavior regarding cause and effect be finer than barley flour.'

"If, as a result of your negative actions, you are reborn in one of the three lower realms, needless to say, you will suffer. Even if you have given up the ten nonvirtuous actions, and through the power of small virtues you are born in the higher realms as a human being, you will endure the sufferings of birth, old age, sickness and death, of having what you do not want and of not having what you want, of separation and gathering,[37] of having more power or less power, of being beaten, and so forth. Likewise, if you are born as demigod you will suffer from constant fighting; if you are born a god you will suffer from the change and fall that go with death[38]—there are inconceivable sufferings!

"The *Supreme Dharma of Intent Mindfulness*[39] states, 'In samsara there is no place in which there is happiness—no place even as small as the tip of a needle.' Thus, once you are born in samsara, you will only reap suffering; you will not find one single instant of true happiness [325b]. Look, therefore, at the 'joys of samsara' and the 'perfections of this life' as a jaundiced person looks at food, or a son regards his father's murderer. Have revulsion toward them; abandon them, utterly.

"Consider the qualities of liberation and omniscience, and long for them as a thirsty person longs for water; desire them ardently, like a lustful man who sees a beautiful woman. Constantly keep the feeling in your heart that you must achieve these qualities at any cost.

"Eh, all of you! There is no chance that you can free yourselves from samsara and achieve Buddhahood relying only on your own strength: you require help. In ordinary life, someone with few resources must rely on more powerful people; likewise, you must rely on a spiritual master and the Three Jewels. If you do so, they will protect you from the terrors of samsara, especially those of the three lower realms, and certainly establish you in liberation and omniscience. Therefore, take refuge and rely on them with all your heart.

"Generating the aspiration for enlightenment is the seed for Buddhahood; therefore, engendering total love and compassion, develop the intention and application of Bodhicitta.

"Without completing the two accumulations one cannot achieve Buddhahood; therefore make mandala offerings. Entailing little difficulty and possessing real meaning, mandala offerings are the best way to perfect the two accumulations.

"Without purifying obscurations one cannot achieve Buddhahood; therefore correctly practice the meditation and recitation of Vajrasattva [326a]. Like a stream, it will cleanse all your negative acts, faults, downfalls, and obscurations.

"Without receiving the guru's blessing, one cannot achieve Buddhahood; therefore, practice Guru Yoga, praying from the very core of your heart. This is a vital point.

"These days some people say, 'There is no need to expend great effort on the preliminary practices. What's the point of so much complication? It's enough just to practice Mahamudra, devoid of all elaborations.' But this is like saying, 'Though I can't chew butter, I shall chew stones.' Don't listen to such nonsense. How can someone who hasn't even reached the shore talk about the sea?[40]

"It is said, 'If the preliminary practice is profound, the main practice will be profound.' It is absolutely necessary to develop the inner experiences and realization related to these preliminaries, if you have not yet done so. If you have developed them already, you must develop them further, without letting them deteriorate. This is something important at all stages of practice.

"You must then receive a ripening empowerment for any deity of the Secret Mantrayana—this is the swiftest way to become enlightened. After that, you must keep pure samayas and vows according to the promises you made when receiving the empowerment.

"Following this, you must familiarize yourself with the path of development and completion stages as much as you can. Above all, for a long time, you must practice the ultimate completion stage: remaining in evenness in the continuum of the nature of mind—void, luminous, free of fixation; all-pervading, open, vast, simple, like the sky.

"When practicing the Dharma you must give up all concern for the affairs of this life. Keep to the lowest position, wear worn-out clothing: give no importance to food, talk, or clothes. Be always a child of the mountains: wear mist as a robe, a rocky cave as a cap. Even if trees fall from the right, boulders roll down from the left [326b], the sky collapses on you from above, or the earth quakes under you, you must maintain the firm determination to remain unwavering, like a stake driven into the ground.

"You also must have fervent devotion toward your spiritual master, love for your vajra brothers and sisters, compassion for all beings, and pure perception towards all teachings. Place all beings above yourself, particularly those who have crossed the threshold of Dharma, and more especially those companions with whom you have received teachings. These three are the lesser, medium and supreme companions. Keep to the humblest position; serve and respect others as much as you can; praise their good qualities; give them victory, and take loss upon yourself.

"When Gyalwa Götsangpa[41] was on the way to Tö with some companions, if there was a heavy load to carry, he would take it, if there was a pleasant place to sit he would make the others take it, and if there was an uncomfortable place he would take it. At night, if there were comfortable beds he would have his companions sleep on them; if there was a cold place he would be the one to take it. If there was good food, he would serve it to others and take the worst for himself, and so forth. Thinking of the conduct of a Bodhisattva like him, I can't help but take refuge!

"Even if we can't be like him, at least we should try. But, instead, when *we* reach a gathering place, the first thing we do is look for the best seat; when starting to eat, we choose the best piece; when selecting a cup to drink from, we want the biggest [327a]; when things are given out, we want the largest share. When people tell us a mixture of pleasant and unpleasant things, we can't bear a single harsh word. If we own possessions in common with others, we cannot bear our share to be less, even by a hundred grams.[42]

"Practitioners like this are fine only while they are just sitting around talking, but whenever they actually encounter difficult circumstances they behave even worse than ordinary people.

"To avert this, keep to the humblest position, as explained above; take a vow to consider everyone before yourself, and put this vow into practice at all times.

"It is very important to dedicate all the virtuous actions you have done in accord with the Dharma for the benefit of others, and for their attainment of unsurpassable enlightenment. You should conclude with the pure aspiration to benefit the Dharma and all beings, and in particular to attain enlightenment swiftly yourself—in order to accomplish great deeds for the teachings and for all beings. If you do so, you will soon achieve these goals: your aims and those of others will be naturally accomplished. I concluded with this song:

Lord root guru, Vajradhara,
Remain above my head, on a lotus and
    moon;
Look with compassion
Upon all your children gathered here;
Grant your blessings that we attain su-
    preme enlightenment.

Fortunate disciples who are the children of
    my heart,
Listen without distraction to your father's
    song.

Like the lotus Udumbara [327b],
A free, well-favored human birth is rarely
    found.

Like a rare and precious jewel,
It can be a source of many accomplishments,
If, having been found, it is used to practice
    the Dharma.

Like an animal being led off to the
    slaughterhouse,
Day after day, you are drawing nearer and
    nearer to your death.

Like a butter-lamp's flame flickering in a
    gust of wind,
The length of your own life is uncertain:
The causes of death are many.

Like a poisonous potion and a life-giving
    elixir,
Black deeds do harm; white deeds benefit.

Like throwing away the poison and
    drinking the elixir,
Give up negative acts and undertake
    positive ones.

Just as no rest can be found on the sharp
    tip of a needle,
There is no happiness to be found in
    samsara.
And, in particular, the sufferings
Of the three lower realms are like
Dwelling in a white-hot pit of fire.

Like the terror of a man being dragged off
    to prison
Is the fear born of considering these things.

Like that desperate longing of a criminal
    kept chained in prison
Is the desire to become free of that suffering.

Like a criminal begging for the mercy of
    the king
Is taking refuge in the Three Jewels in
    order to escape.

Like the seeds that become transformed
    into an autumn harvest,
Is Bodhicitta, the seed of Buddhahood.

Like gold, precious even in very small
   amounts,
Is the mandala offering, a way to
   accumulate merit with very slight
   difficulty.

Like a stream that washes away all stains
Is the meditation and recitation of
   Vajrasattva, the means of purifying evil
   deeds.

Like a precious wish-fulfilling gem
Is the sublime, authentic root guru.

Like setting this gem atop a victory
   banner
Is visualizing the guru above one's head.

Like making a wish with that gem
Is making supplications to the lord guru.

Like the gem granting all wishes
Is the arising of the ordinary and
   extraordinary *siddhis*.

Like the enthronement of a prince as king
Is receiving the four empowerments that
   ripen one's being. [328a]

Like taking a secret shortcut
Is traveling the liberating path of the two
   stages.

Like a vast, empty, luminous sky
Is the natural state of one's own mind.

Like the soaring of a great garuda through
   the sky
Is remaining evenly in that state.

Like rainbows in the midst of space,
All phenomena are apparent yet unreal.

Like "Ever-crying" and "Excellent-wealth,"[43]
Have devotion to your guru.

Like Gyalwa Götsangpa,
Show love to your friends.

Like a mother for her ailing child,
Have compassion for all beings, your mothers.

Like a mother who loves her child,
Care lovingly for all sentient beings.

As exemplified in the lives of the Kadampa
   masters,
Consider everyone as being above yourself.

Like a child of humble extraction,
Always keep to the lowest position.

Like turning the head of your horse uphill,
Dedicate all your merit to enlightenment.

Like planting seeds in a fertile field,
Conclude with pure prayers.

Like the Victorious Shakyamuni,
Attain Buddhahood by practicing the
   Dharma.

Like a wish-fulfilling tree and a
   wish-fulfilling jewel,
Effortlessly benefit others.

Disciples who are like my sons,
If you have these aspirations,
Practice in this way and you will surely
   succeed.

By the merit of this song,
May all monks and nuns, and all my
   disciples, attain enlightenment.

Then I taught them these thirty "alrights" [328b]:

Master, Buddhas and Bodhisattvas,
Take under your protection these
   fortunate children!

Now, listen without distraction
To this advice which will help you later
   on—alright?

The guru is like the guide who leads the
   blind:

Hold onto him and never let him go—
    alright?

His word is like ambrosia, the supreme
    panacea:
Drink it to cure yourself from the illness of
    the obscuring emotions—alright?

Spiritual brothers and sisters are like good
    companions on a journey:
Accompany them as you would beloved
    friends—alright?

This precious human birth is like a
    wish-fulfilling jewel:
Don't waste it—alright?

Human life lasts no longer than the rays of
    the setting sun on a mountain pass:
Practice the Dharma, so as to be ready for
    death—alright?

The consequences of your good and evil
    deeds will follow like your shadow:
They accompany you even through
    death—alright?

Samsara is like living on a cannibal island:
Do something to escape quickly—alright?

Friends and relatives are like the snares of
    samsara:
Don't be so attached to them—alright?

One's homeland is like Mara's prison:
Escape! Leave it far behind—alright?

All beings are like your parents of this life:
Protect them with love and compassion—
    alright?

A vicious enemy is like an autumn flower:
He will vanish all by himself, so don't get
    angry—alright?

Wealth and possessions are like a bee's
    honey:

They get consumed by someone else, so
    don't be attached—alright?

Your many projects are like drawings
    made on water:
There is no way to finish them, so just
    forget them—alright?

Pleasant and unpleasant words are no
    more than echoes:
Don't react to them with pointless joy or
    sadness—alright?

Happiness and suffering alternate like
    summer and winter:
Don't fall prey to elation or depression—
    alright?

A rich person is like a hungry ghost
    guarding a treasure:
Have few desires and be content with what
    you have—alright?

To assume an air of self-importance, like
    an army commander—who needs it?
Keep to the lowest position—alright? [329a].

Religious wealth misused is like poisoned
    water:
Don't keep wanting so many things—
    alright?

Husband and wife are like people who
    come together for a fair:
Don't take anything as permanent and
    don't be too attached—alright?

Anger is like a house on fire:
Extinguish it, or it will scorch your mind—
    alright?

Learning is like a torch which dispels darkness:
Listen to the lama's teachings—alright?

Generosity is like making provision for the
    next life:
Give away all that you possess—alright?

Discipline is like a stairway to liberation:
Guard it as you would your own eyes—
    alright?

Patience is like armor on the battlefield:
Abandon anger and cultivate patience—
    alright?

Diligence is like riding a good horse:
It will take you along the entire path, so
    exert yourself—alright?

Firm inner calm is like a fortress.
Practice undistracted samadhi—alright?

Insight is like the sun illuminating darkness:
Light the torch of wisdom—alright?

The natural state of mind is like the sky:
Rest in that state—alright?

Phenomena are like rainbows appearing in
    space:
Regard them as insubstantial
    apparitions—alright?

Mystical visions are like the allure of a
    beautiful woman:
Don't be attached to them—alright?

The various teachings are all like the fruit
    of a good harvest:
See all of them as pure—alright?

Keep in mind this advice
Called *Thirty Alrights*—alright?

By the power of all merit, symbolized by
    this merit,
May all beings practice the Dharma and
    achieve Buddhahood.

As I spoke, all the monks and other disciples
gathered there felt great enthusiasm [329b].

Then, to inquire about his well-being, I sent the
following letter to Trakar Tulku, Jetsun Chökyi
Wangchuk Rinpoche,[44] a person gifted with
many excellent qualities of the Dharma of Transmission and Realization:

Holder of the treasury of many qualities of
    knowledge and realization,
Jetsun Chökyi Wangchuk,
You have reached the other shore
Of consummate learning and
    accomplishment.

I, the dharma-less Shabkar,
A practitioner who wanders throughout
    the land
With no destination in mind,
A hermit who stays in mountain solitudes,
Offer these words at your pristine lotus
    feet,
With sincere respect of body, speech, and
    mind.

Lord, during countless kalpas,
In the presence of many Buddhas
You generated Bodhicitta,
And, having perfected the two
    accumulations,
Became a Buddha yourself.
Although for you there is no further
    enlightenment to obtain,
In the realm of perception of disciples like me
You manifested again as a spiritual master.

So that your disciples might learn the path
Of your life of perfect liberation, O Jetsun,
In the early years of your life
You attended many teachers, and
Endeavored in study, reflection and
    meditation,
Acting as if there would be
Another enlightenment to be achieved
    after enlightenment.

When I thought about this,
I found great meaning in it,
And saw your amazing life as sublime.

Precious guru of great kindness,
Please continue manifesting such activities!

As for me, your respectful servant,
If I divide my life into three,
Two parts have already gone into hearing
    the Dharma and into distractions.
The time of death is unpredictable and I
    won't be around much longer anyway.
So, for the short remainder of my life—
Like the last rays of the sun setting on a
    mountain pass [330a]—
I may find the path to fulfillment for myself
    and others,
If I completely give up my wandering,
Drastically cut through casual efforts to
    learn this and receive that,
And just stay alone in a pleasant mountain
    wilderness,
In a state of simplicity like the sky, free of
    mental fabrications—
The vast, all-encompassing expanse of
    mind,
Void and luminous, free of clinging to
    reality,
The root of all phenomena, illusions and
    dreams which are samsara and
    nirvana—
Arouse compassion for all beings who do
    not realize this,
And conclude with dedication prayers for
    their benefit.

But again, realizing the great good fortune
    of each encounter with you,
A spiritual master with whom any
    connection is meaningful,
I feel like listening to the Dharma once
    more,
Thinking that if some rare transmissions
    could be saved from extinction
It would benefit the lineage of the
    teachings.

Therefore, at this very moment I fold my
    hands and supplicate
That when I, indolent one, reach your
    place,

You will impart to me the most secret,
    profound, ultimate teaching.
When I meet you, please grant me these
    with loving joy!

Simply to attract the attention of the bees
    of your eyes
To the lotus garden of this letter of mine,
And to please you, master, divine among
    divinities,
I send it with a symbolic present wrapped
    in celestial silk.

He replied with this letter:

Svasti!
In the dense forest of the Hari sandal-
    wood[45]—vast knowledge—
At the feet of a majestic and lofty tree—the
    spiritual master [330b]—
A tree that emits the sweet scent of the
    Three Vows,
And whose branches are bent with the
    weight
Of the fruits of excellence in scriptural
    knowledge and realization,
The thief Stupidity stole all my learning,
Bad companions stripped off my armor of
    virtuous discipline, and
The wind of circumstances carried away
    my clothing of goodness.
It is thus a naked renunciate who addresses
    to you these words.

Well-carried by the wind-chariot,
The twofold accumulation and prayers
    you made during long kalpas,
The sun of your manifest body,
Free from all obscuration—Rahu's
    abysmal maw[46]—
Emanates in a hundred directions
The hundred rays of your activities of the
    Three Wheels,[47]
Dispels the mental darkness of the beings
    to be transformed,
Makes blossom the lotus garden of benefit
    and bliss,
And is thus worthy of a hundred praises.

Having reached the far shore of the ocean
   of learning,
You became rich with the jewel treasury of
   profound meaning.
Utterly beautiful with the Bodhisattva's
   activity,
Ferryman for those who desire liberation,
With loving-kindness
You display fearless generosity
And sublime courage in the four ways of
   gathering disciples.

When about to say, "You are the match
   of . . ."
One finds no one but yourself to compare
   with you.

E ma!
Before the eyes of the Compassionate
   Wati—
The friend of beings who grants
The excellent stream of well-being and
   felicity,
The manifestation of the Lotus-bearer,[48]
Ablaze with miraculously manifested
   marks and signs,
Accomplishing the benefit of beings
   through its inanimate form—
You offered a lamp made of precious
   metal,
Infinite clouds of offerings, and
Vast prayers for the benefit and happiness
   of the teachings and beings [331a].
The fame of these offerings rivaling the
   deeds of Samantabhadra[49]
Has spread to the abode of Brahma.

Most people are tightly bound by stinginess
That ties their throats and clenches their
   fists,
And, ignoring the ill-repute and suffering
   that result from evil deeds,
Are ready to lose their lives for the sake of
   material things.

Although the way you performed these
   excellent deeds
Will give all noble-minded persons

The sublime opportunity to rejoice,
It may cause aches and pains for a few
   others.

The celestial beings are murmuring among
   themselves:
"Why in the past could rich people
Not even think of doing such a thing,
Much less actually do it?"

Who can doubt that, from the banyan seed
Of your amazing twofold accumulation [50]
You will harvest the same glory as the
   Sugata Light-giver? [51]

Whosoever offers a delightful white lotus
   garland
Of auspicious words of rejoicing and praise
As a beautiful ornament to your throat,
Will share with you auspicious connections
   of excellence.

Will you come again to perform joyously
Your wondrous work for a longer time,
For the two stupas that are the ornaments
   of this world,
And for the other great sacred places and
   objects
Of the valley of Nepal, praised by the
   Victorious Ones?

In the mountain wilderness, amidst the
   forests of the Deathless Lord [52]
Where many sages once lived,
In pleasant, tranquil meditation mansions
Perched upon elephant-like rocks,
Entering into the equanimity of a hundred
   samadhis [331b],
Through the practice of the sixfold Vajra
   Yoga [53]
You liberated the host of thoughts that
   conceive samsara and nirvana
And let them assume their true nature, free
   of clinging—the vast expanse of
   sameness.

Sectarian views that make distinctions
   between "good" and "bad" doctrines

Obscure the sun of ultimate truth with the
     thick belief
That they alone hold the Buddha's teaching,
And thus stray far from the pristine path.

The realization that the hundred thousand
     rivers of
The nonsectarian Dharma traditions
Gather without conflict
In the single taste of the deep ocean of
     your mind
Gives rise to waves of free openness
Scattering the white spray of your perfect
     instructions.
How wonderful!

When the letter you wrote,
Which arose freely from the playground of
     your pure vision,
Dressed in white silk, and accompanied by
     two jewels—brother sun and sister
     moon[54]—
Came, with seal unbroken,
I experienced measureless joy,
Drunk with the simultaneous arising of
     bliss and emptiness.

A ho!
How can such unprecedented virtue exist!
How can I ever repay your kindness!

As for myself, the feeble tendril of my
     health
Depends entirely upon the support
Of the tree of the Three Jewels'
     compassion,
And I just go on, living like a beast,
With only three preoccupations of body,
     speech and mind.[55]

In a state where the ripples of deluded
     thoughts never cease,
Wasting the freedom and favorable
     conditions of this life, and
Calling all such fantasies "Dharma,"
I eagerly practice in a way that just brings
     ruin for myself and others:
Looking at myself, I feel utterly depressed.

I do not possess even a particle of the good
     qualities and deeds
That might delight your mind
In which all phenomena arise as infinite
     purity;
But don't be upset with me! [332a].

I prayed that, using the winged feet of
     Dharma,[56] and
Unafraid of the hardship involved in
     sustained practice,
I might myself travel along the swift path
That leads to unchanging great bliss.

However, since I am lax about vows and
     samayas,
And my perseverance is so weak,
The wheels of the chariot of skillful means
     and wisdom shattered.

Now I am left like a stone thrown deep
     into water—
Sunk into despair.

Although you have mastered all the
     essential points of the profound path,
Just as the ocean can never have its fill of
     water,
You seek even more instructions on
     various Dharma traditions:
With folded hands, I rejoice in your
     sublime ways.

Grant me the nectar-like gift of your
     elegant discourses,
Embraced by the unbroken seal of
     nonduality,
Announcing the joyous feast of our
     imminent meeting,
And the ever-presentness of your enlight-
     ened mind.

In peaceful forest valleys
Garlanded thickly with many kinds of
     trees,
Where one can hear the gentle sounds of
     cascading water
And the songs of playful birds.

On the serene slopes of solitary hills
Atop the huge, changeless boulders,
Continually fostering unshakable samadhi,
May you remain, firm as diamond.

This garland of noisy chatter
Is neither meaningful nor agreeable to
    hear;
Yet, simply to make you laugh,
I made up this joyous song [332b].

On this auspicious day of the ascending
    moon,
The messenger emanated by my mind
Sprang forth, quick as lightning,
To bring you this letter, inviolably sealed,
Accompanied by a celestial white scarf,
A book containing a wondrous life-story,
And a piece of bright cloth embroidered in
    gold
With the signs of auspiciousness.

This letter is sent from the dwelling place of the accomplished *siddhas*, the heights of the lofty rocky mountain that has been enjoyed by many ascetic yogins. May it be auspicious!

His letter came with many presents.

One day, I gave all my disciples the following instruction called *The Sharp Needle*, to enable them to remove by themselves the prickly thorns of their defects:

"Although the Victorious Ones and their sons, and especially my root teachers in their invisible realm, must be displeased with me, I beseech them just to glance at my wrong behavior with their wisdom eyes and bless me, so that from now on I may be able to act in accord with the Dharma.

"Hey, you! Since you aren't learned, well-behaved or good-natured, and thus have cheapened the dignified name of 'Dharma practitioner',

you are just like a drum—noisy outside, hollow inside. Turn your mind inward and think about this!

"You have the appearance of a Dharma practitioner. You obtained this free, precious, well-favored human existence; you met a spiritual teacher—all the Buddhas of the three times in one; you received profound and vast teachings, and you crossed the threshold of the Dharma long ago [333a]. Tell us! What practice have you done up to now? What meditation experiences, what realization, have you gained? Even if nothing comes to your mind and you have nothing to tell others, you ought, at least, to have *some* sort of idea about it.

"It is said that the best Dharma practitioners will progress in a matter of days, the middling ones in some months, and the worst ones within some years. What about you? Let's see. Days? Months? Years at least? It seems that instead of getting better, you've gotten much worse.

"The sign of learning, it is said, is serenity and self-control; the sign of having meditated is fewer obscuring emotions. In your case, how much more serene and self-controlled have you become in your body, speech, and mind? Have your obscuring emotions diminished? Just see: haven't your emotions gotten worse? Aren't there many more of them? Aren't they more powerful?

"It is said, 'The best practitioner will welcome death with joy, the medium one will have no fear, and the worst one no regrets.' If you died today, would you be joyful? Fearless? At least you should have no regrets. Yet, observing your behavior, if you happen to die in a day or two, it looks as though you'll die full of regret. Think about it!

"Moreover, it is said, 'If you cling to the things of this life you are not a Dharma practitioner.' But as for you, you keep, deep in your mind, a strong craving for food, clothes, and other things of this world, as well as attachment to your relatives. Not only do you stuff your mouth with the live coals of food offered on behalf of the living and the dead; not only do you misappropriate the belongings and wealth of the guru, the Three Jewels, and the sangha [333b], which you gather from all sides, but you also put these coals into the mouths of your friends and relatives, thus burning everyone—yourself and others. How dare you!

"The Buddha said, 'It is worse to swallow religious wealth than to swallow eggs made of burning iron.' Are you so self-assured that you can think these words of the Buddha to be untrue and that you don't need to take them into account?

"Moreover, it is said:

Like sighted people standing before
    the blind,
The Buddhas and Bodhisattvas
See without veils at all times.

"Therefore, don't misbehave and think they don't know!

"But *you*, you've been thinking and doing all kinds of things: you're just a ball of obscuring emotions, a sack full of wrong actions, a bag of faults, a pouch of misused religious wealth, a servant of the eight worldly concerns. You advance towards virtue like a tired donkey pulling uphill, you run towards evil like a waterfall rushing over a cliff. You cling desperately to this life.

"Right until today your body, speech, and mind have been under the power of the three poisons, and you have spent all your time committing the ten nonvirtuous acts. Still, impudent and bold, you pretend to be a Dharma practitioner! Though you can fool today's laypeople, do you think that you can fool the gurus and the Three Jewels, who have unimpeded wisdom eyes? Do you think that the gurus and the Three Jewels are going to swallow this?

"The Buddha expounded the eighty-four thousand sections of the Dharma as antidotes for the eighty-four thousand obscuring emotions [334a]. Spiritual masters say, 'Whatever Dharma you practice, subdue your emotions as much as you can.' No matter how often they say this and good friends repeat the same thing to you, you don't care at all. Within you, the fire of anger blazes, the water of desire seethes, the mist of

stupidity thickens, the peak of pride towers, the wind of jealousy runs wild, the knot of stinginess tightens—just look at it!

"Aside from everything else, you can't tolerate even a few nasty comments; just see how your face becomes convulsed with fury, how harsh words spew from your mouth. Are you aware that neither the lama nor your friends ever told you to do that? Maybe a demon told you, or a wicked spirit has possessed you, or you have gone mad. If you go on in that way, you are just buying suffering in this life, and the fare for your journey to hell in the next life.

"You betray the lama, broadcast the faults of your friends, defile the dignity of a Dharma practitioner, and injure the image of the Dharma. If you have any reason for doing this, just tell us!

"Moreover, although it is said, 'A lazy person has no Dharma,' all night you sleep like a corpse and all day you are carried away by distractions. You practice for only a few moments, and still hope to become a *siddha*—what a braggart you are! Ha! Ha! [334b].

"The aroma of the Dharma hasn't even touched you. If you sincerely want to practice the Dharma, you must shun the desire for pleasurable food and drink and avoid distraction and laziness. With just the right amount of food in daytime and sleep at night, you must persevere in practice.

"Vajradhara[57] said, 'If you enter the gateway of the Secret Mantrayana and practice it, at best you will achieve Buddhahood in this life itself, in the middle case, in the *bardo* of the moment of death,[58] and in the worst case, if you don't break *samaya*, in seven to sixteen lifetimes.' But *you*, you don't keep any *samaya* at all, and even over the matter of a cup of tea you will say, 'The lama does not care for me,' and you lose faith. When a Dharma friend raises his voice at you, you say, 'I don't deserve that,' and you get angry. Consider just that!

"Is it that you don't keep *samaya* because you are afraid of becoming enlightened? Vajradhara and other Buddhas said that if someone does not keep *samaya*, even if he makes offerings he won't be accepted;[59] if he dies suddenly in an accident, he will be reborn in the Vajra Hell—and not only him, but all those who drank the water of the same valley, since they are stained by the defilement of his broken *samaya*. Do you think that Vajradhara's words are false, or that they are true but don't apply to you? [335a]. Maybe you don't respect his words because you have reached a higher level than his? Or because you are so extremely self-confident? Or because you are possessed by some spirit, and no longer have a heart in your chest? It must be one of these.

"You may go to hell, but please don't take with you all the people who drank the water of your valley! Be kind enough to leave them here where they are, and don't devastate the whole place. Does this make sense to you? If you still don't understand, don't hear and don't acknowledge this, it is certain that a dreadful and potent demon has entered into you—the kind of demon that no one has ever been able to subdue. *A-dzi!!* How terrifying!

"You've already been cast out of worldly society, and now you are thrown like a corpse out of the ranks of Dharma practitioners. In case that corpse of yours regains strength and tries to come back, this time don't keep on destroying the Dharma from within. Why not join up with the non-Buddhists? If they won't have you, put your four limbs on the ground and see if dogs or some other animals will accept you. From today onwards you are expelled from among both religious people and laypeople—go away! You belong nowhere—you're not worldly, you're not religious. If you attempt to rejoin, everyone will spit in your face! Is that face of yours made out of wild yak-hide? Or of a double layer of leather? [335b]. Or is the skin on your forehead extraordinarily thick? Otherwise, shouldn't you feel ashamed?

"Well, if you are a man with a sense of shame, with courage in your heart and a brain in your head; if you have some self-respect, it is time to regret your past actions—not only is it time, it is past time!

"See how all those who are born must die; all that is amassed becomes exhausted; all those who were together are separated—how everything is completely without meaning! Having seen that, if you want to do something meaning-ful, let your mind turn toward the Dharma; let your Dharma turn you to a humble life; turn your humble life toward death; and let your death happen in some mountain solitude. Keep to the lowest position, wear shabby clothes; forget about food, clothes and talk. Wear mist as a mantle, a cave as a hat, and remain always a child of the mountains.

"As a consequence of practicing the Dharma, your three doors must become serene and self-controlled, your obscuring emotions must diminish. All the teachings you know must be put into practice as an antidote to your obscuring emotions. From now on, never give them free rein as you have done. Whichever of these emotions arises—desire, anger, and so on—tackle it with the antidote immediately, as it arises. Be vigorous, discourage them, tame them, uproot them, flatten them, and then destroy them! [336a]. In short, put an end to your negative actions and from now on act in accordance with the lama's instructions, the Dharma, and the Vinaya:

> Master—from the invisible realm
> Look down upon this miserable person!
>
> I'll point out my own defects
> As I'd point out lice with my finger.
> I'll toss my defects out the door
> As I'd pull a thorn out of my foot and toss
>   it away.
>
> You, Shabkar—
> You obtained a free, well-favored human
>   birth,
> You met a lama, the embodiment of all the
>   Buddhas,
> You received his profound and vast
>   instructions.
> As the result of having listened to the
>   Dharma and contemplated its meaning,
> Your body, speech, and mind should have
>   become tame and serene,
> But they didn't—they got worse!
>
> Your obscuring emotions should have
>   diminished;
> But they didn't—they got worse!

Your mind should have evolved,
But it didn't—it got worse!

This is what you are:
A sack stuffed with religious wealth and
    food given by the faithful,
A bull sleeping like a corpse,
A snake filled with hatred,
A bird filled with desire,
A pig filled with stupidity,
A lion filled with pride,
A dog filled with jealousy,
A hungry ghost filled with greed,
A butcher thirsting to inflict torment,
A cannibal reveling in flesh and blood.

Toward the lama—all the Buddhas in
    one—
You lack the devotion that brings tears to
    one's eyes.

Toward your Dharma brothers and sisters
You lack the pure perception to see them
    as deities.

Toward all beings—each of whom was
    once your mother—
You lack the compassion that makes one's
    hair stand on end.

Toward the vast and profound instructions,
You lack the diligence that spurs one to
    practice.

Lacking faith and respect,
You are a longtime *samaya*-breaker [336b].

Lacking pure perception,
You are shameless.

Lacking compassion,
Your heart is rotten.

Lacking meditation practice,
You are utterly lazy.

Not seeing your faults,
You are blind.

Proclaiming others' faults,
You have a big mouth.

You are a stone anchored in the depths of
    hell:
You have collected such bad karma,
O dharmaless accumulator of evil.

You are such a traitor,
Betraying the lama who is all the Buddhas
    of the three times.

You are such a traitor,
Betraying your vajra brothers and sisters
    who keep pure *samaya*.

You are such a perverter of the teachings,
Tarnishing the image of the Dharma.

You are such a charlatan,
Outwardly appearing as a practitioner,
Yet acting against the Dharma,
And complaining about the faults of fellow
    practitioners,

You are the living dead—a zombie, a
    walking corpse.
Even if you are not possessed by Maras,
    you are quite mad.

You stuffed dummy,[60] where did you
    come from?
Man of ill omen, where did you come
    from?

Look at your 'diligence':
Nothing but eating, drinking, and sleeping
    like a corpse!

Look how you stubbornly refuse to walk
    toward virtue,
Balking like an exhausted donkey!

Look at how, faster than anyone,
You cascade on toward evil like a waterfall!

You can't tolerate a single bad word;
Look how your face convulses with rage!

You are a sack of faults and downfalls—
To whom have you given back your vows?

You carry a great weight of evil deeds;
Where are your virtues?

You are a huge bladder of defects;
Who stole all your good qualities?

You have a full load of the eight worldly
    dharmas;
What have you done with holy Dharma?

You are nothing like a Dharma practitioner—
Aren't you ashamed of yourself? [337a].

Old dog without a tail,
Go out and join the other dogs!

Bull with upper teeth[61]
Go and look for a herd of cattle!

In case you insist on staying,
Will you dare to behave as before?

Man—
If you have any self-respect,
A heart in your chest,
Brains in your head, and
Some sympathy for yourself,
Regret your past actions and
Improve your whole behavior.
It's time! It's very late!

See how
All that is born dies,
All that is hoarded runs out,
All that is gathered gets separated,
And everything is without essence:
Meaningless activities should be
    abandoned.

To practice the essential, divine Dharma,
You must exert yourself in accordance
With the words of your lama and
The Victorious Ones.
O lama and Three Jewels, look upon me
    compassionately!

My past actions were wrong.
I regret them from the core of my heart,
I confess them, and promise never to com-
    mit them again.

Grant your blessings
So that I may act in accord with the
    Dharma;
Grant your blessings
So that I may observe the Vinaya;
Grant your blessings
So that I may follow the Sutras;
Grant your blessings
So that I may practice according to the
    Abhidharma;
Grant your blessings
So that I may accomplish the Secret
    Mantrayana!

I then handed these pith instructions, *The
Sharp Needle*, to my disciples, telling them to seek
out the thorns of their defects with the eyes of
discrimination, and remove them. Through this
they succeeded in extracting all the poisonous
thorns of their faults which had produced so
much pain [337b]. Before long, in pleasant mountain solitudes, they were able to perform the happy
dance of a life in harmony with the Dharma.

On his return from U and Tsang, where he had
performed many religious deeds, the treasurer
Depa Wangpo came to meet me. I rejoiced
greatly at all the pleasing news he brought. He
stayed there and rested for a while. After I finished my retreat, my spiritual son Jamyang
Rangdrol and a few others left to raise the victory banner of spiritual practice at the Snow
Mountain of Tö.[62] In farewell, I gave all the men
and women of Kyirong a long-life blessing and
some spiritual advice. I also sang this song:

I pray the lama, the union of all refuges,
To bless me so that my body, speech and
    mind blend with the Dharma.

Kyirong folk,
You won't stay long in this life, soon you
    will die:
Practice the Dharma right now to be ready
    for death!

Kyirong folk,
Wear the lama and the Three Jewels like
    your own head.
All those who do this will be victorious!

Kyirong folk,
Care for your kind parents like your own
    two eyes:
The kindhearted will find happiness!

Kyirong folk,
Be like brothers and sisters
Toward close friends who have your
    welfare at heart:
They will be with you when you need
    them!

Kyirong folk,
Staying with him for a long time,
One would even find fault with a
    Buddha:
Don't look for defects in the lama!

Kyirong folk,
If you make an improper offering, even the
    deities will turn against you:
Do not sacrifice animals to local deities!

Kyirong folk,
To have regrets only after your spouse dies
    is the way of fools:
While you both live, remain in harmony!

Kyirong folk,
Mere words of kindness won't do your
    servants much good [338a]:
With an open heart, give them food and
    clothing!

Kyirong traders,
Don't buy sheep and goats from nomads
To sell them to the Mönpas for slaughter!

Kyirong lamas,
Don't be sectarian,
Dividing the teachings into "good" and
    "bad"!

Kyirong monks,
Don't disgrace your teacher
By behaving in careless ways!

Kyirong rulers,
Do not inflict new taxes
Or punishments upon your subjects!

Kyirong officials,
Don't disgrace the rulers
By treating the people badly!

Kyirong subjects,
Don't conspire to rebel
Against your chiefs!

Kyirong *ngakpas,*
Don't cause the ruin of yourself and
    others
By practicing black magic and casting
    spells!

Kyirong folk,
Don't be hostile to the doctrinal views of
    others:
All are teachings of the Buddha!

Kyirong folk,
Don't steal from each other
Land, houses, and religious property!

Kyirong folk,
If you have too little faith in the lama,
Blessings will never penetrate your being!

Kyirong husbands and wives,
Don't both say the same thing at the same
    time:
It will bore people!

Kyirong folk,
Don't be eager to slaughter:
You will sink to the lowest of the hells!

Kyirong old men,
Don't start a new household:
Having two wives is grounds for
    suffering!

Kyirong folk,
Don't undertake unprofitable business:
If you don't know how to trade, you'll get
    into debt!

Kyirong folk,
Don't be too fond of sleeping and
    eating:
Tend to your livelihood and work your
    fields, and you will prosper [338b].

Kyirong folk,
Don't hanker after wealth:
Leave craving for food and drink to the
    dogs!

Kyirong folk,
Don't entertain a lot of impossible plans:
Without merit, you won't accomplish one
    wish out of a hundred!

Kyirong folk,
When your karma manifests as obstacles,
    put your trust in the lama and the
    Three Jewels:
Your aspirations and purposes will be
    accomplished!

Kyirong folk,
There are plenty of ghosts and spirits in the
    houses of the superstitious:
Don't fuel too many of these meaningless
    thoughts!

Kyirong folk,
There are plenty of enemies for the
    angry:
Don't let anger, that meaningless delusion,
    grow!

Kyirong folk,
There is never satisfaction for the miser:
Don't be obsessed with wealth!

Kyirong folk,
If you are generous with food, you will be
    surrounded by attendants:
Don't give people a hard time over food!

Kyirong folk,
If you make offerings and gifts, good
    fortune will naturally increase:
This life, too, will be a happy one!

Kyirong folk,
Always do prostrations and
    circumambulate the Jowo:
The sublime one will keep you under his
    protection!

Kyirong folk,
Provide authentic hermits and great
    meditators with sustenance:
You will become enlightened along with
    them!

Kyirong folk,
By rejoicing in others' virtuous deeds,
You too will achieve great merit!

Kyirong folk,
If you conclude whatever virtuous act you
    do with dedication prayers,
Its benefit will never wane!

Kyirong folk,
All those who practice the divine Dharma
    in this way
Will be happy from this life onwards!

May all the Dharma protectors and
    celestial beings who delight in virtue
Guard all men and women who act in
    accordance with Dharma.

By singing this song I was able to interrupt the
stream of suffering perpetuated by many meat-
dealers, and establish everyone in virtue
[339a].

A man from Kyirong who faced hard times for lack of money went to Shigatse and told many poor children there, "My place is called Happy Village, Kyirong,[63] because it is such a delightful place to live. If you come there, you, too, will be happy." Deceiving them in this way, he went and came back several times with a number of poor children, and sold thirteen of them as slaves to some local Mönpas. He made their lives miserable, while he lived on the earnings of his trade.

When I arrived, one of the boys the man had kidnapped, knowing that he was about to be sold into slavery, ran away to my place; he was soon followed by the man himself. I gave the man many silver coins, reminding him that it was improper to sell human beings and that he would certainly be punished if the Palace of Ganden[64] heard about it. I taught him some Dharma, explaining to him that, behaving in this way, in his next life he would be reborn in the lower realms. Feeling remorse for his misdeeds, he confessed and offered a promise never to deal in slaves again. All the kindhearted people of Kyirong rejoiced and expressed their gratitude.

That year, at the time when all the people of that area hold many *ganachakra* feast offerings and joyful gatherings, a group of young men and women sang this praise of Gyalwa Rinpoche:[65]

> On the top of the Potala
> The full moon rises—
> Oh! It's not the moon,
> It's the face of the Victorious One!
>
> On the top of the Potala
> A golden flute resounds—
> Oh! It's not a golden flute
> It's the melodious voice of the Victorious One!
>
> Whoever sees the face of the Victorious One
> Will not be born in the lower realms.
> Whoever once hears the voice of the Victorious One
> Will obtain a human existence in his next life [339b].

They sang this and many other songs, danced, and exclaimed, "May auspiciousness prevail! May prosperity reign!"

After Jetsun Chökyi Wangchuk had cut their hair,[66] a few nuns performed an auspicious sacred dance, which he himself had created:

> Let's sing this auspicious song
> Of total, consummate auspiciousness,
> Glowing with auspicious virtue
> Like an auspicious waxing moon!
>
> In the auspicious square of this religious enclosure
> Master and disciples have auspiciously gathered,
> And the Dharma spreads in auspicious happiness.
> Perform your auspicious dance!
>
> This auspicious year is joyful,
> Next year too will be happy and auspicious!
> The auspicious connections are unchanging!
> May auspiciousness prevail for ever!
>
> With one, two, three,
> The splendor of auspiciousness blazes forth!
>
> With two, three, six,
> Our auspicious aspirations are accomplished!

They danced and sang in this way. Many others sang, danced, and played all sorts of music for the pleasure of the men and women gathered there.

Then, a few of us, master and disciples, went to visit Kyirong Samten Ling, the seat of Yongdzin Rinpoche.[67] There I offered a general distribution of tea and money, and received from the abbot, Chözang Rinpoche, the transmission for the cycle of teachings on the Great Compassionate One.[68] We stayed there a few days and were welcomed with great hospitality by the treasurer.

We then proceeded to Riwo Pelbar, the Glorious Blazing Mountain, where Jetsun Milarepa once meditated. There we paid homage to the golden reliquary of the great awareness-holder of Kathok;[69] before it we offered a *ganachakra* feast, butter-lamps, and prayers. Then we went to Ragma Changchup Dzong, the Enlightenment Fort of Ragma, and to Kyangpen Namkha Dzong, the Sky Citadel of Kyangpen [340a], establishing connections with these two holy places.

I then went to visit the benefactors of Drothang and made strong spiritual and material connections with them. From there I went to the hermitage of Trakar Taso,[70] the Horse Tooth White Rock, and met the learned and accomplished Jetsun Chökyi Wangchuk. Staying for a few days, I received from him the transmissions of the *Hundred Instructions*,[71] the *Embodiment of the Three Jewels*[72] and *Guru Yoga*. I offered him a white silken scarf, five arm-spans long, with some gold and silver coins, corals and turquoise. I offered tea, money and a *ganachakra* feast, too, to the community of nuns. The lama gave me provisions for the road and many books.

I then reached Ngari Dzongka. From the retreat hut of Om Phuk Lama, I went to meet the lord of *siddhas*, Chingkarwa Donyö Dorje Rinpoche.[73] I received from him the empowerment of the *Sixteen Spheres of the Kadampa Tradition*[74] and the reading-transmission of *The Teachings of the Kadampa, Father and Sons*,[75] *Metaphors for the Graded Path, the Heap of Jewels*,[76] and *The Ultimate Graded Path, "The Blue Beryl Vase,"*[77] as well as the *Three Cycles of Doha*[78] and the *Long-Life Sadhana of the Northern Continent*.[79] I offered him some gold and silver; in return he gave me presents and many books. Our minds became as one.

Then I went for a few days to the Brocade Cave of Rala,[80] establishing a connection with this sacred place and doing some restoration work. After this, I crossed the pass of Gungthang and stayed a day at a small village monastery called Chamangpo, "Many Birds" [340b],[81] where I was received hospitably. Following this, the treasurer Wangpo and a few of his people left for central Tibet through the Pongrong Valley of the glorious Gungthang Plain, while I and the

others stayed at Chamangpo, teaching the Dharma and singing spiritual songs. Finally, having made prayers of dedication and auspiciousness, we set off for Lapchi.

Notes

1. In 1818
2. For Panchen Lobzang Chökyi Gyaltsen, see chap. 2, note 30.
3. The ninth Dalai Lama, whom Shabkar had met earlier and who passed away in 1815 at the age of nine.
4. For Döpel, see chap. 9, note 53.
5. The regent-king of Tibet, Demo Rinpoche; see chap. 9, note 31.
6. The Hundred Springs (*chu mig brgya rtsa*): a famous place called Muktinath by the Nepalese. Standing at 3810 meters above sea level, and located between Manang and Mustang in northwestern Nepal, it is a pilgrimage site for Buddhists and Hindus. There, one can see stones and springs from which blue flames of natural gas burn continuously.
7. The ancient Tibetan kingdom of Lo Mantang or Mustang, incorporated into Nepal in the late eighteenth century, following the Gurkha war. Ngari Panchen Pema Wangyal (*mnga' ris pan chen padma dbang rgyal*, 1487–1542), as well as many learned Sakya teachers, originated from Mustang. See D. P. Jackson, *The Mollas of Mustang*, LTWA, 1984.
8. *'phen*, a flat hanging, made of pieces of different colored brocade.
9. Concerning the one-day vows, see chap. 1, note 11.
10. Vaishravana (Tib. *rnam thos sras*), the god of wealth.
11. In Tibet, it is a sign of opulence to go on horseback, as compared to just going on foot.
12. A lie that can cause a fully ordained person to lose his vows is pretending to be a realized person when he is not; also claiming falsely to have had visions of deities, to have miraculous powers, etc.
13. The Buddha.
14. The Buddha Bright Lamp (Tib. *sang rgyas mar me 'od*, Skt. *Pradipaprabha*).
15. The Buddha Beneficial Speech (Tib. *sangs rgyas phan bzhed*, Skt. *Hitaishin*).
16. Ngari Dzong (*mnga' ris rdzong*) is Dzongka (*rdzong*

kha), which, according to Trulshik Rinpoche should be spelled *rdzong dga'*. See also Aufschnaiter 1976, hereafter referred to as MI. Dzongka is the main village in Gungthang (*gung thang*).

17. The Luminous Cave (*'od gsal phug*) in Rongphu (*rong phu*). See MI, p. 181.

18. The cave of Standing-on-My-Feet (*rkang tshugs phug*), so called because this was the place where Milarepa first established himself on the solid ground of spiritual practice, i.e., "stood on his own two feet."

19. Kya Ngatsa (*skya snga rtsa*), now called Tsalung (see MI), in Gungthang, at an altitude of 4300 meters.

20. "White Garuda" is a common name given to the *dzomo* by villagers.

21. Wati Zangpo *(wati bzang po)* or the Jowo of Kyirong (*skyid grong jo bo*). A famous sandalwood image of Avalokiteshvara in the form of Khasharpana, which is one of the five statues brought from Nepal by Akaramatishila at the order of King Songtsen Gampo (see chap. 9, note 18). This highly venerated image is said to have spoken several times to the temple keepers and to have given prophecies. People used to come from all over central Tibet to seek its blessing. About the size of a five-year-old child, it was saved by Tibetan refugees and is now preserved by His Holiness the Dalai Lama at Dharamsala in India. Trakar Taso Tulku Chökyi Wangchuk (see note 44 below) wrote a detailed history of the Wati Zangpo (see Bibliography).

22. Some snakes are said to have a jewel in their forehead that is called "snake-essence" (*sbrul gyi snying po*). By extension, "snake-essence" is used to refer to very precious things, here to a rare kind of sandalwood.

23. Bodhnath stupa or Jarung Khashor (*bya rung kha shor*, see note 28) and Svayambunath stupa or Phagpa Shinkun (*'phags pa shing kun*) are two of the three Great Stupas in Kathmandu Valley, Nepal. The third one is the Takmo Lujin (*stag mo lus sbyin*, locally known as "Namobuddha"), erected near the place where the Buddha Shakyamuni, when he was born as a prince in one of his former lives, gave his body to feed a starving tigress.

24. "Prosperity" here is the translation of *g.yang*, which indicates a natural magnificence, the prosperity-yielding power of some objects or places.

25. For *The Golden Garland of Dedications*, see Appendix 5.

26. Exposition (*'chad*), debate (*rtsod*), and composition (*rtsom*): these are said to be the three main activities connected with spreading the Dharma.

27. The Tripitaka: the three baskets of Vinaya,

Sutra and Abhidharma. The are all included in the Tibetan canonical collection called Kangyur (*bka' 'gyur*).

28. This refers to the story of the poultry woman Shamvara who built the stupa of Jarung Kashor (*bya rung kha shor*), the present Bodhnath. When she was dying, she enjoined the four sons she had by four different fathers to complete her work. By the merit of her deeds, she attained Buddhahood and manifested as the protectress Pramoha Devi.

At the completion of the work, each of those who contributed to it made an aspiration-prayer. In accordance with their vows, the first son became the Abbot, Shantarakshita, the second one became the Master, Guru Padmasambhava, the third one became the Dharma King Trisong Detsen, and the fourth one became the wise minister Bami Trihzi (*zhang blon rba mi krhi gzigs*), a Buddhist minister of King Trisong Detsen. The ox who had carried earth and stones did not know how to pray and, feeling that his hard work had been forgotten, made the perverse wish to harm the work of the four sons. He became King Langdharma, who attempted to eradicate Buddhism from Tibet, but failed to do so; he was eventually assassinated by Lhalung Palkyi Dorje, himself the rebirth of a crow who had heard the ox make his wicked vow, and had made a wish to be reborn as a Bodhisattva who would assassinate the apostate king.

The text of the history of the Jarung Khashor (*mchod rten chen po bya rung kha shor gyi lo rgyus thos pas grol ba*) is a *terma* revealed at Samye around the eleventh century by Lhatsun Ngonmo (*lha btsun sngon mo*), who hid it again because the time for its dissemination was not ripe. It was rediscovered again (*yang gter*) probably in 1512 (see GC, vol. 3, p. 50) by Ngakchang Sakya Zangpo (*sngags 'chang shakya bzang po*), who wrote it in its present form. See K. Dowman, *The Legend of the Great Stupa* (1973) and Franz-Karl Ehrhard (1990 and 1991).

Keith Dowman communicated to us the following summary of the conventional history of the Great Stupa: "Both Newari and Tibetan legend place the foundation of the Great Stupa of Bodhnath in antiquity. The Newars believe that the Licchavi king Manadeva (died A.D. 505) built the original stupa as a reliquary for his father, King Vrsadeva, after he had unwittingly killed him. The Tibetan legend implies only that the stupa was built before Trisong Detsen invited Guru Padmasambhava to Tibet in the eighth century. A thirteenth-century Tibetan biography of Padmasambhava (*Padma bka' thang shel brag ma*) provides the first literary reference to the stupa and establishes the earliest Tibetan connection with it. There is no further substantial information concerning Bodhnath until the early sixteenth century, when Shakya Zangpo, a Nyingmapa yogin from Kham, had a vision at Samye, in central Tibet, that induced him to travel to Bodhnath to restore the stupa. However, upon arrival, he had difficulty in identifying the mound of earth that once had been the stupa. Having found the right location, Shakya Zangpo unearthed the stupa and restored it. It is Shakya Zangpo's sixteenth-century reconstruction that is still extant, although its form has been modified. Shakya Zangpo established a line of incarnate lamas in Yolmo (Helambu) who were the caretaker abbots of the stupa. Thereafter the community of Buddhist Tamangs thrived around the stupa, which also became the principal destination for Tibetan pilgrims outside Tibet. In 1855 the abbacy of Bodhnath was given to a Chinese pilgrim, a Nyingma yogin, who gave service as interpreter to Jung Bahadur during the peace talks following the Nepali-Chinese war. Under the second and third Chini Lamas, who also were the Dalai Lama's consuls in Nepal, the abbacy of Bodhnath extended both its spiritual and temporal power. Since the death in 1982 of the last traditional abbot of Bodhnath, the third Chini Lama, much of the spiritual authority has devolved upon the Tibetan lamas who have built monasteries in the vicinity of the stupa."

29. Here the text should be corrected from *sku gzugs* to *sku gsum*.

30. Invincible One (*ma pham pa*) is an epithet of Maitreya. Lord of Secrets (*gsang ba'i bdag po*) refers to Vajrapani.

31. The White Jowo Jamali (*jo bo jamali dkar po*) in the royal city of Yambu (Kathmandu) is the Sveta Matsyendranath, Jamalesvara, the White Avalokiteshvara.

32. Meaning above the earth, on the earth, and below the earth, respectively the realms of the gods, human beings, and nagas.

33. Tsami Lotsawa Sangye Trak (*tsa mi lo tsa ba sangs rgyas grags*). Born in the eastern Tibetan province of Minyak, he traveled to India and studied with the famous *pandita* Abhayakara. He was acclaimed throughout India as the most learned of *panditas* and a fully realized *mahasiddha*, and was the only Tibetan ever to hold the thrones of Vajrasana and Nalanda. (See BD, vol. 4, p. 280).

34. Literally, "spreading your ten fingers on your chest." In Western societies to clutch one's head in one's hands is a stereotyped gesture indicating perplexity or deep reflection; Tibetans indicate the same

by putting their two hands upon their chests.

35. The *Prior Lives of the Buddha* (*skyes rabs*, Skt. *Jataka*): accounts of Lord Buddha's former lives as a Bodhisattva, which form a section of the Tengyur (*bstan 'gyur*).

36. Dagpo Lharje (*dwags po lha rje*, 1079–1153), the Physician of Dagpo, is one of Gampopa's names. See chap. 10, note 45.

37. Separation from what one likes and meeting what one does not like.

38. The fall into the lower states of existence, after the long enjoyment of celestial pleasures.

39. For *The Supreme Dharma of Intent Mindfulness*, see chap. 11, note 76.

40. The text actually says, "How could someone who has never been to Nepal know India?" since for a Tibetan the traditional road to India went through Nepal.

41. Gyalwa Götsangpa Gonpo Dorje (*rgyal ba rgod tshang pa mgon po rdo rje*, 1189–1258), a great saint of the Drukpa Kagyu lineage. He lived the life of a perfect hermit, performed many miracles, and left many inspiring writings on devotion (*mos gus*), pure perception (*dag snang*), and many other aspects of contemplative life.

42. *phul-gang*, the one-tenth of a *'bre* which is roughly one kg.

43. "Ever-crying" (*rtag tu ngu*), Sadaprarudita, and the "Youth Excellent Wealth" (*gzhon nu nor bzang*), Sudhana, are the names of the exemplary disciples who never hesitated to endure any amount of hardship in order to meet their teacher, be accepted by him, and receive his teaching. See Bruyat et al. 1987, 162–66, and Bruyat et al. 1994.

44. Trakar Taso Tulku Chökyi Wangchuk (*brag dkar rta so sprul sku chos kyi dbang phyug*, 1775–1837) was an influential master in the areas along the Nepal-Tibet border. He was a disciple of Trinley Dudjom Gön Nang Chöje (*phrin las bdud 'joms mgon gnang chos rje*, 1726–89), himself a disciple of Kathog Rigdzin Tsewang Norbu (*kah thog rig 'dzin tshe dbang nor bu*, 1698–1755). His reply to Shabkar's letter, as well as a reply to a second letter from Shabkar, is found in vol. Tha of *Trakar Taso Tulku's Collected Writings*, pp. 749–54. (Communicated by Franz-Karl Ehrhard.) Shabkar's second letter, as well the letters mentioned above, is found in DOL 3, folio 88b and in TS 4, p. 694.

45. *Hari* sandalwood: a precious kind of sandalwood.

46. For Rahu, see chap. 6, note 48.

47. The three wheels or activities of a Buddha (*'khor lo rnam gsum*): the wheel of study and reflection

(*thos bsam*), the wheel of meditation (*sgom pa*), and the wheel of activity (*phrin las*).

48. Padmapani: a name of Avalokiteshvara, the Buddha of compassion.

49. Samantabhadra is the Bodhisattva who made boundless offerings by emanating innumerable bodies like himself, each of which made offerings filling the sky. They in turn emanated innumerable bodies that also made offerings, and so on, *ad infinitum*.

50. The tiny seed of the banyan, or *nyagrodha*, gives birth to a giant tree which spreads over a huge area.

51. Buddha Dipankara, the Light Giver (*mar me mdzad*), is the protector of mariners. Sometimes also explained as the one "Who Became Buddha Through a Lamp," thus called because he planted the seed of Buddhahood by offering the light of a single lamp with pure aspiration.

52. This image refers to Indra, also called the Lord of the Deathless Ones (= the God of Gods), who lives in the All-Victorious Mansion in the Thirty-three-fold celestial realm, and rides upon a thirty-two-headed elephant.

53. This refers to the six branches of practice according to the Kalachakra (*dus 'khor sbyor ba yan lag drug*). See DZ, vol. 16 and NS, vol. 2, p. 151.

54. Gold and silver.

55. "One with three preoccupations" (*'dus shes gsum ldan*), i.e., who just eats, sleeps and defecates. A self-derisory epithet.

56. Winged feet, or swift feet (*rkang mgyogs*), one of the eight common *siddhis*, which enables one to cover enormous distances in a short time.

57. The primordial Buddha according to the Vajrayana.

58. For *bardo*, see chap. 4 , note 10.

59. By the Buddhas.

60. *glud*, an effigy which is a rough representation of a person offered as ransom in place of the person himself in a ritual for averting premature death. See chap. 6, note 43.

61. Cattle do not have upper teeth, so a bull with upper teeth is a bull-like human being. A tail-less dog is a dog-like human being.

62. Mount Kailash.

63. Kyirong is a contraction for Kyidrong (*skyid grong*), "Happy Village."

64. The seat of the Tibetan government.

65. Gyalwa Rinpoche (*rgyal ba rin po che*), the Precious Victorious One, an epithet of H.H. the Dalai Lama.

66. When giving them ordination.

67. Yongdzin Rinpoche; see chap. 9, note 33.

68. The Great Compassionate One (*thugs rje chen po*), a name of Avalokiteshvara.

69. Rigdzin Tsewang Norbu (*rig 'dzin tshe dbang nor bu*), 1698–1755, a great luminary of Kathok Monastery who traveled extensively and restored too the Great Stupa of Bodhnath, seventy years before Shabkar gilded its pinnacle. He passed away in Kyirong. See GC, vol. 3, pp. 194–98.

70. Trakar Taso (*brag dkar rta so*) between Kyirong and Dzongka (see MI) is one of the most important meditation places of Milarepa. There he spent nine, or according to others twelve, years in continuous meditation, beginning in 1083. At that location is Milarepa's cave known as the Central Citadel (*dbu ma rdzong*).

71. *The Hundred Instructions* (*khrid brgya*) are one hundred meditative instructions from all spiritual traditions, collected and arranged by Jetsun Kunga Drolcho (*rje btsun kun dga' grol mchog*, 1507–66). See DZ, vol.18, and Shabkar's *Emanated Scriptures of Orgyen*, pp. 454–59.

72. For *The Embodiment of the Three Jewels* (*dkon mchog spyi 'dus*), see ch. 10, note 51. Chökyi Wangchuk's lineage of these teachings spread widely from Kyirong to other mountain areas of northern Nepal, where his tradition is still followed. See Ehrhard (JNRC, 1992).

73. Chingkar Donyö Dorje (*phying dkar don yod rdo rje*), "Meaningful Vajra Clad in White Felt;" see Appendix 2, p. 558.

74. *The Sixteen Spheres* (*thig le bcu drug*) is a renowned *sadhana* that belongs to the pith instructions (*man ngag*) section of the Kadampa tradition. Avalokiteshvara is visualized with sixteen other deities in his heart, one within the other, and each one in a sphere of light.

75. Concerning *Teachings of the Kadampa, Father and Sons*, see chap. 6, note 31.

76. *Metaphors for the Graded Path, "Heap of Jewels"* (*dpe'i lam rim rin chen spungs pa*) was composed by Geshe Potowa (*dge bshes po to ba*, 1031–1105), a great Kadampa master. The text consists of hundreds of metaphors on all aspects of the path.

77. *The Ultimate Graded Path, "The Blue Beryl Vase"* (*don gi lam rim be'u bum sngon po*) was composed by the same author. According to Trulshik Rinpoche, *The Beryl Vase* (*be'u bum*, derived from *bee du rya'i bum pa*, or "Vase of Beryl,") is an image for a precious container in which are kept all the most profound and secret pith instructions. It also refers to the container in which the Tibetan translators used to hide and carry the esoteric instructions and mantras they had received and brought back from India. As communi-

cated by Matthew Kapstein, this is probably a late etymology. Be'u, "calf," in Skt. *Vatsa*, refers metaphorically to "wealth," "precious object."

78. *The Three Cycles of Dohas* (*do ha skor gsum*, T 2263) comprises the three main "songs of realization" of the great *siddha* Saraha. They are the *Doha for the King*, the *Doha for the Queen*, and the *Doha for the Subjects*.

79. For the *Long-Life Sadhana of the Northern Continent*, see chap. 4, note 12.

80. Brocade Cave of Rala (*ra la za 'og phug*), near Dzongka in Gungthang.

81. Many Birds (*bya mang po*) is a place near the Divine Lake of the Rakshas (*lha mtsho srin mtsho*) in Gungthang.

13

Meditation at Lapchi

*How, having gone to Lapchi, an authentic pilgrimage place, the
place sacred to the speech aspect of the Striped Tiger-faced
Dakini, I persevered in practice.*

Always wreathed in clouds and mist, latticed with wondrous rainbows, Lapchi[1] is the holy place of the speech aspect of the *yidam* Chakrasamvara, and one of the three main sacred places on this earth.[2] Its main site is the Cave of the Subjugation of Mara,[3] located in the high solitudes of the Lapchi Snow Range. There many learned and accomplished sages have raised the victory banner of practice and turned the wheel of the Dharma of Realization.[4]

I decided to go there to practice. Accompanied by many disciples, I first came to Betse Doyon Dzong, where we stopped for the night. The next day, on the way, we met some pilgrims who told us that the protector and Dharma King of Tibet, Demo Rinpoche, one of my root teachers whom I treasured like a jewel ornament on my head, had discarded the flower of his body.[5] An unfathomable sadness welled up again and again in my mind, and I sang this song of yearning, calling for his swift rebirth [342b]:

Kye hu!
Incarnation of the Victorious Ones, you
    have gone.
Gem fulfilling all beings' wishes,
You adorned the diadem of the teachings.
Unique, inconceivable ornament of this
    universe,
Because of our extreme lack of merit,
As beings of this decadent age,
You vanished suddenly, like a rainbow in
    the sky.

Master of Tibet, spiritual sovereign,
Sun with a thousand rays of compassion,
Now you have set;
Like the earth helplessly shrouded in
    darkness,
Your disciples are stunned by grief.

Though a torrent of tears washes over our
    faces,
The stain of grief will never leave our
    minds.
Though our fists beat on the drums of our
    chests,
We will never awaken from this sleep of
    despair.

You who were to lead us to Buddhahood
    at death,
Our guide and master, have now gone on
    before us.
Blinded by ignorance,
We are all left behind, unfortunate.

Kye hu! What can be done?
Now, who will show us the way at death?
Kind sovereign of wisdom and love,
From the unmanifest expanse, please
    consider us.

Before unfortunate ones like myself,
Stricken with years and on the threshold of
    death
Leave this life,

May your true reembodiment swiftly
   return.

May I see your golden face once more!
May this, my prayer, be fulfilled!

I then thought, "If even great saints suddenly toss away the flower of their lives at an
early age to inspire spiritual practice in those
who cling to permanence [343a], aren't we miserable ones left behind bound to die soon? Yet, I
feel that if I go to the Snows of Lapchi soon and
meditate at Dudul Phugmoche, the Cave of the
Subjugation of Mara, where Lord Milarepa once
lived, I will have no regrets when I die."

Continuing on quickly, I stayed overnight
near the monastery of Pelgyeling at the Belly
Cave of Nyanang,[6] where the foremost roots of
virtue, harmony and pure discipline prevailed.
Hearing that the abbot of this monastery was
Khenpo Kalzang Khedrup Rinpoche, a teacher
who combined knowledge, virtue and excellence,
I sent ahead this letter:

Sublime spiritual guide,
Holder of the banner of the teachings
Of the diadem of gods and men, the
   Buddha,
You found the sky treasure of knowledge
   and realization.

I, a pilgrim without religion,
Who like a river wanders in all directions,
Who like a fox roams the wilderness,
Who, aimless, has no place to call his
   home,
Offer these words at your feet.

When a thousand thunder-dragons thus
   proclaim your fame
Resounding to all horizons:

"Your body is a mighty, unshakable
   Mount Meru,
Made of the jewels of the twofold
   accumulation.
Your immaculate activities are a sun and
   moon

Illuminating the four continents of those
   calling for help!"

Then my fickle mind, this novice acrobat,
Finds itself dancing for joy again and
   again.

Riding this old horse I've borrowed,
My illusory body,
I have gone round many countries [343b].
Now, with my retinue of beggars,
I have finally reached the realm of your
   benevolence.

Wishing to visit the holy places and to meet
   you,
Spiritual guide who benefits all those you
   encounter,
I will enter your presence with folded hands,
Praying that you will grace me with your
   great kindness.

With the help of such a spiritual guide as
   captain,
I pray that, in the vessel of this precious
   human body,
Rigged with all the freedoms and blessed
   with favorable conditions,
I may sail across the waters of samsara
To the shore of liberation.

To attract a fleeting glance from the bee of
   your eyes
To the lotus field of this letter,
I have filled it with honey of silver,
   wrapped it in silk,
And, bowing down, I offer it to you with
   greatest respect.

He found this letter pleasing and, when I met
him in person, received me with the greatest
kindness and gave me many provisions. To make
a spiritual connection, I requested the transmission for the *Fifty Verses of Devotion to the Guru*[7] and
other texts.

In the female Earth Hare[8] Year known as Nyoden, at the auspicious time of the waxing moon of the fourth month, I reached the heights of the Lapchi snow range, where many great saints of the Kagyu lineage once lived. Far away from the cities of distraction, this abode of *rishis* and celestial beings, this dancing place of the mother dakinis, lies beneath slate mountains and glaciers ever wrapped in clouds and mist.[9]

I did prostrations and offerings to the deities, the dakinis, and dharmapalas who delight in virtue, and I sang this song of praise:

I bow down, make offerings, sing praises,
  and pray
To the gurus, *yidam* deities, and dakinis
  [344a]:
May you grant blessings and realization
To all beings who stay in this place.

Universally renowned, truly wondrous,
The Lapchi snow range is the dwelling
  place
Of the forefathers of the practice lineage,
Who turned the wheel of the Dharma of
  Realization.

The mountain summits are crowned with
  snow,
Their waists girdled by belts of silver mist.
Snow-melt streams appear beneath
  glaciers;
From high, rocky cliffs, water cascades
  down.

On lush green mountain meadows
Blanketed with wild flowers,
Beautiful wild animals gambol, completely
  at ease.
Bees gather and sing their songs
On the fragrant corollas of many-colored
  blossoms.

From deep within the thick green foliage,
Birds send forth their sweet calls.
Within the pleasant caves,
Clouds of celestial beings and dakinis
  gather;

The dharmapalas guard practitioners as
  their own child.

There are many precious statues and relics,
Including the clothes of past Kagyu masters.
Mountains and rocks themselves resemble
  deities,
And bear many miraculous footprints.

The natural beauty is enhanced by the sun
  and moon
Of the temples of Drophen and Pelgyeling,
One to the left and one to the right.
At the upper end of the valley are the
  Lapchi highlands.
At the foot of the mountains, there are
  many patrons among the villagers;
Berries, fruits, edible plants, and bamboo
  abound.

Spirits, evil forces, aggressors and bandits:
One never even hears the names of such
  dangers.
In brief, it is a pure celestial realm,
A pleasant place where awareness is clear,

Practitioner, settle here,
And sublime exalted Dharma will result
  [344b].

Faithful patrons, circumambulate this
  place:
All your bad karma, evil deeds and
  obscurations will be purified.

Wealthy people, make offerings to this
  place:
You will attain the ordinary and
  extraordinary *siddhis*.

May whoever hears these words
Remain in this holy place and attain
  enlightenment.

I made offerings and sang praises to the deities, dakinis, and local Dharma protectors. With the patrons of Lapchi, I offered a sacred feast. They provided me with all the necessities.

Above the great Cave of the Subjugation of Mara on the mountainside was an utterly isolated hermitage known as The Hidden One.[10] I entered a strict solitary retreat there, and my practice progressed.

Following my stay in this holy place, all my wandering thoughts, coarse and subtle, subsided by themselves, naturally giving way to the vast, boundless state that is primordial wakefulness completely free of discursive thoughts, and embellished by clarity, bliss, and emptiness.

One wintry afternoon when I was performing a *ganachakra* feast, I saw this: in front of Lapchi Mountain, in the middle of the sky, were two white clouds. Between them a rainbow arose, broad as a highway, such as I had never seen before. Its far end led into another cloud, toward the Tonting Gyalmo, the Azure Queen Mountain;[11] on the path of the rainbow many deities moved back and forth. That scene lasted for a long time.

From then onwards, in dreams, in meditation experiences, and in reality, I met the Five Sisters of Long Life, the protectors of Tibet, many times, and I was able to accomplish whichever of the four activities I needed. In particular, when I offered a coating of gold to the stupa of Bodhnath in Nepal, I solicited their help, and my aims were accomplished easily and without hindrance [345a].

In this holy place, whenever I offered a *ganachakra*, wondrous rainbow-colored clouds would appear, seen by all. I thought that these were signs that, pleased, the Five Sisters of Long Life were coming time and again.

At that time I thought of going to pay homage to the Diamond Throne of India, Bodhgaya. I mentioned this to my disciples, who said, "If you go, we will all go with you."

Having offered a *ganachakra* feast to the deities of the Three Roots and recited all the related prayers, just before dawn the next day, in a state that was half dream, half vision, the Tiger-faced Dakini appeared to me. She said: "If you go to India, many lives will be endangered. If you stay in Tibet to help beings, you will bring great benefit to the Buddhist teachings and to beings. We dakinis will always accompany you like your shadow; we will never fail you." Having spoken thus, she vanished.

Following her advice, I did not go to India.

Soon after that, one night I dreamed that Lapchi had become a vast, open plain. There came a multitude of Tibetans, Nepalese, Mönpas, Indian *acharyas*, and people of many other races, all speaking different languages. They filled the whole plain, which became like a busy metropolis with people moving back and forth. I saw this as a sign that, in the following years, many people would come and gather there.

The next year, on a late summer day, I went to the plain below the Cave of the Subjugation of Mara.[12] Where the plain meets the hill [345b] was a tree with fully developed foliage and branches facing upwards, divided into two crowns. I asked the monks who were with me to build a throne of stones at the foot of the tree. Then I told them, "In future I must teach the Dharma from this throne," and to create an auspicious connection, sitting upon it, I expounded the Dharma to the treasurer Kalzang Trinley and a few other attendants, quoting these and other scriptural passages:

> Doing no harm whatsoever,
> Practice virtue perfectly,
> Tame your mind completely:
> This is the teaching of the Buddha.

and:

> Good health is the supreme comfort,
> Giving joy is the supreme gift,
> Nirvana is the supreme bliss,
> One who is constant is the supreme friend.

They all were very pleased.

At the Cave of the Subjugation of Mara, in order to enter the actual cave where Jetsun Milarepa stayed one had to crawl through a small entrance at the back of a temple. I thought, "At the

time of Jetsun Mila there must have been another, easier, access." After a search, I found
an entrance right in front, at the foot of the
cave. As we were clearing away fallen rocks
and earth, I discovered the remnants of
Milarepa's stone hearth. When this occurred,
strong faith increased in all those assembled
there. The news spread that the door to the
holy site had been reopened.[13]

I stayed in the cave. At the beginning of
summer, just as I had dreamed earlier, one after
another, many worthy and fortunate disciples
[346a] came there from all directions, and I
turned the Wheel of the Dharma for them under
that tree. In the Cave of the Subjugation of Mara
I lit a wick as thick as my forearm in a huge lamp
that was like an ocean of melted butter. This
butter-lamp burned day and night, warming the
whole cave.

At this time I sent a letter to Khenchen
Yonten Lhundrup Rinpoche of Chubar, a master
filled with loving-kindness and compassion whose
wisdom eyes were wide open. Accompanying
my request for his spiritual protection with some
offerings, I wrote:

> Diadem of all gods and men;
> Foremost among learned, virtuous and
>   noble-minded beings,
> Amidst the holders of the teaching,
> You stand aloft like the pinnacle of a
>   victory banner.
> In front of you, great abbot, supreme
>   spiritual guide,
> I present these words, with the unfeigned
>   respect of my body, speech, and mind.
>
> I, the yogin who, like the wind, never
>   settles anywhere,
> Roam at random through secluded groves
>   and mountain retreats,
> Traveling without preference throughout
>   all countries.
>
> With the stirring stick of your perfectly
>   pure motivation,
> You churned the ocean filled by the great
>   waves of the two accumulations,

> And, wondrously, the mighty Mount
>   Sumeru of your body arose,[14]
> Ablaze with the splendor of the major and
>   minor marks.
>
> On the four steps of skillful gathering,
> You stand, lofty and majestic, ringed
> By the golden mountains of your
>   heart-disciples.
>
> The brilliance of the sun and moon—your
>   virtuous deeds—
> Shines over the four continents—the
>   fortunate beings you assist,
> And dispels the darkness of decline and
>   disharmony.
>
> Their beneficial warmth nourishing all lands,
> The vast lotus garden of the teachings of
>   the Victorious Ones
> Spreads and blossoms in a hundred
>   directions [346b].
>
> Your fame, thundered by the thousand
>   drums of summer,
> Resounds as far as the very realm of
>   Brahma.
> On hearing this, my mind, the dancer
> With its myriad movements, cannot help
>   but dance for joy.
>
> Protected by the compassionate rays of the
>   sun of the Three Jewels
> The humble lotus of my illusory body,
>   your respectful servant,
> Has been spared the dreaded curse of frost;
> It exudes the sweet fragrance of spiritual
>   practice.
>
> If I divide my life into three parts,
> Two have already passed;
> Protect me so that, without obstacles,
> I may spend this last third in lonely places,
> Persevering in the virtuous practice that is
>   meditation.
>
> I pray that, throughout all of my lives,
> I may meet spiritual teachers like you,

And, that, in reality, in meditation
    experiences,
In dreams, I may hear their voices.

I respectfully offer you this letter
From the Cave of the Subjugation of Mara
    in Lapchi,
Where Dharma practitioners wield the
    weapon of the antidotes,
Vanquishing the demon of the obscuring
    emotions.

Pleased, he sent me many presents.
    To request some provisions to sustain my
practice, I wrote this letter to Tashi Dedenpa. A
chieftain from the east of the valley, he had a
strong affinity for the Dharma and great devotion to the spiritual teachers.

Powerful governor, who wears as a diadem
    the guru and the Three Jewels,
You care for your retinue and subjects as
    you would your own children;
You endeavor to perform virtuous deeds
As much as peasants strive to till their
    fields.

With respectful body, speech, and mind,
I, White Foot, a counterfeit practitioner
    without Dharma,
Who, like a wild animal without a home,
Wanders throughout mountain solitudes,
    without a destination,
Present these words at your feet, without
    hypocrisy [347a].

Mighty one blessed with faith, diligence,
    wisdom, and compassion,
By the power of the merit you
    accumulated in the past
You gained this precious human body,
So hard to find in these realms without
    leisure,
Even should one search for eighty
    thousand aeons.

A spiritual guide adorns your head like a
    jewel,

Learning serves as your earring,
Meaningful speech as your necklace,
And the bracelets of generosity embellish
    your arms:
Their amazing brilliance outshines all
    ordinary ornaments.

Master of the seven royal emblems—the
    seven noble qualities[15]—
When you gained sovereignty over the four
    continents—your retinue, subjects and
    territory—
Celestial and human beings sang in praise:
"An unprecedented universal monarch has
    come!"

When the echo of this music reached my ears,
The fresh breeze of complete joy
Swept my capricious mind in all directions,
Like a fluffy piece of cotton wool.

Having traveled through many countries
On the horse of this transitory body
Borrowed for a while from the four elements,
I, your humble servant,
Have now safely reached the holy place of
    Lapchi.

O leader endowed with great merit, here is
    my request:
Having arrived at the Jewel Island, where
    the sublime Dharma prevails,
I now gather the gems of immaculate
    virtue,
In order not to return empty-handed
    [347b].

If, while I practice to the extent of my
    abilities
At Lapchi, the seat of the forefathers of the
    practice lineage,
You could provide me with a few
    provisions to sustain my efforts,
It would be of limitless kindness.

Here in mountain solitudes
I shall invoke the spiritual protection of the
    deities of the Three Roots,

So that the banner of your life may stand
    firm,
And all your wishes be accomplished in
    accordance with the Dharma.

I pray that on the day I achieve
    enlightenment
By the strength of practicing in the
    wilderness,
I may, starting with you, lead to
    Buddhahood
All those with whom I have made a
    connection.

Today, I am respectfully sending these
    humble verses
From the Cave of the Subjugation of Mara
    in Lapchi,
The supreme and extraordinary sacred
    site,
Where gurus, deities, dakinis, and
    protectors gather like clouds.

In reply to my request, he sent me whatever
provisions I needed. Later, he came himself to
see me and requested some teachings to establish
a spiritual connection.

Inspired by the pure solitude of this sacred mountain wilderness, where the mind is clear and
serene, and by the progress it brought to my
practice, I sang this:

In this holy place that is like a paradise,
I pray to the father gurus of the Kagyu
    lineage,
To the *yidam* deities, the mother dakinis,
    and the Dharma protectors of Lapchi:
Bestow the waves of your blessings!

Here is the palace of Chakrasamvara on
    earth,
The supreme gathering ground of the
    mother dakinis.

In this pleasant wilderness of Lapchi,
I, the vagabond, progressed in my
    practice.

Evil deeds, the causes of lower states of
    existence [348a],
And my enemies, the obscuring emotions,
    withdrew by themselves:
Practicing in pleasant solitudes,
I wish to emulate Jetsun Mila's life.

Meeting no one, and with no disturbances,
I have kept pure my *samaya* and my vows:
Practicing in serene solitudes,
I wish to emulate Jetsun Mila's life.

Continually remembering the imminence
    of death,
My clinging to this life diminished:
Practicing in pleasant solitudes,
I wish to emulate Jetsun Mila's life.

Taking refuge, generating Bodhicitta, and
    offering the mandala,
I accumulated the necessary merit:
Practicing in pleasant solitudes,
I wish to emulate Jetsun Mila's life.

Doing prostrations, circumambulations,
And the meditation and recitation of
    Vajrasattva,
I purified my misdeeds and obscurations:
Practicing in pleasant solitudes,
I wish to emulate Jetsun Mila's life.

With my whole heart, I took refuge in my
    root guru,
The union of all protectors:
Practicing in pleasant solitudes,
I wish to emulate Jetsun Mila's life.

Having contact with no one,
My body and voice became free;
By resting evenly in the natural state,
My mind became vast and yet more
    vast:
Practicing in pleasant solitudes,
I wish to emulate Jetsun Mila's life.

As I practiced the path of the development
stage,
My visualizations became clearer.
Cultivating inner heat, bliss and warmth
blazed forth:
Practicing in pleasant solitudes,
I wish to emulate Jetsun Mila's life [348b].

When I practiced *phowa*
I had good signs of results,
When I practiced Chöd,
Visions and meditation experiences arose:
Practicing in pleasant solitudes,
I wish to emulate Jetsun Mila's life.

Even if I die now, I will have no regrets;
Happy, I feel like singing!
Practicing in pleasant solitudes,
I wish to emulate Jetsun Mila's life.

From now on, until I attain Buddhahood,
Emulating Jetsun Milarepa's perfect life,
May I practice the Dharma as he did
In the excellent groves of solitude.

Most of the shrines of this holy place, which
sheltered precious relics and symbols of the
enlightened body, speech and mind, were damaged or had fallen into ruins. The monks of
Lapchi were unable to repair them. I could not
bear to see to see this, and the pure intention
arose to do something beneficial for the Dharma
and for all beings.

Accordingly, in the upper part of the valley,
I built shelters at the feet of the glaciers; in the
lower part I made bridges over the streams; and
in between, I restored the damaged temples.

In the center of the plain where the monastic community dwelt,[16] I built an assembly hall
surrounded by an outer, enclosing wall, and many
new cells for the monks. I set up a golden pinnacle on the roof of the temple. Inside, using
thirteen *dotse* of silver, I fitted the temple with all
the ritual objects for performing offerings. I also

gave new ordination to those monks who had
strayed into being householders.

After completing all this, I sent the following
letter to the hierarchs of Drigung, Father and
Son,[17] under the authority of whom this holy site
and its monasteries were placed [349a]:

Supreme pair of great emanations,
Like the sun and moon rising together
You manifested as spiritual guides who
ceaselessly help beings.

I, your humble servant, Shabkar, an idle
hermit,
Making of my body a lotus,
With the ten petals of my fingers
Raised around the pistil of my head,
Present with immense respect this fragrant
letter
At your immaculate lotus feet.

Supreme protectors,
Perfectly born from the vast ocean of the
twofold accumulation,
Ablaze with the splendor of the major and
minor marks,
Your stainless manifested bodies,
Like the sun and the moon,
Are surrounded by constellations of
learned and accomplished beings.

When I heard the thunder-dragon, the
drum of summer,
Heralding the way you made the light of
the Dharma of sutra and mantra
Shine out toward a hundred horizons,
My mind, with myriad movements,
Could not but dance for joy and faith.

As for myself, your humble servant,
Although my realization is small,
Vast are my energy and aspiration
To raise to the very peak of samsara
The precious victory banner of the practice
lineage.

I restored the supreme site of the Cave of
the Subjugation of Mara at Lapchi,

A monastic estate of the victorious
　　Drigungpas, the Lords of the Three
　　Holy Places,
Praying that you, precious protectors,
My refuge for this life and the lives to
　　come,
Supreme healers who triumph over
The hundred plagues of obscuring
　　emotions,
Great captains who ferry us to the Pure
　　Lands,
May accept me as your disciple throughout
　　my lives.

At present, too, I continue to serve you as
　　much as I can [349b].
Protectors and refuge with whom any
　　connection is meaningful,
May you swiftly establish in the state of
　　Buddhahood
All those who, like me, were left
By the many past Buddhas to wander in
　　samsara.

Until we reach the great land—the lasting
　　bliss of Buddhahood,
Grant us your spiritual protection, so
　　that
All adverse circumstances and obstacles
　　subside,
All favorable circumstances come to pass,
And all our aspirations be accomplished.
Dedicate your prayers to us:
Everything is in your hands!

I have renewed the ordinations of your
　　disciples,
The monks of the holy place of Lapchi.
Protectors, accept us as your followers
From this very day throughout the series of
　　our lives.

Despite my great desire, I have never met
　　you,
For I have been wandering in other lands.
I pray that, before long, I may behold your
　　faces
And drink the nectar of your words.

This insignificant letter of mine, calling for
　　your protection,
Is accompanied by a white scarf as a
　　humble support on which to rest your
　　eyes.
I offer to you from the Cave of the
　　Subjugation of Mara in Lapchi,
Where the doctrine of the practice lineage
　　flourishes.

Extremely pleased by this offering, both the protectors, Father and Son, sent me many presents.

One day, since a pilgrim was returning to Domey,
my homeland, I was able to send the following
letter to my root-teacher Tendzin Nyima
Rinpoche, who was living at the summit of the
central island of the great lake of the Queen
Who Destroyed Ten Thousand, Trishok
Gyalmo:

Treasury of sublime wisdom and
　　tenderness [350a],
Spiritual guide who bears the sweet-
　　sounding name "Sun Who
　　Upholds the Teachings,"
You benefit whoever makes a connection
　　with you.

Your spiritual son, Jampa Chödar,
Prostrating himself in your direction,
From the distant solitudes of the Lapchi
　　mountains
Respectfully offers this letter at your
　　renowned feet.

Just hearing the enchanting news
That despite your ripe old age
You remain in perfect health
Instantly filled my whole being with joy.

Owing to your immense kindness,
Wherever I went, I remained well in body
　　and mind,

Found what I needed to sustain my life,
And progressed in my spiritual practice.

Yet, despite all this,
Like a child deprived of his mother,
Saddened by not having met you for many
    years,
I shed tears again and again.

Like a thirsty person longing for water,
Morning and evening I think of you,
    constantly.
When shall I see you again?
Tormented by longing, I am over-
    whelmed.

Precious protector, lasting refuge,
By the power of your enlightened
    aspiration,
Heeding the faith and devotion of your
    disciples,
You should remain for a long time.

But if, because of our lack of good fortune,
You display the way of passing into
    nirvana
In order to spur on to Dharma practice
Those who cling to permanence and
    always postpone their practice,
We, the miserable ones in your care
Who did not enter the path,
Will be left without shelter and protection,
Like an ant's nest bereft of its covering
    stone.

I myself will be like a bee whose fate is
    sealed
In the season when flowers have already
    withered:
No reason for going, no place to go [350b].

Kye hu!
Knowing what will happen to us after you
    leave,
Wherever we happen to wander,
You must not even show signs of aging and
    sickness,
Let alone of leaving this world.

I supplicate you from my heart—
Please remain for hundreds of years,
Lest we be like travelers
Abandoned by their guide on a
    treacherous path.
Please do not forsake those who trust in
    you!

I, your humble servant, will return soon.

Please grant me your spiritual protection
So that I may meet you again
Without encountering obstacles or
    difficulties on the way.

If I cannot meet you again in this life,
In my next life, wherever you, noble
    teacher,
Attain full Buddhahood,
May I be reborn there as your first disciple.

To several lamas, dignitaries, disciples and
patrons, I also sent letters that can be found
among my *Collected Songs*.[18]

Once, several hundred fortunate disciples,
faithful patrons, and Khampa pilgrims, arriving
from all directions, spontaneously gathered in
Lapchi. For them, I taught in detail on relative
truth (the teachings on the karmic law of cause
and effect) and on absolute truth (the profound
nature of emptiness). Through the four skillful ways
of gathering disciples, I was able to help them.

Gyarong Lama (a person learned in the
scriptures and endowed with realization),
Lobzang Dargye, Yonten Gyatso, Sangye Rinchen, Tendzin Gyurme (a close disciple with
faith and pure thoughts), Lochenpa, Leshing
Drupchen, Gyarong Gelong and others [351a]—
in short, all the devoted disciples and patrons
assembled there—asked for some advice. In reply,
I sang this:

I supplicate you, Lord,
Dharma King Ngakyi Wangpo—
Please grant your blessings.

I, your heart-son, Shabkarpa,
Offer this spiritual song,

Melodious to hear and beneficial to the
minds
Of all the celestial and human beings
assembled here:
Gather around me and listen well.

The source of all good qualities is the
spiritual friend;
Follow him properly, in thought and
actions.

This human birth, free and well-favored, is
difficult to find;
Now that you have it, use it to achieve the
essence of the Dharma.

Our hold on life being so uncertain,
If you want to be joyful at the time of
death,
Now is the time to practice the sublime
Dharma.

The law of karma, of cause and effect,
cannot be escaped;
Give up negative actions and practice
virtue.

Immersed in samsara, you will never find
happiness;
To escape from suffering, set out on the
path.

Travel the path of the three trainings;
Listen to and expound the Tripitaka.

In order swiftly to attain Buddhahood
For the sake of leading all beings, your
mothers, to that level,
Practice the six *paramitas*
With a mind filled with love, compassion,
and Bodhicitta.

When the opportunity arises,
Through the four skillful ways of
gathering
Benefit all sentient beings, your
mothers,
To the best of your ability.

Since the Secret Mantrayana, the direct
path,
Is the swift means to attain supreme
Buddhahood,
Practice the paths of development,
completion, and Great Perfection,
And you will become a Buddha in one
lifetime:
This is certain.

When practicing in this way,
Rely upon secluded forest groves [351b].
Emptying your mind of preoccupation
With this life and the eight worldly
concerns,
Treasure a solitary life of practice.

By the merit of these words,
May all beings, our mothers, quickly attain
Buddhahood,
May goodness prevail in this place
And pervade the entire universe.

This song helped many faithful disciples.

The men and women of Drin Chubar,[19]
and most of the wealthy householders of
Nyanang, were well-known for being miserly
people who never made offerings or gave in
charity. In addition, every year they killed scores
of goats, sheep, and yaks. In brief, they performed many evil actions. By teaching them
the Dharma, I was able to interrupt the stream
of their evil deeds and, finally, gave them this
advice:

Precious and supreme gurus:
Like galaxies of stars,
Wreathe and diadem my head.

Under the protection of the unfailing
Three Jewels,
I sing whatever comes into my mind.

We now have a human birth, free and
well-favored:
A unique opportunity which will not occur
time and again—
Thus the Buddha has said.

We are always facing death.
We have no time to waste.
Practice the divine Dharma!

In this life,
We are all alike
In sharing the human condition.

But in our next lives,
Those who have done good will
Continue to ascend the path of light;
Those who have committed negative
    actions
Will descend into the lower realms—
    pitiful!

You rich misers, even if in this life
You cannot bear giving alms,
At least don't ready yourselves
For the depths of hell in your next lives,
Continuing to slaughter goats, sheep, and
    yaks year after year.

To be born in this southern continent of
    the Rose-apple Tree [352a]
Is the same as arriving at a crossroads—
The point that separates two paths—
One leading up and one going down.
Great is the danger of choosing the wrong
    path, O wealthy ones!

It's just gibberish to teach like this to others
When I can't know with confidence where
    I myself will end up;
Yet, since this advice is given out of pure
    good will toward others,
It deserves your attention, O faithful ones!

If you distrust me, ask learned and
    accomplished beings,
And consider the words of the Victorious
    Ones:
You will gain strong conviction
That Lama Shabkar has told you the truth.

May all the men and women who hear this
    song

Rid themselves of miserliness and all other
    defects.

May the faithful develop generosity;
May everyone practice the sublime
    Dharma!

One day, when I went outside to refresh myself,
what I saw made diverse impressions on my
mind, impressions which I put into this song:

Above the white summit of the dazzling
    snow-peak,
A young cloud rises, stark-white, beautiful.
It seems to be saying,
"This is how one should ascend the path of
    liberation."

Rising up higher and higher,
It disappears into the sky.
Seeing this, I remember the Buddha guru,
And, remembering his kindness, tears well
    up in my eyes.

Under cover of the mountainside forests
    [352b],
Many large and small birds are tirelessly
Feeding their tiny young.
They seem to be saying,
"This is how your parents reared you
    when you were small."

Seeing this, I remember the kindness of my
    parents,
And feel a strong wish to repay their
    kindness.

On the shoulders of mountains, along the
    valleys,
Banks of mist form and vanish like
    mirages.
"This is how your body and wealth are
    impermanent."

After many transformations, they are
    suddenly gone.
Seeing this, I remember impermanence
    and death
And feel a strong wish to give away all I
    have.

Through the combination of hot sun and
    cool rain
A rainbow appears in space, arcing over
    the sky,
Vivid yet unreal.
"This is how everything appears, through
    the combination of causes and
    conditions."

The rainbow vividly appears, then
    disappears into the sky.
Seeing this, I remember relative truth
And feel a strong wish to train in the great
    activity of the Bodhisattvas.

The immense, wide-open sky above,
Empty of all limitations—
"This is emptiness—naked and clear, free
    of all veils and obscurations."

Seeing this, I remember absolute truth
And feel a strong wish to practice
    according to the profound view.

In the open vastness of the sky, free of
    center or periphery,
The sun is shining, illuminating without
    any preference.
"This is how you should benefit beings."

Sending forth its rays almost playfully,
It travels across the four continents.
Seeing this, I think about benefiting
    everyone impartially;
I feel a strong wish to serve the teachings
    and all beings.

Singing various songs, I refreshed myself, walking through forests thick with foliage, flowers, and fruits, under cool archways of bamboo,

thoughts of joy and thoughts of sadness alternating in my mind [353a].

At one point some silver and gold came into my hands. I remembered how, in the past, the poultry woman Shamvara, assisted by her four sons, built the stupa of Bodhnath and placed in its central axis[20] a measureful of Buddha Kashyapa's relics. According to the prayers they made,[21] the poultry woman attained Buddhahood as the oathbound deity, Pramoha Devi, and the four sons became, respectively, the Abbot, the Master, the Dharma King, and the Minister, who spread the teachings of the Buddha far and wide in Tibet.

Reflecting upon their story and the benefits of their deeds, I thought it would be such good fortune if, for the welfare of the teachings and all beings, I could offer a coating of pure gold to the thirteen top rings of the Great Stupa. With this in mind, I sent the following letter to the Gorkha king of Nepal:

"Great lord, Dharma King, like the sun you tower above all beings. With immense respect and countless prostrations I, the yogin hermit Shabkarpa, who now dwell in the highlands of Lapchi Snow Range, the holy place of the speech of Chakrasamvara at the border between the excellent land of Nepal, gathering place of all desirable perfections, and the Snow Land of Tibet, source of all benefit and bliss, present this humble petition before your jeweled throne raised by fearless lions:

"Great king, you are like the wish-fulfilling gem adorning the pinnacle of the unshakable victory banner; you are like a diadem for [353b] the heads of all vassal kings and ministers; you display outstanding kindness to all your subjects and to all countries.

"By the compassion of my gurus and the Three Jewels, the illusory body of your humble servant is well. My spiritual practice, as well as my intention and activities to benefit others, continues to bloom.

"The essence of my request is as follows: the royal palace of Yambu in Nepal is like the spectacular Victorious Mansion on top of wondrous Mount Meru brought to the human world. To the right and left of this marvelous palace are the two most precious and wonderful stupas, more beautiful than the sun and moon shining together. It would be magnificent if, for the sake of the Dharma and sentient beings, a covering of gold laid on copper, similar to that of the Svayambhu stupa, could be offered to the top of the stupa of Bodhnath.

"This Great Stupa of Bodhnath, the unique adornment of this world, and the most eminent object of offering and praise, benefits all those who make a connection with it and, as a wish-fulfilling gem, grants all the aspirations of whoever prays to it—the white flag of its melodious name flutters in all directions, its fame increasing day by day.

"Therefore, with a perfectly pure mind, thinking solely to serve the Dharma and all beings, and in particular to make a new sun of happiness shine over all the inhabitants of Nepal and Tibet [354a], I have conceived the wish to offer to the thirteen Dharma wheels[22] at the summit of the Great Stupa of Bodhnath a perfect garment of precious gold laid on copper, which will radiate rays of splendor and beauty in a hundred directions.

"When, next year, the precious chance to do this arises, I request that you, great Dharma King and lord, and your ministers, all true Bodhisattvas, be pleased to grant your permission, delightful to hear, to realize this aim. I request that you also authorize us to buy the necessary copper from the mines in your kingdom. Kindly extend your assistance for whatever might be required—craftsmen, workers, and any other aspect of the work. Such is my prayer.

"After this great project has been accomplished, I shall use whatever I have as a thanksgiving offering to express my gratitude. I shall join to it my prayers and spiritual protection for you, the Dharma King, and for your ministers, so that the victory banner of your lives remains steadfast and all your temporal and ultimate aspirations may be accomplished.

From the solitude of the Cave of the Subjugation of Mara, in the great holy place of the Lapchi Snow Range, I present you with a silken scarf simply as a support for this letter, and a few particles of gold and silver, not to let it be empty."

I sent this letter through Lama Kalzang Gyalpo. Following this, the great king, having consulted with Colonel Bhimsen[23] and the other royal ministers, granted permission to undertake the work, and said that they would offer their assistance [354b].

While I was staying in Lapchi, my disciple Kunzang Shenphen, someone gifted with faith, diligence and intelligence who had been living alone in the mountains, said to himself, "However much I try, I cannot rid my mind of craving for the comforts of this life. If a Dharma companion takes away a tiny object, a piece of cloth or a morsel of food, that poisonous old corpse of attachment and anger tries to get up on its feet again. Isn't this proof that I've missed some crucial point of the teachings? I must go and ask my lama." In this frame of mind, he came to me and expressed his doubts in a song:

Lord Shabkar, king of all renunciates,
Attachment and greed have ceased to exist
   in your mind.
Turn for an instant your tenderness toward
   me—
A disciple scorched by the desires of this
   life and a craving for comfort.

Protector, for long you have regarded
The glories of samsara as a nest of vipers.

By the strength of your deep revulsion for
   material things,
However much food and wealth may be
   offered to you,
It is like putting grass in front of a lion:
You feel not the slightest desire.

If someone ever took something away from
you,
You would care no more about it than
Seeing a dog running off with a piece of
garbage.

I rejoice in such conduct:
Faith dawns deep in my heart.

Practitioners like me,
Our bellies full of food, warming ourselves
in the sun,
Talk a great deal about renouncing
comfort and concern for this life.

Although this way of talking seems impressive,
If someone takes away anything of ours,
food or clothing,
We grow red-faced with fury,
Abuse spews forth from our mouths;
We are fully prepared to beat that person
with a club.

All of us, your followers,
Have little hope soon to be able [355a]
To cast away concerns for this life as you
have;
Still we hope that, through the guru's
compassion,
It may happen one day.

We ask that you impart to us some
profound instructions
That will clearly teach the crucial points
About banishing from our minds all
worldly concerns.

Through practicing according to your
instructions,
May we swiftly banish preoccupation with
this life's concerns.

I replied: "Listen! Preoccupied by these concerns, making countless plans, you eagerly spin
the wheel of attachment and anger. This is the
result of not having kept in mind impermanence
and death. The remedy is to remember these
two constantly. Therefore, until you have for-

saken all preoccupation with the food and possessions of this life, day and night, day after day,
month after month, year after year, contemplate
the uncertainty of the time of death. Do so with
the same diligence with which you have been
meditating on the nature of mind, and you will
turn away from the affairs of this life." Having
said this, I sang a song about keeping impermanence and death in mind:

I respectfully bow down to my teacher:
The thought that says, "I need nothing
whatsoever!"

The coming of death is unpredictable;
I might even die tonight.

Forgetting that death may come at any
time,
I fell prey to longing for this life's comforts.
Gaze compassionately and bestow your
blessings
Upon this senseless madman!

Faithful, diligent, intelligent and
compassionate
Spiritual son, Kunzang Shenphen, listen to
me!
If you don't keep in mind impermanence
and death,
You will find it hard to give up concern for
the affairs of this life.

If you keep in mind impermanence and
death,
To give up the affairs of this life will be
easy [355b].

If you keep in mind impermanence and
death,
You will long for nothing.[24]

If you keep in mind impermanence and
death,
You will be free from desires.

If you keep in mind impermanence and
death,

You will feel devotion toward spiritual
teachers.

If you keep in mind impermanence and
death,
You will develop pure perception toward
your Dharma friends.

If you keep in mind impermanence and
death,
You will constantly fear unvirtuous actions.

If you keep in mind impermanence and
death,
You will endeavor in actions that are pure
and virtuous.

If you keep in mind impermanence and
death,
An overwhelming world-weariness will fill
your heart.

If you keep in mind impermanence and
death,
You will have strong diligence in practice.

If you keep in mind impermanence and
death,
You will regret your past misdeeds.

If you keep in mind impermanence and
death,
You will vow never to commit those
misdeeds again.

The benefits of remembering
impermanence and death
Are beyond words, beyond description.

Therefore, worthy son, from now on,
Keep in mind impermanence and death
Throughout the six periods of the day and
night.

While recollecting impermanence and
death,
You should especially remember that they
may come at any time.

You have no assurance that, tomorrow,
you will still be alive;
Think, "What is the point of making plans
for the day after?"
And rid your mind of the thoughts of this
life.

Today's sun has already set;
Tonight you may die.
Think, "What's the use of planning for
tomorrow?"
And rid your mind of the thoughts of this
life.

Even if, by the guru's kindness,
You don't die today,
Think, "How foolish to remain idle,"
And resolve to practice the Dharma.

May whoever hears these words,
Banish all concern for this life [356a].

These words hit home to all present; they realized the truth of what I had said. Later, by
bearing constantly in mind the imminence of
death, a complete absence of wants and needs
became their natural frame of mind. Many of
them, men and women, became practitioners
who renounced all activities and preoccupations
pertaining to this life.

One day, Gelong Yeshe Nyentrak, a devout,
pure-minded, generous and diligent practitioner, offered me a silver and gold mandala with a
top ornament and, with the following verses,
requested some spiritual advice:

I bow down to you who perfected the
twofold gathering *(Tsog)*,[25]
Lord of the Four Kayas, no different from
the Sixth *(Druk)* Conqueror, Vajradhara.
Having perfected yourself *(Rang)*,
You free *(Drol)* others from the bonds of
the obscuring emotions.

I offer you all the universe and its wealth;
I offer you my practice.
I openly confess all unwholesome actions I
have done.

I rejoice in the unceasing benefit you bring
 to beings.
I supplicate you to turn the Wheel of the
 Dharma;
I entreat you to extend your life span to a
 hundred kalpas.
I dedicate all merit toward the attainment
 of Buddhahood.

Father! Sublime lord, my happiness began
 when,
By your kindness, I turned my mind to the
 Dharma.
How can I repay such kindness?

In the past, you've given me many
 profound and vast instructions,
Still, I could not rid myself of my wicked
 defects.
Eager to cast them away now,
I beseech you for spiritual advice.

I answered, "Listen! All defects come from not
having let go of concern for the affairs of this life,
so—let go!" I gave him this advice on how to
abandon all worldly affairs—preoccupation with
society, wealth and food—and how to detach his
mind from the things of this life:

I bow down at the feet of the guru, the
 Lord of Dharma,
Grant your blessings that I may be able to
 follow the Dharma! [356b].

Heart-disciple, holder of the sacred
 bond,
You who wish from your heart to practice
 the sacred Dharma, listen:

One's homeland is the source of
 attachment and anger;
Leave your native place far behind.

Alcohol is the root of all evil actions;
Do not drink even a sip of it.

Meat, a sinful food, is the flesh and blood
 of beings, your parents in past lives;

Don't even eat the flesh of animals who
 have died natural deaths.

The greatest trouble can come from
 women;
Don't ever get too intimate with one.[26]

Wanting and attachment are the roots of
 samsara;
Curb your longing for food and clothes.

Miserliness will make you take rebirth
 among hungry ghosts;
Do not be miserly with your wealth.

Hatred is the seed of hell;
Do not allow aggression to arise.

Proliferating thoughts are Mara at work;
Preserve wisdom that is beyond the
 workings of mind.

Compassion is the essence of Dharma;
Cultivate it eagerly.

If you do so, you will be happy,
And ultimately you will reach
 Buddhahood.

On hearing these words, he effortlessly rid himself of all his mental sufferings, shortcomings,
and physical sickness, and enjoyed unceasing
happiness of body and mind. Later he became
an authentic renunciate and achieved excellent
meditative experiences and realization—in short,
he became an exemplary Dharma practitioner
able to benefit others.

On another occasion, one of my close heart-
sons, Phugtra Khenpo, a fortunate being
endowed with knowledge and realization
[357a],[27] offered me some gold and silver along
with all his other possessions, and asked, "Have
you been in good health? Has your meditation

flourished in this sacred place?" I replied with this song expressing my well-being and the progress of my practice:

> I pray from the core of my heart
> To the Dharma King Ngakyi Wangpo,
> Kinder than the Buddha himself:
> Bless me from the expanse of your heart!
>
> In the solitudes of the Cave of the
>   Subjugation of Mara
> On the Lapchi Snow Range,
> The place where many holy beings once
>   lived,
> The gathering place of dakas and dakinis,
> I, the yogin Tsogdruk Rangdrol, have
>   been
> Well in body, free from sickness,
> Well in speech, free from obstruction,
> Well in mind, free from suffering.
>
> By the grace of the sublime guru,
> The warmth of *tummo* blazed forth in my
>   body,
> Spontaneous songs flowed from my lips,
> And the sun of meditation experiences and
>   realization arose in my heart.
>
> By the blessings of this holy place,
> Obscuring emotions and wandering
>   thoughts ceased by themselves,
> Vanishing into the wisdom sphere
> Of bliss, clarity, and non-thought.
>
> On the mirror of contemplative evenness,
> Unobscured and transparent,
> Myriad pure visions arose—
> E ma! Wondrous! Fortunate!
>
> Come here, fortunate beings
> Who aspire to happiness and well-being in
>   this life,
> And long for the Dharma that will benefit
>   your future lives;
> Come, and the sun of joy will shine.
>
> By the merit of uttering these words
> May all beings achieve felicity,

> And, joyfully practicing the Dharma,
> May they attain ultimate joy [357b].

Having sung this, I asked him in return, "Have you been well in the Rocky Cave?" He replied with these verses:

> Sovereign of wisdom and compassion,
> Lord of kindness,
> We are deeply grateful that, in this sacred
>   place,
> Your body is healthy, your speech
>   melodious,
> Your realization blooming,
> And that you raise the victory banner of
>   the teaching,
> Accomplishing the benefit of beings.
>
> As for myself, your humble servant,
> Although by the guru's kindness
> My body is perfectly well,
> Unable to discard the thoughts of this life
> My mind has not become much more
>   content.
>
> Like those who, not having eaten what's al-
>   ready in their bowls, reach for a second
>   helping,
> Not having perfected myself I pretend to
>   be of benefit to others.
>
> Governed by my old father, "Craving for
>   Wealth,"
> I strayed into scores of activities.
> Having grown weary, deep in my heart,
> Remembering you, I came into your
>   presence.
>
> From now on, in accordance with my
>   guru's word,
> I shall give up all concerns for this life.
> Abandoning villages and monasteries,
> I shall wander through wild uninhabited
>   lands.
> Following the example of the saints of the
>   past,
> I shall practice the profound and sublime
>   Dharma.

Glorious and compassionate lama,
Grant me the *siddhi* of casting away
    thoughts of this life.
Bless me to be able to remain in mountain
    solitudes.
Pray that I may fulfill my aspirations.

I replied with a song extolling the virtue of giving
up the affairs of this life for a mountain retreat,
following the example of the Victorious Ones:

I bow down to the masters of the past,
Who banished all concern for this life:
Bless all your followers
To be able to renounce interest in worldly
    life!

Lord of learned ones,
Endowed with the many qualities of
    knowledge and realization,
It is wonderful indeed that you conceived
    the wish
To renounce all affairs of this life.

If you renounce the affairs of this life [358a]
You will have accomplished half of the
    Dharma.

If you renounce the affairs of this life
You will have planted the seeds of
    happiness.

If you renounce the affairs of this life,
You will have severed the root of further
    suffering.

If you renounce the affairs of this life,
Your vows and *samaya* will be pure.

If you renounce the affairs of this life,
Bodhicitta will dawn of itself.

If you renounce the affairs of this life,
Others will help sustain your life of practice.

If you renounce the affairs of this life,
You will succeed in any practice you
    undertake.

If you renounce the affairs of this life,
Meditation experiences and realization will
    arise.

If you renounce the affairs of this life,
You will become a Buddha in one
    lifetime.

If you renounce the affairs of this life,
You will bring immense benefit to beings.

The benefits of renouncing the affairs of
    this life
Cannot be captured in words.

So, Dharma friend,
Renounce this life; practice!

You who benefit whomever you meet:
Having turned your back on the works of
    this life,
Go to a wilderness where no one lives,
And your life will be more wondrous than
    ever.

In wild places where no one lives,
Are pleasant caves in which to stay and do
    practice.

In wild places where no one lives,
One's consoling friends will be birds and
    wild animals.

In wild places where no one lives,
One's nourishment will be wild roots and
    berries.

In wild places where no one lives
Is the marketplace for trading samsara for
    nirvana.

In wild places where no one lives
Is the Hidden Treasure[28] of happiness and
    bliss.

In wild places where no one lives
Is the gathering place of dakas and dakinis
    [358b].

In wild places where no one lives
Are the conditions conducive to
    realization.

In wild places where no one lives
Are places blessed by holy beings.

In wild places where no one lives
Is natural beauty delightful to behold.

There is no possible way to express
The many virtues of staying in remote,
    solitary places
Far removed from human habitation.

Therefore, heir of the Victorious Ones,
Go to a secluded place and practice!

After this, renouncing this life, he went off into
the distant mountains. He dedicated himself to
the practice of Dharma, in all its profound and
vast aspects. His meditation experiences and
realization reached their ultimate point. He thus
became an eminent spiritual master who benefited many sentient beings.

Once, for many days, I gave to several hundred
disciples the transmission and explanation of the
Seven-Point Mind Training, and the *Emanated Scriptures of the Bodhisattvas,*[29] a text that I had composed on the basis of the teachings of Gyalse
Rinpoche[30] and other great teachers, embellishing these teachings with various stories. At its
conclusion, all those gathered there requested
some final advice, so I gave this instruction, called
the *Drop of Ambrosia*:

I pray to the guru, the Three Jewels, and
    the *yidam* deities;
Grant us the waves of your blessings!

From benefiting sentient beings comes
    happiness.
From doing them harm comes suffering;

To harm others is like harming oneself.
To help others is like helping oneself.

To expose others' faults is like exposing
    one's own [359a].
To point out others' good qualities is like
    pointing out one's own.

You will reap the fruit of your actions.
Therefore, at all times,
Following the guru's instructions,
Never harm other beings,
But strive to accomplish their happiness.

However much others may harm you,
Do not harbor the least resentment.
Even when you have a chance to strike back,
Don't do it! Practice compassion.

Even when others shower you with abuse,
Don't abuse them in return.

Don't bring up others' weak points,
    taunting them,
Saying "Hey, you! One-eye!" or "Ha, ha!
    You lost your vows!"

Even when you know that others have
    done wrong and are paying for it,
Don't rub their noses in it, saying, "Serves
    you right!"

When blame falls on you,
Don't try to shift it onto someone else.

About an enemy or anyone you don't like,
Don't think, "I wish he were dead!"

Always praise good qualities you see in
    others,
Be they enemies, friends, or strangers.

Even if, in a large gathering of people,
Someone proclaims your faults, don't get
    angry.

Even if someone takes all your belongings,
Food and wealth, don't bear him a grudge.

Even if someone you have cherished like
    your own child
Regards you as an enemy, show him
    kindness.

Even, though you have committed no
    offense,
If someone ties you up and beats you,
    cultivate patience.

Whatever false accusations are brought
    against you,
See this to be the result of your past
    actions, and do not answer back.

Even if you haven't lied, stolen, or gotten
    drunk,
And someone says you have, don't get
    angry [359b].

It is useless to take as true all that people
    say;
Let them say what they want.

Even if you hear a hundred or a thousand
    unpleasant things,
Demand no explanations.

Even if you are mistreated
In a hundred or a thousand different
    ways,
Pay no heed.

Give gain and victory to others;
Take loss and defeat upon yourself.

Patience is the seed for obtaining the body
    of a Buddha
Endowed with the perfect marks and
    signs,
So cultivate it earnestly.

For those who act like this,
There is nothing ahead but reward:
In the immediate future they will be happy
    and appreciated by all,
And ultimately they will attain
    Buddhahood.

May whoever hears, reads, remembers, or
    comes in contact with this song
Obtain unsurpassable enlightenment!

Emulating the exemplary lives of the
Bodhisattvas, those who were present practiced
these instructions. They became practitioners
with compassionate minds, genuinely cherishing
others more than themselves, and were able to
leave gain to others and take loss upon themselves.

One day, Tendzin Nyima, "Sun Holding
the Teaching," one of my heart-sons, a disciple
gifted with fervent devotion to the guru, checked
himself against this song, the *Drop of Ambrosia*,
and other instructions of his teachers; he discovered within himself many flaws. Sadness and
confusion arose in his mind, and he presented
me with these verses:

Most respectfully I pay homage with body,
    speech, and mind
To the guru, holder of the compassion of
    the Three Jewels.

I shall relate how your disciple Tendzin,
    overwhelmed by the three poisons,
Lacks the excellence of the three secrets.[31]

Although I truly see you as the Buddha
    [360a],
I find it hard to bring myself into
    harmony
With the *Drop of Ambrosia* and your other
    teachings.
Kye ma! Look on me with compassion,
Burdened as I am with evil actions.

Although I understand the need to extract
    the essential meaning
From this precious human existence
Favored with the eight freedoms and the
    ten gifts,
I stupidly fall under the tyranny of the
    eight worldly concerns.
Kye ma! Look on me with compassion,
I who will return from this life
    empty-handed.

Although I've seen the way impermanence
    and death strike,
More and more, I regard what is transient
    as being lasting,
And my meditation on impermanence has
    not progressed.
Kye ma! Look on me with compassion,
I who believe that things are lasting.[32]

Although I understand that the law of
    karma, of cause and effect, is inevitable,
Due to strong habitual patterns formed
    through many wrong acts,
What little virtue I have achieved has been
    vitiated by misdeeds.
Kye ma! Look on me with compassion,
I who, as a consequence, am experiencing
    suffering.

Although I understand the shortcomings of
    samsaric pleasures,
My actions of body, speech, and mind are
    dominated by wrongdoing.
The mere sight of the offerings made by
    the faithful
And those made on behalf the dead,
Makes longing arise in my mind.
Kye ma! Look on me with compassion,
I who use religious gifts as personal gain.

Although I understood how to maintain
    awareness
Of the empty, clear nature of mind, free
    from concepts,
I did not perfect Bodhicitta—caring for
    others more than myself.
Kye ma! Look on me with compassion,
I who think only of my own good.

All your worthy disciples are offering you
    their excellent realization.
I, your miserable son, rotten-hearted
    Tendzin Nyima [360b],
Have nothing to offer but my wretched
    attainment of obscuring emotions!

Henceforth, from the depths of my heart, I
    wish to practice

In accordance with the words and
    meaning of the *Drop of Ambrosia*,
Your supreme teaching on mind training.

Protect me so that I may practice your
    advice
Until the end of my life.
I am in your hands!

I replied, "If you aspire to become a
Bodhisattva, whose immense compassion enables
him always to leave gain and victory to others
and take loss and defeat upon himself, you should
first abandon all thoughts limited to this life and,
staying alone on a secluded mountain, train your
mind in compassion, loving-kindness, and the
twofold Bodhicitta. If you do, I'll tell you in this
song what will occur:

I respectfully bow down to the great
    practitioners,
Who meditate in solitude on Bodhicitta.
Grant your blessing that I stay alone in
    solitary places,
And cultivate determination to attain
    enlightenment.

O most faithful spiritual son,
If it is your heart's desire to cultivate
    Bodhicitta,
Reflect on impermanence and on the flaws
    of sense-pleasures;
Turn your mind away from the activities of
    this life;
Rely on whatever frugal food and simple
    clothes you find.
Try to stay in solitary places.

If you stay alone, there are no adverse
    conditions.
If you stay alone, all conditions are
    harmonious.
If you stay alone, all appearances are
    pleasing.
If you stay alone, your practice of virtue
    will increase.
If you stay alone, faith and respect will be
    born.

If you stay alone, you will keep pure
    samaya.
If you stay alone, you will tame your
    emotions.
If you stay alone, renunciation will dawn
    [361a].
If you stay alone, you will be diligent.
If you stay alone, you will develop
    Bodhicitta.
If you stay alone, the dakinis will gather
    near you.
If you stay alone, the dharmapalas will
    surround you.
If you stay alone, meditation experiences
    and realization will arise.
If you stay alone, you will reach Buddhahood.
If you stay alone, a time will come when
    you are capable of benefiting others.

There is no way fully to describe
The benefits of solitude.
Therefore, Tendzin Nyima,
Meditate like the *rishis.*
Until you have perfected the twofold
    Bodhicitta,
Stay alone and be diligent in your practice.

Following this, staying alone in a secluded place,
he meditated on the thought of enlightenment.
Before long, great compassion was born in his
being. He became a Bodhisattva capable of
exchanging his happiness for others' suffering.

One day, Gelong Yeshe, a disciple with a
good mind and a gentle character who had
entirely discarded the thoughts of this life, presented me with a silver coin and a white ceremonial scarf. Prostrating himself, he requested some
advice from me with the following verses:

Authentic and precious guru,
Kindly turn your mind toward me for an
    instant.
Precious Lord, prostrating myself,
I present these words to you with immense
    respect.

On many occasions, you kindly taught
To all of your respectful disciples

The various steps and levels of the path
    [361b],
From the ways to attend the spiritual
    master
Up to the ultimate nondual state in which
    there is nothing more to be learned.
You also taught all the related
    commentaries
In great detail, in a clear way, easy to
    understand.

Above all, out of your infinite love,
You were so exceedingly kind as to grant
    us all
The vast and profound instructions
Of the Madhyamika, the Great Perfection,
    and Mahamudra,
As well as those on *phowa, prana,* and Chöd.

Still, I request that you bestow with all
    your love
A pith instruction that would serve
As a sharp weapon to slay the relentless
    three poisons,
And a peerless remedy to cure disciples like
    me
Of the plague of ego-clinging.

I confess in your presence whatever
    irrelevancies and improprieties
You may find in this idiot's letter,
And dedicate whatever merit may be
    found in it,
So that all beings may be given protection
    by the gurus.
Since you have consented to be my
    teacher,
Throughout my lives, may I exclusively do
    what pleases you.

In answer, I said, "The most potent remedy
to cure ego-clinging, and the sharpest weapon to
slay the three poisons, is the instruction on emptiness imbued with the essence of compassion."
And I sang this song on absolute Bodhicitta:

Namo guru!
I supplicate all the gurus

Who show us that outward appearances
Are like dreams, empty visions,
Who show us that, inwardly, the nature of
    mind
Is empty and immaculate as the sky.

Grant your blessings that,
Merely by thinking of the introduction to
    the nature of mind,
The wisdom of emptiness may arise in our
    mind-stream—
Naked, vivid.

I, Shabkarpa, free from all aims and
    expectations,
At ease and with a cheerful mind [362a],
Sing this song on emptiness and
    compassion.
Gelong Yeshe, listen without distraction.

All the phenomena of samsara and nirvana,
What appears and what exists,
Are no more than rainbows in an empty
    sky,
Which appear through a conjunction of
    causes and conditions.

No matter how they may appear, they are
    nothing in themselves;
They arise as embellishing ornaments
For the sky-like nature of mind—
    wondrous!

Mind—it has no color, it has no shape.
Look for it: it cannot be found at all—
Emptiness!

Leave mind just as it is—
Vivid clarity!

Immaculate, empty, like the infinite sky—
Let mind remain in that very state,
And let it be—raw, brilliant, awake—
Never obscured, utterly transparent.
Leave mind at ease, open, without aim.

When mind merges with that state
Which, like space, is all-encompassing,

All phenomena are understood with utter
    clarity
And all the enlightened qualities
Of the various paths and stages arise.

Boundless compassion is born
Toward beings who lack such realization.

Through such training in emptiness and
    compassion,
Benefit for other beings naturally occurs.

May void, primordial wakefulness,
Immaculate as the sky, actually arise—
Vivid, free of obscuration—
In the mind-streams of those who hear this
    song.

He practiced in accordance with these words;
perfecting the twofold Bodhicitta, he became a
Bodhisattva who benefited both himself and
others.

One day, my heart-son Jimba Norbu, "Jewel of
Generosity," a fortunate being adorned with the
ornament of the three trainings, thought [362b].
"However much people like me practice the
Dharma, they neither please the Buddhas nor
benefit beings; this must be due to having missed
a crucial point of the Dharma, but which one?"
    Since I had said, "Without compassion, the
root of Dharma is rotten," he had reflected a
great deal on compassion, and it became clear to
him that his flaw was that vast compassion encompassing without preference all sentient beings—good, bad, or neutral—had not yet been
born in him. He offered me these verses (825):

Lord Shabkar, benefiting whomever you
    encounter
You are a hidden Buddha in human form
Who makes no distinction between
    enemies and friends,
No distinction between gold and stone.

Lord and protector, since immense
   compassion
Fills the whole stream of your being,
There is no difference for you
Between loving friends and vicious enemies.

As a mother protects her child,
You protect all—friends, enemies, strangers.
I deeply rejoice in your deeds,
And overflow with respectful faith,
Seeing you as the Buddha himself.

Fettered by ignorance,
Lacking compassion,
I divide my companions into good and
   bad.
Because of attachment to some people and
   aversion toward others,
I can't help criticizing people behind their
   backs.

Since I lack great compassion,
My attachment to food, clothing, and
   money increases.

I can't give gain and victory to others
And can't take loss and defeat upon myself.

I confess my past ignorance,
And from now on, in accordance with the
   guru's words,
I will generate compassion as much as I can.
To do so, diligently,
I will cultivate the means to increase
   compassion,
Accumulate merit, and purify my
   obscurations [363a].

Until compassion is born within me,
I will practice month after month, year
   after year.
I offer you my promise to practice
Throughout the six periods of the day and
   night.

Most kind and compassionate guru,
Grant your blessing that compassion
   blossom in me;

That I may never be apart from
   compassion
Throughout all of my lives.

I answered, "This is it! You have understood. If you search for the one root of all the
teachings, it is compassion. If you aspire to please
Buddhas and sentient beings, put aside for a
while meditating according to other teachings,
and meditate on compassion alone. If you do so,
everything will go well." I expressed this in a
song:

With veneration, I offer perpetual homage
To those who hold the treasure, great
   compassion—
The guru, the Buddhas of the three times,
And the sublime lord of compassion,
   Avalokiteshvara:
Grant your blessings that compassion
   increase within me!

Jimba Norbu, you belong to the family
Of the Bodhisattvas who dwell on the
   bhumis.
Through the great faith and respect you
   have for me,
You have truly recognized the root of
   Dharma.

Wondrous! Fortunate heart-son,
If you want to walk in the footsteps of your
   spiritual father,
Listen to this advice that comes straight
   from his heart:

The extraordinary feature of the Buddha's
   teachings
That other teachings lack, is compassion.
A Buddhist who lacks compassion
Is in no way different from a
   non-Buddhist.

That which makes a practitioner
Superior to a worldly person is
   compassion.
A practitioner who lacks compassion
Is worse than a worldly person.

An evil-doer without compassion
Is no different from a soldier of the
　　Lord of Death.
Lacking love, unable to live in harmony
　　with his companions,
Full of animosity, he picks quarrels [363b];
He won't even give a handful of *tsampa* to
　　those begging at his door;
Instead, he'll toss them cruel insults.

Emptiness without compassion
Is like an empty house without a landlord.
Meditating without compassion is simply
　　to inflict hardship on yourself:
You will never achieve ultimate
　　enlightenment.

A practitioner without compassion
Is disliked by whoever lays eyes on him;
A "great meditator" without compassion
Will never benefit beings.

If you possess the wish-fulfilling gem,
All your wishes will be granted;
If you foster great compassion in your
　　mind-stream,
All other practices will follow.

What is the point of learning countless
　　things?
Better to learn a single one, compassion,
The one Dharma that suffices for all.
Therefore, practice compassion earnestly.

A Dharma practitioner endowed with
　　compassion
Will swiftly reach Buddhahood;
A Dharma practitioner endowed with
　　compassion
Can, more than anyone, benefit others.

Wherever a compassionate being goes,
The land will be filled with goodness
And all aspirations will be accomplished.
Wherever a compassionate being stays,
The land will be blessed and all needs
　　fulfilled.

In brief, if you meditate on compassion
You will benefit both yourself and others.
The benefits and qualities of
　　compassion
Cannot be fully described.

Fortunate spiritual son,
Cultivate compassion day and night!

May the compassion that dwells in your
　　father's heart
Be transferred to all his disciples.
May you remain ever inseparable from
　　great compassion.
May the excellence that is great
　　compassion [364a]
Prevail in the minds of all beings.

Following this he meditated one-point-edly on compassion; before long, his love, compassion, and Bodhicitta increased a hundred, a thousand times, becoming like a treasure-lode. He became a supreme practitioner, a lama respected by all, who naturally set in motion great waves of benefit for the Dharma and all beings.

One day my spiritual son Kalden Rangdrol came from the Snow Mountain[33] and presented me with all the offerings he himself had received from others. I told him, "Here is a lot of wealth, but what do you have to offer me in terms of meditation experiences and realization?" In answer he sang this:

Of all beings, you are the jeweled diadem,
　　O compassionate protector;
Of all attachment may I free myself
　　through your blessing;
Of all the many practices you taught, I was
　　a fortunate recipient;
Of all the experiences which arose in my
　　being, this account I offer to you:

*A*bsolute primordial purity (*ka-dag*),³⁴ the nature of mind, cannot be shown by symbols; and

*B*ecause it has neither color (*kha-dog*) nor characteristics,

*C*annot be apprehended no matter how (*ga-nas*) you regard it.

*D*eluded thoughts of "I" (*nga*) have vanished in the absolute expanse—

*E*mpty words (*ca-co*) and cogitation cannot describe this.

*F*orms (*cha-lugs*) differ, but are in harmony with all Dharma traditions.

*G*oing around to drink tea (*ja*), having a lot of wealth, and the like, are nothing but dreams, illusions.

*H*ere, as a fish (*nya*) remains in water, awareness remains in the absolute expanse, inseparable.

I meditated on the Tathagata (*ta*), and

*J*ust by the strength of this, I met the naked, uncontrived (*tha-mal*) awareness-void.

*K*eeping in mind right now (*da*) this sheer simplicity, even though I am

*L*oaded with years (*na-so*), I am free of worries [364b].

*M*orning star (*pa-sangs*), bright and lofty—this is what my view is like.

*N*ow, through meditation, it has reached its ultimate point (*pha-rol*)— a state of vivid clarity.

*O*bserving a way of behaving that is immaculate, white as cow's (*ba*) milk,

*P*rimordial simplicity (*ma-bcos*) is the self-arisen fruit, ripened by itself.

*Q*uesting over the glaciers of Tsari (*tsa*) and other holy places,

*R*id of distinctions between heat (*tsha*) and cold, joy and suffering, apparent forms and emptiness,

*S*ounding the words of the Victorious Ones (*dza-ya*), the inexpressible sound of emptiness,

*T*enaciously, I practiced like a canal's (*wa*) unbroken flow.

*U*pon my head, like a crown (*zha*), is the guru; his kindness

*V*ested me with the treasure of the Seven Noble Qualities,

*W*ith knowing how to be content with food (*za*-ma) and the rest.

*X*tremely content are we ('*a-cag*) hermits, and we

*Y*earn for nothing but to follow your life of perfect (*ya-rabs*) liberation,

*Z*ealously doing pilgrimage to the holy places of the ranges (*ra-ba*) of the Land of Snows.

Roaming at random through passes (*la*) and valleys, I, the old vagabond,

Encountered no obstacles to my body of flesh (*sha*) and blood.

I gradually cleared all doubts regarding the levels (*sa*) and paths,

And without needing a great (*ha-cang*) variety of artificial objects of concentration,

I realized the dharmakaya; the meaning of *A* was complete in my mind.³⁵

Ha! Ha! We lowly ones are happy!

Hey! Hey! We lowly ones are glad!

This happy song I offer you, sovereign of the Hundred Deities,

On the occasion of seeing your face, golden with happiness, once again.

Having joyfully offered this song at your feet,

May I practice the Dharma, happily, joyfully, blissfully.

I answered with these words:

The pure, immaculate Buddha
Is one's own awareness, the dharmakaya,
Clear, transparent, vivid,
Like the cloudless autumn sky.

"As these verses say, the root of all Dharmas is the true nature of mind, the dharmakaya wisdom that is like an autumn sky of immaculate purity: void, clear, immense, all-pervasive [365a], unobstructed, unfabricated, free of the eight limiting concepts.[36] If one realizes this nature and remains evenly in it, then, as it is said, 'Realization is unchanging, like the sky.' It is excellent that you have had such a realization. I expected such an offering from you, and I have received it.

"Now I have some heart-advice to give you: a sky needs a sun, a mother needs a child, a bird needs two wings. Likewise, emptiness alone is not enough. You need to have great compassion for all beings who have not realized this emptiness—enemies, friends, and strangers. You need to have compassion that makes no distinctions between good and bad. You must understand that compassion arises through meditation, not simply from waiting, thinking that it may come forth by itself from emptiness.

"The same number of years you spent meditating on emptiness, you should now spend meditating day and night on compassion—a compassion a hundred times stronger than that of a mother for a child burnt in a fire, an unbearably intense compassion that arises when thinking about the suffering of sentient beings.

"Once such compassion is born, you must practice until you come to think, with fierce energy, 'Until enlightenment, I shall do whatever is possible to benefit all beings, not omitting a single one—no matter what evil actions they commit, and no matter what difficulties I must endure.'"

And I continued with this spiritual advice:

Master, Lord of wisdom and compassion,
I supplicate you:
Grant your blessings that emptiness
    imbued with compassion
May be born in my mind.

Sky-yogin, endowed with realization
    [365b],
Fortunate son, your realization of
    emptiness
Equals that of your father—
This is wonderful indeed, O noble son!

But your compassion, I think,
Is not equal to his.

In the same way that you meditated on
    emptiness,
You should now meditate on compassion.
Day and night hasten to develop
A compassion equal to that of your father.

Although if you meditate on emptiness,
Compassion may sometimes arise,
Don't be content with this:
With great dedication, cultivate
    compassion itself.

Your compassion should be as genuine
    and irresistible
As that of a mother seeing
Her beloved child's limbs being burned by
    fire.

Having clearly in mind the sufferings
Of all sentient beings who have been your
    parents,
The first of your aims must always be
To generate and nurture in your heart a
    compassion
That can in no way bear others' suffering.
Do so until compassion arises, natural and
    unfabricated.

If some can give up their own bodies
For the sake of a being in torment,
Needless to say, they can give away food
    and clothes.

As a mother never turns her love away
From the most mischievous among her
    children,
But gives him food, clothes, and all her
    care,
A Dharma practitioner filled with
    compassion
Never leaves out one single being
Among the multitude of good and bad
    ones,
But continually cares for them all with
    love.

There is no need to request the
    Compassionate One

To work for sentient beings; he always
 does it.
And once he has started, he will continue
Without discouragement until he reaches
 his ultimate goal.

If the sun of compassion rises
In the vast sky of emptiness,
The right connection is created [366a]
To nurture the vast lotus field of infinite
 beings.

When the infant of compassion is born
To the childless old woman of emptiness,
He is the one destined to care
For his parents and relatives—
All sentient beings.

When the young garuda, the self-arisen
 absolute mind,
Has fully developed the two wings
Of emptiness and compassion,
He will surely soar in the sky of
 omniscience.

Fortunate Kalden Rangdrol, this is why you
Must persevere in meditating on
 compassion.

May emptiness and its essence, great
 compassion,
Be born in your being, my son.

From that very same evening he meditated in
this way. An uncontrived compassion arose in
him; cherishing others more than himself, he
greatly benefited beings.

One day, the learned and accomplished Gelong
Dorje Lopön offered me all his possessions, even
his monastic robes, with these words:

Just as when the Muni, the Bhagavat,
 Came into this world,

So you, precious refuge and protector,
Came to benefit the beings of this
 degenerate age.

I, your humble servant, have the great
 fortune to meet you here,
When, for the sake of beings, you are
 turning
The Dharma wheel of the relative and
 absolute truths:
The law of cause and effect, and the
 profound meaning of emptiness.

If I do not request profound instructions at
 this fortunate time,
From which lama will I request them later?
Therefore, I, Dorje Lopön,
Folding my hands at my heart,
Submit these words to you with utter
 veneration:

I have heard it said that the two truths
 [366b]
Were the heart of the teachings
Of the compassionate Shakyamuni.

I therefore ask that you give me a teaching
In a few simple words that contains the
 whole meaning
And explains how to contemplate the view
 of the two truths.

O protector, I pray that throughout my
 lives
I may be nourished by the nectar of your
 words.
Having thoroughly assimilated the
 meaning of the two truths,
May I benefit myself and others.

In answer to his offering, I said:

You, hidden Bodhisattva endowed with
 pure discipline and *samaya*,
Who, in solitary places, endeavored in
 profound practices,
The two Bodhicittas are now born in your
 being.

You have already mastered the meaning of
    the two truths;
Now you diligently perfect the two
    accumulations.
It is certain that, ultimately, achieving the
    two kayas,
You will perfect the two benefits, your own
    and that of others.

There is little need for me to tell you all
    this,
Nevertheless, simply as a reminder for you
And as a source of help for others,
I shall give a few explanations—listen well.

Regarding the view of the absolute truth,
With the help of your intelligence and the
    scriptures,
You should examine in various ways,
    carefully and repeatedly,
The outer objects apprehended by mind
And the inner mind that apprehends them.
Are these empty or not empty?

When you examine them closely,
There is nothing to be found—
See the nature of all phenomena to be
    empty.

Examining well, in the same way, turn
    your attention
Toward the intellect that was analyzing
    objects:
Does that have any true existence or not?

When both the subject that examines
And the object that has been examined
Have completely vanished into emptiness
    [367a],
Looking toward the nature of that sheer
    emptiness
Without distraction is called "the view."

When you are thus looking at the empty
    nature of mind,
Although there is no object being
    examined
And there is no subject who examines,
Do not confuse this empty nature

With some amorphous state of mind
Devoid of any qualities whatsoever.

When you are practicing, remaining in
    evenness
In a state that is like the sky—
Clear without,
Clear within,
Clear and void—transparent—
Although there is no object of
    meditation,
Although there is no subject who is doing
    meditation,
Without agitation, without drowsiness,
Firmly maintain an alert presence.

When you are preserving the natural state
    of mind
That is sheer, unobstructed emptiness,
Free from such limiting concepts as

    Existence and nonexistence,
    Eternity and nothingness
    Going and coming,
    Sameness and difference,

Although there is no object of analysis
And no subject who is analyzing,
Do not, like some thoughtless child,
Just indulge yourself in unconsidered
    actions.

If the wish-fulfilling jewel of the view
Is polished over and over again with
    meditation
And set at the top of the victory banner of
    action,
It will grant you the fruition you desire, the
    dharmakaya.

Regarding the view in terms of relative
    truth:
With the help of your intelligence and the
    scriptures
You should examine in many ways,
    carefully and repeatedly,
How all phenomena of samsara and
    nirvana
Appear freely, like images in a mirror,

Through the play of various combinations
  of causes and conditions.

Appearing in such conditions,
Phenomena do not possess even the tiniest
  shred of true existence.
Just like a rainbow in the sky,
They are apparent yet empty,
Empty but apparent.

Simply regard the spectacle of empty
  appearances
Without taking this to have any solid,
  independent, true existence [367b].

See how the causes and conditions of
  virtue
Lead to its fruit: happiness.
See how the causes and conditions of
  nonvirtue,
Lead to its fruit: suffering.

Cultivate love and compassion
For those who do not recognize this.

Like a magician transforming one thing
  into another,
You must exchange nonvirtue for virtue,
And for the sake of all beings
Release the great waves of Bodhisattva
  activity.
If you accomplish this perfectly,
The fruit of the rupakaya will ripen.

On hearing these words, all those gathered
there developed strong conviction about relative
truth—the law of cause and effect—and about
absolute truth—profound emptiness. Following
this, many of them emulated the perfect lives of
the Bodhisattvas, uniting view and action harmoniously, not making the mistake of combining the highest view with unseemly conduct.

Once, about five hundred monks and nuns and
a thousand laymen and women came to receive

teaching. All of them, including the local Mönpas,
developed faith and listened to the Dharma. I
recounted the past lives of the Buddha and other
life-stories, and taught the *Graded Path* and mind
training. I also gave them empowerments for the
Secret Mantrayana and instructions on the development and completion stages. I gave them,
too, teachings on *phowa, prana,* and Chöd; as well
as on Mahamudra, the Great Perfection, and
the Dohas.

After having thus turned the wheel of the
vast and profound Dharma of the sutras and
mantras at length, I concluded with this advice:

Wear on your head the wish-fulfilling gem,
The Muni, the Buddha,
And all your wishes will be granted.

Listen time and again to the drum of the
  Dharma,
The *Graded Path of Enlightenment,*
And you will be saved from the lower rebirths.

Drink time and again the peerless nectar,
The mind training of the Mahayana,
And you will be cured of the disease of the
  obscuring emotions [368a].

Bathe time and again in the divine stream
That is the four empowerments,
And the stains of the three doors will be
  washed away.

Never injure, break, or defile
The receptacle of all spiritual qualities,
The golden vase, *samaya.*

The alchemy of the development stage will
  transmute
The iron of your three doors into the gold
  of deities, mantras, and samadhi.
The *tummo* fire of the completion stage will
  refine again and again
The rough ore of the skandhas and cast it
  as the golden image, nonduality.

Having clarified the butter churned from
  the milk of the Sutrayana and
  Mantrayana,

Enjoy with pleasure the medicinal butter of
   Mahamudra.

If you taste the dakinis' profound and
   secret heart-essence,
In this life you will achieve the rainbow
   body.

Train the fledgling wings of your mind.
To fly through the fontanelle window[37] of
   your body's house.

Continuously let mind bask in the sun—
Luminous emptiness free from taking
   things as real—
And lasting bliss will arise.

May this *Drop of Gold*,[38] an advice that
   came from the yogin's heart,
Relieve from their sufferings those who are
   destitute of Dharma.

All those present were heartened by these words.
Having accomplished their own benefit through
their practice, many of them became great disciples who brought to others the stream of these
teachings, thus benefiting the Buddha's teachings and many beings.

At this time, several hundred men and
women, led by a lama from Drakmar, the great
siddha Ngawang Lhundrup, shaved their heads.
Some took novice vows; some took full monastic
vows [368b]. After that, one could see hair all
over the place, stuck into the cracks and cavities
of the slate rocks.

One day, I said to the disciples and patrons
that if they prevented people from hunting birds
and wild animals in the vicinity of the mountain
hermitages and monasteries, this would bring
auspiciousness and prosperity to the country;
long life, good health, happiness and good fortune would come to everyone. I explained to
them in detail the reasons for this. Following my
advice, they circulated letters all around explaining that it was wrong to hunt.

After this, not only did people stop hunting
birds and wild animals, but they also forbade

other hunters and Tilinka warriors to hunt. They
also requested and obtained from the Gorkha
king a decree stating that hunters would be punished. In this way the lives of thousands of birds
and wild animals were saved every year.

From this time, too, all the monks there
received a regular allowance of rice. Sometimes,
we would cook ten to fifteen large bags of rice in
a huge pot, and make it into hundreds of
ganachakra offerings. Not just the people but even
the dogs became quite fat and could not eat all
that they were given.

One day, a lame old man sang something
like this:

A good fortune we have, la!
The Dharma has flourished, la!

The banner of the teachings
Has been unfurled on the palace heights;
The auspicious connection has been
   created
For the teachings to spread further and
   further north.[39]

A good fortune we have, la!
The Dharma has flourished, la!

The sky is filled with stars,
But none are like the sun and the moon.
Were they all like the sun and moon,
The universe would be filled with light
   [369a].

A good fortune we have, la!
The Dharma has flourished, la!

The earth is filled with people,
But none are like you, protector and
   refuge.
Were they all like you, protector and
   refuge,
Happiness would prevail all over the
   world.

A good fortune we have, la!
The Dharma has flourished, la!

With a one, two, three,
The Buddha's teachings have spread here,
   la!

With a four, five, six,
Happiness has come to beings, la!

After he chanted this, doing a little dance, everyone nicknamed him Good Fortune. All the people from Nyanang, the pilgrims, and the traveling merchants sang, played music and danced; everyone was filled with joy.

From this time onwards, many fortunate disciples, both men and women, gathered there every year. Before I gave the first teaching, to celebrate the greatness of the teacher and the Dharma, all the disciples would walk in a procession, headed by the fully ordained monks, who were composed and peaceful, wearing the three monastic robes. They carried variegated banners, canopies, and standards; they blew *gyalings,*[40] trumpets, and conches, and beat drums.

The monks would be followed by the great yogins, with their long hair coiled up on top of their heads in various ways. They would beat the big Chöd drum with their right hands and blow the thighbone trumpet held in their left, proceeding with festive dancing movements.

Then would come the ordained nuns, holding vajras and ringing bells, or playing [369b] the tiny cymbals,[41] followed by the female lay practitioners, the long-haired *jetsunmas,*[42] holding incense and multicolored flowers. Thus they would proceed, in groups of five hundred.

The procession started from the plain down below and ended at the Cave of the Subjugation of Mara where I was staying. Those who arrived first would circumambulate the temple three or four times until the procession ended. They would then invite me to come down. When the procession would reach the teaching place, all the disciples and patrons gathered there would display boundless joy, faith, respect, and pure perception, as though they had arrived in a celestial land of dakas and dakinis. Even now, when I remember this, I feel cheerful.

During the summer, many people having gathered there, I thought of building a stupa. I asked everyone to bring stones and with each person fetching only one stone, to everyone's amazement, that very day the stupa was completed.

In the month of the Pleiades in the female Iron Snake Year[43] known as Khyuchog, the treasurer Kalzang Trinley (someone with great faith, generosity, and intelligence, who always did everything in accord with his teacher's word), Lama Jimba Norbu, the sovereign *siddha* Kalden Rangdrol, Phugtra Khenpo, Dapa Lama, and hundreds of other fortunate disciples left, one after the other, to offer the gold for the pinnacle of the Great Stupa of Bodhnath. I sent to the king and his ministers a new letter that said:

Dharma King Surya Kumar,[44] "Princely
   Sun,"
Who illuminates the whole earth with
   loving-kindness [370a],
And sustains all lands with your beneficial
   warmth,
You are without peer on this earth.

To attract the bee of your mind,
Turning toward you the ten petals of my
   fingers
Raised above my head, the pistil of my
   humble lotus body,
I emit the sweet fragrance of these
   wondrous words:

The unshakable Mount Meru of your
   supreme body,
Formed from the jewels of the twofold
   accumulation,
Resplendent amidst the golden mountains
   of your ministers and vassal kings,
Stands lofty and august above the ocean of
   your subjects.

When the fluttering sound of the white flag
  of your fame,
Flying to all directions, reached my ears,
The white celestial youth of my mind
Whirled joyfully in a dance of faith.

The illusory lotus body of your respectful
  and humble servant
Is well, having victoriously withstood the
  bitter frost of sickness.
The petals of love and compassion opened
  to the ten directions,
Giving off the fragrance of Bodhicitta.

When the dazzling rays of the sun and
  moon
Hit the white summit of the snow glaciers,
The summits turn whiter even than white.

Likewise, I believe, O king and ministers,
  true Bodhisattvas,
That if I submit to you again some words
  in accord with the Dharma,
Your minds, whiter than a conch,
Will grow even stronger in virtue.

Yet, if with my immature intelligence,
Acting as a child giving his parents advice,
I have said anything irrelevant,
Kindly bear with me and do not be
  offended [370b].

We know that it is through your kindness,
  O king and ministers,
That until now all lands in all directions
Have auspiciously been spared from
  epidemics, famines, and wars,
And enjoy peace and well-being.

Great Dharma King and ministers, may
  you continue
To care for your subjects, provinces, and
  kingdoms
As a mother cares for her child.
May you pursue more than ever your
  activities,
Becoming Buddha from the royal throne.[45]

Folding my hands at my heart, I make this
  prayer:

So that a new sun of happiness and
  well-being may shine
Upon all the distant countries,
And especially upon all beings of Nepal
  and Tibet,
I, the penniless renunciate vagabond
Request you, O king and ministers,
To give whatever assistance is needed,
When, within this Year of the Snake,
I offer an exquisite garment of gold
For the pinnacle of the Bodhnath stupa.
This is the prayer I formerly made—
I renew it today, with folded hands.

I, a wandering hermit,
Seek the spiritual protection of the Three
  Jewels
So that you, great Dharma King, your
  ministers and your retinue,
May enjoy health bright as the sun,
Good fortune waxing like the moon,
A retinue of subjects increasing like a
  myriad stars,
Fame resounding to all horizons like the
  turquoise dragon,
And a dominion increasing to the limits of
  the sky:
I dedicate my prayers to the fulfillment of
  these wishes! [371a].

This letter, a divine swan white as a conch,
Unfolding its pure white wings—a silken
  scarf—
And singing a melodious song—my verses
  of praise—
Takes wing across the ocean of your merit,
  O king!

By the merit of making this excellent
  offering,
May the king and ministers care for their
  subjects,
And the subjects respect their king and
  ministers.

May all follow the Dharma; may its
    goodness prevail!

I offered this letter with an immaculate white
scarf.

Then, by the power of past prayers and
aspirations, Lama Kalzang—a faithful, diligent
and wise practitioner who enjoyed the respect of
the Gorkha king—having requested all that was
needed of the king and ministers, and Kazi
Bhimsen and others having been exceptionally
helpful, the work was undertaken.

At this time the Amban[46] became appre-
hensive and sent to the court of Jamyang Gongma Rinpoche[47] a letter about current events. But
the day the messenger left to bring the letter, his
horse stepped into one of Lhasa's refuse pits and
broke its leg, and the man himself dislocated his
arm. The box containing the letter fell to the
ground and broke. The Amban saw this as a bad
omen and asked the noble dignitaries, "What
kind of person is Lama Shabkar? What has he
been doing? Won't we be reprimanded if we
don't notify the emperor?" [371b].

The regent-king and ministers of Tibet said,
"From his youth, Lama Shabkar has been concerned solely with the Dharma and knows nothing of worldly affairs. Since he came to central
Tibet, he has used all his possessions for offerings, for charity, and to serve the monastic community. Particularly, he offered lamps of solid
gold to the Crowned Buddhas of Lhasa and
Samye.

"These days, having in mind the long life of
the Gongma Rinpoche and of the Victorious
Ones, Father and Son,[48] the perpetuation of the
Dharma, and the happiness of beings, in fulfillment of these prayers he is currently offering a
gold coating laid on copper to the thirteen rings
crowning the great Bodhnath stupa in Nepal.
We are told that half of the work has been
completed. If he failed to report this matter to
the emperor, it is only because as a Dharma
practitioner, he is unaware of the protocol to be
observed."

Following this the Amban pondered the
matter and said, "The news must be reported to
the emperor, otherwise he may blame us if any
trouble arises with our foreign neighbors." "In
that case, after having consulted each other, we
must send news," they said.

Accordingly, the Amban, having consulted
with the regent-king and ministers of Tibet, sent
a letter that said:

"The one by the name of Lama Shabkar, an
exemplary Dharma practitioner, has undertaken
to offer a gilded copper garment to the upper
rings of the Bodhnath Stupa in Nepal, with the
intention of benefiting Your Imperial Majesty's
longevity, the Buddhist teachings, and the happiness of all beings. Is he or is he not authorized
to do so?"

All the disciples and benefactors then waited
anxiously, wondering what sort of answer the
emperor would give [372a]. When the answer
finally came it said:

"As he is a Dharma practitioner, ignorant of
worldly customs, we will not reprimand him for
not having sought advice. If one prevents him
from completing the thirteen rings, there is a
danger that the neighboring people may become
uneasy and raise trouble. Therefore, let him do
it. After that, he must come back to Tibet and
involve himself in purely religious matters. He
must not stay in border areas."

Everyone rejoiced greatly at this outcome.

Soon after came the good news that the
offering of the thirteen gold rings had been completed. I offered hundreds of dedication prayers
and, with great joy, voiced this song:

I bow down to the matchless king of the
    Shakyas,
To the Dharma sovereign of the three
    worlds, Tsongkhapa,
To his spiritual sons and the heirs of their
    lineage:
Grant your blessings that I may benefit the
    Dharma and all beings!

I will sing here a melody relating the
    happiness
That, by the grace of the peerless guru,
    now fills my mind.

In the beginning, I attended a hundred
  authentic masters,
Receiving from them many teachings on
  the sutras, tantras, and pith instructions.

In the middle, I went to a hundred
  mountain retreats,
Training myself through practicing all that
  I'd heard.

In the end, I roamed at random through a
  hundred lands,
Giving food, clothes, and Dharma to help
  beings.

Now, for the good of the teachings and of
  all beings,
I have covered the Dharma rings of the
  stupa with gold.
I have made pure prayers to dedicate the
  merit from the accomplishment [372b]
Of more than a hundred great tasks for the
  benefit of the Dharma and all beings.

If I die I am glad, I have offered my
  prayers;
If I live I am glad, I shall work intensively
For the sake of the Dharma and all beings.
When I think of it, I see that all this is the
  result of pure motivation.

My master, all the masters of my lineage:
You have been so very kind!
Now, whether I meet happiness or
  suffering,
I am in your hands—
Keep me under your protection until I
  reach enlightenment.

May all those who rejoice upon hearing of
  these deeds
Obtain the merit they would have earned
If they had performed these deeds
  themselves.

When I sang this, all those present were very
happy.
  Since I was wondering whether I should

travel to perform the consecration of the newly
gilded pinnacle, one evening I prayed to the
precious Dharma King, and the same night I
met him in a dream. He said to me, "This year,
do not go; it will be the same if, directing your
mind, you perform the consecration from here."
Accordingly, I did not go to Nepal.

On the consecration day, some ten thousand people gathered and a vast *ganachakra* feast
was offered. The great *siddha* Kalden Rangdrol
gave a long life empowerment to all. With him,
Lama Jimba Norbu, Phugtra Khenpo, and about
a hundred other masters performed the consecration.

On that same day, from Lapchi, I clearly
visualized performing the consecration and then
threw flowers into the sky [373a]. Through the
auspicious coincidence of my doing this and the
ardent faith of the disciples and patrons, some
persons with good karma and pure perception
saw me, amidst an expanse of rainbow-colored
clouds that filled the sky, actually performing the
consecration at Bodhnath. Everyone saw a mass
of light in the sky, in the middle of rainbow
clouds, and a large vulture which, having circled
many time around the stupa, ascended higher
and higher and flew in the direction of Lapchi.
They said that consecration flowers rained on
the stupa; most of the people there collected
some and kept them as objects of faith.

For this great task, Lama Jimba Norbu had
offered 150 *sho* of gold, the great *siddha* Kalden
Rangdrol 400, the chieftain Tako 108, the chieftain Namgyal 200, Sonam Dargye 150, the householder Norbu 80, and Nagpön Sonam and his
wife 50. With this and all the other offerings,
altogether over 1,000 *sang* of gold were used.
The details can be found in the descriptive list
called the *White Path of Liberation*.[49]

The sun and moon are the two marvels in
  the sky;
The Great Stupas are the two marvels on
  earth.
Other than this pair, universally renowned,
Are there, anywhere else, more sublime
  objects
For circumambulation and offering?

Wondrous accounts relate how
Many wise and accomplished great
    beings
Offered time and again a mantle of
    precious gold [373b]
To the Great Stupa of Svayambhu.

Although they also could have offered
A mantle of gold to the great Bodhnath
    stupa,
It seems they left it to be done by us, future
    disciples,
So that we might have the good fortune to
    accumulate merit.

I mustered all my courage,
And with gods and men lending a hand to
    the work,
For the first time a precious mantle of gold
    has been completed.
Look how its dazzling beams shine toward
    a hundred horizons!

Celestial and human beings abiding on the
    side of virtue, rejoice!
With joyous movements, dance cheerfully!
If you have melodious songs to sing, sing
    them!

There is no meaning in accumulated
    wealth,
But there is meaning in wealth used like
    this.
I offer this discourse to all gods and men;
Full of joy, may they repeat it to each
    other.

I pray, not only from the lips, but from
    deep in my heart,
To all future great Dharma practitioners:
Just as I did for the Dharma rings,
May you cover with precious gold
The middle and the vase-like body of the
    stupa.

I pray that in a future life, I myself
May cover the entire stupa with precious
    gold,

And adorn it with the images of the
    thousand Buddhas of this age
And the infinite deities of the four tantras.

I dedicate all merit accumulated
    throughout the three times,
Symbolized by this, to the benefit of the
    Dharma and of all beings.
By the efficacy of this dedication,
May the Buddha's Dharma expand and
    spread [374a];
May all sentient beings find happiness and
    bliss;
May not even the words "disease," "fam-
    ine," "conflict,"
And "undesirable events" be heard in this
    world;
May there be longevity, good health,
    abundant harvests and prosperous
    herds;
May great auspiciousness pervade the
    whole earth!

While I was benefiting many beings in this holy place, many lepers who had heard about me came—those who had someone to take care of them were carried—to receive a blessing that would cure them. I made them stay many days in this holy place, and with great compassion I recited the mantras of the *Three Protectors*, of the *Multicolored Garuda*, and of the *Adamantine Armor*[50] over some water collected from the glaciers, and had them drink it. I also washed their bodies while performing cleansing rituals, and gave them medicines. Many of them were cured, and people said, "This lama is the Buddha in person; he has marvelous blessing powers." Many more sick men and women came and most of them were cured.

After this episode faith grew stronger than ever in the local patrons; many of them tried their best to abandon negative actions and to endeavor in virtue, in accordance with the teachings I had given them.

I gave many presents to all the hunters that came by, Magars and Yalongs,[51] and having taught them some Dharma, made them promise not to kill any more wild animals. They offered me their hunting dogs, and at one point I had ten or fifteen of them. Fearing that these dogs might kill animals or bite people, I put a few men in charge of them [374b]. Later, I took these dogs to Tibet and gave them to some patrons who never hunted.

Sometimes, thieves, monks or nuns who had broken their vows, Khampas who had killed people, villagers possessed by the devil of drunkenness,[52] fighting couples, or old men and women who had committed evil actions—in short, all sorts of mischievous people—would come. Knowing what they had done, either through having talked with others or through my own insight, I would tell them: " Eh, you! Didn't you kill someone?" or, "Aren't you drinking *chang*?" "Yes, it is true," they would admit, and many of them would prostrate themselves, confess their past actions, and promise not to commit them again.

One day a faithful old woman came, bringing along a big lump of butter. I told her, "It is good that Grandma came bringing a big lump of butter, but didn't Grandpa say 'Don't take the big lump, take the small one'?" Realizing that I knew, the old lady replied, "Yes, he did!" and everyone burst into laughter.

Another time, a patron from the valley, a drunkard, came with a supply of *chang*, and hid it somewhere by the road before coming to me. When he arrived, I told him, "Oh, benefactor, welcome to you! By the way, where did you hide your *chang*?" He thought, "He knows!" and vowed, "From now on, I shall not drink so much."

Similarly, because I would sometimes suddenly say whatever came into my mind from within a state of calm meditation, the faithful used to say, "Knowing all the hidden faults of others, he can tell them without difficulty [375a]. If you ask him for a divination, he says he doesn't know; it is not that he doesn't know, it is just that he doesn't say. But when he does say something, he reveals his unimpeded clairvoyance." Many of them developed faith and respect, perceiving me in a pure way.

Sonam Nyentrak was a devoted disciple living at Changchub Metok, the Enlightenment Flower, a new monastery in the valley. On the thirteenth day of the tenth month of the Iron Snake Year,[53] he dreamed of a twenty-year-old yogin with hair knotted on the top of his head and a mark of ashes between his eyebrows, whom he knew to be the protector Shabkar. The yogin sang this song:

Father, Dharma King, inseparable
From the matchless protector Padmakara—
The lord who embodies the Buddhas of
    the three times—
Dwell in the center of my heart!

Listen for an instant, fortunate son:
This excellent support so hard to obtain, a
    free and fit body,
Will not last for long and is doomed to
    destruction.
Better hasten to practice the sublime
    Dharma.

The root of the path is the spiritual master;
You need an authentic one: make no
    mistake.
This is a vital issue. Ponder it carefully
And follow a qualified teacher.

Among the teachings of Madhyamika,
    Mahamudra, and the Great Perfection,
Which all carry the meaning of the sutras,
    the tantras and pith instructions,
Practice the teachings toward which you
    feel most affinity,
And the sun of happiness will shine on this
    life and the lives to come.

The yogin added, "If you need water, you will find a blessed spring to the right side of Changchub Metok" [375b]. It is said that, following these indications, people searched for and found the spring. All were amazed and confirmed in their faith.

In those days the Buddhists living near the Diamond Throne of India, Bodhgaya, were saying,

"Although now the precious teachings of Lord Buddha are not found to any great extent in India, they flourish in Tibet. During the Great Prayer Festival of the miracle month,[54] amidst a gathering of hundreds of thousands of monks and nuns, there are hundreds of *panditas* thoroughly versed in the five branches of learning, and in mountain caves there are thousands of renunciates who are great meditators endowed with clairvoyance and miraculous powers.

"Among them is the *siddha* Shabkarpa, an emanation of a past *siddha* of India. He is called Shabkarpa, White Foot, because wherever he lays his feet, that whole place becomes white with virtue. Whenever he moves to another mountain retreat, he goes unimpeded through the rocks, with no one knowing where he went. When others beg him for wealth, he takes any ordinary stone, transforms it into gold and gives it away. When faithful people pray to him, he appears to them in reality, in visions, or in dreams. Now he is staying at Lapchi Snow Range."

As they were wondering, "What does he look like? Does anyone want to go and see?" four young *acharyas*[55] said, "If this is a true story, we will go."

They came to Lapchi, and when we met I offered them some presents, silver, gold, and other things [376a]. They did not accept them, saying instead, "We don't need these, we came to see you." They stayed about four days, and when they returned they described how I looked, how I spoke, and so on. It is said that, following this, some faithful faced towards Tibet and prostrated themselves.

Once, a foreign notable[56] residing in Nepal met some of my monks who had gone there on pilgrimage and borrowed a collection of my songs they had with them. He asked a knowledgeable person to read them to him, and while listening he thought, "This person seems to be a real Buddha; teachings like these are certainly beneficial to the ethical principles of a country." Following this, he had my songs translated into his language and sent them overseas to his country's queen to arouse her wonder, mentioning, "This is the kind of delightful composition one finds here."

More than once, some respectable Nepalese and Mönpas, with all their young sons and daughters, would walk for ten or fifteen days to come and meet me. Through an interpreter, I used to teach them the Dharma, particularly on the karmic law of cause and effect. With great faith, many of them would place my feet upon their heads, shed tears and make prayers before returning home.

Some of the Mönpas who came to sell loads of rice would kill and eat many large grasshoppers on the way. I told them, "It is wrong to kill living beings; don't do it, or after death you will go to hell" [376b]. After this many of them gave up killing. I also said, "If you want happiness, pray to Avalokiteshvara and, gathering people, wealth, and food, you will find satisfaction. To pray, recite *Om mani padme hum*," and I taught them the *mani*. Later, when I was back in Tsang, some of them came there singing the *mani*.

After three years had passed, filled with the joy of having completed the offering of the gold mantle to the Bodhnath stupa, and also remembering Tibet, the Land of Snows, I felt a wish to return there, and sang this cheerful song:

Authentic jewel guru,
Remain upon my head as my crest ornament.
I, the renunciate yogin,
Will sing today a song of happiness.

Sole ornament of the southern continent of Jambudvipa,
Sublime object of offerings and circumambulations,
Great and wonderful stupa—
Such is Jarung Khashor.[57]

Wishing to bring benefit to the teaching and bliss to all beings,

I wrapped the whole of the thirteen
    Dharma rings
With a garment of gilded copper,
Turning it all to gold.

Lapchi is without doubt the most
    wonderful
Among the three great holy places.
Although it grieves me to leave behind
This playground of the dakinis,
Where it is good to live,
We yogins, master and disciples,
Will now go to the central provinces of U
    and Tsang:
There the Victorious Ones, Father and
    Son,
Dwell amidst a gathering of divine and
    human perfections.

If some of you have the good karma
To be able to travel to see Lhasa and
    Samye,
Do not stay here; let's go together.

Rejecting worldly life
For the sake of the divine Dharma [377a]
We, the flock of happy practitioners,
Master and disciples,
Singing happy songs,
Are leaving to practice the happy Dharma
In the center of the happy land of Tibet,
Where all the happy pleasures are
    gathered.

The singer of such a happy song,
Is none other than Tsogdruk Rangdrol.
May all those who hear this song
Remain happy for ever!

After this I went on pilgrimage to establish a connection with the places where Jetsun Milarepa stayed in meditation: Drakmar Chonglung, the Red Rock of the Valley of Agates; Potho Namkha Dzong, the Sky Citadel Mountain; and Kyiphuk Nima Dzong, the Pleasant Cave of the Sun Citadel.

At the Red Rock we built five hermitages in one day, and I installed a few retreatants in

them. There Drakmar Lama, a resident of Potho, was most helpful to all of us, master and disciples,

From there we went to make a connection with the holy place of Shelphuk Chushing Dzong, the Crystal Cave Reed Fortress.[58] I served Osang Monastery as best I could, setting a *ganjira*[59] pinnacle of gold-plated copper on the roof of the assembly hall. When we came to the castle of the Po district, the notable Tashi Deden and his son offered us good hospitality.

Proceeding to Chubar Gonpa,[60] we paid homage at the statue of the precious Jetsun made out of his funeral ashes and known as the "Jetsun Meaningful to See."[61] We made large offerings in front of it.

There I met Chubar Khen Rinpoche, Yonten Lhundrup, the heart-son of the Bodhisattva Yongdzin Pandita. Over a period of fifteen days, I received from him the explanations upon the *Quintessential Ambrosia* [377b],[62] a text on mind training; the initiations of the *Opening the Door of the Sky*[63] and of the *Sixteen Spheres*;[64] and the transmission of the *Mahamudra Teachings of the Gedenpas*.[65] In gratitude for these teachings, I presented him with an offering of the symbols of the body, speech, and mind, with some silver and gold, and other offerings. He himself gave me many presents.

From there, I returned to Lapchi. As I was going to leave for central Tibet, the lamas Trinley and Tsogsham from the main monastery, the patrons Dorgyapa and Trinley, and all the local disciples and householders offered a vast *ganachakra* feast. They presented me with me the symbols of the body, speech, and mind, and, several times, made the hundredfold offering.[66] The Khampa merchants who had been to India offered many crystal vases filled with water from the Ganges and a large light-mansion made of glass to house butter-lamp offerings. The lama from Lidepago offered a black antelope's skin and horns.

To Tsogsham Monastery I offered a *ganjira* pinnacle made of gilded copper. To all the local disciples and patrons I gave blessed substances, including precious relics of the hair and clothing of past saints. I gave them, too, many pieces of advice useful for this life and the next. Finally I gave some farewell advice to all the lamas, village heads, old men and women, householders and housewives—all the faithful people of the valley:

I supplicate my gurus and all those of the
    lineage:
Grant your blessings that I practice in
    accord with the Dharma!

Faithful villagers, listen carefully
To this advice from my heart.

Lamas, do not spoil the water of virtue at
    its source
By drinking *chang* and becoming possessed
    by the "bitter devil" [378a].
To engender trust in the minds of virtuous
    monks,
Behave in accord with the Dharma.

Virtuous monks, do not drink *chang*,
Lest you act in disorderly ways;
Rather guard your vows as taught by the
    guru
And behave in accord with the monastic
    precepts.

Chieftains, do not inflict
Unjust punishments on your subjects.
Humble the arrogant and raise the humble.
Care for all with loving-kindness.

Old people, driven by excessive cravings,
Do not indulge in useless gossip.
Satisfied with whatever food you get,
Stay quietly and recite the *mani*.

All of you who live in the same home,
Avoid harsh words and quarrels.
The elders should look after the young ones,
And the young should listen to their elders.

Husbands and wives, do not rudely
Talk back to your elderly parents,
But give them the best of your food
And gently help them to dress or go to bed.

Do not give too much work to your
    servants,

Without even feeding them properly;
Give them food and clothing as you would
    to your children,
And give them time to rest.

Don't let the old dog by your door
Suffer from hunger and cold;
Feed it morning and evening,
Let it sleep in a warm place,
And when you eat, give it something, too.

Do not mercilessly slaughter the *dzomo's*
    calf,
As though you were killing an enemy,
Just because it drinks its own mother's
    milk;
But, with compassion, give it half of the
    milk
And never kill the *tolhu* [67] calves.

Don't let people hunt
The birds and wild animals of your land;
Spare their lives, and the local deities will
    be pleased—
Needless to say, you yourself shouldn't
    hunt.

Do not create senseless animosity and
    quarrels [378b]
With your nearest neighbors;
Rather, whenever anyone is in difficulty,
Be quick to help each other.

Don't let quarrels triggered by a few bad
    people
Spread discord among all,
But settle past disagreements,
And then maintain harmony.

Rich people, don't be so miserly:
You cannot say when death will come.
Every year, offer a generous feast
To all the local folk.

During these feasts,
Avoid harsh words and fights,
And take delight in songs and dances
That rival the pleasures of the gods.

Even if you are happy in this life, it lasts
    only an instant;
Remember that you can't tell when you
    must leave for the next life.
It is senseless to accumulate negative
    actions;
Persevere in the divine Dharma for the
    sake of future lives.

Lamas, chieftains, monks, virtuous
    practitioners,
And patrons—all you faithful people—
I shall not fail to remember you;
On your part, cultivate devotion and
    respect.

I pray that—however difficult it seems—
We may meet again in this life.
But even if we don't,
May we meet in the next life.

These words having made their way into people's
minds, they refrained from evil actions and tried
to do good. As a result of the Dharma being
practiced in this area, crops became abundant
and happiness prevailed.

On the eve of my departure, the old patron
Dresang Tsering, Umze Gyawo, and all the
people from this holy place, who had been continuously providing [379a] me with milk, whey,
butter, and other necessities, offered, together
with many wealthy patrons, a great *ganachakra*
feast, and presented me with a hundred different
offerings. Even the poorest contributed whatever they could.

    Then they said: "Precious protector and
lord, you have already shown great kindness to
us, the people of Lapchi. Still, you must remain
in our monastery for one or two more years. If
not, at least you must give us some profound
advice that would be the same as your being
here." In answer, I gave them much beneficial
advice, and concluded with this:

I pray to my gurus and to all the gurus of
    the lineage:
Grant your blessing that all my thoughts
    may be turned towards the Dharma.

I shall tell you a few things that will benefit
    you in this life and in future ones;
Remember my words, Lapchi folk!

Virtuous monks, preserve your *samayas* and
    vows;
Give up *chang* and women, Lapchi folk!

Laypeople, engage in wholesome deeds;
Don't give yourselves up to the devil of
    drunkenness, Lapchi folk!

Unmarried women, know how to behave
    with reserve;
And you men, don't take advantage of
    them, Lapchi folk!

Merchants, do not cheat others;
Trade with honesty, Lapchi folk!

Give pilgrims good guidance to the holy
    sites;
Do not leave hungry those who need food,
    Lapchi folk!

When offering lamps, do it cleanly;
Don't eat the butter you mean to offer,
    Lapchi folk!

Even if you are at the end of your rope,
Don't steal religious objects to sell them,
    Lapchi folk!

Even if you have nothing to eat or to wear
    [379b],
Do not empty stupas or strip off the
    garments of statues, Lapchi folk!

Everyone is quarreling with everyone else!
Don't look for revenge, Lapchi folk!

Aristocrats, high ranking officials who
    drink *chang* and fight:

Do not poison the spring of rectitude at its
source, Lapchi folk!

If you live quietly, there is no cause for
dispute;
Don't engage in slander, Lapchi folk!

In this holy place that is like a pure
Buddhafield,
Do not kill the *dzomo*'s *tolhu* calf, Lapchi
folk!

Do not let others kill birds and wild animals
In this sublime holy place, Lapchi folk!

Do not cut trees on the hillside
Of the Cave of the Subjugation of Mara,
Lapchi folk!

Don't defile the abode of celestial beings
By cremating the corpses of defiled
people,[68] Lapchi folk!

Every year repair this holy place's temples,
And fix the leaks in the roofs, Lapchi folk!

Do your best to provide the retreatants and
virtuous monks
Of this holy place with the basic necessities,
Lapchi folk!

Those acting in these ways will be happy
and satisfied;
These are the best means to achieve
happiness, Lapchi folk!

As for myself, I will not stay but leave for
distant lands;
As for you, behave as I have said, Lapchi
folk!

We met in this life for an instant;
I pray that in a future life we will meet and
never part again.

These words having done some good for
you, Lapchi folk,
May goodness and prosperity fill the land!

These words having served as a reminder
for all, many gave [380a] up unwholesome actions
in favor of virtuous ones. As a result, the people's
good fortune increased and everyone enjoyed
happiness and peace.

Again, for the sake of the faithful and kind
patrons of Drin, Tsogsham, and Nyanang
Tashigang, I gave many teachings and beneficial
pieces of advice. As we were about to part, I
concluded with this heart-advice:

Lord guru endowed with the three
kindnesses,[69]
Assembly of peaceful and wrathful deities,
I pray you to bless the body, speech, and
mind
Of all those gathered here.
Shower upon them a rain of ordinary and
extraordinary *siddhis*.

To have obtained a human body in this
life
Is like reaching a crossroad,
The point from which one may go up or
down:
Don't take the wrong path, dear patrons.

In the years gone by since you were born,
See how many have died, old and young.
Keep in mind that you can't be confident
That you won't die tomorrow or even
today.

When the merciless Lord of Death arrives,
He will not let you remain in this life even
one day longer;
Unable to take with you your children,
food, and wealth,
You go alone from this life to the next.

Those who practiced the Dharma will
ascend to the higher realms;
Those who practiced negative acts will fall
to the lower realms;
Therefore refrain from negative actions.

To practice the Dharma, you don't need
to have learned all sorts of things:

Make offerings to your root guru and the
  Three Jewels,
Offer your service to the virtuous sangha
  [380b],
And time and time again give to the poor.
Always make prayers, do prostrations and
  circumambulations.

People of Drin, Tsoksham, and Nyanang,
You all have humility, pure hearts, and
  strong faith in the Dharma.
While I remained in Lapchi, you came to me;
I was able to turn your minds to the
  Dharma.
Through this, many of you became good
  practitioners.
When I ponder this, I think, "How
  fortunate that was!"

My affection for all of you became greater
  and greater
As the days we spent together passed by.
Now that it is time to leave, we cannot
  bear to separate;
Yet, shedding tears, we must take leave of
  each other.

If your yearning love does not change,
Even though I shall be gone to distant
  lands,
From time to time—in actuality, in
  meditation, or in dreams—
We shall meet again, faithful friends!

And though most of us may not meet
  again in this life,
I pray that we may meet again in the next.
Keep clearly in your minds
This farewell advice given from my heart;
And wherever I go,
In my mind I shall keep you all.

May all those who hear these words,
Ponder the impermanence of all things,
And, having naturally turned their minds
  toward the Dharma,
Give up negative actions to strive in
  positive ones.

As I sang this, most of those present, shedding many tears, took vows not to kill any living being, to recite the *mani*, and to perform other virtuous deeds. Some pulled off their ornaments and offered them to me, requesting protection and prayers [381a]. Some, prostrating themselves, prayed to meet me throughout their lives.

Finally, almost everybody went back home. When the actual time came to leave, I offered a vast *ganachakra* feast to all the gurus, the *yidam* deities, the dakinis, the dharmapalas, such as the Five Sisters of Long Life, who abide on the side of virtue, and to all the local deities including the owners of the ground—in short, to all those abiding in the highlands of the Lapchi Snow Range.

Lapchi is the seat of the supreme Rishi, the playground of the dakas and dakinis, the happy grove where deities inclined toward virtue gather, the central place where the Wheel of the Dharma of Realization has been set in motion, the perfect mansion where the victory banner of the Muni's teaching is raised, the land where the lineage of spiritual practice spreads far and wide, the secluded spot where contemplation naturally flourishes, the exalted sacred place that is like a celestial field wreathed in wondrous rainbows.

Then I gave food, clothes, money for the journey, and other useful things to all the disciples gathered there. The patrons of Lapchi, too, gave presents and provisions. When we were enjoying the sacramental feast together, I gave the following advice to all the disciples and patrons gathered there:

"Although born in different places, by the power of our past karma and prayers, we gathered at this extraordinary place, coming from all directions without having been summoned [381b]. For three years we established deep spiritual connections, through teachings and offerings. Now we are parting from each other, and it seems unlikely that I will come here again: this is the way everything goes. Especially, this is the way we will depart for the next world at the time of death.

"From now on, wherever you may go, never forget your most kind root guru; pray to him at all times, and never harbor negative thoughts towards him.

"Never forget the vajra brothers and sisters bound to you by pure *samaya;* remember them with real affection; never despise them.

"Never forget impermanence and death; rid your mind of concern for this life; do not hoard food and wealth.

"Never forget to maintain pure perception; have faith and respect for other Dharma traditions; never slander them.

"Never forget compassion; do whatever you can to assist the needy; never harm anyone.

"Never forget the instructions on the nature of mind; continuously sustain the recognition that arose from those instructions; free of pride, explain it to those who haven't realized it.

"Never forget the dedication; conclude each meritorious deed with a dedication prayer offered without conceit.

"Acting in this way, you will bring good fortune wherever you go, all your aspirations will be fulfilled in harmony with the Dharma, and a day will come when the sun of happiness will rise from within to shine on this life and all your future lives.

"May we all—master, disciples, patrons, and all those to whom I am linked—gather in this life whatever we need regarding three things: people, food and wealth. May we achieve three things: bliss, happiness, and esteem. With great happiness may we enjoy the good fortune to practice the Dharma, and through the goodness of being in harmony with the Dharma, may we see the face of the guru again and again [382a].

"When we die, may the gurus, the sublime deities, the wisdom dakinis, and Dharma protectors endowed with wisdom eyes come in reality to show us the path leading to the pure land of Celestial Enjoyment, or to any other Buddhafield to which we aspire.

"May we, in the lives thereafter, actually meet in a pure and blissful Buddhafield; then, never parting from each other, may we happily converse on all sorts of subjects. Using unlimited miraculous powers, may we wander throughout the countless millions of realms, pure and impure, making offering to the Buddhas and requesting the deities of the Three Roots to lead and protect all beings. I have made before, and I shall always

make, prayers to create a perfect connection for the accomplishment of these wishes."

Thus, having prayed from my heart, I added, "Now, just like the flowers of auspiciousness tossed into the sky, we, master and disciples, will be scattered in all directions and be separated by great distances. One can never plan birth and death, so who knows whether we will meet again? Now that we are gathered here together, we think, 'How nice if we could remain together a little longer!'"

Garlands of affectionate thoughts revolved in my mind, inspiring this song:

I pray to the guru and the Three Jewels
     [382b]:
Grant your blessing that I be of benefit to
     both myself and others.

All my spiritual sons and patrons, who
     came from up and down the country,
Gathered for a fleeting instant like a
     marketplace crowd.
Now that the time has come to go our own
     ways again,
All of us are filled with loving attachment
     for each other.

Yet separation from those one is close to
Is the law of this samsaric world;
So no matter how strong our affection,
There is not much to be done.

Fortunate spiritual sons and faithful
     patrons,
From now on, and throughout our series of
     lives,
I shall always keep you within my affection
     and love.
Now it is time for you to return home;
Devote all your energies to the Dharma,
Since you can't know when death will
     come.

I pray that we may meet again in this life,
But even if this does not happen
Because of the great distances that will
     separate us,

May the next life bring us together in a
    Pure Land.
Wherever we go, master and disciples,
May all our aspirations be fulfilled!

Having sung this, my mind remained filled
with sadness. As I was about to depart, our
spiritual brothers and sisters, too, were preparing
to leave. Seeing this, Dorje Lopön, Yeshe
Wangchuk, and all the faithful with pure *samaya*
who were staying in this holy place were struck
with boundless sadness, and, with one voice
offered this sorrowful song:

Wondrous and precious Jetsun,
Protector, you are a past Buddha
Who assumed an ordinary human form
To guide the beings of this decadent age
    [383a].

In the beginning, you attended an
    authentic teacher;
In the middle, you practiced in solitude;
In the end, you strove everywhere for the
    welfare of beings:
Amazing is your life of perfect liberation!

All the Buddhas and Bodhisattvas of the
    ten directions,
All the dakas, dakinis, and Dharma
    protectors,
Gathered like clouds in this great holy
    place
To assist you in your efforts to spread the
    teachings.

This celestial field resembles the
    Akanishtha heaven,
And the sky is always filled with rainbows
    and light.
Here are gathered, without having been
    summoned,
Many fortunate beings you are meant to
    help.

Protector, when for three years
Dwelling on the lion throne,

You turned the Wheel of the vast and
    profound Dharma
For all the celestial and human beings who
    thronged here,
We thought that, having thus met
    Vajradhara himself,
Even if we were to reach the Akanishtha
    heaven,
There would be nothing better to expect.

When we think of this, sadness whirls in
    our hearts,
And tears continually fall from our eyes
    [383b].

Driven on by our karma, all of us will go
    our own ways
To the world of our next life.
Who can say whether we will meet or not?

When we think of this, sadness continually
    wells up in our minds.
All gathering ends in separation—
This is the condition of the samsaric
    world;
This brings sadness, but what is to be
    done?

Kye ma!
Precious guru,
Set off in peace for the sake of beings;
In whatever country you may be staying,
Do not cast us from your heart.

All you vajra brothers and sisters with pure
    samaya,
Set off in peace for your own lands.
In whichever direction you may go,
Hoist the victory banner of practice in
    solitude.

Although there is little hope that we,
The lama and spiritual companions,
Will meet again in this life,
By the guru's compassion may we meet in
    the next life
In a pure celestial field.

When they sang this, there was hardly anyone who wasn't weeping. I then sang a song to establish all the departing disciples in auspiciousness:

Gurus, *Yidams*, Dakinis,
Dharmapalas abiding on the side of
virtue,
Dwelling in the sky amidst masses of
rainbows
Sing out melodious, auspicious tunes!

My guru and those of the lineage
Hold the auspicious blessing that ripens
and frees.
May this single auspiciousness make all
auspicious,
May auspiciousness prevail for all my
spiritual sons!

The peaceful and wrathful *yidam* deities
Hold auspicious ordinary and extraordinary *siddhis*.
May this single auspiciousness make all
auspicious,
May auspiciousness prevail for all my
spiritual sons!

The dakas, dakinis, and dharmapalas
Hold the auspicious Four Activities [384a].
May this single auspiciousness make all
auspicious,
May auspiciousness prevail for all my
spiritual sons!

I, Lama Shabkar, "White Foot,"
Hold the auspicious vast and profound
Dharma.
May this single auspiciousness make all
auspicious,
May auspiciousness prevail for all my
spiritual sons!

The Dharma practitioners, brothers and
sisters, dwelling here
Hold auspicious devotion and *samaya*.
May this single auspiciousness make all
auspicious,

May auspiciousness prevail for all my
spiritual sons!

The pure-minded human and celestial
beings assembled here
Hold the auspicious conditions favorable to
the Dharma.
May this single auspiciousness make all
auspicious,
May auspiciousness prevail for all my
spiritual sons!

All the departing disciples
Hold the auspiciousness of being filled with
exalted perfections.
May this single auspiciousness make all
auspicious,
May auspiciousness prevail throughout the
world!

Thus singing, I threw flowers of auspicious-ness in all directions. Then, I set out on the road. All the patrons and disciples of Lapchi escorted me for some distance. When they were going to turn back, I put white scarves around their necks, and, filled with sadness, sang this song with a soft melody:

Most kind root guru,
Having arisen from the center of my heart,
Remain on the great bliss aperture on the
crown of my head,
And watch over with your compassionate
eyes
All my heart-sons and daughters who are
returning home.

I beseech you to turn toward the Dharma
The minds of all those assembled here
And to divert them from worldliness.

Bless them so that the goodness of being in
harmony with the teachings
Brings us together over and over again.

By the power of our past good karma and
prayers,

We practitioners—master, disciples, and
   all those around us [384b]—
Although born in various lands,
Gathered in this exalted holy place,
And remained together for three years.

We made various connections, spiritual
   and material,
And now we are scattering like people
   departing from a marketplace.
We go now to distant places where,
Even if we look, we will not be able to see
   each other;
Even if we call out, we will not hear each
   other—
So it will be, when going on to the next life.

When great distances lie between us,
   master and spiritual friends,
And the way we used to live together in this
   holy place comes back to our minds,
We will think, "Why couldn't that happen
   again?"
And a time will come for all of us to weep.

At that time, remembering the guru,
Pray to him over and over again,
Remembering our spiritual companions,
Let your tears flow freely.
It is certain that you will then meet the
   guru and companions
In reality, in inner experiences, or in dreams.

When in this life, in the *bardo*, or in the next
   life,
We practitioners, master and disciples,
Long to meet each other once again,
May we actually meet face to face.

May auspiciousness be conferred upon this
   land;
May all diseases of humans and animals be
   pacified;
May everyone enjoy long life and good
   health, abundant crops and prosperous
   cattle;
May the auspiciousness of universal
   happiness prevail!

Each person's mind being filled with thoughts
of his or her companions, overwhelmed by a
boundless sadness, weeping, they left, looking
back many times, the thought of impermanence
written on their faces [385a].

Following this, haunted by the way impermanence strikes, most of them did not even feel
like eating for one or two days, and they broke
into tears many times. Later, they went to various mountain solitudes and lived in accord with
the Dharma. When I heard of this, I was very
pleased.

Notes

1. There are several Tibetan guidebooks to
Lapchi, among which the most extensive was written
by Drigung Chungtsang Konchog Tendzin (1829–
1906; see chap. 11, note 10), hereafter quoted as GL.
A clear and detailed description of the site of Lapchi
and its history, with translation of large parts of the
guide mentioned above, has been presented by Toni
Huber (1989, hereafter quoted as LNY).

   Among the twenty-four holy places (see chap.
11, note 10), Lapchi corresponds to Godhavari. Several other locations are also known as Godhavari,
perhaps the most ancient one of which is situated in
central India (see LNY, note 2). Another one is located
in the Kathmandu Valley, near a spring said to be
the womb of Vajravarahi. It must be remembered
that sacred geography does not follow the same crite-
ria as ordinary geography. Kyabje Dilgo Khyentse
Rinpoche (1910–91), for instance, said that within
any single valley one can identify the entire set of the
twenty-four sacred places. Kyabje Dudjom Rinpoche
(1903–87) also said that sacred places, such as
Uddiyana, can shrink and even disappear when conditions are no longer conducive to spiritual practice.
The twenty-four sacred places are also present in the
innate vajra body of each being. Among these,
Godhavari, or Lapchi, is the left ear.

   It is said that Lapchi was first ruled by a malicious and fierce gandharva (*dri za*) couple, Suravarina
and his consort Viramati, who took Mahadeva as
their object of refuge. Following the subjugation of
Mahadeva (see chap. 11, note 10), the Bodhisattva

Vajrapani (*phyag na rdo rje*) and his consort Vetali (*ro lang ma*) subdued Suravarina and his consort. The Bodhisattva and his consort took possession of the spirits' abode and ornaments. The Bodhisattva transformed them respectively into a celestial palace and into divine attributes. He and his consort enjoyed the meat and drink in which the spirits reveled, as the sacramental substances of *ganachakra* feast offerings. They blessed the *lingam* symbol of Mahadeva as the mandala of the sixty-two deities of the Chakrasamvara mandala.

Lapchi was also blessed by Guru Padmasambhava and by the great physician Yuthok Yonten Gonpo (*g.yu thog yon tan mgon po*), but it became especially famous after the great saint Jetsun Milarepa (1040–1123) spent many years there in solitary meditation. Milarepa "opened" the sacred place by subjugating the local deities and negative forces adverse to the Dharma. Later many other masters came to meditate at Lapchi. Those from the Drigung lineage in particular exerted their spiritual influence on the place over centuries down to the present day (see chap. 11, note 10, as well as GL and Petech 1978).

The central site of Lapchi is said to be a "triple triangle"; the sky above is seen as a triangle, the earth below is triangular, and the rivers in between form a triangle. Among the many sacred mountains around, the central one is said to be the palace of Chakrasamvara. Three other mountains are considered to be the palaces of Avalokiteshvara, Vajrapani, and Manjushri.

2. The three sacred places: Kailash, Tsari, and Lapchi.

3. The Cave of the Subjugation of Mara (*bdud 'dul phug*) is the principal among the four main caves of Lapchi, the three other one being the Crest Cave (*ze phug*), the Revelation of All Secrets (*sbas pa kun gsal*), and the Prophesied Cave of the Great Forest (*lung bstan tshal chen phug*), and the Hidden Cave (*sbas phug*). The Cave of the Subjugation of Mara is one of the "four widely known caves" mentioned in Milarepa's life-story (see Bacot 1925 and Lhalungpa 1984). It was in this cave that Jetsun Milarepa subjugated a host of demons who had attacked him. It is also the place where, blocked by snow that had fallen for eighteen days and nights, he spent six months in complete seclusion, surviving on one measure of *tsampa*. There too, Milarepa performed many miracles and left nearby a footprint in a rock. See Tsang Nyong Heruka's *Hundred Thousand Songs of Milarepa* (*mi la'i mgur 'bum*) and their translation in English by G. C. C. Chang (1977).

Other great saints who meditated in this cave include Milarepa's moon-like disciple Rechung Dorje Trakpa (*ras chung rdo rje grags pa*, 1084–1161), Nyö Lhanangpa (*gnyos lha nang pa*, 1164–1224), the "Mad Yogin of Tsang Ornate with Bones" (*gtsang smyon heruka rus pa'i rgyan can*, 1452–1507), and the "Victorious Hermit of Lapchi," Namkha Gyaltsen (*rgyal la phyi pa nam mkha' rgyal mtshan*, fifteenth century, said to be the mind-aspect incarnation of Milarepa).

4. Dharma of Realization (*rtogs pa'i chos*), as compared to the Dharma of the Scriptural Transmission (*lung gi chos*).

5. For Demo Rinpoche, see chap. 9, note 31. He died of smallpox in 1819. Under his regency Tibet knew a period of peace and prosperity. The regency then fell to a weaker character, Tsemön Lingpa, Ngawang Jampel Tsultrim (*tshe smon gling pa ngag dbang 'jam dpal tshul khrims*), who ruled from 1819 to 1844. See Shakabpa 1976 and 1984.

6. Pelgyeling (*'phel rgyas gling*), the "Place of Increase and Expansion," was named by Milarepa. After Milarepa's death, a monastery was built upon the Garuda Cave, Namkha Ding Phug (*nam mkha' lding phug*), a cave where Milarepa meditated for several years, in the "Nyelam," or more correctly Nyanang (*gnya' nang*) Valley. At the nearby Belly Cave (*grod pa phug*, see PP, NLY, and MI), one can still see the hand- and footprint that Milarepa left miraculously on the rock. Rechungpa's cave lies slightly above Milarepa's cave.

7. *Fifty Verses of Devotion to the Guru* (Skt. *Gurupanchashika*, Tib. *bla ma lnga bcu pa*, T 3721) by Asvaghosha (first century C.E.). An English translation has been published by the Library of Tibetan Works and Archives (1975).

8. In the year of the female Earth Hare, 1819, Shabkar was thirty-eight years old.

9. T. Huber (1989) says, "Like many Tibetan pilgrimage sites it is a place characterized by a rugged natural beauty, quite remote from major centers of human activity. Pilgrims who journey to Lapchi from the expansive steppes and broad valleys of the arid Tibetan plateau experience a dramatic change in the physical environment as they descend deep into the heart of this Himalayan valley with its mantle of vegetation and noisy watercourses."

10. The Hidden One (*sbas pa*; see GL, p. 51, and LNY, p. 55). There are two caves, the upper and the lower Hidden Caves (*sbas pa gong 'og*) where Jetsun Milarepa meditated and had a vision of the mandala of Chakrasamvara that dissolved into him. There,

too, meditated Tertön Changchub Lingpa (*byang chub gling pa*, fourteenth century, who came from the place known as Many Birds, *bya mang po*, and attained the rainbow body). According to GL, p. 54/b, Shabkar stayed in the upper cave, the Revelation of All Secrets (*sbas pa kun gsal*).

11. The Azure Queen Mountain (*mthon mthing rgyal mo*), also known as the Peak of the Five Sisters of Long Life (*tshe ring mched lnga*) and as Gaurishankar in Nepali, is a beautiful snow peak of triangular shape (7146 meters), east of Lapchi. It is considered to be the palace of Tseringma and her sisters.

12. According to GL, p. 53/a, this is the Lower Triangular Plain (*chos 'byung ma thang*), below the Cave of the Subjugation of Mara.

13. GL, p. 56/a says that the actual door of the cave, which Shabkar thus reopened, had been closed by nonhuman beings. According to a personal communication from Toni Huber, the cave itself has an outer and an inner part, separated by a narrow passage with a low roof. The stone hearth of Jetsun Milarepa is the centerpiece and inner sanctum of the cave. The temple is built as a continuation of the outer part of the cave.

14. This is an analogy with the formation of the universe. When the primordial ocean was churned by the winds, Mount Sumeru and the continents rose above its surface.

15. The seven royal emblems are the precious wheel, the precious jewel, the precious queen, the precious elephant, the precious minister, the precious horse, and the precious general. Here, Tashi Dedenpa is endowed with the seven noble riches (see chap. 5, note 13).

16. This small monastery called "The Dharma Enclosure where Virtue Increases" (*chos ra dge 'phel gling*) partially escaped destruction during the Cultural Revolution. It is situated at an altitude of 3900 meters at the upper limit of the forest, in the Lower Triangular Plain (*chos 'byung ma thang*) of Lapchi (see LNY, p. 74). It consists of a small temple surrounded by walls and rooms for the monks that form a monastic courtyard, or "Dharma enclosure" (*chos ra*), about twenty-five meters square. After Shabkar completed the construction, most of the precious images and relics in the valley were transferred and preserved in the temple. Chief among them (GL, p. 57/b) was the "Nasal-blood Image" (*mtshal khrag ma*), a statue of Jetsun Mila made by Rechungpa after Milarepa himself had prepared the clay, mixing it with blood from his nose and veins, and with his saliva. Most of these precious images are no longer extant except for a painted-clay statue of Shabkar. (Personal communication by T. Huber.)

17. The Drigung Father and Son are the senior and the junior incarnates of Drigung Monastery, Drigung Chetsang (*che tshang*) and Chungtsang (*chung tshang*). The former was here Drigung Kyabgön Tendzin Padma Gyaltsen ('*bri gung skyabs mgon bstan 'dzin padma rgyal mtshan*, born in 1770), the twenty-seventh hierarch of Drigung and the reincarnation of Jigten Gonpo (*jig rten mgon po*, 1143–1217). The latter was the reincarnation of Drigung Rigdzin Chökyi Trakpa ('*bri gung chung tshang rig 'dzin chos kyi grags pa*, 1597–1659). See Tendzin Pemai Gyaltsen's *Account of the Various Masters of the 'Bri gung bKa' brgyud pa School*. About their authority over Lapchi, see LNY and chap. 11, note 10.

18. See *Collected Songs* (TS 4, pp. 703–9).

19. Drin Chubar (*brin chu dbar*) is a village and monastery near the junction of the Rongshar (*rong shar*, formerly known as *brin*) and the Manglung (*smang lung*) rivers, to the east of Lapchi. See MI, p. 185.

20. At the center of a stupa one puts a life tree (*srog shing*) as its central axis. It is cut square and placed in the stupa, facing the same way as it grew in the wild. One writes on it various mantras and prayers, and one attaches precious relics to it.

21. "According to the prayer they made . . ." See chap. 12, note 28.

22. The very top of a stupa consists of thirteen Dharma wheels of decreasing diameters, finally surmounted by a moon crescent and a sun. These thirteen "wheels" are sometimes thirteen squares, as in the case of Bodhnath stupa.

23. Kazi Bhimsen Thapa ruled as prime minister of Nepal for thirty-one years (1806–37) under three successive kings. When Shabkar wrote his letter, King Rajendra Bikram Shah (1816–81, dethroned in 1847) was an infant, and the power was in the hands of Bhimsen Thapa and the regent queen grandmother, Tripura Sundari.

24. In the Delhi print, *skyo* should be corrected to *skye*.

25. This is a play on Shabkar's name, "Self-liberation of the Six Senses" (*tshogs drug rang grol*).

26. This advice would refer in the same way to men, if it were given to a woman. It does not deprecate women as such, but rather the obstacles created by becoming entangled in sexual relationships.

27. Knowledge of the scriptures and realization of the meaning they convey.

28. *gter ma*. See Appendix 1.

29. For *Seven-Point Mind Training*, see chap. 1, note

60. For *Emanated Scriptures of the Bodhisattva* (*rgyal sras sprul pa'i glegs bam*), see Appendix 5.

30. Gyalse Ngulchu Thogme, see Translator's Introduction, p. xx.

31. Three secrets. See Author's Introduction, note 18.

32. The next four verses are missing in TS 1, p. 819.

33. Mt. Kailash.

34. The verses follow the order of the Tibetan alphabet, which has thirty letters and starts with *Ka, Kha, Ga, Nga* . . .

35. The letter *A* symbolizes the unborn void nature of all phenomena, the absolute "body" or continuum, the dharmakaya.

36. The eight limiting or conditioning concepts (*spros pa'i mtha' brgyad*): conceiving of reality in terms of existence and nonexistence, eternity and nothingness, going and coming, sameness and difference.

37. The Brahma aperture is the fontanelle at the junction of the cranial bones. From there consciousness leaves the body during *phowa* to merge with the guru's or the Buddha's mind, and to be transferred to a Buddhafield.

38. The *Drop of Gold Heart-Advice* (*snying gtam gser gyi thig pa*) is the name given to this advice on Bodhicitta.

39. See chap. 11, note 13.

40. Gyaling (*rgya gling*), a reed instrument close to the Persian *shanai* and one of the principal ritual instruments in Tibetan Buddhism. See NS, note 1133.

41. Tingshag (*ting shags*), tiny, thick cymbals with a high-pitched sound. They are often made of bell-metal and are mostly used in Kriya Tantra rites, water *torma* offering (*chu gtor*), and burnt offerings (*gsur*) made to the starving spirits.

42. *Jetsunmas* (*rje btsun ma*), the "revered" ones: female Dharma practitioners who have not necessarily taken monastic vows.

43. The year 1821, when Shabkar was forty.

44. King Rajendra Bikram Shah, who has ascended to the throne 1816 at the age of two.

45. "Becoming Buddha from the royal throne" is a common expression of respect to kings, implying that their righteous activities will lead them to Buddhahood.

46. The Amban and assistant Amban were the Chinese emperor's representatives in Lhasa, from 1727 to 1912. The emperor himself was known in Tibet as the Jamyang Gongma, or, in full, "God of the Skies, Exalted Manjushri, Great Lord" (*gnam gyi lha 'jam dbyangs gong ma bdag po chen po*), a title that the fifth Dalai Lama, on the occasion of his visit to Peking

in 1653, conferred upon the Manchu ruler (China being considered to be the Buddhafield of Manjushri). The Ambans at the time of this story were Wen'gan (who stayed at Lhasa from 1820 to 1823) and Linghai (1819 to 1821). See Josef Kolmas (1992). The reasons to the apprehensiveness of the Amban are explained below.

Most of the money circulating in Tibet in the second half of the eighteenth century was Nepalese silver coins. Although some were made of pure silver and some of 50 per cent alloy, they all circulated in Tibet at the same value (see Rhodes 1980). In 1768–69, Prithvi Narayan Shah, chief of Gorkha (a principality thirty miles west of Kathmandu) overthrew the Newari rulers in Kathmandu Valley and conquered most of the other areas of what is now Nepal. He then demonetized the debased coins, which became valued at half of those made of fine silver. This devaluation was not accepted by Tibetans, to whom it would have caused great losses. Trouble broke out in 1786, just after the regent-king of Tibet, Tsemön Ling Ngawang Tsultrim, had been invited to China. In 1788, the Gorkhali army invaded Tibet. In 1789 a treaty was signed in favor of the Gorkhalis, who withdrew their troops.

Returning from China, the Tsemön Ling regent scolded his ministers for their feebleness in dealing with the Gorkhalis, but he died in 1791. In one incident, Tibetan negotiators who had come to Nyanang were killed or taken prisoner by the Gorkhalis in a trap set on the occasion of a religious festival, during which Gorkhali soldiers had disguised themselves as merchants and coolies.

In 1791, a Gorkhali army strong of eighteen thousand men again invaded Tibet as far as Tashi Lhunpo. The Tibetan army counterattacked and pushed the Gorkhali forces back to Nyanang. At that point, thirteen thousand Manchu troops arrived in Tibet and joined the ten thousand Tibetan soldiers. Together they drove the Gorkhalis back to within twenty miles of Kathmandu. In 1792, a treaty was signed between Nepal, Tibet, and China. In Lhasa, the populace began to protest against the presence of the Chinese army, which, they said, had entered Tibet unasked for, and had caused more harm to the Tibetans than the Gorkhalis themselves.

Following this, the two Ambans were removed for misconduct and returned to China. The new Ambans sent to Lhasa retained a little power for some time, but this power vanished soon after the death of Emperor Qianlong in 1796. After a period of intrigue, one of the Ambans was returned to China in chains and the other one exiled to Chinese Turkestan. A few more Ambans were sent to Lhasa. The last one was expelled in 1912, under the thirteenth Dalai Lama. After this, the Chinese lost their influence in Tibet until the 1950 invasion. (See Shakabpa, 1976 and 1984.)

47. The Chinese ruler. This was Emperor Jiaqing, who reigned from 1796 to 1820)

48. The Dalai Lama and the Panchen Lama.

49. *White Path of Liberation* (*dkar chag thar lam dkar po*, see Bibliography).

50. *The Adamantine Armor;* see chap. 2, note 18.

51. *Magars;* see chap. 11, note 4.

52. Literally, the "bitter's devil," because *chang* is a bitter kind of millet beer.

53. In 1821.

54. The Great Prayer Festival (*smon lam chen mo*), which takes place every year at Lhasa during the first month of the lunar calendar, called the miracle month.

55. In Tibetan *Atsara*, a common name for Indian wandering ascetics, or sadhus, which is a distortion of the Sanskrit word *acharya*, meaning "master."

56. This must refer to Brian Hodgson, who lived in Nepal from 1819 to 1842. In 1821 he was assistant to the British Resident in Nepal, Edward Gardner. Hodgson wrote voluminous reports about the culture and politics of Nepal. The queen in question is most likely to have been Queen Victoria, who ascended the throne in 1837. See Hodgson, with introduction by P. Denwood (1972).

57. The Great Stupa of Bodhnath.

58. The Crystal Cave Reed Fortress (*shel phug chu shing rdzong*), west of Chubar. See MI, p. 186.

59. *Ganjira*, a golden pinnacle filled with relics and holy scriptures that is set at the top of monasteries and temples.

60. The place where Jetsun Milarepa passed away, also known as the Retreat Center of Chubar (*chu dbar sgrub sde*). At one time a flourishing retreat center of the Drigung tradition, it was then converted to the Karma Kamtsang tradition by the tenth Karmapa,

who erected there a large temple and a protectors' temple. Then in the fifth Dalai Lama's time, the monastery was converted to the Geluk tradition and renamed Ganden Drophen Ling (*dga' ldan 'gro phan gling*).

61. The "Jetsun Meaningful to See" (*rje btsun mthong ba don ldan*) was one the main relics at Chubar retreat center. It was a statue of Jetsun Milarepa made by Rechungpa of clay mixed with Milarepa's nose-blood and funeral ashes (see note 16). It was later transferred to Lapchi and was lost during the Cultural Revolution. Among other relics also kept there were an ivory statue of Milarepa made by Rechungpa and a stone from Milarepa's cremation hearth, upon which the six-syllables of the *mani* appeared miraculously. Many of the contents of Chubar are preserved in crates at Lambagar, Nepal, just south of Lapchi. These may contain some of the precious relics mentioned above.

62. *The Quintessential Ambrosia* (*blo sbyong bdud rtsi snying po*), written by Yongdzin Pandita Kachen Yeshe Gyaltsen (see chap. 9, note 33).

63. For *Opening the Door of the Sky*, see chap. 3, note 22.

64. For the *Sixteen Spheres*, see chap. 12, note 74.

65. For *Mahamudra Teachings of the Gedenpas* (*dge ldan bka' brgyud rin po che'i phyag chen rtsa ba rgyal ba'i gzhung lam*), by Lobzang Chökyi Gyaltsen (*blo bzang chos kyi rgyal mtshan*), see DZ, vol. 4, pp. 489–98.

66. The hundredfold offering: an offering of one hundred different items. Such a vast offering is traditionally made only in exceptional circumstances.

67. For *tolhu*, see chap. 9, note 9.

68. Only the corpses of Dharma practitioners and special persons were actually cremated in Tibet. Others were given "sky-burial"; their corpses were cut up and fed to the vultures. People believed that the smoke from the cremation of ordinary bodies would defile the sky realm of the local deities and mountain gods.

69. For the three kindnesses, see chap. 5, note 36.

14

Return to Central Tibet

How, returning to the Pure Realm of central Tibet,
I wandered on, benefiting beings

In the Water Stallion Year,[1] called "Many Names," on an auspicious day in the eight month, with many disciples I arrived at Pelgyeling monastery at the Belly Cave of Nyanang.[2] I met the precious Khenpo and the sangha and offered a gilded victory banner and a Dharma-wheel flanked by representations of a stag and a doe for the top of the monastery's temple. Inside the temple, I offered a butter-lamp made from over one hundred silver coins and offered a general distribution of alms and tea.

Going to the main market of Nyanang, I taught the Dharma and gave a long-life empowerment to all the Nepalis and Tibetans there [387a]. This inspired many Nepali merchants—who every year sacrificed three hundred goats, sheep, chickens and other animals to the Hindu gods—to stop these "red offerings" and perform "white" ones only. Most of the butchers, too, made a vow to give up slaughter.

After I had ransomed the lives of a thousand sheep with eleven *dotse*, there was no roundup for the slaughter of sheep in the valley that year. All the sheep whose lives I ransomed were set free in the pastures around Pelgyeling Monastery. Their wool was used for the benefit of the sangha—for making cushions and as a source of income. With nine *dotse*, I bought some thin cloth and some heavy woolen cloth and gave it to those monks who needed robes.

Continuing on my way, I paid homage to the "Speaking Tara" at Leshing, and made offerings and prayers. At Dulung, Baro, and other places in Upper Nyanang, many wealthy families vowed to stop butchering sheep and goats. I thus saved the lives of thousands of animals. As the minds of people in the whole of upper, middle and lower Nyanang turned toward the Dharma, they became imbued with virtue. From Zurtso I reached Lung; I gave a longevity blessing and taught the Dharma to the householders. They presented me with many offerings and I made prayers for dedicating their merit.

I went to pay homage and establish a spiritual connection with the place where the *siddha* Tsang Nyön, the Mad Yogin of Tsang,[3] had meditated. Passing through the central district of Nyanang, I reached Tingri Langkhor[4] and stayed for a while in retreat at the place where Padampa had lived. I read the four large volumes of Padampa's teachings entitled *The Pacification of Suffering*[5] and, through his blessings, derived immense benefit from them [387b].

I turned the Wheel of the Dharma for Shekar Changwa, Sharlung Tsering, and other patrons of Shingri and Tingri. As result of this, some wealthy patrons who had previously been slaughtering two to three hundred sheep a year made a vow henceforth not to kill more than twenty or thirty; those who had been slaughtering twenty or thirty vowed to kill no more than two or three; those who had been killing one or two gave up slaughtering altogether and vowed to eat only the meat they could buy. The flow of evil ceased almost entirely and thousands of sheep were saved.

I then went to the White Snows of Tingri. At the invitation of Tsong-ye, a Chinese official,

and of the Tibetan commander Changlochen, I
performed ceremonies for a few days at their
homes. They offered me an abundance of delicious Chinese food; Chinese games and dances
were held and everyone greatly enjoyed the event.

One day, I taught the Dharma and gave a
longevity blessing to several thousand people
gathered in a meadow down in the valley, thus
conferring auspiciousness on the place. The commander Changlochen came to Samling and was
very helpful.[6] I gave him teaching on the nature
of mind and other instructions. He developed a
strong interest in the Dharma and later accomplished many religious deeds.

When I reached Samling in the holy place
of Gyalkyi Shri, "Splendor of the Conquerors,"
commonly known as Tsibri, the first thing I did
was to sing this praise [388a]:

Lord of the infinity of peaceful and
    wrathful deities,
Father, Dharma King, Ngakyi Wangpo,
Endowed with the kindness of all the
    Victorious Ones:
Bless this son who supplicates you!

"Splendor of the Conquerors!"
Wondrous land praised by the holy beings
    of the past,
Your colorful mountains and rocks
Assume the astonishing forms
Of the deities of the five and the three
    Buddha families,
Of the exalted sixteen arhats and others,
And of various sacred letters and sym-
    bols—how amazing!

In all directions, the lesser mountains, too,
Appear as the eight auspicious symbols
And other offerings to the Victorious
    Ones.

All along the periphery are lakes and
    ponds
Beautifully arrayed, like water offerings.

Any faithful person looking around
Will find the place delightful.

Especially, saintly Dharma practitioners
See this land as a pure celestial field.

This is the very place where many wise
    and accomplished sages of India and
    Tibet,
The Indian Padampa Sangye,
The Tibetans of the Land of Snows, Mila
    and his heirs,
And the victorious lords Götsangpa and
    Yangonpa,
Attained realization within a single lifetime.

Here is the supreme palace of the infinite
    peaceful and wrathful deities,
The gathering place of the gods and the
    Dharma protectors who delight in
    virtue.
If you can pray with veneration
To the deities of the Three Roots who
    abide here [388b],
They will dispel all obstacles and confer
    upon you all *siddhis*.

How can I fully describe the qualities of
    such a place?

Emulating the perfect liberation
Of the forefathers of the Kagyu lineage,
May I, the lowly vagabond, genuinely
    practice the Dharma in this land.

You, fortunate beings of the future
    generations,
Give up all concern with worldly life,
Come here, meditate:
Experiences and realization will dawn.

The patrons who provide for the needs
Of the great meditators,
And the meditators who benefit from the
    help of these patrons,
Hold the fortunate fate of gaining
    Buddhahood together.

The worthy beings with good karma
Who do prostrations, circumambulations,
    and offerings at this place

Give meaning to having obtained this
    precious human birth.

By the merit of having praised this holy
    place,
May both the teachings and their practice
    flourish;
May crops be abundant, goodness prevail,
And may auspiciousness encompass the
    entire land of Tibet.

On various occasions, a thousand renunciates, monks and nuns, gathered there, and several thousand householders came to meet me. The various clans of the area offered me a lot of gold, silver and coins, and two offering-lamps weighing fifty ounces of silver each. The chief merchant Sonam Dargye offered me many *sang* and twenty *sho* of gold. The Khampa Tseten of Kyidrong gave me two domes of translucent crystal to cover butter-lamps [389a]—each worth a hundred silver coins—a pair of binoculars, and a vase filled with water from the Ganges. The chieftain Seh offered me valuables, jewels, and dresses worth seven *dotse*. A Kothang house-holder's daughter who renounced this life offered me her hair ornaments, worth sixty *sang*. Like-wise, day after day, faithful monks, nuns, and laypeople offered me dresses and ornaments, as well as many bags of *tsampa* and pouches of butter, which filled the whole place where we stayed. With all this wealth, I provided supplies for the retreatants staying at Khyemkyichu. Ten to fifteen people were employed to make boxes and loads of tea and butter; still there was some left, which was sold. I also gave food and clothing to the pilgrims who had come from afar.

From time to time, we kneaded ten to thirty bags of *tsampa*, added gum to it, and made it into the shape of a huge Mount Meru, with all its steps and levels. Around it, we arranged many offerings—meat, *chang*, fruits, and all kinds of food—and offered a large *ganachakra* feast. The local people sang and danced, and the atmo-sphere of joy and happiness matched that of heaven.

I repaired the Great Maitreya Temple of Samling. I placed on its terrace a golden wheel, and inside, in front of Maitreya, I offered a huge lamp, filled with an ocean of butter and a wick the size of a forearm, which burned day and night. When one entered, the whole temple was warm, reminding one of the Jowo Temple of Lhasa [389b]. For all this I spent fifteen *dotse*. Then I had the treasurer and many monks go and restore the Stupa of Langkhor, and offered one *dotse* for the work.

Altogether I spent over a year in Tingri. When all the disciples who had come from Tö and the lamas from Mangnang were leaving, I sang for them this heart-advice:

O root guru, immensely kind Vajradhara,
Father, whose name I hardly dare to
    pronounce,
Dharma King Ngakyi Wangpo,
Please remain above my head
Upon a throne raised by lions,
Within a tent of rainbow light.

I, your son, ask in fervent supplication:
Turn the minds of those gathered here
    toward the Dharma;
Bring to an end all thoughts contrary to the
    Dharma.

All of us assembled here were born in
    different places,
Yet, by the power of our good karma and
    pure prayers,
We have gathered here in this eminent
    holy place.

Having made many connections, spiritual
    and material,
We now depart in all directions—
Thus are all things impermanent!

From today onward,
Even if we look, we will not see one another;
Even if we call out, with affection, we
    won't hear each other.
We will have gone off to our respective
    lands.
Separated by great distances,
It will be difficult for us to meet again.

I pray that we may meet in future lives;
Yet, as we have accumulated diverse
    karma, good and evil [390a],
Will we really meet again? I cannot say.
Pondering this, I feel sad from deep within.

This joyous gathering of men and gods in
    this village
Was our own unique encounter.
You who spontaneously assembled here,
Listen to this advice from my heart:

How many people have died, old and
    young,
Since your mother bore you?
See how many of your acquaintances
Now leave this world:
Be aware of the fragility of life.

No one lives forever.
What is not related to Dharma
Is of no use in the next life.
Don't simply store up wealth;
Make offerings; give alms.

Even if you can't practice the Dharma very
    much,
Don't act wrongly. Don't kill,
Confess your faults, and refrain from
    repeating them.

At home, avoid animosity and malicious
    thoughts and actions.
Cultivate compassion, gentleness, and
    generate supreme Bodhicitta.

The very essence of all this
Is that, even if you can't practice the
    Dharma
And cannot reach the higher realms,
At the very least, don't wind up in the hells
Through being weighted down by evil
    actions.
This is crucial; keep it in mind.

Farewell now—
I shall pray for your good health and long
    life.

We, master and disciples, won't remain
    either,
But will wander from one mountain
    solitude to another.

When the wish to see each other arises,
May we meet again and again.
If, because of the distances between us, we
    can't meet again in this life,
May we meet in the land of the next.

May whoever hears or reads this song
    embrace the Dharma [390b];
May Dharma practitioners spread
    throughout the world!

After I had sung this, hundreds of disciples departed every day. Seeing how nothing evades impermanence, I was filled with sadness, and so were all those taking leave of each other. We broke camp and made the circumambulation of the sacred place Gyalkyi Shri, "Splendor of the Conquerors." I offered tea and alms to all the monasteries. I requested a longevity blessing from Neuring Lama Rinpoche, who was a hundred years old, and offered him gold and presents.

During the circumambulation, I taught the Dharma to the local householders. A few wealthy patrons who used to kill four or five hundred sheep a year (using some for their needs and selling the rest at the market in spring), vowed not to kill more than forty or fifty. Most other people who used to kill sheep offered me their promise to eat only meat that was being sold, but never themselves to slaughter sheep at home. In that way I was able to interrupt a stream of wrong deeds, enhance the stream of virtue, and turn everyone's mind towards the Dharma.

Then, I went to Shelkar Chödeh,[7] the "White Crystal Abode of Dharma," and offered, as general property for the monastery, the horse I had been riding on, with its gear. I placed on the top of the monastery a gilded-copper Dharma-wheel and made a general distribution of tea and alms. Everyone was pleased. A few monks invited me to their cells and asked me for teachings to establish a spiritual connection; the wealthy ones among them offered me many *sang*. Traversing the various districts of this province [391a], I reached Tsogo and Drangso. I give a long-life blessing and taught the Dharma to the lady of Tsogo, the chieftain of Tradeh, and a crowd of householders. I sang songs as well, inspiring people to practice the Dharma. Many promised to give up killing and practice virtuous deeds. The wealthy local patrons of the area offered gold, silver, clothing, jewelry, and a large amount of barley. Using this, I made a distribution of tea and money to the monastery of Sungkar Chödeh and offered the barley as provisions for the retreatants of Dechen Phuk, the Cave of Great Bliss.

Then I gave empowerments and taught the Dharma to the wealthy patron Shulung Gonpo and to all the local people. They offered me a lot of food, gold, silver, brocades, jewelry and other valuables. I went to the household of Phumar Bartso, a wealthy, good-hearted person inclined toward the Dharma. I gave teachings and blessings to him and his people, and prayed that auspiciousness might reign. They promised not to kill more than fifty sheep a year, instead of five hundred. They offered us all the tea and butter we could have wished for, as well as amber, corals, turquoise, and gold and silver ornaments. I invited Lama Rinpoche of Gonchang and requested him to give me the empowerments for the *Gathering of the Awareness Holders,* the *Great Compassionate One,* and the *Wrathful Guru* from the *Northern Terma* [391b].[8] I presented him with some silk, gold, and turquoise. When I was on the point of leaving I gave the following advice to all the householders:

Lord guru, my everlasting refuge and
  protector,
Remaining as my crown ornament,
Look upon me with compassion
And on all these disciples and patrons,
And grant your blessing.

Faithful, generous, and intelligent patron
  Phumar Bartso,
Listen to this helpful advice from my heart.

Now that you have gained a precious
  human life,
If you don't hurry to practice the divine
  Dharma,
Remember: in this dark age, life's duration
  is uncertain—
You may even die tonight.

One who has acted virtuously
Will go on to the higher realms of freedom;
One who has acted wrongly,
Will go on to the threefold lower realms.

The power to choose your course
Is now in your hands.
Forsake negative deeds, which will drag
  you down,
And diligently pursue positive deeds, which
  will lead to the higher realms.

Among all unvirtuous actions,
Taking life is the worst;
Give it up as you would give up poison.

Stinginess with your own wealth—
Covetousness toward the wealth of
  others—
Anger and hatred, always senseless—
Jealousy and a competitive mind—
All these you should shun.

With remorse, confess your past misdeeds
And promise not to commit them again.

Among all virtuous actions,
Offerings and generosity are foremost—
Perform them at all times.

Be kind to your servants and attendants;
Be helpful to your neighbors [392a];
Don't beat your cattle and the dog at your
  door,
But take good care of them.

Rejoice in the virtuous acts you did in the
  past
And determine to perform them in future.
Do prostrations and say prayers,

Rest your mind in the state of luminous
  emptiness.
Develop compassion for all beings, your
  mothers,
And make vast dedication prayers.

To practice the divine Dharma one does
  not need much;
These pieces of heart-advice will suffice.

By the merit of thus practicing,
May you find happiness in all of your lives.

They prostrated themselves with great veneration, praying that we might meet many times
again. I then reached the great monastic estate of
the Glorious Sakya. I met the elder Jetsunma
and the throne-holders Kunga Gyaltsen and
Ngodrup Pelbar.[9] I offered them pairs of long
copper trumpets, of cymbals, and of *gyalings*, and
some gold, silver, turquoise, corals, and other
valuables. I requested the empowerments of longevity, of Vajrakilaya, and of the Wrathful Guru.
I filled with butter the lamp of solid gold that I
had earlier entrusted the treasurer Depa Wangpo
to offer there on my behalf, and made extensive
prayers. I made offerings in all the other temples,
and arranged a distribution of tea and alms to
the whole monastic community. I stayed fifteen
days, doing prostrations and circumambulations,
and witnessed the Great Thread-cross ceremony.[10]

From Sakya I went to Chang Lhatse and
stayed for two days in the great landlord
Tanagpa's house. I gave him a long-life blessing.
He offered me tea, butter, silver and many other
things [392b]. Then I reached the Yönpo Valley
of Gyang and stayed there a couple of months.
Hundred of patrons of Gyang Lhatse came to
me, and in the course of time, giving them long-
life blessings and teachings, I could turn their
minds towards the Dharma. They presented me
with many offerings.

Lama Pema Rangdrol, accompanied by
many others, arrived from Domey. Offering me
a hundred Chinese silver coins and many valuables of all kinds, he asked for a longevity blessing. I gave him an empowerment according to

the tradition of the "Sole Mother Queen of the
Siddhas,"[11] establishing auspicious connections
for his long life. I also gave him this advice:

I bow down to the gurus and the Three
  Jewels,
To the *yidam* deities, dakinis, and Dharma
  protectors:
Grant the accomplishment of all our aspi-
  rations.

I became filled with joy when I heard
That, by the compassion of the guru and
  the Three Jewels,
You, the great spiritual son Pema Rangdrol,
Gifted with faith, diligence, intelligence,
  and compassion,
Together with the physician Nyerwa
And other worthy disciples, sons of my
  heart,
Had reached the Pure Realm of U-Tsang
Through the northern road, without
  suffering any harm or trouble,
And, after having paid homage to the two
  Crowned Buddhas of Lhasa,
To Samye and to Tashi Lhunpo, were
  heading for this place.

I, the old man, have not yet died.
I went round many countries and many a
  wilderness—
The precious Snow Mountain, Nepal,
  Lapchi, and others—
And have now again reached central
  Tibet.

As if timely appointments had been made,
Owing to my good karma and past
  prayers,
I was able to visit the Yönpo Valley of
  Gyang,
The great master Padmasambhava's
  supreme place of accomplishment.
Everything, filled with auspiciousness,
  occurred in harmony with the Dharma
  [393a].
Paying homage to that place, I felt great
  joy.

E ma! Worthy spiritual sons of mine,
There are so many things to see
And to which to pay respect
In this Pure Realm of U-Tsang!
Why would you go back home?
Stay for a year or so;
That would be the greatest good fortune.
We would talk at ease and at length,
And I would gradually give some helpful
    heart-advice.

Since, however, you must return this year
To serve your teacher and benefit beings in
    Domey,
Prepare everything carefully for the
    journey.

Just as, now, all of us yogins, master and
    disciples,
Part again, all phenomena are
    impermanent.
Reflect upon this and practice the holy
    Dharma.

If you long wholeheartedly to practice the
    Dharma,
Empty your mind of the eight worldly
    concerns,
Keep pure vows and *samayas*,
And practice diligently according to your
    lama's instructions.

Whenever we, Dharma practitioners,
    master and disciples,
Long to encounter each other during the
    remainder of our lives,
May we meet as we did today.

In these degenerate times, our hold on life
    is so fragile!
If because of great distances between us
We cannot meet in this same life,
May we meet in the next.

After Pema Rangdrol had described the
worthy commitments to the Dharma and sentient beings that called him back to Domey, I
gave him my permission to leave.

With them, I sent a letter to the Dharma
King Ngakyi Wangpo's son, Wang Tashi
Jungne,[12] "Royal Fountainhead of Auspiciousness," asking him to come and visit the holy
places of U and Tsang, in keeping with the
excellent tradition of his forefathers:

I present this letter at the feet of the
    Chingwang, king of Mongolia,
The supreme benefactor of the Buddha's
    teaching [393b],
Whose fame resounds to all horizons
Like the thundering summer dragon.

Prompted by the keen affection I nourish
    for you from afar,
I, Tsogdruk Rangdrol, who am linked with
    you through my good karma and past
    prayers,
Submit these few words to you.

Although both the Dharma King and his
    consort have gone on to another
    Buddhafield,
O supreme being, you now hold the
    kingdom.
Hearing how you have established
The whole land in peace, I feel boundless
    joy.

Owing to the Dharma King's kindness,
I am well in body and mind, free from all
    suffering,
Filled with joy in the Pure Realm of
    U-Tsang.

At the same time I am filled with sadness,
Since both the Dharma King and his
    consort
Have departed for the Pure Realms.
Life is short and fragile:
It is time for you to practice the divine
    Dharma!

King of great fortune,
Following the tradition of your ancestors,
You must come to the Pure Realm of
    central Tibet

With the aim of performing virtuous deeds
  of great magnitude.

If now, when you are young, you don't
  come,
You will regret it when you grow old.
It would be best if you came now.
Come, in the midst of your youth.

In the past, when your supreme mother,
  Abhe,
Came to central Tibet, she made such vast
  offerings
And distributed tea and alms to such an
  extent
That her fame spread across the whole
  land.

You, supreme being, her son,
Ought in the same way to make large
  offerings,
To offer tea, and distribute alms.
Such is my feeling; keep it in your heart.

When the Dharma King and his consort
Came to central Tibet,
They encountered neither hardship nor
  hindrances
And could accomplish all their noble aims.

Owing to the auspicious links they thus
  created,
It is certain that if you come to central
  Tibet [394a]
You will meet no difficulties or obstacles.
All favorable conditions will be gathered,
And you will accomplish your aims.

Earlier, I, the old man, offered
Ceremonies for your long life, to the best of
  my ability.
I shall continue to do so in the most careful
  way,
And pray to meet you before long.

Wherever these words are heard,
May auspiciousness and abundance be
  conferred upon the land,

May people enjoy long lives free of illness,
And may all their aspirations be fulfilled in
  accord with the Dharma.

I sent him this letter with some presents—a
gold coin and a rosary made of turquoise, corals,
and other precious jewels. When Pema Rangdrol
was about to leave, praying that we meet again
and again, I presented him with sacred objects of
body, speech, and mind, a *khatvanga* trident from
India, one silver *dotse*, turquoise, corals and other
precious stones.

At this time, the chief merchant Sonam
Rabgye offered me much gold. Instead of
accepting it, I offered it back to him, telling him
to add whatever was needed and offer a lamp of
solid gold before the speaking image of Guru
Padmasambhava (thus called because it actually
spoke on several occasions) at the top temple of
Riwo Trazang.[13] Accordingly, Sonam Rabgye
made a lamp with twenty *sang* of gold and offered,
too, a fund so that the lamp would always be
replenished with butter and burn day and night.
I also made extensive dedication prayers.

I visited Gyang Bumoche,[14] offered some
butter-lamps [394b], and continued on to
Drangmoche where I offered tea and alms and
stayed overnight. In this area, the Tsangpo River
often flooded and damaged the monastery and
the rest of the valley. The next day, on the way to
Chang Lhatse, I erected a placard with an
exhortation to the Three Protectors[15] and consecrated it, visualizing that the waters were diverted
to another direction, and uttering verses calling
for the power of truth to act. Later, by the compassion of the Three Jewels, the course of the
river changed and the valley and monastery were
safe. "This is a miraculous feat," said the people,
and their faith increased.

I was invited to visit the chieftain Tako, who
offered me a golden *ganjira* pinnacle brought from
China, some gold, silver, *tsampa*, and an abundance
of food and valuables. I placed the *ganjira* atop one
of the temples of Chang Lhatse, and offered tea
and alms to the monastic community. In return,
the monastery gave me much help.

Continuing on to Tsarong I spent a few
days at Mengon, where I offered a longevity

blessing to Chöying Drolma—the patroness of Tsarong,[16] a faithful noblewoman who always carried the Three Jewels as her crown ornament and persevered in virtuous deeds— and to all the local householders. I then gave her teaching on the nature of mind, ending with this advice:

Lord root guru, Vajradhara, through your
  blessing
May inner experiences and realization
  arise.

Listen, faithful Chöying Drolma,
I shall tell you how to maintain the
  recognition of mind's nature:

Rest without making efforts
In the expanse of clear emptiness,
Like a great garuda soaring through the
  skies.

Leave your mind as a brilliant radiance
Like the sun free from clouds.

Let mind's vivid cognition be free of
  clinging
Like a young child looking inside a temple.

Let your mind rest in serene, vast
  calmness,
Like an ocean free of waves [395a].

Let thoughts vanish without a trace,
Like a bird's flight that leaves no trace in
  the sky.

If you meditate as I have explained,
Meditation experiences and realization will
  arise like this:

An experience of transparent emptiness
  will arise,
Ineffable—just as space is ungraspable,
  indefinable.

An experience of clarity will arise,
Indescribable—like the dream of a mute.

An experience of bliss will arise,
Inexpressible—like the blissful pleasure of
  a young girl.

An experience of non-thought will arise,
Conceptless—like a corpse abandoned in a
  charnel ground.

Do not have any attachment
Toward whichever experience arises—
Bliss, clarity, or non-thought.
Simply allow it to remain in its vividness.

If you preserve the natural state of mind in
  this way,
At the moment of death you will be
  liberated in the dharmakaya.

Do not forget this advice, keep it at the
  core of your heart;
May it benefit the minds of all those who
  hear it.

This was helpful to all those assembled there. The elder and younger noblewomen and all the local people offered amber, pearls, corals, turquoises worth two hundred *sang*, and many bags of *tsampa*. Having made pure prayers of dedication, I distributed the *tsampa* to five hundred monks and sent all the butter to Tashi Lhunpo as an offering. Since I sent someone every two or three days, the inhabitants of Shigatse and the monks of Tashi Lhunpo started to ask, "Who are all these people?" "Lama Shabkar is coming; those are his monks," they were told. People wondered [395b], "What does Lama Shabkar look like? We must see him."

On the way to Shigatse, I visited Ngor Monastery,[17] met the throne-holder and, having presented him with some offerings, requested a spiritual connection. I offered tea and alms to all, and placed in the temple a large lamp made out of one *dotse* of Chinese silver.

When finally we reached Shigatse, to my great amazement about three thousand people— monks of Tashi Lhunpo, patrons, and householders—had gathered on both sides of the road to see us coming.

At Shigatse, I stayed at Guru Changma and, for many days, received many visitors, who offered me ceremonial scarves and coins.[18] I went to meet the Refuge and Protector, Panchen Rinpoche, at Tashi Kunkhyap Ling, the Abode of All Encompassing Auspiciousness. I presented to him one horse, two *dotse*, a large crystal dome for covering butter-lamps worth a hundred silver coins, and many other precious things. At Tashi Lhunpo, I offered in front of the golden reliquaries of Panchen Lobzang Yeshe and Panchen Palden Yeshe a large begging bowl gilded with three *sang* of gold, worth five *dotse*, and a big lamp made out of one *dotse* of silver. I offered tea and one coin to each of the thirty-eight hundred monks of the monastery.

One day, Panchen Rinpoche called me into his presence and said, "Bearing in mind the benefit of the Dharma and sentient beings, you restored the Great Stupa of Bodhnath. That was an excellent thing [396a]. Now, the Great Stupa of Many Gates of Auspiciousness, Tashi Gomang, at Chung Riwoche,[19] which was erected by the *siddha* Thangtong Gyalpo, the "King of the Empty Plains," to avert the invasions coming from Mongolia and western Tibet, and to bring peace and benefit to the Dharma in central Tibet, has been damaged by the depredations of time. Its thirteen rings have been destroyed by fire. With a pure motivation, you should go and restore it."

Having accepted his command, I prostrated myself and requested his spiritual protection. Praying to the Three Jewels, he put a long silken scarf around my neck, and when I took leave, said, "Muster your diligence and accomplish this task without discouragement. Today, auspicious connections have been established through your past pure prayers and aspirations; there is no doubt that you will succeed in your endeavor."

Confident in the truth of his words, instead of continuing on my journey I retraced my steps. On the way, I stopped a few days at Kagye, visiting the holy places, and finally reached Chung Riwoche. As I was getting things ready for the restoration work, Kunzang Nyentrak Rinpoche, a lama with a gentle nature from Drönla, who lived in perfect harmony with the Dharma, arrived with many monks. He offered me fifteen

gold *sho*, a hundred coins of silver, pieces of coral and turquoise, and a few silver reliquaries, requesting a spiritual connection. I offered him some teachings and a blessing of longevity. He also asked for advice, and I sang this song:

I bow down at your feet, protector [396b],
Lord guru, Dharma King Ngakyi
    Wangpo.
Gaze lovingly upon us;
Bless me and all my disciples.

O lama from Drönla in the north,
You obtained this precious, jewel-like
    human body,
Met many precious authentic teachers,
And practiced the teachings—how
    fortunate you are!

There is no happiness in samsara.
Especially, there is no meaning in
    accumulating wealth.
Life is short and can end at any time.

Henceforth, give up all concern for this life
And remain in mountain solitudes.

Pray to your lama from the core of your
    heart
And, without fixation, rest your mind in
    luminous emptiness.
Foster compassion for all sentient beings,
    your mothers.

To practice Dharma, one does not need
    many instructions.
Keep these in your heart, dear lama!

I pray to behold your face many times
    again,
From now until we reach enlightenment.

May the Buddha's teaching flourish
And may happiness befall all beings, our
    mothers!

In the fifth month of the Wood-Monkey Year,[20] with the treasurer Kalzang Trinley, Ladakh Khenpo, and the chieftain Tako as supervisors, about six hundred monks, nuns, and pilgrims began the work on the stupa. At one point the number of workers exceeded one thousand. Everyone worked in a playful and joyous mood, and soon the restoration of the entire stupa was completed, from top to bottom, within and without. We placed at the top thirteen rings and a *ganjira* pinnacle, all made of copper covered with gold.

After this, about six hundred monks spent days in the waters of the Tsangpo River piling up stones to raise the sagging iron bridge [397a]. Eventually, in the eighth month, the work was completed. On the festive day when I performed the consecration of the Great Stupa, about three thousand people gathered there—monks, nuns, and laypeople. We offered a *ganachakra* feast with fifty loads of *tsampa*, and I distributed alms to everyone—twenty-five *dotse* worth.

As a contribution for these restorations, Lama Kalden Rangdrol offered fifty *dotse*, Lama Jimba Norbu forty, Lama Gangriwa thirty, and the chieftain Tako a hundred *sho* of gold. Altogether, the disciples, patrons, and devoted householders made offerings amounting to seven hundred *dotse;* they are described in detail in the *Bright Mirror Record.*[21]

First the stupa was perfectly erected,
Second the stupa was perfectly restored,
Third dedication prayers were perfectly
    made:
Thus everything was perfect in the
    beginning, middle, and end.

By the compassion of the Two Victors,
    Father and Son,
By the dedicated faith of the disciples and
    patrons,
And by the power of my pure aspiration,
The restoration of the stupa has been well
    completed, O gods and men!

Skillful craftsmen offered a coat of gold
For the canopy and *ginzara* pinnacle, the
    thirteen rings,
And the thousand Buddha images:
See, how dazzlingly they radiate to all
    horizons!

E ma!
Faithful and skilled craftsmen, if you want
    to make a sacred object [397b]
For the sake of your future rebirths, make
    one like this.
Chiefs, whom the people respect and
    admire,
If you want to fulfill everyone's wishes, do
    something like this.
Wise and accomplished lamas,
If you want to benefit sentient beings and
    the Dharma, do something like this.
Mountain retreatants free of attachments,
If, like me, you are unable to remain in
    mountain retreat, do something like
    this.

By the strength of all meritorious deeds
Performed throughout the three times,
    represented by this one,
May the Buddha's teaching flourish and
    spread;
May all the great beings who hold this
    teaching enjoy excellent health;
May all beings have joy and happiness!

May all, without inequality, gather food,
    wealth, and people;
May all, without effort, enjoy renown and
    well-being;
May all, high or low, find happiness;
May all, without interruption, practice the
    Dharma day and night.

May whoever has made a connection with
    this Great Stupa,
Having perfected the two accumulations
    and rent the two veils,
Enjoy happiness in the present, and
    ultimately,
Having attained Buddhahood, guide all
    sentient beings.

Just as the *siddha* Thangtong Gyalpo
Made prayers and aspirations after
    erecting this stupa,
I now make prayers having performed its
    restoration:
May all these prayers be realized!

In all countries, may there be no illness for
   men and beasts,
May calamities never be heard of;
May people be healthy and live long;
May there be good harvests and abundant
   cattle;
May the auspiciousness of general
   happiness and felicity prevail!

At this point I sent *The Melody of Brahma*, a message to all my worthy disciples and faithful male
and female patrons of the three provinces of
Ngari in western Tibet, saying, "I shall now
return to Domey to help beings [398a]; if you
can, come to see me; if you can't, keep this
advice in mind:

I bow down to the compassionate Buddha,
Who first conceived the thought of
   enlightenment,
Then perfected the two accumulations,
And finally won ultimate Buddhahood.

With utter veneration, I prostrate myself
To the Victors, the Father and the Son,
And to all the great beings
Who skillfully spread the Buddha's
   teachings.

I pray with perpetual devotion
To my root master,
Whose kindness surpasses even that of the
   Buddha:
Protect me until I reach enlightenment!

Many years have passed since
I, the renunciate Tsogdruk Rangdrol,
   came here.
Now, I am old, close to death.
Even if I don't die now, I will not stay;
I am leaving for Domey.

Just as, among worldly people, a departing
   father
Gives a last admonition to his children,

So, with great tenderness, I shall now give
   some last advice
To all of you, faithful ones. Listen!

"Keeping in mind the life-examples of the
holy beings of the past, I have wandered at
random through many lands, pleasant dwellings, and mountain solitudes. A free, happy, and
relaxed renunciate, I have pondered the flaws of
samsara's cycle of births and deaths, and
renounced the affairs of this life.

"In the beginning, I followed an authentic
master and received the depth and breadth of his
instructions [398b]; in the middle, I put these
instructions into practice in mountain retreats;
and in the end I benefited the Dharma and
sentient beings as best I could. Especially, with
the welfare of the Dharma and sentient beings in
mind, I offered a mantle of precious gold to the
thirteen rings of the Great Stupa of Bodhnath.
Likewise, I have now offered a canopy, a pinnacle,
and thirteen rings of gilded copper to the Tashi
Gomang Stupa. If I don't die now but live longer, I
will go to Lower Kham to turn toward the Dharma
the minds of the faithful. Here is my advice while I
am alive, my testament when I am dead:

"Every day of your lives, remember that
phenomena are impermanent, unreliable, and
essenceless. Especially remember that life is short
and that death may strike at any time: the last
part of our lives may last no longer than the sun
setting on a mountain pass. Don't take for granted
that you will live long; instead, having thought,
'If I am going to die within a few days, what is the
best thing to do *now*?' persevere day and night in
Dharma practice—the best provision you can
make for next life. This is a crucial point.

"If you can't practice Dharma intensively,
under no circumstances should you commit evil
deeds such as taking life. At all times, cultivate
compassion for sentient beings, your mothers,
and have a good heart. Make vast aspirations for
the sake of beings. If you do, the sun of happiness
will doubtlessly shine upon this life and all your
lives to come [399a].

"May we—master, disciples, and patrons—
enjoy well-being in this and in future lives. Eventually, meeting in a Pure Realm, may we travel
together to millions of Buddhafields, make offer-

ings to the Buddhas, and bring all beings there. This is the sincere prayer I make.

"With my messengers, I send blessed images to touch on the crowns of your heads, protection cords to put around your necks, sacred substances to put in your mouths, and heart-advice for you to hear. When these reach you, feel the same joy as if we had met in reality!

I fervently pray from my heart
To the Dharma King, Ngakyi Wangpo:
With the eyes of compassion look upon me
And upon all my disciples and patrons;
Grant your blessing.

Disciples, worthy children of my heart,
And you, faithful patrons
Of the Three Provinces of Ngari in western Tibet,
Listen to this beneficial heart-advice.

I, the yogin Shabkarpa,
Wandering at random through various countries,
Staying in delightful mountain retreats,
Left my native land behind
And came to the Pure Realm of U-Tsang.

Thus I spent fifteen years
In the Three Provinces of Ngari in Tö,
And in the four districts of U and Tsang.
During these years, I was able to accomplish many religious activities.
Recalling these, I feel extremely fortunate [399b].

Now that I am old, I thought of staying
In this celestial field of central Tibet.
But this year, many devotees came from Domey
Insisting that I come to benefit beings
In the Three Ranges of Domey.[22]

They repeated their request so earnestly
That, feeling pity for them,
I let a promise escape my lips.

Henceforth, if I don't die and live longer,
In order to help other beings

I will surely, step by step,
Go to distant, secluded mountains,
Such as the Five-peaked Mountain of China.

Once I have gone, it seems that we will not meet again in this life.
Therefore, if we don't meet this one last time,
In the future, it will be difficult
Even to hear news of one another, let alone to meet.
It is like a death.

Just as a kind, loving mother
Always thinks of the child gone off to a distant land
Whom she may not see again, and whom she yearns to meet,
So when I am on the eve of leaving for Domey,
A place in which I shall never see you again,
I would like to meet you once more, disciples and patrons.

Therefore, I entreat those who truly want to see me one last time,
To come, within the Bird Year, to the Pure Realm of central Tibet.

I shall pray that all those who come
Encounter no difficulty at home and on the road,
Find favorable conditions, and see their aspirations fulfilled.

For most of you—those who yearn to come, yet are not able to do so
Because of the long distance to travel or adverse circumstances [400a]—
I am sending this letter and news.

In accordance with the lama's word, persevere in the divine Dharma.
I shall pray for you in such a way
That it will be the same as if you had come and met me.

In all our births to come,
May we, master and disciples, whose
    minds have merged as one,
Meet in the Buddhafield of Pure Joy, in the
    Blissful Buddhafield,
Or in any other Pure Realm of our wishes.

Here I offer you this letter,
These verses of heart-advice, meant to help
    you.

May all those who read it or hear it,
Enjoy a long life free of illness;
May the Dharma and auspiciousness
    increase!

Following this letter, most of my disciples and
patrons did come and we met before my departure for Domey.

On the way back from Chung Riwoche, I
visited most of the districts up to the end of that
valley, such as Tharpa Ling Rinchen Ding. At
Chang Lhatse I also went to the estate of the
chieftain Tako, and to most of the other villages
in the area. To all, I gave teachings and sang
spiritual songs, inspiring them to practice the
Dharma. Before leaving, as the chieftain Tako (a
person of great faith, generosity, and intelligence)
and his wife requested some spiritual advice. I
told them this:

I remember you always and supplicate you,
O divine master whose kindness
Is greater than that of the Buddhas of the
    three times.
Make all our aspirations come true!

Tako, wealthy benefactor of the Dharma,
And you, divine lady gifted with faith [400b],
Listen to this useful heart-advice.

Birth ends in death, gathering in separation,
Accumulation in exhaustion, and rise in
    fall.

There is no substance to samsaric dharmas;
Strive from your heart in the divine
    Dharma.

In the best case, to attain Buddhahood in
    this very life,
As the yogin Jetsun Milarepa did,
Banish all concern with this existence alone
And spend your whole life practicing in
    solitary places.

In the middling case, to go to a
    Buddhafield at death,
Guard your vows and *samayas* purely,
And stay in a monastery, exerting yourself
    in religious practice.

In the least case, to obtain another human
    birth,
Like the householder Anathapindika[23]
Even though you live at home,
Work hard at doing prostrations and
    circumambulations,
And at making offerings, giving charity,
    and saying prayers.

In essence, don't fuel discursive thoughts.
At all times and in all circumstances
Let your mind rest in the state of luminous
    void,
And develop vast compassion and a good
    heart.

I, "White Foot," a wanderer,
Having spoken this helpful advice, set out
    on my way;
You who remain should never forget it
But keep it in mind.

If, because of the great distance between
    us,
We don't meet again in this life,
May we meet in our future lives
And remain together in a Pure Realm.

They did many prostrations and circumambulations, praying that we would meet many
times again, and presented me with many offerings.

From there, I visited Ganden Phuntsokling,[24]
the seat of the omniscient Jonangpa, Jetsun Taranatha, where I offered tea and alms to the monks.

From the wooden blocks there, I had printed a set of the eighteen volumes of Taranatha's writings, and took it with me [401a]. I then paid homage at the great statue of Maitreya at Drophu in Botong Tashigang, and offered tea and alms.

Finally I came back to Tashi Lhunpo, where I met the supreme all-knowing Panchen Lama. I offered him the copper and the other materials left over from the stupa's restoration, as well as two fine horses and all the gold, silver, amber, coral, turquoise, and everything else I had been offered while helping beings along the way. I requested a spiritual connection from him, and with great kindness he gave me a longevity empowerment, and the transmission for the teachings on the *Graded Path* and on *Mind Training* found in the writings of the former Panchens. He also gave me about fifty volumes—the collected writings of Lord Tsongkhapa and his two chief disciples, and the writings of the successive Panchen incarnations—and a painting of Chakrasamvara that had been hanging in his room, a yellow shawl that had belonged to the former Panchen Lama, and many "seven-rebirth pills."[25] He also gave to me, and to four of my students, a monk's jacket, protection cords, ceremonial scarves, and many other presents. Especially he gave me this letter for the general benefit of the Dharma and all beings in Domey:

Here is a proclamation from the Shakya bhikshu, Lobzang Palden Tenpai Nyima Chogle Namgyal, "Intelligent All-Victorious Sun of the Glorious Doctrine," someone with perfect courage for holding and spreading the unbroken tradition of the Fourth Buddha of this fortunate aeon, the Matchless Companion of the Sun:

This is a message for those on this earth who enjoy the mandala of intelligence [401b]—the treasure-lode of this world—and especially for the lamas, teachers, and ordained persons; for the notables who hold the rank, according to the golden edicts of the great Emperor, of Wang,[26] Pi'i ling, Pa'i ling, Gung, Jasag, Miring, Jagi Rukshi, Thabunang, Jesang, Misang, Dorokha, and for the inhabitants, religious and lay, high and low, of the forty-nine districts of Mongolia, of the shore of Lake Trishok Gyalmo, Xining,

Tongkhor, the Six Ranges of Dokham, Golok, Rang Ngen, Arik, and other places:

May the sole source of happiness,
The Buddha's Dharma, long remain.

In accordance with these words, the ground and support for the present happiness and ultimate felicity of all beings is indubitably the precious teachings of the Victorious Ones—the teachings themselves and the realization that stems from them. For the Dharma to remain, the Tripitaka needs to be heard and contemplated by the sangha, and the Three Trainings need to be meditated upon.

The renunciate Shabkar Tsogdruk Rangdrol has been acting in accordance with the Dharma in an exalted way since his youth. Not only that, within our land enclosed by snow peaks, at many extraordinary sacred places and mountain solitudes he has exerted himself in the contemplative practice of the teachings he heard.

More especially, as means to avert foreign invasions, he restored the Great Stupa of Glorious Riwoche erected by Thangtong Gyalpo [402a], which had been damaged over the course of time. As the fruit of his pure prayers and his lofty intelligence, with the purest motivation he has restored the Tashi Gomang Stupa, the temple around it, and whatever else needed repair, exhorting to virtue everyone in upper, central, and western Tibet. To the stupa, above the main structure, he offered thirteen rings and a canopy, all made of gilded copper and executed in the finest and most complete way.

In many monasteries and holy sites, he has placed new victory banners and Dharma-wheels of copper gilt. He has made large offerings, including ritual implements made of precious substances, to the two Jowos—the Crowned Buddhas of Lhasa—the precious golden reliquary of the second Dalai Lama, and other sacred objects and relics of the three kinds. He has made clouds of offerings and given service to all religious communities without making any sectarian distinctions: in essence, he has accomplished splendid and mighty virtuous acts which fulfill the intentions of the Victorious Ones and set the finest kind of example for all beings. He has thus become an object of praise.

Wherever he goes and whatever he does in upper, central, and western Tibet, for the good of all, everyone, high and low, should assist him by providing him food, housing, a place to rest, and whatever else he might need. You must listen to his admonition to give up all acts of enmity, [402b] banditry, theft, and other actions that harm sentient beings and to his entreaties to perform virtuous deeds.

This is to be understood by all. I shall always keep in my prayers, and under my spiritual protection, those who act according to this command. Those who transgress it will, without doubt, suffer fierce punishments from the ocean of oath-bound protectors. Be careful!

This letter, clear in meaning, was written on an auspicious day in the twelfth month of the Wood-Monkey Year,[27] from the Lofty Banner of the All-Victorious Palace, at the great monastery of Tashi Lhunpo.

Having affixed his great seal on this decree, he gave it to me rolled up in three lengths of yellow brocade. When taking leave, I asked him never to cast me out from his spiritual protection and to pray that I might be able to meet him again. He did so, adding, "Come back soon, and we will meet."

Then, accompanied by five hundred monks and nuns, I went to Nyamo where the chieftains Tenpa, Drupchen Chödar, and Chöla were most helpful. I performed a longevity blessing, taught the Dharma, and made prayers of dedication and auspiciousness. Through Rongchung, we then reached Nyemo. The chieftain Köchagpa offered over a hundred bags of *tsampa*, and others made many offerings, too [403a]. We offered a vast *ganachakra* feast and distributed the *tsampa*. Carrying whatever they could, one after the other, all my companions reached Lhasa.

I stayed behind and gave long-life blessings and teachings, inspiring all the householders to practice the Dharma. Many patrons, such as the chieftain Marlam and the administrator of Kalön Thönpa's estate, gave me provisions and valuables; many of them became Dharma practitioners.

I then went to Rina Monastery where I met our root teacher, Orgyen Tendzin Rinpoche,[28] to whom I offered five *sho* of gold. I also offered tea and alms to the monks. Arriving at Lhasa, I stayed at the house of Kalön Zurkhang, who offered me exceptional help—whatever could be needed—and became among all my patrons the one toward whom I felt the greatest gratitude.

At that time, Khenpo Shiwa Tsering suffered from edema and was close to death. I performed many curative ceremonies and gave him some medicine. He recovered. To express his thanks, he offered me two *dotse*, which I contributed for alms to be distributed at the Great Prayer Festival of Lhasa.

One day I went to behold the golden face of the Refuge and Protector, the Dalai Lama Tsultrim Gyatso.[29] I offered him the mandala and sacred objects symbolic of the body, speech, and mind of the Buddhas; a large, transparent glass dome made in a distant country, to place over a butter-lamp; one *dotse* of gold; and other valuables worth five *dotse* [403b]. I requested from him the transmission of the *Prayer to the Lords of the Three Families* and of the *Praise of Dependent Arising*.[30]

Following this I went to meet the regent-king of Tibet, Tsemön Lingpa,[31] and presented with him a pair of binoculars and one *dotse*, asking him for a spiritual connection.

Then I gave a long-life empowerment to my hosts, the family of Kalön Zurkhang. I was also called to the houses of Kalön Thönpa, Samdrup Phodrang, the Dalai Lama's mother Döndrup Drolma, and Khenpo Chakzampa; to all, I gave longevity blessings and taught the Dharma as well as I knew how. Pleased, they presented with me many *dotse*, which I offered for distribution at the Great Prayer Festival of Lhasa. From the Muslims and Nepalese merchants, down to the poor people living in the horn-fence huts,[32] whoever called upon me, I answered their requests, went to their homes, and said prayers of auspiciousness. They offered many silver coins. I also gave this advice for long life to all the patrons:

I bow down with respect to all the deities of longevity,

Who have achieved deathlessness:
Please make firm the lives of all those
Who accomplish spiritual deeds.

To have a long and happy life free of
illness,
Receive blessings of longevity from the lamas,
Pray to the Three Jewels,
Recite the *Drum of Deathlessness*, the *dharani*
of long life,
Offer tea to the monastic communities,
Give alms to the poor,
Respect and serve old people,
Give assistance and medicine to the
sick[404a],
Make the *Hundred Torma Offering* and the
Water Torma Offering, and
Ransom the lives of as many animals as
you can, and set them free.

Don't say bad or harsh words;
Instead, give good advice and make wishes
of auspiciousness.

At all times, whether sitting or moving,
Visualize the guru Amitayus on the top of
your head
And supplicate him fervently,
Thinking that he confers upon you the
siddhi of long life.

Visualize the whole universe as the
Buddhafield of Amitayus,
And yourself and others as Amitayus,
Having forms of light, vivid yet empty;
Consider all sounds to be the resonance of
the *jivantiye* mantra,
And the nature of your mind to be the
deathless dharmakaya.

Recite the *dharani* of longevity as much as
you can,
Make dedication prayers for a long life free
of illness,
And recite verses of auspiciousness.

In our time there are many obstacles to
life,

Therefore do these recitations and you will
live long!

May whoever hears and reads this excellent advice
Enjoy the happiness of a long and healthy
life.

Most of them followed this advice and lived
a long time. Many disciples with good karmic
tendencies, able to help beings and to serve the
Dharma, such as Tendzin Nyima from Tögar
and Tendzin Rangdrol from Nyemo, came at
this time. I gave them empowerments and
instructions, thus setting them on the path of
maturation and liberation. All my monks and
nuns did fasting practices and made many circumambulations of the two Jowos, drawing the
admiration of all the faithful.

After we had stayed one month in Lhasa, I
went to Khardo Samten Ling,[33] the wondrous
seat of my kind root master, the lord of *siddhas*
Khardo Chökyi Dorje Rinpoche [404b]. This
sacred place was first blessed by an heir of Jetsun
Mila's lineage, the precious Shang Yudrak
Gonpo,[34] whose fame resounded in all directions. Having paid great service to the Jowo of
Lhasa and established many monastic communities in this area, Yudrak Gonpo came to stay in
this sacred place of Khardo. He performed splendid deeds for the sake of the Dharma and all
beings, and caused the Kagyu teachings to shine
like the sun.

Then came the fifth Dalai Lama, the protector of Tibet, Avalokiteshvara in human form,
who, having brought everything under his power
in an overwhelming way,[35] made the tradition of
the great lord Tsongkhapa become as bright as
the sun. At the time of the sixth Dalai Lama,
Tsangyang Gyatso, Desi Rinpoche[36] built in
Khardo a residence resembling the gem atop the
victory banner, and the Dalai Lama came and
blessed the place.

Söpa Gyatso,[37] who gained matchless realization through the great prayers he made for
the tradition of the Great Lord, lived in Khardo
for a long time. Exemplifying the perfect lives of
liberation of the Kadampas, he vastly benefited

the Dharma and all beings, established a retreat center, and erected many sacred objects symbolic of the enlightened body, speech, and mind. He took rebirth as Chöden Wangpo, who himself was reborn as the lord of *siddhas*, Chökyi Dorje [405a]. Both of them devoted themselves to the essence of spiritual practice and, as a result, could vastly benefit the Dharma and all beings.

Many other great beings also came to this holy place, conquered the stronghold of unwavering inner calm, and, catapulting the boulder of unerring insight, pulverized their archenemies: the five confusions, the eight worldly dharmas, and the misconception that beings and phenomena are real. Thus Khardo Samten Ling, the "Stone Citadel of Contemplation," lived up to its name.

The place has excellent qualities: facing south, it basks in the sun all year; it remains cool in summer so that mind is clear. Water, firewood, and other necessities abound. At its back is a beautiful and lofty rock mountain; to the east is a colony of vultures, which reminds the renunciates and meditators of death and of the need to remain steadfast in their caves, meditating. Pleasant caves of all sizes form beautiful roofs; from time to time mist wreaths the mountain's neck like a silver scarf. Those gifted with good predispositions stemming from their former purification long to take mist as their clothing and caves as hats. Meadows of medicinal plants are strewn with multicolored flowers in which bees buzz their songs, inviting skilled physicians to collect medicinal leaves, flowers, and fruits [405b].

The place is immaculate, with fragrant odors, bright smooth stones, finely shaped hills, and a lofty summit from which one can see far and wide, inviting the families of noblemen and the young Nepalese merchants to come in the summer for joyful picnics.

The cattle herded by the nomad tribes in the meadows up the hill feed on grasses full of strong medicinal herbs. Drinking the curd and whey that comes from the milk of the cows thus cures most illnesses of wind, bile, and phlegm. As they sit, relax, or wander about the slopes, shepherds sing witty songs, making the practitioners who live on the mountain laugh.

Springs of pure water with eight excellent qualities continuously fill ponds in which tadpoles and other water creatures are gracefully moving. The water is cool, and just a sip of it quenches one's thirst. It is perfectly pure; bathing in it cleanses the body and gives a feeling of well-being one has never felt before.

Amid the crags and on the high meadows, wild sheep, musk deer, and many other wild animals live at ease, their young gamboling playfully. Snow cocks, celestial laughing-thrushes, and many other lovely birds, fly happily from place to place, singing sweetly [406a], bringing such delight to those who arrive here that they feel compelled to stay a few days.

In summer, between the fourth and fifth months, the blue cuckoo arrives. The cuckoo, the king of birds, shows off his beauty as it moves about, calling out sweetly, reminding people of the homelands they've left behind; thinking of home, they also think back to when they spent time talking with their kind old parents. The cuckoo's poignant call also makes meditators, who have renounced this life in order to wander through the mountain wilderness, recall vividly the abode of their root lama and the teachings he gave. "This is what the lama said; those were the spiritual companions with pure *samaya* who were there; such were the spiritual conversations we shared, the jokes we enjoyed." Melancholy arises, and tears well up in their eyes.

There are plenty of edible plants here—nettles, wild garlic, bitter roots, and berries—nourishing and succulent, which makes the hermits recall Milarepa's life and thus appreciate the fortunate opportunity of a simple and austere life.

It is wonderful to see the temples and the sacred relics of body, speech, and mind they shelter—they are supreme objects of offering and prostration, inspiring those who live here to perfect the accumulations of merit and wisdom easily by making offerings, prostrations, and circumambulations [406b]. On the sides of the hills are other pleasant hermitages where one's awareness becomes clear. Those are inhabited by spiritual teachers and companions who practice in harmony with the Dharma and give whatever initiations and instructions beginners may need to dispel obstacles and to progress.

Down in the valley is the pleasant city of Lhasa, where all desirable things, food and wealth, are gathered, ensuring that whatever one needs for one's sustenance will come of its own accord.

Brought together by our pure aspirations and good karma, I, the wandering yogin Shabkarpa, and my disciples came to this perfect place. When, following my teacher's word, I was meditating in the Great Cavern of Brilliant Light where Khardo Söpa Gyatso practiced in the past, I was driven by sheer enthusiasm to sing this praise in verse:

Lama who grants all blessings,
Yidam deities who grant all *siddhis*,
Dakinis who dispel all obstacles:
Rain upon us blessings and *siddhis*.

Near the Emanated Temple of Lhasa,
The peer of the Diamond Throne of
    India;
Near the Potala Palace, the seat of
    Avalokiteshvara,
The protector of the Land of Snows;
Near many monastic communities,
Such as Sera, Ganden, and Drepung,
Lies the secluded hermitage of Khardo
    Samten Ling,
Where the Dharma of spiritual practice
    blooms [407a],
Where many wise and realized beings live,
Where dakinis and Dharma protectors
    assemble,
Where gods who delight in virtue abide.

The many-colored mountainside,
An excellent, unsullied site,
Faces south, offering a vast, open view:
In summer, the fragrant breeze is cooling;
In winter, basking in sun all day, the
    mountainside stays warm.

Behind it, cliffs rise up, lofty and majestic;
On one side is a colony of vultures
That make the mountain hermits think,
"This is the kind of place we need!"

It is wrapped in silvery mists,
And is capped becomingly with many
    caves
That make one want to wear
Mist as a mantle and a cave as a hat.

On the slopes are grasslands
With thickets of medicinal plants
And meadows blanketed with bright
    flowers—
Physicians come here to collect medicinal
    herbs.

The mountain is rich in colors;
Its range unfolds in splendid shapes.
Climbing to the summit, one can see far
    and wide.
This is why noble families and merchants
Come here to enjoy pleasant excursions.

The nomads' cows eat potent medicinal
    herbs,
And therefore drinking their curd and
    whey
Naturally cures most diseases.

Shepherds, here and there on the mountain,
Sing spirited songs that make renunciates
Meditating nearby burst out in laughter.

The pure, fresh, limpid springs nearby
Are enlivened by tadpoles and other tiny
    creatures.
Just by drinking or bathing in this water,
Well-being increases and awareness
    becomes clear.

All kinds of wild animals frolic there
    [407b];
Large and small birds emit sweet calls—
Whoever comes here is enchanted,
And wishes nothing more but to stay on.

In summer, the blue cuckoo parades
His beauty and voices his clear calls.
Remembering the father guru
One cannot help but weep.

Nettles, wild garlic and other edible plants
Provide food for the ascetic,
Making one recall Milarepa's life
And wish to live in a completely simple
    way.

Supreme objects of offering and respect,
Temples shelter relics of body, speech, and
    mind, potent with blessing,
Allowing hermits to offer prostrations and
    circumambulations
Along with their meditation.

In the hermitages, here and there,
Live spiritual teachers and spiritual
    companions
Who give initiations and instructions
To beginners, who need them.

Below lies the pleasant town of Lhasa,
Where all food and desirable things
    abound;
From there faithful and wealthy patrons
Will provide one with sustenance.

E ma! Holy place filled with perfections,
Stone Citadel of Contemplation,
I had the good fortune to come
To your Great Cave of Brilliant Light.

Concentrating on spiritual practice
As my master directed me,
I pray again and again that as the fruit of
    my practice,
I may benefit the Dharma and sentient
    beings.

You who aspire from your hearts
To emulate the example of your forefathers,
And give up all thoughts of this life
To live in harmony with the Dharma,
Come here, and you will succeed!

Faithful ones who want to do pilgrimage,
Physicians who want to collect medicinal
    plants [408a],
Noblemen who want to enjoy delightful
    recreation—

Come here, and good will come about for
    all.

By the merit of having praised this holy
    place,
May Dharma practitioners remain in
    mountain retreats!
May all countries enjoy good harvests!
May everyone practice the Dharma!

I stayed nine months in this place, persevering in practice. In between sessions, I composed the *Amazing Emanated Scripture*,[38] a treatise that leads one to consider the flaws of the five sense pleasures in general, and especially the craving for food, clothing, and sex. It then tells of the need to rid oneself of the preoccupations of this life, to devote oneself to spiritual practice in remote solitudes, and be unattached to body, life, and possessions.

Then Kardri of Tsapo, Tsegön Tsultrim, and many other people from Domey arrived in Khardo. I gave them empowerments and instructions. The main disciples stayed in the monastery and most of the other monks and nuns, living almost like wild animals, stayed at the foot of overhanging cliffs and large boulders.

On the twenty-fifth of the tenth month,[39] when the monastic estates are illuminated, we offered countless butter-lamps on all the nearby rocks, so that the place looked like a sky filled with stars. For a few hours the whole hillside was covered with twinkling lights. People could see it from Lhasa and rejoiced, while, amazed, children exclaimed, "Look up there!"

For a few months after this, I gave one session of teaching daily which was attended by hundreds, sometimes thousands of people [408b]—spiritual masters, disciples, monks and nuns, patrons, laymen and laywomen, who came from all directions. I gave the authorizing blessing for the *Hundred Sadhanas, Source of Jewels*,[40] the empowerment of the *Sixteen Spheres of the Kadampas*,[41] and the transmission and explanations on the *Great Graded Path*, the *Teachings of the Kadampas*, the *Metaphors for the Graded Path*, "*Heap of Jewels*," the *Ultimate Graded Path*, "*The Beryl Vase*,"[42] as well as on the *Emanated Scriptures* I had composed myself. I could thus be helpful to all my disciples and patrons.

The last day of the teachings, on the occasion of the thanksgiving feast, Lama Rabgye from Tö offered seven *dotse* and other valuables, worth altogether fifteen *dotse*. The Dharma practitioner from Ruthok offered two *dotse* and other objects, worth altogether five *dotse*. Lama Rigdzin Orgyen Namgyal offered three *dotse*. At various times, the disciples and patrons offered about seven hundred *sho* of gold, a lot of silver coins, and many *dotse*. I used the gold to make an offering to the regent Tsemön Lingpa, and later to make a general distribution of tea and money at the Great Prayer Festival.

Following this, the reembodiment of the great *siddha* Khardo Rinpoche was enthroned. I offered seven *dotse* and did my best to help with the enthronement. The treasurer and two daughters of the former incarnation were extremely pleased and offered me one of his hats, a complete set of his clothes, seven *thangka* paintings that had been the objects of Kardo Rinpoche's meditation, and many precious relics [409a].

I offered to the main temple of Sera a lamp made out of fifty *dotse* of silver, and made a general distribution of tea and alms. I gave supplies of tea, butter, and *tsampa* to most of the thousands of disciples, monks, nuns, householders, and pilgrims who had gathered at Khardo. From time to time, I offered a *ganachakra* feast, using ten to twenty loads of *tsampa*. Altogether I offered tea and soup thirteen times to the monks of the three monasteries of Sera, Ganden, and Drepung—the supreme field for accumulating merit. That year, I twice offered tea, soup, and a coin to each of the monks participating in the Great Prayer Festival.[43] I gave one coin each to two thousand beggars. For all that I spent over one hundred *dotse*. I dedicated all the merit of this to the flourishing of the Buddha's Dharma—the source of present happiness and ultimate contentment—and to the welfare and felicity of all beings.

One day my attendant Khepa asked me to explain the significance of my hat. I answered with these words:

The name of the hat that I,
The renunciate Tsogdruk Rangdrol, wear
  on my head,
Is the Lotus Cap That Liberates on Sight.

As for the significance of its elements,
Meaningful to whoever beholds them:

Its yellow color signifies
That the Buddha's teaching is alive.

Its lofty height symbolizes [409b]
The loftiness of the Three Jewels.

Its beautiful pinnacle banner of victory
  symbolizes
Raising the victory banner of
  Shakyamuni's teachings.

The rainbow-colored border symbolizes
Its being imbued with the five wisdoms.

The three lotus petals at the front
  symbolize
The attainment of the fruit of the three
  kayas.

The multiple colors also symbolize
The accomplishment of beings' benefit
  through the four activities.

Its slight curve forward symbolizes
Fervent devotion to the spiritual master.

Wearing it upon my head symbolizes
Placing everyone above myself.

May everyone practice the Dharma
In accordance with this meaning.

When it came time for Lama Rabgye to leave, I gave him, as an object of faith, a fine statue of the Crowned Buddha beautifully set with various jewels, for the making of which I had spent a hundred *sang*. As a permanent fund for his monastery, I gave to the practitioner of Ruthok one *dotse* of Chinese silver and a big silver butter-lamp. Likewise, I gave suitable farewell presents to all those who were departing. Most of them went to their own places and raised, in mountain retreats, the victory banner of spiritual practice.

Then, with many monks and nuns, I came down to Lhasa. While I was performing *ganachakra* offerings, the monks and nuns, led by Lama Jimba Norbu, did the long circumambulation around Lhasa, doing full prostrations all the way. They filled the circumambulation path so that other people could hardly find space to walk. Everyone said they did not remember ever having seen so many people circumambulating doing full prostrations. People would also come to watch when we were offering *ganachakra* feasts [410a].

I stayed in Lhasa for five months. My disciples and I completed several thousand fasting practices. The patrons and faithful people of Lhasa provided everyone with sustenance. On the full moon of the fourth month,[44] my monks and nuns bought all the flowers from the Lhasa merchants and offered them to the mandala of the Great Compassionate One, filling it completely.

During my stay in Lhasa, every eighth and fifteenth of the month we would knead loads of *tsampa* and, while doing the long circumambulation, feed some to the dogs. We would also take three or four huge hide bags of white *tsampa* and distribute it to the beggars. To the sick, the blind, and poor cripples, I would give coins. After I had done this several times, both humans and dogs recognized me and would rush toward me whenever they saw me coming.

Because I was trying in these ways to help and protect the poor people and beggars from Upper, Lower and Middle Tibet, most of the beggars would speak of me as their "protector." The other inhabitants of Lhasa, too, would say, "the refuge and protector Shabkarpa."

At that time two Indian sadhus—those ascetics who renounce meat, alcohol, onions, and garlic, are celibate, practice pure conduct, and wander at random from place to place—having

heard of me, came to meet me [410b]. "You don't cling to wealth; you give to the beggars; that is truly excellent. Your way of being is like that of many of our gurus in India. Your conduct is also like ours. We feel happy about that. There are many learned lamas in Tibet, but those with compassion like yours are rare. O Bodhisattva guru, give us your spiritual protection! We pray to meet you again in the blissful paradise of Sukhavati." Having prayed with these words, they prostrated themselves, and touched their heads to my feet. After they left for India, I often wondered what had become of them.

I was told that some old lamas from Sera and Ganden were saying to each other, "These days, below the two Victors, Lama Shabkar has become even more famous than the throne-holder of Ganden. He must have a special power for magnetizing people." A lama remarked, "Magnetizing rituals alone can't achieve such results; his gathering of so many people is due to the Bodhicitta which soaks his being." Another concluded, "Anyway, we don't know the reason, but, however one looks, one cannot find fault with his conduct. So, don't criticize him."

I went to Ganden for two days and paid homage to the great Golden Reliquary. I filled the golden lamp with butter a hundred times. Next, I went to Chimphu [411a] and Drakmar Yama Lung,[45] where I stayed a few days making offerings, prostrations, circumambulations, *ganachakra* feasts, and dedication prayers. I went down to Samye and for fifteen days my monks and nuns did many full prostrations. I made large offerings, praying to benefit the Dharma and sentient beings. During my stay, the governor and his wife, who lived near the Red Stupa, provided me with all I could need. Upon my departure they presented me with the collection of the *Seven Treasuries* and of Gampopa's writings.[46]

I then went to Densathil, the seat of Lord Phagmo Drupa;[47] it is a sublime holy place in southern Tibet. My people and I offered our services to the Tibetan government's dignitary in charge of the restoration of the main temple, and gave one *dotse* as a contribution for the work. About five hundred monks and nuns gathered there; they devoted themselves exclusively to practices of purification and accumulation of merit, doing retreat and recitations. I provided most of them with tea, butter and *tsampa*. From time to time we would knead ten to fifteen loads of *tsampa*, add gum to it, and shape it in the form of Mount Meru. We would arrange many offerings around it and hold a great *ganachakra* feast offering.

It was then that Gangshar Rangdrol, "Self-liberation of All That Arises," a close disciple of the precious and powerful *siddha* of the Great Perfection,[48] came from Domey with my disciple Kunzang Rangdrol, my patron the chieftain Bendhe Thar [411b], and many Mongolian na-trons. With Lama Gangshar offering one *dotse*, alto-gether they offered one hundred *sang*. Bendhe Thar explained to me the reasons why I should come to Domey, and my close disciple Kunzang Rangdrol presented me with this written supplication:

To your body—endowed with the marks and signs born of your perfect twofold gathering *(Tsok)*;
To your speech—endowed with the sixty *(Drug)* branches, fulfilling the hopes of the multitude of beings,
To your mind—all-seeing, the self-liberation *(Rangdrol)* of obscurations;
To your body, speech, and mind, which grant all excellence, I bow down.

Embodiment of the compassion of infinite totally Victorious Ones,
Avalokiteshvara, color of the totally white snow mountains,
Lord Shabkar, protector and refuge of totally obscured beings,
You whose totally resplendent name is renowned throughout the world—
Pay heed to me!

In accordance with each fortunate *(Kalden)* being's own *(Rang)* nature,
You turn the blessed Dharma-wheel of maturation and liberation *(Drol)*,[49]
Realized one, destroyer of illusion *(Trulshik)*,
Spontaneously accomplished vidyadhara *(Lhundrup Rigdzin)*,

Listen for a while to the song of this faithful one.

The essence of this request made by me—
A person in whom good qualities, intelligence, and the like,
Are as rare as gems and as rabbit horns;
Who made the short path of Samantabhadra's *(Kunzang)* wisdom
And self-liberation *(Rangdrol)* into a long one—
Is as follows:

Forsaking my native land and father, mother, and relatives,
Traveling along an arduous road
So that beings could be established in happiness,
I came to central Tibet to invite you, old father [412a].

Sublime Dharma Lord, having come to central Tibet,
You may delight at the land being filled with Dharma practitioners,
But how can you forsake your homeland which is bereft of Dharma?
I feel immense sadness at the many non-dharmic actions committed there.

In the past the mighty Victor Born from the Lake,
Abandoned the king and disciples of Tibet
And went to the southwest continent of Chamara[50]
To subdue the untamed *rakshasas*.

Similarly, precious refuge and protector,
I ask that you part from your disciples and patrons of U-Tsang,
And come this year to Domey, your homeland,
To turn toward the Dharma the minds of the untamed people there.

E ma!
Heed me, precious guru!

If, pleased by the large offerings of gold
    and silver
Made by the disciples of the Three
    Provinces of Ngari in western Tibet,
You forget Domey, which has no gold and
    silver,
Aren't you transgressing the Bodhicitta
    vow?

So many men and women of Domey, reli-
    gious and lay,
Have died in sadness, their minds turned
    toward you.
The hearts of those still alive
Are filled with hope, thinking that this year
You, their ultimate protector, will come.

I do not have anything to request—
    divinations, relics, blessed pills, or
    predictions—
From the two Jowos and from the
    Victorious Dalai and the Panchen;
I only request that you come back this year
    to Amdo.

After having spent seven to ten years in
    Amdo,
If you wish to return to U, Tsang, and Tö
    Ngari,
We, disciples and patrons,
Will take you back to central Tibet [412b].

At your feet,
Protector who loves all beings without
    distinction,
While you sit, surrounded without cease
By spiritual friends whose discipline is
    without flaw
And patrons whose wealth is without end,
I the vagabond Kunzang Rangdrol,
    without Dharma,
Not daring to say this directly, being
    without offerings,
Inscribed these words on paper without
    stain,
And offer them to your eyes, O lama with-
    out peer!

By the merit of this, may you, protector of
    the three worlds,
Come soon from the four districts of
    U-Tsang
To the land of Domey.

May this be an auspicious omen
So that the fortunate beings
Who need to be transformed there
Become established in the splendor of the
    tenth *bhumi*.

I promised to go. Lama Kunzang Rangdrol
decided to stay. After I had given them relics of
the three kinds and provisions for the road, Lama
Gangshar (to whom I offered the text of the
Sangwa Yeshe cycle of Olkha)[51] and the other
patrons left with most of the bundles containing
my books.

From time to time, I turned the Wheel of
the Dharma for the disciples assembled
there, giving them explanations on the *Swift Path*,
the *Seven-Point Mind Training*, the *Coemergent
Mahamudra*, the *Great Perfection That Dispels Darkness*, and other teachings. Then they endeavored
in whichever practices they wished.

In answer to the request of my faithful and
intelligent disciple Yonten Gyatso, "Ocean of
Good Qualities," I sang this song in praise of that
great holy place [413a]:

Father lamas, I supplicate you:
Look with compassion upon all of us
    gathered here.

Densathil is the central seat of the holy
    Kagyu forefathers,
A paradise where infinite peaceful and
    wrathful deities abide,
Where mother dakinis and Dharma
    protectors gather.

The mountains behind this perfect forest
    hermitage
Are like a king seated on his throne;
The rocky mountains on the left, mounds
    of jewels;

The meadowed mountain on the right, a
    majestic elephant;
The Tsangpo river in front, a water offering;
The inner valley, a blooming white lotus;
And the temple at its center, its pistil.

In this temple are kept innumerable sacred
    objects.[52]
The whole place is like the Unsurpassable
    Buddhafield.

Whoever yearns to emulate the lives of the
    Kagyu forefathers
Should plant here the victory banner of
    spiritual practice.
Whoever aspires to obtain the supreme
    and common *siddhis*,
Should make offerings and *ganachakra* feasts
    here.
Whoever wants to purify his or her karma
    and wrongdoings,
Should offer prostrations and
    circumambulations here.

By the merit created by this song,
May the Dharma of the practice lineage
    spread.

Celestial and human beings all rejoiced at
this praise. The householders living below this
holy site asked me to make it rain. I told them
that I did not know the special instructions for
bringing rain, but that I would pray to the Three
Jewels [413b]. With a pure motivation, I supplicated the Three Jewels to bring a beneficial rain.
I then rested in meditation, visualizing that the
blessings of the Victorious Ones of the ten directions, and the merit gathered throughout the
three times by myself and others took the shape
of a huge cloud, filling the whole sky, from which
rain fell in drops as big as spindles. The same
evening it rained heavily, without any thunder-
storm, and everyone's wish was fulfilled. Henceforth, rain always fell whenever needed and the
area enjoyed good harvests.

Drolma Kyidzom, the wife of Dagpo
Drumpa,[53] having offered me some of her jew-

elry and many gifts and provisions, asked me
persistently for a supplication prayer to my past
incarnations. In answer I spoke this:

Many, many aeons ago,
Having swiftly attained perfect
    Buddhahood,
To benefit sentient beings and the
    teachings of the Conqueror,
He manifested in whatever manner was
    appropriate to transform beings.

At the time of the Buddha he was
    Avalokiteshvara,
In the land of India he was
    Manjushrimitra,[54]
In the center of Tibet he became Trenpa
    Namkha,
In the Kagyu tradition he was Milarepa,
In the Kadampa lineage he was the
    glorious Gyalse Thogme,
In the Ganden lineage he was the Lord
    Lodrö Gyaltsen,
In the nonsectarian lineage he manifested
    to beings as Thangtong Gyalpo.

Now he is the protector of beings,
    Shabkarpa [414a].
In future, in the presence of the Lords of
    the Five Families,
In True Joy and every other Buddhafield,
He will be a supreme son
Who will lead all those who have made a
    connection with him
To the Pure Realm of their wish.

To him, who in the past, present, and
    future,
Did, does, and will manifest multiple
    forms, according to need,
Compassionate one, who benefits the
    Dharma and all beings,
Wish-fulfilling gem, refuge, and protector,
    I supplicate you!

Even if one searches the ten directions,
    through millions of universes,

A wish-fulfilling gem is so rare to find,
And when found, is of great meaning:
Even greater is the guru—how fortunate to
     have met him!

From now on, throughout all of my lives,
May I never separate from you, O protec-
     tor,
The nectar of your words having ripened
     and freed my mind-stream,
May I spontaneously accomplish benefit
For myself and for others.

This prayer enhanced the faith of disciples and
patrons.

The daughter of the Dharma King Lhagyari[55] came to practice the Dharma. I gave her
monastic vows and the name Lhaksam Drolma,
"Savioress with Noble Intention." She offered
me most of her jewelry, two boxes for storing
religious implements, a good padded carpet, and
valuables worth altogether one hundred *sang*.
Many others monks and nuns, men and women
from Zangri and Drakichö, became good practitioners. To all, I explained the need for conduct-
ing themselves according to the Vinaya, and
many of them became practitioners who kept
pure vows [414b].
    When the time of my departure approached,
I called together all the monks and nuns, and we
offered a large *ganachakra* feast. They implored
me to care for them in all their future lives. After
having made lengthy protection and dedication
prayers, I concluded with this advice:

Three Jewels, I take refuge in you:
Please grant your blessing!
Wish-fulfilling gem, protectors,
Be my refuge and my guide!

All of us yogins, master and disciples,
Were born in different lands;

Yet by the power of our good karma and
     prayers,
Without being called,
Some came from Ngari in western Tibet,
Some came from Domey in eastern Tibet,
Some came from U and Tsang in central
     Tibet,
And today all are assembled for a fleeting
     moment.
Demonstrating again the impermanence of
     compounded things,
We part and go our ways.

Some will go to secluded mountain
     retreats
To raise the victory banner of practice;
Some will wander at random through
     various lands,
As pilgrims to eminent holy places;
Some will go to their homelands
To meet their kind parents.

Once we have gone to our respective
     destinations,
It is unlikely that we will meet our
     companions again in this life.
Even if we were to look for them, we
     would not be able to see them;
Even if we were to listen for them, we
     would not be able to hear them.

All birth ends in death, meeting in
     separation;
Amassing ends in depletion; rise ends in fall
     [415a].

Everything that exists in samsara
Is unreliable, impermanent, essenceless.

None of us assembled here, men and
     women,
Knows when he or she will die.
Give up thoughts of this life!
Practice the divine Dharma!

Keep in your heart
This heart-advice of the departing yogin!

I pray that you may have long lives, free of
illness.
May the auspiciousness of general happiness prevail!

Most of them felt great sadness, contemplating
deeply the impermanence of all compounded
things.

With the offerings made by the departing
disciples and patrons, I offered a great *ganachakra*
feast, and I gave boots, clothes, provisions, protection cords, and blessed substances to those
going far away. Prompted by sadness, I sang this
song:

Sublime wish-granting gem, protector and
refuge,
Dwell as the ornament of the *chakra* of
great bliss.
Rain upon us, master and disciples, a
shower of ordinary and supreme *siddhis*.

Before long, all the fortunate men and
women gathered here,
Like visitors to a marketplace,
Will separate to go their own ways.

Once gone back to your own homelands,
Because of the great distances
You won't be able to return.
Even if a few of you could come, the way is
full of dangers—
Fierce bandits, wide rivers dangerous to
cross.

I myself long to come back [415b];
But I am now old.
Illness and death may strike at any time.
However if, owing to the compassion of
the Three Jewels,
I don't die soon and have a long life,
I may come back to meet you once again.

Even if I do come back, many of you
Will have grown old and died.
Young people think they will be around for
a while,

But in our times there are many obstacles
to life,
And even the young can't be certain to
survive.

However I consider it,
I feel that we won't meet again.
Pondering this, I feel sad deep inside.

Contemplating the time we've spent
together,
It seems to have lasted but an instant.
Now, when the time comes to go,
Unable to endure parting, we must never-
theless part.

Tears gather in my eyes;
I offer you this heart-advice, good for your
mind,
And these provisions and clothes, good for
your body.
Besides giving you these, there is nothing
else I can do.

When you meet each other
Be full of love and affection,
As when true parents, brothers, and sisters
meet;
Help each other with food, clothes, and
Dharma.

O patrons, remembering your guru,
Assist the poor disciples in need,
The sick and the destitute without protec-
tor.

Just as parents rejoice from their hearts
When they see someone benefiting their
children,
So if you benefit the poor,
I shall surely be happy and joyful.

By the merit of thus pleasing the lama,
The faithful patrons will, until
enlightenment,
Enjoy the splendor of well-being and
happiness.

May gentle love, compassion, and an
  enlightened attitude
Be born in the mind-streams of all [416a].
May countries enjoy good harvests;
May Dharma and auspiciousness flourish.

Having given the disciples much similar advice, I sent most of them to mountain hermitages
elsewhere. They left, their eyes filled with tears
and their minds filled with thoughts of their
master and the spiritual companions left behind.

When I was preparing to leave for Domey,
my fortunate heart-son Kunzang Rangdrol, who
was on his way to mountain solitudes in western
Tibet, sang this farewell song:

Sole ornament of the vast celestial pathway
  above,
Lord of the Twelve Mansions, farewell!

When, before long, you will have gone
  round the three other continents,
And, rising again to illuminate
  Jambudvipa,
Radiate in all directions millions of beams,
I, the white lotus, with all my peers,
Our vivid blossoms fully opened,
Will make an offering to the Three Jewels.
This is my prayer!

Sole ornament of rain clouds in space,
Turquoise-blue dragon, farewell!

When, before long, you have gone round
  the mountains and cliffs,
And, returning amid masses of clouds,
Have roared your sonorous thunder,
I, the peacock, and other twice-born
  birds,[56]
Fully opening and fanning out our
  iridescent plumage,
Will dance in joy.
I pray it will happen so!

Sole ornament of the four districts of U
  and Tsang,
Father lama and your spiritual sons,
  farewell! [416b].

When, before long, you have gone round
  the land of Domey,
And, coming back to the land of U-Tsang,
Expound both spiritual and worldly
  matters,
I, Kunzang, and your spiritual sons and
  daughters,
Resplendent with experiences and
  realization,
Will behold your countenance, protector.
I pray it will happen so!

On the auspicious day this happens,
May auspiciousness encompass the whole
  land!
Through auspiciousness pervading the
  land,
May all act in accordance with the
  Dharma!

Having said this, accompanied by a few
companion, he left to raise aloft the victory banner of spiritual practice in the mountain wilderness of Tö, in western Tibet.

On the day that we, master and disciples,
left Densathil, the whole monastic community
accompanied us to the foot of the mountain
which lies in front of the monastery. When we
were going to part, I sang this song of wishing to
meet them again:

Root teacher, Vajradhara,
Remain as my crest ornament.
For all those gathered here, dispel this life's
  obstacles,
And guide them when they leave for the
  next life.

Just as we yogins, master and disciples,
Having first come together are parting
  now,
So conditioned phenomena are
  impermanent.
Ponder this and practice the divine
  Dharma.

How fortunate that we met this time,
We yogins, master and disciples.

Having parted,
One—we will be separated by great
distances,
Two—I, the yogin, have grown old,
Three—our hold on life is always
uncertain [417a].
The conjunction of these three
Makes it unlikely that we will meet again.

Still, whenever we, master and disciples
who are one in mind,
Long to meet each other during the years
left for us to live,
May we meet in reality.

If we cannot meet in reality,
When that longing arises,
May we meet often in dreams or in
meditation states.
If we can't meet at all in this life,
May we meet in reality in a Buddhafield,
In our next existence.

May auspiciousness prevail in all countries!
May all diseases of men and beasts
disappear!
May all enjoy long and healthy lives!
May crops be abundant, and everyone be
happy!

After this song the monks and nuns went
back with heavy hearts to the monastery. My
disciples and I headed for the estate of Dorje, the
administrator of Zangri, and his wife. On the
way, I offered a general distribution of tea to the
monks of Ngari.[57] They requested spiritual protection. I stayed for a few days at the estate of
Zangri, giving long-life empowerments, teachings, and advice, thus turning everyone's mind
to the Dharma. The patrons, men and women,
offered jewelry, clothes, and silver coins.

I went to visit Zangri Kharmar,[58] the Red
Fortress of the Copper Mountain, the seat of the
Sole Mother, Machik Labdrön. There I made
offerings and aspiration prayers.

We crossed the Tsangpo River in a coracle
[417b] and went to the households of Tsachanga,
Yukhang, and Khenpo Shiwa Tsering. To all I

gave a blessing of longevity and a teaching on the
nature of mind. They offered a thanksgiving
ganachakra feast; those who knew how sang and
danced. On this occasion the faithful lady
Chödrung Sherap Drolma offered this song
requesting spiritual protection:

Refuge and protector whose kindness I
cannot repay,
Jetsun Tsogdruk Rangdrol,
I supplicate you from my heart:
Bless me with your compassion!

Completely filled with fervor,
I, Chödrung Sherap Drolma,
Utter this song with great yearning:
Kindly pay heed to it for an instant.

Contemplating the miseries of samsara
Stirred my mind with weariness and feelings of renunciation.

Contemplating the benefits of liberation,
Gave me faith and turned my aspirations
to virtue.

Gaining certainty in the ineluctable laws of
cause and effect,
I conducted myself without confusing
What should and should not be done.

For the good of all beings, my mothers,
I aspire to enlightenment!

Perpetually visualizing you upon my head,
O wish-granting gem, refuge and protector,
Embodiment of all Victorious Ones,
I offer you my obedience to all your
commands.

O ultimate object of my thoughts,
Jetsun, protector and refuge, think of me!

By the power of whatever merit
I have gathered throughout the three
times,
Meditating in a pleasant wilderness,
Striving one-pointedly in spiritual practice,

Having united my mind with your mind,
O refuge and protector, Vajradhara
    [418a],
May I fulfill the twofold aim: to benefit
    myself and others.

Look upon me with compassion,
Grant me your protection!

In essence, from now on, in all my lives,
May I never be parted from you.
In all my lives, may I be the most supreme
    daughter of your heart,
O lord guru, protector and refuge.

In the immeasurable wondrous celestial
    palace
Of whichever Buddhafield you dwell in,
May I perfect enlightened deeds that
    delight the mind.

Others also sang songs, in an atmosphere of
general joyfulness.

As a farewell present for my return to Domey,
the Khenpo offered me a jerkin that had belonged
to the Victorious Jampel Gyatso,[59] a gold-painted
thangka representing a stupa, a painting representing Buddha Shakyamuni, many small images and pills made of sacred *amrita* substances
from the Sakya lineage, some relics of the Buddha that had multiplied miraculously, and many
other sacred relics. In return, I offered him one
dotse and a long ceremonial scarf of the finest silk
with woven images of Amitayus, the Buddha of
Boundless Life.

Tsachanga and Yukhang, too, offered me
ornaments of gold, silver, turquoise, and corals,
light and heavy woolen material, and many bags
of *tsampa*. Since we had known each other for
such a long time, unable to bear our separation I
stayed for a few more days. Finally, with grief in
our hearts and tears in our eyes, we left.

At Neuring, I visited the holy places of the
valley of La [418b], offering tea and alms. Then
I went to the chieftain Khangsar's house and
gave a long-life blessing and teachings, inspiring
everyone to practice the Dharma. They gave me
much food and many valuables.

I went to Lhagyari and met the precious
Dharma King, his wife, and his children, and
established with them spiritual connections. The
precious Dharma King gave me a blessed image
made of *lima*,[60] thirteen *thangka* paintings representing thirty-four former births of Lord Buddha, many sacred relics and sacramental
substances, and many volumes of the *Sangwa
Yeshe* cycle.[61] Upon taking leave, I requested the
Dharma King's spiritual protection by offering
this song with a ceremonial scarf:

Unfailing lasting refuge
For this life, the *bardo*, and the next life,
Root master, Vajradhara,
With your kind compassion, think of me.

In general, in this dark age, life spans are
    short,
And in particular, there are many
    life-endangering hazards.
This body, like a bubble on the surface of
    water, is so fragile.
However one considers it, death is near.

So, wherever I, a lowly vagabond, go or
    stay,
I beseech you to grant your protection
So that there may be no obstacles to my
    life.
I supplicate you to guide me on the
    ascending path,
When I journey to the world of the next life.

With a countenance more beautiful than
    that of celestial beings,
With a voice more melodious than that of
    celestial Brahma,
With a heart softer than celestial silk,
Celestial guru,[62] farewell!

I pray that, in this life, in the next, and in
    the *bardo*,
I may behold your face and hear your
    voice,
In reality, in dreams or in meditative states.
May it happen in accordance with my
    prayer! [419a].

Thus, praying to meet him again and again, I went to the monastery of Rongchekar. I met the abbot, presented him with some gifts, and offered tea and alms to all. The precious abbot gave me a volume of the *Golden-Hued All-Victorious Vinaya*,[63] and seemed quite sad when I left. I departed with a heavy heart.

The Jetsunma of Lhagyari and her attendant accompanied me as far as the plain below, and then stayed behind, in tears. I, too, was filled with sadness, and glanced back from time to time. Reaching Tsetang, I offered tea and alms at the monastery and paid homage to the speaking image of Jetsun Drolma of Yarlung and to that of Guru Padmasambhava of Sheldrak,[64] making offerings and prayers in front of them. I taught the Dharma and said prayers of auspiciousness for the sake of the governor and the householders. I used their gifts to make offerings at Tranang and distribution of tea and alms at the Great Stupa of Jampaling[65] and at the local monastery. The chieftain Dorje helped us greatly; he offered me statues of the Buddhas of the five families made of *lima*, and all the tea, butter, and *tsampa* we might need [419b].

I then went to Orgyen Mindroling,[66] which, like the source of a river in a glacier, is the source of the teachings of the Ancient Translation tradition of the Mantrayana. I met the heir to the throne and the Jetsunmas,[67] and presented them with many offerings—gold, silver, corals, turquoise, and brocades—requesting teachings to establish spiritual connections. I offered tea and alms to the monastic community and stayed there seven days, doing prostrations and circumambulations. When leaving, I was given many presents. Among all the Nyingma monasteries I have seen, there is none better kept and more pleasant than this one. I would have liked to stay longer.

I then reached Dorje Drak monastery, the life-tree of the Nyingma tradition, and met the precious incarnation.[68] Offering him several *sang*, I requested a spiritual connection, and offered tea and alms to the community.

From there I went to Drak Yangdzong and made offerings. I then met the two sons of Zurkar Thekchen Lingpa.[69] I requested a Dharma connection from the elder son and gave full monastic vows to the younger. Our minds merged as one. Finally, I reached Lhasa.

I stayed at Kalön Zurkhang's house,[70] and made preparations for going to Domey. Khenpo Chakzampa, the Dalai Lama's mother Dondrup Drolma, and many other patrons I had known from before called me to their homes and offered me many farewell presents—sacred objects of the body, speech, and mind, provisions and valuables. On the eve of my departure, I said prayers of auspiciousness at everyone's home, as well as gave them advice for the benefit of this life and the next [420a]. I also gave this admonition to the faithful people of Lhasa:

> I pray to the gurus and the Three Jewels:
> May I and others remain in harmony with the Dharma.
>
> The two Jowos are the prime objects of offering.
> Always offer to them, praise them, respect them, people of Lhasa!
>
> The two Victors, Father and Son, are the ultimate refuge;
> Keep them above your heads, people of Lhasa!
>
> Whoever the regent-king of Tibet might be,
> Observe his laws and edicts, people of Lhasa!
>
> Sera, Ganden, and Drepung are the supreme fields for accumulating merit;
> To them, distribute tea and alms, people of Lhasa!
>
> All beings were your parents of your previous lives;
> Cultivate gentle love and compassion for all, people of Lhasa!
>
> To the beggars and old dogs on the outer circumambulation path,
> Always give alms and food, people of Lhasa!

See how many goats, sheep, and yaks there
    are for slaughter:
Be compassionate; ransom their lives,
    people of Lhasa!

You yourselves can't bear even the prick of
    a needle;
Don't sever others' lives with a knife,
    people of Lhasa!

Countless animals are killed for meat;
Don't relish meat, the most sinful of foods,
    people of Lhasa!

Don't be jealous of important persons;
Place everyone above yourself, people of
    Lhasa!

Don't oppress humble people;
Care for everyone with gentle love, people
    of Lhasa! [420b].

Don't compete with your equals;
Relate harmoniously to all, people of
    Lhasa!

If there are no subjects, who will respect
    the governors?
Don't impose heavy taxes and compulsory
    labor, O chiefs of Lhasa!

If there are no governors, who will protect
    the subjects?
Don't stir up shameless discord, O subjects
    of Lhasa!

If there are no lamas, who will turn the
    Wheel of Dharma?
Disciples must respect their teachers,
    O disciples of Lhasa!

If there are no disciples, for whom will the
    Wheel of Dharma be turned?
Take care of your students,
    O lamas of Lhasa!

All Dharmas are profound;
Don't be sectarian, people of Lhasa!

To all the traditions that flourish in Tibet,
Offer as much service as you can, people of
    Lhasa!

Even if the king orders punishment,
Don't banish or put people in jail,
    O nobles of Lhasa!

Out of craving, animosity, and rivalry,
Don't denounce others to the king,
    O nobles of Lhasa!

At the gathering of the Great Prayer
    Festival,
Don't pick fights and quarrel, people of
    Lhasa

The monks of Sera and Drepung are
    strong indeed;
But don't become killers for hire, O *dobdops*
    of Lhasa![71]

When the governor inflicts penalties on a
    village headman,
Don't transfer the penalty to all the
    subjects, O headmen of Lhasa!

Don't bear grudges against others
Or retaliate when harm is done to you,
    people of Lhasa!

Since pickpockets are a disgrace to society
Don't let pickpockets hang around, people
    of Lhasa!

Even if you can't help but steal small
    things,
At least don't slice holes in robes and cut
    off ornaments, O pickpockets of Lhasa!

If everyone—the high, the medium, and
    the low—observes the law,
The sun of happiness will shine for all,
    people of Lhasa! [421a].

May this discourse benefit people of all
    conditions
In the celestial field of U-Tsang.

Goodness prevailing in all countries and
directions,
May auspiciousness encompass the Three
Worlds.

This helped to establish those with fortunate
karma on the excellent path to the higher realms
and ultimate perfection. Then I went to the
Potala Palace to take leave of the Dalai Lama,
our refuge and protector. I asked him to keep me
under his spiritual protection, and he spoke many
words of loving concern. When I left, he gave me
some light and heavy woolen materials and many
other presents, such as miraculously multiplied
relics of the Buddha and other relics related to
the four patron deities of the Kadampas,[72] as
well as elaborately knotted protection cords and
a long ceremonial scarf of fine silk.

When I went to take leave from the regent-
king of Tibet, he, too, gave me many sacred
relics and farewell presents, and this edict for the
benefit of the Dharma and sentient beings in
Domey:

Here is a proclamation from the one known
as Bhadarkol Husamati Pakshi, the Sherekeh
Thushazin of Ganden,[73] representative of the glorious Nominhan[74] who holds the yellow hat tradition
and the responsibility for Tibet, as granted by the
Great Emperor, Jamyang Gongma:

This is addressed to the lamas, chieftains,
Wangs, Pi'i lis, Pa'i lis, Pa'i sis, Gungs, Jasags,
Tha'i jis, Ja'i sangs,[75] noble persons, and all the
inhabitants—religious and lay, high, low, and
medium—of this great continent of the Rose-
apple Tree in general, and to the inhabitants of
the area of the forty-nine tribes, of the four
districts of Orod [421b], of the banks of Lake
Trishok Gyalmo, of the Six Ranges of Dokham,
of Upper and Lower Amdo, of Chagmo Golok,
of Rang Ngen, and of Bhanak in particular.

The renunciate from Amdo called Tsogdruk
Rangdrol, prompted by his excellent propensi-
ties, conceived a strong feeling of renunciation
that led him to receive many profound instructions on the sutras and tantras from numerous
teachers, and then to strive earnestly in spiritual
practice in mountain solitudes.

Not only does he benefit in a vast way, mate-
rially and spiritually, whomever makes a connection with him, but he also has offered thirteen
rings of copper beautifully gilt with gold to the
Great Stupa of Bodhnath in Nepal and to the
Great Tashi Gomang Stupa in Chung Riwoche.
He also offered butter-lamps made of solid gold
in front of the Jowo Rinpoche at Lhasa, the
Jowo Changchup Sempa at Samye, and the
Golden Reliquary at Ganden and made cloud-
like offerings of butter-lamps in different places.
At Purang Shephel Ling and at Shelkar Chödeh
he placed *ganjira* pinnacles and Dharma-wheels
made of gilded copper. In the great holy place of
Lapchi at the Great Maitreya Temple of Gyalgyi
Shri, and in other places, he restored many
temples [422a]. On the occasion of the ocean-
like gathering of Lhasa's Great Prayer Festival,
he offered great services, making several general
distributions of alms and large offerings. These
are just a few examples of the splendid virtuous
activity through which he benefits others with
impeccable intention.

Wherever he gives spiritual advice, everyone
should welcome it with enthusiasm and be helpful to him, as explained in the scriptures, without
ever causing him harm or acting mischievously
against him. All those who act in accordance
with these words will gather the compassion of
the Three Supreme Jewels, and be kept under
their protection in this and future lives.

This proclamation was written in the year of
the Wood-Mouse, called Kundzin, on the auspicious twenty-fifth of the third month, by
Thubten Namgyal Tsemön Lingpa, who is
associated with the fragrant temple[76] of the
Trulnang Tsuklagkhang of Lhasa.

Having affixed his great seal to this proclamation, he wrapped it in brocade and gave it to
me.

The supreme kalön Zurkhang gave me the
ten volumes of the collected writings of Kunkhyen
Pema Karpo[77] and as much *tsampa* as we needed
for the journey. I went to meet the throne-holder
of Ganden and requested his spiritual protection. He gave me a statue of the Buddha, made
of *lima*, saying, "By offering you this, I proclaim

you Lord of the Dharma." I thought this a most auspicious omen on the eve of my departure.

The day before leaving for Domey, I went to pay homage to the two Shakya Jowos [422b], and made extensive prayers for the sake of the Dharma and all beings. That night I dreamed that flying miraculously in the sky like a bird I went between the sun and the moon and looked in the direction of Domey. Seeing that Tsonying, The Heart of the Lake, and Mugeh Thang, the Plain of Famine,[78] were empty, I thought, "I can work miracles! How excellent if I could transport the Crowned Buddha of Lhasa, with its whole temple, to Tsonying, in the middle of the Blue Lake." With my hand, I miraculously lifted the whole temple and put it down intact on the crest of Tsonying Island. All around the summit of the island, many kinds of trees had grown, on the tops of which flocks of the seven kinds of birds found on the island were singing melodiously and playfully flying around.

Then I thought, "How wonderful if I now transported the whole of the Chinese emperor's treasury to Mugeh Plain." Right away, taking it in my hand, I transported it, and laid it in the middle of Mugeh Plain. From four sides of the treasury, four rivers appeared and flowed in the four cardinal directions. Myriads of human beings and animals joyfully drank their water.

I felt this auspicious dream presaged that I would serve the Dharma and beings of Domey in a great way, both spiritually and materially.

Notes

1. In 1822.

2. For the Belly Cave of Nyanang, see chap. 13, note 6.

3. For the Mad Yogin of Tsang, see chap. 13, note 3.

4. Tingri Langkhor (*ding ri glang 'khor*), which lies west of Tingri Dzong, was established in 1097 by the Indian yogin Padampa Sangye (d. 1117). See Aziz

(1980). The relics and belongings of the saint were preserved there. Most of these were saved from the devastation brought on by the Cultural Revolution and are presently preserved by Dza Trulshik Rinpoche in Nepal. The Langkhor monastery, now in process of restoration, was built above the cave where Padampa meditated.

5. On *Pacification of Suffering*, see chap. 6, note 19.

6. Changlochen was a provincial commander (*mda' dpon*) from a noble family that took its name from a village near Gyantse (see Petech 1973, 200–203). Gyalkyi Shri (*rgyal kyi shri*) is the Tsibri (*rtsib ri*) range, west of Shelkar Dzong (*shel dkar rdzong*) in Latö (*la stod*). See Aufschnaiter (1976).

7. Shelkar Chödeh (*shel dkar chos sde*) is located near Shelkar Dzong (*shel dkar rdzong*), the provincial capital of Tingri, which marks the limit between Tsang (*gtsang*) and Latö (*la stod*).

8. These are known as the Three Cycles of the Northern Terma (*byang gter sgrub skor rnam gsum*) and are the most widely practiced among the rediscovered treasures of Rigdzin Gödem. See chap. 1, note 48.

9. On Sakya Monastery, see chap. 11, note 47. The throne-holders Ngakchang Kunga Gyaltsen (*sngags 'chang kun dga' rgyal mtshan*) and Gonpo Ngodrup Pelbar (*mgon po dngos grub dpal 'bar*) were the two youngest among the four sons of Wangdu Nyingpo (*dbang 'dus snying po*, the thirty-third throne-holder of Sakya, 1765–1806). The Jetsunma is probably one of their sisters.

10. The Great Thread-cross (*mdos chen*) is a huge and most elaborate *mdos* (see chap. 5, note 21) accompanied by large offerings. It is usually performed once a year.

11. The Sole Mother Queen of the Siddhas; see chap. 6, note 44.

12. For Wang Tashi Jungne, see Appendix 3, page 567.

13. Riwo Trazang (*ri bo bkra bzang*), a branch monastery of *rdo rje brag* built near the place where Rigdzin Gödem (*rig 'dzin rgod ldem*, 1337–1408) discovered several of his *termas*.

14. Gyang Bumoche (*rgyang 'bum mo che*) was an immense Tashi Gomang (Many Gates of Auspiciousness) stupa build by the Sakya master Sonam Tashi (*bsod nams bkra shis*, 1352–1412). See Tucci (1973) and Vitali (1990).

15. Placards exhorting the three , protectors of the world—the Bodhisattvas Manjushri, Avalokiteshvara, and Vajrapani—are often made to avert the peril of floods.

16. Tsarong (*tsha rong*): this noble family, whose estate was near Sakya, descends from the famous Tibetan physician, Yuthok Yontan Gonpo. See Petech 1973, pp. 134–38.

17. Ngor Ewam Chöden (*ngor e wam chos ldan*) is the second most important monastery of the Sakya school. It was founded in 1429 by Ngorchen Kunga Zangpo (*ngor chen kun dga' bzang po*, 1382–1444). It became famous for being the seat of the *Lamdre* teachings, and sheltered a rich library that included a large collection of Sanskrit manuscripts.

18. Lit. *skar lnga,* half a *sho,* and *phyed brgyad;* see chap. 1, note 68.

19. Tashi Gomang Stupa of Chung Riwoche (*gcung,* or *cung, ri bo che'i bra shis sgo mang*). The building of the gigantic nine-storey stupa with many chapels, which lasted from 1449 to 1456, is described in Thangtong Gyalpo's biography. See Vitali (1990), Stearns (1980), and Gyatso (1981). The stupa is being renovated after the damage caused during the Cultural Revolution.

20. In 1824.

21. *The Bright Mirror Record* (*dkar chags gsal ba'i me long*), the detailed list and description of the restoration work of the stupa of Chung Riwoche (see note 19 above), written by Shabkar. Seven hundred *dotse* are equivalent to one ton of silver.

22. The Three Ranges of Dokham (*smad mdo khams sgang gsum*) are: 1) Markham in Upper Kham (*smar khams* in *mdo khams*); 2) Yermo Thang in Domey (*g.yer mo thang*-in *mdo smad*) Domey; and 3) Tsongkha Gyi Thang (*tsong kha gyi thang*).
Reference is more often made to the Six Ranges of Dokham (*smad mdo khams sgang drug*), which are: 1) Zalmo Gang (*zal mo sgang*); 2) Tsawa Gang (*tsha ba sgang*); 3) Markham Gang (*smar khams sgang*); 4) Pombor Gang (*spo 'bor sgang*); 5) Mardza Gang (*dmar rdza sgang*); and 6) Minyak Rabgang (*mi nyag rab sgang*). See AC, vol. 1, p. 4 and TC, p. 2160.

23. Anathapindika: one of the most generous benefactors of Lord Buddha. He acquired the Jeta Grove at Shravasti and built in it a residence, or sangharama, where the Buddha and his disciples spent their yearly rainy-season retreat for nineteen years. See SD, pp. 8 and 103.

24. Jonang Ganden Phuntsokling (*jo nang dga' ldan phun tshogs gling*) was founded by Dolpopa Sherap Gyaltsen (*dol po pa shes rab rgyal mtshan,* 1292-1361), who established his hermitage nearby and built there the Great Stupa that Liberates on Sight (*mthong grol chen mo,* see R. Vitali, 1990). The place then became

the seat of the great master Jetsun Taranatha Kunga Nyingpo (*rje btsun ta ra na tha kun dga' snying po,* 1575–1635), and was later forcibly converted to the Geluk tradition. See Kapstein (1992).

25. The seven-rebirth pills (*skye bdun ril bu*) are prepared from sacred substances, including originally, it is said, the flesh of a person reborn seven successive lifetimes as a brahmin. The mere taste of these is said to shut the doors of rebirth in the lower realms of samsara.

26. These are Chinese and Mongolian titles of nobility. According to the *Annals of Kokonor* (see Bibliography), *Chingwang* is Prince of the First Order; *Jun Wang,* Prince of the Second Order; *Pile* (in Chinese, *Pei-le*), Prince of the Third Order; *Bise,* or *Be sim* (in Chinese, *Pei tzu*), Prince of the Fourth Order; and *Gung* or *Kung,* Imperial Duke. *T'ai chi* is the lowest order of Mongolian nobility. A Jasag, pronounced by Tibetans *dzasa* (*dza sag,* or *ja sag,* in Chinese *cha sa k'e*), is the chieftain of a Mongolian "banner," or district (see Appendix 3). A Jasag could hold any of the above ranks or titles (from *Chingwang* to *Gung*). This title was also given to Tibetan notables by Mongol invaders. The banner system of the Mongols in Kokonor was established by an imperial edict after Lobzang Tendzin's rebellion in 1724.

27. In 1824.

28. Orgyen Tendzin (*o rgyan bstan 'dzin*), a chief disciple of Kunzang Dechen Gyalpo, and a teacher of both Chögyal Ngakyi Wangpo and Shabkar. See Appendix 4.

29. The tenth Dalai Lama, Tsultrim Gyatso (*tshul khrims rgya mtsho,* 1816–37), who was then eight years old.

30. On *Praise of Dependent Arising,* see chap. 9, note 49.

31. On Tsemön Lingpa, see chap. 9, note 50.

32. "Horn-fence huts" (*rwa yi khang pa*) refers to people near Drepung who live in tents and huts surrounded with horn fences. Ragyap (*rag rgyab*) is a quarter of Lhasa inhabited by poor people who dispose of corpses.

33. Khardo is located on a hill facing Lhasa, on the way to Phenpo.

34. Shang Rinpoche, Yudrak Gonpo; see chap. 9, note 59.

35. The reference here is to the forcible conversion by the fifth Dalai Lama of most of the Kagyu monasteries, including those built here by Shang Rinpoche.

36. The sixth Dalai Lama, Tsangyang Gyatso

(*tshangs dbyangs rgya mtsho*, 1683–1702) and the regent-king, Desi Sangye Gyatso (*sde srid sangs rgyas rgya mtsho*, 1653–1703).

37. Söpa Gyatso is the first Khardo Rinpoche; see Appendix 2. The Great Lord is Tsongkhapa.

38. For the *Amazing Emanated Scriptures* (*ya mtshan sprul pa'i glegs bam*), see Appendix 5.

39. The Ganden Offering of the Twenty-fifth (*dga' ldan lnga mchod: lnga*, fifth, being an abbreviation for twenty-fifth) is the yearly offering, at Ganden and other monasteries, commemorating the anniversary of the death of Je Tsongkhapa on the twenty-fifth of the tenth lunar month. Many butter-lamps are offered on the roofs of monasteries and houses when night comes.

40. *The Hundred Sadhanas, Source of Jewels* (*sgrub thabs rin 'byung brgya rtsa*), a collection of *sadhanas* gathered and arranged by Jonang Taranatha (see above, note 24).

41. For *The Sixteen Spheres of the Kadampas*, see chap. 12, note 74.

42. For *The Metaphors for the Graded Path* and the *Ultimate Graded Path*, see chap.12, note 76.

43. The Great Prayer Festival (*smon lam chen mo*): up to fifty thousand monks and nuns would gather on this occasion.

44. Saga Dawa *(sa ga zla ba*), the fourth month of the Tibetan lunar calendar. It is a special month for practice and performing virtuous actions, since the birth, enlightenment, and parinirvana of Buddha Shakyamuni all fall in this month.

45. For Drakmar Yama Lung, see chap. 10, note 59.

46. For *The Seven Treasuries* (*mdzod bdun)*, see Translator's Introduction, note 15. For Gampopa's writings, see chap.10, note 45.

47. Phagmo Drupa Dorje Gyalpo (*phag mo gru pa rdo rje rgyal po*, 1110–70) was one the three foremost disciples of Gampopa (see chap. 10, note 45), as well as a disciple of Sachen Kunga Nyingpo (*sa chen kun dga' snying po*, 1092–1158). See BA, pp. 552–63.

The monastery of Densathil (*gdan sa mthil*) lay west of Ngari Tratsang (*mnga' ris grwa tshang*), at the border of Yon and Zangri, in a scenic valley with high cliffs, cascades, and beautiful groves of flowering shrubs and juniper trees. It was founded by Phagmo Drupa (see note below), who used to live there in a small meditation hut made of willow branches. Many disciples soon came to live near the saint. After his death, the place came under rule of the Drigung hierarchs, who built a large monastery. Densathil

became a political center, with the rise of the Phagmo Drupa oligarchy, which reigned over Tibet from 1364 to 1435. It has now been thoroughly destroyed by the Chinese. See Dowman (1988) and Thubten Namkhar (1990).

48. The "*Siddha* of the Great Perfection" probably refers to Do Drupchen Trinley Öser (*rdo grub chen 'phrin las 'od zer*); see Translator's Introduction, note 48.

49. Addressed to Shabkar's chief disciple Kalden Rangdrol (*skal ldan rang grol*), also known as Lhundrup Rigdzin (*lhun grub rig 'dzin*), who was present then.

50. Skt. *Chamara* (Tib. *rnga yab*), the southwestern island of the Rakshasas, from which rises the Glorious Copper-colored Mountain (*zangs mdog dpal ri*), the Buddhafield of Guru Padmasambhava.

51. *Sangwa Yeshe* cycle of Olkha (*'ol kha'i gsang ba ye shes*), the sixteen-volume cycle of teachings focused on the dakini "Secret Wisdom" (*gsang ba ye shes*) according to the visions of Lelung Jedrung Shepai Dorje (*sle lung rje drung bzhad pa'i rdo rje*, b. 1697) from Olkha, based on the *terma* revelations of Minling Terchen (see chap. 1, note 38).

52. Densathil was famous for the precious images, paintings, and relics it sheltered.

53. Dagpo Drumpa (*dwags po bhrum pa*), a noble family from Dagpo established in Lhasa.

54. For this and the other masters mentioned in this prayer, see Translator's Introduction, p. xxi.

55. For Dharma King Lhagyari, see chap. 10, note 5.

56. Birds are said to be twice-born, because they are "born" first in an egg and then a second time from the egg. Similarly, religious practitioners are twice-born, having had both bodily and spiritual births.

57. Ngari Tratsang (*mnga' ris grwa tshang*) is a large Gelukpa monastery founded in 1541 under the auspices of the second Dalai Lama, Gedun Gyatso (*dge 'dun rgya mtsho*, 1475–1542) under the patronage of a king of Guge in Ngari, hence the name of the monastery (see Ferrari 1958, p. 120 n.193). It stands like a fortress on an eminence dominating the entrance to the Yon Valley. See also PP, pp. 238.

58. Zangri Kharmar (*zangs ri mkhar dmar*), the Red Fortress of the Copper Mountain, is thus called because it was built upon a red rock overlooking the northern banks of the Tsangpo River, at the southern extremity of the Copper Mountain. On the cliff-face to the west of the temple (which was destroyed by the Chinese) is the meditation cave of Machik Labdrön (*ma gcig lab sgron*, 1055–1153). See PP.

59. The eighth Dalai Lama, Jampel Gyatso (*rgyal ba 'jam dpal rgya mtsho*, 1758–1804).

60. *Li ma*, bronze alloy with a high percentage of silver and gold.

61. For the *Sangwa Yeshe* of Tertön Dechen Gyalpo, see chap. 10, note 52.

62. The Lhagyari kings are considered to be of celestial origin. See chap. 10, note 5.

63. *Golden-Hued All-Victorious Vinaya* (*'dul ba rnam rgyal gser mdog*). This is the *bstan pa'i rtsa ba rab byung dang khyim pa la phan gdags pa'i las kyi cho ga mtha' gcod dang bcas pa'i 'khrul spong rnam rgyal gser mdog*, an important writing of the fifth Dalai Lama, Ngawang Lobzang Gyatso, on the fundamentals of Buddhist discipline (Ochgat: Tashi Dorje, 1983).

64. *Yar lung shel brag*, the Crystal Rock of Yarlung. See chap. 10, note 59. The famed statue of Guru Padmasambhava that was kept there is said to have been made and blessed at the time of Guru Rinpoche by the great translator Vairocana.

65. Jampaling (*byams pa gling*), a large Gelukpa monastic estate on which stood, before its annihilation by the Chinese, the Great Stupa of the Thousand Images of Maitreya, built by Jampa Lingpa Sonam Namgyal (*'byams pa gling pa bsod nams rnam rgyal*, 1401–75). It was an immense stupa, perhaps the largest in Tibet (with Chung Riwoche), sheltering temples inside at each level. In the ground floor temple was an image of Maitreya fifty meters high.

66. Mindroling (*smin grol gling*) was founded in 1670 by Terdak Lingpa (see chap. 1, note 38) and is one the six principal Nyingma monasteries in Tibet (see Glossary of Enumerations). On the Mindroling tradition, see NS, p. 825.

67. The throne of Mindroling is traditionally held by successive descendants of Terdak Lingpa. The jetsunmas are his female descendants, who have always played an important role in the preservation of the teachings. Many of them have been remarkable teachers themselves.

68. Probably the sixth Rigdzin Chenpo of Dorje Drak, Kunzang Gyurme Lhundrup (*rdor brag 'rig 'dzin chen po kun bzang 'gyur med lhun grub*).

Dorje Drak (*rdo rje brag*) is the main center for the practice of the Northern Terma tradition, the collection of spiritual treasures rediscovered by Rigdzin

Gödem (*rig 'dzin rgod kyi ldem phru can*, 1337–1408; see NS, pp. 780–83). It was Ngari Panchen Pema Wangyal (*mnga' ris pan chen padma dbang rgyal*, 1487–1542) who, following Guru Rinpoche's predictions, first identified the site of Dorje Drak, the "Vajra Rock" (thus called because of a round stone with a blue crossed-vajra on it). The monastery was actually founded by Rigdzin III, Ngakyi Wangpo (*ngag gi dbang po*, 1580–1639), in 1632. See also chap. 9, note 41.

69. Drak Yangdzong (*sgrags yang rdzong*); see chap. 10, note 59. On Zurkar Thekchen Lingpa, see Appendix 4, note 7.

70. This is Zurkhang Tseten Dorje (*bka' blon zur khang tshe gtan rdo rje*, d. 1844), who was a minister in the Tibetan government from 1813 until his death (see Petech 1973, pp. 145–48). The Zurkhang family had also been the benefactors of Rigdzin Jigme Lingpa (*rig 'dzin 'jigs med gling pa*, 1729–98).

71. This refers to the dobdops (*rdob rdob*), the famous guard-monks of the big monasteries around Lhasa, who would sometimes behave in a manner inconsistent with the rules of monastic life, acting almost like mercenaries.

72. Four patron deities of the Kadampas (*bka' gdams lha bzhi*): Buddha Shakyamuni, Avalokiteshvara, Vajra Achala, and Tara.

73. These are the titles of the regent-king of Tibet.

74. *Nominhan* is the Manchu equivalent of the Tibetan *chos rgyal*, "Prince of the Faith," or, as in the present translation, "Dharma King." As communicated by Prof. M. Kapstein, this interesting word comes from the Greek *nomos*—"law, norm"—and *Han*, standing for the Mongolian *Khan*, "chieftain."

75. These are Chinese and Mongolian titles used in Amdo and in the area bordering on China.

76. Gandhola, in Tibetan *dri gtsang khang*, "fragrant mansion," refers to a temple.

77. For Kunkhyen Pema Karpo, see chap. 10, note 19.

78. The Plain of Famine (*mu ge thang*) is a sandy desert near the Ba (*'ba'*) valley, north of Ragya (*rwa rgya*) and northeast of the Gyupar Range (*rgyud par*), beyond the sand dunes of Mangri Chema (*mang ri bye ma*).

15

Return to Domey

*How, having returned to Lower Dokham, I worked
to benefit the Dharma and all beings.*

On the ninth day of the fourth month of the male Earth Mouse Year,[1] called Kundzin, eighteen of us left Lhasa, carrying five hundred volumes of Lord Buddha's words and commentaries, a load of precious relics, over a hundred statues of various sizes, eighty painted scrolls, and provisions for the road.

For a while we were escorted by Lama Jimba Norbu, Lochen, Kalden, and about fifty monks and nuns. On the way we met the two Masters of Taklung, father and son [425a],[2] and the throne-holder of Reting. We offered them presents, asking for teaching to establish a spiritual connection. We stayed at Reting until the Offering to the Cuckoos,[3] doing prostrations and circumambulations.

After I had given them much advice, the monks and nuns accompanied me to a pleasant plain. There I gave them blessings, enjoined the evil forces not to harm them, and sang a song, wishing that we would meet throughout our lives:

Lord protector, wish-fulfilling gem,
Remain upon a lotus and moon seat above
   my head!
With intense devotion, I supplicate you:
May there fall a rain-shower of ordinary
   and extraordinary *siddhis!*

By the power of our pure karma and
   aspirations,
We, master and disciples, gathered on this
   plain for an instant.
Now we must part; we shall go our
   separate ways.

This is impermanence: phenomena are not
   lasting.

The time when we must go on to the next
   life is not certain.
Fortunate sons and daughters,
Dismiss from your minds all concern for
   this life!

Following the life-examples of our spiritual
   forefathers,
Guard your vows and *samayas* as you
   would your eyes.
With love, compassion, and a mind turned
   towards enlightenment,
Practice the Dharma of the sutras and
   tantras
In pleasant and secluded places.

I myself am going back to Domey, my
   native land,
To spread the teachings of Lord
   Shakyamuni,
And to establish fortunate disciples
   [425b]
On the sublime level of Buddhahood.

Like a loving mother and child,
Filled with tenderness for each other,
We cannot bear to part.
Yet, for the good of the teachings and
   beings in Domey,
I shall now leave you behind, disciples of
   Tö and U-Tsang.

485

If, by the compassion of the lord guru and
   the Three Jewels,
I, your father, still have time left before
   death,
I pray to return to the pure celestial realm
   of U-Tsang.

Yet the time of birth and death is
   unpredictable;
If we don't meet again in this life,
May we meet in future lives
And stay together in pure Buddhafields.

Then I added, "You need not accompany
me to the northern plains. Stay here, and until
you lose sight of me, keep praying that we come
together again. As I go, I too shall keep you deep
within my heart. Don't be distressed; we may
meet again. I'm going back to my native land.
You should spend some time in solitary places in
your own regions and raise the victory banner of
spiritual practice: this is the best way to serve the
guru, to repay the kindness of your parents, and
to work for the benefit of sentient beings. Don't
forget this!"

Although nearly unable to tear myself away,
but having to part from them, I departed. There
was no one who was not crying, even Lama
Jimba Norbu, foremost among the disciples; some
were even wailing [426a]. I looked back many
times; there came a point where I saw them as a
distant mass of maroon. I did not have the heart
to go on and, turning toward them, sat for a
while. When, finally, I did go on and lost sight of
them, I felt even sadder. They, too, had stood
weeping as long as I had remained visible and
cried even more when I disappeared from sight.
Reluctantly, they went back home, one after the
other.

I traversed Nakchuka and the countries of the
Tsomoras and the Derge Rishorwas,[4] and worked
to benefit them all. As offerings, I received forty
packhorses and *dzomos*, and many goat-skins filled

with butter. We loaded whatever we had on the
animals and went on, in the company of a government trade official, the Garpön of Xining,
and many big merchants.[5]

We took the long northern route, and when
we reached the Drichu River, over a thousand
bandits from Golok captured us with all the
merchants. After talking to them and showing
them the proclamations from the regent and
from the supreme protector, the Panchen Lama,
the bandits gave back the horses, *dzomos*, and
goods belonging to the Garpön, the cloth trader,
and us. But they stole the loads of all the other
merchants. They broke open the bundles, stole
woolen cloth[6] and other valuables and, leaving
all the religious objects and blessed pills scattered
on the ground, rode off [426b].

The Drichu River was in flood, and we
were unable to cross it; we had to wait near the
banks for a month and ten days. I gave each of
the seventy-three people who had been robbed
some barley soup, to which they added what
little meat they had. Eventually their provisions
were exhausted and everyone was on the verge
of starvation. Moved by compassion, and with
no thought for his own life, my precious heart-
son Kalden Rangdrol went along the river searching for a ford, but when he bravely tested the
ford, the current was so strong that he was swept
away and drowned. Filled with boundless grief, I
uttered these words of lamentation:

I pray to all the teachers
Who displayed the ways of passing into
   nirvana
To inspire Dharma practice
Among procrastinating disciples who think
   that everything lasts.

In the past, too, the Enlightened Teacher,
In order to turn our minds to the Dharma,
Displayed at Kushinagara the appearance
   of death;
And at the same time countless arhats
   passed away.

When Shariputra and Maudgalyayana
   passed away,

Countless arhats did likewise.
The Six Ornaments of the World,
The Two Supreme Ones, and all the
    learned and accomplished beings
Of India and Tibet also left this world.

Following in the footsteps of the past saints,
The Dharma King, Ngakyi Wangpo,
And so many of my own teachers have also
    passed away.
When I think of this, sadness fills my mind.

When Lodrak Marpa's son, Dharma
    Dodeh,
Was thrown by his horse and died,
His father and mother suffered
As though their hearts had been torn from
    their chests [427a].

Likewise, out of compassion for those who
    had lost everything,
This precious master went to search for a
    ford
And lost his life to the river.

Kye ma!
Sublime wish-fulfilling gem,
You have been swept off suddenly by the
    raging torrent.
Intense grief wells up within me;
Tears I can't control pour down like rain.

Having pondered the impermanence of
    things,
I shall practice the divine Dharma,
And dedicate all the merit of my practice
To my spiritual daughters and sons.

By the truth of my song,
May the precious lama
Be reborn in a celestial field.

Overwhelmed by sadness, I shed many tears.
By the strength of his compassion, soon after
Kalden Rangdrol's death a ford appeared in the
river. Many of my patrons from Banak Khasum,
the "Three Black Camps,"[7] who were on their
way to central Tibet arrived on the other side of

the Drichu River. We called out to them. In their
midst were some ferrymen who had brought
many horses and *dzos*, and who crossed to fetch
the survivors of the robbery. Everyone was able
to reach the other side of the river safe and
sound.

We then met the omniscient Kusho Nye
and Bensar Rinpoche. When we came upon
Norbu, of the Khyam family, and other faithful
men and women, patrons from Banak Khasum,
we rejoiced beyond expression. I stayed with
them for a day and gave them a long-life empowerment, as well as many blessed substances
[427b]. They gave us butter and *tsampa*, eighteen
bundles of tea, and horses to carry them. All
those now-destitute victims of the bandits, who
had almost died of starvation, realized that they
owed their lives and safe return to these patrons,
and remembered their kindness forever.

Continuing on our way to Domey, we encountered a group headed by the Khenpo and
the Nangso, two high officials of the central government; they were returning to Lhasa.[8] They,
too, gave us much tea, butter, and *tsampa*. Owing
to the kindness of these people, more than seventy survivors were able to continue their journey with sufficient food and clothing.

One day, the chief of the caravan left an
attendant behind, near a place called Choneh. I
felt great pity for him and, stopping by the road,
sent my disciple Drupchen half a day's walk to
fetch him. With difficulty, we continued on.

As we reached the top of the pass of Hato,
we saw the Kokonor, the Blue Lake. The sight of
it brought to my mind the memory of my root
teacher, Tendzin Nyima Rinpoche, who had
lived there before, and inspired these words:

True and precious guru,
My constant refuge in this and future lives,
Lord protector, look on me with compas-
    sion
From the Blissful Paradise; bless me.

In the past, in the wilderness of the Blue
    Lake,
The authentic guru was in good health;
I was young myself.

Thinking that I would meet the guru again
Later in my life, I went to central Tibet;
When I was in the Pure Realm of U-
    Tsang,
Not meeting him for many years, I longed
    to see him
Like someone parched with thirst [428a].

Having traveled by the long northern road;
Today, arriving within sight of the Blue
    Lake,
I learn that the guru is no more—
He has gone on to another Buddhafield.

Distress and weariness whirl in my mind.
What joy if he were here now!
I long to meet and serve him—
To see him, even for an instant,
Would make me as happy as reaching the
    bhumi of Perfect Joy.

Kye ma! How unfortunate I am—
Master and disciple did not meet again.

When I remember you dwelling
In the wilderness of the Blue Lake, tears fill
    my eyes;
I prostrate myself many times in your
    direction
And ask that you look upon me with
    compassion.

When the time comes for me to die,
May you, my guru, come,
To lead me without hindrance
To the Blissful Buddhafield.

May we then travel to many Pure Realms,
Make offerings to all the Buddhas,
And return to this impure world
To guide all beings!

As we neared the shore of the lake, we sat for
a while to rest. Led by Lharampa, the Mongolian monks and those who had been robbed said,
"Your compassion saved our lives!" Everyone
felt completely relieved; they were happy to be
alive. As a gesture of gratitude, they offered me

some silver, which I returned to them. By this
time, everyone felt so close to one another that,
when we separated to go our own ways, we
parted in tears [428b].

Reaching the shore of the Blue Lake, I was
happy to meet many friends, disciples and
patrons, including the Chöd practitioner of
Tromtsa and other disciples from Arik. As an
object of faith, I gave to the Chöd practitioner a
painting related to the mind treasure of Khardo
Rinpoche; it was sealed on the back by both the
master and his son.

I accepted an invitation from fifty nomads
of Derge and went to their camp near Arik.
They gave me many horses, *dzos*, and yaks. I
myself gave them many precious pieces of robes
of past saints and other sacred relics.

At this time, my spiritual son, the powerful
siddha Pema Rangdrol, accompanied by his father
Aka and a few other people, came to the Blue
Lake carrying a letter and a ceremonial scarf
from Pöntsang Chingwang Rinpoche,[9] but I had
I had already left for Xining. They went to wait
for me near Gomeh, while I myself was approaching Xining via Tongkhor.

In Xining, I told the Amban everything that
had happened; he said with great warmth, "It is
remarkable that you were able to save from
starvation so many who had been robbed, to
provide them with food and clothing, and to
bring them back. I am very happy about that."
He gave me tea, clothes, and other gifts.

Following this, I went to Kumbum, where I
met the throne-holder. As a funeral offering for
Lama Kalden Rangdrol, I presented a few horses
and *dzos* to the lamas of Kumbum and requested
their spiritual protection [429a]. I also offered
tea and three hundred silver coins to the monastic congregation. At the precious Golden Reliquary,[10] I offered a rosary of coral adorned with
various jewels, and a silver lamp made of six
ounces of Chinese silver. I also lit a hundred
butter-lamps, praying for the benefit of the
Dharma and all beings. We stayed and rested
there for thirteen days, doing prostrations and
circumambulations.

Then I went across to Dhitsa, where the
many *ngakpas* took good care of me. There I met

the accomplished *siddha* Pema Rangdrol and his retinue. He offered me a horse, a load of butter, a letter of greetings and a scarf from Chingwang Rinpoche, and other letters, all of which brought me great joy. To return his greetings I offered him a scarf; some particularly sacred objects related to body, speech, and mind; blessed substances and relics that had multiplied miraculously; a monk's jerkin; and a jeweled rosary. To Chingwang Rinpoche I sent blessed substances of the body, speech, and mind, multiplying relics of Lord Buddha, some corals and a ceremonial scarf. Very pleased, he later sent to me at Tashikhyil fifty *sang* of silver.

Many people from Gomeh came to meet me at the entrance to the Machu Valley. Some wealthy people offered me horses; I ended up with three of them, four loads of black tea bricks, and many ceremonial scarves. Then I came up the valley and went to see the temple of the Crowned Buddha of Trika. I stayed there a few days, making offerings [429b]. The enclosure of the Crowned Buddha's temple grew crowded with thousands of people from the Trika area, monks, laymen and women. I received them all, taught them the foundations of the Dharma, and gave the transmission of the *dharanis* of the Three Lords, the *Miktsema* prayer, and the Vajra Guru and longevity mantras. Finally I sang this song:

Compassionate Buddha, I supplicate you—
Look upon us, your followers!

I shall now sing of the benefit of virtue:
Listen to me with a joyous, undistracted mind!

If you offer even a single flower or incense stick
To the Three Jewels, you will be reborn in the Immutable Buddhafield.

If you offer butter-lamps, in your next life you will have a beautiful appearance
And obtain the clairvoyance of celestial beings.

If you offer service to the sangha,
In your future lives you will be a great king.

If you offer fields and crops,
You will enjoy the increasing bliss of the higher realms and Pure Lands.

If you serve your parents, you will never be disparaged,
And in your next life you will surely go to the higher realms.

If you give food, you will have a beautiful complexion and a long life, and
You will be gifted with great strength and enjoy abundance of food and wealth.

If you give drink, you will have all sense-faculties intact,
And, when thirsty, you will find something delicious to drink.

If you give clothes, you will have a beautiful appearance and fine complexion,
And will have good clothing in all of your lives.

If you give a horse, you will achieve the four bases of miraculous powers,
And will be able to go wherever you wish [430ab].

If you give a cow, you will have strength and fine color,
And a great abundance of milk, curd, butter, and other riches.

If you give food to a large anthill,
You will be reborn as the king of a vast country.

If you give the Dharma, you will obtain clairvoyance;
You will remember your former births and swiftly attain Buddhahood.

If you repair a boat, a path, or a bridge,
From life to life you will go from bliss to
    bliss, and be respected by all.

If you erect sacred objects related to the
    body, speech, and mind,
Your life span and merit will increase;
In the present, you will be happy;
Ultimately you will attain Buddhahood.

If you offer prostrations and
    circumambulations,
You will be reborn as a universal monarch
As many times as the number of dust
    particles beneath your prostrate body.

If you recite the *mani*,
You will be free from sickness and will
    remember your former lives;
At death you will be reborn in Sukhavati.

If you have great compassion, you will
    have a long life, progress in the
    Dharma,
And, not remaining in the peace of
    nirvana,
You will become a guide for beings.

May all men and women who hear this
    song,
Practice virtue and swiftly attain
    Buddhahood.

All the people from Tromlha who were gathered there rejoiced greatly and were confirmed in their faith.

At that time the community of yogins of Nub Khamra came to greet me and offered many bricks of black tea. In return I offered them a painted scroll from central Tibet as an object of faith. About a hundred people—some on horseback, some on foot—came from my homeland, Shohong Lakha, to receive me, led by the chieftains Tralo and Tselo. When we met, everyone rejoiced.

Continuing on, I went to pay homage to the local deity of Trika [430b]. I offered some brocade, two rings of gold and silver, and some turquoise and corals, beseeching the deity to act for the sake of the Dharma and all beings. I met, too, the two Jamgon Lamas, senior and junior, as well as Kusho Shabdrung Karpo. I offered them sacred objects related to the body, speech, and mind, relics that had multiplied miraculously, and other sacred substances, along with a bowl in divine *dzab* wood[11] and a rosary. To establish spiritual connections, I requested some teaching from them; on their part, they gave me some horses, clothes, and many other presents and provisions.

I then went to visit the monasteries of Deshung district in Trika and offered some relics. I taught the local men and women, and said prayers of dedication and auspiciousness. Faithful people offered me barley, coins, pieces of cloth and ceremonial scarves—over three hundred items altogether. I gave these to Kumbum Monastery as reimbursement for the coins I had distributed earlier.

After this I reached the Yellow Valley of Rekong. At the pass of Thang, the treasurer and other main attendants of the Omniscient One of Shar, from the great monastery of Rongpo, had come to welcome me with many horsemen.[12] Accompanied by them, I reached Rongpo Gön. The day I entered the monastery, many rainbows appeared in the sky; they were seen by both Tibetans and Chinese. Everyone said it was an auspicious sign, and the faithful rejoiced.

When I entered the presence of the Precious Omniscient One of Shar [431a], I offered him a full set of robes, the skin of a *krishnasara* antelope[13] with its two horns, a longevity vase made of gilded copper (with a stopper carved with an image of Amitayus), a finely painted set of three scrolls from central Tibet representing the Sixteen Arhats, eighty-eight volumes of the collected writings of various teachers, and one horse, one mule, and twenty-five yaks, all with their saddles. I requested from him the transmission of the *dharanis* of the Three Lords, the *dharani* of longevity, and the prayer known as the *Ground of Good Qualities*. I venerated him as my root teacher, thinking of him always present above my head as a crown jewel.

I also met all the other lamas of Rongpo: Khenchen Tulku, Yershong Tulku, Rongpo Tsang, Kusho Samdrup, Changse Tsang, the senior and junior Dzongkar, the senior and junior Dechen, and others. I asked them for some teachings to form spiritual bonds with them, and I offered one yak with its saddle to each of the senior attendants. With ten large packages of tea, I offered tea to all the monks of the monastery.

Lamas, chieftains, monks and nuns, and men and women of Rekong by the tens of thousands came to meet me. I gave audience for many days. Almost all the lamas and chieftains asked me, "From the time you first left our country until now, which holy places have you visited, which extraordinary lamas and sacred objects have you met, what sort of things have you seen? Today, you must recount all this for us in great detail" [431b]. I told them at length how I had visited the great holy places and practiced there, how I had met many teachers and paid homage to many sacred objects, and how in different countries I had seen people dressed in all sorts of ways. Finally, I summarized everything in these verses:

Masters, grant your blessings
That I accomplish all my aims!

I, the yogin Tsogdruk Rangdrol,
Became weary of samsaric affairs,
And, leaving my native land,
Went to the monastery of Doby.
There, I met Yongdzin Arik Geshe,
And from him received the full monastic vows.
I understood that discipline was the root of the Dharma
And acted in accordance with the Vinaya, not eating in the evening, for example.

Then I went to Little Mongolia
And met the Dharma King Ngakyi Wangpo.

I received instructions that unite sutra and tantra,
And preserved the Three Vows as though they were my own eyes.

I went to the wilderness of Tseshung
And practiced for five years.
Through the kindness of the Dharma King and his consort
Everything went well; my experiences and realization flourished.

I went to the wilderness of Tsonying Island
And practiced for three years.
In meditation experiences and in dreams,
I heard teachings from the gurus and deities.
I was happy on this delightful island,
Where seven kinds of birds sing.

I went to the glaciers of Machen
And practiced for nine months.
I saw the faces of many deities
In reality, visions and dreams [432a].

On my way back, events turned out well
When I happened to ride on a wild *drong*.

I went to Trakar Drel Dzong
And meditated for six months.
I saw on the rocks of this sacred place
Many naturally formed figures of deities.
From the patrons of the Three Black Camps,
Provisions fell upon me like rain.

The death of my mother
Led me to the Pure Realm of U-Tsang.
In Lhasa I paid homage to the two Crowned Buddhas,
Which I perceived as the Buddha himself.

I met the Precious Victorious One,[14]
Whom I saw as the Lotus-bearer in person.
The Potala Palace of the Victorious One
Has extraordinary walls which seem to have grown by themselves.

The beautiful dress and ornaments of the
    Lhasa people
Seemed to me to be those of celestial
    beings.
At the Great Prayer Festival
I saw all sorts of amazing scenes.

I saw the Great Golden Reliquary of
    Ganden,
The most supreme object of offering and
    prostrations,
And perceived it as if meeting
The Victorious One, Lobzang Trakpa, in
    person.

I went to glorious Samye, the
    Inconceivable,
And saw the Triple-Styled Central
    Temple.
Remembering the graciousness of the
    Abbot, the Master and the King,[15]
Boundless faith grew in me.
During the Sutra Offering at Samye,[16]
I saw many wondrous happenings.

I made the pilgrimage of the Tsari
    Ravines,
Where I experienced both happiness and
    hardship.
Seeing some Lhopas wearing small
    cymbals
Attached to their ears made me laugh
    [432b].

The Turquoise Palace Lake of Tsari
Seemed to be laid out as a mandala of
    turquoise.
I saw great *siddhas* remain on glaciers
    overnight
Wearing a single cotton garment.
Practicing there for one year,
I had various visions and spiritual
    experiences.

On my way back, I went to Shar Dagla
    Gampo
And saw the abode of the Physician of
    Dagpo.

I remained there about four months,
Contemplating the life-stories of Kagyu
    masters of the past.

I went to Tashi Lhunpo
And met Panchen Rinpoche,
Whom I saw as the lord of the Blissful
    Realm in person.
The roofs of the temples
Were shining like golden suns—
Such a great and pleasant monastery
Is indeed a wonder in the world.

I went to Tö Ngari
And saw the three silver-crowned Buddhas.
The inhabitants of Purang have great faith
    in the Dharma,
And many of them gave me all I needed to
    sustain me.

I went to the White Snows of Mount
    Kailash
And remained in retreat for three years.
At the door of my cave, I expounded the
    Dharma,
Accomplishing the good of others as well
    as my own.

The snow-white summit of Mount Kailash
Is like a stupa of crystal.
There are many gold mines.
Crystal-sugar and molasses can be bought.

I went to the land of Lo
And visited the Hundred Springs,
Where one can see fire continually burning
On the waters and in the cracks of the
    earth and rocks.

I went to the border between Nepal and
    Tibet,
Where I saw the self-arisen Wati Zangpo
    [433a].[17]
By the blessings of this sublime image,
Everyone there enjoyed happiness.

I journeyed into Nepal
And paid homage at the two Great Stupas.

It is a delightful paradise, with green grass
And colorful flowers, even in the winter.
There, women adorn their noses with
    golden rings.

I went to the Snows of Lapchi
And practiced there for three years.
By the blessings of the deities and the
    dakinis,
I constantly saw rainbow clouds.

I came back to central Tibet,
And, as before, encountered spiritual
    teachers and sacred objects.
By accomplishing the good of others,
My own benefit was accomplished as well.

I finally returned to Lower Dokham,
And today, in celebration of our meeting
Within the auspicious and harmonious
    sphere of the Dharma,
I have offered you these agreeable words

May this song benefit the minds
Of all those who hear it.
Virtue prevailing all over the country,
May everyone practice the Dharma!

These stories about the lands of Tö, U, Tsang,
and others, satisfied everyone.

I went to meet Kusho Magsar Rinpoche[18] who,
having fallen ill, was on the verge of death. Soon
after we met each other, he passed away with a
joyful heart, but my mind was sad beyond measure [433b]. For his funeral, I offered a horse, a
dzo, and a large white porcelain cup, as well as
some brocades; I performed dedication prayers, comforted everyone, and looked after his monastery.

I met Drupwang Namkha Rinpoche[19] and
Götse Tulku. One of my spiritual sons from the
early days, Alak Dechen, invited me to his home,
and offered me objects symbolic of body, speech,
and mind, as well as a large-sized bell,[20] five

head each of horses and cattle, a hundred large
pieces of cloth, and a hundred ceremonial scarves.
I accepted these and said prayers to dedicate the
merit. Then I went to the end of Gowu, the
auspicious and pleasant place where Jetsun
Kalden Gyatso had meditated in the past, and
stayed there a few days.

During that time, three tribes from Lingya
and seven from Lower Jam were feuding. The
whole area was seething with unrest; about eighteen people had already been killed. When I
heard about it, I went there and blessed them all,
after which the demon instigating their quarrel—their spiteful thoughts and violence—qui-
eted down. Having talked to them in accord with
both the Dharma and the customs of this world,
I settled them down.

Having left the chief Tralo as my temporary representative, we all, master and disciples,
went to Shelgon, the Crystal Monastery, and
met Kusho Chumar Rinpoche. I offered him
symbols of body, speech, and mind, and requested some teaching from him to create a
spiritual connection between us. Treating us as
guests coming from afar, he gave us all the provisions we needed. When I took leave, he gave me
a mule, a lot of cloth, and some silk.

When I returned from Shelgon, I was able
to settle the feud between Lingya and Lower
Jam once and for all; many human lives were
saved [434a].

As the river of Serkha had become muddy
and was running dry, problems and repeated
quarrels arose among the local people. I blessed
the river, and from that year onwards, it broad-
ened and flowed without cease. For the first
time, an abundance of trees and shrubs flourished there. People said that this was a miraculous deed, and their faith became stronger than
ever. This ended, too, all reason for people to
quarrel and kill each other about sharing the
water.

Then, taking the White Road, I reached
Shohong Lakha and my own village, Nyengya. I
met my two sisters, my nephews, and other relatives, and all the people around were extremely
pleased to see me. The whole village gave a feast,
after which everyone asked me to their homes.

They offered me eighteen horses and head of cattle, and forty bags of barley.

I went to my mother's house, which was deserted and had fallen into ruins. In one corner was a small shed with no one but a lone, half-paralyzed woman. When she saw me, she cried. I felt great pity for her; the image of my old mother rose in my mind. Now, not only was my mother no more, but even her home no longer existed. Tears gathered in my eyes; filled with sadness, thinking, "It's really true that all things are impermanent," I sang this song [434b]:

Gurus, Buddhas and Bodhisattvas,
Having seen with your wisdom eyes
Wherever in the six realms my mother
    may be,
Lead her to the pure Blissful Buddhafield.

At the time that I lived here,
I myself was young, and my mother was
    not old.
I then went off to other lands—
But I thought that I would meet her once
    again
In the clear light of this world.

When my kind mother stayed at home,
I, the son, left for distant places.
By the time that I returned,
My mother had gone on to the next world:
The reunion of mother and son did not
    occur.

Thinking of this, I remember my mother.
What joy if she were here now!
How I wish that mother and son
Could meet again once more!
If we could meet but for an instant,
How happy would be the reunion of the
    living with the dead!

Kye ma!
Everything that exists in samsara
Is fleeting, impermanent, essenceless.

My mother is no more—that's how it is.
Even her house did not outlast her.

Both my mother and her home have given
    me
The teachings on impermanence
And the transience of illusory phenomena.

Contemplating this, I, the yogin,
Feel sadness deep within my mind;
I want to relinquish pointless activities;
I want to practice the divine, purposeful
    Dharma.

As result of practicing this holy Dharma,
May the two of us, mother and son,
Be reunited in our next lives in a pure
    Buddhafield,
Talk together joyfully,
Make offerings to all the Buddhas,
And guide all sentient beings.

Sadness welled up from the depths of my being [435a]. I thought, "My work in my homeland is over; who knows when my life's work will be finished?" This reflection strengthened my diligence in performing positive actions.

After some time the ailing woman died. I erected a temple and a stupa on the site where my home had been. There, I gave teaching on *mani*, setting into motion the stream of virtue. Following this, all the local people never stopped doing prostrations, circumambulating, and making daily offerings, morning and evening.

Following this, I went to Tashikhyil Hermitage.[21] The caretakers of the monastery, the senior and junior lamas of Shohong, the chieftain Norbu, and all the men and women of the locality, came to see me and requested the initiation of the Great Compassionate One. On the day I gave it, the sky was filled with rainbows; seeing this, everyone felt stronger faith than ever. They offered me all the tea, butter, and *tsampa* I could use.

My Dharma friend Chogden, a sky-like yogin who had destroyed illusion and attained sublime realization, asked for some condensed spiritual advice on the way to maintain recognition of the nature of mind. In answer I said:

"Aku Chogden, listen well! Your body and everything that exists in samsara and nirvana— the universe and the beings in it—are just words, names; they do not have an atom of existence on their own; they are primordially void, like the sky. Manifest phenomena are but an architecture of various causes and conditions that came into being on the basis of our various good and bad actions, through the process of interdependent arising. Like a rainbow in the sky, the reflection of the moon in water, or an image in a mirror, although they do not exist, they appear; they are empty even though they are apparent [435b]. This entire illusory display of unreal void-appearances is fabricated by mind, appears in mind, and remains in the expanse of mind.

"The nature of mind is an infinite, all-encompassing and unobstructed expanse, void and luminous, free of taking things as real, and devoid of fabrication—like the sky. To remain in total ease and openness within this natural expanse of mind is to become a glorious sky-like yogin for whom there is no difference between friend and enemy, gold and stone, the present life and future lives." I continued with this song:

I continually supplicate the accomplished
    guru
Whose realization is as vast as the sky:
Watch over me with your compassionate
    eyes
And bless me so that your mind and mine
    fuse into one.

The source of all phenomena of samsara
    and nirvana
Is the nature of mind—void, luminous,
All-encompassing, vast as the sky.

When remaining in that state of sky-like
    vastness,
Relax into its openness; remain in that very
    openness,
Merge with that sky-like state:
Naturally, it will become more and more
    relaxed—
Excellent!

If you become accomplished
In this method of integrating mind with
    view,[22]

Your realization will naturally become
    vast.

Just as the sun shines unobstructed within
    the sky,
Compassion will infallibly shine on all
    unrealized beings [436a].
If an heir of the yogin Longchen Rabjam's
    lineage
Sings a spiritual song, he will sing in this
    way.

O yogin, destroyer of illusion, endowed
    with supreme realization,
If you want to maintain awareness of the
    nature of mind, follow this song.

I pray that, after death, you may be
    liberated in the absolute body,
And benefit beings with your manifest
    body.

After hearing this song, Chogden relaxed in unobstructed openness, and as he remained in this state his realization of the natural brilliance and vastness of mind increased greatly. From then on, no matter where he was, his perceptions remained completely free and at ease. Knowing how to get along with everyone, he was always joyful. Later, when he passed away, he did so with pure joy, in the state of the great openness and freedom of the absolute nature. A limpid sky and other excellent signs indicated that at the moment of death he had achieved liberation in the dharmakaya.

Having held a meeting, the local patrons decided to repair the monastery, which was in a poor condition. All the faithful men and women from the Upper and Lower Shohong all the way to Tsodu in Lingya came; many people began to work. All the nomads from Awartheu, Kangtsa, Lhashi and other places came in crowds to join us, bringing supplies of tea, butter, milk, curd, and cheese. While villagers and nomads were carrying on the restoration work [436b], the Vajradhara lama, Kusho Serkhang Rinpoche, came and offered many horses and cattle as a contribution to the restoration.

Having blessed this place of veneration by setting foot there, he said, "I had a good dream last night; I dreamed that the whole hill of Tashikhyil was covered with temples and hermitages, right to the top." Later, his prediction came true. An outstanding Dharma and *samaya* connection was established between us, and our minds mingled as one.

At that time too, many lamas and spiritual teachers—Kusho Hortsang, Changlung Tulku, Alak Tragpoche, and others—came, offered many horses and cattle, and asked for teaching. Complying with their wishes, I offered them initiations, transmissions, and explanations on the profound path of Chöd, and whatever other teachings they wanted. Over several months, I gave several initiations, such as the Avalokiteshvara initiation of the *Sixteen Spheres*[23] from the Kadampa tradition, and initiations of Vajrasattva and of Vajra Kilaya, as well as blessings for longevity and prosperity. I gave transmissions and explanations to the congregation of yogins and to many laymen and laywomen. I also gave many of them monastic vows.

In this way I was able to turn everyone's mind toward the Dharma. Many male and female disciples, such as Lodrö of Gomeh, the Gelong of Khagya, the sculptor of Mangra, Rigdrol the Mongolian, and others, completely relinquished the ordinary affairs of this life. Hundreds of monks, nuns, and *ngakpas* such as the hidden yogin Pema Rigdzin, the hermit of Tongsa, Rinchen Dorje, and so on, either devoted their whole lives to spiritual practice or stayed several months or years in retreat [437a].

When help was welcome for the restoration of the temple, my relative Aku Menpa offered a horse with its saddle, carpet, and bridle, a full set of clothes, a big bundle of tea, and two lumps of butter, one big and one small. His attendant, Gelong Tenpa Dargye, contributed one big bundle of tea, two ounces of silver, five bags of barley, and a few wide pieces of cloth, all of

which proved very useful. I gave them both the transmission and explanations of the *Condensed Meaning of the Graded Path*[24] and the transmission of the *Transference That Leads to Enlightenment Without Meditation.* I gave them many miraculously multiplied relics of the Buddha, and other blessed substances.

When the outer works of the temple had been completed, the mask makers Jamyang Tashi and Trogyal Bum and the sculptor Sonam Rinchen made the statues and other sacred objects inside. Both the outside and the inside were decorated with various paintings. A monastic congregation was then installed.

To pay for this, I spent nine packets of red and yellow gold leaves, and gave five hundred lengths of cloth to the artists and the same to the carpenters; altogether I must have spent the equivalent of more than a thousand ounces of silver.

Having more or less settled at Tashikhyil, I deposited there most of the precious things I had brought from U and Tsang. I gave the rest of the statues and *thangka* paintings to neighboring monasteries [437b]. I used the miraculously multiplied relics and other precious relics I had to fill statues and other sacred objects symbolic of enlightened body, speech, and mind that had been erected in some one hundred and eight temples. As time passed, I also gave some to many faithful people. The whole region became filled with these three kinds of sacred objects.

After having performed the consecration of the temple, I offered a feast and sang a song in praise of the place:

> I pay homage to all the Victorious Ones of
>   the past
> Who attained Buddhahood by dwelling in
>   solitary places:
> Bless us, your followers, practitioners of the
>   Dharma,
> That we be able to remain in mountain
>   retreat.
>
> South of the king of mountains, the central
>   Meru,
> North of the Diamond Throne of India,

East of the Pure Realm of U-Tsang,
South of the lofty Mount Kyeri in
    Tsongkha,
Is the Yellow Valley of Rekong,
Containing the Eight Places of the
    Accomplished Ones and their
    surroundings.[25]
The highlands bear vast forests and
    berry-shrubs,
And the meadowed hillsides are blanketed
    with flowers.
At the border between rural and nomadic
    areas,
On a lofty hill with a wide summit,
Stands the great holy place called
    Tashikhyil—
A place foretold by the saints of the past,
The seat of many learned and
    accomplished sages,
The paradise where deities and dakinis
    gather.

Its excellent qualities are obvious,
But if you wish to know what they are:
The ground is like an eight-petaled lotus,
The sky is like an eight-spoked wheel,
The shape of the mountain
Is that of a standing elephant [438a].
The temple of the Blissful Paradise
Is like the gem on the elephant's head.
The temple of the Vidyadharas,
The temple of Maitreya, and the others,
Are like its jewel and gold ornaments.

On the mountain slopes one can recognize
    the eight auspicious symbols
And the seven emblems of royalty.

First, to the east is the lofty Drapchen,
Second, to the south is the formidable
    Nyenmar,
Third, to the west is the luxuriant Gödzong,
Fourth, to the north is the ruddy Jadrön.[26]
All face towards Tashikhyil,
As though protecting it.

All around, the garland of forests
Unfolds like a circle of benefactors;

The two rivers to the right and left
Are like white scarves softly laid across
    mountains and valleys.

Cuckoos and laughing-thrushes sing out in
    clear tones.
Wild animals amble here and there, utterly
    at ease.
There are plenty of wild berries,
Nettles, garlic, and other edible plants.
There are plenty of green slopes, cool leafy
    shades,
And meadows illuminated with flowers.

In the valleys, *tsampa* and bread are
    plentiful;
And among the nomads curd, whey,
    butter, and cheese abound.
Whatever else one needs is easily found
In the nearby valleys and the nomads'
    pastures.
No one is imperiled by enemies, robbers or
    wild beasts.

This sublime place where all desirable
    things are gathered
Resembles an abode of the gods of the
    realm of desire.
Of all the secluded places near here,
This is the most pleasant [438b].

For those who live here,
There will be no obstacles to practice
And the sun of experience and realization
    will shine.

By the virtue of having mentioned some of
    the qualities of this holy place,
May the magnificence of the teachings of
    the practice lineage
Fill the whole of this secluded place,
And these teachings spread and increase.

As I sang this, everyone became happy. At
this time, Kusho Tsendrok Khen Rinpoche,[27]
someone with universal knowledge of both the
new and the ancient traditions, and one of the
teachers of the Manchu emperor, was living in

the royal palace of China. I sent him a letter with a drum for the practice of Chöd, embellished with representations of the eight cemeteries; a thighbone trumpet covered with silver inlaid with turquoise and corals; a fine *phurba* of gilded copper; earth from many holy places; various kinds of relics; and a white ceremonial scarf. In reply he favored me with these verses:

Lord of *siddhas*, Wheel of the Teaching,[28]
Manifest dance of the Holder of the Lotus
    Flower,[29]
Emanation sprung from the compassionate
    power of Victorious Ones and their
    sons,
To you who bring bliss and benefit to all
    beings,
Here speaks your close friend, truly the
    portrait of a fox,
Tarrying in oblivious ignorance,
Wearing the showy fur of the eight worldly
    concerns
That will make for the death of perfect
    virtue.[30]

My ten fingers of unshakable, spontaneous
    faith
Rise by themselves above my head [439a]
To toss from your longtime, devoted
    friend,
The bouquet of this poem.

Born from the majesty of your twofold
    accumulation,
The full array of your body's marks and
    signs
Is the dazzling orb of the Lord of the
    Emerald Steeds[31]
That radiates throughout the ten directions
    of space the beams of your twofold
    activity,[32]
Wholly illuminating the excellent path of
    the sutras and tantras that ripen and
    free
And establish in glorious bliss the swarm of
    fortunate bees
That feed on the lotus garden of the
    Muni's teachings:

The glory of such deeds blazes up to the
    peak of samsaric existence.

As a sign of our indestructible friendship,
Built up by our births, our prayers, and our
    karma,
Is it not wondrous that, though the width
    of a whole country lies between us,
We are together at the time of spiritual
    work?

The sacred relics, Chöd drum, thighbone
    trumpet and *phurba*,
Which rolled down from the mountain of
    your benevolence
As auspicious omens for the performance
    of the Four Activities,
Blossomed and filled with joy my mind's
    spring.

The flower of my life is now a bit withered;
Having been spared by the killing touch of
    frost,
It lingers amidst endless ripples of
    meaningless distraction.

Henceforth, just as the king of the Shakyas
    conceived the thought of enlightenment,
I shall follow the perfect career of the great
    beings
Who developed ardent courage
To transform others, especially those
    hardest to tame [439b].

It seems difficult to find a way of acting
Attuned to the minds of the beings of our
    times.
Most of the learned and accomplished
    sages
Have passed away or gone into the easy
    rest of their own practice.
I request that you increase even further
    your peerless aspiration
To work for the sake of others,
Remaining alive a long time in the glory of
    the benefit and bliss you bring to others.
Never cast me out of the expanse of your
    kindness.

The stream of the words I offer you having
    overflowed,
It could not be contained in the white
    conch of this immaculate paper;
May this water, now calmly collected in
    the lake of your messenger's mind,
Be allowed to flow into the river of your
    heart![33]

On this day, from the Yung monastery, I
respectfully offer you this letter laid upon a
celestial scarf, a dress, a hat and a belt.

When I received this letter, which he had sent
with great enthusiasm, I felt as much joy as though
meeting him in person.

One night I dreamt that I came to a place said to
be the Paradise Arrayed in Turquoise Petals[34]—
a vast and even plain, perfect in all aspects,
ringed with different kinds of trees with beautiful
leaves, flowers, and fruits. In the middle of the
plain stood a lofty three-story pavilion entirely
made of jewels, the beauty of which was enhanced
by a glittering golden dome, just like paintings of
Buddhafields.

As I arrived on the path that encircled the
pavilion, there came three young maidens doing
circumambulations. One of them kept on looking at me and asked, "Don't you recognize me?"
"No," I said, "I don't" [440a]. She continued,
"Son, I am your mother! After I died, I came
here. It has been many years since I've seen you.
It is good that we've met again. You've grown
old, my son."

The image of my mother in her old age was
vivid in my mind and I cried. My mother, too,
could not hold back her tears. Then I asked,
"Who are these two other girls?" and she mentioned the names of two old women of our village who were always reciting prayers to Drolma.
The girls, too, looked at me and cried. When I
recalled the faces of the two old grandmothers,
more tears filled my eyes. "It is really good that

you are all happy now! But where do you usually
stay?" I asked. "We live in the Western Blissful
Buddhafield; we came this morning to circumambulate and offer prostrations to Jetsun Drolma.
For the moment, you must continue benefiting
beings; later we will meet again, in whichever
Buddhafield you attain." With that, the three
girls continued their circumambulations. As I
was thinking myself to do some, I woke up.

I realized that what had become of my old
mother and her friends, the two old ladies, was
thanks to their having said many prayers to
Drolma, and I felt great joy.

That year, just before the autumn, I went to
Gartse Monastery at the invitation of its monastic community [440b]. They presented me with
a hundred different offerings, starting with a big
bundle of tea. Some monks from wealthy families asked me to their cells and offered me bundles
of tea also. I then proceeded to Shuknyin Hermitage, where Kusho Gartse gave me one bundle
of tea and two lengths of thick woolen cloth.[35]
The junior lama of Gartse gave me one horse,
one *dzo*, and two lengths of woolen cloth; the old
lama Tendzin gave me a large bundle of tea; all
the monks and neighbors, too, offered me a lot of
provisions and other things. I made a distribution of money and tea to all the monks, offerings
to the two main lamas, and requested teaching
from them. From then on, we were to accomplish many religious tasks, helping each other as
friends.

Then, one after the other, I visited the nomadic areas of Awartheu, Kangtsa, Lhashi, Rang
Ngen, Gengya, and Luchu Thang. They gave us
a thrilling welcome; everywhere it was all, "The
gods have come! Glory has come!" and so on.
They sent parties of horsemen to receive me,
cooked and made tea in common, and requested
teachings. To each group I gave empowerments
for longevity and prosperity, and whatever teaching they wanted. Everyone's mind was turned
toward the Dharma, and in great faith both the

rich and the poor made offerings. The offerings came to eighty horses and head of cattle, seven big bundles of tea, thirty-three large and small hide-pouches of butter, thirty-one lengths of white felt,[36] and many pieces of wool, cotton, and ceremonial scarves.

From Lhashi I went to meet Taksang Lhamö Ser Tri Rinpoche, a Bodhisattva who was dwelling on the *bhumis* [441a]. I offered him a horse and requested some teaching. Then I went to Nyimalung Monastery and met Alak Hortsang, who gave me horses and cattle in great number. On my part, as substitute for a general distribution of alms and tea, I offered to the monastery several horses and head of cattle.

Going to Gengya, I visited the great holy site of Trakar, the White Rock, and remained for many days in the guest house attached to it. Establishing a connection with this holy place, I met the Dakini of Trakar, offered her the symbols of body, speech, and mind, and requested some teaching from her. As the equivalent of a tea offering, I offered one horse to the monastery. I stayed there for two days, doing prostrations and circumambulating the temple.

Just before the winter, I came back home and gave initiations and teachings to benefit the people of Shohong Chi. I was offered a hundred and fifty large and small bags of wheat and barley, and nearly thirty horses and other animals. During the winter I went to the various districts of Shohong Lakha, taught the Dharma, and gave empowerments. On the occasion of a general feast, people sang songs like this one sung by Nam Lhagyal:

> One garment gives warmth to all beings—
> The sun of Jambudvipa.
> One food sustains all beings—
> The white *tsampa*.
> One chief can rule all his provinces—
> The Manchu ruler.

And the singer Tse Wangyal sang:

> High mountains? Tsongkha Kyeri is high:
> Even birds must fly around it, not over it;

> Wide rivers? Machu Luma is wide [441b]:
> When crossing, one starts above and ends
>   far down;

> Great rulers? The Manchu ruler is great:
> People are still paying attention this year
> To what he was saying last year.

Two girls sang in unison:

> When the sun emerges from behind the
>   mountain,
> See how sunny and shady slopes both grow
>   warm.

> When the moon rises high in the
>   firmament,
> See how mountains and plains both grow
>   clear.

> When the protector and refuge comes back
>   from U,
> See how old and young faces all grow
>   happy.

A young boy sang:

> The lama is a winter sun—
> Day after day he shines brighter.
> The treasurer is a cairn on the mountain
>   pass—
> Day after day he grows richer.[37]
> Monks are stars in the sky—
> Day after day their numbers increase.

These songs and dances filled everyone with joy. The chieftain Tralo offered me a silver *dotse* and five bags of barley; the chieftain Tselo, twenty-five bags of barley, ten ounces of silver, and one piece of brocade; and with everyone, rich and poor, offering me whatever they had amassed, the offerings came to thirty horses and other animals, and over three hundred bags of barley, big and small.

I spent the rest of the winter in retreat at Tashikhyil. When the warmth of spring came back, I turned the Wheel of the Dharma, expounding the *Graded Path*, mind training, instructions on the nature of mind, and other teachings. I also sang a song explaining the need for compassion, the root of all Dharma:

Avalokiteshvara, mighty Great Treasure of
   Compassion
From my heart I invoke your blessing [442a].
By this blessing, may compassion be born
   in my mind
And in the minds of all beings under the
   sky.

If a man has compassion, he is a Buddha;
Without compassion, he is a Lord of
   Death.

With compassion, the root of Dharma is
   planted,
Without compassion, the root of Dharma
   is rotten.

One with compassion is kind even when
   angry,
One without compassion will kill even as
   he smiles.

For one with compassion, even his enemies
   will turn into friends,
Without compassion, even his friends turn
   into enemies.

With compassion, one has all Dharmas;
Without compassion, one has no Dharma
   at all.

With compassion, one is a Buddhist,
Without compassion, one is worse than a
   heretic.

Even if meditating on voidness, one needs
   compassion as its essence.
A Dharma practitioner must have a
   compassionate nature.

Compassion is the distinctive characteristic
   of Buddhism.

Compassion is the very essence of all
   Dharmas.

Great compassion is like a wish-fulfilling
   gem.
Great compassion will fulfill the hopes of
   self and others.

Therefore, all of you, practitioners and
   laypeople,
Cultivate compassion and you will achieve
   Buddhahood.

May all men and women who hear this
   song,
With great compassion benefit all beings!

This song benefited everyone's mind [442b]; many became Dharma practitioners and, with the love of a mother for her child, cared with intense compassion for all suffering beings.

In the summer, accompanied by Kusho Gartse Rinpoche, the old lama Tendzin, and many chieftains and disciples, I went to settle a feud that had been going on for eighteen years between the people of Doby and Seychang, and that had led to the loss of the lives of over eighty men and horses, with still more killing going on. Neither envoys from China nor lamas and officials from Tibet had succeeded in settling the dispute. Speaking to both parties, I brought them to an agreement.

In this region was a stupa known as Namdag Chenmo, the Great Pure One, which contained a begging bowl made of lapis lazuli filled with small relics of the Buddha Kashyapa. It had become damaged, and I restored it. On the day of the thanksgiving feast for the consecration, sitting at the feet of the Great Stupa, I taught the Dharma. Everyone, even the Chinese, Mongols and Muslim Salars,[38] listened with faith. Later, people said, "The words of our Kachu Buddha[39] and those of the Lama Shabkar from Tibet are identical."

Then the Dotheye[40] of Xining came on a tour. He had heard that I used to feed many beggars and especially that I had taken care of and safely brought back many people who had been robbed by Golok bandits, and that I had thus benefited the country. When he reached Yadzi, he called me into his presence and said [443a], "I am very pleased to hear all this news about you; you are truly a good Dharma practitioner." He gave me a piece of brocade, some black tea, and a mirror, adding, "Henceforth, continue to benefit beings. In particular, tell each bandit group from Banak Khasum and Nyakyarul to stop robbing and to respect the command of the emperor. This will benefit those places. If you come to visit the Five-peaked Mountain, I shall help you." At my request, he freed many prisoners at Yadzi and everyone, even the Salars, became filled with faith and respect.

Then I went to Shardzong, the Eastern Fortress, where Jetsun Kalden Gyatso had meditated; I stayed there many days to establish a connection with this holy place. I also erected a stupa of piled-up stones, and beside the monastic community I built a walled enclosure for holding religious debates. Within it, I erected a mansion sheltering a statue of the Protector of Nechung, whom I supplicated to increase the prosperity of the monastery.

I gave a long-life empowerment and taught the Dharma to all the villagers, who became filled with faith. Many of them offered me food, animals, and possessions. I myself gave service to the monastic community. I also brought back many bags of barley to Tashikhyil, where they were very useful.

From Tashikhyil, I went first to Lingya. Giving teachings and empowerments, singing spiritual songs—through various means I turned everyone's mind towards the Dharma and inspired strong faith in them. They offered me about a hundred bags of wheat and two hundred large and small bags of barley [443b].

At that time my fortunate disciple Gyurme and my good friend the retreatant Toptsang left together on pilgrimage to the Five-peaked Mountain of China. I visited one by one all the districts of the upper, middle and lower parts of the Golden Valley of Rekong—the ten districts of Lower Jam, Nyang, Dardrong, Changchup, Kyitsang, Tsodu, Gyalpo, Trang Yar, Nang, Sedo Runyin, Chuma, Shalang, Lhönchö, Hornag Lakha, the seven districts of Rongpo, the four parts of Gyatre, and so on. To all the male and female patrons I explained the Dharma and gave empowerments.

In particular, I gave them much advice regarding the affairs of this world, following which all dissension and quarrels ceased. I began many projects that were the sources of virtuous activity. Especially in the places where there were no temples, no *mani* prayer-wheels, and no stupas, I urged them to erect holy edifices and objects related to the body, speech, and mind of the Buddhas.

All the benefactors, rich and poor, of the north and south sides of Rekong, filled with faith, offered many provisions and animals: one thousand and thirty bags of barley, horses, yaks, *dris,* and oxen (two hundred head altogether), thirteen big and small skin-bags of butter; five big bundles of tea, two *dotse* of silver; red woolen bags,[41] lengths of cloth of various colors and several thousand ceremonial scarves. On that occasion I offered the following prayer for the fulfillment of whatever the disciples and patrons wished [444a]:

> May the blessings of the Three Jewels enter your minds!
> May accumulated virtue ripen for the sake of the whole universe and its inhabitants!
> May the outer universe be a pure Buddhafield!
> May the inhabitants be only celestial beings!
> May grass grow where there was no grass!
> May water gush forth where there was no water!
> May trees grow where there were no trees!
> May crops be abundant where they were scant!
> May children be born to the childless!

May wealth come to those in need!
May fools become intelligent!
May monks and yogins spread the
    Dharma to those without religion!
May lama, disciples, and patrons meet
    again!
May they meet within the auspicious
    harmony of the Dharma!
May they meet while accomplishing
    virtuous deeds!
May they meet accomplishing their own
    good and that of others!
May men and beasts enjoy happiness in
    their old age.
May all fathers and mothers give
    themselves to the Dharma when
    they grow old!
May they all enter the path when they die!
May all wishes be effortlessly
    accomplished!

This prayer greatly pleased the benefactors, who prayed, too, that it might all happen that way.

While I was at Yarnang Dambu Trakar, I met Kusho Dzong Ngön Rinpoche when he came there [444b].[42] He offered me a lot of provisions and animals, including horses, clothing, and a white conch. In return, I offered him many sacred objects and the three kinds of blessed substances, as well as some teaching to establish a spiritual connection. I told him, "Your aims are the welfare of the beings and the teachings; as a means to accomplish this, it would be very good if you built a temple to Maitreya," and he did so.

At that time, too, I met the senior and the junior Alak of Gartse. I offered them a long-life empowerment and some blessed substances; in return they presented me with horses, clothes, and many other things, and took good care of me. Our minds mingled as one.

Once, when the junior Alak was helping in the construction of a house for retreat at the entrance to the holy place of Dambu Trakar, he

fell from the roof—a height of three storeys—without suffering any harm. Everyone was amazed that he wasn't hurt and proclaimed, "By the compassion and protection of the lord guru, he displayed a miraculous sign of accomplishment. How amazing!" Some said, "Don't tell the villagers that Alak fell, tell them he flew!" and everyone laughed. Later we met time and again, and erected together many sacred objects and buildings.

As I went to Magsar, my fortunate spiritual son Khandro called me for the consecration of a temple devoted to the Great Compassionate One, "King of the Sky."[43] On the occasion of the thanksgiving ceremony, he offered me a horse and a *dzo*, a skin-bag of butter, and one hundred pieces of cloth. I dedicated the merits with many prayers.

I then went to Kohudeh, where I met the powerful *siddhas* of the Great Perfection, father and son [445a].[44] I offered them many precious objects, including miraculously multiplying relics, and requested teachings from them to make a spiritual connection. In return they gave me horses, clothes, tea, butter, and other useful things.

Then, at Rongpo Gonchen, at the time of the great annual Chinese prayer festival,[45] I had some bread baked with more than forty bags of wheat, and distributed these to the assembly with tea and soup. Before the Omniscient Manjushri, I placed a set of seven large brass offering bowls and a butter-lamp made out of one hundred and eight silver coins. At Lukra Pekar Chöling, I built a large temple to shelter the principal images: a statue of the Crowned Buddha and one of Manjushri. To cover the expense, I used over a hundred bags of barley and ten of wheat, as well as thirteen packets of ten thousand pieces of yellow and red paper.[46] As wages I offered eighteen big bundles of tea for the sculptors and five hundred large pieces of cloth for the carpenters. Tea, butter, and many other goods were also used for expenses.

Arriving at the Jokhang Temple of Sakarshar, I offered forty silver coins and five big bundles of tea. As a contribution for the Rongpo temple of Kusho Tsendrok Khen Rinpoche, I offered thirty-three bags of wheat and barley.

For the repair of the Maitreya temple at Gartse, I offered twenty-five bags of barley to the treasurer of Kusho Sey Rinpoche. For the making of thirty-one paintings depicting the *One Hundred Episodes of Lord Buddha's Former Lives* [445b],[47] I offered thirty horses and other animals, twelve bags of wheat and barley, and nineteen *sang* of silver. In addition, I offered fifteen pieces of brocade for the frames and ten lengths of cloth for the lining on the back. On various occasions I also gave over a hundred bags of barley to beggars.

During the following summer, my fortunate spiritual son, the learned Achung, went to do a retreat at Namdzong, the "Sky Citadel," after which his practice, meditation experiences, and realization developed greatly. The Khenpo and the cook Kunga Tendzin, who had stayed at Tashikhyil meanwhile, completed the remaining work on the temples. Accompanied by Orgyen, Drupchen, and the other monks, we were escorted by a hundred horsemen from the Upper and Lower Shohong La up to the Golden Valley above Great Bend, where we stayed for a day. People organized horse races and all kinds of singing and dancing. Then all the horsemen went back.

With a large party, I went to the nomadic area of Changlung. The population there requested a longevity blessing; I gave them empowerments and teachings, and enjoined the bandits to obey the laws. I went to everyone's tents, rich and poor, said prayers of auspiciousness, and dedicated the merit. I was offered horses, cattle, and excellent butter.

I then proceeded to nomad areas of Dopa, where many people came on horseback to welcome me. Horse races and all sorts of games were held. At the request of those gathered there, I gave a longevity empowerment and a blessing of Jambhala to four or five hundred people, taught the Dharma, and sang spiritual songs. Many bandits promised to cease robbing; thus I helped revive and enforce the laws against banditry [446a]. All the wealthy families called me to their tents; I said prayers for bringing prosperity and auspiciousness, and dedication prayers. They offered me many horses and cattle, and much butter and cheese. Having received forty head of

horses and cattle and fourteen loads of butter at Changlung and Dopa, I brought them to Tashikhyil for the use of the temple and other works.

Then I went to Gonshul, Chipa, Meshul, and Gartse. At each place I taught the Dharma and gave empowerments. Everyone, out of faith, offered silver *dotse* and many head of horses and cattle. Then I went to Tseshung, in Mongolia, and met Kusho Lakha Rinpoche. I offered him many sacred objects and substances, including multiplying relics of great blessing, as well as many books, some flour, *tsampa*, horses, and clothes, and requested some teaching from him. With great kindness he gave me a hundred silver coins, a hundred pieces of cloth, thirteen horses and *dzos*, and four saddles; he also gave many sheep to those who were accompanying me. I met Kusho Depa Tsang from Labrang, offered him flour, *tsampa*, horses, and clothes, and requested teaching from him to make a spiritual connection. He gave me one dress and a scarf.

Then I met Pöntsang Chingwang Rinpoche, and offered him flour, *tsampa*, horses, and clothes, with relics of the three kinds and long-life pills. In return he gave me a plate, some brocades, and a ceremonial scarf [446b]. We vowed to meet again.

Then fighting broke out between the tribes of Banak Khasum and the two tribes of Hor. Because of this, I had to return quickly to the site of the fighting, and could not visit the many patrons from Mongolia who had invited me.

On my way back, I reached Upper Namo Wen in Hor. Many people mounted on horses, led by the chieftain of Hor, came to welcome me. The whole population requested teachings, and I gave empowerments for long life and prosperity to a crowd of over a thousand people. After giving them plenty of advice on spiritual and temporal matters, I sang this song:

> O guru who knows the spiritual and the
> temporal,
> Grant me your blessing!
>
> I shall sing some beneficial advice that
> springs from my heart:
> Listen with joy, O people of this world!

At the beginning of the teaching, welcome it with a smile,
At the conclusion of the teaching, keep on smiling!

The meaning and need of a teaching must be clear,
And the teaching itself must be of just the right length.

Delicious good food has its appeal; give some to others.
A treasure has enemies; keep it in a safe place.

A council is a source of prosperity; consult one another.
A discourse entails meaning; listen to its argument!

If you steal, you'll end up as a beggar;
If you rob, you'll die by the sword;
If you quarrel, you'll end up regretting it.
If you kill someone, you'll wind up in the hells.

Do not befriend short-tempered people;
Do not ask advice from the evil-minded;
Do not trust someone you don't know well;
Don't confide in people unnecessarily [447a].

If you are eloquent, preach before the assembly of men and gods;
If you have good clothes, parade them in the marketplace;
If you are a good son, bring about peace in the country;
If you practice the Dharma, do it when you are young.

Do not keep company with women of easy virtue, lest you cause gossip.
Do not rear hawks and cats; you will gather sin.
Do not eat food that does not agree with you; you will get sick.
Do not sleep in fearsome places; demons and spirits will harm you.

Welcome with smiles the faithful friend you need.
If you ask for advice, ask from experienced elders.
The wealthy must know how to be satisfied.
The poor must know how to eat within their means.

Do not say what hurts others.
Do not stay near an enemy who hates you.
When it is time to eat, let the elders begin.
Do not grimace if the food is not delicious.
Do not gorge yourself on succulent food and *chang*.
When it's time to work, the younger ones should begin it.

If you make offerings to the deities and the Three Jewels,
Your aspirations will be fulfilled;
If you rely upon the lord guru, you will succeed in the divine Dharma;
If you meditate, experiences and realization will arise;
If you have great love and compassion, you will help beings.

May whoever hears this song
Know both the Dharma and the world.

After I had sung this, everyone became filled with faith and respect. The sun shone upon the clouds, a rainbow appeared, and a fine rain fell gently. At that moment, a turquoise dragon alighted on the ground, drank some water, and rose again into the sky with roars of thunder. Everyone watched and said, "Extraordinary!" [447b]. Some old people added: "We heard the rumbling of the turquoise dragon filling the sky, but we never thought we would see the dragon itself. This year, it alit on the ground and we saw it. We heard the fame of the Precious Protector resounding throughout Tö and sunny U-Tsang like dragon's thunder, but we never thought that we would ever meet him. This year he came to our place and we met him. If that is not good fortune, what is? In this life nothing better could happen to us!"

They all felt extremely happy.

Following this, I gave a lot of gifts to many fierce bandit chiefs, made them promise not to rob anymore, and enforced the law on banditry. Having stopped the fighting between Banak and the two other tribes, I gradually brought them to an agreement. Many people came to offer me horses, *dzos*, *dris*, yaks, multicolored leather boxes,[48] woolen bags, fox-skins, butter, and cheese.

I gave food and clothing to all the monks who were accompanying me, and to everyone else, including the Chinese beggars. To pay for this, I gave away seventy-five horses and other animals, large and small. To the wonder of all the patrons I gave a horse each to some people who had been killing marmots, and made them swear never to hunt anymore.

At this time I made this stainless prayer for the sake of all beings, myself and others:

"By the merit I and others have accumulated throughout the three times, symbolized by these present deeds, may there be food for the hungry, clothes for those who have none [448a], companions for those who are alone, a child for the childless, a horse for those who have no horse, a mount for those on foot, and a house for the homeless. May all beings thus find happiness.

"Again, by the merit accumulated by myself and others throughout the three times, may those who have no spiritual guide find one, may those without Dharma find it, may those without a spiritual friend meet one, may those without a place of retreat find one, and may those without means of subsistence find some, so that they may all become able to follow the Dharma and achieve enlightenment.

Throughout all of my lives,
May I benefit beings;

May I never be born as someone
Who harms others instead of helping them.

Throughout all of my lives, may I be born
As someone who brings benefit to beings.

If beings are happy, may I be their friend
    in happiness;
If they suffer, may I be their friend in
    suffering.

May the thought that disregards the
    welfare of others
Never arise in my mind.

May I work for the sake of all beings,
As long as a single one remains.
May my work for them end only
When they are all established in
    Buddhahood.

By the merit of so doing,
May I myself reach Buddhahood
    effortlessly.

May all my aspirations and those of others
Be accomplished according to our wishes
    [448b].
May this prayer come true
Just as I have said."

I then went to Böngya. Many people on horses came to welcome me; they ran horse races. The people asked that I give some teaching; I gave empowerments and explained the Dharma to all, turning their minds toward the sublime teachings.

I responded to the invitations of all the faithful who invited me to their homes, and said for them prayers and wishes of auspiciousness. They offered me horses, cattle, and sheep, and much butter and cheese. I sent seventy horses and cattle, twenty-two sheepskin pouches of butter, and sixteen silver coins to Rongpo Gonchen, with a hundred horses, *dzos*, *dris*, and yaks, twenty loads of butter, many ceremonial scarves, and fifty silver *sang*, to be distributed among the eigh-

teen retreat centers of Rekong and all the monasteries, large and small, up to Dobi Monastery
in Marnang.

I sent many monks to Labrang Tashikhyil
with large offerings to make a general distribution of money and tea. There were all sorts of
people among my monks, and it happened that
one of them, whom I had sent because he was
familiar with the place, was a *samaya*-breaker
who had been expelled from the Labrang, a fact
of which I had not been aware. When those who
had earlier expelled him recognized him, they
did not let him make the offerings and sent him
back, saying that they wouldn't drink from the
hand of a monk who had broken *samaya*. Some
people who were ignorant of the reasons why
this had happened said that the monks had
refused to drink out of sectarianism [449a]. Whatever the truth, it was an obstacle to my virtuous
intention. I felt sad to have been unable to make
this distribution, and left some money to make a
general tea offering later on.

Then I went to visit, one by one, the patrons
Lheba, Palchog, Dushul, and others. They all
came to welcome me on horses. Arriving at their
homes, I taught the Dharma, gave empowerments, and was invited everywhere. Many of
them offered silver coins in packets of fifty, and
numerous horses, cattle, and sheep. Then I went
to two places in Upper Mangra, Dratsa Chador
and Benshul. People came to welcome me on
the way with food. They made a common offering of fifty pieces of sweet cheese and of melted
butter. At their request, I gave them empowerments and spiritual instructions, and went to
their homes. They offered many horses and cattle.

Then the powerful *siddha* Pema Rangdrol,
with all the patrons from Khyamru Kangtsa in
Lower Mangra, came to fetch me. I went to his
residence, where he held a great feast and offered me hundreds of sweet buttered cheeses. I
gave elaborate empowerments for longevity and
prosperity to a gathering of several thousand
people from Tromlha, and gave them teachings
on the truth of the karmic law of cause and effect.
Having given them advice on the affairs of this
life, I sang this song:

Crest jewel above all celestial and human
  beings [449b],
Wish-fulfilling gem, refuge and protector,
I ask that you look down on us with
  compassion, and grant your
  blessing on us all—
Disciples and patrons, men and women.

I shall give you advice
Beneficial for this life and the next;
Listen to me without distraction, dear patrons.

For this life, if you wish there to be peace
  in all regions,
It is fine to respect the laws of the Manchu
  ruler.

For the next life, if you aspire to happiness
  and well-being,
It is excellent to respect the laws of cause
  and effect expounded by Lord Buddha.

Pray from your heart to the guru,
Unfailing refuge for this life and the next;
His blessings will enter you.

From your heart take refuge in the
  undeceiving Three Jewels;
All your aspirations will be accomplished.

There is no one kinder than your old parents;
Show them your gratitude and you will
  gain merit, son or daughter.

To kill goats, sheep, and yaks while
  performing virtuous ceremonies
  for the dead
Goes totally against the Dharma—never
  do that!

During marriage celebrations, many
  unwholesome activities are carried out.
Never hold big wedding feasts.

Whether or not they are guilty,
Don't accuse the humble in order to take
  their possessions.

Rather than mistakenly handing over
    innocents to the Chinese,
Let trespassers and bandits go free.

When you must face the worst,
Don't pay a pauper to take your place.[49]

Robbers and thieves are the grounds of
    animosity;
It's best that, everywhere, their activities
    should cease.

Do not indulge in senseless and sinful
    actions [450a]
Such as hunting marmots when summer
    comes.

Being unable yourself to bear a tiny
    scratch,
Never raise a knife to men, horses, or dogs.

Do not create causes of epidemics for man
    and cattle
By annoying the fierce ones,[50] who are like
    poison ivy.

The demon of alcohol brings failure,
    squandering of wealth, and indigence;
By no means should you become addicted
    to it.

Rulers: a bad example given to others will
    rebound on yourself;
Don't make bad judgments and bad laws.

Powerful ones, don't oppress the humble
By exploiting your power.

Never take a wife who beats the servants,
Lest you end up with a violent and
    bellicose woman.

Better to be scolded and beaten by one's
    loving parents
Than to be spoken well of by malicious
    neighbors.

Better not to have any helpers and servants
    at all

Than to have many who don't listen to a
    thing you say.

Better to remain childless
Than to have a son who creates problems
    and contention.

Better to have no wife than to marry a
    demoness
Who quarrels with husband, family, and
    servants.

Better to throw them out the door
Than to keep at home children who
    misbehave.

Spread some sand on the kitchen fires
Of the cantankerous old men who
    constantly boil the soup of endless
    complaints.

Praise the nice old ladies
Who always have a smile for everyone
    [450b].

If your life is spent in the happiness of
    Dharma practice,
It will have been meaningful to have
    obtained a human body.

May the minds of all the patrons, men and
    women, who hear this song
Turn toward the holy Dharma.

May auspiciousness and abundance prevail
    in this land
And the earth be covered with wealth and
    cattle.

On hearing this song, everyone became filled
with faith; many bandits and thieves gave up
their activities; the laws on robbery and theft
were enforced. I instituted the regular observance of one-day vows, the fasting practice, and
the Offering of the Twenty-Fifth,[51] of the Tenth,
and the other auspicious days.[52] The great *siddha*
Pema Rangdrol presented me with fifteen horses
and cattle, and fifty sheep, of which I offered half
back to him.

Then, one after the other, I went to the districts in Kangtsa Khyam in the Mangra province, which were under the authority of the Shabdrung of Hrinag Tharshul in Rang Ngen. There I gave my blessings and protection to all, performed *phowa* for the old men and women, and recited dedication prayers and wishes of auspiciousness. Every day, people would come and offer forty of fifty head of horses and cattle, as well as many sheep. I also received many silver *dotse*. With this, I offered to Ragya Monastery fifty horses, *dzos*, *dris* and yaks large and small, eight loads of butter, and six bags of barley. To Lhamo Dechen Monastery I offered fifty horses, *dris*, *dzos*, and yaks, ten loads of butter, and ten silver coins for distributing tea and soup. Before the great Crowned Buddha of Trika I placed a large butter-lamp worth two hundred silver coins [451a], lighted a thousand lamps, and made vast prayers. To each of the thirty-six monasteries of the Trika district I offered one *dzo* and one *sang* of silver. About twenty horses and *dzos* went to people who came to gather funds for various monasteries.

Since my two disciples Khepa and Tshegön were restoring the temple of Achung Namdzong, I offered a horse and two loads of butter and cheese. I met Dechen Pönlop Rinpoche, offered him a horse and some brocade, and requested a teaching to establish a spiritual connection. I met the reincarnation of Arik Geshe Rinpoche, offered him some precious relics and a horse, and requested his spiritual protection. Machak Tulku came to meet me and I offered him the empowerment and reading transmission of the *Sixteen Spheres*. He presented me with a horse, which I offered back to him.

That winter, many of those accompanying me stayed at Chuzang; I myself stayed in retreat at Madram Machak Monastery, on the banks of the Machu River. As a contribution to the monastic community, I offered horses and some cattle—seven head altogether. In the main temple I erected a statue of the Great Lord.[53] That year, too, many monks came by, one after the other, to raise funds for their monasteries. Altogether, I gave them eighty horses, *dzos*, *dris*, and yaks.

I bought seven *dotse* and thirteen horses' worth of *tsampa* and gave it to the many beggars of Chuzang. As this still wasn't enough, I also gave over a hundred sheep to be traded away, thus saving more than hundred beggars from certain death by starvation [451b].

Then I wrote for my disciples and benefactors in U, Tsang, and Ngari provinces this letter of advice called the *White Banner of Praise*, and sent it with my disciple Tashi Lhunpo, who was going to the Pure Realm of U-Tsang, via Kham and Lokha:

> Supreme objects of offering and
> prostration,
> Sole ornament of the universe, the two
> Shakya Jowos and the two Victors,
> Father and Son,
> I supplicate you: look upon us with
> compassion
> And bless us so that our aspirations will be
> fulfilled in harmony with the Dharma!
>
> At the beginning I received instructions
> from a spiritual master,
> In the middle I practiced in a mountain
> hermitage,
> And in the end I established disciples and
> patrons in virtue.
> Thus I, Shabkarpa, "White Foot,"
> Practiced virtue in the beginning, middle,
> and end.
>
> The white flag that heralds
> The many excellent dharmic deeds I've
> performed
> In the five years since returning to Domey
> From the Pure Realm of U-Tsang,
> Waves in all directions.
>
> Fortunate disciples and faithful patrons
> Dwelling in Ngari, U, and Tsang,
> All celestial and human beings delighting
> in virtue,
> Listen without distraction and with joyful
> minds.

By the compassion of the glorious guru
    and the Three Jewels,
And of the merit I and others have
    accumulated in the three times,
I persevered in these white deeds
For the happiness and well-being of you all
    [452a].

Although we all, master and disciples,
Met with many hazards on the way,
By the grace of the Victorious Ones,
    Father and Son,
We reached Dokham safe and sound.

By expounding the Dharma—chiefly the
    law of cause and effect—
To religious and laypeople and the
    chieftains of this area,
I was able to put an end to robbery and
    theft in Upper Rekong
And to all the feuds and disputes in Lower
    Rekong.

Today, since there are no more attacks
    and thefts in the area of Rongpo,
A new sun of unprecedented peace and
    happiness has arisen there,
And happy tales resound in the ten
    directions.

There people offered me food, cattle, and
    wealth, according to their means.
As soon as these had been offered to me,
Without storing or accumulating it, I used
    it
To serve the spiritual teachers around,
Making offerings to sacred objects of the
    body, speech, and mind of the Buddhas,
Making distributions of money and tea to
    the monastic communities,
Giving alms to thousands of needy
    beggars,
And buying animals to free them and save
    their lives.

Particularly, having in mind the prosperity
    of the Dharma and all beings,

As well as the long life of the two Victors,
    Father and Son,
I restored many damaged temples and
    sacred objects,
And in monasteries and villages built
    temples where there were none
    [452b]—
Altogether a hundred and eight temples,
Ten thousand statues, large and small, as
    symbols of the Buddha's body,
One thousand volumes of sutras, tantras,
    and commentaries, as symbols of the
    Buddha's speech,
And over a hundred stupas, large and
    small, as symbols of the Buddha's mind.

Besides this, many hermitages were built in
    secluded places,
People molded many hundreds of
    thousands of small statues and *tsa-tsas*,
And many stayed in retreat and practiced
    the Dharma.
In brief, directly or indirectly
I was able to bring great benefit to the
    Dharma and to many beings.

The sheer joy of celestial and human
    beings who delight in virtue
And particularly of my gurus, spiritual
    companions,
Disciples and patrons, by tens and hun-
    dreds of thousands,
Expands as a billowing cloud of offerings.
May all those—gods and humans abiding
    on the side of virtue—
Who hear or read this narration
Told with a mind that cares not for fame,
Rejoice in complete happiness,
And they will have the fortune to earn
    equal merit!

If I don't die and my life continues for one
    or two more years,
I shall do my best to benefit
The Dharma and the beings in this place.
When all my religious activities are
    complete,

Once more, together with good
companions,
I have it in mind to come to U-Tsang,
The supreme paradise of abundance and
accumulated merit,
And meet the two Crowned Buddhas, the
two Victorious Ones, Father and Son,
And the disciples and patrons of Sera,
Drepung and Ganden [453a].

I pray that in accordance with my wish,
Quickly reaching U,
I may make offerings to the Jowo, the
Wish-fulfilling Gem,
Serve the two Victorious Ones, Father and
Son,
And benefit the Dharma and all beings.

In the Year of the Dragon, in central
Tibet,
Through the auspicious omen of the
rumbling of the summer drum's
glad tidings,
May rain be timely, crops be abundant
and cattle prosper;
May all countries enjoy happiness.

By the grace of the two Victorious Ones,
our lords, our refuge,
By the faith and devotion of disciples and
patrons,
And by the strength of my perfectly pure
wishes,
May all our aspirations quickly be fulfilled!

I also sent a missive called the *Song of the Nightingale*, a spiritual song called the *Gentle Call of the Blue Cuckoo*, a song of excellent aspiration called the *Melodious Lute and Flute*, and the supreme teaching of the *Sublime Drumbeat of the Golden Radiance*.[54] These appear in my Collected Songs. It was said that when these reached the hands of my disciples and patrons, they felt boundless joy, as though meeting me in person.

The next year my spiritual sons Drupchen, Onpo, Kardri, Tayen, and others stayed at Chuzang and built a temple with an image of the crowned Buddha [453b]. For this we spent the equivalent of three *dotse* of gold leaf, paint, and varnish, twenty horses, *dzos*, yaks, and *dris*, fifty sheep, and thirteen silver coins as wages for the artists, and twenty horses and head of cattle and twenty-five silver coins for the carpenters. With many disciples I went from Chuzang to the Bhel area. We met Gyaza Tripa Rinpoche of Serlag Monastery, the holder of the throne of Gyaza. As a contribution to the construction of the new monastery, I offered him fifteen horses and head of cattle, half a large load of tea, and a load of butter; I requested teaching to make a spiritual connection.

Then I went successively to the area of my old patrons Bongtag Benlo, Chökyap, the Bache Rinchen Jam family, Kalo (the chief of Gyaza), the governor Chönyon, and the chieftain of Khonag. To all of them I gave longevity empowerments and Dharma teachings, and said prayers for them. People came to offer many *dotse* of silver, clothes, and head of cattle and sheep. The list of the offerings made by the nomads included thirteen hundred horses, *dzos*, *dris*, and yaks large and small, seventeen hundred sheep, one hundred and eighty skins of butter, one hundred loads of cheese, ten big bundles of tea, thirty-three *dotse*, seventy whole pieces of dyed leather, and sixty pairs of boots of the same material, forty fox-skins, over five hundred lengths of cloth and printed woolen material [454a], and several thousand large and small ceremonial scarves.

At that time, for the sake of disciples and patrons, I uttered this blessing for perfect auspiciousness:

Om Svasti!

May there be the perfection of a sky filled
with Buddhas!
May there be the perfection of the air filled
with the Dharma!
May there be the perfection of the earth
covered by the Sangha!

May there be the perfection of the Three
Jewels, our objects of refuge!

May there be auspiciousness high in the
sky!
May there be auspiciousness down on the
earth!
May there be auspiciousness in the vast
atmosphere in between!
May auspiciousness encompass sky, earth,
and everywhere!

In the sky, may there be the auspiciousness
of timely rainfalls!
In the air, may there be the auspiciousness
of rainbow-clouds!
On earth, may there be the auspiciousness
of good crops and cattle!
May there be the auspiciousness of the
rising sun of happiness!

May there be the auspiciousness of father,
mother, and children gathered together!
May there be the auspiciousness of men,
cattle, and food gathered together!
May there be the auspiciousness of food,
clothing, and Dharma gathered
together!
May there be the auspiciousness of
happiness, well-being, and renown
gathered together!
May there be the auspiciousness of the
joyous feast of gods and men!
May there be the auspiciousness of
melodious songs!
May there be the auspiciousness of
cheerful dancing!
May there be the auspiciousness of joy
increasing everywhere! [454b].

May there be the auspiciousness of bliss
equal to that of the celestial realms!
May there be the auspiciousness of
well-being like that of the golden age!
May there be the auspiciousness of
perpetual joy and contentment!
May there be the auspiciousness of
everything being perfect!

After I said this, grass grew in all arid places,
and water surged forth where there had been no
water before; these and other auspicious things
happened in the district of Bhel Mangra, arous-
ing in everyone greater faith and respect than
ever.

I then met the reembodiment of the omniscient Shingsa Rinpoche[55] and offered him a
horse. I met Alak Gonpo of Labrang and the
reembodiment of Jetsun Jamyang Gyatso
Rinpoche, and offered each of them a horse. I
met too the reembodiment of Gyal Khenchen
Rinpoche, my most kind root teacher, who had
taken rebirth in the family of Aku Bendhe of
Gyaza. I offered him fifteen horses and *dzos*, fifty
sheep, and ten *sang* of silver, with some loads of
tea, butter and cheese. I offered Tsang Monastery thirty *dzos*, *dris*, yaks, and horses, and four
loads of butter and one big package of tea.

Then a feud broke out between the people
of Rekong and the three districts of Banak
Khasum. Chang Tse Khen Rinpoche and myself
went to conciliate the two sides. We succeeded in
pacifying the quarrel and bringing things back to
the Dharma; thus many lives were saved.

After this I came back to the hermitage of
Tashikhyil and stayed there in retreat. While in
retreat I composed the *Wondrous Emanated Scriptures*,[56] which explains the need to give up meat,
alcohol, and women. It makes one reflect upon
the negativity associated with their enjoyment
and quotes excerpts from many scriptures [455a].

In summer, remembering the places where
my root guru of unfaltering kindness, the Dharma
King Ngakyi Wangpo, and his consort, had first
stayed, I felt a great desire to go there. Accordingly, I proceeded through Sazang. First I met
Rinpoche's son, inquired about his health, and
presented my offerings to him. He himself gave
me some brocades and other presents.

Then I met Kusho Lakha Rinpoche, a
Bodhisattva who had reached the *bhumis*, and
staying over a month in his presence, I received
from him the empowerments and transmissions
for both the *Rigdzin Dupa*, *The Gathering of the
Vidyadharas* and the *Khandro Dechen Gyalmo*, *The
Sky-faring Queen of Great Bliss*, from the cycle of the
Longchen Nyingthig, *The Heart Essence of the Great*

Expanse.[57] In return, I offered him the empowerment of the *Sixteen Spheres of the Kadampas,* and the
blessings and transmission of the collections of
sadhanas called the *Source of Jewels.*[58] I also offered
him three volumes of the *Sealed Visions,*[59] and
other useful books, as well as some fine *tsampa.*
He gave me fifteen horses and cattle, fifty sheep,
thirty length of cloth, tea, butter and all sorts of
helpful things.

After this I met the supreme reembodiment
of Jetsun Sonam Trakpa, the Dharma heir of the
teachings of the profound path of Chöd. I offered
him some *tsampa* and requested from him the
transmission for the text of the *Profound Pacifying
Path of Cutting Through.*[60] We had many discussions which pleased him [455b]. He gave me
presents and provisions.

Following this I responded to the invitations
of the chieftain Tsige, of the chieftain of Mongolia, and of many other faithful patrons. I gave
them longevity blessings and Dharma teachings.
In conclusion, I sang this song of advice on
worldly and religious ethics:

I bow down to the Omniscient One:
Look with compassion upon me and all
beings!

Listen to this beneficial advice
On both divine and human dharmas.

When any newcomer arrives, as soon as
you see him,
Ask after his health with a smiling face.

Any guest who comes must be received like
a deity;
Offer him some tea and *chang*, and talk
with him in a pleasant way.

Speak suitably and with measure,
Not saying everything that crosses your
mind.

Gentle speech and a broad mind will
accomplish
Every aim, whether for yourself or for
others.

Explain the reasons: if you don't give clear
explanations,
Even your own father won't understand.

Give good advice: if you don't teach the
good and the bad in detail,
Even your own child won't listen.

Give food and clothes to those around you,
servants and relatives.
If you don't, even your own son won't stay
around.

Become skilled in either religious or
worldly matters:
No one learns without effort.

Don't consider an outsider as an enemy:
Make a friend of him; that will be good for
you.

Keep to the humblest position and you will
be respected by all:
The greatness of a good person does not
need an enthronement.

Even when persons of bad character put
themselves forward,
In others' eyes they are merely objects of
shame and derision.

Just mouthing kind words won't please
your relatives;
Be sincerely eager to do what benefits
them [456a].

A big mouth will not defeat an enemy;
Better subdue him through gentleness and
skillful means.

Great miserliness will not accumulate wealth;
You must know how to give and receive.

Even if the wife is wise in giving counsel,
It looks better if the husband decides.

Treat a good friend well,
And he will be with you in a time of need.

Remain unruffled both in success and in
   adversity.

Do not decide on issues you've not thought
   out completely;
Otherwise, who knows where you'll end up.

Do not talk about something before it is
   finished,
For it is difficult to know how things will
   turn out.

Do not revile the bad;
They may improve later.

Do not praise the good prematurely;
They might do evil later.

Don't scold or beat your servants fiercely,
Or there won't be a single person left
   around you.

Do not exercise power ruthlessly.
People will resent it and retaliate.

Do not denigrate your friends or expose
   their faults;
It will hurt their feelings.

Work for the cause of the community
And your own good will come of itself.

In essence, take care about even the
   smallest aspects of the law of
   cause and effect,
And the well-being of gods and men will
   follow naturally.

May whoever hears this excellent advice
Be of benefit to his fellow human beings!

As I sang this, everyone's thoughts turned to the
Dharma. Many people offered horses, cattle,
cheese, and butter.
   I proceeded to Thayenchi, the pleasant secluded grove of Tseshung [456b], and stayed
there for a week. I repaired my retreat hut and

had an arm-size statue of Lord Buddha erected
inside it, for the making of which I gave one *dzo*
to the sculptor. While I stayed there, many people
came from Tsang Arik to meet me and offered
much butter and cheese. I taught the Dharma
and said prayers of dedication. I installed my
spiritual sons Rigdrol and Khampa Drupchen in
retreat and left an annual allowance for them.
   I then went to the upper end of the sunny
slopes where the Dharma King and his consort
lived when they first came. I offered prostrations
and prayers, and remembering my guru, sang
this song of grief and longing:

Gurus whom I met and heard,
You have dissolved your manifest bodies
   into absolute space
And now dwell in the invisible expanse:
Think upon me with compassion and bless
   me!

The gurus of my homeland,
Whose faces I saw, whose voices I heard:
What joy if they were here now!
I yearn to meet them, to serve them!

Today, not one of them remains;
They have all departed for other Pure
   Realms,
And I, unfortunate, am left behind
With none of my gurus still in this world.

Thinking and thinking, my tears pour
   down like rain.
I remember my gurus one by one
And think, "This one is no more; that one
   is gone."
Thinking and thinking, my mind reels with
   sadness.

Above all, as soon as I think of the Dharma
   King and his consort,
Remembering their faces, the sound of
   their voices,
The way they acted, and their immense
   kindness [457a],
Sadness and grief overwhelm my mind.

Left behind, I am close to death.
Before it comes, I shall practice the divine
    Dharma,
And pray that in the next life I may meet
    my gurus
In the pure Buddhafields.

As I sang this, I remembered my lamas, one by one.
Particularly, when remembering vividly the Dharma
King and his consort, an unfathomable sadness
swept through my mind and I shed many tears.

On my way back, I came to the Shukdu retreat
center of Upper Rekong and stayed there a few
days to establish a connection with that holy
place. The patrons from Khasog Lakha, Karon-
khok, Tsenmo Thang, and other nearby villages
and nomad grounds invited me and I visited
them all. They offered me many horses and
other animals. I said some prayers and wishes of
auspiciousness; having gathered all the people of
the area I taught the Dharma and sang spiritual
songs, thus turning everyone's minds to the
Dharma.

   Then I visited Dzong Kar and Dzong Ngön,
the "White and the Blue Fortresses,"[61] as well as
Dechen Gonpa, the "Monastery of Great Bliss."
I offered butter-lamps in the temple and made a
general offering of money and tea to the monks.
As a contribution to the Maitreya temple built
by Kusho Dzong Ngön, I offered one horse and
many precious relics. In return, he gave me
sacred objects related to body, speech and mind,
together with horses, clothes, and corals.

   Having returned to Tashikhyil, I entered
into retreat. During this retreat I composed the
Emanated Scripture of Pure Vision,[62] in which I
explained the need to develop pure perception,
faith, and respect toward all the great and holy
lamas who did not reject sense-pleasures, but
enjoyed them as ornaments, as well as toward all
the yogin practitioners of the two stages of the
Mantrayana [457b].[63]

After this, for one year I again went to the
area of Hrinag and Chenza for the sake of the
nomads there. I gave empowerments for long-
life and prosperity to the Hrinag lamas and all
the patrons, gave teachings on the law of karma,
and sang them this song of beneficial advice:

I bow down to those knowledgeable in
    temporal and spiritual ethics:
Grant your blessing that I may be able to
    distinguish right from wrong.

Human and celestial beings, for the sake of
    your happiness
Listen to this beneficial song of mine.

Do not be contemptuous toward those in
    difficulty;
Misfortune may come to you one day.

Do not show off when everything goes
    well;
Good fortune comes to others also.

Don't make those who gave wrong advice
    feel guilty;
You too will make mistakes.

Don't demand gratitude in return for your
    help;
Let your generosity fade away
    unrecognized.

A person is judged by the gentleness of his
    speech and of his actions;
Try to act in harmony with all.

If you neither lie nor deceive,
Wherever you go, you will find food and
    clothing.

If you speak little and you are honest,
Wherever you stay people will like you.

If your wants are few and you know how
    to be content,
Everyone will be your friend.

Do not put power into the hands of a base
  person;
He will get everyone into trouble.

Give the highest rank to a good person
  [458a];
There will be happiness for yourself and
  others.

Teach your children everything you
  know;
Ultimately both parent and child will be
  happy.

Do whatever pleases your kind guru and
  your parents;
All your aspirations will be fulfilled.

Place everyone above yourself—superiors,
  equals and inferiors;
Celestial and human beings will all
  rejoice.

If with kind intentions you do good to
  others,
Your own happiness will come of its own
  accord.

Someone as good-natured as a celestial
  being
Will be esteemed wherever he goes.

In brief, whatever you do,
Take as witness the law of karma.
Doing so, you will be happy in this life
And in the next one you will obtain a
  human or a celestial existence.

May this song benefit the mind
Of all who hear it.
May goodness prevailing in all directions,
Long-life, good health, and happiness be
  enjoyed by all.

Having sung this, I calling for blessings and
made prayers of auspiciousness for the benefit of
the area. From then on, illnesses of both humans

and cattle subsided, and good grass grew on the
plain of Chenza, where there had been none
before. Consequently, all the patrons became
filled with faith and respect. They also offered
me a hundred horses and seventy sheep. Bandits
vowed not to rob and kill, and many people
committed themselves to perform virtuous
actions.

At that time the bursar Orgyen and a few people
accompanying him were departing for the Pure
Realm of U-Tsang to make offerings there. As
offerings, I sent with them ten *dotse* of Chinese
silver, carpets, some dyed leather, corals, turquoise, a lot of brocade [458b] and ceremonial
scarves, and thirty-three horses and *dzos*. I also
offered to all the disciples and patrons of U-
Tsang, high, medium, and low, this *Garland of
Jewels*, an excellent discourse reminding them
about virtue:

> I supplicate the two Victorious Ones,
>   Father and Son,
> Crest ornaments for all sentient beings:
> Look compassionately upon human and
>   celestial beings,
> And grant your blessings
> So that I become able to benefit both
>   others and myself.
>
> Even though it is explained by a dull-
>   witted person like me,
> Lend an ear to this discourse, wise
>   U-Tsang folk!
>
> This human life, free and well-favored, is
>   more precious than a wish-fulfilling
>   gem;
> Don't let it be pointlessly wasted, U-Tsang
>   folk!
>
> In this degenerate age, life is short and the
>   time of death is unpredictable;

Don't be so concerned with this life,
   U-Tsang folk!

Human life soon exhausts itself in futile
   distractions;
Prepare for the levels and paths in the next
   life, U-Tsang folk!

If you take the Three Jewels as your refuge,
You will be happy in this life and in the next;
Take refuge at all times, U-Tsang folk!

Make offering, praises, and prayers
To the two wish-fulfilling Crowned
   Buddhas, U-Tsang folk!

The patron deity of Tibet is the mighty
   Avalokiteshvara;
Recite the *mani*, U-Tsang folk!

The two Victorious Ones, Father and Son,
   are your objects of refuge for this life
   and the next;
Pray to them from your heart, U-Tsang
   folk!

The words of the Victorious One provide
   the means for lasting happiness;
Act as the Muni taught, U-Tsang folk!

The one who establishes the country in
   peace is the emperor [459a];
Respect his laws, U-Tsang folk!

If you do whatever the guru says, all your
   aspirations will be accomplished;
Fulfill all his wishes, U-Tsang folk!

The supreme field for accumulating merit
   is the sangha;
Make offerings to Sera, Ganden, and
   Drepung, U-Tsang folk!

Good fortune will come to children if they
   respect their parents;
Always respect them as if they were deities,
   U-Tsang folk!

By doing prostrations and circumambulations,
Illness, evil influences, and wrongdoing are
   purified;
Circumambulate Lhasa and Samye,
   U-Tsang folk!

If you store whatever you acquire, it will be
   lost to enemies and demons;
Don't hoard but give away, U-Tsang folk!

Favoring the rich, some lamas and chiefs
Make biased decisions and enact wrong
   laws;
Don't behave in this way, U-Tsang folk!

When the king's and ministers' decisions
   are just,
The subjects must not rebel, U-Tsang folk!

If the best people are given high rank, they
   will be good to all;
Place them at the top, U-Tsang folk!

If inferior people reach the top, they will
   abuse everyone;
Don't give them high positions, U-Tsang
   folk!

Scolding from one's parents is better than
   praise
From neighbors filled with ill-will and
   craving, U-Tsang folk!

To say whatever you think leads to
   quarrels;
Don't say unnecessary things, U-Tsang
   folk!

Servants, perform all your duties in a
   useful way [459b];
Don't indulge in stealing and lying,
   U-Tsang folk!

For the long life of the two Victors, Father
   and Son,
Save animals from slaughter, U-Tsang
   folk!

If killings are many, rainfall will be scarce;
Don't move around too much in summer,
    U-Tsang folk!

Buddhist *ngakpas*, if you fight with Bönpos,
    obstacles will rise;
Beware of this, U-Tsang folk!

Control your anger and hatred;
They destroy all merit and are the causes
    for rebirth in the hells, U-Tsang folk!

Do extensive prayers of dedication;
They increase your merit and are the
    cause of attaining Buddhahood,
    U-Tsang folk!

This wondrous discourse, the *Garland of
Jewels*,
I send to you as an excellent present,
    U-Tsang folk!

Good people, wear it as a garland;
It will be the best of your ornaments,
    U-Tsang folk!

In whatever lands this discourse resounds,
May whoever hears it find happiness and
    bliss!
May auspiciousness and good harvests
    prevail,
And the new ears of abundant crops cover
    the whole earth!

I also sent a respectful letter to the two
Victors, a prayer to the two Crowned Buddhas,
a pith instruction called *The Golden Scalpel*, and a
melancholy song called *The Many-stringed Lute*.
They are found in my Collected Songs.[64]
    I then went to Upper Gurong, where I taught
the Dharma and benefited beings. The patrons
of both Upper and Lower Gurong offered me
five mules with saddles, saddle carpets, and har-
nesses; ten *dzomos*, *dris*, yaks, and oxen; and thirty
goats and sheep [460a]. The temple at Mani
Thang in Gurong had been burned down by
armies of Chinese Salars, who later committed
themselves to rebuild the temple. I offered a

statue of Lord Buddha made of precious *lima*
alloy, sacred relics, and earth and water that
came from various parts of the world.
    Then going to Shingkar, to Gurteng, and to
Nangra, I bestowed empowerments and gave
teaching, turning the minds of all towards the
Dharma. I paid homage and made offerings to
the image of the Buddha that had been consecrated by the Dharma Lord Do Rinpoche and
that is the main sacred object of the Golden
Temple of Nangra. I urged all the patrons to
have a fence built by the army around the temple.
I also repaired a large stupa.
    After this, I proceeded towards Lo Dorje
Drak[65] and paid homage to the famed *Prajnaparamita* of Lowa, which had been written in gold
by dakinis who had transformed themselves into
vultures. I also consecrated the stupa of Kyaring.
    Then I went to Ri Nyingpo, where I stayed
many days. I gave teachings on the nature of
mind to many faithful yogins. I repaired the back
of the Temple of the Great Dharma Wheel, and
helped the abbot, Konchog, and the other monks
staying there.
    I went to Trulche and Doring, and per-
formed the consecration of the Mani Temple.
Going to many districts in the areas of Hor
Pashi, Hrinag, Kyamtsang, Totsang, Shodzom
Lakha, Keu Chu, and so on, I gave long-life
empowerments, taught the Dharma, and also
sang this spiritual song [460b]:

Gurus and the Three Jewels filled with
    grace,
Bless the body, speech and mind of those
    gathered here!

Listen to this song, which tells
What chieftains, faithful men and women
    need.

One—to say good things,
Two—to have good thoughts within,
Three—to always tell the truth,
Four—to ponder everything carefully,
Five—to be impartial, and
Six—to want little for yourself:
These are what a chief needs.

One—great generosity,
Two—a fierce and impressive appearance,
Three—an unwavering mind,
Four—the grit to face an adversary, should
    one arise,
Five—a stable mind in a strong body, and
Six—a sense of moderation:
These are what a man needs.

One—an excellent descent,
Two—a great sense of modesty and
    shyness,
Three—knowledge of how to run a
    household,
Four—ability in dealing with all people,
Five—not to form ties with other men,
Six—to see her spouse as a deity:
These are what a woman needs.

This song on the six things that
Chiefs, men and women need to have
Has been sung by Tsogdruk Rangdrol;
May it benefit all those who hear it!

After hearing this song, everyone's mind
was turned toward the Dharma. Filled with faith,
men and women offered me four mules, two
dzomos, forty cows and bulls, two hundred bags of
barley [461a], fifteen mats of white felt, eighteen
bricks of black tea, thirteen rifles, thirty porcelain
cups, and many pieces of turquoise and coral.
Then I offered thirty *dris* and yaks, two loads of
butter, and fifty sheep to Dechen Gonpa, the
Monastery of Great Bliss. As a contribution for
the repair of the Temple of the Crowned Buddha, I offered a hundred silver coins with tea,
butter, and *tsampa*. To all the small and big
monasteries around, I offered two, three, or four
horses and head of cattle, forty in all.

A feud had occurred at Mapha Ri between the
tribes of Adarchaka and Sheshin, causing the
killing of many people. I went there and settled
their dispute through various means.

One day I had gone for a stroll at Shisar—
the location that had been the cause of the feud.
I was sitting in the cool shade of the hollow trunk
of a large tree, when an old Chinese Mongol
came, and stared at me for a long time. Finally
he said, "Hey! I've heard of you before, but I
never thought I would meet you. What a pleasure it is to meet you today! In the past when one
spoke of a 'good lama', one would speak of Arik
Geshe; these days people are speaking of you,
Alak Shabkar. I don't have any wealth, but please
come and have a cup of tea at my place."

I went, and having drunk some tea and
eaten a piece of bread I told him [461b], "We
don't know when we will die. Have a good heart;
don't be cruel to people at home. If you don't die
too soon, you will find some wealth and the end
of your life will be without hardship. When your
children have grown up, life will be pleasant for
both parents and children." Before leaving, I
said some prayers of dedication.

As I sang verses of auspiciousness, a Chinese
woman who was there became moved by faith
and started to weep. The old man escorted me
and said, "Alak, come again from time to time!"
and I replied, "Yes, yes, if I don't die I will come.
Be well!" and he added, "Be well too, Alak!" and
went back to his house.

My close disciple Tendzin Nyima had built
a new temple on the plain of Adarchaka. For
that I contributed eighteen horses and other
cattle, one bundle of ten thousand yellow paper
sheets, and three bundles of one thousand, as
well as much *tsampa*, butter, and tea. The chief of
Adarchaka offered one mule, a rifle, a *shanglang*
cymbal[66] and a package of black tea. Kyargö
offered a horse and many turquoise and corals.
Other local people, too, offered a lot of food,
wheat and barley, cattle and other valuables.

Then I went to Chakyung Gonpa, the Garuda
Monastery. I offered forty horses, *dzos*, *dris* and yaks
large and small, as well as four loads of butter and
four bundles of black tea. Also, I made a general
distribution of tea and alms to the monks.

I sent two of my disciples, Drupchen and
Neten, to bring the following letter to both the
all-knowing Kusho Changkya[67] and Chuzang
Rinpoche [462a]:

Supreme Omniscient Changkya and
Chuzang Rinpoche, O glory of the southern
continent Jambudvipa, you rise like the radiant
sun and moon together in the infinite sky that
has neither center nor periphery. I, the vagabond yogin Shabkar, respectfully offer countless
prostrations at your feet adorned with golden
wheels.

Fulfilling our prayers, both of you, precious
and supreme objects of refuge, remain in good
health and, out of your vast aspirations, show
the greatest possible kindness to beings, displaying the great waves of your activities for the sake
of the teachings and sentient beings. By the
compassion of the guru and the Three Jewels, I
am well in body and mind, and, like a small bird
trying to imitate an eagle, looking up at the lives
of the great saints of the past I train in the
Bodhisattva's activity as best I can.

For the sake of the Dharma and all beings,
according to your aspirations, both of you, precious lords and objects of refuge, have built
without hindrance a temple more wonderful
than any before, filled with sacred objects [462b].
With one voice, celestial and human beings claim
that it is just as though the Rasa Tsuglakhang
Temple of Lhasa, erected by King Songtsen
Gampo in the Pure Realm of U-Tsang, had
been transported with all its sacred objects, to
become the glory of the beings that need to be
benefited in Domey. Hearing this pleasant news
resound in the ten directions of space, not once
but many times, like the rumble of the summer
thunder-dragon, my faith, my respect, my pure
perception, and my desire to meet you increase
like the waters of a lake in summertime. With
great delight I rejoice, and not just in words.

Again I pray with folded hands that for the
sake of the Dharma and all beings you live long,
and that your pure activities continue to increase
year after year. I shall always offer, to the best of
my ability, prayers for your long lives, O great
beings who hold the life-tree of the teaching.

Supreme objects of refuge! Always nurture
in the expanse of your vast and profound mind
the spiritual protection that you extend to me
and my peers, who are and will be your disciples
throughout our lives, until enlightenment.

Heed me! Heed me!

Today I offer you this letter along with two
good horses, one mule, and a pair of immaculate ceremonial scarves, from the holy place of
the Garuda, on this auspicious month and date.

Again I said in verse:

In the vast sky without center or periphery,
Radiant, like the sun and moon rising together
    [463a],
You shine beautifully, O glory of this southern
    continent of the Rose-apple Tree.

I, the carefree happy yogin who roams
    carelessly
Through mountain wildernesses,
Offer countless prostrations with utter respect
At your lotus feet, O my protectors.
Folding hands at my heart, I present you with
    these words:

You both achieved Buddhahood long ago,
Yet, for the sake of those beings to be helped in
    this degenerate age,
You assumed with great kindness the form of
    holders of the three saffron robes,
And have worked for the benefit of the
    Dharma and all living beings.

By the compassion of the gurus and the Three
    Jewels
I am well in body and in mind.
Like a small bird trying to imitate an eagle,
I struggle to follow the lives of the saints of the
    past.

When I heard time and again, resounding like
    the summer thunder-dragon,
The delightful news that, within no time,
You had completed the construction of a
    temple
Which was as though the magically arisen
    Rasa Temple,
Erected long ago at the time of the Dharma
    King,
Had been transported with all its contents to
    Lower Dokham,
Again and again, faith, respect, pure perception,
Rejoicing and the wish to meet you arose.

Now comes the core of my request, O lords,
  exalted objects of refuge:
Live long and increase even further
Your activity for the Dharma and all beings—
This is the prayer I repeatedly make,
Not merely paying lip service [463b].

I beg your spiritual protection,
So that I and all your disciples, my peers,
Be accepted by you and never part from you,
My refuge, my protectors,
Throughout our lives, until we reach
  enlightenment.

So that my request for your protection may not
  be without any support,
I offer you three horses and mules, together
  with immaculate scarves,
Most respectfully, on this auspicious date and
  month,
From the Monastery of the Garuda, source of
  all benefit and bliss.

When the messengers who had gone to carry this letter came back and gave me all the news and details, my desire to meet these two great beings increased even more.

For a while I remained there, making offerings to the Golden Reliquary of the Garuda Monastery and other sacred objects, meeting the lamas, requesting their spiritual protection, and doing prostrations and circumambulations.

Then I went to Dosho and a few other districts, and helped beings. Many people offered me great quantities of wheat, barley, and silver coins. I also went to pay homage to the Lhachen Palbar, the "Mahadeva Ablaze with Glory" of Shongchen, and made prayers and offerings. After this, accompanied by a few people, I went up and stayed overnight at Serkhang, the "Golden Mansion." The next morning, starting early from the peak on the right side, we went round Tsongkha Kyeri Mountain. We started by walking and rode mules on the other side of the mountain, finally reaching Chuzang.

There we met the all-knowing Kusho Changkya. I offered him a statue of Amitayus, the Buddha of Eternal Life, a copy of the *Treasury of the Sublime Vehicle*,[68] and the mule I had been riding on, with its saddle and harness. I requested from him the transmission of the commentary on the mind-training teaching known as *The Wheel of Sharp Weapons* [464a].[69]

I met Kusho Chuzang Rinpoche too, offered him apparel and requested a spiritual connection. I met the tulku of the precious throne-holder of Gyanak, offered him apparel, and asked his protection.

On the occasion of the celebration marking the completion of the new temple, Kusho Changkya Rinpoche, the venerable Chuzang, Gyanak Sertri Tulku, the venerables Shar, Ragor, and Jedrung, and many other great lamas went to make a purifying offering of fragrant smoke on the pass above the Kyela Cairn. After that, tents having been pitched down on the plain, a great feast was given. Complying with the command of the supreme refuge Changkya Rinpoche to sing a spiritual song, I sang about the Five Perfections:

Lord gurus who bestow blessings,
Yidam deities who grant accomplishments,
Assembly of dakinis who dispel obstacles,
Remain as ornaments on the wheel crown-
  ing my head,
And shower a rain of blessings and *siddhis*
Upon all the virtue-loving human and
  celestial beings assembled here.

Here, at a time of perfect joy and happiness,
I shall sing a cheering and joyous song.

The place is a wondrous Pure Realm,
The Lord is the Vajradhara Changkya,
The retinue consists of the pure and
  fortunate disciples,
The teachings are the unsurpassable
  Dharma of the Great Vehicle,
And the time is the zenith of the golden
  age.
Everything is truly perfect and auspicious!
  [464b].

In this sublime, all-perfect, sacred place,
Gurus and tutelary deities gather like
  clouds;

Dakas and dakinis are vivid as rainbows;
Guardians and protectors of the Dharma
    flash like lightning;
Blessings and *siddhis* shower down like rain;
Fame and glory rumble like thunder;
Enjoyment and abundance brim like a lake;
Happiness and satisfaction shine like the
    sun;
Meditative experiences and realization
    wax like the moon:
Everything is truly perfect and auspicious!

May this all-perfect song
Bring happiness and well-being to all who
    hear it;
Through all-perfect happiness and
    well-being
May the auspiciousness of practicing the
    divine Dharma prevail!

Then, modifying slightly the *Wondrous Happy Song* that I had sung earlier on the occasion of a *ganachakra* feast, I sang this:

To receive wondrous blessings,
We have our own gurus and those of the
    lineage.
We don't need to look for other blessings.
How happy we are!

To attain ordinary and supreme *siddhis*
We have the assembly of the peaceful and
    wrathful deities.
We don't need to look for other *siddhis;*
How happy we are!

To dispel obstacles and unfavorable
    circumstances
We have the dakinis and dharmapalas of
    the three planes.
We don't need to look for other guardian
    deities;
How happy we are!

To attain enlightenment in one lifetime,
We have the instructions of the Secret
    Mantrayana, which ripen and free
    [465a].

There is no doubt that we will become
    enlightened;
How happy we are!

As companions in accomplishing
    unsurpassable enlightenment,
We have vajra brothers and sisters of pure
    samaya.
Together we will attain Buddhahood;
How happy we are!

As the supreme field for accumulating
    merit,
We have erected sacred objects of the
    body, speech, and mind.
All our wishes will be accomplished;
How happy we are!

On hearing this happy song,
May our gurus, brothers, and sisters be
    pleased,
May all celestial and human beings who
    delight in virtue rejoice;
May all be auspicious in this land.

Hearing this, the lamas, notables, and everyone else there were very pleased. Changkya Rinpoche presented me with a long ceremonial scarf.

Though these two great teachers had already performed one hundred and eight consecration ceremonies, they asked me to perform one, too, and to say prayers of auspiciousness, which I did. Extremely pleased, they gave me one *dotse* of Chinese silver, one horse, two pieces of brocade, a rosary ornamented with corals and two long ceremonial silk scarves. I accepted these except for the silver, which I offered back to them. I also made a thousandfold offering[70] in the temple, a general distribution of tea to the monks, and alms to the beggars. I sealed all with pure prayers for the long life of the two protectors and other prayers [465b]. I uttered a command to the Chinese spirits not to cause any harm to the masters' relatives. I gave them a protecting bless- ing, which kept them well.

Although some patrons from the area of Palri invited me to visit them, I told them, "I cannot come now, but I will try to come later," and did not go. Then I thought that it would be quite convenient to go with Changkya Rinpoche on pilgrimage to the Five-peaked Mountain of China. I told this to this great being, who replied, "According to your aspirations you benefited beings from central Tibet to Domey. If you forsake helping others here and go to the Five-peaked Mountain, you will indeed pay homage to a holy place, but you won't be able to continue benefiting others. The reason for this is that you know neither Chinese nor Mongolian, and, not being able to communicate with people, even if you meet them, it will be just like one animal meeting another.

"In the past you have been able to help all those who live in Rongpo, Rekong, and on both sides of the Machu River. These are people who could not be tamed by the countless Buddhas who have already come on this earth; they are tough people who don't stay home and who kill many people with little reason. If you can continue to help them for a few more years, it will be a hundred times more beneficial than to go to the Five-peaked Mountain. You have reached a ripe old age; it is very hot in China [466a]. Who knows if the conditions there will suit your health? One cannot be sure that there won't be some obstacles to your life. Since in your own country the water agrees with you,[71] and you benefit beings more and more, it seems to me that it would be best for you to remain here."

Echoing this, the Omniscient One of Shar said, "Don't go to other places. By the power of your past prayers and aspirations, and by the skillfulness of the means you have displayed in the present time, you have helped Upper, Middle and Lower Rekong. If, for a few more years, without feeling disheartened, you continue to benefit and tame the wild people of these places, not only it will be an inexhaustible cloud of offering to the Buddhas of the three times, but it will please the teachers of this decadent age, such as myself." In accordance with their words, I gave up the idea of going to the Five-peaked Mountain.

When I came back to benefit beings at Khagang in Mapha Ri, I received this missive in verse from Alak Lhönchö, the eminent spiritual son of Jetsun Serkhang Rinpoche:

At the feet of the great holder of the
   mantra teachings,
The one who has seen inherent primordial
   mind,
Luminous and devoid of concepts,
Who has realized the illusory nature of
   whatever arises,
The yogin free from doing and not-doing,
   accepting and rejecting [466b],
An insignificant old beggar monk will
   speak frankly to you.

Having seen the mad dance of the eight
   worldly concerns,
And the condition of samsara—a pit of
   burning coals—
An intense weariness and renunciation
   shook your being,
And, entering the door of the teachings,
You reached the very summit of the Secret
   Mantras.

Alone, like a wounded deer,
You roamed from wilderness to wilderness,
And having cleared away all doubts
   through study, reflection, and
   meditation,
Your meditation experiences and
   realization became vast as space,
You freed yourself from the chains of
   clinging to subject and object.

Naturally your action became free of doing
   and not-doing, accepting and rejecting.
Moved by irresistible loving-kindness and
   purity of intention,
You strive in all ways to aid all beings and
   teachings without distinction;
Gathering disciples through the four ways,
You ripen and free them;
Paying boundless honor to the sacred
   objects of body, speech, and mind,
You serve and help all monastic
   communities;
You pacify quarrels through skillful
   means,
And bathe all things in the radiance of the
   jewel of pure perception.

I too rejoice at your amazing life and deeds
With all of my heart.

We are now at the most degenerate point
   of a degenerate age.
At this time, when the hidden faults of this
   dark age are on the increase,
When harm is returned for good,
Though people may deceive and slander you,
Don the armor of patience
And the indomitable courage of cherishing
   others more than yourself.

To benefit the Dharma and all beings [467a],
Leading an utterly perfect life in the image
Of Samantabhadra, Manjushri,
   Avalokiteshvara, and others,
I request that you remain in this world for
   an ocean of kalpas.

Protect me so that, through my virtuous
   thoughts and actions, however small,
Such as doing a few prayers, recitations
   and the like,
I may serve the Dharma and all beings,
And attain unsurpassable enlightenment.

I respectfully offer these requests with a
   scarf and a few presents.
By this merit, may all sentient beings—our
   mothers—find happiness.

In answer I sent him some news and our mutual
pure perception increased.

Hail had damaged the crops at Khagang. After I
gave a blessing, no more hailstorms came that
way. At that time I gave this oral advice to my
disciples and patrons, sons and daughters of
Shakyamuni's spiritual lineage:

May all the supreme beings who have
   come in the past
Grant their blessings.

The sublime protector of beings,
   Nagarjuna, said:
Taking support of the Dharma of human
   beings,
The celestial realm is not far.
Taking support of the Dharma of celestial
   and human beings,
Liberation is near.

Accordingly, if you follow the Dharma
   tradition of celestial and human beings
You will achieve the ultimate excellence of
   liberation.
Therefore, first of all, to obtain the
   excellent condition of celestial and
   human beings.
Maintaining a sense of shame and
   propriety
Always avoid the ten negative actions [467b].
Toward your parents, relatives, and all
   beings,
Look with the eyes of love and affection.

Encourage everyone to practice the
   sublime Dharma
And turn them away from wrong actions.

Offer to the guru and the Three Jewels;
Give to those who have nothing.
Serve the old; respect your parents.

Be helpful to the guest coming from afar;
Care for those who are chronically ill.

Repair damaged boats, bridges, and roads;
Build river embankments and shelters.

Guide people across perilous paths, rivers,
And areas where enemies and brigands
   abound.

Ransom the lives of goats, sheep, birds,
Game and fish which are about to be
   killed.

Pray with folded hands, walk round, and
   bow down
To stupas, temples, and sacred images.

Looking at them with admiring eyes and
   making offerings,
Restore old monuments and repair those
   that are damaged or destroyed.

Making no distinctions between strangers
   and those who are dear,
With equanimity and gentleness inspire
   everyone to practice Dharma.

Doing away with anger, quarrels, and
   arguments,
Remain in harmony with everyone's mind.

Though someone may say unpleasant
   things to you,
Do not utter harsh words in return.

Always be broad-minded and
   good-natured;
Do not harm others, help them
   as much as you can.

Never deceive, defraud or pretend;
Always keep an honest mind.

Never forget kindness done to you;
Be well-disposed and grateful for ever.

Do not upset others' minds, cut off
   jealousy,
And get rid of rivalry, craving, hatred and
   dispute.

When you happen to be rich, don't be
   haughty;
Don't disdain others.

When you happen to be poor, don't be
   disheartened [468a];
See it as the mere result of your past actions.

The temporal and the spiritual are for the
   most part in agreement,[72]
So act in harmony with both society and
   the Dharma.
In brief, give up nonvirtue and accomplish
   virtue,

And always have a kind mind.
This is the way noble worldly people
Lead their perfect lives.

May this nectar-like admonition
Be useful to me and to everyone else.

This advice benefited the minds of all. I then
came back toward Marnang Tsho-nga. The devoted *ngakpa* Tamdrin and the other *ngakpas* of
Tsho-nga's community gave me a fine welcome.
After I taught the Dharma, many people gave
up wrong actions and practiced virtue. Many
people, too, erected sacred objects of the body,
speech, and mind, such as the stupa of Gurchung.
For these, I gave many miraculously multiplied
relics of Lord Buddha and other precious relics.

Out of great faith, the patrons on both banks
of the Machu offered me three horses, thirty
dzomos, *dris*, yaks, cows, and bulls; twenty goats
and sheep; five bundles of tea; ten mats of white
felt; a hundred bags of barley; and many cups
and ceremonial scarves. Of these, I offered thirty
horses, *dzos*, *dris*, yaks, cows and bulls to the
various monasteries on both banks of the river.

I also began building one hundred and eight
temples in separate monasteries and villages, and
making several hundred volumes of the holy
scriptures, stupas, and *mani* wheels.[73] To pay for
these, I offered an almost incalculable number of
bars of silver, horses, *dzos*, *dris*, yaks, cows, bulls,
goats, and sheep [468b]; bundles of tea, lengths
of cloth, brocade, ceremonial scarves, and bags
of barley and wheat. I offered this prayer for
everyone:

"By virtue of the meritorious deeds I and
others have performed throughout the three
times, symbolized by these present ones, may the
precious Dharma of the Buddha spread, expand
and prevail in all directions, places, and circumstances. In particular, may boundless happiness
and contentment befall the totality of beings
under the sky.

"More especially, may all the disciples, patrons, and I live as long as the sun and moon;
may our merit become like Mount Meru, the
king of mountains; may our fame fill the skies;
may our activity for the sake of beings equal that

of the Buddha; may the word 'suffering' not even be heard; may we never be parted from bliss and joy even for an instant.

"May I be able one day to dispel all the sufferings of beings. May I be able one day to establish in wealth all those stricken by poverty. May the day come when I am able to give my flesh and blood for the welfare of beings. May I become able one day to remain in the hell realm and bring some good there. May the day come when I am able to fulfill all the hopes of beings with the bounty of samsara and nirvana [469a]. May the day come when I become enlightened, a Buddha, able to remove forever the suffering of beings. May I never enjoy harming others rather than benefiting them. May the day come when all beings will become happy through the exchange of my happiness for their suffering.

May all beings have happiness;
May they be free of all suffering;
May they never be separated from happiness;
May they abide in boundless equanimity!"

Thus in accordance with the Eight Wishes of the Bodhisattvas and the Four Boundless Ones, I made an excellent concluding connection with this stainless prayer. I also offered for the assembly hall of Gartse monastery a silver lamp made with thirty *sang* of silver, and for the temple of Tashikhyil a set of offering bowls made with twenty-five silver *sang* worth of bell-metal.

I offered too many ritual objects to Bhupshol, Dungkar Shagpa, and other temples in various places. I offered garments and long silken scarves to many statues, and ended with aspiration prayers.

I brought back seven hundred sheep to Tashikhyil, and kept them there, saving their lives. I used their wool as a resource for the monastery, and gave the other sheep that were offered to me to the people who were coming to collect donations for their monasteries, with the condition that the sheep would not be killed.

For many years, I looked after sixty to seventy humble monks, nuns and beggars at Tashikhyil who were homeless and had no one to take care of them [469b].

Every year on the fifteenth day of the fourth month, I would gather several hundred religious and lay devotees for a fasting practice. During the third week of the fourth month, I would sponsor a five-day ceremony of the Eight Classes of Herukas, performed by nineteen hundred *phurba* mantra-practitioners of Rekong.[74]

As an endowment for tea and butter to be distributed during this ceremony, I offered over a hundred *dzomos* and *dris*. As if to confirm the saying which goes, "Wealth is a flag that calls forth enemies and demons," all these animals were taken by cattle rustlers from Achog in Tsa. Some thousand *phurba*-holding *ngakpas* performed a *phurba* ritual; their powers being feared by everyone in the region, the thieves brought back all the animals and begged for forgiveness.

From then on, thinking that hoarding is not in accord with the Dharma, I gave everything away as offerings and charity. Again, just as the saying goes, "No more wealth, no more enemies"; free from enemies, thieves and bandits, I enjoyed complete tranquility. Patrons from Shohong and Dzamling provided for my sustenance. Every year I received alms of barley in the autumn and of butter in the spring. Besides this, people would help me as best they could and gave me donations for prayers for the dead and other things.

One day, Kathok Lama Rinpoche came from Chuzang. I invited him to the Tashikhyil Hermitage and received him in the finest fashion. He gave the empowerment of the peaceful and wrathful deities to the assembly of *ngakpas*, and to about thirty of us, master and disciples he gave the complete empowerments and reading transmission of the *Nyingthig Ya Shi*, the *Four Heart-Essences*.[75] In thanks, I presented him with a statue of Tara, a copy of the *Graded Path of the Jewel Ornament of Liberation*, a stupa in the Kadampa style [470a], one horse, one mule, and four *dzos* with saddles.

After that, Serkhang Rinpoche, a Bodhisattva dwelling at a level where he benefited all who made a connection with him, came to Rongpo. I met him and offered him, as sign of homage, a statue of the Great Compassionate One and a copy of Drukpa Kunleg's life-story, together with two horse blankets. Then, when he gave the empowerments of *Guhyasamaja* and *Chakra-samvara* to the whole assembly of the main monastery of Rongpo, I sat among them to receive these teachings.

People from Nyenthok invited him to give a blessing of the Great Compassionate One, which I received too. One day I went into his presence; he spoke to me at length and showed me great kindness. He gave me some yellow brocade, a red shawl, many plates of sugar and fruit, two long silken scarves, and a copy of the teachings on mind training called the *Rays of the Sun*.[76]

After I had returned to Tashikhyil and was staying there, he sent Lobzang Dargye, a holder of the three trainings, as well as Jampa, Khedrup, and others—six monks who had completely renounced worldly life. According to the Kagyu tradition, I gave them the transmission and detailed explanations upon Mahamudra, the Six Yogas of Naropa, the *Three Cycles of Oral Lineage*,[77] the *Nine Cycles of the Formless Dakini*,[78] and all the related yogic exercises. Then, the great spiritual son Lobzang Dargye asked for some spoken advice [470b]; I gave him this *Great Wondrous Advice*:

> The Teacher, the Buddha,
> Who loved all beings like his only child,
>   said:
>
>> To benefit beings
>> Is to benefit me.
>> To harm beings
>> Is to harm me.
>>
>> Just as a mother rejoices
>> When someone is helpful to her
>>   child,
>> My heart is gladdened
>> When someone is helpful to any
>>   sentient being.
>>
>> Just as a mother is distressed
>> When someone harms her child,

>> My heart is distressed
>> When someone harms any sentient
>>   being.
>>
>> Therefore, never do harm and
>>   violence,
>> And always strive to bring benefit
>>   and happiness.

He also said:

>> Incense, flowers, lamps, and the like
>> Are not the best offerings to the
>>   Buddha.
>> The best offering to the Buddha,
>> Is to benefit all sentient beings.
>>
>> Therefore, to make an offering to
>>   the Buddha,
>> Benefit all sentient beings.
>> This offering will delight the
>>   Buddhas
>> And make all sentient beings happy.
>>
>> There is no better way to please the
>>   Victorious Ones
>> Than to gladden the hearts of
>>   sentient beings.

If you ponder these verses of the Buddha,
There is a very deep point to be understood:
If we please the Buddha
He will accept us with joy,
And once he has accepted us,
We will be continuously happy and
  fulfilled.

There is no virtue greater than this:
To gladden the hearts of Buddha and all
  beings [471a].
And a time will come when, without
  making great efforts,
Our own accumulations will be complete,
And we ourselves will become Buddhas.

This instruction for bringing satisfaction to
  both oneself and others
Is wonderful indeed!

May this *Great Wondrous Advice*
Benefit the minds of all who hear it.

This was my advice.

From time to time, I used to go to the Eight Great Places of the Accomplished Ones of Rekong, as well as to the places where Jetsun Kalden Gyatso meditated and other secluded sites. I would stay in retreat in each of these places, in some for one month, in some half a month, in some seven days, establishing a connection with these holy sites, performing "Calling for the Descent of Blessings," and reciting prayers and wishes for auspiciousness. I made a small retreat hut in every place where there had been none, and sang this song in praise of mountain solitudes:

I pray to the eight *siddhas*
Who came in the past to the eight holy places
Of the Golden Valley of Rekong:
Bless me to be able to remain continuously in mountain retreats.

E ma! The golden days of old are gone.
Kye ma! The evil times have dawned.

All the wise beings of the past have gone
And a crowd of fools is born.

The silken knot—the divine Dharma—has been untied,
And the binding of the sheaf—human ethics—has been cut.

The golden yoke of the royal laws has been broken,
And the ocean of the chiefs' counsel has dried up.

The pattern has vanished from the skins of tiger-like heroes,

And virtuous women have thrown away the mantle of modesty [471b].

The noble traditions of the elite are not being maintained,
And vulgar behavior is encouraged.

Without thinking carefully about ultimate benefit
People only make careful reckoning of immediate profit.

Not holding onto excellent traditions,
They set a plethora of bad examples.

Not heeding the scriptural authority of the learned,
They make a great fuss about the discourses of fools.

Now, when people are not imitating the good
But emulating the inferior,
Is the time to follow the examples
Of the perfect lives of past saints
And give up all concerns of this life;
Now is the time to devote oneself to the profound practice
In places where the past *siddhas* dwelled.

E ma!
In the pleasant groves of wild mountain solitudes
Where wise and accomplished beings
Attained supreme realization,
One is not distracted by the affairs of this life.

As gods and goddesses play
In the pleasant gardens of Indra's paradise,
Birds and wild animals frolic insouciantly
In thickets and meadows where medicinal herbs grow in abundance.

As Buddhas and Bodhisattvas dwell
In their wondrous pure Buddhafields,
Holy Dharma practitioners
Dwell in the cool shade of delightful forests.

In the Eight Sacred Places of the Accom-
plished Ones
And in those where the precious Kalden
Gyatso practiced,
The sun of experiences and realization rises
In the minds of those who pursue
unsurpassable enlightenment.

Therefore it would be good for the
fortunate ones
Among the monks, Bönpos, and *ngakpas*,
To hoist the victory banner of
accomplishment
In the great sacred places of their own land
[472a].

May all practitioners who hear this song
Not stay in their homelands,
But, relying on places of total solitude,
Devote themselves to the essence of
practice.

After this, most of the monks and nuns, Bönpos,
and *ngakpas* around went into retreat in these
holy places, and devoted themselves to recitation
and *sadhana* practice.

In the villages, yearly gatherings were instituted to recite the *mani*. Also, at home, everyone
did a lot of spiritual practice with body, speech,
and mind. Under these fortunate circumstances,
the whole province was rendered sparkling white
by the holy Dharma. For the benefit of all the
men and women of Amdo I then sang a song
called the *Garland of Vital Points of Human Ethics*:

I entreat the blessing of the gracious gurus
So that I may accomplish my aspirations
In accordance with the Dharma.

Observe spiritual values
And ethical values will naturally be
accomplished;
Always practice the divine Dharma, Amdo
folk!

Do not postpone immaculate, virtuous
Dharma;
Practice it as soon as possible, Amdo folk!

If your aspirations are just for food and
comforts,
You won't go far in the Dharma.
Be strong-minded about bearing hardships
for the sake of practice, Amdo folk!

Even if you do something difficult for
someone else,
Don't keep on whining about having done
it, Amdo folk!

No matter who requests teachings, even a
leper or a beggar,
Expound the Dharma willingly, Amdo
folk! [472b].

Though some may ask you questions just
to test your realization,
Teach them in the best possible way,
Amdo folk!

Without consideration for illusory material
wealth,
Fill up the whole place with the Dharma,
Amdo folk!

Regarding all that truly should be kept
secret,
Remain completely mute, Amdo folk!

Attachment and hatred are the hail-demon
that wreaks ruin on the harvest of Dharma;
Have neither attachment for those who are
dear to you
Nor hatred for those who are not, Amdo folk!

When you have food and wealth, don't be
stingy;
Use it and give it to others, Amdo folk!

When you have little food and no wealth,
don't get into debt;[79]
Know how to eat and drink wisely, Amdo
folk!

Do not show an unkind face to anyone;
Welcome everyone with a smile, Amdo
folk!

In villages and also in monasteries
There is always plenty of useless gossip;
Never listen to slander, Amdo folk!

In the highlands and also in the lowlands
There are plenty of enemies and robbers;
Be cautious and watchful, Amdo folk!

Never put your trust in shameless people;
Associate with the reliable, Amdo folk!

In hard times do not count on men,
But pray to the deities, Amdo folk!

Wherever you go, wherever you stay,
Be in harmony with all, Amdo folk!

Even if you have great attachment for your
    own things,
Never covet another's possessions, Amdo
    folk!

Even if you are skilled and wise,
Ask everyone's opinion, Amdo folk!

Even if you have built up a fortune by
    yourself,
Don't show off in public, Amdo folk! [473a].

Even if everyone holds you in high esteem,
Don't become infatuated with your
    greatness, Amdo folk!

Even if you are acknowledged as a spiritual
    teacher,
Don't disdain those who are less
    renowned, Amdo folk!

Even from afar, bow down and show
    marks of respect
To others' teachers and chiefs, Amdo folk!

When you encounter someone of equal status,
Place him above yourself, Amdo folk!

Whatever you do, have little craving;
Know how to be content with what you
    have,

And always keep a humble position, Amdo
    folk!

In brief, be always respectful to your
    superiors,
Kind to your inferiors,
And in harmony with your equals, Amdo
    folk!

Act thus in accordance with the Dharma:
You will enjoy happiness and everyone's
    confidence, Amdo folk!

From now on and throughout all my lives,
May I myself be skilled in benefiting all
    beings.

May all who read, hear, remember, or
    merely touch the written words of this
    song
Realize their aims and those of others in
    this very life.

May goodness prevail in all countries, may
    crops be abundant,
May a great auspiciousness cover the
    whole earth.

This song opened the minds of most of the religious and laypeople gathered there.

I went and stayed for a few days in each of the districts. When I took leave, all the patrons escorted me for a while, and when we were going to part I gave them my blessing, protection[80] and advice, put around their necks farewell scarves, and sang for them, men and women, this song of helpful advice that starts with "Upon my head, in a vast tent of rainbows . . ." [473b].

Upon my head, in a vast tent of rainbows,
Upon a throne raised by eight lions,
Dwells my lord root guru, Vajradhara,

Great in kindness, whose name I barely
  dare to pronounce,
My father, the King of Dharma, Ngakyi
  Wangpo.

I, his son, supplicate with fervor:
May you turn to the Dharma the minds of
  all those present here;
May all their perceptions alien to Dharma
  cease.

By the power of our past prayers and
  karma,
We, people of various origins, gathered
  here for a fleeting moment—
Some coming from the realm of U-Tsang,
Some from the directions of Kham and
  Domey—
And established perfect connections through
  Dharma, food and material things;
Yet, before long we will disperse.

Like this, everything is impermanent.
There isn't a single being who will remain
  in this life,
And when going to the land of the next life
Nothing but the Dharma will help at all.

You patrons, men and women, assembled
  here,
Remember that death may come at any
  time,
And without entertaining excessive
  attachment for the affairs of this life,
Endeavor in the sublime Dharma to
  prepare for the paths and levels in the
  next life.

Even if you can't practice the Dharma,
  beware of sin,
And have good thoughts at all times.
Wherever I myself may go,
I'll always keep you within my spiritual
  protection
For this life and the life thereafter.

Now, farewell, men and women patrons;
I, the yogin, will not stay, but go.

May we meet again and again
Before the end of this very life [474a].
Yet, since in this degenerate age life is
  uncertain,
If, separated by great distances, we don't
  meet again,
May we meet in the land of the next life.

This is farewell advice given from my heart
To all the devout patrons;
May all men and women who hear this song
Be joyful and happy at all times.
May good omens and prosperity prevail in
  this land;
May auspiciousness encompass the three
  realms!

All those gathered there felt completely tired
of samsara, and felt an urge to escape from it.
Faith burst forth in their minds, and made tears
well up in their eyes and all the hair on their
body stand on end. Praying that we might meet
many times again in this life and all our future
lives, they did prostrations, respectfully walked
round me, and departed for home.

That year a new retreat place had been established at Amnye Jadrön. I went and stayed there
for seven days. One day, remembering my kind
root teacher Jetsun Jamyang Gyatso Rinpoche, I
went to see the stupa containing his relics and
found it had collapsed into an earthen heap.
Realizing the impermanent nature of all conditioned things, I became overwhelmed with sadness, and, remembering my precious lama with
all my heart, I bowed down, touched the heap of
earth with my head, and wept helplessly [474b].
Then I offered a *ganachakra*, supplicated him many
times, and made vast prayers. Prostrating myself
and reverentially walking round the stupa many
times, I stayed a long time. Before leaving, I
touched my head again against the mound of
earth and uttered this song of longing for the
gracious guru:

Kind lord, precious lama,
Who bore the sweet-sounding name
"Ocean of Serene Melody,"
I, your son, supplicate you with great
    fervor;
Look upon me from invisible space!

Before, I met the body of the guru.
His body did not remain, but left this world.

Later, I met the relics of the guru;
The stupa that contained them fell apart.

At last, I meet a mere mound of earth.

Now, as I go wandering on to distant
    lands,
How shall I ever encounter even this
    earthen heap again?

Thinking of this, again and again,
I remember you, my supremely kind
    master.

As soon as you come into my mind
Tears stream down my face, beyond
    control.

Today, I, your son who clings to
    permanence,
Can see that all compounded things do not
    last;
Impermanent, they are doomed to
    disintegrate,
Just as I've seen here.

In particular, this illusory body of mine,
A compound of the four elements,
Is doomed to dissolution,
Just as I've seen here.

For the swiftly vanishing remnant of this
    life,
Like the sun setting swiftly over a
    mountain pass,
Not indulging in the affairs of this life,
I will practice Dharma for the sake of the
    next.

Compassionate lord, master,
In whichever of the infinity of Buddhafields
    you now dwell [475a],
Comfort the mind of your son on the brink
    of death.
In whichever Buddhafield you are—take
    me there,
And once reunited, may we two, father
    and son,
Never part again.

By your blessings, glorious lord guru,
May the years in this land always be
    good.[81]

As I sang this, the few disciples and patrons who
were there felt strong disillusionment with this
world, and were filled with awe and faith.

On the way back I performed the consecration of the retreat place and pronounced verses
of auspiciousness. Then I came back to the
secluded place of Tashikhyil, blessed by the feet
of past saints. I entered into a year's retreat and,
like the Great Compassionate One, "Repose of
the Mind," I remained in the state of luminous
radiance, the true nature of mind.

Soldiers from Rekong raided and destroyed the
monastery of Upper Tashi Gephel. The abbot,
Khen Rinpoche, a person who always fulfilled
his guru's commands, together with all his disciples rebuilt the monastery and erected a huge
statue of Buddha Maitreya. For that purpose
they spent a bundle of ten thousand gold leaves
and seven bundles of one thousand; twenty horses,
dzos and *dris*; thirty sheep; forty-five bags of *tsampa*;
ten sheepskin bags of butter; and two large
bundles of tea.

Similarly, Alak Tendzin Nyima, Rabjung,
and Nuchi rebuilt the monastery of Lower
Gurong, which had been burnt down by Chinese soldiers [475b]. For that they spent two
hundred and eighty lengths of cloth, about forty
bags of *tsampa*, eight sheepskin bags of butter,

and over half a large bundle of tea. Many monks, led by the treasurer Drupchen and Tendzin, made one hundred thousand *tsa-tsas* and a line of stones, engraved with the *mani*, next to Tashikhyil Monastery where I was living. By doing so they were fortunate enough to purify their obscurations and accumulate merit.

Eating only one meal a day, I remained evenly in the natural state. As post-meditation practice, I opened hundreds of different doors of concentration, practicing long-life *sadhanas*, development and completion stages, emanations and transformations,[82] and other practices.

At one point I had the following thought: "There is a saying that goes, 'When one reaches fifty, life is gone; when the cock sings, night is gone.' Now I am fifty-six, my hair has turned grey and my eyes red; all the signs announcing death have descended upon me. Now my body is still free of illness and my mind free of suffering; my intelligence is still clear and my tongue agile; so if I have anything to give to my disciples, anything to tell them, I must give it and tell it now." Accordingly, I sang a song—my advice while I was alive and my last will and testament for the time of my death:

> I bow down and make offerings, praises
>   and prayers
> To the gurus who bestow the waves of
>   blessing,
> To the *yidam* deities who grant accomplish-
>   ments,
> To the dakinis who dispel obstacles [476a]:
> Always look with compassion
> Upon myself, my disciples and benefactors.
> Grant the blessings of your body, speech,
>   and mind,
> And the supreme and ordinary *siddhis!*
>
> Having pondered the unpredictability of
>   the time of death,
> I, the yogin Tsogdruk Rangdrol,
> Will, while I am still alive,
> Give to my disciples what they need.
>
> To the disciple whose vows and *samayas* are
>   perfectly pure,

> Who has few needs and is easily contented,
> Who has sharp intelligence and great
>   diligence,
> I give a place where the past saints
>   meditated.
>
> To the disciple who, like the Victorious
>   Ones of the past,
> Has given up all the affairs of this life
> And is able to stay in solitude,
> I give the victory banner of the lineage of
>   spiritual practice.
>
> To the disciple who, having practiced,
>   tamed his mind,
> Cultivated loving-kindness, compassion,
>   and Bodhicitta,
> And is able to benefit others,
> I give the golden wheel for expounding the
>   teachings.
>
> To the disciple who from childhood has
>   had faith, compassion,
> Great capacity for study, reflection, and
>   meditation,
> As well as sharp intelligence,
> I give the treasury of the pith instructions
>   of sutra and tantra.
>
> To the disciple who, having studied and
>   reflected impartially in his youth,
> Acquired a pure perception of all the
>   doctrinal views
> And is free of sectarianism,
> I give the jewels of the Madhyamika,
>   Mahamudra, and Mahasandhi.
>
> To the miserable masterless disciple,
> Who has no predisposition for the
>   Dharma,
> And does not possess the wealth of merit,
> I give the food and possessions that bring
>   fleeting happiness.
>
> I, the renunciate Tsogdruk Rangdrol [476b],
> Having remembered the imminence of
>   death,
> Leave this will to all my disciples

While I still enjoy all my faculties of
     expression.

You disciples who once had a strong faith
     in the Dharma,
And after a few years developed strong
     faith in wealth,
Busying yourselves with trade, exorcisms,
     and village ceremonies,
Do not disgrace the Dharma.

You disciples who once devoted yourselves
     to the practice of Dharma,
And after a while began to hoard
And keep accounts for every needle and
     thread,
Do not trade away the lineage of spiritual
     practice.

You disciples who once worked for the
     benefit of others,
And after a few years began to work for
     yourselves
And to be jealous of other practitioners,
Don't make the teachings meaningless.

You disciples who once devoted yourselves
     to study, reflection, and meditation,
And, after some years turned into
     sectarians
And disparaged others' traditions,
Don't accumulate bad karma by throwing
     away the Dharma.

You disciples who once kept pure monastic
     vows,
And after a few years came to rely on
     women and liquor,
Don't behave in an even less disciplined
     way
Than ordinary laymen.

You disciples who have been left behind,
When after some days your mourning is
     over
And you start to quarrel about food and
     money,
Do not betray your teacher.

Everyone must die, certainly;
At the time of death, what's certain to
     benefit
Is the sublime Dharma—nothing else.
So, all of you, practice the supreme
     Dharma!

While I am alive, this is my advice,
When I die, this will be my testament.
This is my ultimate admonition:
Act according to it and all will go well.

May this benefit the minds of all the
     faithful men and women who hear it;
In the next life, may I lead all those
With whom I have had a connection in
     this one,
May crops and cattle prosper throughout
     the land [477a],
May Dharma, auspiciousness, and all
     excellent qualities
Increase like the waxing moon.

This advice did some good to the minds of
most of the disciples; later many of them gave
up worldly affairs to wander in mountain solitudes.

One day, having come to remain in the even,
natural state of mind, I rested for a long time
simply enjoying the taste of the samadhi of bliss,
clarity, and absence of thoughts. At the end I
thought, "How nice if all my faithful disciples
could just remain like this in the natural state of
all things, without having to do intentional meditation," and I sang a song upon my meditation
experience, the *Guru and Triple Gem* song:

   Guru and wish-fulfilling triple gem,
   Shower blessings and *siddhis* upon us like
        rain!

   All appearances are vast openness,
   Blissful and utterly free.

With a free, happy mind
I sing this song of joy.

When one looks toward one's own mind—
The root of all phenomena—
There is nothing but vivid emptiness,
Nothing concrete there to be taken as real.

It is present as transparent, utter openness,
Without outside, without inside—
An all-pervasiveness
Without boundary and without direction.

The wide-open expanse of the view,
The true condition of mind,
Is like the sky, like space:
Without center, without edge, without aim.

By leaving whatever I experience
Relaxed in ease, just as it is,
I have arrived at the vast plain
That is the absolute expanse [477b].

Dissolving into the expanse of emptiness
That has no limits and no boundary,
All vision, all sound,
My own mind, and the sky all merge.

Not once did the notion arise
Of these being separate and distinct.

In the absolute expanse of awareness
All things are blended into that single
    taste—
But, relatively, each and every phenom-
    enon is distinctly, clearly seen.
Wondrous!

Deeply intoxicated with the bliss
Of radiant clarity—vivid, brilliant,
    immaculate—
From my heart, I wished to dance with joy.

Toward all the beings under the skies
Who have failed to realize this,
All-pervading compassion spontaneously
    dawned;
The urge to sing this song arose of itself.

Without entering into the narrow
    rock-gorge
Which is mind watching for stillness and
    movement,
Without being caught in the snare of
    "view" and "meditation" created by the
    intellect,
Without flying into the dark clouds of dull
    states of mind,
Without plunging into the storm of
    agitated thinking,
The great garuda, my own mind,
Flew freely into the wide-open sky of the
    absolute expanse.

Eyes completely open, encompassing a
    hundred horizons,
Utterly at ease, the garuda of mind wings
    its way—
What delight!

In the expanse of sky-like evenness,
All phenomena, all the appearances and
    sounds
Of samsara and nirvana are apparent yet
    empty;
They are empty, and yet they appear.

Although they appear, phenomena are
    empty,
Free of the limiting concept "truly
    existent."
Although they are empty by nature,
    phenomena do appear,
Free of the limiting concept "nonexistent."
In the vast space of the view
That is itself spontaneously free
From the two limiting concepts—belief in
    permanence or in nothingness [478a]—
This joyous song burst forth by itself.

Even more vast than the sky is the view,
    emptiness;
There, the sun of love and the moon of
    compassion arose
And again and again I made boundless
    prayers
To benefit the teachings and beings.

May all disease and epidemics of disease,
All famine, and all wars be ended,
And may all have happiness and joy.

Following this, I related everything to an understanding of voidness in which all phenomena are like illusions, like dreams. In this way, I had little difficulty in accumulating merit and purifying my obscurations, as a way to perfect easily the two accumulations. I persevered as much as I could in all Bodhisattva actions. With a strong intent, I dedicated all merit toward present and ultimate aims, and concluded with pure prayers, adorning them with many verses of auspiciousness.

Notes

1. In 1828.

2. Taklung Shabdrung (*stag lung zhabs drung*) and his son. The Shabdrung lineage of the throne-holders of Taklung was hereditary. If the Shabdrung was too young to take care of the monastery, either of the two main incarnate lamas of Taklung, Matrul (*ma sprul*) and Tsetrul (*rtse sprul*), would be the throne-holder.

3. Every spring, when the cuckoos returning from their winter migration reached Reting (*rwa sgreng*) in great numbers, vast offerings of food were made to them; many people would come for this occasion.

4. Derge Rishorwas (*sde dge ri shor ba*), literally, "those from Derge who ran away to the mountains," designates nomad tribes who left Derge and settled in northeastern Tibet.

5. Caravans of Tibetan merchants used to travel up to the Chinese border—to and from Tachienlu and Xining—exchanging herbal medicine and woolen clothes for tea, horses and mules. Because of the arduous nature of the long journey and the danger of bandits, the traders made the trip only once a year. To check the disputes that often arose because of the lack of security and price regulation, trade agents (*tshong dpon*) were appointed by the regent-king of Tibet. These agents would accompany the yearly caravan, protect it with a small military escort under their command, administer the trading camps, and

regulate prices. The Garpön (*sgar dpon*) is the governor of Xining.

6. *snam bu* is a thick woollen material and *ther ma* is a finer wool serge.

7. Correct *sgra* to *sbra* (a tent made of yak's hair and thus usually black).

8. The Khenpo (*mkhan po*) and the Nangso (*nang so*) were two Tibetan dignitaries posted at the court of the Manchu emperor in Beijing. They came every year up to Nakchuka to meet the Tsipön (*rtsis dpon*), the head of the finances, who himself came from Lhasa. (In that year, 1828, the envoy was Tsipön Phala. See Petech 1973, 82 and 237.)

9. For Tashi Jungne, the son of Chögyal Ngakyi Wangpo, see Appendix 3.

10. Kumbum Jampa Ling (*sku 'bum byams pa gling*) was founded in 1560 by Gompa Rinchen Tsondru (*sgom pa rin chen brtson 'grus*) at the birthplace of Tsongkhapa. Kumbum (*sku 'bum*), the Hundred Thousand Icons, refers to one hundred thousand images of Manjushri, the Buddha of wisdom, which appeared naturally on the leaves of a tree said to have sprung from a drop of umbilical blood at Tsongkhapa's birth. The Golden Reliquary (*gser gdung*) contains some relics of Je Tsongkhapa. See AC, vol. 2, pp. 311–21.

11. *dzab*, a highly prized wood used to make bowls. It is a rare growth, or gall, which occurs upon certain kinds of trees. After the bowl has been made, it is varnished several times with the milky sap of a poisonous plant.

12. It is a tradition to come and welcome a respected teacher at some distance from the monastery. Horsemen, sometimes hundreds of them, each wearing a special white hat called the "welcome hat" (*phebs bsu zhwa mo*), then lead the lama in procession to the monastery.

13. *Krishnasara*, a kind of golden spotted antelope said to be very compassionate incarnations of Bodhisattvas who have attained the eighth *bhumi*.

14. The Dalai Lama, an emanation of Padmapani (Avalokiteshvara), the Lotus-holder.

15. The Abbot Shantarakshita, the Master Padmasambhava, and the King Trisong Detsen.

16. The annual religious dance festival of the tenth day, the Tsechu Cham of Samye, which originated as a vast offering ceremony based upon the sutra section of the Kangyur and thus is known as the Sutra Offering (*mdo sde mchod pa*).

17. For Wati Zangpo, see chap. 12, note 21.

18. Magsar Rinpoche (*dmag gsar rin po che*). Possibly the hermit of Magsar (*dmag gsar mtshams pa*; see RO,

p. 652), who traveled to central Tibet where he met Kardo Rinpoche (one of Shabkar's teachers; see Appendix 2) and embraced the Nyingma tradition.

19. *A lag nam mkha'*; see Appendix 6.

20. Thekchen (*theg chen*), a large-sized bell used by the chant leader of the monks.

21. On Tashikhyil, see Author's Introduction, note 22.

22. *mnyam par bzhag pa* refers to integrating one's mind with the view.

23. For *The Sixteen Spheres*, see chap. 12, note 74.

24. For *The Condensed Meaning of the Graded Path*, see chap. 1, note 59.

25. Apart from the Eight Places of the Accomplished Ones (see chap. 1, note 4), there are also eighteen others related sacred places in Rekong (see AC, vol. 2, p. 303)

26. This and the following are names of local deities (*sa dag*) who give their names to the mountain where they reside. "Ruddy" (*dmar yag*) is a common epithet given to the tiger. Lofty and impressive red cliffs abound in the Tashikhyil Hermitage area.

27. Tsendrok Khen Rinpoche, Lobzang Dargye (*mtshan dgrogs mkhan chen blo bzang dar rgyas*, d. 1834) became the teacher of the Chinese emperor in Beijing and was the twenty-sixth hierarch of Thösam Nampar Gyalwai Ling (*thos bsam rnam par rgyal ba'i gling*), a monastery founded by Kalden Gyatso. See RO, p. 236.

28. Wheel of the Teaching (*bstan pa'i 'khor lo*): one of Manjushri's names, here given to Shabkar.

29. Meaning that Shabkar is an emanation of Padmapani, Avalokiteshvara.

30. This refers to the story from the sutras of the fox who fell into a pot of blue dye and became unrecognizable. The other animals crowned him their king, as they had never seen such an impressive animal. One night, however, when the other foxes were barking under the full moon, the "king" forgot his ruse and started to bark. His subjects realized that he was nothing but an ordinary fox and chased him away.

31. For the Lord of the Emerald Steeds, see chap. 6, note 50.

32. Both temporal and spiritual activities.

33. By asking all the details of this messenger.

34. Paradise Arrayed in Turquoise Petals; see chap. 1, note 34.

35. *phrug*, a long strip of thick woollen material, of a kind mostly woven in Tsang, central Tibet.

36. *phying dkar*, a thick felt made by laying the raw wool on large surfaces on the ground, sprinkling water on it, and beating it. It is made into capes used against rain and snow.

37. Travelers always add a stone to the cairn when crossing the pass.

38. The Salars are a Muslim tribe of Amdo.

39. Kachu (*bka' bcu*), or "ten scriptures," refers to a teacher who knows by heart and can fully explain ten major basic Buddhist treatises. Although there were quite a few learned lamas bearing this title, the highly honorific name of Kachu Buddha (*bka' bcu sangs rgyas*) could possibly refer to Jetsun Kalden Gyatso (1607–77; see chap.1, note 2), who was also known as Kachu Rinpoche (*bka' bcu rin po che*), or to Alak Kachu (*A lag bka' bcu*, 1667–1744). See RO, p. 185.

40. *do the ye*, an official.

41. *da dmar:* some informants speak of saddlebags made of red woolen cloth.

42. Alak Dzong Ngon (*a lag dzong sngon*), a disciple of Dola Jigme Kalzang (*mdo bla 'jigs med skal bzang*, see Appendix 3). See also RO, p. 483.

43. King of the Sky (*nam mkha'i rgyal po*): an aspect of Avalokiteshvara.

44. This refers to Chöying Topden Dorje, the founder of Kohudeh Dzogchen Namgyal Ling Monastery. See Appendix 2 and RO, p. 651.

45. Held at the Chinese New Year.

46. Tribam (*khri bam*). Informants suggested either "ten thousand gold leaves" or "ten thousand leaves of red and yellow paper," which seems more likely.

47. A series depicted in a text in verse known as the *Wish-fulfilling Tree* (*dpag bsam 'khri shing*, T 4155) by Kshemendra, which is often used as a model for paintings. A prose version, *The One Hundred Episodes of Lord Buddha's Former Lives* (*skyes rabs brgya rtsa ma*) or *Hundred Rebirths*, was written by the third Karmapa Rangjung Dorje (*rang 'byung rdo rje*, 1284–1339).

48. *bhu la*, leather boxes with multicolored patches.

49. This refers to the practice of bribing or coercing a poor person to go to jail or to war as a substitute for oneself.

50. Fierce ones (*'dregs pa*), here referring to the nagas, spirits, and gods of the locality, who live in lakes, trees, rocks, etc. If harmed, as when trees are cut, for instance, they may bring sickness to the people and epidemics to the cattle.

51. For the Offering of the Twenty-Fifth, see chap. 14, note 39.

52. These are the tenth day of the lunar month, dedicated to Guru Padmasambhava; the twenty-fifth, dedicated to the dakinis; the fifteenth and thirtieth, dedicated to Lord Buddha Shakyamuni; and the eighth, dedicated to the Medicine Buddha.

53. Tsongkhapa.

54. *The Song of the Nightingale* (*spring yig ka la pinka'i sgra dbyangs*) appears in TS 4 p.774; *The Gentle Call of the Blue Cuckoo* (*khu byug sngon mo'i skad snyan*), in TS 4, p. 777; *The Melodious Lute and Flute* (*gdangs snyan pi wang gling bu*) in TS 4, p. 780; and *The Sublime Drumbeat of the Golden Radiance* (*dam chos gser 'od dam pa'i rnga sgra*) in TS 4, p. 780. The title of the latter song is inspired by a sutra and a *dharani* bearing the same name, which are part of the *gzungs 'dus* (a collection of *dharanis* and short sutras drawn from the *bka' 'gyur*).

55. The incarnation of Shingsa Rinpoche (*shing bza' rin po che;* see chap. 5, note 15) was Lobzang Tenpai Wangchuk Tsultrim Phuntsok (*blo bzang bstan pa'i dbang phyug tshul khrims phun tshogs;* see Jigme Gyaltsen, p. 11).

56. For the *Wondrous Emanated Scriptures* (*rmad byung sprul pa'i glegs bam*), see Appendix 5.

57. *The Heart Essence of the Great Expanse* (*klong chen snying thig*) is the cycle of the mind *termas* of Rigdzin Jigme Lingpa. See Translator's Introduction, note 43.

58. For *The Hundred Sadhanas, Source of Jewels,* see chap. 14, note 40.

59. *The Secret Biography, "Sealed Visions"* (*gsang ba'i rnam thar dag snang rgya can*), is the cycle of twenty-five sections of teachings received in visions as mind *terma* by the fifth Dalai Lama, Ngawang Lobzang Gyatso (*ngag dbang blo bzang rgya mtsho,* 1617–82, see NS, pp. 819–24), arranged as an esoteric autobiography.

60. *Profound Pacifying Path of Cutting Through* (*zhi ba lam zab gcod*). This text of the *gcod* practice (see Author's Introduction, note 32) has not been identified.

61. *The Blue Citadel of the Great Gate* (*sgo chen rdzong sngon*), in *sha la* Valley (see Rock 1956, 90).

62. For the *Emanated Scriptures of Pure Vision* (*dag snang sprul pa'i legs bam*), see Appendix 5.

63. For the development and the completion stages (*bskyed rim* and *rdzogs rim*), see chap. 3, note 1.

64. The melancholy song called *The Many-stringed Lute* (*skyo mgur pi wang rgyud mang*) and the pith instruction *The Golden Scalpel* (*man ngag gser gyi thur ma*) are found in TS 4, on pp. 785 and 788, respectively.

65. Lo Dorje Drak (*lo rdo rje brag*), a place blessed by Lhalung Palkyi Dorje (*lha lung dpal gyi rdo rje*) and the Three Learned Men (*mkhas pa mi gsum;* see chap. 2, note 5). See AC, vol. 2, p. 198.

66. Shanglang (*shang lang*), a single cymbal with a piece of horn inside, played as one would a bell. Mostly used by Bönpos, it is also used by Buddhists in some special ceremonies, such as the ritual offering to the protector King Pehar.

67. Kusho Changkya, the immediate reembodiment of the erudite Changkya II, Rolpa Dorje (*lcang skya rol pa rdo rje* a.k.a. *ye shes bstan pa'i sgron me,* 1717–86), who was brought to Peking at the age of six and later became a teacher of the emperor of China.

68. *The Treasury of the Sublime Vehicle* (*theg mchog mdzod*), the longest of the *Seven Treasuries* of Gyalwa Longchen Rabjam (see Translator's Introduction, note 15). A masterly exposition of the nine vehicles of the Nyingma tradition.

69. *The Wheel of Sharp Weapons* (*blo sbyong tshon cha'i 'khor lo;* see DZ, vol. 4) is a teaching on mind training composed by Dharmarakshita. It was brought to Tibet by his disciple Atisha, who translated it from Sanskrit into Tibetan with his own disciple Drom Tönpa Gyalwe Jungne (*'brom ston pa rgyal ba'i 'byung gnas,* 1004–64). An English translation has been published by the Library of Tibetan Works and Archives, Dharamsala, 1976.

70. An offering of one thousand of each of the seven traditional offerings: water, flowers, incense, lamps, perfume, food, and music.

71. According to Tibetan medicine, the qualities of the water in various places greatly affect people's health, and encountering a different kind of water when moving to a new place is a major cause of falling ill.

72. Meaning that the worldly values of honesty, altruism, a good temper, etc., go hand in hand with spiritual values.

73. *Mani* wheels: huge cylinders, often containing more than one hundred million printed mantras, which are painted with saffron water and rolled vertically around the axis of the wheel. These wheels are built in villages or monasteries so that monks and laypeople may always turn them by pushing, or by pulling an attached strap. Some are also set in streams and rivers and turn day and night through a device using the strength of the current.

74. "Fifteen" has been corrected to "nineteen"; see RO, p. 642. Once the great *ngakpa* (mantra practitioner) Namkha Jigme (*nam mkha' 'jigs med;* see Translator's Introduction, note 20) offered a *phurba* dagger to each *ngakpa* in the Rekong area, one thousand nine hundred altogether. Since then, the *ngakpa* community of Rekong became known as the "One Thousand Nine Hundred *Phurba* Holders."

75. *The Four Heart-Essences* (*snying thig ya bzhi*): the most profound cycle of Great Perfection teachings, written by Gyalwa Longchen Rabjam (*rgyal ba klong chen rab 'byams,* 1308–63). It contains the *Khandro Nyingthig* (*mkha' 'gro snying thig*) of Guru Rinpoche,

found in *terma* by Pema Ledreltsel (see chap. 3, note 16), and continued by Longchen Rabjam in the *Khandro Yangtig (mkha' 'gro yang tig)*; the *Vima Nyingthig (bi ma snying thig)* of Vimalamitra, given in vision to Chetsun Senge Wangchuk (*lce btsun seng ge dbang phyug*) and continued by Longchen Rabjam in the *Lama Yangtig (bla ma yang tig)*; and the quintessence of all these expressed by Longchen Rabjam in the *Zabmo Yangtig (zab mo yang tig)*.

76. The mind training called *The Rays of the Sun (blo sbyong nyi ma 'od zer)*, written by Namkha Pel (*nam mkha' dpal*, 1170-1226).

77. The *Three Cycles of Oral Transmission (snyan brgyud skor gsum)* are the three main lineages of the Oral or Whispered Transmission of the Chakrasamvara teachings of the Kagyu tradition. The three are: 1) the *Oral Transmission of Gampopa, Dagpo Nyengyu (dwags po snyan brgyud)*, the most extensive form; 2) the *Oral Transmission of Rechungpa, Rechung Nyengyu (ras chung snyan brgyud)*, the middle form; and 3) the *Oral Transmission of Ngamdzong, Ngamdzong Nyengyu (ngam rdzong snyan brgyud)*, the condensed form. See DZ, vols. 7 to 10.

78. For the *Nine Cycles of the Formless Dakini*, see chap. 11, note 45.

79. *log dom* should be corrected to *lag dom*.

80. *bka' bsgo*, an injunction or command given by the teacher to all the negative forces not to harm the person who has requested this protection.

81. *lo* is for *lo tog*, which means crops, harvests, but in a more general way refers to the yearly resources from growing crops as well as from raising cattle or any other occupation.

82. Transformations (*sprul bsgyur*); see chap. 6, note 28.

Conclusion

Conclusion of the Life-Story in Prose

[480a] By the power of merit accumulated in the past, in this life, I obtained a sound human body endowed with all the freedoms and favorable conditions. From childhood until now, touching my head to the dust of their feet, I have attended hundreds of spiritual teachers. From them I received time and again many vast and profound instructions uniting sutra and tantra.

I have done spiritual practice in hundreds of mountain retreats, from the White Snows of Kailash in Upper Tibet, to The Heart of the Lake, Tsonying Mahadeva, in Lower Dokham. I have also been to hundreds of villages and monasteries, benefiting as much as possible the teachings and all beings.

From the ages of twenty-one to forty I kept unbroken the precept of not eating after noon. I did the fasting practice more than three hundred times. I recited one million times the hundred-syllable mantra[1] and the *mani* ten million times, as well as many other mantras and prayers. From the ages of twenty to thirty I mainly practiced to perfect myself, and from the ages of thirty to fifty I worked mainly for the good of others.

I spent altogether nine years in the Three Provinces of Ngari[2] in western Tibet, in the Four Districts of U-Tsang[3] in central Tibet, and in the Three Heights of Dokham[4] in eastern Tibet, tirelessly working for beings.

I always kept purely the three vows [480b]. Giving up meat, garlic, onions, and tobacco, I lived on the three whites[5] and the three sweets, and on tea, butter, and *tsampa*. Wherever I went in Upper, Middle, and Lower Tibet, I told everyone there, men and women:

"There is no certainty as to when we will die. It may well happen tonight, tomorrow, or the day after. You must consider carefully the law of karma, cause and effect. If, as someone who has committed many negative deeds, you haven't taken this law into account and die suddenly, you will be reborn in the hell realm, while those who have practiced virtue will be reborn in the higher realms; therefore you must beware of negative actions and exert yourself in virtuous ones.

"Above all, you must constantly train your mind to be loving, compassionate, and filled with Bodhicitta. You must give up eating meat, for it is very wrong to eat the flesh of our parent sentient beings. If you are unable to give up eating meat, only take meat under the three permissive conditions,[6] and by no means should you accept meat of an animal that has been killed for you.

"Keeping pure vows and *samayas*, you should study, reflect and meditate in a proper way upon the vast and profound teachings of both sutra and tantra.

After earnestly teaching in Upper, Middle, and Lower Tibet, I had over one hundred great learned and accomplished disciples, who were mindful of the law of cause and effect, maintained pure discipline, and had good hearts; who realized the natural state; who had thoroughly assimilated the practices of the development and completion stages and had visions of their *yidam*; and who were aware of the happiness and the suffering, the good and bad qualities of others, and were thus able to benefit both the Dharma and all beings.

I had over three hundred disciples who were practitioners who trained in the Bodhicitta practice of cherishing others more than themselves, were filled with compassion, and never ate meat [481a].

I had one thousand eight hundred disciples—monks, nuns, and hermits—who, coming from all directions and all lands, lived in the mountains, kept pure vows and *samayas*, and gave up all concern for the affairs of this life.

Finally, I had countless disciples who were monks and nuns dwelling in monasteries, disciples who worked hard at making offerings, prostrations, circumambulations, prayers and recitations; village *ngakpas* who practiced recitation and meditation upon the *yidam* deities; and laymen and laywomen who took temporary vows and vows of fasting, and recited the *mani*.

I was fortunate enough to be able to ransom the lives and set free tens and hundreds of thousands of goats, sheep, yaks, birds, and other wild animals, and to save over five hundred people who were on the verge of death—beggars, pilgrims, people coming from afar, people who had long been sick, condemned prisoners, and people who had been trying to kill each other in feuds.

Having returned to Domey, using spiritual and worldly skillful means, along with wealth, I settled eighteen great feuds, in which many people had been killed, thus putting a halt to the line of those waiting to enter the hells.

In brief, directly and indirectly I was able to bring vast benefit to the Dharma and sentient beings.

Wherever I worked for others, I would mentally call for the descent of auspiciousness on all the places I saw; call for a rain of blessings over all the mountain retreats I saw; consecrate all the sacred objects I saw; give empowerment to all the people I saw, and pray for all those who had died [481b].

I felt loving-kindness when seeing someone bereft of happiness, compassion when seeing someone suffering, joy when seeing someone happy and free of suffering, and evenness when seeing someone free of attachment and hatred. While traveling I would continually repeat:

> May all beings have happiness and the
>   causes of happiness;
> May all beings be free from suffering and
>   the causes of suffering,
> May all beings never be parted from the
>   happiness free from suffering,
> May all beings remain in the evenness free
>   from attachment and aversion.

To conclude every action done in accordance with the Dharma, I would say prayers dedicating all merit, so that the precious teachings of the Buddha—the source of all temporal benefit and ultimate happiness—would spread vastly, and that in this way the sun of happiness and fulfillment would shine on sentient beings. I prayed that, by the power of my dedication, in all lands and particularly in the places I was visiting, the rain would be timely, crops good, and cattle prosperous, that diseases of men and beasts cease, that life span and merit would increase, that everyone might enjoy happiness and comfort in this life and the next, and that, ultimately, meeting in a Buddhafield we would all have the good fortune to attain Buddhahood together.

CONCLUSION OF THE LIFE-STORY IN VERSE

Peerless victorious Shakyamuni,
Inseparable from the King of Dharma,
  Lord Chökyi Wangpo [482a],
Remain always as the ornament of the
  chakra at the crown of my head,
And let fall an inexhaustible rain of
  blessings and *siddhis*.

Grant your blessing so that all those
Who see, hear, remember, or touch

The outer, inner, and secret accounts of
my life-story and my songs
May find happiness now and swiftly attain
the level of Buddhahood.

Composed by an ignorant uneducated
man, my life-story
Is not likely to please the learned,
Yet for the sake of the faithful
I shall summarize it once more in a song.

Listen with joy, fortunate ones gifted with
good karma
Who wish to emulate the lives of perfect
liberation
Of the past Buddhas and Bodhisattvas,
And of all the learned and realized beings
Down to your own present root guru.

In my past lives, having laid a foundation
with discipline,
Helped by generosity and the other *paramitas*,
And having made connections through
stainless aspiration prayers,
I obtained this precious human body so
hard to find.

A predisposition toward the Dharma
having awakened in me at an early age,
I had great faith in the guru and the Three
Jewels.

Growing up, with correct motivation and
conduct,
I attended many spiritual teachers
Who were able to benefit whoever made a
connection with them,
And received the transmission of many
teachings on sutra and tantra,
Together with pith instructions and advice.

I kept all the *pratimoksha* vows, the
Bodhisattva vows, and those of the
Mantrayana;
I gave up meat, *chang*, garlic, onion, and
tobacco,
And sustained myself on the three whites,
the three sweets, and tea, butter, and
tsampa [482b].

From up in the White Snows of Kailash in
central Tibet,
Down to Mahadeva, The Heart of the Lake,
I raised the victory banner of the traditions
of teaching and practice
In many supreme mountain retreats and
other secluded places.

I went to many places in the Upper,
Middle and Lower provinces,
Expounding the vast and profound
Dharma
To fortunate disciples endowed with good
karma,
Establishing them on the path to the
higher realms and ultimate excellence.

I had a hundred and eight great spiritual
sons, wise and accomplished,
Who, having perfected themselves, were
able to benefit others;
Over three hundred practitioners who,
having attained
Consummate loving-kindness, compassion
and Bodhicitta, ceased eating meat;
One thousand eight hundred great
meditators, men and women,
Who gave up all concern for this life and
practiced in solitudes;
Tens of thousands of monks and nuns
dwelling in monasteries
Who worked hard at prostrations,
offerings, circumambulations, and
other virtuous actions;
And countless *ngakpas*, village practitioners
and householders
Who fasted, did recitations, practiced
sadhanas, and chanted the *mani*.

I ransomed the lives of several hundred
thousand animals,
Goats, sheep, birds, fish, and other wild
animals.
I protected and saved the lives of five
hundred people
Afflicted by hunger, cold, sickness, evil
influences and enemies.
I settled eighteen major feuds in which
men and horses were being killed,

Thus halting the line of those who were
    going to hell.

In brief, by the compassion of my gurus
    and the Three Jewels
Great benefit was brought to the Dharma
    and all beings.
To conclude every action I did in
    accordance with Dharma,
I made vast dedications and prayers [483a].

I established auspicious links with
    whomever I encountered,
For their present happiness and so that
Ultimately we might attain Buddhahood
    together.
Now, although I have reached a ripe old
    age,
I work unstintingly for the benefit of both
    others and myself.

That, in brief, is the story of my life
From birth until this fifty-sixth year of mine.
You disciples to come in future generations
Follow the example of the life of your
    teacher and,
As true heirs of the victorious Shakyamuni,
May you benefit the Dharma and all living
    beings.

As true heirs, sons and daughters of the
    master Padmakara,
May you be rich in the Dharma of the
    Canonical Transmission,
Revealed Treasures and Pure Visions.[7]

As true heirs, sons and daughters of the
    peerless Jowo Je,[8]
May all the holy scriptures arise as spiritual
    instructions.

As true heirs, sons and daughters of the
    victorious Lobzang Trakpa,
May you be embellished by the jewel
    ornament of the Three Trainings.

As true heirs, sons and daughters of Sakya
    Pandita,

May you be matchless in expounding the
    scriptural tradition.

As true heirs, sons and daughters of Jetsun
    Milarepa,
May you have great perseverance in the
    hardships of spiritual practice.

As true heirs, sons and daughters of the
    sole father, Padampa of India,
May you transform all adverse circum-
    stances into the spiritual path.

As true heirs, sons and daughters of the
    sole mother, Machik Lapkyi Drönma,
May you sever the root of ego-clinging and
    the obscuring emotions.

May all beings who see, hear, remember,
    or touch me,
Attain temporal happiness and ultimate
    Buddhahood.
For all who read my life-story and songs
    [483b]
May the doors of the three lower realms be
    shut.
May all who hear my life-story and songs
Obtain in their next life a human or
    celestial birth.
May all who remember or simply touch
    my life-story and songs
Be reborn in the same realm where I will
    have been reborn.

May all those who, when asked, recite my
    life-story and songs
Be filled with blessings and achieve
    liberation.
May the aspirations of those who act
    according to my life-story and songs
Be accomplished in harmony with the
    Dharma.
Wherever my life-story and songs are
    found, in monasteries and villages,
May they fulfill all needs and aspirations
    like a wish-fulfilling jewel.
Wherever my life-story and songs are
    carried,

May the Dharma, general auspiciousness,
and excellent virtue blossom.

With these verses of aspiration, I thus added a final ornament.[9]

Having thus completed the detailed account of my life, in prose and in verse, one day I gave the transmission for it, reading it to many disciples and patrons. All the fortunate beings, gods and men, who were gathered there were filled with faith, respectful fervor, pure perception, and an intense feeling of renunciation. Many of them were moved to such an extent that all the hairs on their body stood on end and tears streamed from their eyes.

On that occasion the Hermit of Nyang said, "Precious refuge and protector, how kind you have been to tell us your life-story in such detail! [484a]. The more one thinks of it, the more it seems impossible to accomplish in one lifetime benefit for oneself and others as you have done, effortlessly. However, we, your followers, shall try to emulate at least part of your perfect life; therefore, always keep us under your spiritual protection."

All the other people present there, rejoicing greatly, and singing songs of praise, circumambulated me and offered prostrations.

COLOPHON

Thus the detailed life-story of the Great Vajradhara Shabkar, White Foot, the refuge and protector of all sentient beings in this decadent time—a life-story known as *The King of Wish-Granting Jewels which Fulfills the Hopes of Fortunate Disciples Who Seek Liberation* has been told, at the request of all his fortunate disciples and faithful patrons, men and women, by the yogin Tsogdruk Rangdrol, who wanders without preference throughout many lands, and roams through many mountain solitudes without having any particular destination in mind. It was composed at Tashikhyil, a secluded place where the mind is happy and awareness is clear, located on a high mountain on the border between villages and nomad pastures, above vast forests of medicinal trees, below highland meadows bedecked with flowers. It was written down by my spiritual son Sangye Rinchen, someone gifted with faith, diligence, intelligence and compassion. May it bring limitless benefit to the Dharma and to all sentient beings. May all be auspicious!

TRANSLATORS' COLOPHON

Thus ends the first part of the spiritual biography of Lama Shabkar, "White Foot," protector of beings. The story of the remainder of his life until he died in 1851 at the age of seventy comprises another volume.

The first draft of the translation of this wondrous life-story was completed in the divine valley of Gangten in Bhutan, wreathed in the golden sunrays of His Holiness Dilgo Khyentse Rinpoche's compassionate wisdom, in the summer of 1987 by the wretched French vagabond Konchog Tendzin Kunkhyab Rangdrol and his Dharma brothers and sisters.

The final draft was finished at Orgyen Kunzang Chöling, Darjeeling, the seat of the Lord of the Mandalas, Kyabje Kangyur Rinpoche, on the eighth day of the eighth Tibetan month, 8 October 1989.

The final English version was completed with Lodrö Garma on the auspicious twenty-fifth day of Saga Dawa in the Iron Sheep Year, 7 June 1991, under the cool shadow of the snow-white Jarung Khashor Stupa, Bodhnath, reading by the brilliant light-rays reflected by the Great Stupa's thirteen-wheel pinnacle, which Lord

Shabkar himself had caused to be covered with the mantle of gold that still shines to this day.

May all merit gathered throughout the three times by all beings, symbolized by the merit of this present act, be dedicated to the present happiness and ultimate enlightenment of all sentient beings, the long life of the spiritual masters, and the blossoming of the teachings!

Sarva Mangalam

Notes

1. *yig brgya*, the hundred syllable mantra of Vajrasattva.

2. The Threefold Division of Ngari in Tö *(stod mnga' ris skor gsum)*:

According to CN, p. 23, they are: 1) the Dharma Land of Mang Yul *(mang yul chos kyi skor)*; 2) the Auspicious Bönpo Land of Guge *(gu ge g.yung drung bon gi skor)*; and 3) the Snow Land of Purang *(pu rang / spu hreng gangs kyi skor*, sometimes spelled *spu rangs* and *pu hrang)*.

Alternately, these three have been defined as 1) Guge Ya'i Kor *(gu ge g.ya' yi skor)*, the Slate Land of Guge; 2) Purang Khang gi Kor *(spu hreng gangs kyi skor)*, the Snow Land of Purang; 3) Ruthop Chap gi Kor *(ru thob chab kyi skor)*, the Water Land of Ruthop.

According to AC, vol. 1, p. 3, the three divisions are:

1) Purang, Mang Yul, and Zanskar *(spu hreng, mang yul, zangs dkar)*, making the first division; 2) Li, Gilgit, and Balti *(li, bru sha, sbal ti)*, making the second division; and 3) Shang Shung, Triteh and Lower Tö *(zhang zhung, khri te / bri ste, stod smad)*, making the third division.

Tö *(stod)* and Latö *(la stod)* are sometimes confused. Tö refers traditionally to the western part of Tibet at large, as opposed to U-Tsang *(dbu gtsang)* and Domey *(mdo smad)*, and is the same as Ngari. Latö is the western part of Tsang and includes the districts of Nyanang *(gnya' nang)*, Tingri *(ding ri)*, Pungrong *(spung*

rong), and Shelkar *(shel dkar)*. People from Latö call themselves Töpas *(stod pa)*, "the people of Tö," which adds to the confusion, but they are not considered as such by inhabitants of Ngari. One also distinguishes North Latö *(byang la stod)* and South Latö *(lho la stod;* see TC, p. 2745), which were two of the thirteen divisions of Tibet *(bod khri skor gcu sum)*.

3. The Four Districts of U-Tsang *(bar dbus gtsang ru bzhi)*: According to AC, vol. 1, p. 4. and CN, p. 97, initially, during the reign of Songtsen Gampo the Four Regions in U and Tsang were described as follows:

In U *(dbus)*: 1) Uru *(dbu ru)* all the regions on the left banks of the Kyichu River, and of the Tsangpo River, after Chaksam, where the Kyichu and Tsangpo meet; 2) Yoru *(g.yo ru)*, the regions on the right banks of these two rivers.

In Tsang *(gtsang)*: 3) Yeru *(g.yas ru)*, the Right Region (on the right bank of the Tsangpo which flows from Mt. Kailash) and 4) Ru lag *(ru lag)* on the left bank of the Tsangpo.

More recently, they have been described as in U: 1) Puru *(spus ru)* and 2) Gungru *(gung ru)*; in Tsang: 3) Yeru *(g.yas ru)* and 4) Yönru *(g.yon ru)*.

4. For the Three Ranges of Dokham, see chap.14, note 22.

5. "The three whites" are milk, curd, and butter; "the three sweets" are sugar, honey and molasses.

6. For the "three permissive conditions," see Appendix 5, note 7, and Shabkar's *Emanated Scriptures of Compassion (snying rje sprul pa'i glegs bam)*.

7. The long Canonical Transmission *(ring brgyud bka' ma)*, the direct lineage of the Revealed Treasures *(nye brgyud gter ma)*, and the profound Pure Visions *(zab mo dag snang)*: see Appendix 1.

8. Jowo Je *(jo bo rje)* is Lord Atisha; see Translator's Introduction, note 12.

9. There are two conclusions in the autobiography. The first one concludes the set of summaries in verse, which appear one at the end of each chapter; these summaries have not been translated in this edition. The second is the conclusion of the life-story in prose. Ordinarily only one, the second, would be needed in this translation, but because both conclusions have their own particular content and flavor, and therefore their own interest, we have translated them both.

Appendix 1

Introduction to the teachings dealt with in the biography

In the course of telling the story of his life, Shabkar teaches us, through his songs and through his own example, the entire path of Buddhist practice. He highlights the significance and value of human life, the meaning of impermanence and the imminence of death, the ineluctable laws of karma, the unsatisfactory condition of samsara, and the necessity of developing a determination to renounce worldly affairs and accomplish spiritual goals.

He explains the benefits of relying upon an authentic master, the need to cultivate compassion, devotion, and pure vision, and, finally, the unsurpassable view of the infinite purity of all phenomena, which allows the actualization of one's innate Buddha-nature. Not only does Shabkar explain all this, but he does so in a way which makes one feel that with the right amount of personal effort and confidence in the teachings, one could follow in his "white footsteps."

These teachings, however, do not appear in the autobiography in the same order as they would in a traditional graded exposition of the path. For the sake of clarity, we will therefore present an overview of their general structure.

Some elements of Buddhist philosophy and practice purportedly reached remote Tibet as early as the fifth century (see Translator's Introduction). However, the major advent of Buddhism occurred in the eighth century, when King Trisong Detsen (b. 730 or 742) invited the Indian abbot Shantarakshita to Tibet, and, soon afterwards, the incomparable tantric master Padmasam-

bhava. Under the latter's guidance, over a hundred great Indian *panditas* and an equivalent number of Tibetan translators translated into Tibetan most of the Buddhist Canon.

This period is known as the Early Translation, Ngagyur (*snga 'gyur*). The upholders of the vast and rich spiritual tradition which flourished in its wake are known as the Ancient Ones, or Nyingma (*rnying ma*). Although the monastic tradition was nearly eradicated during the persecution waged by King Langdarma, the Nyingma tradition survived through lineages of highly realized lay yogins (see NS, p. 523).

In the late tenth century, a second wave of translation occurred, spearheaded by the great translator Rinchen Zangpo (957–1055). The various lineages that sprang from it belong to the New Translation period (*gsar ma*). These include the traditions of the Kadam (and its later development, the Geluk), Sakya, Kagyu, Shangpa Kagyu, Chöd and Shije, Kalachakra, and Orgyen Nyendrub.[1] These traditions, old and new, are often called the Eight Chariots of Spiritual Accomplishment (*sgrub brgyud shing rta brgyad*). The main instructions of these eight schools were collected by Jamgon Kongtrul Lodrö Thaye (1813–99) in the *Treasury of Spiritual Instructions* (DZ).

Firmly grounded in the Mind Training (*blo sbyong*) of the Kadam-Geluk tradition with its emphasis on renunciation and compassion, Shabkar's main practices were those of the Nyingma lineage, particularly the *terma* tradition of revealed spiritual treasures stemming from Padmasambhava.

Guru Padmasambhava's lineage maintains a complete tradition of both sutra and mantra, arranged into nine vehicles that incorporate all aspects of Buddhist theory and practice. Although all teachings and paths have but one goal, there are as many paths and vehicles to reach Buddhahood as there are different natures and capacities in sentient beings. This is why the Buddha and all the accomplished masters following him taught a variety of methods to suit varying needs. The *Lankavatara Sutra* says:[2]

> As long as there are deluded minds,
> There will be no limit to the number of vehicles.
> Once delusion comes to an end,
> There will be neither vehicles nor sentient beings.

The Nyingma tradition distinguishes nine main vehicles for realization, or *yanas*. They do not represent separate, altogether different, approaches: each of them is a step toward the next, which naturally includes the preceding ones. Just as all rivers merge into one ocean, as all paths lead to a single summit, so all vehicles ultimately fuse into one as they culminate in Buddhahood, the Radiant Vajra Essence (*'od gsal rdo rje snying po*) of the Great Perfection (*rdzogs chen*).

The following summary of the view, meditation, action, and result of these nine vehicles is based on Shechen Gyaltsap Pema Namgyal's *Concise Meaning of the Nine Vehicles,*[3] and on Khenpo Yonten Gyatso's commentary on Jigme Lingpa's *Treasury of Spiritual Qualities.*[4]

A *yana* is defined as a "vehicle or support that allows one to reach the path's final destination." It is a means of spiritual development. Before summarizing the main features of each of the nine vehicles, one must first establish the distinction between worldly or mundane vehicles, which cannot take one beyond samsara, and supramundane vehicles, which can lead one first to freedom from samsara and, ultimately, to enlightenment.

WORLDLY VEHICLES

There are two kinds of worldy or mundane vehicles, which, according to their result, are considered to be unmistaken or mistaken. The first is the "vehicle followed by human and celestial beings" (*lha mi'i theg pa*), which allows rebirth in the highest forms of existence within samsara but cannot deliver one from samsara altogether. We will consider here briefly its view, meditation, action, and fruit.

View: Here, the practitioner acknowledges the suffering of the lower realms of samsara, and recognizes the laws of karma, of cause and effect (that negative acts will inevitably bring suffering and positive acts happiness), and the existence of past and future rebirths. In this respect his understanding is considered to be correct. His aim, however, is limited to avoiding rebirth in the lower realms and gaining rebirth as a human being or as one of the three kinds of celestial beings.[5]

Meditation: Striving to reach his goal, he practices the four contemplations (*bsam gtan*) and merges with the four formless states.

Action: To achieve this he avoids the ten nonvirtuous actions (killing, stealing, and sexual misconduct; telling lies, slandering, gossiping, and saying harsh words; envy, ill will, and erroneous views) and actively practices their opposites, the ten virtuous acts, while cultivating loving-kindness, compassion, sympathetic joy, and evenness—the four boundless thoughts.

Fruit: According to the strength of his meditation and the extent of his virtuous deeds, the practitioner will take rebirth in any of the higher realms of samsara, from the human realm up to the realm of formless gods.

Among the followers of the second kind of worldly vehicles, the mistaken ones, there are some who thoroughly lack understanding and ignore the karmic laws of cause and effect, as well as some with wrong understanding, such as nihilists who assume that there are no past and future lives and are principally concerned with seeking power and pleasure in this present life. Others, the eternalists for instance, assume that there is a permanent, independent, all-powerful creator, himself without cause, who decides the fate of beings and who produces impermanent phenomena despite being permanent himself. In short, the followers of these vehicles lack the views and means effective for achieving liberation.

THE NINE VEHICLES
FOR REALIZATION

In the supramundane vehicles, one takes the support of the Three Jewels—the Buddha, the Dharma, and the Sangha—and one trains in ethical discipline, concentrated meditation, and penetrating insight, which can deliver one from the bonds of samsara.

These nine vehicles comprise the three vehicles of the sutras—those of the shravakas, the pratyekabuddhas and the Bodhisattvas—and the six vehicles of the Kriya, Upa, Yoga, Mahayoga, Anuyoga, and Atiyoga tantras. They can also be grouped into three vehicles, Hinayana, which includes the first two, Mahayana the third, and Vajrayana the last six.

THE HINAYANA

The Hinayana path is based on renunciation. Its practice is motivated by the wish to liberate oneself alone. When considered on its own, it may be called "lesser vehicle"; when integrated into the whole path of the three vehicles, it is regarded as the "fundamental vehicle."

THE SHRAVAKAS

A shravaka (*nyan thos*, literally, a "listener") is someone who fears the sufferings of samsara. Concerned with his own liberation, he listens to the teachings of the Buddha, realizes the suffering inherent in all conditioned phenomena, and meditates upon the Four Noble Truths—suffering, the cause of suffering (the obscuring emotions), the extinction of suffering, and the path to attain this extinction.

View: A shravaka understands that there is no truly existent "self" inherent in an individual, but maintains that phenomena have a real basis in indivisible particles and moments of consciousness, which are held to be truly existent. Such views define the Vaibhasika school (*bye brag smra ba*).

Meditation: On the basis of flawless ethics and self-discipline, lay or monastic, the practitioner listens to the teachings, ponders their meaning, and assimilates this meaning through meditation. Applying antidotes, such as considering the unpleasant aspects of objects of desire, he conquers the conflicting emotions (*kleshas*), and attains inner calm (*samatha*). By cultivating insight (*vipasyana*), he comes to understand that an individual possesses no truly existent, independent "self."

Action: He practices the twelve ascetic virtues[6] and acts chiefly to achieve personal liberation.

Fruit: Beginning with the stage of "stream-enterer" and continuing with the stages of "once-returner" who will be reborn only one more time, and of "non-returner" who will no longer be reborn into samsara, he liberates himself and eventually becomes an arhat, "one who has destroyed his adversary" (*dgra bcom pa*), referring to the vanquishing of the obscuring emotions.

THE PRATYEKABUDDHAS

A pratyekabuddha (*rang sangs rgyas*, "who became Buddha by himself") can attain the level of an arhat without relying upon a teacher in this lifetime (although he has met teachers in former lifetimes). He meditates on dependent origination (*rten 'brel*), the natural process through which everything arises and appears. Phenomena come into existence through the combination of causes and conditions. No phenomenon appears without a cause, none are made by an uncaused creator.

Acquainting himself with the fact of death, he becomes weary of the condition of samsara and, pondering the causes of suffering and death, he investigates the twelve links of dependent origination to find that the misery of samsara originates in ignorance.

View: He realizes that individuals and indivisible particles of matter are devoid of true existence, yet he still clings to moments of consciousness as constituting real entities. Thus he realizes fully the selflessness of the individual and partly the selflessness of phenomena. This view characterizes the Sautrantika school (*mdo sde pa*).

Meditation: He contemplates the twelve interdependent links, first in reverse order: seeing bones in a cemetery, he reflects upon death (12), and finds out that it follows old age, which itself is the outcome of birth (11). Birth is the result of the drive toward existence (10), which arises from grasping (9), which rises from craving (8), which arises from feeling (7), which arises from contact (6), which arises from the six senses (5), which arise from name and form (4), which arise from consciousness (3), which arises from karmic dispositions (2), which arise from ignorance (1). Following the chain in its direct order from ignorance to death, the pratyekabuddha understands that ignorance, the clinging to phenomena as real, is the source of all suffering in samsara.

Fruit and Action: Practicing for his own, limited deliverance, the pratyekabuddha does not teach others verbally, but inspires faith in them through the display of miracles, such as flying through the sky and transforming the upper half of his body into fire and the lower half into water, etc. Eventually he becomes an arhat. Since shravakas and pratyekabuddhas practice primarily for their own sakes, they cannot attain complete Buddhahood and benefit innumerable sentient beings, as does a Bodhisattva.

THE MAHAYANA

The Mahayana practitioner is motivated by the altruistic intention to liberate others from suffering and bring them to Buddhahood. The Mahayana, or Great Vehicle, surpasses the Hinayana in many essential aspects. A Bodhisattva recognizes the lack of true existence both of the individual and of all phenomena. Vowing to attain enlightenment for the sake of others, he develops limitless compassion for all suffering beings, yet his compassion is united with wisdom, the perfect realization of emptiness.

Having examined phenomena and recognized their empty nature, the Bodhisattva regards everything as being like a dream or an illusion. However, his understanding of absolute truth does not lead him to ignore relative truth: with loving-kindness and compassion, he keeps his actions in perfect accord with the karmic law of cause and effect and works tirelessly to benefit beings. Realizing the ultimate nature, which is free from clinging and from all limiting conditions, he rests in the great evenness, the nondual absolute truth.

View: The view involves correct understanding of the lack of reality of both the individual and all phenomena. Various levels of understanding this view, and of defining the absolute and the relative truth, are found in the Mahayana schools of Cittamatra and Madhyamaka.

The Cittamatrin (*sems tsam pa*) says that all phenomena are the products of mind, and therefore unreal, but postulates that, in terms of absolute truth, self-cognizant, nondual awareness truly exists.

The Madhyamaka (*dbu ma*) has two main schools, Svatantrika (*rang rgyud pa*) and Prasangika (*thal 'gyur pa*). The first one considers that, in terms of absolute truth, phenomena have no true existence whatsoever; but in terms of relative truth, phenomena appear through the combination of causes and conditions, perform their function, and have a verifiable conventional existence.

The second school asserts that, from both an absolute and a relative point of view, phenomena are totally devoid of existence and cannot be characterized by any concept such as "existent," "nonexistent," "both existent and nonexistent," or "neither existent nor nonexistent." For the Prasangikas, absolute truth is the nondual pristine wisdom of the Buddhas, free from conceptual elaboration.

Meditation: On the four "paths of learning" one practices the thirty-seven branches of enlightenment. Having recognized that the potential for achieving Buddhahood, the Tathagatagarbha, is present within oneself, one aspires to reach enlightenment. Through inner-calm meditation (*shamatha*) one pacifies all clinging to outer perceptions and develops a serene samadhi. Through insight meditation (*vipasyana*) one ascertains that all outer phenomena are unreal, like illusions, and that all inner clingings and dualistic notions of subject-object are void. According to the Great Middle Way, resting free of taking things as real in the evenness of the absolute nature—in which there nothing to subtract and nothing to add—one unites inner-calm meditation and insight.

Action: In post-meditation, one benefits beings, considering others as dearer than oneself. For this, one practices the six *paramitas*—generosity, morality, patience, effort, meditation, and insight—to which one adds skillful means, strength, prayer, and pristine wisdom, thus defining ten paramitas altogether. When these all become permeated with wisdom, the other *paramitas* are transformed from ordinary virtues into transcendent activities.

Fruit: Eventually, when a Bodhisattva attains the path of "no more learning" and the eleventh spiritual level, or *bhumi*, he becomes a fully enlightened Buddha. Having fulfilled his own aspirations by realizing the dharmakaya (the absolute body), for the sake of others he manifests the rupakaya (the body of form which includes the sambhogakaya and the nirmanakaya) and performs his compassionate activity for sentient beings until the end of samsara.

THE VAJRAYANA

The Vajrayana path is based on pure perception and is motivated by the aspiration to free swiftly oneself and others from delusion through skillful means. The Mahayana chiefly considers that the Buddha nature is present in every sentient being like a seed, or potentiality. The Vajrayana considers that this nature is fully present as wisdom or pristine awareness, the undeluded aspect and fundamental nature of the mind. Therefore, while the former vehicles are known as "causal vehicles," the Vajrayana is known as the "resultant vehicle." As it is said, "In the causal vehicles one recognizes the nature of mind as the cause of Buddhahood; in the resultant vehicle one

regards the nature of mind as Buddhahood itself." Since the "result" of the path, Buddhahood, is primordially present, one only needs to actualize it or divest it of its veils. The Vajrayana is also said to be unobscured, to provide many skillful means, to be without difficulty, and to be intended for beings of highest faculties.

The various levels of the Madhyamaka philosophy consider relative truth as either false, impure, and rejectable, or as simply nonexistent. Here, the Vajrayana is able to make use of relative truth as a path by seeing phenomena as the unlimited display of primordial purity. The six classes of Vajrayana tantras teach this in an increasingly direct and profound way.

The gateway to the Vajrayana is the empowerment, or *abhisheka*, which is given by the spiritual master. It empowers one to practice the Vajrayana teachings and thus to achieve ordinary and supreme spiritual attainments, or *siddhis*. The tantras and their related vehicles are categorized into three outer and three inner tantras, according to the level of their view, meditation, action, and fruit.

THE THREE OUTER TANTRAS

KRIYA. Although one has gained some understanding of absolute truth, in relative truth one still seeks accomplishment as something to be gained from outside. Kriyatantra (*bya rgyud*, the tantra of activity), emphasizes ritual cleanliness: cleanness of the mandala and the sacred substances, and physical cleanliness of the practitioner, who practices ablutions and changes clothes three times a day, and eats the three white and the three sweet foods.[7]

View: The view is based on the two truths. Absolute truth is the wisdom of mind's ultimate nature, which is pure, luminous and void. It is free of four limiting concepts: existence and nonexistence, appearance and emptiness. Relative truth can be viewed in two ways: according to the Madhyamaka, it is completely fictitious while, according to the view of the tantras, it is perfect, since phenomena are perceived as constituting the mandala of enlightened deities.

Meditation: The deity that is the object of one's meditation is considered as a lord whom the practitioner, usually visualizing himself in his ordinary form, supplicates to be granted *siddhi* in the same way as a servant or a subject would supplicate a master. Contemplating absolute truth, without any specific object of focus, is also practiced.

Action: Action focuses on cleanliness, concentration, fasting, and mantra recitation.

Fruit: Realization of the Three Kayas and Five Wisdoms of perfect Buddhahood is attained in seven human lifetimes.

UPA. It is called Upatantra (*spyod rgyud*), "practice tantra," or Ubhayatantra (*gnyis ka'i rgyud*), "dual-tantra," because it practices the view of the next vehicle, Yogatantra, along with the action, or conduct, of the former, Kriyatantra. The *abhisheka* consists of the empowerment of the Five Buddha Families. Realization can be gained in five lifetimes.

YOGA. This *yana* is the Yogatantra (*rnal 'byor rgyud*)y or "tantra of union with the nature." It is thus called because it emphasizes inner practice more than outer conduct. The *abhisheka* adds to that of Upa the blessing of the vajra master.

View: In absolute truth one realizes the non-conceptual ultimate nature and its expression, luminosity. As result of this realization, within the "perfect" relative truth, phenomena appear as the "mandala of adamantine space" (*vajradhatu mandala*).

Meditation: In formal meditation one visualizes oneself as a deity and invites from the Buddhafield a wisdom deity similar to oneself, which usually remains in the space before one. The relationship between the deity and the practitioner is that of equals or friends. In objectless meditation, one merges one's perception of phenomena with the absolute nature beyond characteristics and one rests in evenness: phenomena are thus seen as the play of wisdom manifesting as deities.

Action: One still strives toward accomplishment through achieving the "good" and eschewing the "bad"; one gives chief importance to the yoga of the deity and one strives to benefit others.

Fruit: Realization is attained in three lifetimes.

THE THREE INNER TANTRAS

The view is to see all phenomena as being primordially perfect; one thus realizes the "great purity" and the "great evenness." Deities are visualized in union, symbolizing the indivisibility of emptiness and compassion, wisdom and means. The wisdom nature of the deity is considered to be inseparable from one's own nature. Action transcends accepting and rejecting. The fruit is Buddhahood in one lifetime.

There are three inner tantras: Mahayoga is like the ground, or basis; all phenomena are recognized as the magical display of mind-as-such, the union of emptiness and appearances. Anuyoga is like the path; it allows one to realize that phenomena are the nondual manifestation of space and primordial wisdom. Atiyoga is like the fruit and allows one to realize the natural presence of primordial wisdom, beyond beginning and ending.

MAHA. Mahayoga is called the "great yoga" (*rnal 'byor chen po*) because it brings realization of non-duality. Its gateway consists of four main empowerments: the vase, the secret, the wisdom, and the symbolic (or word) empowerment. These purify the defilements of the body, speech and mind, as well as their subtle obscurations, and enable one to realize the Four Kayas.

View: Awareness, free from all conceptual limitations, is here considered as absolute truth and is inherently endowed with all enlightened qualities. All phenomena—the outer universe, the various psychophysical elements of the body, as well as thoughts—arise as a mandala which stands for relative truth. The two truths, emptiness and phenomena, are inseparable, like gold and its color.

Meditation: Mahayoga emphasizes the development stage (*bskyed rim*), which focuses on the process of visualization. One sees oneself as a deity—the manifestation of one's own wisdom nature. The outer world is seen as a Buddhafield and the beings therein as male and female deities.

These methods help one to recognize the primordial, unchanging purity of phenomena, which is the true condition of things. One also practices the completion stage (*rdzogs rim*) related to the channels (*nadi*), energy (*prana*) and essence (*bindu*). Formless meditation is merging one's mind with the profound, absolute nature.

Action: In the path of action, through the confidence born from skillful means, such as devotion and pure perception, without rejection or attachment one uses samsaric experiences as catalysts to foster one's practice.

Fruit: Realization is attained within this lifetime, or in the ensuing *bardo*, the transitional state between death and rebirth.

ANU. Anuyoga emphasizes the completion stage (*rdzogs rim*) and the mandala as being contained within one's own vajra-body. Having realized the non-duality of the expanse of emptiness and of pristine wisdom, through "union" and "liberation" (*sbyor grol*), one attains accomplishment. Anuyoga is called the "ensuing yoga" (*rjes su mal 'byor*) because it focuses on the path of wisdom-desire which follows the experience of bliss. Its gateway, the empowerment, comprises thirty-six sections.

View: All phenomena are understood as the play of one's own mind. The uncreated aspect of mind, transcending all conditions, is the called the "immaculate expanse of the mother Samantabhadri," the mandala of the primordial nature. Its all-pervading and unobstructed manifestation, which is mind's self-display, is the "wisdom father Samantabhadra," the naturally present mandala. These two aspects have the same nature: this is called the "child of great bliss," in which the absolute expanse and of pristine wisdom are united, representing the indivisible nature of all mandalas.

Meditation: One practices the path of skillful means (*thabs lam*), which focuses on the channels, energies, and vital essences of one's vajra-body. Practicing the yogas of the "upper door" and the "lower door," one swiftly realizes one's inherent wisdom. One also practices the Path of Liberation (*grol lam*) without elaboration. Having merged with the depth of nonconceptual simplicity, without intentional meditation, one lets everything remain in the absolute nature, just as it is. In formal, elaborate practice, through uttering a mantra once, the mandala with its deities arises with perfect clarity, instantly, like a fish leaping out of water.

Action: This primarily involves resting in evenness. One also speaks of three actions: the "sky-like action," which comes through realizing the nonduality of the absolute expanse of emptiness (*dbyings*) and pristine wisdom (*ye shes*); the "king-like action," also called the "action resembling wood burning in a bonfire," which comes through mastering the five poisons as five wisdoms; and the "uninterrupted river-like action," which comes through realizing the sameness of samsara and nirvana.

Fruit: Within one lifetime, one actualizes the Body of Great Bliss, which embodies the Four Kayas.

ATI. The extraordinary feature of Atiyoga is that one maintains lucid recognition of the ultimate nature of mind: pure, vividly clear, perfect in itself. It is luminosity which is naturally present, self-existing primordial wisdom, without any alteration or fabrication, beyond taking or rejecting, hope and fear. This is the "ultimate yoga" (*shin tu mal 'byor*), far surpassing all the lower vehicles (all of which entail striving, fabrication, and effort). Atiyoga is also known as Dzogchen, the Great Perfection, meaning that *all* phenomena are naturally perfect in their primordial purity.

Its gateway is the empowerment of the "efflorescence of awareness."[8] According to the *Secret Heart Essence* (*gsang ba snying thig*), one receives four empowerments: elaborate, unelaborate, very unelaborate, and utterly unelaborate.

View: All phenomena, within both samsara and nirvana, are perfect in primordial Buddhahood, the great sphere of dharmakaya, the self-existing pristine wisdom beyond search and effort.

Atiyoga has three classes:

According to the mind class (*sems sde*), all perceived phenomena are none other than the play of mind-as-such (*sems nyid*), the inexpressible, self-existing wisdom.

According to the space class (*klong sde*), the self-existing wisdom and all the phenomena sprung from its continuum never stray from the expanse of Samantabhadri: they have always been pure and liberated.

According to the most extraordinary of the three, the class of pith instructions (*man ngag sde*), in the true nature of samsara and nirvana there are no obscurations to be rid of and no enlightenment to be acquired. To realize this allows an instant arising of the self-existing wisdom beyond intellect.

The first class is meant for individuals who are concerned with the workings of mind, the second for individuals whose minds are like the sky, and the third for individuals who transcend all effort.

Meditation: In the mind class, having recognized that all phenomena are the indescribable dharmakaya, the self-existing wisdom, one rests in the continuum of the awareness-void in which there is nothing to illuminate, nothing to reject, and nothing to add. The enlightened mind is like infinite space, its potential for manifestation is like a mirror, and the limitless illusory phenomena are like multifarious reflections in the mirror. Since everything arises as the play of the enlightened mind, one does not need to obstruct the arising of thoughts; one simply remains in the natural condition of mind-as-such.

In the space class, having recognized that all phenomena never leave the expanse of Samantabhadri and are primordially pure and free, one abides in the continuum of the ultimate nature (*chos nyid*), without targets, effort, or search. There is no need to use antidotes: being void, thoughts and perceptions vanish by themselves. Phenomena are like stars naturally arrayed as ornaments in the firmament of the absolute nature: one needs not consider, as one does in the mind class, that they arise as the play of awareness. Everything is the infinite expanse of primordial liberation.

In the class of pith instructions, having recognized that mind-as-such is primordially pure emptiness, one practices Trekchö, leaving mind and all phenomena in their natural state of pris-

tine liberation. Then, having discovered the naturally present mandala of one's body, one practices Thögal and sees the very face of the naturally present luminosity, the pristine wisdom which dwells within oneself.

Without leaning either toward the "clarity" aspect of the mind class or toward the "void" aspect of the space class, without considering either the self-liberation of thoughts (as in the mind class), or the way of letting them be in emptiness (as in the space class), one simply rests in the confident realization of primordial purity, which is inexpressible, beyond intellect, and of which phenomena are the natural radiance.

Trekchö, "cutting through hardness [or concreteness]," refers to breaking through the solidity of mental clinging, and Thögal, "direct leap," refers to going directly to the highest point of realization. These two are related respectively to primordial purity (*ka dag*) and to spontaneous presence (*lhun grub*). These extraordinary practices are found only in the teachings of the Great Perfection. It is said that the first eight vehicles use mind (*sems*) as the path, and that only the ninth uses awareness (*rig pa*) as the path.

Action: Since everything that arises is the play of the absolute nature, one acts within the continuum of nondual evenness, without taking and rejecting, free from clinging and fixation.

Fruit: One dwells right now on the level of the Ever-perfect, Samantabhadra. Having mastered outer phenomena, they are realized as infinite Buddhafields; having mastered the inner aggregates of one's illusory body, this body can turn into radiant light; having mastered the innermost expanse of awareness, one puts an end to delusion. One has neither hope of attaining Buddhahood, nor fear of falling into samsara. As it is said:

> The fruit of the Great Perfection
> Is primordially present as the Buddha
>   nature.
> It does not need to be obtained:
> It is ripe within oneself.

As said above, the nine vehicles do not represent separate paths. Each of them is a step toward the next; all vehicles ultimately culminate in the Great Perfection.

THE THREE VOWS

The practice of these nine vehicles involves vows, precepts, and commitments. There are many divisions to these, but, in essence, they fall under three sets of vows (*sdom gsum*).

The *pratimoksha vows* of the Hinayana concern all the lay and monastic precepts of ethical conduct taught by Lord Buddha in the Vinaya. Discipline and the keeping the vows protect the mind from conditions that generate negativity and emotional entanglements.

The *Bodhisattva vows* of the Mahayana are embodied in the generation, cultivation, and preservation of Bodhicitta,[9] the vow to dedicate all one's thoughts, words and actions toward the benefit of others and to lead all beings to complete enlightenment.

The *samayas* are the precepts and commitments of the Vajrayana, which formalize the all-important bonds with one's guru, fellow disciples, and spiritual practice. There are many levels of *samayas* according to the outer and inner tantras.

KAHMA, TERMA, AND DANANG

The Nyingma tradition has been blessed by countless enlightened masters and is very rich in spiritual lineages. Its three main streams of transmission are the long canonical lineage, *kahma* (*ring brgyud bka' ma*), the short lineage of spiritual treasures, *terma* (*nye brgyud gter ma*), and the profound pure visions, *dagnang* (*zab mo dag snang*).

The first is the "long" lineage of the canonical scriptures, which have been transmitted without interruption from master to disciple, from the primordial Buddha, Samantabhadra, through Guru Padmasambhava and other great Awareness Holders.

The second is the "short," or direct, lineage of the revealed treasures concealed by Guru Padmasambhava for the sake of future generations, and represents the quintessence of the *kahma*. When the Lotus-born Guru, Padmasambhava, bestowed the ripening empowerments and liberating instructions upon the Tibetan king Trisong Detsen, the dakini Yeshe Tsogyal and the other twenty-five main disciples, he entrusted many teachings to each of them and miraculously concealed these as spiritual treasures in various places—temples, images, sky, rocks, and lakes. Then, he prophesied that, in the future, these disciples would reincarnate, reveal these teachings from their place of concealment, and spread them for the sake of beings.

Such reincarnate lamas are called "treasure masters," or tertöns (*gter ston*). In due time, a tertön experiences visions or signs indicating how and where to discover his or her destined *terma*. In the case of "mind-treasure" (*dgongs gter*), the teachings are not physically unearthed but arise in the tertön's mind by the blessing of Guru Rinpoche. Many such masters have appeared throughout the centuries, down to the present day.

In the third stream of transmission, the pure visions, Guru Padmasambhava appears in reality to the tertön and speaks to him in person.

Although this brief introduction to the Buddhist path structured into nine vehicles reflects the approach of the Nyingma tradition, it is by no means contradictory to that of other schools of Tibetan Buddhism. In several of his writings, Shabkar quotes Panchen Lobzang Yeshe, who said:

> The various doctrinal views found in the
> provinces of U, Tsang, and Ngari
> Are all the very teachings of the Victorious
> One.
> How fine if, not allowing the demon of
> sectarianism to ignite animosity,
> The radiance of the jewel of pure
> perception would encompass all.

Notes

1. Respectively *bka' gdams* and *dge lugs, bka' brgyud, shangs pa bka' brgyud, sa skya, gcod* and *zhi byed, dus 'khor* or *sbyor drug,* and *o rgyan bsnyen sgrub.*

2. The *Lankavatara-sutra*, Tib. *lang kar gshegs pa'i mdo*, T 107.

3. *The Jewel Lute, a Concise Explanation of the Nine Vehicles* (*snga 'gyur theg dgu'i tshogs bshad mdor bsdus nor bu'i tambura*), as well as *The Jewel Ladder, a Concise Exposition of the Nine Vehicles* (*snga 'gyur theg pa rim dgu'i rnam gzhag mdor bsdus su brjod pa rin po che'i them skas*) by Shechen Gyaltsap Gyurme Pema Namgyal (*zhe chen rgyal tshab 'gyur med padma rnam rgyal*, 1871–1926). Respectively in volumes Tha and Da of his collected works.

4. The commentaries on Jigme Lingpa's Yonten Dzö (*yon tan rin po che mdzod kyi 'grel ba zla ba'i sgron me* for the sutra section, and *nyi ma'i 'od zer* for the mantra section) were written at the end of the nineteenth century by Khenpo Yonten Gyatso (*mkhan po yon tan rgya mtsho*) of Gemang Monastery in Dzachuka (*rdza*

chu kha dge mang dgon pa). The latter was a close disciple of Patrul Rinpoche (*dpal sprul*) and Onpo Tendzin Norbu (*dbon po bstan 'dzin nor bu*). In *rnying ma bka' ma*, vols. 38–40.

5. For this and subsequent enumerated categories, see the Glossary of Enumerations.

6. For the twelve ascetic virtues (*sbyangs pa'i yon tan bcu gnyis*), see NS, vol. 2, p. 169.

7. See Conclusion, note 6.

8. *rig pa'i rtsal dbang*, a most profound empowerment which introduces one to the nature of awareness beyond conditioned mind, and makes one realize that thoughts are but the display of awareness.

9. Concerning Bodhicitta, see Author's Introduction, note 6.

Appendix 2

Shabkar's spiritual teachers

In the Translator's Introduction, we have briefly presented three masters Shabkar acknowledged as his main teachers: Jampel Dorje, Jamyang Gyatso, and Chögyal Ngakyi Wangpo. However, following his nonsectarian approach, Shabkar received teachings from many other masters as well, wherever his wandering through mountain wildernesses and holy places took him.

In Urgeh, for instance, he received the transmission for the lineage of Chöd (see chap. 3, fol. 38b). In Tsari, he received many teachings according to the Kagyu tradition (see chap. 10), and in central Tibet he forged close connections with the ninth and tenth Dalai Lamas, and the seventh Panchen Lama (see chaps. 9 and 14). At Sakya, he received important empowerments from Ngakchang Kunga Gyaltsen and Gonpo Ngodrup Pelbar, sons of Wangdu Nyingpo (1765–1806), the thirty-third throne-holder of the Sakya lineage, who had been a teacher of Chögyal Ngakyi Wangpo (see chap. 6, fol. 78a). We will consider here a few other masters who were influential in Shabkar's spiritual quest.

TERTÖN SONAM NYENTRAK
At Urgeh, together with Chögyal Ngakyi Wangpo, Shabkar received many transmissions from Tertön Sonam Nyentrak, said be an emanation of Drogmi Lotsawa and the fifth descendant of Dudul Dorje (see chap. 4, fol. 44a). Little is known about this tertön, but, according to Shabkar's autobiography, in which he is frequently mentioned, he appears to have been an influential teacher in the Rekong area. (See, for instance, chap. 8, fol. 160a and chap. 9, fol. 180a). Through this master, Shabkar became connected with the lineage of Kathok, the oldest Nyingma Monastery in Kham (see NS, pp. 688ff.).

KHARDO CHÖKYI DORJE
Khardo Chökyi Dorje Rinpoche (*mkhar rdo chos kyi rdo rje*, died c. 1820) was a highly realized lama, initially of the Geluk tradition, who later became a Nyingma master and revealed some mind treasures (*dgongs gter;* see Appendix 1). He was a reincarnation of Khardo Söpa Gyatso (*mkhar rdo bzod pa rgya mtsho*, b. 1672), a main disciple of the hermit Drupkhangpa Gelek Gyatso (*sgrub khang pa dge legs rgya mtsho*, 1641–1713). Söpa Gyatso deliberately renounced the world at the early age of seven and, after some formal studies, devoted himself entirely to the contemplative life at the age of seventeen, practicing the *Great Graded Path.*[1] Later in his life, he founded the retreat center of Khardo and wrote many instructions on contemplative practice (see BD, vol. 5, pp. 361–69). His next reincarnation was Chöden Wangpo (*chos ldan dbang po*), the immediate predecessor of Chökyi Dorje.

As seen in chap. 9, fol. 198a, Shabkar received the transmission of several of this master's mind treasures and felt "just as though meeting the Dharma King Terdak Lingpa and other tertöns of the past." A few writings of Khardo Rinpoche survive to this day. As described in chap. 14, fol. 408b, when Khardo Rinpoche's reincarnation was found, Shabkar helped the late master's family during the enthronement ceremonies, which took place in 1823.

CHINGKAR DONYÖ DORJE

Chingkar Donyö Dorje,[2] "Meaningful Vajra Clad in White Felt," an important master in the lineage of the famed *Yangti Nagpo* cycle of Dungtso Repa (see chap. 4, note 17), was both a teacher and a disciple of Shabkar, a not uncommon occurrence among spiritual masters in Tibet. Like Khardo Rinpoche, Chingkar begun his studies in Gelukpa monasteries and eventually became a great yogin of the Nyingma tradition.

Shabkar met Chingkar at Ngari Dzong Kar (see chap. 12, fol. 340a) and received several teachings from him. The oral tradition, as related by Trulshik Rinpoche, has this to say about the relation between these two masters:

"Chingkar Donyö Dorje first became a Geshe of Sera Monastery. He then had a vision of Guru Rinpoche, prophesying that he would discover spiritual treasures. Following this prediction, Donyö Dorje abandoned the monastic life and became a yogin. For that reason he was despised, and for some time unable to spread the teachings.

"When Guru Rinpoche gave the *Yangti Nagpo* teachings to King Trisong Detsen, Yeshe Tsogyal and Vairocana, he had predicted that an emanation of Vairotsana would reveal them in the future. Accordingly, of the Three Roots of the *Yangti Nagpo*, Dungtso Repa (see chap. 4, note 17) found the *Yidam* (deva) section. Chingkar Donyö Dorje, a reincarnation of Dungtso Repa, found the *Lama* (guru) section and the *Khandro* (dakini) section. He revealed several *termas* connected with the *Yangti Nagpo*. Donyö Dorje's tertön name was Guyang Lodeh Dechen Do-ngak Lingpa (*gu yangs blo bde bde chen mdo sngags gling pa*), the 'Serene Relaxed One', but he was also known as the 'Crazy Tekya' *(rtas sky smyon pa).*[3]

When Shabkar came to Betse Doyön Dzong in Mangyul and taught the Dharma, Chingkar Donyö Dorje sat there, unnoticed among the crowd, along with his consort and children. At one point, Shabkar remained silent for a little while and then said, 'There is someone here

greater than I.' As people wondered who he could be referring to, Shabkar pointed to the anonymous beggar yogin and invited him to sit on the seat next to him. By recognizing him in this way, Shabkar enabled Donyö Dorje to increase his activities for the benefit of beings and to spread the *termas* he had discovered. Shabkar and Donyö Dorje became very close and exchanged teachings, thus becoming connected to each other as both master and disciple."

Chingkar Donyö Dorje's reembodiment was Trulshik Kunzang Thongdrol (*'khrul zhig kun bzang mthong grol*, see *Yangti Nagpo*, vol. 1, p. 446), whose subsequent reembodiment is the present Trulshik Rinpoche, Ngawang Chökyi Lodrö (*ngag dbang chos kyi blo gros*, b. 1924), also known as Kunzang Trinley Drodul Tsel (*kun bzang phrin las 'dro 'dul rtsal*).

In his *Collected Songs*, fol. 145/b,[4] Chingkar often speaks of Shabkar as one of his five principal teachers. It was Shabkar who gave him the empowerment of the *Khandro Nyingthig*, and thus enabled him to attain the final realization of the Great Perfection, the level of the "exhaustion of phenomena in the absolute nature" (*chos nyid zad sa*). He also says (ibid., fol. 33):

> In the Flower Cave at glorious Chimphu,
> In the presence of Kunkhyen Jigme
>   Lingpa,
> I received the Heart Essence of the Three
>   Roots, the core of the Great
>   Perfection—
> The seed of Dzogchen was sown.

> Later, in Tsang Tö at Ngangrim Dedrol,
> In the presence of the second Buddha,
>   Jetsun Kutsampa,
> The seedling of Dzogchen thrived.

> At the supreme Scintillating Glacier,
> I met the hidden Buddha called "Sky"[5]—
> There, the flower of the luminous
>   Dzogchen blossomed.

> Finally, owing to my good karmic
>   potential,

TABLE 1

SHABKAR'S MAIN TEACHERS AND DISCIPLES

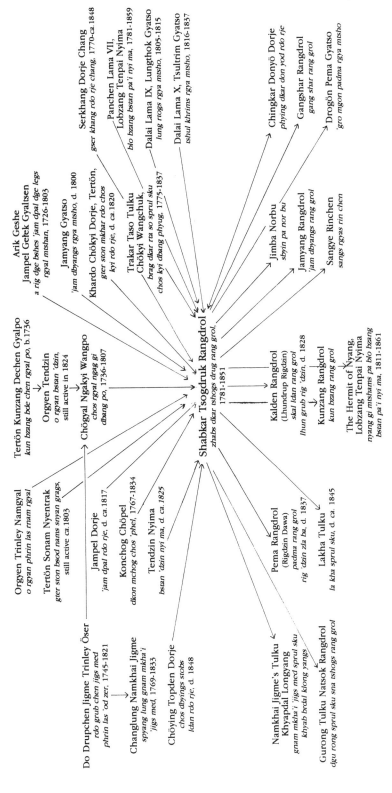

TABLE 2   KHANDRO NYINGTHIG LINEAGE

Kuntuzangpo
kun tu bzang po
↓
Dorje Sempa
rdo rje sems dpa'
↓
Garab Dorje
dga' rab rdo rje
↓
Sri Singha
↓
Guru Padmasambhava

gives the Khandro Nyingthig
in visions to Longchenpa
and names him Drime Özer,
dri med 'od zer,

Yeshe Tsogyal
ye shes mtsho rgyal, 8th-9th cent.

Lhacham Pematsel
lha lcam padma gsal
King Trisong Detsen's daughter

gives the Khandro Nyingthig
in visions to Longchenpa and
names him Dorje Dziji,
rdo rje gzi brjid

reincarnated as

Pema Ledreltsel,[1]
padma las 'brel rtsal, 1291-1315/9?,
a.k.a Pangangpa Rinchen Tsultrim Dorje
spang sgang pa rin chen tshul 'khrims rdo rje
discovers the yellow scroll in 1313 at
Danglung Tramo in Dakpo (*dvags po dangs lung khra mo*)
and entrusts it to

Dharma protectress
Shenpa Sodrupma,
shan pa srog sgrub ma,
offers the Khandro Nyingthig to

Tulku Lekden
sprul sku legs ldan, 1290-1366, a.k.a
Shoi Gyalse Lekpa, *sho'i rgyal sras legs pa*

Gyalwa Longchenpa
rgyal ba klong chen pa, 1308-1363

Naldjor Öser Gocha
rnal 'byor 'od zer go cha,
brings the Khandro
Nyingthig scriptures to
Longchenpa

Karmapa III, Rangjung Dorje
karma pa rang byung rdo rje, 1284-1339

Yungtön Dorje Pal
g.yung ston rdo rje dpal, 1284-1365
first of seven disciples who received
the transmission from Rangjung Dorje

Khedrup Khyapdal Lhundrup
mkhas grub khyab gdal lhun grub

Lama Orgyenpa
bla ma o rgyan pa

Gyalse Tulku Trakpa Özer,
Longchenpa's son and reembodiment of Tulku Lekden
rgyal sras sprul sku 'grags pa 'od zer, 1356-1409

Rinpoche Ösel Rangdrol
rin po che 'od gsal rang grol

Sangye Onpo Trulshik Sherap Gyatso
sangs rgyas 'on po 'khrul shig shes rab rgya mtsho

Gyalse Dawa Trakpa
rgyal sras zla ba 'grags pa
Trakpa Özer's son
↓
Drupchen Kunzang Dorje
grub chen kun bzang rdo rje

(CONT)

Drupchen Kunzang Dorje
grub chen kun bzang rdo rje
↓
Chöje Kunga Gyaltsen Palzang
chos rje kun dga' rgyal mtshan dpal bzang, 1497-1568
↓
Tulku Natsok Rangdrol
sprul sku sna tshogs rang grol, 1494-1570
reembodiment of Ratna Lingpa, 1403-1478
↓
Peling Tulku Tendzin Trakpa
pad gling sprul sku bstan 'dzin grags pa
↓
Nyötön Khedrup Do-ngak Tendzin
smyos ston mkhas grub mdo sngags bstan 'dzin, 1576-1628
reembodiment of Natsok Rangdrol and father of
↓
Nyötön Sangdak Trinley Lhundrup
smyos ston sang bdag 'phrin las lhun grub, 1611-1662
father of Minling Terchen
↓
Sotön Thukchog Öbar
so ston thugs mchog 'od 'bar
↓
Minling Terchen Gyurme Dorje
smin gling gter chen
'gyur med rdo rje, 1646-1714

Gyalse Zangpo Pal.[2]
rgyal sras bzang po dpal
= ? Gampo Zangpo Dorje
sgam po bzang po rdo rje, 1634-ca.1700
↓
Rigdzin Palden Tashi
rig 'dzin dpal ldan bkra shis
still active *ca.*1730
↓
Dorje Namgyal
rdo rje rnam rgyal
= ? Tsodu Ngakchang Dorje Namgyal,
'tsho 'du sngags 'chang rdo rje rrnam rgyal
(Shabkar's father) [3]
↓
Jampel Dorje
'jam dpal rdo rje, d. 1817

Gyalse Rinchen Namgyal
rgyal sras rin chen rnam rgyal, 1694-1758
↓
Drupwang Shri Natha
grub dbang srinatha
↓
Rigdzin Jigme Lingpa
rig 'dzin 'jigs med gling pa, 1729-1798
↓
Dzogchenpa Kunzang Shenpen,
first Do Drupchen
rdzogs chen pa kun bzang gzhan phan, 1745-1821
↓
Chögyal Ngakyi Wangpo
chos rgyal ngag gi dbang po, 1736-1807

Shabkar Tsogdruk Rangdrol
zhabs dkar tshogs drug rang grol, 1781-1851
↓
Chingkar Donyö Dorje
phying dkar don yod rdo rje

The Lord of Yogins, Tsogdruk Rangdrol,
Made ripen the fruit of Dzogchen, the
     secret doctrine.

Shabkar's lineage of the *Khandro Nyingthig*
(see chap. 3, note 16) is detailed in DOL 3 (fol.
109/b), and represented in table 2. It is also
quoted in one of Chingkar's Dzogchen writings,
the *Guyang Nyingthig*,[6] which spread widely in
Amdo and elsewhere. In the colophon of this text,
Chingkar also speaks of Shabkar as "the ultimate
renunciate, the monarch of the wise and accomplished masters, the Vajradhara Tsogdruk Rangdrol," and presents him as the main person who
requested the composition of the text. The spiritual transmission of Chingkar's writings and
visionary teachings is still alive today, owing
especially to the efforts of Trulshik Rinpoche.

Later in his life, having returned to Amdo,
Shabkar met two masters for whom he expressed
great admiration. One was a Nyingmapa,
Chöying Topden Dorje, and the other a Gelukpa,
Serkhang Dorje Chang.

CHÖYING TOPDEN DORJE

Chöying Topden Dorje (*chos dbyings stobs ldan rdo
rje*, 1787?–1848) was a Nyingmapa master
renowned for his tantric powers and his realization of the Great Perfection. He was a disciple
the first Do Drupchen, Jigme Trinley Öser,
Kunzang Shenpen (see Translator's Introduction, note 48), and founded the monastery of
Kohudeh Dzogchen Namgyal Ling,[7] where he
taught Jigme Lingpa's *Longchen Nyingthig* cycle.

Around 1833, Shabkar read some of Tobden
Dorje's writings, including the *Treasury of Sutra
and Tantra*,[8] and was moved by faith. He sent a
song of praise to the master, whom he calls
Kushog Dzogchen Rinpoche, the Precious Master of the Great Perfection. Shabkar went to
meet Tobden Dorje at Gartse. He was received
with great pomp and ceremony, and Tobden
Dorje compelled him to take his own seat.
Shabkar then requested from Topden Dorje a
longevity blessing and the transmission of the
Treasury of Sutras and Tantras.

When Topden Dorje died in 1848, Shabkar
performed all the funeral rituals and comforted
the master's consort and two sons. From the
colophon of the *Treasury of Sutra and Tantra* one
reckons that this master was born around 1787.
He composed thirteen volumes of writings (see
RO, p. 651). His immediate reincarnation, Dzogchen Tenpai Gyaltsen, was recognized in the
Kokonor area.

SERKHANG DORJE CHANG

The Vajradhara Serkhang (*gser khang rdo rje 'chang*)
was a remarkable Gelukpa master who spent
most of his life in mountain retreats. He exemplified the pure life-style of his Kadampa forefathers at a time when many Gelukpa monasteries
in Amdo had become large institutions sheltering monks who had often ceased to follow the
renunciate's ideals (as Shabkar notes in SH 2,
pp. 310–12).

Shabkar expressed great admiration for this
master, who returned the sentiment, declaring
Shabkar a "Lord of the Buddha's Teachings"
(GL2, fol. 302).

According to AC, vol. 2, pp. 151–54 and
RO, p. 241, Serkhang Lobzang Tendzin Gyatso
(*gser khang blo bzang bstan 'dzin rgya mtsho*) was born
in 1780 and recognized by Arik Geshe (see above)
to be the reincarnation of Rayo Jamyang Tendzin
Gyatso (*ra yo 'jam dbyangs bstan 'dzin rgya mtsho*).
After studying at Ragya Monastery, he spent
many years in retreat places such as Göpo Dzong,
Tsonying Island and Serkhang, the place which
lent him his name. He also made a pilgrimage to
Wu Tai Shan, the Five-peaked Mountain of
China. He died around 1848 (see TS 2, p. 410–
11). In his *Emanated Scriptures of Orgyen*, Shabkar
mentions a biography of this master.[9]

Notes

1. For *The Great Graded Path* (*lam rim chen mo*), see
chap. 3, note 8.

2. Chingkar Donyö Dorje (*phying dkar don yod rdo rje*) or "Meaningful Vajra Clad in White Felt." Compassionate teachers like Patrul Rinpoche and Shechen Gyaltsap Pema Namgyal, who emphasized the practice of Bodhicitta, abstained from wearing or using animal furs and skins, and preferred using white felt for their coats and carpets.

3. Crazy Tekya (*rtas skya smyon pa*): *rtas skya* is written in a mystic dakini script and has no ordinary intelligible meaning. As communicated by Trulshik Rinpoche, because he was refused the consort he needed for the discovery of the *Guru Sadhana* (*gu ru bla sgrub*), Donyö Dorje (*don yod rdo rje*) could not reveal it fully and write it down. Soon afterward, the maiden who should have been his consort died. The parents felt great regret and contacted the yogin, who said that the auspicious connection had been missed. It is said that he brought the girl back to life for a few moments and gave her instructions, adding that he would guide her in the *bardo*. After these events, Donyö Dorje concealed the Yellow Scroll (*shog ser*) for the Guru Sadhama in a mask, to be discovered again as a *yang gter*. His immediate reembodiment, the former Trulshik Rinpoche, Thongdrol Dorje (*mthong grol rdo rje*), found this Yellow Scroll when he came to Nepal with Dzatrul Ngawang Tendzin Norbu (*rdza sprul ngag dbang bstan 'dzin nor bu*, 1867–1940, the present Trulshik Rinpoche's root teacher) to perform the reconsecration of the Bodhnath stupa. Thongdrol Dorje also wrote expanded versions of the other *sadhanas* of the Three Roots.

4. A copy of a manuscript of the *Collected Songs* of Chingkar Donyö Dorje, entitled *ma bcos gnyug ma'i zog smyon gu yangs blo bde'i shugs 'byung nyams glu'i 'phreng ba 'gag med rdo rje'i sgra dbyangs* (147 folios), kept at Nubri in northern Nepal, was kindly made available to us by Franz-Karl Ehrhard.

5. This refers to Namkha Wangchuk (*nam mkha' dbang phyug*), who gave to Chingkar the name Guyang Lodeh (*gu yangs blo bde*). Ibid., fol. 88/b.

6. *Guyang Nyinthig, The Heart Essence of Openness and Ease* (*rdzogs pa chen po snying thig gi khrid yig go bde bklag chog tu bkod pa lhun grub rtogs pa'i rang sgra kun bzang thugs*

mdzod gu yangs snying gi thig le). Fine wooden blocks for this work have recently been carved under the guidance of Trulshik Rinpoche at Thupten Chöling in Sharkhumbu, Nepal. See also Ehrhard, *Flügelschläge des Garuda*, p. 37.

7. For Kohudeh Dzogchen Namgyal Ling (*ko'u sde rdzogs chen rnam rgyal gling*), see RO, p. 651.

8. *The Precious Treasury of Sutra and Tantra* (*mdo rgyud rin po che'i mdzod*) was composed in 1838, when Chöying Tobden Dorje was fifty-one years old. See GL, vol. 2, p. 186.

9. The biography of *gser khang rin po che*, called *thams cad mkhyen par bsgrod pa'i them skas*. See fol. 16/b of Shabkar's *o rgyan sprul pa'i glegs bam*.

Notes to Table 2

1. For Pema Ledreltsel (*padma las 'brel rtsal*), see NS, note 614 and BM, p. 152. For Tulku Lekden, see BM, p. 153, TN, pp. 520–22, and other references summarized in Ehrhard 1990, 109 n.94. Regarding the other masters of this lineage, the sources are GT, vol. 2, pp. 27–62 and pp. 79–109; the *zhus lan bdud rtsi gser phreng* and the *lo rgyus rin po che'i phreng ba* from the *mkha' 'gro snying thig*, pt. 1, vol. 7 of Longchenpa's Nyingthig Yazhi (*snying thig ya bzhi*); BM, pp. 152–61, and NS, p. 595. Other ramifications of the Khandro Nyingthig lineage are described in GT, vol. 2, pp. 110–14 and in Thondup 19884, 34–35.

2. This is possibly Gampo Zangpo Dorje (*sgam po bzang po rdo rje*, born around 1634, passed away before 1700) for several reasons: 1) he is counted among the chief disciples of Minling Terchen (see GC, vol. 4, pp. 118–25 and NS, p. 833); 2) he is a disciple of Tertön Nyima Trakpa and so is Rigdzin Palden Tashi, the next master in the lineage; 3) Rigdzin Palden Tashi was also a disciple of Nyima Trakpa's son, Gyalse Orgyen Tendzin (*rgyal sras o rgyan bstan 'dzin*, 1701–27/28) who was the immediate reembodiment of Zangpo Dorje. See GC, vol. 4, p. 444.

3. On Tsodu Ngakchang Dorje Namgyal, said to be Shabkar's father, see chap. 1, note 12.

Appendix 3

Chögyal Ngakyi Wangpo's ancestry

The following is an account of the ancestry of the Dharma King Chögyal Ngakyi Wangpo, known in historical records as Chingwang Ngawang Dargye (*ching wang ngag dbang dar rgyas*).

Tendzin Chögyal (*bstan 'dzin chos rgyal*, 1592–1654), otherwise known as Gushri Khan, left his pasture lands in Urumchi to establish himself near Lake Kokonor. He had three queens and ten sons. His descendants in the region of Kokonor and along the banks of the Machu River became known as the Barungar (Right Banner) of the Orod Mongols.

The Mongolian nation was divided into a series of principalities or "banners" (Tib. *dpon khag*, Mong. *khoshun*). Each was ruled by a Jasag (*ja sag*, pronounced *dzasa* by Tibetans), who could belong to any of the various ranks of the Mongolian nobility, from that of Chingwang, king or prince of the first order, to that of *Gung*, or duke. These "banners" were in turn subdivided into "arrows" (Tib. *mda'*, Mong. *sumun*), originally a group of 150 adult men and their families. See Howorth (1876), Ahmad (1970), and Ho-chin Yang (1969). Thirty-three "banners" and a hundred and one "arrows" are mentioned by Sumpa Khenpo as existing in the Kokonor area.

As Konchog Tenpa Rabgye points out (AC, vol. 1, pp. 56–105), there exist several different, often contradictory, accounts of Gushri Khan's genealogy. The clearest records of the rulers of the right, or southern, bank of the Machu River

are given by Konchog Tenpa Rabgye, by Konchog Gyaltsen, in his *History of China, Tibet, and Mongolia* (*rgya bod sog gi lo rgyus*), and by Muge Samten (a scholar of Labrang Tashikhyil) in his recent article *dris lan li dwangs rang sgra*. See also table 3.

Gushri Khan's fifth son, Tsering Elduchi (*tshe ring el du chi*), ruled over a vast territory: the whole of Choneh (*co ne*), Upper and Lower Rekong (*reb kong stod smad*), Ngawa (*rnga ba*), and Rado (*rwa mdo*). Tsering Elduchi's eldest son, Khandro Lobzang Tenkyong (*mkha' 'gro blo bzang bstan skyong*), conquered the entire Six Ranges of Kham (*mdo khams sgang drug*, see chap. 14, note 23) and adjacent regions up to Dartsedo (*dar rtse mdo*, Tachienlu or Kanding) in the east. He eventually settled in the Dzachukha area (*rdza chu kha*) and adopted the Nyingma tradition of Tibetan Buddhism. Other chieftains were displeased by this and had him assassinated.

Lobzang Tenkyong was succeeded by his younger brother, Dar Gyalpo Shokthu (*dar rgyal po shog thu*), who first settled near Lake Kokonor and later in Balshung (*'bal gzhung*) and Tseshung (*rtse gzhung*), a place to the southeast of the Machu River where Shabkar stayed for many years in retreat. Dar Gyalpo also extended his territories to include most of Amdo and Kham, up to Konjo (*go jo*). During his reign the region enjoyed a period of great prosperity.

Of Dar Gyalpo's five sons, the most influential was Wang Gyalpo Junang Tsewang Tendzin

TABLE 3   CHÖGYAL NGAKYI WANGPO'S GENEALOGY

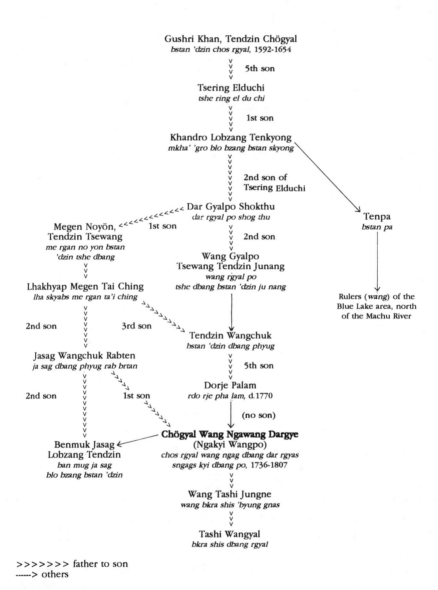

Gushri Khan, Tendzin Chögyal
bstan 'dzin chos rgyal, 1592-1654

5th son

Tsering Elduchi
tshe ring el du chi

1st son

Khandro Lobzang Tenkyong
mkha' 'gro blo bzang bstan skyong

2nd son of
Tsering Elduchi

Dar Gyalpo Shokthu
dar rgyal po shog thu

Megen Noyön,   1st son
Tendzin Tsewang   2nd son
me rgan no yon bstan
'dzin tshe dbang

Tenpa
bstan pa

Wang Gyalpo
Tsewang Tendzin Junang
wang rgyal po
tshe dbang bstan 'dzin ju nang

Lhakhyap Megen Tai Ching
lha skyabs me rgan ta'i ching

Rulers (*wang*) of the
Blue Lake area, north
of the Machu River

2nd son   3rd son

Tendzin Wangchuk
bstan 'dzin dbang phyug

Jasag Wangchuk Rabten
ja sag dbang phyug rab brtan

5th son

2nd son   1st son

Dorje Palam
rdo rje pha lam, d.1770

(no son)

Benmuk Jasag
Lobzang Tendzin
ban mug ja sag
blo bzang bstan 'dzin

Chögyal Wang Ngawang Dargye
(Ngakyi Wangpo)
chos rgyal wang ngag dbang dar rgyas
sngags kyi dbang po, 1736-1807

Wang Tashi Jungne
wang bkra shis 'byung gnas

Tashi Wangyal
bkra shis dbang rgyal

>>>>>>> father to son
------> others

(*wang rgyal po tshe dbang bstan 'dzin ju nang*, or *jo nang*), the son of his middle wife. Junang also proved to be a powerful monarch, and enlarged his frontiers as far as Golok Dzamthang (*mgo log 'dzam thang*). It was he who offered land to the first Jamyang Shepa[1] and helped him to build the large monastery of Labrang Tashikhyil in 1708. Later, at the height of its prosperity, this monastery counted four thousand monks and fifty incarnate Lamas. King Junang had three queens, one of whom, Chungurza Namgyal Drolma, gave birth to a son, Dondrup Wangyal (*don grub dbang rgyal*). The latter, however, died young. Junang therefore adopted as his heir Tendzin Wangchuk (*bstan 'dzin dbang phyug*), the third son of his elder brother Lha Kyap Mergen Tai Ching (*lha skyabs me rgan ta'i ching*).

Tendzin Wangchuk's youngest son, Dorje Palam (*rdo rje pha lam*), inherited the title of Ching-wang at an early age, since both his parents and two of his elder brothers died during his infancy. However, he died without issue in 1770, and was succeeded by a cousin, the son of Jasag Wangchuk Rabten (*ja sag dbang phyug rab brtan*).[2] This son was Ngawang Dargye, Chögyal Ngakyi Wangpo (*ngag dbang dar rgyas chos rgyal ngag gi dbang po*, 1736–1807), Shabkar's teacher.

Following the death of King Junang, a series of bloody feuds broke out among the rulers of the Kokonor area, with the result that by the time Ngawang Dargye inherited the throne, the power of the Wang rulers was reduced to the region of Sogpo, south of Rekong. Nevertheless, Ngawang Dargye received the title of Chingwang and eventually ruled over two to three thousand families (as compared with the thirty thousand acknowledging the authority of Junang).

Ngawang Dargye devoted most of his life to spiritual activities; eventually he asked his brother, Benmuk Jasag Lobzang Tendzin (*ban mug ja sag blo bzang bstan 'dzin*), to administer most of the domestic affairs. It so happened, however, that Lobzang Tendzin fell foul of the central Tibetan government and was deprived of the title of Chingwang.

After his death, Ngawang Dargye was succeeded by his son, Wang Tashi Jungne (*wang bkra shis 'byung gnas*). According to AC (vol. 2, p. 123), the latter had three sons, one of whom, Tashi Wangyal (*bkra shis dbang rgyal*), ascended the throne. The Ven. Tulku Thondup, however, tells us of a different oral tradition:

"Tashi Jungne became the disciple of Dola Jigme Kalzang,[3] a great Nyingmapa master, himself one of the main disciples of the first Do Drupchen, Jigme Trinley Öser. After having been invited to Tashi Jungne's court, Dola Jigme went to China. There he encountered a thief who was going to be tortured to death by being made to ride an iron horse which, like a cast iron oven, was being slowly heated red hot by a fire within. Seeing this, in order to spare the thief, Dola Jigme immediately claimed that he had committed the theft. He was seized, and died on the iron horse. When they heard that their master had died in China, Dola Jigme's disciples blamed Tashi Jungne, thinking he was responsible for their master going to China. One of them, Alak Dzong Ngön, put a curse on Tashi Jungne so that he could have no male descendants. The oral sources claim that Tashi Jungne had only daughters, who themselves had no sons."

Tashi Jungne's descendants are now living near Rekong, in Amdo. One of them married Apa Alo (a relative of the fifth Jamyang Shepa), who became a very popular secular leader in Amdo until his death in 1988.

Notes

1. Jamyang Shepa Ngawang Tsondru (*'jam dbyangs bzhad pa ngag dbang brtson 'grus*, 1648–1722).

2. TC, p. 3277, specifies that *bla ma dar rgyas* ascended the throne of the Dzungars in 1750. This seems, however, to be an early date, since Dorje Palam, Ngawang Dargye's predecessor, died in 1770.

3. Dola Jigme Kalzang Chökyi Lodrö (*rdo bla 'jigs med skal bzang chos kyi blo gros*). Together with Do Drupchen Trinley Öser (see Translator's Introduction, note 48), Dola Jigme recognized the tulku of Palge, Samten Puntshok (*dpal dge bsam gtan phun tshogs*), who became the celebrated master Dza Patrul Rinpoche, Orgyen Jigme Chökyi Wangpo (*dpal sprul o rgyan 'jigs med chos kyi dbang po*, 1808–87).

Appendix 4

Kunzang Dechen Gyalpo and the "Wish-fulfilling Gem, Hayagriva and Varahi"

The first and foremost spiritual empowerment (*dbang*) that Shabkar received from Chögyal Ngakyi Wangpo was that of the *Wish-fulfilling Gem, Hayagriva and Varahi* (*rta phag yid bzhin nor bu*), a spiritual treasure revealed by Kunzang Dechen Gyalpo. Following this empowerment, Shabkar spent five years in Tseshung Hermitage practicing this cycle of teachings, which covers the entire spiritual path from the preliminaries to the Great Perfection. It was during this period of intense practice that Shabkar's meditative experiences and ultimate realization gradually unfolded (see chap. 4, fol. 41b). Later on, the *Wish-fulfilling Gem, Hayagriva and Varahi* remained the innermost empowerment and instructions that Shabkar bestowed upon his close disciples. Today, this is perhaps the only *terma* of Dechen Gyalpo for which the transmission has remained unbroken.

Kunzang Dechen Gyalpo was also known, at different times and in different places, as Mönlam Dorje, Ngawang Dorje, Karak Tertön, Kongpo Terchen, and Drukthang Tertön.[1] He was the immediate reincarnation of Ratön Tertön Topden Dorje,[2] a master whose *termas* were also practiced by Shabkar. The ramifications of Dechen Gyalpo's lineage (see table 4) reveal close connections with other important spiritual lineages, such as Jigme Lingpa's *Longchen Nyingthig*, which Shabkar's teacher, Chögyal Ngakyi Wangpo, held too.

Kunzang Dechen Gyalpo was born in 1736 in an area below the White Vulture Pass (*rgod dkar la*) at Samye. He studied at Samye and at Palri Monastery (*dpal ri mgon*) at Chongye (*'phyong rgyas*).

His principal spiritual teachers were Kunzang Öser, Chubri Drupchen Kunzang Rangdrol, and especially Rigdzin Thukchog Dorje,[3] who became his root master and whom he served for many years. At the age of five or six, Dechen Gyalpo had a vision of Guru Padmasambhava. It is said that he was forever afterwards accompanied by dakinis, who followed him like his shadow. At the age of twelve he found the list of the *termas* he was to discover, and at the age of twenty-six he revealed the *Five Essential Cycles of the Five Families* (*rigs lnga snying po'i skor lnga*) from the sacred site of Rolpu on the border between Upper Kongpo and Lower Dagpo. Following this he revealed many other spiritual treasures in Powo, Kongpo, Dagpo, Tsari, Samye, Drigung, and elsewhere.[4] At Tsechen Drolma Lhakhang (*rtse chen sgrol ma lha khang*), near Gyantse, he revealed profound instructions that had been concealed by Atisha. Altogether he rediscovered eighteen spiritual treasures.

Dechen Gyalpo became the teacher of the regent-king of Tibet, Demo Rinpoche,[5] who invited him to perform the "Taming the Ground" ritual (*sa 'dul*) on the occasion of the restoration of Samye in 1770.

Dechen Gyalpo performed many miracles. To extract a *terma* from a high cliff at the Grove of the Secret Mantras, Sang-ngak Gatsel (*gsang sngags dga' tshal*), in inner Tsari, he flew through the sky like a bird. In other places he left imprints of his hands and feet in rocks. In Dagpo, a statue of Gampopa took off its hat and spoke to him. When he went to pay homage to the Jowo

TABLE 4

LINEAGE OF THE RTA PHAG YID BZHIN NOR BU
AND RELATED LINEAGES

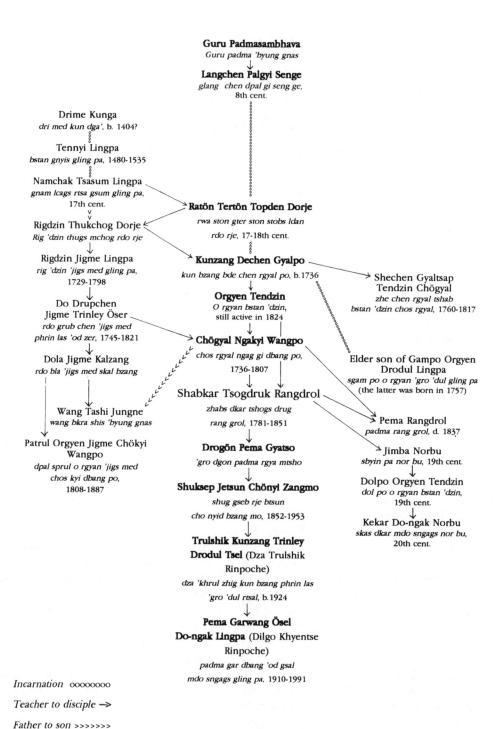

Guru Padmasambhava
Guru padma 'byung gnas

Langchen Palgyi Senge
glang chen dpal gi seng ge,
8th cent.

Drime Kunga
dri med kun dga', b. 1404?

Tennyi Lingpa
bstan gnyis gling pa, 1480-1535

Namchak Tsasum Lingpa
gnam lcags rtsa gsum gling pa,
17th cent.

Rigdzin Thukchog Dorje
Rig 'dzin thugs mchog rdo rje

Ratön Tertön Topden Dorje
rwa ston gter ston stobs ldan
rdo rje, 17-18th cent.

Rigdzin Jigme Lingpa
rig 'dzin 'jigs med gling pa,
1729-1798

Kunzang Dechen Gyalpo
kun bzang bde chen rgyal po, b.1736

Shechen Gyaltsap
Tendzin Chögyal
zhe chen rgyal tshab
bstan 'dzin chos rgyal, 1760-1817

Do Drupchen
Jigme Trinley Öser
rdo grub chen 'jigs med
phrin las 'od zer, 1745-1821

Orgyen Tendzin
O rgyan bstan 'dzin,
still active in 1824

Chögyal Ngakyi Wangpo
chos rgyal ngag gi dbang po,
1736-1807

Elder son of Gampo Orgyen
Drodul Lingpa
sgam po o rgyan 'gro 'dul gling pa
(the latter was born in 1757)

Dola Jigme Kalzang
rdo bla 'jigs med skal bzang

Shabkar Tsogdruk Rangdrol
zhabs dkar tshogs drug
rang grol, 1781-1851

Wang Tashi Jungne
wang bkra shis 'byung gnas

Pema Rangdrol
padma rang grol, d. 1837

Patrul Orgyen Jigme Chökyi
Wangpo
dpal sprul o rgyan 'jigs med
chos kyi dbang po,
1808-1887

Drogön Pema Gyatso
'gro dgon padma rgya mtsho

Jimba Norbu
sbyin pa nor bu, 19th cent.

Shuksep Jetsun Chönyi Zangmo
shug gseb rje btsun
cho nyid bzang mo, 1852-1953

Dolpo Orgyen Tendzin
dol po o rgyan bstan 'dzin,
19th cent.

**Trulshik Kunzang Trinley
Drodul Tsel** (Dza Trulshik
Rinpoche)
dza 'khrul zhig kun bzang phrin las
'gro 'dul rtsal, b.1924

Kekar Do-ngak Norbu
skas dkar mdo sngags nor bu,
20th cent.

**Pema Garwang Ösel
Do-ngak Lingpa** (Dilgo Khyentse
Rinpoche)
padma gar dbang 'od gsal
mdo sngags gling pa, 1910-1991

Incarnation oooooooo

Teacher to disciple —>

Father to son >>>>>>>

Rinpoche statue in Lhasa, many tiny relics (*ring bsrel*) fell from the statue's heart onto his head, and he received further prophecies.

The seventh Dalai Lama, Kalzang Gyatso (1708–57), was prophesied to be his principal spiritual heir, but the auspicious connections between them were not to be completely fulfilled. His other Dharma heirs were the thirteenth Karmapa Dudul Dorje (1733–97), Shamar Trisur Garwang Gyatso (b. around 1735),[6] Thekchen Lingpa Drodön Tarchin (d. 1775/6),[7] Gampo Drodul Lingpa (see below), the second Shechen Gyaltsap, Pema Sang-ngak Tendzin Chögyal (1760–1817),[8] and many others. His main patrons were the Lhagyari king of E Rigpai Jungne (*e rig pa'i 'byung gnas*) and other notables of Dagpo and Kongpo. He passed away in Kongpo, where he had settled after he had been offered Drukthang Monastery (see note 1). Many relics the size and shape of sesame seeds, as well as naturally formed images of deities, were found among his bones and ashes.

According to GC, vol. 4, p. 143, Dechen Gyalpo passed away after Shamar IX Trisur Garwang Gyatso, which means not before 1791 (Garwang Gyatso lived fifty-eight years and could not have been born before 1733, since Shamar VIII died in 1732).

According to the *Necklace of Jewels* (ND), Kunzang Dechen Gyalpo's next incarnation was the eldest son of Orgyen Drodul Lingpa[9] (the fifth Gampopa, b. 1757), one of his chief disciples. This incarnation revealed some *termas*, but died young.

An oral tradition, related to us by Ven. Khetsun Sangpo, who is a native of Bartang,[10] near Karak, presents some little-known aspects of Dechen Gyalpo's life-story.

"In his youth, Dechen Gyalpo was a humble shepherd on the slopes of Jomo Karak, at a place called Yangdrong Shika (*yang grong gzhi kha*) in Bartang (*bar thang*). Soon he developed into a realized *siddha* blessed with many visions and signs of accomplishment. For a long time he lived in a cave called Dechen (*bde chen*, 'Great Bliss'), where Guru Padmasambhava had spent six months in meditation at the edge of the eternal snows on the secluded heights of Jomo Karak's western slopes. On account of this, Dechen Gyalpo became renowned as Karak Tertön. Several statues, preserved in this area until the Chinese invasion,[11] depicted him as an impressive, large, bearded lama, not unlike Minling Terchen Gyurme Dorje.

"Some say that when, in the latter period of his life, Dechen Gyalpo's fame as a spiritual teacher had spread far and wide, some peasants from his valley who had come to meet him in southern Tibet were amazed—and somewhat disappointed—to discover that the great master they had come to meet was none other than the shepherd they had known. But others say that this anecdote stemmed from a confusion with a similar event that happened to Thangtong Gyalpo when he resided at Chuwori."

The *Taphag Yishin Norbu (rta phag yid bzhin nor bu)* belongs to the larger cycle of the *Khandro Sangwa Yeshe (mkha' 'gro gsang ba ye shes)*. The account of its discovery is found in the *terma* texts[12] and in the *Torch of Wisdom* (TW, pp. 8–20), a commentary on them written by Chögyal Ngakyi Wangpo, of which the following is a summary:

Langchen Palgyi Senge was Yeshe Tsogyal's companion while she practiced Vajra Kilaya at Paro Taktsang in Bhutan. After numerous rebirths, he appeared as Ratön Tertön Rigdzin Topden Dorje, whose immediate reincarnation, born in the Fire Dragon Year (1736), was the treasure rediscoverer Dechen Gyalpo Tsel. At the age of thirty-two (in the Pig Year, 1767), when Dechen Gyalpo was in strict retreat at Chuwori, a beautiful woman, magnificently dressed and adorned, appeared to him at dawn on the fifteenth of the eighth month and said, "In the east, in the cave called Sang Yak Drak, you will receive a prophecy from Guru Rinpoche."

First, Dechen Gyalpo suspected that this was a hallucination, but the woman reappeared many times, urging him to go. Finally, he went to this place and at dawn, on the fifteenth of the *rawa* month[13] of the Earth Mouse Year (1768), Dechen Gyalpo's brother, Rigden Yinrik, told the tertön, "I can see many things appearing in the sky." At that very moment, Dechen Gyalpo had an experience of intense bliss and saw Guru Pema Gyalpo, one of the eight manifestations of

Guru Padmasambhava, in the sky, encircled by an expanse of five-colored rainbow light. On either side of him were the Lady Mandarava, dressed as a nun, and Yeshe Tsogyal, dressed as a Tibetan laywoman. They were surrounded by myriads of dakas and dakinis who made offerings, danced, and sang, assuming innumerable attitudes and expressions. Moreover, King Pehar appeared at the head of a wonderful procession, waving fragrant incense. All the sky was filled, as if by clouds, with gods and rakshas of the eight classes.[14]

Seeing this, Dechen Gyalpo prayed fervently, and Guru Pema Gyalpo said:

A ho!
Listen, supreme son who is like my own
  heart.
I, Padmakara of Uddiyana,
Never fail to fulfill karmic connections.
Let my words dissolve into your heart,
  noble son;
The time has come to reawaken your
  excellent potential!

In the sublime hidden land of Pemakö, the
  Lotus Array,[15]
To the right of the throne upon which I
  dwell in the form of the Medicine
  Buddha
Is a treasure that was meant for Topden
  Dorje.
Yet because of the scant merit of beings in
  this dark age,
The profound requisite conditions did not
  manifest for him.
Now is the time for this *siddhi*
To be granted to you, his next rebirth.
Pray from your heart that it will benefit
  beings!

By the power of our past prayers,
The actual Yellow Scroll,[16] endowed with
  pure and perfect karmic links,
Will be brought to you by dakinis
From Pemakö's divine land.

Northeast of here, at the Treasure Chest,[17]
Tsogyal will be holding the Yellow Scroll.

She herself will utter the symbolic words
And decipher the symbolic writings.

These teachings will spread to Tibet,
  Mongolia, and China,
And bring immeasurable benefit to beings.

Then Pema Gyalpo predicted that auspicious connections would be established if the tertön could find a dakini who was an incarnation of Shakyadevi [one of Guru Rinpoche's five main consorts]; he also gave many other predictions. For seven days after this, rainbows filled the sky.

Later, in Yeshe Tsogyal's Secret Cave at Shotö Terdrom in Drigung, Dechen Gyalpo, having fulfilled all of Guru Rinpoche's predictions and auspicious connections, received the *terma* in direct transmission (*snyan brgyud*), amidst many miraculous signs. When he practised the *sadhana* related to the *terma*, he dreamt that he went to Zangdok Palri and received empowerment from Thekchen Lingpa, whom he perceived as inseparable from Guru Rinpoche.

In the *Crystal Mirror* (CM), a manual for practicing the *Taphag Yishin Norbu* written by one of Shabkar's chief disciples, Gurong Tulku Natsok Rangdrol, the transmission of the *terma* in Shotö Titro (same as Terdrom) and its propagation are related in the following way:

While Dechen Gyalpo was practicing for a long time at Chuwori and other sacred places, living on alms, he received repeated predictions from the gurus and dakinis. When he was thirty-three years old, he came to the Secret Cave of Tsogyal at Shotö Titro. On the fifteen of the month of the sheep (sixth month) in the female Earth Ox Year (1769), while he was offering a large *ganachakra* feast, he beheld Guru Padmasambhava and his consort appearing in a sky filled with rainbows. As Guru Padmasambhava gave him the direct oral transmission (*snyan brgyud*)[18] of the profound terma, rainbow canopies shone in all directions, the air was filled with extraordinary fragrances, and many other miraculous signs occurred.

When Dechen Gyalpo practiced this spiritual treasure he had many visions and meditation experiences, such as receiving empowerments from Guru Padmasambhava and the wisdom dakinis. Keeping to the injunction of Guru Padmasambhava and his consort, he kept his *terma* secret for ten years. When the time was ripe for establishing his fortunate disciples on the path of maturation and liberation, following the repeated requests of the *terma* guardians and the Dharma protectors, on the first day of the first month of the male Earth Dog Year (1778) he undertook a special spiritual practice on top of Chuwori Mountain. On the twenty-second, in the morning, he offered an elaborate *ganachakra* feast. When he supplicated the guardians of the *terma*, there appeared, on a mass of clouds, a resplendent blue dakini, naked and without ornaments. She held in her right hand an arrow of long life, and in her left hand a mirror and a treasure box. This was the sign that the *terma* could now be propagated.

Through these profound teachings, he set countless male and female disciples on the path of ripening and liberation. Among these was his spiritual son Orgyen Tendzin Rinpoche, who had been prophesied to be the heir to this spiritual treasure. Orgyen Tendzin gave the complete transmission to the glorious Dharma King Chögyal Ngakyi Wangpo, who had been predicted to be the mind incarnation of Guru Padmasambhava and the *terma*'s next spiritual heir.

When Ngakyi Wangpo practiced the Three Roots of the *terma*, he had visions of the mandala and the deities, and many miraculous signs occurred: sparks and smoke came from the *tormas*, and vessels of *amrita* and *rakta* overflowed. The Dharma King subsequently disseminated these teachings widely in Tibet, Mongolia, and China. His main spiritual heir was Shabkar.

In this way, the lineage of the *Taphag Yishin Norbu* has come down to the present, unbroken (see table 4). In a song,[19] the Dharma King invokes this spiritual lineage:

Samantabhadra and consort,
Vajrasattva,
Great wisdom dakini Lekyi Wangmo,
Humchenkara, Lapkyi Drönma,
Pejung, Tsogyal, Palseng, Dechen Gyal,

Orgyen Tendzin and all the other glorious root and lineage gurus—
With your extraordinary blessings,
Make a rain of *siddhis* fall,
And bless this fortunate disciple's three doors as the three vajras.

According to this supplication, the transmission thus passed from the primordial dharmakaya Buddha, Samantabhadra, and his dharmakaya consort Samantabhadri, to the sambhogakaya Buddha Vajrasattva, and then to the wisdom dakini Lekyi Wangmo.[20] It then went to the dakini Lapkyi Drönma who, according to TW (p. 139) and to the *Necklace of White Lotuses* (NW),[21] is said to reside to the east of the Great Holy Mountains of China.[22]

From Guru Padmasambhava the lineage passed to his chief consort and disciple, the princess of Karchen, Yeshe Tsogyal, a human emanation of Jetsun Drolma and Vajrayogini, who wrote down and helped to conceal most of the *termas* that Guru Rinpoche had taught to his disciples. It then passed to Palgyi Senge, one of Guru Rinpoche's twenty-five main disciples. Guru Rinpoche entrusted the teachings of the *Taphag Yishin Norbu* to him and predicted that, in a future rebirth, Palgyi Senge would reveal these teachings and propagate them for the sake of beings. This prophesied rebirth was the treasure discoverer Terchen Dechen Gyalpo, whose spiritual heir was Orgyen Tendzin. According to NW, Orgyen Tendzin is said to have lived at Dechen Ling, Rina Monastery.[23] CM states unambiguously that Ngakyi Wangpo[24] received the transmission from Orgyen Tendzin. There is no mention of Ngakyi Wangpo meeting Dechen Gyalpo, although he was the latter's contemporary.

Ngakyi Wangpo transmitted these teachings to Shabkar Tsogdruk Rangdrol. In chapter 9, Shabkar says that in 1824, at Rina Monastery,[25] he received from Orgyen Tendzin the transmission of "the New Termas." This certainly refers to Dechen Gyalpo's revelations, and probably to the *Taphag Yishin Norbu*.

Through Shabkar the lineage of *Taphag Yishin Norbu* spread widely. One line of transmission has come down to the present day through

Shabkar's heart-son Pema Gyatso;[26] the great woman teacher Shuksep Jetsun Rigdzin Chönyi Zangmo (1852–1953); and Dza Trulshik Rinpoche, Kunzang Trinley Drodul Tsel (born in 1924), an emanation of the great translator Vairocana.[27] It then passed to H.H. Dilgo Khyentse Rinpoche, Pema Garwang Ösel Dongak Lingpa (1910–91), who was the emanation of King Trisong Detsen and of the great *pandita* Vimalamitra.[28] Other lines of this transmission are said to have survived in Amdo, and remain to be investigated.

At the request of several disciples, especially of Shabkar himself, Ngakyi Wangpo wrote *The Torch of Wisdom That Dispels the Darkness of Ignorance* (TW), a lucid explanation of the practice of *Taphag Yishin Norbu*. This explanation covers the complete spiritual path from the preliminary practices up to the highest teachings of the Great Perfection. A manuscript copy of this text, in Shabkar's own handwriting, was enshrined in a golden stupa containing some bones and other relics of Shabkar at Pelek Gonpa in central Tibet.[29] Some relatives of Lopön Khyentse, a disciple of Dza Trulshik Rinpoche, saved and concealed these relics when the reliquary was destroyed by the Chinese invaders. Later, Lopön Khyentse offered this manuscript to Trulshik Rinpoche, who in turn presented it to H.H. Dilgo Khyentse Rinpoche, in whose library it is now preserved.[30]

Most of the available material on the *Sangwa Yeshe* cycle, of which the *Taphag Yishin Norbu* is one part, is presently kept in the library of Trulshik Rinpoche in Sharkhumbu (see Bibliography). A large number of these texts originated from the library of Kyabje Kangyur Rinpoche in Darjeeling.

In our days, it is through the efforts of the Ven. Trulshik Rinpoche that these teachings remain alive for practitioners.

Notes

1. For Kunzang Dechen Gyalpo (*kun bzang bde chen rgyal po*), see GC, vol. 3, pp. 222–27; for Mönlam Dorje (*smon lam rdor rje*), see TN, pp. 634/2 to 636/2. On Karak Tertön (*kha rag gter ston*), see p. 571 of this work. For Kongpo Terchen (*kong po gter chen*) and Ngawang Dorje (*ngag dbang rdo rje*), see SG (the biography of the second Shechen Gyaltsap, Pema Sangnak Tendzin Chögyal), folios 6/a, 45/b, 53/b, 102/b and 112/b. For Drukthang Tertön (*'brug thang gter ston*), see ND, p. 327/4–5, p. 341/4, p. 345/6. Drukthang is the name of a monastery in Kongpo that was offered to Dechen Gyalpo by Chöling Tulku Jigten Wangchuk (*chos gling sprul sku 'jig rten dbang phyug*, see TN, p. 636). In ND, p. 361/5, mention is also made of a *Complement to the History of Treasure Revealers* (*gter ston rnam thar 'phrod 'thud*), written by Drupwang Yung Gon Dorje (*grub dbang g.yung mgon rdo rje*), which ends with an account of Dechen Gyalpo's life.

2. For Ratön Tertön (*rwa ston gter ston*), see Translator's Introduction, note 41.

3. Kunzang Öser (*kun bzang 'od zer*), Chubri Drupchen Kunzang Rangdrol (*lcub ri*, or *rtsub ri?, grub chen kun bzang rang grol*). For Rigdzin Thukchog Dorje (*rig 'dzin thugs mchog rdo rje*), see Translator's Introduction, note 42.

4. At Gawalung (*dga' ba lung*) in Powo (*spo bo*), Orgyen Dzong (*o rgyan rdzong*) in Rishö (*ri shod*), Phugmoche (*phug mo che*) in Puri (*spu ri*), Tsechen Drak (*rtse chen brag*), Sang-ngak Gatsel (*gsang sngags dga' tshal*) in Tsari (*tsa nang*), Samye Chimphu (*bsam yas mchims phu*), Samye Tamdrin Ling (*rta mgrin gling*), Yamalung (*g.ya ma lung*) near Samye, Shotö Terdrom or Titro (*gzho stod gter sgrom* or *ti sgro*) in Drigung, at Chakpori (*lcags po ri*), Chuwori (*chu bo ri*), Dzakar in Upper Dagpo (*dwags stod dza dkar*), Gyaltago in Lower Dagpo (*dwags smad rgyal rta mgo*), Karzug Trang in Kongpo (*kong po dkar zug 'phrang*).

5. Demo Rinpoche Gelek Gyatso (*de mo rin po che, dge legs rgya mtsho*, d. 1777) himself had visions of Guru Padmasambhava, Thangtong Gyalpo, and others (see GC, vol. Ga, p. 227). He received the full transmission of Dechen Gyalpo's *termas*.

6. Shamar Trisur Garwang Gyatso (*zhwa dmar khri zur gar dbang rgya mtsho*). See GC, vol. 4, pp. 133–37. Wondrous signs indicated that he was the reincarnation of the eighth Shamar, Palchen Chökyi Dondrup (1695–1732), and he was enthroned at Yangpachen. However, when another reincarnation was recognized, he left the throne and remained at Namseling (*rnam sras gling*); hence his title of "retired" Shamar (*zur pa*). His main teacher was Gampo Kunzang Ngedön Wangpo (*sgam po kun bzang nges don dbang po*). He displayed a vast activity for the benefit of the Dharma and sentient beings, and lived fifty-eight years.

7. Thekchen Lingpa Karma Drodön Tarchin (*theg chen gling pa karma 'gro don mthar phyin*, 1700–75/76, see GC, vol. Ga, p. 218), also known as Tertön Drime Lingpa (*gter ston dri med gling pa*), born in Zurkar as a descendant of Tertön Dechen Lingpa (*bde chen gling pa*). He was the incarnation of Guru Padmasambhava's disciple Gyalwa Chöyang (*rgyal ba mchog dbyangs*) and the immediate incarnation of Rongpa Tertön Dudul Lingpa (*rong pa gter ston bdud 'dul gling pa*). He became a disciple of Rigdzin Thukchog Dorje (*rig 'dzin thugs mchog rdo rje*), from whom he received the transmission of the *Kunzang Nyingthig* (*kun bzang snying thig*) of Tennyi Lingpa (*bstan gnyis gling pa*, 1480–1535). He was gifted with clairvoyance and had visions in which he remembered his former births as Melong Dorje (*me long rdo rje*, 1243–1303), Dechen Lingpa (*bde chen gling pa*), Dudul Lingpa (*bdud 'dul gling pa*), and others. He lived a contemplative life in solitary places and revealed several *termas* in Trak Yangdzong (*sgrags yang rdzong*) and other places. His main disciples were Jigme Lingpa (*rig 'dzin 'jigs med gling pa*), Kunzang Dechen Gyalpo (*kun bzang bde chen rgyal po*), Trati Ngakchang (*bkra ti sngags 'chang*), Chaksampa Tendzin Yeshe Lhundrup (*lcags zam pa bstan 'dzin ye shes lhun grub*), and the seventh Dalai Lama (*skal bzang rgya mtsho*). His descendants are still found at Zurkar Lhadeng (*zur mkhar lha sdeng*).

8. For Pema Sangnak Tendzin Chögyal (*padma gsang sngags bstan 'dzin chos rgyal*, 1760–1817), see SG. Dechen Gyalpo recognized Tendzin Chögyal to be an incarnation of the famous *siddha* of Vajra Kilaya, Langlap Changchup Dorje (*langs lab byang chub rdo rje*), see NG fol. 6a. The list of teachings received by Tendzin Chögyal from Dechen Gyalpo has much in common with the transmissions that Shabkar himself received from Chögyal Ngakyi Wangpo and other teachers of the same lineage. These teachings included the new *termas* of Dechen Gyalpo and those of Thekchog Dorje, Ratön Tertön, Namchak Tsasum Lingpa, and Dungtso Repa. See NG, 52/b to 53/a.

9. Dagla Gampo Orgyen Drodul Lingpa (*dwags la sgam po'i mchog sprul o rgyan 'gro 'dul gling pa*, 1757-?), also known as Jampel Trinley Wangpo (*'jam dpal phrin las dbang po*) and Tertön Dorje Gyalpo (*gter ston rdo rje rgyal po*, see GC, vol. 4, pp. 137–48 and ND, pp. 339–46). On Dechen Gyalpo's incarnation, see ND, pp. 345–46.

10. Bartang (*bar thang*) is a locality on the slopes of Jomo Karak overlooking the Tsangpo River.

11. There was an especially beautiful statue at the nunnery of Rinchen Ding (*rin chen lding*), a monastery where Kalden Rangdrol (*skal ldan rang grol*), one of Shabkar's closest disciples, lived for some time.

12. See in the bibliography the various materials related to the *rta phag yid bzhin nor bu*.

13. The first month of each of the four seasons is a *ra wa zla ba*.

14. The gods and rakshas of the eight classes (*lha srin sde brgyad*); see CN, p. 285.

15. Pemakö (*padma bkod*), one of the main sacred "hidden lands" (*sbas yul*) connected with Vajrasattva and Guru Padmasambhava. It is located in southeast Tibet, north of the Indian state of Arunachal Pradesh.

16. *Termas* are very often discovered in the form of a yellow scroll (*shog ser*) on which are written a few syllables in symbolic dakini script (*mkha' 'gro brda yig*). These letters can only be deciphered by the tertön to whom the legacy of the spiritual treasure belongs, and are unintelligible to anyone else.

17. Shotö Terdrom at Drigung (*'bri gung gzho stod gter sgrom*); see NW, fols. 1b and 5b.

18. As explained by H.H. Dilgo Khyentse Rinpoche, in pure visions (*dag snang*) the tertön has a vision of Guru Padmasambhava or another saint from the lineage. In the direct oral transmission (*snyan brgyud*, lit. "hearing transmission"), Guru Padmasambhava appears and speaks as a real person to the tertön.

19. Chapter 6, fol. 78b.

20. The dakini Lekyi Wangmo (*mkha' 'gro las kyi dbang mo*), who received the Vajrayana teachings from Vajrasattva and transmitted them to the first human guru of this lineage, Humchenkara, one of the eight Vidyadharas of India. She also entrusted to Guru Padmasambhava, here Pemajungney (Skt. Padmakara, the "One Originated from the Lotus"), the transmission of the *Eight Commands, the Union of the Sugatas* (*bka' brgyad bde gshegs 'dus pa*).

21. The text for conferring the empowerment of the *rta phag yid bzhin nor bu*, written by Trulshik Rinpoche.

22. There seems to be no reason for identifying her with Machik Lapkyi Drönma (*ma gcig lab gyi sgron ma*, 1055–1143?), the famed incarnation of Yeshe Tsogyal who became the consort and chief disciple of Padampa Sangye and spread the teachings of Chöd in Tibet. However, if the dakini mentioned at this point were Machik, this would offer an example of *cholori (co lo ris)*, a form of lineage prayer in which the order is not based on chronology but upon a mystical order stemming from the visionary inspiration of the saint who wrote the prayer.

23. Dechen Ling, Rina Monastery (*bde chen gling ri sna dgon*). According to Ven. Khetsun Sangpo, this monastery is located by the Kyichu River, east of Lhasa.

24. Who in NW, too, is referred to as Karma Guru Ngakyi Wangpo (*ka rma gu ru ngag gi dbang po*).

25. See NW and chapter 9 of this biography, fol. 199b.

26. The "great disciple and protector of beings Pema Gyatso" (*bu chen 'gro mgon padma rgya mtsho*) is not mentioned in Shabkar's autobiography. As seen in *The Story of a Tibetan Yogini, Shuksep Jetsun* (K. Yeshi and T. Tsering, 1991), he was the main teacher of the famed woman master Shuksep Jetsun Chönyi Zang-mo (*shug gseb rje btsun cho nyid bzang mo*, 1852–1953). He was active in Kyirong (*skyid grong*). He must have been quite young when he received the transmission from Shabkar, and lived to a ripe old age since, not long before his death, he met the thirteenth Dalai Lama (1876–1933). He met Shabkar possibly in Kyirong in 1818–19, and most likely before the saint's return to Amdo in 1825. The biography of the Shuksep Jetsun gives no indication that Pema Gyatso traveled to Amdo.

27. Dza Trulshik Rinpoche, Kunzang Trinley Drodul Tsel (*kun bzang phrin las 'dro 'dul rtsal*), or Ngawang Chökyi Lodrö (*ngag dbang chos kyi blo gros*), born in 1924.

28. H.H Dilgo Khyentse Rinpoche: *Padma gar dbang 'od gsal mdo sngags gling pa.* See Translator's Introduction, note 8. His many other names include Tashi Paljor (*bkra shis dpal 'byor*), Rabsel Dawa (*rab gsal zla ba*), and Gyurme Thekchog Tenpai Gyaltsen (*'gyur med theg mchog bstan pa'i rgyal mtshan*).

29. Pelek Gonpa (*spe legs dgon pa*), the "Exemplary Monastery," so called after the remarkable stone house built there by Sangye Lama (*gter ston sangs rgyas bla ma*), the first of all tertöns. The monastery is built on the large cave of *bde chen skyid phug*, where Ra Lotsawa stayed, and is situated west of Sakya.

30. A facsimile of Shabkar's manuscript has been reproduced by Lama Ngodrup and Sherap Drimed, 1979.

Appendix 5

Shabkar's writings

In addition to having improvised a vast number of inspired songs related to the contemplative life, Shabkar was a prolific writer. His style is among the clearest and most beautiful found in Tibetan literature. Shabkar writes in the lively, often colloquial manner that later characterized Patrul Rinpoche's works such as his *Words of My Perfect Teacher (kun bzang bla ma'i zhal lung)*. Colorfully and effectively, he articulates a fresh exposition of the truths underlying the contemplative life, weaving together stories from traditional scriptures and anecdotes from recent times to make the Dharma a living reality in one's own life. Although the author's erudition is daunting, his main focus is not theoretical knowledge but bringing the essence of the teachings to life.

The evocative titles of his works—*The Mountain of Gold*, *The Songs Arisen on the Mirror of Mind*, *The Many-stringed Lute*—open the reader's mind to the teachings they contain. The expression *Emanated Scriptures* appears in the titles of nine of Shabkar's major works. In his autobiography (chap. 10), Shabkar explains, "I called these teachings 'emanated' to indicate their authenticity. They are as though emanated from earlier scriptures, just as one butter-lamp is lit from another." Shabkar's writings never remain frozen in one literary style or confined to one viewpoint. His series of *Emanated Scriptures* succeeds in capturing and conveying the savor and the essential teachings of all the main streams of Tibetan Buddhism.

Shabkar's works never fall into being mere imitations. While he makes free use of quotations from past masters, his explanations are strikingly

original, and are expressed in his own vigorous, lucid manner without lapsing into pedantry. This style became characteristic of a number of writers of the nineteenth century, a time of Renaissance in Tibetan Buddhism.

Although no listing (*dkar chag*) of Shabkar's collected works seems to have been written in the master's time, most of his works are referred to in his autobiography or in his other writings. In 1988 Jigme Thekcho included a partial list of Shabkar's writings in his *History of the Great Monastery of Rongpo*.[1] In 1993 Pal Gyalkar presented an extensive list, with abstracts, of the master's works, and an excellent analysis of his style.[2] The latter is so far the best study in the Tibetan language on Shabkar's literary production. A few of Shabkar's works described in this Appendix, however, appear in neither of these two lists.[3]

Excellent wood blocks existed at Tashikhyil Hermitage in Amdo for almost the entire corpus of Shabkar's works Through the efforts of Sangye Rinchen, one of Shabkar's close disciples, most of them were copied and carved during Shabkar's lifetime. Shortly after the master's death, Sangye Rinchen completed his task by carving both another volume of *Collected Songs* and the second part of Shabkar's autobiography (see Translator's Introduction). These wood blocks were burned during the Cultural Revolution, but printed volumes made from them were hidden and saved. Several volumes of manuscripts in Shabkar's own handwriting have also been preserved at Tashikhyil Hermitage and nearby.[4] Wood blocks for several volumes were carved too at Shuksep

Monastery under the inspiration of Shuksep Jetsun Rigdzin Chönyi Zangmo (1852–1953, see Appendix 4). Only a few prints have survived.

According to an oral communication from Khetsun Sangpo Rinpoche, several manuscript copies of Shabkar's works were preserved at Rinchen Ding in Barthang (*bar thang rin chen lding*) at the foot of Jomo Karak Mountain, in central Tibet, where Shabkar's close disciple Kalden Rangdrol lived for several years. This monastery and its treasures have been destroyed.

A few manuscripts of Shabkar's writings have come down through his disciple Jimba Norbu, who stayed with Shabkar when the master was at Mount Kailash, Lapchi, and other places. A number of Jimba Norbu's lineage-holders have kept these manuscripts at Dolpo Tarap in Nepal.

A important part of the available manu-· scripts and xylographs has been collected and reprinted in India under the inspiration of the late H.H. Dilgo Khyentse Rinpoche (see Bibliography). The Qinghai Nationalities Press in Amdo, Tibet, also reprinted the two autobiographies and two volumes of songs.

The xylographic edition of Shabkar's writings seems to have been arranged in ten volumes, designated with Tibetan letters from Ka through Ta, the last volume being marked Om. This collection begins with the two volumes of Shabkar's autobiography, continues with general Mahayana teachings, and ends with Vajrayana and Dzogchen teachings. Yet, in the absence of a complete set of xylographs, we are not able to ascertain the order of the *Collected Works* according to the Tashikhyil edition. With the exception of the autobiographies and the collections of songs, Shabkar's writings are therefore listed below chronologically, according to indications given in their colophons and in the present autobiography. Whenever known, the letter assigned to each text in the Tashikhyil edition is shown in parentheses.

THE AUTOBIOGRAPHIES

PART I

The King of Wish-Granting Jewels (*Ka*), the full title of which is *snyigs dus 'gro ba yongs kyi*

skyabs mgon zhabs dkar rdo rje 'chang chen po'i rnam par thar pa rgyas par bshad pa skal bzang gdul bya 'thar dod rnams kyi re ba skong ba'i yid bzhin gyi nor bu bsam 'phel dbang gi rgyal po. First part of volume Ka of the Tashikhyil edition, 485 fols. [SH 1]. Dolanji: Tsering Wangyal, 1975. Also published as vols. 1 and 2 of the *Collected Works of Zhabs dKar Tshogs Drug Rang Grol* (hereafter abbreviated as *Collected Works*). Paro: Lama Ngodrup and Sherap Drimey, 1980. Also Xining: Qinghai Nationalities Press (*mtsho sngon mi rigs dpe mdzod khang*) 1985. 1097 pp. [TS 1].

PART II

The Wish-fulfilling Gem (*Ka*), *'gro mgon zhabs dkar ba'i sku tshe'i smad kyi rnam thar thog mtha'i bar du dge ba yid bzhin nor bu dgos 'dod kun 'byung*. 345 fols. Completed by a section written by Changlung Tulku Khyapdal Longyang (*spyang lung sprul sku khyab brdal klong yangs*). Second part of volume Ka of the Tashikhyil edition [SH 2]. Published as vol. 3 of the *Collected Works*. Paro: Lama Ngodrup and Sherap Drimey, 1983. Also Xining: Qinghai Nationalities Press, 1986, 645 pp. [TS 2]

Early Autobiography

The actual biography, *rnam thar dngos*. Manuscript in *dbu med*, 50 fols. kept at Khakar Gonpa, Tarap Dolpo, Nepal. NGMPP, reel no. L 408/10.

Autobiographical Song

Beginning with the verse *pha yul rgya mtsho nang nas thon/ mi med ri khrod mkha' la 'phags/ tshogs drug rang grol nyi gzhon gyi/ rnam thar dri med 'od zer* . . . Manuscript in *dbu med*, 3 fols. kept at Khakar Gonpa, Tarap Dolpo, Nepal. NGMPP, reel no. L 408/9.

The contents and genesis of the two autobiographical volumes and of the early autobiography have been discussed in the Translator's Introduction. Part I covers Shabkar's life until the age of fifty-six, and Part II, from the age of fifty-six to seventy. The section written by Changlung Tulku Khyapdal Longyang includes facts and miraculous events not mentioned in the autobiographies, and describes as well the last moments of the master's life. An esoteric autobiography of Shabkar (*gsang ba'i rnam thar*) is known to exist in Amdo.

The Festival of Melodious Songs

bya btang tshogs drug rang grol gyis rang dang skal ldan gdul bya la mgrin pa gdams pa'i dang mdzod nas glu dbyangs dga' ston 'gyed pa rnams. Volume Kha of the Tashikhyil edition. Xining: Qinghai Nationalities Press. Vol. 1, 1987, 846 pp. [TS 3] Vol. 2, 1988, 872 pp. [TS 4]. TS 3 has also been reproduced from a print of the Tashikhyil edition and published as volume 4 of the *Collected Works*, 380 fols. Paro: Lama Ngodrup and Sherap Drimey, 1983.

Early one morning at Amnye Machen (see chap. 7, fol. 13ab), Shabkar had a vision of a king who told him, "It is very wonderful that you adhere to the life-style of our holy predecessors, singing songs of the sacred teachings. I name you 'Bard of the Land of Snows'. It is most kind of you to leave thousands of songs as the heritage of Tibet. They will bring immense benefit to faithful disciples."

Shabkar is often compared to Milarepa, not only for his way of life and his spiritual accomplishments, but also for his amazing ability to improvise extemporaneous songs. From down-to-earth advice on ethics and conduct, through highly ornate poetry sent to spiritual masters and kings, up to songs setting forth the vastness of the Dzogchen view, each song has a particular flavor. In whatever style he chooses to adopt, the Bard of Tibet effortlessly displays his mastery of all facets of Tibetan literary art.

The collections of songs are a mine of information about both Shabkar's activities and his disciples. Several smaller collections were gathered at every sacred place where Shabkar spent time: Lake Kokonor, Tsari, Mount Kailash, Lapchi, etc. (See below under Miscellaneous Writings). Later, many of the songs were incorporated in the two autobiographies (see Translator's Introduction, p. xix). Yet, there were still enough written songs left to fill two more volumes. The complete edition, which contains over a thousand songs, has been published by the Qinghai Nationalities Press.

PRINCIPAL WRITINGS

The Flight of the Garuda

'od gsal rdzogs pa chen po'i khregs chod lta ba'i glu dbyangs sa lam ma lus myur du bgrod pa'i rtsal ldan mkha' lding gshog rlabs (fols. 1–29), together with *'od gsal rdzogs pa chen po'i lhun grub thod rgal gyi glu dbyangs ting 'dzin sgo 'phar brgya phrag cig car 'byed pa'i lde mig* (fols. 30–55), and *thod rgal gyi gnad kyi zhal shes mgur dbyangs bdud rtsi'i bum bzang* (fols. 55–61). Part of volume Ta of the Tashikhyil edition. Wood blocks have also been carved at Tashijong Khampagar, Kangra, India (75 fols.).

Composed at Tsonying Island when the author was around twenty-six (1807), this is perhaps Shabkar's most famous work. In twenty-three short songs addressed to his disciples, it introduces—with striking beauty, simplicity, and clarity—the profound view, meditation and practice of Dzogchen, the Great Perfection.

The *Flight of the Garuda* (*mkha' lding gshog rlabs*), which gives its name to the collection, is the first part of a trilogy; it focuses on the Trekchö section of Dzogchen practice, which leads directly to realization of the ultimate nature of mind. It has been translated into English by E. Schmidt (1987) and by Keith Dowman (1993), and in part into German by Franz-Karl Ehrhard (1990). The latter also offers a detailed analysis of the text and its background. The second part, in eighteen songs, presents the fundamentals of Thögal, the ultimate practice of Dzogchen. The third part, in three songs, elucidates actual instructions for that visionary practice, based on the oral tradition. Because of their highly esoteric nature these last two parts were not included in the above translations.

The Torch That Illuminates the Graded Path

mi shes mun pa thug po sel ba'i lam rim gsal ba'i sgron me. 61 fols. Tashikhyil edition. Paro: Lama Ngodrup and Sherap Drimey, 1983.

In 1808, on Tsonying Island, Shabkar had a dream: he ascended a long crystal staircase to the top of a jewel mountain, upon which he met a lama of resplendent dignity. "One never tired of looking at him; the mere sight of his face put an end to mind's delusion." This lama was Guru Padmasambhava appearing in the form of Tsongkhapa.[5] He was teaching the *Condensed Graded Path* to a retinue of disciples; at the end of the teaching, he gave the book to Shabkar. (See chap. 6, fol. 117a)

Inspired by this dream, disciples requested that Shabkar compose a teaching in verse on the graded path (*lam rim*), easy to comprehend and to practice. In answer to their request, he wrote *The Torch That Illuminates the Graded Path* (*lam rim gsal ba'i sgron me*). Shabkar's intention was to write an intermediate version of the *Graded Path* teachings of Tsong-khapa—shorter than the lengthy *Great Graded Path* (*lam rim chen mo*), yet more detailed than the *Condensed Meaning of the Graded Path* (*lam rim bsdus don*). Composed in verses of fifteen syllables each, this treatise is the most formal of Shabkar's works.

The Beneficial Sun, A Dharma Discourse

> *chos bshad gzhan phan nyi ma*, composed in 1811, at Chölung near Lhasa. Part of volume Ja of Tashikhyil edition, 122 fols. Also manuscript in *dbu med*, 166 fols. Paro: Lama Ngodrup and Sherap Drimey, 1983.

"Scholars," says Shabkar, "can deliver a stream of teachings in a profound and elegant way that delights the learned, but might provide no help to ordinary, uneducated people. Such people sometimes emerge from a long session of teachings with nothing to keep in mind and nothing to pass on to others. They can only say, 'The master spoke at length, but we did not understand what he said. We would like to practice, but we don't know how to begin.'"

In order to benefit everyone, even the most uneducated people, Shabkar composed this text. He said, "When my disciples kept on asking for these teachings, I had no book from which to draw stories and quotations; yet like a generous person who turns his bag inside out and pours all the contents onto a cloth spread on the ground,

without holding anything back, I wrote down everything that came into my mind and called it *The Beneficial Sun.*"

The structure of this text is typical of several other writings of Shabkar that focus on Mahayana training. Beginning with the basic law of karma, cause and effect, he explains how negative thoughts and actions lead to suffering and positive ones bring happiness. He also explains the value of human existence: to misuse or squander this life is like filling a jeweled golden vase with filth. Through vividly depicting the sufferings of animals, he stresses the evils of hunting, fishing, butchering animals, and eating meat.

Having emphasized the essential role of loving-kindness, compassion, and Bodhicitta as the very essence of the Mahayana path, Shabkar exhorts everyone to be altruistic and open-minded, to have a good heart, and to renounce selfishness and all the deluded pursuits of this ephemeral world. Finally, he explains the importance of dedicating the merits of virtuous actions to the benefit of others.

The Beneficial Moon, The Beneficial Jewel and *The Offering Cloud of Samantabhadra*

> *chos bshad gzhan phan zla ba*, composed at Tsari in 1812. Tashikhyil edition, 171 fols. Also manuscript in *dbu chen* of 178 fols., kept in Kyermi, Humla, Nepal. NGMPP, reel no. E 2723/11 to 2724/1.

> *chos bshad gzhan phan nor bu*, composed at Tsari in 1812. Tashikhyil edition, 247 fols.

> *chos bshad kun bzang mchod sprin*, composed at Tsari in 1812. Tashikhyil edition, 86 fols.

These three texts were composed at Tsari in 1812. For the benefit of disciples living in solitary mountain retreats, Shabkar wrote *The Beneficial Moon* (*chos bshad gzhan phan zla ba*), studding it with sayings of the saints of the Kagyu lineage. Among all of Shabkar's writings, this text offers the strongest incentive to give up the ordinary affairs of this world. It presents nonattachment and renunciation as the keys to spiritual progress and happiness. If no inner transformation comes out of study, meditation and action, it is because of desiring the pleasures of this life. Shabkar exhorts us to go to a secluded mountain retreat without postponing our spiritual practice any further. A novice practitioner who practices in bustling places stacks all the odds against his or her success on the spiritual path. On the contrary, solitary places allow even vulnerable beginners to foster their progress without hindrance. Although the welfare of beings must be their only preoccupation, immature practitioners should not hasten to help or teach others before they have developed a stable realization. Shabkar wrote the *Beneficial Jewel* and the *Samantabhadra Offering-Cloud* (*chos bshad gzhan phan nor bu* and *chos bshad kun bzang mchod sprin*) in response to disciples who asked for a text that would expound the Buddhadharma according to a nonsectarian point of view and generate faith, respect, and pure perception.

The Emanated Scriptures of the Kadampas

> *bka' gdams sprul pa'i glegs bam.* Part of vol. Kha of Tashikhyil edition, 233 fols. Also, manuscript in *dbu med* of 171 fols. Paro: Lama Ngodrup and Sherap Drimey, 1983.

By Shabkar's own account, this work—composed at Mount Kailash around 1815—was intended to make the meaning of the Kadampas' *Graded Path* easily intelligible to ordinary people. The text is a perfect example of Shabkar's above-mentioned colorful style. Beginning with renunciation and culminating with the six *paramitas*, it abounds with stories and anecdotes illustrating teachings on the practices for various individuals with limited, medium, and superior faculties. It may be considered a lively, expanded version of *The Torch That Illuminates the Graded Path.*

The Emanated Scriptures of Manjushri

> *'jam dbyangs sprul pa'i glegs bam.* Tashikhyil edition, 155 fols. Also manuscript in *dbu can*, 109 fols., published as vol. 5 of the *Collected Works.* Paro: Lama Ngodrup and Sherap Drimey, 1984.

Composed at the Cave of Miracles (*rdzu 'phrul phug*) close to Mount Kailash around 1815, this compendium of spiritual instructions is written in the form of questions and answers between Shabkar and his disciples. It presents the essence of the Great Graded Path, Mind Training, Mahamudra, Dzogchen, and the Dohas.[6] In a hundred folios containing twenty-two pieces of advice, Shabkar states in a clear and effective way the essentials of spiritual practice: the need to renounce the world, to rely on a spiritual master, and to unite meditation on emptiness with compassion. He also explains how to practice meditation and maintain at all times the insight thus gained, how to practice absolute Bodhicitta and realize the union of appearance and emptiness, how to merge one's mind with the guru's mind, how to liberate thoughts as they arise; and how to cultivate nonsectarian pure perception toward all the different teachings. Shabkar's style here is crisp and concise, as if he had intended to define each step of the contemplative life in the most brief, yet complete, way for practitioners.

The Emanated Scriptures of the Bodhisattva

> *rgyal sras sprul pa'i glegs bam.* Tashikhyil edition, 181 fols.

According to Shabkar's reference in chap. 11 (fol. 263a), one may assume that this text was composed at Mount Kailash around 1815. In chap. 13 (fol. 358b), Shabkar also mentions giving the transmission for this text in 1819 at Lapchi. This volume, in seven sections, derives its name from its basis in the life and teachings of the great Bodhisattva Ngulchu Gyalse Thogme Zangpo, an emanation of Avalokiteshvara and a prior incarnation of Shabkar (see Translator's Introduction, p. xx).

The Marvelous Emanated Scriptures

> *ngo mtshar sprul pa'i glegs bam.* Tashikhyil edition, 163 fols. Also manuscript in *dbu med*, 109 fols. Paro: Lama Ngodrup and Sherab Drimey, 1985.

Composed at Shephel Ling Monastery in Purang, western Tibet, during the winter of 1817–18, this volume is, in Shabkar's words, "based on the teachings and stories found in the discourses of Buddha Shakyamuni and in various writings of learned and accomplished sages of India and Tibet."

It opens with a praise to the Twelve Deeds of the Buddha, then goes on to describe how, during his past lives, the Bodhisattva, who was to become the Awakened One, first developed the wish to attain enlightenment for the sake of all sentient beings. It tells of thirty-four former existences of Buddha Shakyamuni—of how he accumulated merit and wisdom over the course of three kalpas, and was willing to endure immense hardship in order to receive even a few words of the teachings.

The second part of the text exhorts readers to emulate the example of this peerless being. With examples and stories, it emphasizes the importance of reflecting on impermanence and death, and explains in great detail the law of karma, of cause and effect. The third and fourth parts, once again with the help of didactic stories, explain how lay people can live in harmony with the Dharma. This text became very popular in central Tibet.

The Amazing Emanated Scriptures

ya mtshan sprul pa'i glegs bam. Tashikhyil edition, 67 fols. Also manuscript in *dbu can,* 88 fols. Darjeeling: Lama Dawa and Chopal Lama, 1984.

Composed at Khardo Samten Ling Hermitage near Lhasa in 1825, this treatise leads one to consider the five sense-pleasures and the problems that attachment to them creates, particularly attachment to food, clothing, and sex. It then tells of the need to rid oneself of the preoccupations of this life and to give oneself over to spiritual practice in solitary places, unattached to one's body, one's life, or one's possessions, explaining the joy that such renunciation brings about.

The Wondrous Emanated Scriptures

rmad byung sprul pa'i glegs bam. Part of vol. Cha of Tashikhyil edition, 112 fols. Also, manuscript in *dbu can,* 119 fols. Darjeeling: Lama Dawa and Chopal Lama, 1984.

This text was composed at Tashikhyil Hermitage after Shabkar's return from central Tibet. It opens with a powerful admonition against eating meat, one of Shabkar's favorite themes. Shabkar quotes at length several Mahayana sutras, especially the *Lankavatara Sutra* (often said to be "the quintessence of the Buddha's words"), in which the Buddha says, "Those who practice loving-kindness should consider all sentient beings as their own children; therefore, they must give up eating meat." The sixth chapter of this sutra is entirely devoted to condemnation of the eating of meat.

Contrary to common belief, not only the sutras but also the tantras condemn meat-eating. The *Tantra of the Great Compassionate One Who Dredges the Depths of Samsara* (*thugs rje chen po 'khor ba dong sprug gi rgyud*), for instance, says that the result of eating meat is rebirth in the hell realm for one kalpa. If one eats the meat of an animal one has killed oneself or asked someone to kill for oneself, one will be reborn in the hell realm for a hundred thousand kalpas.

Many great saints of the past have denounced meat-eating. The "divine madman" Drukpa Kunleg, seeing monks going to buy meat at the autumn market, exclaimed, "Here is a den of wolves, here is a den of wolves!" And Milarepa said, "Having slaughtered innocent animals, one eats their flesh and drinks intoxicants: all the conditions come together for rebirth in the hell realm."

The second section of the text depicts the negative effects of drinking. It quotes Guru Padmasambhava and Lord Buddha, who said, "Whoever drinks a drop of alcohol is not my disciple." The third section discusses sex, presenting it as a compulsive craving that leads to all kinds of negative behavior. The concluding section depicts the dreadful karmic consequences of killing any living being.

The Emanated Scriptures of Pure Vision

dag snang sprul pa'i glegs bam. Part of vol. Tha of Tashikhyil edition, 135 fols. Published as vol. 5 of the *Collected Works.* Paro: Lama Ngodrup and Sherap Drimey, 1984.

This text stands somewhat apart from Shabkar's other works. In many of his writings, Shabkar emphasizes the approach of Mind Training, including renunciation of worldly pleasures, since such an approach is suited to most practitioners. Here, Shabkar explains the fundamentals of the path that utilizes sense-pleasures and bliss as catalysts for spiritual progress. He clearly delineates the conditions that must be fulfilled by the exceptional practitioners who can perform such practices in a valid way.

Shabkar wrote this text when his disciples requested that he compose a teaching that would universally inspire pure vision toward Vajrayana yogins. In the colophon Shabkar mentions that he first conceived the wish to write such a text when he saw, during his travels, that many people thoughtlessly criticized practitioners of the Vajrayana who did not renounce meat, alcohol, and sex. In the introduction he states, "Although many individuals in this age appear to be merely indulging their worldly desires, one does not have the capacity to judge them, so it is best to train in pure vision."

With the help of many quotations he defends the Nyingma tradition against its detractors, warning that it is a serious fault to disparage an authentic tradition because of prejudice and ignorance. He also shows that all views and traditions are mutually noncontradictory and lead to the same goal.

Sense-pleasures, says Shabkar, are like fire: if one does not know how to use them, one gets burned. Yet, for a genuine Vajrayana practitioner, bliss and the experiences of the five senses are offerings to the Three Roots and effect swift progress toward realization. It is craving and attachment that make one fall into the lower realms, not sense-pleasure itself.

Shabkar also explains at length that one should treat one's human body properly, using proper food and clothing to sustain one's life and use it solely to practice the Dharma. One needs to renounce worldly concerns but not to mistreat one's body. Extreme asceticism is inappropriate.

Shabkar also explains the reasons why the Vajrayana must be kept secret, and concludes, "Since one cannot judge the actions of Bodhisattvas and great *siddhas*, one must cultivate pure perception toward them. Yet, immature disciples should not thoughtlessly try to imitate them."

The Mountain of Gold

rang gzhan thams cad 'tshengs pa'i gdams ngag gser gyi ri bo. 47 fols. Tashikhyil edition.

This instruction, composed at Tashikhyil Hermitage around 1845, refers to various activities related to the preparation for spiritual practice and what comes after it. It emphasizes the benefit of cleaning temples, of displaying sacred images, and of arranging offerings properly and beautifully. These, and others, are the various methods that allow one to perfect the twofold accumulation of wisdom and merit. The text then tells how to behave and perform virtuous practices in between meditation sessions and, finally, how to dedicate any merit through prayers of aspiration.

The Emanated Scriptures of Orgyen

bstan 'gro yongs la phan pa'i o rgyan sprul pa'i glegs bam. 106 fols. Vol. Om of Tashikhyil edition. Dolanji: Tsering Wangyal, 1975.

Once, in his old age, Shabkar had a vision of Guru Padmasambhava. In this vision he told Guru Rinpoche, "I have prayed to you throughout my life, yet before now I was not blessed by a vision of you." Guru Rinpoche replied, "Don't you remember the vision you had on The Heart of the Lake Island? That was me." Thus he indicated that it was he who had appeared to Shabkar in the form of Tsongkhapa. Following this vision of Guru Padmasambhava, Shabkar wrote the *Emanated Scriptures of Orgyen* at Tashikhyil Hermitage around 1845 (see SH, vol. 2, p. 349).

The first section describes how our universe—with its countless realms, Buddhas, and sentient beings—appeared within the unchanging primordial emptiness, like a rainbow appearing in space or the reflection of the moon upon the surface of a lake. Shabkar then explains how various impure and pure perceptions, samsara and nirvana, came about through the process of dependent arising. In infinite Buddhafields and in every atom of the universe, infinite Buddhas manifest infinite forms to meet the aspirations and capacities of beings and free them from ignorance and suffering. Shabkar shows how, with pure perception, one can consider the whole phenomenal world as the manifestation of Guru Padmasambhava.

The second section is chiefly devoted to demonstrating the authenticity of the tantras and *termas* of the Nyingma tradition. Shabkar shows that *termas* are found in all lineages of Indian and Tibetan Buddhism, not exclusively in the Nyingma lineage, and he quotes great masters from various schools who indicate that the *terma* tradition is especially needed and appropriate for this "final age."

The third section describes how Lord Atisha Dipamkara and Tsongkhapa Lobzang Trakpa were both emanations of Padmasambhava. The second Dalai Lama, Gedun Gyatso, for instance, wrote,

> Awareness Holder, the Lord of Siddhas, Padmakara,
> Crest Ornament of five hundred [*panditas*], the glorious Dipamkara,
> Mighty Vajra Bearer, the exalted Lobzang Trakpa:
> I bow down to you who display the dance of various emanations.

Arik Geshe (see Translator's Introduction, p. xxix n. 46), a great nonsectarian Gelukpa master, also said, "To be able to practice the Dharma is due to the unique kindness of Guru Padmasambhava, who bound under oath all negative forces in Tibet."

Having thus quoted many masters from all schools, Shabkar lays special emphasis on the important relationship between the Nyingma master Lodrak Drupchen Lekyi Dorje and Tsongkhapa.[7] The oral tradition also says that Lekyi Dorje described Tsongkhapa as someone who attained instant realization (*gcig char ba*).[8] Tsongkhapa used to ask Lekyi Dorje questions to clarify profound aspects of his spiritual practice. Lekyi Dorje, who had frequent visions of Vajrapani, the "Lord of Secrets," would present these queries to Vajrapani, and convey the latter's answers to Tsongkhapa. These answers are pure Dzogchen teachings, highly similar in word and content to those of Padmasambhava's *Khandro Nyingthig* (see chap. 3, note 16). When he first encountered Lekyi Dorje, Tsongkhapa was on his way to India to meet Indian *panditas* in order to clarify his understanding of the doctrine. However, according to some prophecies he received, Lekyi Dorje persuaded Tsongkhapa to remain in Tibet. This event had an immense impact on the unfolding of the history of Tibet.

The fourth section is a final encouragement to disentangle oneself from the bonds of samsara and quickly reach Buddhahood: maintaining pure vision toward all teachings, one must follow the life-examples of all the masters of the past.

The Stream of Ambrosia, An Excellent Discourse

legs bshad bdud rtsi'i chu rgyun. Manuscript in *dbu med* kept at Tashikhyil Hermitage. We did not have access to this text.

The Self-Arising Sun

legs bshad nyi ma rang shar. 116 fols.

A text focused on the "view" of emptiness, mentioned by Pal Gyalkar (1993).

The Emanated Scriptures of Compassion

snying rje sprul pa'i glegs bam. Part of vol. Cha of Tashikhyil edition, 61 fols.

This is Shabkar's last major work (together with the second part of his autobiography), composed at Tashikhyil Hermitage around 1846 (see SH, vol. 2, p. 363). It opens with a beautiful hymn to compassion, adorned with many quotations that Shabkar collected throughout his life. It continues with two sections in which he again condemns uncompromisingly the eating of meat by Buddhist practitioners. On the Mahayana path, says Shabkar, eating meat, at the cost of great suffering for animals, is unacceptable.[9] In the *Sutra of The Great Nirvana* (*Mahaparinirvana-sutra*), the Buddha said, "The eating of meat annihilates the seed of compassion," and in the *Lankavatara Sutra* he taught, "If, bereft of compassion and wisdom, you eat meat, you have turned your back on liberation. . . . Meat is food for ferocious beasts, improper to eat."

Shabkar articulates here the most sweeping indictment against meat-eating found in Tibetan literature. This was particularly relevant at a time when the prediction the Buddha made in the *Lankavatara Sutra* had already become a reality: "In the future, meat-eaters, speaking out of ignorance, will say that the Buddha permitted the eating of meat, and that he taught there was no sin in doing so."

MISCELLANEOUS WRITINGS

Words of Advice to Self and Others

rang gzhan gyi sems la phan pa'i gsung nye mkho kha shas. Manuscript in *dbu med*, 202 fols. NGMPP, reel no. L 178/3.

The manuscript of this collection was lost in the fire that destroyed Thangboche Monastery (Nepal) in 1988. Fortunately, it has been preserved on microfilm through the efforts of the Nepal German Manuscript Preservation Project (NGMPP).

The Tsari Songs

bya btang tshogs drug rang grol gyis phyogs med ri khrod 'grims pa'i tshe rang gzhan chos la bskul ba'i phyir glu dbyangs blangs tshul rim pa. Manuscript in *dbu med*, 44 fols. NGMPP, reel no. L 315/9. (Folio 17 missing.)

The contents and arrangement of this *dbu med* manuscript preserved in Trulshik Rinpoche's library are almost identical to the section on *Tsari Songs* in TS 4, but it contains a few short pieces not found in TS 4.

Songs Arisen in the Mirror of Mind

bya btang tshogs drug rang grol gyis sems nyid me long gsal la mgur dbyangs gzugs brnyan gang shar rnams yi ge'i gzugs su bris pa. Manuscript in *dbu med* from Dolpo Tarap in northwest Nepal, 76 fols. [DOL 1].

This manuscript contains seventy-nine pieces: thirteen songs that were incorporated into the beginning of the eleventh chapter of the autobiography, sixty-two songs which were incorporated in *The Collected Songs* (TS 4), and four songs that are found in neither of these two. This collection was gathered by Orgyan Tendzin (*o rgyan bstan 'dzin*), a disciple of Jimba Norbu (*sbyin pa nor bu*; see Appendix 6) active in Dolpo Tarap. For a discussion on DOL 1, 2, 3 and the genesis of Shabkar's autobiography, see the Translator's Introduction, p. xix.

Short Biography with the Kailash Songs

rje btsun tshogs drug rang grol gyi rnam thar bsdus pa dang gangs rir mdzad pa'i mgur ma. Manuscript in *dbu med* from Dolpo Tarap in northwest Nepal, 43 fols. [DOL 2].

This second manuscript from Dolpo contains forty-one songs and pieces of advice. Out of these, ten were incorporated in the eleventh chapter of the autobiography, twenty-one were incorporated in the *Collected Songs* (TS 4), and ten are not found elsewhere.

The Many-Stringed Lute

bya btang tshogs drug rang grol gyis phyogs med rgyal khams 'grim pa'i tshe dad can snang 'gyur ba'i thabs mgur dbyangs pi wang rgyud mangs. Manuscript in *dbu med* from Dolpo Tarap in northwest Nepal, 117 fols. [DOL 3].

Out of the sixty pieces contained in this collection, fifteen have been incorporated in TS 4, eight in chapter 11, twenty in chapter 12, and four in chapter 13. The few pieces original to this collection include a devotional prayer to Jimba Norbu composed by Shabkar at Lapchi, as well as prayers to the lineage of the Mahamudra teachings, the lineage of Nagarjuna's Profound View (*zab mo lta brgyud*), and of the lineage of the *Dzogchen Khandro Nyingthig* (*rdzogs chen mkha' 'gro snying thig*). One also finds a supplication for Shabkar's long life offered by the government of Tibet (*zhung dga' ldan pho brang*). The collection ends with an appeal to benefactors for the restoration of the Tashi Gomang stupa at Chung Riwoche (*gcung ri bo che'i bkra shis sgo mang*), which must have been written in 1824 (see chap. 14).

The Biography of Namkha Jigme

grub pa'i dbang phyug dam pa dpal chen nam mkha' 'jigs med mchog gi rnam par thar pa snying por dril ba skal bzang thar pa 'khrid pa'i ded dpon. 51 fols.

This biography of Changlung Namkha Jigme, 1769–1833 (see Appendix 6), is mentioned by Pal Gyalkar (1993).

The Arrow of Scriptures and Reason

dug don lung dang rigs pa'i mda' mo. 12 fols., MGMPP, reel no. L 26318.

This short text explains the harmful effects of smoking tobacco. Tibetan Buddhism, and, in particular, the Nyingmapa school, is one of the only religious traditions that consider smoking tobacco as a major source of obstacles to spiritual practice. See also Dudjom Rinpoche (1978).

The Swift Gathering of Blessing

bla ma'i gsol 'debs byin rlabs myur 'jugs. Manuscript in *dbu med*, 2 fols. A prayer to Shabkar, composed at Mt. Kailash.

The Swift Path of Guru Yoga

myur lam bla ma'i rnal 'byor. Manuscript in *dbu med*, 4 fols. A general *guru yoga* applicable to all teachers, composed at Mt. Kailash.

The Blazing Jewel That Grants All Wishes

smon lam 'dod 'byung nor bu 'od 'bar. A prayer to accompany lamp-offerings. Mentioned in chap. 9, fol. 200b, this piece was probably composed in Lhasa around 1810–11 and has not been found.

The White Path of Liberation

dkar chag thar lam dkar po. A description of the offering of a coat of gold to the Great Stupa of Bodhnath, Kathmandu, Nepal in 1821. Not found.

The Bright Mirror Record

dkar chag gsal ba'i me long. The detailed list and description of the restoration work of the Great Tashi Gomang stupa of Chung Riwoche (*cung ri bo che'i bkra shis sgo mang mchod rten chen po*), in Tö, composed at Chung Riwoche in 1824 (see chap. 14, fol. 397a). Not found.

The Golden Garland of Dedications

bsngo ba gser gyi phreng ba. A prayer used for dedicating virtuous deeds. (See chap. 12, fol. 314a). Not found.

The Golden Scapel

legs bshad gser gyi thur ma, composed at Tashikhyil Hermitage. Wood-block print from Lhasa, carved in 1842 or 1902, 27 fols., and manuscript in *dbu chen*, 22 fols.

One of the most famous short Dzogchen instructions for recognizing the fundamental nature of mind.

The Spontaneously Arising Sun of Happiness

chos spyod smon lam rim pa bde skyid nyi ma rang sha, 14 fols.

A liturgical text arranged for the daily recitation of basic Buddhist practices such as taking refuge, generating loving-kindness, compassion, and Bodhicitta, as well as the dedication of merit.

The Wish-Fulfilling Gem and *The Heart Jewel,* two mind teachings.

sems khrid yid bzhin nor bu, composed at Kuntuzangpo Forest Hermitage, manuscript in *dbu med*, 8 fols., and *sems khrid snying gi nor bu*, wood-block print, 5 fols.

The Axe to Cut Through Taking Self and Phenomena as Real

zab lam gcod kyi ngag 'don bdag 'dzin gcod pa'i sta re. Manuscript in *dbu med*, 4 fols. NGMPP, reel no. L 309/5.

A liturgical text for the practice of Chöd (see Author's Introduction, note 32).

Consecration Ritual

rab gnas bsdus pa, 2 fols. Manuscript in *dbu can* preserved at Serang Gonpa, Nepal. NGMPP, reel no. L 342/3.

Prayer

Beginning with the words, "*bla ma dkon mchog gsum la phyag 'tshal lo.*" 2 fols.

This is a prayer used for dedicating virtuous deeds to the benefit of all sentient beings, the continuation of the Buddhist teachings, and the longevity of spiritual masters.

Notes

1. In his *History of the Great Monastery of Rongpo* (RO, p. 646), Jigme Thekcho, speaks of twenty-two major works of Shabkar: nine "Emanated Scriptures" (*sprul pa'i glegs bam*), three "Excellent Discourses" (*legs bshad*), three "Dharma Discourses" (*chos bshad*), three "Songs on the View" (*lta mgur*), and four "Autobiographical Songs" (*rnam mgur*). However, he does not identify them individually.

The nine "Emanated Scriptures" have been reviewed above. The three "Excellent Discourses" are *The Self-arising Sun* (*legs bshad nyi ma rang shar*), *The Golden Scalpel* (*legs bshad gser gyi thur ma*), and *The Offering-Cloud of Samantabhadra* (*legs bshad kun bzang mchod sprin*).

In his autobiography, Shabkar mentions four, not three, "Dharma Discourses": *The Beneficial Sun* (*chos bshad gzhan phan nyi ma*), *The Beneficial Moon* (*chos bshad gzhan phan zla ba*), *The Beneficial Jewel* (*chos bshad gzhan phan nor bu*) and *The Offering-Cloud of Samantabhadra* (*chos bshad kun bzang mchod sprin*).

The three "Songs on the View" may correspond to the trilogy of *The Flight of the Garuda*. The identification of the four "Autobiographical Songs" is also unclear, although here and there in the autobiography Shabkar offers summaries of his life (for example, in chapters 11 and 15).

2. Pal Gyalkar (1992) speaks of twenty-five major works. To Jigme Thekcho's catalog, he adds a list of miscellaneous writings:

The Biography of Namkha Jigme (*grub pa'i dbang phyug dam pa dpal chen nam mkha' 'jigs med mchog gi rnam par thar pa snying por dril ba skal bzang thar pa 'khrid pa'i ded dpon*), *The Torch That Illuminates the Graded Path* (*lam rim gsal ba'i sgron me*), *A Treatise on the View* (*legs bshad nyi ma rang shar*), *The Many-stringed Lute* (*springs yig pi wang rgyud mangs*), *Opening the Door of Compassion* (*snying rje sgo 'byed*), *Opening the Door of Faith* (*dad pa'i sgo 'byed*), *The Song to Rejoice Lobzang* (*blo bzang dgyes pa'i glu dbyangs*), (*grangs 'drin me tog phreng ba blo gsal gzhon nu'i mgul rgyan*), *The Song of Remembering My Mother* (*a ma dran pa'i mgur*), *The Spontaneously Arising Sun of Happiness* (*bde skyid nyi ma rang shar*), *The Instruction That Alone Frees All* (*gdams pa gcig shes kun grol*), *Commentary upon the Three Sentences that Strike to the Vital Point* (*tshig gsum gnad rdegs kyi 'grel ba*), *Advice to My Disciples* (*bu slob zhal gdams*), and *Advice to My Benefactors* (*yon bdag zhal gdams*).

3. These include *The Mountain of Gold* (*gdams ngag gser gyi ri bo*), and a few of the miscellaneous works.

4. Communicated to H.H. Dilgo Khyentse

Rinpoche by Alak Sherap, who was in charge of Tashikhyil Hermitage until his death in 1992, and by Matthew Kapstein, on the basis of interviews with students of Alak Namkha.

5. Shabkar did not realize this at the time of his vision, but understood later when he had a vision of Guru Padmasambhava himself (see *o rgyan sprul pa'i glegs bam*, p. 575).

6. *Doha*, mystical songs of the great *siddhas*.

7. On the relation between Lhodrak Drupchen and Tsongkhapa, see Ehrhard (1989).

8. Communicated by the late Khenpo Trinle Wangyal from Gemang monastery in Dzachuka (*rdza chu kha dge mang dgon*).

9. According to some Hinayana treatises, meat-eating is tolerated to a certain extent, under the so-called "three conditions": 1) that one has not killed the animal oneself; 2) that one has not ordered its killing; 3) that it has not been purposely killed for one's own consumption.

The Mahayana view understands that meat is sold purely because of consumer demand. Therefore, only the meat of animals who have died of natural or accidental causes is suitable to be eaten, a rare occurrence. In Mahayana sutras it is explained that applying the "three conditions" to oneself is a method that should result in one's becoming more aware and responsible, and thus help one to stop eating meat. It is not intended to suggest that, even though these "three conditions" may have been met, eating meat is suitable for a Buddhist practitioner.

Appendix 6

Shabkar's disciples

In Buddhist teachings, it is said that, just as bees swarm around a flower filled with nectar, disciples will gather around a master replete with wisdom and compassion. This was certainly the case with Shabkar, who inspired fervent devotion in the many disciples who flocked to him.

Shabkar never changed his ascetic life-style, which was always that of a wandering renunciate. However, after his fame spread through Tibet, when he was walking from one holy place to another he would sometimes be followed by hundreds of disciples and beggars, and be awaited by thousands of people who came to see him passing by and to seek his blessing.

At the end of his autobiography Shabkar says, "I had over one hundred great, learned and accomplished disciples who were mindful of the law of cause and effect, maintained pure discipline and had good hearts; who realized the natural state; who thoroughly assimilated the practices of the developing and completion stages and had visions of their *yidam;* who were aware of the happiness and the suffering of others, as well as their own good and bad qualities, and were thus able to benefit both the Dharma and sentient beings.

"I had over three hundred disciples who were practitioners trained in the Bodhicitta practice of cherishing others more than themselves, were filled with compassion, and never ate meat. I had one thousand eight hundred disciples—monks, nuns, and hermits—who, coming from all directions and all lands, lived in the mountains, kept pure vows and *samayas,*

and gave up all concern for the affairs of this life.

"Finally, I had countless disciples who were monks and nuns living in monasteries, disciples who worked hard at making offerings, prostrations, circumambulations, prayers, and recitations; village *ngakpas* who practiced at recitation and meditation on the *yidam* deities; and laymen and women who took temporary vows and vows of fasting, and recited the *mani.*"

Only a small fraction of Shabkar's spiritual heirs are mentioned in his autobiography and in his other writings, such as the *Collected Songs.* It appears, from these texts, that Shabkar's chief disciples were Pema Rangdrol and Kalden Rangdrol in Amdo, and Jimba Norbu in western Tibet. In his *History of the Great Monastery of Rongpo* (RO, p. 646), Jigme Thekchog speaks of six main disciples by the name of Rangdrol: Kalden Rangdrol, Pema Rangdrol, Kunzang Rangdrol, Natsok Rangdrol, Gangshar Rangdrol, and Jamyang Rangdrol. (This enumeration, however, refers to disciples from Amdo.) Shabkar's lineage has also been passed on through important disciples from central and western Tibet. A few details about Shabkar's main disciples are presented below.

PEMA RANGDROL

Pema Rangdrol, otherwise known as Sengzang Gyatso and Rigdzin Dawa, had also been a close disciple of the Dharma King Ngakyi Wangpo. Shabkar refers to him as "great spiritual son" (*bu chen*) or as "lord of the accomplished ones" (*grub dbang*), saying, "The great spiritual son, Lama Pema Rangdrol, had received many instructions and empowerments from Chögyal Rinpoche . . . I also gave him many transmissions, instructions, and much personal advice—although this was like using a butter-lamp to light up the daytime. Later, he went on to the Golden Valley of Rekong, and there, in the solitude of the heights of Tashikhyil, a place foretold by deities and gurus, he concentrated on practice for many years. In this way, he produced immeasurable benefit for the Dharma and for all sentient beings. The details can be found in his biography."[1]

Throughout his life, in Amdo and in central Tibet, Pema Rangdrol visited Shabkar many times to receive his guidance. When Pema Rangdrol died in 1837, Shabkar performed the funeral ceremonies and erected a stupa containing the disciple's relics (see TS 2, pp. 183–84 and 202). Pema Rangdrol's reincarnation was born into the family of Alak Khandro and was active in the areas of Kyamru and Kangtsa.

KALDEN RANGDROL

Kalden Rangdrol, also referred to in this autobiography as Lhundrup Rigdzin, was one of Shabkar's earliest and closest disciples. He accompanied his teacher for most of his life, from Amdo to Mount Kailash and Lapchi. Shabkar sent him to Nepal as his representative for the consecration of the newly gilded Great Stupa of Bodhnath (see chap. 13, fol. 369b) and speaks of him as "great *siddha*" and "precious heart-son." It is to him that Shabkar sang his famous advice on compassion (chap. 13, fol. 365) that begins:

> Sky-yogin, endowed with realization,
> Fortunate son, your realization of
>   emptiness
> Equals that of your father—
> This is wonderful indeed, O noble son!
> But your compassion, I think,
> Is not equal to his.
> In the same way that you meditated on
>   emptiness,
> You should now meditate on compassion.

On his way back to Amdo with Shabkar in 1828, Kalden Rangdrol lost his life while searching for a ford in the Drichu River to save from starvation a hundred people who had been robbed by Golok bandits (see chap. 15, fol. 426b).

KUNZANG RANGDROL

Originally from Dzogeh in Amdo, Kunzang Rangdrol came to meditate near Shabkar at Tsonying Island. He also went to meet Shabkar in Tsari, and is often mentioned in the autobiography as one of Shabkar's closest disciples. In chapter 9, Shabkar says, "After staying one year in central Tibet, he returned to Domey. There he practiced the two stages of the Secret Mantrayana and the profound path of Chöd, and became a realized sky-like yogin who brought delusion to an end."

NATSOK RANGDROL

This is Gurong Tulku Natsok Rangdrol, a figure who often appears in the second part of Shabkar's autobiography. He wrote *The Crystal Mirror*, an important guide to the *Wish-fulfilling Gem*, *Hayagriva and Varahi* (see Bibliography).

GANGSHAR RANGDROL

This could be the lama of whom Shabkar speaks in chap. 11, fol. 239a: "In the summer, Lama Neten, who was from Marmig in the northern steppes and whose secret name was Gangshar Rangdrol, 'Self-liberation of Whatever Arises,' arrived at this sacred place. He had consciously taken rebirth for the sake of the nomads of the northern steppes who had neither protector nor refuge." In chap. 14, fol. 14a, Shabkar speaks of Gangshar Rangdrol as "a close disciple of the precious and powerful *siddha* of the Great Perfection," which presumably refers to Do Drupchen Jigme Trinley Öser (1745–1821). In his *Beneficial Moon* Shabkar also quotes extensively the songs of a Gangshar Rangdrol but gives no indications allowing identification of this author.

JAMYANG RANGDROL

In chapter 12, Shabkar, then staying at Kyirong, speaks of Jamyang Rangdrol as one of his close disciples. Later (see fol. 210), Shabkar also says, "Jamyang Rangdrol and a few others left to raise the victory banner of spiritual practice at the Snow Mountain of Tö . . ."

JIMBA NORBU

A detailed manuscript autobiography of Jimba Norbu is kept in Tarap, Dolpo, Nepal (see Bibliography). Shabkar's main disciple in western and central Tibet, Jimba Norbu entered Shepel Ling Monastery, in Purang, when he was ten years old and took novice vows from Jimba Dargye (*sbyin pa dar rgyas*). He then went to central Tibet and received full monastic ordination from the seventh Panchen Lama, Lobzang Tenpai Nyima (*blo bzang bstan pa'i nyi ma*, 1781–1854). He studied at Sera and then met the throne-holder of Ratreng (*rwa sgreng khri chen*), who gave him many teachings and initiations on Madhyamaka, Mahamudra, and Dzogchen, but soon passed away. Finally, at Mount Kailash, Jimba Norbu met Shabkar, who was to become his lifelong teacher, and remained near him for several years. When Shabkar went to Nepal, he sent Jimba Norbu to Droshö (*dro shod*) to do a three-year retreat. Following this, Shabkar entrusted Jimba Norbu with the task of going to Nepal to gild the top of the Bodhnath stupa. After spending some more years with his master, Jimba Norbu accomplished the Tsari pilgrimage. He came once more into Shabkar's presence at Densathil, where the master gave him his final instructions before leaving for Amdo in 1828. Their final parting occurred near Ratreng. Jimba Norbu, in tears, compared Shabkar's departure to that of Guru Padmasambhava leaving Tibet for the southwest continent of Chamara. After spending some months in retreat, Jimba Norbu went to Draktsa Cave (*brag rtsa phug*), Yeshe Tsogyal's cave in Drigung Terdrom in which Kunzang Dechen Gyalpo had revealed the *terma* of the *Wish-fulfilling Gem, Hayagriva and Varahi*. He then returned to western Tibet through Lodrak (where he visited the place where Lodrak Drupchen met Tsongkhapa) and Ralung.

The autobiography ends abruptly after Jimba Norbu takes leave of the Panchen Lama at Tashi Lhunpo and heads westward. Jimba Norbu already had disciples of his own when he was practicing and studying with Shabkar and he later became a charismatic teacher in western Tibet. His autobiography is rich in songs and teachings in prose, the style of which, clear and inspiring, is reminiscent of Shabkar's own.

Although his initial training was in the Geluk tradition, Jimba Norbu predominantly makes use of the style and vocabulary of the Dzogchen teachings of the Nyingma tradition.

CHANGLUNG TULKU KHYAPDAL LONGYANG

Changlung Tulku Khyapdal Longyang (*spyang lung sprul sku khyab brdal klong yangs*; see RO, p. 640–41; spelled *lcang lung* in AC) was the reembodiment of Changlung Namkha Jigme (*spyang lung nam mkha' 'jigs med*, 1769–1833) who founded the Garuda Monastery (*khyung dgon*, which is not to be confused with the large Gelukpa monastery of *bya khyung*, nearby in Domey). Namkha Jigme traveled to central Tibet and Kham, where he received and transmitted Nyingma teachings, especially those of the Mindroling tradition, of Nyima Trakpa's *termas*, and of the *Longchen Nyingthig* cycle. It is said that when he recited the hundred-syllable mantra of Vajrasattva, the sound of his heartbeat became the same as the sound of the mantra and that the mantra could be heard resounding from his chest. According to H.H. Dilgo Khyentse Rinpoche, he was also a disciple of Do Drupchen Jigme Trinley Öser (1745–1821). He became an accomplished master of the Palchen Dupa practice from the *Longchen Nyingthig* and recited the mantra of this *yidam* two hundred million times at one of the Eight Places of Accomplishment of Rekong. Shabkar wrote a biography of this master (see Pal Gyalkar 1993). Namkha Jigme had three immediate reincarnations, one in Kyung Gön (*khyung dgon*), one in Adarchaka (*a dar chags ka*) and one in Gurong (*dgu rong*; see RO, p. 642 and AC, vol. 2, p. 298). Khyapdal Longyang, the first of these three, was one of Shabkar's close disciples. He is often mentioned in the second part of the autobiography (TS 2) as Namkha Jigme Tulku or as Alak Namkha. Alak Namkha's reincarnation was a disciple of Jamyang Khyentse Chökyi Lodrö (1893–1959), who also recognized the next incarnation. The present Alak Namkha is a respected teacher in the Rekong area.

Among Shabkar's other eminent disciples are the following: Nyangkyi Tsampa, the "Hermit of Nyang," Lobzang Tenpai Nyima (*nyang mtshams pa blo bzang bstan pa'i nyi ma*, 1811–61), who was a learned and influential master in the Rekong area (see Author's Introduction, note 24); Chingkar Donyö Dorje, who considered himself to be Shabkar's disciple but was at the same time one of his teachers (see Appendix 2); Drogön Pema Gyatso, who was the teacher of the Shuksep Jetsun, owing to whom the lineage of the *Wish-fulfilling Gem, Hayagriva and Varahi* is still extant today (see Appendix 4); and Sangye Rinchen, a resident of Tashikhyil Hermitage, who copied and directed the carving on wooden blocks of most of Shabkar's writings.

Today, Shabkar's spiritual heritage is alive throughout Amdo province and in the mountain areas between Tibet and Nepal. In Nepal, India, and other parts of the world, his lineage has been preserved and spread by Ven. Trulshik Rinpoche, Ven. Tenga Rinpoche (who holds the transmission for this autobiography), and by H.H. Dilgo Khyentse Rinpoche.

Notes

1. Chap. 5, fol. 57a. Shabkar also mentions a biography of Pema Rangdrol in T2, p. 203. This work, however, has not been found.

List of
Abbreviations

AC — *A mdo'i chos 'byung deb ther rgya mtsho*, by Konchog Rabgye.

BA — *The Blue Annals*, by Gö Lotsawa Shonnu Pel, translated by G. N. Roerich.

BD — *Biographical Dictionary of Tibet and Tibetan Buddhism*, by Khetsun Sangpo.

BM — *Buddha Mind*, by Tulku Thondup Rinpoche.

CM — *The Crystal Mirror*, by Gurong Tulku.

Collected Works: — *The Collected Works of Zhabs dkar tshogs drug rang grol*.

DOL 1 — *Songs Arisen on the Mirror of Mind*, by Shabkar, manuscript I from Dolpo Tarap.

DOL 2 — *Short Biography and Kailash Songs*, by Shabkar, manuscript II from Dolpo Tarap.

DOL 3 — *The Many-stringed Lute*, by Shabkar, manuscript III from Dolpo Tarap.

DZ — *gdams ngag mdzod* [The treasury of precious instructions of Tibetan Buddhism], by Jamgön Kongtrul.

GC — *gur bkra chos 'byung* [History of the Nyingma tradition], by Guru Tashi.

GL — *Guide to Lapchi*, by Konchog Tendzin.

GT — *A Guide-book to Tsari*, by E. De Rossi Filibeck.

JK — *The Collected Works (gsung 'bum) of 'jam dbyangs mkhyen brtse'i dbang po*.

LNY — "A Pilgrimage to La-phyi," by T. Huber, 1989.

LTWA — Dharamsala: Library of Tibetan Works and Archives.

MI — "Lands and Places of Milarepa," by P. Aufschnaiter.

MK — *Guide to Mt. Kailash, Lake Manasarovar, and the Sacred Pretapuri*, by Chöying Dorje, 1990.

ND — *nor bu rdo shel* [The necklace of jewels], by Rigdzin Kunzang Ngedön Long Yang.

NG — *rnam grangs rgya mtsho* [Concepts and categories of Buddhist philosophy], by Nyakla Pema Rigdzin.

NGB — *rnying ma rgyud 'bum* [Collected tantras of the Nyingmapa].

NGMPP — Nepal German Manuscript Preservation Project.

NS   *The Nyingma School of Tibetan Buddhism. Its Fundamentals and History,* by Dudjom Rinpoche. Translated by G. Dorje and M. Kapstein.

NW   *The Necklace of White Lotus,* by Trulshik Rinpoche.

PP   *The Power-places of Central Tibet,* by K. Dowman (1988)

RO   *rong po dgon chen gyi gdan rabs* [History of the Great Monastery of Rongpo], by Jigme Thekchog, 1988.

RT   *rin chen gter mdzod* [The treasury of rediscovered teachings], by Jamgön Kontrul.

SG   *gsang sngags bstan 'dzin chos rgyal gyi rnam thar* [Life of the second Shechen Gyaltsap, Pema Sangnak Tendzin Chögyal].

T   Tohuku's catalogue of the *bka' 'gyur* and *bstan 'gyur.*

TC   *tshig mdzod chen mo* [Great Tibetan-Chinese Dictionary].

TH   *The Literary Transmission of the Traditions of Thang-stong rGyal-po: A Study of Visionary Buddhism in Tibet,* by J. Gyatso.

TN   *The Lives of the Hundred Treasure-Discoverers,* by Jamgön Kongtrul.

TS 1   *zhabs dkar rnam thar stod cha* [The autobiography of Shabkar, first part], Qinghai Nationalities Press.

TS 2   *zhabs dkar rnam thar smad cha* [The autobiography of Shabkar: second part], Qinghai Nationalities Press.

TS 3   *zhabs dkar mgur 'bum stod cha.* [The collected songs of Shabkar, vol. 1], Qinghai Nationalities Press.

TS 4   *zhabs dkar mgur 'bum smad cha* [The collected songs of Shabkar, vol. 2], Qinghai Nationalities Press.

TW   *The Torch of Wisdom,* by Chögyal Ngakyi Wangpo.

WL   *The White Lotus Garland,* by Trulshik Rinpoche.

Glossary of Enumerations

TWO

TWO ACCUMULATIONS (*tshogs gnyis*). The accumulations of merit (*bsod nams*) and wisdom (*ye shes*), which lead to the realization of the Two Bodies or Kayas of a Buddha.

TWO BENEFITS (*don gnyis*). The present and ultimate benefit of self and others.

TWO BODIES OR KAYAS (*sku gnyis*). The dharmakaya (*chos kyi sku*), or absolute body, and the rupakaya (*gzugs kyi sku*), or body of form.

TWO CROWNED BUDDHAS (*jo bo rnam gnyis*). The Jowo Rinpoche (*jo bo rin po che*), or Jowo Shakyamuni, which is in the Jokhang, the main temple of Lhasa (also known as *ra sa 'phrul snang gtsug lag khang*); and the Jowo Mikyö Dorje (*jo bo mi bskyod rdo rje*), which is kept in the temple of Ramoche (*ra mo che*). These statues, the most venerated in Tibet, were brought to Lhasa by the two wives of Songtsen Gampo, the Nepalese princess Bhrikuti (*lha gcig khri btsun*), who founded the Jokhang, and the Chinese princess Wengchen Kungchu, who founded Ramoche.

TWO STAGES (*rim gnyis*). The development stage (*bskyed rim*) during which one visualizes deities and recites their mantras, followed by the completion stage (*rdzogs rim*), with or without formal representations.

TWO SUPREME ONES (*mchog gnyis*). Nagarjuna and Asanga, two among the Six Ornaments of the World.

TWOFOLD THOUGHT OF ENLIGHTENMENT (*byang chub kyi sems gnyis*). Bodhicitta, the thought or mind of enlightenment, is defined as the intention to achieve Buddhahood for the sake of all beings. It has two aspects, relative and absolute. The relative mind of enlightenment (*kun rdzob byang chub kyi sems*) is itself divided into two steps: the wish to attain ultimate perfection to become able to free all beings from suffering (*smon pa'i sems bskyed*), and the entry into spiritual practice in order to actualize this wish (*'jug pa'i sems bskyed*). The absolute mind of enlightenment (*don dam byang chub kyi sems*) is the realization of emptiness and the recognition that the Buddha-nature abides in every sentient being.

TWO TRUTHS (*bden pa gnyis*). Absolute truth and relative truth. Absolute truth (*don dam bden pa*) is beyond concepts and definitions. Relative truth (*kun rdzob bden pa*) is considered as deceptive and devoid of any true existence; or, according to the Mantrayana, as the display of innate wisdom, the infinite purity of all phenomena.

TWO VEILS (*sgrib gnyis*). The veil created by the obscuring emotions (*nyon mongs pa'i sgrib*) and the veil masking ultimate knowledge (*shes bya'i sgrib*). They prevent one from achieving enlightenment.

THREE

THREE ACTIVITIES CONNECTED WITH SPREADING THE DHARMA (*chos kyi las gsum*). Exposition (*'chad*), debate (*rtsod*), and composition (*rtsom*)

THREE BASKETS (Skt. *Tripitaka*, Tib. *sde snod gsum*). Vinaya (*'dul ba*), sutra (*mdo*) and abhidharma (*mngon pa*). They are included in the Tibetan canonical collection called *Kangyur*.

THREE BODIES OR KAYAS (*sku gsum*). The dharmakaya (*chos kyi sku*), or absolute body; the sambhogakaya (*longs spyod rdzogs pa'i sku*), or body of enjoyment; and the nirmanakaya (*sprul pa'i sku*), or manifested body. They correspond to the empty nature of mind and of all phenomena; the luminous clarity of wisdom; and the unobstructed manifestation of compassion. These are known as the three bodies (*trikaya*) of a Buddha.

THREE CLASSES WITHIN ATIYOGA (*rdzogs chen sde gsum*). 1) the mind class (*sems sde*), 2) the space class (*klong sde*), and 3) the class of pith or extraordinary instructions (*man ngag sde*).

THREE CONDITIONS FOR THE PURITY OF MEAT (*gnas gsum dag pa'i sha*). There are three conditions that make the eating of meat less evil: 1) that one has not oneself killed an animal for meat, 2) or asked someone to kill it, 3) or taken the meat of an animal that has been killed specifically for oneself, even though one did not ask for it to be slaughtered. These are defined according to Hinayana sutras. According to Mahayana sutras the eating of meat, at the cost of animals' suffering, is unacceptable (see Appendix 5, note 6, and *Emanated Scriptures of Compassion*).

THREE CONFIDENCES (*yid ches gsum*). 1) The confidence that the goal of the practice resides in oneself (*bsgrub bya rang la bzhugs pa yid ches*), 2) the confidence in the extraordinary instructions that allow one to attain this goal (*sgrub byed kyi man ngag la yid ches*), and 3) the confidence in the spiritual master (*bla ma la yid ches*).

THREE DIAMOND-HARD, OR VAJRA-LIKE, RESOLUTIONS (*rdo rje gsum*). 1) The vajra of unswerving determination: no matter what our parents, friends, or anyone else may think or say, no matter what adverse conditions there may be, nothing can deter us from our resolve to practice the Dharma. 2) The vajra of indifference to what others may think of us: Once we have achieved our goal—to practice Dharma— even if people have a poor opinion of us, criticize us for "wasting our time," or slander us, we should not care about it in the least. 3) The vajra of wisdom: awareness of the ultimate truth, which should accompany us at all times.

THREE DIVISIONS OF NGARI IN TÖ (*stod mnga' ris skor gsum*). According to CN, p. 23, they are: 1) The Dharma Land of Mang Yul (*mang yul chos kyi skor*); 2) The Auspicious Bönpo Land of Guge (*gu ge g.yung drung bon gi skor*); and 3) The Snow Land of Purang (*spu hreng gangs kyi skor*), variously spelled *spu rangs* and *pu hrang*.

Alternately, these three have been defined as 1) Guge Ya'i Kor (*gu ge g.ya' yi skor*), the Slate Land of Guge; 2) Purang Khang gi Kor (*spu hreng gangs kyi skor*), the Snow Land of Purang; 3) Ruthop Chap gi Kor (*ru thob chab kyi skor*), the Water Land of Ruthop.

According to AC, vol. 1, p. 3, the three divisions are 1) Purang, Mang Yul, and Zanskar (*spu hreng, mang yul, zangs dkar*), making the first division; 2) Li, Gilgit, and Balti (*li, bru sha, sbal ti*), making the second division; and 3) Shang Shung, Triteh and Lower Tö (*zhang zhung, khri te /bri ste, stod smad*), making the third division.

THREE DOORS (*sgo gsum*). Body, speech, and mind.

THREE FAMILIES, LORDS OF THE (*rigs gsum mgon po*). The Buddhas Manjushri, Avalokiteshvara, and Vajrapani, the respective manifestations of wisdom, compassion, and power.

THREE FUNDAMENTAL ASPECTS OF THE BUDDHIST TEACHINGS. 1) Renunciation (*nges byung*), the root of the Hinayana and therefore the foundation of all subsequent vehicles, 2) compassion (*snying rje*), the driving force of the Mahayana, and 3) pure vision (*dag snang*), the extraordinary outlook of the Vajrayana.

THREE INNER TANTRAS (*nang rgyud sde gsum*). The tantras of Mahayoga, Anuyoga, and Atiyoga.

THREE KINDNESSES OF A SPIRITUAL MASTER (*bka' drin gsum*). To mature the disciple with an empowerment (*dbang bskur*), to expound the tantras (*rgyud bshad*), and to bestow pith instructions (*man ngag ston*).

THREE KINDS OF CELESTIAL BEINGS (*lha gsum*). The gods of the realms of desire, form, and no-form.

THREE LOWER REALMS (*ngan song gsum*). The realms of the denizens of the hells, of the tormented spirits, and of the animals.

THREE PLACES (*sa gsum*). The realms of the celestial beings above the earth, of human beings upon the earth, and of the nagas below the earth.

THREE POISONS or *kleshas* (*dug gsum*). Desire, hatred, and confusion.

THREE RANGES OF DOKHAM (*smad mdo khams sgang gsum*). 1) Markham in Upper Kham (*smar khams* in *mdo khams*); 2) Yermo Thang in Lower Kham, Amdo (*g.yer mo thang* in *mdo smad*); and 3) Tsongkha Gyi Thang (*tsong kha gyi thang*).

THREE ROOTS (*rtsa ba gsum*). The guru (*bla ma*); the deva, or meditational deity (*yi dam*); and the dakini (*mkha' 'gro*). They are the roots, respectively, of blessings, of spiritual accomplishment, and of enlightened activity.

THREE SECRETS (*gsang ba gsum*). The vajra body, vajra speech, and vajra mind of an enlightened being.

THREE STRENGTHS OF THE LION (*seng ge'i rtsal gsum*). Miraculous transformations (*rdzu 'phrul*), swiftness (*myur mgyogs*), and the possession of wings made of wind (*rlung gshog*).

THREE SUFFERINGS (*sdug bsngal rnam pa gsum*). The suffering upon suffering (as when losing one's parents and then falling very sick); the suffering of change (as when going to a happy picnic and being bitten by a snake); and the all-pervading, latent suffering inherent in all forms of conditioned existence.

THREE SWEETS (*mngar gsum*). Sugar, honey and molasses.

THREE TRAININGS (*bslab pa gsum*). Ethical discipline (*tshul khrims*), contemplation (*ting nge 'dzin*), and wisdom (*shes rab*).

THREE VOWS (*sdom gsum*). The *pratimoksha vows* of the Hinayana, which concern all the lay and monastic precepts of conduct taught by Lord Buddha in the Vinaya; the *Bodhisattva vows* of the Mahayana, which are embodied in the generation, cultivation and preservation of the twofold thought of enlightenment, or Bodhicitta; and the *samayas*, which are the precepts and commitments of the Vajrayana. *Samayas* formalize and acknowledge the all-important bonds with one's guru, one's fellow disciples, and one's practice.

THREE WHEELS OR ACTIVITIES OF A BUDDHA (*'khor lo rnam gsum*). The wheel of study and reflection (*thos bsam*); the wheel of meditation (*sgom pa*); and the wheel of activity (*phrin las*).

THREE WHITES (*dkar gsum*). Milk, curd, and butter.

THREE WORLDS (*khams gsum*). The world of desire (*'dod pa'i khams*), the world of form (*gzugs kyi khams*), and the world of no-form (*gzugs med kyi khams*).

FOUR

FOUR ACTIVITIES (*las bzhi*). Performed for the sake of others by accomplished yogins: *pacifying* sickness, obstacles, mental obscurations, and ignorance; *enriching* merit, life span, glory, prosperity, and wisdom; *bringing under control* the good qualities, life force, and powerful energies of the three worlds; and *subjugating wrathfully* outer and inner negative forces, and obstacle-makers.

FOUR ATTRACTIVE QUALITIES OF A BODHISATTVA, OR FOUR WAYS OF GATHERING BEINGS WHO NEED TO BE BENEFITED (*bsdu ba'i dngos po bzhi*). 1) To please them with presents (*sbyin pa*), 2) to please them by saying gentle things suited to their minds (*snyan par smra ba*), 3) to teach them in accordance with their needs and capacities (*don spyod pa*), 4) to behave and practice in accordance with what one teaches (*don mthun pa*).

FOUR BASIC PRACTICES OF THE KAGYU LINEAGE 1) The view—of Mahamudra (*phyag rgya chen po*), 2) the meditation—the Six Yogas of Naropa (*naro chos drug*), 3) the action—the Six Cycles of Even Taste (*ro snyoms skor drug*), 4) the profound path—Guru Yoga (*lam zab bla ma'i rnal 'byor*).

FOUR BOUNDLESS THOUGHTS (*tshad med bzhi*). Boundless loving-kindness, boundless compassion, boundless sympathetic joy, and boundless equanimity. They are boundless because the number of beings to whom they apply is boundless, the motivation to benefit them is boundless, the virtues of doing so are boundless, and the excellence of the result is boundless.

FOUR BRANCHES OF APPROACH AND ACCOMPLISHMENT (*bsnyen sgrub yan lag bzhi*). These four belong to the development stage (*bskyed rim*), during which one visualizes wisdom deities and recites their mantras. First one "approaches" or "serves" (*bsnyen*) the deity by familiarizing oneself with the practice; one "approaches

further" (*nye bsnyen*) by undertaking mantra recitation, visualization, etc.; one "accomplishes" (*sgrub*) the deity by mastering these practices; and, finally, one achieves the "great accomplishment" (*sgrub chen*) by becoming one with the deity's wisdom nature. See YZ, vol. 40, pp. 121ff.

FOUR CLASSES OF TANTRA (*rgyud sde bzhi*). Kriya, Upa, Yoga, and Anuttara.

FOUR CONTEMPLATIONS (*bsam gtan bzhi*). The first involves both discursive thoughts (*rtog pa*) and examination (*dpyod pa*). The second is sheer examination devoid of discursive thoughts. The third is free from both examination and discursive thoughts. The fourth is attention (*yid la byed pa*) united with bliss (*dga' ba*). See YZ, vol. 39, pp. 400–402.

FOUR DHARMAS OF TRAINING IN VIRTUE (*dge sbyong gi chos bzhi*). Not returning anger for anger, insult for insult, slander for slander, blow for blow.

FOUR DISTRICTS OF U AND TSANG (*bar dbus gtsang ru bzhi*). Initially, during the reign of King Songtsen Gampo, the Four Regions in U and Tsang were described as follows:

In U (*dbus*): 1) Uru (*dbu ru*), all the regions on the left banks of the Kyichu River, and of the Tsangpo River, after Chaksam, where the Kyichu and Tsangpo meet; 2) Yoru (*g.yo ru*), the regions on the right banks of these two rivers.

In Tsang (*gtsang*): 3) Yeru (*g.yas ru*), the Right Region (on the right bank of the Tsangpo, which flows from Mt. Kailash), and 4) Ru lag (*ru lag*), on the left bank of the Tsangpo.

More recently, they have been described as

In U: 1) Puru (*spus ru*) and 2) Gungru (*gung ru*)

In Tsang: 3) Yeru (*g.yas ru*) and 4) Yönru (*g.yon ru*).

For a discussion of this, see AC, pt. 1, p. 4, and CN, p. 97.

FOUR ELEMENTS (*'byung ba bzhi*). Earth (*sa*), water (*chu*), fire (*me*), wind (*rlung*), and space (*nam mkha'*).

FOUR EMPOWERMENTS (*dbang bzhi*). 1) The vase empowerment (*bum dbang*), 2) the secret empowerment (*gsang dbang*), 3) the wisdom empowerment (*shes rab ye shes kyi dbang*), and 4) the precious word empowerment (*tshig dbang rin po che*).

    Within Atiyoga (*rdzogs chen*), the four empowerments are 1) elaborate (*spros bcas*), unelaborate (*spros med*), very unelaborate (*shin tu spros med*), and utterly unelaborate (*rab tu spros med*).

FOUR FORMLESS STATES (*gzugs med kyi gnas bzhi*). Infinite space (*nam mkha' mtha' yas*), infinite consciousness (*rnam shes mtha' yas*), nothing at all (*ci yang med pa*), and neither perception nor non-perception (*'du shes med 'du shes med min*). See YZ, vol. 39, p. 403.

FOUR GUESTS (*mgron po bzhi*). 1) The Three Jewels, the Buddhas and Bodhisattvas who elicit faith and respect, 2) the protectors of the Dharma, who are endowed with excellent qualities, 3) sentient beings, who deserve our compassion, and 4) negative harmful spirits, to whom we must repay karmic debts.

FOUR LIMITING CONCEPTS (*spros pa'i mtha' bzhi*). Conceiving of reality in terms of existence and nonexistence, eternity and nothingness.

FOUR MAIN TRADITIONS OF TIBETAN BUDDHISM (*bod kyi chos lugs chen po bzhi*). Nyingma (*rnying ma*), Kagyu (*bka' brgyud*), Sakya (*sa skya*), and Geluk (*dge lugs*).

FOUR MAJOR TRANSGRESSIONS OF THE MONASTIC VOWS (*pham pa bzhi*). To kill a human being, to steal (to take what is not given), to break celibacy, and to lie about one's spiritual attainment (pretending to have attained a high spiritual level, to have experienced visions, etc.). These four are called "defeats" (*pham pa*),

because they make one completely lose one's ordination.

FOUR NOBLE TRUTHS (*bden pa bzhi*). 1) The truth of suffering, 2) of the origin of suffering (the obscuring emotions), 3) of the cessation of suffering, and 4) of the path to achieve this cessation.

FOUR ORNAMENTS (*rgyan bzhi*). Four classical themes on old brocades—the elephant *hastina*, symbolizing strength; the deer *sharana*, symbolizing compassion; the sea monster *patrana*, which purified desire; and the garuda *karuna*, which purified ignorance.

FOUR PREFERENCES OF THE NOBLE ONES (*'phags pa'i rigs bzhi*). Simple food, simple clothing, simple dwelling-place, simple possessions.

FOUR ULTIMATE AIMS (*gtad pa bzhi*). To let one's mind turn toward the Dharma; to let one's Dharma turn oneself to a humble life; to turn one's humble life toward death; and to let one's death happen in a solitary cave.

FOUR VISIONS OF THÖGAL PRACTICE (*thod rgal kyi snang ba bzhi*). 1) The vision of the absolute nature becoming manifest (*chos nyid mngon sum*), 2) the vision of the experience of increasing appearances (*nyams gong 'phel*), 3) the vision of awareness reaching its greatest magnitude (*rig pa tshad phebs*), and 4) the vision of the exhaustion of phenomena in dharmata (*chos nyid zad pa*).

FIVE

FIVE BUDDHA FAMILIES (*rgyal ba rigs lnga*). Buddha (in the center), Vajra (in the east), Ratna (in the south), Padma (in the west), and Karma (in the north).

FIVE DEGENERATIONS (*snyigs ma lnga*). The "age of residues" (*snyigs dus*) is characterized by a degeneration in 1) the life span (*tshe*), 2) the general karma (*las*), 3) the view (*lta ba*), and 4) the faculties of beings (*sems can*), as well as by 5) an increase of the obscuring emotions (*nyon mongs*).

FIVE GREAT TREASURIES (*mdzod chen rnam pa lnga*). Five collections of essential teachings on Buddhist theory and practice collected or written by Jamgön Kongtrul Lodrö Thaye (1813–99). These five are 1) the *All-encompassing Treasury of Knowledge* (*shes bya kun la khyab pa'i mdzod*, 4 vols.), an encyclopedia of Buddhist wisdom and knowledge; 2) the *Treasury of Precious Instructions* (*gdams ngag mdzod*, 18 vols.), which gathers the pith instructions of the eight main lineages of Tibetan Buddhism (see Eight Chariots of the Dharma); 3) the *Mantra Treasury of the Oral Lineage* (*bka' brgyud sngags mdzod*, 8 vols.), which gathers some fundamental teachings of the Nyingma *kahma* and the main teachings for the practice of the Kagyu lineage; 4) the *Precious Treasury of Rediscovered Teachings* (*rin chen gter mdzod*, 63 vols.), which gathers the most important rediscovered teachings (*gter ma*) of the Nyingma tradition, and incorporates what is extant of the *Extraordinary Treasury* (*thun mong ma yin pa'i mdzod*), Jamgön Kongtrul's own revealed teachings (*gter ma*); 5) the *Vast Treasury of Teachings* (*rgya chen bka'i mdzod*, 16 vols.), which comprises the remaining works of Jamgön Kongtrul.

FIVE POISONS (*dug lnga*). 1) Desire-attachment (*'dod chags*), 2) hatred (*zhe sdang*), 3) lack of discernment (*gti mug*), 4) pride (*nga rgyal*), and 5) jealousy (*phrag dog*).

FIVE SCIENCES (*thun mong rigs pa lnga*). Languages, crafts, medicine, astrology, and philosophy.

FIVE STEPS OF THE PRELIMINARY PRACTICE (*sngon 'gro*). 1) The taking of refuge, with prostrations (*skyabs 'gro*), 2) generation of Bodhicitta (*sems bskyed*), 3) meditation on Vajrasattva and recitation of the hundred-syllable mantra (*rdor sems sgom bzlas*), 4) offering of the mandala (*mandal*), and 5) guru yoga (*bla ma'i 'byor*). This practice entails 110,000 repetitions of each of these steps.

FIVE WISDOMS (*ye shes lnga*). 1) The wisdom of the absolute expanse (*chos dbyings ye shes*), 2) the mirror-like wisdom (*me long ye shes*), 3) the all-discerning wisdom (*so sor rtog pa'i ye shes*), 4) the wisdom of sameness (*mnyam nyid ye shes*), and 5) the all-accomplishing wisdom (*bya ba grub pa'i ye shes*).

FIVEFOLD MAHAMUDRA (*phyag chen lnga ldan*). According to the Drigung Kagyu tradition: 1) The Great Seal of Bodhicitta (*byang sems phyag chen*); 2) the Great Seal of the Deity's form (*lha sku'i phyag chen*); 3) the Great Seal of Fervent Devotion (*mos gus phyag chen*); 4) the Great Seal of the True Nature (*gnas lugs phyag chen*); and 5) the Great Seal of Dedication (*bsngo ba'i phyag chen*).

SIX

SIX BARDOS (*bar do*). *Bardo*, "intermediate" or "transition" state, commonly refers to the transitional state between death and the next rebirth. Texts discuss six *bardos*: the *bardos* of birth and life (*skye gnas rang bzhin gyi bar do*); of meditative concentration (*bsam gtan gyi bar do*); of the dream-state (*rmi lam gyi bar do*); of the moment of death (*'chi kha'i bar do*); of the absolute nature (*chos nyid bar do*); and of taking a new existence (*srid pa'i bar do*).

SIX BRANCHES OF PRACTICE, ACCORDING TO THE KALACHAKRA (*dus 'khor sbyor ba yan lag drug*). Composure (*sor-sdud*), contemplation (*bsam gtan*), breath control (*srog 'dzin*), awareness of the complete deity (*sku ril bur 'dzin pa*), subsequent recollection of this (*rjes su dran pa*), and contemplation (*ting nge 'dzin*). See NS, vol. 2, p. 151, and DZ, vol. 16.

SIX CHARACTERISTICS PARTICULAR TO HUMAN BEINGS. The four elements of earth, water, fire, and wind, along with the spiritual channels (*rtsa*) and vital essence (*thig le*), are the six characteristics that make a human being a suitable vessel for receiving the four empowerments (*dbang*, or Skt. *abhisheka*), and consequently for practicing the Vajrayana. Celestial beings from the form realm and the formless realm have subtle elements only, or none, and lack the proper support of the channels (*rtsa*), energies (*rlung*), and vital essences (*thig le*) for receiving the second and third empowerments.

SIX CLASSES OF VAJRAYANA TANTRAS (*rgyud sde drug*). Kriya, upa, yoga, maha, anu and ati.

SIX DHARMAS (*chos drug*). Also known as Six Yogas of Naropa. 1) Inner heat (*gtum mo*), 2) illusory body (*sgyu lus*), 3) dream (*rmi lam*), 4) luminosity (*'od gsal*), 5) transference of consciousness (*'pho ba*), 6) intermediate or transition state (*bar do*).

SIX ORNAMENTS OF THE WORLD (*'dzam gling rgyan drug*). Six great Indian *panditas*, namely Nagarjuna, Asanga, Dignaga, Aryadeva, Vasubandhu, and Dharmakirti.

SIX RANGES OF DOKHAM (*smad mdo khams sgang drug*). According to AC, vol. 1, p. 4, these are 1) Zalmo Gang (*zal mo sgang*), 2) Tsawa Gang (*tsha ba sgang*), 3) Markham Gang (*smar khams sgang*), 4) Pombor Gang (*spo 'bor sgang*), 5) Mardza Gang (*dmar rdza sgang*) and 6) Minyak Rabgang (*mi nyag rab sgang*). See also CN, p. 176.

SIX REALMS/CLASSES OF SENTIENT BEINGS (*'gro ba rigs drug*). 1) Celestial beings (*lha*), 2) antigods or demi-gods (*lha ma yin*), 3) human beings (*mi,*) 4) animals (*dud 'gro*), 5) tormented spirits (*yi dwags*), and 6) denizen of the hells (*dmyal ba*).

SIX SENSE PERCEPTIONS (*tshogs drug gi snang ba*). Sights, sounds, smells, tastes, tactile sensations, and mental events.

SEVEN

SEVEN-BRANCH PRAYER (*yan lag bdun pa*). 1) Prostration as an antidote to pride, 2) offering as an antidote to miserliness, 3) confession and repentance as an antidote to the three poisons, 4) joy at others' happiness and virtues as an antidote to jealousy, 5) the request that the Wheel of Dharma be turned as a purification

for having abandoned the Dharma in the past, 6) the prayer that the Buddhas, Bodhisattvas and spiritual masters remain in this world as a purification for having upset one's teacher, and 7) dedication of merit as an antidote to wrong views.

SEVEN NOBLE RICHES OR QUALITIES (*'phags pa'i nor bdun*). Faith, discipline, generosity, learning, a sense of moral shame in front of others, a sense of ethical conscience in regard to oneself, and intelligence. One also speaks of faith, which is like a river; discipline, which is like a flower; generosity, which is like a jewel; learning, which is like an ocean; *samaya*, which is like a crystal; a sense of moral shame, which is undeceiving like one's own parents; and wisdom, which is like the sun.

SEVEN-POINT POSTURE OF VAIROCANA (*rnam snang chos bdun*). 1) The legs should be crossed in the Vajrasana, the so-called "lotus posture," the right foot over the left thigh. 2) The hands, closed into fists and with the thumb pressing the base of the fourth finger, are placed on the thighs at the juncture with the pelvis, and the elbows are then locked straight. (One variation of this is to place the hands palms up, right over left, on the lap, with elbows bent out to the sides; another is to place both hands palms down, relaxed, on the knees.) 3) The shoulders should be raised and rolled slightly forward. 4) The abdomen should be pushed forward. 5) The spine should be kept straight and erect, "like a pile of golden coins." 6) The chin should be tucked in slightly. 7) The eyes should be kept without blinking and unwaveringly focused at a distance of twelve fingers' breadth ahead of the tip of the nose. See Shechen Gyaltsap's *kun mkhyen zhal lung*, p. 41.

EIGHT

EIGHT ASPIRATIONS OF A BODHISATTVA (*byang chub sems dpa'i rtog pa brgyad*). 1) To become able to dispel all the sufferings of beings, 2) to establish in wealth all those stricken by poverty, 3) to become able to give one's flesh and blood for the welfare of beings, 4) to remain in the hell realm and bring some good there, 5) to fulfill the hopes of beings with the bounty of samsara and nirvana, 6) to attain enlightenment, and remove forever the suffering of beings 7) never to enjoy harming others rather than benefiting them, and 8) to want all beings to become happy through the exchange of one's happiness for their suffering.

EIGHT CHARIOTS OF THE PRACTICE LINEAGES (*sgrub brgyud shing rta brgyad*). Nyingma (*rnying ma*), Kadam (*bka' gdams*), Sakya (*sa skya*), Kagyu (*bka' brgyud*), Shangpa Kagyu (*zhangs pa bka' brgyud*), Shiche and Chöd (*zhi byed* and *gcod*), Kalachakra or Jordrug (*dus 'khor* or *sbyor drug*), and Orgyen Nyengyu (*o rgyan bsnyen brgyud*). For a collection of instructions and empowerments related to these eight chariots, see DZ.

EIGHT CLASSES OF GODS AND RAKSHAS (*lha srin sde brgyad*). According to the Yamantaka tantra (*gshin rje gshed kyi rgyud*, see TC, p. 3090) these are *gshin rje, ma mo, srin po, gnod sbyin, mi'am ci, sa bdag, btsan,* and *bdud*. In his *sde brgyad gser skyems,* Nub Sangye Yeshe enumerates six different series of these eight classes. See NS, vol. 2, pp. 158–59.

EIGHT CLASSES OF HERUKAS OR MEANS FOR ATTAINMENT (*sgrub pa bka' brgyad*). 1) Yamantaka, the wrathful Manjushri, the deity of body (*'jam dpal sku*); 2) Hayagriva, the deity of speech (*padma gsung*); 3) Vishuddha, the deity of mind (*yang dag thugs*); 4) Vajramrita, the deity of enlightened qualities (*bdud rtsi yon tan*); 5) Vajra Kila, the deity of action (*phur ba 'phrin las*); 6) Matarah, the deity of calling and dispatching (*ma mo rbod gtong*); 7) the worldly deities of offering and praise (*'jig rten mchod bstod*); and 8) the worldly deities of wrathful mantras (*mod pa drag sngags*).

EIGHT FREEDOMS (*dal ba brgyad*) AND TEN FAVORABLE CONDITIONS (*'byor ba bcu*) CONDUCIVE TO PRACTICING THE DHARMA. First are the freedoms from eight obstacles to practicing the Dharma, which are to be born 1) in a hell

realm, 2) among the *pretas,* or tormented spirits, 3) as an animal, 4) among savages, 5) as a long-living god, 6) holding totally erroneous views, 7) in a dark kalpa, during which no Buddha has appeared in the world, 8) with impaired sense faculties.

Second, among the ten favorable conditions, there are five conditions that depend on ourselves (*rang 'byor lnga*): to be born as 1) a human being, 2) in a place where the Dharma flourishes, 3) with complete sense faculties, 4) without the karma of living in a way totally opposite to the Dharma, 5) and having faith in what deserves it. There are five conditions that depend upon others (*gzhan 'byor lnga*): 1) A Buddha should have appeared in the world, 2) and have taught the Dharma, 3) the Dharma should have remained until our days, 4) we should have entered the Dharma, 5) and have been accepted by a spiritual teacher.

EIGHT LIMITING, OR CONDITIONING, CONCEPTS (*spros pa'i mtha' brgyad*). Conceiving of reality in terms of existence and nonexistence, eternity and nothingness, going and coming, sameness and difference.

EIGHT PLACES OF THE ACCOMPLISHED ONES (*grub thob gnas brgyad*). The Eight Sacred Sites of the Accomplished Ones, located in the Golden Valley of Rekong, are eight places prophesied by Guru Padmasambhava where eight great yogins of his lineage practiced, attained realization, and performed many miracles.

In AC, vol. 2, pp. 304–12, the eight (or nine) places are identified as follows: In the center is Balgi Khargong Lakha (*'bal gyi mkhar gong la kha*), the meditation place of the Bodhisattva of Bol (*'bol gyi byang chub sems dpa'*).

In the east is Taklung Shelgi Riwo (*stag lung shel gyi ri bo*), the meditation place of Shelgi Odeh Gung Gyal (*shel gyi 'o de gung rgyal*).

In the southeast is Lhadrak Karpo, in the Upper part of Chang (*spyang phu'i lha brag dkar po*), where Kalden Gyatso had a vision of Kasarpani and of the Sixteen Arhats. In the vicinity is Ratse Phug (*rwa rtse phug*), the meditation place of Masö Shili Urwa (*ma gsod zhi li 'ur ba*).

In the south, in Dambu, is Drakar Serkhang (*'dam bu'i brag dkar gser khang*), the meditation place of the great Brahmin Litrö (*bram ze chen po li khrod*).

In the southwest is Thamug Dzongmar Gonpa (*mtha' smug rdzong dmar dgon pa*), the meditation place of Athu Ngakpa Yu Ngok (*a mthu'i sngags pa g.yu rngogs*).

In the west is Sheldel Chökyi Potrang (*shel del chos kyi pho brang*), the meditation place of Tönpa Odeh Shampo (*ston pa 'o de sham po*). AC mentions that this is actually an extra, or ninth, place.

In the northwest is Kyagang Nemö Bangwa or Dori Palkyi Ritse (*skya sgang gnas mo'i bang ba*, or *do ri dpal gyi ri rtse*), the meditation place of Seyi Gyalwa Changchup (*bse yi rgyal ba byang chub*), where there are many sacred images that have appeared naturally on the rocks.

In the north is Gongmo Gurkhang Draktsa (*gong mo'i gur khang brag rtsa*), the meditation place of the Bönpo master Drenpa Namkha (*dran pa nam mkha'*).

In the northeast is Chuchik Shel (*bcu gcig shel*), the meditation place of Kathok Dorje Wangpo (*ka thog rdo rje dbang po*; see notes 5 and 6), Chöpa Rinpoche, and Jetsun Kalden Gyatso (see note 2).

In RO, pp. 46–58, nine places where eight *siddhas* meditated are identified in a slightly different way. The spelling of the names of the places and of the *siddhas* also vary.

EIGHT LAY PRECEPTS (*bsnyen gnas kyi sdom pa*). A lay ordination of precepts taken for twenty-four hours, from dawn to dawn. These include avoiding 1) taking life, 2) taking what is not given, 3) sexual intercourse, 4) telling lies, 5) drinking liquor, 6) dancing, wearing garlands, using perfumes, playing worldly music, 7) sleeping on a high and ornamented bed, and 8) eating after noon.

EIGHT QUALITIES OF PERFECT WATER (*chu yan lag brgyad ldan*). Water which is cool, sweet, light, soft, clear, pure, and which is neither upsetting to the stomach nor irritating to the throat.

EIGHT VIDYADHARAS OR AWARENESS-HOLDERS OF INDIA (*rgya gar rig 'dzin brgyad*). Vimalamitra, Humkara, Manjushrimitra, Nagarjuna, Padmasambhava, Dhanasamskrita, Rambuguhya-Devacandra, and Shantigarbha. See NS, vol. 1, pp. 475–83.

EIGHT WORLDLY CONCERNS (*'jig rten chos brgyad*). Happiness and suffering, gain and loss, praise and criticism, fame and obscurity.

NINE

NINE ACTIONS OF THE THREE DOORS (*bya ba dgu phrugs*). The outer, inner, and secret activities of body, speech, and mind, which a yogin will give up when engaging in Thögal practice. *Three concern the body:* 1) outwardly, all worldly, distracting activities, 2) inwardly, all ordinary virtuous deeds such as prostrations and circumambulations, and 3) secretly, all unnecessary movements that scatter one's practice. *Three concern speech:* 1) outwardly, all worldly, deluded conversations, 2) inwardly, all liturgies and recitations, and 3) secretly, any talking whatsoever. *Three concern the mind:* 1) outwardly, all worldly, deluded thoughts, 2) inwardly, all mental activity focused on visualizations of the development and the completion stages, and 3) secretly, all movements of the mind. (See Jamgön Kongtrul's *snying thig ma bu'i khrid yig*, in DZ, vol. Kha, pp. 196–97.)

NINE GRADED VEHICLES (*theg pa rim pa dgu*). The three sutric vehicles of the Sravakas, the Pratyekabuddhas and the Bodhisattvas, followed by the six vehicles of Kriya, Upa, Yoga, Mahayoga, Anuyoga, and Atiyoga tantras. They can also be grouped into three vehicles, Hinayana which comprises the first two, Mahayana the third, and Vajrayana the last six. For explanations of their approaches, similarities and differences, see Appendix 1.

TEN

TEN BENEFITS OF LIVING IN ISOLATED PLACES, according to the *King of Samadhi Sutra*. 1) One's activities will be fewer and fewer, 2) one will be far removed from noise and distractions, 3) one will be free from quarrels, 4) one will also be free from harm, 5) one will not let obscuring emotions increase, 6) one will not create causes for discord, 7) one will always enjoy perfect tranquility, 8) one will keep one's body, speech, and mind under control, 9) one will live in a way that is conducive to liberation, and 10) one will quickly reach complete freedom.

TEN DHARMA ACTIVITIES (*chos spyod bcu*). 1) Writing commentaries and spiritual instructions, if one is qualified to do so, 2) making offerings (of the mandala, the seven branches, etc.), 3) giving to the needy, 4) listening to the teachings, 5) reading the holy scriptures, 6) committing their meaning to memory, 7) explaining this meaning to others, 8) reciting one's daily prayers, 9) pondering over the teachings one has received, 10) assimilating them through contemplation and meditation. See Kongtrul's *rgya chen bka'i mdzod*, vol. 12, p. 238.

TEN NONVIRTUOUS ACTIONS (*mi dge ba bcu*). Killing, stealing, and sexual misconduct; telling lies, slandering, gossiping and saying harsh words; envy, ill will, and erroneous views. These three groupings comprise the wrongdoings, respectively, of body, speech and mind.

TEN PARAMITAS (*pha rol du phyin pa bcu*). 1) Generosity (*sbyin pa*), 2) ethical discipline (*tshul khrims*), 3) patience (*bzod pa*), 4) effort (*brtson 'grus*), 5) concentration (*bsam gtan*), 6) insight (*shes rab*), 7) means (*thabs*), 8) aspiration-prayer (*smon lam*), 9) strength (*stobs*), and 10) primordial wisdom (*ye shes*)

TEN SPIRITUAL STAGES OR *BHUMIS* (*sa bcu*). The stages through which a Bodhisattva passes before attaining full Buddhahood, the eleventh *bhumi*. These are 1) Perfect Joy (*rab tu dga' ba*), 2) Immaculate (*dri ma med pa*), 3) Illuminat-

ing (*'od byed pa*), 4) Brilliant (*'od 'phro ba*), 5) Hard to Conquer (*sbyang dka' ba*), 6) Manifest (*mngon du gyur pa*), 7) Far-reaching (*ring du song ba*), 8) Immutable (*mi g.yo ba*), 9) Excellent Intelligence (*legs pa'i blo gros*), and 10) Cloud of the Dharma (*chos kyi sprin*).

TEN VIRTUOUS DEEDS (*dge ba'i las bcu*). *Three of the body:* 1) To protect life, 2) to be honest, 3) to maintain proper sexual conduct. *Four of speech:* 1) to tell the truth, 2) to avoid gossip 3) to avoid slander, 4) to speak gentle words that bring happiness to others. *Three of the mind:* 1) to rejoice in the good fortune of others, 2) to have only thoughts that are beneficial to others, 3) to have correct views.

TWELVE

TWELVE ASCETIC VIRTUES (*sbyangs pa'i yon tan bcu gnyis*). 1) To wear clothing found in a garbage heap (*phyag dar khrod pa*), 2) to own only three monastic robes (*chos gos gsum pa*), 3) to wear clothes and boots made of felt (*phying pa ba*), 4) to eat one's meal at a single sitting (*stan gcig pa*), 5) to live only on alms (*bsod snyoms pa*), 6) not to eat after midday (*zas phyis mi len pa*), 7) to live in secluded places (*dgon pa ba*), 8) to live under trees (*shing drung ba*), 9) to live in the open air (*bla gab med pa*), 10) to live in cemeteries (*dur khrod pa*), 11) to sleep in a sitting posture (*tsog pu ba*), and 12) to stay wherever one happens to be (*gzhi ji bzhin pa*). See TC, p. 2023.

TWELVE DEEDS PERFORMED BY AN ENLIGHTENED BUDDHA (*mdzad pa bcu gnyis*). 1) Descending from Tushita Heaven (*dga' ldan gnas nas 'pho ba*), 2) entering the womb of his mother (*lhums su bzhugs pa*), 3) taking birth (*sku bltams pa*), 4) becoming skilled in worldly arts and demonstrating physical prowess (*bzo la mkhas par ston pa dang gzhon nu'i rol rtsed*), 5) enjoying his retinue of queens (*btsun mo'i 'khor gyis rol pa*), 6) renouncing the world (*rab tu 'byung ba*), 7) practicing austerities and renouncing them (*dka' ba spyad pa*), 8) going to the Bodhi-tree (*byang chub snying por gshegs pa*), 9) subduing Mara (*bdud btul*), 10) attaining full enlighten-ment (*mngon par sangs rgyas pa*), 11) turning the Wheel of the Dharma (*chos kyi 'khor lo bskor*), 12) passing into the ultimate peace beyond suf-fering (Skt. *parinirvana*, Tib. *mya ngan las 'das pa*).

EIGHTEEN

EIGHTEEN FREEDOMS AND FAVORABLE CONDITIONS (*dal 'byor bco brgyad*). These are the Eight Free-doms (*dal ba brgyad*) and Ten Favorable Con-ditions (*'byor ba bcu*) conducive to practicing the Dharma.

EIGHTEEN HELLS (*dmyal khams bco brgyad*). These include the eight hot hells (*tsa dmyal*), the eight cold hells (*grang dmyal*), the ephemeral hells (*nyi tshe ba*), and the surrounding hells (*nye 'khor ba*). See Bruyat (1987, pp. 67–76).

TWENTY-FOUR

TWENTY-FOUR GREAT SACRED PLACES (*gnas chen nyer gzhi*). According to the Hevajra Tantra (see Snellgrove 1959, 1:70) these are: Jalandhara, Oddiyana, Paurnagiri, Kamarupa, Malaya, Sindhu, Nagara, Munmuni, Karunyapataka, Devikota, Karmarapataka, Kulata, Arbuta, Godavari, Himadri, Harikela, Lampaka, Kani, Saurasta, Kalinga, Kokana, Caritra, Kosala, and Vindhyakaumarapaurika.

Other sources, such as the *sadhana* (*sgrub thabs*) of the *Queen of Great Bliss* (*yum bka' bde chen rgyal mo*) from the *Longchen Nyingthig* (see Tulku Thondup 1985), give a different enumeration of these twenty-four sacred places. They abide on the vajra-body inherent in every sentient being, which is symbolized here by the body of Vajrayogini. These twenty-four are divided in three groups:

a) Eight celestial abodes (Skt. *khagacharya*, Tib. *mkha' spyod*): 1) The crown of the head is Jalandhara, 2) in between the eyebrows is Pulliramalaya, 3) the nape is Arbuta, 4) the *urna* (the hair at the center of the forehead) is Rameshvara, 5) the right ear is Oddiyana, 6) the left ear is Godavari, 7) the eyes are Devikota, and 8) the shoulders are Malava.

b) Eight earthly abodes (Skt. *gocharya*, Tib. *sa spyod*): 9) the throat is Lampaka, 10) the underarms and kidneys are Kamarupa, 11) the two breasts are Odra, 12) the navel is Trish-anku, 13) the nose-tip is Koshala, 14) the palate is Kalinga, 15) the heart is both Kanchi-ka and 16) Himalaya (Himavat).

c) Eight underground abodes (Skt. *bhu-garbha*, Tib. *sa 'og gi gnas brgyad*): 17) the genitals are Pretapuri, 18) the anus is Grihadeva, 19) the thumbs and big toes are Maru, 20) the thighs are Saurashtra, 21) the calves are Suvar-nadvipa, 22) the sixteen other fingers and toes are Nagara, 23) the knees are Kulata, and 24) the ankles are Sindhu.

Bibliography

I

SHABKAR'S COLLECTED
WRITINGS
(See Appendix 5)

II

TIBETAN SOURCES

Chabpel Tsewang Phuntsok (*chab spel tshe dbang phun tshogs*, comp.). *rlangs kyi po ti bse ru rgyas pa.* Vol. 2 of *gangs can rig mdzod* series. Lhasa: Tibet People's Press (*bod ljongs mi dmangs dpe skrun khang*), 1986.

Chingkar Dönyö Dorje (*phying dkar don yod rdo rje*). *rdzogs pa che po snying thig gi khrid yig go bde bklag chog tu bkod pa lhun grub rtogs pa'i rang sgra kun bzang thugs mdzod gu yangs snying gi thig le* [The heart essence of openness and ease]. Printed from wooden blocks carved under the direction of Dza Trulshik Rinpoche at Thupten Chöling (*thub bstan chos gling*) in Sharkhumbu, Nepal. 96 fols.

——. *O rgyan thugs sprul dpal he ru ka grub dbang phying dkar ba'i bka'* [The spiritual songs of Chingkar Dönyö Dorje]. Manuscript in *dbu med*, 146 fols.

Chökyi Nangwa, the eighth Gyalwang Drukpa (*rgyal dbang 'brug pa kun gzigs chos kyi snang ba*). *rtsa ri gnas bshad rgyas par bshad pa'i le'u* [The extensive guide to Tsari]. In *Rare Tibetan Texts from Nepal*. Dolanji: Tashi Dorje, 1976.

Chöying Dorje (*gangs ri ba chos dbyings rdo rje*). *gangs mtsho gnas gsum gyi lo rgyus* [Guide to Mt. Kailash, Lake Manasarovar, and Pretapuri]. Vol. 1 of *bod ljongs nang bstan*. Lhasa: 1990. [MK]

Chöying Topden Dorje (*chos dbyings stobs ldan rdo rje*). *mdo rgyud rin po che mdzod* [The treasury of sutras and tantras]. Chengdu: Sichuan Nationalities Press, 1989.

Dudjom Rinpoche, Jigdral Yeshe Dorje (*bdud 'joms 'jigs bral ye shes rdo rje*). *rnying ma chos 'byung (gangs ljongs rgyal bstan yongs rdzogs kyi phyi mo snga 'gyur rdo rje theg pa'i bstan pa rin po che'i ji ltar byung ba'i tshul dag cing gsal bar brjod pa lha dbang g.yul las rgyal ba'i rnga bo che'i sgra dbyangs* [History of the Nyingma school of Tibetan Buddhism]. In *Collected Writings and Revelations of H. H. bDud-'joms Rin-po-che 'Jigs-bral Ye-shes rDo-rje*, vol. 1.

——, ed. *rnying ma bka' ma rgyas pa* [The expanded redaction of the Nyingma canon]. 58 vols. Kalimpong: Drubjung Lama, 1982–87.

——. *The Harmful Effects of Tobacco*, translated by Konchog Tendzin. St Léon-sur-Vézère: Editions Padmakara, 1978.

Dungtso Repa "the Later" (*dung mtsho ras pa phyi ma*). *yang ti nag po gser gyi 'bru cig pa*. 3 vols. Dalhousie: Damchoe Sangpo, 1979.

Gegyepa Tendzin Dorje (*dge rgyas pa bstan 'dzin rdo rje*). "*yer pa lha ri snying po'i dben gnas kyi chags rabs lo rgyus*" [History of Drak Yerpa]. In fascicle

1 of *bod ljongs nang bstan*, pp. 27–31. Lhasa: 1988.

Gonpo Wangyal, comp. *chos kyi rnam grangs shes bya'i nor gling 'jug pa'i gru gzings* [Glossary of enumerations]. Chengdu: Sichuan Nationalities Press, 1986.

Guru Tashi (*gu ru bkra shis*, also known as *stag gsang mkhas mchog ngag dbang blo 'gros*). *bstan pa'i snying po gsang chen snga 'gyur nges don zab mo'i chos kyi 'byung ba gsal bar byed pa'i legs bshad mkhas pa dga' byed ngo mtshar gtam gyi rol mtsho* [History of the Nyingma tradition], commonly known as Gurtra Chöjung (*gur bkra chos 'byung*), 5 vols. Paro: Published for H.H. Dilgo Khyentse Rinpoche by Lama Ngodrup and Sherab Drimey, Kyichu Temple, 1986 [GC]. Also published in one volume by *bod kyi shes rig dpe skrun khang*, 1990, and in two volumes by the *bod ljongs mi dmangs dpe skrun khang* (in the latter edition the author is misidentified as *thub bstan 'od gsal bstan pa'i nyi ma*), 1992.

Jamgön Kongtrul, Lodrö Thaye (*'jam mgon kong sprul blo gros mtha' yas*). *rin chen gter mdzod chen mo* [The treasury of rediscovered teachings]. Tsurphu edition, 73 vols. Paro: Lama Ngodrup and Sherab Drimey, for H.H. Dilgo Khyentse Rinpoche, 1976–80. [RT]

———. *gdams ngag mdzod* [The treasury of precious instructions of Tibetan Buddhism]. 18 vols. Paro: Lama Ngodrup and Sherab Drimey, for H.H. Dilgo Khyentse Rinpoche, 1979–82. [DZ]

———. *rgya chen bka'i mdzod* [The vast treasury of teachings]. Paro: Lama Ngodrup and Sherab Drimey, for H.H. Dilgo Khyentse Rinpoche, 1975–76.

———. *gter ston brgya rtsa'i rnam thar* [The lives of the hundred treasure discoverers]. In vol.1 of the *rin chen gter mdzod*. [TN]

Jamyang Khyentse Wangpo. *The Collected Works (gsung 'bum) of the great 'jam dbyangs mkhyen brtse'i dbang po*, 13 vols. Gangtok: Gonpo Tseden, 1977–80. [JK]

———. In vol. Da (*Tsha* according to American Library of Congress's catalogue). *gangs can bod kyi yul du byon pa'i gsang sngags gsar rnying gi gdan rabs mdor bsdus ngo mtshar padmo'i dga' tshal* [A brief history of the successive Mantrayana masters related to traditions of the New and the Ancient Translations], pp. 315–521.

Jamyang Khyentse Wangpo and Jamyang Loter Wangpo (*'jam dbyangs mkhyen brtse'i dbang po* and *'jam dbyangs blo gter dbang po*, comp.). *sgrub thabs kun btus* [Compendium of *sadhanas*]. 14 volumes. Dehra Dun: G.T.K. Lodoy et al., 1970.

Jigme Gyaltsen (*'jigs med rgyal mtshan*). *rwa rgya dga' ldan bkra shis 'byung gnas kyi lo rgyus mdo tsam brjod pa 'jam mgon bla ma dgyes pa'i mchod sprin* [History of Ragya Monastery]. Manuscript, 31 pages.

Jigme Thekchog (*'jigs med theg mchog*). *rong po dgon chen gyi gdan rabs rdzogs ldan gtam gyi rang sgrags* [History of the Great Monastery of Rongpo]. Xining: Qinghai Nationalities Press, 1988. [RO]

Jimba Norbu (*sbyin pa nor bu*). *'khri pa rtsad chod kyi bya ba nga sbas pa'i rnal 'byor chen po sbyin pa nor bu'i rnam thar . . .* [end of the title missing] [Jimba Norbu's autobiography]. Manuscript in *dbu med*, 247 fols. kept at Khakar Gonpa, Tarap Dolpo, Nepal. NGMPP, reel no. L 408/11.

Karma Mingyur Wangyal (*karma mi 'gyur dbang rgyal*). *gter ston brgya rtsa'i mtshan sdom gsol 'debs chos rgyal bkra shis stobs rgyal gyis mdzad pa'i 'grel pa lo rgyus gter ston chos 'byung* [History of the one hundred and eight treasure rediscoverers]. Darjeeling: Taklung Tsetrul Pema Wangyal, 1978.

Kathok Situ Chökyi Gyatso (*ka thog si tu chos kyi rgya mtsho*). *gangs ljongs dbus gtsang gnas bskor lam yig* [An account of a pilgrimage to central Tibet during the years 1918 to 1920]. Tashijong: Sungrab Nyamso Gyunphel Parkhang, 1972.

Khetsun Sangpo. *Biographical Dictionary of Tibet and Tibetan Buddhism*. 14 vols. Dharamsala: Library of Tibetan Works and Archives, 1981–92. [BD]

Konchog Gyaltsen (*dbal man dkon mchog rgyal mtshan*). *rgya bod sog gi lo rgyus nyung ngur brjod pa byis pa 'jug pa'i 'bab stegs*, pp. 480–665 of *Collected Works*, vol. 4. New Delhi, 1974.

Konchog Tenpai Rabgye (*dkon mchog bstan pa'i rab rgyas*). *Histoire du Bouddhisme dans l'Amdo*, or *deb ther rgya mtsho* [also known as *The Ocean Annals*, a religious history of Amdo], 4 vols. Delhi and Paris: École Pratique des Hautes Études à la Sorbonne. Also Gansu: Gansu Nationalities Press (*ken su'u mi rigs dpe skrun khang*), 1991. [AC]

Konchog Tendzin Chökyi Lodrö, Drigung Chungtsang VI ('*bri gung chung tshang dkon mchog bstan 'dzin chos kyi blo gros*). *gangs ri chen po ti se dang mtsho chen ma dros pa bcas kyi sngon 'byung lo rgyus mdor bsdus su brjod pa'i rab byed shel dkar me long* [Guide to Mt. Kailash].

——. *gsang lam sgrub pa'i gnas chen nyer bzhi'i ya rgyal gau-da-wa-ri 'am 'brog la phyi gangs kyi ra ba'i sngon byung gi tshul las brtsams pa'i gtam gyi rab tu phyed pa nyung ngu rnam gsal*. In *Two popular Tibetan Guides to the Pilgrimages to Mt. Kailash and to Lake Manasarovar and to the Lapchi Glacier or Godavari*. Delhi: Damchoe Sangpo, 1983. [GL]

Kunga Kewang (*kun dga' mkhas dbang*). *yul rma chen gangs ri'i gnas kyi rten bshad gdul bya'i 'gro blo'i dad brgya'i padmo 'byed pa'i nyin byed snang ba* [Guide to Amnye Machen]. Manuscript in *dbu can*, 12 fols.

Lelung Shepai Dorje (*sle lung bzhad pa'i rdo rje*). *dam can bstan srung rgya mtsho'i rnam par thar pa cha shas tsam brjod pa sngon med legs bshad* [History of the Dharma protectors]. 2 vols. Paro: Lama Ngodrup and Sherab Drimey for H.H. Dilgo Khyentse Rinpoche, 1978.

Lodrak Drupchen (*lho brag grub chen*). *The Collected Works (gsung 'bum) of lho brag grub chen nam mkha' rgyal mtshan*. Thimphu: Kunzang Topgyel, 1985.

Longchen Rabjam (*klong chen rab 'byams*). *mdzod bdun* [The seven treasuries]. 6 vols. Gangtok: Dodrup Rinpoche, 1970.

Muge Samten (*dmu dge bsam brtan*). *dris lan li dwangs rang sgra*. Pp. 100–22 in fascicle 3 of *rigs gnas lo rgyus dpyad yig bdams bsgrigs*. Chinese Tibetan Cultural Printing Press (*rga ba bod rigs rang skyongs khul*), May 1987.

Namchag Tsa Sum Lingpa (*nam lcags rtsa gsum gling pa*). *Rediscovered Treasures of Namchag Tsa Sum Lingpa (gnam lcags rtsa gsum gling pa'i zab gter)*. 12 vols. Kathmandu: Lama Ngodrup, 1989.

Ngawang Sonam Gyaltsen, Ngor Khangsar Khenpo (*ngor khang gsar mkhan po ngag dbang bsod nams rgyal mtshan*). *History of the 'Khor-chags Jo-bo Image and Temple (lhar bcas 'gro ba'i mchis sdong jo bo dngul sku mched gsum sngon byung gi gtam rabs brjod pa rin chen bedur sngon po'i pi wam*). Dharamsala: *bod ljong mnga' ris rigs gzhung gces skyong khang*, 1988.

Nyakla Pema Rigdzin (*sa smad bla ma nyag bla padma rig 'dzin*). *chos thams cad kyi spyir btang dka' ba'i gnas kyi brjed byang gsal bar ston pa rnam grangs rgya mtsho'i gter* [Concepts and categories of Buddhist philosophy]. Gangtok: Lama Dodrup Sangay, 1977.

Nyingma Gyubum (*rnying ma rgyud 'bum*). *Collected Tantras of the Nyingmapa*. 36 vols. Thimpu: Dilgo Khyentse Rinpoche, 1982. [NGB]

Orgyen Lingpa (*gter ston o rgyan gling pa*). *padma bka' thang* [The life of Guru Padmasambhava]. Chengdu: Sichuan Nationalities Press, 1987.

Orgyen Samten Lingpa (*O rgyan bsam gtan gling pa*). *mtsho snying mahadewa'i gnas yig* [The guide to Tsonying Island]. Manuscript, 7 fols.

Pal Gyalkar (*dpal rgyal mkhar*). "*rje zhabs dkar ba'i mgur glu'i bsam blo'i rang bzhin skor rags gleng ba.*" *krung go'i bod kyi shes rig* 4 (1989): 132–40.

——. "*bya gtang chen po zhabs dkar tshogs drug rang grol ba'i phyag rtsom gyi che ba bzhad pa'i me tog,*" In *bod kyi shes rig dpyad rtsom phyogs bsgrigs blo gsal bung ba 'dren pa'i dpyid kyi pho nya*, vol. 3, pp. 1–56. Beijing: China Tibetology Publishing House (*krung go'i bod kyi shes rig dpe skrun khang*), 1992.

Palden Yeshe (*dpal ldan ye shes*). *rgyal sras rin po che thogs med pa'i rnam thar bdud rtsi'i thigs pa* [The drop of ambrosia; or, The perfect liberation of the Precious Bodhisattva Thogme, a hagiography of Gyalse Thogme]. In *Instructions and minor writings of the bka' gdams pa master rgyal sras thogs med bzang po dpal*, 23 fols. Thimphu: Kunzang Topgay, 1985.

Patrul Rinpoche (*dpal dge sprul sku o rgyan 'jigs med chos kyi dbang po*). *zhabs dkar sprul sku myur 'byon gsol 'debs* [Prayer for the swift rebirth of Shabkar]. In *Ngagyur Nyingmay Sungrab*, 43:38–41. Gangtok: Sonam Kazi, 1969.

———. *kun bzang bla ma'i zhal lung* [The words of my perfect teacher, an explanation of the preliminary practices according to the *klong chen snying thig* tradition]. In *Ngagyur Nyingmay Sungrab*, vol. 42. Gangtok: Sonam Kazi, 1969.

Pema Karpo (*kun mkhyen padma dkar po*). *gnas chen tsa ri tra'i ngo mtshar snang ba pad dkar legs bshad* [The guidebook of the holy place of Caritra.] In *Collected Works of kun mkhyen padma dkar po*, vol. 4. Darjeeling: 1973. Also, Delhi: Lama Sherab Gyatso, 1982.

Phuntsok Tsering. *bod gyi lo rgyus zhib 'jug la nye bar mkho ba'i lo rgyus don chen re'u mig ketaka* [A compendium of historical dates]. Lhasa: Tibet Nationalities Press, 1987.

Ratna Lingpa, Tertön. *Collected Rediscovered Teachings of Ratna gling-pa*. 19 vols. Darjeeling: Taklung Tsetrul Pema Wangyal, 1977–79.

Rigdzin Kunzang Ngedön Long Yang (*rig 'dzin kun bzang nges don klong yangs*). *bod tu byung ba'i gsang sngags snga 'gyur gyi bstan 'dzin skyes mchog rim byung gyi rnam thar nor bu'i do shal* [The necklace of jewels, a concise history of the Nyingmapa tradition of Tibetan Buddhism]. Dalhousie: Damchoe Sangpo, 1976. [NJ]

Shakya Sangpo (*sngags 'chang shakya bzang po*). *mchod rten chen po bya rung kha shor gyi lo rgyus thos pas grol ba* [History of the Jarung Khashor (Bodhnath stupa) in Nepal]. Edited by Dalama Namgyal Dorje. Berkeley, 1967.

Sangye Chöphak (*sangs rgyas chos 'phags*). *rje btsun bla ma padma gsang sngags bstan 'dzin chos rgyal gyi rnam par thar pa skal bzang gdung sel* [Life of the second Shechen Gyaltsap, Pema Sangnak Tendzin Chögyal]. Manuscript in *dbu med*, 232 fols., kept at Shechen Monastery in Kham.

Shakabpa, Tsepon, W. D. *bod kyi srid don rgyal rabs* [Tibetan political history]. 2 vols. Kalimpong: Shakabpa House, 1976.

Shechen Gyaltsap, Gyurme Padma Namgyal (*zhe chen rgyal tshab 'gyur med padma rnam rgyal*). *snga 'gyur theg dgu'i tshogs bshad mdor bsdus nor bu'i tambura* [The jewel lute, a concise explanation of the nine vehicles], and *snga 'gyur theg pa rim dgu'i rnam gzhag mdor bsdus su brjod pa rin po che'i them skas* [The jewel ladder, a concise exposition of the nine vehicles]. Respectively in volumes Tha and Da of *The Collected Works of zhe chen rgyal tshab padma rnam rgyal*, 18 vols. Paro: Lama Ngodrup, 1975–90.

———. *rdo rje theg pa'i thun mong gi sngon 'gro spyi la sbyor chog pa'i khrid kyi rgyab yig kun mkhyen zhal lung rnam grol shing rta*. In volume Ja of the *Collected Works*, in 364 fols.

Sölo (*bsod blo*). "*mi la ras pa'i rnam thar' dang zhabs dkar ba'i rnam thar gnyis bsdur nas rags tsam dbyad pa.*" *bod ljongs zhib 'jug* 4 (1990): 44–60.

Sumpa Khenpo Yeshe Paljor (*gsum pa mkhan po ye shes dpal 'byor*). *mtsho sngon gyi lo rgyus sogs bkod pa'i tshangs glu gsar snyan*. Satapitaka (New Delhi: International Academy for Indian Culture) 12, no. 2 (1960): 425–58. [Partly translated as the *Annals of Kokonor*, see below].

Trakar Taso Tulku Chökyi Wangchuk (*brag dkar rta so sprul sku chos kyi dbang phyug*). *'phags mchog thugs rje chen po rang byung wati bzang po'i rnam thar ngo mtshar rmad du byung ba'i gtam dad pa'i nyin byed phyogs brgyar dren pa'i rta ljang*. Manuscript in sixty-five folios, kept in Nubri, Nepal.

Yontan Gyatso, Khenpo (*mkhan po yon tan rgya mtsho*). *yon tan rin po che mdzod kyi 'grel ba zla ba'i sgron me* and *nyi ma'i 'od zer* [Commentary on Jigme Lingpa's Yontan Dzö]. In *rnying ma bka'* ma, vols. 38–40. Kalimpong: Drubjung Lama, 1982–87. [YZ]

Tendzin Pemai Gyaltsen, the fourth Drigung Chetsang (*'bri gung che tshang bstan 'dzin padma'i rgyal mtshan*). *nges don bstan pa'i snying po mgon po 'bri gung pa chen po'i gdan rabs chos kyi byung tshul gser gyi phreng ba* [A detailed historical account of the various masters of the 'Bri Gung Bka' Brgyud Pa school]. Bir: Tsondu Senghe, 1977.

Thubten Namkhar (*thub bstan gnam mkhar*). "*gdan sa mthil dgon pa'i lo rgyus rags gleng*" [A brief account of the history of Densathil Monas-tery]. *lho kha'i rtsom rig sgyu rtsal* 1 (1990): 67–69.

Tsang Nyon Heruka (*gtsang smyon heruka*). *rnal 'byor gyi dbang phyug dam pa rje btsun mi la ras pa'i rnam par thar pa dang thams cad mkhyen pa'i lam ston* [The life-story of Milarepa and the *Collection of Songs of Spiritual Experience* of Milarepa]. Xylographs carved at Apho Rinpoche's monastery, Manali, India.

Zhang Yisun et al. *bod rgya tshig mdzod chen mo* [Great Tibetan-Chinese Dictionary]. 3 vols. Beijing: Nationalities Press, 1985. [TC]

III
TERMAS OF KUNZANG DECHEN GYALPO
AND RELATED MATERIALS

Chögyal Ngakyi Wangpo (*chos rgyal ngag gi dbang po*). *gter gsar rdzogs chen gyi khrid rim ma rig mun sel ye shes sgron me* [The torch of wisdom that dispels the darkness of ignorance]. Manuscript in *dbu med* in Shabkar's own handwriting. Paro: Lama Ngodrup and Sherab Drimey, 1979. [TW]

Gurong Tulku, Natsok Rangdrol (*dgu rong sprul sku sna tshogs rang grol*). *gter gsar rta phag yid bzhin nor bu'i bsnyen sgrub kyi yi ge rab gsal shel dkar me long* [The crystal mirror]. Manuscript in *dbu med*, 34 fols. [CM]

Kalden Rigdrol (*skal ldan rigs grol*). *rdzogs pa chen po ma rig mun sel gyi sngon 'gro'i zur rgyan.* Manuscript in *dbu med*, 12 fols. NGMPP, reel no. L 309/2.

Kyapdal Lhundrup (*khyab brdal lhun grub*). *yang gsang rta phag gi las byang dngos grub rgya mtsho las lhan thabs gang ga'i chu rgyun gtsang ma'i spel ba.* Manuscript in *dbu med*, 26 fols. NGMPP, reel no. L 308/11.

——. *rta phag yid bzhin nor bu'i bskyed rdzogs.* Manuscript in *dbu med*, 2 fols. NGMPP, reel no. L 309/6.

——. *rol grangs tshangs pa'i rnga sgra dgyes pa'i mchod sprin ma dge (rta phag yid bzhin nor bu'i cho ga).*

Manuscript in *dbu med*, 5 fols. NGMPP, reel no. L 309/4.

——. *rta phag yid bzhin nor bu'i zhi ba'i sbyin bsreg sdig sgrib nyes ltung bsreg byed ye shes 'od snang.* Manuscript in *dbu med*, 12 fols. NGMPP, reel no., L 309/6 and 309/11.

——. *rigs drug gi 'dug stangs dang snang bzhi'i 'dug stangs shog khra gnyis.* Manuscript in *dbu med*, 3 fols. NGMPP, reel no. L 309/11.

Kunzang Dechen Gyalpo (*kun bzang bde chen rgyal po*). *yang gsang rta phag gi las byang dngos grub rgya mtsho.* Manuscript in *dbu med*, 11 fols. NGMPP, reel no. L 308/7.

——. *rta phag yid bzhin nor bu'i rtsa rlung seng ge'i nyams rtogs bde chen 'od 'bar.* Manuscript in *dbu med*, 12 fols. NGMPP, reel no. L 309/6.

——. *ma cig gsang ba ye shes las rta phag gi dbang bskur zab mo'i rim pa.* 5 fols. NGMPP, reel no. L 308/12 and 7.

——. *ma cig gsang ba ye shes las padma rgyal po'i dbang bskur gyi las rim nag 'gros bklag tu bkod pa.* 12 fols. NGMPP, reel no. L 308/17.

——. *ma cig gsang ba ye shes las dbang gi dkyil 'khor bca' gzhi.* 9 fols. NGMPP, reel no. L 308/17.

------. *ma cig gsang ba ye shes las nang sgrub bcom ldan 'das dzam lha'i rjes gnang bskur ba'i rim pa.* 7 fols. NGMPP, reel no. L 308/7.

Lobzang Tsultrim (*blo bzang tshul khrims*). *yang gsang rta phag gi las byang dngos grub rgya mtsho'i rnam bshad bsnyen bsgrub dang 'brel bas 'dod dgu'i bang mdzod.* Manuscript in *dbu med,* 100 fols. NGMPP, reel no. L 308/18 and 309/1.

Ngonchung Rangdrol (*sngon chung rang grol*). *'pho ba spyi gtsug 'ja' gur ma.* Manuscript in *dbu med,* 3 fols. NGMPP, reel no. L 309/4.

Tenrab (*bstan rab*). *gter gsar yid bzhin nor bu'i bsnyen yig nyams chung yid kyi mun sel.* Manuscript in *dbu med,* 6 fols. NGMPP, reel no. L 309/2.

Trulshik Rinpoche, Ngawang Chökyi Lodrö (*'khrul zhig ngag dbang chos kyi blo sgros*). *gter ston rig 'dzin chen po kun bzang bde chen rgyal po rtsal gyi zab gter yang zab rta phag yid bzhin nor bu'i dbang chog ye shes bdud rtsi'i bum bzang.* Manuscript in *dbu med,* 33 fols. NGMPP, reel no. L 308/14. [WL]

------. *rta phag yid bzhin nor bu'i las byang dngos grub rgya mtsho dang zur rgyan 'dod 'byung nor bu bklag chog tu bkod pa pundarika'i do shal* [The necklace of white lotuses]. Manuscript in *dbu med,* 25 fols. NGMPP, reel no. L 308/15 and 11, in 17 fols. [NW]

Tsondru (*brtson 'grus*). *ma cig gsang ba ye shes las rig 'dzin bla ma'i sgrub thabs las byang nag 'gros su bkod pa.* Manuscript in *dbu med,* 8 fols. NGMPP, reel no. L 309/3.

------. *ma cig gsang ba ye shes las mkha' 'gro'i las byang me tog 'phreng mdzes.* Manuscript in *dbu med,* 9 fols. NGMPP, reel no. L 309/3.

IV
SOURCES IN
WESTERN LANGUAGES

Ahmad, Zahiruddin. *Sino-Tibetan Relations in the Seventeenth Century.* Serie Orientale Roma, vol. 40. Rome: Istituto Italiano per il Medio ed Estremo Oriente (Is.M.E.O), 1970.

Aufschnaiter, Peter. "Lands and Places of Milarepa." *East and West* 26 (1976): 175–89. [MI]

Aziz, Barbara N. "The work of Pha-dam-pa sangs-rgyas as revealed in Ding-ri folklore." In *Tibetan Studies in Honour of Hugh Richardson,* edited by M. Aris and Aung San Suu Kyi, 21–29. Warminster, 1980.

------. "Indian Philosopher as Tibetan Folk Hero." *Central Asiatic Journal* 23, nos. 1–2 (1979): 19–37.

Bacot, Jacques, trans. *Le poète tibétain Milarépa.* Paris: Brossart, 1925.

Bailey, F. M. *No Passport to Tibet.* London: 1957.

Barraux, Roland. *Histoire des Dalaï Lamas, quatorze reflets sur le Lac des Visions.* Paris: Albin Michel, 1993.

Batchelor, Stephen, et al. *The Tibet Guide.* 2d rev. ed. Boston: Wisdom, 1991.

Blondeau, Anne-Marie. "mKhyen brtse'i dbang po: La Biographie de Padmasambhava selon la tradition du bsGrags-pa Bon, et ses sources." *Orientalia Iosephi Tucci Memoriae Dicata,* Seria Orientale Roma, 56, no. 1 (1985): 111–58.

Bruyat, Christian, et al., trans. *Le Chemin de la Grande Perfection* [translation of Patrul Rinpoche's Kunzang Lamai Shelung, *kun bzang bla ma'i zhal lung*].St Léon-sur-Vézère: Editions Padmakara, 1987. Translated into English under the title *The Words of My Perfect Teacher.* London: Harper and Row, 1994.

Buffetrille, Katia. "Le Grand Pélérinage de l'A myes rma chen au Tibet: Tradition Écrite, Réalités Vivantes." In *Mandala and Landscapes,* edited by A. W. MacDonald. Delhi: DK Printworld, 1994. [Includes a translation of the *Guide to Amnye Machen;* see above.]

Chang, G. C. C. *The Hundred Thousand Songs of Milarepa*. 2 vols. New York: University Books, 1962. Boulder: Shambhala, 1977.

De Rossi Filibeck, E. "A Guide-Book to Tsari." In *Reflections on Tibetan Culture*, edited by L. Epstein. Seattle, 1989. [GT]

Dilgo Khyentse Rinpoche. *The Wish-fulfilling Jewel. The Practice of Guru Yoga according to the Longchen Nyingthig Tradition*. Boston: Shambhala, 1988.

———. *La Sagesse aux Cent Miroirs. Commentaire sur les Cent Conseils de Padampa Sanguié au peuple de Tingri*. Peyzac-le-Moustier: Editions Padmakara, 1994.

Dowman, Keith, trans. *The Legend of the Great Stupa* [translation of the *mchod rten chen po bya rung kha shor gyi lo rgyus thos pas grol ba*]. Berkeley, Calif.: Dharma Publishing, 1973.

———. "A Buddhist Guide to the Power Places of the Kathmandu Valley." *Kailash* (Kathmandu) 8, nos. 3–4 (1981): 183–291.

———. *The Power-places of Central Tibet: The Pilgrim's Guide*. London and New York: Routledge and Kegan Paul, 1988. [PP]

———. *The Flight of the Garuda*. Boston: Wisdom, 1993.

Dudjom Rinpoche. *The Nyingma School of Tibetan Buddhism. Its Fundamentals and History*. Translated and edited by Gyurme Dorje and Matthew Kapstein. Boston: Wisdom, 1991. [NS]

Ehrhard, Franz-Karl. *Flügelschläge des Garuda. Literar- und ideengeschichtliche Bermerkungen zu einer Liedersammlung des rDzogs-chen*. Stuttgart: Franz Steiner Verlag. 1990.

———. "The 'Vision' of rDzogs-chen: A text and its histories." In *Proceedings of the 5th Conference of the International Association for Tibetan Studies*. Naritasan: 1989.

———. "The Stupa of Bodhnath: A Preliminary Analysis of the Written Sources." *Ancient Nepal: Journal of the Department of Archeology* (Kathmandu), no. 120 (Oct.–Nov.1990).

———. *Views of the Bodhnath Stupa*. Kathmandu: 1991.

———. "Two Documents on the Tibetan Ritual Literature and Spiritual Genealogy." *Journal of the Nepal Research Center (JNRC)* 9 (1992).

Eimer, Helmut. "The Development of the Biographical Tradition concerning Atisha (Dipamkarasrijnana)." *The Journal of Tibet Society* 2 (1982): 41–51.

Ferraci, A. *mKyen brtse's Guide to the Holy Places of Central Tibet*. Edited by L. Petech. Serie Orientale Roma, vol. 16. Rome: Is. M.E.O, 1958.

Fletcher, H. R. *A Quest of Flowers*. Edinburgh: 1975.

Frye, Stanley, trans. *The Sutra of the Wise and the Foolish* [translation from the Mongolian of the *Damamuka-nama-sutra*]. Dharamsala: Library of Tibetan Works and Archives, 1981.

———. *A Drop of Nourishment for the People* [translation from the Mongolian of the *Nitasastrajantuposanabindu* (Tib. *lugs kyi bstan bcos skye bo gso ba'i thig pa*)]. Dharamsala: Library of Tibetan Works and Archives, 1981.

Goodman, Steven D. "The Klong chen snying thig: An Eighteenth-Century Tibetan Revelation." Ph.D. diss., University of Saskatchewan, 1983.

Guenther, Herbert V., trans. *The Life and Teachings of Naropa*. Oxford: Clarendon Press, 1963.

———, trans. *Kindly Bent to Ease Us*, by Gyalwa Longchenpa, parts 1–3. Emeryville, Calif.: Dharma Publishing, 1975-1976.

Gyatso, Janet. "The Literary Transmission of the Traditions of Thang-stong rGyal-po. A Study of Visionary Buddhism in Tibet." Diss., University of California at Berkeley, 1981. [TH]

———. "The Development of the *gcod* tradition." In *Soundings in Tibetan Civilization*, edited by B. N. Aziz and M. Kapstein, 320–41. New Delhi: Manohar, 1985.

Ho-Chin Yang. *The Annals of Kokonor* [translation of part of Sumpa Khenpo's *mtsho sngon gyi lo rgyus*]. The Hague: Mouton; Bloomington: Indiana University Press, 1969.

Hodgson, Brian H. *Essays on the Languages, Literature, and Religion of Nepal and Tibet.* Introduction by Philip Denwood. New Delhi. Manjusri Publishing House, 1972.

Hookham, Shenphen K.. *The Buddha Within.* Albany: State University of New York Press, 1991.

Howorth, H. H.: *History of the Mongols.* 4 vols. London: 1976.

Huber, Toni. "A Pilgrimage to La-phyi: A study of sacred and historical geography in southwestern Tibet." Masters diss., University of Canterbury, 1989.

——. "Traditional Environmental Protectionism in Tibet Reconsidered." *The Tibet Journal* 16, no. 3 (Autumn, 1991): 63–77.

——. "A Pilgrimage to La-phyi: The Sacred and Historical Geography of a Holy Place in South-Western Tibet." In *Mandala and Landscapes,* edited by A.W. MacDonald. Delhi: DK Printworld, 1994.

——. "Where Exactly Are Caritra, Devikota and Himavat? A Sacred Geography Controversy and the Development of Tantric Buddhist Pilgrimage Sites in Tibet." *Kailash, A Journal of Himalayan Studies* (Kathmandu) 18 (1992).

——. "A Tibetan Map of Lho-kha in the South-Eastern Himalayan Borderlands of Tibet." *Imago Mundi* 44 (1992).

Jackson, David P. *The Mollas of Mustang.* Dharamsala: Library of Tibetan Works and Archives, 1984.

Kapstein, Matthew: "The Shangs-pa bKa'-brgyud: An unknown tradition of Tibetan Buddhism." In *Tibetan Studies in Honour of Hugh Richardson,* edited by M. Aris and Aung San Suu Kyi, 138–44. Warminster, 1980.

——. "The Purificatory Gem and its Cleansing: A late Tibetan polemical discussion of apocryphal texts." *History of Religions* 28, no. 3 (1988/89): 217–44.

Karma Thinley (*karma 'phrin las*). *The History of the Sixteen Karmapas of Tibet.* Boulder: Shambhala, 1978.

Karsten, J. "Some notes on the House of lHa rGya ri." In *Tibetan Studies in Honour of Hugh Richardson,* edited by M. Aris and Aung San Suu Kyi, 153–68. Warminster, 1980.

Kolmas, Joseph. "The Ambans and Assistant Ambans." Paper handed out at the International Association for Tibetan Studies, 6th International Conference, Fagernes, 1992.

Lamotte, Étienne. *Histoire du Bouddhisme Indien.* Vol. 43. Louvain: Bibliothèque du Muséon, 1958.

Lhalungpa, L. P., trans. *The Life of Milarepa,* by Tsang Nyön Heruka. New York: E. P. Dutton, 1977. Boston: Shambhala, 1984.

——, trans. *Mahamudra, The Quintessence of Mind and Meditation,* by Takpo Tashi Namgyal. Boston: Shambhala, 1986.

Martin, D. "For Love or Religion? Another Look at a 'Love Song' by the Sixth Dalai Lama." In *Zeitschrift der deutschen Morgenländishen Gesellschaft,* 1988, 349–63.

Petech, L. *China and Tibet in the Early 18th Century.* 2d ed. Leiden: E. J. Brill, 1972.

——. *Aristocracy and Government in Tibet.* Serie Orientale Roma, vol. 45. Rome: Is. M.E.O, 1973.

——. "The 'Bri-gung-pa Sect in Western Tibet and Ladakh." In *Proceedings of the Csoma De Koros Memorial Symposium,* edited by L. Ligeti, 313–26. Latrafured Hungart, 1976. Budapest, 1978.

Rhodes, N. G. "The development of currency in Tibet." In *Tibetan Studies in Honour of Hugh Richardson,* edited by M. Aris and Aung San Suu Kyi, 261–68. Warminster, 1980.

Rock, J. F. "The Amnye Machen Range and Adjacent Regions."In *Serie Orientale Roma* 12:33–50. Rome: Istituto Italiano per il Medio ed Estremo Oriente (Is.M.E.O), 1956.

Roerich, George N., trans. *The Blue Annals* [translation of Gö Lotsawa Shonnu Pel (*'gos lo tsa ba gzhon nu dpal*), *deb ther sngon po*]. 2d ed. Delhi: Motilal Banarsidass,1976. [BA]

Rowell, Galen. *Mountains in the Middle Kingdom: Exploring the High Peaks of China and Tibet.* San Francisco: Sierra Club Books, 1984.

Ruegg, David S. "The Jo-nang pas: A School of Buddhist Ontologists according to the Grub mtha' shel gyi me long." *Journal of the American Oriental Society* 83 (1963): 73–91.

Schmidt, Erik Pema Kunzang, trans. *The Flight of the Garuda.* [translation of the *mkha' lding gshog rlabs*]. Kathmandu: Rangjung Yeshe, 1984.

Shakabpa, Tsepon, W. D. *Tibet, a Political History.* New Haven: Yale University Press, 1967.

Smith, E. Gene. Foreword to the "Tibetan Chronicle of Padma-dkar-po." In *Sata-Pitaka Series* 75, edited by Lokesh Chandra. New Delhi: 1968.

———. Foreword to *Kongtrul's Encyclopedia of Indo-Tibetan Culture*, edited by Lokesh Chandra. Sata-Pitaka Series. New Delhi: 1970.

———. Foreword to the *yang ti nag po gser gyi 'bru gcig pa'i chos skor.* In *Smanrtsis Shesrig Spendzod*, vol. 41. Leh: 1972.

Snellgrove, D. L.: *The Hevajra Tantra.* Pts. 1 and 2. London Oriental Series, vol. 6. London: Oxford University Press, 1961

Snodgrass, A.: *The Symbolism of the Stupa.* Ithaca, N.Y.: Seap, 1985.

Sorensen, Per K.: "Divinity Secularized: An inquiry into the nature and form of the songs ascribed to the sixth Dalai Lama." In *Wiener Studien Zur Tibetologie und Buddhismuskunde.* Wien: 1990.

Stearns, Cyrus: *The Life and Teachings of the Tibetan Mahasiddha Thang-stong rGyal-po, 'King of the Empty Plain',* Master's thesis, University of Washington, 1980.

Takpo Tashi Namgyal (*dwags po bkra shis rnam rgyal*). *phyag chen zla ba'i 'od zer.* Translated into English by L. P. Lhalungpa under the title *Mahamudra, The Quintessence of Mind and Meditation.* Boston: Shambhala, 1986.

Tempa Gyaltsen Negi, A., Evelyne Borremans, and O. L. Chökyi Dawa, trans. *Machik Labdrön.* Brussels: Editions Dharmachakra, 1990.

Thondup, Tulku Rinpoche. *The Tantric Tradition of the Nyingmapa: The Origin of Buddhism in Tibet.* Marion: Buddhayana Foundation, 1984 (Khandro Nyingthig, pp. 33ff.).

———. *Hidden Teachings of Tibet: An Explanation of the Terma Tradition of the Nyingma School of Buddhism.* London: Wisdom, 1986.

———. *Buddha Mind: An Anthology of Longchen Rabjam's Writings on Dzogpa Chenpo.* Ithaca, N.Y.: Snow Lion, 1989. [BM]

Tsarong, T. J. *Handbook of Traditional Tibetan Drugs.* Kalimpong: Tibetan Medical Publications, 1986.

Tsepak Rigzin. *Tibetan-English Dictionary of Buddhist Terminology.* Dharamsala, India: Library of Tibetan Works and Archives, 1986.

Tucci, Giuseppe. *Transhimalaya.* Genève: Nagel, 1973.

Ui, H. et al., eds. *A Complete Catalogue of the Tibetan Buddhist Canon, Bkah-hgyur and Bstan-hgyur.* Sendai: Tohoku Imperial University Library, 1934. [T]

Vitali, R.: *Early Temples of Central Tibet.* London: Serindia, 1990.

Vostrikov, A. I. *Tibetan Historical Literature.* In *Soviet Indology Series, Bd. 4*, translated by Harish Chandra Gupta. Calcutta: Indian Studies, Past and Present, 1970.

Willis, Janice D., ed. *Feminine Ground. Essays on Women and Tibet.* Ithaca, N.Y.: Snow Lion, 1987.

———. "On the nature of rnam thar: Early dge lugs pa *siddhas'* biographies." In *Soundings in*

Tibetan Civilization, edited by B. N. Aziz and M. Kapstein, 304–19. New Delhi: Manohar, 1985.

Yeshe Tsogyal. *The Lotus Born Guru. The Life Story of Padmasambhava*. Revealed by Nyang Ral Nyima Öser. Translated by Erik Padma Kunzang. Boston: Shambhala, 1993.

Yeshi, Kim, and Acharya Tashi Tsering: "The Story of a Tibetan Yogini, Shungsep Jetsun." In *Chö-Yang*, the Year of Tibet edition. Dharamsala: 1991.

Yuthok, Dorje Yudon: *House of the Turquoise Roof.* Ithaca, N.Y.: Snow Lion, 1990.

Maps

Shabkar's autobiography provides a mine of information concerning the location of places that are not found on available maps. Besides this autobiography, our main sources have been the map of Amdo in Tenpai Rabgye (AC) for map 2; the map of Tibet (Information Office, Gangchen Kyishong, Dharamsala), for maps 1 to 4; Peter Kessler (personal communications) for maps 2 to 6; Mike Farmer (NS and personal communications) for maps 2 to 4; Toni Huber (LNY and personal communication) for map 4 and insert in map 3; Keith Dowman (PP) for maps 3 and 4; Stephen Batchelor (1991) for maps 3 and 4; Peter Aufschnaiter (MI) for map 5; Swami Pranavananda (Calcutta, 1949) and Chöying Dorje (NK) for map 6. We have also consulted several other maps and sketches including *Stanford's* map of South-Central Tibet (1987) and *Mandala Graphic Arts'* map of Kathmandu to Tibet.

The areas covered by maps 2 to 6 are indicated by dotted lines.

MAP 1

General map showing the traditional borders of Tibet before the Communist Chinese invasion. After 1959, Tibet was split into three parts. Amdo (Domey) was made the new province of Qinghai; Kham was attached to the existing Chinese province of Szechuan, and the rest of Tibet was named the so-called "Autonomous Region of Tibet."

MAP 2

Domey (*mdo smad*) or Amdo *(a mdo)*, the native province of Shabkar. See Author's Introduction, chaps. 1 to 8, and 15.

Blue Lake = Lake Kokonor; Heart of the Lake = Tsonying Island; White Rock Monkey Fortress = Trakar Drel Dzong; Tigress Fort = Takmo Dzong; Abode of the Hundred Thousand Maitreyas = Jampa Bumling; Three Black Camps = Banak Khasum.

MAP 3

U *(dbus)*, or Central Tibet, with an insert detailing the area of Tsari. See chaps. 9, 10, and 14.

Seven Households of Lo = Lomi Kyimdun

MAP 4

Tsang *(gtsang)* province. See chaps. 11, 12, and 13.

Splendor of the Conquerors (Gyalkyi Shri) = Tsibri.

MAP 5

Details of the areas of Lapchi, Nyanang, Kyirong, Gungthang, and Lo Mantang. See chaps. 12 and 13.

Azure Queen Mountain = Tonting Gyalmo, Gaurishankar; Brocade Cave of Rala = Rala Zaog Phuk; Cave of the Subjugation of Mara = Dudul Phuk; Cavern of Brilliant Light = Ösel Phuk; Chamangpo = Many Birds; Happy Village = Kyirong; Horse Tooth White Rock = Trakar Taso; Hundred Springs = Chumik Gyatsa or Muktinath; Red Rock = Trakmar; Sky Citadel = Namkha Dzong.

MAP 6

Mt. Kailash and Lake Manasarovar area. See chap. 11.

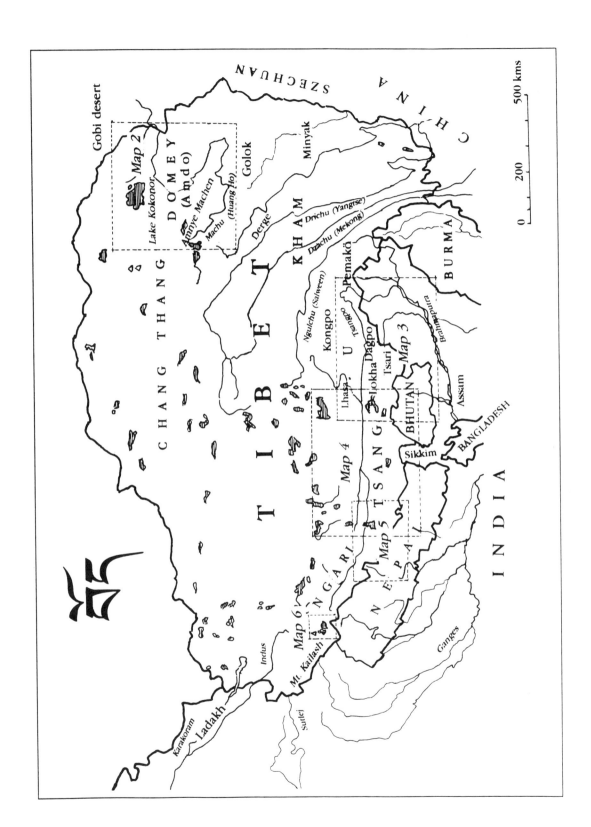

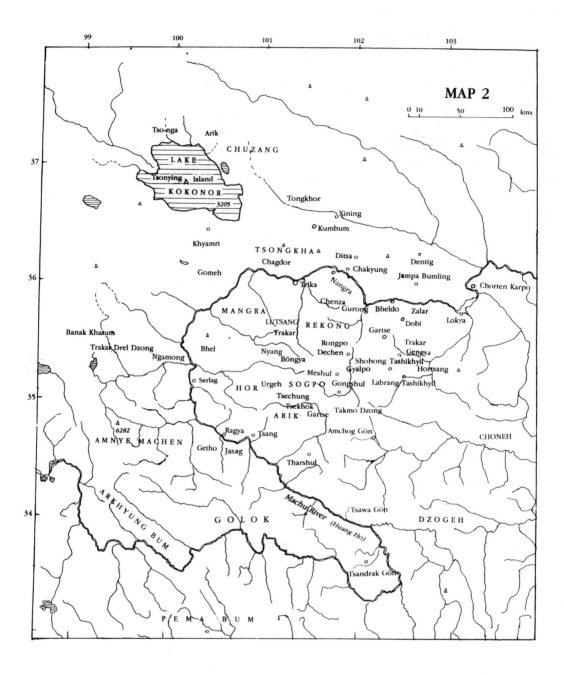

MAP 2

0 10   50   100   kms

99   100   101   102   103

Tso-nga   Arik   C H U Z A N G

LAKE

37   Tsonying   Island

K O K O N O R   3205   Tongkhor

Xining

Kumbum

Khyamri   T S O N G K H A   Ditsa   Dentig

Chagdor   Chakyung   Jampa Bumling

36   Gomeh   Trika   Nangra   Chorten Karpo

Chenza   Gurong   Bheldo   Zalar

MANGRA   LUTSANG   R E K O N G   Dobi   Lokya

Banak Khasum   Trakar   Gartse

Trakar Drel Dzong   Bhel   Rongpo   Trakar

Ngamong   Nyang   Dechen   Gengya

Böngya   Shohong Tashikhyil   Hortsang

Meshul   Gyalpo

Serlag   Urgeh S O G P O   Gongshul   Labrang Tashikhyil

35   H O R   Tsechung

Tsekhok

6282   A R I K · Gartse   Takmo Dzong   C H O N E H

A M N Y E   M A C H E N   Ragya   Tsang   Amchog Gön

Getho   Jasag

Tharshul

A R   K H Y U N G   B U M   Machu River   Tsawa Gön

34   G O L O K   (Huang Ho)   D Z O G E H

Tsandrak Gön

P E M A   B U M

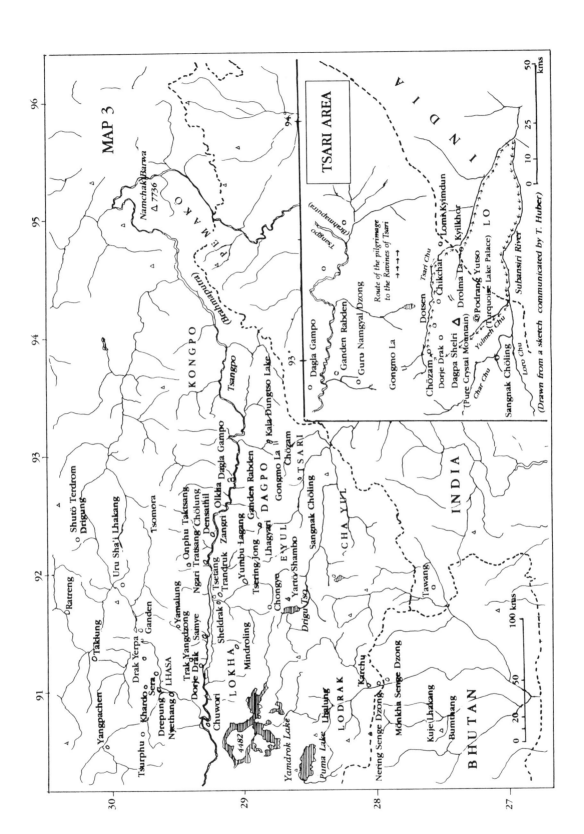

MAP 3

Namchak Barwa △7736

PEMAKO

KONGPO

(Brahmaputra)

Tsangpo

Yangpachen

Tsurphu o Khardo o Drak Yerpa o Ganden
Drepung o Sera o
Nyethang o LHASA

Ratreng

Takdung

Uru Sha'i Lhakang

Tsomora

Shutö Terdrom o Drigung

Yamalung o Onphu Taktsang o
Ngari Tratsang Chölung Densathil

Trak Yangdzong Samye
Dorje Drak o
Chuwori

LOKHA

Mindroling

Sheldrak o Tsetang o Olkha Dagla Gampo
Trandruk Zangri

Yumbu Lagang Ganden Rabden
Tsering Jong Lhagyari DAGPO
Gongmo La
Chongye o EYUL Chözam
Yartö Shambo II TSARI

Drigu Tso

4482

Yamdrok Lake

Puma Lake Lhalung

LODRAK

Karchu

Nering Senge Dzong
Mönkha Senge Dzong

Kuje Lhakang
Bumthang

Sangnak Chöling

CHAYUL

Tawang

INDIA

BHUTAN

Kala Dungtso Lake

100 kms

0 20 50

0 50 100 kms

TSARI AREA

o Dagla Gampo

Tsangpo
(Brahmaputra)

o Ganden Rabden

o Guru Namgyal Dzong

Gongmo La

Chözam o Dotsen Tsari Chu Lomk Kyimdun o
Dorje Drak o o Chikchar Kyilkhor
Dagpa Shelri △ Drolma La
(Pure Crystal Mountain) o Podrang Yutso
Yulmet Chu (Turquoise Lake Palace)

Char Chu LO

Sangnak Chöling Loro Chu Subansiri River

Route of the pilgrimage
to the Ravines of Tsari

INDIA

0 10 25 50
kms

(Drawn from a sketch communicated by T. Huber)

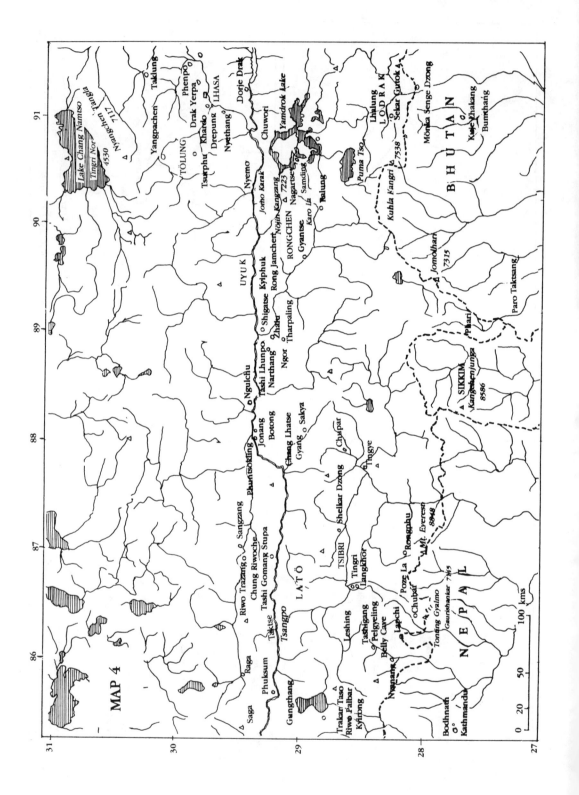

MAP 4

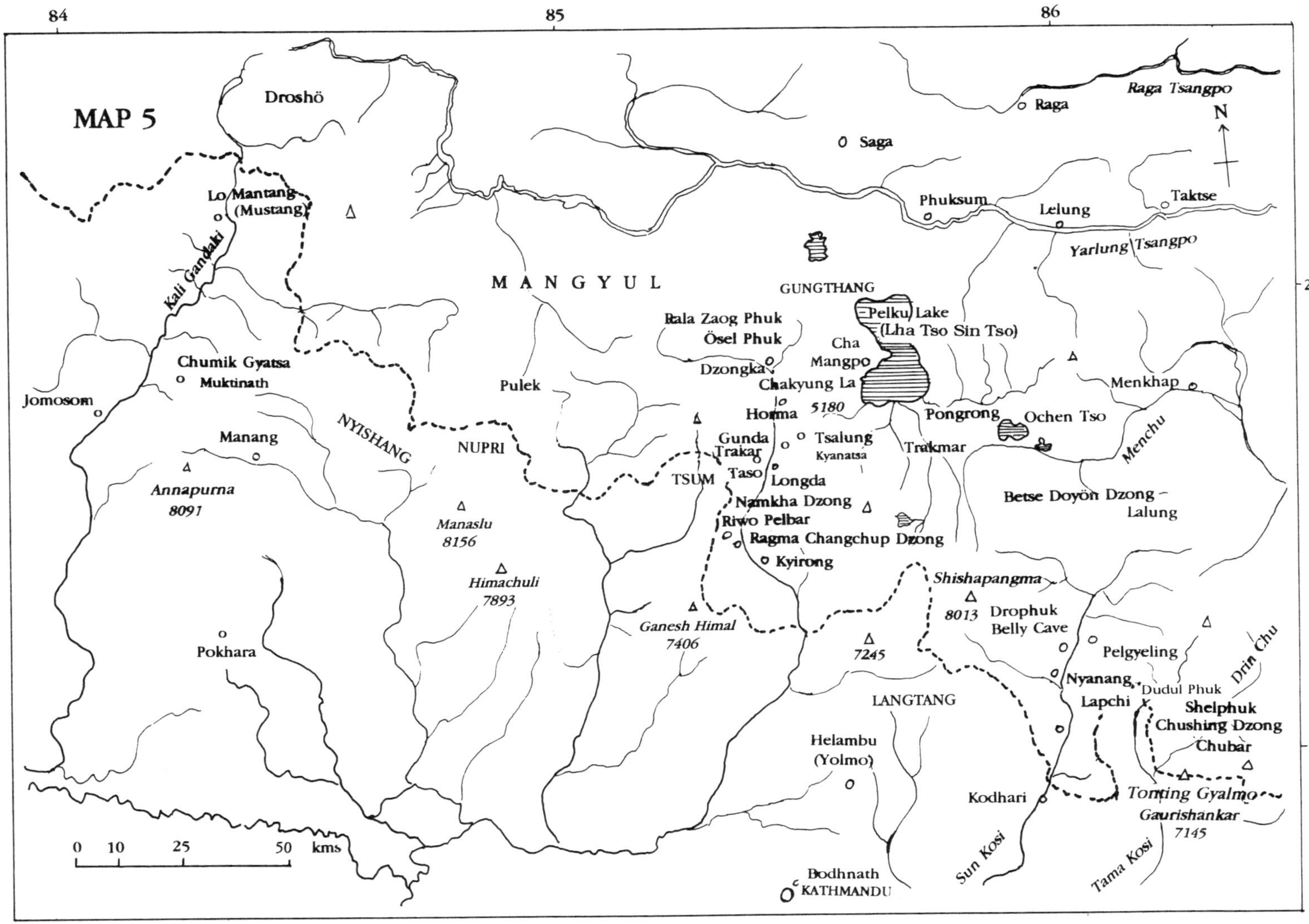

MAP 5

N

Raga Tsangpo
Raga
Taktse
Lelung
Phuksum
Saga
Droshö

Yarlung Tsangpo
Menkhap
Menchu
Pongrong Ochen Tso
Betse Doyön Dzong
Lalung

Pelku Lake
(Lha Tso Sin Tso)
Cha
Mangpo
Chakyung La
5180
Trakmar
Tsalung
Kyanatsa
Longda
Taso
Namkha Dzong
Riwo Pelbar
Ragma Changchup Dzong
Kyirong

Bala Zaog Phuk
Ösel Phuk
Dzongka
Horma
Gunda
Trakar

GUNGTHANG

MANGYUL

Pulek

NUPRI

TSUM

Ganesh Himal
7406

Manaslu
8156

Himachuli
7893

NYISHANG

Manang

Annapurna
8091

Lo Manrang
(Mustang)
Chumik Gyatsa
Muktinath

Kali Gandaki

Jomosom

Pokhara

Shishapangma
8013
Drophuk
Belly Cave

7245

LANGTANG

Helambu
(Yolmo)

Bodhnath
KATHMANDU

Pelgyeling
Nyanang, Dudul Phuk
Lapchi
Shelphuk
Chushing Dzong
Chubar
Tomting Gyalmo
Gaurishankar
7145

Drin Chu

Kodhari

Sun Kosi

Tama Kosi

0 10   25   50 kms

86   85   84

29   28

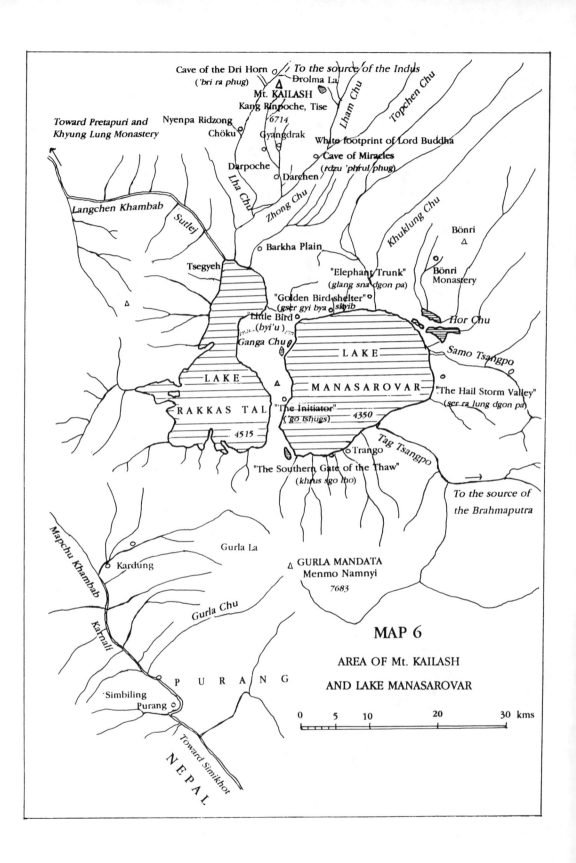

Cave of the Dri Horn
('bri ra phug)
To the source of the Indus
Drolma La
Mt. KAILASH
Kang Rinpoche, Tise
6714
Nyenpa Ridzong
Chöku
Gyangdrak
White footprint of Lord Buddha
Cave of Miracles
(rdzu 'phrul phug)
Toward Pretapuri and
Khyung Lung Monastery
Darpoche
Darchen

Langchen Khambab
Sutlej
Lha Chu
Zhong Chu
Khuklung Chu
Bönri
Bönri
Monastery

Barkha Plain
Tsegyeh
"Elephant Trunk"
(glang sna dgon pa)

"Golden Bird shelter"
(gser gyi bya skyib)
"Little Bird"
(byi'u)
Ganga Chu
LAKE
MANASAROVAR
Hor Chu
Samo Tsangpo
"The Hail Storm Valley"
(ser ra lung dgon pa)

LAKE
RAKKAS TAL
"The Initiator"
('go tshugs)
4350
4515

Tag Tsangpo
Trango
"The Southern Gate of the Thaw"
(khrus sgo lho)

To the source of
the Brahmaputra

Mapchu Khambab
Karnali
Gurla La
Kardung
GURLA MANDATA
Menmo Namnyi
7683

Gurla Chu

MAP 6

AREA OF Mt. KAILASH

AND LAKE MANASAROVAR

P U R A N G

Simbiling
Purang

0   5   10   20   30 kms

Toward Simikhot
N E P A L

Table of Songs, Letters, Teachings, and Major Events

(Unless otherwise specified the songs, letters and teachings are Shabkar's)

LETTERS

TEACHINGS IN PROSE

MAJOR EVENTS

General Index

Numbers in bold indicate main references

A and *Hang*, syllables visualized in Tummo practice, 282
Abhisheka *(dbang)*. *See* Empowerment
Absolute body *(chos sku)*. *See* Dharmakaya
Absolute expanse *(chos dbyings)*. *See* Dharmadhatu
Absolute nature *(chos nyid)*. *See* Dharmata
Absolute nature becoming manifest *(chos nyid mngon sum)*, 51
Absolute truth *(don dam bden pa)*, 101, **257**, 404, 407, **424**, 425, 550. *See also* Truth
Abuse, not returning, 414
Acceptance and rejection, 89, 552
Accumulation of merit and wisdom. *See* Merit and wisdom
Ache Lhamo *(a ce lha mo)*, dance rituals, xxi
Activities/actions
    distinguishing between virtuous and nonvirtuous, 247
    four *(las bzhi)*, 24n. 35, 441, **598**
    negative/nonvirtuous *(mi dge ba'i las)*, 338, 372, 548
        definition, 326, 354
        killing, the worst of, 451
        purification of, 373
        results of, 166, 351, 354
        ten *(mi dge ba bcu)*, 213, 326, 327, 339, 372, **548**
    nine, of the body, speech, and mind *(bya ba dgu phrugs)*, given up during Thögal practice, 282, 344n. 15, 603
    of this life, 372
    ten spiritual *(chos spyod bcu)*, 387, 425
    ten virtuous/positive *(dge ba bcu)*, 327, 352, **548**
        definition of, **24**n. 32, 326, 355
        results of, 166, 354
    worldly, xiii, xiv, xvii, **27**, 409, **411**, 547
Adverse circumstances. *See* Circumstances
Advice
    to Dharma practitioners, 19, **68**, 88, 89, 97,

146, 234, 261, 281, 289, 293, 302, 305, 310, 311, 318, **321**, **336**, 338, **353–57**, **371–75**, 404, 414, 456
    from a flower, 56
    on giving up concern for this life, 66
    on human ethics, 529
    to a king, 352
    pointing out the defects of Dharma practitioners, 381–85
    to retreatants, 302
    on worldly and religious ethics, 513
    on worldly wisdom, 385, **435**, 451, 504, 507, 524
Age of residues/dark, degenerate age *(snyigs dus)*, 3, 8
    five degenerations of the, 11n. 12, 97
Alcohol, drinking, as causes of negative actions 286, 411
    incompatible with Buddhist practice 582
All-encompassing *(khyab gdal)*, mind of the Buddhas, 259
All-pervasiveness *(zang thal)*, 535
Alms, living on, 291
Alms-seekers, and meat-eating, 195
Altruism *(gzhan phan)*, 140
Amorphous states of mind *(lung ma bstan)*, 256, 424
Amrita *(bdud rtsi)*, 573
Anger, 296, 376, 382, 525, 529
    antidotes to, **301**
    one's archenemy, 333
    controlling, 387
    as destroying kalpas of merit, 355
    freeing, 89
    negative effects of, 301
Animal(s), 325
    preventing the hunting of, 349, 432
    protection of, 139
    ransoming the lives of, **xxx** n. 53, 328, 349, 351, 353, 355, 433, 447, 517, 524, 542
    sacrifice of, 198, 386

Bonnet Bell-flower (Lat. *Codonopsis*). *See* Black Naga's Devil

Brahma aperture (Skt. *brahmanandra, tshangs bu*), 445n. 37

Brown or Snow Bear, Dremong *(dred mong, Lat. Ursus isabellinus)*, 179, 203n. 1

Buddhafield(s). *See Index of Places*

Buddhahood *(sangs rgyas)*, 63n. 6, 65, 327, 361, 373, 550, 551. *See also* Enlightenment
    in this life, at death, or in sixteen lifetimes, 382
    in one lifetime, 330, 351, 552
    in one, three, five, or seven lifetimes, 552
    primordially present qualities of, 92n. 32

Buddha-nature/Tathagatagarbha *(bde gshegs snying po)*, xvi, **xvii**, 550
    actualization of, 547
    present in every sentient being, 11n. 6, 551

Buddhist teachings *(sangs rgyas kyi bstan pa)*
    spreading north, 426
    three fundamental aspects of, xvii, 597

Business, giving up, 358

Butter-lamp(s), 101, 329
    golden, 231
        dedication prayer engraved upon a, 365
    karmic result of offering, 489
    offered at Nyanang, 447
    offered on the 25th of 10th month, anniversary of Tsongkhapa's death, 466

Calendar, Tibetan, 23n. 16

Calligraphy, ultimate, metaphors on, 88

Calm-state meditation *(zhi gnas)*. *See* Shamatha

Campu, style of classical Sanskrit poetry, ix

Canonical Transmission *(bka' ma)*, 544, **555**

Caravans, 536n. 5

"Casting oneself out, taking, and finding," three of the ten cardinal treasures of past saints, 309

Cauldron, story of two black men and, 80

Causal links. *See* Interdependent links

Cause and effect. *See* Karma

Causes and conditions *(rgyu rkyen)*, the source of all phenomena, 407

Celestial beings *(lha)*, 325

Central channel *(dbu ma)*, 131, 263
    isolating the *(dbu ma 'dzugs skor)*, a yogic exercise, 271n. 44
    untying its knots with the two lateral channels, 63n. 6

Chakra(s)/wheel *('khor lo)*, sacred diagrams for protection and liberation, 20, 21, **24**n. 40, 36n. 27, 195, 282, 283, 284
    that liberates the cities *(grong khyer grol ba'i 'khor lo)*, 33, 36n. 27

Chang, a fermented beverage, 35n. 2, 196, 328, 432, 435

Channels, energies, and vital essences *(rtsa rlung thig le)*, 64n. 20, 50, 283, 284, 553. *See also* Central channel

Chariots of the Practice Lineage, Eight *(sgrub brgyud shing rta brgyad)*, xvii, 547

Chatter *(ngag 'khyal)*. *See* Gossip.

Che-gye (phyed brgyad), a coin, 26n. 68

Child of the mountains, being a, 373

Children, loving ones and troublemakers, 142

Chinese canker *(rgya rma)*, venereal disease, 157, 177n. 3

Chöd *(gcod)*, "cutting through" (ego-clinging), a system of practice spread in Tibet by Machik Lapdrön, **12**n. 32, 71, 152n. 30, 190, 241n. 57, 302, 425, 513, 547
    practitioners of, 112, 133

Circumambulation(s), 217, 219, 249, 305, 308, 352, 355, 463, 490
    benefit of, 245
    to purify negative acts, 123
    at Tara's Paradise Arrayed with Turquoise Petals, 499
    of Tingri, 450

Circumstances/conditions, adverse/difficult *('gal rkyen/rkyen ngan)*, 290, 522
    overcoming, 81
    a test for the practitioner, 374
    used to progress on spiritual path, 205, 544

Cittamatra *(sems tsam pa)*, 550

Clairvoyance *(mngon shes)*, 258, 432, 489
    in perceiving the old Lama crossing the frozen lake, 127

Clarity *(gsal ba)*, 58
    of mind, 257

Cleaning temples, merit accrued from, 583

Cleanliness, three kinds of *(gtsang spra gsum)*, in Kriya tantra practice, 551

Clearing hindrances away *(bgegs sel)*, ritual, 121

Clinging *('dzin pa)*
    dual, to subject and object *(gnyis 'dzin)*, xxii, 523, 551
    to permanence *(rtag 'dzin)*, 280
    to phenomena as real *(bden 'dzin)*, 550

Coins
    that allow one to fly, in Shabkar's dream, 262
    Nepal-Tibet dispute about, 445n. 46
    Tibetan, 26n. 68

Combining and Transfer *(bsre 'pho)*, a practice of the Kagyu tradition, 269n. 24

Comforts, clinging to, 333

Companions. *See* Spiritual companions

Compassion *(snying rje)*, xv, 97, 169, 263, 296, 300, 326, 330, 373, 384, 416, 490, 547
    arising within the realization of emptiness, 535
    best weapon against anger, 333
    boundless *(snying rje tshad med)*, 92n. 40

SELECTED TERMS IN TIBETAN TRANSLITERATION

Index of Persons, Deities, and Sacred Images

Abhayakara (*mi 'jigs pa'i 'byung gnas*, c. 1100), an Indian master, 391n. 33

Abhe, Rigdzin Wangmo (*rig 'dzin dbang mo*), wife of Chögyal Ngakyi Wangpo, 45, 97, 100, 148, 266

    bidding farewell to Shabkar 49

Acharyas, Indian masters, 398, 446n. 55

    coming to visit Shabkar, 433

Ajatashastru (*ma skyes dgra*), King, a disciple and patron of Buddha Shakyamuni, 289

Aka, Pema Rangdrol's father, 488

Akaramatishila, a miraculously emanated bhikshu, **239**n. 18, 390n. 21

Akshobhya (*mi bskyod pa/mi 'khrugs pa*), Buddha of the Vajra Family, 299, 344n. 28

Aku, uncle, a polite way of addressing a lama or a notable in Amdo, 23n. 15

Aku Bendhe of Gyaza (*rgya za'i a khu bendhe*), 512

Aku Menpa (*a khu sman pa*), a relative of Shabkar, 496

Alak (*a lags*), the equivalent of "Rinpoche" in Amdo, a way of addressing religious dignitaries, 11n. 16

Alak Dechen (*a lags bde chen*, 18–19th cent.), 4, 53, 493

Alak Dzong Ngön (*a lags dzong sngon*, 18–19th cent.).
    See Dzong Ngön Rinpoche

Alak Gedun Sherap (*a lags dge 'dun shes rab*, 18–19th cent.), 209, 211

Alak Gonpo (*a lags mgon po*, 18–19th cent.), 181, 512

Alak Hortsang (*a lags hor tshang*, 18–19th cent.), 500

Alak Kachu (*a lags bka' bcu*, 1667–1744), 537n. 39

Alak Lhönchö (*a lags blon chos*, 18–19th cent.), 523

Alak Namkha (*a lags nam mkha'*, 18–19th cent.), 591.
    See also Changlung Tulku

Alak Sherap (*a lags shes rab*, d. 1992), 12n. 22

Alak Tragpoche (*a lags drag po che*, 18–19th cent.), 496

Alak Tsöndru (*a lags brtson 'grus*, 18–19th cent.), 211, 231, 241n. 54

Ama Khandroma (*a ma mkha' 'gro ma*), said to be a human descendant of the dakini guardian of Tsari, 270n. 38

Amban, Chinese representative in Tibet, **429**n. 4, 445
    at Xining, 488

Amitabha (*'od dpag med*) the Buddha of the Lotus Family, 23n. 21, 226, 253, 364
    as the source for the emanation of Guru Padmasambhava, xxvi n. 17
    and Avalokiteshvara, 35n. 15
    supplication to, on behalf of a dying woman, 79

Amitayus (*tshe dpag med*), the Buddha of Boundless Life, 153n. 44, 463, 476

Amogasiddhi (*don yod grub pa*), the Buddha of the karma family, 253

Ananda (*kun dga' bo*), the closest disciple and attendant of Buddha Shakyamuni, 8

Anathapindika (*mgon med zas sbyin*), a patron of Buddha Shakyamuni, 460, 481n. 23

Ancestors of Shabkar, 15

Apa Alo (*a pha a lo*), 567

Apo Yag (*a po yag*), ancestor of Shabkar, 16

Arhat (*dgra bcom pa*), one who has vanquished his enemies, the obscuring emotions (*kleshas*). The highest level attained by sravakas and pratyekabuddhas, 275, 487, 549, **550**

Arik Geshe (*a rig dge bshes 'jam dpal dge legs rgyal mtshan*, or *rgyal mtshan 'od zer*, 1726–1803), a preeminent master from Domey, who gave monastic ordination to Shabkar, xxi, **xxix**n. 46, 33, 78, 88, 491, 519, 562, 584
    passing away of, 88
    reincarnation of, 509

Aryadeva (*'phags pa lha*, c. 450 B.C.?), disciple of Nagarjuna and one of the "six ornaments of India," in Tsongkhapa's dream, 240n. 49

Asuras, demi-gods (*lha ma yin*), 343n. 10

Asvaghosha (*rta dbyangs*), an Indian master, 323

Atisha Dipamkara Shri Jnana (982–1054), the great Indian *pandita* who founded the Kadampa school in Tibet, xv, xviii, **xxv**n. 12, 3, 25n. 60,

Index of Places

679

Index of Tibetan Works

Cited by the author
or quoted in notes and appendices

PART II
TITLES IN ENGLISH TRANSLATION